Economics Principles and Practices

Features and Benefits

Dynamic Instructional Strategies	**. . . present a clear and comprehensive coverage of economics.** • Engaging section introductions include a Guide to Reading and In the News. • BusinessWeek Newsclip provide opportunities for students to discuss current issues in the world of business. • The Chapter Visual Summary offers a concise outline of important chapter topics and can be used to preview, review, or summarize chapter content.
A Strong Reading Strand	**. . . encourages active reading and learning for students of all reading levels.** • Point-of-use activities and questions engage students in interacting with the content. • Content Vocabulary, Academic Vocabulary, Section Preview, and Reading Strategy prepare students to organize key content as they read.
Differentiated Instruction	**. . . makes *Economics Principles and Practices* accessible to students of all learning levels.** • Differentiated Instruction activities and strategies can be found in the Teacher Wraparound Edition, the Unit Resource Booklets, the Differentiated Instruction Activities ancillary, and online. • Big Ideas and Main Ideas help students sort out, understand, and retain course information and get the most value out of the Student Edition. • The Skills Handbook contains Critical Thinking and Economics Skills lessons that help all levels of students.
Standardized Test Preparation	**. . . gives students the opportunity to practice for state and national exams.** • Chapter assessments provide a variety of standardized test practice, including Open-ended Short Response and Open-ended Extended Response. • Section Assessments help students learn how to successfully approach test questions.
A Variety of Economics Activities and Features	**. . . are essential for student success and get students excited about economics.** • Personal Finance and Skills Handbooks show students how to use essential tools, such as graphs, tables, and interest rates. • The Careers feature presents information on various jobs related to economics from the *Occupational Outlook Handbook* published annually by the Bureau of Labor Statistics. • Case Study and Debate in Economics features help students apply what they have learned as they investigate and debate high-interest topics. • Profiles in Economics highlight the contributions of key figures in today's society.
Teacher Resources	**. . . provide convenient strategies to help new and experienced teachers.** • The Resource Manager provides tools and strategies to help you prepare for each unit. • Blackline Masters provide background and support for teacher planning, reviewing, reinforcement, enrichment, and extension, interdisciplinary connections, and assessment. • *Dinah Zike's Reading and Study Skills Foldables* booklet provides interactive graphic organizers to help students organize and process information as they read.
Technology	**. . . provides time-saving software products to help you creatively engage your students and reduce your prep time.** • *TeacherWorks Plus™* DVD contains the Interactive Teacher Edition, all ancillaries and transparencies, *editable* blackline masters, and the most powerful and easy-to-use lesson planner. • *Presentation Plus! with MindJogger Checkpoint* DVD contains a PowerPoint™ presentation of the textbook, all program transparencies, and the interactive MindJogger quiz game. • Economics Online provides lesson plans, updates, economics activities, and links to other resources at glencoe.com

Improving Active Reading and Study Skills

Dinah Zike's

FOLDABLES™

Foldables are easy-to-make, three-dimensional, interactive graphic organizers that students create out of simple sheets of paper. The Teacher Classroom Resources includes *Dinah Zike's High School Economics Reading and Study Skills*. This booklet provides you with step-by-step instructions for using Foldables in your classroom. Each Foldable is designed to be used as a study guide for the main ideas and key points presented in a chapter. Foldables can also be used for a more in-depth investigation of a concept, an idea, an opinion, an event, or a person or place studied in a chapter. These unique hands-on tools for studying and reviewing were created exclusively for Glencoe by education specialist Dinah Zike.

Why Use Foldables in Social Studies?

Because they:

• organize, display, and arrange information, making it easier for students to grasp social studies concepts, theories, facts, opinions, questions, research, and ideas.

• are student-made study guides that are compiled as students listen for main ideas, read key points, or conduct research.

• provide a multitude of creative formats in which students can present projects, research, interviews, and inquiry-based reports.

• replace teacher-generated writing or photocopied sheets with student-generated print.

• incorporate the use of such skills as comparing and contrasting, recognizing cause-and-effect, and finding similarities and differences.

• continue to "immerse" students in previously learned vocabulary, concepts, information, generalizations,

ideas, and theories, providing them with a strong foundation that they can build upon with new observations, concepts, and knowledge.

• can be used by students or teachers to easily communicate data through graphs, tables, charts, models, and diagrams, including Venn diagrams.

• allow students to make their own journals for recording observations, research information, primary and secondary source data, surveys, and so on.

• can be used as alternative assessment tools by teachers to evaluate student progress or by students to evaluate their own progress.

• integrate language arts, the sciences, and mathematics into the study of social studies.

• provide a sense of student ownership or investiture in the social studies curriculum.

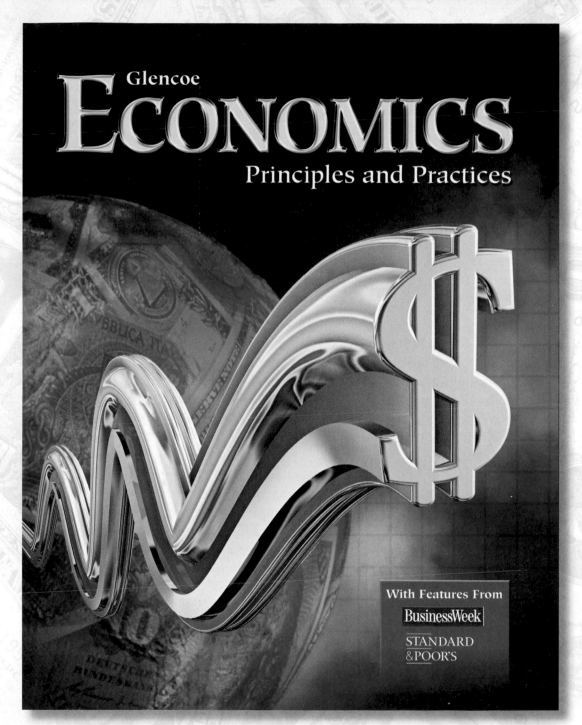

Glencoe
ECONOMICS
Principles and Practices

With Features From
BusinessWeek

STANDARD
&POOR'S

Gary E. Clayton, Ph.D.

Glencoe

New York, New York   Columbus, Ohio   Chicago, Illinois   Woodland Hills, California

About the Author

GARY E. CLAYTON, Ph.D., is Professor and Chair of the Economics and Finance Department at Northern Kentucky University. He received his Ph.D. in economics from the University of Utah and an honorary doctorate from the People's Friendship University of Russia in Moscow. Dr. Clayton has authored several textbooks and a number of articles, has appeared on numerous radio and television programs, and was a guest commentator for economic statistics on NPR's Marketplace. Dr. Clayton won the Freedoms Foundation Leavey Award for Excellence in Private Enterprise Education in 2000. Other awards include a national teaching award from the National Council on Economic Education (NCEE) and NKU's 2005 Frank Sinton Milburn Outstanding Professor award. Dr. Clayton has taught international business and economics to students in England, Austria, and Australia. In 2006 he helped organize a micro loan development project in Uganda.

Contributors

BusinessWeek is the most widely read business publication in the world and is the only weekly business news publication in existence. *BusinessWeek* provides incisive and comprehensive interpretation of events by evaluating the news and its implications for the United States, regional, and world economies.

STANDARD &POOR'S

Standard & Poor's is a leading source of data, news, and analyses on regional, national, and global economic developments. Standard & Poor's information is used by industrial firms, financial institutions, and government agencies for setting policy, managing financial positions, planning production, formulating marketing strategies, and a range of similar activities. Standard & Poor's data services represent the single most sophisticated source of information for organizations that need to understand the impact of the path of economic growth and of government fiscal and monetary policies on their activities.

The McGraw·Hill Companies

 Macmillan/McGraw-Hill Glencoe

Copyright © 2008 by The McGraw-Hill Companies, Inc. All rights reserved. Printed in the United States of America. Except as permitted under the United States Copyright Act, no part of this publication may be reproduced or distributed in any form or by any means, or stored in a database or retrieval system, without prior written permission from the publisher.

Send all inquiries to:
Glencoe/McGraw-Hill
8787 Orion Place
Columbus, OH 43240

ISBN: 978-0-07-874765-6 *(Teacher Wraparound Edition)*
MHID: 0-07-874765-1 *(Teacher Wraparound Edition)*
ISBN: 978-0-07-874764-9 *(Student Edition)*
MHID: 0-07-874764-3 *(Student Edition)*

1 2 3 4 5 6 7 8 079/043 12 11 10 09 08 07

Consultants / Reviewers

Academic Consultants

Lawrence R. Dale, Ph.D.
Director, Northeast Arkansas
    Center for Economic
    Education
Arkansas State University
Jonesboro, Arkansas

Julie Heath, Ph.D.
Chair, Department of Economics
University of Memphis
Memphis, Tennessee

Jane S. Lopus, Ph.D.
Director, Center for Economic
    Education
California State University,
    East Bay
Hayward, California

Kathy Parkison, Ph.D.
Professor of Economics
Indiana University–Kokomo
Kokomo, Indiana

Mark J. Perry, Ph.D.
Professor of Finance and
    Economics
University of Michigan–Flint
Flint, Michigan

Teacher Reviewers

James Artese
Bogan High School
Chicago, Illinois

David A. Bleakley
Freehold Township
    High School
Freehold, New Jersey

Richard A. Dollison
W.P. Davidson High School
Mobile, Alabama

Lorraine "Lori" J. Dumerer
R.L. Turner High School
Carrollton, Texas

Lisa C. Herman Ellison
Kokomo High School
Kokomo, Indiana

Tenika L. Holden
Charles Herbert Flowers
    High School
Springdale, Maryland

Carrie P. Howell, Ph.D.
Stewart County High School
Dover, Tennessee

Carl K. Lett, Jr.
Oak Mountain High School
Birmingham, Alabama

Sandra L. Mangen
Beavercreek High School
Beavercreek, Ohio

Andre Martinez
Tulare Union High School
Tulare, California

Matt Pedlow
Jackson High School
Jackson, Michigan

Michael B. Raymer
Starr's Mill High School
Fayetteville, Georgia

Laura Rhea
Louisville Male Traditional
    High School
Louisville, Kentucky

David L. Schreiber
Maggie L. Walker Governor's
    School
Richmond, Virginia

Janet C. Tavares
Apponequet Regional
    High School
Lakeville, Massachusetts

Alice L. Temnick
Cactus Shadows High School
Cave Creek, Arizona

Anna Ruth Vanlandingham
Lake Mary High School
Lake Mary, Florida

Mark Wallace
Gateway High School
Monroeville, Pennsylvania

Tom Woodruff, Ed.D.
Rogers High School
Rogers, Arkansas

Table of Contents

UNIT 1

Fundamental Economic Concepts 2

Table of Contents

Table of Contents

Features

Economics ONLINE

All essential content is covered in the Online Student Edition. Use our Web site glencoe.com for these additional resources:

- Chapter Overviews
- Student Web Activities
- Self-Check Quizzes
- In Motion graphics

Features

Profiles in Economics

DEBATES IN ECONOMICS

CAREERS

Charts, Graphs, and Maps

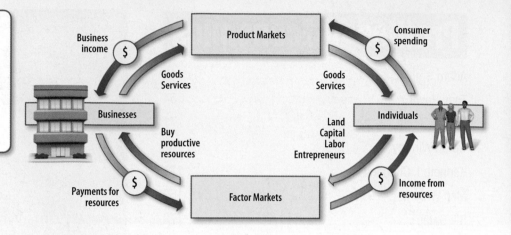

Graphs In Motion

Entries in blue indicate In Motion graphics. These graphs and charts have been specially enhanced on the StudentWorks™ Plus CD-ROM and on glencoe.com.

THE RATE OF INFLATION AND THE CONSUMER PRICE INDEX, 1965–2006

Recession years

Source: Bureau of Labor Statistics

Charts, Graphs, and Maps

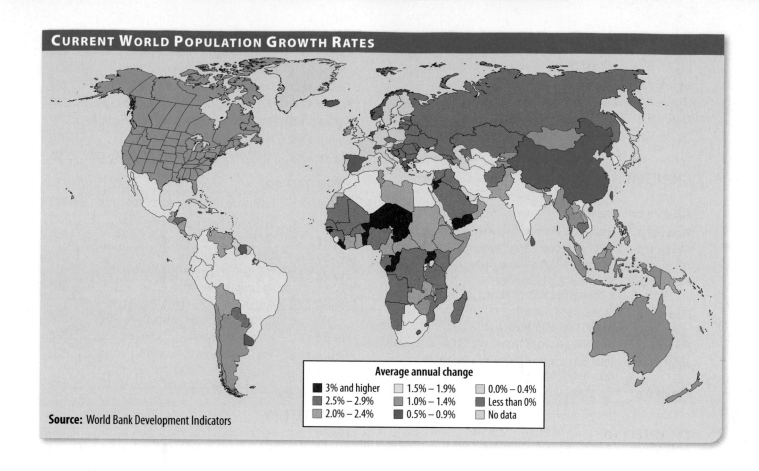

CURRENT WORLD POPULATION GROWTH RATES

Average annual change

- ■ 3% and higher
- ■ 2.5% – 2.9%
- ■ 2.0% – 2.4%
- □ 1.5% – 1.9%
- ■ 1.0% – 1.4%
- ■ 0.5% – 0.9%
- ■ 0.0% – 0.4%
- ■ Less than 0%
- □ No data

Source: World Bank Development Indicators

SCAVENGER HUNT

Economics: Principles and Practices contains a wealth of information. The trick is to know where to find it. If you go through this scavenger hunt, either alone, with a fellow student, or with your teacher or parents, you will quickly learn how the textbook is organized and how to get the most out of your reading and study time. Let's get started!

1. How many units and chapters are in the book? 5 units and 18 chapters

2. What is the difference between the glossary and the index? glossary defines vocabulary; index provides page references

3. All sections of a chapter open with a primary source—a news item or other article related to the content in the section. Where else can you find primary sources in the textbook? BusinessWeek Newsclip and Debates in Economics

4. How can you find out how each Main Idea in the book relates to your life? Read the Economics & You below the Main Idea.

5. If you want to quickly find all the maps, charts, and graphs about supply or demand, where in the front of the book do you look? Table of Contents

6. What is the quickest way to find information on detailed, specific topics such as gross domestic product and the national debt? look in the index

7. Where can you find the topic Sources of Government Revenue summarized in a visual way? Visual Summary

8. What are the key terms for Chapter 8, Section 3, and how are they highlighted in the text? listed in the Guide to Reading, and boldfaced and highlighted in yellow in the text

9. The Web site for the book appears four times in each chapter. Find all of the references of one chapter. How can the Web site help you? provides overviews, practice tests, and additional activities and resources

10. Which of the book's special features provides information about how the global economy affects you and your community? The Global Economy & You

The Economics America and Economics International Program

National Council on Economic Education

March 26, 2007
Leading the Campaign for Economic and Financial Literacy

Dear Educator,

We commend this textbook to teachers. The Principles and Practices of sound, standards-based Economics are needed for our students and our society, now, more than ever. These lessons are correlated with the Voluntary National Content Standards in Economics written and published by the National Council on Economic Education.

Economics is no longer (if it ever was) the "dismal science." It is an essential set of reasoning and decision-making skills for surviving, let alone, thriving, in a challenging, competitive global economy.

As we confront the issues of the increasing number of personal bankruptcies, uncontrolled credit card debt, ignorance of the value of saving and investing, and the inability of many of our students and their families to grasp the repercussions of international trade, these public concerns magnify the need for increasing economic literacy in our young adults and for enhancing economic education in our nation's schools.

The challenge was expressed nearly sixty years ago in the founding of the National Council on Economic Education (NCEE): "There is no aspect of education more important than that which makes all our citizens intelligent and truly informed about the economic system in which they live and work."

In principle and in practice, teaching standards-based economics is an excellent thing to be doing.

Respectfully,

Robert F. Duvall
President & Chief Executive Officer

T16

In 1994 the United States Congress designated economics as one of the nine core subjects to be taught in America's schools. As a result, the National Council on Economic Education developed the *Voluntary National Content Standards in Economics* for use in economics curricula.

Economics: Principles and Practices provides extensive coverage for the 20 voluntary content standards. For a complete discussion of the standards, you can reach the National Council on Economic Education through the Internet at www.ncee.net, or at 1-800-338-1192.

For each standard, students will understand:	*Economics: Principles and Practices* Chapter and Section Coverage
1 Scarcity Productive resources are limited. Therefore, people cannot have all the goods and services they want; as a result, they must choose some things and give up others.	**Chapter 1** Section 1 Scarcity and the Science of Economics Section 3 Economic Choices and Decision Making **Chapter 18** Section 3 Applying the Economic Way of Thinking
2 Marginal Cost/Benefit Effective decision making requires comparing the additional costs of alternatives with the additional benefits. Most choices involve doing a little more or a little less of something; few choice are "all or nothing" decisions.	**Chapter 1** Section 3 Economic Choices and Decision Making **Chapter 5** Section 3 Cost, Revenue, and Profit Maximization **Chapter 15** Section 3 Economics and Politics
3 Allocation of Goods and Services Different methods can be used to allocate goods and services. People, acting individually or collectively through government, must choose which methods to use to allocate different kinds of goods and services.	**Chapter 2** Section 1 Economic Systems **Chapter 17** Section 3 The Transition to Capitalism
4 Role of Incentives People respond predictably to positive and negative incentives.	**Chapter 6** Section 1 Prices as Signals **Chapter 18** Section 2 Global Problems and Economic Incentives
5 Gain from Trade Voluntary exchange occurs only when all participating parties expect to gain. This is true for trade among individuals or organizations within a nation, and among individuals or organizations in different nations.	**Chapter 16** Section 1 Absolute and Comparative Advantage Section 2 Barriers to International Trade Section 3 Foreign Exchange and Trade Deficits **Chapter 18** Section 1 Globalization: Characteristics and Trends

6	**Specialization and Trade** When individuals, regions, and nations specialize in what they can produce at the lowest cost and then trade with others, both production and consumption increase.	**Chapter 16** Section 1 Absolute and Comparative Advantage
7	**Markets—Price and Quantity Determination** Markets exist when buyers and sellers interact. This interaction determines market prices and thereby allocates scarce goods and services.	**Chapter 6** Section 1 Prices as Signals Section 2 The Price System at Work **Chapter 16** Section 3 Foreign Exchange and Trade Deficits
8	**Role of Price in Market System** Prices send signals and provide incentives to buyers and sellers. When supply or demand changes, market prices adjust, affecting incentives.	**Chapter 4** Section 1 What Is Demand? Section 2 Factors Affecting Demand Section 3 Elasticity of Demand **Chapter 5** Section 1 What Is Supply? Section 2 The Theory of Production Section 3 Cost, Revenue, and Profit Maximization **Chapter 6** Section 1 Prices as Signals Section 2 The Price System at Work **Chapter 18** Section 2 Global Problems and Economic Incentives
9	**Role of Competition** Competition among sellers lowers costs and prices, and encourages producers to produce more of what consumers are willing and able to buy. Competition among buyers increases prices and allocates goods and services to those people who are willing and able to pay the most for them.	**Chapter 7** Section 1 Competition and Market Structures Section 2 Market Failures
10	**Role of Economic Institutions** Institutions evolve in market economies to help individuals and groups accomplish their goals. Banks, labor unions, corporations, legal systems, and not-for-profit organizations are examples of important institutions. A different kind of institution, clearly defined and enforced property rights, is essential to a market economy.	**Chapter 3** Section 1 Forms of Business Organization Section 3 Nonprofit Organizations **Chapter 8** Section 1 The Labor Movement **Chapter 11** Section 1 Savings and the Financial System

11 **Role of Money** Money makes it easier to trade, borrow, save, invest, and compare the value of goods and services.	**Chapter 14** Section 1 Section 2	The Evolution, Functions, and Characteristics of Money The Development of Modern Banking
12 **Role of Interest Rates** Interest rates, adjusted for inflation, rise and fall to balance the amount saved with the amount borrowed, which affects the allocation of scarce resources between present and future uses.	**Chapter 14** Section 3 **Chapter 15** Section 2	The Federal Reserve System and Monetary Policy Stabilization Policies
13 **Role of Resources in Determining Income** Income for most people is determined by the market value of the productive resources they sell. What workers earn depends, primarily, on the market value of what they produce and how productive they are.	**Chapter 8** Section 2 Section 3 **Chapter 12** Section 3	Wages and Labor Disputes Employment Trends and Issues Poverty and the Distribution of Income
14 **Profit and the Entrepreneur** Entrepreneurs are people who take the risks of organizing productive resources to make goods and services. Profit is an important incentive that leads entrepreneurs to accept the risks of business failure.	**Chapter 1** Section 1 **Chapter 3** Section 2	Scarcity and the Science of Economics Business Growth and Expansion
15 **Growth** Investment in factories, machinery, new technology, and in the health, education, and training of people can raise future standards of living.	**Chapter 11** Section 2 Section 3 **Chapter 12** Section 2 **Chapter 17** Section 1 Section 2	Financial Assets and Their Markets Investing in Equities and Options Population and Economic Growth Economic Development Achieving Economic Development

16 **Role of Government**

There is an economic role for government in a market economy whenever the benefits of a government policy outweigh its costs. Governments often provide for national defense, address environmental concerns, define and protect property rights, and attempt to make markets more competitive. Most government policies also redistribute income.

Chapter 2
Section 1   Economic Systems
Section 2   Evaluating Economic Performance
Section 3   American Free Enterprise

Chapter 3
Section 3   Nonprofit Organizations

Chapter 6
Section 3   Social Goals and Market Efficiency

Chapter 7
Section 2   Market Failures
Section 3   The Role of Government

Chapter 9
Section 1   The Economics of Taxation
Section 2   Federal, State, and Local Revenue Systems
Section 3   Current Tax Issues and Reforms

Chapter 10
Section 1   The Economics of Government Spending
Section 2   Federal, State, and Local Government Expenditures

Chapter 17
Section 3   The Transition to Capitalism

Chapter 18
Section 2   Global Problems and Economic Incentives

17 **Using Cost-Benefit Analysis to Evaluate Government Programs**

Costs of government policies sometimes exceed benefits. This may occur because of incentives facing voters, government officials, and government employees; because of actions by special interest groups that can impose costs on the general public; or because social goals other than economic efficiency are being pursued.

Chapter 6
Section 2   The Price System at Work

Chapter 16
Section 2   Barriers to International Trade

Chapter 15
Section 2   Stabilization Policies
Section 3   Economics and Politics

Macroeconomy—Income/Empoyment, Prices

A nation's overall levels of income, employment, and prices are determined by the interaction of spending and production decisions made by all households, firms, government agencies, and others in the economy.

Chapter 12
Section 1   Measuring the Nation's Output and Income
Section 2   Population and Economic Growth

Chapter 13
Section 1   Business Cycles and Fluctuations
Section 2   Inflation
Section 3   Unemployment

Chapter 15
Section 1   Macroeconomic Equilibrium
Section 3   Economics and Politics

Chapter 17
Section 1   Economic Development

Unemployment and Inflation

Unemployment imposes costs on individuals and nations. Unexpected inflation imposes costs on many people and benefits some others because it arbitrarily redistributes purchasing power. Inflation can reduce the rate of growth of national living standards because individuals and organizations use resources to protect themselves against the uncertainty of future prices.

Chapter 12
Section 3   Poverty and the Distribution of Income

Chapter 13
Section 1   Business Cycles and Fluctuations
Section 2   Inflation
Section 3   Unemployment

Monetary and Fiscal Policies

Federal government budgetary policy and the Federal Reserve System's monetary policy influence the overall levels of employment, output, and prices.

Chapter 10
Section 1   The Economics of Government Spending
Section 3   Deficits, Surpluses, and the National Debt

Chapter 14
Section 3   The Federal Reserve System and Monetary Policy

Chapter 15
Section 1   Macroeconomic Equilibrium
Section 2   Stabilization Policies
Section 3   Economics and Politics

Voluntary National Content Standards in Economics

Economics: Principles and Practices incorporates the 20 **Voluntary National Content Standards** developed by the **National Council on Economic Education.**

Standard 1 Scarcity

Productive resources are limited. Therefore, people cannot have all the goods and services they want; as a result, they must choose some things and give up others.

Related concepts: Capital Resources, Choice, Consumer Economics, Consumers, Goods, Human Resources, Natural Resources, Opportunity Cost, Producers, Production, Productive Resources, Scarcity, Services, Wants, Entrepreneurship, Inventors, Entrepreneur, Factors of Production

Standard 2 Marginal Cost/Benefit

Effective decision making requires comparing the additional costs of alternatives with the additional benefits. Most choices involve doing a little more or a little less of something; few choices are "all or nothing" decisions.

Related concepts: Decision Making, Profit Motive, Benefit, Costs, Marginal Analysis, Profit, Profit Maximization, Cost-Benefit Analysis

Standard 3 Allocation of Goods and Services

Different methods can be used to allocate goods and services. People acting individually or collectively through government must choose which methods to use to allocate different kinds of goods and services.

Related concepts: Economic Systems, Market Structure, Supply, Command Economy, Market Economy, Traditional Economy

Standard 4 Role of Incentives

People respond predictably to positive and negative incentives.

Related concepts: Choice, Incentive

Standard 5 Gain from Trade

Voluntary exchange occurs only when all participating parties expect to gain. This is true for trade among individuals or organizations within a nation, and usually among individuals or organizations in different nations.

Related concepts: Barriers to Trade, Barter, Exports, Imports, Voluntary Exchange, Exchange, Exchange Rate

Standard 6 Specialization and Trade

When individuals, regions, and nations specialize in what they can produce at the lowest cost and then trade with others, both production and consumption increase.

Related concepts: Division of Labor, Production, Productive Resources, Specialization, Factor Endowments, Gains from Trade, Relative Price, Transaction Costs, Factors of Production, Full Employment

Standard 7 Markets–Price and Quantity Determination

Markets exist when buyers and sellers interact. This interaction determines market prices and thereby allocates scarce goods and services.

Related concepts: Market Structure, Markets, Price Floor, Price Stability, Quantity Demanded, Quantity Supplied, Relative Price, Exchange Rate

Standard 8 Role of Price in Market System

Prices send signals and provide incentives to buyers and sellers. When supply or demand changes, market prices adjust, affecting incentives.

Related concepts: Non-price Determinants, Price Floor, Price Stability, Supply, Determinants of Demand, Determinants of Supply, Law of Demand, Law of Supply, Price Ceiling, Substitute Good, Price

Standard 9 Role of Competition

Competition among sellers lowers costs and prices, and encourages producers to produce more of what consumers are willing and able to buy. Competition among buyers increases prices and allocates goods and services to those people who are willing and able to pay the most for them.

Related concepts: Market Structure, Non-price Competition, Levels of Competition

Standard 10 Role of Economic Institutions

Institutions evolve in market economies to help individuals and groups accomplish their goals. Banks, labor unions, corporations, legal systems, and not-for-profit organizations are examples of important institutions. A different kind of institution, clearly defined and enforced property rights, is essential to a market economy.

Related concepts: Legal and Social Framework, Mortgage, Borrower, Interest, Labor Union, Legal Forms of Business, Legal Foundations of a Market Economy, Nonprofit Organization, Property Rights, Banking, Economic Institutions

Voluntary National Content Standards in Economics

Standard 11 Role of Money

Money makes it easier to trade, borrow, save, invest, and compare the value of goods and services.

Related concepts: Exchange, Money Management, Money Supply, Currency, Definition of Money, Money, Characteristics of Money, Functions of Money

Standard 12 Role of Interest Rates

Interest rates, adjusted for inflation, rise and fall to balance the amount saved with the amount borrowed, which affects the allocation of scarce resources between present and future uses.

Related concepts: Interest Rate, Monetary Policy, Real vs. Nominal, Risk, Investing, Savers, Savings

Standard 13 Role of Resources in Determining Income

Income for most people is determined by the market value of the productive resources they sell. What workers earn depends, primarily, on the market value of what they produce and how productive they are.

Related concepts: Human Resources, Derived Demand, Functional Distribution of Income, Labor, Labor Market, Marginal Resource Product, Personal Distribution of Income, Wage, Aggregate Demand (AD), Aggregate Supply (AS), Demand, Prices of Inputs, Functional Distribution

Standard 14 Profit and the Entrepreneur

Entrepreneurs are people who take the risks of organizing productive resources to make goods and services. Profit is an important incentive that leads entrepreneurs to accept the risks of business failure.

Related concepts: Taxation, Costs, Costs of Production, Entrepreneur, Risk, Taxes, Cost-Benefit Analysis, Innovation, Entrepreneurship, Inventors

Standard 15 Growth

Investment in factories, machinery, new technology, and in the health, education, and training of people can raise future standards of living.

Related concepts: Incentive, Interest Rate, Opportunity Cost, Production, Technological Changes, Trade-off, Trade-offs Among Goals, Human Capital, Intensive Growth, Investment, Physical Capital, Productivity, Risk, Standard of Living, Economic Efficiency, Economic Equity, Economic Freedom, Economic Growth, Economic Security, Investing, Business, Businesses and Households, Factors of Production, Health and Nutrition, Savers, Savings, Stock Market

Standard 16 Role of Government

There is an economic role for government in a market economy whenever the benefits of a government policy outweigh its costs. Governments often provide for national defense, address environmental concerns, define and protect property rights, and attempt to make markets more competitive. Most government policies also redistribute income.

Related concepts: Externalities, Income, Natural Monopoly, Role of Government, Taxation, Bonds, Income Tax, Maintaining Competition, Monopolies, Property Rights, Public Goods, Maintaining Regulation, Taxes, Regulation, Government Expenditures, Government Revenues

Standard 17 Using Cost-Benefit Analysis to Evaluate Government Programs

Costs of government policies sometimes exceed benefits. This may occur because of incentives facing voters, government officials, and government employees; because of actions by special interest groups that can impose costs on the general public; or because social goals other than economic efficiency are being pursued.

Related concepts: Cost-Benefit Analysis, Benefit, Costs, Special Interest Group, Barriers to Trade

Standard 18 Macroeconomy—Income/Employment, Prices

A nation's overall levels of income, employment, and prices are determined by the interaction of spending and production decisions made by all households, firms, government agencies, and others in the economy.

Related concepts: Gross Domestic Product (GDP), Macroeconomic Indicators, Nominal Gross Domestic Product (GDP), Per Capita Gross Domestic Product (GDP), Potential Gross Domestic Product (GDP), Real Gross Domestic Product (GDP), Circular Flow

Standard 19 Unemployment and Inflation

Unemployment imposes costs on individuals and nations. Unexpected inflation imposes costs on many people and benefits some others because it arbitrarily redistributes purchasing power. Inflation can reduce the rate of growth of national living standards because individuals and organizations use resources to protect themselves against the uncertainty of future prices.

Related concepts: Types of Unemployment, Causes of Inflation, Consumer Price Index (CPI), Deflation, Labor Force, Unemployment, Unemployment Rate, Inflation

Standard 20 Monetary and Fiscal Policy

Federal government budgetary policy and the Federal Reserve System's monetary policy influence the overall levels of employment, output, and prices.

Related concepts: Inflation, National Debt, Tools of the Federal Reserve, Discount Rate, Federal Budget, Fiscal Policy, Monetary Policy, Open Market Operations, Reserve Requirements, Budget, Budget Deficit, Central Banking System, Budget Surplus, Causes of Inflation

Economics: Principles and Practices is organized so that it can be adjusted easily for alternative lengths or varied course emphases. The models on the following pages are based on the 20 **Voluntary National Content Standards** developed by the **National Council on Economic Education (NCEE).**

Voluntary National Content Standards

- Scarcity
- Marginal Cost/Benefit
- Allocation of Goods and Services
- Role of Incentives
- Gain from Trade
- Specialization and Trade
- Markets—Price and Quantity Determination
- Role of Price in Market System
- Role of Competition
- Role of Economic Institutions
- Role of Money

- Role of Interest Rates
- Role of Resources in Determining Income
- Profit and the Entrepreneur
- Growth
- Role of Government
- Using Cost-Benefit Analysis to Evaluate Government Programs
- Macroeconomy—Income/Employment, Prices
- Unemployment and Inflation
- Monetary and Fiscal Policy

Chapter or Section	Standards Addressed	Length of Study in Days
Chapter 1 What Is Economics?	• Scarcity • Marginal Cost/Benefit • Profit and the Entrepreneur	5
Chapter 2 Economic Systems and Decision Making	• Allocation of Goods and Services • Role of Government	5
Chapter 3 Business Organizations	• Role of Economic Institutions • Profit and the Entrepreneur • Role of Government	5
Chapter 4 Demand	• Role of Price in Market System	6
Chapter 5 Supply	• Marginal Cost/Benefit • Role of Price in Market System	6
Chapter 6 Prices and Decision Making	• Role of Incentives • Markets—Price and Quantity Determination • Role of Price in Market System • Role of Government • Using Cost-Benefit Analysis to Evaluate Government Programs	6
Chapter 7 Market Structures	• Role of Competition • Role of Government	6
Chapter 8, Section 2 Wages and Labor Disputes	• Role of Resources in Determining Income	2
Chapter 8, Section 3 Employment Trends and Issues	• Role of Resources in Determining Income	2
Chapter 12, Section 3 Poverty and the Distribution of Income	• Role of Resources in Determining Income • Unemployment and Inflation	2
		Total Days: 45

Chapter or Section	Standards Addressed	Length of Study in Days
Chapter 1 **What Is Economics?**	• Scarcity • Marginal Cost/Benefit • Profit and the Entrepreneur	4
Chapter 2 **Economic Systems and Decision Making**	• Allocation of Goods and Services • Role of Government	5
Chapter 3, Section 1 **Forms of Business Organization**	• Role of Economic Institutions	2
Chapter 8 **Employment, Labor, and Wages**	• Role of Economic Institutions • Role of Resources in Determining Income	5
Chapter 9 **Sources of Government Revenue**	• Role of Government	6
Chapter 10 **Government Spending**	• Role of Government • Monetary and Fiscal Policy	6
Chapter 11 **Financial Markets**	• Role of Economic Institutions • Growth	6

Chapter or Section	Standards Addressed	Length of Study in Days
Chapter 12 **Macroeconomic Performance**	• Role of Resources in Determining Income • Growth • Macroeconomy—Income/Employment, Prices • Unemployment and Inflation	6
Chapter 13 **Economic Instability**	• Macroeconomy—Income/Employment, Prices • Unemployment and Inflation	6
Chapter 14 **Money, Banking, and the Fed**	• Role of Money • Role of Interest Rates • Monetary and Fiscal Policy	6
Chapter 15 **Economic Stabilization Policies**	• Marginal Cost/Benefit • Role of Interest Rates • Using Cost-Benefit Analysis to Evaluate Government Programs • Macroeconomy—Income/Employment, Prices • Monetary and Fiscal Policy	6
		Total Days: 58

Chapter or Section	Standards Addressed	Length of Study in Days
Chapter 1 What Is Economics?	• Scarcity • Marginal Cost/Benefit • Profit and the Entrepreneur	7
Chapter 2 Economic Systems and Decision Making	• Allocation of Goods and Services • Role of Government	8
Chapter 3, Section 1 Forms of Business Organization	• Role of Economic Institutions	7
Chapter 4, Section 1 What Is Demand?	• Role of Price in Market System	2
Chapter 5, Section 1 What Is Supply?	• Role of Price in Market System	2
Chapter 6, Section 1 Prices as Signals	• Role of Incentives • Markets—Price and Quantity Determination • Role of Price in Market System	2
Chapter 12 Macroeconomic Performance	• Role of Resources in Determining Income • Growth • Macroeconomy—Income/ Employment, Prices • Unemployment and Inflation	8
Chapter 13 Economic Instability	• Macroeconomy—Income/ Employment, Prices • Unemployment and Inflation	8

Chapter or Section	Standards Addressed	Length of Study in Days
Chapter 14 **Money, Banking, and the Fed**	• Role of Money • Role of Interest Rates • Monetary and Fiscal Policy	8
Chapter 15 **Economic Stabilization Policies**	• Marginal Cost/Benefit • Role of Interest Rates • Using Cost-Benefit Analysis to Evaluate Government Programs • Macroeconomy—Income/ Employment, Prices • Monetary and Fiscal Policy	8
Chapter 16 **International Trade**	• Gain from Trade • Specialization and Trade • Markets—Price and Quantity Determination • Using Cost-Benefit Analysis to Evaluate Government Programs	8
Chapter 17 **Developing Countries**	• Allocation of Goods and Services • Growth • Role of Government • Macroeconomy—Income/ Employment, Prices	8
Chapter 18 **Global Economic Challenges**	• Scarcity • Role of Incentives • Gain from Trade • Role of Price in Market System • Role of Government	6
		Total Days: 82

Chapter or Section	Standards Addressed	Length of Study in Days
Chapter 1 What Is Economics?	• Scarcity • Marginal Cost/Benefit • Profit and the Entrepreneur	7
Chapter 2 Economic Systems and Decision Making	• Allocation of Goods and Services • Role of Government	7
Chapter 3 Business Organizations	• Role of Economic Institutions • Profit and the Entrepreneur • Role of Government	7
Chapter 4 Demand	• Role of Price in Market System	7
Chapter 5 Supply	• Marginal Cost/Benefit • Role of Price in Market System	7
Chapter 6 Prices and Decision Making	• Role of Incentives • Markets—Price and Quantity Determination • Role of Price in Market System • Role of Government • Using Cost-Benefit Analysis to Evaluate Government Programs	7
Chapter 7 Market Structures	• Role of Competition • Role of Government	7
Chapter 11 Financial Markets	• Role of Economic Institutions • Growth	7

Chapter or Section	Standards Addressed	Length of Study in Days
Chapter 13 Economic Instability	• Macroeconomy—Income/ Employment, Prices • Unemployment and Inflation	7
Chapter 16 International Trade	• Gain from Trade • Specialization and Trade • Markets—Price and Quantity Determination • Using Cost-Benefit Analysis to Evaluate Government Programs	7
Chapter 18 Global Economic Challenges	• Scarcity • Role of Incentives • Gain from Trade • Role of Price in Market System • Role of Government	7
Personal Finance Handbook	• Scarcity • Marginal Cost/Benefit • Role of Incentives • Role of Money • Role of Interest Rates	5
		Total Days: 82

Chapter or Section	Standards Addressed	Length of Study in Days
Chapter 1 What Is Economics?	• Scarcity • Marginal Cost/Benefit • Profit and the Entrepreneur	8
Chapter 2 Economic Systems and Decision Making	• Allocation of Goods and Services • Role of Government	8
Chapter 3 Business Organizations	• Role of Economic Institutions • Profit and the Entrepreneur • Role of Government	8
Chapter 4 Demand	• Role of Price in Market System	9
Chapter 5 Supply	• Marginal Cost/Benefit • Role of Price in Market System	9
Chapter 6 Prices and Decision Making	• Role of Incentives • Markets—Price and Quantity Determination • Role of Price in Market System • Role of Government • Using Cost-Benefit Analysis to Evaluate Government Programs	9
Chapter 7 Market Structures	• Role of Competition • Role of Government	9
Chapter 8 Employment, Labor, and Wages	• Role of Economic Institutions • Role of Resources in Determining Income	9
Chapter 9 Sources of Government Revenue	• Role of Government	8
Chapter 10 Government Spending	• Role of Government • Monetary and Fiscal Policy	8
Chapter 11 Financial Markets	• Role of Economic Institutions • Growth	9

Chapter or Section	Standards Addressed	Length of Study in Days
Chapter 12 Macroeconomic Performance	• Role of Resources in Determining Income/Growth • Macroeconomy—Income/Employment, Prices • Unemployment and Inflation	9
Chapter 13 Economic Instability	• Macroeconomy—Income/Employment, Prices • Unemployment and Inflation	9
Chapter 14 Money, Banking, and the Fed	• Role of Money/Role of Interest Rates • Monetary and Fiscal Policy	9
Chapter 15 Economic Stabilization Policies	• Marginal Cost/Benefit • Role of Interest Rates • Using Cost-Benefit Analysis to Evaluate Government Programs • Macroeconomy—Income/Employment, Prices • Monetary and Fiscal Policy	9
Chapter 16 International Trade	• Gain from Trade • Specialization and Trade • Markets—Price and Quantity Determination • Using Cost-Benefit Analysis to Evaluate Government Programs	9
Chapter 17 Developing Countries	• Allocation of Goods and Services • Growth/Role of Government • Macroeconomy—Income/Employment, Prices	8
Chapter 18 Global Economic Challenges	• Scarcity/Role of Incentives • Gain from Trade/Role of Government • Role of Price in Market System	8
Personal Finance Handbook	• Scarcity/Role of Money • Marginal Cost/Benefit • Role of Incentives • Role of Interest Rates	5
		Total Days: 180

Using the Teacher Wraparound Edition

To Teachers:

Welcome to the the Teacher Wraparound Edition of *Economics: Principles and Practices.* We have created this teacher edition based on input from experienced teachers and educational consultants. Our goal is to provide you with teaching strategies and activities, which are labeled for you at point of use. The following pages will show the structure of the Teacher Wraparound Edition.

Student-Based Instruction

Point-of-Use
- Strategies and activities apply directly to student content.

Differentiated Instruction
- Leveled activities and options for differentiated instruction help meet the needs of all your students, including English language learners.

Review and Reinforcement
- Reading and critical thinking skills are reinforced throughout the lesson.

Assessment and Intervention
- Section Reviews and Chapter Assessments gauge student mastery of content.
- Additional resources provide intervention options.

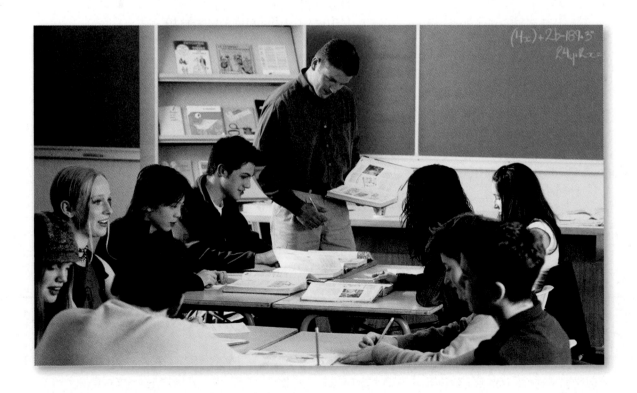

Planning and Teaching the Unit

Unit Planning Guides appear at the beginning of each unit.

Pacing Chart

Provides time management suggestions for teaching the unit

Author Note

Highlights author's ideas for teaching the unit

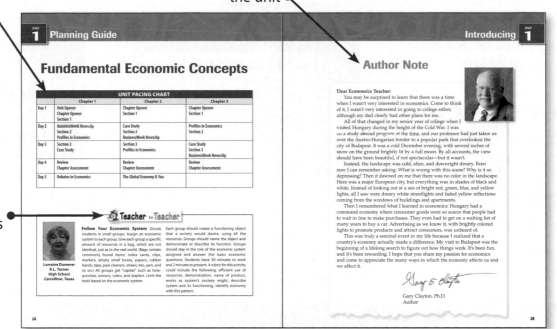

Teacher to Teacher

Includes activities from the classrooms of successful teachers

Unit Objectives

Lists objectives for student learning

Making It Relevant

Relates student knowledge to the unit

Unit Overview

Provides a brief overview of unit content

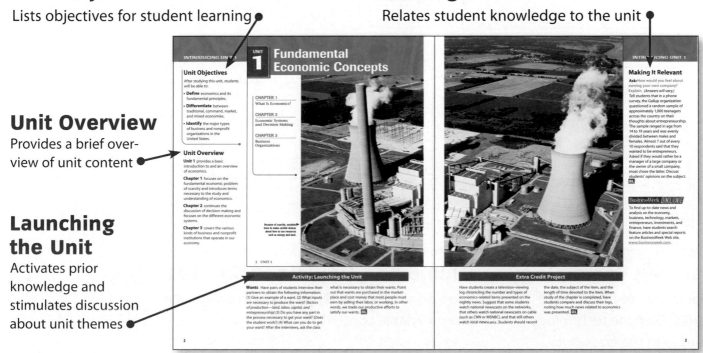

Launching the Unit

Activates prior knowledge and stimulates discussion about unit themes

Using the Teacher Wraparound Edition

Planning the Chapter

Chapter Planning Guides provide a snapshot of the scope of resources available to enhance and extend learning in each chapter.

Incorporating Resources

Utilizes a structured lesson plan to incorporate additional resources

Leveled Activities

Organizes resources by appropriate ability levels

*Spanish Resources

Provides resources for English language learners

Additional Resources

Identifies resources for supplementing the chapter

Teaching Technology

Explains how to incorporate different Glencoe technology resources in the classroom

Online and Downloadable Learning

Engages students and parents with online and downloadable content

Teaching the Chapter

The Big Ideas and Essential Question at the beginning of the chapter help you teach the most important chapter contents.

The BIG Ideas

Big Ideas are major themes, issues, concepts, questions, or ideas that are tied to the Voluntary National Content Standards in Economics that help students organize information and understand economic themes.

Economics & You Video

Engage students with the content using a short video

Foldables

Dinah Zike's Foldables™ help students organize information and prepare for assessments

Economics Online

Provides additional chapter resources

Using the Teacher Wraparound Edition

Lesson Structure

Each lesson in *Economics: Principles and Practices* is presented in a structured lesson plan: Focus, Teach, Assess, and Close.

FOCUS

Includes a Bellringer activity to help your students think about the lesson topic

Guide to Reading

Provides pre-reading strategies to improve comprehension

Resource Manager

Provides a list of teacher edition and supplemental resources that supports lesson content and reinforces skills

TEACH

Stimulates learning and interest using leveled activities

ASSESS

Identifies assessment resources

CLOSE

Gauges comprehension of section content

Answers

Lists the answers to Student Edition questions

Understanding the Brackets and Letters

Brackets

Brackets on the reduced Student Edition page correspond to teaching strategies and activities in the Teacher Wraparound Edition. As you teach the section, the brackets show you exactly where to teach these strategies and activities.

Letters*

The letters on the reduced Student Edition page identify the type of strategy or activity. See the key below to learn about the different types of strategies and activities.

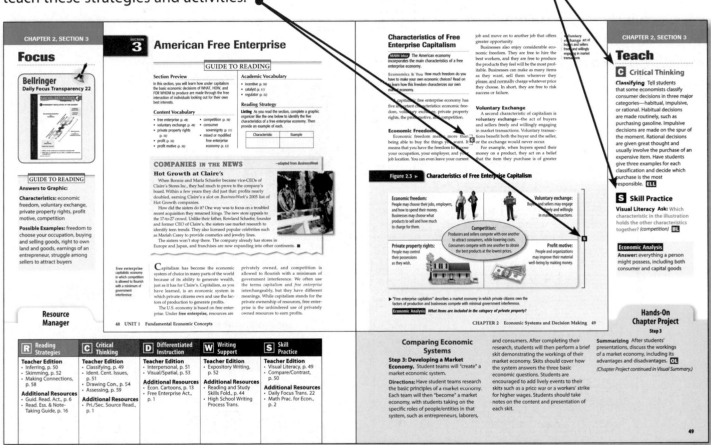

KEY for Using the Teacher Wraparound Edition

R **Reading Strategy** activities help you teach reading skills and vocabulary.

C **Critical Thinking** strategies help students apply and extend what they have learned.

D **Differentiated Instruction** activities provide differentiated instruction for students learning to speak English, along with suggestions for teaching various types of learners.

S **Skill Practice** strategies help students practice economic analysis and skills.

W **Writing Support** activities provide writing opportunities to help students comprehend the text.

* Letters are followed by a number when there is more than one of the same type of strategy or activity on the page.

Hands-On Chapter Projects

Extend student learning with unique interactive projects in each chapter. The Hands-On Chapter Projects allow students to take concepts and put them to practical use. Activities are progressive and require teamwork. Students conceptualize, plan, and execute their vision in a hands-on approach that makes economics come alive.

Steps

Each lesson includes a self-contained activity, with one lesson building on knowledge gained from previous lessons.

Hands-On

Students utilize diverse learning styles and creativity and work cooperatively to create a final project for each lesson.

Results

The Hands-On project culminates in a summary activity that ties the other activities in the chapter together.

Differentiated Instruction

Each section of the Teacher Wraparound Edition of *Economics: Principles and Practices* provides differentiated instruction activities to meet the diverse needs of every student.

Differentiated Instruction

Innovative ideas meet each student's interests and learning styles through point-of-use activities

Additional Support

Provides suggestions for incorporating additional resources based on students' different learning abilities

Leveled Activities

Extends instruction beyond the text by suggesting activities related to content on the page

Dynamic Features

Use the creative features in the textbook to dig deep into the fascinating issues and people covered in the text.

Debates in Economics

Teaches students to analyze different points of view on current issue in economics

Case Study

The case studies show students how economics is an integral part of their daily lives.

Profiles in Economics

Profiles make economics relevant to students.

Using the Teacher Wraparound Edition

Chapter Summary and Assessment

Visual Summary
Summary activities help students to synthesize major chapter themes

Math Practice
Allows students to apply what they have learned in the chapter

Reviews
Students have ample opportunity to check their understanding of chapter content

Critical Thinking
Challenge students with Visual Analysis and Critical Thinking questions

The BIG Ideas in ECONOMICS

As you read *Economics: Principles and Practices*, you will be given help in sorting out all the information you encounter. This textbook organizes economic concepts around Big Ideas. These Big Ideas are the keys that will help you unlock all of the concepts you will study. By recognizing the Big Ideas and how they relate to the different concepts, you will better understand how economics affects you, your family, and your community today and in the future.

▶ **Scarcity is the basic economic problem that requires people to make choices about how to use limited resources.**

As much as we would like to do and buy anything we want at any time, this is not always possible because there are not enough resources to produce all the things people would like to have. Scarcity forces us to make choices about what, how, and for whom we produce.

▶ **Every society has an economic system to allocate goods and services.**

All societies develop economic systems to provide for the wants and needs of their citizens. In the market economy of the United States, buyers and sellers make economic decisions in their best interest.

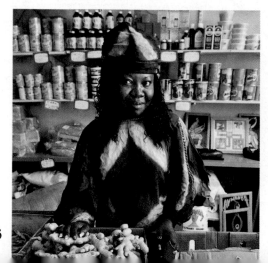

▶ **The profit motive acts as an incentive for people to produce and sell goods and services.**

In a market economy, people open businesses because they hope to be successful and make a profit. They are free to produce any good or service they wish. They can also decide on their own at what prices to offer these goods and services.

▶ **Buyers and sellers voluntarily interact in markets, and market prices are set by the interaction of demand and supply.**

Sellers are free to choose what to sell, and buyers are free to choose what to buy in a market economy. The price for a product is set by the forces of demand and supply.

▶ **Governments strive for a balance between the costs and benefits of their economic policies to promote economic stability and growth.**

The federal government uses a number of economic policies to further economic growth. The government tries to limit the negative effects of its policies while expanding the benefits.

▶ **Governments and institutions help participants in a market economy accomplish their financial goals.**

There are a number of organizations that help people accomplish their financial goals. Governments develop regulations, and institutions such as banks and nonprofits offer ways to save and grow money.

▶ **Economists look at a variety of factors to assess the growth and performance of a nation's economy.**

Over time, economists have devised different ways to measure economic performance. These measures range from factors that affect individuals to those that assess the economies of countries, regions, and the world.

▶ **The labor market, like other markets, is determined by supply and demand.**

The forces of supply and demand influence labor as much as any other market. Factors such as skills required and competition for various jobs determine wages.

▶ **All levels of government use tax revenue to provide essential goods and services.**

We have to pay taxes at the local, state, and federal levels. The governments, in turn, use these revenues to provide goods and services that the market economy does not offer.

▶ **Trade and specialization lead to economic growth for individuals, regions, and nations.**

The more we practice a particular skill, the better we tend to get at it. The same is true in economics. When companies, regions, or nations specialize in the production of goods and services, they become better at it and both the seller and the buyer profit.

▶ **The study of economics helps us deal with global economic issues and global demand on resources.**

Scarcity is an issue not just on a local or national level—it provides challenges on a global scale. Understanding how economics works helps us learn how we can address global problems such as population growth, pollution, and limited resources.

Using The **BIG** Ideas

You will find Big Ideas at the beginning of each chapter of your text. You are asked questions that help you put it all together to better understand how economic concepts are connected— and to see why economics is important to you.

Academic Vocabulary

How Can I Help My Students Learn Academic Vocabulary?

What Is Academic English?

Academic English is the language used by the power elite. Academic vocabulary is the basis for academic English. It is the language used in academics, business, and courts of law. It is the type of English used in professional books, including textbooks, and it contains specific linguistic features that are associated with academic disciplines like social studies. Proficiency in reading and using academic English is especially related to long-term success in all parts of life.

By reinforcing academic vocabulary and academic English, teachers can help learners to access authentic, academic texts—not simplified texts that dummy down the content. In this way, they can provide information that will help build their students' background knowledge rapidly.

What Is Academic Vocabulary?

By the time children have completed elementary school, they must have acquired the knowledge needed to understand academic vocabulary. How many words should they acquire to be able to access their textbooks? A basic 2,000-word vocabulary of high-frequency words makes up 87% of the vocabulary of academic texts. Eight hundred other academic words comprise an additional 8% of the words. Three percent of the remaining words are technical words. The remaining 2% are low-frequency words. There may be as many as 123,000 low-frequency words in academic texts.

Why Should Students Learn Academic Vocabulary?

English learners who have mastered a basic 2,000-word vocabulary are ready to acquire the majority of general words found in their academic texts.

Knowledge of academic words combined with continued acquisition of general words can significantly boost an English learner's comprehension level of academic texts. English learners who learn and practice these words before they graduate from high school are likely to be able to master academic material with more confidence and speed. They waste less time and effort in guessing words or consulting dictionaries than those who only know the basic 2,000 words that characterize general conversation.

Also, consider academic success in terms of measurement and assessment—high school exit exams, the SAT, the ACT, and the GRE—with regard to word mastery. All demand an understanding of academic vocabulary.

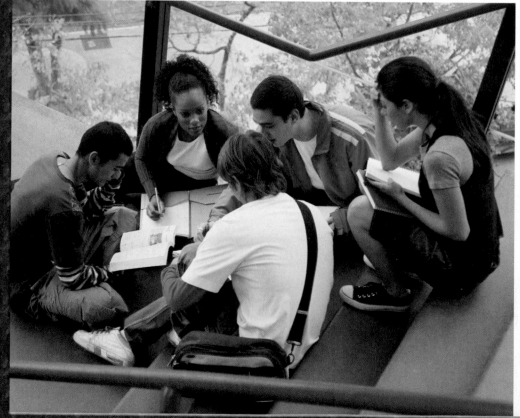

How Do I Include Academic Vocabulary and Academic English in My Teaching?

Teachers can provide their students with rich samples of academic vocabulary and help students understand and attend to the academic English of their text.

To develop academic English, learners must have already acquired a large amount of basic proficiency in the grammar of everyday English.

Academic English should not be taught overtly but rather within contexts that make sense. In terms of instruction, teaching academic English includes providing students with access to core curriculum—in this case, social studies.

Academic English arises not only from knowledge of a linguistic code and cognition but also from social practices in which academic English is used to accomplish communicative goals. The acquisition of academic vocabulary and grammar is necessary to advance the development of academic English.

Tips for Teaching Academic Vocabulary:

✔ **Expose Students to Academic Vocabulary** You do not need to call attention to words students are learning because they will acquire them subconsciously.

✔ **Do Not Correct Students' Mistakes When Using the Vocabulary Words** All vocabulary understanding and spelling errors are developmental and will disappear once the student reads more.

✔ **Help Students Decode the Words Themselves** Once they learn the alphabet, they should be able to decode words. Decoding each word they don't recognize will help them more than trying to focus on sentence structure. Once they can recognize the words, they can read "authentic" texts.

✔ **Do Not Ignore the English Learner in This Process** They can learn academic vocabulary before they are completely fluent in oral English.

✔ **Helping Students Build Academic Vocabulary Leads to Broader Learning** Students who have mastered the basic academic vocabulary are ready to continue acquiring words from the rest of the groups. To help determine which words are in the 2,000-word basic group, refer to West's General Service List of English Words, 1953. The list is designed to serve as a guide for teachers and as a checklist and goal list for students. For additional information about the list, visit: http://www.vuw.ac.nz/lals/research/awl/.

Guidelines for Teaching Academic Vocabulary

1. Direct and planned instruction
2. Models—that have increasingly difficult language
3. Attention to form—pointing out linguistic features of words
4. Practice
5. Motivation
6. Instructional feedback
7. Assessment—on a regular basis

Classroom Activity

Writing About the Global Economy

Give students an impromptu writing assignment. Ask them to write a short essay about one of the topics listed below in the left column. Have students use as many of the academic vocabulary words in the right column as they can in their essay. Give students a time limit for their writing. When completed, ask student volunteers to share their writing. Note what academic vocabulary words they use.

Topic	Academic Vocabulary
The Benefits of Trade	source
	overseas
	benefit
	adapt
	complex
Globalization	technology
	culture
	cooperate
	interact
	network

Meeting the Diverse Needs of Our Students

by Douglas Fisher, Ph.D.

Today's classroom contains students from a variety of backgrounds with a variety of learning styles, strengths, and challenges. As teachers we are facing the challenge of helping students reach their educational potential. With careful planning, you can address the needs of all students in the social studies classroom. The basis for this planning is universal access. When classrooms are planned with universal access in mind, fewer students require specific accommodations.

What Is a Universal Access Design for Learning?

Universal design was first conceived in architectural studies

when business people, engineers, and architects began making considerations for physical access to buildings. The idea was to plan the environment in advance to ensure that everyone had access. As a result, the environment would not have to be changed later for people with physical disabilities, people pushing strollers, workers who had injuries, or others for whom the environment would be difficult to negotiate. The Center for Universal Design at www.design.ncsu.edu/cud defines Universal Design as *the design of products and environments to be usable by all people, to the greatest extent possible, without the need for adaptation or specialized design.*

Universal Design and Access in Education

Researchers, teachers, and parents in education have expanded the development of built-in adaptations and inclusive accommodations from architectural space to the educational experience, especially in the area of curriculum.

In 1998, the National Center to Improve the

Tools of Educators (NCITE), with the partnership of the Center for Applied Special Technology (CAST), proposed an expanded definition of universal design focused on education:

In terms of learning, universal design means the design of instructional materials and activities that allows the learning goals to be achievable by individuals with wide differences in their abilities to see, hear, speak, move, read, write, understand English, attend, organize, engage, and remember.

How Does Universal Design Work in Education?

Universal design and access, as they apply to education and schooling, suggest the following:

✔ **Inclusive Classroom Participation**
Curriculum should be designed with all students and their needs in mind. The Glencoe/McGraw-Hill social studies texts and materials were designed with a wide range of students in mind. For example, understanding that English learners and students who struggle with reading would be using this textbook, vocabulary is specifically taught and reinforced. Similarly, the teacher-support materials provide multiple instructional points to be used depending on the needs of the students in the class. Further, the text is written

such that main ideas are identified for all learners. Activating prior knowledge is also taken into consideration by the text. Connections between what students know and think about are made within the text.

✔ **Maximum Text Readability** In universally designed classrooms that provide access for all students, texts use direct language, clear noun-verb agreements, and clear construct-based wording. In addition to these factors, the Glencoe social studies text uses embedded definitions for difficult terms, provides for specific instruction in reading skills, uses a number of visual representations, and includes note-taking guides.

✔ **Adaptable and Accommodating** The content in this textbook can be easily translated, read aloud, or otherwise changed to meet the needs of students in the classroom. The section and end-of-chapter assessments provide students with multiple ways of demonstrating their content knowledge while also ensuring that they have practice with thinking in terms of multiple-choice questions. Critical thinking and analysis skills are also practiced.

How Is Differentiated Instruction the Key to Universal Access?

To differentiate instruction, teachers must acknowledge student differences in background knowledge and current reading, writing, and English language skills. They must also consider student learning styles and preferences, interests, and needs, and react accordingly. There are a number of general guidelines for differentiating instruction in the classroom to reach all students, including:

✔ **Link Assessment With Instruction** Assessments should occur before, during, and after instruction to ensure that the curriculum is aligned with what students do and do not know. Using assessments in this way allows you to plan instruction for whole groups, small groups, and individual students. Backward planning, where you establish the assessment before you begin instruction, is also important.

✔ **Clarify Key Concepts and Generalizations** Students need to know what is essential and how this information can be used in their future learning.

In addition, students need to develop a sense of the Big Ideas—ideas that transcend time and place.

✔ **Emphasize Critical and Creative Thinking** The content, process, and products used or assigned in the classroom should require that students think about what they are learning. While some students may require support, additional motivation, varied tasks, materials, or equipment, the overall focus on the end product should be stressed.

✔ **Include Teacher- and Student-Selected Tasks** A differentiated classroom includes both teacher- and student-selected activities and tasks. At some points in the lesson or day, the teacher must provide instruction and assign learning activities. In other parts of the lesson, students should be provided choices in how they engage with the content. This balance increases motivation, engagement, and learning.

Classroom Activity

Display a map of imperialism in Africa around 1914. Be sure your map notes which European powers controlled what countries. Discuss with students the general information on the map. Then have them list each country under the correct European power that controlled it.

To differentiate this activity:

- Ask students to imagine they are living at the time of the Boer War. Have students write an editorial to a British newspaper regarding the situation in South Africa.
- Have students tabulate the number of countries controlled by each European power. Have them take the data and create a bar graph that shows who were the most active imperialistic powers at the time.
- Have students compose a ballad about the presence of the British in India, from an Indian's point of view.
- Have students create and present a dialog that might have taken place between a native African and a European during the late 1800s.
- Have students create a map—using whatever material they choose—that shows the major physical features of Africa.
- Have students choose a country of modern Africa with an unstable government to research. Have them write a three-page paper discussing the potential economic growth that could occur there if a stable government were installed.
- Have students list each city they see on the map and write in which country they were located.

How Do I Support Individual Students?

The vast majority of students will thrive in a classroom based on universal access and differentiated instruction. However, wise teachers recognize that no single option will work for all students and that there may be students who require unique systems of support to be successful.

Tips For Instruction

The following tips can support your efforts to help all students reach their maximum potential.

✔ Survey students to discover their individual differences. Use interest inventories of their unique talents so you can encourage contributions in the classroom.

✔ Be a model for respecting others. Adolescents crave social acceptance. The student with learning differences is especially sensitive to correction and criticism, particularly when it comes from a teacher. Your behavior will set the tone for how students treat one another.

✔ Expand opportunities for success. Provide a variety of instructional activities that reinforce skills and concepts.

✔ Establish measurable objectives and decide how you can best help students meet them.

✔ Celebrate successes. Make note of and praise "work in progress."

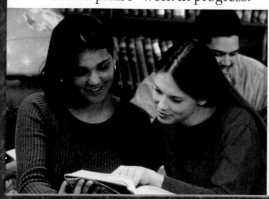

✔ Keep it simple. Point out problem areas if doing so can help a student effect change. Avoid overwhelming students with too many goals at one time.

✔ Assign cooperative group projects that challenge all students to contribute to solving a problem or creating a product.

How Do I Reach Students With Learning Disabilities?

✔ Provide support and structure. Clearly specify rules, assignments, and responsibilities.

✔ Practice skills frequently. Use games and drills to help maintain student interest.

✔ Incorporate many modalities into the learning process. Provide opportunities to say, hear, write, read, and act out important concepts and information.

✔ Link new skills and concepts to those already mastered.

✔ If possible, allow students to record answers on audiotape.

✔ Allow extra time to complete assessments and assignments.

✔ Let students demonstrate proficiency with alternative presentations, including oral reports, role plays, art projects, and musical presentations.

✔ Provide outlines, notes, or tape recordings of lecture material.

✔ Pair students with peer helpers, and provide class time for pair interaction.

How Do I Reach Students With Behavioral Challenges?

✔ Provide a structured environment with clear-cut schedules, rules, seat assignments, and safety procedures.

✔ Reinforce appropriate behavior and model it for students.

✔ Cue distracted students back to the task through verbal signals and teacher proximity.

✔ Set goals that can be achieved in the short term. Work for long-term improvement in the big areas.

How Do I Reach Students With Physical Challenges?

✔ Openly discuss with the student any uncertainties you have about when to offer aid.

✔ Ask parents or therapists and students what special devices or procedures are needed and whether any special safety precautions need to be taken.

✔ Welcome students with physical challenges into all activities, including field trips, special events, and projects.

✔ Provide information to assist class members and adults in their understanding of support needed.

How Do I Reach Students with Visual Impairments?

✔ Facilitate independence. Modify assignments as needed.

✔ Teach classmates how and when to serve as visual guides.

✔ Limit unnecessary noise in the classroom if it distracts the student with visual impairments.

✔ Provide tactile models whenever possible.

✔ Foster a spirit of inclusion. Describe people and events as they occur in the classroom. Remind classmates that the student with visual impairments cannot interpret forms of nonverbal communication.

✔ Provide taped lectures and reading assignments for use outside the classroom.

✔ Team the student with a sighted peer for written work.

How Do I Reach Students With Hearing Impairments?

✔ Seat students where they can see your lip movements easily and where they can avoid any visual distractions.
✔ Avoid standing with your back to the window or light source.
✔ Use an overhead projector so you can maintain eye contact while writing information.
✔ Seat students where they can see speakers.
✔ Write all assignments on the board, or hand out written instructions.
✔ If the student has a manual interpreter, allow both student and interpreter to select the most favorable seating arrangements.
✔ Teach students to look directly at each other when they speak.

How Do I Reach English Learners?

✔ Remember, students' ability to speak English does not reflect their academic abilities.
✔ Try to incorporate the students' cultural experience into your instruction. A bilingual aide may be helpful.
✔ Avoid making references that could be construed as cultural stereotypes.
✔ Preteach important vocabulary and concepts.
✔ Encourage students to preview text before they begin reading.
✔ Remind students not to ignore graphic organizers, photographs, and maps since

there is much information in these visuals.
✔ Use memorabilia and photographs whenever possible to build background knowledge and understanding. An example of this would be coins in a foreign currency or a raw cotton ball to reinforce its importance in history.

How Do I Reach Gifted Students?

✔ Make arrangements for students to take selected subjects early and to work on independent projects.
✔ Ask "what if" questions to develop high-level thinking skills. Establish an environment safe for risk taking.
✔ Emphasize concepts, theories, ideas, relationships, and general-izations about the content.
✔ Promote interest in the past by inviting students to make connections to the present.
✔ Let students express themselves in alternate ways, such as

creative writing, acting, debates, simulations, drawing, or music.
✔ Provide students with a catalog of helpful resources, listing such things as agencies that provide free and inexpensive materials, appropriate community services and programs, and community experts who might be called upon to speak to your students.
✔ Assign extension projects that allow students to solve real-life problems in their communities.

Classroom Activity

Students respond to a subject better when they can make a personal connection to it. With the growing number of students who are Latino or come from other parts of the world, explaining geography through a worldwide theme such as volcanoes can draw them into an awareness of the world as a whole rather than the region from which they came. To develop this awareness and an understanding of latitude and longitude, first display a large world map. Have students research the longitude and latitude of 15 major volcanoes around the world. The library or Internet can provide this information. Have them pinpoint these locations on the map with markers and answer the following:

• What patterns do you see in volcanic activity?
• What causes volcanic activity?
• Where might more volcanoes appear?
• Where in the world are volcanoes still active?

As a follow-up, suggest students go to http://volcano.und.nodak.edu/vwdocs/kids/legends.html to find legends about the origins of some of these volcanoes. Encourage students to share what they find with the class.

Douglas Fisher is a professor at San Diego State University, San Diego, CA.

Backward Mapping

How Can My Instruction Help Students Succeed in a Standards-Based System?

by Emily M. Schell, Ed.D.

Content standards articulate what students should know and be able to do in every social studies classroom. Effective instructional planning based in the standards and maximizing available resources is essential for meaningful teaching and learning of social studies. Planning instruction with educational goals in mind makes for the most effective teaching.

How Do I Map My Curriculum?

Mapping the curriculum from beginning to end, and from the end to the beginning—backward mapping—makes for solid instruction. Mapping out the curriculum allows teachers to achieve several goals. These goals include a better understanding of the standards and content-specific objectives, organization and pacing of the curriculum, and focused assessment related to specific goals and objectives.

✔ **Begin the Process of Curriculum Mapping** To begin, teachers analyze the body of content standards for one grade level. They then compare and contrast these standards to additional sources of information that support effective teaching and learning at that grade level and in that subject area. This process works best with same-grade colleagues who bring varying perspectives and expertise to teaching this subject. As a result of this collaboration, strengths and weaknesses of the standards become apparent. Teachers will have a better understanding of the standards and identify concerns and questions for follow-up while mapping.

✔ **Analyze the Organization of the Standards-Based Content** Most social studies teachers agree with researchers that history is best taught in chronological order. However, some grade-level standards either do not or cannot present the content in chronological order. Rich discussions about themes and concepts tend to emerge, and teachers identify meaningful methods for presenting complex and overlapping information. In this way students will see the connections that transcend chronology.

✔ **Identify the Content and Order of Teaching** A plan is developed to present certain content first, then second, then third, and so on. Folding in content that is either missing from the standards or essential in building background knowledge with students enters the curriculum map as well. Outside resources brought into the classroom are good supplements.

✔ **Separate Overlapping Units** Identify areas of instruction for the topics, themes, Big Ideas, or concepts. It is at this stage that backward planning is introduced for the development of instructional units, which will support the grade-level curriculum map. The instruction must support the planned assessment.

✔ **Map Curriculum at Each Grade Level** Curriculum planning should be shared among grade levels. Teachers will have a better understanding of what knowledge and skills students bring to their coursework if they take into consideration what has been learned previously.

How Do I Use Backward Mapping?

After a year-long course of study is mapped out, each unit must be further developed through backward mapping. You will start with the end in mind—knowing your curricular goals and objectives at the outset, which are often found in the content standards and articulated in the curriculum maps.

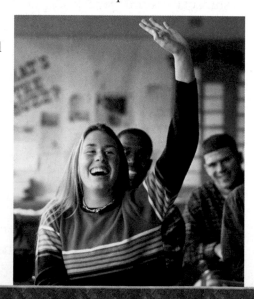

Once goals have been determined, teachers develop assessments that will show progress toward those goals and objectives. In the final step of this backward mapping process, teachers determine meaningful teaching and learning strategies and identify useful resources that support the assessment.

To use backward mapping in developing your units of instruction, consider the following steps:

Step One: Know Your Targets

First, identify exactly what students must know and do in this unit. Analyze content standards and any other resources that support curricular goals and objectives for this unit. As you plan, ask yourself:

✔ What do I want my students to know as a result of this unit?
✔ What skills will students develop during the course of this unit?
✔ How do I describe these goals clearly and concisely to my students so they understand where we should be at the end of this unit?
✔ What essential knowledge will students need to access to make sense of this information?
✔ Do my instructional goals align with strategies identified in the curriculum map?
✔ Have I introduced any Big Ideas that are pertinent to this content?

Step Two: Identify and Develop Assessments

✔ Second, consider the multiple forms of formal and informal assessments that will help you determine to what degree each student has achieved the stated goals and objectives seen in Step One. Some assessments are embedded throughout the instructional unit, while others

come at the end of the unit. Some assessments are performance-based, while others are not. Some are authentic applications of information and skills, while others require the formal recall of information. Ask yourself:

✔ What do I want to know and see from each student?
✔ What are the best methods for students to demonstrate what they know and can do based on the goals and objectives?
✔ How many assessments do I need to determine what students know and can do?
✔ How will I balance informal and formal assessments?
✔ How will I assess students with diverse learning styles, skills, and abilities?
✔ How can I prepare and support students?
✔ How will these assessments promote student progress in social studies?
✔ At what time(s) during the unit will I administer these assessments?

Step Three: Develop Meaningful Instruction

After the assessments for the unit have been determined, consider the meaningful and effective teaching strategies that will support learning and student achievement on assessments. While developing lesson plans for instruction, ask yourself:

✔ How will students learn what they are expected to know?
✔ How will I engage students in the studies of this unit?
✔ In what ways might students relate or connect to this information?
✔ What research-based strategies will be most effective with my students and in these studies?

✔ How will I differentiate my instruction to meet the diverse needs of my students?
✔ How will I scaffold or provide access to the curriculum for my English learners?
✔ What vocabulary requires attention in this unit?
✔ How much time will I have to effectively teach this unit?
✔ How will I use the textbook and other resources to support the goals and objectives for this unit?
✔ What lessons will I develop?
✔ In what sequence will I teach these lessons during this unit?
✔ How will these lessons support the assessments from Step Two?

Step Four: Locate and Manage Resources

Effective teaching and learning of social studies requires the use of multiple forms of text and varied resources. Consider what you have available in your classroom, including your textbook, and identify resources you will add in order to teach this unit successfully. Ask yourself:

✔ What parts of the textbook are required for the lessons determined in Step Three?
✔ What ancillary materials are needed for the lessons in this unit?
✔ What Web sites will I recommend to students to support these lessons?
✔ Do I need to contact guest speakers or obtain outside resources?
✔ What literature resources are available to support this unit?

Emily Schell is Visiting Professor, San Diego State University, and Social Studies Education Director, SDSU City Heights Educational Collaborative, San Diego, CA.

Teaching Maps, Graphs, and Charts

How Can I Use Visuals to Improve Students' Reading Comprehension?

Maps, graphs, and charts are visual tools. By using images rather than words, these tools present complex information in an easy-to-understand format. Teach students the following generalized viewing strategies, and encourage them to apply these strategies as they study each chapter.

✔ **Asking Questions** Students should start by looking over the graphic and asking themselves questions, such as "What is my purpose for looking at this image?" Then students can identify questions they hope to answer, such as "What is being compared?" or "What are the most important features?"

✔ **Finding Answers** Next, students should use the graphic's structural features, such as the title, labels, colors, and symbols, to help them find the answers to their questions. If the source of the graphic is available, students should also determine its reliability.

✔ **Drawing Conclusions** After studying the visual, students should summarize its main points and draw conclusions.

✔ **Connecting** Before moving on, students should relate what they learned from the visual with what they gained from reading the text selection. Students can examine how the visual supports or extends the meaning of the text.

Maps

Maps show the relative size and location of specific geographic areas. There are as many different kinds of maps as there are uses for them. Two of the most common general purpose maps are political maps and physical maps. Political maps show human-made boundaries, such as state and country borders. Physical maps show physical features, such as mountains and lakes. Special purpose maps might show historical change, cultural features, population, land use, or climate.

Parts of Maps

All maps contain parts that assist in interpreting the information. Help students learn to identify the following map parts.

✔ **Title** The map title identifies the area shown on the visual. The title can also identify a map's special focus.

✔ **Map Key** The map key, or legend, explains the symbols presented on the map, thus unlocking the map's information.

✔ **Compass Rose** A compass rose is a direction marker. It is a symbol that points out where the cardinal directions—north, south, east, and west—are positioned.

✔ **Scale** A measuring line, often called a scale bar, indicates the relationship between the distances on the map and the actual distances on Earth. Distance on a map can be determined by measuring the distance between points, then multiplying that measure by the number of miles or kilometers specified in the map scale ratio.

✔ **Latitude and Longitude** Mapmakers use lines of latitude and longitude to pinpoint exact locations on maps and globes. The imaginary horizontal lines that circle the globe from east to

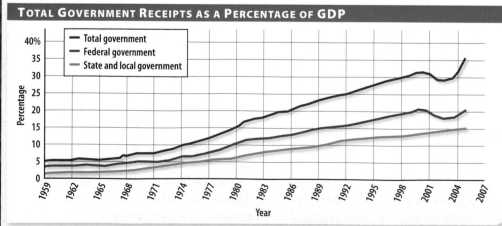

TOTAL GOVERNMENT RECEIPTS AS A PERCENTAGE OF GDP

Legend:
— Total government
— Federal government
— State and local government

Percentage (y-axis): 0, 5, 10, 15, 20, 25, 30, 35, 40%
Year (x-axis): 1959, 1962, 1965, 1968, 1971, 1974, 1977, 1980, 1983, 1986, 1989, 1992, 1995, 1998, 2001, 2004, 2007

Source: *Economic Report of the President, 2006*

west are lines of latitude, also called parallels. The imaginary vertical lines are lines of longitude, also called meridians. Both parallels and meridians are measured in degrees.

Graphs

Graphs are a way of showing numbers or statistics in a clear, easy-to-read way. Because graphs summarize and present information visually, readers have an easier time understanding the data and drawing conclusions. The most common types of graphs are bar graphs, line graphs, circle graphs, and pictographs.

✔ **Bar Graphs** A bar graph shows how two or more subjects or statistics compare. It provides information along two sides or axes. The horizontal axis is the line across the bottom of the graph. The vertical axis is the line along the side. The bars may be either vertical or horizontal. In most cases the labels on one axis show quantity, while the labels on the opposite axis show the categories of data being compared.

✔ **Line Graphs** A line graph shows change over time. Like a bar graph, it organizes information along the horizontal and vertical axes. The horizontal axis usually shows passing time, such as months, years, or decades. The vertical axis usually shows quantity or amount. Sometimes more than one set of data is shown in a line graph. A double-line graph, for instance, plots data for two related quantities, which

may be represented in different colors or patterns.

✔ **Circle Graphs** A circle graph, also called a pie graph, shows how each part or percentage relates to the whole. A circle graph enables a viewer to make comparisons between parts and to analyze the relationship of each part to the whole.

✔ **Pictograph** A pictograph uses rows of small symbols or pictures, each representing a particular amount. Like a bar graph, a pictograph is useful for making comparisons.

Charts

While all charts present information or data in a visual way, the type of chart is often dictated by the nature of the information and by the chart-maker's purposes.

✔ **Tables** Tables show information, including numerical data, in columns and rows. This organized arrangement facilitates comparisons between categories of information. Labels are usually located at the top of each column and on the left-hand side of the table.

✔ **Diagrams** Diagrams are specialized drawings. They can show steps in a process; point out parts of an object, organization, or idea; or explain how something works. Arrows or lines may join parts of a figure and can show relationships between parts or the flow of steps.

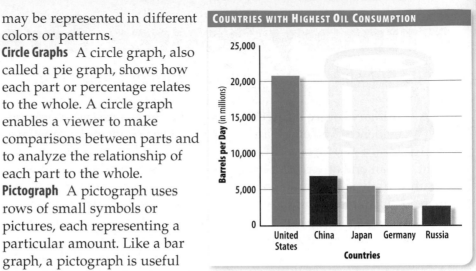

COUNTRIES WITH HIGHEST OIL CONSUMPTION

Classroom Activity

Create a Graph

Graphs can be difficult to interpret and understand. Help students by having them create their own graph. To help students begin thinking about graphs, separate students into small groups. Then explain that each group should take a quick survey of classmates and make a graph to show their survey results. Suggest that students make either a bar graph, line graph, circle graph, or pictograph to show their data. To prompt students' thinking, ask the following questions:

- *Do you play on a sports team? Which sport(s)?*
- *What do you plan to do after high school?*
- *About how much time do you spend watching TV each day? About how much time did you spend on TV when you were 10 years old? When you were five years old?*

After students are done graphing their data, invite each group to share its work. Discuss the types of graphs students made and their reasons for choosing them. Each group should then take the graph that another group has prepared and transfer the information into another type of graph.

Primary Source Strategies

How Do I Use Primary Sources in My Classroom?

A primary source is direct evidence of an event, an idea, a period, or a development. It is an oral or written account obtained from actual participants in an event. Examples of primary sources include the following:

✔ official documents (records, statistics)
✔ political declarations, laws, and rules for governance
✔ speeches and interviews
✔ diaries, memoirs, and oral histories
✔ autobiographies
✔ recipes and cookbooks
✔ advertisements and posters
✔ letters

Physical objects, such as tools and dishes, can be primary sources; so can visual evidence in the form of fine art, photographs, maps, films, and videotapes. Primary sources can also include songs and audio recordings.

Why Use Primary Sources in Your Classroom?

Using primary sources to teach transforms the study of social studies from a passive process to an active one. Students become investigators—finding clues, formulating hypotheses and drawing inferences, making judgments, and reaching conclusions. Bringing primary sources into the classroom stimulates students to think critically about events, issues, and concepts rather than just memorizing dates, names, and generalizations reached by others. Thinking critically then becomes a habit that can help students become good citizens.

How Do I Introduce Students to Primary Sources?

Carefully explain the nature of primary sources when you introduce them to students. Although primary sources contain valuable clues, be sure to alert students that primary sources contain biases and prejudices and must be approached with caution. Every primary source reflects the creator's point of view to some degree. Students must consider the authorship and why the primary source was written.

Choosing Primary Sources

Provide exposure to a variety of source types, including historic photographs, folk or popular music, financial records or household accounts, as well as letters, journals, and historic documents.

When choosing print sources, consider the interests and reading levels of your students. Many texts contain challenging vocabulary and unfamiliar sentence structure. You may need to create a reader's guide that defines key vocabulary and paraphrases the main points of the reading.

Some documents may be too long. Decide whether using an excerpt will provide enough information for students to draw conclusions. Depending upon the topic and your instructional objectives, you may need to provide several different primary sources to expose students to a variety of perspectives.

Decide how students will access the primary sources: through the Internet, the library, a museum, or other print resources. Consider the possibility of an Internet virtual field trip for students. Moving from URL to URL, students can visit museum sites and other Web pages to view artifacts; interpret economic or census data; and read journals, letters, and official documents.

Interpreting a Primary Source

Before students interpret a primary source, they need to know the

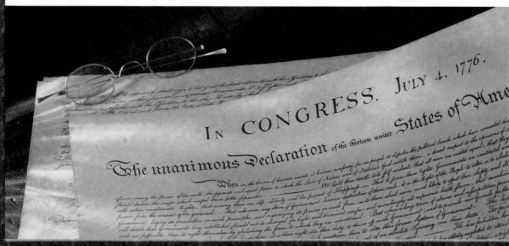

context into which the source fits. Then they can use questions and guidelines, such as those below, to help them analyze and interpret the primary source.

Print Sources

- ✔ Who created the source, and what was the purpose for doing so?
- ✔ Did the writer personally experience or witness the event(s)?
- ✔ At what point did the writer record the information—as it happened or afterward? How long after?
- ✔ Who was the intended audience?
- ✔ Was the writer trying to record facts, express an opinion, or persuade others to take action?
- ✔ What is the author's main message?
- ✔ What values does the document convey?
- ✔ What bias does it reflect?
- ✔ What information about the topic can you gather from this document?
- ✔ Compare this document with what you know about the topic. Does it confirm those ideas or introduce a new perspective?
- ✔ How might other accounts about this topic support or modify the message this source delivers?

Visual Sources

- ✔ Who created the source, and what was the purpose for doing so?
- ✔ What does the image show?
- ✔ What mood does the image convey?
- ✔ Who or what dominates the image or catches your eye?
- ✔ How does the view impact the message?

- ✔ What details can you learn from the image?
- ✔ What is excluded from view?
- ✔ What bias does the visual reflect?
- ✔ What information about the topic can you gather from this visual?
- ✔ How might other visuals about this topic support or modify the message this one delivers?

Audio Sources

- ✔ Who created the source? What was the purpose for creating this source?
- ✔ What is the main idea of the audio?
- ✔ What mood does the recorder's voice convey?
- ✔ What bias does the audio text reflect?
- ✔ What information about the topic can you gather from this audio source?
- ✔ Compare the information in this source with what you already know about the topic. Does it confirm those ideas or introduce a new perspective?
- ✔ How might other sources about this topic support or modify the message that this one delivers?

Exploring Information

Provide a variety of primary sources related to a topic or time period. Have students compare and contrast the items, analyzing the information, making inferences, and drawing conclusions about the period.

Prereading Activities

Present a primary source for students to study at the beginning of a new chapter or topic. Have students analyze the source, using the questions and guidelines presented previously. Then have students make predictions about what they might learn in the upcoming lessons.

Evaluation Activities

Have students evaluate a primary source and tell how it supports or refutes what they learned in the textbook. Alternately, have students read a primary source document that provides one perspective on a topic, and have students write their own account, presenting another perspective or opinion.

Classroom Activity

Use this activity to explore the use of primary sources. This activity is especially beneficial when a less-proficient reader is paired with a more-proficient reader.

1. Before class, make a list of student reading partners. Make sure one of the two is a good reader.
2. Have students read a primary source document (or part of a primary source document), taking turns as they go. They should "mark" any words that they do not understand.
3. After each paragraph, the student pair should stop and paraphrase what it says in their own words.
4. Students should look up unfamiliar words they've marked and create an illustrated dictionary entry for each term (over the course of the year or semester).
5. Ask student pairs to present their paraphrased primary source to the rest of the class.

Test-Taking Strategies

How Can I Help My Students Succeed on Tests?

It's not enough for students to learn social studies facts and concepts—they must be able to show what they know in a variety of test-taking situations.

How Can I Help My Students Do Well on Objective Tests?

Objective tests may include multiple choice, true/false, and matching questions. Applying the following strategies can help students do their best on objective tests.

Multiple-Choice Questions

✔ Students should read the directions carefully to learn what answer the test requires— the best answer or the right answer. This is especially important when answer choices include "all of the above" or "none of the above."

✔ Advise students to watch for negative words in the questions, such as *not, except, unless, never,* and *so forth.* If the question contains a negative, the correct answer choice is the one that does not fit.

✔ Students should try to mentally answer the question before reading the answer choices.

✔ Students should read all the answer choices and cross out those that are obviously wrong. Then they should choose an answer from those that remain.

True/False Questions

✔ It is important that students read the entire question before answering. For an answer to be true, the entire statement must be true. If one part of a statement is false, the answer should be marked False.

✔ Remind students to watch for words like *all, never, every,* and *always.* Statements containing these words are often false.

Matching Questions

✔ Students should read through both lists before they mark any answers.

✔ Unless an answer can be used more than once, students should cross out each choice as they use it.

✔ Using what they know about grammar can help students find the right answer. For instance, when matching a word with its definition, the definition is often the same part of speech (noun, verb, adjective, and so forth) as the word.

How Can I Help My Students Do Well on Essay Tests?

Essay tests require students to provide thorough and well-organized written responses, in addition to telling what they know. Help students use the following strategies on essay tests.

✔ **Analyze** To analyze means to systematically and critically examine all parts of an issue or event.

✔ **Classify or Categorize** To classify or categorize means to put people, things, or ideas into groups, based on a common set of characteristics.

✔ **Compare and Contrast** To compare is to show how things are similar, or alike. To contrast is to show how things are different.

✔ **Describe** To describe means to present a sketch or an impression. Rich details, especially details that appeal to the senses, flesh out a description.

✔ **Discuss** To discuss means to systematically write about all sides of an issue or event.

✔ **Evaluate** To evaluate means to make a judgment and support it with evidence.

✔ **Explain** To explain means to clarify or make plain.

✔ **Illustrate** To illustrate means to provide examples or to show with a picture or other graphic.

✔ **Infer** To infer means to read between the lines or to use knowledge and experience to draw conclusions, make a generalization, or form a prediction.

✔ **Justify** To justify means to prove or to support a position with specific facts and reasons.

✔ **Predict** To predict means to tell what will happen in the future, based on an understanding of prior events and behaviors.

- ✔ **State** To state means to briefly and concisely present information.
- ✔ **Summarize** To summarize means to give a brief overview of the main points of an issue or event.
- ✔ **Trace** To trace means to present the steps or stages in a process or event in sequential or chronological order.

Read the Question

The key to writing successful essay responses lies in reading and interpreting questions correctly. Teach students to identify and underline key words in the questions and to use these words to guide them in understanding what the question asks. Help students understand the meaning of some of the most common key words, listed in the chart on the previous page.

Plan and Write the Essay

After students understand the question, they should follow the writing process to develop their answer. Encourage students to follow the steps below to plan and write their essays.

1. Map out an answer. Make lists, webs, or an outline to plan the response.
2. Decide on an order in which to present the main points.
3. Write an opening statement that directly responds to the essay question.
4. Write the essay. Expand on the opening statement. Support key points with specific facts, details, and reasons.
5. Write a closing statement that brings the main points together.
6. Proofread to check for spelling, grammar, and punctuation.

How Can I Help My Students Prepare for Standardized Tests?

Students can follow the steps below to prepare for standardized assessments they are required to take.

- ✔ **Read About the Test** Students can familiarize themselves with the format of the test, the types of questions that will be asked, and the amount of time they will have to complete the test. Emphasize that it is very important for students to budget their time during test-taking.
- ✔ **Review the Content** Consistent study throughout the school year will help students build social studies knowledge and understanding. If there are specific objectives or standards that are tested on the exam, help students review these facts or skills to be sure they are proficient.
- ✔ **Practice** Provide practice, ideally with real released tests, to build students' familiarity with the content, format, and timing of the real exam. Students should practice all the types of questions they will encounter on the test—multiple choice, short answer, true or false, and extended response.
- ✔ **Pace** Students should pace themselves differently depending on how the test is administered. If the test is timed, students should not allow themselves to become stuck on any one question. As students practice, they should try to increase the number of questions they can answer correctly. If the test is untimed, students should work slowly and carefully. If students have trouble with an item, they should mark it and come back to it later.
- ✔ **Analyze Practice Results** Help students improve test-taking performance by analyzing their test-taking strengths and weaknesses.

Spend time discussing students' completed practice tests, explaining why particular answers are right or wrong. Help students identify what kinds of questions they had the most difficulty with. Look for patterns in errors and then tailor instruction to review the appropriate test-taking skills or social studies content.

Classroom Activity

Below is an example of an activity to incorporate assessment review in the classroom. Frequently reviewing graded tests is a great way for students to assess their test-taking skills. It also gives teachers the opportunity to teach test-taking strategies and review content. As the class rereads each test question, guide students to think logically about their answer choices. Show students how to:

1. Read each question carefully to determine its meaning.
2. Look for key words in the question to support their answers.
3. Recognize synonyms in the answer choices that may match phrases in the question.
4. Narrow down answer choices by eliminating ones that don't make sense.
5. Anticipate the answer before looking at the answer choices.
6. Circle questions of which they are unsure and go back to them later. Sometimes a clue will be found in another question on the test.

Alternative Assessment Strategies

How Can I Go Beyond Tests to Assess Students' Understanding of Social Studies Facts and Concepts?

In response to the growing demand for accountability in the classroom, educators must use multiple assessment measures to accurately gauge student performance. In addition to quizzes, tests, essay exams, and standardized tests, assessment today incorporates a variety of performance-based measures and portfolio opportunities.

Performance assessment is a way of teaching and learning that involves both process and product. It is not just a testing strategy. Performance assessment activities provide hands-on approaches to learning concepts. Through activities students are able to actually experience these concepts rather than just reading and listening about them. These activities also help students become aware of diverse audiences for their work. Students are also involved in developing the process that leads to the finished product.

Performance assessment tasks are based on what is most essential in the curriculum and what is interesting to the student.

What Are Some Typical Performance-Based Assessments?

There are many kinds of performance-based assessments. They all share one common characteristic—they challenge students to create products that demonstrate what they know. One good way to present a performance assessment is in the form of an open-ended question.

Writing

Performance-based writing assessments challenge students to apply their knowledge of social studies concepts and information in a variety of written ways. Writing activities are most often completed by one student, rather than by a group.

✔ **Journals** Students write from the perspective of a historical character or a citizen of a particular historical era.

✔ **Letters** Students write a letter from one historical figure to another or from a historical figure to a family member or other audience.

✔ **Position Paper or Editorial** Students explain a controversial issue and present their own opinion and recommendations, supported with strong evidence and convincing reasons.

✔ **Newspaper** Students write a variety of stories from the perspective of a reporter living in a particular historical time period. This could also involve the writing of editorials or letters to the editor.

✔ **Biographies and Autobiographies** Students write about historical figures either from the third person point of view (biography) or from the first person (autobiography).

✔ **Creative Stories** Students integrate historical events into a piece of fiction, incorporating the customs, language, and geography of the period.

✔ **Poems and Songs** Students follow the conventions of a particular type of song or poem as they tell about a historical event or person.

✔ **Research Reports** Students synthesize information from a variety of sources into a well-developed research report.

Oral Presentations

Oral presentations allow students to demonstrate their social studies literacy before an audience. Oral presentations are often group efforts, although this need not be the case.

✔ **Simulations** Students hold simulations, or reenactments, of actual events, such as trials, acts of civil disobedience, battles, speeches, and so forth.

✔ **Debates** Students debate two or more sides of a historical policy or issue. Students can debate from a contemporary perspective or in a role play in which they assume a viewpoint held by a historical character.

✔ **Interview** Students conduct a mock interview of a historical character or bystander.

- ✔ **Oral Reports** Students present the results of research efforts in a lively oral report. This report may be accompanied by visuals.
- ✔ **Skits and Plays** Students use historical events as the basis for a play or skit. Details should accurately reflect customs, language, and the setting of the period.

Visual Presentations

Visual presentations allow students to demonstrate their social studies understandings in a variety of visual formats. Visual presentations can be either group or individual projects.

- ✔ **Model** Students make a model to demonstrate or represent a process, a place, an event, a battle, an artifact, or a custom.
- ✔ **Museum Exhibit** Students create a rich display of materials around a topic. Typical displays might include models, illustrations, photographs, videos, writings, and audiotaped explanations.
- ✔ **Graph or Chart** Students analyze and represent historical data in a line graph, bar graph, table, or other chart format.
- ✔ **Drawing** Students represent or interpret a historical event or period through illustration, including political cartoons.
- ✔ **Posters and Murals** Posters and murals may include maps, time lines, diagrams, illustrations, photographs, and written explanations that reflect students' understandings of historical information.
- ✔ **Quilt** Students sew or draw a design for a patchwork quilt that shows a variety of perspectives, events, or issues related to a key topic.

- ✔ **Videotapes** Students film a video to show historical fiction or to preserve a simulation of a historical event.
- ✔ **Multimedia Presentation or Slide Show** Students create a computer-generated multimedia presentation containing historical information and analysis.

How Are Performance Assessments Scored?

There are a variety of means used to evaluate performance tasks. Some or all of the following methods may be used.

- ✔ **Scoring Rubrics** A scoring rubric is a set of guidelines for assessing the quality of a process and/or product. It sets out criteria used to distinguish acceptable responses from unacceptable ones, generally along a scale from excellent to poor. Rubrics may be used as guidelines as the students prepare their products. They are also commonly used for self-assessment.
- ✔ **Models of Excellent Work** Teacher-selected models of excellent work concretely illustrate expectations and help students set goals for their own projects.
- ✔ **Student Self-Assessment** Common methods of self-assessment include ranking work in relation to the model, using a scoring rubric, and writing their own goals and then evaluating how well they have met the goals they set for themselves. Regardless of which method or methods students use, they should be encouraged to evaluate their behaviors and processes, as well as the finished product.

- ✔ **Peer or Audience Assessment** Many of the performance tasks target an audience other than the classroom teacher. If possible, the audience of peers should give the student feedback. Have the class create rubrics for specific projects together.
- ✔ **Observation** As students carry out their performance tasks, you may want to formally observe students at work. Start by developing a checklist, identifying all the specific behaviors and understandings you expect students to demonstrate. Then observe students as they carry out performance tasks and check off the behaviors as you observe them.
- ✔ **Interviews** As a form of ongoing assessment, you may want to conduct interviews with students, asking them to analyze, explain, and assess their participation in performance tasks. When projects take place over an extended period of time, you can hold periodic interviews as well as exit interviews. In this way the interview process allows you to gauge the status of the project and to guide students' efforts along the way.

The Stock Market Game™

More THAN A GAME
AN *education* FOR LIFE

What is the Stock Market Game?

The Stock Market Game (SMG) is a comprehensive, engaging real-world program that advances student academic achievement in the core disciplines and enhances understanding of investment concepts among learners of all ages.

The SMG program is a national investor education program targeting students in grades 4–12. It is administered locally by SMG Coordinators at local councils for economic education, not-for-profit organizations, universities, and Newspaper in Education programs.

How does it work?

Students work cooperatively in teams of three to five to invest a virtual $100,000 in stocks and mutual funds listed on the three major U.S. markets: the New York Stock Exchange, the NASDAQ, and the American Stock Exchange.

In the SMG program, students are in full control of the creation and management of their virtual team portfolio, including company research, stock and fund selection, and whether to buy, sell, or hold.

How do I get more information?

Information about the SMG program is available on our Web site at *www.stockmarketgame.org* or by calling the **Foundation for Investor Education** at (212) 618-0519.

Are curriculum materials provided?

The SMG program's teaching materials distinguish it from other trading simulations. SMG is an educational program. Once a teacher has registered teams, he or she receives an ID and password that provides instant access to lesson plans, technical guides, and support material in the SMG's online Teacher Support Center.

What's the cost?

Fees associated with participating in the SMG program are determined by local distributors, so they may vary from region to region. Please visit The Stock Market Game Web site (*www.stockmarketgame.org*) for the most up-to-date information about your local SMG program.

Who sponsors the SMG Program?

The Stock Market Game is a trademarked program of the Foundation for Investor Education (FIE), an affiliate of the Securities Industry and Financial Markets Association (SIFMA). SMG is supported nationally and locally by securities industry firms, SIA Districts, the National Council on Economic Education, Newspapers in Education, and other organizations involved in economic and financial literacy education.

Foundation for Investor Education

120 Broadway, 35th Floor,
New York, NY 10271-0080

212-618-0519
212-968-0901 fax
smg@sifma.com

The Challenge

The Federal Reserve Banks invite high school teams to enter the Fed Challenge. This multilevel national competition is designed to bring real-world economics into the classroom.

Goals

- To increase understanding of the Federal Reserve's role in setting U.S. monetary policy
- To develop students' research, cooperation, presentation, and critical-thinking skills
- To promote interest in economics, not only as a subject for undergraduate and postgraduate study but as the basis for a career
- To foster a closer relationship between schools and participating Federal Reserve Banks

How It Works: Presentations and Judges' Q&A

The Fed Challenge is a **25-minute performance-based assessment** conducted at participating Federal Reserve Banks and branches. Each performance consists of two parts: a **15-minute presentation**—inspired by the work of the Federal Open Market Committee (FOMC)—and a **10-minute question-and-answer session.**

High school teams (only one per school), made up of five students each, gather research to make a presentation, including the following:
- An analysis of economic and financial conditions (as of the day of the presentation)
- A near-term forecast of economic, financial, and international conditions of critical importance in developing monetary policy (e.g., unemployment, inflation, output, etc.)
- Identification of risks to the economy that should be of special concern for monetary policy makers
- A recommendation to increase, decrease, or leave unchanged the level of short-term interest rates

Following the presentation, a panel of judges—typically made up of Federal Reserve staff members, financial professionals, and educators—question the team about its analysis, forecast, and recommendation, and about the Federal Reserve's role in developing and implementing monetary policy.

Scoring

Judges will score teams based on five criteria:
1. Knowledge of the Federal Reserve's role in developing and implementing monetary policy
2. Responses to judges' questions
3. Quality of the presentation
4. Quality of the research and analysis
5. Evidence of teamwork and cooperation

All rounds of the Fed Challenge—from district competitions to a NATIONAL championship—use the same scoring rubric and adhere to the following rules: Students may refer to, but not read from, notes or scripts. Each team member must play a substantial role in making the presentation. More than one team member may answer a judge's question. While huddling to formulate a response to a judge's question is permitted, teams are cautioned that lengthy and excessive huddling will result in points being deducted, to the extent that it significantly limits the number of questions posed.

Awards, Prizes, and Endorsements

Citibank has established the **Citibank Scholarships and Grants for the Fed Challenge.** As a result, the team that wins the National Championship will be awarded $50,000, composed of $35,000 in scholarships ($7,000 per team member), a $5,000 achievement award (for the teacher), and a $10,000 grant to set up an in-school economics laboratory.

Each of the other national finalist teams will take home a total of $25,000, composed of $20,000 in scholarship money ($4,000 per student), a $2,000 achievement award (for the teacher), and a $3,000 grant to set up an in-school economics laboratory.

The **McGraw-Hill Companies** will sponsor a reception in Washington, D.C., for all students and teachers of Federal Reserve District champion teams.

Registration and More Information

- Outside the 212 area code, call toll free 1-877-FED-CHLG (1-877-333-2454)
- In area codes 212, 718, 516 and 914, call 212-720-1836
- Web site: www.federalreserveeducation.org/teachers/ FedChallenge/FedChallenge_intro.htm

Sample Fed Challenge Questions

Questions from Fed Challenge judges generally are from the following categories:

- Questions based upon the presentation
- Interpretive questions
- Hypothetical questions
- Program learning or evaluative questions

The following questions from previous competitions provide examples of these types of questions.

1. On the fiscal policy side, how would the passage of a federal balanced budget measure affect the Fed's monetary policy decisions? Do you think balancing the federal budget is an important goal?

2. What is the impact of the nation's trade deficit on U.S. growth prospects?

3. What did you learn from participating in the Fed Challenge?

4. What is the primary goal of monetary policy? What do you think the goal(s) should be?

5. In your own words, explain the Phillips Curve. What is it and what does it show? Why do some economists question the validity of the Phillips Curve? Is there any justification to question its validity?

6. The CPI (consumer price index) and PPI (producer price index) are recognized measures of inflation. Why in your presentation did you include capacity utilization as a measure of inflation?

7. How would movement in the unemployment rate, wages, salaries, benefits, and total compensation figure into your analysis of an inflationary trend? Are you worried about recent gas and food price movements? Explain the concept of Core CPI and why it is important.

8. Should all FOMC (Federal Open Market Committee) members be appointed by the U.S. president and confirmed by the U.S. Senate?

9. Talk about the issues involved in trying to balance inflation and unemployment in the short run and in the long run.

10. The most recent rate hike resulted in letters of protest from several members of Congress. How would you respond to criticism that the Fed is not considering the consequences of unemployment, which may arise from rate hikes?

Fundamental Economic Concepts

UNIT PACING CHART			
	Chapter 1	**Chapter 2**	**Chapter 3**
Day 1	Unit Opener Chapter Opener Section 1	Chapter Opener Section 1	Chapter Opener Section 1
Day 2	BusinessWeek Newsclip Section 2 Profiles in Economics	Case Study Section 2 BusinessWeek Newsclip	Profiles in Economics Section 2
Day 3	Section 3 Case Study	Section 3 Profiles in Economics	Case Study Section 3 BusinessWeek Newsclip
Day 4	Review Chapter Assessment	Review Chapter Assessment	Review Chapter Assessment
Day 5	Debates in Economics	The Global Economy & You	

Teacher to Teacher

Lorraine Dumerer
R.L. Turner
High School
Carrollton, Texas

Follow Your Economic System Divide students in small groups. Assign an economic system to each group. Give each group a specific amount of resources in a bag, which are not identical, just as in the real world. (Bags contain commonly found items: index cards, clips, markers, empty small boxes, papers, rubber bands, tape, pipe cleaners, straws, ties, yarn, and so on.) All groups get "capital" such as hole-punches, scissors, rulers, and staplers. Limit the tools based on the economic system.

Each group should create a functioning object that a society would desire, using all the resources. Groups should name the object and demonstrate or describe its function. Groups should stay in the role of the economic system assigned and answer the basic economic questions. Students have 30 minutes to work and 2 minutes to present. A rubric for this activity could include the following: efficient use of resources, demonstration, name of product, works as system's society might, describe system and its functioning, identify economy with this pattern.

Author Note

Dear Economics Teacher:

You may be surprised to learn that there was a time when I wasn't very interested in economics. Come to think of it, I wasn't very interested in going to college either, although my dad clearly had other plans for me.

All of that changed in my senior year of college when I visited Hungary during the height of the Cold War. I was on a study-abroad program at the time, and our professor had just taken us over the Austro-Hungarian border to a popular park that overlooked the city of Budapest. It was a cold December evening, with several inches of snow on the ground brightly lit by a full moon. By all accounts, the view should have been beautiful, if not spectacular—but it wasn't.

Instead, the landscape was cold, alien, and downright dreary. Even now I can remember asking: What is wrong with this scene? Why is it so depressing? Then it dawned on me that there was no color in the landscape. Here was a major European city, but everything was in shades of black and white. Instead of looking out at a sea of bright red, green, blue, and yellow lights, all I saw were dreary white streetlights and faded yellow reflections coming from the windows of buildings and apartments.

Then I remembered what I learned in economics: Hungary had a command economy where consumer goods were so scarce that people had to wait in line to make purchases. They even had to get on a waiting list of many years to buy a car. Advertising as we know it, with brightly colored lights to promote products and attract consumers, was unheard of.

This was truly a seminal event in my life because I realized that a country's economy actually made a difference. My visit to Budapest was the beginning of a lifelong search to figure out how things work. It's been fun, and it's been rewarding. I hope that you share my passion for economics and come to appreciate the many ways in which the economy affects us and we affect it.

Gary E. Clayton

Gary Clayton, Ph.D.
Author

UNIT 1 Fundamental Economic Concepts

Unit Objectives

After studying this unit, students will be able to:

- **Define** economics and its fundamental principles.
- **Differentiate** between traditional, command, market, and mixed economies.
- **Identify** the major types of business and nonprofit organizations in the United States.

Unit Overview

Unit 1 provides a basic introduction to and an overview of economics.

Chapter 1 focuses on the fundamental economic problem of scarcity and introduces terms necessary to the study and understanding of economics.

Chapter 2 continues the discussion of decision making and focuses on the different economic systems.

Chapter 3 covers the various kinds of business and nonprofit institutions that operate in our economy.

Because of scarcity, societies ▶ have to make careful choices about how to use resources such as energy and land.

Activity: Launching the Unit

Wants Have pairs of students interview their partners to obtain the following information: (1) Give an example of a want. (2) What inputs are necessary to produce the want? *(factors of production—land, labor, capital, and entrepreneurship)* (3) Do you have any part in the process necessary to get your want? (Does the student work?) (4) What can you do to get your want? After the interviews, ask the class what is necessary to obtain their wants. Point out that wants are purchased in the marketplace and cost money that most people must earn by selling their labor, or working. In other words, we trade our productive efforts to satisfy our wants. **OL**

Making It Relevant

Ask: How would you feel about owning your own company? Explain. *(Answers will vary.)* Tell students that in a phone survey, the Gallup organization questioned a random sample of approximately 1,000 teenagers across the country on their thoughts about entrepreneurship. The sample ranged in age from 14 to 19 years and was evenly divided between males and females. Almost 7 out of every 10 respondents said that they wanted to be entrepreneurs. Asked if they would rather be a manager of a large company or the owner of a small company, most chose the latter. Discuss students' opinions on the subject. **BL**

BusinessWeek ONLINE

To find up-to-date news and analysis on the economy, business, technology, markets, entrepreneurs, investments, and finance, have students search feature articles and special reports on the BusinessWeek Web site, www.businessweek.com.

Extra Credit Project

Have students create a television-viewing log chronicling the number and types of economics-related items presented on the nightly news. Suggest that some students watch national newscasts on the networks, that others watch national newscasts on cable (such as CNN or MSNBC), and that still others watch local newscasts. Students should record the date, the subject of the item, and the length of time devoted to the item. When study of the chapter is completed, have students compare and discuss their logs, noting how much news related to economics was presented. **OL**

Planning Guide

Key to Ability Levels	Key to Teaching Resources
BL Below level **AL** Above level	📁 Print Material 💿 DVD
OL On level **ELL** English Language Learners	💿 CD-Rom 🖨 Transparency

Levels					Resources	Chapter Opener	Section 1	Section 2	Section 3	Chapter Assess
BL	OL	AL	ELL							
					FOCUS					
BL	OL	AL	ELL	🖨	**Daily Focus Skills Transparencies**		1, 5, 23	4, 65	2, 97	
					TEACH					
BL	OL		ELL	📁	**Guided Reading Activities***		p. 1	p. 2	p. 3	
BL	OL	AL	ELL	📁	**Economic Content Vocabulary Activities***		p. 1	p. 1	p. 1	
	OL	AL		📁	**Critical Thinking Activities**		p. 1	p. 1	p. 1	
BL	OL		ELL	📁	**Reading Essentials and Note-Taking Guide***		p. 1	p. 4	p. 7	
		AL		📁	**Enrichment Activities**				p. 1	
	OL	AL		📁	**Free Enterprise Activities**		p. 1			
BL	OL	AL	ELL	📁	**Primary and Secondary Source Readings**			p. 3		
BL	OL	AL	ELL	📁	**Economic Cartoons**			p. 8		
BL	OL	AL	ELL	📁	**Hands-On Economics**		p. 1			
BL	OL	AL	ELL	🖨	**Economic Concepts Transparencies, Strategies, and Activities**		p. 1	p. 5	pp. 3, 5	
BL	OL	AL	ELL	📁	**Math Practice for Economics**				p. 1	
BL	OL		ELL	📁	**High School Reading in the Content Area Strategies and Activities**	✓	✓	✓	✓	✓
BL	OL	AL	ELL	🖨	**High School Writing Process Transparencies**	✓	✓	✓	✓	✓
BL	OL	AL	ELL	📁	**Writer's Guidebook**	✓	✓	✓	✓	✓
BL	OL	AL	ELL	💿	**StudentWorks Plus CD-ROM**	✓	✓	✓	✓	✓
BL	OL	AL	ELL	💿	**Vocabulary PuzzleMaker CD-ROM**	✓	✓	✓	✓	✓

*Also available in Spanish

- Interactive Lesson Planner
- Interactive Teacher Edition
- Fully editable blackline masters
- Economics & You videos

- Differentiated Lesson Plans
- Printable reports of daily assignments
- Standards tracking system

Levels					Resources	Chapter Opener	Section 1	Section 2	Section 3	Chapter Assess
BL	OL	AL	ELL							
					TEACH (continued)					
BL	OL	AL	ELL		**Economics & You Video Program DVD— *What is Economics?***	✓	✓	✓	✓	✓
BL	OL	AL	ELL		**Graph Coach CD-ROM**	✓	✓	✓	✓	✓
Teacher Resources					**Differentiated Instruction Strategies**	✓	✓	✓	✓	✓
					Success with English Learners	✓	✓	✓	✓	✓
					Presentation Plus! CD-ROM	✓	✓	✓	✓	✓
					ASSESS					
BL	OL	AL	ELL		**Section Quizzes and Chapter Tests**		p. 5	p. 6	p. 7	pp. 9, 13
BL	OL	AL	ELL		**Authentic Assessment Strategies and Activities**		p. 1			
BL	OL	AL	ELL		***ExamView® Assessment Suite* CD-ROM**		1-1	1-2	1-3	Ch. 1
BL	OL	AL	ELL		**Interactive Tutor Self-Assessment CD-ROM**		1-1	1-2	1-3	
					CLOSE					
BL			ELL		**Reteaching Activities***		p. 1	p. 1	p. 1	
BL	OL		ELL		**Reading and Study Skills Foldables**		p. 43	p. 43	p. 48	
BL	OL	AL	ELL		**Graphic Organizer Transparencies**		p. 37	p. 35		

*Also available in Spanish

Activity
Using the Glencoe Web Site

Student Web Activities

Technology Product

The Glencoe Web site provides Web activities to students that reinforce and enrich chapter content. The Student Web Activities

- introduce topics relevant to chapter content, along with links to Web sites that provide information about the topics;
- prompt students to complete tasks specific to the activity;
- assess student comprehension of the material.

Objectives

The Student Web Activities help students

- learn online research and study skills;
- practice reading and comprehension skills.

Steps

Provide students with the following steps to complete the activities:

- Locate the Web page for the textbook being studied on the Glencoe Web site glencoe.com.
- Click on **Student Center** under the textbook title.
- In the Student Center, select a unit from the Unit Resources menu and a chapter from the Chapter Activities menu using the drop-down arrows.
- Click on the **Student Web Activities** link.
- Have students complete the activity on the page, clicking on the featured Web link for the chapter selected and answering the activity questions.

Provide students with an e-mail address to submit their answers for grading.

Economics ONLINE

	Student	Teacher	Parent
Beyond the Textbook	●	●	●
Chapter Overviews	●	●	●
ePuzzles and Games	●		●
Concepts in Motion	●		●
Multi-Language Glossaries	●		●
Online Student Edition	●	●	●
Self-Check Quizzes	●		●
Student Web Activities	●		●
Study Central™	●		●
Time Current Events	●	●	●
Teaching Today		●	
Vocabulary eFlashcards	●		●
Web Activity Lesson Plans		●	

Glencoe Media Center

> glencoe.com

Study-To-Go
- Vocabulary eFlashcards
- Self-Check Quizzes

> **Audio/Video**
- Student Edition Audio
- Spanish Summaries
- Economics & You Videos

READING SUPPORT FROM
JAMESTOWN EDUCATION

- **Timed Readings Plus in Social Studies** helps students increase their reading rate and fluency while maintaining comprehension. The 400-word passages are similar to those found on state and national assessments.

- **Reading in the Content Area: Social Studies** concentrates on six essential reading skills that help students better comprehend what they read. The book includes 75 high-interest nonfiction passages written at increasing levels of difficulty.

- **Reading Social Studies** includes strategic reading instruction and vocabulary support in Social Studies content for both ELLs and native speakers of English. www.jamestowneducation.com

---

Reading List Generator CD-ROM

GLENCOE BOOKLINK 3

Use this database to search more than 30,000 titles to create a customized reading list for your students.

- Reading lists can be organized by students' reading level, author, genre, theme, or area of interest.

- The database provides Degrees of Reading Power™ (DRP) and Lexile™ readability scores for all selections.

- A brief summary of each selection is included.

Leveled reading suggestions for this chapter:
For students at a Grade 10 reading level:
- *Oprah Winfrey: Rising Above, Reaching Out,* by Henry Billings and Melissa Billings

For students at a Grade 11 reading level:
- *Influential Economists,* by Marie Bussing-Burks

For students at a Grade 12 reading level:
- *How Cool Is Comics Lit,* by Charles McGrath

* Review suggested books before assigning them.

NCEE

National Council on Economic Education

Voluntary Standards Emphasized in Chapter 1

Content Standard 1 Productive resources are limited. Therefore, people cannot have all the goods and services they want; as a result, they must choose some things and give up others.

Content Standard 2 Effective decision making requires comparing the additional costs of alternatives with the additional benefits. Most choices involve doing a little more or a little less of something: few choices are "all or nothing" decisions.

Content Standard 14 Entrepreneurs are people who take the risks of organizing productive resources to make goods and services. Profit is an important incentive that leads entrepreneurs to accept the risks of business failure.

Resources Available from NCEE
- Virtual Economics®: An Interactive Center for Economic Education Version 3.0
- Capstone: The Nation's High School Economics Course
- Focus: High School Economics, Second Edition
- Economics in Action

To order these materials, or to contact your State Council on Economic Education about workshops and programs, call 1-800-338-1192 or visit the NCEE Web site at store.ncee.net.

The BIG Idea

As students study the chapter, remind them to consider the chapter-based Big Idea. The **Essential Question** in the chapter launch activity below ties in to the Big Idea and helps students think about and understand important chapter concepts. In addition, the Hands-On Chapter Project relates the content from each section to the Big Idea. The steps in each section build on each other and culminate in the Wrap-Up Activity on the Visual Summary page.

Economics & You Video
To generate student interest and provide a springboard for class discussion, access the Economics & You Topic 1 video, **What is Economics?**, at glencoe.com or on the video DVD.

FOLDABLES **Study Organizer**
Dinah Zike's Foldables are three-dimensional, interactive graphic organizers that help students practice basic writing skills, review key vocabulary terms, and identify main ideas. Have students complete this chapter's Foldable activity or activities in *Dinah Zike's Reading and Study Skills Foldables* booklet. **OL**

Economics ONLINE
Introduce students to chapter content and key terms by having them access *Chapter 1—Chapter Overviews* at glencoe.com.

CHAPTER 1

What Is Economics?

Why It Matters

Congratulations on being selected to head up the prom committee! Now you must decide on location, music, and refreshments. What factors do you need to consider when making your choices? In groups of four, determine your budget and identify possible locations, music providers, and food. Read Chapter 1 to learn how your prom selections, like all economic decisions, require you to make choices about how to best use limited resources.

The BIG Idea

Scarcity is the basic economic problem that requires people to make careful choices about how to use limited resources.

Because of limited resources, ▶ consumers must make choices.

Economics ONLINE **Chapter Overview** Visit the *Economics: Principles and Practices* Web site at glencoe.com and click on *Chapter 1—Chapter Overviews* to preview chapter information.

4   UNIT 1

Activity: Launching the Chapter

Categorizing Have students brainstorm a list of common needs and wants such as food items, clothing, or entertainment expenses. Divide students into small groups and assign each group several of the items on the list. Ask them to explain why each item proves important to many people. **Essential Question:** How do limitations on people's time and income affect these needs and wants? *(Students may suggest that these limitations cause people to first focus on acquiring the things they need, before devoting additional time and income to the things they want.)* Have students also use Internet resources and financial magazines to obtain pictures of the items on their list. Students should then create a poster listing needs and wants. **OL**

SECTION 1
Scarcity and the Science of Economics

GUIDE TO READING

Section Preview

In this section, you will learn why scarcity is the basic economic problem that faces every society and why scarcity requires us to make choices.

Content Vocabulary

- scarcity (p. 6)
- economics (p. 6)
- need (p. 6)
- want (p. 6)
- factors of production (p. 8)
- land (p. 8)
- capital (p. 8)
- capital good (p. 8)
- labor (p. 8)
- entrepreneur (p. 9)
- gross domestic product (GDP) (p. 9)

Academic Vocabulary

- resource (p. 6)
- comprehensive (p. 10)

Reading Strategy

Listing As you read the section, complete a graphic organizer like the one below by listing and describing the three economic choices every society must make.

Economic Choices

Focus

Bellringer
Daily Focus Transparency 1

GUIDE TO READING

Answers to Graphic: what to produce; how to produce; for whom to produce

PEOPLE IN THE NEWS

—moneycentral.msn.com

Teens in the Red

Like a lot of hard-working women, Andrea Alba has moments of financial despair. Between juggling three jobs, paying her bills and trying to get out of debt, she feels overwhelmed. "I just want to pay everything off," she says. "I wish I didn't have to struggle so much." But Alba is no debt-weary baby boomer. She's only 19 and a couple of years out of high school.

Her financial burdens may be heavier than other teens: She pays her own college tuition and also helps pay the rent and utilities at home. But the sinker was signing that first credit card application before she had even graduated from high school. "It was fine at first," she says. "I used it mainly for gas. Then it just got deeper and deeper." Within a year and a half of her 18th birthday, Alba was $2,500 in the hole. ■

You may wonder if the study of economics is worth your time and effort. As you learned in the news story, though, many young people find out about economic issues the hard way. They discover, however, that a basic understanding of economics can help them make sense of the world they live in.

The study of economics helps us in many ways, especially in our roles as individuals, as members of our communities, and as global citizens. The good news is that economics is not just useful. It can be interesting as well, so don't be surprised to find that the time you spend on this topic will be well spent.

Personal Finance Handbook

See pages R10–R13 for more information on credit cards.

Resource Manager

R Reading Strategies	C Critical Thinking	D Differentiated Instruction	W Writing Support	S Skill Practice
Teacher Edition • Making Connections, p. 7 • Det. Importance, p. 9 **Additional Resources** • Guid. Read. Act., p. 1 • Read. Ess. & Note-Taking Guide, p. 1 • Free Ent. Act., p. 1	**Teacher Edition** • Det. Cause/Effect, p. 6 • Theorizing, p. 7 **Additional Resources** • Authentic Assess., p. 1 • Econ. Concepts Trans., Strat. & Act., p. 1 • Hands-on Econ., p. 1	**Teacher Edition** • Special Ed., p. 6 • ELL, pp. 8, 9 **Additional Resources** • Daily Focus Trans. 1, 5, 23 • Reteach. Act., p. 1	**Teacher Edition** • Expository Writing, pp. 8, 10 **Additional Resources** • High School Reading in the Content Area Strat. and Act.	**Teacher Edition** • Analyzing Graphs, pp. 9, 11 **Additional Resources** • Graph. Org. Trans., p. 19 • Reading and Study Skills Fold., p. 43

Teach

C Critical Thinking

Determining Cause and Effect Ask: What effect do limited resources and unlimited wants have on the economy? *(They create scarcity.)* **OL**

D Differentiated Instruction

Special Education Ask: What is the difference between a need and a want? *(A need is a requirement for living; a want is just something we would like to have.)* Have students bring to class photographs or magazine clippings that illustrate needs and wants. Then have students organize the clippings into a two-column chart labeled "needs" and "wants." **BL**

Economic Analysis

Answer: because most people seem to want more than they already have

---

✓**Reading Check** **Answer:** A need is necessary for survival; a want is not.

Differentiated Instruction

Authentic Assessment Strategies and Activities, p. 1

---

scarcity fundamental economic problem of meeting people's virtually unlimited wants with scarce resources

economics social science dealing with how people satisfy seemingly unlimited and competing wants with the careful use of scarce resources

need basic requirement for survival, including food, clothing, and shelter

want something we would like to have but is not necessary for survival

The Fundamental Economic Problem

MAIN Idea Societies do not have enough productive resources to satisfy everyone's wants and needs.

Economics & You Can you remember a time when you saved money to buy something expensive? Was the item a necessity or something that you simply wanted to own? Read on to find out how this relates to the core concepts of economics.

Have you ever noticed that very few people are satisfied with the things they have? For example, someone without a home may want a small one; someone else with a small home may want a larger one; someone with a large home may want a mansion. Whether they are rich or poor, most people seem to want *more* than they already have. In fact, if each of us were to make a list of all the things we want, it would most likely include more things than we could ever hope to obtain.

Scarcity

The fundamental economic problem facing all societies is that of scarcity. **Scarcity** is the condition that results from society not having enough **resources** to produce all the things people would like to have.

As **Figure 1.1** shows, scarcity affects almost every decision we make. This is where economics comes in. **Economics** is the study of how people try to satisfy seemingly unlimited and competing wants through the careful use of relatively scarce resources.

Needs and Wants

Economists often talk about people's needs and wants. A **need** is a basic requirement for survival, such as food, clothing, and shelter. A **want** is simply something we would like to have but is not necessary for survival. Food, for example, is needed for survival. Because many foods will satisfy the need for nourishment, the range of things represented by the term *want* is much broader than that represented by the term *need*.

TINSTAAFL

Because resources are limited, everything we do has a cost—even when it seems as if we are getting something "for free." For example, do you really get a free meal when you use a "buy one, get one free" coupon? The business that gives it away still has to pay for the resources that went into the meal, so it usually tries to recover these costs by charging more for its other products. In the end, you may actually be the one who pays for the "free" lunch!

Realistically, most things in life are not free, because someone has to pay for producing them in the first place. Economists use the term *TINSTAAFL* to describe this concept. In short, it means There Is No Such Thing As A Free Lunch.

✓**Reading Check** **Contrasting** What is the difference between a need and a want?

Figure 1.1 ▶ **Scarcity**

Unlimited wants **Limited resources**

SCARCITY

Choices

WHAT to produce | **HOW to produce** | **FOR WHOM to produce**

▶ Scarcity is the fundamental economic problem that forces consumers and producers to use resources wisely.

Economic Analysis *Why is scarcity a universal problem?*

Scarcity

Objective: Understand the basic economic questions facing the economic system of every nation.

Focus: Ask students to brainstorm a list of economic decisions that businesses must make.

Teach: Review the procedure outlined in the activity and guide a discussion about the results.

Assess: Discuss students' responses on their self-evaluations.

Close: Have students identify similar examples of scarcity in the business world.

Differentiated Instruction Strategies

BL Ask students to identify two factors of production used to make several common products.

AL Have students describe how a change in the amount of Play-Doh might change their product's price.

ELL Help students list products that they might create with the Play-Doh.

Three Basic Questions

> **MAIN Idea** Scarcity forces every society to answer the basic questions of WHAT, HOW, and FOR WHOM to produce. 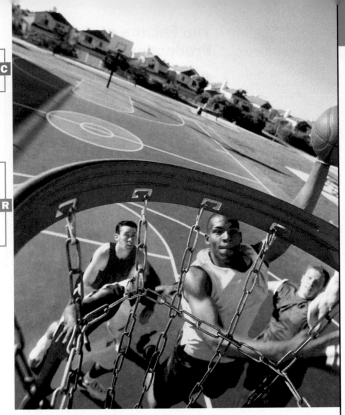 **C**

Economics & You When you write a report, you usually answer the who, what, when, where, and why questions. Read on to learn about the three basic questions in economics.

Because we live in a world of relatively scarce resources, we have to make careful economic choices about the way we use these resources. Figure 1.1 presents three basic questions we need to answer as we make these choices. **R**

WHAT to Produce

The first question is WHAT to produce. For example, should a society direct most of its resources to the production of military equipment or to other items such as food, clothing, or housing? Suppose the decision is to produce housing. Should the limited resources be used to build low-income, middle-income, or upper-income housing? A society cannot have everything its people want, so it must decide WHAT to produce.

HOW to Produce

A second question is HOW to produce. Should factory owners use automated production methods that require more machines and fewer workers, or should they use fewer machines and more workers? If a community has many unemployed people, using more workers might be better. On the other hand, in countries where machinery is widely available, automation can often lower production costs. Lower costs make manufactured items less expensive and, therefore, available to more people.

FOR WHOM to Produce

The third question is FOR WHOM to produce. After a society decides WHAT and HOW to produce, it must decide who will receive the things produced. If a society decides to produce housing, for

WHAT to Produce Societies need to decide whether to include parks in housing areas or to produce more housing. *How do the three questions help societies make choices about scarce resources?*

example, should it be the kind of housing that is wanted by low-income workers, middle-income professional people, or the very rich? If there are not enough houses for everyone, a society has to make a choice about who will receive the existing supply.

These questions concerning WHAT, HOW, and FOR WHOM to produce are never easy for any society to answer. Nevertheless, they must be answered as long as there are not enough resources to satisfy people's seemingly unlimited wants and needs.

✓ **Reading Check** **Analyzing** Why are societies faced with the three basic questions of WHAT, HOW, and FOR WHOM?

CHAPTER 1 What Is Economics? 7

C **Critical Thinking**

Theorizing Ask: What problems do you think society might face in trying to decide what, how, and for whom to produce? *(Answers will vary but may include the problem of meeting many needs with limited resources.)* **OL**

R **Reading Strategy**

Making Connections
Ask: What resources have you noticed are less abundant than in previous years? How has this change affected your family's use of the resource? *(Answers will vary but may include water, electricity, and gasoline. Students' families may use these resources carefully, such as by carpooling or conserving water.)* **AL**

Caption Answer: The three questions focus on using scarce resources to meet people's needs.

✓ **Reading Check** **Answer:** because the world has scarce resources and societies need to make careful choices about the way they use these resources

---

Leveled Activities

BL **Reteaching Activities, p. 1**

OL **Hands-On Economics , p. 1**

AL **Free Enterprise Activities, p. 1**

D Differentiated Instruction

English Language Learners

Explain that in the context of economics, words such as *capital* and *labor* have meanings different than those with which students may be most familiar. Ask students to write these terms on a sheet of paper and draw several illustrations that demonstrate the meaning of each term, as described in the text. **ELL**

W Writing Support

Expository Writing

Point out the image representing *land* at the bottom of the page. Instruct students to write a brief paragraph that identifies the resources that could be considered *land* in the photograph, and explains why the resources identified fit this categorization. *(Answers may include trees, plants, minerals, and so on.)* **BL**

Economic Analysis

Answer: land, capital, labor, entrepreneurs

Additional Support

---

factors of production productive resources that make up the four categories of land, capital, labor, and entrepreneurs

land natural resources or other "gifts of nature" not created by human effort

capital or capital goods tools, equipment, and factories used in the production of goods and services

labor people with all their efforts, abilities and skills

The Factors of Production

MAIN Idea Four factors of production—land, capital, labor, and entrepreneurs—must be present to produce goods and services.

Economics & You When you were younger, did you ever sell something or have a paper route to make money? Read on to find out how this relates to the factors of production.

People cannot satisfy all their wants and needs because productive resources are scarce. The **factors of production,** or resources required to produce the things we would like to have, are land, capital, labor, and entrepreneurs. As shown in **Figure 1.2,** all four are required to produce goods and services.

Land

In economics, **land** refers to the "gifts of nature," or natural resources not created by people. "Land" includes deserts, fertile fields, forests, mineral deposits, livestock, sunshine, and the climate necessary to grow crops. Because a finite amount of natural resources are available at any given time, economists tend to think of land as being fixed, or in limited supply.

Capital

Another factor of production is **capital,** sometimes called **capital goods**—the tools, equipment, machinery, and factories used in the production of goods and services. Capital is unique because it is the result of production. A bulldozer, for example, is a capital good used in construction. When it was built in a factory, it was the result of production involving other capital goods. The computers in your school that are used to produce the service of education also are capital goods.

Labor

A third factor of production is **labor**—people with all their efforts, abilities, and skills. This category includes all people except a unique group of individuals called entrepreneurs, whom we single out because of their special role in the economy. Historically, factors such as birthrates, immigration, famine, war, and disease have had a dramatic impact on the quantity and quality of labor.

Figure 1.2 ▶ The Factors of Production

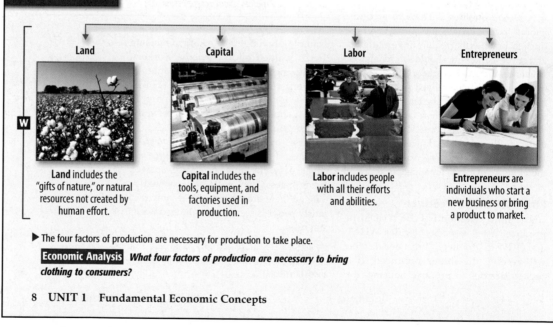

Land | **Capital** | **Labor** | **Entrepreneurs**

Land includes the "gifts of nature," or natural resources not created by human effort.

Capital includes the tools, equipment, and factories used in production.

Labor includes people with all their efforts and abilities.

Entrepreneurs are individuals who start a new business or bring a product to market.

▶ The four factors of production are necessary for production to take place.

Economic Analysis *What four factors of production are necessary to bring clothing to consumers?*

8 UNIT 1 Fundamental Economic Concepts

Activity: Hands-On Economics

Scarcity and the Factors of Production Tell students that just as consumers are faced with scarcity of goods and services, entrepreneurs must deal with scarcity of the other three factors of production—land, capital, and labor. Have students imagine that they are entrepreneurs in the business of producing and selling CDs. Inform them that the price of the raw material used for making CDs has doubled. Encourage students to make economic predictions about what will happen in the CD business. *(Possible answers: Fewer CDs will be produced. The price of CDs will go up. Consumers will purchase fewer CDs.)* **OL**

The Global Economy & YOU

Global Entrepreneurs Drive the Economy

Every time you get paid for baby-sitting, mowing the lawn, or being the deejay at an event, you have joined the "force"—the global entrepreneurial force, that is. A vast majority of the more than 20 million businesses in the United States are owned by entrepreneurs. Most either work alone or have a few employees.

Until recently, the United States led in the percentage of adult entrepreneurs, with an estimated 11.3 percent of Americans starting a new business each year. Today, the small country of Jordan has just over half a million entrepreneurs, but it can boast the highest percentage of individuals attempting to go it alone. That's nearly one in every five adults. The bar graph here illustrates the percentage of the adult population in select countries who are starting new businesses.

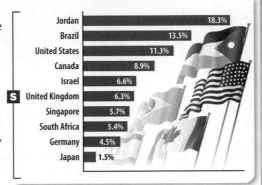

Jordan	18.3%
Brazil	13.5%
United States	11.3%
Canada	8.9%
Israel	6.6%
United Kingdom	6.3%
Singapore	5.7%
South Africa	5.4%
Germany	4.5%
Japan	1.5%

Source: 2004 Global Entrepeneurship Monitor (GEM) www.gemconsortium.org

Entrepreneurs

Some people are singled out because they are the innovators responsible for much of the change in our economy. Such an individual is an **entrepreneur**, a risk-taker in search of profits who does something new with existing resources. Entrepreneurs are often thought of as being the driving force in an economy because they are the people who start new businesses or bring new products to market.

Production

Everything we make requires the four factors of production. The desks and lab equipment used in schools are capital goods. Teachers and other employees provide the labor. Land includes the property where the school is located as well as the iron ore and timber used to make the building. Finally, entrepreneurs are needed to organize the other three factors and make sure that everything gets done.

✓Reading Check **Interpreting** What would happen if one of the factors of production was missing?

The Scope of Economics

MAIN Idea Economics analyzes how societies satisfy wants through careful use of relatively scarce resources.

Economics & You So far, you have learned about the basics of economics. Read on to learn how economists help us make sense of this information.

Economics is the study of human efforts to satisfy seemingly unlimited and competing wants through the careful use of relatively scarce resources. Economics is also a *social science* because it deals with the behavior of people as they deal with this basic issue. The four key elements to this study are description, analysis, explanation, and prediction.

Description

One part of economics describes economic activity. For example, we often hear about **gross domestic product (GDP)**—the dollar value of all final goods, services, and structures produced within a country's borders in a 12-month period. GDP is the

entrepreneur
risk-taking individual in search of profits

gross domestic product (GDP)
dollar value of all final goods, services, and structures produced within a country's borders during a one-year period

📖 Skills Handbook
See page R50 to learn about Using Bar Graphs.

Hands-On Chapter Project
Step 1

W Writing Support

Expository Writing Have students write a paragraph naming the four key elements of economics and explaining how they are interrelated. **OL**

✓**Reading Check** **Answer:**
because it deals with the behavior of people as they try to satisfy their wants with relatively scarce resources

Assess

🔘 Use the Interactive Tutor Self-Assessment CD-ROM to review Section 1, and then assign the Section 1 Review as homework or as an in-class activity.

Close

Identifying Have students identify and explain the fundamental economic problem. **OL**

SECTION 1 Review

---

most **comprehensive** measure of a country's total output and a key measure of a nation's economic health. Economics also describes jobs, prices, trade, taxes, and government spending.

Description allows us to know what the world looks like. However, description is only part of the picture, because it leaves many important "why" and "how" questions unanswered.

Analysis

Economics analyzes the economic activity that it describes. Why, for example, are the prices of some items higher than others? Why do some people earn higher incomes than others? How do taxes affect people's desire to work and save?

Analysis is important because it helps us discover why things work and how things happen. This, in turn, will help us deal with problems that we would like to solve.

Explanation

Economics also involves explanation. After economists analyze a problem and understand why and how things work,

they need to communicate this knowledge to others. If we all have a common understanding of the way our economy works, some economic problems will be easier to address or even fix in the future. When it comes to GDP, you will soon discover that economists spend much of their time explaining why the measure is, or is not, performing in the manner that is expected.

Prediction

Finally, economics is concerned with prediction. For example, we may want to know whether our incomes will rise or fall in the near future. Because economics is the study of both what is happening and what tends to happen, it can help predict what may happen in the future, including the most likely effects of different actions.

The study of economics helps us become more informed citizens and better decision makers. Because of this, it is important to realize that good economic choices are the responsibility of all citizens in a free and democratic society.

✓**Reading Check** **Explaining** Why is economics considered to be a social science?

SECTION 1 Review

Vocabulary
1. **Explain** the significance of scarcity, economics, need, want, factors of production, land, capital, capital good, labor, entrepreneur, and Gross Domestic Product (GDP).

Main Ideas
2. **Identifying** What three basic questions must every society answer, and why?
3. **Organizing** Use a graphic organizer similar to the one below to identify and describe the factors of production.

Factor	Description
Land	

Critical Thinking
4. **The BIG Idea** How can studying economics help us make better choices about how to use scarce resources?
5. **Synthesizing Information** Do you pay to drink from the water fountains at school? Explain why the water is not really free by stating who actually pays for it.
6. **Analyzing Visuals** Look at Figure 1.2. Identify and categorize the factors of production for a business you know, such as your place of employment. What would happen if one of these factors was no longer available?

Applying Economics
7. **Scarcity** How does scarcity affect your life? Provide several examples of items you had to do without because of limited resources, and explain how you adjusted to this situation.

10   UNIT 1   Fundamental Economic Concepts

Answers

1. All definitions can be found in the section and the Glossary.
2. Societies must answer three questions—what to produce, how to produce it, for whom to produce—to help them make careful economic choices about the way they use resources.
3. **Land:** gifts of nature or natural resources. **Capital:** tools, equipment, factories used in production. **Labor:** people, their efforts and abilities. **Entrepreneurs:** people who start new businesses or bring a product to market

4. **Possible answer:** It helps us make choices about using scarce resources in responsible, logical, productive ways.
5. There is no charge to drink from water fountains at school, but the water is paid for by the school district with tax money from citizens.
6. Answers will vary but should identify the factors of production for a particular business. Students should recognize that if one of the factors was unavailable, there would be no production.

7. Answers will vary but should include examples of items students did without because of limited resources. Students should explain how they adjusted to the situation.

Entrepreneurs are willing to take risks because they hope to reap great rewards. These rewards may come more quickly for some than for others. Kevin Plank, founder and CEO of Under Armour Inc., proves that it takes sweat to be a successful entrepreneur.

Under Armour—No Sweat

Eleven years ago, Kevin A. Plank was a walk-on football player at the University of Maryland who relished throwing his body at hulking opponents. But he hated how the cotton T-shirts under his uniform got sopping wet with sweat or rain. By then, cycling outfits and football undershorts were made with moisture-wicking synthetic fabrics. Plank, a starter during kickoffs and punts, wondered why not gridiron T-shirts, too? He tore the content label off a pair of his wick-away shorts, bought the same material from a fabric store, and gave a tailor $460 to sew seven shirts. "I set out to build a better football undershirt," he says.

Plank's teammates loved the tees. So he drove to New York's garment district, had hundreds more samples made, and dubbed his invention "Under Armour." Now, at 33, Plank is the multimillionaire head of an athletic apparel powerhouse. . . .

Yet it didn't happen as fast as Plank originally expected. "At 23, I was probably the smartest guy in the world," he jokes. . . . "But I learned early on [that] this is not about one blast of exposure or one person wearing the product."

Operating at first out of his grandmother's Georgetown house, Plank spent four years tirelessly pitching his product to college and NFL teams. "We convinced these big tough football players to start wearing tight-fitting synthetic shirts, which was completely new and different," he says. . . .

The pros' acceptance brings Under Armour an authenticity that advertising alone can't create. . . . That cachet also gives Plank license to charge $40 for a short-sleeve T-shirt.

—Reprinted from *BusinessWeek*

UNDER ARMOUR REVENUE

Sources: Businessweek.com, www.123jump.com

Examining the Newsclip

1. **Identifying** How did Kevin Plank get his idea for a new product?
2. **Analyzing** How does Plank exemplify the characteristics of an entrepreneur?

CHAPTER 1 What Is Economics? **11**

BusinessWeek

Teach

S Skill Practice

Analyzing Graphs Ask: What was the total amount of Under Armour's increase in revenue between 2002 and 2005? *(about $225 million)* Have students work with a partner to create a graph showing the amount of revenue increase for each year. **OL**

BusinessWeek ONLINE

To find up-to-date news and analysis on the economy, business, technology, markets, entrepreneurs, investments, and finance, have students search feature articles and special reports on the BusinessWeek Web site, www.businessweek.com.

Examining the Newsclip

Answers:
1. He hated how cotton T-shirts under his football uniform got wet with sweat or rain.
2. He had an idea, created something new with existing resources, and started a successful, new business.

Additional Support

Extending the Content

Lockertag™ Technology One of the most recognizable trademarks of Under Armour is Lockertag™. It earned that status by going one step further than fulfilling its original purpose of creating a shirt out of moisture-wicking fabric: It removed the awkward garment labels from inside the shirts, and it provided space for the owner's jersey number to be clearly written on each piece of clothing. Taking the steps to increase comfort and individualize garments for clothing owners has made Lockertag™ an even more recognizable trademark for Under Armour. It helps fulfill Under Armour's goal of allowing players to focus on the game, without the distraction of uncomfortable clothing.

Focus

Basic Economic Concepts

Bellringer
Daily Focus Transparency 4

FOCUS ACTIVITIES
Transparency 4

PRODUCTS, GOODS, AND SERVICES

ECONOMIC PRODUCTS
Economic products are goods and services that are useful, relatively scarce, and transferable to others.

GOODS
Goods are items that are economically useful or satisfy an economic want. A computer is an example of a good.

SERVICES
Services are jobs that are performed for someone. Selling a computer is an example of a service.

CONSUMER GOODS
Consumer goods are goods intended for final use by individuals. A VCR player is an example of a consumer good.

CAPITAL GOODS
Capital goods are goods used to produce other goods and services. A machine used to manufacture a computer is an example of a capital good.

1. What is the difference between a good and a service?
2. What are the two basic types of goods?

Daily Focus Transparency

GUIDE TO READING

Answers to Graphic:
productivity; investing in human capital; division of labor and specialization; economic interdependence

Resource Manager

GUIDE TO READING

Section Preview
In this section, you will learn about some key economic terms and concepts.

Content Vocabulary

- good *(p. 13)*
- consumer good *(p. 13)*
- durable good *(p. 13)*
- nondurable good *(p. 13)*
- service *(p. 13)*
- value *(p. 14)*
- paradox of value *(p. 14)*
- utility *(p. 14)*
- wealth *(p. 14)*
- market *(p. 15)*
- factor market *(p. 15)*
- product market *(p. 15)*
- economic growth *(p. 16)*
- productivity *(p. 16)*
- human capital *(p. 16)*
- division of labor *(p. 17)*
- specialization *(p. 17)*
- economic interdependence *(p. 17)*

Academic Vocabulary

- transferable *(p. 13)*
- accumulation *(p. 14)*
- mechanism *(p. 15)*

Reading Strategy

Describing As you read the section, describe the factors that lead to economic growth.

Economic Growth

PRODUCTS IN THE NEWS

— Asbury Park Press and the New York Times

Comic Books a Big Business

America may have started the worldwide comics craze when U.S. soldiers scattered them around in foreign countries during World War II. Today, they are a global phenomenon—the most widely read literature in the world. According to one published report, 40 percent of all printed material in Japan consists of comics. In the United States, 375 new comic books are sold every month.

The comic-book industry as a whole has had a healthy year. Industry analysts from the Comic Buyer's Guide reported new comics sales of more than $149 million for the first half of 2005, up 6 percent from the period a year earlier. Marvel Entertainment, a publicly traded company that filed for bankruptcy protection in December 1996 and reorganized in July 1998, has recovered strongly in recent years, largely on the strength of its success with movies based on X-Men and Spider-Man. ■

When you hear the word *economics,* you probably think of "big business"—large corporations that run banks and petroleum refineries, or companies that make automobiles, computers and, yes, even comic books. Economics does include big business, but it also includes much more.

Like other social sciences, economics has its own vocabulary and uses terms such as *recession, commodity,* or *utility.* To understand economics, a review of key terms is necessary. Fortunately, most economic terms are widely used, and you will already be familiar with many of them.

12   UNIT 1   Fundamental Economic Concepts

R Reading Strategies	**C** Critical Thinking	**D** Differentiated Instruction	**W** Writing Support	**S** Skill Practice
Teacher Edition • Questioning, p. 13 • Making Inferences, p. 14 **Additional Resources** • Guid. Read. Act., p. 2 • Read. Ess. & Note-Taking Guide, p. 4 • Pri./Sec. Source Read., p. 3	**Teacher Edition** • Ident. POV, p. 14 • Contrasting, p. 15 • Pred. Consequences, p. 16 **Additional Resources** • Crit. Think. Act., p. 1 • Econ. Concepts Trans., Strat. & Act., p. 5	**Teacher Edition** • Kinesthetic, p. 16 • Visual/Spatial, p. 18 **Additional Resources** • Daily Focus Trans. 4, 65 • Econ. Cont. Vocab. Act., p. 1	**Teacher Edition** • Personal Writing, p. 17 **Additional Resources** • High School Writing Process Trans. • Reading and Study Skills Fold., p. 43	**Teacher Edition** • Visual Literacy, pp. 13, 15 • Analyzing Charts, p. 16 **Additional Resources** • Graph. Org. Trans., p. 18 • Econ. Cartoons, p. 8

Goods, Services, and Consumers

MAIN Idea Economic products are goods or services that are useful, relatively scarce, and transferable.

Economics & You Every time you buy something in a store, you act as a consumer. Read on to learn more about this and other basic economic vocabulary.

Economics is concerned with economic products—goods and services that are useful, relatively scarce, and **transferable** to others. Economic products help us satisfy our wants and needs. Because they are both scarce and useful, they command a price.

Goods

There are different types of economic products. The first one is a **good**—a useful, tangible item, such as a book, car, or compact disc player, that satisfies a want. When manufactured goods are used to produce other goods and services, they are called capital goods. An example of a capital good would be a robot welder in a factory, an oven in a bakery, or a computer in a high school. Goods intended for final use by individuals are **consumer goods.**

Any good that lasts three years or more when used on a regular basis is called a **durable good.** Durable goods include both capital goods, such as robot welders, and consumer goods, such as automobiles. A **nondurable good** is an item that lasts for fewer than three years when used on a regular basis. Food, writing paper, and most clothing items are examples of nondurable goods.

Services

The other type of economic product is a **service,** or work that is performed for someone. Services include haircuts, home repairs, and forms of entertainment such as concerts. They also include the work that doctors, lawyers, and teachers perform. The difference between a good and a service is that a good is tangible, or something that can be touched, while a service is not.

Consumers

Consumers are the people who use goods and services to satisfy their wants and needs. As consumers, people indulge in consumption, the process of using up goods and services in order to satisfy wants and needs.

✓**Reading Check** Interpreting How are goods, services, and consumers related?

good tangible economic product that is useful, relatively scarce, and transferable to others

consumer good good intended for final use by consumers rather than businesses

durable good a good that lasts for at least three years when used regularly

nondurable good a good that wears out or lasts for fewer than three years when used regularly

service work or labor performed for someone

Consumer Goods These students are using computers in their school computer lab. *Would you consider computers as durable goods or nondurable goods, and why?* **S**

13

Teach

R Reading Strategy

Questioning Ask: When purchasing a particular good, what question could you ask yourself to help identify the best product? *(Possible answers: How much will I use a particular product? How long do I want a particular product to last?)* **OL**

S Skill Practice

Visual Literacy In addition to the computer, have students identify another consumer good shown in the image. **Ask:** Is the good durable or nondurable? *(Students may identify clothing and eye glasses as nondurable goods.)* **OL**

Caption Answer: Computers are durable goods because they last longer than three years.

✓**Reading Check Answer:** Consumers use goods and services to satisfy their wants and needs.

Additional Support

Activity: Collaborative Learning

Categorizing Have students work together in small groups of three or four. Ask each group to create a table with three headings: Durable Goods, Nondurable Goods, Services. Then ask them to list the goods and services that they use as consumers under the relevant heading on the table. For each durable and nondurable good, have students circle items that are capital goods and draw a square around items that are consumer goods. Invite volunteers to explain their group's decisions. Keep a class tally of the number of responses in each heading. **BL**

Teacher Tip

Adjusting for Students' Learning Styles Suggest that visual, kinesthetic, and English language learners illustrate their tables with images of each good and service. Students might draw pictures or cut out images from magazine advertisements.

R Reading Strategy

Making Inferences Ask: Why do you think that some goods are more valuable than others? *(To have monetary value, a good must be scarce and have utility for the person purchasing it. Some goods that have utility are more scarce than others, which makes them more valuable.)* **OL**

C Critical Thinking

Identifying Point of View

Ask: What was Adam Smith's view of the relationship between a country's wealth, its material possessions, and its people? *(Adam Smith believed that a nation's wealth consisted of material possessions and its people. If material possessions were taken away, the people could restore the possessions. If a country's people were taken away, the nation's wealth would deteriorate.)* **OL**

✓**Reading Check** **Answer:** For something to have value, it must have utility.

---

value monetary worth of a good or service as determined by the market

paradox of value apparent contradiction between the high monetary value of a nonessential item and the low value of an essential item

utility ability or capacity of a good or service to be useful and give satisfaction to someone

wealth sum of tangible economic goods that are scarce, useful, and transferable from one person to another

---

Value, Utility, and Wealth

MAIN Idea The value of a good or service depends on its scarcity and utility.

Economics & You Has anyone ever thought you paid too much for something? Read on to learn how the value of an item is determined.

In economics, **value** refers to a worth that can be expressed in dollars and cents. Why, then, does something have value, and why are some things more valuable than others? To answer these questions, it helps to review a problem Adam Smith, a Scottish social philosopher, faced back in 1776.

The Paradox of Value

Adam Smith was one of the first people to describe how markets work. He observed that some necessities, such as water, had a very low monetary value. On the other hand, some nonnecessities, such as diamonds, had a very high value. Smith called this contradiction the **paradox of value.** Economists knew that scarcity was necessary for something to have value. Still, scarcity by itself could not fully explain how value is determined.

Utility

It turned out that for something to have value, it must also have **utility,** or the capacity to be useful and provide satisfaction. Utility is not something that is fixed or even measurable, like weight or height. Instead, the utility of a good or service may vary from one person to the next. One person may get a great deal of satisfaction

---

Did You Know?

▶ **Value** Economists aren't the only ones obsessed with value. Do a simple Google search of "value," and you'll get nearly 2 million hits. You'll get approximately a quarter million if you search for "measure of value," and nearly 140,000 if you search for "measuring value." Maybe that's why economists simply define *value* as "a worth that can be expressed in dollars and cents."

---

from a home computer; another may get very little. One person may enjoy a rock concert; another may not.

Value

For something to have monetary value, economists decided, it must be scarce *and* have utility. This is the solution to the paradox of value. Diamonds are scarce and have utility, thus they possess a value that can be stated in monetary terms. Water has utility but is not scarce enough in most places to give it much value. Therefore, water is less expensive, or has less monetary value, than diamonds.

The emphasis on monetary value is important to economists. Unlike moral or social value, which is the topic of other social sciences, the value of something in terms of dollars and cents is a concept that everyone can easily understand.

Wealth

In an economic sense, the **accumulation** of products that are tangible, scarce, useful, and transferable from one person to another is **wealth.** A nation's wealth is comprised of all tangible items—including natural resources, factories, stores, houses, motels, theaters, furniture, clothing, books, highways, video games, and even basketballs—that can be exchanged.

While goods are counted as wealth, services are not, because they are intangible. However, this does not mean that services are not useful or valuable. Indeed, when Adam Smith published his famous book *The Wealth of Nations* in 1776, he was referring specifically to the abilities and skills of a nation's people as the source of its wealth. For Smith, if a country's material possessions were taken away, its people, through their efforts and skills, could restore these possessions. On the other hand, if a country's people were taken away, its wealth would deteriorate.

✓**Reading Check** **Summarizing** How are value and utility related?

14 UNIT 1 Fundamental Economic Concepts

Differentiated Instruction

Critical Thinking Activities, p. 1

What Is the Main Idea?

Objective: Understand the importance of finding the main idea of a passage or feature.

Focus/Teach: Discuss how finding main ideas can help students understand a text. Then have students read the passage and answer the questions.

Assess: Review the answers to questions 1 through 5 as a class.

Close: Ask students to explain how a main idea is different from a supporting detail.

Differentiated Instruction Strategies

BL Have students explain how main ideas assist readers.

AL Have students write a paragraph about Adam Smith's idea of wealth, with at least three supporting details.

ELL Ask students to create a main idea and supporting details graphic organizer using the activity passage.

The Circular Flow of Economic Activity

MAIN Idea The economic activity in markets connects individuals and businesses.

Economics & You When you receive a paycheck, do you understand how you fit in the larger economy? Read on to learn about the flow of economic activity.

The wealth that an economy generates is made possible by the circular flow of economic activity. The key feature of this circular flow is the **market,** a location or other **mechanism** that allows buyers and sellers to exchange a specific product. Markets may be local, national, or global—and they can even exist in cyberspace.

Factor Markets

As shown in **Figure 1.3,** individuals earn their incomes in **factor markets,** where the factors of production are bought and sold.

This is where entrepreneurs hire labor for wages and salaries, acquire land in return for rent, and borrow money. The concept of a factor market is a simplified but realistic version of the real world. For example, you participate in the factor market when you work and sell your labor to an employer.

Product Markets

After individuals receive their income from the resources they sell in a factor market, they spend it in **product markets.** These are markets where producers sell their goods and services. Thus, the wages and salaries that individuals receive from businesses in the factor markets returns to businesses in the product markets. Businesses then use this money to produce more goods and services, and the cycle of economic activity repeats itself.

✓ **Reading Check** **Explaining** What roles do factor markets and product markets play in the economy?

market meeting place or mechanism that allows buyers and sellers to come together

factor market market where the factors of production are bought and sold

C

product market market where goods and services are bought and sold

C Critical Thinking

Contrasting Ask: What are the major differences between factor markets and product markets? *(In factor markets, factors of production are bought and sold, and individuals earn incomes. In product markets, producers sell goods and services to individuals using income they receive from businesses.)* **OL**

S Skill Practice

Visual Literacy Discuss the diagram with the class. Then have students construct a similar diagram that represents their own economic activity if they have a job or the activity of a family member if they do not. **AL**

✓ **Reading Check** **Answer:** They create economic activity that connects individuals and businesses.

Economic Analysis

Answer: Consumers spend income from factor markets on goods and services sold in product markets.

Figure 1.3 ▶ **The Circular Flow of Economic Activity**

Charts In MOtion
See StudentWorks™ Plus or glencoe.com.

▶ The circular flow diagram shows the high degree of economic interdependence in our economy. In the diagram, the factors of production and the products made from them flow in one direction. The money consumers spend on goods and services flows in the opposite direction.

Economic Analysis *As a consumer, what role do you play in the circular flow of economic activity?*

CHAPTER 1 What Is Economics? 15

Leveled Activities

BL **Guided Reading Activities, p. 2**

OL **Economic Concepts Transparencies, Strategies, and Activities, p. 5**

AL **Primary and Secondary Source Readings, p. 3**

D Differentiated Instruction

Kinesthetic Write "human capital" on the board, and have students illustrate the concept. Encourage them to think of their personal skills and abilities, their health, how they learn, and what motivates them. Invite students to label their illustrations and present them to the class. **BL**

C Critical Thinking

Predicting Consequences

Ask: What might happen if individuals don't invest in their own education? *(Possible answer: They will have trouble getting a job and making a living.)* **OL**

S Skill Practice

Analyzing Charts Ask students to draw a conclusion based on the information in the chart. *(Possible answer: Achieving higher education increases an individual's income.)* **OL**

Economic Analysis

Answer: Education improves people's skills and abilities, which benefits both employers and their employees.

Hands-On Chapter Project

Step 2

Modeling an Economic Decision

Step 2: Identifying Basic Economic Concepts. Students will answer basic economic questions about their T-shirt business.

Directions: Ask student groups to work together to answer the following questions about their T-shirt business:

---

economic growth increase in a nation's total output of goods and services over time

productivity measure of the amount of output produced with a given amount of productive factors

human capital sum of people's skills, abilities, health, knowledge and motivation

Personal Finance Handbook

See pages R16–R19 for more information on education.

Productivity and Economic Growth

> **MAIN Idea** A nation's economic growth is due to several factors.

Economics & You Have you decided yet what you will do after graduating from high school? Read on to learn how investing in more education now can give you a higher lifetime income.

Economic growth occurs when a nation's total output of goods and services increases over time. This means that the circular flow becomes larger, with more factors of production, goods, and services flowing in one direction and more payments in the opposite direction. Productivity is the most important factor contributing to economic growth.

Productivity

Everyone in a society benefits when scarce resources are used efficiently. This is described by the term **productivity,** a measure of the amount of goods and services produced with a given amount of resources in a specific period of time.

Productivity goes up whenever more can be produced with the same amount of resources. For example, if a company produced 5,000 pencils in an hour, and it produced 5,100 in the next hour with the same amount of labor and capital, productivity went up. Productivity is often discussed in terms of labor, but it applies to all factors of production.

Investing in Human Capital

A major contribution to productivity comes from investments in **human capital,** the sum of people's skills, abilities, health, knowledge, and motivation. Government can invest in human capital by providing education and health care. Businesses can invest in training and other programs that improve the skills of their workers. Individuals can invest in their own education by completing high school, going to technical school, or attending college.

Figure 1.4 shows that investments in education can have substantial payoffs. According to the table, high school graduates earn substantially more than nongraduates, and college graduates make even more than

---

Figure 1.4 ▶ **Effect of Education on Income**

▶ Education is one way to invest in human capital.

Economic Analysis *How does this type of investment pay off for both employers and their employees?*

Education	Average income	
	Males	Females
Less than 9th grade	$19,746	$11,492
9th to 12th grade (no diploma)	$23,747	$13,343
High school graduate or equivalent	$34,700	$20,325
Some college, no degree	$43,531	$25,111
Associate degree	$45,800	$29,031
Bachelor's degree	$65,523	$37,373
Master's degree	$83,189	$48,945
Professional degree	$126,728	$63,322
Doctorate degree	$103,939	$67,676

Source: U.S. Department of Commerce, Bureau of the Census, 2006

16 UNIT 1 Fundamental Economic Concepts

- Are you producing a good or a service? If it is a good, is it durable or nondurable? Explain.
- What consumers will you target with your product?
- Describe the value of your product.
- Describe three ways in which you can increase your business's productivity and achieve growth.
- What other kinds of businesses will you need to depend on to make and sell your product?

Comparing Have groups compare their answers with one another. Allow them time to revise or change their answers, if necessary. **OL**

(Chapter Project continued in Section 3.)

high school graduates. Educational investments require that we make a sacrifice today so we can have a better life in the future, and few investments generate higher returns.

Division of Labor and Specialization

Division of labor and specialization can improve productivity. **Division of labor** is a way of organizing work so that each individual worker completes a separate part of the work. In most cases, a worker who performs a few tasks many times a day is likely to be more proficient than a worker who performs hundreds of different tasks in the same period.

Specialization takes place when factors of production perform only tasks they can do better or more efficiently than others. The division of labor makes specialization possible. For example, the assembly of a product may be broken down into a number of separate tasks (the division of labor). Then each worker can perform the specific task he or she does best (specialization).

One example of the advantages offered by the division of labor and specialization is Henry Ford's use of the assembly line in automobile manufacturing. Having each worker add one part to the car, rather than a few workers assembling the entire vehicle, cut the assembly time of a car from a day and a half to just over 90 minutes—and reduced the price of a new car by more than 50 percent.

Economic Interdependence

The U.S. economy has a remarkable degree of **economic interdependence.** This means that we rely on others, and others rely on us, to provide most of the goods and services we consume. As a result, events in one part of the world often have a dramatic impact elsewhere.

This does not mean that interdependence is necessarily bad. The gains in productivity and income that result from specialization almost always offset the costs associated with the loss of self-sufficiency.

✓**Reading Check** **Analyzing** What role does specialization play in the productivity of an economy?

> **division of labor** division of work into a number of separate tasks to be performed by different workers

> **specialization** assignment of tasks to the workers, factories, regions, or nations that can perform them more efficiently

> **economic interdependence** mutual dependency of one person's, firm's, or region's economic activities on another's **W**

Skills Handbook
See page R40 to learn about Analyzing Information.

W **Writing Support**
Personal Writing Have students write about ways that they are dependent on others or how others are dependent on them. Then have students circle which examples show economic interdependence and explain why. **OL**

✓**Reading Check** **Answer:** It allows people to become more efficient by performing tasks that they can do better than others; this makes the economy more productive.

Assess

Use the Interactive Tutor Self-Assessment CD-ROM to review Section 2, and then assign the Section 2 Review as homework or as an in-class activity.

Close

Making Connections Have students choose a product and identify its value and utility. **OL**

SECTION 2 Review

Vocabulary
1. **Explain** the significance of good, consumer good, durable good, nondurable good, service, value, paradox of value, utility, wealth, market, factor market, product market, economic growth, productivity, human capital, division of labor, specialization, and economic interdependence.

Main Ideas
2. **Explaining** How do goods and services differ?
3. **Organizing** Use a graphic organizer similar to the one below to describe the different transactions that take place in product markets.

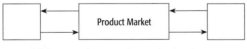

4. **Describing** How is economic growth related to productivity?

Critical Thinking
5. **The BIG Idea** How is value related to scarcity and utility?
6. **Drawing Conclusions** Why is investing in human capital beneficial?
7. **Analyzing Visuals** Look at Figure 1.3. How can individuals increase the flow of circular activity? What effect would this increase have on the other parts of the economy?
8. **Inferring** How might major events such as labor strikes affect you and your community? Select a possible event and write a brief paragraph about the potential effects.

Applying Economics
9. **Specialization** Provide at least three examples each of specialized workers and specialized capital that are used in your school to provide the service of education. How would productivity change if they were not available to your school?

CHAPTER 1 What Is Economics? 17

Review **SECTION 2**

Answers

1. All definitions can be found in the section and the Glossary.
2. Goods are tangible products, and services are work or labor performed for someone.
3. Organizers should illustrate the following transactions: Consumers spend money on goods and services. Businesses use this income to produce goods and services for consumers.
4. High productivity results in economic growth.

5. The value of a good or service depends on its scarcity and utility.
6. **Possible answer:** It makes employees more skilled, which increases a company's productivity.
7. Individuals could spend more of their income on goods and services. That increase would put more income into businesses, which would produce more goods and services for the individuals.

8. Answers will vary but should include the concept that during a labor strike, people produce fewer goods to sell and usually have less money to spend.
9. Answers will vary, but students may say that the quality of education would drop if specialized workers (such as teachers and school nurses) and specialized capital (such as government grants and school levies) were not available.

Teach

D Differentiated Instruction

Visual/Spatial Have students create a two-column chart, with the first column listing Adam Smith's new economic ideas and the second column describing each new idea. *(Division of labor: labor becomes more productive as each worker becomes more skilled at a single job. "Invisible hand": the belief that competition and individual self-interest would invisibly guide resources to their most productive uses. Wealth of nations: the sum of goods produced by labor.)* **OL**

Examining the Profile

Answers:

1. the importance of the division of labor, the idea of the "invisible hand" guiding resources, and the definition of the wealth of nations
2. Answers will vary but may include that factories use division of labor.

Additional Support

Profiles in Economics

Adam Smith (1723–1790)

- introduced the idea that the division of labor led to the great prosperity of Britain
- defined the wealth of a nation as the sum of the goods produced by its people

Division of Labor

Adam Smith did not set out to become an economist. In fact, he focused on philosophy when, at age 14, he earned a scholarship to attend Glasgow University. Travels throughout Europe and talks with notable thinkers helped Smith turn his attention to economics. In 1776 he published his most influential book, *An Inquiry into the Nature and Causes of the Wealth of Nations,* in which he observed that labor becomes more productive as each worker becomes more skilled at a single job. This made him the first to introduce and recognize the importance of the "division of labor."

Invisible Hand

D Smith's most important contribution was the notion that competition and individual self-interest would somehow act as an "invisible hand" to guide resources to their most productive uses. He suggested that the role of government should be limited to enforcing contracts, granting patents and copyrights to encourage inventions and new ideas, and providing public works, such as roads and bridges.

Wealth of Nations

Smith also put forth the new idea that the "wealth of nations" should be defined as the sum of the goods produced by labor, not the personal financial wealth of those who owned them. Competition in markets, along with the division of labor and the invisible hand, would lead to increased productivity and output. Smith's doctrine of laissez-faire (French for "let it be") marked the beginning of modern economic thought, and it still serves as the basis of our free market economy.

Adam Smith studied to become a philosopher. Yet today he is best known for his support of a free market economy.

Examining the Profile

1. **Summarizing Ideas** What ideas did Adam Smith contribute to economic thought?
2. **Synthesizing** Explain how Smith's ideas are evident in the workings of the American economy.

Activity: Collaborative Learning

Division of Labor Have students work together in small groups to form a fictitious business that manufactures a product such as computers, shoes, automobiles, or microwaves. Using the division of labor idea, have each group write an organizational plan for their business, where each group member is assigned a single job to perform. Groups should ensure that every position has a job description that contributes to the success of the company. When groups have completed their plans, have volunteers present them to the class and predict how division of labor will influence their company's productivity. After each presentation, have a class discussion on how division of labor benefits each fictitious company. **OL**

SECTION 3
Economic Choices and Decision Making

GUIDE TO READING

Section Preview
In this section, you will learn that you face trade-offs and opportunity costs whenever you make an economic decision.

Content Vocabulary
- trade-off *(p. 20)*
- opportunity cost *(p. 20)*
- production possibilities frontier *(p. 21)*
- economic model *(p. 23)*
- cost-benefit analysis *(p. 24)*
- free enterprise economy *(p. 24)*
- standard of living *(p. 24)*

Academic Vocabulary
- alternative *(p. 20)*   • assumption *(p. 23)*

Reading Strategy
Identifying As you read this section, complete a graphic organizer similar to the one below by identifying the ways in which you can make economic choices and what these strategies allow you to learn.

Problems	Strategy	Purpose
Trade-offs	Decision-making grid	

Focus

Bellringer
Daily Focus Transparency 2

GUIDE TO READING

Possible Answers to Graphic:
Trade-offs: decision-making grid; helps evaluate choices
Opportunity cost: decision-making grid; helps in deciding the next best alternative
Comparing choices: cost-benefit analysis; helps make choices with the highest return for the dollar spent

PEOPLE IN THE NEWS
—BusinessWeek

The Grease Pits of Academia

Students at Belmont Abbey College may have a head start in the race for post-graduation jobs—at least jobs that go *VROOM!* Starting this fall, the 1,000-student school outside Charlotte, N.C., will offer the nation's first four-year bachelor's degree in Motorsports Management. Students will study such topics as sports marketing and racing management.

"The program will be NASCAR-focused but will have a broad application to all portions of the motor sports industry," says Philip Bayster, head of the school's business department. Charlotte, the NASCAR epicenter, is home to about 250 racing teams and 25 specialized media and marketing firms.

Pay is anything but the pits. Annual salaries for the region's 14,000 motor sports jobs, not including drivers, average $72,000. ■

What will you do after graduating from high school? Get a job? Go to college? If you choose to work, you will benefit by receiving a paycheck right away. If you decide to earn a college degree—like the NASCAR-focused degree at Belmont Abbey College—you may give up four years of earning potential. The benefit, however, is that your income after college will be greater than the income you will earn with just a high school diploma.

Because resources are scarce, everyone has to make choices. To become a good decision maker, you need to know how to identify the problem and then analyze your alternatives. Finally, you have to make your choice in a way that carefully considers the costs and benefits of each possibility.

CHAPTER 1   What Is Economics?   19

Resource Manager

R Reading Strategies	**C** Critical Thinking	**D** Differentiated Instruction	**W** Writing Support	**S** Skill Practice
Teacher Edition • Using Context Clues, p. 21 • Making Connections, p. 23 **Additional Resources** • Guid. Read. Act., p. 3 • Read. Ess. & Note-Taking Guide, p. 7	**Teacher Edition** • Making Connections, p. 21 • Compare/Contrast, p. 24 **Additional Resources** • Math Prac. for Econ., p. 1 • Econ. Concepts Trans., Strat. & Act., p. 5	**Teacher Edition** • Logical/Math., p. 22 • Verbal/Linguistic, p. 24 • Intrapersonal, p. 25 **Additional Resources** • Enrichment Act., p. 1 • Reading and Study Skills Fold., p. 48	**Teacher Edition** • Persuasive Writing, p. 20 • Personal Writing, p. 23 • Expository Writing, p. 31 **Additional Resources** • Writer's Guidebook	**Teacher Edition** • Analyzing Charts, p. 20 • Visual Literacy, p. 26 • Analyzing Info., p. 30 **Additional Resources** • Daily Focus Trans. 2, 97

Teach

W Writing Support

Persuasive Writing Instruct students to think of a recent economic choice they made and the trade-offs involved in that choice. Then, direct them to write a short persuasive essay in which they explain their choice and attempt to convince others that they made the correct choice. **OL**

S Skill Practice

Analyzing Charts Ask: Would you have made the same decision as Jesse? Why or why not? *(Students may have made a different decision because the criteria would have been different for them.)* **OL**

√Reading Check **Answer:** The opportunity cost refers to the cost of the next-best alternative. Trade-offs include all of the other alternative choices.

Economic Analysis

Answer: They mean opportunity cost, or the cost of the next-best alternative.

Additional Support

---

trade-off alternative that is available whenever a choice is to be made

opportunity cost cost of the next-best alternative use of money, time, or resources when making a choice

Trade-Offs and Opportunity Cost

MAIN Idea Economic choices involve trade-offs and the careful evaluation of opportunity costs.

Economics & You When you go shopping, you usually have to make choices, because you cannot afford to buy everything you want. Read on to learn about the terms economists apply to these decisions.

There are alternatives and costs to everything we do. In a world where "there is no such thing as a free lunch," it pays to examine these concepts closely.

Trade-Offs

Every decision we make has its **trade-offs,** or alternative choices. One way to help us make decisions is to construct models such as the grid in **Figure 1.5.** This grid shows how Jesse decides to spend a $100 gift.

Jesse likes several **alternatives:** a video game, concert tickets, an MP3 player, and a replica NFL jersey. At the same time, he realizes that each item has advantages and disadvantages. Some of the items can be used more than once, and some might require his parents' consent. Some even have additional costs such as batteries.

To help with his decision, Jesse can draw a grid that lists his alternatives and several criteria by which to judge them. Then he evaluates each alternative with a "yes" or "no." In the end, Jesse chooses the jersey because it satisfies more of his criteria than any other alternative.

Using a decision-making grid is one way to analyze an economic problem. It forces you to consider a number of alternatives and the criteria you'll use to evaluate the alternatives. Finally, it makes you evaluate each alternative based on the criteria you selected.

Opportunity Cost

People often think of cost in terms of dollars and cents. To an economist, however, cost means more than the price tag on a good or service. Instead, economists think broadly in terms of **opportunity cost,** the cost of the next-best alternative. When Jesse decided to purchase the jersey, his opportunity cost was the MP3 player—the next-best choice he gave up. In contrast, trade-offs are all of the other alternatives that he could have chosen.

Even time has an opportunity cost, although you cannot always put a monetary value on it. The opportunity cost of reading this economics book, for example, is the history paper or math homework that you could not do at the same time.

√Reading Check **Summarizing** How are trade-offs and opportunity cost related?

Figure 1.5 ▶ **Jesse's Decision-Making Grid**

Alternatives	Criteria				
	Costs $100 or less?	Durable?	Will parents approve?	Future expense unnecessary?	Can use anytime?
Video game	yes	yes	no	yes	no
Concert tickets	yes	no	yes	no	no
MP3 player	yes	yes	yes	no	yes
NFL jersey	yes	yes	yes	yes	yes

▶ A decision-making grid lists alternatives and criteria to help evaluate choices.

Economic Analysis *What do economists mean when they talk about costs?*

Extending the Content

Trade-Offs of Higher Education
As many high school students approach graduation, they must weigh the trade-offs of attending college or immediately entering the workforce. In 2004, 67 percent of students completing high school chose to enroll in college. This percentage has increased from 49 percent in 1972. In making these choices, high school graduates must weigh both the cost of attending college, as well as the potential earning power they will gain by acquiring a college education. For the academic year 1984–1985, the average cost of undergraduates' tuition, room, and board was about $4,500. By 2004–2005, that figure had increased to more than $13,000. However, the earning power of workers with a college degree also proved significantly higher than that of workers with a high school diploma or GED. In 2004, males with a bachelor's degree or higher earned about 67 percent more than workers who had only completed high school.

Production Possibilities

MAIN Idea Economies face trade-offs when deciding what goods and services to produce.

Economics & You You just learned that you face trade-offs and opportunity costs when making choices. Read on to learn how opportunity cost applies to countries as well as individuals.

To illustrate opportunity cost, economists use the **production possibilities frontier,** a diagram representing various combinations of goods and services an economy can produce when all its resources are in use. In the example in **Figure 1.6,** a mythical country called Alpha produces two goods—cars and clothing.

Identifying Possible Alternatives

Even though Alpha produces only two goods, the country has a number of alternatives available to it. For example, it could choose to use all of its resources to produce 70 units of cars and 300 units of clothing, which is shown as point **a** in Figure 1.6. Or it could shift some of its resources out of car production and into clothing, thereby moving to point **b.** Alpha could even choose to produce at point **c,** which represents all clothing and no cars, or at point **e,** which is inside the frontier.

Alpha has many alternatives available to it, which is why the figure is called a production "possibilities" frontier. Eventually, though, Alpha will have to settle on a single combination such as point **a, b,** or any other point on or inside the curve, because its resources are limited.

Fully Employed Resources

All points on the curve such as **a, b,** and **c** represent *maximum* combinations of output that are possible if all resources are fully employed. To illustrate, suppose that Alpha is producing at point **a,** and the people would like to move to point **d,** which represents the same amount of cars, but more clothing. As long as all resources are fully employed at point **a,** there are no extra

resources available to produce the extra clothing. Therefore, point **d** cannot be reached, nor can any other point outside the curve. This is why the figure is called a production possibilities "frontier"—to indicate the maximum combinations of goods and services that can be produced.

The Cost of Idle Resources

If some resources were not fully employed, then it would be impossible for Alpha to reach its maximum potential production. Suppose that Alpha was producing at point **b** when workers in the clothing industry went on strike. Clothing production would fall, causing total output to change to point **e.** The opportunity cost of the unemployed resources would be the 100 units of lost clothing production.

Production at point **e** could also be the result of other idle resources, such as factories or land that are available but not being used. As long as some resources are idle, the country cannot produce on its frontier—which is another way of saying that it cannot reach its full production potential.

production possibilities frontier diagram representing the maximum combinations of goods and/or services an economy can produce when all productive resources are fully employed

Figure 1.6 ► Production Possibilities Frontier

THE PRODUCTION POSSIBILITIES FRONTIER

► The production possibilities frontier shows the different combinations of two products that can be produced if all resources are fully employed.

Economic Analysis *Why can production take place on or inside the frontier?*

R Reading Strategy

Using Context Clues Ask: What is the meaning of the term *frontier* when used by economists? *(Answers may include a boundary or a limit. Countries have a boundary or limit when considering the maximum combination of goods and services that can be produced.)* **OL**

C Critical Thinking

Making Connections Have students imagine a scenario in which it would be useful for a company to construct a production possibilities frontier. Ask volunteers to share their scenarios with the class. *(Possible answer: A company is producing CDs and cassettes. They are thinking of eliminating cassettes and just producing CDs, but they want to see all the production possibilities before making their decision.)* **OL**

Economic Analysis
Answer: Production on or inside the frontier indicates the maximum combinations of goods and services that can be produced.

Differentiated Instruction

Math Practice for Economics, p. 1

Analyzing Trade-Offs

Objective: Understand the costs involved whenever a choice is made.

Focus/Teach: Ask students to brainstorm possible purchases that involve choices. Then review the decision-making grid, and have students answer the activity questions.

Assess: Discuss the reasons behind students' choices.

Close: Ask students why it is important to analyze trade-offs when they are making economic decisions.

Differentiated Instruction Strategies

BL Have students summarize the concept of trade-offs.

AL Ask students to write a brief paragraph explaining how knowing about trade-offs will influence their decision making in the future.

ELL Have students fill out a decision-making grid as they complete the activity.

D Differentiated Instruction

Logical/Mathematical Tell students that Gerard has two choices for a summer job— a manufacturing job that pays $10.25 per hour or a landscaping job that pays $8.65 per hour. At the landscaping company, he could work and have lunch with three of his closest friends.
Ask: For one 40-hour workweek, what would be the opportunity cost, in dollars, of accepting the landscaping job? *($64.00)* What would be the opportunity cost of accepting the manufacturing job? *(not working or eating lunch with his friends every day)* **OL**

Economic Analysis

Answer: zero

Economic Analysis

Answer: having more resources or increased productivity

✓**Reading Check** **Answer:** by representing potential output at a given point in time

---

Figure 1.7 ▶ **Opportunity Cost**

OPPORTUNITY COST

▶ When the production for one item increases, the production of other items decreases. In the example shown, the opportunity cost for producing and additional 10 units of clothing is the 30 cars given up.

Economic Analysis *If Alpha decided to produce units of clothing at point c, what would be the opportunity cost in cars?*

Figure 1.8 ▶ **Economic Growth**

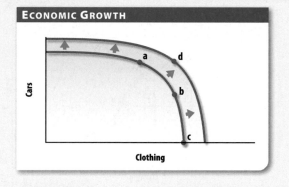

ECONOMIC GROWTH

▶ The only way to expand the production possibilities frontier is to attain economic growth.

Economic Analysis *What factors make it possible for the economy to grow?*

D Opportunity Cost

Suppose that Alpha was producing at point **a** and that it wanted to move to point **b**. This is clearly possible as long as point **b** is not outside the production possibilities frontier. However, Alpha will have to give something up in return. As shown in **Figure 1.7,** the opportunity cost of producing the 100 additional units of clothing is the 30 units of cars given up.

As you can see, opportunity cost applies to almost all activities, and it is not always measured in terms of dollars and cents. For example, you need to balance the time you spend doing homework and the time you spend with your friends. If you decide to spend extra hours on your homework, the opportunity cost of this action is the time that you cannot spend with your friends. You normally have a number of trade-offs available whenever you make a decision, and the opportunity cost of the choice you make is the value of the next best alternative that you give up.

Economic Growth

The production possibilities frontier represents potential output at a given point in time. Eventually, however, changes may cause the production possibilities frontier to expand. The population may grow, the stock of capital may expand, technology may improve, or productivity may increase. If any of these changes occur, then Alpha will be able to produce more in the future.

The effect of economic growth is shown in **Figure 1.8.** Economic growth, made possible by having more resources or increased productivity, causes the production possibilities frontier to move outward. Economic growth will eventually allow Alpha to produce at point **d,** which it could not do earlier.

✓**Reading Check** **Synthesizing** How can the production possibilities frontier be used to illustrate economic growth?

Leveled Activities

BL **Reading Essentials and Note-Taking Guide, p. 7**

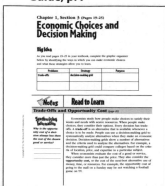

OL **Economic Concepts Transparencies, Strategies, and Activities, p. 3**

AL **Enrichment Activities, p. 1**

Thinking Like an Economist

MAIN Idea **MAIN Idea** Economists use a strategy called cost-benefit analysis to evaluate choices.

Economics & You When you work a complicated math problem, do you ever look at a simplified example to better understand the process? Read on to learn how economists use models to understand complex economic activities.

Because economists study how people satisfy seemingly unlimited and competing wants through the careful use of scarce resources, they are concerned with strategies that will help people make the best choices. Two strategies are building models and preparing a cost-benefit analysis.

Build Simple Models

One of the most important strategies is to build economic models. An **economic model** is a simplified equation, graph, or figure showing how something works. Simple models can often reduce complex situations to their most basic elements. To illustrate, the production possibility frontiers in this section and the circular flow diagram in Figure 1.3 on page 15 are examples of how complex economic activity can be explained by a simple model.

Another basic model is the production possibilities frontier that is illustrated in Figure 1.6 on page 21. Realistically, of course, economies are able to produce more than two goods or services, but the concepts of trade-offs and opportunity costs are easier to illustrate if only two products are examined. As a result, simple models such as these are sometimes all that economists need to analyze or describe an actual situation.

It is important to realize that models are based on **assumptions,** or things we think are true. In general, the quality of a model is no better than the assumptions on which it is based, but a model with simple assumptions is usually easier to understand. In the case of the production possibilities frontier,

for example, we assumed that only two goods could be produced. This made the model easier to illustrate and still allowed us to discuss the concepts of trade-offs and opportunity costs.

It is also important to keep in mind that models can be revised to make them better. If an economic model helps us to make a prediction that turns out to be right, the model can be used again. If the prediction is wrong, the model might be changed to make better predictions the next time.

> **economic model** simplified version of a complex concept or behavior expressed in the form of an equation, graph, or illustration

CAREERS

Economist

The Work

* Collect and analyze data, observe economic trends

* Advise businesses and other organizations on such topics as energy costs, inflation, imports, and employment levels

* Study economic conditions in the United States or in other countries to estimate the economic effects of new legislation or public policies

Qualifications

* Strong computer and quantitative skills

* Ability to conduct complex research, write reports, and prepare statistical data

* Bachelor's degree, with a focus on economics and statistics, accounting, or calculus

* Master's degree required for most economists in the private sector

Earnings

* Median annual earnings: $72,780

Job Growth Outlook

* Slower than average

Source: *Occupational Outlook Handbook, 2006–2007 Edition*

R Reading Strategy

Making Connections Ask students to think about the ways in which economists might gather the data they use to study specific parts of the economy. Then, direct students to make a list of these methods. Students may suggest methods such as statistical analysis, polling and interviews, and surveys or questionnaires. Invite students to explain how these approaches to gathering data might help economists develop economic models. **OL**

W Writing Support

Personal Writing Have students write a paragraph expressing their thoughts on the following question: *Does an economist's model have value if data collected shows that his or her theory is incorrect?* Students should clearly state their opinions on the topic and provide reasonable explanations for their beliefs. *(Answers will vary, but students may suggest that such a model does have value because it points the way for further study of the issue.)* **AL**

Hands-On Chapter Project

Step 3

Modeling an Economic Decision

Step 3: Evaluating Trade-Offs and Opportunity Costs. Students will identify trade-offs and determine opportunity costs associated with changes in production.

Directions: Explain to students that their T-shirt business must now decide whether to produce hats also. Have students compose a list of possible trade-offs associated with this decision. Inform students that they will evaluate the

opportunity costs associated with producing hats by making a production possibilities curve. Direct students to construct such a curve using the data in the following table.

Number of T-Shirts and Hats Produced

T-Shirts	Hats
500	0
400	175
300	300
200	350
100	400
0	500

Describing When each group has completed its production possibilities chart, ask group members to use their finished work to describe the opportunity costs of producing several quantities of hats. **OL**

(Chapter Project continued in Visual Summary.)

C Critical Thinking

Comparing and Contrasting

Ask: How are economic models and cost-benefit analyses alike and different? *(They are both strategies that help people make the best economic choices. An economic model uses graphs, equations, or illustrations to explain concepts. A cost-benefit analysis compares an action to its benefits.)* **OL**

D Differentiated Instruction

Verbal/Linguistic Have students research to find out what elements are used to measure a country's standard of living (for example, poverty rate and personal income). Have students use their findings to comment on the standard of living in the United States. **OL**

Caption Answer: to investigate projects that give the highest return per dollar spent

✓**Reading Check** **Answer:** It reveals the choice with the lowest cost and the highest benefits.

Additional Support

Cost-Benefit Analysis Before making any major financial decisions, it is a good idea to weigh the benefits against the costs. *How might a business use cost-benefit analysis?*

SO WHAT ABOUT RAISING MY ALLOWANCE, DAD?

WELL, SINCE YOU DON'T DO YOUR CHORES, MY COST-BENEFIT ANALYSIS WOULD INDICATE THAT YOUR ALLOWANCE HAS COSTS BUT NO BENEFITS. THEREFORE, YOUR BUDGET INCREASE IS DENIED.

I LIKED YOU BETTER BEFORE THE MANAGEMENT CLASS.

cost-benefit analysis way of thinking about a choice that compares the cost of an action to its benefits

free enterprise economy market economy in which privately owned businesses have the freedom to operate for a profit with limited government intervention

standard of living quality of life based on ownership of necessities and luxuries that make life easier

Apply Cost-Benefit Analysis

Most economic decisions can be evaluated with **cost-benefit analysis,** a way of comparing the costs of an action to the benefits received. This is what Jesse did when he devised a decision-making grid. This decision can be made subjectively, as when Jesse selected the jersey, or it can be made more objectively, especially if the costs of the various alternatives are different.

To illustrate, suppose that you have to make a decision, and you like choices A and B equally. If B costs less, it would be the better choice because you would get more satisfaction per dollar spent. Businesses make investment decisions in exactly this manner, choosing to invest in projects that give the highest return per dollar spent or, in other words, the best cost-benefit ratio.

Take Small, Incremental Steps

Finally, it also helps to take small, incremental steps toward the final goal. This is especially valuable when we are unsure of the exact cost involved. If the cost turns out to be larger than we anticipated, then the resulting decision can be reversed without too much being lost.

✓**Reading Check** **Explaining** How does cost-benefit analysis help make economic decisions?

24   UNIT 1   Fundamental Economic Concepts

The Road Ahead

MAIN Idea The study of economics helps people become better citizens.

Economics & You As you become old enough to vote, are you also becoming more aware of current events? Read on to learn how economic issues affect politics.

The study of economics does more than explain how people deal with scarcity. Economics also includes the study of how things are made, bought, sold, and used. It provides insight as to how incomes are earned and spent, how jobs are created, and how the economy works on a daily basis. The study of economics also gives us a better understanding of the workings of a **free enterprise economy**—one in which consumers and privately owned businesses, rather than the government, make the majority of the WHAT, HOW, and FOR WHOM decisions.

Topics and Issues

The study of economics will provide you with a working knowledge of the economic incentives, laws of supply and demand, price system, economic institutions, and property rights that make the U.S. economy function. Along the way, you will learn about topics such as unemployment, the business cycle, inflation, and economic growth. You will also examine the role of business, labor, and government in the U.S. economy, as well as the relationship of the United States economy with the international community.

All of these topics have a bearing on our **standard of living**—the quality of life based on the ownership of the necessities and luxuries that make life easier. As you study economics, you will learn how to measure the value of our production and how productivity helps determine our standard of living. You will find, however, that the way the American people make economic decisions is not the only way to make these decisions.

Activity: Interdisciplinary Connection

Science Tell students that determining value can be very difficult when economic decisions are related to environmental concerns. When the Northern Spotted Owl was declared a threatened species, the owls' nesting sites and surrounding locations became protected by the government. This helped the chances for the owls' survival, but it greatly impacted the logging industry in parts of the northwest. Because fewer trees could be cut down, logging decreased dramatically. Many workers lost their jobs in an area with few other economic opportunities. Have students report on another case in which environmental government policy impacted the economy. Discuss how the value of the environment might be weighed against other economic concerns. **OL**

Economists have identified three basic kinds of economic systems. We will analyze these systems and how their organization affects decision making in the next chapter.

Economics for Citizenship

The study of economics helps us become better decision makers—in our personal lives as well as in the voting booths. Economic issues are often debated during political campaigns, so we need to understand the issues before deciding which candidate to support.

Most of today's political problems have important economic aspects. For example, is it important to balance the federal budget? How can we best keep inflation in check? What methods can we use to strengthen our economy? The study of economics will not provide you with clear-cut answers to all of these questions, but it will give you a better understanding of the issues involved.

Understanding the World Around Us

D The study of economics helps us understand the complex world around us. This is particularly useful because the world is not as orderly as your economics textbook, for example. Your book is neatly divided into sections for study. In contrast, society is dynamic, and technology and other innovations always lead to changes.

Economics provides a framework for analysis—a structure that helps explain how things are organized. Because this framework describes the incentives that influence behavior, it helps us understand why and how the world changes.

In practice, the world of economics is complex and the road ahead is bumpy. As we study economics, however, we will gain a much better appreciation of how we affect the world and how it affects us.

✓Reading Check **Determining Cause and Effect**
How do you think our society would be different if citizens did not study economics?

Economics
ONLINE
Student Web Activity Visit the *Economics: Principles and Practices* Web site at glencoe.com and click on *Chapter 1— Student Web Activities* to learn more about how economics affects our lives.

D **Differentiated Instruction**

Intrapersonal Ask students to consider past economic decisions, such as buying a gift or finding a job. Then have them write a journal entry in response to this question: *How can studying economics help you personally?* OL

✓Reading Check **Possible Answer:** Our society as a whole might not make good decisions for groups or individuals.

Assess

⊙ Use the Interactive Tutor Self-Assessment CD-ROM to review Section 3, and then assign the Section 3 Review as homework or as an in-class activity.

Close

Making Connections Have students imagine that they have won $100 in a raffle. Ask them how the knowledge of trade-offs and opportunity cost can help them decide what to do with the money. OL

SECTION 3 Review

Vocabulary
1. **Explain** the significance of trade-off, opportunity cost, production possibilities frontier, economic model, cost-benefit analysis, free enterprise economy, and standard of living.

Main Ideas
2. **Illustrating** Imagine you have $50 to spend. What one item would you buy? Complete the graphic organizer below to illustrate your final choice, the opportunity cost of your choice, and the trade-offs.

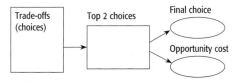

3. **Explaining** What decision-making strategies do economists recommend using?

Critical Thinking
4. **The BIG Idea** Why is it important for governments to understand trade-offs and opportunity costs? Explain in a brief paragraph.

5. **Synthesizing** How does economics play a part in politics?

6. **Analyzing Visuals** Study the production possibilities frontier in Figure 1.6 on page 21. What does it mean when the frontier shifts outward? What possible causes exist for such a shift?

Applying Economics
7. **Economic Way of Thinking** Search the newspaper and identify a major economic issue facing your community or state. Identify possible solutions and prepare a decision-making grid to evaluate the alternatives. What decision would you make? Write a short essay in which you explain your choice.

CHAPTER 1 What Is Economics? 25

Review SECTION 3

Answers

1. All definitions can be found in the section and the Glossary.
2. Answers will vary, but students should illustrate how analyzing trade-offs and opportunity costs can help them make economic decisions.
3. building economic models and preparing a cost-benefit analysis

4. **Possible answer:** Understanding trade-offs and opportunity cost helps governments decide what goods and services to produce.
5. **Possible answer:** Economic issues are often debated in political campaigns. Voters may decide which candidates to support by understanding their positions on economic issues.

6. It means that resources have been shifted from the production of one good to another. Possible causes will vary but may include that demand for one of the goods has increased.
7. Answers will vary but should demonstrate the student's understanding of decision-making grids to evaluate alternatives.

Teach

S Skill Practice

Visual Literacy Ask: Which store carries the most expensive jeans? The least expensive jeans? *(Banana Republic; Old Navy)* What is the difference in the price of the most expensive jeans and the least expensive jeans? *($98.50)* **OL**

Analyzing the Impact

Answers:

1. Each of their brands now has a unique identity that is carried out in the store environment and marketing agenda.

2. Answers will vary but should identify aspects of the site's design that reflect the brand's target audience.

Additional Support

CASE STUDY
Gap, Inc.

Search for the Perfect Jeans

We all have them. And if you don't, you are probably looking for them—the perfect pair of jeans. Preferably, they are faded, soft, and perfect. In 1969, Don and Doris Fisher opened the first Gap store in San Francisco "to make it easier to find" that perfect pair. This store was only the beginning. Gap, Inc., expanded its consumer market through Banana Republic, Old Navy, and, most recently, Forth and Towne.

Average Price of Jeans:

Gap: $58
Banana Republic: $68 to $128
Old Navy: $29.50 to $34.50
Forth & Towne: $54 to $78

GAP REVENUES

Net sales in billions

- Gap U.S.
- Banana Republic
- Old Navy
- Gap International
- Forth & Towne

Source: www.gapinc.com

Something for Every "Body"

Why did a single retail shop morph into four different brands? In the 1990s, Gap seemed to be losing its edge. A boastful rival claimed to Gap's then-CEO Mickey Drexler that "he could create a cheap Gap knockoff that one day would be bigger than Gap itself." Drexler liked the idea and ran with it himself. Enter Old Navy.

Just as each body requires a different pair of jeans—be it boot cut or low rise—each Gap, Inc., brand has a unique identity that is carried out in the store environment and marketing agenda. For example, budget-conscious consumers can peruse the deals at Old Navy while standing on concrete floors and listening to loud music. Down the street at Banana Republic, a more sophisticated crowd is checking out

the season's trendiest fashions at "approachable prices." Meanwhile, at Forth and Towne, the target is the female baby boomer. These 35-and-over women are treated to chandeliers and lavish fitting rooms stocked with bottled water and chocolates.

Retail Success

The economics and marketing savvy behind the retailer's rise to success are pretty simple: provide a product of value at different price levels in order to reach the maximum number of consumers. It seems to be working. With more than 3,000 stores and 2005 revenues topping out at $16 billion, Gap, Inc. operates under the notion that every "body" deserves that perfect pair of jeans.

Analyzing the Impact

1. **Summarizing** How did Gap, Inc., tackle the economic problem of consumers having to make choices?

2. **Analyzing** Investigate each brand's Web site. How does each site's design reflect the brand's target audience?

Extending the Content

Gap Facts In 1969 Doris and Don Fisher opened the first Gap clothing store. By the next year, the San Francisco outlet boasted $2 million in sales. The Fishers quickly opened a number of other Gap stores in the 1970s to capitalize on the brand's popularity. In 1976 the Gap went public, offering 1.2 million shares of stock. Less than eleven years later, the company's annual sales topped $1 billion. By 1998, the company had Gap stores in all 50 states. The company now operates more than 3,100 stores throughout the United States, Canada, the United Kingdom, France, Ireland and Japan, and employs more than 150,000 people.

STUDY TO GO **Study anywhere, anytime!** Download quizzes and flash cards to your PDA from glencoe.com.

▶ **Scarcity** Because of scarcity, society needs to decide how to distribute limited resources to satisfy seemingly unlimited wants and needs.

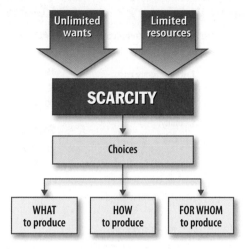

Unlimited wants → **SCARCITY** ← Limited resources

Choices

WHAT to produce | **HOW to produce** | **FOR WHOM to produce**

▶ **Factors of Production** Four factors of production are required to produce the things we would like to have.

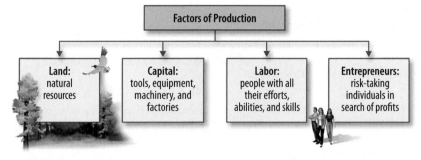

Factors of Production

Land: natural resources | **Capital:** tools, equipment, machinery, and factories | **Labor:** people with all their efforts, abilities, and skills | **Entrepreneurs:** risk-taking individuals in search of profits

▶ **Trade-offs and Opportunity Costs** All economic decisions require us to make choices among alternatives. Trade-offs are all the available alternatives. The opportunity cost is the next-best alternative we give up.

Trade-offs (choices) → **Top 2 choices** → **Final choice** / **Opportunity cost**

CHAPTER 1 What Is Economics? 27

Assessing Ask students to think about needs that all people have and then consider people's most common wants. Have a volunteer record students' responses on the board. Then lead a class discussion about the most significant wants that people seek to acquire. **Ask:** How do you think people determine what their most important wants will be? *(Answers will vary, but students may suggest that people determine what these wants will be based on factors such as the items' practicality, affordability, status, value, and so on.)* **BL**

Personal Writing Direct students to write an essay in which they explain how their economic choices might change if they found themselves with twice the amount of financial resources they currently have. Ask them to consider whether they would allocate more money to spending, saving, and so on, and encourage them to explain the reasoning behind their decisions. **OL**

Hands-On Chapter Project
Step 4: Wrap Up

Modeling an Economic Decision

Step 4: Bringing It All Together. Students will synthesize what they learned in previous steps.

Directions: Have students resume work in their groups. Instruct each group to compile their work throughout the chapter into a booklet. The booklet should include their summary reports from Step 1, their answers to the questions posed in Step 2, and the production possibilities charts from Step 3.

Then, review the Big Idea with students by asking volunteers to explain how the problem of scarcity and the concept of limited resources affected each step in the T-shirt business plan. **OL**

Assessment & Activities

ExamView®
Assessment Suite

This easy-to-use software includes extensive question banks and allows you to create fully customized tests that can be administered in print or online.

Review Content Vocabulary

1. b	2. j
3. h	4. g
5. f	6. e
7. i	8. a
9. d	10. c

Review Academic Vocabulary

11.–17. Students' sentences will vary but should demonstrate understanding of each term's meaning in an economic context.

Review the Main Ideas

18. Cause: not having enough resources to produce all of the things that people would like to have. Effects: careful decisions have to be made about how to use resources.

19. They are all required to produce goods and services.

20. describing an economic activity; analyzing the economic activity; explaining the activity to other people; predicting what may happen in the future

21. Consumers: People who use goods and services to satisfy their wants and needs. **Goods:** Tangible products that are useful, relatively scarce, and transferable to others. **Services:** Acts of work or labor performed for someone.

Review Content Vocabulary

Use the key terms from the list below to complete the sentences that follow.

a. capital goods	**f.** opportunity cost
b. consumer goods	**g.** scarcity
c. economics	**h.** services
d. factors of production	**i.** utility
e. human capital	**j.** value

1. Economic products designed for final use by people are called _____ .

2. The _____ of a CD player can be expressed in dollars and cents.

3. Haircuts and appliance repairs are examples of _____ .

4. _____ arises because society does not have enough resources to produce all the things people would like to have.

5. The _____ of going to a football game instead of working would include the money not earned at your job.

6. _____ is the sum of the skills, abilities, health, and motivation of people.

7. _____ is another name for the capacity of a product to be useful.

8. The only factors of production that are themselves the result of earlier production are _____ .

9. Land, capital, labor, and entrepreneurs are _____ .

10. _____ is the study of how people use limited resources to satisfy unlimited wants.

Review Academic Vocabulary

On a separate sheet of paper, use each of these terms in a sentence that reflects the term's meaning in the chapter.

11. resource	15. mechanism
12. comprehensive	16. alternative
13. transferable	17. assumption
14. accumulation	

28   UNIT 1   Fundamental Economic Concepts

Review the Main Ideas

Section 1 *(pages 5–10)*

18. Identify the cause and effects of scarcity.

19. Explain how the factors of production relate to one another.

20. Describe the key elements of studying economics.

Section 2 *(pages 12–17)*

21. Define *goods, services,* and *consumers* and describe the relationship among the three, using a graphic organizer similar to the one below.

```
        ┌──────────────┐
        │ Consumers:   │
        └──────┬───────┘
        ┌──────┴───────┐
   ┌────────┐      ┌──────────┐
   │ Goods: │      │ Services:│
   └────────┘      └──────────┘
```

22. Describe the paradox of value.

23. Explain how the circular flow of economic activity generates wealth in an economy.

24. Identify two ways to increase productivity.

Section 3 *(pages 19–25)*

25. Describe how economists view the term *cost.*

26. Identify the economic concept illustrated by the production possibilities frontier.

27. Describe how economic models help economists develop strategies that help people make economic choices.

28. Explain why economic education is important.

Critical Thinking

29. The BIG Idea You have learned that scarcity is the fundamental economic problem for societies. Write a short paragraph explaining how scarcity affects you and your family on a daily basis.

22. the fact that some necessities have a very low monetary value and some nonnecessities have a very high value

23. Individuals earn their income in factor markets, where factors of production are bought and sold. They spend their income in product markets. Businesses use this money to produce more goods and services.

24. to produce more with the same amount of resources; to invest in human capital

25. the next-best alternative

26. the various combinations of goods and services that an economy can produce when all of its resources are in use

27. Economists can use models to analyze or describe an actual situation, which helps people make economic choices.

28. It helps us become better decision makers.

Critical Thinking

29. Answers will vary, but students should identify the personal effects of scarcity.

Economics ONLINE **Self-Check Quiz** Visit the *Economics: Principles and Practices* Web site at glencoe.com and click on *Chapter 1—Self-Check Quizzes* to prepare for the chapter test.

Assessment and Activities **CHAPTER 1**

30. Determining Cause and Effect Copy the two diagrams of the production possibilities frontiers shown below. Then write captions that explain what each diagram is showing.

31. Understanding Cost-Benefit Analysis How would you apply the concept of cost-benefit analysis to the decision whether to finish high school? To further your education beyond high school? To purchase a computer? Explain your results in a few sentences.

32. Evaluating Alternatives Refer to the chapter opener activity on page 4 and evaluate the alternatives in *one* of the three categories (location, music, refreshments). What criteria will you use? What are the trade-offs? On a separate sheet of paper, illustrate your decision in a decision-making grid similar to the one below.

Alternatives	Criterion 1	Criterion 2	Criterion 3	Criterion 4

Writing About Economics

33. Persuasive Writing Research a recent school funding levy for your school district that was not approved. Find out what changes the school district had to implement to adjust to the reduced funding levels and reduced resources available to schools. Write a two-page paper in which you evaluate the choices.

Math Practice

34. A city administrator with a $100,000 annual budget is trying to decide between fixing potholes or directing traffic after school at several busy intersections. Studies have shown that 15 cars hit potholes every week, causing an average of $200 in damages. Collisions at the intersections are less frequent, averaging one per month at an average cost of $6,000, although none have caused injuries or deaths. Use this information to answer the following questions.

    a. What are the annual costs from the pothole damage?

    b. What are the annual costs due to damage from collisions?

    c. Given the size of the annual budget, make your recommendation as to which project should be undertaken. Explain your answer in terms of dollar benefits per dollar spent.

Thinking Like an Economist

35. Use a problem-solving process to gather information about the alternatives, trade-offs, and opportunity costs facing the city administrator in the previous question. Consider the advantages and disadvantages of implementing the possible solutions. Prepare a written summary.

Interpreting Cartoons

36. Critical Thinking Look at the cartoon below. How does the message of this cartoon relate to the concepts presented in this chapter?

www.CartoonStock.com

Thinking Like an Economist

35. Answers will vary but should demonstrate use of a problem-solving process to consider advantages and disadvantages of implementing possible solutions.

Interpreting Cartoons

36. Answers will vary but should demonstrate an understanding of trade-offs and opportunity costs.

---

30. Answers will vary, but students should note that in the first diagram, the production of cars is shown increasing while the production of clothing stays the same. In the second diagram, the production of cars stays the same while the production of clothing increases.

31. Answers will vary, but students should demonstrate understanding of the cost-benefit analysis in each given situation.

32. Answers will vary, but students should illustrate their decision in a decision-making grid.

Writing About Economics

33. Answers will vary but should demonstrate an understanding of how to evaluate choices.

Math Practice

34. a. $10,400
    b. $72,000
    c. Answers will vary but should explain dollar benefits per dollar spent.

Focus

Ask students to use an online inflation calculator to determine how much 25 cents per hour in 1938 would equal today. (You might suggest that they visit www.minneapolisfed.org.) Have students write a paragraph explaining whether they think the 1938 minimum wage was fair. *(Students who believe that it was not fair may point out that the 1938 wage is equivalent to less than $4.00 per hour today. Students who believe it was fair may point out that Depression-era businesses could not afford to pay more than 25 cents per hour.)*

Teach

S Skill Practice

Analyzing Information

Ask: Does this graph support Dreier and Candaele's argument? Why or why not? *(Possible answer: The graph supports their argument because it shows that the purchasing power of the minimum wage is nearing its lowest value since 1950.)* **OL**

Additional Support

DEBATES IN ECONOMICS

Should the Minimum Wage Be Increased?

The minimum wage was created in 1938 by the Fair Labor Standards Act (FLSA), debuting at 25 cents per hour. Even though it has been raised many times since then, it remains the subject of debate. Unions and antipoverty organizations typically spearhead campaigns to increase the minimum wage, saying it will help the nation's working poor without affecting employment. Business organizations typically oppose a hike in the minimum wage, arguing that it will increase unemployment.

Who is right? As you read the selections, ask yourself: Should the minimum wage be increased?

PRO A MORAL MINIMUM WAGE

. . . 1968 [was] the last year that the minimum wage was above the nation's poverty line. . . . If the minimum wage were pegged at $9.50, millions . . . would be lifted out of poverty. The largest group of beneficiaries would be children, whose parents would have more money for rent, food, clothing and other basic necessities.

Business leaders still trot out economists to claim that raising the minimum wage will destroy jobs and hurt small businesses. But the evidence, based on studies of the effects of past increases in both the federal and state minimum-wage levels, . . . shows otherwise. Because the working poor spend everything they earn, every penny of a minimum-wage increase goes back into the economy, increasing consumer demand and adding at least as many jobs as are lost. Most employers actually gain, absorbing the increase through decreased absenteeism, lower recruiting and training costs, higher productivity and increased worker morale.

—*Peter Dreier, director of the Urban & Environmental Policy program at Occidental College; and Kelly Candaele, founding member of the Peace Institute at California State University, Chico*

MINIMUM WAGE PURCHASING POWER LOW BY HISTORICAL STANDARDS

The Inflation-Adjusted Value of the Minimum Wage

S

Source: Author's calculations based on the U.S. Department of Labor.

30   UNIT 1   Fundamental Economic Concepts

Extending the Content

Minimum Wage in the States As of 2007 the federal minimum wage was $5.15 per hour. However, millions of Americans earning minimum wage that year received a higher hourly rate of pay than $5.15. This is because more than half of the states have set minimum wage rates that are higher than the federal rate. When state and federal laws set differing wage rates, the higher standard applies. Thus, in states such as New York, Massachusetts, Oregon, and California, workers earning the minimum wage received more than $7.00 per hour. Kansas, on the other hand, had a state minimum wage of $2.65 per hour. Louisiana, Mississippi, Alabama, Tennessee, and South Carolina had no minimum wage law as of 2007.

CON WAGE HIKE WOULD COST JOBS

Raising the federal minimum wage by $1.50 an hour will reduce job opportunities for those who need it most, new entrants to the job market with the least skills or experience. Raising the minimum wage hurts all American consumers and workers, by artificially inflating the cost of entry-level jobs, which is passed on through higher prices and lower real wages.

The convenience store industry offers a compelling employment opportunity, with competitive wages, flexible schedules, and career development. Most convenience stores offer wages far above the minimum—in 2001, the average was $9.28 an hour. However, our industry strongly opposes an increase in the federal minimum wage because it will discourage the creation of entry-level jobs and hurt small businesses. With higher costs of health care and other benefits, and lower profit margins, convenience store owners and petroleum marketers cannot sustain an increase in the minimum wage.

NACS members want to do what's best for their own employees without government interference. And NACS members are very concerned about the inevitable result of a higher minimum wage—a 'ripple effect' of higher prices throughout the economy.

If Congress really wants to help low-income workers, there are much more constructive things that can be done, such as reducing payroll taxes, cutting the capital gains tax, and eliminating unnecessary and burdensome regulations.

—*Allison Shulman, director, National Association of Convenience Stores, government affairs*

Raising the federal minimum wage from $5.15 to $6.65 an hour would:

- Cost private-sector employers $30.2 billion over four years
- Impose $2.1 billion in unfunded mandates on state and local governments

Source: Congressional Budget Office

Analyzing the Issue

1. **Identifying** What arguments do Dreier and Candaele make in support of increasing the minimum wage?
2. **Explaining** Why does Shulman believe that raising the minimum wage will hurt convenience stores and other small businesses?
3. **Deciding** With which opinion do you agree? Explain your reasoning.

CHAPTER 1   What Is Economics?   31

Assess/ Close

W Writing Support

Expository Writing Have students select a time in U.S. history when Congress raised the minimum wage. Instruct students to research and then write about the economic effects of the minimum wage increase they selected. OL

Analyzing the Issue

Answers:
1. An increase would lift millions of Americans out of poverty, spark consumer spending, create jobs, and lower employer expenses.
2. It will discourage the creation of entry-level jobs and force businesses to absorb greater expenses that would lower profit margins.
3. Answers will vary but should be logical and well supported.

Additional Support

Activity: Interdisciplinary Connection

Art Organize the class into small groups. Instruct students in each group to decide among themselves which position on the minimum wage issue they support. Have groups then prepare sketches for a visual advertising campaign promoting the position they support. Ideas for campaigns include posters, bumper stickers, web banners, T-shirt logos, billboards, placards, mugs, and so on. Ask groups to present the sketches of their visual ad campaigns to the class. After groups have presented, have students discuss the strengths and weaknesses of each ad campaign. They might consider whether the campaign is eye-catching and unique and whether it appeals to a diverse group of viewers. Then ask the class to vote on which ad campaign they think would be most effective. OL

Key to Ability Levels

BL Below level **AL** Above level
OL On level **ELL** English
Language Learners

Key to Teaching Resources

Print Material | DVD
CD-Rom | Transparency

BL	OL	AL	ELL		Resources	Chapter Opener	Section 1	Section 2	Section 3	Chapter Assess
					FOCUS					
BL	OL	AL	ELL		**Daily Focus Skills Transparencies**		6, 7, 85	8	22	
					TEACH					
BL	OL		ELL		**Guided Reading Activities***		p. 4	p. 5	p. 6	
BL	OL	AL	ELL		**Economic Content Vocabulary Activities***		p. 2	p. 2	p. 2	
	OL	AL			**Critical Thinking Activities**		p. 2			
BL	OL		ELL		**Reading Essentials and Note-Taking Guide***		p. 10	p. 13	p. 16	
		AL			**Enrichment Activities**			p. 2		
	OL	AL			**Free Enterprise Activities**		p. 1		p. 1	
BL	OL	AL	ELL		**Primary and Secondary Source Readings**			pp. 1, 15	pp. 1, 15	
BL	OL	AL	ELL		**Economic Cartoons**				p.13	
BL	OL	AL	ELL		**Economic Concepts Transparencies, Strategies, and Activities**		p. 7			
BL	OL	AL	ELL		**Math Practice for Economics**				p. 2	
BL	OL	AL	ELL		**Reinforcing Economic Skills**		p. 11			
BL	OL		ELL		**High School Reading in the Content Area Strategies and Activities**	✓	✓	✓	✓	✓
BL	OL	AL	ELL		**High School Writing Process Transparencies**	✓	✓	✓	✓	✓
BL	OL	AL	ELL		**Writer's Guidebook**	✓	✓	✓	✓	✓
BL	OL	AL	ELL		**StudentWorks Plus CD-ROM**	✓	✓	✓	✓	✓
BL	OL	AL	ELL		**Vocabulary PuzzleMaker CD-ROM**	✓	✓	✓	✓	✓

*Also available in Spanish

- Interactive Lesson Planner
- Interactive Teacher Edition
- Fully editable blackline masters
- Economics & You videos

- Differentiated Lesson Plans
- Printable reports of daily assignments
- Standards tracking system

Levels					Resources	Chapter Opener	Section 1	Section 2	Section 3	Chapter Assess
BL	OL	AL	ELL							
TEACH (continued)										
BL	OL	AL	ELL		Economics & You Video Program DVD— *Economic Systems and the American Economy*	✓	✓	✓	✓	✓
BL	OL	AL	ELL		**Graph Coach CD-ROM**	✓	✓	✓	✓	✓
Teacher Resources					**Differentiated Instruction Strategies**	✓	✓	✓	✓	✓
					Success with English Learners	✓	✓	✓	✓	✓
					Presentation Plus! CD-ROM	✓	✓	✓	✓	✓
ASSESS										
BL	OL	AL	ELL		**Section Quizzes and Chapter Tests**		p. 17	p. 18	p. 19	pp. 21, 25
BL	OL	AL	ELL		**Authentic Assessment Strategies and Activities**			p. 2		
BL	OL	AL	ELL		*ExamView® Assessment Suite* **CD-ROM**		2-1	2-2	2-3	Ch. 2
BL	OL	AL	ELL		**Interactive Tutor Self-Assessment CD-ROM**		2-1	2-2	2-3	
CLOSE										
BL			ELL		**Reteaching Activities***		p. 2	p. 2	p. 2	
BL	OL		ELL		**Reading and Study Skills Foldables**		p. 44		p. 44	
BL	OL	AL	ELL		**Graphic Organizer Transparencies**		pp. 9, 19			

*Also available in Spanish

Activity Using CyberScout

Research Using Browse Famous People

Technology Product

CyberScout is a convenient and dynamic search engine that provides several easy ways to locate information outside the McGraw-Hill Learning Network. CyberScout only searches Web sites that have been reviewed by teachers, so the information students find is always appropriate and accurate.

Objectives

After students learn to use CyberScout, they will be able to

- research information on famous people in economics;
- exercise research and study skills;
- practice writing skills.

Steps

- From the McGraw-Hill Learning Network home page (www.mhln.com), click on **For Students**.
- Choose **CyberScout** below **Homework Help.**
- Click on a subject area link to narrow the search.
- The CyberScout page will display a set of subcategories.
- Click the **Browse Famous People** button at the bottom of the page.
- The CyberScout page displays a set of names related to the subject area. Click a name.
- The CyberScout page displays a set of results.
- Click the link to a Web site of interest.
- Students will be redirected to the Web site in a new window.
- Students navigate through the chosen Web site to gain information on a topic and take notes.

Economics ONLINE

	Student	Teacher	Parent
Beyond the Textbook	●	●	●
Chapter Overviews	●	●	●
ePuzzles and Games	●		●
Concepts in Motion	●		●
Multi-Language Glossaries	●		●
Online Student Edition	●	●	●
Self-Check Quizzes	●		●
Student Web Activities	●		●
Study Central™	●		●
Time Current Events	●	●	●
Teaching Today		●	
Vocabulary eFlashcards	●		●
Web Activity Lesson Plans		●	

Glencoe Media Center

❯ glencoe.com

Study-To-Go
- Vocabulary eFlashcards
- Self-Check Quizzes

❯ **Audio/Video**
- Student Edition Audio
- Spanish Summaries
- Economics & You Videos

READING SUPPORT FROM JAMESTOWN EDUCATION

- **Timed Readings Plus in Social Studies** helps students increase their reading rate and fluency while maintaining comprehension. The 400-word passages are similar to those found on state and national assessments.

- **Reading in the Content Area: Social Studies** concentrates on six essential reading skills that help students better comprehend what they read. The book includes 75 high-interest nonfiction passages written at increasing levels of difficulty.

- **Reading Social Studies** includes strategic reading instruction and vocabulary support in Social Studies content for both ELLs and native speakers of English. www.jamestowneducation.com

Reading List Generator CD-ROM

GLENCOE BookLink 3

Use this database to search more than 30,000 titles to create a customized reading list for your students.

- Reading lists can be organized by students' reading level, author, genre, theme, or area of interest.
- The database provides Degrees of Reading Power™ (DRP) and Lexile™ readability scores for all selections.
- A brief summary of each selection is included.

Leveled reading suggestions for this chapter:

For students at a Grade 10 reading level:
- *That One Man's Profit Is Another's Loss,* by Michel de Montaigne

For students at a Grade 11 reading level:
- *The Haunted Land: Facing Europe's Ghosts After Communism,* by Tina Rosenberg

For students at a Grade 12 reading level:
- *Small Is Beautiful: Economics as if People Mattered,* by E. F. Schumacher

* Review suggested books before assigning them.

NCEE

National Council on Economic Education

Voluntary Standards Emphasized in Chapter 2

Content Standard 3 Different methods can be used to allocate goods and services. People acting individually or collectively through government, must choose which methods to use to allocate different kinds of goods and services.

Content Standard 16 There is an economic role for government in a market economy whenever the benefits of a government policy outweigh its costs. Governments often provide for national defense, address environmental concerns, define and protect property rights, and attempt to make markets more competitive. Most government policies also redistribute income.

Resources Available from NCEE
- Virtual Economics®: An Interactive Center for Economic Education Version 3.0
- Capstone: The Nation's High School Economics Course
- Civics and Government: Focus on Economics, Second Edition
- Focus: Economic Systems

To order these materials, or to contact your State Council on Economic Education about workshops and programs, call 1-800-338-1192 or visit the NCEE Web site at store.ncee.net.

CHAPTER

2 Economic Systems and Decision Making

Why It Matters

Take a closer look at the way your high school is organized. Who makes the decisions on lesson plans? Who plans out events that take place during the year? Who makes financial decisions, and how? Are parents and voters involved in the educational system? Obtain information from your school district office or the library to create a chart that lists the rights and responsibilities of people in your school district to meet the needs of education. Read Chapter 2 to learn about the different economic systems that societies set up to meet their specific economic needs.

The BIG Idea

Every society has an economic system to allocate goods and services.

In a market economy, individuals ▶ can freely make all economic choices, including opening a store.

Economics ONLINE **Chapter Overview** Visit the *Economics: Principles and Practices* Web site at glencoe.com and click on *Chapter 2–Chapter Overviews* to preview chapter information.

32 UNIT 1

Activity: Launching the Chapter

Comparing Have students recall the different stores that they have visited in the past week. Ask them to consider the products that were on sale at those stores and then think about who made the decision to make those products available to consumers. **Essential Question:** Why is the question of who decides which products to sell to consumers important? *(The people who decide what to produce and sell help set prices, which* impacts the lifestyles of citizens.) Write the names of three different countries on the board, and have students discuss who makes these economic decisions in those nations. **OL**

GUIDE TO READING

Section Preview

In this section, you will learn about the different types of economic systems that govern WHAT goods and services to produce, HOW to produce them, and FOR WHOM to produce them.

Content Vocabulary

- economic system *(p. 33)*
- traditional economy *(p. 34)*
- command economy *(p. 35)*
- market economy *(p. 37)*
- market *(p. 37)*
- capitalism *(p. 38)*
- mixed economy *(p. 39)*
- socialism *(p. 39)*
- communism *(p. 39)*

Academic Vocabulary

- stagnation *(p. 35)*
- allocate *(p. 36)*
- emphasizing *(p. 36)*

Reading Strategy

Comparing and Contrasting As you read the section, complete a graphic organizer like the one below to identify ways in which a market economy differs from, and is similar to, a command economy.

Market Economy

Similarities

Command Economy

Bellringer
Daily Focus Transparency 6

GUIDE TO READING

Answers to Graphic:

Market Economy: people make decisions based on their own self-interest; high degree of freedom; private ownership of resources

Command Economy: central authority makes economic decisions and owns resources; low degree of freedom

Similarities: both must decide *what, how,* and *for whom* to produce; both face scarcity

COMPANIES IN THE NEWS
—Global Business Today

McDonald's and Hindu Culture

For thousands of years, India's Hindu culture has revered the cow. Hindu scriptures state that the cow is a gift of the gods to the human race. . . . [The cows] are everywhere, ambling down roads, grazing in rubbish dumps and resting in temples—everywhere, that is, except on your plate, for Hindus do not eat the meat of the sacred cow.

. . . McDonald's responded to this cultural food dilemma by creating an Indian version of its Big Mac—the "Maharaja Mac"—which is made from mutton. . . . According to the head of McDonald's Indian operations, "We had to reinvent ourselves for the Indian palate." ■

When companies want to do business in other countries, they need to adjust their business plans to meet local customs. This is what McDonald's corporation had to do when it expanded to India. While India's economy shares many characteristics with the United States, many of its business practices are based on a more traditional economic system.

All societies use an **economic system**—an organized way of providing for the wants and needs of their people. The way societies organize themselves determines the type of economic system they have. Three major kinds of economic systems exist—traditional, command, and market economies. In practice, however, almost all economies, like that of India, combine elements of all three.

economic system
organized way in which a society provides for the wants and needs of its people

Resource Manager

R Reading Strategies	**C** Critical Thinking	**D** Differentiated Instruction	**W** Writing Support	**S** Skill Practice
Teacher Edition • Using Context Clues, p. 34 • Making Connections, p. 36 • Act. Prior Know., p. 38 **Additional Resources** • Guid. Read. Act., p. 4 • Read. Ess. & Note-Taking Guide, p. 10	**Teacher Edition** • Drawing Con., p. 35 • Analyzing Visuals, p. 38 • Speculating, p. 41 • Designing, p. 42 **Additional Resources** • Econ. Concepts Trans., Strat. & Act., p. 7	**Teacher Edition** • Logical/Math., p. 35 • ELL, p. 37 • Interpersonal, p. 39 **Additional Resources** • Reading and Study Skills Fold., p. 44 • Daily Focus Trans. 6, 7, 85 • Free Ent. Act., p. 1	**Teacher Edition** • Narrative Writing, p. 34 • Persuasive Writing, p. 39 **Additional Resources** • High School Reading in the Content Area Strat. and Act.	**Teacher Edition** • Compare/Contrast, p. 36 • Visual Literacy, p. 40 • Using Tables and Charts, p. 40 **Additional Resources** • Graph. Org. Trans., pp. 5, 10

Teach

R Reading Strategy

Using Context Clues
Ask: What does the term *custom* mean as it is used in the text? *(an action that has been done by others in the past)* What words and phrases provide clues to this meaning? *(Possible answers: "habit," "does the bride toss the bouquet at a wedding," "traditional culture")* **BL**

W Writing Support

Narrative Writing Have students write a short story about a young person who lives in a traditional economy. Stories should include a description of the trade that the person learns from his or her parents. Invite students to illustrate their stories with drawings or magazine images. **OL**

Caption Answer: In a traditional economy, the questions *what, how,* and *for whom* to produce are answered by habit or custom.

Hands-On Chapter Project

Step 1

Comparing Economic Systems

In this project, students will write and perform skits illustrating the types of economic systems.

Step 1: Developing a Traditional Economy. Student teams will "create" traditional economic systems.

Directions: Divide the class into teams of five to seven students, and have each team sit together in the classroom. Have each team select one traditional economy in the world to research. Based on their findings, each team will then "become" a traditional economy, with students taking on the specific roles of people in the traditional system, such as village leader, hunter, and hunter's offspring. Students will perform a brief skit for the class demonstrating how their traditional economy functions. Skits should cover how the system answers the three basic economic questions. Students may wish to embellish their skits with

dramatic events such as a young woman in a village challenging the traditional structure or the introduction of a new technology. Students should take notes on the content and presentation of each skit.

Summarizing After the skits are performed, discuss the positives and negatives of a traditional economy. **OL**

(Chapter Project continued in Section 2.)

Economics ONLINE

Student Web Activity Visit the *Economics: Principles and Practices* Web site at glencoe.com and click on *Chapter 2–Student Web Activities* for an activity on the economies of traditional societies.

---

traditional economy economic system in which the allocation of scarce resources and other economic activities are based on ritual, habit, or custom

---

Traditional Economies

MAIN Idea Traditional societies use ritual, habit, or customs to answer the basic questions of WHAT, HOW, and FOR WHOM to produce.

Economics & You Does your family have a tradition that has been passed down from generation to generation? Read on to learn how traditions govern the economies of some societies.

R Many of our actions spring from habit and custom. Why, for example, does the bride toss the bouquet at a wedding? Such practices have become part of our traditional culture.

Characteristics

In a society with a **traditional economy,** the use of scarce resources—and nearly all other economic activity—stems from ritual,

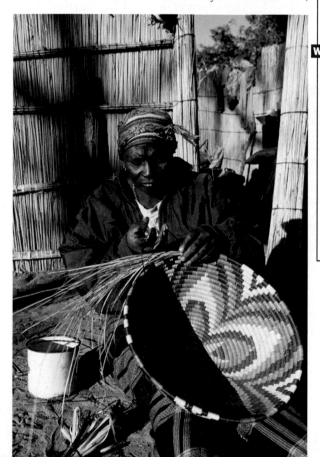

Traditions This woman in Botswana weaves a basket based on methods handed down by her ancestors. *What are the main characteristics of a traditional economy?*

habit, or custom. Habit and custom also dictate most social behavior. Individuals are generally not free to make decisions based on what they want or would like to have. Instead, their roles are defined by the customs of their elders and ancestors.

Examples

Many societies—such as the central African Mbuti, the Australian Aborigines, and other indigenous peoples around the world—have traditional economies. The Inuit of northern Canada in the 1800s provide an especially interesting case of a traditional economy.

For generations, Inuit parents taught their children how to survive in a harsh climate, make tools, fish, and hunt. Their children, in turn, taught these skills to the next generation. When the Inuit hunted, it was traditional to share the spoils of the hunt with other families. If a walrus or bear was taken, hunters divided the kill evenly into as many portions as there were heads of families in the hunting party. The hunter most responsible for the kill had first choice, the second hunter to help with the kill chose next, and so on. Because the Inuit shared freely and generously with one another, members of the hunting party later shared their portions with other families who had not participated.

The result was that the hunter had the honor of the kill and the respect of the village, rather than a physical claim to the entire animal. Because of this tradition of sharing, a village could survive the long, harsh winters as long as skilled hunters lived in the community. This custom was partially responsible for the Inuit's survival for thousands of years.

Advantages

The main advantage of a traditional economy is that everyone knows which role to play. Little uncertainty exists over

The Global Economy & YOU

The Great Wal [Mart] of China

What do you and 1 billion Chinese consumers have in common? Access to a Wal-Mart store. China's membership in the World Trade Organization has opened the door for capitalist companies to do business in this communist country. Now a growing number of Wal-Marts—48 and counting—cater to China's upper-middle class. Chinese consumers are pleased with the cleanliness and convenience Wal-Mart has to offer. Joe Hatfield, president and CEO of Wal-Mart Asia, explains that while Chinese grocers use fans to scatter flies, "They hold us to a higher standard than others and to set the expectations for others to follow."

While each new store creates roughly 500 new jobs, the retailer's presence in China does not come without controversy. Opponents deride the company's low wages—between $84 and $96 per month—and argue that Wal-Mart encourages exploitation of Chinese workers. Headlines detailing the power struggle between the All-China Federation of Trade Unions (ACFTUS) and Wal-Mart have drawn attention to the retailer's anti-union stance in a Communist country. Meanwhile, the world watches as China seeks to balance modern and traditional ways, as well as capitalist and communist ideologies.

WHAT to produce. If you are born into a family of hunters, you hunt. If you are born into a family of farmers, you farm. Likewise, little uncertainty exists over HOW to produce, because you do things much the same way your parents did. Finally, the FOR WHOM question is determined by the customs and traditions of the society. In some societies, you would provide for your immediate family. In others, such as the Inuit, you would share what you have hunted with all families of the village. In other words, tradition dictates how people live their lives.

Disadvantages

The main drawback of a traditional economy is that it tends to discourage new ideas and new ways of doing things. The strict roles in a traditional society have the effect of punishing people who [C] act differently or break the rules. The lack of progress leads to economic **stagnation** and a lower standard of living than in other economic systems.

✓Reading Check **Describing** What are the advantages and disadvantages of a traditional economy?

Command Economies

MAIN Idea Command economies rely on a central authority to make most of the economic decisions.

Economics & You As you make career decisions, does the government or other authority tell you what to do? Read on to find out how decisions are made in a command economy.

In a **command economy,** a central authority makes the major decisions about WHAT, HOW, and FOR WHOM to produce. A command economy can be headed by a king, a dictator, a president, or anyone else who makes the major economic decisions.

Characteristics

In a pure command economy, the government makes the major economic decisions. This means that the government decides if houses or apartments will be [D] built. It also decides on the best way to build them, as well as who will receive them.

Most command economies severely limit private property rights. People are not allowed to own their homes, businesses, and

command economy economic system with a central authority that makes the major economic decisions

CHAPTER 2   Economic Systems and Decision Making   35

Extending the Content

Bartering An element of the traditional economic system—barter—remains a major part of the global economy of the twenty-first century. Barter involves the exchange of goods and services. According to the World Trade Organization, $8.4 billion of all international trade in 2004 was conducted on a non-cash basis. That figure represents 15% of the total value of international transactions made that year.

Consumer Goods Command economies often limit the production of consumer goods. The result is sparsely stocked shelves, such as in this store in Pyongyang, North Korea. *Why might command economies lack consumer goods?*

other productive resources, although they may have some personal items and tools.

Individual freedom also is limited. For example, if the government wants engineers rather than social workers, then its universities will train more engineers. This limits individual choices because people have to live within the government's restrictions.

Finally, government officials tend to favor themselves when making economic decisions. The result is that some of the country's money often goes to luxury goods like houses, cars, and extravagant vacations for these officials.

Examples

Because they tend to be unproductive, few pure command economies exist today. North Korea and Cuba are modern examples, but in the 1970s and 1980s, the communist bloc countries of the former Soviet Union had command economies.

In the former Soviet Union, for example, the State Planning Commission determined needs, set goals, and established production quotas for major industries. If it wanted growth in heavy manufacturing, it would **allocate** resources to that sector. If it wanted to strengthen national defense, it directed resources to military production.

Advantages

The main strength of a command system is that it can change direction drastically. The former Soviet Union went from a rural agricultural society to an industrial nation in a few decades by **emphasizing** the growth of heavy industry. During this period, the central planning agency shifted resources on a massive scale.

Another advantage of command economies, especially those represented by the former Soviet Union, is that many health and public services are available to everyone at little or no cost.

Disadvantages

Pure command economies have their disadvantages. One is that they ignore the basic wants and needs of consumers. In the Soviet Union, for example, generations of people were forced to do without consumer goods and adequate housing. Similarly, the current North Korean government has put a strong emphasis on defense. In the meantime, the North Korean people have been suffering years of hunger. At times, the government even had to accept aid from international sources.

A second disadvantage is that the system gives people the incentive to fill their quotas instead of producing a good product. At one time in the former Soviet Union, quotas for electrical motors were measured in tons of output. Soviet workers then filled their quotas by producing the world's heaviest electrical motors.

A third weakness is that a command economy requires a large decision-making bureaucracy. In the former Soviet Union, an army of clerks, planners, and other administrators was needed to operate the system. This structure slowed decision making and raised the cost of production.

Yet a fourth weakness is that the planning bureaucracy lacks the flexibility to deal with minor day-to-day problems. As a result, command economies tend to lurch from one crisis to the next—or collapse completely, as did the former Soviet Union.

Finally, rewards for individual initiative are rare in a command economy. Each person is expected to perform a job in a factory or on a farm according to the decisions made by central planners.

✓Reading Check **Analyzing** What are the major problems with a command economy?

Market Economies

MAIN Idea In a market economy, consumers and businesses jointly answer the questions of WHAT, HOW, and FOR WHOM to produce.

Economics & You Name one or two things you like about the economic system in the United States. Read on to learn about the advantages of a market economy.

In a **market economy,** people make decisions in their own best interest. In economic terms, a **market** is an arrangement that allows buyers and sellers to come together to exchange goods and services. A market might be in a physical location, such as a farmers' market, or on an Internet site, such as eBay. Regardless of its form, a market can exist as long as a mechanism is in place for buyers and sellers to meet.

Characteristics

A market economy is characterized by a great deal of freedom. People can spend their money on the products they want most, which is like casting dollar "votes" for those products. This tells producers which products people want, thus helping them answer the question of WHAT to

market economy economic system in which supply, demand, and the price system help people make economic decisions and allocate resources

market meeting place or mechanism that allows buyers and sellers to come together (also see page 15)

Market Economies In a market economy, people have the freedom to start any business they wish. *How do the two entrepreneurs in the cartoon reflect this freedom of choice?*

"Forget lemonade. The real money's in bottled water."

CHAPTER 2   Economic Systems and Decision Making   37

D Differentiated Instruction

English Language Learners Tell students that the woman in the cartoon is speaking figuratively, not literally; thus, students should not take her comment at face value. Ask students to replace "The real money's in bottled water" with a sentence that conveys a more literal meaning. *(Possible answers: More profits are to be made in bottled water. We can make more money selling bottled water.)* **ELL**

Caption Answer: Each person is choosing to make a different product.

✓Reading Check **Answer:** ignores consumer wants and needs; gives incentive to fill quotas instead of making good products; needs a large bureaucracy; cannot handle minor problems; rarely rewards individual initiative

Additional Support

Activity: Technology Connection

The Electronic Marketplace Have students use print or online sources to research how technology changed the concept of the marketplace. Ask students to write a report about how exchanging goods today contrasts with how goods were exchanged in the early years of the United States. For example, people today buy and sell goods online, whereas in 1800 they used carts or barges to deliver goods to sell at a physical marketplace. **OL**

R Reading Strategy

Activating Prior Knowledge
Ask: What are some products that have fallen out of favor in the United States? Challenge students to write down as many of these products as they can.
Ask: Why aren't these goods as widely produced as they used to be? *(Possible answers: VCRs, because DVDs last longer, provide better pictures, and take up less space. Vinyl record albums, because CDs are more convenient and compact.)* **OL**

C Critical Thinking

Analyzing Visuals **Ask:** Why are there six information boxes on the chart? *(The chart organizes information about three systems according to two factors: advantages and disadvantages. 3 × 2 = 6)* **BL**

Economic Analysis

Answer: market economy; because it is responsive and efficient

---

capitalism
economic system in which private citizens own and use the factors of production in order to generate profits

Skills Handbook
See page **R45** to learn about **Comparing and Contrasting.**

produce. Businesses are free to find the best production methods when deciding HOW to produce. Finally, the income that consumers earn and spend in the market determines FOR WHOM to produce.

Market economies also feature the private ownership of resources. A market economy is often described as being based on **capitalism**—an economic system where private citizens own the factors of production. The term *capitalism* draws attention to the private ownership of resources, while the term *market economy* focuses on where the goods and services are exchanged. As a result, the two terms focus on different features of the same economy.

Examples

Many of the most prosperous economies in the world, such as the United States, Japan, South Korea, Singapore, Australia, Great Britain, and parts of Western Europe, are based on markets and capitalism. While there are significant differences among them, these economies share the common elements of markets and the private ownership of resources to seek profits.

Advantages

The first advantage of a market economy is its high degree of individual freedom. People are free to spend their money on almost any good or service they choose. They also are free to decide where and when they want to work, or if they want to invest further in their own education and training. At the same time, producers are free to decide whom they want to hire, which inputs they want to use, as well as the way they want to produce.

The second advantage of a market economy is that it adjusts gradually to change over time. Prior to 2005, for example, gasoline prices were low, so people tended to buy large gas-guzzling SUVs. When the price of gas rose sharply in that year, SUV sales fell, and smaller, more fuel-efficient vehicles became popular.

A third advantage is the relatively small degree of government interference. Except for certain concerns such as national defense, environmental protection, and some care for the elderly, the government normally tries to stay out of the way of buyers and sellers.

Figure 2.1 ► **Comparing Economic Systems**

	Traditional	Command	Market
Advantages	• Sets forth certain economic roles for all members of the community • Stable, predictable, and continuous life	• Capable of dramatic change in a short time • Many basic education, health, and other public services available at little or no cost	• Individual freedom for everyone • Able to adjust to change gradually • Lack of government interference • Decentralized decision making • Incredible variety of goods and services • High degree of consumer satisfaction
Disadvantages	• Discourages new ideas and new ways of doing things • Stagnation and lack of progress • Lower standard of living	• Does not meet wants and needs of consumers • Lacks effective incentives to get people to work • Requires large bureaucracy, which consumes resources • Has little flexibility to deal with day-to-day changes • Lacks room for individual initiative	• Rewards only productive resources; does not provide for people too young, too old, or too sick to work • Does not produce enough public goods such as defense, universal education, or health care • Workers and businesses face uncertainty as a result of competition and change

► Every society has an economic system. The type of system that is best for a society depends on its ability to satisfy people's wants and needs and to fulfill its economic goals.

Economic Analysis *Which economic system do you think is best able to provide for the wants and needs of individuals, and why?*

Differentiated Instruction

Economic Concepts Trans., Strat. and Act., p. 7

Economic Systems

Objective: Recognize that the U.S. Constitution provides a framework for our market economy.

Focus: Have students predict what would happen if there were no laws protecting private property.

Teach: Have students read the transparency and respond to the questions.

Assess: Ask student pairs to go over each other's answers.

Close: Have students summarize how the Constitution functions as an economic document.

Differentiated Instruction Strategies

BL Have small groups use a web diagram to summarize the definition of an economic system.

AL Ask students to write an essay on the importance of private property rights.

ELL Tell student pairs to make a chart listing the three economic systems and each system's decision-making process.

A fourth advantage is that decision making is decentralized. Billions, if not trillions, of individual economic decisions are made daily. Collectively, people make the decisions that direct scarce resources into the uses consumers favor most, so everyone has a voice in the way the economy runs.

A fifth advantage of the market economy is the variety of goods and services. You can find ultrasound devices to keep the neighbor's dog out of your yard, or you can download music and video to your cell phone. In short, if a product can be imagined, it is likely to be produced in hopes that people will buy it.

A sixth advantage is the high degree of consumer satisfaction. In a market economy, the choice one group makes does not affect the choices of other groups. If 51 percent of the people want to buy classical music, and 49 percent want to buy rap music, people in both groups can still get what they want.

Disadvantages

The market economy does not provide for everyone. Some people may be too young, too old, or too sick to earn a living or to care for themselves. These people would have difficulty surviving in a pure market economy without assistance from family, government, or charitable groups.

A market economy also may not provide enough of some basic goods and services. For example, private markets do not adequately supply all of the roads, universal education, or comprehensive health care people would like to have. This is because private producers concentrate on providing products they can sell for a profit.

Finally, a market economy has a high degree of uncertainty. Workers might worry that their company will move to another country in search of lower labor costs. Employers may worry that someone else will produce a better or less expensive product, thereby taking their customers.

✓**Reading Check** **Identifying** What are the main characteristics of a market economy?

Mixed Economies

MAIN Idea Most economies in the world today feature some mix of traditional, command, and market economies.

Economics & You You just learned about traditional, command, and market economies. Read on to learn how most societies combine elements of each.

While textbooks identify neat categories like traditional, command, and market economies, the real world is not so orderly. Most countries have **mixed economies**—systems that combine elements of all three types. When we consider political systems as well as economic systems, the picture gets even more complicated.

For example, **socialism** is a mixed economic and political system in which the government owns and controls some, but not all, of the basic productive resources. In socialistic countries, the government also provides some of the basic needs of its people, such as education and health care.

An extreme form of socialism is **communism**—a political and economic system where all property is collectively—not privately—owned. In a communist system, labor is organized for the common advantage of the community, and everyone consumes according to their needs. In practice, however, communist governments have become so involved in economic decisions that they are often called command economies.

Characteristics

If government or tradition, as well as markets, answer *some* of the questions of WHAT, HOW, and FOR WHOM to produce, then a society has a mixed economy. The type of political system in a mixed economy is less important than the way basic economic decisions are made.

For example, some mixed economies have a political system based on democracy, and others do not. The state's involvement in economic decisions also can vary. Some governments provide only for basic needs such as defense, a justice system, and

W **mixed economy** economic system that has some combination of traditional, command, and market economies

socialism political and economic system in which the government owns and controls some factors of production

communism economic and political system in which all factors of production are collectively owned and controlled by the state

CHAPTER 2 Economic Systems and Decision Making 39

D **Differentiated Instruction**

Interpersonal Organize students into small groups, and have them brainstorm answers to the following question: How might the government help with some of the disadvantages of a market economy? *(Possible answers: provide universal health care; help the sick and the elderly through programs such as Medicare and Social Security; offer unemployment insurance to reduce insecurity)* OL

W **Writing Support**

Persuasive Writing Have students write several paragraphs arguing why they believe that a market economy, command economy, or mixed economy is superior. AL

✓Reading Check **Answer:** freedom; consumers tell businesses what to produce through spending; private ownership of resources

Leveled Activities

BL **Graphic Organizer Transparencies, p. 5**

OL **Critical Thinking Activities, p. 2**

AL **Reinforcing Economic Skills, p. 11**

Visual Literacy Ask: Why do the arrows point away from socialism in both directions? *(Socialism is a middle ground between capitalism and communism.)* **OL**

S2 **Skill Practice**

Using Tables and Charts
Ask: If you were to list China, North Korea, Cuba, and the United States under the systems on the chart, where would you put them? *(North Korea and Cuba would be under communism; China would be to the right of communism, almost under socialism; the United States would be far to the right of socialism but not directly under capitalism.)* **OL**

Economic Analysis

Answer: Under socialism only some resources are government owned and operated and only some industries are planned. Under communism all resources are government owned and operated and all industries are planned.

Additional Support

Figure 2.2 ▶ The Spectrum of Mixed Economies

Charts In MOtion
See StudentWorks™ Plus or glencoe.com.

▶ In mixed economies, government involvement can range from providing basic public goods to making most economic decisions.

Economic Analysis *What distinguishes socialism from communism?*

COMMUNISM	SOCIALISM	CAPITALISM
Directed by command		Directed by the free market

Ownership of resources

| All productive resources are government owned and operated. | Basic productive resources are government owned and operated; the rest are privately owned and operated. | Productive resources are privately owned and operated. |

Allocation of resources

| Centralized planning directs all resources. | Government plans ways to allocate resources in key industries. | Capital for production is obtained through the lure of profits in the market. |

Role of government

| Government makes all economic decisions. | Government directs the completion of its economic plans in key industries. | Government may promote competition and provide public goods. |

universal education. The more socialistic a country is, the more it will make major economic decisions, often with the claim that this is done for the betterment of the people. Some governments intervene only in certain key sectors or industries and leave the rest to markets. If the government intervenes too much, a mixed economy can turn into a command economy.

Examples

There is a wide range of mixed economies. China has a mixture of traditional, command, and market economies. While tradition has a strong influence in rural areas, the government makes many of the major economic decisions and owns many of the factors of production. China is changing, however. In recent years the government has allowed some private ownership of resources, and capitalism is beginning to flourish.

In Norway, the government owns the basic petroleum industry. It uses the revenue from the sale of oil to other nations to keep its domestic gas prices low, finance education, maintain roads, and provide social welfare for its citizens. Because the government controls just one industry, the mixed economy is based on capitalism and markets with some elements of socialism.

Cuba and North Korea today are very similar to the former Soviet Union, where a socialist government controlled resources to provide for all the people. However, the ownership and control of resources were so extensive that many economists thought of the country as a command economy.

Advantages

One advantage of a mixed economy is that it provides assistance for some people who might otherwise be left out. All societies

40   UNIT 1   Fundamental Economic Concepts

Activity: Collaborative Learning

Monitoring Write on the board the advantages and disadvantages of a mixed economic system. Have students copy the list. Then ask small groups of students to find examples of each advantage and disadvantage in newspapers and magazines or on television or radio news programs. Suggest that groups present their findings in pictorial essays titled "Mixed Economies: Advantages and Disadvantages." Call on group representatives to share their essays with the class. **OL**

include some people who are too young, too old, or too sick to provide for themselves, for example, and most societies have traditions that address some of these concerns.

If the society has a democracy, voters can use their electoral power to affect the WHAT, HOW, and FOR WHOM decisions even if the government owns no productive resources. For example, the government can pass laws to provide aid for those most in need or to fund road construction.

Under socialism, the FOR WHOM question is addressed more directly. Ideally, those who are not fortunate or productive enough to take care of themselves still share certain benefits, such as free or low-cost public housing, transportation, medical care, and education.

Disadvantages

While mixed economies tend to provide more services, the costs for these benefits can mean higher costs for citizens overall. Germany, for example, offers a wide range of benefits, but it also has a high tax rate. During economic downturns, when the government collects fewer taxes, less money is available for these programs. The German government has discussed placing limits on benefits, such as unemployment and welfare, because of lower revenues.

In some socialist countries, the availability of services may be limited or the quality may deteriorate over time. Today, for example, Cuba claims that it has free health care for everyone, but the care is substandard for everyone except high-ranking members of the Communist Party and those willing to pay for services in dollars.

Historically, both socialism and communism have proved to be less efficient than capitalism. For example, if workers receive government guarantees of jobs, more workers may be hired in a plant than are necessary, driving up production costs.

Because socialism has proved to be so inefficient, many socialistic countries today allow more capitalist development. This is especially true in China, where the emergence of capitalism has helped the country to become one of the major economic powers in the world today.

✓Reading Check **Explaining** How can you explain the range of mixed economies in the world?

C Critical Thinking

Speculating Ask: Why else might socialism be less efficient than capitalism? *(Possible answers: People are not rewarded for hard work. Central planners cannot efficiently make the number of economic decisions needed to serve current population levels.)* **OL**

✓Reading Check **Answer:** People are different around the world, and they develop different solutions to problems. They also have different histories and priorities.

Assess

💿 Use the Interactive Tutor Self-Assessment CD-ROM to review Section 1, and then assign the Section 1 Review as homework or as an in-class activity.

Close

Making Connections Have students write about how a recent purchase would have been different if it had been made in a traditional, command, or market system. **OL**

SECTION 1 Review

Vocabulary
1. **Explain** the significance of economic system, traditional economy, command economy, market economy, market, capitalism, mixed economy, socialism, and communism.

Main Ideas
2. **Describing** Use a graphic organizer like the one below to describe how economic systems answer the basic economic questions.

	WHAT, HOW, and FOR WHOM?
Traditional economy	
Command economy	
Market economy	
Mixed economy	

3. **Explain** how a command economy differs from the other economic systems.

Critical Thinking
4. **The BIG Idea** Why do market economies tend to be more efficient than traditional or command economies?
5. **Analyzing Visuals** Look at the chart on page 40. Why does the top row show arrows on the left and right?
6. **Inferring** Why are market economies more innovative than either traditional or command economies?
7. **Analyzing** How does a traditional economy differ from a mixed economy like that of the United States today?

Applying Economics
8. **Mixed Economy** List specific examples to illustrate why the U.S. economy is categorized as a mixed economy.

Answers

1. All definitions can be found in the section and the Glossary.
2. **Traditional economy:** All decisions made according to tradition and custom.
   Command economy: Questions answered by central planners in the government.
   Market economy: Consumers decide *what*, businesses decide *how*, and *for whom* is according to who is willing and able to pay.
   Mixed economy: Consumers decide *what* (government is also a consumer); businesses decide *how*, with regulation from government; *for whom* is according to who is willing and able to pay, although some people are helped by the government.
3. Under a command economy, all productive resources and most other properties are owned collectively.
4. because they are able to respond to change and because they provide incentives to be efficient and innovative
5. The arrows indicate that there is a spectrum rather than concrete divisions.
6. because they welcome change and improvement and provide incentives that reward them
7. In a traditional economy, habit or custom answers the economic questions. In a mixed economy, the government or tradition, as well as markets, answer some of the economic questions.
8. Answers will vary but should reflect an understanding of mixed economies.

CASE STUDY
The Home Depot®

Fast Rise to Riches

In 1978, co-founders Bernie Marcus and Arthur Blank tapped into America's love of "big" and bargains when they started a chain of retail warehouses stacked floor to ceiling with everything a builder or homeowner could want or need. Thus The Home Depot® was born.

NEWS FLASH
Rethinking Pink
Other predominantly "male" markets are also reaching out to women, and not just by changing a product's color to pink. Harley-Davidson has created a section on its Web site for its growing female base. When Apple introduced its multicolored iPod Mini, it experienced a 74 percent jump in sales.

Lagging Sales

In the early 2000s, however, Home Depot's largest competitor, Lowe's, gained sales faster. Its secret? Focusing on women customers. The home-improvement market is huge, estimated at a quarter of a trillion dollars. Roughly one-fourth of that (over $50 billion) consists of purchases made by women. Hardware retailers big and small began courting women—with features such as brighter lighting, wider aisles, and easy-to-reach shelves.

NET SALES FOR THE HOME DEPOT AND LOWE'S, 1996–2005

Legend: Home Depot, Lowe's

Y-axis: Billions of dollars (0, 20, 40, 60, 80, 100)
X-axis: Years (1996, 1997, 1998, 1999, 2000, 2001, 2002, 2003, 2004, 2005, 2006)

Source: www.homedepot.com and www.morningstar.com.

"Do It Herself"

The Home Depot decided to jump on the bandwagon, but it took this courtship one step further. It set up nationwide Do-It-Herself Workshops, taught by experienced Home Depot associates who offer hands-on demonstrations and step-by-step instructions for completing a project. The first workshop took place in May 2003. A little over a year later, more than 200,000 women had attended one of the Do-It-Herself remodeling workshops.

Today The Home Depot is the world's second-largest retailer, after Wal-Mart. As of spring 2006, the company operated 2,054 stores in 50 states, the District of Columbia, Puerto Rico, U.S. Virgin Islands, 10 Canadian provinces, and Mexico.

Analyzing the Impact

1. **Summarizing** How did The Home Depot market its stores toward women?

2. **Making Inferences** Think about recent television and magazine advertisements. Which gender do you feel marketers were targeting? Describe five products and the "hook" used to capture the consumer's attention.

Activity: Collaborative Learning

Entrepreneurship Organize students into small groups, and have them imagine that they are entrepreneurial teams, like the founders of Home Depot. Have them choose an idea for a new business and then outline the tasks that need to be accomplished to get the new business started. Have students write a series of e-mails to each other, communicating how they imagine their work on the tasks might progress. They can then put the e-mails together into a journal describing how the business began. **OL**

SECTION 2 — Evaluating Economic Performance

GUIDE TO READING

Section Preview

In this section, you will learn how economic freedom, economic security, and economic equity are related to the level of satisfaction people have with their economic systems.

Content Vocabulary

- minimum wage *(p. 44)*
- Social Security *(p. 45)*
- inflation *(p. 45)*
- fixed income *(p. 45)*

Academic Vocabulary

- adverse *(p. 45)*
- accommodate *(p. 46)*

Reading Strategy

Differentiating As you read the section, identify seven major economic and social goals by completing a graphic organizer like the one below.

Economic and Social Goals

Bellringer
Daily Focus Transparency 8

COMPANIES IN THE NEWS
—Newsweek

Fruits That Go Fizz

Schoolkids in Oregon are trying something new at lunch: carbonated fruit that the Fizzy Fruit Co. hopes will lead to effervescent profits. Founder Galen Kaufman discovered his product when he ate a pear that had been stored in dry ice, which is made of carbon dioxide. The pear was fizzy and sweet, and ever since, Kaufman's been trying to commercialize the idea.

Not a few exploded kitchen experiments later, Kaufman has found his market. School-lunch supplier Sodexho has been serving the fruit in a pilot project at 14 Oregon schools, and it is expected to be in about 500 schools nationally by next month. Fizzy Fruit will also soon be sold in vending machines and at convenience stores. The trick is in the packaging. Because the fruit loses its fizz within about 20 minutes of being exposed to air (think of a soda bottle left uncapped), it's got to be wrapped tight. ■

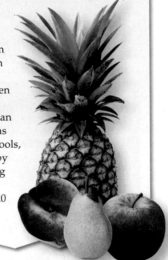

When Galen Kaufman discovered that fruit could fizz, he made it his goal to market the idea. Economic systems also have goals. These goals provide a way to guide economic decisions. They can also help people measure how well the system is working to meet its goals.

If our economic system fails to achieve our goals, we may decide to seek changes. We could demand laws to modify the system until our needs are met. In the United States, efforts to meet our economic and social goals have caused the economy to evolve slowly over time.

GUIDE TO READING

Answers to Graphic: economic freedom, economic efficiency, economic equity, economic security, full employment, price stability, economic growth

Resource Manager

R Reading Strategies	C Critical Thinking	D Differentiated Instruction	W Writing Support	S Skill Practice
Teacher Edition • Making Connections, p. 46 **Additional Resources** • Guid. Read. Act., p. 5 • Read. Ess. & Note-Taking Guide, p. 13	**Teacher Edition** • Det. Cause/Effect, p. 44 **Additional Resources** • Authentic Assess., p. 2 • Pri./Sec. Source Read., p. 1 • Quizzes and Tests, p. 17	**Teacher Edition** • ELL, p. 44 • Naturalist, p. 45 **Additional Resources** • Pri./Sec. Source Read., p. 15 • Enrichment Act., p. 2	**Teacher Edition** • Personal Writing, p. 44 **Additional Resources** • Writer's Guidebook • Econ. Content Vocab., p. 2	**Teacher Edition** • Visual Literacy, p. 45 • Using Tables and Charts, p. 47 **Additional Resources** • Daily Focus Trans. 8 • Reteaching Act., p. 2

Teach

W Writing Support

Personal Writing Ask students to write a letter to a figure from American history, expressing their thoughts and feelings on how the person embodied or contributed to American economic freedom. **AL**

C Critical Thinking

Determining Cause and Effect Ask: What effect does efficiency have on the number of goods available? (*Higher efficiency produces a larger number of goods.*) **OL**

D Differentiated Instruction

English Language Learners Ask: What is the difference between *equity* and *equality*? (*Equity means "fairness"; equality means "the same."*) Have students write a sentence using each word. **ELL**

Caption Answer: One person's desires or actions may interfere with another's.

---

minimum wage lowest legal wage that can be paid to most workers

Economic and Social Goals

MAIN Idea Americans share several major economic and social goals.

Economics & You As you approach graduation, what kinds of goals have you set for your future? Read on to learn about the economic goals of the nation.

In the United States, people share many broad economic and social goals. While it might be difficult to find all of our goals listed in any one place, they are repeated many times in statements made by friends, relatives, community leaders, and elected officials. We can categorize those statements into seven major economic and social goals.

Economic Freedom

Americans traditionally place a high value on the freedom to make their own economic decisions. They like to choose their own occupations, employers, and uses for their money. Business owners like the freedom to choose where and how they

Economic Freedom Americans are free to open any business they choose, such as this music store. **How might the goal of economic freedom conflict with other goals?**

produce. The belief in economic freedom, like the belief in political freedom, is one of the cornerstones of American society.

Economic Efficiency

Most people recognize that resources are scarce and that factors of production must be used wisely. If resources are wasted, fewer goods and services can be produced and fewer wants and needs can be satisfied. Because economic decision making must be efficient, economic efficiency is also one of our major goals.

Economic Equity

Americans have a strong tradition of justice, impartiality, and fairness. Many people, for example, believe in equal pay for equal work. As a result, it is illegal to discriminate on the basis of age, sex, race, religion, or disability in employment. At the national level, we have established the **minimum wage**—the lowest legal wage that can be paid to most workers. While not everyone supports it, the minimum wage does put a floor on the amount of income that some workers earn.

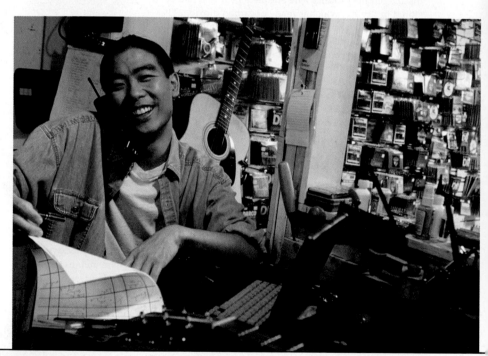

Differentiated Instruction

Authentic Assessment Strategies and Activities, p. 2

The Goals of the Economy

Objective: Describe the goals and characteristics of the U.S. free enterprise system.

Focus: Ask students to suggest goods or services that they wish the government would provide.

Teach: Review the procedure outlined in the activity.

Assess: Use the rubric to assess students' work.

Close: Have students identify other examples of the government seeking to accomplish economic goals.

Differentiated Instruction Strategies

BL Give students a chart listing the meanings of each segment of the Preamble.

AL Have students write essays explaining one U.S. economic goal and how the government helps accomplish it.

ELL Have students explain the difference between a *goal* and a *characteristic*.

Most people believe that advertisers should not be allowed to make false claims about their products. Many states even have "lemon laws" that allow new car buyers to return cars with too many defects.

Economic Security

Americans desire protection from such **adverse** economic events as layoffs and illnesses. As a result, many states have set up programs to help workers who lose their jobs through no fault of their own, and many employers have insurance plans to cover the injuries and illnesses of their workers. At the national level, Congress has set up **Social Security**—a federal program of disability and retirement benefits that covers most working people.

More than 90 percent of all American workers participate in the Social Security system. Retirees, survivors, disabled persons, and Medicare recipients are eligible for benefits. Survivors are spouses and children of deceased persons covered by Social Security. Medicare also provides health insurance for persons 65 or older.

Full Employment

When people work, they earn income by producing goods and services for others. Without jobs, people cannot support themselves or their families, nor can they produce output for others. As a result, most people want their economic system to provide as many jobs as possible. The goal of full employment even became law when Congress passed the Employment Act of 1946 in an effort to avoid the widespread joblessness before World War II.

Price Stability

Another goal is to have stable prices. If **inflation**—a rise in the general level of prices—occurs, workers need more money to pay for food, clothing, and shelter. People who live on a **fixed income**—an income that does not increase even though prices go up—find that bills are harder to pay and planning for the future is more difficult.

Did You Know?

➤ **On Easy Street?** The earliest reported recipient of Social Security was Ernest Ackerman, a retired Cleveland motorman. Ackerman retired one day after the Social Security program began. In return for the nickel withheld from his pay for this one day, he received a lump-sum payment of 17 cents, barely higher than the smallest payment ever of 5 cents. Such lump sum payments were made until 1942, with an average payment of $58.06. Ida May Fuller from Ludlow, Vermont, became the first recipient of monthly Social Security benefits.

High rates of inflation can even discourage business activity. During times of inflation, interest rates on loans tend to increase along with the prices of goods and services. If interest rates get too high, they can discourage both borrowing and spending by businesses. Price stability adds a degree of certainty to the future for businesses and consumers alike.

Economic Growth

The last major goal of most Americans is economic growth. Most people hope to have a better job, a newer car, their own home, and a number of other things in the future. Overall growth enables more people to have more goods and services. Because the nation's population is likely to increase, economic growth is necessary to meet everyone's needs.

Future Goals

The seven goals we have discussed so far are the ones on which most people seem to agree. As our society evolves, however, it is possible for new goals to develop. Do people feel that a cleaner environment is important enough to be added to the list of goals? Should we add the preservation of endangered species such as the California Channel Islands fox? In the end, we are the ones who decide on the goals that are most important to us, and it is entirely possible that our goals could change in the future.

S

D

✓**Reading Check** **Interpreting** What major themes can you identify in the list of seven economic goals?

Social Security federal program of disability and retirement benefits that covers most working people

inflation rise in the general level of prices

fixed income income that does not increase even though prices go up

S **Skill Practice**

Visual Literacy Ask students to create a poster about one of the seven major economic and social goals. Students can use magazine and newspaper photos to illustrate their chosen goal. Have students write a short sentence explaining how each photo represents the goal. **OL**

D **Differentiated Instruction**

Naturalist **Ask:** How might the goal of protecting the environment conflict with the goals of efficiency or full employment? *(Possible answer: Protecting the environment might mean limiting the use of resources such as timber, which would cost jobs, or regulating the amount of pollution that firms could produce, which might drive some firms out of business.)* **OL**

✓**Reading Check** **Possible Answer:** fairness; safety; improvement

Hands-On Chapter Project

Step 2

Comparing Economic Systems

Step 2: Developing a Command Economy. Student teams will "create" a command economic system.

Directions: Have students reassemble into their teams and select and study one of the few remaining command economies in the world. Each team will then "become" a command economy, with students taking on the specific roles of people/entities in

that system, such as dictator, government planners, and workers. After completing their research, have students perform a brief skit for the class demonstrating the workings of their command economy. Skits should cover how the system answers the three basic economic questions. Suggest that teams include major events like famine, drought, lack of needed resources, or five-year plans. Students should take notes on the content and presentation of each skit.

Summarizing After students' presentations, discuss how a command system functions and why so few nations in the world today operate as command economies. **OL**

(Chapter Project continued in Section 3.)

R Reading Strategy

Making Connections

Ask: What are some other ways that Americans have modified the free enterprise economy? *(Possible answers: Government provides social goods such as schools and police and fire protection. Products such as cigarettes and alcohol have age limits on them. Only drugs approved by the FDA can legally be sold.)* **OL**

✓**Reading Check** **Answer:** Some goals conflict with each other.

Assess

💿 Use the Interactive Tutor Self-Assessment CD-ROM to review Section 2, and then assign the Section 2 Review as homework or as an in-class activity.

Close

Organizing Have students use information from the text to create a chart of American economic goals. Ask students to list three specific examples for each goal. **OL**

SECTION 2 Review

🗒 **Skills Handbook**

*See page **R48** to learn about **Problems and Solutions.***

Resolving Trade-Offs Among Goals

MAIN Idea Conflicts among goals can be solved by comparing the cost of a goal to its benefit.

Economics & You You learned earlier about trade-offs when deciding how to spend a monetary gift of $100. Read on to find out how trade-offs also apply to economics goals.

⋯⋯⋯⋯

People often have different ideas about how to reach a goal, or the goals themselves might conflict. Even our economic policies have opportunity costs.

For example, a policy that keeps foreign-made shoes out of the United States could help achieve the goal of full employment in the domestic shoe industry, but it could work against individual freedom if people have fewer choices of shoes to buy.

Even an increase in the minimum wage involves a conflict of goals. On one hand, supporters of the increase argue that an increase is the equitable, or "right," thing to do. Opponents argue that an increase may cause fewer workers to be hired. In addition, it restricts the freedom of employers to pay wages that they think are fair.

How are trade-offs among goals resolved? In most cases, people compare their estimate of the costs to their estimate of the benefits, and then vote for political candidates who back their position. If the majority of voters feel that the minimum wage is too low, then it will be raised. The minimum wage then tends to stay at this new level until the majority of people feel that it needs to be changed again.

People, businesses, and government are usually able to resolve conflicts among goals. Fortunately, the economic system of the United States is flexible enough to allow choices, **accommodate** compromises, and still satisfy the majority of Americans.

R In a democratic society, government reflects the will of a majority of its people. As a result, many government functions reflect people's desire to modify the economic system to achieve their economic goals. A program such as Social Security, as well as laws dealing with child labor and the minimum wage, reveal how Americans have modified their free enterprise economy. This system most likely will undergo further change as the goals and objectives of the American people change.

✓**Reading Check** **Explaining** Why do trade-offs among goals exist?

SECTION 2 Review

Vocabulary

1. **Explain** the significance of minimum wage, Social Security, inflation, and fixed income.

Main Ideas

2. **Explain** why it is important for a nation to set economic and social goals.

3. **Determining Cause and Effect** Use a graphic organizer like the one below to illustrate how economic and social goals may conflict with one another.

Critical Thinking

4. **The BIG Idea** How does an increase in the minimum wage involve a conflict of goals?

5. **Inferring** What can Americans do to influence the economic goals of the nation?

6. **Applying** How do laws against false or misleading advertising promote the goal of economic equity?

Applying Economics

7. **Economic Security** Interview a friend or relative who is retired or approaching retirement to find out if he or she believes the government has achieved the goal of economic security for its senior citizens, and why. Write a paragraph to describe these views and explain why you agree or disagree with them.

46   UNIT 1   Fundamental Economic Concepts

Answers

1. All definitions can be found in the section and the Glossary.
2. Goals serve as benchmarks that help us determine whether our economic system meets most, if not all, of our needs.
3. The action helps achieve the goals of economic security or full employment while working against the goal of economic efficiency.
4. Increasing the minimum wage promotes the goal of economic equity by providing workers with higher paying jobs. It conflicts

with the goals of economic freedom and economic efficiency by setting a wage that might be higher than what the market would pay.
5. People can weigh the costs and benefits and then exercise their right to vote.
6. Making false claims reduces the consumer's ability to make sound choices. Such actions give the seller an unfair advantage over the consumer. Having laws that prevent this ensures fairness.

7. Answers may include opinions related to issues such as Social Security, Medicare, Medicaid, senior housing, and taxes. Students should explain whether they agree or disagree with the views.

W e do not usually associate economic efficiency with fun. In the past few years, though, some companies have found a new and unusual tool to make job training more efficient—and more fun.

On-the-Job Video Gaming

Laura Holshouser's favorite video games include *Halo, Tetris*, and an online training game developed by her employer. A training game? That's right. The 24-year-old graduate student, who manages a Cold Stone Creamery ice-cream store in Riverside, Calif., stumbled across the game on the corporate Web site in October.

It teaches portion control and customer service in a cartoon-like simulation of a Cold Stone store. Players scoop cones against the clock and try to avoid serving too much ice cream. The company says more than 8,000 employees, or about 30% of the total, voluntarily downloaded the game in the first week. . . .

The military has used video games as a training tool since the 1980s. Now the practice is catching on with companies, too. . . . Corporate trainers are betting that games' interactivity and fun will hook young, media-savvy employees like Holshouser and help them grasp and retain sales, technical, and management skills. . . .

$736	Cost of traditional training per employee
8,000	Number of employees who download the game in the first week
$5,888,000	Cost of traditional training for 8,000 employees
$500,000	Average cost of corporate training game

Companies like video games because they are cost-effective. Why pay for someone to fly to a central training campus when you can just plunk them down in front of a computer? Even better, employees often play the games at home on their own time. . . .

Games are especially well-suited to training technicians. . . . Last year, Cisco rolled out six new training games—some of them designed to teach technicians how to build a computer network. It's hard to imagine a drier subject. Not so in the virtual world. In one Cisco game, players must put the network together on Mars. In a sandstorm. . . . Sounds suspiciously like fun.

—Reprinted from *BusinessWeek*

Examining the Newsclip

1. **Summarizing** How has on-the-job video gaming made workers and companies more efficient?
2. **Analyzing** How do companies make video training games appealing for their employees?

Teach

S Skill Practice

Using Tables and Charts
Ask: According to the chart, how much money would a company save by using video games for training? *($5,388,000)* **OL**

BusinessWeek ONLINE

To find up-to-date news and analysis on the economy, business, technology, markets, entrepreneurs, investments, and finance, have students search feature articles and special reports on the BusinessWeek Web site, www.businessweek.com.

Examining the Newsclip

Answers:
1. It is less expensive and it encourages employees to play the games on their own time.
2. **Possible answer:** They use fun and interesting graphics, unusual settings, and elements of competition.

Additional Support

Activity: Hands-On Economics

Designing Have small groups of students write an outline of a video game that would help employees learn an aspect of a job typically held by a teenager (for example, baby-sitting, retail, food service, yard work, dog walking, and so on). Students should begin by identifying the overall job and then the major tasks involved in the job. Encourage students to think about how they could make the game educational and fun for employees. Ask groups to present their outlines to the class. Then have students vote on their favorite video game idea. **OL**

Focus

Bellringer
Daily Focus Transparency 22

GUIDE TO READING

Answers to Graphic:

Characteristics: economic freedom, voluntary exchange, private property rights, profit motive, competition

Possible Examples: freedom to choose your occupation, buying and selling goods, right to own land and goods, earnings of an entrepreneur, struggle among sellers to attract buyers

Resource Manager

SECTION 3
American Free Enterprise

GUIDE TO READING

Section Preview
In this section, you will learn how under capitalism the basic economic decisions of WHAT, HOW, and FOR WHOM to produce are made through the free interaction of individuals looking out for their own best interests.

Content Vocabulary
- free enterprise (p. 48)
- voluntary exchange (p. 49)
- private property rights (p. 50)
- profit (p. 50)
- profit motive (p. 50)
- competition (p. 50)
- consumer sovereignty (p. 51)
- mixed or modified free enterprise economy (p. 53)

Academic Vocabulary
- incentive (p. 50)
- catalyst (p. 51)
- regulator (p. 52)

Reading Strategy
Listing As you read the section, complete a graphic organizer like the one below to identify the five characteristics of a free enterprise economy. Then provide an example of each.

Characteristic	Example

COMPANIES IN THE NEWS
—adapted from BusinessWeek

Hot Growth at Claire's

When Bonnie and Marla Schaefer became vice-CEOs of Claire's Stores Inc., they had much to prove to the company's board. Within a few years they did just that: profits nearly doubled, earning Claire's a slot on *BusinessWeek*'s 2005 list of Hot Growth companies.

How did the sisters do it? One way was to focus on a troubled recent acquisition they renamed Icings. The new store appeals to the 17-to-27 crowd. Unlike their father, Rowland Schaefer, founder and former CEO of Claire's, the sisters use market research to identify teen trends. They also licensed popular celebrities such as Mariah Carey to provide cosmetics and jewelry lines.

The sisters won't stop there. The company already has stores in Europe and Japan, and franchises are now expanding into other continents. ∎

---

free enterprise capitalistic economy in which competition is allowed to flourish with a minimum of government interference

Capitalism has become the economic system of choice in many parts of the world because of its ability to generate wealth, just as it has for Claire's. Capitalism, as you have learned, is an economic system in which private citizens own and use the factors of production to generate profits.

The U.S. economy is based on free enterprise. Under **free enterprise**, resources are privately owned, and competition is allowed to flourish with a minimum of government interference. We often use the terms *capitalism* and *free enterprise* interchangeably, but they have different meanings. While capitalism stands for the private ownership of resources, free enterprise is the unhindered use of privately owned resources to earn profits.

R Reading Strategies	**C** Critical Thinking	**D** Differentiated Instruction	**W** Writing Support	**S** Skill Practice
Teacher Edition • Inferring, p. 50 • Skimming, p. 52 • Making Connections, p. 58 **Additional Resources** • Guid. Read. Act., p. 6 • Read. Ess. & Note-Taking Guide, p. 16	**Teacher Edition** • Classifying, p. 49 • Ident. Cent. Issues, p. 51 • Drawing Con., p. 54 • Assessing, p. 59 **Additional Resources** • Pri./Sec. Source Read., p. 1	**Teacher Edition** • Interpersonal, p. 51 • Visual/Spatial, p. 53 **Additional Resources** • Econ. Cartoons, p. 13 • Free Enterprise Act., p. 1	**Teacher Edition** • Expository Writing, p. 52 **Additional Resources** • Reading and Study Skills Fold., p. 44 • High School Writing Process Trans.	**Teacher Edition** • Visual Literacy, p. 49 • Compare/Contrast, p. 50 **Additional Resources** • Daily Focus Trans. 22 • Math Prac. for Econ., p. 2

Characteristics of Free Enterprise Capitalism

MAIN Idea The American economy incorporates the main characteristics of a free enterprise economy.

Economics & You How much freedom do you have to make your own economic choices? Read on to learn how this freedom characterizes our own market economy.

A capitalistic free enterprise economy has five important characteristics: economic freedom, voluntary exchange, private property rights, the profit motive, and competition.

Economic Freedom

Economic freedom means more than being able to buy the things you want. It means that you have the freedom to choose your occupation, your employer, and your job location. You can even leave your current job and move on to another job that offers greater opportunity.

Businesses also enjoy considerable economic freedom. They are free to hire the best workers, and they are free to produce the products they feel will be the most profitable. Businesses can make as many items as they want, sell them wherever they please, and normally charge whatever price they choose. In short, they are free to risk success or failure.

Voluntary Exchange

A second characteristic of capitalism is **voluntary exchange**—the act of buyers and sellers freely and willingly engaging in market transactions. Voluntary transactions benefit both the buyer and the seller, or the exchange would never occur.

For example, when buyers spend their money on a product, they act on a belief that the item they purchase is of greater

voluntary exchange act of buyers and sellers freely and willingly engaging in market transactions

Figure 2.3 ▶ Characteristics of Free Enterprise Capitalism

Economic freedom:
People may choose their jobs, employers, and how to spend their money. Businesses may choose what products to sell and how much to charge for them.

Voluntary exchange:
Buyers and sellers may engage freely and willingly in market transactions.

Competition:
Producers and sellers compete with one another to attract consumers, while lowering costs. Consumers compete with one another to obtain the best products at the lowest prices.

Private property rights:
People may control their possessions as they wish.

Profit motive:
People and organizations may improve their material well-being by making money.

▶ "Free enterprise capitalism" describes a market economy in which private citizens own the factors of production and businesses compete with minimal government interference.

Economic Analysis *What items are included in the category of private property?*

Teach

C Critical Thinking

Classifying Tell students that some economists classify consumer decisions in three major categories—habitual, impulsive, or rational. Habitual decisions are made routinely, such as purchasing gasoline. Impulsive decisions are made on the spur of the moment. Rational decisions are given great thought and usually involve the purchase of an expensive item. Have students give three examples for each classification and decide which purchase is the most responsible. **ELL**

S Skill Practice

Visual Literacy Ask: Which characteristic in the illustration holds the other characteristics together? *(competition)* **BL**

Economic Analysis

Answer: everything a person might possess, including both consumer and capital goods

---

Hands-On Chapter Project
Step 3

Comparing Economic Systems

Step 3: Developing a Market Economy.
Student teams will "create" a market economic system.

Directions: Have student teams research the basic principles of a market economy. Each team will then "become" a market economy, with students taking on the specific roles of people/entities in that system, such as entrepreneurs, laborers, and consumers. After completing their research, students will then perform a brief skit demonstrating the workings of their market economy. Skits should cover how the system answers the three basic economic questions. Students are encouraged to add lively events to their skits such as a price war or a workers' strike for higher wages. Students should take notes on the content and presentation of each skit.

Summarizing After students' presentations, discuss the workings of a market economy, including its advantages and disadvantages. **OL**

(Chapter Project continued in Visual Summary.)

R Reading Strategy

Inferring Ask: Why is it economically efficient and necessary for people to keep the rewards they earn? *(Possible answer: If they can keep their rewards, they will work harder and be willing to take risks.)* **OL**

S Skill Practice

Comparing and Contrasting

Tell students that some industries, such as fast-food restaurants, are highly competitive, while others have little competition (for example, some cities have a single cable TV provider). Have students identify one example of a competitive industry and one example of an industry with little competition. Ask them to compare and contrast the two industries. **OL**

✓ Reading Check Answer:
A buyer gives up money for a good she thinks is worth more than the money, while the seller gives up the good for money that she thinks is worth more than the good.

---

private property rights fundamental feature of capitalism that allows individuals to own and control their possessions as they wish

profit extent to which persons or organizations are better off financially at the end of a period than they were at the beginning

profit motive incentive that encourages people and organizations to improve their financial and material well-being

competition the struggle among sellers to attract consumers

S❘ Personal Finance Handbook

See pages R6–R9 for more information on saving and investing.

---

value than the money they give up—or they would not make the purchase. When sellers exchange their products for cash, they believe that the money they receive is more valuable than the product they sell—otherwise they would not make the sale.

Private Property Rights

Another major feature of capitalism is **private property rights,** which allow people to own and control their possessions as they wish. People have the right to use or even abuse their property as long as they do not interfere with the rights of others.

Private property gives people the **incentive** to work, save, and invest. When people are free to do as they wish with their property, they are not afraid to accumulate, improve, use, or lend it. They also know they can keep any rewards they might earn.

Profit Motive

Under free enterprise capitalism, people are free to risk any part of their wealth in a business venture. If it goes well, they will earn rewards for their efforts. If it goes poorly, however, they could lose part or all of their investment.

Profit is the extent to which persons or organizations are better off financially at the end of a specific period than they were at the beginning. The **profit motive**—the incentive that encourages people and organizations to improve their material well-being—is largely responsible for the growth of a free enterprise system.

Competition

Capitalism thrives on **competition**—the struggle among sellers to attract consumers. Competition is possible because individual entrepreneurs have the freedom to produce the products they think will be the most profitable. Free enterprise capitalism allows competition to flourish, benefiting both producers and consumers alike.

✓ Reading Check Summarizing How does voluntary exchange work in the free enterprise economy?

The Role of the Entrepreneur

MAIN Idea Entrepreneurs are the driving force of the free enterprise system.

Economics & You Can you think of a successful entrepreneur and the business he or she runs? Read on to learn why entrepreneurs are important in a free enterprise economy.

The entrepreneur plays one of the most important roles in the free enterprise economy. The entrepreneur organizes and manages land, capital, and labor in order to seek the reward called profit.

Entrepreneurs are the people who start up new businesses such as restaurants, automobile repair shops, Internet stores, and video arcades. They include people who may have worked for others at one time, but who decided to quit and start their own businesses. Entrepreneurs want to "be their own boss" and are willing to take risks to make their dreams come true.

Many entrepreneurs fail. Others survive and manage to stay in business with varying degrees of success. A few, and only a very few, manage to become fantastically wealthy. Well-known entrepreneurs include Robert Johnson, founder of BET,

Robert Johnson

Primary and Secondary Source Readings, p. 15

Differentiated Instruction

Budding Entrepreneurs

Objective: Learn about the skills needed to run a successful business.

Focus: Ask students to brainstorm qualities of successful business owners.

Teach: Have students read the article and then answer the questions that follow.

Assess: Discuss as a class the answers to the questions.

Close: Ask students to write a paragraph about whether entrepreneurial skills are inborn or can be taught.

Differentiated Instruction Strategies

BL Have students list qualities that the entrepreneurs share.

AL Ask students to explain which of the three individuals in the article impressed them the most and why.

ELL Have students look up unfamiliar words in a dictionary and then write sentences using the words.

Bill Gates, who founded Microsoft, and Mary Kay Ash, who founded Mary Kay Cosmetics.

Despite the high rate of failure among entrepreneurs, the dream of success is often too great to resist. The entrepreneur is both the spark plug and the **catalyst** of the free enterprise economy. When an entrepreneur is successful, everybody benefits. The entrepreneur is rewarded with profits, a growing business, and the satisfaction of a job well done. Workers are rewarded with more and better-paying jobs. Consumers are rewarded with new and better products. The government is rewarded with a higher level of economic activity and larger tax receipts that can be used to build roads, schools, and libraries for people not even connected with the original entrepreneur.

It does not stop there. Successful entrepreneurs attract other firms to the industry who rush in to "grab a share" of the profits. To remain competitive and stay in business, the original entrepreneur may have to improve the quality of the product or cut prices, which means that customers can buy more for less. In the end, the entrepreneur's search for profits can lead to a chain of events that brings new products, greater competition, more production, higher quality, and lower prices for consumers.

✔**Reading Check** Analyzing Why are entrepreneurs considered both spark plugs and catalysts of the free enterprise economy?

The Role of the Consumer

MAIN Idea The economy in the United States adapts to consumers' wants.

Economics & You When you go shopping and cast your dollar "votes," do you realize that you are helping to answer the question of WHAT to produce? Read on to learn how consumers help decide what products are offered in a free market economy.

Consumers have power in the economy because ultimately they determine which products are produced. If consumers like a new product, the producer will be rewarded with profits. If consumers do not buy it, the firm may lose money or even go out of business. The term **consumer sovereignty** recognizes the role of the consumer as sovereign, or ruler, of the market. The phrase "the customer is always right" reflects this power.

In recent years, producers have had outstanding successes with products ranging from video games to Internet search engines such as Google. Other products—including "Crystal" Pepsi, celery-flavored Jell-O, and Dr. Care's aerosol toothpaste (which kids discovered they could spray around the bathroom)—were rejected.

In addition, consumers' wants change constantly as people are exposed to new ideas and products. Today, Americans purchase more home computers every year than TV sets, even though computers were

consumer sovereignty role of consumer as ruler of the market when determining the types of goods and services produced

Skills Handbook

See page **R40** to learn about **Analyzing Information.**

Entrepreneurs and Consumers
Some entrepreneurs, like Robert Johnson, develop corporations for consumers nationwide, while others serve local customers. *How do consumers influence the economy?*

photo: Hot dog stand in Los Angeles

D **Differentiated Instruction**

Interpersonal Have each student describe to a partner a business that a teenager could open. Then tell students to ask these questions about his or her partner's business:

- What are the start-up costs?

- How much time would you need to devote to the business?

- Who are your target customers?

Have partners present each other's answers to the class. **OL**

C **Critical Thinking**

Identifying Central Issues Have student pairs develop a list of economic rights and responsibilities of consumers. Ask pairs to share their ideas. **OL**

✔**Reading Check** **Answer:** Entrepreneurs act as spark plugs by energizing the economy. They also act as catalysts by causing economic events to happen.

Caption Answer: By casting dollar "votes," consumers decide what products get produced.

Leveled Activities

BL Reading Essentials and Note-Taking Guide, p. 16

OL Economic Cartoons, p. 13

AL Math Practice for Economics, p. 2

R Reading Strategy

Skimming Have students skim the section on "The Role of Government" to find the answer to this question: **What are four functions of the government in the U.S. economy?** *(to protect, provide, regulate, and consume)*
BL

W Writing Support

Expository Writing Have students select one of the economic roles of the government and then use historical and current materials to research whether the role changed over time. Students should write a report about their findings, including visuals such as charts and graphs where appropriate. **OL**

✓**Reading Check** **Answer:** They determine which products are produced; they are the rulers of the market.

Additional Support

Teacher Tip

Working With Web Sites
You may wish to provide students with the addresses for your city and state government Web sites. Help below-level learners navigate to the employment section of each site.

---

barely known just 25 years ago. They buy products all over the world and frequently use the Internet to research products and make purchases.

The dollars consumers spend in the marketplace are the "votes" that give them a say in what is, and what is not, produced. Because of this, consumers play an important role in the American free enterprise economy.

✓**Reading Check** **Summarizing** What role do consumers play in a free enterprise system?

CAREERS

Construction and Building Inspector (Zoning Officer)

The Work

* Examine the construction or repair of buildings, sewer and water systems, dams, bridges, highways, and streets to ensure compliance with building codes, zoning regulations, and contract specifications

* Review blueprints, write reports and detailed logs, and schedule inspections

Qualifications

* Profound knowledge of construction materials and practices

* Experience with survey instruments, metering devices, and test equipment

* Degree or certificate in building inspection with an emphasis on blueprint reading, construction technology, drafting, mathematics, and English and Spanish

* Background in engineering or architecture or a degree from a community college

Earnings

* Median annual earnings: $43,670

Job Growth Outlook

* Faster than average

Source: *Occupational Outlook Handbook, 2006–2007*

R The Role of Government

MAIN Idea The economic role of the U.S. government is decided by its citizens.

Economics & You What economic roles do you think federal, state, and local governments play in your life? Read on to learn how the government has modified our country's economic system.

The role of government—whether national, state, or local—stems from the desires, goals, and aspirations of its citizens. Government has become involved in the economy because the citizens want it that way. Consequently, government has **W** become a protector, provider, **regulator**, and consumer. In general, the role of government in the economy is justified whenever the benefits outweigh the costs.

Protector

As protector, the United States government enforces laws such as those against false and misleading advertising, unsafe food and drugs, environmental hazards, and unsafe automobiles. It also enforces laws against abuses of individual freedoms. Employers, for example, cannot discriminate against workers because of their age, gender, race, or religion.

Provider

All levels of government provide goods and services for citizens. The national government supplies a system of justice and national defense. It provides subsidies to parts of the economy, such as agriculture. In addition, it gives funding to state and local governments for some programs such as road construction. State governments provide education, highways, and public welfare. Local governments provide parks, libraries, sanitation, and bus services.

Regulator

In its role as a regulator, the national government is charged with preserving competition in the marketplace. It also oversees communications, interstate commerce, and

---

Activity: Technology Connection

The Role of Government Have students visit three government Web sites, preferably of different levels of government. For example, they might visit a city Web site, a state Web site, and the federal government Web site. Have them search the careers/jobs/employment sections of the sites for jobs that show government fulfilling the roles discussed in the text. Have students find three job examples for each role and then share their findings in a class discussion. **OL**

even entire industries, such as banking and nuclear power. Many state governments oversee insurance rates, while local governments regulate economic activity with building and zoning permits.

The regulatory role of government is controversial. Most businesses do not like to be told how to run their affairs. Consumers, however, do not always know when they are at risk from hazards, such as potential poisoning from unsafe food preparation or false and misleading advertising from some companies. As a result, they want the government to monitor and regulate such activities.

D

Consumer

The tasks of protecting, providing, and regulating are expensive. All levels of government, like any business, consume scarce resources to fulfill their role. Government has grown so much in recent years that it is now the second-largest consuming unit in the economy, after the consumer sector, eclipsing spending by all private businesses combined. You will learn later

in this textbook how the government collects and spends the money required to accomplish these tasks.

Modified Free Enterprise

Perhaps an unintended consequence of government's role as protector, provider, regulator, and consumer is the emergence of the **mixed,** or **modified free enterprise economy.** In this economy, people and businesses carry on their economic affairs freely, but they are subject to some government intervention and regulation.

Some people prefer to have no government involvement in the economy, but this is not possible. After all, some services, such as national defense and a system of laws and justice, cannot be supplied by the private sector alone. Unfortunately there is no clear answer to the question of how much government involvement is necessary, but if it changes, it will be because the voting public wants it that way.

✓**Reading Check** Explaining Why do Americans want government to play a role in the economy? Use specific examples.

mixed or **modified free enterprise economy** economy where people carry on their economic affairs freely but are subject to some government intervention and regulation

D **Differentiated Instruction**

Visual/Spatial Have students search for examples of advertising that could be misleading. Have them construct a poster showing the examples they find with captions that explain why each ad might be misleading. **OL**

✓**Reading Check** **Possible Answer:** It can reduce the disadvantages of a market system. For example, it can reduce insecurity through its role as provider, and it can decrease consumer risks through its role as regulator.

Assess

Use the Interactive Tutor Self-Assessment CD-ROM to review Section 3, and then assign the Section 3 Review as homework or as an in-class activity.

Close

Drawing Conclusions Ask: How would life be different if the government did not play certain roles in the economy? **OL**

SECTION 3 Review

Vocabulary
1. **Explain** the significance of free enterprise, voluntary exchange, private property rights, profit, profit motive, competition, consumer sovereignty, and mixed or modified free enterprise economy.

Main Ideas
2. **Describe** the five major characteristics of a free enterprise system by completing a graphic organizer like the one below.

Free Enterprise System

3. **Explain** the differences in the roles of entrepreneurs, consumers, and the government.

Critical Thinking
4. **The BIG Idea** When consumers cast their "votes" in a free enterprise economy, how do they influence what is and is not produced?

5. **Analyzing Visuals** Look at the photo on page 51. How are the consumers demonstrating their sovereignty?

6. **Drawing Conclusions** How is the protection of private property rights necessary to the other characteristics of free enterprise?

7. **Analyzing** Explain why entrepreneurs are the driving force of the free enterprise system.

Applying Economics
8. **Voluntary Exchange** Cite at least three examples of voluntary exchanges you made this week. How are you better off by having made the exchanges? Did the person with whom you exchanged gain too? How?

CHAPTER 2 Economic Systems and Decision Making 53

Review **SECTION 3**

Answers

1. All definitions can be found in the section and the Glossary.
2. economic freedom, voluntary exchange, private property rights, profit motive, and competition
3. Entrepreneurs take the initiative to combine the other resources to start businesses. Consumers decide what is to be produced by casting their dollar votes. Government serves as a consumer, regulator, provider, and protector.

4. Consumers buy products that they like, providing profits to the firms that make the products. Consumers do not buy products that they dislike, causing firms to lose money and possibly go out of business.
5. The consumers are getting the goods that they want.
6. **Possible answer:** If private property rights are not protected, the profit motive cannot work because people cannot keep the rewards for their work. Competition would

not exist because there would be no incentive for it. Exchanges would not be voluntary; whoever was the biggest and strongest would be able to take everything.
7. Entrepreneurs organize and manage the factors of production. They seek profits by opening new businesses, selling new products, and improving older ones.
8. Students' answers should include a discussion of how both parties benefited from each voluntary exchange.

Teach

C Critical Thinking

Drawing Conclusions
What characteristic did Tony Hawk's daily skateboarding illustrate? *(determination)* Is this a characteristic that an entrepreneur needs? Why or why not? *(Possible answer: Yes, entrepreneurs need determination because they often face setbacks that they must overcome.)* **OL**

Examining the Profile

Answers:
1. He has used his name to promote skateboarding-related products, such as skateboards, clothes, and video games.
2. He worked closely with developers to ensure that the video game he was going to brand was authentic.

Additional Support

Profiles in Economics

Tony Hawk (1968–)

- professional athlete at age 14 and best skateboarder in the world by age 16
- owner of a successful business empire based on resurgence of skateboarding and name recognition

Making a Name

C Tony Hawk did not set out to become a businessman. When his brother gave him his first skateboard at age nine, all he wanted to do was have some fun. But he was determined that he would learn how to ride it. This determination—and 6 hours of skateboarding a day—led to success. By age 16, Hawk was the best skateboarder in the world. He also opened a skateboarding company, Birdhouse Projects, that brought him his first big financial success.

The Hawk Takes Off

While Hawk had made a name for himself, skateboarding itself faded in popularity, and with it Hawk's company. Then ESPN decided to broadcast the X Games in 1995. The show's immense success revitalized the skateboarding phenomenon and brought Hawk's name into the mainstream. At the end of his competitive career in 1999, Hawk had won 73 first-place competition titles, created some 80 new tricks, and pioneered a new form of vertical skateboarding.

Hawk's skills piqued the interest of software developer Activision. In 1998 the company approached him with an idea for his own skateboarding video game. Hawk wanted to "make sure that the skating aspect is authentic." He met weekly with the game developers, nixing unrealistic moves and refining aerial stunts. The next year, "Tony Hawk's Pro Skater" flew off the shelves. The Pro Skater games eventually sold 20 million copies and gave Hawk over $6 million a year in royalties.

In 2002 Hawk launched the Boom Boom HuckJam tour, an extreme sports event that brings the world's best skateboarders, BMX bikers, and motocross racers to arenas around the country. On top of that, his combined brands, which today include skateboards, clothes, shoes, video games, and action figures, generate about $300 million a year in retail sales.

When Tony Hawk first started skateboarding, he saw it as a fun way to spend some time. Just three years later, he signed with his first sponsor, and today he has turned it into a multi-million-dollar business.

Examining the Profile

1. **Drawing Conclusions** How has Tony Hawk used his sport to develop into an entrepreneur?
2. **Making Inferences** How do you know that Hawk is careful about which products he brands? Explain.

54 UNIT 1 Fundamental Economic Concepts

Activity: Hands-On Economics

Name Branding Have students identify a special talent or skill that they have or would like to have that could serve as a basis for a business. Ask students what special considerations might arise because the product bears their name. How would they ensure that the product met the highest of standards? Have each student write a one-page business plan describing the business and addressing these concerns. Invite students to include a drawing showing how they would like their name to appear on their products. **OL**

STUDY TO GO

Study anywhere, anytime!
Download quizzes and flash cards to your PDA from glencoe.com.

▶ **Economic Systems** Most countries have a mix of three different types of economic systems.

Traditional	Command	Market	Mixed
• Most economic activities based on ritual, habit, or customs • Everyone knows which role to play • Little innovation	• Government makes all major economic decisions • Private property severely limited • Can be adjusted quickly to meet a country's demands • Does not meet all of consumers' wants and needs • Is inefficient and discourages innovation	• People make economic decisions based on supply, demand, and the price system • High degree of individual freedom and innovation • Does not provide for the basic needs of everyone	• Provides a mix of all three economic systems • Government involvement varies • Government provides help to some people who might otherwise be left out • Systems like socialism and communism are less efficient than capitalism

▶ **Economic and Social Goals** In the United States, we share several economic and social goals.

Economic and Social Goals:
- Economic freedom
- Economic efficiency
- Economic equity
- Economic security
- Full employment
- Price stability
- Economic growth

▶ **Free Enterprise** The U.S. economic system is based on the free enterprise system and is characterized by competition and private ownership of resources.

Characteristics	Role of Entrepreneurs	Role of Consumers	Role of Government
• Economic freedom • Voluntary exchange • Private property rights • Profit motive • Competition	• Organize land, capital, and labor in order to seek profit • Accept the risk of loss • Decide HOW to produce • Are innovators and catalysts	• Decide WHAT is produced by how they spend their money • Spur development of new products by changing their wants	• As protector, provider, and regulator, ensures and enforces that economic and social goals are carried out • Is a large consumer in the economy

CHAPTER 2 Economic Systems and Decision Making **55**

Personal Writing Direct students to choose one of the economic and social goals and write about a personal experience involving the goal. **OL**

Determining Importance
Ask: Which event in American history was most significant in developing and enhancing the U.S. economic system? Why? *(Possible answer: the writing of the Constitution; it established the rights and protections that enable the U.S. economic system to function)* **AL**

Evaluating Have students list what they think are the top five problems that exist in the U.S. economy today. Have a volunteer write the suggested problems on the board. Have other volunteers identify what role the government would play if it took on the problem. Conduct a poll to find which problems students think are the most important. **BL**

Hands-On Chapter Project
Step 4: Wrap Up

Comparing Economic Systems

Step 4: Make the Comparisons.
Student teams will synthesize what they learned in Steps 1–3.

Directions: Using the notes that students compiled on the skits, have students write essays reviewing the performances of other teams' skits. Essays should focus on how the skits demonstrated the different functioning of the three economic systems. Students should include specific scenes or bits of dialogue that they observed that highlighted these differences. After students have completed their essays, discuss as a class how the different economic systems impact the societies in which they operate. **OL**

CHAPTER
2
Assessment & Activities

ExamView®
Assessment Suite

This easy-to-use software includes extensive question banks and allows you to create fully customized tests that can be administered in print or online.

Review Content Vocabulary

1. c	**2.** d
3. f	**4.** a
5. e	**6.** g
7. b	**8.** h

Review Academic Vocabulary

9.–16. Students' sentences will vary but should demonstrate understanding of each term's meaning in an economic context.

Review the Main Ideas

17. All economic activity is conducted according to ritual, custom, or tradition.

18. does not meet consumer wants, lacks incentives to get people to work, requires a large bureaucracy, has little flexibility to deal with small changes, and discourages individuality and new ideas

19. Individuals and firms make decisions by interacting and communicating through markets and prices.

20. There is help for people who might be left out. Voters can influence economic decisions. A disadvantage is that there are greater costs to citizens.

21. Individuals can choose their occupation and employer. Businesses can produce, sell, and price goods and services however they want.

22. workers who have lost their jobs, the elderly, the sick, the disabled

Review Content Vocabulary

On a separate sheet of paper, write the letter of the key term that best matches each statement below.

a. capitalism
b. command economy
c. consumer sovereignty
d. economic system

e. private property rights
f. profit motive
g. traditional economy
h. voluntary exchange

1. the idea that buyers and sellers rule the market
2. a society's organized way of providing for its people's wants and needs
3. the incentive that encourages people and organizations to try to improve their material well-being
4. an economic system in which the factors of production are owned by private citizens
5. the right and privilege to control one's own possessions
6. an economic system in which ritual, habit, and custom dictate most economic and social behavior
7. an economic system in which a central authority makes economic decisions
8. the act of buyers and sellers freely conducting business in a market

Review Academic Vocabulary

On a separate sheet of paper, define and illustrate each of the following terms. See the sample below.

Term	Definition	Illustration
• Incentive	• Something that encourages or motivates	

9. allocate
10. emphasize
11. stagnation
12. adverse

13. catalyst
14. regulator
15. accommodate
16. incentive

Review the Main Ideas

Section 1 *(pages 33–41)*

17. Describe the main characteristics of a traditional economy.

18. Identify the five major weaknesses of a command economy.

19. Explain who makes economic decisions in a market economy.

20. Describe the advantages and disadvantages of a mixed economy.

Section 2 *(pages 43–46)*

21. Describe how individuals and businesspeople benefit from economic freedom.

22. Discuss who benefits from economic security.

23. Explain how a society resolves conflicts between economic and social goals.

Section 3 *(pages 48–53)*

24. Describe the five major characteristics of free enterprise.

Free Enterprise

25. Explain why entrepreneurs are thought to have important roles in the economy.

26. Describe how consumers have influenced the success of products in recent years.

27. List the five major roles that the government plays in the economy.

---

23. Citizens weigh benefits against costs and then vote for the candidates who best represent their desires.

24. economic freedom (freedom of individuals and businesses to determine work-related issues), voluntary exchange (act of buyers and sellers freely and willingly engaging in market transactions), private property rights (allow people to own and control their possessions), profit motive (incentive that encourages people and organizations to improve their material well-being), and

competition (the struggle among sellers to attract consumers)

25. They combine the other factors of production and manage the resulting businesses.

26. When consumers like a product, they buy it and therefore make it profitable.

27. protector, provider, regulator, and consumer

Economics ONLINE **Self-Check Quiz** Visit the *Economics: Principles and Practices* Web site at glencoe.com and click on *Chapter 2–Self-Check Quizzes* to prepare for the chapter test.

Assessment and Activities

CHAPTER 2

Critical Thinking

28. **The BIG Idea** Some people believe that the profit motive conflicts with the goals of economic security and equity. Do you agree? Why or why not?

29. **Understanding Cause and Effect** How has the development of modern transportation and communication systems affected the type of economy that exists in the United States?

30. **Making Inferences** What incentive does owning private property give people?

31. **Making Comparisons** Reproduce the following diagram on a separate sheet of paper. Then, in the spaces indicated, identify several elements of command and tradition in the U.S. economy that make it a mixed, or modified private enterprise, economy.

Analyzing Visuals

32. **Critical Thinking** Look at the chart on page 40. Explain how government involvement differs under communism, socialism, and capitalism. Where on the spectrum does the economy of the United States fit, and why?

Math Practice

33. If the typical minimum-wage employee works 40 hours a week and has two weeks' unpaid vacation, how much will that person earn in a year if the minimum wage is $5.15/hour? How much extra will that person earn for every $0.25 increase per hour in the wage?

Thinking Like an Economist

34. **Critical Thinking** Not all societies have market economies. Some have command or traditional economies. Use the discussion of opportunity cost and cost-benefit analysis in Chapter 1 on pages 20 and 24 to explain why you would or would not like to live in a society with a different economic system. Prepare a decision grid similar to the one on page 20 to help you with your analysis. Write a paragraph that summarizes your conclusion.

Applying Economic Concepts

35. **Tradition** Most people tip for service in restaurants, but not for service at clothing stores or gas stations. Explain how this illustrates economic behavior by tradition rather than by market or command.

36. **Economic and Social Goals** Compare the figures below and then answer the questions that follow.

a. If the diagram in Figure 1 represents "needs" and "wants," how would you label the two diagrams in the figure? Explain your choice.

b. If the two circles in Figure 2 represent the goals of economic security and economic equity, where would you place a federal policy such as the minimum wage law—in area A, B, or C? Explain your choice.

c. If you were to change "Economic security" to "Economic efficiency" in Figure 2, would this change your placement of the minimum wage policy? How?

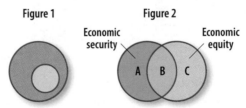

The U.S. economy fits between socialism and capitalism because it has a mixed economy.

Math Practice

33. Annual income: $10,300; $500 annual additional income per $.025/hour increase

Thinking Like an Economist

34. Answers will vary but should use a decision grid and summary to describe the advantages and disadvantages of the different economic systems.

Applying Economic Concepts

35. **Possible answer:** It is a custom to tip at restaurants and not clothing stores or gas stations. Tipping is not a government requirement (command), and it is not done because it is in the customer's best interest (market).

36. **a.** Needs are smaller than wants, so students should label the smaller circle "needs."

b. Since the minimum wage increases both security and equity, it should be placed in area B.

c. Yes. The minimum wage interferes with efficiency, and so it would need to be moved to area C, indicating that it increases equity only.

Critical Thinking

28. Answers will vary, but students should demonstrate a clear understanding of the two goals.

29. It has increased the level of government involvement in the economy through its regulatory function.

30. the incentive to work, save, invest, and be successful

31. Answers will vary but may include traditional economy: any products or choices based on habits or customs such as father/son businesses and greeting cards for traditional holidays; command economy: banning certain products, setting prices, regulatory actions, defense; market economy: any example illustrating interaction of individuals and businesses.

Analyzing Visuals

32. Government makes all economic decisions under communism and far fewer decisions under socialism. Under capitalism government promotes competition and provides public goods.

Focus

Teach

R Reading Strategy

Making Connections
Have students study the table and the graph on this page.
Ask: What connections can you make between the PC Software Market graph and the Software Piracy table? (*Possible answer: Both the graph and the table show that software piracy occurs at a much higher rate in developing countries; the piracy rate is lowest in developed nations.*) **OL**

Additional Support

Pirating Intellectual Property

A major feature of capitalism is the concept of private property rights—the freedom to own and control your possessions as you wish. Another major feature is the profit motive—taking a risk with your labor, property, or money in order to reap financial gains. Unfortunately, in our global economy the risks you take don't always result in rewards—at least for you.

Stolen Profits

Pirates of intellectual property reduce profits in some industries by as much as 50 percent. The term *intellectual property* (IP) refers to creations of the mind: inventions, literary and artistic works, symbols, names, images, and designs. Piracy of CDs, software, and clothing designs has expanded in recent years, along with counterfeit money and prescription medications. The illegal trade in pirated and counterfeit goods costs the legal world economy an estimated $630 billion per year.

SOFTWARE PIRACY*			
Highest piracy rates		**Lowest piracy rates**	
Vietnam	92%	Germany	29%
Ukraine	91%	Finland	29%
China	90%	Japan	28%
Zimbabwe	90%	Switzerland	28%
Indonesia	87%	Denmark	27%
Russia	87%	United Kingdom	27%
Nigeria	84%	Sweden	26%
Tunisia	84%	Austria	25%
Algeria	83%	New Zealand	23%
Kenya	83%	United States	21%

*Percentage of software pirated versus paid for
Source: *Second Annual BSA and IDC Global Software Piracy Study,* 2005

Case Study: China

In Silk Alley, a street in Beijing, bargain hunters can find just about anything on the cheap, including inexpensive knockoffs of Gucci, Chanel, Prada, and North Face products. Chinese piracy has made a significant dent in American music, movie, and software profits. In 2004 alone, U.S. companies lost an estimated $40 billion to IP piracy, the majority of which allegedly took place in China.

In the past, China blamed its flourishing culture of piracy on a myriad of issues. Yet the Chinese government also fostered a culture of piracy by maintaining that intellectual property was not an individual right, but a benefit to the state.

Now that the country is a member of the World Trade Organization, China must follow market-economy rules. It did a remarkable job of cracking down on its own domestic pirates, who have attempted to profit from the 2008 Beijing Olympics. U.S. officials now want to see similar efforts to protect U.S. intellectual property.

R

PC SOFTWARE MARKET

Billions of dollars* (y-axis: $60, 50, 40, 30, 20, 10, 0)

Legend: ■ 2004 Paid for ■ 2004 Pirated

Developed countries: $52, $22
Developing countries: $7, $12

*retail value

Source: *Second Annual BSA and IDC Global Software Piracy Study,* 2005

58 UNIT 1 Fundamental Economic Concepts

Extending the Content

Fighting Back Against IP Piracy in China For several years, companies in the United States and Europe had little success in stopping intellectual property pirates in China from robbing them of billions of dollars. Suing Chinese companies in China usually ended in failure. Courts, government officials, and reporters in the home city of the company being sued invariably sided with the defendants. Recently, however, Chinese premier Wen Jiabao has promised that his nation will better protect IP rights. Encouraged by this pledge, foreign companies are taking a more aggressive approach to asserting their legal rights in China. These companies have learned that bringing suit in a city outside a Chinese company's home region and generating international media coverage yields better results. In 2007, Starbucks won a high-profile case in China against a Shanghai coffee chain that used a name and logo similar to that of the U.S. company.

Worldwide Problem

Piracy has become a worldwide problem and affects the bottom line of companies everywhere. IP theft also raises unemployment rates and lowers tax revenues, especially in developing countries. Losses in tax revenue are more costly than one might think. Experts estimate that in four years, a 10 percent drop in the global piracy rate would add roughly 2.4 million new jobs, $400 billion in profits, and $67 billion in tax revenues world-wide.

What Does It Mean For You?

C While you might think that software piracy does not affect you directly, this is far from the truth. Companies that lose profits from IP theft often pass the cost of piracy on to you—the honest consumer. For every song or movie downloaded or sold illegally, businesses must charge paying customers more to cover their production costs. In addition, government revenue that could go to your education, parks, or better roads instead is funneled into law enforcement to prevent IP piracy. But perhaps the biggest loser in IP piracy is creativity. After all, if you were an artist or designer, would you be willing to spend your money as well as months or years of your life to develop a new product, only to have it copied and your profits taken away by someone else?

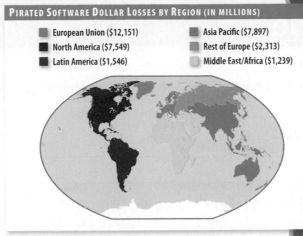

PIRATED SOFTWARE DOLLAR LOSSES BY REGION (IN MILLIONS)

- European Union ($12,151)
- North America ($7,549)
- Latin America ($1,546)
- Asia Pacific ($7,897)
- Rest of Europe ($2,313)
- Middle East/Africa ($1,239)

Source: *Second Annual BSA and IDC Global Software Piracy Study, 2005*

photo: A bulldozer destroying pirated CDs, DVDs, and videos in Moscow, Russia

Analyzing the Issue

1. **Identifying** What economic policy allowed IP piracy to grow in China?
2. **Describing** What is the relationship between piracy rates and developing countries?
3. **Applying** Check your local newspaper, news magazines, or Internet news sources for recent articles about intellectual property theft. How does IP piracy affect your state?

Assess/ Close

C Critical Thinking

Assessing Have students select a U.S. company that has been affected by IP piracy. Ask students to research the effects of the IP pirates and then prepare a report assessing the impact of IP piracy on the company. Reports should include examples of the products pirated, statistics quantifying the losses, and strategies the company has used to protect its rights. **OL**

Analyzing the Issue

Answers:
1. the policy of maintaining that intellectual property is not an individual right, but a benefit to the state
2. It is an inverse relationship. Piracy rates are higher in developing countries and lower in developed countries.
3. Students should assess how IP piracy affects their state.

Additional Support

Activity: Technology Connection

Designing Organize the class into small groups. Instruct each group to choose an item that has commonly been pirated (for example, CDs, DVDs, computer software, clothing designs, and so on). Have groups design a new technological device or procedure that would prevent or reduce the piracy of their item. Encourage students to research efforts that companies have already used to prevent piracy of different types of items. Have groups create a sketch, diagram, or computer program that illustrates the specifications and functioning of their new anti-piracy device or procedure. Ask groups to present their ideas to the class. Have the class take notes during group presentations and then speculate on the effectiveness of each device or procedure in a class discussion. **OL**

Planning Guide

Key to Ability Levels

BL Below level   **AL** Above level
OL On level   **ELL** English Language Learners

Key to Teaching Resources

Print Material   DVD
CD-Rom   Transparency

Levels					Resources	Chapter Opener	Section 1	Section 2	Section 3	Chapter Assess
BL	OL	AL	ELL							
FOCUS										
BL	OL	AL	ELL	🖨	**Daily Focus Skills Transparencies**		16, 19	17	18	
TEACH										
BL	OL		ELL	📁	**Guided Reading Activities***		p. 7	p. 8	p. 9	
BL	OL	AL	ELL	📁	**Economic Content Vocabulary Activities***		p. 3	p. 3	p. 3	
	OL	AL		📁	**Critical Thinking Activities**		pp. 3, 17			
BL	OL		ELL	📁	**Reading Essentials and Note-Taking Guide***		p. 19	p. 22	p. 25	
		AL		📁	**Enrichment Activities**			p. 3		
	OL	AL		📁	**Free Enterprise Activities**		p. 3			
BL	OL	AL	ELL	📁	**Economic Cartoons**		p. 26			
BL	OL	AL	ELL	🖨	**Economic Concepts Transparencies, Strategies, and Activities**			pp. 3, 9	p. 5	
BL	OL	AL	ELL	📁	**Math Practice for Economics**		p. 3			
BL	OL		ELL	📁	**High School Reading in the Content Area Strategies and Activities**	✓	✓	✓	✓	✓
BL	OL	AL	ELL	🖨	**High School Writing Process Transparencies**	✓	✓	✓	✓	✓
BL	OL	AL	ELL	📁	**Writer's Guidebook**	✓	✓	✓	✓	✓
BL	OL	AL	ELL	💿	**StudentWorks Plus CD-ROM**	✓	✓	✓	✓	✓
BL	OL	AL	ELL	💿	**Vocabulary PuzzleMaker CD-ROM**	✓	✓	✓	✓	✓

*Also available in Spanish

- Interactive Lesson Planner
- Interactive Teacher Edition
- Fully editable blackline masters
- Economics & You videos

- Differentiated Lesson Plans
- Printable reports of daily assignments
- Standards tracking system

Levels					Resources	Chapter Opener	Section 1	Section 2	Section 3	Chapter Assess
BL	OL	AL	ELL							
TEACH *(continued)*										
BL	OL	AL	ELL		Economics & You Video Program DVD—*Business Organizations*	✓	✓	✓	✓	✓
BL	OL	AL	ELL		Graph Coach CD-ROM	✓	✓	✓	✓	✓
Teacher Resources					Differentiated Instruction Strategies	✓	✓	✓	✓	✓
					Success with English Learners	✓	✓	✓	✓	✓
					Presentation Plus! CD-ROM	✓	✓	✓	✓	✓
ASSESS										
BL	OL	AL	ELL		Section Quizzes and Chapter Tests		p. 29	p. 30	p. 31	pp. 33, 37
BL	OL	AL	ELL		Authentic Assessment Strategies and Activities		p. 3			
BL	OL	AL	ELL		*ExamView*® *Assessment Suite* CD-ROM		3-1	3-2	3-3	Ch. 3
BL	OL	AL	ELL		Interactive Tutor Self-Assessment CD-ROM		3-1	3-2	3-3	
CLOSE										
BL			ELL		Reteaching Activities*		p. 3	p. 3	p. 3	
BL	OL		ELL		Reading and Study Skills Foldables		p. 45	p. 45		
BL	OL	AL	ELL		Graphic Organizer Transparencies		p. 31			

*Also available in Spanish

Integrating Technology

Activity
Using Skillbuilder Interactive Workbook CD-ROM

Comparing and Contrasting

Technology Product

Glencoe's *Skillbuilder Interactive Workbook CD-ROM* provides self-paced instruction, practice, and assessment of key skills your students need in social studies, including comparing and contrasting. The *Skillbuilder Interactive Workbook*

- lets students learn, practice, and assess their knowledge of social studies skills.
- lists key terms and a glossary where appropriate.
- includes a **Management System** to create class rosters and monitor student progress.

Objectives

The *Skillbuilder Interactive Workbook* help students

- learn and practice comparing and contrasting;
- identify areas for reinforcement.

Steps

Provide students with the following information:

- Select **Comparing and Contrasting** from the Main Menu page. Then select one of the options.
- The **Instruction** option on the Activities page provides a step-by-step tutorial to learn the skill being taught, along with an audio component.
- The **Guided Practice** section presents comprehension questions to review the material covered in the Instruction section. Questions include multiple choice, true/false, fill-in-the-blank, and drag-and-drop types.
- The **Assessment** section includes 10 questions that test student mastery of the skill.

Have students complete the activity and use the Management System to monitor their progress.

Economics ONLINE

	Student	Teacher	Parent
Beyond the Textbook	●	●	●
Chapter Overviews	●	●	●
ePuzzles and Games	●		●
Concepts in Motion	●		●
Multi-Language Glossaries	●		●
Online Student Edition	●	●	●
Self-Check Quizzes	●		●
Student Web Activities	●		●
Study Central™	●		●
Time Current Events	●	●	●
Teaching Today		●	
Vocabulary eFlashcards	●		●
Web Activity Lesson Plans		●	

Glencoe Media Center

⟩ glencoe.com

Study-To-Go
- Vocabulary eFlashcards
- Self-Check Quizzes

⟩ **Audio/Video**
- Student Edition Audio
- Spanish Summaries
- Economics & You Videos

- **Timed Readings Plus in Social Studies** helps students increase their reading rate and fluency while maintaining comprehension. The 400-word passages are similar to those found on state and national assessments.

- **Reading in the Content Area: Social Studies** concentrates on six essential reading skills that help students better comprehend what they read. The book includes 75 high-interest nonfiction passages written at increasing levels of difficulty.

- **Reading Social Studies** includes strategic reading instruction and vocabulary support in Social Studies content for both ELLs and native speakers of English. www.jamestowneducation.com

Reading List Generator CD-ROM

Use this database to search more than 30,000 titles to create a customized reading list for your students.

- Reading lists can be organized by students' reading level, author, genre, theme, or area of interest.

- The database provides Degrees of Reading Power™ (DRP) and Lexile™ readability scores for all selections.

- A brief summary of each selection is included.

Leveled reading suggestions for this chapter:
For students at a Grade 10 reading level:
- *Top Entrepreneurs and Their Businesses,* by Robert B. Pile

For students at a Grade 11 reading level:
- *Be Your Own Boss: Small Businesses,* by Ernestine Giesecke

For students at a Grade 12 reading level:
- *Business Builders in Cosmetics,* by Jacqueline C. Kent

* Review suggested books before assigning them.

National Council on Economic Education

Voluntary Standards Emphasized in Chapter 3

Content Standard 10 Institutions evolve in market economies to help individuals and groups accomplish their goals. Banks, labor unions, corporations, legal systems, and not-for-profit organizations are examples of important institutions. A different kind of institution, clearly defined and enforced property rights, is essential to a market economy.

Content Standard 14 Entrepreneurs are people who take the risks of organizing productive resources to make goods and services. Profit is an important incentive that leads entrepreneurs to accept the risks of business failure.

Content Standard 16 There is an economic role for government in a market economy whenever the benefits of a government policy outweigh its costs. Governments often provide for national defense, address environmental concerns, define and protect property rights, and attempt to make markets more competitive. Most government policies also redistribute income.

Resources Available from NCEE
- Virtual Economics®: An Interactive Center for Economic Education Version 3.0
- Learning, Earning and Investing, High School
- Focus: Institutions and Markets
- Financing Your Future

To order these materials, or to contact your State Council on Economic Education about workshops and programs, call 1-800-338-1192 or visit the NCEE Web site at store.ncee.net**.**

The BIG Ideas

As students study the chapter, remind them to consider the chapter-based Big Ideas. The **Essential Question** in the chapter launch activity below ties in to the Big Ideas and helps students think about and understand important chapter concepts. In addition, the Hands-On Chapter Project relates the content from each section to the Big Ideas. The steps in each section build on each other and culminate in the Wrap-Up Activity on the Visual Summary page.

 Economics & You Video To generate student interest and provide a springboard for class discussion, access the Economics & You Topic 3 video, **Business Organizations,** at glencoe.com or on the video DVD.

FOLDABLES Study Organizer **Dinah Zike's Foldables** are three-dimensional, interactive graphic organizers that help students practice basic writing skills, review key vocabulary terms, and identify main ideas. Have students complete this chapter's Foldable activity or activities in *Dinah Zike's Reading and Study Skills Foldables* booklet. **OL**

Economics ONLINE

Introduce students to chapter content and key terms by having them access *Chapter 3 —Chapter Overviews* at glencoe.com.

CHAPTER 3 Business Organizations

Why It Matters

You have an idea for a new product and you want to set up a company to market it. You need $5,000 to get started with production and advertising. Use what you have already learned about the factors of production to create a list of resources you will need and where to find them. Read Chapter 3 to learn about the different ways to organize a business.

The BIG Ideas

1. The profit motive acts as an incentive for people to produce and sell goods and services.

2. Governments and institutions help participants in a market economy accomplish their financial goals.

▶ Businesses can be owned by individuals such as this flower shop owner, by two or more partners, or by many stockholders of a large company.

Economics ONLINE Chapter Overview Visit the *Economics: Principles and Practices* Web site at glencoe.com and click on *Chapter 3–Chapter Overviews* to preview chapter information.

60 UNIT 1

Activity: Launching the Chapter

Speculating Have a volunteer read aloud the Big Ideas. Ask students whether they agree with the statement that earning money plays a big part in why people decide to produce and sell goods and services. **Essential Question: What other reasons might people have for starting their own businesses?** *(Answers may include the desire for independence or prestige or the desire to satisfy a consumer need.)*

Encourage students to look for reasons why people start their own businesses, along with the costs and benefits involved with the decision, as they read this chapter. **OL**

SECTION 1

Forms of Business Organization

GUIDE TO READING

Section Preview

In this section, you will learn about the advantages and disadvantages of various forms of business organization.

Content Vocabulary

- sole proprietorship (p. 62)
- proprietorship (p. 62)
- unlimited liability (p. 63)
- inventory (p. 64)
- limited life (p. 64)
- partnership (p. 64)
- general partnership (p. 64)
- limited partnership (p. 64)
- corporation (p. 67)
- charter (p. 67)
- stock (p. 67)
- stockholder (p. 67)
- shareholder (p. 67)
- dividend (p. 67)
- common stock (p. 67)
- preferred stock (p. 68)
- bond (p. 69)
- principal (p. 69)
- interest (p. 69)
- double taxation (p. 69)

Academic Vocabulary

- comprise (p. 62)
- entity (p. 63)

Reading Strategy

Contrasting As you read about business organizations, complete a graphic organizer similar to the one below to show how the three types of business organizations differ from one another.

Business Organizations → Proprietorship, Partnership, Corporation

---

Focus

Bellringer
Daily Focus Transparency 16

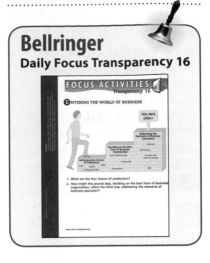

GUIDE TO READING

Answers to Graphic:

Proprietorship: owned and run by a single person

Partnership: jointly owned by two or more persons

Corporation: business organization recognized by law as a separate legal entity with all the rights of an individual

---

COMPANIES IN THE NEWS
—adapted from BusinessWeek

Selling to a Different Beat

Marc Weinstein's Amoeba Music store stocks 2.5 million titles, half of which are rare and used vinyl records. With genres ranging from jazz and hip-hop to Hungarian folk music and Pakistani *qawwali*, Amoeba is Weinstein's alternative to music megastores.

Amoeba's 1990 launch in Berkeley, California, was risky. Still, Weinstein and his two partners staked $325,000 in loans and savings on their vision. The risk yielded sales of $10,000 on opening day. Today the business has stores in Los Angeles and San Francisco. And while most of the industry faces declining sales, Amoeba's sales continue to rise.

For Weinstein and company, the vision is evolving. Soon Amoeba will have its own record label and launch a Web site for music downloads. ■

There are three main forms of business organization in the economy today—the sole proprietorship, the partnership, and the corporation. Each offers its owners significant advantages and disadvantages.

The type of business an entrepreneur decides on can have real consequences. If Marc Weinstein and his co-founders had organized as a corporation instead of a partnership, then the corporation would have to please its stockholders. Instead, the business was organized as a partnership, which allows the partners to set their own criteria for success.

Resource Manager

R Reading Strategies	**C** Critical Thinking	**D** Differentiated Instruction	**W** Writing Support	**S** Skill Practice
Teacher Edition • Using Context Clues, p. 62 • Sequencing Info., p. 67 • Identifying, p. 67 **Additional Resources** • Guid. Read. Act., p. 7 • Read. Ess. & Note-Taking Guide, p. 19	**Teacher Edition** • Making Inferences, p. 62 • Analyzing, p. 64 • Drawing Con., p. 69 • Problem-Solving, p. 71 **Additional Resources** • Authentic Assess., p. 3 • Free Ent. Act., p. 3 • Math Prac. for Econ., p. 3	**Teacher Edition** • ELL, p. 63 • Special Ed., p. 64 • Interpersonal, p. 65 • Verbal/Linguistic, p. 66 **Additional Resources** • Daily Focus Trans. 16, 19 • Econ. Cartoons, p. 26	**Teacher Edition** • Narrative Writing, p. 63 • Personal Writing, p. 65 • Expository Writing, pp. 68, 70 **Additional Resources** • High School Writing Process Trans. • Crit. Think. Act., pp. 3, 17	**Teacher Edition** • Reading Graphs, p. 62 • Interpreting Political Cartoons, pp. 66, 69 • Visual Literacy, p. 68 **Additional Resources** • Graph. Org. Trans., p. 31 • Reading and Study Skills Fold., p. 45

Teach

R Reading Strategy

Using Context Clues Tell students that the word *sole* in the term *sole proprietorship* is an adjective that means "one and only" or "single." **Ask:** What are other terms that use *sole* as an adjective? *(Possible answers: sole ownership, sole survivor, sole heir)* **OL**

C Critical Thinking

Making Inferences Ask: What are some personal qualities that a sole proprietor might need to form a successful proprietorship? *(Answers may include intelligence, determination, self-confidence, flexibility, a sense of humor, commitment, and optimism.)* **OL**

S Skill Practice

Reading Graphs Ask: Which business type is most common in the United States? *(sole proprietorships)* Which business type brings in the most profits? *(corporations)* **OL**

Economic Analysis

Answer: corporations

Differentiated Instruction

---

sole proprietorship or proprietorship business owned and run by a single person who has the rights to all profits and unlimited liability for all debts of the firm

Skills Handbook
See page **R50** for more information on *Using Bar and Circle Graphs.*

Sole Proprietorships

MAIN Idea Sole proprietorships are easy to start, but owners have unlimited liability.

Economics & You Have you ever dreamed of starting your own business? Read on to learn what it takes to own a business.

R The most common form of business organization in the United States is the **sole proprietorship** or **proprietorship**—a business owned and run by a single individual. Because proprietorships are basically one-person operations, they **comprise** the smallest form of business and have the smallest fraction of total sales. As **Figure 3.1** shows, they are also relatively profitable, as they bring in about one-fifth of the total profits earned by all businesses.

C Forming a Proprietorship

The sole proprietorship is the easiest form of business to start because it involves almost no requirements except for occasional business licenses and fees. Most proprietorships are ready for business as soon

as they set up operations. You could start a proprietorship simply by putting up a lemonade stand in your front yard. Someone else could decide to mow lawns or open a restaurant. A proprietorship can be run on the Internet, out of a garage, or from an office in a professional building.

Advantages

As you have learned, a sole proprietorship is easy to start up. If someone has an idea or an opportunity to make a profit, he or she only has to decide to go into business and then do it.

Management also is relatively simple. Decisions do not require the approval of a co-owner, boss, or other "higher-up." This flexibility means that the proprietor can make an immediate decision if a problem comes up.

A third advantage is that the owner can keep the profits of successful management without having to share them with other owners. The owner also has to accept the possibility of a loss, but the lure of profits makes people willing to take risks.

Figure 3.1 ▶ Business Organizations

Number of organizations
8.5%
19.9%
71.6%

Sales
4.6%
11.8%
83.6%

Net income (profit)
20.9%
25.7%
53.4%

○ Corporations   ● Partnerships   ● Sole proprietorships

Source: *2006 Statistical Abstract of the United States.*

▶ Businesses in the United States can be organized as sole proprietorships, partnerships, or corporations. Their numbers, sales, and profits vary widely. Corporations make up only 20 percent of businesses, yet they account for over half of the total net income.

Economic Analysis *Which business organization accounts for the largest amount of sales?*

Critical Thinking Activities, p. 3

Categorizing Information About Business Organizations

Objective: Analyze sole proprietorships and partnerships.

Focus: Ask students to describe sole proprietorships and partnerships.

Teach: Have students categorize the phrases in the chart.

Assess: Review answers individually, and ask students to explain their choices.

Close: Have students choose what they think is the main advantage and disadvantage for each organization.

Differentiated Instruction Strategies

BL Have students discuss how important they think "ease of starting up" (item 2) is to new business owners.

AL Ask students whether they would rather work alone or with a partner, and why.

ELL Have students create a short glossary of five terms used in the activity.

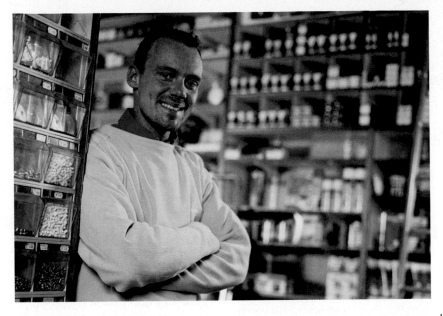

Sole Proprietorship
Anyone can start a business as a sole proprietor, as this pharmacist has done. *What are the advantages of sole proprietorships?*

W **Writing Support**

Narrative Writing Have students write a short story about a person who achieves his or her dream of owning a business. Remind students to include a conflict, such as financial trouble or competition from a larger business. **AL**

D **Differentiated Instruction**

English Language Learners
Help students understand the concept of unlimited liability. Divide them into pairs, and have one student play the part of a proprietor. The other student will play the part of the investor who loaned the proprietor money to start the business. Have pairs act out the consequence of a failed business for the proprietor.
Ask: Why is unlimited liability a disadvantage of a proprietorship? *(If the business fails, the owner's personal property might be taken away to pay off his or her debt.)* **ELL**

Caption Answer: easy to start, management relatively simple, owner can keep profits for self, no separate business income taxes, psychological satisfaction from being one's own boss, easy to get out of business

Fourth, the proprietorship does not have to pay separate business income taxes because the business is not recognized as a separate legal **entity.** The owner still must pay individual income taxes on profits taken from the sole proprietorship, but the business itself is exempt from any tax on income.

Suppose, for example, Mr. Winters owns and operates a small hardware store in a local shopping center and a small auto repair business in his garage next to his home. Because neither business depends on the other, and because the only thing they have in common is Mr. Winters's ownership, the two businesses appear as separate and distinct economic activities. For tax purposes, however, everything is lumped together at the end of the year. When Mr. Winters files his personal income taxes, the profits from both businesses are combined with any wages and salaries from other sources. He does not pay taxes on either of the businesses separately.

Another advantage of the proprietorship is the psychological satisfaction many people get from being their own boss. These people often have a strong desire to see their name in print, have dreams of great wealth or community status, or simply want to make their mark in history.

A sixth advantage is that it is easy to get out of business. All the proprietor has to do is pay any outstanding bills and then stop offering goods or services for sale.

W **unlimited liability** requirement that an owner is personally and fully responsible for all losses and debts of the business

Disadvantages

The main disadvantage of a proprietorship is that the owner of the business has **unlimited liability.** This means that the owner is personally and fully responsible for all losses and debts of the business. If the business fails, the owner's personal possessions may be taken away to satisfy business debts. **D**

As an example, let us revisit the earlier case of Mr. Winters, who owns and operates two businesses. If the hardware business should fail, his personal wealth, which includes the automobile repair shop, may be legally taken away to pay off debts arising from the hardware store.

A second disadvantage of a proprietorship is the difficulty of raising financial capital. Generally, a large amount of

CHAPTER 3 Business Organizations **63**

Leveled Activities

BL **Graphic Organizer Transparencies, p. 31**

OL **Authentic Assessment Strategies and Activities, p. 3**

AL **Free Enterprise Activities, p. 3**

D Differentiated Instruction

Special Education Encourage students to use context clues to decode and comprehend unfamiliar words. Ask them to begin a list of words with which they are unfamiliar, such as *efficiency*. Then pair them with a partner, and have them guess at the meaning of the words based on the context. *(Unfamiliar words might include* managerial, fringe benefits, *and* ceases.*)* **BL**

C Critical Thinking

Analyzing Ask: Why might a business *not* want to have a large inventory of parts and supplies on hand? *(Possible answer: It costs money and takes up space to store parts and supplies.)* **AL**

✓Reading Check Answer:
owner has unlimited liability and may have limited managerial experience; difficult to raise financial capital, attract qualified employees, and stock adequate inventory; business has limited life

---

Additional Support

Teacher Tip

Assembling Resources You may want to provide students with a newspaper, local telephone book, Chamber of Commerce guide, or other directory of local businesses. Students may also be able to locate new local businesses on the Internet.

---

inventory stock of finished goods and parts held in reserve

limited life situation in which a firm ceases to exist when an owner dies, quits, or sells the business

partnership unincorporated business owned and operated by two or more people who share the profits and responsibility for debts

general partnership form of partnership where all partners are equally responsible for management and debts

limited partnership form of partnership where one or more partners are not active in the daily running of the business and have limited responsibility for debts

---

money is needed to set up a business, and even more may be required for its expansion. However, banks and other lenders are often reluctant to lend money to new or very small businesses. As a result, the proprietor often has to raise financial capital by tapping savings, using credit cards, or borrowing from friends and family.

D The size and efficiency of a proprietorship also are disadvantages. A retail store, for example, may need to hire several employees just to stay open during normal business hours. It may also have to carry a minimum **inventory**—a stock of finished goods and parts in reserve—to satisfy customers or to keep production flowing smoothly. Because of limited financial capital, the proprietor may not be able to hire enough personnel or stock enough inventory to operate the business efficiently.

A fourth disadvantage is that the proprietor often has limited managerial experience. The owner-manager of a small company may be an inventor who is highly qualified as an engineer but lacks the "business sense" or the time needed to oversee the growth of the company. This owner may have to hire others to do the types of work—manufacturing, sales, and accounting—at which he or she is not an expert.

A fifth disadvantage is the difficulty of attracting qualified employees. Because proprietorships tend to be small, employees often have to be skilled in several areas. In addition, many top high school and college graduates are more likely to be attracted to positions with larger, well-established firms than small ones. This is especially true when larger firms offer *fringe benefits*—employee benefits such as paid vacations, sick leave, retirement, and health or medical insurance—in addition to wages and salaries.

A sixth disadvantage of the sole proprietorship is **limited life.** This means that the firm legally ceases to exist when the owner dies, quits, or sells the business.

✓Reading Check Describing What are the major disadvantages of a sole proprietorship?

Partnerships

MAIN Idea In a partnership, each partner fully shares responsibility for the operation of the business and all profits or losses.

Economics & You Have you ever had a partner for a school project? How did you handle individual tasks, and how were grades assigned? Read on to find out about issues associated with partnerships.

A **partnership** is a business that is jointly owned by two or more persons. It shares many of the same strengths and weaknesses of a sole proprietorship. As shown in Figure 3.1, partnerships are the least numerous form of business organization in the United States, accounting for the second smallest proportion of sales and net income.

Types of Partnerships

The most common form of partnership is a **general partnership,** in which all partners are responsible for the management and financial obligations of the business. In a **limited partnership,** at least one partner is not active in the daily running of the

---

Activity: Hands-On Economics

Making Connections Organize students into several small groups. Ask each group to locate and contact a new small business in the community. Have the groups interview the owners of the businesses to discover what steps they took to start their businesses. Have groups find out why the owners wanted to start their own businesses, what challenges the owners faced, and what skills the owners felt were needed for success. Have groups report their findings to the class. **OL**

business. Likewise, the limited partner only has limited responsibility for the debts and obligations of the business.

Forming a Partnership

Like a proprietorship, a partnership is relatively easy to start. Because more than one owner is involved, formal legal papers called *articles of partnership* are usually drawn up to specify arrangements between partners. Although not always required, these papers state ahead of time how the expected profits (or possible losses) will be divided.

The articles of partnership may specify that the profits be divided equally or by any other arrangement suitable to the partners. They also may state the way future partners can be added to the business, and the way the property of the business will be distributed if the partnership ends.

Advantages

Like the sole proprietorship, one advantage of the partnership is its ease of startup. Even the costs of the articles of partnership, which normally involve attorney fees and a filing fee for the state, are minimal if they are spread over several partners.

Ease of management is another advantage. Each partner usually brings a different area of expertise to the business: one might have a talent for marketing, another for production, another for bookkeeping and finance, and yet another for shipping and distribution. While partners normally agree ahead of time to consult with each other before making major decisions, partners generally have a great deal of freedom to make minor ones.

A third advantage is the lack of special taxes on a partnership. As in a proprietorship, the partners withdraw profits from the firm and then pay individual income taxes on them at the end of the year. Partners have to submit special schedules to the Internal Revenue Service detailing their profits from the partnership, but this is for informational purposes only and does not give a partnership any special legal status.

Fourth, partnerships can usually attract financial capital more easily than proprietorships. They are generally larger and

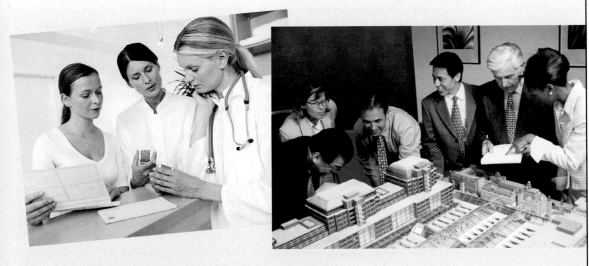

Partnerships Businesses owned by two or more people are called partnerships. Lawyers, doctors, and architects often form partnerships to limit overhead costs. *How are partnerships founded?*

CHAPTER 3 Business Organizations 65

Hands-On Chapter Project
Step 1

Creating a Business Plan

In this project, students will write a business plan for a firm that is suitable to the skills of team members.

Step 1: Brainstorming and Evaluating Ideas.
Students will gather into teams and brainstorm ideas for a business they could start.

Directions: Organize the class into an equal number of teams with about five or six members each. Tell teams that their task will be to choose and plan a business that

they could start right now with the set of skills that group members possess. Have them begin by brainstorming a list of possible businesses and then debating each suggestion's suitability. Students should make a chart of pluses and minuses for each of several suggestions as a way of evaluating each possibility. They may also want to discuss the availability of resources, potential profit, special challenges, possible help they could use, and how each of the elements of business operation will be addressed. Their goal by the end of the

working period is to generate a list of finalists and evaluate the advantages and disadvantages of each idea.

Categorizing Have students categorize each suggestion as providing a product or a service. **OL**

(Chapter Project continued in Section 2.)

Liability In a partnership, all partners take on responsibility for the debts of the business. *How do general partnerships and limited partnerships differ?*

"Congratulations on becoming a partner - your share of company losses are $200,000."

have a better chance of getting a bank loan. The existing partners could also take in new partners who bring financial capital with them as part of their price for joining.

A fifth advantage of partnerships is the more efficient operations that come with their slightly larger size. In some areas, such as medicine and law, a relatively small firm with three or four partners might be just the right size for the market. Other partnerships, such as accounting firms, may have hundreds of partners offering services throughout the United States.

A sixth and final advantage is that partnerships often find it easier to attract top talent than proprietorships. Because most partnerships offer specialized services, top graduates seek out stable, well-paying firms to apply their recently acquired skills.

Disadvantages

The main disadvantage of the *general partnership* is that each partner is fully responsible for the acts of all other partners. If one partner causes the firm to suffer a huge loss, each partner is fully and personally responsible for the loss. This is similar to the unlimited liability feature of a proprietorship, but it is more complicated because more owners are involved. As a result, most people are extremely careful when they choose a business partner.

In the case of the *limited partnership*, a partner's responsibility for the debts of the business is limited by the size of his or her investment in the firm. If the business fails and debts remain, the limited partner loses only the original investment, leaving the general partners to make up the rest.

Another disadvantage is that the partnership, like the proprietorship, has limited life. When a partner dies or leaves, the partnership must be dissolved and reorganized. However, the new partnership may try to reach an agreement with the older partnership to keep its old name.

A third disadvantage is the potential for conflict between partners. Sometimes partners discover that they do not get along, so they have to either learn to work together or leave the business. If the partnership is large, these types of problems can easily develop, even though initially everyone thought they would get along.

✓**Reading Check** **Contrasting** What are the differences between a general partnership and a limited partnership?

Extending the Content

Sole Proprietorships and Partnerships
Although sole proprietorships and partnerships account for only a small part of total business sales, they still play a very important role in the overall economy. These relatively small operations usually have close personal ties with their customers and often are the first to notice—and respond to—changes in consumer demand. In addition, small businesses are able to produce certain specialty items—fine jewelry, for example—more economically than larger companies.

Corporations

MAIN Idea Corporations are one of the most important forms of business and can easily raise large amounts of financial capital.

Economics & You Do you know someone who works for a corporation? Read on to learn how corporations are organized.

Corporations account for only about one-fifth of the businesses in the United States, as shown in Figure 3.1, although they are responsible for a majority of all sales. A **corporation** is a form of business organization recognized by law as a separate legal entity with all the rights of an individual. This status gives the corporation the right to buy and sell property, to enter into legal contracts, and to sue and be sued.

Forming a Corporation

Unlike a sole proprietorship or partnership, a corporation is a very formal and legal arrangement. People who want to *incorporate,* or form a corporation, must file for permission from the national government or the state where the business will have its headquarters. If approved, a **charter**—a government document that gives permission to create a corporation—

is granted. The charter states the company's name, address, purpose, and other features of the business.

The charter also specifies the number of shares of **stock,** or ownership certificates in the firm. These shares are sold to investors, called **stockholders** or **shareholders.** As shown in **Figure 3.2,** stockholders then own a part of the corporation. The money gained from the sale of stock is used to set up the corporation. If the corporation is profitable, it may eventually issue a **dividend**—a check that transfers a portion of the corporate earnings—to each stockholder.

Corporate Structure

When investors purchase stock, they become owners with certain ownership rights. The extent of these rights depends on the type of stock purchased: common or preferred.

Common stock represents basic ownership of a corporation. The owner of common stock usually receives one vote for each share of stock. This vote is used to elect a board of directors, which in turn directs the corporation's business by setting broad policies and goals. The board also hires a professional management team to run the business on a daily basis.

corporation form of business organization recognized by law as a separate legal entity

charter written government approval to establish a corporation

stock certificate of ownership in a corporation

stockholders or shareholders people who own a share or shares of stock in a corporation

dividend check that transfers a portion of the company profits to stockholders, usually quarterly

common stock most frequently used form of corporate ownership, with one vote per share for stockholders

Figure 3.2 ► **Stock Ownership**

CERTIFICATE OF STOCK
Terrestrial Computers of America Inc.
1 share

1/200th

► If a corporation has 200 shares of stock, and if you could divide the firm into 200 equal parts, the owner of a single share of stock would own 1/200th of the corporation.

Economic Analysis *How does common stock differ from preferred stock?*

CHAPTER 3   Business Organizations   67

Activity: Interdisciplinary Connection

History Tell students that state charters issued during the 1800s, for the most part, greatly restricted the powers of corporations. By the end of the century, however, courts and legislatures, yielding to pressure from business interests, began to ease controls on corporate activities. Exposés of business corruption by muckraking journalists at the turn of the century stirred demands for renewed restrictions. As a result, federal and state

governments passed laws regulating practically every aspect of corporate operations. Invite students to research and report on one of these historical events, such as Upton Sinclair and America's meat-packing industry or Ida Tarbell and Standard Oil. Have students present their findings in oral presentations. **OL**

preferred stock form of corporate ownership without vote, in which stockholders get their investments back before common stockholders

Preferred stock represents nonvoting ownership shares of the corporation. Because the stock is nonvoting, preferred stockholders do not have the right to elect members to the board of directors. However, preferred stockholders receive their dividends before common stockholders receive theirs. If a corporation goes out of business, preferred stockholders get their investment back before common stockholders get theirs back.

In theory, a stockholder who owns a majority of a corporation's common stock can elect board members and control the company. In some cases, the common stockholder might elect himself or herself, or even other family members, to the board of directors.

In practice, this is not done very often because most corporations are so large and the number of shares held by the typical stockholder is so small. Most small

stockholders either do not vote or they turn their votes over to someone else. This is done with the use of a *proxy,* a ballot that gives a stockholder's representative the right to vote on corporate matters.

Although corporations differ in size and industry, they generally organize in similar ways. As **Figure 3.3** shows, the day-to-day operations of a corporation are divided into different departments headed by vice presidents, who in turn report to the president of the company. Neither the president nor the other employees of the corporation have direct contact with the owners, or shareholders, of the company.

Advantages

The main advantage of a corporation is the ease of raising financial capital. If the corporation needs more capital, it can sell additional stock to investors. The revenue

Charts In Motion
See StudentWorks™ Plus or glencoe.com.

Figure 3.3 ▶ Corporate Structure

▶ This organizational chart shows the chain of command of a typical organization. It also outlines the basic components of the business, such as sales, production, and payroll.

Economic Analysis *Who reports directly to the vice president of production?*

- Owners, the shareholders, elect the
- Board of directors, who select the
- President, who hires the
- Vice president, sales
- Vice president, production
- Vice president, finance
- Domestic
- International
- Quality control
- Research and development
- Payroll

Activity: Technology Connection

can then be used to finance or expand operations. A corporation may also borrow money by issuing bonds. A **bond** is a written promise to repay the amount borrowed at a later date. The amount borrowed is known as the **principal.** While the money is borrowed, the corporation pays **interest,** the price paid for the use of another's money.

A second and very important advantage is that the corporation provides *limited liability* for its owners. This means that the corporation itself, not its owners, is fully responsible for its obligations. To illustrate, suppose a corporation cannot pay all of its debts and goes out of business. Because of limited liability, stockholder losses are limited to the money they invested in stock. Even if other debts remain, stockholders are not responsible for them.

S

Some firms will incorporate just to take advantage of the limited liability. For example, suppose Mr. Winters, who owns the hardware store and the auto repair business, now decides to set up each business as a separate corporation. If the hardware business should fail, his personal wealth, which includes stock in the automobile repair business, is safe. Mr. Winters may lose all the money invested in the hardware business, but that would be the extent of his loss.

From a broader economic perspective, limited liability enables firms to undertake potentially profitable ventures which are inherently risky. For example, corporations rather than individuals usually introduce new medicines because of the limited liability feature.

A third advantage of a corporation is that the directors of the corporation can hire professional managers to run the firm. This means that the owners, or stockholders, can own a portion of the corporation without having to know much about the business itself.

Another advantage is unlimited life, meaning that the corporation continues to exist even when ownership changes. Because the corporation is recognized as a separate legal entity, the name of the company stays the same, and the corporation continues to do business.

Cornered
by Mike Baldwin

TAX DEPARTMENT

DOUBLE

WHAMMY

WHAMMY

Double Taxation Shareholders have to pay corporate taxes and income taxes on their dividends. *Why are people interested in owning stock when they have to pay so much in taxes?*

This leads to a fifth advantage, the ease of transferring ownership of the corporation. If a shareholder no longer wants to be an owner, he or she simply sells the stock to someone else who then becomes the new owner. As a result, it is easier for the owner of a corporation to find a new buyer than it is for the owner of a sole proprietorship or a partnership.

C

Disadvantages

Because the law recognizes the corporation as a separate legal entity, the corporation must keep detailed sales and expense records so that it can pay taxes on its profits. This leads to the first disadvantage, the **double taxation** of corporate profits. Double taxation means that stockholder dividends are taxed twice. They are taxed the first time when the corporation pays taxes on its profits. Then they are taxed a

bond formal contract to repay borrowed money with interest

principal amount borrowed when getting a loan or issuing a bond

interest payment made for the use of borrowed money

double taxation taxation of dividends both as corporate profit and as personal income

CHAPTER 3   Business Organizations   69

S **Skill Practice**

Interpreting Political Cartoons Have a volunteer explain the cartoon. *(The cartoon illustrates the concept of double taxation of corporate profits. The box labeled "Whammy" represents corporate taxes, and the stacked boxes labeled "Whammy" and "Double" represent corporate taxes and income taxes on their dividends.)* **AL**

C **Critical Thinking**

Drawing Conclusions Tell students that when stockholders want to sell their stocks, they might contact people called stockbrokers. Stockbrokers are people who connect buyers and sellers of stock. **Ask:** Why do you think stockholders might hire the services of stockbrokers? *(Possible answer: Stockbrokers usually know people who want to buy the stockholder's stock. Therefore, it is easier for the stockholder to find a new buyer through a stockbroker.)* **OL**

Possible Caption Answer: Stocks are easy to sell and have the potential for making the owner large amounts of money.

Additional Support

Extending the Content

Bankruptcy If a firm files for bankruptcy under Chapter 7, it simply liquidates and goes out of business. If it files for bankruptcy under Chapter 11, it is given one year to reorganize and is allowed to stay in business. Individuals with regular incomes may file bankruptcy under Chapter 13, which is less complicated and less expensive than filing under Chapter 11. Chapter 13 is not available to corporations or partnerships.

W Writing Support

Expository Writing Have students review business periodicals to locate articles about public and privately held corporations. Ask students to write a few paragraphs on their findings, using the key terms introduced in the discussion on corporations in this section. **OL**

✓**Reading Check** **Answer:** Corporations provide limited liability for their owners. This means that the corporation itself is fully responsible for its obligations.

Assess

Use the Interactive Tutor Self-Assessment CD-ROM to review Section 1, and then assign the Section 1 Review as homework or as an in-class activity.

Close

Summarizing Have students list the three forms of business organizations and summarize the advantages and disadvantages of each. **OL**

SECTION 1 Review

Did You Know?

➤ **What's a public corporation anyway?** It's one that has "gone public," which means anyone with a little extra cash can buy stock and own a part of the company. A *privately held corporation*, on the other hand, sells shares only to a select group of people. Sometimes that group may consist of a few family members. The Securities and Exchange Commission (SEC) was set up in 1934 to regulate the sale of stock by public corporations.

Skills Handbook

See page **R41** for more information on **Evaluating Information.**

second time when investors, as the owners of the corporation, report their dividends as personal income.

Another disadvantage of the corporate structure is the difficulty and expense of getting a charter. Depending on the state, attorney's fees and filing expenses can cost several thousand dollars.

A third disadvantage of the corporation is that the owners, or shareholders, have little voice in how the business is run. Shareholders vote for the board of

directors, and the directors turn day-to-day operations over to a professional management team. The result is a separation of ownership and management. This is different from the proprietorship and partnership, where ownership and management are usually one and the same.

Finally, the fourth disadvantage is that corporations are subject to more government regulation than other forms of business. Corporations must register with the state in which they are chartered. If a corporation wants to sell its stock to the public, it must register with the federal Securities and Exchange Commission (SEC). It will also have to provide financial information concerning sales and profits to the general public on a regular basis. Even an attempt to take over another business may require federal government approval.

✓**Reading Check** **Evaluating** Why do many business owners prefer corporations over other forms of business organization?

SECTION 1 Review

Vocabulary

1. **Explain** the significance of sole proprietorship, proprietorship, unlimited liability, inventory, limited life, partnership, general partnership, limited partnership, corporation, charter, stock, stockholder, shareholder, dividend, common stock, preferred stock, bond, principal, interest, and double taxation.

Main Ideas

2. **Discuss** the advantages and disadvantages of the corporation.

3. **Describing** Use a graphic organizer like the one below to describe the characteristics of proprietorships, partnerships, and corporations.

Business Form	Characteristics
Proprietorship	
Partnership	
Corporation	

Critical Thinking

4. **The BIG Idea** How do partnerships support the profit motive of entrepreneurs?

5. **Analyzing Visuals** Look at Figure 3.3 on page 68. What is the relationship between the owners and the employees of the corporation?

6. **Drawing Conclusions** When a corporation wants to introduce a potentially profitable but risky product, it frequently sets up a separate company that has its own corporate structure. Why do you think the corporation does this?

Applying Economics

7. **Partnerships** Assume that you and a friend want to start a partnership to run your own business, such as a music store. Draw up one-page articles of partnership that outline how you will address financial issues of the partnership.

Answers

1. All definitions can be found in the section and the Glossary.

2. Advantages: easy to raise financial capital, limited liability for owners, professional managers can be hired to run the firm, unlimited life status, easy to transfer ownership. Disadvantages: double taxation, difficult and expensive to get a charter, shareholders have little voice in how the business is run, subject to more government regulations than other forms of business.

3. **Proprietorship:** owned and run by a single person who has rights to all the profits and unlimited liability for all the firm's debts. **Partnership:** owned and operated by two or more people who share the profits and responsibilities of the debts. **Corporation:** recognized by law as a separate legal entity, owned by many people called stockholders.

4. **Possible answer:** Members of a partnership may be motivated by sharing profits equally.

5. The owners have no direct contact with the employees of a corporation.

6. **Possible answer:** to take advantage of the limited liability feature that protects its owners

7. Answers will vary but should demonstrate knowledge of how to address financial issues of a partnership.

Profiles in Economics

Andrea Jung (1958–)

- first female chief executive officer (CEO) in Avon Products' 118-year history
- ranked #5 on *Fortune* magazine's "50 Most Powerful Women in Business"

The Avon Lady

When promoted to Avon's top spot in 1999, Andrea Jung was charged with modernizing and restructuring what many considered to be a hopelessly antiquated company. Women have been selling Avon cosmetics directly to customers since 1886, but in the Internet era, this hands-on business model became a liability. If women had no Avon representative in their area, they had no way to purchase the products from the catalog—until Andrea Jung took charge.

The Mobilization Campaign

Jung faced a problem. Putting Avon products in retail stores or offering them online put the company in direct competition with its own army of 5 million independent sales representatives in 140 countries. Working closely with the "reps" was paramount to Jung. So when Jung took the company online, she made sure it directed users to local reps. She also gave the reps the opportunity to purchase kiosks in malls and other retail venues as franchises. Fluent in Mandarin Chinese, she helped strengthen Avon's presence in China and other countries, such as Russia. She also updated and innovated products and introduced a new line, called Mark™ that was tailored to the increasing number of younger, college-aged reps and their customers. These changes and others caused a rebound in Avon stock, led to increases in annual revenues from $5.3 billion to more than $8 billion, and made Jung a corporate celebrity.

Jung also had an impact within the company. Avon has more women in management—86 percent—than any other Fortune 500 company. Jung serves as a mentor to other women in the company. She encourages questions and rewards success. Although she is a private person, Jung has learned to be more open with Avon reps and motivate them to enact the changes she sees ahead.

C

After graduating from Princeton with a degree in English literature, Andrea Jung wanted to spend just two years in retail before pursuing a law degree. Instead, she turned retail into a career—and Avon into a global success.

> ### Examining the Profile
>
> 1. **Summarizing** What changes did Jung make to Avon's marketing strategy?
> 2. **For Further Research** What career steps did Jung take that allowed her to move from a degree in English literature to a top management position?

CHAPTER 3   Business Organizations   **71**

Teach

C Critical Thinking

Problem-Solving Ask: What problem did Jung face when she became CEO at Avon? *(modernizing and restructuring an antiquated company)* What steps did she take to solve the problem? *(She took the company online, gave representatives the opportunity to purchase kiosks in malls and other retail venues, strengthened Avon's international presence, updated and innovated products, and introduced a new line for younger customers.)* What other possible solutions can you think of? *(Possible answer: Recruit celebrities to represent the line.)* **OL**

> ### Examining the Profile
>
> **Answers:**
> 1. She took the company online, worked closely with the Avon sales representatives, marketed new products, and offered franchises.
> 2. Students should research Jung's career path online or in print materials.

Additional Support

Activity: Collaborative Learning

Comparing Organize students into small groups, and have each group choose and then research another woman who has appeared on *Fortune* magazine's "50 Most Powerful Women in Business" list. Ask students to write a summary of the woman's life and work, based on their research. As a class, discuss similarities between Andrea Jung and the women that student groups researched. Have a volunteer write common characteristics on the board. Ask students to draw conclusions about how succeeding in business may or may not be different for women versus men. **OL**

Focus

Bellringer
Daily Focus Transparency 17

GUIDE TO READING

Section Preview

In this section, you will learn how businesses grow through merging with other companies or by reinvesting profits in themselves.

Content Vocabulary

- merger (p. 72)
- income statement (p. 73)
- net income (p. 73)
- depreciation (p. 73)
- cash flow (p. 73)
- horizontal merger (p. 75)
- vertical merger (p. 75)
- conglomerate (p. 76)
- multinational (p. 76)

Academic Vocabulary

- internally (p. 75)
- dominant (p. 75)

Reading Strategy

Comparing As you read the section, complete a graphic organizer similar to the one below by comparing a vertical merger to a horizontal merger.

Vertical merger

Similarities

Horizontal merger

GUIDE TO READING

Answers to Graphic:

Vertical merger: combines companies in different stages of manufacturing or marketing; may take place to protect companies from potential loss of suppliers

Horizontal merger: combines companies that produce the same kind of product

Similarities: reasons for merging (to grow faster, to become more efficient, to acquire or deliver a better product)

COMPANIES IN THE NEWS
—Newsweek

Reinvesting for Monster Growth

How does a booming company spark new growth the year *after* its sales nearly double? If you're Hansen Natural, maker of Monster Energy drinks, you start by signing a two-year endorsement deal with Ricky Carmichael, the Michael Jordan of motocross and super-cross racing. It's good for business when "R.C." hoists a can of Monster on the victory stand.

. . .[A] big endorsement deal is just one way Hansen hopes to build on its growth. CEO Rodney Sacks [and fellow South African-born company president Hilton Schlosberg] wants to roll out new products that reach . . . the key male market of 18- to 25-year-olds. In addition to regular Green Monster, there's . . . Monster Assault in a camouflage can aimed at teens and a Lost Energy brand targeting surfers and skateboarders. ∎

merger combination of two or more businesses to form a single firm

When Hansen Natural decided to sign up a celebrity to endorse its products, the company hoped to increase profits by expanding its markets and sales. Investing these profits in new plant, equipment, and products is one way a business can grow.

Another way a business can expand is by engaging in a **merger**—a combination of two or more businesses to form a single firm. Yet mergers can be risky because they often combine very different corporate cultures, and there is no guarantee that consumers will like the resulting products. Even so, the payoffs can be huge, so the temptation to merge is always attractive to businesses.

Resource Manager

R Reading Strategies	**C** Critical Thinking	**D** Differentiated Instruction	**W** Writing Support	**S** Skill Practice
Teacher Edition • Reading Charts, pp. 73, 75 • Organizing, p. 76 **Additional Resources** • Guid. Read. Act., p. 8 • Read. Ess. & Note-Taking Guide, p. 22	**Teacher Edition** • Compare/Contrast, p. 75 • Analyzing, p. 76 • Differentiating, p. 77 **Additional Resources** • Econ. Concepts Trans., Strat. & Act., p. 9	**Teacher Edition** • ELL, p. 73 • Logical/Math., p. 74 **Additional Resources** • Daily Focus Trans. 17 • Econ. Cont. Vocab. Act., p. 3 • Enrichment Act., p. 3	**Teacher Edition** • Expository Writing, p. 74 • Descriptive Writing, p. 75 **Additional Resources** • High School Reading in the Content Area Strat. and Act.	**Teacher Edition** • Reading Graphs, p. 78 **Additional Resources** • Reading and Study Skills Fold., p. 45 • Reteaching, p. 3

Growth Through Reinvestment

> **MAIN Idea** Business owners can use their profits to update and expand their firms.

Economics & You Do you know a local business that has expanded in recent years? Read on to learn how business owners reinvest cash flow for growth.

Most businesses use financial statements to keep track of their business operations. One of the most important of those is the **income statement**—a report showing a business's sales, expenses, net income, and cash flows for a period of time, such as three months or a year. We can use the income statement to show how a business can use some of the revenue it receives from sales to grow through reinvestment.

Estimating Cash Flows

An income statement such as the one in **Figure 3.4** shows a firm's **net income**—the funds left over after all of the firm's expenses, including taxes, are subtracted from its sales. These expenses include the cost of inventory, wages and salaries, interest payments, and all other payments the firm must make as part of its normal business operations.

One of the most important of these payments is **depreciation**—a noncash charge the firm takes for the general wear and tear on its capital goods.

Depreciation is called a *noncash charge* because the money stays in the firm rather than being paid to someone else. For example, interest may be paid to a bank, wages may be paid to employees, or payments may be made to suppliers to provide some of the inputs used in production. However, the money allocated to depreciation never goes anywhere. Since this money stays in the business, the firm treats it as a form of income. Because of this, firms usually prefer to take as much depreciation as possible. As you can see in the figure, an incease in depreciation would lower the earnings before tax but increase the cash flow.

The **cash flow**—the sum of net income and noncash charges, such as depreciation—is the *bottom line*, a more comprehensive measure of profits. This is because the cash flow represents the total amount of new funds generated from operations.

Reinvesting Cash Flows

If the business has a positive cash flow, the owners can then decide how to allocate it. The board of directors of a corporation

---

income statement report showing a firm's sales, expenses, net income, and cash flows for a certain period, usually three months or a year

net income common measure of business profits determined by subtracting all expenses, including taxes, from revenues

depreciation gradual wear on capital goods

cash flow total amount of new funds a business generates from operations

---

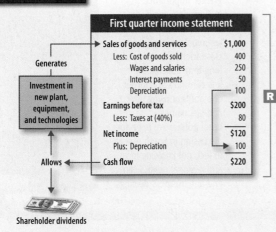

Figure 3.4 ▶ Growth Through Reinvestment

Generates → Investment in new plant, equipment, and technologies → Allows → Shareholder dividends

First quarter income statement

Sales of goods and services	$1,000
Less: Cost of goods sold	400
Wages and salaries	250
Interest payments	50
Depreciation	100
Earnings before tax	**$200**
Less: Taxes at (40%)	80
Net income	**$120**
Plus: Depreciation	100
Cash flow	**$220**

Charts In MOtion
See StudentWorks™ Plus or glencoe.com.

▶ Businesses use income statements to record sales and expenses. Cash flow includes the net income plus depreciation. Any cash flow not paid out to stockholders as dividends is money that businesses can use for reinvestment.

Economic Analysis *Which of the items on the income statement represents the real measure of profits for the business?*

CHAPTER 3   Business Organizations   73

CHAPTER 3, SECTION 2

Teach

D Differentiated Instruction

English Language Learners
To help students understand the concept of depreciation, have them name capital goods needed in a clothing manufacturing business. *(Possible answer: machines that make patterns, cut the material, and sew the garments)* Explain that the machines gradually deteriorate, or depreciate, with use. **ELL**

R Reading Strategy

Reading Charts Ask: What are two things that a business can do with its cash flow? *(pay shareholder dividends or invest in a new plant, equipment, or technologies)* **OL**

Economic Analysis
Answer: the cash flow

Hands-On Chapter Project
Step 2

Creating a Business Plan

Step 2: Choosing a Business. Students will choose a business and begin writing a business plan.

Directions: During the first part of the session, have student groups choose their business. During the second part of the session, in preparation for writing a business plan, have each group assign one or two members to study the following topics. The study teams should prepare a short report on how the start-up business should handle each:

- Expenses
- Advertising
- Record Keeping
- Risk
- Type of Business Organization
- Opportunities for Growth and Expansion

Encourage students to refer to the text as they analyze the elements of business operation and the types of business organizations. As homework, have students draft elements of a business plan to share with the group.

Formulating Questions Have each student make a list of three questions that the group could ask a business-development expert about their chosen business. **OL**

(Chapter Project continued in Section 3.)

D Differentiated Instruction

Logical/Mathematical

Have students research a major American corporation's growth over the years. Then ask them to create a time line illustrating the growth. Have volunteers share their time lines with the class. **OL**

W Writing Support

Expository Writing Assign students a foreign country (such as China) or an area of the world (such as Latin America). Have students use books and Web sites to develop a guide for conducting business in their assigned area. Remind students that their primary audience is business travelers, so students should address issues that might arise from common business transactions and situations. **OL**

✓ Reading Check **Answer:** The firm can produce additional products, which generates additional sales and a larger cash flow.

Differentiated Instruction

Economic Concepts Trans., Strat. and Act., p. 9

74

---

may declare a dividend to be paid directly to shareholders as a reward for their investments. The owners of a proprietorship or partnership may keep some cash flow as the reward for risk-taking. The remainder of the funds could then be reinvested in new plant, equipment, or technologies.

When cash flows are reinvested in the business, the firm can produce additional products. This generates additional sales and an even larger cash flow during the next sales period. As long as the firm has positive cash flows, and as long as the reinvested funds are larger than the wear and tear on equipment, the firm will grow.

Finally, the concept of cash flow is also important to investors. In fact, if investors want to know about the financial health of a firm, a positive cash flow is one of the first things they look for.

✓ Reading Check **Summarizing** What is the benefit of reinvesting cash flow in a business?

The Global Economy & YOU

Know Your Manners

As American businesses expand into other countries, they face a question that has nothing to do with actual business: how to interact with people from a different culture. You too may someday find yourself working in another country or traveling abroad to meet with businesspeople. How will you know what to do and say?

Many books and Web sites offer advice on customs to Americans doing business in other countries. Here are some things to keep in mind as you travel around the globe:

- Gift-giving is an important part of Japanese business protocol. Present your gift with both hands and note that it is of no large value. This tells your business partner that you value the relationship more than the gift itself.
- In Argentina, it is not unusual for a business associate to arrive 30 to 40 minutes late to a meeting.

- The amount of time you spend in negotiations will often determine the importance of a business arrangement in India. More time implies greater importance.
- In Germany, avoid using first names. These are reserved for family and close friends. Even among long-time colleagues, it is common to address one another using titles and last names.
- Local politics are open for discussion in South Africa. In fact, not knowing local and regional politics can end any business dealings.

Growth Through Mergers

MAIN Idea Mergers allow firms to quickly grow in size.

Economics & You Can you think of any recent mergers and the issues those mergers raised? Read on to learn about the various types of mergers.

When two companies merge, one gives up its separate legal identity. For public recognition purposes, however, the name of the new company may reflect the identities of both. When Chase National Bank and Bank of Manhattan merged, the new company was called the Chase Manhattan Bank of New York. Later it changed its name to the Chase Manhattan Corporation to reflect its geographically expanding business. Finally, after merging with JP Morgan, it settled on JPMorgan Chase. Likewise, Procter & Gamble kept the brand name *Gillette* after it bought the company.

Economic Institutions and Incentives

Objective: Understand the importance of economic institutions and incentives.

Focus: Discuss types of institutions and how they respond to economic incentives.

Teach: Have students examine the transparency and answer the questions that follow.

Assess: Review the answers to questions 1 through 5.

Close: Ask students to explain the relationship between economic institutions and incentives.

Differentiated Instruction Strategies

BL Have students make a chart showing the types of economic institutions.

AL Have students choose an economic institution and predict what it will look like in 200 years.

ELL Have students write sentences using the words *evolve* and *incentive*.

Figure 3.5 ▶ Types of Mergers

▶ Horizontal mergers combine two or more firms that produce the same kind of product. Vertical mergers bring together firms involved in different stages of manufacturing or marketing.

Economic Analysis *How does a company benefit from a vertical merger?*

VERTICAL MERGER

Hickory Tree Farms
+
Boston Baseball Bat, Inc.
+
Fast Delivery, Inc.
=
Boston Baseball Bat, Inc.

HORIZONTAL MERGER

Nickel Savings Bank + People's Building & Loan Association = Nickel Savings & Loan Association

R Reading Strategy

Reading Charts Ask: What connects the companies involved in the vertical merger? *(They are all involved in making baseball bats or bringing them to market.)* **OL**

W Writing Support

Descriptive Writing Have students choose two companies that they would like to see merge. Ask students to write several paragraphs describing the type of merger and how the culture of the merged company might change, including its advertising and product or service. **AL**

C Critical Thinking

Comparing and Contrasting Have each student choose a large business and a small business in the community to compare (for example, a large grocery chain versus a small neighborhood market). Tell students to create a chart with headings such as *Price, Selection, Knowledgeable Staff, Speed of Service*, and so on, as a part of their report. **OL**

Economic Analysis

Answer: It may grow faster and become more efficient.

Types of Mergers

There are two types of mergers, both of which are illustrated in **Figure 3.5**. The first is a **horizontal merger,** which takes place when firms that produce the same kind of product join forces. One such example is the bank merger of JP Morgan and Chase Manhattan to form JPMorgan Chase.

When companies involved in different stages of manufacturing or marketing join together, it results in a **vertical merger.** One example of a vertical merger is the formation of the U.S. Steel Corporation. At one time it mined its own ore, shipped it across the Great Lakes, smelted it, and made steel into many different products. Vertical mergers take place when companies seek to protect against the potential loss of suppliers.

Reasons for Merging

Mergers take place for a variety of reasons. A business may seek a merger to grow faster, to become more efficient, to acquire **W** or deliver a better product, to eliminate a rival, or to change its image.

For example, some managers find that they cannot grow as fast as they would like using the funds they generate **internally.** As a result, one firm may consider merging with another firm. Sometimes a merger makes sense, and other times it may not, but the desire to become a larger company in the industry—if not the largest—is one reason that mergers take place.

Efficiency is another reason for mergers. When two firms merge, they no longer need two presidents, two treasurers, and two personnel directors. The new company can have more retail outlets or manufacturing capabilities without significantly increasing management costs. In addition, the new company may be able to get better discounts by making volume purchases, and it may be able to make more effective use of its advertising. Sometimes the merging firms can achieve two objectives at once—such as **dominant** size and improved efficiency.

C horizontal merger combination of two or more firms producing the same kind of product

vertical merger combination of firms involved in different stages of manufacturing or marketing

CHAPTER 3 Business Organizations 75

Leveled Activities

BL Reading Essentials and Note-Taking Guide, p. 22

OL Reading and Study Skills Foldables, p. 45

AL Economic Content Vocabulary Activities, p. 3

C Critical Thinking

Analyzing Ask: What may be the consequences of a store that sells snowboards merging with a store that sells surfboards? Would this likely be a responsible use of both businesses? Explain. *(Possible answer: A store in a cold climate would sell many snowboards but few surfboards. A store on the coast would sell many surfboards but few snowboards. Merging would likely not be responsible, as most places warm enough for surfing do not get cold enough for snow, and vice versa.)* **OL**

R Reading Strategy

Organizing Ask students to create a chart listing the similarities and differences of conglomerates and multinationals. *(Possible answer: Both are corporations and large in size. Differences include that they have a different scope, with multinationals operating in different countries, paying taxes in the countries where it has operations, and being a citizen of several countries at the same time.)* **OL**

Economic Analysis

Answer: six

Additional Support

Figure 3.6 ▶ **Conglomerate Structure**

▶ A conglomerate is a firm with at least four businesses that make unrelated products, none of which is responsible for a majority of its sales. General Electric is a U.S. conglomerate with products ranging from aircraft engines to movies.

Economic Analysis *How many different industries can you identify in the list of GE products?*

- 8.5%
- 28.1%
- 10.5%
- 8.5%
- 20.2%
- 24.2%

○ Commercial finance
◑ Consumer finance
● Health care
◐ Industrial
◑ Infrastructure
● NBC Universal

Source: www.ge.com, 2006

photo on top: Engineer working on GE aircraft engine
photo on bottom: Entrance to NBC Universal Studios

conglomerate
firm with four or more businesses making unrelated products, with no single business responsible for a majority of its sales

multinational
corporation producing and selling without regard to national boundaries and whose business activities are located in several different countries

Some mergers are driven by the desire to acquire new product lines. When a telecommunications company such as AT&T buys a cable TV company, for example, it can offer faster Internet access and telephone service in a single package.

Sometimes firms merge to catch up with, or even eliminate, rivals. Royal Caribbean Cruises acquired Celebrity Cruise Lines and nearly doubled in size to become the second largest cruise line behind Carnival.

Finally, a company may use a merger to *lose* its corporate identity. For example, ValuJet merged with AirWays to form AirTran Holdings Corporation. The new company flew the same planes and routes as the original company, but AirTran hoped the name change would help the public forget ValuJet's tragic Everglades crash in 1996 that claimed 110 lives.

Conglomerates

A corporation may become so large through mergers and acquisitions that it turns into a conglomerate. A **conglomerate** is a firm that has at least four businesses,

each making unrelated products and none responsible for a majority of its sales.

Diversification is one of the main reasons for conglomerate mergers. Some firms hope to protect their overall sales and profits by not "putting all their eggs in one basket." Isolated economic events, such as bad weather or a sudden change of consumer tastes, may affect some product lines but not all of them at the same time.

In recent years, the number of conglomerates in the United States has declined. In Asia, however, conglomerates remain strong. Samsung, Gold Star, and Daewoo are still dominant in Korea, as are Mitsubishi, Panasonic, and Sony in Japan.

Multinationals

Other large corporations have become international in scope. A **multinational** is a corporation that has manufacturing or service operations in a number of different countries. In effect, it is a citizen of several countries at one time. A multinational is likely to pay taxes in each country where it has operations and is subject to the laws of each. General Motors,

Activity: Hands-On Economics

U.S. Mergers Organize students into groups, and provide each group with a list of recent mergers in the United States—for example, America Online and Time Warner, Exxon and Mobil, Citicorp and Travelers Corp., SBC Communications and Ameritech, and AT&T and TCI. Have students choose a merger and then use print or online sources to determine the type of merger and the reasons that the two companies merged. Students should also explore the results of the merger. Have groups present their findings in an oral presentation. **OL**

Nabisco, British Petroleum, Royal Dutch Shell, Mitsubishi, and Sony are examples of multinational corporations that have attained worldwide economic importance.

Multinational corporations are important because they have the ability to move resources, goods, services, and financial capital across national borders. A multinational with its headquarters in Canada, for example, could sell bonds in France. The proceeds could then be used to expand a plant in Mexico that makes products for sale in the United States. A multinational may also be a conglomerate if it makes unrelated products, but it is more likely to **C** be called a multinational if it conducts operations in several different countries.

Multinationals are usually welcome in a nation because they transfer new technology and generate new jobs in areas where jobs are needed. Multinationals also produce tax revenues for the host country, which helps that nation's economy.

At times, multinationals have been known to abuse their power by paying low wages to workers, exporting scarce natural resources, or interfering with the development of local businesses. Some critics point out that multinational corporations are able to demand tax, regulatory, and wage concessions by threatening to move their operations to another country. Other critics are concerned that multinationals may alter traditional ways of life and business customs in the host country.

Most economists, however, welcome the lower-cost production and higher-quality output that global competition brings. They also believe that the transfer of technology that eventually takes place will raise the standard of living for everyone. On balance, the advantages of multinationals far outweigh the disadvantages.

Skills Handbook

See page **R42** to learn about **Making Inferences**.

✓Reading Check **Contrasting** How do conglomerates and multinationals differ?

See page **R42** to learn about **Making Inferences**.

CHAPTER 3, SECTION 2

C Critical Thinking

Differentiating Ask: How can a multinational corporation also be a conglomerate? *(If a multinational makes unrelated products, it is a conglomerate.)* **OL**

✓Reading Check **Answer:** Multinational corporations have operations in a number of different countries. A conglomerate has at least four businesses, each making unrelated products and none responsible for a majority of its sales.

Assess

Use the Interactive Tutor Self-Assessment CD-ROM to review Section 2, and then assign the Section 2 Review as homework or as an in-class activity.

Close

Making Connections Ask students to discuss the statement "The world is shrinking," in relation to multinationals and the global economy. **OL**

Review SECTION **2**

SECTION 2 Review

Vocabulary
1. **Explain** the significance of merger, income statement, net income, depreciation, cash flow, horizontal merger, vertical merger, conglomerate, and multinational.

Main Ideas
2. **Describe** how a firm can generate funds internally to grow and expand.

3. **Explain** the basic difference between a conglomerate and a multinational corporation.

4. **Identifying** Use a graphic organizer like the one below to identify the reasons businesses merge.

Reasons for mergers

Critical Thinking
5. **The BIG Idea** How could a merger between two large cellular phone companies provide better products in a more efficient manner?

6. **Analyzing Visuals** Look at Figure 3.6 on page 76. Explain how the diversification of General Electric illustrates the saying: "Don't put all your eggs in one basket."

7. **Inferring** What are the possible benefits and drawbacks of multinationals to their host countries?

Applying Economics
8. **Horizontal Mergers** Research the ownership of radio stations in a nearby metropolitan area. Are any owned by the same company? Do the stations have the same types of broadcasts or the same advertising? Write a one- to two-page paper about your findings. In your paper, explain why a company would want to own multiple stations in the same geographical market.

Answers

1. All definitions can be found in the section and the Glossary.
2. Firms can take their profits and reinvest them to produce additional products.
3. A conglomerate is a firm that has at least four businesses, each making unrelated products and none responsible for a majority of its sales. A multinational has manufacturing and service operations in a number of different countries.

4. to grow faster, to become more efficient, to acquire new product lines, to catch up with or eliminate rivals, to lose its corporate identity
5. **Possible answer:** The new company could have more manufacturing capabilities without increasing management costs.
6. They have several different businesses that make different products, so if something happens that hurts one product, the others should still be safe.

7. Possible benefits include new technologies, new jobs, and tax revenues for the host countries. Possible drawbacks include the abuse of power by paying low wages to workers, exporting scarce natural resources, and interfering with the development of local businesses.
8. Answers will vary, but students will likely find that many radio stations are owned by the same company and that they have similar advertising.

Teach

S Skill Practice

Reading Graphs Ask: Which country has the highest population? *(United States)* Which country has more stores per person? *(Japan)* Invite students to draw a conclusion based on information in the graph. *(Possible answer: 7-Elevens are popular with Japanese citizens.)* **OL**

Analyzing the Impact

Answers:

1. They are located in 17 countries and U.S. territories.

2. Japanese 7-Eleven stores offer high-quality food, in addition to banking services, dry-cleaning drop-off, parcel post, mobile-phone recharging, photocopying, and voter registration. American 7-Elevens offer basic food and may not offer the same services.

Additional Support

Case Study

7-Eleven

"Convenience" Is Born

In 1927 an employee of the Southland Ice Company in Dallas, Texas, began selling milk, bread, and eggs from the ice dock on Sundays and evenings when grocery stores were closed. This sparked the idea for the convenience store. In 1946 the stores were renamed 7-Eleven to reflect their new hours: 7 A.M. to 11 P.M.

Japan Borrows the Idea

In the early 1970s, Toshifumi Suzuki, a young Japanese executive, came to the United States to look into franchising Denny's restaurants in Japan. He was more impressed by the 7-Elevens he saw. With its densely populated cities and small commercial lots, Japan was perfectly suited to the convenience-store format. In 1974 Suzuki opened a chain of stores under the 7-Eleven name.

Since then, the retailer has changed the way the country shops and eats. Many stores offer banking services, dry-cleaning drop-off, parcel post, mobile-phone recharging, photocopying, and even voter registration. They also stock cheap, high-quality foods, such as gourmet rice balls, exotic salads, and other delicacies customized to local tastes.

Technology, coordinated deliveries, and inventory control have boosted efficiency. The company uses a satellite-based ordering system that includes detailed weather reports. This way, managers know to order more cold noodles on warm days or more fresh produce on rainy days, when customers want to avoid a trip to the grocery store. Today 7-Eleven is Japan's most profitable retailer.

7-ELEVENS IN THE UNITED STATES AND JAPAN

*Number of stores includes 7-Eleven stores in Canada

The Student Buys the Teacher

While 7-Eleven Japan boomed, its U.S. counterpart declined. In the late 1980s, 7-Eleven Japan and its parent company, Ito-Yokado, helped turn around the U.S. stores. They improved the U.S. distribution network and introduced new sandwiches, bakery items, and coffees. In 1991, Ito-Yokado bought 70 percent of the American company outright. Today nearly 30,000 7-Eleven stores generate total sales of more than $43 billion in 17 countries and U.S. territories.

Analyzing the Impact

1. **Drawing Conclusions** How do you know that 7-Eleven is a multinational corporation?

2. **Comparing and Contrasting** In what ways do 7-Elevens in Japan differ from their U.S. counterparts?

Extending the Content

Facts About 7-Eleven

1. July 11 (7/11) is the "birthday" of the 7-Eleven chain.

2. With nearly 1,200 locations, California has more 7-Elevens than any other state.

3. Most U.S. customers visit a 7-Eleven store about 17 times a month.

4. Each year 7-Eleven sells about 60 million freshly baked donuts and pastries and 33 million gallons of fountain drinks.

5. In 1949, 7-Eleven ran the first television commercial by any convenience store— a cartoon featuring a singing owl and rooster.

SECTION 3 Nonprofit Organizations

GUIDE TO READING

Section Preview

In this section, you will learn about the economic benefits that cooperatives and other nonprofit organizations bring to their members.

Content Vocabulary

- nonprofit organization (p. 79)
- cooperative (p. 80)
- co-op (p. 80)
- credit union (p. 80)
- labor union (p. 81)
- collective bargaining (p. 81)
- professional association (p. 81)
- chamber of commerce (p. 81)
- Better Business Bureau (p. 82)
- public utility (p. 83)

Academic Vocabulary

- analyze (p. 80)
- devoting (p. 80)

Reading Strategy

Describing As you read the section, complete a graphic organizer similar to the one below by describing the benefits of nonprofit organizations.

Organization	Benefits
Community organization	
Consumer cooperative	

Focus

GUIDE TO READING

Possible Answers to Graphic:

Community organization: assists consumers with health care, education, and social services

Consumer cooperative: offers its members products at lower prices than regular businesses

Service cooperative: offers its members services rather than goods

Producer cooperative: helps members promote and sell their products

---

PEOPLE IN THE NEWS —adapted from American Red Cross *News* online

Katrina Volunteer Vacation

Last semester, they studied textbook disasters. Over their winter break, they helped feed and comfort Hurricane Katrina victims.

Each day, Nellie Afshar, Jemma Binder, Dawn Birk, Zachary Joyce, and graduate student Jessica Walsh from the State University of New York at New Paltz rose before dawn, helped load supplies, spent all day dispensing hot meals in flood-ravaged areas, and then pitched in to clean their vehicles afterward.

Their service fulfilled a field work requirement for a disaster studies practicum, part of SUNY's new disaster studies minor, but the experience was more than that for these students. "You couldn't get me up at 6 A.M. for any other reason," said Joyce, 21. "I wouldn't get up at 6 A.M. to make money. This is the best work I've ever done." ■

Most businesses use scarce resources to produce goods and services in hopes of earning a profit for their owners. Other organizations operate on a "not-for-profit" basis. A **nonprofit organization** works in a businesslike way to promote the collective interests of its members rather than to seek financial gain for its owners.

The American Red Cross is one example of a nonprofit. Like other nonprofits, it relies on volunteers such as the SUNY students for much of its work. In this way, nonprofits and other community and civic organizations can perform useful services with minimal expense and without regard to earning a profit.

nonprofit organization economic organization that operates like a business but does not seek financial gain

CHAPTER 3 Business Organizations **79**

Resource Manager

R Reading Strategies	C Critical Thinking	D Differentiated Instruction	W Writing Support	S Skill Practice
Teacher Edition • Organizing, p. 82 **Additional Resources** • Guid. Read. Act., p. 9 • Read. Ess. & Note-Taking Guide, p. 25	**Teacher Edition** • Making Decisions, p. 82 • Det. Cause/Effect, p. 83 **Additional Resources** • Econ. Concepts Trans., Strat. & Act., p. 5	**Teacher Edition** • Special Ed., p. 80 **Additional Resources** • Econ. Cont. Vocab. Act., p. 3 • Quizzes and Tests, p. 29	**Teacher Edition** • Persuasive Writing, p. 81 **Additional Resources** • Writer's Guidebook	**Teacher Edition** • Visual Literacy, p. 81 • Reading a Time Line, p. 84 **Additional Resources** • Daily Focus Trans. 18 • Reteaching Act., p. 3

Teach

D Differentiated Instruction

Special Education Have students skim for a main idea in the subsection titled "Cooperatives." Have them tell in their own words what the subsection is about. Next, have students read the first sentence of each paragraph in the subsection. Point out that main ideas are often, but not always, stated in the first sentence of paragraphs. Students should then state the main idea of this subsection. **BL**

Economic Analysis

Answer: A consumer cooperative buys bulk amounts of goods on behalf of its members. A service cooperative provides services to its members, rather than goods. A producer cooperative helps members promote and sell their products.

✓**Reading Check** **Answer:** Cooperatives carry on various economic activities to benefit their members.

Additional Support

---

cooperative or co-op nonprofit association performing some kind of economic activity for the benefit of its members

credit union nonprofit service cooperative that accepts deposits, makes loans, and provides other financial services

---

Community Organizations and Cooperatives

MAIN Idea A variety of nonprofit organizations provide a wide range of goods and services to communities and members.

Economics & You Have you volunteered for a community organization? Read on to find out how such organizations help their communities.

Community Organizations

Community organizations include schools, churches, hospitals, welfare groups, and adoption agencies. Many of these organizations are legally incorporated to take advantage of unlimited life and limited liability. They are similar to profit-seeking businesses but do not issue stock, pay dividends, or pay income taxes.

Figure 3.7 ▶ Cooperatives

Consumer Cooperatives
Housing cooperatives
Discount price clubs
Bulk foods store

Service Cooperatives
Credit unions
Insurance companies
Babysitting services

Producer Cooperatives
Farmers marketing cooperatives

▶ Cooperatives are voluntary associations of people formed to carry on some kind of economic activity that will benefit their members.

Economic Analysis *How do the three kinds of cooperatives differ?*

If their activities produce revenues in excess of expenses, they use the surplus to further their work.

Like for-profit businesses, nonprofit organizations use scarce factors of production. Their work is difficult to **analyze** economically because the value of their efforts is not easy to measure. Still, the large number of these organizations shows that they are important to our economic system.

D Cooperatives

A common type of nonprofit organization is the **cooperative,** or **co-op.** A cooperative is a voluntary association formed to carry on some kind of economic activity that will benefit its members. As **Figure 3.7** shows, cooperatives can have a variety of goals. Cooperatives fall into three major categories: consumer, service, and producer.

The *consumer cooperative* is a voluntary association that buys bulk amounts of goods such as food or clothing on behalf of its members. Members usually help keep the cost of the operation down by **devoting** several hours a week or month to the operation. If successful, the co-op is able to offer its members products at prices lower than those charged by regular businesses.

A *service cooperative* provides services such as insurance, credit, or child care to its members, rather than goods. One example is a **credit union,** a financial organization that accepts deposits from, and makes loans to, employees of a particular company or government agency.

Like consumers, producers also can have co-ops. A *producer cooperative* helps members promote or sell their products. In the United States, most cooperatives of this kind are made up of farmers. The co-op helps the farmers sell their crops directly to central markets or to companies that use the members' products. Some co-ops, such as the Ocean Spray cranberry co-op, market their products directly to consumers.

✓**Reading Check** **Explaining** How does a cooperative work?

Activity: Collaborative Learning

Expository Writing Point out that the first successful cooperative in the United States—the Philadelphia Contributionship for the Insurance of Houses from Loss of Fire—was organized by Benjamin Franklin in 1752. It is still operating today, making it the oldest continuously operating cooperative in the country. Have students work in pairs to research the development of cooperatives in the United States, from their beginnings in the mid-1700s to the present day. Students should present their findings in a written report that discusses how the focus of cooperatives has expanded over the years. **OL**

Labor Unions
Workers may join a labor union that represents their interests. *How do labor unions help their members?* **S**

Labor, Professional, and Business Organizations

....

MAIN Idea Some nonprofit organizations are formed to promote the interests of workers and consumers.

Economics & You You just learned about nonprofit organizations that help consumers and communities. Read on to find out about groups that support workers and businesses.

....

Nonprofit organizations are not just limited to co-ops and civic groups. Many other groups also organize this way to promote the interests of their members.

Labor Unions

One important economic institution is the **labor union,** an organization of workers formed to represent its members' interests in various employment matters. The union participates in **collective bargaining** when it negotiates with management over issues such as pay, working hours, health care coverage, vacations, and other job-related matters. Unions also lobby for laws that will benefit and protect their workers.

The largest labor organization in the United States is the American Federation of Labor-Congress of Industrial Organizations (AFL-CIO), an association of unions whose members include workers in many different jobs. Other unions, such as the National Education Association for teachers, are independent and represent workers in specific industries.

Professional Associations

Some workers belong to professional societies, trade associations, or academies. Such a **professional association** consists of people in a specialized occupation interested in improving the working conditions, skill levels, and public perceptions of the profession. **W**

The American Medical Association (AMA) and the American Bar Association (ABA) are examples of organizations that include members of specific professions. These groups influence the licensing and training of their members, set standards for conduct, and are actively involved in political issues. Other professional associations represent bankers, teachers, college professors, police officers, and hundreds of other professions.

Business Associations

Businesses also organize to promote their collective interests. Most communities have a local **chamber of commerce,** an organization that promotes the welfare of its member businesses. The typical chamber sponsors activities ranging from educational programs to lobbying for favorable business legislation.

Industry or trade associations represent specific kinds of businesses. Trade associations are interested in shaping the

labor union
organization that works for its members' interests concerning pay, working conditions, and benefits

collective bargaining
negotiation between union and company representatives over pay, benefits, and other job-related matters

professional association
nonprofit organization of professional or specialized workers seeking to improve working conditions, skill levels, and public perception of its profession

chamber of commerce
nonprofit organization of local businesses formed to promote their interests

CHAPTER 3 Business Organizations **81**

S Skill Practice

Visual Literacy Ask: How is the saying "there is power in numbers" illustrated by the image? *(Possible answer: The image shows members of a labor union, probably at a political rally of some sort. By uniting members, labor unions are able to have more impact and influence than separate individuals not affiliated with a union.)* **AL**

W Writing Support

Persuasive Writing Have students interview a professional in their community (for example, a teacher, doctor, lawyer, or police officer) about his or her professional association. Have them inquire about the association's licensing and training, standards for conduct, and representation on political issues. Then have students write a persuasive essay on why they think professionals should or should not belong to a professional association. **OL**

Caption Answer: They negotiate with management over job-related matters and lobby for laws that will benefit and protect their members.

Leveled Activities

BL Reteaching Activities, p. 3

OL Guided Reading Activities, p. 9

ELL Reading Essentials and Note-Taking Guide, p. 25

C Critical Thinking

Making Decisions Ask: How might the Better Business Bureau help a consumer decide where to have his or her car serviced? *(Possible answer: The consumer can check out local car repair businesses with the Better Business Bureau to find out whether other consumers have registered complaints about the business. This would help the consumer find a business with a strong customer service record.)* **OL**

R Reading Strategy

Organizing Have students create a two-column chart on the roles that government plays in helping the market economy operate efficiently. Under the headings "Direct Role" and "Indirect Role," students should list examples of how the local, state, or national government helps link consumers and resources. **OL**

✓**Reading Check** **Answer:** They influence the licensing and training of members, set standards for conduct, and are involved in political issues.

Hands-On Chapter Project

Step 3

Better Business Bureau business-sponsored nonprofit organization providing information on local companies to consumers

government's policy on such economic issues as free enterprise, imports and tariffs, the minimum wage, and new construction.

Some business associations help protect the consumer. The **Better Business Bureau** is a nonprofit organization sponsored by local businesses. It provides general information on companies, maintains records of consumer inquiries and complaints, and offers consumer education programs.

✓**Reading Check** **Summarizing** How do professional associations help their members?

CAREERS

Sociologist

The Work

* Study the development, interaction, and behavior of social groups, including various social, religious, and business organizations

* Gather firsthand information from people and derive conclusions that can lead to formulating policies that impact educators, lawmakers, administrators, and others committed to resolving social problems

* Knowledge of society and social behavior may be used by companies in product development, marketing, and advertising

Qualifications

* Strong mathematical skills, quantitative research and analysis skills, and the ability to communicate ideas clearly

* Objectivity, an open mind, and systematic work habits

* Master's degree, with a Ph.D. required of sociologists teaching at the university level

Earnings

* Median annual earnings: $57,870

Job Growth Outlook

* Slower than average

Source: *Occupational Outlook Handbook, 2006–2007 Edition*

82 UNIT 1 Fundamental Economic Concepts

Government

MAIN Idea The government provides some goods and services while helping to make sure the economy runs smoothly.

Economics & You You read earlier about the role of the government in economic policy. Read on to learn more details about that role.

Although you may not think of it that way, your local, state, or national government actually is a nonprofit economic organization. Sometimes government plays a direct role in the economy, while at other times the role is indirect.

Direct Role of Government

Many government agencies produce and distribute goods and services to consumers, giving government a direct role in the economy. The role is "direct" because the government supplies a good or service that competes with private businesses.

One example of direct involvement is the Tennessee Valley Authority (TVA). The TVA supplies electric power for most of Tennessee and parts of Alabama, Georgia, Kentucky, North Carolina, Virginia, and Mississippi. This power supplier competes directly with other, privately owned, power companies.

Another example is the Federal Deposit Insurance Corporation (FDIC), which insures deposits in our nation's banks. Because the insurance the FDIC supplies could be provided by privately owned insurance companies, the FDIC is also an example of the direct role of government.

Perhaps the best-known government corporation is the U.S. Postal Service (USPS). Originally an executive department called the Post Office Department, the USPS became a government corporation in 1970.

Many of these federal agencies are organized as government-owned corporations. Like privately owned businesses, these corporations have a board of directors that hires a professional management team to oversee daily operations. These corporations charge

---

Creating a Business Plan

Step 3: Writing the Business Plan.
Students will write their business plans.

Directions: Have students share their ideas for the business plan. Then, with one student acting as secretary, have the group write the plan, devoting a paragraph to each of the elements listed in Step 2, as well as projected earnings, employees needed, necessary inventory, and uses of future profits. When the draft is completed, have the group arrange for a final version to be made. (To avoid one or a few students doing most of the work, you may want to have each group member write a section as homework.)

Analyzing Visuals Ask groups to discuss types of visuals that they could use to make the information in their business plans accessible and clear. Have them decide on one visual to include in their finished plan and assign a group member to create it. **OL**

(Chapter Project continued in Visual Summary.)

fees for their products and services, and the revenue goes back into the "business." Unlike private corporations, however, Congress supplies funds to cover any losses the public corporation may incur.

State and local governments also play a direct role in the economy. State governments provide colleges and universities, retirement plans, and statewide police protection. Local governments provide police and fire protection, rescue services, and schools. At the same time, all levels of government help develop and maintain roads, libraries, and parks.

Indirect Role of Government

The government plays an indirect role when it acts as an umpire to help the market economy operate smoothly and efficiently. One such case is the regulation of **public utilities**, municipal or investor-owned companies that offer products such as water, sewerage, and electric service to the public.

Because many public utilities have few competitors, consumers often want government supervision. For example, the federal government established regulatory control over the cable television industry in 1993 because it felt that some operators were charging too much. Without competition, utilities with exclusive rights in certain areas have little incentive to offer services at reasonable rates.

The government also plays an indirect role when it grants money to people in the form of Social Security checks, veterans' benefits, financial aid to college students, rent subsidies, and unemployment compensation. Such payments give the recipients of these funds a power they otherwise might not have—the power to "vote" by making their demands known in the market. This power influences the production of goods and services, which in turn affects the allocation of scarce resources. **C**

Economics ONLINE
Student Web Activity Visit the *Economics: Principles and Practices* Web site at glencoe.com and click on *Chapter 3–Student Web Activities* for an activity on nonprofit organizations.

public utility company providing an essential service such as water or electricity to consumers

✓**Reading Check** **Evaluating** Do you think one government role is more important than another? Why?

C Critical Thinking

Determining Cause and Effect **Ask:** What effect does receiving payments from the government have on its recipients? *(Possible answer: It gives recipients the power to make their demands known in the market.)* **OL**

✓**Reading Check** **Possible Answer:** No; both roles are important in connecting consumers and resources to help the economy run smoothly.

Assess

💿 Use the Interactive Tutor Self-Assessment CD-ROM to review Section 3, and then assign the Section 3 Review as homework or as an in-class activity.

Close

Determining Importance Have students discuss this question: *Which type of business organization—sole proprietorship, partnership, or corporation—is the most important to the American economy?* **OL**

SECTION 3 Review

Vocabulary
1. **Explain** the significance of nonprofit organization, cooperative, co-op, credit union, labor union, collective bargaining, professional association, chamber of commerce, Better Business Bureau, and public utility.

Main Ideas
2. **Describe** the roles that federal, state, and local governments play in the economy.

3. **Identifying** Use a graphic organizer like the one below to identify the different types of nonprofit organizations.

Nonprofit organizations

Critical Thinking
4. **The BIG Idea** Compare and contrast the purposes of the following nonprofits: American Red Cross, American Medical Association, and Teachers' Credit Union.

5. **Analyzing Visuals** Look at Figure 3.7 on page 80. Select one of the cooperatives and explain the benefits it offers its members.

6. **Inferring** What motivates individuals to join professional associations and unions?

7. **Drawing Conclusions** Explain why the government, rather than private firms, operates agencies such as the TVA and the FDIC.

Applying Economics
8. **Nonprofit Organizations** Identify a nonprofit organization in your community. Discuss with an official or volunteer of the organization how the loss of nonprofit status would affect its activities and services. Write a paragraph about your findings.

CHAPTER 3 Business Organizations **83**

Answers

1. All definitions can be found in the section and the Glossary.
2. The federal government provides goods and services such as the U.S. Postal Service. The state government provides goods and services such as colleges and universities and statewide police protection. The local government provides goods and services such as local police and fire protection. All three levels help develop and maintain roads, libraries, and parks.

3. community, labor, professional, business, government
4. **Possible answer:** They all provide services to consumers and their members. The American Red Cross provides rescue services to victims of disasters. The American Medical Association is interested in improving the working conditions, skill levels, and public perceptions of the medical community. The Teachers' Credit Union accepts deposits from and makes loans to its members.

5. Answers will vary but should illustrate an understanding of cooperatives.
6. **Possible answer:** to try to improve their working conditions or skill levels
7. **Possible answer:** Only the government has access to the resources and capital needed to carry out business that is of such a wide scope.
8. Answers will vary but should indicate how nonprofit status affects an organization's activities and services.

Running a cooperative doesn't make being in business easier. In fact, it may be especially difficult to secure high prices for members while remaining competitive in the market. Ocean Spray Cranberries Inc., one of the largest producer cooperatives in the United States, has made it work.

Ocean Spray's Creative Juices

Randy C. Papadellis has a corporate mandate that would make many CEOs blanch. . . . The chief executive officer of juice giant Ocean Spray Cranberries Inc. leads a cooperative that's owned by about 800 cranberry and grapefruit farmers. Papadellis has to buy all the fruit his farmers produce—about two-thirds of the world's cranberry crop—and buy it at the highest possible price. . . .

It's a dilemma that has sparked frenetic cranberry-fueled creativity. After spurring supermarkets to add juice aisles in the 1960s, Ocean Spray followed with hits including the first juice boxes, low-calorie cranberry drinks, and white cranberry juice. Now Craisins, the dried-fruit snack made from husks that used to be thrown away but are now reinfused with juice, have exploded in popularity. Ocean Spray is spinning out variations—chocolate-covered Craisins, anyone?—as fast as it can. The company's food product segment has doubled during the past two years, and total sales have grown 12%, to $1.1 billion. . . . Ocean Spray remains No. 1 in juices. . . .

Of course, past success isn't any guarantee of future results. . . . The cooperative is supposed to pay farmers the commodity price for fruit plus a dividend reflecting the profits of the Ocean Spray brand. But in 2000 overproduction sent the price of raw cranberries crashing from over $60 a barrel to under $20. . . . Papadellis quickly realized that the farmers needed to decide whether or not the cooperative still made sense. . . .

After weeks of arguing the pros and cons, and with a buyout offer on the table from Pepsi, the farmers opted for Papadellis' vision of a more focused Ocean Spray that would stay independent. . . . The plan not only improved the bottom line but also won back the trust of the farmers. . . .

—Reprinted from *BusinessWeek*

1930 Cooperative formed by 3 cranberry growers

1963 First juice blend introduced

1976 Membership expands to include grapefruit growers

1981 First company to introduce juice boxes

2004 Members vote down a joint venture with PepsiCo

2006 Ocean Spray cooperative has over 900 members

| 1930 | 1940 | 1950 | 1960 | 1970 | 1980 | 1990 | 2000 | 2010 |

84 UNIT 1 Fundamental Economic Concepts

Examining the Newsclip

1. **Summarizing** What is the purpose of the Ocean Spray Cranberry Inc. cooperative?

2. **Analyzing** How does the organizational structure of the cooperative reflect member interests?

Extending the Content

Bouncing Cranberries Ocean Spray evaluates the quality of cranberries by their color, size, and freshness—and by the way they bounce. This unusual indicator was discovered by New Jersey grower John "Peg-Leg" Webb, whose wooden leg led him to pour his berries down from the loft of his barn where he stored them. He soon noticed that only the freshest berries bounced to the bottom, while the soft and bruised ones were left behind. As a result of Webb's findings, a cranberry bounce board separator was developed to pick out the low-quality berries. Ocean Spray still uses this device today.

STUDY TO GO Study anywhere, anytime! Download quizzes and flash cards to your PDA from glencoe.com.

Visual Summary CHAPTER 3

▶ **Business Organizations** Three main forms of business organizations exist in the United States today.

Sole proprietorships	Partnerships	Corporations
• Owned and run by a single owner	• Two or more owners	• Owners purchase stock but do not run the company
• Easy to set up and operate with few or no requirements	• Requires legal papers	• Formal and legal arrangement
• Owner responsible for all operations but reaps all earnings	• Can attract different talents as partners	• Easier to raise capital
• Owner has unlimited liability	• Relatively easy to raise capital	• Owners taxed twice
	• All partners are equally liable	• Limited liability

▶ **Growth** A company can reinvest its profits or merge with another firm in order to grow.

REINVESTMENT

Net income + Depreciation = Cash flow → Reinvest in new plant, equipment, or technology → More products → Increase in cash flow

MERGERS

Horizontal: Firms produce the same kind of products

Vertical: Firms involved in different stages of production

▶ **Nonprofit Organizations** Some organizations work in a businesslike way to promote the interests of their members. Unlike businesses, these nonprofit organizations do not seek to earn a profit.

Community or civic organizations	Cooperatives
• Range from schools to churches and hospitals	• Consumer cooperatives provide goods to their members at lower prices
• Most are legally incorporated, with unlimited life and limited liability	• Service cooperatives offer specific services to members
• Provide goods and services while trying to improve the quality of life for people	• Producer cooperatives help members sell their products

Other organizations	Government
• Labor unions represent their members in employment matters	• Has a direct role in the economy by providing some goods and services
• Professional associations seek to improve the skills, working conditions, and public perception of their members	• Has an indirect role in the economy by acting as a regulator and a provider of benefits
• Business associations support specific businesses or trade groups	

Problem-Solving Remind students that sole proprietorships and partnerships are the two main types of unincorporated businesses in the United States. **Ask:** What conditions might lead a sole proprietor to change the business to a partnership? *(Possible answers include needing more business capital, wanting more help in running the business, or wanting to spend less time on the business.)* **Then ask:** What conditions might lead a partnership to change the business to a sole proprietorship? *(Possible answers include needing to earn more money by not sharing profits with a partner, not getting along with a partner, or wanting to shrink the business to demand less time.)* **OL**

Drawing Conclusions Have students look at the Reinvestment chart. **Ask:** How can reinvesting in new technology increase a business's profits? *(Possible answer: New technology can lead to more efficient processes that increase production. Increased production results in higher profits.)* **AL**

Hands-On Chapter Project

Step 4: Wrap Up

Creating a Business Plan

Step 4: Critiquing a Business Plan. Students will study and critique another group's business plan, and then present their own plan.

Directions: Have groups exchange completed business plans with another group. Have the groups read and evaluate the plan, making notes on strengths and weaknesses and listing suggestions. Then have each group present its own plan to the class, using the visual it prepared in Step 3.

Evaluating Information Have students discuss their own plans and the plans they reviewed and learned about in class. Write these and other questions you choose on the board to guide students' discussions:

• What strengths did you find?
• What potential weaknesses did you identify?
• What is the greatest challenge your group faced? How did you address it?

• What would you do differently if you wrote another business plan? **OL**

Assessment & Activities

ExamView®
Assessment Suite

This easy-to-use software includes extensive question banks and allows you to create fully customized tests that can be administered in print or online.

Review Content Vocabulary

1. c	2. c
3. d	4. c
5. a	6. c
7. d	8. d
9. b	10. d
11. b, c	12. a, b
13. a, b, c	14. a, b, c

Review Academic Vocabulary

15.–20. Crossword puzzles will vary but should demonstrate understanding of each term's meaning in an economic context.

Review the Main Ideas

21. They are easy to start and manage. The owner can keep the profits and does not have to pay business income taxes.
22. Strengths: easy to start up, management is simple, no special taxes, financial capital is easy to attract, operations are more efficient, can attract talented employees. Weaknesses: each partner is fully responsible for the acts of other partners, has limited life, potential for conflict between partners.
23. Stocks are ownership certificates in the firm. Bonds are written promises to repay the amount borrowed at a later date.
24. Businesses obtain cash flow from operations and dispose of it by keeping it or reinvesting it.

Review Content Vocabulary

On a separate sheet of paper, classify each of the numbered terms below into the following categories. Some terms may apply to more than one category.

a. sole proprietorships
b. partnerships
c. corporations
d. nonprofit organizations

1. bond
2. stock
3. cooperative
4. dividend
5. unlimited liability
6. charter
7. labor union
8. professional association
9. limited partner
10. credit union
11. limited liability
12. limited life
13. merger
14. cash flow

Review Academic Vocabulary

Design a crossword puzzle using the terms below. Use a synonym or antonym (specify which) as your clue. For example, clues for "limited" could be "endless (ant.)" or "restricted (syn.)."

15. entity
16. comprise
17. internally
18. dominant
19. analyze
20. devoting

Review the Main Ideas

Section 1 (pages 61–70)

21. **Explain** why sole proprietorships are attractive for entrepreneurs wanting to start a new business.
22. **Identify** the strengths and weaknesses of a partnership.
23. **Describe** the difference between owning stocks and owning bonds.

Section 2 (pages 72–77)

24. **Describe** how a business obtains, and then disposes of, its cash flow.
25. **Discuss** the difference between a horizontal and a vertical merger.
26. **Explain** why a corporation might choose to become a conglomerate.

Section 3 (pages 79–83)

27. **Discuss** the difference between a nonprofit and other forms of business organizations.
28. **Describe** the purpose of a labor union.
29. **Identifying** Use a graphic organizer like the one below to identify examples of the direct and the indirect roles of government.

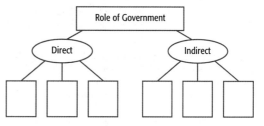

Critical Thinking

30. **The BIG Idea** If you were planning to open a business such as a sportswear store or lawn service, which form of business organization would you prefer—sole proprietorship, partnership, or corporation? Explain.

25. Horizontal mergers take place between firms that produce the same kind of product. Vertical mergers take place between firms that are in different stages of manufacturing or marketing.
26. so it can diversify and protect overall sales and profits
27. A nonprofit organization works to promote the interests of its members rather than to seek financial gain for its owners. Other forms of businesses seek financial gain for their owners.

28. to represent its members' interests in various employment matters
29. **Direct:** Tennessee Valley Authority, Federal Deposit Insurance Corporation, U.S. Postal Service **Indirect:** regulates public utilities, regulates investor-owned companies, grants money to people

Critical Thinking

30. Answers will vary but should show knowledge of business forms.

Economics ONLINE **Self-Check Quiz** Visit the
Economics: Principles and Practices Web site at glencoe.com and click
on *Chapter 3—Self-Check Quizzes* to prepare for the chapter test.

**Assessment
and Activities**

**CHAPTER
3**

31. Drawing Conclusions Do you think mergers are beneficial for the U.S. economy? Defend your response.

32. Analyzing Cite a case in your community where a cooperative would fulfill a definite economic need. Explain why you think so, and then describe what kind of cooperative you would set up.

33. Comparing and Contrasting What is the difference between the unlimited liability of proprietorships and partnerships, and the limited liability of corporations?

34. Understanding Cause and Effect What advantages might a multinational corporation bring to a host nation?

Math Practice

35. Examine the table that follows. Then answer the following questions.

Sole proprietorships, 1990–2002				
	1990	1995	2000	2002
Business receipts	731	807	1,021	1,030
Business deductions	589	638	806	809
Net income				

a. What is the net income for each of the years listed? How did you find the answer?

b. In what year did sole proprietorships have the largest net income?

c. In what year did sole proprietorships have the largest net income as a percentage of business receipts? How did you find your answer?

Applying Economic Concepts

36. Business Organizations Return to your list from the Why It Matters activity on page 60. Now that you have learned about the different business forms, review the resources on your list and decide how you will organize your new business. Prepare an oral report and present your decision and rationale to the class.

Thinking Like an Economist

37. Identify two ways a firm's cash flow can be used. Explain why these uses are a trade-off, and explain the opportunity costs of these choices in terms of the firm's future growth.

Analyzing Visuals

38. Look at Figure 3.5 on page 75. Describe in your own words each type of merger. Then discuss the benefits of each.

Writing About Economics

39. Expository Writing Use the library or the Internet to research a conglomerate. Then write a paper describing where the company is headquartered, where its manufacturing plants are located, and where it sells its products. Also include reasons why the firm chose those particular locations.

Interpreting Cartoons

40. Look at the cartoon below. What message is the cartoonist trying to deliver? How does the cartoon relate to what you have learned about proprietorships and corporations?

CHAPTER 3   Business Organizations   **87**

Applying Economic Concepts

36. Answers will vary, but students should demonstrate knowledge about the different business forms.

Thinking Like an Economist

37. Answers will vary but should show knowledge of cash flow, trade-offs, and opportunity costs.

Analyzing Visuals

38. Answers will vary. Benefits of horizontal mergers may include more efficient operations, faster growth, and the elimination of rivals. Benefits of vertical mergers may include more efficient operations, acquiring new product lines, and faster growth.

Writing About Economics

39. Answers will vary, but students should demonstrate knowledge about the company they research.

Interpreting Cartoons

40. Students will likely recognize that the message is that proprietorships sometimes have difficulty competing against large corporations or specialty firms. Students should then comment on how this relates to what they have learned about proprietorships and corporations.

31. Answers will vary, but students should give reasons for their opinion.

32. Answers will vary, but students should describe the cooperative that they would set up and support their opinion.

33. Unlimited liability holds the owners of proprietorships and partnerships personally and fully responsible for all losses and debts of the business. Corporations are fully responsible for their obligations, providing limited liability for their owners.

34. transfers new technology, creates new jobs, produces tax revenues

Math Practice

35. a. 1990, $142; 1995, $169; 2000, $215; 2002, $221; subtracted business deductions from business receipts
b. 2002
c. 2002; by dividing net income by business receipts

Microeconomics: Prices and Markets

UNIT PACING CHART				
	Chapter 4	**Chapter 5**	**Chapter 6**	**Chapter 7**
Day 1	Unit Opener Chapter Opener Section 1	Chapter Opener Section 1	Chapter Opener Section 1	Chapter Opener Section 1
Day 2	BusinessWeek Newsclip Section 2 Profiles in Economics	Case Study Section 2 Profiles in Economics	Case Study Section 2 BusinessWeek Newsclip	Profiles in Economics Section 2 BusinessWeek Newsclip
Day 3	Section 3 Case Study	Section 3 BusinessWeek Newsclip	Section 3 Profiles in Economics	Section 3 Case Study
Day 4	Review Chapter Assessment	Review Chapter Assessment	Review Chapter Assessment	Review Chapter Assessment
Day 5	The Global Economy & You		Debates in Economics	

Teacher to Teacher

Erin Johnston
South Caldwell
High School
Hudson, North
Carolina

The Model J Materials: 1 yardstick (the chassis); 1 empty garbage bin (the engine); 1 chair (the driver's seat); 4 large cans (the tires); 2 soft drink cans, flattened lengthwise (the gas and brake pedals); 4 paper cups (the headlights and taillights); 1 paper plate (the steering wheel); 1 stop watch and someone to keep "production time" (middle management); tape (nuts and bolts).

The workforce assembles the Model J as follows: (1) Lay the yardstick on the floor. (2) Place empty bin at one end to indicate front of car. (3) Place chair over opposite end of yardstick. (4) Place large cans in location of wheels. (5) Place brake and gas pedals on proper side of the chassis. (6) Tape taillights to top of seat.

(7) Tape headlights to front of engine. Tell students that to stop the clock, one member of their "workforce" must sit in the seat, hold the steering wheel, and make a horn sound.

Have a student record the production time for each round. Then have two different students work together to produce a Model J in round 2. Do not give them instructions on how to divide the labor. For round 3, assign 13 students a specialized task. Make sure that students follow the same order for each round. Students should see that the production time goes down with each round, although you may have to add "governmental" controls to ensure that this happens. Discuss the differences in production time.

Author Note

Dear Economics Teacher:

Economists love the free enterprise system. In fact, there is no better way to organize the way in which we use our scarce resources. The free enterprise system, along with its demand, supply, competition, prices, and private ownership of property, is the most prolific wealth-generating system in the world!

One of the most fascinating things about our economy is that it seems to almost run itself. Little coordination and direction are needed once the basic foundation is in place—a foundation typified by a large number of buyers and sellers, plenty of information, and generally adequate competition.

You might be interested to know that the free enterprise system we have today is not something that economists—or anyone else for that matter—actually invented. Instead, the system is one that more or less evolved. Changes have been so slow that they are almost imperceptible. Capitalism, for example, has what economists would call "large-scale tendencies"—meaning that firms tend to merge in an attempt to grow, which in turn reduces the number of firms needed for competition. We see this in almost every industry, from automobiles to banking to retail.

Economists may warn that increased industry concentration is hindering competition, yet this is often offset by business community announcements that profits are going up. Which view is correct, and should anything be done about it?

This is where economics comes in. If we can understand how the economy actually works, we can introduce changes that influence some of the evolutionary direction. As you go through the chapters, you'll discover that I try to describe how things work, and then provide enough background so that you and your students can make your own decisions. This is the task of this book, and I hope it is one that appeals to you as well.

Gary E. Clayton

Gary Clayton, Ph.D.
Author

UNIT 2

Microeconomics:
Prices and Markets

Unit Objectives

After studying this unit, students will be able to:

• **Discuss** demand and the factors that cause changes in it.

• **Explain** the concept of supply and the theory of production.

• **Explain** how supply and demand interact to determine price.

• **Describe** how competition and different market structures affect prices.

Unit Overview

Unit 2 examines major markets with respect to the degree of competition within each type and how this affects buyers and sellers.

Chapter 4 explains the concept of demand.

Chapter 5 discusses supply, the theory of production, and profit maximization.

Chapter 6 brings supply and demand together in a relationship focusing on prices and explains how the price system operates.

Chapter 7 introduces competition and market structures. It also discusses market failures and the government's role in the economy.

► Buyers and sellers in a music store show how supply and demand play out in the market.

88   UNIT 2

Activity: Launching the Unit

Local Competition Ask students to select a business in their community that they patronize. Have them write a short analysis of the business by responding to the following questions: (1) What is the name and location of the business? (2) Why do you purchase from this business? *(convenience, price, service, quality of product)* (3) What is the competition for the business? *(stores nearby, malls, mail order)* (4) How does the business compete? *(price competition, sales, advertising, special service)* Have students share their analyses with the class. **OL**

Making It Relevant

Ask: How much does a baseball glove cost? Answers should vary, suggesting that prices for baseball gloves differ widely. Discuss with students the possible reasons for the different prices. *(Possible answers: brand name, type of glove, type of store, quality of leather)*

Suggest to students that the price of a baseball glove depends on demand for that glove relative to supply. In turn, the other factors can influence demand. For example, advertising may increase demand for a particular brand name, thus affecting the price. **OL**

BusinessWeek ONLINE

To find up-to-date news and analysis on the economy, business, technology, markets, entrepreneurs, investments, and finance, have students search feature articles and special reports on the BusinessWeek Web site, www.businessweek.com.

Extra Credit Project

Have students research and write about a product or service for which they believe there will be a high demand in the twenty-first century. Students should explain why they think such a high demand will exist and use the Internet and financial magazines to make predictions about the product or service's potential growth. Have students create charts and graphs to support their positions. **AL**

Planning Guide

Key to Ability Levels	
BL Below level	**AL** Above level
OL On level	**ELL** English Language Learners

Key to Teaching Resources	
Print Material	DVD
CD-Rom	Transparency

Levels				Resources	Chapter Opener	Section 1	Section 2	Section 3	Chapter Assess
BL	OL	AL	ELL						
FOCUS									
BL	OL	AL	ELL	Daily Focus Skills Transparencies		10, 11	3, 9	12	
TEACH									
BL	OL		ELL	Guided Reading Activities*		p. 10	p. 11	p. 12	
BL	OL	AL	ELL	Economic Content Vocabulary Activities*		p. 4	p. 4	p. 4	
	OL	AL		Critical Thinking Activities			p. 4		
BL	OL		ELL	Reading Essentials and Note-Taking Guide*		p. 28	p. 31	p. 34	
		AL		Enrichment Activities			p. 4		
BL	OL	AL	ELL	Primary and Secondary Source Readings		pp. 5, 7	p. 7	p. 9	
BL	OL	AL	ELL	Economic Cartoons		p. 5	p. 8		
BL	OL	AL	ELL	Math Practice for Economics			p. 6	p. 4	
BL	OL		ELL	High School Reading in the Content Area Strategies and Activities	✓	✓	✓	✓	✓
BL	OL	AL	ELL	High School Writing Process Transparencies	✓	✓	✓	✓	✓
BL	OL	AL	ELL	Writer's Guidebook	✓	✓	✓	✓	✓
BL	OL	AL	ELL	StudentWorks Plus CD-ROM	✓	✓	✓	✓	✓
BL	OL	AL	ELL	Vocabulary PuzzleMaker CD-ROM	✓	✓	✓	✓	✓

*Also available in Spanish

TeacherWorks *Plus*
All-In-One Planner and Resource Center

- Interactive Lesson Planner
- Interactive Teacher Edition
- Fully editable blackline masters
- Economics & You videos

- Differentiated Lesson Plans
- Printable reports of daily assignments
- Standards tracking system

Levels					Resources	Chapter Opener	Section 1	Section 2	Section 3	Chapter Assess
BL	OL	AL	ELL							
TEACH *(continued)*										
BL	OL	AL	ELL		Economics & You Video Program DVD—*What is Demand?*	✓	✓	✓	✓	✓
BL	OL	AL	ELL		**Graph Coach CD-ROM**	✓	✓	✓	✓	✓
Teacher Resources					**Differentiated Instruction Strategies**	✓	✓	✓	✓	✓
					Success with English Learners	✓	✓	✓	✓	✓
					Presentation Plus! CD-ROM	✓	✓	✓	✓	✓
ASSESS										
BL	OL	AL	ELL		**Section Quizzes and Chapter Tests**		p. 45	p. 46	p. 47	pp. 49, 53
BL	OL	AL	ELL		**Authentic Assessment Strategies and Activities**		p. 4	p. 4		
BL	OL	AL	ELL		*ExamView® Assessment Suite* **CD-ROM**		4-1	4-2	4-3	Ch. 4
BL	OL	AL	ELL		**Interactive Tutor Self-Assessment CD-ROM**		4-1	4-2	4-3	
CLOSE										
BL			ELL		**Reteaching Activities***		p. 4	p. 4	p. 4	
BL	OL		ELL		**Reading and Study Skills Foldables**		p. 51	p. 51	p. 51	
BL	OL	AL	ELL		**Graphic Organizer Transparencies**		p. 29			

*Also available in Spanish

Activity Using CyberScout

Researching Using Keyword

Technology Product

CyberScout is a convenient and dynamic search engine that provides several easy ways to locate information outside the McGraw-Hill Learning Network. CyberScout only searches Web sites that have been reviewed by teachers, so the information students find is always appropriate and accurate.

Objectives

After students learn using CyberScout, they will be able to

- research topics and issues in economics using CyberScout;
- exercise research and study skills;
- practice writing skills.

Steps

- From the McGraw-Hill Learning Network home page (www.mhln.com), click on **For Students**.
- Choose **CyberScout** below **Homework Help**.
- Enter a keyword or phrase in the **Keyword** field and click on the **Go** button.
- Click on the link to a Web site of interest.
- Students will be redirected to the Web site in a new window.
- Students navigate through the chosen Web site to gain information on their topic and take notes.

Economics ONLINE

	Student	Teacher	Parent
Beyond the Textbook	●	●	●
Chapter Overviews	●	●	●
ePuzzles and Games	●		●
Concepts in Motion	●		●
Multi-Language Glossaries	●		●
Online Student Edition	●	●	●
Self-Check Quizzes	●		●
Student Web Activities	●		●
Study Central™	●		●
Time Current Events	●	●	●
Teaching Today		●	
Vocabulary eFlashcards	●		●
Web Activity Lesson Plans		●	

Glencoe Media Center

❯ glencoe.com

Study-To-Go
- Vocabulary eFlashcards
- Self-Check Quizzes

❯ **Audio/Video**
- Student Edition Audio
- Spanish Summaries
- Economics & You Videos

READING SUPPORT FROM JAMESTOWN EDUCATION

- **Timed Readings Plus in Social Studies** helps students increase their reading rate and fluency while maintaining comprehension. The 400-word passages are similar to those found on state and national assessments.

- **Reading in the Content Area: Social Studies** concentrates on six essential reading skills that help students better comprehend what they read. The book includes 75 high-interest nonfiction passages written at increasing levels of difficulty.

- **Reading Social Studies** includes strategic reading instruction and vocabulary support in Social Studies content for both ELLs and native speakers of English. www.jamestowneducation.com

Reading List Generator CD-ROM — GLENCOE BookLink 3

Use this database to search more than 30,000 titles to create a customized reading list for your students.

- Reading lists can be organized by students' reading level, author, genre, theme, or area of interest.
- The database provides Degrees of Reading Power™ (DRP) and Lexile™ readability scores for all selections.
- A brief summary of each selection is included.

Leveled reading suggestions for this chapter:
For students at a Grade 10 reading level:
- *Exploring Careers*, by U.S. Department of Labor

For students at a Grade 11 reading level:
- *The Success of the Navajo Arts and Crafts Enterprise,* by Lenora Begay Trahant

For students at a Grade 12 reading level:
- *Business Builders in Fast Food,* by Nathan Aaseng

* Review suggested books before assigning them.

NCEE

National Council on Economic Education

Voluntary Standards Emphasized in Chapter 4

Content Standard 8 Prices send signals and provide incentives to buyers and sellers. When supply or demand changes, market prices adjust, affecting incentives.

Resources Available from NCEE
- Virtual Economics®: An Interactive Center for Economic Education Version 3.0
- Capstone: The Nation's High School Economics Course
- Focus: High School Economics, Second Edition
- Mathematics and Economics: Connections for Life, Grades 9–12

To order these materials, or to contact your State Council on Economic Education about workshops and programs, call 1-800-338-1192 or visit the NCEE Web site at store.ncee.net**.**

The BIG Idea

As students study the chapter, remind them to consider the chapter-based Big Idea. The **Essential Question** in the chapter launch activity below ties in to the Big Idea and helps students think about and understand important chapter concepts. In addition, the Hands-On Chapter Project relates the content from each section to the Big Idea. The steps in each section build on each other and culminate in the Wrap-Up Activity on the Visual Summary page.

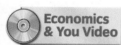
Economics & You Video To generate student interest and provide a springboard for class discussion, access the Economics & You Topic 4 video, **What is Demand?,** at <u>glencoe.com</u> or on the video DVD.

FOLDABLES Study Organizer **Dinah Zike's Foldables** are three-dimensional, interactive graphic organizers that help students practice basic writing skills, review key vocabulary terms, and identify main ideas. Have students complete this chapter's Foldable activity or activities in *Dinah Zike's Reading and Study Skills Foldables* booklet. **OL**

Economics ONLINE Introduce students to chapter content and key terms by having them access *Chapter 4 —Chapter Overviews* at <u>glencoe.com</u>.

CHAPTER
4 Demand

Why It Matters

Think about the items you bought during the past two months. What influenced your purchases? Did you need the items, or did you buy them because you wanted them? Make a list of the items, and next to each one write why you bought it. Then add for each item whether you would have bought more if the price had been lower, or fewer had the price been higher. Read Chapter 4 to learn how economists interpret your actions.

The BIG Idea

Markets exist when buyers and sellers interact, and market prices are set by the interaction of demand and supply.

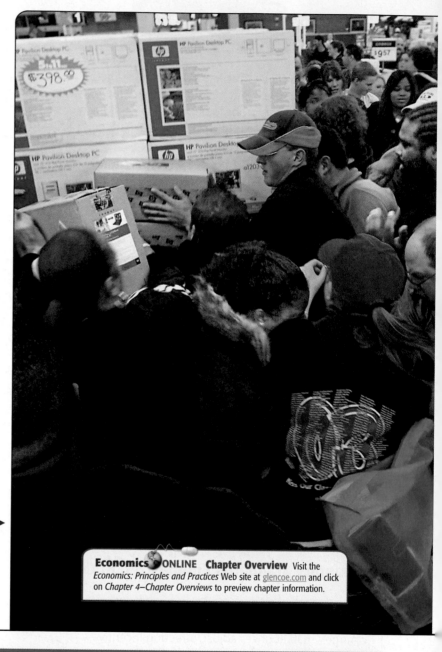

When prices go down for ▶ products, such as the computers in this computer store, consumers demand more of them.

90 UNIT 2

Economics ONLINE **Chapter Overview** Visit the *Economics: Principles and Practices* Web site at <u>glencoe.com</u> and click on *Chapter 4–Chapter Overviews* to preview chapter information.

Activity: Launching the Chapter

Predicting Have students research and write about two products: one that they expect to increase in popularity in the next few years and one that they expect to decrease in popularity. For each product, students should explain why they expect the popularity of the product to change in the way they predict.
Essential Question: What causes desire, or demand, for a product to rise or fall? *(Possible answers: changing tastes and preferences;*

changes in income; increase or decrease in how many people want a product) Students may also use Internet resources and financial magazines to make predictions about the two products. Have students create charts and graphs to support their positions. **OL**

SECTION 1

What Is Demand?

GUIDE TO READING

Section Preview

In this section, you will learn that you express demand for a product when you are willing and able to purchase it.

Content Vocabulary

- demand (p. 91)
- microeconomics (p. 91)
- market economy (p. 92)
- demand schedule (p. 92)
- demand curve (p. 93)
- Law of Demand (p. 93)
- market demand curve (p. 94)
- marginal utility (p. 95)
- diminishing marginal utility (p. 95)

Academic Vocabulary

- prevail (p. 92)
- inversely (p. 93)

Reading Strategy

Identifying As you read this section, use a web diagram similar to the one below to identify the characteristics of demand.

Characteristics of Demand

Focus

Bellringer
Daily Focus Transparency 10

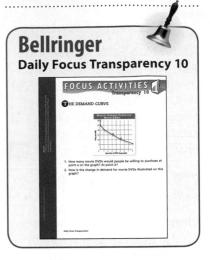

FOCUS ACTIVITIES
Transparency 10
THE DEMAND CURVE

1. How many movie DVDs would people be willing to purchase at point a on the graph? At point b?
2. How is the change in demand for movie DVDs illustrated on this graph?

Daily Focus Transparencies

GUIDE TO READING

Answers to Graphic: the desire, ability, and willingness to buy a product; involves the variables of price and quantity; quantity demanded varies inversely with price

PRODUCTS IN THE NEWS

–adapted from
The Columbus Dispatch

Wrist Watch

It's all in the wrist. Actually, this spring, it's all *on* the wrist.

Skinny bracelets and subtle strands of bling are being replaced by chunky looks with boldness and color, often worn in multiples.

"Last year, everything was thin; now, 'big' is being demanded everywhere," said Toni Miller Dunleavy, owner of Etc. Gifts and Accessories.

Big and brash wrist frosting takes its newest form with Wonder Woman-esque cuffs. . . . Other popular choices include wide, flexible "liquid metal" (a la chain mail) and oversize bangles strung with colored beads or seashells—or even bottle caps or typewriter keys.

Meanwhile, those slim bangles from years past shouldn't be tossed: A piling of 8, 10, or more easily makes the wearer a member of the bigger-is-better bracelet brigade. ■

When we talk about the "demand" for a product, we mean more than the desire to simply have or to own the item. In order for demand to be counted in the marketplace, desire must be coupled with the ability and willingness to pay for it. Only those people with **demand**—the desire, ability, and willingness to buy a product—can compete with others who have similar demands.

Demand, like many of the other topics discussed in Unit 2, is a microeconomic concept. **Microeconomics** is the part of economic theory that deals with behavior and decision making by individual units, such as people and firms. Collectively, our microeconomic concepts help explain how prices are determined and how individual economic decisions are made.

demand
combination of desire, ability, and willingness to buy a product

microeconomics
part of economics that studies small units, such as individuals and firms

CHAPTER 4 Demand 91

Resource Manager

R Reading Strategies	**C** Critical Thinking	**D** Differentiated Instruction	**W** Writing Support	**S** Skill Practice
Teacher Edition • Act. Prior Know., p. 92 **Additional Resources** • Guid. Read. Act., p. 10 • Read. Ess. & Note-Taking Guide, p. 28 • Pri./Sec. Source Read., p. 5	**Teacher Edition** • Det. Cause/Effect, p. 93 • Theorizing, p. 95 **Additional Resources** • Authentic Assess., p. 4 • Quizzes and Tests, p. 45	**Teacher Edition** • ELL, p. 92 • Logical/Math., p. 93 **Additional Resources** • Reading and Study Skills Fold., p. 51 • Econ. Cartoons, p. 5	**Teacher Edition** • Expository Writing, p. 94 • Persuasive Writing, p. 96 **Additional Resources** • Writer's Guidebook	**Teacher Edition** • Using Tables and Charts, p. 92 • Using Line Graphs, p. 94 **Additional Resources** • Graph. Org. Trans., p. 29 • Daily Focus Trans. 10, 11

Teach

R Reading Strategy

Activating Prior Knowledge

Ask: What are the three basic questions? *(WHAT, HOW, and FOR WHOM)* What is their purpose? *(Answering the questions helps people make careful decisions about using limited resources.)* **OL**

D Differentiated Instruction

English Language Learners

Explain that *variables* is a math term referring to quantities that may change. Often, in a relationship between variables, one is unknown and changes as the other variable changes. Give students the example of height varying with age. **ELL**

S Skill Practice

Using Tables and Charts

Ask: How many CDs does the consumer demand at a price of $20? *(1)* $5? *(8)* **BL**

Economic Analysis

Answer: As the price of the CDs decreases, the quantity demanded increases.

---

market economy
economic system in which people and firms make all economic decisions *(also see page 37)*

demand schedule
a table that lists how much of a product consumers will buy at all possible prices

An Introduction to Demand

MAIN Idea Demand is a concept specifying the different quantities of an item that will be bought at different prices.

Economics & You Do you buy more of an item when the price goes down, or less of it when the price goes up? Read on to see how this behavior illustrates the concept of demand.

R In a **market economy** people and firms act in their own best interests to answer the basic WHAT, HOW, and FOR WHOM questions. Demand is central to this process, so an understanding of the concept of demand is essential if we are to understand how the economy works.

Demand Illustrated

D Fortunately, the concept of demand is easy to understand because it involves only two variables—the price and quantity of a specific product at a given point in time. For example, we might want to know how many people would want to see a movie on a given afternoon if the price was $5. Or we might want to know how many would want to view it if the price was $10.

The answers would depend on a number of things, including the number of people living in the area, the number and types of other movies that were playing at the same time, and of course the popularity of the movie itself. But in the end, everything would be measured in terms of prices and quantities.

The Individual Demand Schedule

To see how an economist would analyze demand, look at **Panel A** in **Figure 4.1**. It shows the amount of a product that a consumer, whom we'll call Mike, would be willing and able to purchase over a range of possible prices that go from $5 to $30. The information in Panel A is known as a **demand schedule.** The demand schedule shows the various quantities demanded of a particular product at all prices that might **prevail** in the market at a given time.

Figure 4.1 ▶ **The Demand for Compact Digital Discs**

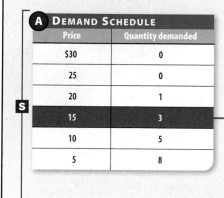

A DEMAND SCHEDULE	
Price	Quantity demanded
$30	0
25	0
20	1
15	3
10	5
5	8

B DEMAND CURVE

▶ The demand schedule and the demand curve both show the quantity of CDs an individual consumer demands at every possible price. Note how the three CDs demanded at a price of $15 are plotted as point **a** on the demand curve.

Economic Analysis *Why is the demand curve downward sloping?*

How the Furby Flies

PRIMARY & SECONDARY SOURCES Reading 4
HOW THE FURBY FLIES

Primary and Secondary Source Readings, p. 7

Objective: Understand some reasons why demand can increase dramatically.

Focus/Teach: Ask students to brainstorm a list of products in high demand. Then have students complete the activity.

Assess: Have students exchange papers to grade each other's answers.

Close: Have students identify other products that have been scarce in stores due to popularity.

Differentiated Instruction Strategies

BL Ask students to draw a graphic organizer to show the sequence of events in the article.

AL Direct students to write a description of the causes and effects of the Furby craze.

ELL Show students pictures of the products mentioned in the article.

Demand and Prices If the prices of CDs drop, consumers will be better able and more willing to buy them. *How does this situation reflect the Law of Demand?*

As you can see, Mike would not buy any CDs at a price of $25 or $30, but he would buy one if the price fell to $20, and he would buy three if the price was $15, and so on. Just like the rest of us, he is generally willing to buy more units of a product as the price gets lower.

The Individual Demand Curve

The demand schedule in Panel A of Figure 4.1 can also be shown graphically as the downward-sloping line in **Panel B.** All we have to do to is to transfer each of the price-quantity observations in the demand schedule to the graph, and then connect the points to form the curve. Economists call this the **demand curve,** a graph showing the quantity demanded at each and every price that might prevail in the market. **C**

For example, point **a** in Panel B shows that Mike purchased three CDs at a price of $15 each, while point **b** shows that he will buy five at a price of $10. The demand schedule and the demand curve are similar in that they both show the same information—one in the form of a table and the other in the form of a graph.

✓**Reading Check** **Interpreting** How do you react to a change in the price of an item? How does this illustrate the concept of demand?

The Law of Demand

MAIN Idea There is an inverse relationship between the price of an item and the quantity demanded.

Economics & You When you go shopping, do you try to catch sale days? Read on to find out how an economic "law" describes your behavior.

The prices and quantities in Figure 4.1 point out a feature of demand: for practically every good or service that we might buy, higher prices are associated with smaller amounts demanded. Conversely, lower prices are associated with larger amounts demanded. This is known as the **Law of Demand,** which states that the quantity demanded varies **inversely** with its price. When the price of something goes up, the quantity demanded goes down. Likewise, when the price goes down, quantity demanded goes up. **D**

Why We Call It a "Law"

Expressing something as a "law" may seem like a strong statement for a social science like economics to make, but there are two reasons why economists prefer to do so. First, the inverse relationship between price and quantity demanded is something

demand curve
a curve that shows the quantities demanded at all possible prices

Law of Demand
rule stating that consumers will buy more of a product at lower prices and less at higher prices

S **Personal Finance Handbook**
See pages R4–R5 for more information on budgeting.

CHAPTER 4 Demand 93

C **Critical Thinking**

Determining Cause and Effect Ask: What causes a change in demand? *(a change in price)* **BL**

D **Differentiated Instruction**

Logical/Mathematical
Have students construct three imaginary demand schedules for three products of their choice. Then have them graph each of the schedules. Students should pair with another student to check each other's schedules and graphs. **OL**

Caption Answer: The situation shows consumers buying more at lower prices, which reflects the inverse relationship specified by the Law of Demand.

✓**Reading Check** **Answer:** Answers will vary, but most students will agree that they will buy more at lower prices, which illustrates the Law of Demand.

Leveled Activities

BL **Reteaching Activities, p. 4**

OL **Graphic Organizer Transparencies, p. 29**

AL **Primary and Secondary Source Readings, p. 5**

Skill Practice

Using Line Graphs Ask: How many CDs would Mike buy at a price of $20? *(1)* How many would Julia buy at the same price? *(2)* How can you determine the number of CDs that would be bought in the market at a price of $20? *(Possible answer: Add together Mike's and Julia's quantities.)* **OL**

Writing Support

Expository Writing Have students write about a time when they observed the Law of Demand working. Students can write about purchases they have made or purchases they have observed others making. **OL**

Economic Analysis

Answer: The first two curves each show what one person would buy at various prices. The third curve shows the quantities demanded by the entire market.

✓ **Reading Check** **Answer:** It slopes downward to the right, reflecting the inverse relationship between price and quantity stated in the Law of Demand.

Hands-On Chapter Project

Step 1

Making Decisions About Demand and Elasticity

In this project, students will create a presentation to stockholders outlining the progress of a business over the course of a year.

Step 1: Identifying Demand for a Product. Students will choose a product and survey classmates to determine demand schedules.

Figure 4.2 ▶ Individual and Market Demand Curves

▶ The market demand curve shows the quantities demanded by everyone in the market who is interested in purchasing a product. Point **a** on the market demand curve represents the three CDs Mike and Julia each would purchase at a price of $15 for a total of six CDs.

Economic Analysis *How do the three demand curves differ?*

Graphs In MOtion
See StudentWorks™ Plus or glencoe.com.

Skills Handbook

See page **R49** to learn about **Using Line Graphs.**

market demand curve a curve that shows how much of a product all consumers will buy at all possible prices

that we find in study after study, with people almost always stating that they would buy more of an item if its price goes down, and less if the price goes up.

Second, common sense and simple observation are consistent with the Law of Demand. This is how people behave in everyday life—they normally buy more of a product at lower prices than they do at higher ones. All we have to do is to note the increased purchases at the mall whenever there is a sale. This is why economics is a social science: because it is the study of the way we behave when things around us change.

The Market Demand Curve

So far we have discussed a particular individual's demand for a product. Sometimes, however, we are more concerned with the **market demand curve,** the demand curve that shows the quantities demanded by everyone who is interested in purchasing the product. **Figure 4.2** shows the market demand curve **D** for Mike and

his friend Julia, the only two people whom (for simplicity) we assume to be willing and able to purchase CDs.

To get the market demand curve, all we do is add together the number of CDs that Mike and Julia would purchase at every possible price. Then, we simply plot the prices and quantities on a separate graph. To illustrate, point **a** in Figure 4.2 represents the three CDs that Mike would purchase at $15, plus the three that Julia would buy at the same price. Likewise, point **b** represents the quantity of CDs that both would purchase at $10.

The market demand curve in Figure 4.2 is very similar to the individual demand curve in Figure 4.1. Both show a range of possible prices that might prevail in the market at a given time, and both curves are downward sloping. The main difference between the two is that the market demand curve shows the demand for everyone in the market.

✓ **Reading Check** **Explaining** How does the market demand curve reflect the Law of Demand?

Directions: In a general class discussion, brainstorm a list of products that class members buy. Organize the class into small groups, and tell each group to imagine that they are forming a business. Students should then choose from the list a product that they would like to sell and set a range of three to five possible prices that they might charge for it. Group members should then survey ten classmates to see what quantities they would buy at each of the prices. Have each group compile the data into a demand schedule.

Summarizing Direct each group to use their demand schedules to graph a demand curve for their product. **OL**

(Chapter Project continued in Section 2.)

Demand and Marginal Utility

MAIN Idea As we buy more of an item, we get less satisfaction from each additional purchase.

Economics & You When you buy clothes, why do you prefer a variety of colors and styles to identical items? Read to see how this relates to marginal utility.

As you may recall from Chapter 1, economists use the term *utility* to describe the amount of usefulness or satisfaction that someone gets from the use of a product. **Marginal utility**—the extra usefulness or additional satisfaction a person gets from acquiring or using one more unit of a product—is an important extension of this concept because it explains so much about demand.

The reason we buy something in the first place is because we feel that the product is useful and will give satisfaction. However, as we use more and more of a product, we

encounter **diminishing marginal utility**, the principle which states that the extra satisfaction we get from using additional quantities of the product begins to decline.

Because of our diminishing satisfaction, we usually are not willing to pay as much for the second, third, fourth, and so on, as we did the first unit. This is why our demand curve is downward-sloping, and this is why Mike and Julia won't pay as much for the second CD as they did for the first.

Diminishing satisfaction happens to all of us at some time. For example, when you buy a drink because you are thirsty, you get the most satisfaction from the first purchase. Since you are now less thirsty, you get less satisfaction from the second purchase, and even less from the next, so you are not willing to pay as much for the second and third purchases.

✓**Reading Check** **Describing** How does the principle of diminishing marginal utility explain the price we pay for another unit of a good or service?

marginal utility additional satisfaction or usefulness a consumer gets from having one more unit of a product

diminishing marginal utility decrease in satisfaction or usefulness from having one more unit of the same product

C Critical Thinking

Theorizing **Ask:** What problems might economists have in trying to measure marginal utility? Explain. *(Possible answer: Marginal utility is difficult to measure because it is subjective. If 20 people were asked how much satisfaction they received from a second soft drink, each one might give a different answer.)* **AL**

✓**Reading Check** **Answer:** If we get less satisfaction from more of a product, we won't be willing to pay as much for another unit of the product.

Assess

💿 Use the Interactive Tutor Self-Assessment CD-ROM to review Section 1, and then assign the Section 1 Review as homework or as an in-class activity.

Close

Making Connections Have students give an example of how price or diminishing marginal utility changed their decision to buy a good or service. **OL**

SECTION 1 Review

Vocabulary
1. **Explain** the significance of demand, microeconomics, market economy, demand schedule, demand curve, Law of Demand, market demand curve, marginal utility, and diminishing marginal utility.

Main Ideas
2. **Describing** What is the relationship between the demand schedule and the demand curve?

3. **Determining Cause and Effect** Using a graphic organizer like the one below, explain how a change in price changes the quantity demanded of an item.

Critical Thinking
4. **The BIG Idea** How does the principle of diminishing marginal utility explain the slope of the demand curve?

5. **Inferring** Although people buy more of a product when the seller lowers the price, some items such as luxury goods are not offered at a lower price. Why?

6. **Analyzing Visuals** Look at the demand schedules on page 94. Assume that Julia is willing to purchase different quantities at the same prices, and write down the new demand. Then plot a new market demand curve that incorporates the changed demand.

7. **Using Graphs** Create your own demand schedule for an item you currently purchase. Next, plot your demand schedule on a demand curve. Be sure to include labels.

Applying Economics
8. **Diminishing Marginal Utility** Using what you have learned about diminishing marginal utility, find examples from your own experience and explain how they support this concept.

Review SECTION 1

Answers

1. All definitions can be found in the section and the Glossary.
2. The demand curve is a graphical representation of the information given in a demand schedule.
3. As price increases, quantity demanded decreases. As price decreases, quantity demanded increases.
4. The principle of diminishing marginal utility tells us that the more of a product we consume, the less satisfaction we will get from additional units. If we are getting less

satisfaction, we will be willing to pay less money for those additional units, which would produce an inverse relationship between price and quantity.

5. **Possible answer:** Sellers offer products at the price at which they can make the most profit. Luxury goods can command high prices.

6. Answers will vary, but the new demand schedule should follow the Law of Demand and the resulting curve should slope downward to the right.

7. Answers will vary, but demand schedules should reflect an inverse relationship between price and quantity demanded.

8. Answers will vary but should include personal experiences that reflect the principle of diminishing marginal utility.

BusinessWeek NEWSCLIP

Oscar Mayer, one of the brands of Kraft Foods Inc., first launched its Lunchables product line in 1988. The pre-packaged lunches quickly became popular, and today these snacks are available in many different flavor combinations. They also have come under attack by critics. Kraft is finding ways to satisfy these critics and keep consumer demand high.

Slimmer Kids, Fatter Profits?

Charles Davis, a Kraft food maven, is on a health kick. But then, he has no choice. Making cheese healthier is complicated. Add too much calcium, and it starts to taste chalky. Take out too much fat, and the cheese emerges from mechanical graters like Play-Doh. "It becomes a big glob instead of having good shredding integrity," says Charles W. Davis, vice-president of global technology and quality for convenient meals at Kraft Foods Inc.

Davis can tell you all about finding that delicate balance between what tastes good and what's good for you. Since 2004, the 48-year-old chemist has been leading a team of scientists, technicians, and engineers working to improve the nutritional content of Kraft's popular Lunchables Lunch Combinations line, a process known industrywide as reformulation.

That means he has spent an inordinate amount of time experimenting not only with cheese but also with the juice drinks, crackers, deli meats, and fruit snacks that make up these all-in-one meals. If you count all 41 varieties of Lunchables, Davis has cut calories by an average of 10%, fat by 24%, and sodium by 20%.

Why do Davis and hundreds of other people throughout the company do nothing else but experiment in their kitchen labs all day? Because their employer has no choice. Kraft, the nation's largest food manufacturer, and its competitors risk becoming this decade's cigarette companies: vilified for pushing junk to children, restricted by often-conflicted regulators, challenged in court.

—Reprinted from *BusinessWeek*

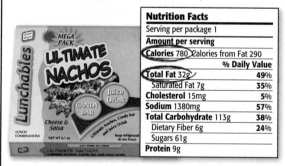

Examining the Newsclip

1. **Understanding Cause and Effect** Why did Kraft decide to reformulate a product that was already popular?
2. **Making Inferences** What might happen to demand for the Lunchables products if Kraft did not respond to consumer demands?

96   UNIT 2   Microeconomics: Prices and Markets

Activity: Interdisciplinary Connection

Health Tell students that competition forces businesses to follow consumer desires. Direct students to find two TV or print advertisements for products that have been reformulated to be "healthier." Have students research the products to find out how much they have changed (for example, students might compare and contrast each product's past and present nutrition information). Have students write several paragraphs analyzing the product changes and determining whether the reformulated products should truly be labeled "healthier." Call on volunteers to share their findings with the class. **OL**

SECTION 2 Factors Affecting Demand

GUIDE TO READING

Section Preview

In this section, you will learn about the factors that cause changes in demand.

Content Vocabulary

- change in quantity demanded *(p. 98)*
- income effect *(p. 98)*
- substitution effect *(p. 98)*
- change in demand *(p. 99)*
- substitutes *(p. 100)*
- complements *(p. 101)*

Academic Vocabulary

- principle *(p. 98)*
- illustrated *(p. 98)*

Reading Strategy

Listing As you read about the determinants of demand, list each on a table similar to the one below and provide an example of each.

Determinants of Demand		
Determinant	Example	Effect on demand

GUIDE TO READING

Possible Answers to Graphic:

Determinant: consumer income. **Example:** getting a raise. **Effect on demand:** income rising increases demand.

Determinant: consumer tastes. **Example:** fashion. **Effect on demand:** can increase demand for fashionable clothing and decrease demand for unfashionable clothing.

COMPANIES IN THE NEWS —*TIME*

McMakeover Deluxe

McDonald's is getting a makeover. The fast-food force has launched its first restaurant redesign in 30 years. More than 6,000 locations will feature the new look by year's end.

Customers will have three zones to choose from, based on their dining needs. Counter seating will serve eat-and-run customers. Those looking to linger will find soft lighting and plush chairs. Mingling teens can cram tables together in a flexible seating area.

"It's something McDonald's should have done years ago," says restaurant analyst Howard Penney. The design suggests a certain coffee chain, but Penney says it could give McDonald's an edge over fast-food rivals. ■

Why would McDonald's go to the trouble and expense of redesigning its restaurants? The company realizes that consumer demand is changing. This means the company has to change too, or it risks losing business to competitors that better meet customer demand. Such changes in demand have an effect on both the demand schedule and the demand curve.

When it comes to demand, there are two types of changes. When the price of a product changes while all other factors remain the same, we have a change in the quantity demanded. Sometimes other factors change while the price remains the same—similar to the change in consumer taste in our news story. When this happens, we see a change in demand.

Resource Manager

R Reading Strategies	C Critical Thinking	D Differentiated Instruction	W Writing Support	S Skill Practice
Teacher Edition • Making Connections, pp. 98, 100 • Analyzing Text Structure, p. 99 **Additional Resources** • Guid. Read. Act., p. 11 • Read. Ess. & Note-Taking Guide, p. 28	**Teacher Edition** • Making Inferences, p. 98 • Dist. Fact/Opinion, p. 102 **Additional Resources** • Crit. Think. Act., p. 4 • Daily Focus Trans. 3, 9	**Teacher Edition** • Interpersonal, p. 99 • ELL, p. 100 **Additional Resources** • Econ. Cartoons, p. 8 • Pri./Sec. Source Read., p. 7 • Enrichment Act., p. 4	**Teacher Edition** • Narrative Writing, p. 100 • Expository Writing, p. 102 **Additional Resources** • High School Writing Process Trans.	**Teacher Edition** • Making Inferences, p. 101 **Additional Resources** • Reading and Study Skills Fold., p. 51 • Math Prac. for Econ., p. 6

Teach

C Critical Thinking

Making Inferences Tell students that inflation is a rise in the general level of prices. **Ask:** What kind of income effect do you think inflation would produce? *(It would make consumers feel poorer.)* How might it affect quantity demanded? *(Consumers will likely buy smaller quantities.)* **AL**

R Reading Strategy

Making Connections Ask students to list five goods that they use. Then have them list other goods they would buy more of if the prices of the original goods rose and the substitution effect took hold. **OL**

Economic Analysis

Answer: because people are willing to buy more items when prices are low and less items when prices are high

✓**Reading Check** **Answer:** by a movement from one point to another on the same curve

Differentiated Instruction

change in quantity demanded movement along the demand curve showing that the amount someone is willing to purchase changes when the price changes

income effect that part of a change in quantity demanded due to a change in the buyer's real income when a price changes

substitution effect that part of a change in quantity demanded due to a price change that makes other products more or less costly

Change in the Quantity Demanded

MAIN Idea Only a change in price can cause a change in quantity demanded.

Economics & You When you shop for an item, do you also consider prices of related items? Read on to learn how demand accounts for this behavior.

Look at **Figure 4.3** to see what happens when only the price changes and everything else remains constant. Point **a** on the demand curve shows that six CDs are demanded at a price of $15. When the price falls to $10, 10 CDs are demanded. This movement from point **a** to point **b** is a **change in quantity demanded**—a change that is graphically represented as a movement *along* the demand curve. When the price goes up, fewer CDs are demanded. When the price goes down, more are

Figure 4.3 ▶ **Change in the Quantity Demanded**

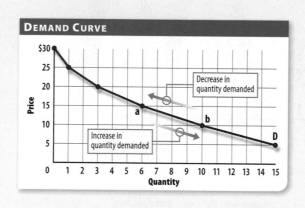

DEMAND CURVE

▶ Only a change in price can cause a change in quantity demanded. When the price goes down, the quantity demanded increases. When the price goes up, the quantity demanded decreases. Both changes appear as a movement along the demand curve.

Economic Analysis *Why do price and quantity demanded move in opposite directions?*

demanded. As we will see, the income and substitution effects also help us understand this **principle.**

The Income Effect

When the price of a product drops, consumers pay less and, as a result, have some extra income to spend. For example, we can see from Figure 4.3 that consumers spent $90 to buy six CDs when the price was $15 per CD. If the price drops to $10, they would spend only $60 on the same quantity, leaving them $30 "richer" because of the drop in price. They may even spend some of this extra income on more CDs. As a result, part of the increase from 6 to 10 units purchased, shown as the movement from point **a** to point **b** on the demand curve, is due to consumers feeling richer.

If the price had gone up, consumers would have felt a bit poorer and would have bought fewer CDs. This illustrates the **income effect,** the change in quantity demanded because of a change in price that alters consumers' real income.

The Substitution Effect

A lower price also means that CDs will be relatively less expensive than other goods and services such as concerts and movies. As a result, consumers will have a tendency to replace a more costly item— say, going to a concert—with a less costly one—more CDs. The **substitution effect** is the change in quantity demanded because of the change in the relative price of the product. Together, the income and substitution effects explain why consumers increase their consumption of CDs from 6 to 10 when the price drops from $15 to $10.

Whenever a price change causes a change in quantity demanded, the change appears graphically as a movement *along* the demand curve. The change in quantity demanded, as **illustrated** in Figure 4.3, can be either an increase or a decrease, but in either case the demand curve itself does not shift.

✓**Reading Check** **Describing** How is a change in the quantity demanded illustrated on the demand curve?

Graphing the Law of Demand

Authentic Assessment Strategies and Activities, p. 4

Objective: Graph the demand curve and identify factors leading to shifts in demand.

Focus/Teach: Review the graphs shown in the chapter. Then divide students into groups and have them complete the activity.

Assess: Review the answers as a class. Then have each group present its product.

Close: Have each student summarize the determinants of demand.

Differentiated Instruction Strategies

BL Have students explain why the demand curves shift right or left.

AL Have students choose one of the scenarios and write what would happen to the demand curve.

ELL Have students give their own examples for each of the factors affecting demand.

Figure 4.4 ▶ **Change in Demand**

▶ A change in demand occurs when people decide to purchase different amounts of a product at the same price. When we plot the numbers from the demand schedule, we get two separate demand curves. An increase in demand appears as a shift of the demand curve to the right. A decrease in demand appears as a shift to the left.

Graphs In MOtion
See StudentWorks™ Plus or glencoe.com.

Economic Analysis *What might cause a change in demand for CDs?*

A DEMAND SCHEDULE		
Price	D	D'
$30	0	1
25	1	3
20	3	6
15	6	10
10	10	15
5	15	20

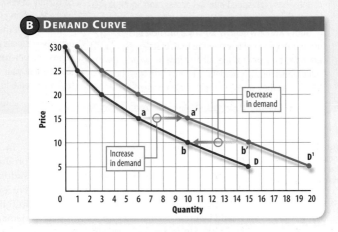

B DEMAND CURVE

Change in Demand

MAIN Idea Several factors can cause the demand curve to shift.

Economics & You Can you remember something fashionable that quickly went out of style? Read on to learn how changing consumer tastes affect demand.

Sometimes other factors change while the price remains the same. When this happens, people may decide to buy *different* amounts of the product at the same prices. This is known as a **change in demand.** As a result, the entire demand curve shifts—to the right to show an increase in demand, or to the left to show a decrease in demand. Therefore, a *change in demand* results in an entirely new demand curve, while a *change in quantity demanded* is a movement along the original demand curve.

A change in demand is illustrated in the schedule and graph in **Figure 4.4.** Note that

Panel A has a third column showing that people are willing to buy different amounts at each and every price. At a price of $15, for example, consumers are now willing to buy 10 CDs instead of 6, moving from point **a** to point **a´**. When this information is transferred to the graph, the demand curve appears to have shifted to the right.

When demand changes, a new schedule or curve must be constructed to reflect the new quantities demanded at all possible prices. Demand can change because of changes in the determinants of demand: consumer income, consumer tastes, the price of related goods, expectations, and the number of consumers.

Consumer Income

Changes in consumer income can cause a change in demand. An increase in income means people can afford to buy more at all possible prices. Suppose, for example, that

change in demand shift of the demand curve when people buy different amounts at every price

CHAPTER 4 Demand **99**

Leveled Activities

D Differentiated Instruction

English Language Learners
Tell students that an item's *popularity* grows when more and more people like it. **Ask:** What foods are popular in your school's cafeteria? What makes them popular? *(Answers will vary, but students will likely recognize that the foods are popular because the majority of students enjoy eating them.)* **ELL**

W Writing Support

Narrative Writing Have students write a short story about how a rumor or an unfavorable report affects the demand of a product or service. For example, students might imagine how a negative report on death rates might affect a hospital. **AL**

R Reading Strategy

Making Connections Have students suggest more examples of substitute goods. Write the list on the board. *(Possible answers: Coke and Pepsi; beef and chicken; minivans and SUVs.)* Remind students to consider their own behavior when thinking about how a change in the price of a related product will affect demand. **OL**

Hands-On Chapter Project
Step 2

The Global Economy & YOU

Digital Demand in South Korea

When a financial crisis hit Asia over a decade ago, South Koreans decided to invest in technology to spur economic development. Today over 70 percent of the country has high-speed Internet access, and South Korea boasts the world's largest Wi-Fi network.

South Koreans eagerly embrace the new technology, using it in ways unknown in the United States. For example, they pay for the subway fare by swiping their cell phones through readers. Students access Webcast tutorials as they study for their version of the SAT.

The increasing demand for new technology is most evident in cell phones. South Koreans replace their cell phones as often as every six months. That puts pressure on companies to constantly develop upgraded models with new and exciting features.

It also has turned South Korea into a nation-wide focus group on cell phones. The phone you purchase today may well have features that your South Korean peers tested for you 6 to 12 months earlier.

---

substitutes
competing products that can be used in place of one another

Mike and Julia get a raise, which allows them to buy more CDs. Instead of Mike and Julia each buying 3 for a total of 6 when the price is $15, they can now each buy 5—for a total of 10. If we plot how many CDs would be purchased at every possible price in the market as demand curve D^1 in Figure 4.4, then it appears as if the curve has shifted to the right.

Exactly the opposite could happen if there was a decrease in income and Mike and Julia bought less. The demand curve would then shift to the left, showing a decrease in demand.

Consumer Tastes

Consumers sometimes change their minds about the products they buy. Advertising, fashion trends, and even changes in the season can affect consumer tastes. For example, when a product is successfully advertised, its popularity increases and people tend to buy more of it. As a result, the demand curve shifts to the right.

On the other hand, people will buy less of a product if they get tired of it. This is exactly what happens when a rumor or unfavorable report about a product appears. When fewer people want the product at all possible prices, the demand curve shifts to the left, showing a decrease in demand.

In addition, the development of new products can have a dramatic and relatively sudden impact on consumer preferences. For example, when music CDs were first introduced on the market, they reduced the demand for cassette players and tapes, shifting the demand curves for both to the left. When the iPod and similar devices arrived, the demand for CDs and CD players decreased.

Sometimes the change in consumer tastes and preferences is relatively rapid, and sometimes the change occurs more slowly. In recent years, for example, consumer concerns about health have slowly increased the demand for healthful foods.

Substitutes

A change in the price of related products can cause a change in demand. Some products are known as **substitutes** because they can be used in place of other products. For example, if people treat butter and margarine as substitutes, a rise in the price of butter will cause an increase in the demand for margarine. Likewise, a rise in the price of margarine would cause the demand for butter to increase. In general, the demand for a product tends to increase if the price of its substitute goes up. The demand for a product tends to decrease if the price of its substitute goes down.

Making Decisions About Demand and Elasticity

Step 2: Identifying Relevant Demand Determinants. Students will determine which demand determinants they might manipulate to increase demand.

Directions: Have students return to their previous groups, review the information in the section, and discuss how each determinant might apply to their product. For example, they should identify what products might be substitutes or complements and whether

fashion or health information might apply. Have groups plan an advertising campaign aimed at manipulating one of the determinants in the hopes of increasing demand for their product.

Designing Have groups write ad copy, draw pictures, or choose a photo to represent their ad campaign. **OL**

(Chapter Project continued in Section 3.)

Complements

Other related goods are known as **complements,** because the use of one increases the use of the other. Personal computers and software are two complementary goods. When the price of computers decreases, consumers buy more S computers *and* more software. If the price of computers spirals upward, consumers would buy fewer computers and less software. Thus, an increase in the price of one good usually leads to a decrease in the demand for its complement.

Expectations

The way people think about the future can affect demand. For example, suppose that a company announces a technological breakthrough in television picture quality. Even if the new product might not be available for a year, some consumers might hold off buying a TV today due to their expectations. Purchasing less at every price would cause demand to decline, illustrated by a shift of the demand curve to the left.

Of course, expectations can also have the opposite effect on market demand. For example, if the weather service forecasts a bad year for crops, people might stock up on some foods before these items actually become scarce. The willingness to buy more because of expected future shortages would cause demand to increase, shown by a shift S of the demand curve to the right.

Number of Consumers

A change in income, tastes, and prices of related products affects *individual* demand schedules and curves—and hence the *market* demand curve. The market demand curve can also change if there is a change in the number of consumers.

Suppose that Devan, one of Mike's and Julia's friends, decides to purchase CDs. We would add the number of CDs that Devan would buy at all possible prices to those for Mike and Julia. The market demand curve would shift to the right to reflect an increase in demand. If Mike or Devan should leave the market, the total number of CDs purchased would decrease, shifting the market demand curve to the left.

✓**Reading Check** **Explaining** How do changes in consumer income and tastes affect the demand curve?

Economics ONLINE
Student Web Activity Visit the *Economics: Principles and Practices* Web site at glencoe.com and click on *Chapter 4–Student Web Activities* for an activity on change in demand.

complements products that increase the use of other products

S Skill Practice

Making Inferences List the following products on the board: peanut butter, hamburger, CD player, car, TV. Have students suggest complements for the products. *(Possible answers: peanut butter: bread, jelly; hamburger: bun, ketchup, cheese; CD player: CDs, headphones; car: gasoline; TV: cable service)* OL

✓**Reading Check** **Answer:** If people make more money or come to like a product, demand goes up; if consumers make less money or no longer like a product, demand goes down.

Assess

💿 Use the Interactive Tutor Self-Assessment CD-ROM to review Section 2, and then assign the Section 2 Review as homework or as an in-class activity.

Close

Summarizing Have students list and briefly explain the factors that cause a change in demand. OL

Review **SECTION 2**

SECTION 2 Review

Vocabulary
1. **Explain** the significance of change in quantity demanded, income effect, substitution effect, change in demand, substitutes, and complements.

Main Ideas
2. **Explaining** What is the difference between a change in quantity demanded and a change in demand?
3. **Describing** Using a graphic organizer similar to the one below, describe the determinants of market demand.

Determinants of market demand

Critical Thinking
4. **The BIG Idea** How and why does a change in price affect the demand for substitutes? Provide an example.
5. **Analyzing Visuals** Look at Figure 4.4 on page 99. Assume that a new CD format will come out soon. What do you think will happen to the market demand curve D? Explain.
6. **Interpreting** Locate an article in your newspaper illustrating at least one determinant of demand. Write a brief explanation of the effect of the determinant(s).

Applying Economics
7. **Change in Demand** Name a product that you recently purchased because it was on sale. Identify one substitute and one complement for the product and describe how your demand for the substitute and complement changed because of the sale.

Answers

1. All definitions can be found in the section and the Glossary.
2. A change in quantity demanded is a change in a single quantity that occurs as a result of a change in price; a change in demand is a change in all the quantities demanded at all possible prices.
3. consumer income (increase or decrease in how much people make); consumer tastes (change in what people like and dislike); substitutes (products that can be used in place of other products); complements (products whose use increases the use of other products); expectations (the way people think about the future); number of consumers (increase or decrease in number of people interested in purchasing a product)
4. When the price of a good rises, it becomes less attractive to consumers, as per the Law of Demand. This encourages consumers to buy substitutes for the good, which constitutes a change in demand for the substitute. Students' examples will vary.
5. It will likely shift to the left, indicating a decrease in demand as the result of consumers buying the new CD format instead.
6. **Possible answer:** Doctors discover that a food is very beneficial to health. Consumer preferences for that food increase, as does demand.
7. Answers will vary but should illustrate substitutes and complements and how they are affected by a sale price.

Teach

C Critical Thinking

Distinguishing Fact from Opinion Ask: What is one fact and one opinion given in the feature? *(Answers will vary but may include as a fact that Winfrey moved to Chicago in 1984. An opinion might be the description of Oprah as "likable" in the caption.)*
OL

W Writing Support

Expository Writing Have students make an annotated time line of Winfrey's career, highlighting the achievements discussed in the feature. **BL**

Examining the Profile

Answers:

1. Winfrey is the first woman to produce and own her own talk show and the first African American woman to own a major television and film studio.
2. Answers will vary but may include ambition, determination, and confidence.

Additional Support

Most people know Oprah Winfrey as a talk show host. Over the years, though, the likable Winfrey has developed many other talents to become one of the wealthiest, most successful, and most influential women in America.

c Profiles in Economics

Oprah Winfrey (1954–)

- first woman in history to produce and own her own talk show
- first African American woman—and third woman in history—to own a major television and film studio

The Gift of Gab

Oprah Winfrey grew up in deep poverty. As a troubled teenager, she went to live with her father, who encouraged her education. Four years later Winfrey received a scholarship to attend Tennessee State University. At the same time, she got her first media job as a radio news announcer. Two years later Winfrey became cohost of a talk show—and found her calling. Winfrey felt comfortable talking in front of cameras, and viewers responded to her easygoing attitude by making her program the number-one talk show in the Baltimore market.

In 1984 Winfrey relocated to Chicago to take over the failing talk show **W** *A.M. Chicago.* Just as in Baltimore, the audience responded to her relaxed manner by watching in increasing numbers. Within two years, the show, renamed *The Oprah Winfrey Show,* became nationally syndicated, and today viewers watch her in more than 100 countries. The syndication deal made Winfrey the highest-paid entertainer at the time, with estimated earnings of over $37 million in 1987.

Building a Media Empire

Winfrey used this money and her personal ambition to build a wide-ranging business empire. In 1986 she established her own company, Harpo Inc. (*Harpo* is *Oprah* spelled backward.) A production company and movie studio grew from that venture. Since then, Winfrey has become cofounder of the Oxygen television network and branched out into print media through the publications *O, The Oprah Magazine,* and *O at Home.*

Success has allowed Winfrey to spend a portion of her income on charities that support education and help families. That portion is rising. *Forbes* magazine listed Winfrey as the first African American woman to become a billionaire. Her annual income, estimated at over $225 million by 2006, has increased ever since.

Examining the Profile

1. **Drawing Conclusions** Why is Oprah Winfrey considered to be one of the most powerful women in America?
2. **Analyzing** What characteristics helped Winfrey become a successful talk show host and entrepreneur?

102   UNIT 2   Microeconomics: Prices and Markets

Teacher Tip

Arranging Student Groups
When dividing students into groups, be sure to mix students of differing abilities and backgrounds. In particular, be sure to include a student with strong math skills in each group.

Activity: Collaborative Learning

Demographics Have students work together in small groups to calculate Oprah's influence in quantitative terms. Share this information with them: Oprah's show has reached as many as ten million people daily in more than 190 cities in 112 countries. On average, when the *Oprah Winfrey Show* airs, about 7 percent of households with televisions are tuned into it. Have students research the populations of five countries as well as the number of households with televisions. They should then calculate how many people in those countries are reached on an average day by Oprah's show. **OL**

SECTION 3 — Elasticity of Demand

GUIDE TO READING

Section Preview

In this section you will learn about the factors that influence the size of a change in quantity demanded.

Content Vocabulary

- elasticity (p. 103)
- demand elasticity (p. 104)
- elastic (p. 104)
- inelastic (p. 104)
- unit elastic (p. 105)

Academic Vocabulary

- technical (p. 106)
- adequate (p. 108)

Reading Strategy

Describing As you read about price elasticity, complete a web diagram like the one below to describe what effect a change in price has on quantity demanded if the demand curve is elastic, inelastic, or unit elastic.

Change in Price

COMPANIES IN THE NEWS
—www.entertainmentculture.com

Netflix, Blockbuster Battle It Out

Netflix and Blockbuster continue to battle head to head in the online movie rental arena. The monthly rental prices have dropped for DVD entertainment delivered to your door, ordered online. . . . Entertainment culture at its best, it seems—lots of competition and that is normally a better price point for the consumer.

[Reed Hastings, the CEO of Netflix, says,] "One of the reasons our last year has been so successful is the market's elasticity in response to our price cuts one year ago. . . . Obviously, if there's enough elasticity to make additional price cuts work, this would increase the economic pressure on video stores, and the additional store closures would further increase Netflix growth for many years ahead."

In 2006, Netflix expects to grow to 5.65 million subscribers with pretax net income between $50 million and $60 million. ■

You can find cause-and-effect relationships everywhere, and they are especially important to businesses. For example, Netflix had hoped that lower prices would entice customers to rent more movies and thus increase its overall revenues. The gamble paid off. Company CEO Reed Hastings credited the market's demand elasticity for the company's success.

Elasticity is a general measure of responsiveness—an important cause-and-effect relationship in economics. It tells us how a dependent variable, such as quantity demanded, responds to a change in an independent variable, such as price. Elasticity is a general concept that can also be applied to other measures such as income or supply.

elasticity
a measure of responsiveness that shows how one variable responds to a change in another variable

CHAPTER 4 Demand 103

R Reading Strategies	C Critical Thinking	D Differentiated Instruction	W Writing Support	S Skill Practice
Teacher Edition • Det. Importance, p. 106 • Monitoring, p. 107 **Additional Resources** • Guid. Read. Act., p. 12 • Read. Ess. & Note-Taking Guide, p. 28 • Pri./Sec. Source Read., p. 9	**Teacher Edition** • Predicting, p. 104 • Making Inferences, p. 105 • Drawing Con., p. 110 • Problem-Solving, p. 115 **Additional Resources** • Math Prac. for Econ., p. 4	**Teacher Edition** • ELL, p. 104 • Special Ed., p. 108 • Adv. Learners., p. 109 • Auditory/Musical, p. 110 **Additional Resources** • Econ. Cont. Vocab. Act., p. 4 • Reading and Study Skills Fold., p. 51	**Teacher Edition** • Expository Writing, p. 106 • Narrative Writing, p. 108 **Additional Resources** • High School Reading in the Content Area Strat. and Act.	**Teacher Edition** • Comparing Data, p. 104 • Using Tables and Charts, p. 105 • Interpreting Political Cartoons, p. 107 • Visual Literacy, p. 114 **Additional Resources** • Reteaching, p. 4

Teach

D Differentiated Instruction

English Language Learners

Guide students in pronouncing the term *elastic*. Help them understand the meaning by showing them a piece of elastic and how it stretches. Extend their understanding by pointing out that the prefix *in-* means "without." **Ask:** Which stretches, or changes, more—something that is elastic or inelastic? *(something that is elastic)* **ELL**

C Critical Thinking

Predicting Ask students to suggest other products where demand may be inelastic. Make a list on the board. As you continue the section, have students discuss the validity of their suggestions. **AL**

S Skill Practice

Comparing Data Have students compare the data shown in the two graphs. **Ask:** Which graph shows the greatest change in expenditure? *(the elastic demand graph)* **OL**

Additional Support

---

demand elasticity a measure that shows how a change in quantity demanded responds to a change in price

elastic type of elasticity where a change in price causes a relatively larger change in quantity demanded

inelastic type of elasticity where a change in price causes a relatively smaller change in quantity demanded

---

Demand Elasticity

MAIN Idea When the price of an item changes, the change in quantity demanded can vary a little or a lot.

Economics & You If there was a huge sale on table salt, would you stock up? Read on to learn how elasticity describes your response to the price change.

Consumers react to a change in price by changing the quantity demanded, although the size of their reaction can vary. This response is known as **demand elasticity**—the extent to which a change in price causes a change in the quantity demanded.

D Elastic Demand

Economists say that demand is **elastic** when a given change in price causes a relatively larger change in quantity demanded. To illustrate, look at how price and quantity demanded change between points **a** and **b** on the demand curve in **Panel A** of **Figure 4.5.**

As we move from point **a** to point **b,** we see that price declines by one-third, or from $3 to $2. At the same time, the quantity demanded doubles from two to four units. Because the percentage change in quantity demanded is relatively larger than the percentage change in price, demand between those two points is elastic.

This type of elasticity is typical of the demand for products like green beans, corn, or other fresh garden vegetables. Because prices of these products are lower in the summer, consumers increase the amount they purchase during that time. When prices are considerably higher in the winter, consumers tend to buy canned or frozen products instead.

Inelastic Demand

For other products, demand may be **inelastic,** which means that a given change in price causes a relatively smaller change in the quantity demanded. We can see the case of inelastic demand in **Panel B** of Figure 4.5. In this case, the one-third drop in price from point **a′** to **b′** causes quantity demanded to increase by only 25 percent, or from two to two and one-half units.

This is typical of the demand elasticity for a product like table salt. A change in the price for salt does not bring about much change in the quantity purchased. Even if the price was cut in half, the quantity

---

Figure 4.5 ▶ **Demand Elasticity and the Total Expenditures Test**

A **ELASTIC DEMAND**

Expenditure $6 = $3 per 2 units
Expenditure $8 = $2 per 4 units

B **INELASTIC DEMAND**

Expenditure $6 = $3 per 2 units
Expenditure $5 = $2 per 2.5 units

104   UNIT 2   Microeconomics: Prices and Markets

Extending the Content

Analyzing Policy Since raising the price of a product reduces quantity demanded, it is often suggested that harmful goods such as cigarettes should be heavily taxed. Taxing would raise the price that consumers would have to pay, therefore reducing the number of cigarettes bought. But how successful this policy would actually be is determined by the price elasticity of demand for cigarettes. If demand is inelastic, the tax will not cause cigarette buying to decrease significantly. However, if it is elastic, the tax will have a real impact on smoking. One study shows that the elasticity of demand for cigarettes is .35, or inelastic. However, this study dealt with people of all ages who smoke. Another study looked only at teenage smoking and found that demand for cigarettes by this age group is elastic. Therefore, raising taxes on cigarettes could significantly decrease teenage smoking.

demanded would not increase by much because people can consume only so much salt. Similarly, if the price doubled, we would still expect consumers to demand about the same amount, because people spend such a small portion of their budget on salt.

Unit Elastic Demand

Sometimes demand is **unit elastic,** so that a given change in price causes a proportional change in quantity demanded. When demand is unit elastic, the percentage change in quantity equals the percentage change in price. For example, a five percent drop in price would cause a five percent increase in quantity demanded. Unit elastic demand is shown in **Panel C** of Figure 4.5.

Examples of unit elasticity are difficult to find because the demand for most products is either elastic or inelastic. Unit elasticity is more like a middle ground that separates the other two categories of elasticity: elastic and inelastic.

✓Reading Check **Comparing** What is the difference between elastic and inelastic demand?

The Total Expenditures Test

MAIN Idea The total expenditures test is used to estimate the demand elasticity of a product.

Economics and You You just learned about demand elasticity. Read on to find out how businesses apply elasticity when setting prices.

To estimate elasticity, it is useful to look at the impact of a price change on total expenditures, or the amount that consumers spend on a product at a particular price. This is sometimes called the total expenditures test.

Determining Total Expenditures

We find total expenditures by multiplying the price of a product by the quantity demanded for any point along the demand curve. To illustrate, the total expenditure under point **a** in Panel A of Figure 4.5 is $6, which is determined by multiplying two units times the price of $3. Likewise, the total expenditure under point **b** in Panel A is $8, or $2 times four units. By observing the change in total expenditures when the price changes, we can test for elasticity.

unit elastic type of elasticity where a change in price causes a proportional change in quantity demanded

▶ Panels A, B, and C show how quantity demanded responds to a price change for products with elastic, inelastic, and unit elastic demand. Panel D summarizes these changes in a chart.

Economic Analysis *Why is an understanding of elasticity important for a business?*

C Critical Thinking

Making Inferences Explain to students that an actual number value for elasticity is found by dividing the percent change in quantity demanded by the percent change in price. **Ask:** *Why might the term* unit *be used to label a quantity change that, percentage-wise, is equal to a price change? (If you divide a number by an equal number, the answer is one.)* **AL**

S Skill Practice

Using Tables and Charts
Ask: *How will a decrease in price affect expenditures on an elastic good? (Expenditures will rise.) On an inelastic good? (Expenditures will fall.)* **BL**

✓Reading Check **Answer:**
Elastic: a price change causes a larger change in quantity demanded. Inelastic: a price change causes a smaller change in quantity demanded.

Economic Analysis
Answer: so it will know how one variable will respond to a change in another variable

Additional Support

Activity: Hands-On Economics

Restaurant Revenues Present students with the following scenario: You own a restaurant that is fully booked during the weekends. In mid-week, however, you rarely have enough bookings to stay open. To make more money during this slow period, you decide to cut dinner prices by one-third—from $15 to $10—on Wednesdays and Thursdays.

Ask: Do you think this action will increase your revenues? Suggest that students draw graphs similar to those in Figure 4.5 to illustrate their answers. Call on volunteers to present and discuss their graphs. **OL**

R Reading Strategy

Determining Importance
Ask: Which qualification do you think is the most important for this job? *(Possible answer: the ability to identify products that will sell)* **OL**

W Writing Support

Expository Writing Have students write two paragraphs explaining what steps they could take to raise revenues in a business of their choice. Tell students to give extensive consideration to the issue of elasticity. **OL**

Differentiated Instruction

Math Practice for Economics, p. 4

Three Results

The relationship between changing prices and total expenditures is summarized in the four panels of Figure 4.5 on the previous page. The figure shows how a decrease in price from $3 to $2 impacts total expenditures for each of the demand curves. In each case, the change in expenditures depends on the elasticity of the demand curve.

CAREERS

Buyer

The Work

* Purchase merchandise for resale to the public

* Study sales records, inventory levels of current stock, determine foreign and domestic suppliers, and determine supply and demand for products and materials

* Choose suppliers, negotiate the lowest price, and award contracts

* Stay informed about new products and trends, attend trade shows, assist in sales promotions and advertising campaigns, check on displays

Qualifications

* Ability to plan, analyze data provided by suppliers, make decisions quickly, work under pressure, and identify products that will sell

* Good communication, negotiation, and mathematical skills

* Knowledge of supply-chain management

* Bachelor's degree with a business emphasis

Earnings

* Median annual earnings: $42,230

Job Growth Outlook

* Slower than average

Source: *Occupational Outlook Handbook, 2006–2007 Edition*

The demand curve in Panel A is elastic. When the price drops by $1 per unit, the increase in the quantity demanded is large enough to raise total expenditures from $6 to $8. The relationship between the change in price and total expenditures for the elastic demand curve is described as "inverse." In other words, when the price goes down, total expenditures go up.

The demand curve in Panel B is inelastic. In this case, when the price drops by $1, the increase in the quantity demanded is so small that total expenditures fall below $6. For inelastic demand, total expenditures decline when the price declines. Finally, the demand curve in Panel C is unit elastic. This time, total expenditures remain unchanged when the price decreases from $3 to $2.

Determining Elasticity

The relationship between the change in price and the change in total expenditures is shown in **Panel D** of Figure 4.5. If the changes in price and expenditures move in opposite directions, demand is elastic. If they move in the same direction, demand is inelastic. If there is no change in expenditure, demand is unit elastic.

Even though all the price changes we just discussed were decreases, the results would be the same if prices had gone up instead of down. If the price rises from $2 to $3 in Panel A, spending falls from $8 to $6. Prices and expenditures still move in opposite directions, as shown in the table.

Elasticity and Revenues

While this discussion about elasticity may seem **technical** and somewhat unnecessary to you, knowledge of demand elasticity is extremely important to most businesses. Suppose, for example, that you run your own business and want to do something that will raise your revenues. You could try to stay open longer, or you could try to advertise in order to increase sales. You might, however, also be tempted to raise the price of your product in order to increase total revenue from sales.

Recognizing Demand and Elastic Demand

Objective: Understand how elasticity affects total expenditure.

Focus/Teach: Ask students to name a good that they have bought at different prices. Have them speculate on how their purchases affected total revenues.

Assess: Have students check each other's answers.

Close: Ask students why it is important to know your product or service's elasticity of demand before changing its price.

Differentiated Instruction Strategies

BL Have pairs explain how price changes affect expenditures for goods with different elasticities.

AL Ask students how a business owner might use the concept of elasticity.

ELL Have students make flash cards to coach themselves on the effects of elasticity on expenditures.

www.CartoonStock.com

Total Expenditures and Demand Elasticity Some consumers, such as the painter in this cartoon, buy more than they need when items go on sale. ***What kind of demand elasticity is depicted in this cartoon, and what happened to total expenditures for green paint?***

THEY HAD A SALE ON ELECTRIC GREEN

This might actually work in the case of table salt or medical services, because the demand for both products is generally inelastic. However, what would happen if you sold a product with elastic demand? If you raise the price, your total revenue—which is the same as consumer expenditures—will go down instead of up. This outcome is exactly the opposite of what you intended!

This is exactly why some businesses experiment with different prices when they introduce a new product to the market. They may adjust prices repeatedly to see how customers respond to new prices. If a business can determine a new product's demand elasticity, it can find the price that will maximize total revenues. This is why demand elasticity is more important than most people realize.

✓ Reading Check **Explaining** What happens to the total expenditures for a product with elastic demand when its price goes up?

Determinants of Demand Elasticity

MAIN Idea The answers to three questions help determine a product's demand elasticity.

Economics and You Can you think of an item you delayed buying because it was too expensive? Read on to learn how your decision to wait is a way to determine the elasticity of a product.

What makes the demand for a specific good elastic or inelastic? To find out, we can ask three questions about the product. The answers will give us a reasonably good idea about the product's demand elasticity.

Can the Purchase Be Delayed?

Sometimes consumers cannot postpone the purchase of a product. This tends to make demand inelastic, meaning that the quantity of the product demanded is not especially sensitive to changes in price.

🖐 Skills Handbook

See page R36 to learn about Determining Cause and Effect.

CHAPTER 4 Demand **107**

S **Skill Practice**

Interpreting Political Cartoons **Ask:** What economic concept does this cartoon illustrate? Explain. *(elastic demand; the man bought several cans of electric green paint because it was on sale)* **OL**

R **Reading Strategy**

Monitoring Tell students that asking themsel ves questions as they read can help them check their understanding of a text. Have students check their comprehension by asking the following question as they read the bracketed paragraph: Why do some businesses experiment with different prices when they introduce a new product? *(Businesses sometimes experiment because they don't know the product's elasticity. Changing price is one way to find out.)* **OL**

Caption Answer: elastic; they went up

✓ Reading Check **Answer:** They go down.

Leveled Activities

107

D Differentiated Instruction

Special Education Ask: Can purchasing table salt be delayed? *(no)* Are there adequate substitutes for butter? *(yes)* To help students answer these questions, suggest that they use a blank sheet of paper to cover the areas of the chart that they aren't using. **BL**

W Writing Support

Narrative Writing Have students write a short story about someone who has inelastic demand for a product but is faced with a significant price change. Students can use medicine or drugs but could also invent examples of their own, such as the gas needed to get to a job interview or a special gift for an important person. **OL**

Economic Analysis

Answer: The purchase can be delayed, there are adequate substitutes, and the purchase is likely to take up a large portion of the budget. For all these reasons, demand for a luxury good would tend to be elastic.

Hands-On Chapter Project

Step 3

Figure 4.6 ▶ Determinants of Demand Elasticity

▶ The elasticity of demand can usually be estimated by examining the answers to three key questions. All three answers do not have to be the same in order to determine elasticity, and in some cases the answer to a single question is so important that it alone might override the answers to the other two.

Economic Analysis *If you applied the three questions to a luxury product, what would be the elasticity of demand for that product?*

PRODUCTS							
Determinants of elasticity **If yes: elastic** **If no: inelastic**	**Fresh tomatoes, corn, or green beans**	**Table salt**	**Gasoline from a particular station**	**Gasoline in general**	**Services of medical doctors**	**Insulin**	**Butter**
Can purchase be delayed?	Yes	No	Yes	No	No	No	Yes
Are adequate substitutes available?	Yes	No	Yes	No	No	No	Yes
Does purchase use a large portion of income?	No	No	Yes	Yes	Yes	No	No
Type of elasticity	Elastic	Inelastic	Elastic	Inelastic	Inelastic	Inelastic	Elastic

For example, persons with diabetes need insulin to control the disorder. An increase in its price is not likely to make diabetes sufferers delay buying and using the product. The demand for tobacco also tends to be inelastic because the product is addictive. As a result, a sharp increase in price will lower the quantity purchased by consumers, but not by very much. The change in quantity demanded is also likely to be relatively small for these products when their prices go down instead of up.

W If the products were corn, tomatoes, or gasoline from a particular station, however, people might react differently to a price change. If the prices of these products were to increase, consumers could delay buying any of these items without suffering any great inconvenience.

Figure 4.6 summarizes some of these observations. If the answer to the question "Can the purchase be delayed?" is yes, then the demand for the product is likely to be elastic. If the answer to the question is no, then demand is likely to be inelastic.

Are Adequate Substitutes Available?

If **adequate** substitutes are available, consumers can switch back and forth between the product and its substitute to take advantage of the best price. If the price of beef goes up, buyers can switch to chicken. With enough substitutes, even small changes in the price of a product will cause people to switch, making the demand for the product elastic. The fewer substitutes available for a product, the more inelastic the demand.

Sometimes only a single adequate substitute is needed to make demand elastic. For example, in the past there were few substitutes for sending a letter through the post office. Then fax machines allowed messages to be transmitted over phone lines. Today many people use e-mail on the Internet or send instant messages on their cell phones. Because of all these alternatives, it is more difficult for the U.S. Postal Service to increase its total revenues by raising the price of a first-class stamp.

Making Decisions About Demand and Elasticity

Step 3: Comparing Demand Schedules With the Determinants of Elasticity.

Students will use their demand schedules to calculate elasticity and then analyze their product with the determinants of elasticity.

Directions: Have students calculate elasticity of demand for their product using the total expenditure test and the demand schedules they made when surveying classmates. Then

have students evaluate their product according to the determinants of elasticity listed in the text. Students should summarize their comparison in a paragraph. If the two elasticities are different, students should write another paragraph in which they choose and defend which elasticity they will use when writing their price and sales histories. **OL**

(Chapter Project continued in Visual Summary.)

Note that the size of the market is important. For example, the demand for gasoline from a particular station tends to be elastic because consumers can buy gas at another station. If we ask about the demand for gasoline in general, however, demand is much more inelastic because there are few adequate substitutes for gasoline.

Does the Purchase Use a Large Portion of Income?

The third determinant is the amount of income required to make the purchase. If the amount is large, then demand tends to be elastic. If the amount of income is small, demand tends to be inelastic.

Finally, you may have noticed that the answers to our three questions is not always "yes" or "no" for each of the products shown in Figure 4.6. For example, some products such as salt may be easy to classify, since each of the answers is "no." However, we have to use our judgment on others. For

example, the demand for the services of medical doctors tends to be inelastic even though they require a large portion of income. This is because most people prefer to receive medical care right away rather than taking the time to look for adequate substitutes.

✓ **Reading Check** **Identifying** Can you think of other goods with inelastic demand? Why is the demand for those goods inelastic?

D **Differentiated Instruction**

Advanced Learners Point out to students that, while the demand for some products may seem inelastic, over time demand may grow somewhat more elastic. Have students find examples of such products. (*Possible answer: rise in gas prices in the 1970s eventually made demand more elastic*) **AL**

✓ **Reading Check** **Possible Answer:** food in general—no adequate substitutes; pencils—small portion of budget

Assess

💿 Use the Interactive Tutor Self-Assessment CD-ROM to review Section 3, and then assign the Section 3 Review as homework or as an in-class activity.

Close

Making Connections Have students list the five most elastic products they buy and the five most inelastic products they buy. **OL**

SECTION 3 Review

Vocabulary
1. **Explain** the significance of elasticity, demand elasticity, elastic, inelastic, and unit elastic.

Main Ideas
2. **Describing** How do consumers react to price changes on products with elastic, inelastic, and unit elastic demand?
3. **Explaining** How do total expenditures relate to the demand elasticity for products?
4. **Organizing** Use a graphic organizer like the one below to describe the three determinants of demand elasticity.

Determinant	Description

Critical Thinking
5. **The BIG Idea** Why is the demand for airplane tickets inelastic for last-minute ticket purchases?

6. **Understanding Cause and Effect** A hamburger stand raised the price of its hamburgers from $2.00 to $2.50. As a result, its sales of hamburgers fell from 200 per day to 180 per day. Was the demand for its hamburgers elastic or inelastic? Why?
7. **Analyzing Visuals** Based on Figure 4.6 on page 108, create your own chart for the following products: an MP3 player, electricity, a gallon of milk, an ink pen, and a pound of onions. Explain.
8. **Drawing Conclusions** Airlines in the United States generally do not offer reduced round-trip airfares during holidays such as Easter, Thanksgiving, and Christmas. What can you conclude about the elasticity of demand for airplane travel at these times?

Applying Economics
9. **Elasticity of Demand** Interview an owner or manager of a local business about the effects of recent price increases for a product. Is the demand for these goods or services elastic or inelastic? Why?

Review **SECTION 3**

Answers

1. All definitions can be found in the section and the Glossary.
2. When a price changes on an elastic good, consumers make proportionally greater changes in quantity demanded. For an inelastic good, the change in quantity is proportionally smaller than the change in price. The changes are proportionally the same for a good with unit elasticity.
3. For a given price change, total expenditures will rise or fall depending on the elasticity of demand for a product.
4. **Determinant:** Can purchase be delayed? If yes, demand will be more elastic. **Determinant:** Are adequate substitutes available? If yes, demand will be more elastic. **Determinant:** Does the purchase use a large portion of income? If yes, demand will be more elastic.
5. The purchase probably cannot be delayed, nor will there be good substitutes available.
6. Inelastic; prices rose from $2.00 to $2.50 and total expenditures rose from $400 to $450.
7. Answers will vary but should reflect the determinants of elasticity for each product.
8. **Possible answer:** Because people desire so strongly to travel at those specific times, the purchase cannot be delayed and there are few adequate substitutes. Therefore, demand will be relatively inelastic.
9. Answers will vary, but students should draw conclusions about a product's elasticity.

Focus

D Differentiated Instruction

Auditory/Musical Have students write a journal entry detailing their experiences with the iTunes Store or handheld music devices. **OL**

Teach

C Critical Thinking

Drawing Conclusions

Ask: How does Apple's digital rights management technology affect the elasticity of demand for iPods? *(It makes the demand less elastic.)* **OL**

Analyzing the Impact

Answers:

1. The iPod was smaller and could hold more songs. Also, it gave users access to the iTunes Store. Subsequent innovations kept the iPod in the dominant position.
2. Apple continues to innovate, making the iPod ever smaller and more adaptable.

Additional Support

CASE STUDY

The iPod

The Idea

Handheld music devices date back to the 1970s, when Sony introduced the Walkman. So why has the iPod dominated the MP3 market in the early 2000s?

When the iPod hit store shelves in November 2001, other MP3 players were already on the market. Yet they were larger than the 6.5-ounce iPod, and they could not hold nearly as many songs. The iPod was an instant hit.

APPLE'S REVENUE 2000–2006*

Revenue (in billions), $0–$24

Years: 2001, 2002, 2003, 2004, 2005, 2006*

Source: www.apple.com   *2006 earnings projected

Innovation

Technology set off the iPod in other ways. The mechanical scroll wheel allowed easy scrolling and navigation. FireWire allowed much faster transfer of music from the computer to the iPod.

In 2003 Apple CEO Steve Jobs announced that the iTunes software, formerly used to store and play digital music on a Mac, would become a gateway to the online iTunes Store. The owners of iPods now were able to download songs for just 99¢ each. While Apple makes only about .10¢ per

sale, it generates many more iPod sales. On top of that, music from the iTunes Music Store can be played only on Apple devices because of Apple's digital rights management technology. This tempts more people to purchase iPods.

Staying Ahead of the Pack

Apple continues to innovate. In January 2004, Apple introduced the iPod mini. Its "click wheel" removed the need for buttons. Newer models can hold ever larger volumes of data, while tiny flash-memory chips keep the player size small. Today's iPods can store up to 10,000 songs, hold hundreds of photos, and play entire movies. Adapters connect iPods with car or home stereo systems. By constantly updating, Apple has been able to keep its huge market share ever since the iPod was introduced.

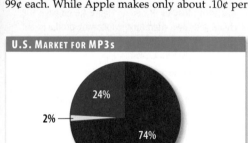

U.S. MARKET FOR MP3s

24%
2%
74%

● Apple   ○ Sony   ● All others

Source: *BusinessWeek*

Analyzing the Impact

1. **Summarizing** What features allowed Apple's iPod to dominate the market?
2. **Drawing Conclusions** How does Apple continue to stay ahead of the competition?

Extending the Content

iPod Innovations Apple has now partnered with Nike in such a way as to decrease elasticity for both the iPod Nano and Nike running shoes. The companies have developed a Sport Kit that enables athletic shoes to communicate with the iPod, so that athletes can get real-time feedback and commentary on their workouts. The kit includes a sensor that goes in the running shoe and a receiver that goes in the iPod, enabling the iPod to provide audible updates on the runner's speed, distance, and calories burned. Workouts can be customized according to goals, and the athlete's weight can be entered to more accurately measure burned calories. The kit can also be calibrated according to gait, running surface, incline, or temperature. Although it is a luxury, there are as yet no substitutes for this device. Hence, one can expect demand for the good to be inelastic.

STUDY TO GO

Study anywhere, anytime! Download quizzes and flash cards to your PDA from glencoe.com.

▶ **Law of Demand** The Law of Demand states that when the price goes up, quantity demanded goes down. When the price goes down, quantity demanded goes up.

When the price goes up . . .

quantity demanded goes down . . .

When the price goes down . . .

quantity demanded goes up . . .

▶ **Change in Demand** When a change in demand occurs, people want to buy different amounts of a product at the same price. A change in demand can happen for several reasons.

Consumer tastes

Consumer income

Price of substitutes

Change in Demand

Number of consumers

Expectations

Price of complements

▶ **Demand and Elasticity** Changes in price and total expenditures help determine the demand elasticity of a product.

Type of Demand	Change in Price	Change in Expenditure	Movement of Price and Expenditure
Elastic	↓	↑	Opposite
Inelastic	↓	↓	Same
Unit elastic	↓	No change	

CHAPTER 4 Demand **111**

Assessing Ask students to think about the goods that they purchase. Using information from the text, have them make a judgment as to which good has the most elastic demand and the most inelastic demand. Have students write a paragraph about each good, explaining why the good has certain demand characteristics. **OL**

Personal Writing Tell students to write an essay in which they choose three products that they currently purchase and describe how a change in each determinant of demand would affect the amount of the good that they purchase. **OL**

Hands-On Chapter Project

Step 4: Wrap Up

Making Decisions About Demand and Elasticity

Step 4: Bringing It All Together.
Students will synthesize what they learned in Steps 1–3.

Directions: Instruct each group to outline the progress of business practices and sales for their product over the course of a year, as if they were reporting to imaginary stockholders. Groups should choose an initial price, with the resulting quantity sold given by the market demand schedule. Students should then predict what would happen to demand following their ad campaign, and choose a new price that might result. Students should use their decisions regarding elasticity when determining the new quantity and total expenditure (sales figures) that would result. Presentations should include copy, graphs, visuals, and any events that might have happened, such as the product being put on sale, seasonal variations, and so on. Groups should use their reports to make oral presentations to the class, as if the class constituted a stockholder's meeting. **OL**

Assessment and Activities

ExamView®
Assessment Suite

This easy-to-use software includes extensive question banks and allows you to create fully customized tests that can be administered in print or online.

Review Content Vocabulary

1.	e	2.	d
3.	b	4.	g
5.	h	6.	c
7.	i	8.	a
9.	j	10.	f

Review Academic Vocabulary

11.–16. Students' sentences will vary but should demonstrate understanding of each term's meaning in an economic context.

Review the Main Ideas

17. A demand schedule shows the quantities demanded of a good at all prices. A demand curve is a graph showing the same information.

18. The law expresses the inverse relationship that exists between price and quantity demanded.

19. The principle says that the more of a product we consume, the less satisfaction we will receive from consuming additional units. The demand curve indicates that we will purchase additional units of a good only if the price drops.

20. Income effect: When the price of a good drops, consumers have extra income and might buy more of the good, increasing demand. Substitution effect: If the price of a good rises, consumers will buy cheaper substitutes, decreasing demand.

112

Review Content Vocabulary

On a separate sheet of paper, match the letter of the term best described by each statement below.

a. demand
b. demand elasticity
c. change in demand
d. demand curve
e. Law of Demand
f. complement
g. elastic demand
h. substitutes
i. marginal utility
j. unit elastic demand

1. statement that more will be demanded at lower prices and less at higher prices

2. graph that shows the quantity demanded at all possible prices in the market at a given time

3. measure of responsiveness relating change in quantity demanded to a change in price

4. a given change in price causes a relatively larger change in quantity demanded

5. products that can be used in place of one another

6. a principle illustrating that consumers demand different amounts at every price, causing the demand curve to shift to the left or the right

7. additional satisfaction or usefulness as more units of a product are acquired

8. the desire, ability, and willingness to buy a product

9. a given change in price causes a proportional change in quantity demanded

10. product that increases the use of another product

Review Academic Vocabulary

On a separate sheet of paper, use each of these terms in a sentence that reflects the term's meaning in the chapter.

11. prevail
12. inversely
13. principle
14. illustrate
15. technical
16. adequate

Review the Main Ideas

Section 1 *(pages 91–95)*

17. **Describe** a demand schedule and a demand curve. How are they alike? How do they differ?

18. **Discuss** what is meant by the Law of Demand.

19. **Explain** how the principle of diminishing marginal utility is related to the downward-sloping demand curve.

Section 2 *(pages 97–101)*

20. **Explain** the difference between the income effect and the substitution effect.

21. **Identify** and describe the five factors that can cause a change in individual demand, using a graphic organizer similar to the one below.

Section 3 *(pages 103–109)*

22. **Describe** the difference between elastic demand and inelastic demand.

23. **Explain** how the total expenditures test can be used to determine demand elasticity.

24. **Identify** and then describe the determinants of demand elasticity.

Critical Thinking

25. **The BIG Ideas** Assume that demand for pizza has been steady for some time. How do you think the market demand curve for pizza would be affected by (1) an increase in everyone's pay, (2) a successful pizza advertising campaign, (3) a decrease in the price of hamburgers, and (4) new people moving into the community? Explain your answers.

21. consumer income (how much people make); consumer tastes (what people like and dislike); substitutes (products that can be used in place of other products); complements (products whose use increases the use of other products); expectations (how people view the future); number of consumers (people interested in purchasing a product)

22. Elastic demand: quantity demanded responsive to price changes. Inelastic demand: quantity demanded not responsive to price changes.

23. Total expenditure will change in the opposite direction of price with elastic demand. Expenditure will change in the direction of price with inelastic demand.

24. If a purchase can be delayed, adequate substitutes are available, and the purchase uses a large portion of income, demand will be elastic.

Critical Thinking

25. Answers will vary but should recognize that 1, 2, and 4 would shift the curve right and 2 would shift the curve left.

Economics ONLINE Self-Check Quiz Visit the
Economics: Principles and Practices Web site at glencoe.com and click
on *Chapter 4–Self-Check Quizzes* to prepare for the chapter test.

Assessment
and Activities

CHAPTER
4

26. Determining Cause and Effect Razor blades are complementary goods for razor handles, while electric razors are substitutes. Copy the demand curves below on a sheet of paper. Then show how the rise in the cost of razor handles, if they were sold separately, would affect the demand curves for its complementary and its substitute products.

27. Making Generalizations Do you think the Law of Demand accurately reflects most people's behavior regarding certain purchases? Explain.

28. Synthesizing Assume that you are a business owner. How would you use your knowledge of demand elasticity to determine the price of your product?

Math Practice

29. Mindy is trying to estimate the elasticity of demand for a product she wants to sell at a craft fair. She has been told that she can expect to sell 10 items if she charges a price of $10, six items if she charges a price of $20, and 18 items at a price of $5.

a. Make a demand schedule to show the quantities demanded at each price, and plot a demand curve.

b. At which price would the total expenditures by consumers be greatest for the product? At what price would expenditures be the smallest?

Analyzing Visuals

30. Look at Figure 4.2 on page 94. Suppose that Avi, a friend of Mike's and Julia's, is also willing to buy CDs. Create a new market demand schedule by adding the numbers that you think Avi is willing to purchase at different prices. Then draw a market demand curve reflecting the new numbers.

Thinking Like an Economist

31. Write a paragraph describing a business you might like to own. Describe the product your business makes. Then use the three determinants of demand elasticity to predict the elasticity of demand for that product. Explain the pricing policy you would use to get consumers to maximize their expenditures on that product.

Interpreting Cartoons

32. Critical Thinking Look at the cartoon below. What do you think Snoopy's doghouse represents? What message is the cartoonist trying to convey? Explain whether or not he found a good way to discuss the topic.

CHAPTER 4 Demand 113

Math Practice

29. a. The demand schedule should show a quantity of 10 partnered with a price of $10, 6 with $20, and 18 at $5.

b. Total expenditures would be greatest at a price of $20 and smallest at a price of $5.

Analyzing Visuals

30. Answers will vary, but Avi's demand schedule should follow the Law of Demand and use the same prices as those used for Mike and Julia. The market demand curve should also use the same prices, with Avi's quantities added to the sum of Mike's and Julia's quantities.

Thinking Like an Economist

31. Answers will vary, but students should demonstrate understanding of elasticity, its determinants, and how to use elasticity to predict the effects of price changes on total expenditures on a product.

Interpreting Cartoons

32. Answers will vary but should convey that the price given has no realistic relationship with the actual value of the doghouse.

26. A rise in the cost of razor handles would decrease the demand for razor blades, as they are complementary goods. The demand curve for razor blades would shift to the left. A rise in the cost of razor handles would make electric razors more attractive, as they are substitutes. The demand curve for electric razors would shift to the right.

27. Answers will vary, but students should mention diminishing marginal utility, the substitution effect, and the income effect.

28. Knowing demand elasticity of a product enables a business owner to price her product so as to maximize total revenue from it. If the good is inelastic, the owner could raise prices. If the good is elastic, lowering prices would increase revenue.

Focus

Tell students that oil is a fossil fuel, meaning that it is formed from plant and animal remains. Have small groups discuss what the implications are for nations with economies dependent upon fossil fuels. *(Students should realize that as a fossil fuel, oil is a nonrenewable resource. If global consumption continues to increase, oil supplies will someday run out.)*

Teach

S Skill Practice

Visual Literacy Ask: What does this graphic reveal about oil consumption in China? *(It has increased rapidly and will continue to increase rapidly.)* What does the graphic suggest about the future oil consumption of other industrializing nations? Explain. *(The graphic reveals that the industrializing nation of China will consume a much larger amount of oil in the future. This suggests that oil consumption will increase in other industrial nations as well.)* **OL**

**Additional
Support**

China's Thirst for Gas

Hurricanes in the Gulf of Mexico, deteriorating pipelines in Alaska, and conflict in Iraq can cause gasoline prices to rise by restricting supply. Often the events we see in the headlines affect the supply of oil available to consumers, but changes in the level of world demand for petroleum products also affects the price of oil.

China's Growing Demand

U.S. demand for petroleum products has been high for decades. The United States is the largest consumer of oil, using about a quarter of the world's petroleum. This is quickly changing. Emerging nations are becoming thirsty for oil, and China is at the top of that list.

How did such a rapid change happen? In the past, China has not needed much petroleum. As the country is industrializing, however, it needs more and more fuel to satisfy its growing energy needs. In fact, as the graph of oil consumption between 1995 and 2025 shows, China's consumption is increasing much more rapidly than U.S. consumption.

PROJECTED OIL CONSUMPTION, UNITED STATES AND CHINA (1994–2025)

1995   2005   2025

1 barrel = 1 million barrels/day   ▮ United States   ▮ China

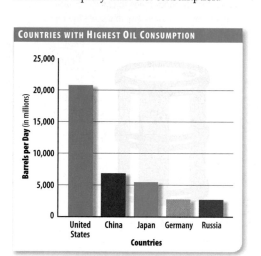

COUNTRIES WITH HIGHEST OIL CONSUMPTION

Barrels per Day (in millions)

25,000
20,000
15,000
10,000
5,000
0

United States   China   Japan   Germany   Russia

Countries

While China still consumes considerably less petroleum than the United States, it has been responsible for over 25 percent of the growth in world petroleum consumption since 1994 and 30 percent of growth since 2000. This increase was enough to make China the second biggest consumer in the world market in 2003, and its demand is not expected to slow down soon.

Worldwide Impact

China's growing energy needs have worldwide repercussions. The nation's increasing demand has helped to push up prices for crude oil. In 2005 the International Monetary Fund (IMF), which promotes economic growth and cooperation, expressed concern that high oil prices could bring about a worldwide slowdown in economic growth because of these increased energy needs.

114   UNIT 2   Microeconomics: Prices and Markets

Extending the Content

Carbon Emissions According to recent scientific reports, China is on course to soon overtake the United States as the world's leading emitter of carbon dioxide. The projections are based on China's rapid increases in oil, gas, and coal consumption. The burning of those three fuels for heat, power, and transportation produces carbon dioxide. Since most scientists view carbon dioxide as a major contributor to global warming, the recent trends in China have caused concern around the world. Thirty-five developed nations have agreed to a United Nations plan to cut their emissions. These countries have called on the world's two leading carbon emitters, the United States and China, to make similar cuts.

EFFECTS OF HIGHER OIL PRICES

Higher prices for food and items in stores because of higher transportation cost

Higher prices for plastics, paints, and other products made with petroleum

Higher Oil Prices

Cuts in school programs because of higher transportation costs

Higher prices at the gas pump

Assess/ Close

C Critical Thinking

Problem-Solving Have students brainstorm possible solutions to the problem of increased global demand for petroleum. (*Possible answer: development of alternative energy sources such as wind or solar power*) Ask students to write and deliver a speech proposing a future course of action based on the solution they think will be most effective. **OL**

What Does It Mean for You?

Why should you care whether China is increasing its demand for petroleum? Simply put, any increase in demand for oil on the world market can lead to rising prices for a variety of goods and services in the United States because so many other products are linked to energy costs.

The results of all these increased costs are manifold. You may see a cut in school programs to pay for higher transportation costs. The products you buy in stores may become more expensive. And of course the price of gas you put into your car may increase. If you are on a limited or fixed budget, like most students, such increases will leave you with less money to spend on other things. As you see, China's higher demand for petroleum has a direct impact on you and your wallet.

Analyzing the Issue

1. **Identifying** Why has China's demand for petroleum increased in recent years?
2. **Describing** What is the effect of increased oil prices on your or your family's budget?
3. **Applying** Check your local newspaper, news magazines, or Internet news sources for recent reports about global issues affecting oil prices. On a separate piece of paper, summarize the issues discussed in these articles and describe how they affect you.

Analyzing the Issue

Answers:
1. As China industrializes, it consumes more petroleum to satisfy its growing energy needs.
2. Students should note that they impact the cost of goods and services.
3. Students should describe the personal effects of global oil prices.

Additional Support

Activity: Collaborative Learning

Analyzing Organize the class into small groups. Instruct each group to select an industrializing nation not already mentioned in this feature. You may wish to assign nations to avoid overlap. Have groups use reliable print or online resources to research the past and projected oil consumption of their assigned nation. Ask groups to prepare a visual presentation (possible formats include charts, posters, video, and PowerPoint) that explains oil production and consumption trends of their country. Visuals should also analyze how these trends will impact the global oil market in the future. After each group has presented, lead the class in a discussion about the likely effects of the world's changing energy needs. **OL**

Teacher Tip

Comparing and Contrasting After the presentations, create a bar graph on the board showing the oil consumption of the nations that students studied. Refer to the graph during the class discussion about the world's energy needs.

Key to Ability Levels

BL Below level		**AL** Above level	
OL On level		**ELL** English Language Learners	

Key to Teaching Resources

Print Material		DVD	
CD-Rom		Transparency	

Levels					Resources	Chapter Opener	Section 1	Section 2	Section 3	Chapter Assess
BL	OL	AL	ELL							
					FOCUS					
BL	OL	AL	ELL	🖼	**Daily Focus Skills Transparencies**		3, 14	3	24	
					TEACH					
BL	OL		ELL	📁	**Guided Reading Activities***		p. 13	p. 14	p. 15	
BL	OL	AL	ELL	📁	**Economic Content Vocabulary Activities***		p. 5	p. 5	p. 5	
	OL	AL		📁	**Critical Thinking Activities**		p. 5			
BL	OL		ELL	📁	**Reading Essentials and Note-Taking Guide***		p. 37	p. 40	p. 43	
		AL		📁	**Enrichment Activities**		p. 5			
BL	OL	AL	ELL	📁	**Primary and Secondary Source Readings**		p. 9		p. 9	
BL	OL	AL	ELL	📁	**Economic Cartoons**		p. 7			
BL	OL	AL	ELL	📁	**Hands-On Economics**				p. 5	
BL	OL	AL	ELL	📁	**Math Practice for Economics**		p. 5		p. 5	
BL	OL	AL	ELL	🖼	**Economics Forms and Financial Pages Transparencies, Strategies, and Activities**		p. 17			
BL	OL	AL	ELL	📁	**Reinforcing Economic Skills**			p. 15		
BL	OL		ELL	📁	**High School Reading in the Content Area Strategies and Activities**	✓	✓	✓	✓	✓
BL	OL	AL	ELL	🖼	**High School Writing Process Transparencies**	✓	✓	✓	✓	✓
BL	OL	AL	ELL	📁	**Writer's Guidebook**	✓	✓	✓	✓	✓
BL	OL	AL	ELL	💿	**StudentWorks Plus CD-ROM**	✓	✓	✓	✓	✓
BL	OL	AL	ELL	💿	**Vocabulary PuzzleMaker CD-ROM**	✓	✓	✓	✓	✓

*Also available in Spanish

Teacher Works Plus
All-In-One Planner and Resource Center

- Interactive Lesson Planner
- Interactive Teacher Edition
- Fully editable blackline masters
- Economics & You videos

- Differentiated Lesson Plans
- Printable reports of daily assignments
- Standards tracking system

Levels					Resources	Chapter Opener	Section 1	Section 2	Section 3	Chapter Assess
BL	OL	AL	ELL							
TEACH (continued)										
BL	OL	AL	ELL		Economics & You Video Program DVD—*What is Supply?*	✓	✓	✓	✓	✓
BL	OL	AL	ELL		Graph Coach CD-ROM	✓	✓	✓	✓	✓
					Differentiated Instruction Strategies	✓	✓	✓	✓	✓
	Teacher Resources				Success with English Learners	✓	✓	✓	✓	✓
					Presentation Plus! CD-ROM	✓	✓	✓	✓	✓
ASSESS										
BL	OL	AL	ELL		Section Quizzes and Chapter Tests		p. 57	p. 58	p. 59	pp. 61, 65
BL	OL	AL	ELL		Authentic Assessment Strategies and Activities		p. 5			
BL	OL	AL	ELL		*ExamView® Assessment Suite* CD-ROM		5-1	5-2	5-3	Ch. 5
BL	OL	AL	ELL		Interactive Tutor Self-Assessment CD-ROM		5-1	5-2	5-3	
CLOSE										
BL			ELL		Reteaching Activities*		p. 5	p. 5	p. 5	
BL	OL		ELL		Reading and Study Skills Foldables		p. 52	p. 46	p. 46	
BL	OL	AL	ELL		Graphic Organizer Transparencies		p. 29			

*Also available in Spanish

Activity
Using PuzzleMaker™ 3.1

Online Word Search Puzzles

Technology Product

Glencoe's Vocabulary PuzzleMaker™ 3.1 CD-ROM is an easy-to-use program that lets you create your own puzzles based on the glossary for classroom use. The PuzzleMaker allows you to

- create word search puzzles based on content vocabulary and academic vocabulary that is specific to what is taught in the classroom;
- create online (LAN-based, or local area network) or paper word search puzzles.

Objectives

After students complete the word search puzzles, they will be able to

- recall academic vocabulary terms based on the clues provided for a puzzle;
- reinforce their understanding of the vocabulary.

Steps

- Run PuzzleMaker™ 3.1. On the main menu, click on **Create a New Puzzle.**
- Select the *Puzzle Database* for the vocabulary.
- The *PuzzleMaker Wizard* will take you through selecting a puzzle type and grid type.
- Then select one or more chapters from the list. Indicate whether you want the words selected randomly or manually.
- Select the language and words you wish to use within the maximum for the puzzle. Click **Finish.**
- Save your word search puzzle to a location that is easily accessible by your students with PuzzlePlayer™ 3.1, or print copies for your students to complete.
- Use PuzzlePlayer™ 3.1 to review the puzzles after your students have worked on and saved them.

Economics ONLINE

	Student	Teacher	Parent
Beyond the Textbook	●	●	●
Chapter Overviews	●	●	●
ePuzzles and Games	●		●
Concepts in Motion	●		●
Multi-Language Glossaries	●		●
Online Student Edition	●	●	●
Self-Check Quizzes	●		●
Student Web Activities	●		●
Study Central™	●		●
Time Current Events	●	●	●
Teaching Today		●	
Vocabulary eFlashcards	●		●
Web Activity Lesson Plans		●	

Glencoe Media Center

❯ glencoe.com

Study-To-Go
- Vocabulary eFlashcards
- Self-Check Quizzes

❯ **Audio/Video**
- Student Edition Audio
- Spanish Summaries
- Economics & You Videos

- **Timed Readings Plus in Social Studies** helps students increase their reading rate and fluency while maintaining comprehension. The 400-word passages are similar to those found on state and national assessments.

- **Reading in the Content Area: Social Studies** concentrates on six essential reading skills that help students better comprehend what they read. The book includes 75 high-interest nonfiction passages written at increasing levels of difficulty.

- **Reading Social Studies** includes strategic reading instruction and vocabulary support in Social Studies content for both ELLs and native speakers of English. www.jamestowneducation.com

Use this database to search more than 30,000 titles to create a customized reading list for your students.

- Reading lists can be organized by students' reading level, author, genre, theme, or area of interest.

- The database provides Degrees of Reading Power™ (DRP) and Lexile™ readability scores for all selections.

- A brief summary of each selection is included.

Leveled reading suggestions for this chapter:
For students at a Grade 10 reading level:
- ***Networking to Find a Job,*** by Stuart Schwartz & Craig Conley

For students at a Grade 11 reading level:
- ***Futurelife: The Biotechnology Revolution,*** by Alvin Silverstein & Virginia Silverstein

For students at a Grade 12 reading level:
- ***Our Own Devices: The Past and Future of Body Technology,*** by Edward Tenner

* Review suggested books before assigning them.

National Council on Economic Education

Voluntary Standards Emphasized in Chapter 5

Content Standard 2 Effective decision making requires comparing the additional costs of alternatives with the additional benefits. Most choices involve doing a little more or a little less of something: few choices are "all or nothing" decisions.

Content Standard 8 Prices send signals and provide incentives to buyers and sellers. When supply or demand changes, market prices adjust, affecting incentives.

Resources Available from NCEE
- Virtual Economics®: An Interactive Center for Economic Education Version 3.0
- Capstone: The Nation's High School Economics Course
- Focus: High School Economics, Second Edition
- Mathematics and Economics: Connections for Life, Grades 9–12

To order these materials, or to contact your State Council on Economic Education about workshops and programs, call 1-800-338-1192 or visit the NCEE Web site at store.ncee.net**.**

The BIG Ideas

As students study the chapter, remind them to consider the chapter-based Big Ideas. The **Essential Question** in the chapter launch activity below ties in to the Big Ideas and helps students think about and understand important chapter concepts. In addition, the Hands-On Chapter Project relates the content from each section to the Big Ideas. The steps in each section build on each other and culminate in the Wrap-Up Activity on the Visual Summary page.

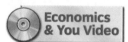

Economics & You Video To generate student interest and provide a springboard for class discussion, access the Economics & You Topic 5 video, **What is Supply?,** at glencoe.com or on the video DVD.

FOLDABLES™ Study Organizer

Dinah Zike's Foldables are three-dimensional, interactive graphic organizers that help students practice basic writing skills, review key vocabulary terms, and identify main ideas. Have students complete this chapter's Foldable activity or activities in *Dinah Zike's Reading and Study Skills Foldables* booklet. **OL**

Economics ONLINE

Introduce students to chapter content and key terms by having them access *Chapter 5 —Chapter Overviews* at glencoe.com.

CHAPTER 5 Supply

Why It Matters

In order to earn some extra money, you are considering opening a lawn or babysitting service. Brainstorm the resources you would need. What specific services would you offer? What prices would you charge? What information do you need to determine answers to these and other questions? Read Chapter 5 to find out about the factors that influence how businesses make production decisions.

The BIG Ideas

1. Buyers and sellers voluntarily interact in markets, and market prices are set by the interaction of demand and supply.

2. The profit motive acts as an incentive for people to produce and sell goods and services.

▶ Firms base their supply of products on production costs and the price they can charge for the product.

Economics ONLINE Chapter Overview Visit the *Economics: Principles and Practices* Web site at glencoe.com and click on *Chapter 5—Chapter Overviews* to preview chapter information.

116   UNIT 2

Activity: Launching the Chapter

Speculating Have students brainstorm products that they purchase regularly, including the prices of those products. Then ask whether there has ever been a change in the price they pay for a product. Have a volunteer read aloud the Big Ideas. Ask students to explain how market prices set by demand and supply relate to profit motive. **Essential Question: How do firms make decisions about their supply of** products and the prices they charge for them? *(Students may suggest that a firm's production of goods and the price for those goods is determined by demand.)* As they read this chapter, encourage students to look for guidelines that suppliers use in making decisions about production, pricing, and profits. **OL**

SECTION 1
What is Supply?

GUIDE TO READING

Section Preview
In this section, you will learn that the higher the price of a product, the more of it a producer will offer for sale.

Content Vocabulary
- supply (p. 117)
- Law of Supply (p. 117)
- supply schedule (p. 118)
- supply curve (p. 118)
- market supply curve (p. 119)
- quantity supplied (p. 119)
- change in quantity supplied (p. 119)
- change in supply (p. 120)
- subsidy (p. 122)
- supply elasticity (p. 124)

Academic Vocabulary
- various (p. 118)
- interaction (p. 120)

Reading Strategy
Describing As you read the section, complete a graphic organizer similar to the one below by describing the causes for a change in supply.

Change in Supply

—www.forbes.com

COMPANIES IN THE NEWS

Flu Shot Gold Rush

Last year, the U.S. flu shot market was so unappealing that only two players were producing injectable vaccine—leading to a serious shortage when one of them, Chiron, had to shut down its plant. Now, it seems, non-U.S. firms are rushing to make influenza vaccine.

Today, CSL Limited, a $2 billion biopharmaceutical firm based in Melbourne, Australia, is announcing plans to invest more than $60 million to enter the U.S. flu shot business. It expects to compete with Sanofi-Aventis, GlaxoSmithKline and Novartis, which plans to buy Chiron. . . . CSL [hopes to] be able to move 20 million doses, giving it a 10% to 15% market share. ■

The concept of supply is based on voluntary decisions made by producers, whether they are proprietorships working out of their homes or large corporations. A producer might decide to offer one amount for sale at one price and a different quantity at another price. **Supply,** then, is defined as the amount of a product that would be offered for sale at all possible prices that could prevail in the market.

Because producers receive payment for their products, it comes as no surprise that they will offer more at higher prices. This forms the basis for the **Law of Supply,** the principle that suppliers will normally offer more for sale at high prices and less at lower prices. The promise of high prices, and hopefully high profits, is what lured the company in the news story into entering the U.S. market.

supply amount of a product offered for sale at all possible prices

Law of Supply principle that more will be offered for sale at higher prices than at lower prices

---

Focus

Bellringer
Daily Focus Transparency 14

FOCUS ACTIVITIES
Transparency 14

CHANGES IN SUPPLY AND EQUILIBRIUM

"Rather amazingly, equilibrium is reached through thousands of individual decisions. It is the price and quantity levels to which the forces of the market naturally gravitate. No one tells anyone else what to do...

The bottom line is that we have to ask just what difference all of this makes since [the supply-demand model] obviously is a vast oversimplification of our economic behavior. The answer is that the tendencies [that] the graphs and schedules portray really are typical behaviors."

—Elaine Schwartz, economist

1. According to this quote, what is equilibrium?
2. If the economic model of supply and demand is "a vast oversimplification," why do economists use it?

GUIDE TO READING

Possible Answers to Graphic:
cost of resources—change in the cost of productive inputs can cause change in supply; productivity—can go up or down depending on workers, which also affects supply; technology—can affect supply by lowering cost of production or increasing productivity; taxes and subsidies—taxes going up or down can affect supply; expectations—people's expectations of future prices can affect supply

Resource Manager

R Reading Strategies	C Critical Thinking	D Differentiated Instruction	W Writing Support	S Skill Practice
Teacher Edition • Identifying, p. 121 • Monitoring, p. 124 • Summarizing, p. 125	**Teacher Edition** • Analyzing, pp. 119, 121 • Det. Cause/Effect, p. 121	**Teacher Edition** • Logical/Math., p. 120 • Kinesthetic, p. 123 • ELL, p. 124	**Teacher Edition** • Personal Writing, p. 118 • Narrative Writing, p. 122	**Teacher Edition** • Visual Literacy, p. 118 • Analyzing Graphs, pp. 119, 126
Additional Resources • Guid. Read. Act., p. 13 • Read. Ess. & Note-Taking Guide, p. 37	**Additional Resources** • Authentic Assess., p. 5 • Pri./Sec. Source Read., p. 9 • Enrichment Act., p. 5	**Additional Resources** • Econ. Cartoons, p. 7 • Math Prac. for Econ., p. 5 • Crit. Think. Act., p. 5	**Additional Resources** • Writer's Guidebook • Reading and Study Skills Fold., p. 52	**Additional Resources** • Graph. Org. Trans., p. 29 • Daily Focus Trans. 3, 14

Teach

W Writing Support

Personal Writing Have students imagine that they manufacture sneakers. At some point in the manufacturing process, the price of a pair of sneakers goes up to $800 a pair. Have each student write a paragraph explaining why he or she is choosing to supply more sneakers. **OL**

S Skill Practice

Visual Literacy Ask: How does the supply curve compare to the demand curve you read about in the previous chapter? *(It slopes in the opposite direction.)* **BL**

Economic Analysis

Answer: For the Law of Supply, quantity varies directly with the price, rather than inversely as with the Law of Demand.

Additional Support

---

supply schedule
a table showing how much a producer will supply at all possible prices

supply curve
a graph that shows the different amounts of a product supplied over a range of possible prices

An Introduction to Supply

MAIN Idea Supply can be illustrated by a supply schedule or a supply curve.

Economics & You Earlier you learned how to illustrate demand using schedules and graphs. Read on to learn how to illustrate supply.

All suppliers of products must decide how much to offer for sale at **various** prices—a decision made according to what is best for the individual seller. What is best depends, in turn, upon the cost of producing the goods or services. The concept of supply, like demand, can be illustrated in the form of a table or a graph.

The Supply Schedule

The **supply schedule** is a listing of the various quantities of a particular product supplied at all possible prices in the market. **Panel A** of **Figure 5.1** presents a hypothetical supply schedule for CDs. It shows the quantities of CDs that will be supplied at various prices, other things being equal.

If you compare it to the demand schedule in Panel A of Figure 4.1 on page 92, you will see that the two are remarkably similar. The main difference between them is that for supply, the quantity goes up when the price goes up—rather than down as in the case of demand.

The Individual Supply Curve

The data presented in the supply schedule can also be illustrated graphically as the upward-sloping line in **Panel B** of Figure 5.1. To draw it, all we do is transfer each of the price-quantity observations in the schedule over to the graph, and then connect the points to form the curve. The result is a **supply curve,** a graph showing the various quantities supplied at all possible prices that might prevail in the market at any given time.

All normal supply curves have a positive slope that goes up from the lower left-hand corner of the graph to the upper right-hand corner. This shows that if the price goes up, the quantity supplied will go up too.

Figure 5.1 ▶ **Supply of Compact Discs**

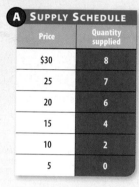

Price	Quantity supplied
$30	8
25	7
20	6
15	4
10	2
5	0

▶ The supply schedule and the supply curve both show the quantity of CDs supplied in the market at every possible price. Note that a change in the quantity supplied appears as a movement along the supply curve.

Economic Analysis *How does the Law of Supply differ from the Law of Demand?*

Activity: Hands-On Economics

Illustrating Ideas Draw a two-column table on the board with "Pay Per Hour" and "Students Willing to Work" as column headings. In the "Pay" column, list the figures $1 through $10. State that you need help to clean the classroom. Ask who would be interested in the job at a wage of $1 an hour.

Record the number in the "Students Willing to Work" column, and then repeat the process for all other hourly rates. Tell students that they have provided an example of the Law of Supply. Have students use the data in the chart to construct a graph similar to Figure 5.1. **ELL**

Figure 5.2 ► Individual and Market Supply Curves

Graphs In Motion
See StudentWorks™ Plus
or glencoe.com.

▶ The market supply curve shows the quantities supplied by all firms that offer the product for sale in a market. Point **a** on the market supply curve represents the four CDs that Firm A would supply and the two CDs that Firm B would supply, at a price of $15, for a total of six CDs.

Economic Analysis *Why are the supply curves upward sloping?*

SUPPLY CURVE OF FIRM A

SUPPLY CURVE OF FIRM B

MARKET SUPPLY CURVE

While the supply schedule and curve in Figure 5.1 represent the voluntary decisions of a single, hypothetical producer of CDs, we should realize that supply is a very general concept. In fact, you are a supplier whenever you look for a job and offer your services for sale. Your economic product is your labor, and you would probably be willing to supply more labor for a high wage than for a low one.

The Market Supply Curve

The supply schedule and curve in Figure 5.1 show the information for a single firm. Frequently, however, we are more interested in the **market supply curve,** the supply curve that shows the quantities offered at various prices by all firms that offer the product for sale in a given market.

To obtain the data for the market supply curve, add the number of CDs that individual firms would produce, and then plot them on a separate graph. In **Figure 5.2,** point **a** on the market supply curve represents six CDs—four supplied by the first firm and

two by the second—that are offered for sale at a price of $15. In the same way, point **b** on the curve represents a total of nine CDs offered for sale at a price of $20.

A Change in Quantity Supplied

The **quantity supplied** is the amount that producers bring to market at any given price. A **change in quantity supplied** is the change in amount offered for sale in response to a change in price. In Figure 5.1, for example, four CDs are supplied when the price is $15. If the price increases to $20, six CDs are supplied. If the price then changes to $25, seven units are supplied.

These changes illustrate a change in the quantity supplied, which—like the case of demand—shows as a movement *along* the supply curve. Note that the change in quantity supplied can be an *increase* or a *decrease*, depending on whether more or less of a product is offered. For example, the movement from **a** to **b** in Figure 5.1 shows an increase because the number of products offered for sale goes from four to six when

market supply curve a graph that shows the various amounts offered by all firms over a range of possible prices

quantity supplied amount offered for sale at a given price

change in quantity supplied change in amount offered for sale when the price changes

S Skill Practice

Analyzing Graphs Ask: Why is quantity supplied plotted on the horizontal axis? *(Possible answers: because the price is supplied on the vertical axis; because the quantity is the variable being controlled)* **AL**

C Critical Thinking

Analyzing Have students explain the relationship between individual supply curves and market supply curves. *(Possible answer: Individual supply curves illustrate information from single, individual firms. Market supply curves illustrate information from all firms that offer a product for sale.)* **OL**

Economic Analysis

Answer: because the Law of Supply states that more will be offered for sale at high prices than low prices

Additional Support

CHAPTER 5 Supply **119**

Activity: Collaborative Learning

Predicting Organize students into teams of three to play the Supply Curve Game. Choose two teams and give each team two flashcards—one saying LEFT and the other saying RIGHT. Present scenarios such as the following: If the price for raw materials used in making CDs falls, will the supply curve for CDs shift left or right? Team members should display

their flashcards with the correct answer. If any team member displays the flashcard incorrectly, that team is disqualified and a new team joins the game. Continue the game until all teams have competed. **OL**

Teacher Tip

Grouping Students As you make assignments, create groups where students have mixed achievement levels, avoid putting friends together in a group, and place only one special needs student in each group.

D Differentiated Instruction

Logical/Mathematical

Tell students that the Jolly Music Company has three employees. Two work 40-hour weeks, and one works a 25-hour week. Each worker just received a raise from $8.40 an hour to $9.92 an hour. **Ask:** What is the company's old and new weekly labor costs? What is the amount of the increase? *(old: $882; new: $1,041.60; increase: $159.60)* How might this increase affect supply? *(Fewer products might be offered for sale.)* **OL**

✓ Reading Check **Answer:** He may produce fewer bicycles.

Economic Analysis

Answer: A change in quantity supplied is caused by a change in price. A change in supply is caused by a change in the determinants of supply.

---

change in supply situation where different amounts are offered for sale at all possible prices in the market; shift of the supply curve

the price goes up. If the movement along the supply curve had been from point **b** to point **a,** there would have been a decrease in quantity supplied because the number of products offered for sale went down. It makes no difference whether we are talking about an individual supply curve or a market supply curve. In either case, a change in quantity supplied takes place whenever a change in price affects the amount of a product offered for sale.

In a market economy, producers usually react to changing prices in just this way. While the **interaction** of supply and demand usually determines the final price of the product, the producer normally has the freedom to adjust production up or down. Take oil as an example. If the price of oil falls, the producer may offer less for sale, or even leave the market altogether if the price goes too low. If the price rises, the producer may offer more output for sale to take advantage of the better prices.

✓ Reading Check **Synthesizing** How might a producer of bicycles adjust supply when prices decrease?

D Change in Supply

MAIN Idea Several factors can contribute to a change in supply.

Economics & You Can you think of a time when you wanted to buy something, but the product was sold out everywhere? Read on to learn about factors that can affect supply.

Sometimes something happens to cause a **change in supply,** a situation where suppliers offer different amounts of products for sale at all possible prices in the market. This is not the same as the change in quantity supplied illustrated in Figure 5.1, because now we are looking at situations where the quantity changes even though the price remains the same.

For example, the supply schedule in **Figure 5.3** shows that producers are now willing to offer more CDs for sale at every price than before. Where 6 units were offered at a price of $15, now there are 13. Where 11 were offered at a price of $25, 18 are now offered, and so on.

Figure 5.3 ► **A Change in Supply**

A SUPPLY SCHEDULE		
Price	S	S¹
$30	13	20
25	11	18
20	9	16
15	6	13
10	3	9
5	0	3

► A change in supply means that suppliers will supply different quantities of a product at the same price. When we plot the numbers from the supply schedule, we get two separate supply curves. An increase in supply appears as a shift of the supply curve to the right. A decrease in supply appears as a shift of the supply curve to the left.

Economic Analysis *How do change in supply and change in quantity supplied differ?*

Differentiated Instruction

Economics Forms and Fin. Pages Trans., Strat. and Act., p. 17

X–Y Axis Line Graph

Objective: Create an X–Y line graph and interpret its data.

Focus/Teach: Review supply curves with students. Guide them in interpreting the activity data and plotting the numbers on each axis.

Assess: Ask students to compare their supply curves to the one in the activity. Do they slope in the same direction? If not, why?

Close: Have students summarize what happens to supply when the price of corn goes up.

Differentiated Instruction Strategies

BL Have students plot three points from the Supply Schedule in Figure 5.3.

AL Ask students why the supply of corn was greatest at a price of $3.50/bushel.

ELL Have students create a cause-and-effect graphic organizer using the corn supply data.

Technology In this Ford manufacturing plant, robots assemble the body of a new Fusion sedan. *What effect does the introduction of new technology have on the supply curve?*

When both old and new quantities supplied are plotted in the form of a graph, it appears as if the supply curve has shifted to the right, showing an *increase in supply*. For a *decrease in supply* to occur, less would be offered for sale at all possible prices, and the supply curve would shift to the left.

Changes in supply, whether increases or decreases, can occur for several reasons. As you read, keep in mind that all but the last reason—a change in the number of sellers—affects both the individual and the market supply curves.

Cost of Resources

A change in the cost of productive inputs such as land, labor, and capital can cause a change in supply. Supply might increase because of a decrease in the cost of inputs such as labor or packaging. If the price of the inputs drops, producers are willing to produce more of a product, thereby shifting the supply curve to the right.

An increase in the cost of inputs has the opposite effect. If labor or other costs rise, producers would not be willing to produce as many units. Instead, they would offer fewer products for sale, and the supply curve would shift to the left.

Productivity

Productivity goes up whenever more output is produced using the same amount of imput. When management trains or motivates its workers, productivity usually goes up. Productivity should also go up if workers decide to work harder or more efficiently. In each case, more output is produced at every price, which shifts the supply curve to the right.

On the other hand, if workers are unmotivated, untrained, or unhappy, then productivity could decrease. The supply curve then shifts to the left because fewer goods are produced at every possible price.

Technology

New technology tends to shift the supply curve to the right. The introduction of a new machine or a new chemical or industrial process can affect supply by lowering the cost of production or by increasing productivity. For example, improvements in the fuel efficiency of jet aircraft engines have lowered the cost of providing passenger air service. When production costs go down, the producer is usually able to produce more goods and services at all possible prices in the market.

CHAPTER 5 Supply 121

Subsidies Some subsidies pay for farmers not to farm some land to avoid overproduction.
Why does the federal government pay such subsidies?

Did You Know?

Many U.S. farmers now use computers, the Internet, and e-mail to get information about the supply of crops that will come to market, prices offered, yield per acre, and other data. This information helps farmers decide how much to plant and where to sell their products. State agricultural departments and universities have Web sites to help farmers use electronic information effectively.

W Writing Support

Narrative Writing Ask students to imagine what it would be like to get paid a subsidy for studying and going to school. Have them write an essay describing the impact of this on students, teachers, and the government. Remind students that their essays should have a plot structure, including characters, a conflict, and a resolution. **OL**

Caption Answer: to help the market economy operate efficiently

Additional Support

subsidy government payment to encourage or protect a certain economic activity

New technologies do not always work as expected, of course. Equipment can break down, or the technology—or even replacement parts—might be difficult to obtain. This would shift the supply curve to the left. These examples are exceptions, however. New technologies are usually expected to be beneficial, or producers would not be interested in them.

Taxes and Subsidies

Firms view taxes as a cost of production, just as they do raw materials and labor. If a company pays taxes on inventory or pays fees for a license to produce, the cost of production goes up. This causes the supply curve to shift to the left. However, if taxes go down, then production costs go down as well. When this happens, supply normally increases and the supply curve shifts to the right.

Did You Know?

▶ **Technology and Supply** New technology can affect supply. But did you realize that supply can also affect technology? When supplies are low and prices are high, companies have an incentive to use technology to develop substitute products they can sell for less. If the price of oil gets too high, for example, there is more of an incentive to develop new technologies for solar, geothermal, or wind power.

W A **subsidy** is a government payment to an individual, business, or other group to encourage or protect a certain type of economic activity. Subsidies lower the cost of production, encouraging current producers to remain in the market and new producers to enter. When subsidies are repealed, costs go up, producers leave the market, and the supply curve shifts to the left.

Historically, many farmers in the milk, cotton, corn, wheat, and soybean industries received subsidies to support their income. Some farmers would have quit farming without these subsidies. Instead, the subsidies kept them in business and even attracted additional farmers into the industry—thereby shifting the market supply curve to the right.

Expectations

Expectations about the future price of a product can also affect supply. If producers think the price of their product will go up, they may make plans now to produce more later on. When the new production is ready, the market supply curve will increase, or shift to the right.

On the other hand, producers may expect lower future prices. In this case, they may try to produce something else or even stop producing altogether—causing the supply curve to shift to the left.

Extending the Content

Babysitter Shortage For generations, teenagers have worked as babysitters to earn extra spending money. Yet lately there has been a babysitter shortage in some parts of the country. Possible reasons might include a decrease in teenagers' free time due to homework and other activities or even a lower teenager-to-child ratio nationwide. Whatever the reason,

babysitter shortages—and the law of supply—have helped some teenagers cash in. "It's a case of supply and demand," one father of three said. "The babysitters know they have the control. You have to start calling weeks in advance."

Just like any other example of the law of supply, when the number of available babysitters gets smaller, the price for those

sitters goes up. Some teens have even reported that beyond a pay increase, their babysitting clients have started to provide them extra snacks to sweeten the deal. Other parents, desperate to keep their babysitter working for them, have started paying the teenager for every Saturday night—whether or not their kids actually needed a sitter.

Expectations can also affect the price a firm plans to pay for some of the inputs used in production, so expectations can affect a business in a number of different ways. This is often compounded by events in the news, so expectations tend to change relatively frequently.

Government Regulations

When the government establishes new regulations, the cost of production can change, causing a change in supply. For example, when the government requires new auto safety features such as air bags or emission controls, cars cost more to produce. Producers adjust to the higher production costs by producing fewer cars at every possible price.

In general, increased—or tighter—government regulations restrict supply, causing the supply curve to shift to the left. Relaxed government regulations allow producers to lower the cost of production, which results in a shift of the supply curve to the right.

Number of Sellers

All of the factors we have discussed so far can cause a change in an individual firm's supply curve and, consequently, the market supply curve. It follows, therefore, that a change in the number of suppliers can cause the market supply curve to shift to the right or left.

As more firms enter an industry, the supply curve shifts to the right because **D** more products are offered for sale at the same prices as before. In other words, the larger the number of suppliers, the greater the market supply. However, if some suppliers leave the market, fewer products are offered for sale at all possible prices. This causes supply to decrease, shifting the curve to the left.

In the real world, sellers are entering and leaving individual markets all the time. You see this in your own neighborhood when one store closes and another opens in its place.

Changes in technology can also impact the number of sellers. For example, recently the Internet has attracted a large number of new businesses, as almost anyone with some Internet experience and a few thousand dollars can open an online store. Because of the ease of entry into these new markets, selling a product is no longer just for the big firms.

✓ Reading Check **Explaining** Why do factors that cause a change in individual supply also affect the market demand curve?

Personal Finance Handbook
See pages *R20–R23* for more information on getting a job.

CAREERS

Retail Salesperson

The Work
* Demonstrate products and interest customers in merchandise in an efficient and courteous manner
* Stock shelves, take inventory, prepare displays
* Record sales transactions and possibly arrange for product's safe delivery

Qualifications
* Ability to tactfully interact with customers and work under pressure
* Knowledge of products and the ability to communicate this knowledge to the customer
* Strong business math skills for calculating prices and taxes
* No formal education required, although opportunities for advancement may depend on a college degree

Earnings
* Median hourly earnings (including commissions): $8.98

Job Growth Outlook
* Average

Source: *Occupational Outlook Handbook, 2006–2007 Edition*

CHAPTER 5   Supply   123

D Differentiated Instruction

Kinesthetic Tell students they represent suppliers and that the number of suppliers affects the market supply curve, causing it to shift. Choose a few students to represent suppliers in an industry. Then add students to the small group and ask what change occurred. *(Suppliers were added.)* Create a graph on the board and have a volunteer chart the change, noting that the market supply curve shifted right. Then have some students leave the group of suppliers. Ask the class how the change affected the supply of products offered for sale. *(It decreased.)* Have a volunteer chart the change, noting that the market supply curve will shift left. Tell students this is how the number of sellers affects the market supply. **BL**

✓ Reading Check **Answer:**
Factors that change individual supply affect quantity supplied. Consequently, the market demand curve will respond to those changes.

Additional Support

Activity: Interdisciplinary Connection

Geography Tell students that geography helps determine the supply of products and affects the unequal distribution of the factors of production. Students should recognize obvious geographical influences on supply, such as climate, growing season, and proximity to transportation routes. For example, the supply of pineapples is relatively limited in the continental United States because of geographical influences. Pineapples are tropical plants and cannot be widely grown in the 48 continental states. Have students identify geographical influences on the supply of products in their region. Have them choose one particular product, analyze the geographical influences that affect its supply, and present their findings to the class. **OL**

R Reading Strategy

Monitoring Have students explain Table D: Determining Elasticity in their own words. *(Possible answer: Elastic means an increase in price leads to a larger increase in output. Unit elastic means an increase in price causes a similar change in output. Inelastic means an increase in price causes a smaller change in output.)* **OL**

D Differentiated Instruction

English Language Learners
Bring three different strengths of rubber bands to class. Demonstrate elastic supply with the more relaxed band, adding that there is a larger increase in output. Demonstrate inelastic supply with the tightest band, adding that there is a smaller increase in output. Demonstrate unit elastic with the medium strength of band, adding that the change in output is similar in proportion to price increase. **ELL**

Economic Analysis

Answer: quantity supplied and price changes

Hands-On Chapter Project

Step 1

Graphing the Law of Supply

In this project, students will produce a graphic presentation of a production schedule to find a firm's total profits.

Step 1: Identifying How a Change in Supply Affects a Supply Schedule.
Students will determine the factors that contribute to a change in supply and illustrate that change on a supply schedule.

Figure 5.4 ▶ Elasticity of Supply

▶ The elasticity of supply is a measure of how quantity supplied responds to a price change. If the change in quantity supplied is more than proportional to the price change, supply is elastic; if it is less than proportional, it is inelastic; and if it is proportional, it is unit elastic.

Economic Analysis *Which factors determine whether a firm's supply curve is elastic or inelastic?*

D DETERMINING ELASTICITY

Type of elasticity	Change in quantity supplied due to a change in price
Elastic	More than proportional
Unit elastic	Proportional
Inelastic	Less than proportional

supply elasticity
a measure of how the quantity supplied responds to a change in price

Elasticity of Supply

MAIN Idea The response to a change in price varies for different products.

Economics & You You learned earlier that demand can be elastic, inelastic, or unit elastic. Read on to learn about the elasticity of supply.

Just as demand has elasticity, supply also has elasticity. **Supply elasticity** is a measure of the way in which the quantity supplied responds to a change in price. If an increase in price leads to a proportionally larger increase in output, supply is elastic. If an increase in price causes a proportionally smaller change in output, supply is inelastic. If an increase in price causes a proportional change in output, supply is unit elastic.

As you might imagine, there is very little difference between supply and demand elasticities. If quantities of a product are being purchased, the concept is demand elasticity. If quantities of a product are being brought to market for sale, the concept is supply elasticity. In both cases, elasticity is simply a measure of the way quantity adjusts to a change in price.

Three Elasticities

Figure 5.4 illustrates three examples of supply elasticity. The supply curve in **Panel A** is elastic because the change in price causes a proportionally larger change in quantity supplied. Doubling the price from $1 to $2 causes the quantity brought to market to triple from two to six units.

124   UNIT 2   Microeconomics: Prices and Markets

Directions: Organize the class into small groups of three or four. Instruct group members to imagine that they are partners in a fictitious company that supplies a product of their own choosing. Groups will create a name for their company and decide on a product to produce. They will then create a supply schedule for their company and identify one factor that will change their supply schedule. Have groups graph the results.

Summarizing Direct each group to use their completed graphs to write a brief report summarizing how changes in supply affect the supply schedule. **OL**

(Chapter Project continued in Section 2.)

Panel B shows an inelastic supply curve. In this case, a change in price causes a proportionally smaller change in quantity supplied. When the price doubles from $1 to $2, the quantity brought to market goes up only 50 percent, or from two units to three units.

Panel C shows a unit elastic supply curve. Here a change in price causes a proportional change in the quantity supplied. As the price doubles from $1 to $2, the quantity brought to market also doubles.

Determinants of Supply Elasticity ℝ

The elasticity of a producer's supply curve depends on the nature of its production. If a firm can adjust to new prices quickly, then supply is likely to be elastic. If the nature of production is such that adjustments take longer, then supply is likely to be inelastic.

The supply curve for nuclear power, for example, is likely to be inelastic in the short run. No matter what price is being offered, electric utilities will find it difficult to increase output because of the huge amount of capital and technology needed—not to mention the issue of extensive government regulation—before nuclear production can be increased.

However, the supply curve is likely to be elastic for many toys, candy, and other products that can be made quickly without huge amounts of capital and skilled labor. If consumers are willing to pay twice the price for any of these products, most producers will be able to gear up quickly to significantly increase production.

Unlike demand elasticity, the number of substitutes has no bearing on supply elasticity. In addition, neither the ability to delay the purchase nor the portion of income consumed are important. Instead, only production considerations determine supply elasticity. If a firm can react quickly to a changing price, then supply is likely to be elastic. If the firm takes longer to react to a change in prices, then supply is likely to be inelastic.

✓ Reading Check   Comparing How are the elasticities of supply and demand similar? How do they differ?

R **Reading Strategy**

Summarizing Have students write a paragraph summarizing the information in the subsection. *(Answers will vary but should include the concept that the elasticity of a producer's supply curve depends on the nature of its production.)* **OL**

✓ Reading Check **Answer:** They both measure the way quantity adjusts to a change in price. Supply elasticity measures quantity supplied; demand elasticity measures quantity demanded.

Assess

💿 Use the Interactive Tutor Self-Assessment CD-ROM to review Section 1, and then assign the Section 1 Review as homework or as an in-class activity.

Close

Making Connections Invite students to discuss how supply helps shape profits and employment in a market economy. **OL**

Review SECTION 1

SECTION 1 Review

Vocabulary

1. **Explain** the significance of supply, Law of Supply, supply schedule, supply curve, market supply curve, quantity supplied, change in quantity supplied, change in supply, subsidy, and supply elasticity.

Main Ideas

2. **Determining Cause and Effect** Use a graphic organizer like the one below to explain how a change in the price of an item affects the quantity supplied.

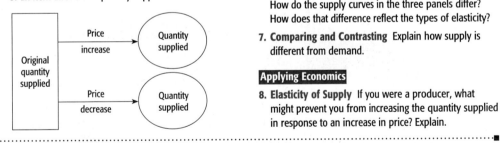

3. **Explaining** What is the difference between a change in supply and a change in quantity supplied?

4. **Describing** How does the quantity supplied change when the price doubles for a unit elastic product?

Critical Thinking

5. **The BIG Idea** Explain why the supply curve slopes upward.

6. **Analyzing Visuals** Look at Figure 5.4 on page 124. How do the supply curves in the three panels differ? How does that difference reflect the types of elasticity?

7. **Comparing and Contrasting** Explain how supply is different from demand.

Applying Economics

8. **Elasticity of Supply** If you were a producer, what might prevent you from increasing the quantity supplied in response to an increase in price? Explain.

CHAPTER 5 Supply   125

Answers

1. All definitions can be found in the section and the Glossary.

2. Organizers should show the quantity supplied going up when there is a price increase in the original quantity supplied. The quantity supplied goes down when there is a price decrease in the original quantity supplied.

3. A change in supply means that different amounts will be offered for sale at every price. It results from factors other than price. A change in quantity supplied results from an increase in the price of a good or service.

4. The quantity supplied will also double.

5. All normal supply curves show that if price increases, quantity supplied increases.

6. They have different lengths and angles, illustrating an increase in price. The elastic supply curve is the longest and slopes up gently, covering four quantity units. The inelastic supply curve is the shortest and slopes at the sharpest angle, covering one quantity unit. The unit elastic supply curve is shorter in length than the elastic supply curve and slopes up at a sharper angle, covering two quantity units.

7. Supply describes the actions of producers, while demand represents the buyer's side.

8. Answers will vary but should mention a shortage of additional resources, such as insufficient workforce or storage space. Students may also address elasticity.

125

Teach

S Skill Practice

Analyzing Graphs

Ask: In what year was ethanol production the greatest? *(2005)* In what year did production fall by millions of gallons? *(1996)* How much more was produced in 2005 than in 1999? *(2,500 millions of gallons)* **OL**

Analyzing the Impact

Answers:

1. Advantages: Ethanol yields more energy than it takes to produce it, the industry has created U.S. jobs, and ethanol will reduce U.S. dependence on foreign oil. Disadvantages: Few service stations supply it, it contains less energy than gasoline, and it can be used only in flexible-fuel vehicles.

2. The increased cost of oil is increasing the supply of ethanol.

Additional Support

CASE STUDY
"Green" Suppliers

From Black Gold to Golden Corn?

As the world supply of oil is spread among developing nations and becomes increasingly expensive, Americans are looking for alternative fuels. One option is ethanol, a renewable energy source made from corn and other plants. Ethanol suppliers and automakers are touting E85—a mixture of 15 percent gasoline and 85 percent ethanol—as a cleaner, domestic substitute for America's gas tanks.

Aventine and VeraSun

Aventine Renewable Energy, Inc., is just one ethanol supplier that is banking on the potential of plants. So far it's paying off. Aventine reported net income of $32 million on revenues of $935 million in 2005. That is an increase of 10 percent from 2004.

Another ethanol supplier, VeraSun Energy Corp., has teamed up with General Motors and Ford to make E85 more available. Revenues for VeraSun look promising—from $194 million in 2004 to $111 million in just the first quarter of 2006.

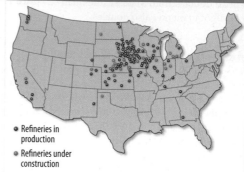

U.S. ETHANOL REFINERIES

● Refineries in production
● Refineries under construction

Source: Renewable Fuels Association

Drawbacks vs. Benefits

Ethanol does have some drawbacks. Only about 600 of the 180,000 U.S. service stations supply it. You also have to fill up more often, because ethanol contains less energy than gasoline. In addition, you have to drive a flexible-fuel vehicle (FFV) to use it.

On the upside, ethanol yields about 26 percent more energy than it takes to produce it. Such a high yield is possible because sunlight is "free" and farming techniques have become highly efficient. As for the labor force, the ethanol industry supported the creation of more than 153,000 U.S. jobs in 2005. Perhaps the greatest benefit of increased ethanol supply will be reducing U.S. dependence on foreign oil.

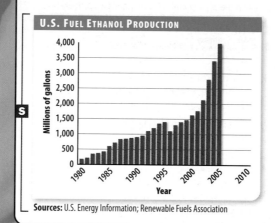

U.S. FUEL ETHANOL PRODUCTION

Millions of gallons (y-axis: 0, 500, 1,000, 1,500, 2,000, 2,500, 3,000, 3,500, 4,000)
Year (x-axis: 1980, 1985, 1990, 1995, 2000, 2005, 2010)

Sources: U.S. Energy Information; Renewable Fuels Association

Analyzing the Impact

1. **Comparing and Contrasting** What are the advantages and disadvantages of E85?

2. **Drawing Conclusions** What is the relationship between the increased cost of oil and the supply of ethanol?

Activity: Hands-On Economics

Government and Renewable Resources Review what students already know about renewable and nonrenewable resources. *(Renewable resources can be reused in the future, whereas we have a limited supply of nonrenewable resources.)* Ask students to brainstorm a list of renewable and nonrenewable energy sources. Write their answers on the board.

(Renewable sources might include wind-generated electricity, ethanol, and solar power; nonrenewable sources might include coal and natural gas.) Divide the class into small groups, and have each group brainstorm answers to this question: *How can the government encourage the use of renewable sources of energy?* Each group should list at least four ideas and then

present their thoughts to the class. After student presentations, lead a class discussion about the possible advantages and disadvantages of government involvement in individual and business use of energy sources. **OL**

The Theory of Production

GUIDE TO READING

Section Preview

In this section, you will learn how a change in the variable input called "labor" results in changes in output.

Content Vocabulary

- production function *(p. 128)*
- short run *(p. 128)*
- long run *(p. 129)*
- total product *(p. 129)*
- marginal product *(p. 129)*
- stages of production *(p. 129)*
- diminishing returns *(p. 130)*

Academic Vocabulary

- hypothetical *(p. 128)*
- contributes *(p. 130)*

Reading Strategy

Listing As you read about production, complete a graphic organizer similar to the one below by listing what occurs during the three stages of production.

Stage I	Stage II	Stage III

Focus

Bellringer
Daily Focus Transparency 3

GUIDE TO READING

Answers to Graphic:

Stage I: marginal product of each additional worker increases

Stage II: total production keeps growing but by smaller amounts; each additional worker is making a diminishing, but still positive, contribution

Stage III: marginal products of additional workers are negative

COMPANIES IN THE NEWS

—*TIME*

The Hole in the Pipeline

On December 5 [2005], known as Blank Monday in the surfing world, the $4.5 billion industry's core snapped like a board caught in the Banzai Pipeline. Reason? The closure of Gordon (Grubby) Clark's four-decade virtual monopoly on polyurethane blanks, the raw material for most surfboards. (Shapers then customize them for surfers.) Clark's company produced 80% of blanks worldwide, and his sudden exit left surfers treading water as board prices doubled and deliveries were cut off.

One man's wipeout, though, could be another's dream wave. Harold Walker and Gary Linden have quadrupled Walker Foam's staff and are scouting for a new factory, hoping to produce 800 blanks a day by July, up from 125 now. ■

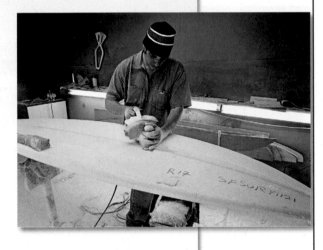

Changes in manufacturing, such as the fourfold increase in staff described in the news story above, happen all the time in any type of business. In fact, if you have ever worked in the fast food industry, you already know that the number of workers is the easiest factor of production for a business to change.

How many times, for example, have you or one of your friends been called in when the business got busy, or were sent home when sales slowed down? Because it is so easy for firms to change the number of workers it employs whenever demand changes, labor is often thought of as being the *variable* factor of production.

CHAPTER 5   Supply   127

Resource Manager

R Reading Strategies	C Critical Thinking	D Differentiated Instruction	W Writing Support	S Skill Practice
Teacher Edition • Det. Importance, p. 128 **Additional Resources** • Guid. Read. Act., p. 14 • Read. Ess. & Note-Taking Guide, p. 40	**Teacher Edition** • Det. Cause/Effect, p. 129 • Analyzing, p. 131 **Additional Resources** • Econ. Content Vocab. Act., p. 5	**Teacher Edition** • Visual/Spatial, p. 130 **Additional Resources** • Reteaching Act., p. 5 • Reinforcing Econ. Skills, p. 15	**Teacher Edition** • Descriptive Writing, p. 129 **Additional Resources** • High School Reading in the Content Area Strat. and Act.	**Teacher Edition** • Using Tables and Charts, p. 128 **Additional Resources** • Reading and Study Skills Fold., p. 46 • Quizzes and Tests, p. 58

Teach

R Reading Strategy

Determining Importance
Ask: Why is the use of the production function important in business? *(It allows businesses to gauge whether additional input will result in extra output.)* **OL**

S Skill Practice

Using Tables and Charts
Direct students to the small print at the bottom of the table in Figure 5.5. **Ask:** Why is a short run useful for changes in labor? *(Output resulting from changes in labor can be evaluated using shorter periods, such as on a daily basis. Output resulting from changes in other variables, such as land or capital, requires longer periods of evaluation.)* **OL**

Economic Analysis
Answer: because the marginal product shows a certain pattern in each stage of production

---

production function a graph showing how a change in the amount of a single variable input changes total output

short run production period so short that only the variable inputs (usually labor) can be changed

The Production Function

MAIN Idea The production function shows how output changes when a variable input such as labor changes.

Economics & You You have learned that changes in demand or supply can be illustrated with graphs. Read on to learn how changes in input are illustrated.

Production can be illustrated with a **production function**—a figure that shows how total output changes when the amount of a single variable input (usually labor) changes while all other inputs are held constant. The production function can be illustrated with a schedule, such as the one in **Panel A** of **Figure 5.5**, or with a graph like the one in **Panel B**.

Both panels list **hypothetical** output as the number of workers changes from zero to 12. According to the numbers in Panel A,

if no workers are used, there is no output. If the number of workers goes up by one, output rises to 7. Add another worker and total output rises to 20. We can use this information to construct the production function that appears as the graph in Panel B, where the number of variable inputs is shown on the horizontal axis, and total production on the vertical axis.

The Production Period
When economists analyze production, they focus on the **short run**, a period so brief that only the amount of the variable input can be changed. The production function in Figure 5.5 reflects the short run because only the total number of workers changes. No changes occur in the amount of machinery, technology or land used. Thus, any change in output must be caused by a change in the number of workers.

Figure 5.5 ▶ Short-Run Production

Graphs In MOtion
See StudentWorks™ Plus or glencoe.com.

A THE PRODUCTION SCHEDULE			
Number of workers	Total product	Marginal product*	Regions of production
0	0	0	Stage I
1	7	7	
2	20	13	
3	38	18	
4	62	24	
5	90	28	
6	110	20	Stage II
7	129	19	
8	138	9	
9	144	6	
10	148	4	
11	145	−3	Stage III
12	135	−10	

* All figures in terms of output per day

B THE PRODUCTION FUNCTION

▶ Short-run production can be shown both as a schedule and as a graph. In Stage I, total output increases rapidly with each worker added. In Stage II, output still increases, but at a decreasing rate. In Stage III output decreases.

Economic Analysis *How does marginal product help identify the stages of production?*

Differentiated Instruction

Making Predictions

Objective: Understand the importance of using past events to predict future trends.

Focus: Discuss how making accurate predictions can help students understand trends.

Teach: Have students study the graph and answer the questions that follow.

Assess: Review the answers as a class.

Close: Ask students to give a real-life example showing how past events can help predict future trends.

Differentiated Instruction Strategies

BL Ask students to explain why it is important to base predictions on data.

AL Have students explain how predicting trends might help a business.

ELL Have groups create a fictitious graph of profits and losses over five years. Then have them predict what will happen in the future.

Other changes take place in the **long run,** a period long enough for the firm to adjust the quantities of *all* productive resources, including capital. For example, a firm that reduces its labor force today may also have to close down some factories later on. These are long-run changes because the amount of capital used for production changes.

Total Product

The second column in Figure 5.5 shows **total product,** or the total output produced by the firm. As you read down the column, you will see that zero units of total output are produced with zero workers, seven are produced with one worker, and so on.

Again, this is a short-run relationship, because the figure assumes that only the amount of labor varies while the amount of other resources used remains unchanged. Now that we have total product, we can easily see how we get our next measure.

Marginal Product

The measure of output shown in the third column in Figure 5.5 is an important concept in economics. The measure is **marginal product,** the *extra* output or change in total product caused by adding one more unit of variable input.

As we see in the figure, the marginal product, or extra output, of the first worker is 7. Likewise, the marginal product of the second worker is 13. If you look down the column, you will see that the marginal product for every worker is different, with some even being negative.

Finally, note that the sum of the marginal products is equal to the total product. For example, the marginal products of the first and second workers is 7 plus 13, or 20—the same as the total product for two workers. Likewise, the sum of the marginal products of the first three workers is 7 plus 13 plus 18, or 38—the total output for three workers.

✓Reading Check Analyzing Why does the production function represent short-run production?

Short Run When companies want to make quick changes in output, they usually change the number of workers. *Why is a change in the number of workers considered a short-run change?*

Stages of Production

MAIN Idea The stages of production help companies determine the most profitable number of workers to hire.

Economics & You If you were a business owner, how would you decide on the number of workers you would hire? Read on to find out how the production function could help you.

In the short run, every firm faces the question of how many workers to hire. To answer this question, let us take another look at Figure 5.5, which shows three distinct **stages of production:** increasing returns, diminishing returns, and negative returns.

Stage I—Increasing Marginal Returns

Stage I of the production function is the phase in which the marginal product of each additional worker increases. This happens because as more workers are added, they can cooperate with each other to make better use of their equipment.

long run
production period long enough to change the amounts of all inputs

total product
total output or production by a firm

marginal product
extra output due to the addition of one more unit of input

stages of production
phases of production that consist of increasing, decreasing, and negative marginal returns

CHAPTER 5 Supply **129**

C Critical Thinking

Determining Cause and Effect
Ask: How does changing one variable affect the other variable inputs of a firm? Explain. *(It will eventually cause the other variables to change because output has changed.)* **OL**

W Writing Support

Descriptive Writing Have students write several paragraphs describing how the three stages of production are different. Remind students to include details from the text. **OL**

Caption Answer: because the change happens in a very brief period

✓Reading Check **Answer:** because it illustrates the changes of one variable in a brief period

Hands-On Chapter Project

Step 2

Graphing the Law of Supply

Step 2: Creating a Production Schedule. Students will create a production schedule for their business. They will graph the production function reflecting a short run where only the total number of workers changes.

Directions: Ask student groups to work together to complete the following steps in creating a production schedule:

• Decide how many units will be produced with one worker in your company.

• Decide a hypothetical output as the number of workers changes.

• Determine the marginal product, remembering that the sum of the marginal products is equal to the total products.

• Determine the stages of production.

Determining Importance Have members of the group take one part of the production schedule and explain its importance to the other members. Then have the group write a statement explaining the importance of the production schedule to their company. **OL**

(Chapter Project continued in Section 3.)

129

D Differentiated Instruction

Visual/Spatial Have student pairs choose a specific product and create a visual presentation depicting how the marginal product changes in the three stages of production. Have pairs explain their visuals to the class. **OL**

✓Reading Check **Answer:** The marginal products of additional workers are negative.

Assess

Use the Interactive Tutor Self-Assessment CD-ROM to review Section 2, and then assign the Section 2 Review as homework or as an in-class activity.

Close

Summarizing Have students use their own words to write a summary of the production function. **OL**

---

diminishing returns stage where output increases at a decreasing rate as more units of variable input are added

As we see in Figure 5.5, the first worker produces 7 units of output. The second is even more productive, with a marginal product of 13 units, bringing total production to 20. As long as each new worker **contributes** more to total output than the worker before, total output rises at an increasing rate. According to the figure, the first five workers are in Stage I.

When it comes to hiring workers, companies do not knowingly produce in Stage I. When a firm learns that each new worker increases output more than the last, it tries to hire yet another worker. Soon, the firm finds itself in the next stage of production.

Stage II—Decreasing Marginal Returns

In Stage II, the total production keeps growing, but it does so by smaller and smaller amounts. Each additional worker, then, is making a diminishing, but still positive, contribution to total output.

Stage II illustrates the principle of decreasing or **diminishing returns**—the stage where output increases at a diminishing rate as more variable inputs are added. In Figure 5.5, Stage II begins when the sixth worker is hired, because the 20-unit marginal product of that worker is less than the 28-unit marginal product of the fifth worker. The stage ends when the tenth worker is added, because marginal products are no longer positive after that point.

Stage III—Negative Marginal Returns

If the firm hires too many workers, they will get in each other's way, causing output to fall. Stage III, then, is where the marginal products of additional workers are negative. For example, the eleventh worker has a marginal product of *minus* three, and the twelfth's is *minus* 10, causing output to fall.

Because most companies would not hire workers if this would cause total production to decrease, the number of workers a firm hires can only be found in Stage II. As we will see in the next section, the exact number of workers to be hired also depends on the revenue from the sale of the output. For now, however, we can say that the firm in Figure 5.5 will hire from 6 to 10 workers.

✓Reading Check **Interpreting** What is unique about the third stage of production?

SECTION 2 Review

Vocabulary

1. **Explain** the significance of production function, short run, long run, total product, marginal product, stages of production, and diminishing returns.

Main Ideas

2. **Describing** How does the length of the production period affect the output of a firm?

3. **Explaining** Use a graphic organizer like the one below to explain how marginal product changes in each of the three stages of production.

Stage of production	Marginal product
I	
II	
III	

Critical Thinking

4. **The BIG Idea** Explain how a change in inputs affects production.

5. **Analyzing Visuals** Look at Figure 5.5 on page 128. Explain what happens to marginal product when production moves from Stage II to Stage III.

6. **Sequencing Information** You need to hire workers for a project and add one worker at a time to measure the added contribution of each worker. At what point will you stop hiring workers? Relate this process to the three stages of the production function.

Applying Economics

7. **Diminishing Returns** Provide an example of a time when you entered a period of diminishing returns or even negative returns. Explain why this might have occurred.

Answers

1. All definitions can be found in the section and the Glossary.
2. In the short run, only the amount of the variable input can be changed. In the long run, a firm can adjust the quantities of all productive resources.
3. I: product increases; II: product decreases; III: product is negative

4. Initially, increasing inputs leads to increased production. Eventually, continuing to increase inputs leads to declining production.
5. Total product begins to decline. In Stage III, adding additional workers causes output to fall.
6. You will stop hiring when the first additional worker reduces total output, which is Stage III of the production function.

7. Student examples should demonstrate an understanding of how increasing inputs may lead to diminishing or negative returns. For example, studying four or five hours straight may be less effective than studying two hours.

ENTREPRENEUR

Profiles in Economics

Kenneth I. Chenault (1952–)

- first African American to be CEO of a top-100 company
- responsible for continuing American Express's 155-year-old tradition of "reinvention" during global change

Stepping Stones

Kenneth Chenault did not start his career in business. Instead, he earned an undergraduate degree in history and a law degree at Harvard. He had keen instincts for business, however, and worked for a management consulting firm before joining American Express in 1981.

At first, Chenault was responsible for strategic planning. His intelligence and hard work moved him up the corporate ranks. Each promotion brought him new challenges and opportunities.

Tools of Success

In 2001 Chenault became chairman and CEO of American Express. When the terrorist attacks of 9/11 brought a downturn for the company, Chenault acted fast to adjust to market conditions. He changed the focus of American Express from telephone and mail to the Internet. He also cut the workforce by 15 percent. "We had to focus on the moderate and long-term," he explained. "In volatile times, leaders are more closely scrutinized. If you cannot step up in times of crisis, you will lose credibility."

Returning to Basics

Four years later, Chenault decided to refocus on "plastic." American Express sold off its many financial planning services and regrouped around its core business—credit cards, corporate travel cards, and "reloadable" traveler's checks. In addition, a 2004 Supreme Court decision on an antitrust suit ended Visa's and Mastercard's control over U.S. bank cards—a $2.1 trillion business. This opened the door for U.S. banks to issue American Express cards.

As chairman and CEO of American Express, Kenneth Chenault believes the key to success in the global economy is adaptability. "It's not the strongest or the most intelligent who survive, but those most adaptive to change."

C

Examining the Profile

1. **Summarizing** How did Chenault's decisions improve American Express?
2. **Evaluating** Do you agree with Chenault's claim that being adaptable to change is the most important strategy for a successful business?

CHAPTER 5 Supply 131

Teach

C Critical Thinking

Analyzing Have students describe Chenault's actions when 9/11 brought a downturn for American Express. *(He took fast action to help his company adjust by changing the focus of American Express from telephone and mail to the Internet. He also cut the workforce by 15 percent.)* **Ask:** How did his actions relate to his belief that adaptability is the key to success? *(His changes helped American Express survive the changing market and kept them successful in the global economy.)* **OL**

Examining the Profile

Answers:

1. His decisions regrouped and focused the company on its core business, which strengthened it. They also kept the company strong during a volatile time.
2. Answers will vary, but students should be able to express an opinion on Chenault's claim.

Additional Support

Activity: Collaborative Learning

Categorizing Have students work together in small groups to create a two-column chart with the headings "Personal" and "Professional." Then have students list steps that Chenault took in his personal life that made him a successful CEO. Next, have them list steps that Chenault took in his professional life that made American Express successful. If time allows, have students do further research on Chenault using print or online resources and then add more examples to their charts. After groups have completed their charts, have students write a concluding statement on how Chenault's beliefs about adaptability and success have shaped his personal and professional life. **OL**

Focus

Bellringer
Daily Focus Transparency 24

FOCUS ACTIVITIES
Transparency 24

COSTS, REVENUES, AND PROFITS

Units Sold	Fixed Costs
×	+
Average Price Per Unit	Variable Costs
TOTAL REVENUE	− TOTAL COSTS = PROFIT or LOSS

1. How are total costs calculated? Total revenues?
2. How is profit related to costs and revenues?

Daily Focus Transparencies

GUIDE TO READING

Answers to Graphic:

Total revenue is: the total amount earned by a firm from the sale of its products. **Possible Ex.:** Seven units sold at $15 each = $105 total revenue.

Marginal revenue is: extra revenue from the sale of one more unit of output. **Possible Ex.:** Five workers producing 90 units of output = $1,350 total revenue. Adding another worker increases output by 20 units and total revenue jumps to $1,650. This results in a marginal revenue of $15.

Resource Manager

SECTION 3
Cost, Revenue, and Profit Maximization

GUIDE TO READING

Section Preview
In this section, you will learn how businesses analyze their costs and revenues, which helps them maximize their profits.

Content Vocabulary

- fixed costs *(p. 133)*
- overhead *(p. 133)*
- variable costs *(p. 133)*
- total cost *(p. 134)*
- marginal cost *(p. 134)*
- e-commerce *(p. 135)*
- break-even point *(p. 135)*
- total revenue *(p. 136)*
- marginal revenue *(p. 136)*
- marginal analysis *(p. 137)*
- profit-maximizing quantity of output *(p. 137)*

Academic Vocabulary

- conducted *(p. 135)*
- generates *(p. 136)*

Reading Strategy

Explaining As you read the section, complete a graphic organizer similar to the one below by explaining how total revenue differs from marginal revenue. Then provide an example of each.

| Total revenue is: | → | Example: |
| Marginal revenue is: | → | Example: |

COMPANIES IN THE NEWS
—BusinessWeek

FedEx Saves the Day

As soon as Motion Computing Inc. in Austin, Texas, receives an order for one of its $2,200 tablet PCs, workers at a supplier's factory in Kunshan, China, begin assembling the product. When they've finished, they individually box each order and hand them to a driver from FedEx Corp., who trucks it 50 miles to Shanghai, where it's loaded on a jet bound for Anchorage before a series of flights and truck rides finally puts the product into the customer's hands. Elapsed time: as little as five days. Motion's inventory costs? Nada. Zip. Zilch. "We have no inventory tied up in the process any-where," marvels Scott Eckert, Motion's chief executive. "Frankly, our business is enabled by FedEx."

There are thousands of other Motion Computings that, without FedEx, would be crippled by warehouse and inventory costs. ■

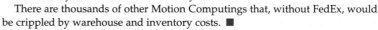

The news story above features a problem that all businesses, nonprofit organizations, and even individuals face—that of having to deal with the costs of running an organization. Scott Eckert could have decided to build a warehouse to store an inventory of tablet PCs waiting for future orders. Instead, he builds the tablet PCs one order at a time and uses a shipping company to deliver orders immediately.

Anyone who is in charge of a business or a nonprofit organization spends a lot of time with costs. The task may be to identify the costs, and at other times it may be to reduce them. Our first task here, however, is to classify the costs.

R **Reading Strategies**	C **Critical Thinking**	D **Differentiated Instruction**	W **Writing Support**	S **Skill Practice**
Teacher Edition • Identifying, p. 133 • Visualizing, p. 136 **Additional Resources** • Guid. Read. Act., p. 15 • Read. Ess. & Note-Taking Guide, p. 43	**Teacher Edition** • Defending, p. 134 • Hypothesizing, p. 135 • Form. Quest., p. 136 **Additional Resources** • Math Prac. for Econ., p. 5	**Teacher Edition** • ELL, p. 133 • Intrapersonal, p. 135 • Logical/Math., p. 138 **Additional Resources** • Reading and Study Skills Fold., p. 46	**Teacher Edition** • Expository Writing, pp. 136, 137 **Additional Resources** • High School Writing Process Trans. • Pri./Sec. Source Read., p. 9	**Teacher Edition** • Analyzing Graphs, p. 134 **Additional Resources** • Reteaching Act., p. 5

Measures of Cost

> **MAIN Idea** Businesses analyze fixed, variable, total, and marginal costs to make production decisions.

Economics & You Are you involved in student government? Organizing events can often cost more than you might have originally thought. Read on to find out about the costs that organizations face.

Because businesses want to produce efficiently, they must keep an eye on their costs. For purposes of analysis, they use several measures of cost.

Fixed Costs

The first measure is **fixed costs**—the costs that an organization incurs even if there is little or no activity. When it comes to this measure of costs, it makes no difference whether the business produces nothing, very little, or a large amount. Total fixed costs, sometimes called **overhead**, remain the same.

Fixed costs include salaries paid to executives, interest charges on bonds, rent payments on leased properties, and state and local property taxes. Fixed costs also include depreciation—the gradual wear and tear on capital goods through use over time. A machine, for example, will not last forever, because its parts will wear out slowly and eventually break.

Variable Costs

Other costs are **variable costs,** or costs that change when the business's rate of operation or output changes. While fixed costs are generally associated with machines and other capital goods, variable costs are usually associated with labor and raw materials. For example, wage-earning workers may be laid off or work overtime as output changes. Other examples of variable costs include electric power to run machines and freight charges to ship the final product.

For most businesses, the largest variable cost is labor. If a business wants to hire one worker to produce seven units of output per day, and if the worker costs $90 per day, the total variable cost is $90. If the business wants to hire a second worker to produce additional units of output, then its total variable costs are $180, and so on.

---

fixed costs costs that remain the same regardless of level of production or services offered

overhead broad category of fixed costs that includes rent, taxes, and executive salaries

variable costs production costs that change when production levels change

Teach

R Reading Strategy

Identifying Ask: What are four types of costs that affect a business's decisions about production? *(fixed, variable, total, marginal)* Have students list the definition of each cost as they read. **BL**

D Differentiated Instruction

English Language Learners Review with students the difference between fixed costs and variable costs. Then invite the principal to the class to discuss the cost of running the school. After the principal's talk, ask students to make charts using "Fixed Costs" and "Variable Costs" as headings. Have students place in the proper category the various costs noted by the principal. **ELL**

Caption Answer: It changes when the business's rate of operation or output changes.

Additional Support

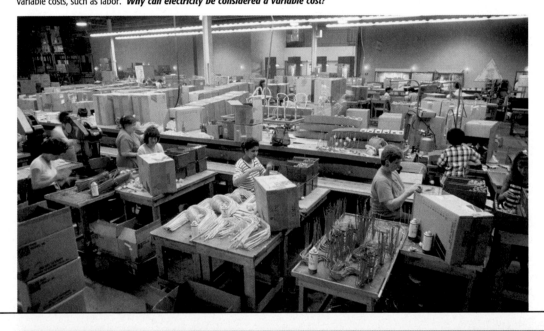

Costs Businesses need to consider both fixed costs, such as rent and taxes, and variable costs, such as labor. *Why can electricity be considered a variable cost?*

Activity: Interdisciplinary Connection

Language Arts In everyday usage, the words *cost* and *price* are often used interchangeably. For example, when someone says, "The cost of living is going up," he or she is comparing the prices of goods and services today with prices during an earlier time. For economists, however, the terms *price* and *cost* are distinct. Economists define *price* as the amount consumers are willing and able to pay for goods and services. *Cost* is expressed in terms of opportunity cost, or that which is given up to do something else. To accountants, cost entails all the expenses directly related to doing business, while business managers define it as anything that reduces profits. Have students write a brief paragraph on how they and their peers use the two terms as consumers. **OL**

S Skill Practice

Analyzing Graphs Ask: What is the most number of workers that can be hired before negative returns cause output to fall? *(10)* How many new workers will give the greatest total profit? *(8)* Why do the numbers in the total fixed cost column stay the same? *(Fixed costs remain the same regardless of the level of production or services offered.)* **OL**

C Critical Thinking

Defending Ask students whether they agree with this statement and why: *The most useful measure of cost is marginal cost.* **OL**

Economic Analysis

Answer: Total cost is the sum of the fixed and variable costs. Marginal cost is the extra cost incurred when producing one more unit of output.

✓Reading Check **Answer:** No; fixed costs remain the same regardless of the business's rate of output.

Differentiated Instruction

Hands-On Economics, p. 5

Figure 5.6 ▶ Production, Costs, and Revenues

▶ When we add the costs and revenues to the production schedule, we can find the firm's profits. Note that fixed costs don't change. Marginal cost and marginal revenue are used to determine the level of productivity with the maximum level of profits.

Economic Analysis *How do total costs differ from marginal costs?*

PRODUCTION SCHEDULE				COSTS				REVENUES		PROFIT
Regions of production	Number of workers	Total product	Marginal product	Total fixed cost	Total variable cost	Total cost	Marginal cost	Total revenue	Marginal revenue	Total profit
	0	0	0	$50	$0	$50	--	$0	--	−$50
Stage I	1	7	7	50	90	140	$12.86	105	$15	−35
	2	20	13	50	180	230	6.92	300	15	70
	3	38	18	50	270	320	5.00	570	15	250
	4	62	24	50	360	410	3.75	930	15	520
	5	90	28	50	450	500	3.21	1,350	15	850
Stage II	6	110	20	50	540	590	4.50	1,650	15	1,060
	7	129	19	50	630	680	4.74	1,935	15	1,210
	8	138	9	50	720	770	10.00	2,070	15	1,300
	9	144	6	50	810	860	15.00	2,160	15	1,300
	10	148	4	50	900	950	22.50	2,220	15	1,270
Stage III	11	145	−3	50	990	1,040	--	2,175	15	1,135
	12	135	−10	50	1,080	1,130	--	2,025	15	895

total cost the sum of fixed costs and variable costs

marginal cost extra cost of producing one additional unit of production

Total Cost

Figure 5.6 shows the **total cost** of production, which is the sum of the fixed and variable costs. Total cost takes into account all of the costs a business faces in the course of its operations. If the business decides to use six workers costing $90 each to produce 110 units of total output, then its total cost will be $590—the sum of $50 in fixed costs *plus* $540 of variable costs.

Skills Handbook

See page **R51** *to learn about* **Using Tables and Charts.**

C Marginal Cost

The most useful measure of cost is **marginal cost**—the *extra* cost incurred when producing one more unit of output.

In fact, marginal cost is more useful than total cost because it shows the change in total variable costs when output increases.

Figure 5.6 shows that the addition of the first worker increases total product by seven units. Because total variable costs increased by $90, each additional unit of output has a marginal cost of $12.86, or $90 divided by seven. If a second worker is added, 13 more units of output will be produced for an additional cost of $90. This means that the extra, or marginal, cost of producing each new unit of output is $90 divided by 13, or $6.92.

✓Reading Check **Analyzing** If a firm's total output increases, will the fixed costs increase? Explain.

134   UNIT 2   Microeconomics: Prices and Markets

Learning from Supply and Demand Curves

Objective: Understand the relationship among demand, supply, and price.

Focus/Teach: Ask students to define each term. Review the graphs, and then have students answer the activity questions.

Assess: Discuss students' reasoning for their choices.

Close: Ask students to list other goods that are affected by even slight changes in supply or demand.

Differentiated Instruction Strategies

BL Fill in the graphs for students before they answer the activity questions.

AL Ask students how fixed, variable, total, and marginal costs apply to the crude oil industry.

ELL Assign small groups a term or concept from the activity to explain to the class.

Applying Cost Principles

MAIN Idea Fixed and variable costs affect the way a business operates.

Economics & You Have you or anyone you know purchased something on the Internet? Read on to find out about the costs of doing business online.

The types of cost a firm faces may affect the way it operates. That is why owners analyze the costs they incur when they run their business.

Costs and Business Operation

For reasons largely related to costs, many stores are flocking to the Internet, making it one of the fastest-growing areas of business today. Stores do this because the overhead, or the fixed costs of operation, on the Internet is so low. Another reason is that a firm does not need as much inventory.

People engaged in **e-commerce**—an electronic business **conducted** over the Internet—do not need to spend a large sum of money to rent a building and stock it with inventory. Instead, for just a fraction of the cost of a typical store, the e-commerce business owner can purchase Web access along with an e-commerce software package that provides everything from Web catalog pages to ordering, billing, and accounting software. Then, the owner of the e-commerce business store inserts pictures and descriptions of the products for sale into the software and loads the program.

When customers visit the "store" on the Web, they see a range of goods for sale. In some cases, the owner has the merchandise in stock; in other cases, the merchant simply forwards the orders to a distribution center that handles the shipping. Either

way, the fixed costs of operation are significantly lower than they would be in a typical retail store.

Break-Even Point

Finally, when a business knows about its costs, it can find the level of production that generates just enough revenue to cover its total operating costs. This is called the **break-even point.** For example, in Figure 5.6, the break-even point is between 7 and 20 units of total product, so at least two workers would have to be hired to break even.

However, the break-even point only tells the firm how much it has to produce to cover its costs. Most businesses want to do more—they want to maximize the amount of profits they can make, not just cover their costs. To do this, they will have to apply the principles of marginal analysis to their costs and revenues.

✓**Reading Check** **Contrasting** What are the differences between an e-commerce store and a traditional business?

CHAPTER 5 Supply **135**

---

e-commerce electronic business conducted over the Internet

break-even point production level where total cost equals total revenue

E-Commerce Companies such as Amazon.com have been able to offer a wide range of products while keeping their overhead low. *What helps e-commerce firms to reduce cost?*

D Differentiated Instruction

Intrapersonal Have students make a list in their journals of e-commerce businesses that they or their family visit on the Web. Next, ask students to share their preference of shopping—traditional, e-commerce, or both—and why. **OL**

C Critical Thinking

Hypothesizing **Ask:** What might happen if a business does not know its break-even point? Explain. *(If a business does not understand how much revenue it must generate to cover its total operating costs, it may lose money and fail.)* **OL**

Caption Answer: low overhead

✓**Reading Check** **Answer:** E-commerce stores do not have to pay rent or keep large inventories. Traditional stores have a greater overhead.

Leveled Activities

BL Reteaching Activities, p. 5

OL Math Practice for Economics, p. 5

AL Primary and Secondary Source Readings, p. 9

135

C Critical Thinking

Formulating Questions

Before reading the subsection, have students write two questions they have about the topic. After reading, have students try to find the answers to their questions in the text. If they can't find them, have students research to find the answers. **OL**

W Writing Support

Expository Writing Have students write a paragraph explaining the two key measures of revenue that businesses use, including a description of each kind of revenue and how it is calculated. **OL**

R Reading Strategy

Visualizing Have students define the term *generates*. *(creates or produces)* **Ask:** What could you visualize to help you remember the meaning of *generates*? *(Possible answer: a factory producing stacks of money)* **BL**

Hands-On Chapter Project

Step 3

Graphing the Law of Supply

Step 3: Adding Information to the Production Schedule. Students will create costs columns, revenue columns, and a profit column for their business.

Directions: Have students follow these steps to add their schedules:

1. Estimate total fixed costs and variable costs columns.
   - Compute the total cost by adding the fixed and variable columns.

The Global Economy & YOU

It *Is* a Small World . . . After All

If you can't find a product at a local store, you can browse millions of Internet sources to find what you're looking for. It's a simple process that, like any other transaction, involves a buyer and a seller. The Internet serves as a neutral venue for buyers and sellers to come together. What makes this such a unique global process is the efficient shipping that allows you to receive your product in a matter of days from such faraway places as China, the United Kingdom, and Australia.

Previously a luxury, shipping goods from country to country—and continent to continent—has expanded the global marketplace with overnight and express mail options. Companies such as DHL, FedEx, and UPS work around the clock—and around the world—delivering packages to businesses and consumers. FedEx, for example, operates 120 flights weekly to and from Asia, including 26 out of China alone.

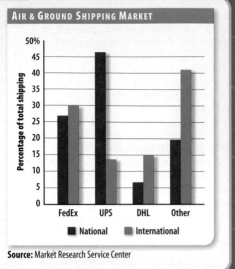

AIR & GROUND SHIPPING MARKET

Percentage of total shipping

- National
- International

Source: Market Research Service Center

---

total revenue total amount earned by a firm from the sale of its products

marginal revenue extra revenue from the sale of one additional unit of output

C Marginal Analysis and Profit Maximization

MAIN Idea Businesses compare marginal revenue with marginal cost to find the level of production that maximizes profits.

Economics & You You just learned about the importance of costs to a business. Read on to learn how businesses use this information to maximize their profits.

W Businesses use two key measures of revenue to find the amount of output that will produce the greatest profits. The first is total revenue, and the second is marginal revenue. The marginal revenue is compared to marginal cost to find the optimal level of production.

Total Revenue

The **total revenue** is all the revenue that a business receives. In the case of the firm shown in Figure 5.6 on page 134, total revenue is equal to the number of units sold

multiplied by the average price per unit. So, if seven units are sold at $15 each, the total revenue is $105. If 10 workers are hired and their 148 units of total output sell for $15 each, then total revenue is $2,220. The calculation is the same for any level of output in the table.

Marginal Revenue

The more important measure of revenue is **marginal revenue,** the extra revenue a business receives from the production and sale of one additional unit of output. You can find the marginal revenue in Figure 5.6 by dividing the change in total revenue by the marginal product.

R For example, when the business employs five workers, it produces 90 units of output and **generates** $1,350 of total revenue. If a sixth worker is added, output increases by 20 units and total revenues increase to $1,650. If we divide the change in total revenue ($300) by the marginal product (20), we have marginal revenue of $15.

- Determine the marginal cost by dividing the variable cost of one unit by the marginal product of each new worker added.

2. Calculate the total revenue column. It is equal to the number of units sold multiplied by the average price per unit.

3. Find the marginal revenue by dividing the change in total revenue by the marginal product if one worker is added.

4. Conduct a marginal analysis to determine whether additional benefits are greater than the extra costs. This is done by adding more variable inputs (workers) and comparing the extra benefit (marginal revenue) to the additional cost (marginal cost).

5. Calculate the total profits by subtracting the total cost from the total revenue.

6. Decide the profit-maximizing quantity of output by identifying marginal cost and marginal revenue as the same. **OL**

(Chapter Project continued in Visual Summary.)

As long as every unit of output sells for $15, the marginal revenue earned by the sale of one more unit will always be $15. For this reason, the marginal revenue appears to be constant at $15 for every level of output in Figure 5.6. In reality, this may not always be the case, as businesses often find that marginal revenues vary.

Marginal Analysis

Most people, as well as most businesses, use **marginal analysis**, a type of decision making that compares the extra benefits of an action to the extra costs of taking the action. Marginal analysis is useful in a number of situations, from our own individual decision making to production decisions made by corporations.

In the case of our own individual decision making, it is usually best for us to take small, incremental steps to determine if the additional benefits from each step are greater than the additional costs. A business does the same thing. It adds more variable inputs (workers) and then compares the extra benefit (marginal revenue) to the additional cost (marginal cost). If the extra benefit exceeds the extra cost, then the firm hires another worker.

W Profit Maximization

We can now use marginal analysis to find the level of output that maximizes profits for the business represented in Figure 5.6. The business would hire the sixth worker, for example, because the extra output would cost only $4.50 to produce while generating $15 in new revenues.

Having made a profit with the sixth worker, the business would hire the seventh and eighth workers for the same reason. While the addition of the ninth worker neither adds to nor takes away from total profits, the firm would have no incentive to hire the tenth worker. If it did, it would quickly discover that profits would go down, and it would go back to using nine workers.

When marginal cost is less than marginal revenue, more variable inputs should be hired to expand output. Eventually, the **profit-maximizing quantity of output** is reached when marginal cost and marginal revenue are equal, as shown in the last column in Figure 5.6. Other levels of output may generate equal profits, but none will be more profitable.

✓Reading Check Summarizing Why do people, especially business owners, use marginal analysis?

Economics ONLINE
Student Web Activity Visit the *Economics: Principles and Practices* Web site at glencoe.com and click on *Chapter 5—Student Web Activities* for an activity on the operation of a company.

marginal analysis decision making that compares the extra costs of doing something to the extra benefits gained

profit-maximizing quantity of output level of production where marginal cost is equal to marginal revenue

W Writing Support

Expository Writing Tell students that the U.S. Constitution established a climate for profit maximizing by supporting property rights, enforcing contracts, giving the federal government control over monetary matters, and not creating trade barriers among states. Ask students to research and write about the Constitution and laws that affect business's drive to maximize profits. **AL**

✓Reading Check **Answer:** to compare the extra benefits of an action to the extra costs of taking the action

Assess

⊙ Use the Interactive Tutor Self-Assessment CD-ROM to review Section 3, and then assign the Section 3 Review as homework or as an in-class activity.

Close

Making Connections Ask: How could this chapter help a person starting a business? **OL**

Vocabulary
1. **Explain** the significance of fixed costs, overhead, variable costs, total cost, marginal cost, e-commerce, break-even point, total revenue, marginal revenue, marginal analysis, and profit-maximizing quantity of output.

Main Ideas
2. **Identifying** Use a graphic organizer like the one below to identify examples of both fixed and variable costs.

3. **Explaining** What is the difference between break-even output and profit-maximizing quantity of output?

Critical Thinking
4. **The BIG Idea** Explain how businesses use marginal analysis to maximize profits.

5. **Analyzing Visuals** Look at Figure 5.6 on page 134. Using the numbers in the figure, write a paragraph to explain in your own words how many workers this company should hire and why it should make this decision. Provide specific examples based on the information in the table.

6. **Inferring** If the total output of a business increases, what will happen to fixed costs? To variable costs?

Applying Economics
7. **Total Cost** Many plants use several shifts of workers in order to operate 24 hours a day. How do a plant's fixed and variable costs affect its decision to operate around the clock?

Answers

1. All definitions can be found in the section and the Glossary.
2. Fixed costs include rent or mortgage, property taxes, executive salaries, truck/car payments, and depreciation on capital goods. Variable costs include wages, electricity, shipping costs, and raw materials.
3. The break-even point is the production level where total cost equals total revenue. The profit-maximizing quantity of output is the production level where marginal cost is equal to marginal revenue.

4. Marginal analysis compares the extra benefits of an action to the extra costs of taking the action. When marginal cost and marginal revenue are equal, businesses know that they've reached the maximum level of profits.
5. Students' paragraphs will vary but should identify the optimal number of workers as 10. At this level, workers are still making a positive impact on output; with the addition of one more worker, the total product begins to decrease.

6. Fixed costs will not change. Variable costs will increase as output increases.
7. Fixed costs have no bearing because they remain constant. Variable costs will increase as output increases. Businesses must compare marginal costs and marginal revenue to decide the optimal number of hours to operate.

Teach

D Differentiated Instruction

Logical/Mathematical

Ask: How much would you spend at each store if you bought all four items? *(Wal-Mart: $44.48; Target: $53.86; Steve & Barry's: $31.92)* **OL**

BusinessWeek *ONLINE*

To find up-to-date news and analysis on the economy, business, technology, markets, entrepreneurs, investments, and finance, have students search feature articles and special reports on the BusinessWeek Web site, www.businessweek.com.

Examining the Newsclip

Answers:

1. makes cut-rate deals with landlords, avoids import duties and quotas by buying from factories in Africa, and accepts longer lead times when buying direct from overseas factories
2. They keep overhead low.

Additional Support

BusinessWeek NEWSCLIP

Profit maximization is the goal of all American businesses. Many increase profits by keeping costs as low as possible. One company has taken cost-cutting to new "lows": Steve & Barry's University Sportswear.

Steve & Barry's Rules the Mall

Steven Shore and Barry Prevor love to fill a void — about 3.5 million square feet of it. That's how much space Steve & Barry's University Sportswear took in U.S. shopping centers last year, the most of any mall-based chain.

The co-CEOs soaked up that space by opening 62 supermarket-sized stores, almost doubling their outlets in one year, to 134. The privately held chain, which lures shoppers with casual clothing priced at $7.98 or less—a 40% discount to prices at Wal-Mart Stores Inc. and Target Corp.—plans to operate more than 200 stores by yearend.

. . . How can Steve & Barry's charge so little? One reason: the cut-rate deals it negotiates with land-lords. Most of its stores are in middle-market malls, which have seen rising vacancies. . . .

Low rents are hardly the only way the men keep costs low. While malls usually give new tenants allowances of $20 to $30 a square foot to build interiors, the popularity of Steve & Barry's has allowed the chain to command [allowances] as high as $80, considerably more than actual costs. . . .

Steve & Barry's also saves money in purchasing. It buys direct from overseas factories, like many others, but cuts costs by accepting longer lead times. It also saves by offering steady production throughout the year rather than seasonal ramp-ups. The chain cuts expenses further by deft navigation of import quotas and duties. . . . That's why it buys more from factories in Africa and less from China than many rivals—most African countries face neither U.S. quotas nor duties. Advertising isn't an expense Steve & Barry's wrestles with, either—it relies mostly on word of mouth.

—Reprinted from *BusinessWeek*

Item	Store	Price
Carpenter jeans	Wal-Mart	$14.88
	Target	16.99
	S&B's	7.98
Polo shirt	Wal-Mart	9.83
	Target	11.99
	S&B's	7.98
Baseball cap	Wal-Mart	7.00
	Target	11.89
	S&B's	7.98
Hooded sweatshirt	Wal-Mart	12.77
	Target	12.99
	S&B's	7.98

Sources: www.walmart.com, www.target.com, www.steveandbarrys.com

Examining the Newsclip

1. **Summarizing** How has Steve & Barry's University Sportswear cut costs?

2. **Making Connections** How do the cost-cutting steps help Steve & Barry's increase its profits?

138 UNIT 2 Microeconomics: Prices and Markets

Extending the Content

Friends and Business Partners Steve and Barry knew each other long before they became business partners in a unique venture that had them opening hundreds of stores across the United States. They were first childhood friends in New York. As teenagers, they started screen-printing T-shirts and selling them at nearby flea markets for $1.00 each. In 1985 Steve and Barry opened a collegiate apparel store at the University of Pennsylvania, where students could purchase collegiate-licensed clothing for lower prices than were found at the campus bookstore. The business partners soon opened locations at other universities and in shopping malls across the country. Today, Steve & Barry's carries the largest collection of collegiate-licensed items in the nation. They have expanded their inventory to include men's, women's, and children's casual clothing. The company also now sells licensed apparel from U.S. brands such as World Wrestling Entertainment (WWE), Ford, Kellogg's, Hershey's, and Marvel Comics.

Visual Summary

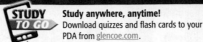

Study anywhere, anytime!
Download quizzes and flash cards to your PDA from glencoe.com.

Visual Summary

CHAPTER
5

▶ **Law of Supply** When the price of a product goes up, quantity supplied goes up. When the price goes down, quantity supplied goes down.

When the price goes up . . .

quantity supplied goes up.

When the price goes down . . .

quantity supplied goes down.

▶ **Production Function** The production function helps us find the optimal number of variable units (labor) to be used in production. As workers are added in Stage I, production increases at an increasing rate. In Stage II, production increases at a decreasing rate because of diminishing returns. In Stage III, production decreases because more workers cannot make a positive contribution.

THE PRODUCTION FUNCTION

Total product (y-axis: 20, 40, 60, 80, 100, 120, 140, 160)
Variable input: number of workers (x-axis: 0, 1, 2, 3, 4, 5, 6, 7, 8, 9, 10, 11, 12, 13)
Stage I, Stage II, Stage III

▶ **Cost and Revenue** While businesses have several types of costs, they can find the profit-maximizing quantity of output by comparing **marginal cost** to their **marginal revenue**.

Cost

Fixed cost: always the same and always has to be paid

Variable cost: varies depending on level of production

Marginal cost (MC): extra cost per additional unit of output

If MC = MR

Profit-maximizing quantity of output

Revenue

Marginal revenue (MR): extra revenue from one additional unit of output

Total revenue: revenue based on number of units multiplied by average price per unit

CHAPTER 5 Supply **139**

Contrasting Have students look at the production function and describe the shape of the curve as it goes from one stage to the next. Then have them explain the reason that the curve changes in this way. *(Answers will vary, but students should be able to verbalize that the curve rises sharply during Stage I, rises more gently in Stage II, and slopes downward in Stage III. The sharp rise in Stage I indicates increases at a consistently higher rate. Stage II indicates slower increases at a higher rate. Stage III indicates decreases.)* **AL**

Problem-Solving Remind students that when the marginal cost is equal to the marginal revenue, profit-maximizing quantity of output is reached. **Ask:** What steps can a company take if marginal cost is less than marginal revenue? *(Expand output by hiring workers, increasing production, and so on.)* How would that help equalize marginal cost and marginal revenue? *(Expanding output would increase marginal cost, eventually increasing it to become equal with marginal revenue.)* **OL**

Hands-On Chapter Project
Step 4: Wrap Up

Graphing the Law of Supply

Step 4: Bringing It All Together.
Students will synthesize what they learned in previous steps.

Directions: Have students resume work in their groups. Instruct each group to compile their work throughout the chapter into a booklet. The booklet should include their graphs and summary reports from Step 1 and the steps in creating a production schedule from Steps 2

and 3. Then have students use the materials to make a final production schedule graph. Review the Big Ideas with students by asking volunteers to explain how the production of goods and services is motivated by a firm's profit motive. Have students respond by writing several lines in their notebooks. **OL**

![ExamView Assessment Suite]

This easy-to-use software includes extensive question banks and allows you to create fully customized tests that can be administered in print or online.

Review Content Vocabulary

1. c
2. d
3. b
4. j
5. g
6. e
7. f
8. a
9. i
10. h
11. l
12. k

Review Academic Vocabulary

13.–18. Sentences should show that students have a clear understanding of the academic vocabulary in an economic context.

Review the Main Ideas

19. the amount of a good or service that the producer is willing and able to provide
20. individual curve relates to a single firm; market curve relates to all firms producing the same product
21. Descriptions will vary, but students should identify these factors: cost of resources; productivity; technology; taxes and subsidies; expectations; government regulations; number of sellers.
22. **Elastic:** change in price causes relatively large change in quantity supplied. **Inelastic:** change in price causes relatively smaller change in quantity supplied. **Unit elastic:** change in price causes proportional change in quantity supplied.
23. total product: total output produced by the firm; marginal product: extra

Review Content Vocabulary

On a separate sheet of paper, write the letter of the key term that best matches each definition below.

a. change in quantity supplied
b. diminishing returns
c. fixed costs
d. marginal analysis
e. marginal product
f. marginal revenue
g. production function
h. Law of Supply
i. total cost
j. change in supply
k. overhead
l. total product

1. a production cost that does not change as total business output changes
2. decision making that compares the additional costs with the additional benefits of an action
3. associated with Stage II of production
4. situation where the amount of products for sale changes while the price remains the same
5. a graphical representation of the theory of production
6. the additional output produced when one additional unit of input is added
7. change in total revenue from the sale of one additional unit of output
8. change in the amount of products for sale when the price changes
9. the sum of variable and fixed costs
10. principle that more will be offered for sale at high prices than at lower prices
11. total output produced by a firm
12. total fixed costs

Review Academic Vocabulary

On a separate sheet of paper, write a paragraph about "supply" that uses all of the following terms.

13. interaction
14. various
15. hypothetical
16. contributes
17. conducted
18. generates

Review Main Ideas

Section 1 (pages 117–125)

19. **Describe** what economists mean by *supply*.
20. **Distinguish** between the individual supply curve and the market supply curve.
21. **Describe** the factors that can cause a change in supply.
22. **Identify** the three types of elasticity, using a graphic organizer similar to the one below.

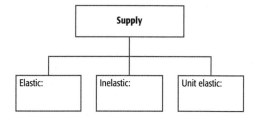

Section 2 (pages 127–130)

23. **Explain** the difference between total product and marginal product.
24. **Describe** the three stages of production.

Section 3 (pages 132–137)

25. **Describe** the relationship between marginal cost and total cost.
26. **Explain** the difference between fixed and variable costs.
27. **Discuss** why businesses analyze their costs.
28. **Explain** how businesses determine their profit maximization output.

Critical Thinking

29. **The BIG Idea** Imagine that gas prices have increased to $5.00 per gallon. What will happen to the supply of fuel-efficient cars in the short run and in the long run? Explain.
30. **Determining Cause and Effect** Explain why e-commerce reduces fixed costs.

---

output caused by adding one more unit of variable output
24. Stage I (increasing marginal returns), Stage II (decreasing marginal returns), Stage III (negative marginal returns)
25. Total costs equal fixed plus variable costs. Marginal costs equal the increase in total variable costs from producing one more unit of output.
26. Fixed costs do not change; variable costs change with a change in output.
27. to make production decisions concerning efficiency

28. They determine the point where their marginal revenue equals marginal costs.

Critical Thinking

29. Answers will vary but should note that in the short run, there is no change. In the long run, there will be an increase.
30. It does not require a lot of money to rent a building and stock inventory.

Economics ONLINE   **Self-Check Quiz**   Visit the *Economics: Principles and Practices* Web site at glencoe.com and click on *Chapter 5–Self-Check Quizzes* to prepare for the chapter test.

Assessment and Activities   CHAPTER **5**

31. Making Generalizations Why might production functions tend to differ from one firm to another?

32. Interpreting Return to the chapter opener activity on page 116. Now that you have learned about supply, review the questions you answered at the beginning of the chapter. How would you revise your earlier decisions on services and prices, and why?

33. Understanding Cause and Effect According to the Law of Supply, what will happen to the number of products a firm offers for sale when prices go down? What will happen if the cost of production increases while prices remain the same?

34. Drawing Conclusions Use a graphic organizer like the one below to illustrate what will happen to supply in each of the situations provided.

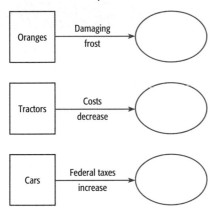

Applying Economic Concepts

35. Marginal Analysis Think about a recent decision you made in which you used the tools of marginal analysis. Describe in detail the problem, the individual steps you took to solve the problem, and the point at which you stopped taking further steps. Explain why you decided to make no further changes.

36. Overhead Overhead is a concern not just for businesses, but also for individuals. What overhead costs do you have to take into consideration if you want to own a car?

Thinking Like an Economist

37. Label the following actions according to their placement in the stages of production:

  a. After many hours of studying, you are forgetting some of the material you learned earlier.

  b. You are studying for a test and learning rapidly.

  c. After a few hours, you are still learning but not as fast as before.

Analyzing Visuals

38. Making Connections Look at Panel B in Figure 5.5 on page 128. Describe the shape of the curve as it goes through the three different stages. How does the shape correspond to the total product and the marginal product listed in Panel A?

Writing About Economics

39. Persuasive Writing Research the way government regulates a business or industry in your region. Write a short paper discussing how you think the regulation affects the supply curve of the product both for the firm and for the industry.

Math Practice

40. Using the schedule below as a starting point, create a supply schedule and a supply curve that shows the following information: American automakers are willing to sell 200,000 cars per year when the price of a car is $20,000. They are willing to sell 400,000 when the price is $25,000 and 600,000 at a price of $30,000.

Price	Quantity supplied
$20,000	200,000
$25,000	

36. Answers will vary but may include the costs of car insurance, gasoline, and oil changes.

Thinking Like an Economist

37. a. Stage III
  b. Stage I
  c. Stage II

Analyzing Visuals

38. In Stage I, the curve rises sharply. In Stage II, the curve still rises but not as sharply. In Stage III, the curve drops to previous levels. In relation to total product, the marginal product numbers increase greatly in Stage I, increase less in Stage II, and reflect negative numbers in Stage III.

Writing About Economics

39. Answers will vary but should illustrate an understanding of the relationship between government regulations and the supply curve.

Math Practice

40.

Supply Schedule

Price	Quantity Supplied
$20,000	200,000
$25,000	400,000
$30,000	600,000

Students' supply curves should indicate an upward direction, illustrating an increase in both price and quantities supplied.

31. Production functions tend to differ because the mix of inputs, the quality of inputs, and/or the quantity of inputs differs from firm to firm. Firms reach the points of diminishing or negative returns at different points because the businesses themselves vary.

32. Answers will vary, but students will likely revise their predictions now that they are more knowledgeable about supply and pricing.

33. If prices go down, suppliers will offer less for sale at lower prices. If the cost of production increases while prices remain the same, suppliers will offer less for sale.

34. Oranges: supply drops. **Tractors:** supply increases. **Cars:** supply drops.

Applying Economic Concepts

35. Answers will vary, but students should demonstrate a clear understanding of how marginal analysis operates in their decisions.

Key to Ability Levels		Key to Teaching Resources	
BL Below level	**AL** Above level	📁 Print Material	💿 DVD
OL On level	**ELL** English Language Learners	💿 CD-Rom	🖨 Transparency

Levels					Resources	Chapter Opener	Section 1	Section 2	Section 3	Chapter Assess
BL	OL	AL	ELL							
					FOCUS					
BL	OL	AL	ELL	🖨	**Daily Focus Skills Transparencies**		25	13	26	
					TEACH					
BL	OL		ELL	📁	**Guided Reading Activities***		p. 16	p. 17	p. 18	
BL	OL	AL	ELL	📁	**Economic Content Vocabulary Activities***		p. 6	p. 6	p. 6	
	OL	AL		📁	**Critical Thinking Activities**		pp. 6, 11	p. 11		
BL	OL		ELL	📁	**Reading Essentials and Note-Taking Guide***		p. 46	p. 49	p. 52	
		AL		📁	**Enrichment Activities**			p. 6		
BL	OL	AL	ELL	📁	**Hands-On Economics**			p. 5		
BL	OL	AL	ELL	🖨	**Economic Concepts Transparencies, Strategies, and Activities**			pp. 13, 15		
BL	OL	AL	ELL	📁	**Math Practice for Economics**		p. 8	p. 8		
BL	OL	AL	ELL	🖨	**Economics Forms and Financial Pages Transparencies, Strategies, and Activities**			p. 15		
BL	OL	AL	ELL	📁	**Reinforcing Economic Skills**			p. 4		
BL	OL		ELL	📁	**High School Reading in the Content Area Strategies and Activities**	✓	✓	✓	✓	✓
BL	OL	AL	ELL	🖨	**High School Writing Process Transparencies**	✓	✓	✓	✓	✓
BL	OL	AL	ELL	📁	**Writer's Guidebook**	✓	✓	✓	✓	✓
BL	OL	AL	ELL	💿	**StudentWorks Plus CD-ROM**	✓	✓	✓	✓	✓
BL	OL	AL	ELL	💿	**Vocabulary PuzzleMaker CD-ROM**	✓	✓	✓	✓	✓

*Also available in Spanish

Teacher Works *Plus*
All-In-One Planner and Resource Center

- Interactive Lesson Planner
- Interactive Teacher Edition
- Fully editable blackline masters
- Economics & You videos

- Differentiated Lesson Plans
- Printable reports of daily assignments
- Standards tracking system

Levels					Resources	Chapter Opener	Section 1	Section 2	Section 3	Chapter Assess
BL	OL	AL	ELL							
TEACH (continued)										
BL	OL	AL	ELL	🔒	Economics & You Video Program DVD— *The Price System at Work*	✓	✓	✓	✓	✓
BL	OL	AL	ELL	💿	Graph Coach CD-ROM	✓	✓	✓	✓	✓
Teacher Resources				📁	Differentiated Instruction Strategies	✓	✓	✓	✓	✓
				📁	Success with English Learners	✓	✓	✓	✓	✓
				💿	Presentation Plus! CD-ROM	✓	✓	✓	✓	✓
ASSESS										
BL	OL	AL	ELL	📁	Section Quizzes and Chapter Tests		p. 69	p. 70	p. 71	pp. 73, 77
BL	OL	AL	ELL	📁	Authentic Assessment Strategies and Activities				p. 9	
BL	OL	AL	ELL	💿	*ExamView® Assessment Suite* CD-ROM		6-1	6-2	6-3	Ch. 6
BL	OL	AL	ELL	💿	Interactive Tutor Self-Assessment CD-ROM		6-1	6-2	6-3	
CLOSE										
BL			ELL	📁	Reteaching Activities*		p. 6	p. 6	p. 6	
BL	OL		ELL	📁	Reading and Study Skills Foldables		p. 53	p. 48	p. 53	

*Also available in Spanish

Activity
Using the McGraw-Hill Learning Network

Researching World Book™ Select

Technology Product
World Book Select offers thousands of detailed articles chosen from the *World Book Encyclopedia* and covers all curricular areas. World Book Select allows students to research national and international topics and issues in economics and other curriculum areas.

Objectives
After students learn to use World Book Select, they will be able to
- develop and expand research and study skills;
- practice reading and writing skills.

Steps
Give students the following directions to use World Book Select:
- From the McGraw-Hill Learning Network home page (www.mhln.com), click on **For Students.**
- Choose **World Book Select** below **Homework Help.**
- Click the letter for the encyclopedia volume you want to use.
- On the search page for the volume selected:
  - click the title of a featured article on the right side of the page; or
  - click on a topic from the list on the left side of the page; then click on the title of an article of interest on the right.
- Read the article and take notes.

Economics ONLINE

	Student	Teacher	Parent
Beyond the Textbook	●	●	●
Chapter Overviews	●	●	●
ePuzzles and Games	●		●
Concepts in Motion	●		●
Multi-Language Glossaries	●		●
Online Student Edition	●	●	●
Self-Check Quizzes	●		●
Student Web Activities	●		●
Study Central™	●		●
Time Current Events	●	●	●
Teaching Today		●	
Vocabulary eFlashcards	●		●
Web Activity Lesson Plans		●	

Glencoe Media Center

〉 glencoe.com

Study-To-Go
- Vocabulary eFlashcards
- Self-Check Quizzes

〉 **Audio/Video**
- Student Edition Audio
- Spanish Summaries
- Economics & You Videos

- **Timed Readings Plus in Social Studies** helps students increase their reading rate and fluency while maintaining comprehension. The 400-word passages are similar to those found on state and national assessments.

- **Reading in the Content Area: Social Studies** concentrates on six essential reading skills that help students better comprehend what they read. The book includes 75 high-interest nonfiction passages written at increasing levels of difficulty.

- **Reading Social Studies** includes strategic reading instruction and vocabulary support in Social Studies content for both ELLs and native speakers of English. www.jamestowneducation.com

Reading List Generator CD-ROM

Use this database to search more than 30,000 titles to create a customized reading list for your students.

- Reading lists can be organized by students' reading level, author, genre, theme, or area of interest.

- The database provides Degrees of Reading Power™ (DRP) and Lexile™ readability scores for all selections.

- A brief summary of each selection is included.

Leveled reading suggestions for this chapter:
For students at a Grade 10 reading level:
- *How Do They Package It?,* by George Sullivan

For students at a Grade 11 reading level:
- *The World of Power and Energy,* by Frank Ross

For students at a Grade 12 reading level:
- *Food, Inc.: Mendel to Monsanto—The Promises and Perils of the Biotech Harvest,* by Peter Pringle

* Review suggested books before assigning them.

NCEE

National Council on Economic Education

Voluntary Standards Emphasized in Chapter 6

Content Standard 4 People respond predictably to positive and negative incentives.

Content Standard 7 Markets exist when buyers and sellers interact. This interaction determines market prices and thereby allocates scarce goods and services.

Content Standard 8 Prices send signals and provide incentives to buyers and sellers. When supply or demand changes, market prices adjust, affecting incentives.

Content Standard 17 Costs of government policies sometimes exceed benefits. This may occur because of incentives facing voters, government officials, and government employees, because of actions by special interest groups that can impose costs on the general public, or because social goals other than economic efficiency are being pursued.

Resources Available from NCEE
- Virtual Economics®: An Interactive Center for Economic Education Version 3.0
- Capstone: The Nation's High School Economics Course
- Focus: High School Economics, Second Edition
- Advanced Placement Economics: Teacher Resource Manual, Third Edition

To order these materials, or to contact your State Council on Economic Education about workshops and programs, call 1-800-338-1192 or visit the NCEE Web site at store.ncee.net.

The BIG Ideas

As students study the chapter, remind them to consider the chapter-based Big Ideas. The **Essential Question** in the chapter launch activity below ties in to the Big Ideas and helps students think about and understand important chapter concepts. In addition, the Hands-On Chapter Project relates the content from each section to the Big Ideas. The steps in each section build on each other and culminate in the Wrap-Up Activity on the Visual Summary page.

Economics & You Video To generate student interest and provide a springboard for class discussion, access the Economics & You Topic 11 video, **The Price System at Work,** at glencoe.com or on the video DVD.

FOLDABLES Study Organizer **Dinah Zike's Foldables** are three-dimensional, interactive graphic organizers that help students practice basic writing skills, review key vocabulary terms, and identify main ideas. Have students complete this chapter's Foldable activity or activities in *Dinah Zike's Reading and Study Skills Foldables* booklet. **OL**

Economics ONLINE

Introduce students to chapter content and key terms by having them access *Chapter 6 —Chapter Overviews* at glencoe.com.

CHAPTER 6 Prices and Decision Making

Why It Matters

Have you ever wondered why famous athletes and entertainers make millions of dollars each year? Imagine that you are one of these athletes or entertainers and will be interviewed on a major television program. Knowing that the interviewer will ask you why you make so much money, prepare a list of 5 to 10 reasons that explain why you are worth your salary. Read Chapter 6 to learn about how economic systems allocate goods and services.

The BIG Ideas

1. Markets exist when buyers and sellers interact, and market prices are set by the interaction of demand and supply.

2. Governments strive for a balance between the costs and benefits of their economic policies to promote economic stability and growth.

Every day prices help buyers ▶ make decisions about the quantities of goods and services they buy.

Economics ONLINE **Chapter Overview** Visit the *Economics: Principles and Practices* Web site at glencoe.com and click on *Chapter 6–Chapter Overviews* to preview chapter information.

142 UNIT 2

Activity: Launching the Chapter

Categorizing Have students make a list of the goods and services they have purchased over the past week. Next, ask them to list the factors they believed affected the prices of the items they bought. **Essential Question: How might the government have influenced the prices of items you bought during the last week?** *(Possible answers: government funds reduced the price of school lunches; a recent* *increase to the minimum wage caused a local pizza restaurant owner to raise the price of pizza.)* Organize the class into pairs. Have each pair interview a local business owner about the factors that influence the prices of certain items he or she sells. Ask students to present the results of their interviews to the class. **OL**

SECTION 1 — Prices as Signals

GUIDE TO READING

Section Preview
In this section, you will learn that prices act as signals that help us allocate scarce resources.

Content Vocabulary
- price *(p. 143)*
- rationing *(p. 145)*
- ration coupon *(p. 145)*
- rebate *(p. 146)*

Academic Vocabulary
- neutral *(p. 144)*
- criteria *(p. 145)*

Reading Strategy
Explaining As you read the section, complete a graphic organizer similar to the one below by explaining the advantages of prices.

Advantages of Prices

Focus

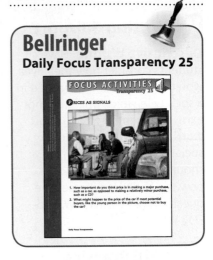

Bellringer
Daily Focus Transparency 25

FOCUS ACTIVITIES
Transparency 25
PRICES AS SIGNALS

1. How important do you think price is in making a major purchase, such as a car, as opposed to making a relatively minor purchase, such as a CD?
2. What might happen to the price of the car if most potential buyers, like the young person in the picture, choose not to buy the car?

Daily Focus Transparencies

GUIDE TO READING

Answers to Graphic: neutral; flexible; familiar and easy to understand; no cost of administration

---

PRODUCTS IN THE NEWS
—New Orleans Times-Picayune

Katrina Fallout

The local real estate market soared after Hurricane Katrina, with home prices recording double-digit increases and the number of sales remaining surprisingly strong. . . .

During the final four months of 2005—the months after Katrina—the average sale price in the metropolitan area was $215,769, or 21 percent higher than the average price of all homes sold in 2004. . . .

The strong real estate figures send the clearest signal yet that the New Orleans housing market is not dead. In fact, they might make the city more appealing than ever to national investors . . . looking to snatch up bargain properties they can sell down the road for a profit. ■

Life is full of signals that help us make decisions. For example, when we pull up to an intersection, we look to see if the traffic light is green, yellow, or red. We look at the other cars to see if any have their blinkers on, signaling their intentions to turn. While these are clear and obvious signals, there are other, more hidden ones. Pain, for example, signals you that something is wrong with your body. But have you ever thought about signals in economics?

It turns out that something as simple as a **price**—the monetary value of a product as established by supply and demand—is a signal that helps us make economic decisions. Prices give information to buyers and sellers. High prices signal buyers to buy less and producers to produce more. Low prices signal buyers to buy more and producers to produce less. Even housing prices, as we read in the news story above, send signals.

price monetary value of a product as established by supply and demand

CHAPTER 6 Prices and Decision Making **143**

Resource Manager

R Reading Strategies	C Critical Thinking	D Differentiated Instruction	W Writing Support	S Skill Practice
Teacher Edition • Inferring, p. 145 **Additional Resources** • Guid. Read. Act., p. 16 • Reading Ess. & Note-Taking Guide, p. 46	**Teacher Edition** • Speculating, p. 146 • Theorizing, p. 147 **Additional Resources** • Crit. Think. Act., pp. 6, 11	**Teacher Edition** • Adv. Learners, p. 145 **Additional Resources** • Math Prac. for Econ., p. 8 • Reading and Study Skills Fold., p. 53	**Teacher Edition** • Descriptive Writing, p. 144 • Personal Writing, p. 147 **Additional Resources** • Writer's Guidebook	**Teacher Edition** • Analyzing Info., p. 144 **Additional Resources** • Reteach. Act., p. 6 • Econ. Content Vocab. Act., p. 6

Teach

W Writing Support

Descriptive Writing Have students consider how their lives would be different if they lived in a society in which prices did not exist. Ask them to write a short story describing this fictional society. Tell students that they should include in their stories how the society addresses the questions of WHAT, HOW, and FOR WHOM. **OL**

S Skill Practice

Analyzing Information

Ask: How do you think the profit margin for laptops sold in 2000 differed from the profit margin for laptops sold in 2006? *(Profit margin per unit sold was much higher in 2000 than in 2006.)* What was the reason for that difference? *(Laptop prices were much higher in 2000 than in 2006.)* **OL**

✓**Reading Check** **Answer:** People make purchasing decisions based on prices; this results in the allocation of goods and services.

Differentiated Instruction

Critical Thinking Activities, p. 6

Advantages of Prices

MAIN Idea Prices help the economy run smoothly by providing a good way to allocate resources.

Economics & You Have you ever seen news reports about rising prices for building materials after a hurricane? Read on to learn how the price system helps us deal with natural disasters.

W Prices help producers and consumers decide the three basic questions of WHAT, HOW, and FOR WHOM to produce. Without prices, the economy would not run as smoothly, and allocation decisions would have to be made some other way. Prices perform this function well for several reasons.

First, in a competitive market economy, prices are **neutral** because they favor neither the producer nor the consumer. Since prices are the result of competition between buyers and sellers, they represent compromises that both sides can live with.

Second, prices in a market economy are flexible. Unforeseen events such as natural disasters and war affect the prices of many items. Buyers and sellers then react to the new level of prices and adjust their consumption and production accordingly. Before long, the system functions as smoothly again as it had before. The ability of the price system to absorb unexpected "shocks" is one of the strengths of a market economy.

Third, most people have known about prices all their lives. As a result, prices are familiar and easy to understand. There is no ambiguity over a price—if something costs $1.99, then we know exactly what we have to pay for it. This allows people to make decisions quickly and efficiently, with a minimum of time and effort.

Finally, prices have no cost of administration. Competitive markets tend to find their own prices without outside help or interference. No bureaucrats need to be hired, no committees formed, no laws passed, or other decisions made. Even when prices adjust from one level to another, the changes are usually so gradual that people hardly notice.

✓**Reading Check** **Summarizing** In what way do prices perform the allocation function?

The Global Economy & YOU

Mobility on the Cheap

Americans are constantly in motion. The popularity of cell phones and laptop computers illustrates this point. Luckily for on-the-go consumers, the prices of these mobile products are falling. The average cost of a laptop in 2000 was more than $2,000. Each year, the average price has dropped by several hundred dollars.

Competition has played the biggest role in the downward spiral of profits for laptop makers. In 2006, the profit margin for most laptops was only $50. This meager profit means that manufacturers are aiming for high sales volume rather than high profit margins. They are also counting on consumers to spend more on expensive accessories, such as service plans, docking stations, and batteries.

How does this competitive market impact you? Consumers can expect lower prices and a wider selection. In addition, the competition ensures innovation, as manufacturers search for the gadget or accessory that none of us can do without.

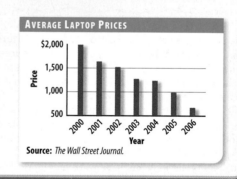

AVERAGE LAPTOP PRICES

Source: *The Wall Street Journal.*

Comparing Rationing and the Price System

Objective: Understand the differences between the price system and the rationing system.

Focus/Teach: Ask students to describe how people acquire goods in a price system and in a rationing system. Then have them complete the activity.

Assess: Call on volunteers to share their answers.

Close: Have students write two paragraphs summarizing the characteristics of the price system and those of the rationing system.

Differentiated Instruction Strategies

BL Have students explain how a person acquires a good under the rationing system.

AL Have students add a phrase to each column in the chart.

ELL Ask students to look up the word *ration* in a dictionary and then write a sentence using that word.

Allocations Without Prices

MAIN Idea Rationing has disadvantages that are not present in the price system.

Economics & You How would you allocate goods like cars or food if there were no prices? Read on to learn about the problems associated with other systems.

Prices help us make the everyday economic decisions that allocate scarce resources. But what would life be like without a price system? Would intelligence, good looks, or even political connections determine the allocations?

These **criteria** may seem far-fetched, but this happens in countries with command economies. When the Baltimore Orioles played an exhibition baseball game in Cuba several years ago, there were not enough stadium seats for the local baseball fans who wanted to attend. Fidel Castro then solved the FOR WHOM questions by giving the seats to Communist Party members—whether or not they were baseball fans.

Rationing This clerk in a grocery store in Cuba accepts ration coupons as payment for the products people are buying. *How are ration coupons allocated?*

Rationing

Without prices, another system must be used to decide who gets what. One method is **rationing**—a system under which a government agency decides everyone's "fair" share. Under such a system, people receive a **ration coupon,** a ticket or a receipt that entitles the holder to obtain a certain amount of a product. The coupon can be given to people outright, or the government can charge a modest fee that is less than the product's market value. Rationing has been widely used during wartime, but it can lead to problems.

R

Problems with Rationing

The first problem with rationing is that almost everyone feels his or her share is too small. During the energy crisis of the early 1970s, the government made plans for, but never implemented, gasoline rationing. One problem was determining how to allocate **D** the rationing coupons in a way that everyone would see as fair. A number of ways to allocate gas coupons were debated, but the issue of fairness was never resolved.

A second problem is the administrative cost of rationing. Someone must pay the salaries and the printing and distribution costs of the coupons. In addition, no matter how much care is taken, some coupons will be stolen, sold, or counterfeited and used to get a product intended for someone else.

A third problem is the negative impact on the incentive to produce. What if you were paid with ration coupons and you received the same number of coupons as your coworkers? Without the possibility of earning more coupons, you might lose some of your incentive to work.

✓**Reading Check** **Contrasting** What are the differences between the price system and rationing?

rationing system of allocating goods and services without prices

ration coupon permit allowing holder to receive a given amount of a rationed product

📖 **Skills Handbook**

See page **R43** to learn about *Comparing and Contrasting.*

R **Reading Strategy**

Inferring **Ask:** What types of governments do you think are most likely to make allocations based on rationing? Why? *(totalitarian; those governments generally control purchasing decisions)* **OL**

D **Differentiated Instruction**

Advanced Learners Have students use print or online resources to research a time in U.S. history when the government implemented rationing. Ask students to write a paper on the topic they selected. **AL**

Caption Answer: The government decides what is "fair."

✓**Reading Check** **Answer:** Price system: people make their own purchasing decisions based on the prices of goods and services. Rationing system: government agency decides what and how many goods and services people will receive.

Hands-On Chapter Project

Step 1

Evaluating Prices

In this project, students will set and evaluate the prices of cookies that they will bake and sell.

Step 1: Setting Prices. Students will set prices for cookies based on their estimates of production costs and potential demand.

Directions: Organize the class into four groups. Assign one of the following cookie types to each group: chocolate chip, peanut butter, sugar, and oatmeal raisin. Ask each group to research what it would cost them to produce four dozen of their assigned cookies for a class bake sale. Remind students to include advertising expenses (such as posters and markers) as well as the cost of ingredients when making their calculations. Next, have student groups evaluate the potential demand for their cookie (for example, they could poll students at their school to determine the level of interest in their assigned cookie type).

Summarizing Direct each group to synthesize the information they have gathered about production costs and potential demand to determine a price for their cookie that they believe will yield a profit.. **OL**

(Chapter Project continued in Section 2.)

C Critical Thinking

Speculating Ask: How do you think the actions of automakers would have been different if oil prices had dropped between 2005 and 2006? *(Students will likely say that SUVs would have continued to sell, so changes in price and production would not have occurred.)* **OL**

✓**Reading Check** **Answer:** Price increases in a certain market lower demand, which causes manufacturers to shift resources to more profitable markets.

Assess

⊙ Use the Interactive Tutor Self-Assessment CD-ROM to review Section 1, and then assign the Section 1 Review as homework or as an in-class activity.

Close

Categorizing Have students create a chart that categorizes the different functions that prices perform. **OL**

SECTION
1 Review

---

rebate partial refund of a product's original price

Prices as a System

MAIN Idea Prices connect all markets in an economy.

Economics & You Have you noticed ads for rebates on SUVs when gas prices soar? Read on to learn how these rebates are one way in which prices allocate resources between markets.

Because of the difficulties with nonprice allocation systems, economists overwhelmingly favor the price system. In fact, prices do more than help individuals make decisions: they also serve as signals that help allocate resources between markets.

Consider the way in which higher oil prices affected producer and consumer decisions when the price of oil went from under $35 to over $70 a barrel in 2005 and 2006. Because the demand for oil is basically inelastic, people spent a greater part of their income on energy. Higher energy costs left them with less to spend elsewhere.

The SUV market was one of the first to feel the effects of high prices. Because most of these vehicles got poor gas mileage, people bought fewer SUVs, leaving dealerships with huge inventories. To move these inventories,

some manufacturers offered consumers a **rebate**—a partial refund of the original price of the product. The rebate was the same as a temporary price reduction, because consumers were offered thousands of dollars back on each new car they bought. Other dealers offered zero-interest financing.

Finally, automakers had to reduce their
C production of these vehicles. Ford Motor Company, for example, closed plants, laid off workers, and tried to sell more fuel-efficient cars. Many automobile workers who lost their jobs eventually found new ones in other industries. In the end, the result of higher international oil prices was to shift productive resources out of SUV production into other products. Although the adjustment process was painful for many in the industry, it was a natural and necessary shift of resources for a market economy.

In the end, prices do more than convey information to buyers and sellers in a market: they also allocate resources between markets. This is why economists think of prices as a "system"—part of an informational network—that links all markets in the economy.

✓**Reading Check** **Identifying** How do prices allocate resources between markets?

SECTION
1 **Review**

Vocabulary
1. **Explain** the significance of price, rationing, ration coupon, and rebate.

Main Ideas
2. **Describing** What are the advantages of prices?
3. **Identifying** Use a graphic organizer like the one below to identify the problems associated with rationing.

Problems of Rationing

4. **Explaining** Why are prices an efficient way to allocate goods and services?

Critical Thinking
5. **The BIG Idea** Describe how prices help allocate scarce resources by answering the questions of WHAT, HOW, and FOR WHOM to produce.
6. **Analyzing Visuals** Look at the photograph on page 145. What effect does rationing seem to have on the number and variety of items in the store?
7. **Understanding Cause and Effect** Assume that there is a gasoline shortage and your state has imposed rationing. Write a paragraph about how this might affect you, your family, and your community.

Applying Economics
8. **Rationing** List five items you would like to buy. How does the price of each item affect your decision to allocate scarce resources—your money and your time?

Answers

1. All definitions can be found in the section and the Glossary.
2. Prices favor neither the producer nor the consumer; prices are flexible; people are familiar with prices; prices have no administrative cost.
3. almost everyone wants a larger share; high administrative cost; declining incentive to produce
4. They have no administrative costs and competitive markets tend to find their own prices without outside help or interference.

5. Prices tell manufacturers what to produce by indicating which products they can sell at a profit. The price producers have to pay for resources guides their decisions about how to produce items. The willingness of people to buy an item at a certain price answers the "for whom" question of production.
6. Answers may vary, but students should recognize that the number and variety of items in the store appear limited.

7. Students' paragraphs should demonstrate an understanding of how a rationing system functions and the problems that could potentially result.
8. Students should present economically sound evaluations of how the prices of their listed items affect their decisions regarding the allocation of their scarce resources of money and time.

CASE STUDY

'I Bought It on eBay'

The World's Online Marketplace

Since its introduction in 1995, eBay has given rise to the phrase "I bought it on eBay." Buyers and sellers flock to the online auction site to bid on and sell everything from snow and math tutoring to collectibles and used cars.

The Perfect Price

The site serves as an online forum where supply meets demand in a seamless process. Sellers enjoy the advantages of a huge customer base and little overhead. They also have the option to list a "reserve," or minimum price. All of these features help maximize profits. Buyers appreciate the ability to browse millions of items, shop from home, and counter-offer with their own bid. **W**

Because eBay does not produce, sell, or distribute any of the products offered on its Web site, it makes money by charging a modest listing fee and commission for each item sold. In 2005 the number of registered eBay members topped 100 million, including potential buyers in more than 30 countries.

EUROPEANS EARNING AT LEAST 25% OF THEIR INCOME FROM EBAY BUSINESS

Britain
Germany
France
Italy
Spain

0 10 20 30 40 50 60 70
Thousands

Source: eBay Inc.

To some members, eBay is a great place to sell an item they no longer need or want, such as a baby stroller or CD. For others, eBay has turned from a hobby into a career. In 2005 more than 700,000 people in the United States earned full- or part-time income on eBay. Many sellers in Europe—especially Britain and Germany—also rely on eBay to make money. **C**

eBay Express

In 2006 eBay faced serious competition from Google and Yahoo for a larger share of the e-commerce market. The company's response was eBay Express, which allows shoppers to purchase products immediately without waiting a week for an auction to close. The hope is that a brand new audience will tap into the eBay experience.

EBAY REVENUES 2001–2005

$5

Revenue (in billions)

4

3

2

1

2001 2002 2003 2004 2005
Year

Source: moneycentral.msn.com

Analyzing the Impact

1. **Summarizing** How is price determined for an item on eBay?
2. **Explaining** What change did eBay make to attract more shoppers?

CHAPTER 6 **Prices and Decision Making** 147

Extending the Content

Customer Satisfaction With Online Auctions Many people thinking about selling or purchasing an item through eBay may have concerns about fraud or other problems with the transaction process. The results of a recent national survey may assuage some of their fears. According to a poll by the University of Michigan and ForeSee Results, customer satisfaction with online auctions stood at 78 percent in 2006. eBay led all companies in that category with an 80 percent satisfaction rating. Customer satisfaction with e-commerce overall—including online retail, auction, brokerage, and travel companies—was at 80 percent. To compare, customer satisfaction with the traditional offline retail sector was more than five points lower at 74.4.

Focus

Bellringer
Daily Focus Transparency 13

GUIDE TO READING

Answers to Graphic:

Surplus/Effects: prices fall until demand increases and supply is reduced

Shortage/Effects: prices increase until demand falls and supply can increase

Resource Manager

The Price System at Work

GUIDE TO READING

Section Preview
In this section, you will learn how economic models help us understand prices in competitive markets.

Content Vocabulary
- economic model (p. 149)
- equilibrium price (p. 149)
- surplus (p. 150)
- shortage (p. 151)

Academic Vocabulary
- voluntary (p. 149)
- fluctuates (p. 153)

Reading Strategy
Describing As you read the section, complete a graphic organizer similar to this by describing how a surplus and a shortage affect prices, demand, and supply.

Surplus → Effects

Shortage → Effects

COMPANIES IN THE NEWS
—adapted from *The Miami Herald*

Want Prime Seats? Get Ready to Bid

Bids on the best seats in the house for Madonna's concert . . . could start at the face-value price of $350. Do I hear $450? Going once, going twice . . . Sold! To the person online.

Tired of competition from scalpers, Ticketmaster and its clients are now auctioning "premium seats" to concerts, sports meets, and other events. The practice, dubbed "dynamic pricing," allows customers to set their own prices. Competitors see it differently, saying the practice allows Ticketmaster to scalp its own tickets. (Scalping is a second-degree misdemeanor under Florida state law, punishable by up to 60 days in jail and a $500 fine.)

. . . Dynamic pricing endorses a free market economic principle: namely, that the market determines the fair value of a ticket. ∎

One of the most appealing features of a competitive market economy is that everyone who participates has a hand in determining prices. This is why economists consider prices to be neutral and impartial.

The process of establishing a price, as you read in the news story above, can be complicated—or even contentious—because buyers and sellers have exactly the opposite hopes and desires. Buyers want to find good buys at low prices. Sellers hope for high prices and large profits. Neither can get exactly what they want, so some adjustment is necessary to reach a compromise.

Will consumers pay too much for tickets? Most economists would argue that as long as the process is competitive and the transaction voluntary, then the price will be about right under a bidding system.

R Reading Strategies	**C** Critical Thinking	**D** Differentiated Instruction	**W** Writing Support	**S** Skill Practice
Teacher Edition • Academic Vocab., p. 149 • Outlining, p. 152 **Additional Resources** • Guid. Read. Act., p. 17 • Reading Ess. & Note-Taking Guide, p. 49 • Enrichment Act., p. 6	**Teacher Edition** • Ident. POV, p. 150 • Det. Cause/Effect, p. 151 • Interpreting, p. 154 • Assessing, p. 155 **Additional Resources** • Econ. Concepts Trans., Strat. and Act., pp. 13, 15	**Teacher Edition** • Verbal/Linguistic, p. 150 • ELL, p. 153 **Additional Resources** • Econ. Forms and Financial Pages Trans., Strat. and Act., p. 15 • Crit. Think. Act., p. 11 • Daily Focus Trans. 13, 14	**Teacher Edition** • Narrative Writing, p. 152 **Additional Resources** • High School Writing Process Trans. • Reading and Study Skills Fold., p. 48	**Teacher Edition** • Evaluating Info., p. 149 • Analyzing Cartoons, p. 151 **Additional Resources** • Reinforcing Econ. Skills, p. 4 • Hands-On Econ., p. 5 • Math Prac. for Econ., p. 8

The Price Adjustment Process

MAIN Idea In a market economy, prices seek their own equilibrium.

Economics & You You learned earlier that the price system is flexible. Read on to find out how prices adjust to changes in the economy.

Because transactions in a market economy are **voluntary,** the compromise that settles the differences between buyers and sellers must be to the benefit of both, or the compromise would not occur. **R**

A Market Model

To show how the adjustment process works, we use the supply and demand illustration shown in **Figure 6.1**—one of the more popular "tools" used by economists. The figure illustrates how we can use an **economic model** to analyze behavior and predict outcomes.

The data in the figure show the demand for and supply of CDs at various prices. You are already familiar with these numbers, because they are the same ones you saw when you learned about demand in Chapter 4 and supply in Chapter 5. **Panel A** combines information from the market demand schedule in Figure 4.2 on page 94 and the market supply schedule in Figure 5.2 on page 119. **Panel B** shows both the market demand curve and the market supply curve, again from those two earlier figures.

Separately, each of these graphs represents the demand or supply side of the market. When the curves are combined, we have a complete model of the market, which will allow us to analyze how the interaction of buyers and sellers results in a price agreeable to all market participants.

Note that the supply and demand curves intersect at a specific point. This point is called the **equilibrium price**, the price at which the number of units produced equals the number of units sold. It means that at this price there is neither a surplus nor a shortage of the product in the market. But how does the market reach this equilibrium price, and why does it settle at $15 rather

economic model a simplified version of a complex behavior expressed in the form of an equation, graph, or illustration *(also see page 23)*

equilibrium price price where quantity supplied equals quantity demanded

Teach

R Reading Strategy

Academic Vocabulary
Have students write a paragraph explaining why the actions of buyers and sellers in a market can be considered voluntary. *(Answers will vary but should include that no one is forcing buyers or sellers to buy/sell items.)* **BL**

S Skill Practice

Evaluating Information Have students compare data in the graph with their knowledge of current CD prices. **Ask:** How realistic is the graph in reflecting the current CD market? *(Answers will vary but may include that the graph is realistic in that CD prices generally hover around $15. CDs at $30 would not sell well, whereas there would be increased demand for CDs priced at $5.)* **OL**

Economic Analysis

Answer: It is the price at which there is neither a surplus nor a shortage of a given product.

Figure 6.1 ► **Market Equilibrium**

A MARKET DEMAND AND SUPPLY SCHEDULES

Price	Quantity demanded	Quantity supplied	Surplus/shortage
$30	0	13	13
25	1	11	10
20	3	9	6
15	6	6	0
10	10	3	−7
5	15	0	−15

B MARKET DEMAND AND SUPPLY CURVES

S

► The schedules provide the quantities demanded and the quantities supplied at different prices. The last column lists the surpluses or shortages at each price. When the demand and supply at each price are plotted, they show that the curves intersect at a price of $15. This is the equilibrium price.

Economic Analysis *Why is the equilibrium price important?*

Additional Support

Activity: Interdisciplinary Connection

Mathematics Supply and demand curves can be written as equations. Have your students graph the following equations on graph paper (with *P* on the vertical axis and *Q* on the horizontal axis).

- Supply: $P = 14 - 2Q$
- Demand: $P = 2 + Q$

Ask students to find the equilibrium price *P* and quantity *Q*. Next have them find the equilibrium price and quantity algebraically by solving the two equations for *P* and *Q*. *(P = 6, Q = 4)* **OL**

Teacher Tip

Reviewing Equations Before beginning this activity, take a few moments to review with students the elements of an equation and how to solve it.

C Critical Thinking

Identifying Points of View
Ask: Do you think it is common for sellers to offer a new product at a price well above what turns out to be the equilibrium price? Why or why not? *(Answers will vary. Students responding "yes" may reason that sellers, wanting to maximize profits, will sell a product at as high of a price that buyers are willing to pay. If the initial price turns out to be too high, sellers can always lower it later.)* **OL**

D Differentiated Instruction

Verbal/Linguistic Have students reflect upon the items they have purchased in their lifetimes. Ask them to identify a product that, although too expensive when it first came out, they were able to afford after the price eventually dropped. Have students write and deliver a short oral report describing the experience. **OL**

Economic Analysis
Answer: Sellers set the price at a level higher than buyers were willing to pay.

Additional Support

---

surplus situation where quantity supplied is greater than quantity demanded at a given price

Skills Handbook
See page **R53** to learn about **Comparing Data.**

Surplus
We start on Day 1 with sellers thinking that the price will be $25. If you examine the supply schedule in Panel A of Figure 6.1, you see that suppliers will produce 11 units for sale at that price. However, the suppliers soon discover that buyers will purchase only one CD at a price of $25, leaving a surplus of 10.

A **surplus** is a situation in which the quantity supplied is greater than the quantity demanded at a given price. The 10-unit surplus at the end of Day 1 is shown in column four of Panel A in Figure 6.1 as the difference between the quantity supplied and the quantity demanded at the $25 price. It is also shown graphically in **Panel A** of **Figure 6.2** as the horizontal

than some other price? To answer these questions, we have to examine the reactions of buyers and sellers to different market prices. When we do this, we assume that neither the buyer nor the seller knows the final price, so we'll have to find it using trial and error.

distance between the supply and demand curves at a price of $25.

This surplus shows up as unsold products on suppliers' shelves, and it begins to take up space in their warehouses. Sellers now know that $25 is too high, and they know that they have to lower their price if they want to attract more buyers and dispose of the surplus.

Therefore, the price tends to go down as a result of the surplus. The model cannot tell us how far the price will go down, but we can reasonably assume that the price will go down only a little if the surplus is small, and much more if the surplus is larger.

Shortage
Suppliers are more cautious on Day 2, so they anticipate a much lower price of $10. At that price, the quantity they are willing to supply changes to three CDs. However, as **Panel B** in Figure 6.2 shows, this price turns out to be too low. At a market price of $10, only three CDs are supplied and 10 are demanded—leaving a shortage of seven CDs.

Figure 6.2 ▶ Surpluses and Shortages

▶ A surplus occurs when sellers produce more units than buyers will purchase at a given price. A shortage is the result of buyers wanting to purchase more units than sellers offer at a given price. Surpluses will cause prices to drop, and shortages will cause prices to rise until prices reach an equilibrium.

Economic Analysis Why did the surplus shown in Panel A occur?

Graphs In MOtion
See StudentWorks™ Plus or glencoe.com.

Activity: Hands-On Economics

Identifying Surpluses and Shortages
Have students visit an area shopping mall and look for examples of surpluses and shortages, listing 5 to 10 items for each concept. Encourage students to visit a range of stores and include a range of products in their counts. Note that almost any sale or clearance item can be an example of a surplus, while rain checks or sold-out items signal a shortage. If students encounter difficulty identifying shortages,

they may want to interview salespeople about their experiences with shortages. **Ask:** Did the stores visited have more surpluses or more shortages? Ask students to write short essays in which they examine the prices and other determinants related to the items they found. They should also hypothesize as to why the surplus or shortage occurred. **OL**

© Mike Baldwin / Cornered

Music World

GREATEST HITS $20

GREATEST MISSES $5

Mike Baldwin/CartoonStock

Equilibrium Price Supply and demand determine the final price of a product. *Why does the price differ for the CDs in the cartoon?*

S

S Skill Practice

Analyzing Cartoons After students answer the caption question, have them make a list of other items that the cartoonist could have used to convey the same message. *(Possible answers: best-selling and bargain bin books; hit DVDs and box-office bombs)* **BL**

C Critical Thinking

Determining Cause and Effect **Ask:** What are some factors that could disturb an equilibrium market? *(Possible answers: new competitors entering the market; technological improvements to a product; drop in wages; inflation)* **OL**

Caption Answer: The $20 CDs are popular sellers; the $5 CDs are not.

✓Reading Check Answer: Surpluses cause sellers to lower prices while shortages cause sellers to raise prices. This process continues until there are no surpluses or shortages and an equilibrium price is reached.

A **shortage** is a situation in which the quantity demanded is greater than the quantity supplied at a given price. When a shortage happens, producers have no more CDs to sell, and they end the day wishing that they had charged a higher price for their products.

As a result of the shortage, both the price and the quantity supplied will go up in the next trading period. While our model does not show exactly how much the price will go up, we can assume that the next price will be less than $25, which we already know is too high.

Equilibrium Price

If the new price is $20 on Day 3, the result will be a surplus of six CDs. This surplus will cause the price to drop again, but probably not below $10, which already proved to be too low. However, if the price drops to $15, the market will have found its equilibrium price. As you learned earlier, the equilibrium price is the price that "clears the market" by leaving neither a surplus nor a shortage at the end of the trading period.

While our economic model of the market cannot show exactly how long it will take to reach equilibrium, the temporary surpluses and shortages will always be pushing the price in that direction. Whenever the price is too high, the surplus will tend to force it down. Whenever the price is too low, the shortage will tend to force it up. As a result, the market tends to seek its own equilibrium.

When the equilibrium price of $15 is finally reached, it will tend to remain there because the quantity supplied is exactly equal to the quantity demanded. Something could come along to disturb the equilibrium, but then new shortages, new surpluses, or both would appear to push the price toward its new equilibrium level.

C

Think of how much more difficult it would be to reach an equilibrium price if we did not have markets to help us with these decisions. You already learned that prices are neutral, flexible, understood by everybody, and free of administrative costs. It would be difficult to find another system that works equally well at setting the equilibrium price at exactly $15 and the equilibrium quantity at exactly six units. Also, when markets set prices, everybody has a hand in determining the outcome.

shortage situation where quantity supplied is less than quantity demanded at a given price

✓Reading Check **Summarizing** How do surpluses and shortages help establish the equilibrium price?

CHAPTER 6 Prices and Decision Making **151**

Hands-On Chapter Project

Step 2

Evaluating Prices

Step 2: Determining an Equilibrium Price. Students will seek to find an equilibrium price for cookies they are selling.

Directions: Have students return to the groups previously established. Instruct groups to bake a batch of cookies of the type that was assigned to them in Step 1. Ask each group to set up a table in a hallway during lunch period or after school, placing only six of their cookies on sale for 10 cents apiece. The next day have students offer three dozen of their cookies for sale at $1 apiece. On the third day (they may wish to bake a fresh batch of cookies by this point) have students place two dozen of their cookies on sale for 30 cents apiece. On the fourth day, have students choose how many and at what price to sell cookies based on what they believe is the equilibrium price. Students should record customer response for each sale day. You may wish to vary prices, number of cookies sold, or number of sale days for this activity.

Comparing Instruct groups to write a report comparing the results of their bake sale with the case study on CDs in this section. Student reports should include their theories on why their results were similar to or different from the case study. **OL**

(Chapter Project continued in Section 3.)

R Reading Strategy

Outlining Have students outline the subsection, taking note of the most important ideas and concepts. Provide students with examples of an outline to use as a guide. **BL**

W Writing Support

Narrative Writing Have students identify a business, other than farming, that sometimes experiences fluctuations in supply (for example, gas stations and grocery stores). Ask students to write a short story about an entrepreneur in that business who must deal with certain supply fluctuations. Tell students to explain in their stories the factors that caused the fluctuations and how they affected supply and prices. **OL**

Economic Analysis

Answer: Students will likely say an economic upturn or downturn, or a change in income, or a change in number of consumers.

Economics ONLINE

Student Web Activity Visit the *Economics: Principles and Practices* Web site at glencoe.com and click on *Chapter 6–Student Web Activities* for an activity on prices.

Explaining and Predicting Prices

MAIN Idea Changes in supply and demand can result in changes in prices.

Economics & You What happens to prices of concert tickets for bands that have become popular? Read on to find out how changes in demand affect prices.

Economists use their market models to explain changes in prices. A change in price is normally caused by a change in supply, a change in demand, or changes in both. Elasticity is also important when predicting how prices are likely to change.

Change in Supply

Consider agriculture, which often experiences wide swings in prices from one year to the next. A farmer may keep up with all the latest developments and have the best advice experts can offer, but the farmer can never be sure what price to expect for the

crop. For example, a soybean farmer may put in 500 acres of beans, hoping for a price of $9 a bushel. However, the farmer also knows that the actual price may end up being anywhere from $5 to $20.

Weather is one of the main reasons for variations in agricultural prices. If it rains too much after planting, the seeds may rot or be washed away and the farmer must replant. If it rains too little, the seeds may not sprout. Even if the weather is perfect during the growing season, rain can still interfere with the harvest. The weather, then, often causes a change in supply.

The result, shown in **Panel A** of **Figure 6.3,** is that the supply curve for agricultural products is likely to shift, causing the price to go up or down. At the beginning of the season, the farmer may expect supply to look like curve **S.** If a bumper, or record, crop is harvested, however, supply may look like **S¹.** If severe weather strikes, supply may look like **S².** In either case the price of soybeans is likely to change dramatically.

Figure 6.3 ▶ Changes in Prices

A FOOD PRICES
B ENERGY PRICES

▶ The supply and demand curves are both inelastic. Panel A illustrates how a change in supply due to weather can cause a large change in food prices. Panel B shows that a large price change will also take place if there is a change in demand.

Economic Analysis *What would cause a change in the market demand for food?*

Differentiated Instruction

Economic Concepts Trans., Strat., and Act., p. 13

Markets and Prices

Objective: Understand how prices are determined in a market.

Focus: Ask students to write a definition in their own words for *market* and *price*.

Teach: Have students examine the transparency and answer the questions on the activity sheet.

Assess: Review the answers as a class.

Close: Ask students to write a paragraph explaining the relationship between markets and prices.

Differentiated Instruction Strategies

BL Have students answer the question in Suggested Activity a.

AL Have students answer the question in Suggested Activity b.

ELL Have students draw a diagram illustrating in some way the concepts of markets and prices.

Change in Demand

A change in demand, like a change in supply, can affect the price of a good or service. All of the factors we examined in Chapter 4—changes in income, tastes, prices of related products, expectations, and the number of consumers—affect the market demand for goods and services. One example is the demand for oil.

In **Panel B** of Figure 6.3, a modest increase in demand, illustrated by a shift from **D** to **D¹**, causes a large increase in the price. This is exactly what happened in 2005 and 2006 when economic growth in the U.S. economy and the rest of the world, especially China and India, increased the demand for energy. Because both the supply and the demand for oil are inelastic, the price of oil increased dramatically. On the other hand, if the world economy had declined instead, demand would have shifted to **D²**, bringing the price of oil down.

Change in Supply *and* Demand

In the real world, changes in both supply and demand often affect prices. For example, we know that strong economic growth in 2005 caused the demand curve for oil to increase (or shift to the right), which drove prices up.

To make matters worse, hurricanes Katrina and Rita tore through the Gulf of Mexico, destroying and disabling hundreds of drilling platforms, refineries, and storage facilities. This caused the supply of oil to decrease (or shift to the left), driving the price of gasoline even higher. The resulting combination of increased demand and decreased supply gave the U.S. economy some of the highest energy prices it had seen since the 1970s.

The Importance of Elasticity

Whenever supply or demand for a product **fluctuates,** the elasticity of the two curves affects the size of the price change. To illustrate, both curves are relatively inelastic in Figure 6.3. If you look at Panel A, **D**

you can see that the change in price is relatively large when supply changes. Panel B shows that the change in price is also large when demand shifts. If one or both curves are elastic, though, the change in price will be smaller.

Fortunately, as we saw in Chapters 4 and 5, there are ways for us to determine the elasticity of both supply and demand. This means that we can predict how prices are likely to change if we know the elasticity of each curve and the underlying factors that cause the supply and demand curves to change.

CAREERS

Real Estate Agent

The Work

* Assist in renting, selling, and buying property for clients
* Obtain listings (owner agreements to place properties for rent or sale), advertise the property, and show the property to prospective renters and buyers

Qualifications

* Knowledge of fair-market values, zoning laws, local land-use laws, housing and building codes, insurance coverage, mortgage and interest rates
* Highly ambitious, flexible schedule, extensive social and business connections
* High-school diploma, at least 18 years old, state real estate license
* College courses in real estate, finance, business administration, statistics, economics, law, and English helpful

Earnings

* Median annual earnings (including commissions): $35,670

Job Growth Outlook

* Average

Source: *Occupational Outlook Handbook, 2006–2007 Edition*

CHAPTER 6 Prices and Decision Making 153

D Differentiated Instruction

English Language Learners
Organize the class into pairs before asking the following questions. **Ask:** What are three objects that could be used to illustrate the concept *fluctuate*? *(Possible answer: a swing, a yo-yo, a bouncing ball)* What are three objects that could be used to illustrate the concept *elastic*? *(Possible answer: a rubber band, a waistband in sweatpants, a metal spring)* Call on pairs to share their examples with the class. **ELL**

Did You Know?

In 1990 the median price for an existing home in the United States was $92,000. Five years later this figure had climbed to $110,500, and in 2000 it was at $139,000. In 2005 the median price for an existing home had reached $219,000, representing a 138% increase in only 15 years.

Leveled Activities

BL Reteaching Activities, p. 6

OL Economic Concepts Transparencies, Strategies, and Activities, p. 15

AL Reinforcing Economic Skills, p. 4

C Critical Thinking

Interpreting Ask: What is ironic about what is happening in the cartoon? *(A customer is using a seller's own product to identify a better price on the same product sold by a competitor.)* **BL**

Caption Answer: Price systems are more efficient in them.

✓**Reading Check** **Answer:**
Elasticity limits the changes in prices that occur for a good when its supply or demand fluctuates.

Assess

💿 Use the Interactive Tutor Self-Assessment CD-ROM to review Section 2, and then assign the Section 2 Review as homework or as an in-class activity.

Close

Outlining Ask students to make an outline of the section. **OL**

Competitive Markets
In competitive markets, sellers need to adjust their prices to attract buyers.
Why do economists like competitive markets?

C

HERMAN®
by Jim Unger

"Well look at that! The store across the street has the same binoculars for $15 less."

Prices and Competitive Markets

Economists like to see competitive markets because the price system is more efficient when markets are competitive. A perfectly competitive market requires a set of ideal conditions and outcomes that are seldom found in the real world, but fortunately markets don't have to be perfect to be useful. As long as prices are allowed to adjust to new levels in response to the pressures exerted by surpluses and shortages, prices will perform their role as signals to both consumers and producers.

The great advantage of competitive markets is that they allocate resources efficiently. As sellers compete to meet consumer demands, they are forced to lower the prices of their goods. This in turn encourages them to keep their costs down. At the same time, competition among buyers helps prevent prices from falling too far.

In the final analysis, a competitive market economy is one that "runs itself." There is no need for a bureaucracy, planning commission, or other agency to set prices, because the market tends to find its own equilibrium. In addition, the three basic economic questions of WHAT, HOW, and FOR WHOM to produce are decided by the participants—the buyers and sellers—in the market.

✓**Reading Check** **Explaining** How does the elasticity of a good affect its price?

SECTION 2 Review

Vocabulary
1. **Explain** the significance of economic model, equilibrium price, surplus, and shortage.

Main Ideas
2. **Determining Cause and Effect** Use a graphic organizer like the one below to show how a change in demand or supply affects the price of a product.

Demand/Supply → Increases → Price _____ / _____
Demand/Supply → Decreases → Price _____ / _____

3. **Explaining** How does the elasticity of supply and demand for a product affect the size of a price change?

Critical Thinking
4. **The BIG Idea** Explain why competitive markets allocate resources efficiently.

5. **Making Inferences** What do merchants usually do to sell items that are overstocked? What does this tell you about the equilibrium price for the product?

6. **Understanding Cause and Effect** What will happen to the price you pay for concert tickets if a popular group has to move its show to a smaller facility? Why?

7. **Analyzing Visuals** Look at Figure 6.2 on p. 150. Create a graph showing what will happen at a price of $20.

Applying Economics
8. **Equilibrium Price** Select a product that appears in newspaper ads of several different stores. Note the various prices and indicate whether any of these prices are sale prices. What does the information tell you about the equilibrium price of the product you selected?

Answers

1. All definitions can be found in the section and the Glossary.
2. **Price** (top): increases/decreases
   Price (bottom): decreases/increases
3. If supply and demand for a product are inelastic, a change in price will be relatively large. If supply and demand are elastic, a change in price will be relatively small. If one is elastic and the other inelastic, a moderate price change will result.

4. As sellers compete with each other, they are forced to lower prices to attract customers. This encourages them to limit production costs. Competition among buyers helps prevent prices from falling too far.
5. Merchants usually lower the prices of overstocked items. A surplus indicates that the equilibrium price for an item is lower than the original price charged by the merchant.

6. Ticket prices will increase because the supply is reduced, while demand remains high.
7. Students' graphs should identify a surplus of 6 at a price of $20.
8. Answers will vary. If a product is on sale everywhere, this indicates that its original price was higher than its equilibrium price. If stores are generally charging the same price for an item, this indicates that it is selling at or near the equilibrium price.

The beauty of the supply and demand system lies in its ability to set prices. If demand is high and supply low, prices skyrocket and producers increase supplies. Simple, right? What happens, though, if suppliers are unable keep up with rapidly growing demand?

What's Raining on Solar's Parade?

The solar power industry has been on a tear, growing at more than 30% per year for the last six years. It's poised to reach a surprising milestone within two years, when it will gobble up more silicon for its electricity-generating panels than semiconductor makers use in all their chips and devices. . . .

So what's the problem? "Global demand is stronger than the existing supply," says Lee Edwards, president and CEO of BP Solar. His company and others can't buy enough of the ultrapure polysilicon now used in 91% of solar panels. The raw material shortage has slashed growth for the industry from more than 50% in 2004 to a projected 5% in 2006.

The shortage has caused prices for polysilicon to more than double over the last two years. As

Economics 101 teaches, that should prompt producers to expand capacity. But for suppliers such as Michigan-based Hemlock Semiconductor Corp., the world's largest producer, the decision hasn't been easy. For one thing, the company was badly burned in 1998. It had just built a new facility in response to pleas from semiconductor makers when Asia went into a slowdown. Demand for silicon plunged, and the factory had to be shuttered. . . .

Hemlock finally decided that the industry is real, but only after solar companies agreed to share the risk by signing contracts to buy the future output. So in December the company began an expansion worth more than $400 million that will increase silicon production by 50%. Competitors are following suit.

—Reprinted from *BusinessWeek*

DEMAND AND PRICE OF SILICON

- Demand for polysilicon in semiconductors
- Demand for polysilicon in solor photovolting
- Price of polysilicon

Thousands of metric tons — Price per kilogram

Year: 2003, 2004, 2005†, 2006, 2007*, 2008

Sources: Riper Jaffray, www.renewableenergyaccess.com
* 2007 figure for price is estimated.
† 2005–2008 figures for demand are estimated.

Examining the Newsclip

1. **Understanding Cause and Effect** How did the shortage of polysilicon affect its price?
2. **Analyzing** Why was Hemlock Semiconductor Corp. at first reluctant to increase the production of polysilicon?

CHAPTER 6   Prices and Decision Making   155

BusinessWeek

Teach

C Critical Thinking

Assessing Ask: What risk is Hemlock taking with its recent action? *(expanding its silicon production beyond demand)* Do you think the corporation made a wise move? *(Students responding "yes" may point out that demand has grown and solar companies have agreed to buy Hemlock's output. Students responding "no" may point out that new technology or an economic downturn could reduce demand.)* **OL**

BusinessWeek ONLINE

To find up-to-date news and analysis on the economy, business, technology, markets, entrepreneurs, investments, and finance, have students search feature articles and special reports on the BusinessWeek Web site, www.businessweek.com.

Examining the Newsclip

Answers:
1. caused it to more than double
2. It had earlier expanded production but demand fell.

Additional Support

Activity: Collaborative Learning

Understanding Demand Fluctuations
Organize the class into small groups. Direct groups to review recent newspapers, magazines, and Internet news Web sites to find articles about a product for which demand has significantly increased or decreased in recent years. Have groups prepare a multimedia presentation that explains why the demand fluctuation has occurred, how the fluctuation has impacted the price of the product, and how businesses have responded to these trends. **OL**

Teacher Tip

Adding to the Content As a way of introducing this activity, you may want to have a local business owner or manager visit the class to describe his or her business's response to demand fluctuations.

Focus

Bellringer
Daily Focus Transparency 26

FOCUS ACTIVITIES
Transparency 26

Ⓐ GRICULTURAL PRICE SUPPORTS

AMERICAN FARM INCOME

Other income
$30.5 billion

Government payments
$13.3 billion

Crops
$124 billion

Livestock
$124.6 billion

Total: $292.4 billion

Source: Statistical Abstract of the United States

1. How much money did the government pay directly to farmers?
2. What percentage of farm income did government payments account for?

Daily Focus Transparencies

GUIDE TO READING

Answers to Graphic:

Price ceiling: supply decreases as sellers shift resources to more profitable ventures

Price floor: demand decreases; for example, employers might hire fewer workers if the minimum wage is raised

---

Resource Manager

SECTION 3
Social Goals and Market Efficiency

GUIDE TO READING

Section Preview

In this section, you will learn that governments sometimes use policies that interfere with the market in order to achieve social goals.

Content Vocabulary

- price ceiling *(p. 157)*
- minimum wage *(p. 158)*
- price floor *(p. 158)*
- target price *(p. 159)*
- nonrecourse loan *(p. 159)*
- deficiency payment *(p. 159)*

Academic Vocabulary

- arbitrarily *(p. 157)*   • stabilize *(p. 159)*

Reading Strategy

Explaining As you read the section, complete a cause-and-effect chart similar to the one below by explaining the effects of price ceilings and price floors.

Policy	Effects
Price ceiling	
Price floor	

ISSUES IN THE NEWS   —*The Washington Times*

Minimum Wage Rise Hurts Students

Maryland small business owners are bemoaning higher labor costs as the state's minimum wage increases today from the federal threshold of $5.15 per hour to $6.15.

. . . "A dollar an hour is a huge jump—people have no idea how that affects your payroll," said Mike Kostinsky, who owns Sorrento of Arbutus, a pizza restaurant in Arbutus, Md.

. . . Mr. Kostinsky, whose family has owned Sorrento for 41 years, said he typically adds four or five high school students at minimum wage during the summer to allow his 30 or so permanent employees to take vacations. As a result of the wage increase, "I won't let anybody go, but I probably won't hire anybody else," he said. ∎

In Chapter 2 we examined seven broad economic and social goals that most people seem to share. We also observed that these goals, while commendable, are sometimes in conflict with one another. These goals also have been partially responsible for the increased role that government plays in our economy.

Attempts to achieve one of these goals—economic security—occasionally result in legislation such as the increase in the minimum wage in Maryland described in the news story above. While the legislation is clearly beneficial to some people, it can be detrimental to others. What is common to all of these situations, however, is that the outcome—wage control—can only be achieved by interfering with the price system and distorting the allocations made in the market.

R Reading Strategies	**C** Critical Thinking	**D** Differentiated Instruction	**W** Writing Support	**S** Skill Practice
Teacher Edition • Det. Importance, p. 158 • Monitoring, p. 160 **Additional Resources** • Guid. Read. Act., p. 18 • Reading Ess. & Note-Taking Guide, p. 52	**Teacher Edition** • Evaluating, p. 159 • Differentiating, p. 162 **Additional Resources** • Econ. Content Vocab. Act., p. 6 • Authentic Assess., p. 9	**Teacher Edition** • Intrapersonal, p. 158 • Interpersonal, p. 161 **Additional Resources** • Reading and Study Skills Fold., p. 53 • Quizzes and Tests, p. 71	**Teacher Edition** • Persuasive Writing, pp. 157, 167 • Expository Writing, p. 159 **Additional Resources** • High School Reading in the Content Area	**Teacher Edition** • Analyzing Charts, p. 157 • Analyzing Cartoons, p. 160 • Using Tables and Charts, p. 166 **Additional Resources** • Reteach. Act., p. 6

Distorting Market Outcomes

MAIN Idea Price ceilings and price floors prevent prices from allocating goods and resources.

Economics & You Do you think the minimum wage helps you or other people who are looking for jobs? Read on to learn how the minimum wage can affect the job market.

One common way to achieve social goals is to have the government set prices at "socially desirable" levels. When this happens, prices are not allowed to adjust to their equilibrium levels, and the price system cannot transmit accurate information to other buyers and sellers in the market.

Price Ceilings

Some cities, especially New York City, have a long history of using rent controls to try to make housing more affordable. This is an example of a **price ceiling,** a maximum legal price that can be charged for a product.

The case of a price ceiling is shown in **Figure 6.4.** Let us assume that without the ceiling, the market would establish monthly rents at $900, which is an equilibrium price because 2.0 million apartments would be supplied and rented at that rate. If authorities think $900 is too high, and if they want to achieve the **W** social goals of equity and security for people who cannot afford these rents, they can **arbitrarily** establish a price ceiling at $600 a month.

No doubt renters would love the lower price and might demand 2.4 million apartments. Landlords, on the other hand, would try to convert some apartments to other uses, such as condominiums and office buildings that offer higher returns. Therefore, the supply might only reach 1.6 million apartments at $600 per month, leaving a permanent shortage of 800,000 apartments.

Are consumers better off? Perhaps not. More than likely, the better apartments will be converted to condos or offices—leaving the poorer ones to be rented. In addition, 800,000 people are now unhappy because they cannot get an apartment, although they are willing and able to pay for one. Prices no longer allocate apartments. Instead, landlords resort to long waiting lists or other nonprice criteria such as excluding children and pets to discourage applicants.

Rent controls also freeze a landlord's total revenue and threaten his or her profits. As a result, the landlord tries to lower costs by providing the absolute minimum upkeep. In addition, landlords have little incentive to add additional units if they feel rents are too low. Some apartment buildings may even be torn down to make way for shopping centers, factories, or high-rise office buildings.

The price ceiling, like any other price, affects the allocation of resources—but not in the way intended. The attempt to limit rents makes some people happy, until their

price ceiling highest legal price that can be charged for a product

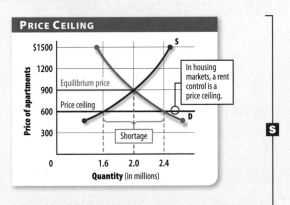

Figure 6.4 ▶ Price Ceilings

PRICE CEILING

In housing markets, a rent control is a price ceiling.

▶ A price ceiling of $600 leaves 800,000 people permanently without apartments. Without the ceiling, an additional 400,000 people would have found an apartment at $900.

Economic Analysis *Why does government sometimes impose restrictions such as price ceilings on the market?*

Teach

W Writing Support

Persuasive Writing Instruct students to research rent controls in a large U.S. city such as New York. Ask students to write a persuasive essay in which they argue that rent controls are or are not an effective method of promoting social equality and security among citizens. **AL**

S Skill Practice

Analyzing Charts Ask: What would likely happen if the government raised the price ceiling by $400? Explain. *(Apartment prices would increase to $900, and apartment unit supply would increase to accommodate 400,000 more people. The new $1,000 price ceiling would have little additional effect since it is more than the equilibrium price.)* **OL**

Economic Analysis

Answer: to try to achieve social equality and security for people who cannot afford equilibrium prices

Additional Support

Activity: Hands-On Economics

Price Controls Organize the class into pairs. Instruct pairs to conduct research to identify an example of a price control that was once in place in their city or county. Controls on gas prices during the 1970s and Nixon's price controls (1971–1974) are possible examples. Students may be able to find people who can recall the price controls enacted during the Korean War and World War II. Have students interview at least three people who were impacted by the price control they identify. Encourage students to talk to at least one producer and one consumer during their interviews, if possible. Ask each pair to write a report describing the local impact of the price control they selected. **OL**

R Reading Strategy

Determining Importance

Ask: What important points about the minimum wage are made in this subsection? *(It may increase unemployment; it may promote equality; it may not be relevant in some areas.)* **OL**

D Differentiated Instruction

Intrapersonal Ask students to think about how the minimum wage may affect them now or in the future. Then have them write an essay on their thoughts and opinions. **OL**

Economic Analysis

Answer: workers who keep their jobs and whose wages are raised by the price floor benefit; people who are not hired because of employer cutbacks on hiring

✓Reading Check **Answer:** Price ceilings keep certain products affordable but limit their supply. Price floors increase income but lower demand for services.

minimum wage lowest legal wage that can be paid to most workers

price floor lowest legal price that can be paid for a product

buildings begin to deteriorate. Others, including landlords and potential renters on waiting lists, are unhappy from the beginning. Finally, some productive resources—those used to build and maintain apartments—slowly move out of the rental market.

R Price Floors

Other prices are sometimes considered too low, so the government takes steps to keep them higher. The **minimum wage,** the lowest legal wage that can be paid to most workers, is such a case. The minimum wage in fact is a **price floor,** or lowest legal price that can be paid for a good or service.

Figure 6.5 uses a minimum wage of $5.15 per hour as an illustration of a price floor. At this wage, the supply curve shows that 14 million people would want to offer their services. According to the demand curve for labor, however, only 10 million would be hired, leaving a surplus of 4 million workers without jobs.

Figure 6.5 ▶ Price Floors

▶ At a price floor of $5.15 per hour, 10 million workers will be hired. At the equilibrium price of $4.00 per hour, 2 million more people would find jobs.

Economic Analysis *Who benefits from price floors? Who is placed at a disadvantage?*

158   UNIT 2   Microeconomics: Prices and Markets

The figure also shows that without the minimum wage, the actual demand and supply of labor would establish an equilibrium price of $4.00 per hour. At this wage, 12 million workers would offer their services and the same number would be hired—which means that there would be neither a shortage nor a surplus in the labor market.

Most economists argue that the minimum wage actually increases the number of people who do not have jobs because employers hire fewer workers at higher wages. In the case of Figure 6.5, the number of people who lose jobs amounts to 2 million—the difference between the 12 million who would have worked at the equilibrium price and the 10 million who actually work at the higher wage of $5.15 per hour.

Is the minimum wage good or bad for the economy? Certainly the minimum wage is not as efficient as a wage set by supply and demand, but not all decisions in our economy are made on the basis of efficiency. The basic argument in favor of the minimum wage is that it raises poor people's incomes and provides a small measure of equity—one of our seven major economic and social goals. A federal minimum wage is evidence that the small measure of equity provided by the minimum wage is preferred to the loss of efficiency.

Finally, it could be argued that the minimum wage is irrelevant because it is actually lower than the lowest wages paid in many areas. Consider the wages in your area, for example. More than likely, most employers pay wages higher than the minimum wage and would not lower them even if the minimum wage were eliminated. Do you think that your employer would pay you less if he or she were allowed to do so? Your response will provide a partial answer to the question.

✓Reading Check **Analyzing** What are the negative and positive aspects of price ceilings and price floors?

Authentic Assessment Strategies and Activities, p. 9

Government's Role in Pricing

Objective: Understand the motives for and consequences of government policies that influence prices.

Focus: Ask students to brainstorm possible ways that the government influences prices.

Teach: Have the students complete the activity.

Assess: Ask students to vote on the debate winners as described in step 7.

Close: Lead the class in a discussion of the questions in step 8 of the Procedure.

Differentiated Instruction Strategies

BL Have students describe a possible government motive for each of the resolutions in step 1.

AL Ask students to write a short paper supporting the position they argued against during the debate.

ELL Have students create a poster supporting their group's debate position.

Differentiated Instruction

Agricultural Price Supports

MAIN Idea Government programs to help stabilize prices for farmers have both positive and negative effects.

Economics & You Do you remember learning in your history class about the plight of farmers during the Great Depression? Read on to find out how the government tried to help farmers.

During the Great Depression of the 1930s, prices plummeted everywhere. Farmers, however, had an even more difficult time because they were having the "bumper yields" illustrated in Panel A of Figure 6.3 on page 152 that pushed prices even lower. Because both the demand for and supply of food were inelastic, farm prices fell much further than other prices in the economy.

To help farmers, the federal government established the Commodity Credit Corporation (CCC), an agency in the Department of Agriculture. The CCC then used a **target price,** which is essentially a price floor, to help **stabilize** farm prices.

Loan Supports

Under one CCC support program, a farmer borrowed money from the CCC at the target price and pledged his or her crops as security in return. The farmer then used the loan to plant, maintain, and harvest the crops. When they were ready for harvest, the farmer had two choices: either sell the crop in the market and use the proceeds to repay the CCC loan, or keep the proceeds of the loan and let the CCC take possession of the crop. The farmer could get at least the target price because the loan was a **nonrecourse loan**—a loan that carries neither a penalty nor further obligation to repay if not paid back.

Deficiency Payments

While the CCC loan program helped farmers, it created new problems because the U.S. Department of Agriculture soon owned enormous stockpiles of food. The deparment had to resort to storing surplus wheat in rented warehouses or on open ground. Surplus milk was made into cheese and stored in underground caves. The military received some of the food, while public schools received other food that they could use in their "free lunch" programs. Still the surpluses grew, leaving politicians to consider how they could support farm prices and avoid holding large surpluses at the same time.

The solution was a new government-program that combined the competitive market with price supports. Farmers sold their crops on the open market for the best price they could get based on demand and supply. The CCC then gave farmers a **deficiency payment**—a check the government sends to producers to make up the difference between the market price and the target price.

target price price floor for agricultural products set by the government to stabilize farm income

nonrecourse loan agricultural loan that carries no penalty or further obligation if it is not repaid

deficiency payment cash payment making up the difference between the market price and the target price

Figure 6.6 ▶ Deficiency Payments

DEFICIENCY PAYMENTS

Target price

Market price

The farmer is paid the difference between the target and the market price.

▶ Under the CCC deficiency payment program, a target price such as $4 per bushel of wheat was set. At this price farmers would produce and sell 10,000 bushels. With 10,000 bushels produced, buyers would pay $2.50 per bushel in the marketplace, so the CCC would need to give an additional payment of $1.50 per bushel to farmers to hit the target price.

Economic Analysis *How much would the farmer have produced and earned without the deficiency payment program?*

CHAPTER 6, SECTION 3

W Writing Support

Expository Writing Have students use reliable print or Internet resources to research what life was like for farmers during the Great Depression. Ask students to write a report on this subject (they may focus on a single family's experiences if they wish). Tell students to include in their reports how government programs, such as the ones described on this page, affected the farmers. **AL**

C Critical Thinking

Evaluating Ask: Why might some people have opposed the CCC's programs during the Great Depression? *(Possible answers: concern about excessive government involvement in the economy; concern about higher taxes; concern that farmers were getting more help than workers in other sectors)* **OL**

Economic Analysis

Answer: 9,000 bushels at $3 per bushel

Leveled Activities

BL Guided Reading Activities, p. 18

OL Reading Essentials and Note-Taking Guide, p. 52

AL Economic Content Vocabulary Activities, p. 6

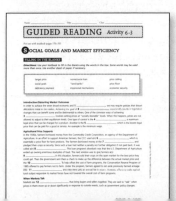

S Skill Practice

Analyzing Cartoons Ask: Do you think this cartoon is generally in favor of or generally critical of the government's support of agriculture? Explain. *(critical; the cartoon implies that farmers are being paid to do nothing and are becoming lazy)* **OL**

R Reading Strategy

Monitoring Instruct students to ask themselves questions about the text on this page. Then have students look for answers to their questions. *(For example: What is the government doing with the land in the "land bank"? It is being saved for future use.)* Ask students to think of at least one question for each heading on the page. **OL**

Caption Answer: an area larger than the state of New York

✓**Reading Check Answer:** American agriculture is more dependent than ever on subsidies and price supports.

Hands-On Chapter Project
Step 3

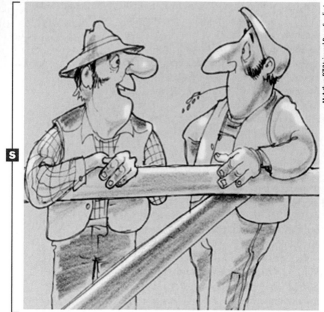

"...and here I was... only just getting used to being paid for NOT doing things."

Federal Land Bank The government currently pays some farmers to not farm in an effort to reduce production and to support farm income. *How much land is in the land bank program?*

R Conservation "Land Banks"

The loan support and deficiency payment programs of the 1930s continued for several decades. By the 1980s, though, two factors combined to make these programs increasingly expensive to maintain. For one, agricultural output increased dramatically because of increased farm productivity. In addition, there were simply too many farmers involved in agriculture. Many experts concluded that the solution was to get some farmers to stop farming.

The result was the Conservation Reserve Program of 1985 that paid farmers to *not* farm. To enroll in the program, acreage where crops previously grew was set aside in a "land bank" to save the land for future use. The U.S. Department of Agriculture would then pay the farmer an annual fee as long as the land was not farmed. While the program was expensive for taxpayers, it has since become very popular with farmers and today accounts for nearly 10 percent of total farm subsidies.

Reforming Price Supports

In an effort to make farming responsive to the market forces of supply and demand, Congress passed the Federal Agricultural Improvement and Reform (FAIR) Act in 1996. Under FAIR, "loan rates" took the place of target prices, and temporary cash payments replaced price supports and deficiency payments. Lawmakers hoped that when the law expired, farmers would be experienced enough with the laws of supply and demand to no longer need help.

However, the new payments turned out to be larger than the ones they replaced, and the overall cost of the U.S. farm support programs actually went up. Then, when FAIR was about to expire in 2002, Congress replaced it with the Farm Security and Rural Investment Act of 2002, which provided for even larger price support payments that would last through 2007.

Continued Agricultural Support

Today, American agriculture is more dependent than ever on subsidies and price supports. In addition to subsidizing basic commodities like rice, corn, sugar, and cotton, crops such as peanuts, sunflower seeds, and mohair are also covered. The amount of land that farmers are paid to not farm has grown to be larger than the state of New York.

Whether this is good or bad depends on your perspective. If you are a taxpayer supplying the funds for these payments, you might think that the government spends too much on these programs. If you are a farmer receiving payments, you are probably glad that the government is supporting the goal of economic security.

✓**Reading Check** Summarizing What has been the effect of agricultural price supports?

Evaluating Prices

Step 3: Evaluating Effects. Students will evaluate how price ceilings or price floors affect cookie sales.

Directions: Assign a price ceiling to two of the previously established groups. Tell these two groups that they must sell their cookies at a price no more than 15 cents below the equilibrium price they determined in Step 2. Assign price floors to the other two groups. Tell these groups that they must charge a price per cookie no less than 15 cents above the equilibrium price they determined in Step 2. Have students bake and sell their cookies with the price ceilings and price floors in place.

Comparing Have groups write a report comparing the results of their cookie sale at the controlled price with the results of their sale at equilibrium price. Student reports should include an explanation for any differences. **OL**

(Chapter Project continued in Visual Summary.)

When Markets Talk

MAIN Idea Markets send signals when prices change in response to events.

Economics & You Have you heard stories in the news about changes in the stock market when a new government policy was announced? Read on to find out how markets "talk."

Markets are impersonal mechanisms that bring buyers and sellers together. Although markets do not talk in the usual sense of the word, they do send signals in that they speak collectively for all of the buyers and sellers who trade in the markets. Markets are said to "talk" when prices in them move up or down significantly in reaction to events that take place elsewhere in the economy.

Suppose the federal government announced that it would raise taxes to pay off some of the federal debt. If investors thought this policy would not work or that other policies might be better, they might decide to sell some of their stocks and other investments to buy gold. As a result, stock prices would fall, and the price of gold would rise. In a sense, the market would "talk" by voicing its disapproval of the new tax policy.

In this example, individual investors made decisions on the likely outcome of the new policy and sold stocks for cash or gold. Together, investor actions were enough to influence stock prices and to send a signal to the government that investors did not favor the policy. If investors' feelings were divided about the new policy, some would sell while others bought stocks. As a result, prices might not change, and the message would be that, as yet, the market had not made up its mind.

✓Reading Check **Examining** Can you think of any other examples of markets "talking"? Explain.

Skills Handbook
See page **R35** to learn about **Identifying the Main Idea.**

D ## Differentiated Instruction

Interpersonal Have small groups use news Web sites or print sources to find an article about markets "talking" in response to an event. Ask groups to perform a skit illustrating the event and the market "talk" that followed. **OL**

✓Reading Check **Possible Answer:** a market fluctuation that occurs after the president announces an overseas military operation

Assess

💿 Use the Interactive Tutor Self-Assessment CD-ROM to eview Section 3, and then assign the Section 3 Review as homework or as an in-class activity.

Close

Problem-Solving Have students identify a government policy they would like to see implemented that will influence the market. Ask them to explain the positive results they believe this policy will bring about. **OL**

SECTION 3 Review

Vocabulary
1. **Explain** the significance of price ceiling, minimum wage, price floor, target price, nonrecourse loan, deficiency payment.

Main Ideas
2. **Determining Cause and Effect** Use a graphic organizer like the one below to illustrate how price floors affect quantity demanded and supplied.

Quantity demanded ← Price floor → Quantity supplied

3. **Explaining** Why did the federal government establish agricultural price support programs?

4. **Describing** How do markets speak collectively for buyers and sellers?

Critical Thinking
5. **The BIG Idea** Explain why a government would consider imposing a price ceiling or price floor.

6. **Analyzing Visuals** Look at Figure 6.4 on p. 157. How does the price ceiling affect the relationship between quantity supplied and quantity demanded? Why does the price ceiling make this relationship permanent?

7. **Predicting** What would happen if the government eliminated all farm subsidies?

Applying Economics
8. **Price Floor** Interview 10 classmates who have part-time jobs. Identify where they work and who gets paid at, below, or above the federal minimum wage. Use that information to predict how increasing the federal minimum wage by $1.00 per hour would impact employment for teenagers in your area.

Review **SECTION 3**

Answers

1. All definitions can be found in the section and the Glossary.
2. **Quantity demanded:** decrease
   Quantity supplied: increase
3. because farm prices fell and farmers were struggling to make a living
4. Buyers and sellers interact in a market. A significant movement of prices reflects the collective actions of buyers and sellers in a market, which thus "speaks" for these buyers and sellers.
5. A government might impose a price ceiling or a price floor to better promote social equity and security for certain groups.
6. The price ceiling creates a shortage because quantity demanded exceeds quantity supplied. This relationship is permanent because producers cannot respond to increased demand by raising prices, nor is there any incentive for them to increase quantity supplied.
7. **Possible answers:** farmers would try to produce more to make up for the loss of subsidy income; farm prices would fall with the increased production, causing farmers to go out of business; fewer farmers would reduce competition, allowing the remaining farm producers to raise prices.
8. If most students already earn more than the minimum wage, then the increase will have little effect. If most students earn less than the minimum wage, then some teenagers would lose job opportunities since employers would hire fewer of them at the higher wage level.

Teach

C Critical Thinking

Differentiating Ask: How do you think Margaret Whitman is different from most other CEOs? *(Answers may include her willingness to listen to customers and employees, her preference for asking questions rather than issuing orders, and her practice of reading e-mails from customers.)* **OL**

Examining the Profile

Answers:

1. listening to customers and responding to their demands, sharing information with employees

2. Answers will vary. Students answering "yes" may explain that valuing customer and employee opinions will make companies more responsive to current trends. Students answering "no" may explain that most companies do not function like an online auction site and thus cannot be run like eBay.

Additional Support

Teacher Tip

Computer-Savvy Students
Poll students to find out who has prior experience with eBay. Then organize groups so that at least one of these students (or a computer-savvy student) is in each group.

ENTREPRENEUR

Profiles in Economics

Margaret (Meg) Whitman (1956–)

- ranked by *Fortune* magazine as the "Most Powerful Woman in Business" in 2005
- turned eBay into one of the fastest-growing companies in U.S. history

Excellence Leads eBay

As president and CEO of eBay Inc. since 1998, Meg Whitman runs the world's leading Internet auction site. Although eBay was invented by software engineer Pierre Omidyar in 1995, it has been Whitman's leadership and branding expertise that made the site a household name.

The year Whitman took over eBay, the company earned about $6 million. Seven years into her leadership, the company's revenues grew to $4.6 *billion.* Her secret? She works quickly to fix problems, such as removing counterfeit items for auction and instituting PayPal to help streamline the payment process. She asks questions instead of issuing orders, and she shares what she learns with her employees. She also listens to customers and employees and seeks their feedback.

The Power of All of Us

Business analysts agree that Whitman's success has more to do with her willingness to listen than anything else. As she says, "Our army of users figures out what's hot before we even know." That attitude keeps Whitman in the chat room instead of the boardroom. She reads hundreds of e-mails from users every day, and her "Voice of the Customer" program has been known to reverse business decisions based on user complaints. She trusts what she calls "The Power of All of Us" to sustain a community of users that will essentially guide itself. When eBay management thought car sales would be too complicated and risky, the eBay community demanded the capability. Because Whitman was open to the suggestion, more than 1 million cars have now been sold on eBay. If Meg Whitman were to have a feedback profile similar to the ones kept by the buyers and sellers on eBay, her rating would be high indeed.

When Meg Whitman became CEO, many of the items auctioned on eBay were small collectibles like Star Wars toys. Today eBay sells everything consumers demand. Says Whitman, "It is the users who build the company."

Examining the Profile

1. **Summarizing** What management techniques have made eBay so successful?
2. **Drawing Conclusions** Do you think Whitman's philosophy of "The Power of All of Us" could work in other industries? Explain.

162 UNIT 2 Microeconomics: Prices and Markets

Activity: Technology Connection

Using an Online Auction Site
Organize the class into small groups. Have each group select an item owned by one of its students that he or she would like to sell. Instruct the groups to register at the eBay Web site and place the item up for sale. Students should survey like items on the Web site to get an idea of the price they should start the bidding at. After placing the item for sale, students should monitor the item's price activity. **Ask: Does the item demonstrate high demand?** After selling the item, ask groups to prepare a report describing their experiences and expressing their opinions about using eBay. **OL**

Visual Summary

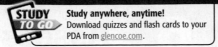

▶ **Allocation of Resources** Prices are signals that help buyers and sellers make economic decisions. Without prices, societies must find other ways to allocate resources.

With Prices:
- Prices serve as link between producers and consumers
- Allocation easy because prices are neutral, flexible, and have no cost

Allocation of resources

Without Prices:
- Must find another system such as rationing
- Allocation difficult because of problems with fairness, high cost of administration, and less incentive for people to work

▶ **Market Equilibrium** When buyers and sellers can freely make production and purchase decisions, the price of a product will move toward market equilibrium. At this point, the quantity supplied is exactly equal to the quantity demanded.

MARKET DEMAND AND SUPPLY CURVES

▶ **Social Goals and Prices** The social goals of equity and security sometimes can be achieved only by giving up parts of other goals. Price ceilings or price floors can help achieve these goals, but they may result in fewer goods and services offered overall.

PRICE CEILING

In housing markets, a rent control is a price ceiling.

PRICE FLOOR

In labor markets, a minimum wage is a price floor.

Analyzing Ask students to create a graph showing market demand and supply curves based on the following figures:

Price	Demand	Supply
$22	60,000	20,000
$24	50,000	28,000
$26	44,000	32,000
$28	36,000	36,000
$30	30,000	40,000
$32	24,000	46,000

Ask: Which prices will result in surpluses? *($30 and $32)* Which prices will result in shortages? *($22, $24, and $26)* **BL**

Defending Have students take on the roles of Congress members participating in a floor debate about a bill that would raise the minimum wage by $1.00 per hour. Direct students to write a speech expressing their views on the bill. Students may wish to suggest a modification to the bill rather than accepting or rejecting it outright. Remind students that the speech is intended to win the support of other members. **OL**

Hands-On Chapter Project

Step 4: Wrap Up

Evaluating Prices

Step 4: Bringing It All Together.
Students will synthesize what they learned in previous steps.

Directions: Have students resume work in their groups. Ask students to compare the price prediction they made in Step 1 with the actual equilibrium price for their cookies as determined in Step 2. Then, instruct each group to create graphs charting the supply and demand curves for their cookie sales in Step 2, and then for their cookie sales in Step 3 with the price control. Finally, ask groups to prepare a "business report" to be presented orally to the class. The report should explain the accuracy of their Step 1 prediction, their sales numbers in Steps 2 and 3, and an assessment of the factors that influenced their market results. **OL**

Assessment & Activities

Review Content Vocabulary

1. c
2. a
3. d
4. e
5. b
6. f

Review Academic Vocabulary

7. Puzzles will vary but should demonstrate understanding of each term's meaning in an economic context.

Review the Main Ideas

8. prices are neutral, prices are flexible, people are familiar with prices, prices have no administrative costs

9. People question the fairness of a rationing system; rationing has a high administrative cost.

10. Prices favor neither the producer nor the consumer.

11. the price at which the number of units produced equals the number of units sold

12. Shortages reveal that the price is below equilibrium level. Surpluses indicate that the price is above equilibrium level.

13. Answers will vary but should identify the three factors as a change in supply, a change in demand, and a change in both supply and demand.

14. Price controls prevent the market from adjusting prices to eliminate shortages and surpluses.

Review Content Vocabulary

Use the terms below to identify the missing cause or effect in the following situations.

a. rationing   d. equilibrium price
b. surplus   e. price ceiling
c. shortage   f. price floor

1. **Cause:** The government tries to keep prices down by legislating a price ceiling. **Effect:** _____

2. **Cause:** The government wants to allocate scarce goods and services without the help of a price system. **Effect:** _____

3. **Cause:** A reasonably competitive market experiences brief, minor shortages and surpluses. **Effect:** _____

4. **Cause:** _____ **Effect:** New York City has many apartments with very low rents but also has a shortage of apartment units.

5. **Cause:** A market is at equilibrium, but the product falls out of style before producers can reduce production. **Effect:** _____

6. **Cause:** _____ **Effect:** Farmers receive higher prices for milk and cheese but also experience a surplus.

Review Academic Vocabulary

7. Create the clues for the crossword puzzle below. Your clues should relate to the chapter content.

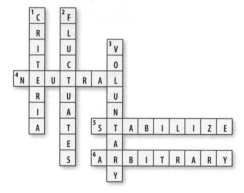

164   UNIT 2   Microeconomics: Prices and Markets

Review the Main Ideas

Section 1 (pages 143–146)

8. **Describe** four advantages of using price as an allocating mechanism.

9. **Discuss** why allocating resources without prices is difficult.

10. **Explain** why prices are neutral.

Section 2 (pages 148–154)

11. **Explain** what is meant by the term *market equilibrium*.

12. **Describe** the role of shortages and surpluses in competitive markets.

13. **Identify** three causes of a price change in a market, using a graphic organizer like the one below. Add examples and identify the possible results for each.

Section 3 (pages 156–161)

14. **Explain** why shortages and surpluses are not temporary when price controls are used.

15. **Identify** and describe two of the programs that have been used to stabilize farm incomes.

16. **Explain** what is meant by the statement that "markets talk."

Critical Thinking

17. **The BIG Idea** Explain why and how a reasonably competitive market is always moving toward equilibrium.

18. **Making Generalizations** Some people argue that providing price supports to farmers is unfair to consumers. In a short paper, describe the positive and negative results of these price supports. Then explain why you support or oppose such programs.

15. **Possible answer:** deficiency payments—farmers received government money to make up the difference between market price and target price; Conservation Reserve Program—farmers paid not to farm.

16. When prices increase or decrease, the market is "voicing" the collective opinion of buyers and sellers.

Critical Thinking

17. Surpluses cause producers to lower prices to sell more items. Shortages cause producers to raise prices. These pressures continue until equilibrium is reached.

18. Positive results include security for farmers, stability of domestic food supply, and stronger agricultural sector. Negative results include higher taxes, higher prices, and inefficient use of resources.

Economics ONLINE   Self-Check Quiz Visit the
Economics: Principles and Practices Web site at glencoe.com and click
on Chapter 6—Self-Check Quizzes to prepare for the chapter test.

Assessment
and Activities

CHAPTER
6

19. Making Predictions Suppose that your state wanted to make health care more affordable for everyone. To do this, state legislators put a series of price controls—price ceilings—in place that cut the cost of medical services in half. In short paragraphs, explain your answers to the following questions:

a. What would happen to the demand for medical services at the new, lower price?

b. What would happen to the supply of medical services that doctors would be willing to provide at the new, lower price?

c. What considerations would new doctors take into account when they decide where to set up their practice? Explain the reasons for your answers.

20. Synthesizing You were invited to speak to a middle school class about the activities available at your school. You brought 20 ballpoint pens with the high school logo, but there were 30 students in the class. What kind of nonprice rationing system would you devise to fairly allocate the scarce item?

21. Predicting Assume that the price of school lunches has become too high, and you need to set a price ceiling to remedy the problem. What would the consequences of such a policy be for both students and the school?

Math Practice

22. A shoe store is having a sale. The first pair of shoes sells for $40. The second pair sells for half price, or $20. The next pair sells for half of that, and so on. Create a table like the one below that tracks the total cost of the shoes as each pair is added. Stop when the selling price of the last pair of shoes is less than $1.50.

Number of pairs	Total cost
1	

Analyzing Visuals

23. Examine the figure below, then answer the questions that follow.

PRICE ADJUSTMENT PROCESS

a. What is the quantity demanded at a price of $20? At $15?

b. What is the quantity supplied at a price of $10? At a price of $20?

c. How large is the shortage or surplus at $5? Explain your answer.

d. If the price started at $5 today, what would likely happen to the price tomorrow? Why?

Thinking Like an Economist

24. Economists like to use cost-benefit analysis to assess the merits of any program. Use this decision-making strategy to evaluate the desirability of continuing rent control. Write a paragraph describing your strategy and results.

Writing About Economics

25. Persuasive Writing Research newspapers and news magazines for recent articles about the minimum wage. Using what you have learned about price floors and the information in the articles, decide whether you favor or oppose raising the minimum wage. Write a 2-page paper outlining your views.

CHAPTER 6   Prices and Decision Making   165

Math Practice

22.

Number of pairs	Total cost
1	$40.00
2	$60.00
3	$70.00
4	$75.00
5	$77.50
6	$78.75

Analyzing Visuals

23. a. 3; 6

b. 3; 9

c. There is a shortage of 15; consumers demand 15 items but producers supply zero at that price.

d. Assuming that the demand is 1, the price would increase to at least $25. Producers would try to capitalize on the great demand and maximize their profits.

Thinking Like an Economist

24. Answers will vary but should demonstrate use of the cost-benefit analysis strategy to evaluate the positives and negatives of rent control.

Writing About Economics

25. Answers will vary. Students should support their opinions with logical arguments and information found in recent news articles.

19. a. Demand for medical services would increase.

b. Supply for medical services would decrease.

c. New doctors would assess if they can make a profit in a given location. They may consider moving their practice to another state.

20. Students' answers should demonstrate an understanding of rationing. Possible allocation options include drawing numbers, school trivia contest, or using attendance as a basis for distribution.

21. Providers of school lunches may reduce their supply. At the same time student demand would increase, creating a shortage of school lunches.

DEBATES IN ECONOMICS

Focus

Before they read the selections, have students brainstorm reasons that college athletes should be paid. Write these ideas in a column on the board. Next, have students brainstorm reasons that college athletes should not be paid. Write these ideas on the board in another column. After they finish reading the section, ask students to review the reasons listed on the board, and pick the position they believe is best supported.

Teach

S Skill Practice

Using Tables and Charts Have students review and compare the NCAA Revenues and Expenditures charts. **Ask:** Do you think the figures in the charts support one of the two positions? Why or why not? *(Possible answer: The figures support the con position because total expenditures nearly match total revenues.)* **OL**

Additional Support

DEBATES IN ECONOMICS

Should College Athletes Be Paid?

College athletes—particularly basketball and football players—rake in millions of dollars for their universities and the National Collegiate Athletic Association (NCAA). Some people argue that these athletes deserve to be compensated for their role in generating this revenue, whereas others maintain that free-ride scholarships and the potential to "go pro" are more than enough compensation.

Can you sift through the debate to determine whether college athletes should receive more than a free college education for their efforts? As you read the selections, ask yourself: Should college athletes be paid?

PRO COLLEGE ATHLETES SHOULD BE PAID

Vince Young fakes the pass, pulls the ball down and runs for the game-winning touchdown in the national championship game. Those connected with Texas are smiling as one of the greatest players in its storied history has led the Longhorns to a national title. The higher-ups at the school had reason to smile much earlier. . . With the chance to claim a national title also came $3.5 million from the [Bowl Championship Series] directly to Texas and another $14.9 million distributed among the Big 12 conference teams.

The problem is, the athletes who help schools and conferences make that money do not see a dime of it. They may receive scholarships, but so do students who don't help the school make money in any way. . . . If schools can profit off of student athletes, why should those athletes not be paid for helping schools make money? . . .

Paying [college athletes] would improve quality of play by keeping borderline professional athletes in college. Also, it would help those same players develop their skills so they could make more money at the professional level.

—*Andrew Zivic, writer for* iMPrint Magazine

NCAA REVENUES	
• CBS broadcast and marketing rights, including Division I men's basketball tournament	$453,000,000
• ESPN broadcast rights for 21 championships, including Division I women's basketball, baseball, ice hockey, and softball	$13,000,000
• Other broadcast rights	$4,450,000
• Division I men's basketball tickets	$27,870,000
• Tickets for other Division I championships	$13,175,000
• Tickets for Division II and III championships	$705,000
• Investments, fees, and services	$8,790,000
• Membership dues	$1,010,000

Source: IndyStar.com, 2005–2006 NCAA Revenues

166   UNIT 2   Microeconomics: Prices and Markets

Extending the Content

Challenging the Tax-Exempt Status of the NCAA In 2006 Representative Bill Thomas, chair of the House Ways and Means Committee at the time, proposed revoking the NCAA's tax-exempt status. Citing corporate sponsorships, massive television revenues, costly state-of-the-art athletic facilities, and soaring coaches' salaries, Thomas raised the issue that college athletics are now functioning like professional sports. The representative wrote a letter to the NCAA asking how highly commercialized sports further the colleges' education purposes. Thomas pointed out that more than 35 college coaches receive annual salaries of at least $1 million and that universities spend up to $600,000 per men's basketball player each academic year. NCAA spokesman Erik Christianson defended his organization by explaining that athletics are a part of higher education and that colleges "educate student-athletes; they are students first."

CON COLLEGE ATHLETES SHOULD NOT BE PAID W

As my opening kick against this notion, please accept the obvious premise that college athletes do trade on their skill for financial gain. This gain is realized in the form of a scholarship. . . . Four (or five) years on a free ride at, say, the University of Michigan can cost a person well over 100,000 [dollars]. . . .

How much loot-gathering should be attributed to the play of [a] backup left guard? How about the second-string corner? Should there be a salary scale that bestows a stipend commensurate with the player's productivity? What a hayride that would be to administrate. . . .

Another problem with paying or subsidizing college athletes is the danger of tipping an already unbalanced playing surface. While it's assumed that most Division I schools are rolling in dough, reality finds many athletic departments in the red. At more than a few schools, some of the low-revenue sports often are sacrificed. Schools with huge football revenues—such as Michigan, Texas, Ohio State, and USC—would have an even bigger advantage if paying players became an option.

—*Randy Hill, writer for FOXSports.com*

NCAA Expenditures

* The NCAA maintains that 95 percent of its money is returned to the membership via direct payments or event services.

• Division I athletic departments and conferences	$129,435,000
• Division I conferences, based on performance in the men's basketball tournament	$122,800,000
• Division I academic support; need-based emergency aid for players; "student-athlete opportunity fund"	$55,357,000
• Division I championships and other programs, including team travel and officials	$55,100,800
• Division II and III expenditures	$39,411,000
• Association-wide expenses, including insurance, enforcement, communications, and legal services	$87,779,400
• General administration	$22,836,800
• Legal contingencies; president's reserve; endowment	$9,280,000

Source: IndyStar.com, 2005–2006 NCAA Revenues

Analyzing the Issue

1. **Identifying** What are the arguments in favor of paying college athletes to play?
2. **Summarizing** What reasons does Hill give against paying college athletes?
3. **Deciding** With which opinion do you agree? Explain your reasoning.

CHAPTER 6 Prices and Decision Making **167**

Activity: Collaborative Learning

Analyzing Information Organize students into small groups of three students each. Have each group interview 10 different college athletes about the issue debated in this feature. Instruct students that no more than two athletes interviewed can be from the same sport. Also, groups should select five male athletes and five female athletes to interview. Tell students to ask their subjects whether they think athletes should be paid and how they think such a change would affect them. Ask each group to present the results of their interviews to the class. Then, as a class, synthesize the data from all of the groups. Discuss any variations among the athletes' opinions based on individual sport or gender. AL

Planning Guide

Key to Ability Levels		Key to Teaching Resources	
BL Below level	**AL** Above level	📁 Print Material	💾 DVD
OL On level	**ELL** English Language Learners	💿 CD-Rom	🖋 Transparency

Levels					Resources	Chapter Opener	Section 1	Section 2	Section 3	Chapter Assess
BL	OL	AL	ELL							
					FOCUS					
BL	OL	AL	ELL	🖋	**Daily Focus Skills Transparencies**		20, 21	72	22	
					TEACH					
BL	OL		ELL	📁	**Guided Reading Activities***		p. 19	p. 20	p. 21	
BL	OL	AL	ELL	📁	**Economic Content Vocabulary Activities***		p. 7	p. 7	p. 7	
	OL	AL		📁	**Critical Thinking Activities**		p. 7			
BL	OL		ELL	📁	**Reading Essentials and Note-Taking Guide***		p. 55	p. 58	p. 61	
		AL		📁	**Enrichment Activities**		p. 7			
	OL	AL		📁	**Free Enterprise Activities**		p. 6		p. 2	
BL	OL	AL	ELL	📁	**Primary and Secondary Source Readings**				pp. 37, 39	
BL	OL	AL	ELL	📁	**Economic Cartoons**		p. 11	p. 26	pp. 2, 4	
BL	OL	AL	ELL	🖋	**Economic Concepts Transparencies, Strategies, and Activities**		p. 17	p. 21	p. 23	
BL	OL	AL	ELL	📁	**Math Practice for Economics**		p. 7			
BL	OL		ELL	📁	**High School Reading in the Content Area Strategies and Activities**	✓	✓	✓	✓	✓
BL	OL	AL	ELL	🖋	**High School Writing Process Transparencies**	✓	✓	✓	✓	✓
BL	OL	AL	ELL	📁	**Writer's Guidebook**	✓	✓	✓	✓	✓
BL	OL	AL	ELL	💿	**StudentWorks Plus CD-ROM**	✓	✓	✓	✓	✓
BL	OL	AL	ELL	💿	**Vocabulary PuzzleMaker CD-ROM**	✓	✓	✓	✓	✓

*Also available in Spanish

- Interactive Lesson Planner
- Interactive Teacher Edition
- Fully editable blackline masters
- Economics & You videos

- Differentiated Lesson Plans
- Printable reports of daily assignments
- Standards tracking system

Levels					Resources	Chapter Opener	Section 1	Section 2	Section 3	Chapter Assess
BL	OL	AL	ELL							
TEACH *(continued)*										
BL	OL	AL	ELL		Economics & You Video Program DVD— *Competition and Monopolies*	✓	✓	✓	✓	✓
BL	OL	AL	ELL		Graph Coach CD-ROM	✓	✓	✓	✓	✓
Teacher Resources					Differentiated Instruction Strategies	✓	✓	✓	✓	✓
					Success with English Learners	✓	✓	✓	✓	✓
					Presentation Plus! CD-ROM	✓	✓	✓	✓	✓
ASSESS										
BL	OL	AL	ELL		Section Quizzes and Chapter Tests		p. 81	p. 82	p. 83	pp. 85, 89
BL	OL	AL	ELL		Authentic Assessment Strategies and Activities			p. 12		
BL	OL	AL	ELL		*ExamView® Assessment Suite* CD-ROM		7-1	7-2	7-3	Ch. 7
BL	OL	AL	ELL		Interactive Tutor Self-Assessment CD-ROM		7-1	7-2	7-3	
CLOSE										
BL			ELL		Reteaching Activities*		p. 7	p. 7	p. 7	
BL	OL		ELL		Reading and Study Skills Foldables		p. 54			
BL	OL	AL	ELL		Graphic Organizer Transparencies		p. 17			

*Also available in Spanish

Activity Using *StudentWorks™ Plus*

Read and Listen Simultaneously

Technology Product

Glencoe's *StudentWorks™ Plus* CD-ROM contains everything your students need, including the complete Student Edition, text in audio, access to all student workbooks, and links to online activities and resources.

- Students can read chapters with Adobe Acrobat Reader software, which is opened automatically by the *StudentWorks™ Plus* program.
- The complete textbook is available with audio via the *StudentWorks™ Plus* CD-ROM.
- Students can read and listen simultaneously with page-by-page audio, which can improve content comprehension for all your students.
- Use this component with struggling readers or to emphasize an important concept.

Objectives

Using *StudentWorks™ Plus* will help your students

- practice their reading skills;
- improve their listening comprehension.

Steps

Provide students with the following information:

- Launch *StudentWorks™ Plus*.
- Select **Student Edition with Audio** from the launch screen.
- Use the bookmarks along the left side to navigate to the desired chapter or use the **Page Navigator** link in the bookmarks to link to the exact page number in the Student Edition.
- Click on the audio icon located on each page in the upper left corner to launch the audio.
- Read along with the audio.

Economics ONLINE

	Student	Teacher	Parent
Beyond the Textbook	●	●	●
Chapter Overviews	●	●	●
ePuzzles and Games	●		●
Concepts in Motion	●		●
Multi-Language Glossaries	●		●
Online Student Edition	●	●	●
Self-Check Quizzes	●		●
Student Web Activities	●		●
Study Central™	●		●
Time Current Events	●	●	●
Teaching Today		●	
Vocabulary eFlashcards	●		●
Web Activity Lesson Plans		●	

Glencoe Media Center

> glencoe.com

Study-To-Go
- Vocabulary eFlashcards
- Self-Check Quizzes

> **Audio/Video**
- Student Edition Audio
- Spanish Summaries
- Economics & You Videos

- **Timed Readings Plus in Social Studies** helps students increase their reading rate and fluency while maintaining comprehension. The 400-word passages are similar to those found on state and national assessments.

- **Reading in the Content Area: Social Studies** concentrates on six essential reading skills that help students better comprehend what they read. The book includes 75 high-interest nonfiction passages written at increasing levels of difficulty.

- **Reading Social Studies** includes strategic reading instruction and vocabulary support in Social Studies content for both ELLs and native speakers of English. www.jamestowneducation.com

Reading List Generator CD-ROM

Use this database to search more than 30,000 titles to create a customized reading list for your students.

- Reading lists can be organized by students' reading level, author, genre, theme, or area of interest.

- The database provides Degrees of Reading Power™ (DRP) and Lexile™ readability scores for all selections.

- A brief summary of each selection is included.

Leveled reading suggestions for this chapter:

For students at a Grade 10 reading level:
- *Hearing the Pitch: Evaluating All Kinds of Advertising,* by Carlienne Frisch

For students at a Grade 11 reading level:
- *Government and the Environment: Tracking the Record,* by Thomas G. Aylesworth

For students at a Grade 12 reading level:
- *Foreign Oil Dependence,* by James Haley

* Review suggested books before assigning them.

National Council on Economic Education

Voluntary Standards Emphasized in Chapter 7

Content Standard 9 Competition among sellers lowers costs and prices, and encourages producers to produce more of what consumers are willing and able to buy. Competition among buyers increases prices and allocates goods and services to those people who are willing and able to pay the most for them.

Content Standard 16 There is an economic role for government in a market economy whenever the benefits of a government policy outweigh its costs. Governments often provide for national defense, address environmental concerns, define and protect property rights, and attempt to make markets more competitive. Most government policies also redistribute income.

Resources Available from NCEE
- Virtual Economics®: An Interactive Center for Economic Education Version 3.0
- Capstone: The Nation's High School Economics Course
- Focus: High School Economics, Second Edition
- Advanced Placement Economics: Teacher Resource Manual, Third Edition
- Focus: Institutions and Markets
- Focus: Understanding Economics in U.S. History

To order these materials, or to contact your State Council on Economic Education about workshops and programs, call 1-800-338-1192 or visit the NCEE Web site at store.ncee.net**.**

The BIG Ideas

As students study the chapter, remind them to consider the chapter-based Big Ideas. The **Essential Question** in the chapter launch activity below ties in to the Big Ideas and helps students think about and understand important chapter concepts. In addition, the Hands-On Chapter Project relates the content from each section to the Big Ideas. The steps in each section build on each other and culminate in the Wrap-Up Activity on the Visual Summary page.

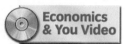 **Economics & You Video** To generate student interest and provide a springboard for class discussion, access the Economics & You Topic 7 video, **Competition and Monopolies,** at glencoe.com or on the video DVD.

FOLDABLES *Study Organizer* **Dinah Zike's Foldables** are three-dimensional, interactive graphic organizers that help students practice basic writing skills, review key vocabulary terms, and identify main ideas. Have students complete this chapter's Foldable activity or activities in *Dinah Zike's Reading and Study Skills Foldables* booklet. **OL**

Economics ONLINE

Introduce students to chapter content and key terms by having them access *Chapter 7 —Chapter Overviews* at glencoe.com.

CHAPTER 7 Market Structures

Why It Matters

A developer has acquired the large piece of vacant land across the street from your house and plans to build a large shopping mall on the property. How might you benefit from the mall? How might it negatively impact your life? Read Chapter 7 to learn about market structures and economic growth.

The BIG Ideas

1. The profit motive acts as an incentive for people to produce and sell goods and services.

2. Economists look at a variety of factors to assess the growth and performance of a nation's economy.

3. Governments strive for a balance between the costs and benefits of their economic policies to promote economic stability and growth.

When many companies offer ▶ similar products, each firm tries to differentiate its goods to attract customers.

Economics ONLINE **Chapter Overview** Visit the *Economics: Principles and Practices* Web site at glencoe.com and click on *Chapter 7–Chapter Overviews* to preview chapter information.

Activity: Launching the Chapter

Analyzing Have students select a company that recently opened for business in their area. Ask students to write a brief report on the goods or services that company provides, and note which other businesses provide the same goods and services in the area. Instruct students to conclude their reports by explaining why they think the owners of the business decided to open in that particular location.

Essential Question: How are competition and the profit motive related? *(People open businesses to earn profits. Competition forces entrepreneurs to keep prices low enough to attract customers. However, prices must remain high enough to ensure profits.)* Ask for volunteers to share the names of the companies they selected. Discuss as a class how each new business could affect the market for the goods and services that it sells. **OL**

Competition and Market Structures

GUIDE TO READING

Section Preview

In this section, you will learn that market structures include perfect competition, monopolistic competition, oligopoly, and monopoly.

Content Vocabulary

- laissez-faire (p. 169)
- market structure (p. 169)
- perfect competition (p. 170)
- imperfect competition (p. 172)
- monopolistic competition (p. 173)
- product differentiation (p. 173)
- nonprice competition (p. 173)
- oligopoly (p. 174)
- collusion (p. 174)
- price-fixing (p. 175)
- monopoly (p. 175)
- natural monopoly (p. 176)

- economies of scale (p. 176)
- geographic monopoly (p. 176)
- technological monopoly (p. 176)
- government monopoly (p. 177)

Academic Vocabulary

- theoretically (p. 170)
- equate (p. 177)

Reading Strategy

Identifying As you read the section, complete a graphic organizer similar to the one below by identifying the characteristics of different market structures.

Market Structure	Characteristics
Perfect competition	

Focus

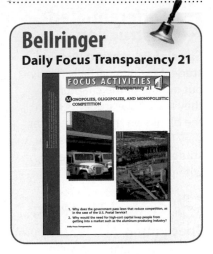

Bellringer
Daily Focus Transparency 21

ISSUES IN THE NEWS

—The Washington Post

Profits, Prices Spur Oil Outrage

Exxon Mobil Corp. reported $8.4 billion in first-quarter profit yesterday, as members of Congress, outraged over high gasoline prices, hastened to propose measures that would boost taxes on oil firms, open new areas to drilling and provide rebates to taxpayers but would not necessarily alter prices at the pumps.

"What you have today is an oligopoly, effectively, and I think it's a disaster for the American people," said Senator Dianne Feinstein.

Federal Reserve Chairman Ben S. Bernanke cautioned Congress on the various proposals being floated. "I would like to let the market system work as much as possible to generate new supplies. . . ." ■

When Adam Smith published *An Inquiry into the Nature and Causes of the Wealth of Nations* in 1776, the average factory was small, and businesses were competitive. *Laissez-faire,* the French term that means "allow them to do," was the prevailing philosophy that limited government's role to protecting property, enforcing contracts, settling disputes, and protecting firms against foreign competition.

Conditions are much different today. An industry, or the supply side of the market, has many firms of different sizes producing slightly different products. These conditions help determine **market structure,** or the nature and degree of competition among firms doing business in the same industry. Economists group firms into four different market structures that reflect the competitive conditions in those markets.

laissez-faire
philosophy that government should not interfere with business activities

market structure
nature and degree of competition among firms in the same industry

GUIDE TO READING

Answers to Graphic:

Perfect competition: large number of well-informed independent buyers and sellers who exchange identical products

Monopolistic competition: same as perfect competition except that products are generally similar

Oligopoly: a few large sellers dominate; products may have distinct features

Monopoly: a single seller of a particular product

Resource Manager

R Reading Strategies	**C** Critical Thinking	**D** Differentiated Instruction	**W** Writing Support	**S** Skill Practice
Teacher Edition • Inferring, p. 171 • Summarizing, p. 172 • Using Word Parts, p. 174 **Additional Resources** • Guid. Read. Act., p. 19 • Read. Ess. & Note-Taking Guide, p. 55	**Teacher Edition** • Speculating, p. 170 • Ident. Central Issues, p. 173 • Det. Cause/Effect, p. 174 • Form. Quest., p. 178 **Additional Resources** • Crit. Think. Act., p. 7 • Econ. Concepts Trans., Strat. and Act., p. 17	**Teacher Edition** • Special Ed., p. 170 • ELL, p. 171 • Auditory/Musical, p. 173 • Visual/Spatial, p. 176 **Additional Resources** • Econ. Cartoons, p. 11 • Free Ent. Act., p. 6 • Enrichment Act., p. 7	**Teacher Edition** • Personal Writing, p. 172 • Persuasive Writing, p. 174 • Narrative Writing, p. 176 **Additional Resources** • Writer's Guidebook • Reading and Study Skills Fold., p. 54	**Teacher Edition** • Analyzing Graphs, p. 171 • Using Tables and Charts, p. 175 • Evaluating Info., p. 177 **Additional Resources** • Daily Focus Trans. 20 • Graph. Org. Trans., p. 9 • Math Prac. for Econ., p. 7

Teach

D Differentiated Instruction

Special Education Provide students with a partially filled out outline of the chapter. As they read, have students fill in the blanks on the outline. After they finish the chapter, have students compare outlines with partners. **BL**

C Critical Thinking

Speculating Ask: What would happen if consumers did not have easy access to information about products and services? *(Possible answer: Sellers would exploit the consumers' lack of knowledge to raise prices.)* **OL**

Caption Answer: The products are identical, the buyer is acting independently, and the buyer is free to make a business transaction if he wishes.

Additional Support

---

perfect competition market structure with many well-informed and independent buyers and sellers who exchange identical products

D Perfect Competition

MAIN Idea Perfect competition is an ideal market situation used to evaluate other market structures.

Economics & You You learned earlier about industries. Read on to find out how perfect competition is the ideal market structure in an industry.

Perfect competition is a market structure characterized by a large number of well-informed independent buyers and sellers who exchange identical products. It represents a **theoretically** ideal situation that is used to evaluate other market structures. In order for a market to have perfect competition, it needs to meet five necessary conditions that other market structures lack.

Necessary Conditions

The first condition is that there must be a large number of buyers and sellers. No single buyer or seller is large enough or powerful enough to single-handedly affect the price.

The second condition is that buyers and sellers deal in identical products. With no difference in the products, there is no need for brand names and no need to advertise, which keeps prices low. With no differences between products, one seller's merchandise is just as good as another's.

The third condition is that each buyer and seller acts independently. This ensures that sellers compete against one another for the consumer's dollar, and that consumers compete against one another to obtain the best price.

The fourth condition is that buyers and sellers are reasonably well-informed about products and prices. Well-informed buyers shop at the stores that have the lowest prices. Well-informed sellers match the lowest prices of their competitors to avoid losing customers.

The fifth condition is that buyers and sellers are free to enter into, conduct, or get out of business. This freedom makes it difficult for producers in any industry to keep the market to themselves. Producers have to keep prices competitive, or new firms can take away some of their business. Collectively, these conditions help ensure the competition that is necessary to keep prices low and quality high.

Profit Maximization

Under perfect competition, market supply and demand set the equilibrium price for the product. Because the price is determined in the market, and because each firm by itself is too small to influence the market price, the perfect competitor is often called

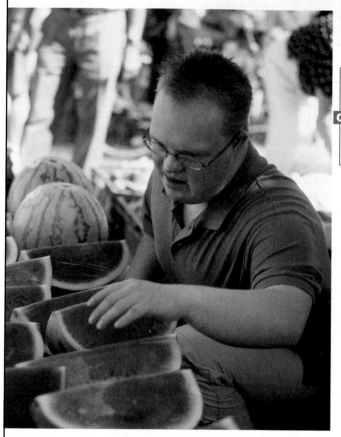

Perfect Competition A farmers' market comes closest to satisfying the conditions for a perfectly competitive market. *What conditions for perfect competition are met in this photograph, and how?*

Activity: Extending the Content

Agriculture and Perfect Competition
Few markets today meet the conditions of the perfectly competitive market model. However, the grain market for number two yellow corn—a standard product that does not vary—closely fits this description. There are many farmers who grow and sell number two yellow corn, as well as a large number of buyers. The farmers do not advertise or band together to control price.

There is open communication between buyers and sellers about the market price. The grain market for number two yellow corn, however, falls short of satisfying the fifth condition for perfect competition: ease of access to the market. Entry is limited because it takes a sizeable investment to start a farm focused on the growing of grain.

Figure 7.1 ▶ Perfect Competition and Profit Maximization

▶ Under perfect competition, the market forces of supply and demand establish the equilibrium price. The perfectly competitive firm treats this price as its demand curve and its marginal revenue (MR) because the firm will receive $15 for each and every unit it sells.

Graphs In MOtion
See StudentWorks™ Plus or glencoe.com.

Economic Analysis *What would happen to total profits if the firm used 10 workers instead of 9?*

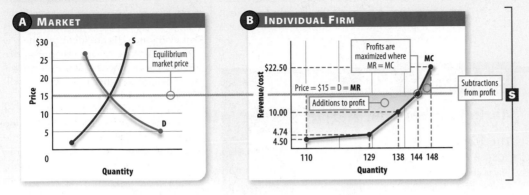

a "price taker." The firm then must find the level of output it can produce that will maximize its profits.

To understand how this is done, it helps to examine **Figure 7.1.** This figure shows the relationship between the perfectly competitive firm and its industry. In **Panel A,** supply and demand set the equilibrium market price at $15 per unit of output. Because the firm in **Panel B** receives $15 for the first and every additional unit it sells, the market price is the same as the firm's marginal revenue curve (MR).

In order to show a graphical example, the firm in Figure 7.1 is the same one that appeared earlier in Figure 5.6 on page 134. While the number of workers are not shown in Figure 7.1, the total production, marginal cost, and marginal revenue are the same in both figures.

When it comes to determining the profit maximizing quantity of output in Figure 7.1, the logic of marginal analysis is the same as before. For example, Panel B in the figure above tells us that the firm would make a profit on the 110th unit of output because it would only cost $4.50 to produce and could be sold for $15. As long as the marginal cost of producing one more unit of output is less than the marginal revenue from the sale of that output, the firm would continue to hire more workers and expand its output.

Given its marginal cost and marginal revenue conditions, the firm shown in Figure 7.1 would find it profitable to hire enough workers to expand production until 144 units of output are produced. Of course, total output would continue to go up if the firm hired more workers and expanded production. However, total profits would start to go down because the marginal cost of production would then become increasingly larger than the $15 marginal revenue from sales.

In the end, the profit maximizing quantity of output is found where the marginal cost of production is equal to the marginal revenue from sales, or where MC = MR. This occurs at 144 units of output. Other levels of output may generate equal profits, but none will generate more.

CHAPTER 7   Market Structures   **171**

S Skill Practice

Analyzing Graphs Ask: What is the difference between marginal cost and marginal revenue at the quantity of 129? *($10.26)* **OL**

R Reading Strategy

Inferring Ask: What would happen if the firm in the graph tried to charge a price greater than $15? *(Consumers would buy from other firms, and sales for the firm in the graph would drop.)* **AL**

D Differentiated Instruction

English Language Learners Have students list three words from this spread that they are not familiar with (such as *marginal*). Next, have them exchange lists with a partner. Ask each student to look up the definitions of the words on the list and then explain orally to his or her partner what the words mean. **ELL**

Economic Analysis

Answer: The firm would hire more workers and increase output.

Hands-On Chapter Project

Step 1

Analyzing American Market Structures

In this project, students will examine the four market structures by making posters, conducting surveys, and writing laws and policies.

Step 1: Comparing Market Structures.
Student groups will compare the different market structures in the American economy.

Directions: Organize the class into at least six different small groups. Tell students that each group will create a large collage-type poster for each of the four market structures in the American economy (perfect competition, monopolistic competition, oligopoly, monopoly). Groups should identify specific businesses and industries that fit with each of the different market structures. Student should then select images, such as company logos, office buildings, and customers buying products, to cut out and place on a large poster board. Posters should also include text describing how the images relate to the specific market structure that they represent.

Display the completed posters in the classroom. Have a spokesperson from each group explain the information presented on the group's poster. Allow students from other groups to ask questions about the poster.

Summarizing Have students write a short paper summarizing what they learned about the different market structures from their own work and the work of other groups. **OL**

(Chapter Project continued in Section 2.)

R Reading Strategy

Summarizing Tell students: Use your own words to summarize the reasons why perfect competition keeps prices low. *(Summaries should include the following: no need for advertising; no reason for one seller to charge a higher price; buyers will always purchase from the seller with the lowest price; new sellers can enter easily.)* **BL**

W Writing Support

Personal Writing Have students write a one-page essay giving their thoughts and feelings about the role of economic competition in a political democracy. Students might attempt to link the freedom of interaction that occurs under perfect competition with the political freedoms granted in a democracy, or they might note that economic competition implies equality of opportunity. **AL**

✓ **Reading Check** **Answer:** Although perfect competition rarely exists, its advantages serve as a yardstick against which other structures are measured.

Differentiated Instruction

imperfect competition market structure that does not meet all conditions of perfect competition

A Theoretical Situation

Few perfectly competitive markets exist because it is difficult to satisfy all five necessary conditions. Local vegetable farming, sometimes called "truck" farming, comes close.

In these markets many sellers offer nearly identical products. Individual sellers are generally unable to control prices, and both buyers and sellers have

reasonable knowledge of most products and prices. Finally, anyone who wants to enter the business by growing tomatoes, corn, or other products can easily do so.

When markets are perfectly competitive, several things combine to keep prices low. For example, when everyone is dealing with identical products, there is no need to advertise, which keeps the cost down. Second, when the products that everyone sells are identical, there is no reason for one seller to charge a price higher than anyone else. If the seller does try to charge a higher price, buyers will simply go elsewhere.

R Third, if there are a large number of independent buyers and sellers, then no single buyer is big enough to push the price down and no single seller is big enough to force the price up. As a result, buyers will always try to purchase from the seller with the lowest price.

Finally, if it is easy for sellers to enter or leave the market, then new sellers can always come in if they think they can make a profit. Likewise, sellers who cannot match the new competition are free to leave.

Imperfect Competition

Although perfect competition is rare, it is important because economists use it to evaluate other, less competitive, market structures. **Imperfect competition** is the name given to any of three market structures—monopolistic competition, oligopoly, and monopoly—that lacks one or more of the conditions required for perfect competition. Most firms and industries in the **W** United States today fall into one of these categories. When we examine imperfect competition, we will see that it results in less competition, higher prices for consumers, and fewer products offered. This is why perfectly competitive markets are theoretically ideal situations that can be used to evaluate other market structures.

CAREERS

Market Researcher

The Work
* Gather, record, and analyze facts about products and sales using company or government records, published materials, statistical files, and other sources
* Print and circulate questionnaires or survey people over the phone or door-to-door to help companies forecast future sales trends, design new products, and develop advertising strategies

Qualifications
* Strong analytical and writing skills
* Experience with computerized data
* College courses in marketing, statistics, English composition, speech, psychology, and economics
* Bachelor's degree, with many positions requiring a master's or Ph.D.

Earnings
* Median annual earnings: $53,810

Job Growth Outlook
* Faster than average

Source: *Occupational Outlook Handbook, 2006–2007 Edition*

✓ **Reading Check** **Describing** Why does perfect competition serve as a theoretical market structure?

Math Practice for Economics, p. 7

Competing in the Marketplace

Objective: Understand how competition affects prices.

Focus: Have students brainstorm current examples of monopolies and competitive markets.

Teach: Have students complete the exercises in the activity.

Assess: Make sure that students have the correct answers and understand the calculations behind them.

Close: Have students write a paragraph explaining how monopolies and competition affect prices.

Differentiated Instruction Strategies

BL Have student groups devise strategies for what the farmer could do to maximize profits in the future.

AL Ask students to create a similar exercise with different products and prices.

ELL Have students write sentences using the words *monopoly*, *competition*, and *equilibrium*.

GREAT NEW TASTE! BETTER THAN EVER.

CEW! Coke

Product Differentiation
Monopolistic competitors must find ways to attract the attention of buyers. *How does the advertisement on this billboard differentiate this product from other colas?*

Monopolistic Competition

MAIN Idea Monopolistic competition shares all the conditions of perfect competition except the same goods or services.

Economics & You How many stores do you know that offer similar products? Read on to learn how this reflects monopolistic competition.

Monopolistic competition is the market structure that has all the conditions of perfect competition except for identical products. Under monopolistic competition, products are generally similar and include things such as designer clothing, cosmetics, and shoes. The *monopolistic* aspect is the seller's ability to raise the price within a narrow range. The *competitive* aspect is that if sellers raise or lower the price enough, customers will ignore minor differences and change brands.

Product Differentiation

Monopolistic competition is characterized by **product differentiation**—real or perceived differences between competing products in the same industry. Most items produced today—from the many brands of athletic footwear to personal computers—are differentiated.

Nonprice Competition

To make their products stand out, monopolistic competitors try to make consumers aware of product differences. They do this with **nonprice competition**—the use of advertising, giveaways, or other promotions designed to convince buyers that the product is somehow unique or fundamentally better than a competitor's.

In a monopolistically competitive industry, advertising is important. This explains why producers of designer clothes spend so much on advertising and promotion. If a seller can differentiate a product in the mind of the buyer, the firm may be able to raise the price above its competitors' prices. Because advertising is expensive, it raises the cost of doing business for the monopolistic competitor, and hence the price the consumer pays.

Profit Maximization

The profit maximizing behavior of the monopolistic competitor is no different from that of other firms. The firm will expand its production until its marginal cost is equal to its marginal revenue, or where MC = MR. If the firm's advertising convinces consumers that its product is better, then it can charge a higher price. If not, the firm must charge less.

Finally, it is easy for firms to enter the monopolistically competitive industry. Each new firm makes a product only a little different from others on the market. The result is a large number of firms producing a variety of similar products.

✓Reading Check **Comparing** How is profit maximization in a monopolistic firm different from that of a perfect competitor?

monopolistic competition market structure that meets all conditions of perfect competition except identical products

product differentiation real or imagined differences between competing products in the same industry

nonprice competition sales strategy focusing on a product's appearance, quality, or design rather than its price

CHAPTER 7 Market Structures **173**

C Critical Thinking
Identifying Central Issues
List the following products on the board: soda, bottled water, perfume, aspirin. Ask students to name their favorite brands of these items and explain their choices. Point out that this is an illustration of product differentiation, because student preferences were based on slight differences among brands. **OL**

D Differentiated Instruction
Auditory/Musical Ask students to think of advertising jingles that have influenced them to buy a product. Have each student sing, hum, or identify one such song and explain its effectiveness. **BL**

Caption Answer: It claims that the cola has a new taste.

✓Reading Check **Answer:** It's not; the firm still maximizes profits at the output where marginal cost equals marginal revenue.

Leveled Activities

BL Reading and Study Skills Foldables, p. 54

OL Free Enterprise Activities, p. 6

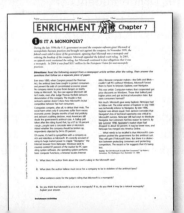

AL Enrichment Activities, p. 7

R **Reading Strategy**

Using Word Parts Have students research the origins and meaning of the two parts of the word *oligopoly* and then explain its meaning. (*It is a Greek word. Olig means "few"; poly means "many." Hence, oligopoly means "few sellers, many buyers."*) **AL**

W **Writing Support**

Persuasive Writing Have students choose a product made by an oligopoly and write a brief essay in which they argue for the superiority of their preferred brand. (For example, students may argue that McDonald's has the best cheeseburgers, based on taste, price, and convenience.) **OL**

C **Critical Thinking**

Determining Cause and Effect **Ask:** What is the effect of a company in an oligopoly making a product change? (*The other companies in the oligopoly will make the same change.*) **BL**

Additional Support

The Global Economy & YOU

Poco, Heart, and Wisdom

If you invent a product, remember that an important part of selling it is the brand name. In the global economy, Western brands sometimes get lost in translation. The real genius in selling overseas is to capture foreign consumers' attention with a Western product, but relate it to their lives and culture in a familiar way.

PepsiCo, for example, sells its popular Lays potato chips in China. It also introduced a local brand of potato chips called Poco. In addition to changing the name of the chips, PepsiCo adjusted the flavor to satisfy local tastes.

German carmaker Volkswagen used its slogan, "For the love of the automobile," as a springboard for the Asian market. Savvy marketing gurus took this catchy slogan and attached it to the Chinese-language written character for *heart.* The VW brand campaign includes 16 total characters, including those for *compassion, loyalty,* and *wisdom,* and associates the characters with VW automobiles. The VW Golf model represents *loyalty,* for example, whereas the Passat is a blend of *heart* and *goal.*

---

oligopoly market structure in which a few large sellers dominate the industry

collusion agreement, usually illegal, among producers to fix prices, limit output, or divide markets

Personal Finance Handbook

See pages R30–R31 for more information on buying a car.

Oligopoly

MAIN Idea Oligopoly describes a market in which a few sellers dominate an industry.

Economics & You What products can you think of that are sold by a small number of sellers? Read on to learn about oligopolies.

Oligopoly is a market structure in which a few very large sellers dominate the industry. The product of an oligopolist may have distinct features, as do the many makes and models of cars in the auto industry; or it may be standardized, as in the steel industry. As a result, oligopoly is further from perfect competition than monopolistic competition.

In the United States, many markets are already oligopolistic, and many more are becoming so. For example, Burger King, McDonald's, and Wendy's dominate the fast-food industry. A few large corporations control other industries, such as the domestic airline and automobile industries.

Interdependent Behavior

Because oligopolists are so large, whenever one firm acts, the other firms in the industry usually follow—or they run the risk of losing customers. For example, when Chrysler introduced the first minivan, other companies soon followed.

The tendency of oligopolists to act together often shows up in their pricing behavior, such as copying a competitor's price reduction in order to attract new customers. For example, if Ford or General Motors announces zero-interest financing or thousands of dollars back on each new car purchased, its competitors will match the promotion almost immediately. In extreme cases this can lead to a price war, or a series of price cuts that result in unusually low prices.

Because oligopolists usually act together when it comes to changing prices, many firms prefer to compete on a nonprice basis by enhancing their products with new or different features. Automobile companies do this every year when they introduce models. If an oligopolist finds a way to enhance a product, its competitors are at a disadvantage for a period of time. After all, it takes longer to develop a new physical attribute for a product than it does to match a price cut.

Sometimes the interdependent behavior takes the form of **collusion,** a formal agreement to set specific prices or to otherwise behave in a cooperative manner. One form

174 UNIT 2 **Microeconomics: Prices and Markets**

Activity: Collaborative Learning

Local Oligopolies Divide students of mixed abilities into groups of four. Have them identify a business in the community that is part of an oligopoly. Have students observe the business as well as research it through print and online resources. Then have groups present an oral report describing the competitive strategies employed by the business. For their reports, student might look for advertisements and evaluate them for effectiveness and purpose. (For example, does the ad seek to expand market share by product differentiation, or does it seek to increase overall demand for the product?) Students might evaluate product quality of their producer vs. that of other producers, or they might observe strategies such as location and price. Students should evaluate the business's place in the oligopoly. For example, does it distribute a good made under oligopoly conditions? (car dealership, gas station) Or does it actually produce a good or service under oligopoly conditions? (one of two or three doctors in town; one of two or three Italian restaurants in town) **OL**

of collusion is **price-fixing,** or agreeing to charge the same or similar prices for a product. In almost every case these prices are higher than those determined under competition. The firms also might agree to divide the market so that each is guaranteed to sell a certain amount. Because collusion usually restrains trade, it is against the law.

Profit Maximization

The oligopolist, like any other firm, maximizes its profits when it finds the quantity of output where its marginal cost is equal to its marginal revenue, or where MC = MR. The oligopolist will then charge the price consistent with this level of sales.

Because of all the nonprice competition, the product's final price is likely to be higher than it would be under monopolistic competition, and much higher than it would be under perfect competition. Nonprice competition is always expensive for a firm, and these expenses usually come back to the consumer in the form of higher prices.

✓**Reading Check** **Explaining** Why do oligopolists frequently appear to act together?

Monopoly

▪▪▪▪▪**MAIN Idea** A monopoly is a market with only one seller for a particular product.

Economics & You Did you ever play the game of Monopoly? Read on to learn how this game reflects the problems caused by having one seller in the market.

At the opposite end of the spectrum from perfect competition is monopoly. A **monopoly** is a market structure with only one seller of a particular product. This situation—like that of perfect competition—is an extreme case. In fact, the American economy has very few, if any, cases of pure monopoly— although the local cable TV operator or telephone company may come close.

Even the telephone company, however, faces competition from other communication companies, from the United States Postal Service, and from Internet providers that supply e-mail and telephone services. Local cable providers face competition from video rental stores, satellite cable systems, and the Internet. Consequently, when people talk about monopolies, they usually mean near-monopolies.

price-fixing agreement, usually illegal, by firms to charge the same price for a product

monopoly market structure with a single seller of a particular product

S **Skill Practice**
Using Tables and Charts
Ask: In which market structures is product differentiation important? *(monopolistic competition and oligopoly)* In which market structure do firms have limited influence over price? *(monopolistic competition)* **BL**

Did You Know?

The game of Monopoly was invented by an unemployed engineer named Charles Darrow. Hoping to profit from his idea, Darrow presented his game to Parker Brothers in 1934. The company rejected it but eventually reconsidered and bought the rights to Darrow's game.

✓**Reading Check** **Answer:** Because they are so large, they must follow the actions of other firms or risk losing customers.

Economic Analysis
Answer: monopolistic competition and oligopoly

Additional Support

Figure 7.2 ▶ **Characteristics of Market Structures**

	Number of firms in industry	Influence over price	Product differentiation	Advertising	Entry into market	Examples
Perfect competition	Many	None	None	None	Easy	Perfect: None Near: Truck farming
Monopolistic competition	Many	Limited	Fair amount	Fair amount	Easy	Gas stations Women's clothing
Oligopoly	Few	Some	Fair amount	Some	Difficult	Automobiles Aluminum
Pure monopoly	One	Extensive	None	None	Almost impossible	Perfect: None Near: Water

▶ The term *market structure* refers to the nature and degree of competition among firms operating in the same industry. Individual market structures, listed on the left, are determined by the five characteristics listed in the columns above.

Economic Analysis *In which market structure does nonprice competition play a major role?*

Activity: Hands-On Economics

Technology and Monopoly In this activity, students will explore the relationship between technology and monopolies. Ask students to take notes on at least one way that they use modern technology. Then have students write a report explaining how this interaction relates to the economic concept of monopoly. Examples that students could write about include: placing an order with Amazon.com (weakens the geographic monopoly of a local bookstore); using a computer with Windows (strengthens the Microsoft monopoly); paying for and downloading a song onto an iPod (abiding by the song's copyright protection). **OL**

W Writing Support

Narrative Writing Have students write a fictional story describing a futuristic society in which there is only one university, doctor, and grocery store—in fact, there is only one of everything. Stories should focus on how living among such monopolies impacts the daily lives of individuals. **OL**

D Differentiated Instruction

Visual/Spatial Have students contribute to a list of natural monopolies that you write on the board. Then have students choose one of the monopolies and draw a picture or make a collage that illustrates what the community would look like if the product or service was supplied by competitors instead of a regulated monopoly. **ELL**

Caption Answer: There are no other sellers in the area.

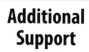

Additional Support

Teacher Tip

Researching Supreme Court Cases Students might find Supreme Court opinions online. Suggest that they visit the Legal Information Institute (www.law.cornell.edu) or the U.S. Supreme Court (www.supremecourt.us.gov).

Monopolies A geographic monopoly exists when there is only one seller of a product in a particular area. *What would indicate that this gas station has a geographic monopoly?*

natural monopoly market structure where average costs of production are lowest when a single firm exists

economies of scale situation in which the average cost of production falls as a firm gets larger

geographic monopoly market structure in which one firm has a monopoly in a geographic area

technological monopoly monopoly based on a firm's ownership or control of a production method, process, or other scientific advance

We have few monopolies today because Americans traditionally have disliked them and have tried to outlaw them. Another reason is that new technologies often introduce products that compete with existing monopolies. The development of the fax machine allowed businesses to send electronic letters that competed with the U.S. Postal Service. Later, e-mail became even more popular than the fax. Today, telephone service over the Internet is yet another technology challenging phone monopolies.

Types of Monopolies

Sometimes the nature of a good or service dictates that society would be served best by a monopoly. A **natural monopoly**—a market situation where the costs of production are minimized by having a single firm produce the product—is one such case.

Natural monopolies often can provide services more cheaply than several competing firms could. For example, two or more competing telephone companies serving the same area would be inefficient if each company needed its own telephone poles and lines.

Public utility companies fall into this category because it would be wasteful to duplicate the networks of pipes and wires that distribute water, gas, and electricity throughout a city. To avoid these problems, the government often gives a public utility company a *franchise*—the exclusive right to do business in a certain area without competition. By accepting such franchises, the companies also accept a certain amount of government regulation.

The justification for the natural monopoly is that a larger firm can often use its personnel, equipment, and plant more efficiently. This results in **economies of scale**, a situation in which the average cost of production falls as the firm gets larger. When this happens, it makes sense for the firm to be as large as is necessary to lower its production costs.

Sometimes a monopoly exists because of a specific location. A drugstore operating in a town too small to support two or more such businesses becomes a **geographic monopoly**. This is a monopoly based on the absence of other sellers in a certain geographic area. Similarly, the owner of the only gas station on a lonely interstate highway exit also has a type of geographic monopoly.

A **technological monopoly** is a monopoly that is based on ownership or control of a manufacturing method, process, or other scientific advance. The government may grant a *patent*—an exclusive right to manufacture, use, or sell any new and useful invention for a specific period—to the inventor. Inventions are covered for 20 years; however, a product's design can be patented for shorter periods, after which it becomes public property available for the benefit of all. Art and literary works are protected through

Activity: Interdisciplinary Connection

Civics Tell students that in early 2007, the Supreme Court heard arguments in a case in which AT&T sued Microsoft for patent infringement. Software patents in general are a significant issue in the case. Have students research this case or other similar cases, such as *MercExchange* v. *eBay* or *NTP* v. *Research in Motion*. Students should examine why the judicial system is necessary for maintaining patents and

write reports on their findings. Reports should include analysis of the importance to progress and growth of maintaining intellectual property rights. **AL** a *copyright*—the exclusive right of authors or artists to publish, sell, or reproduce their work for their lifetime plus 50 years.

Still another kind of monopoly is the **government monopoly**—a monopoly owned and operated by the government. Government monopolies are found at all three levels of government—national, state, and local. In most cases they involve products or services that private industry cannot adequately supply.

Many towns and cities have monopolies that oversee water use. Some states control alcoholic beverages by requiring that they be sold only through state stores. The federal government controls the processing of weapons-grade uranium for military and national security purposes.

Profit Maximization

Monopolies maximize profits the same way other firms do: they **equate** marginal cost with marginal revenue to find the profit-maximizing quantity of output. Even so, there are differences between the

monopolist and other profit-maximizing firms—especially the perfect competitor.

First, the monopolist is much larger than the perfect competitor. This is because there is only one firm—the monopolist—supplying the product, rather than thousands of smaller ones. Second, both because of its large size and the lack of meaningful competition, the monopolist is able to behave as a "price maker." This differs from the perfect competitor, who faces competition and is a price taker.

Because there are no competing firms in the industry, there is no equilibrium price facing the monopolist. In order for the monopolist to maximize its profits, it will do exactly as all the other firms have done: it will equate MC with MR because this method always shows the level of output that produces the highest total profits. The result will be a very high price—higher than would be charged under conditions of perfect competition, monopolistic competition, or oligopoly.

✓Reading Check **Analyzing** Why do natural monopolies sometimes result in economies of scale?

government monopoly
a monopoly owned and operated by the government

See page **R41** to learn about **Drawing Conclusions**.
📖 **Skills Handbook**

S Skill Practice
Evaluating Information
Ask: Do you think it is fair for copyrights to last for the lifetime of the author plus 70 years? Explain. *(Answers will vary but will likely reference the importance of art and literature to the public vs. the individual rights of each author.)* **OL**

✓Reading Check **Answer:**
Sometimes a larger firm can use its personnel, equipment, and plant more efficiently.

Assess

💿 Use the Interactive Tutor Self-Assessment CD-ROM to review Section 1, and then assign the Section 1 Review as homework or as an in-class activity.

Close

Identifying Have students list three specific companies that operate in each of the three market structures described in this chapter. **OL**

SECTION 1 Review

Vocabulary
1. **Explain** the significance of laissez-faire, market structure, perfect competition, imperfect competition, monopolistic competition, product differentiation, nonprice competition, oligopoly, collusion, price-fixing, monopoly, natural monopoly, economies of scale, geographic monopoly, technological monopoly, and government monopoly.

Main Ideas
2. **Explaining** Why is the perfect competitor often called a "price taker"?

3. **Identifying** Use a graphic organizer like the one below to identify the characteristics of imperfect competition.

Imperfect Competition

Critical Thinking
4. **The BIG Idea** Describe the four basic market structures and explain how they differ from one another.

5. **Differentiating** Which characteristics of firms selling designer clothing are monopolistic? Which are competitive? Write a brief paragraph explaining your answer.

6. **Inferring** If Americans traditionally dislike monopolies, why do some monopolies exist today? What types of monopolies are they, and what are their characteristics?

7. **Analyzing Visuals** Compare the photos of the farmers on page 170 and the gas station on page 176. How do market conditions differ for these sellers?

Applying Economics
8. **Product Differentiation** Search your local newspaper for local clothing stores ads. You should find at least two different ads. Describe how the advertisements succeed or fail to differentiate the products.

CHAPTER 7 Market Structures **177**

Review SECTION 1

Answers

1. All definitions can be found in the section and the Glossary.
2. because there are so many buyers and sellers that none can influence price; they must take the price that the market gives
3. few firms; less competition; higher prices; fewer products
4. perfect competition: many buyers and sellers acting independently, identical products, good information; monopolistic competition: many sellers, product differentiation, nonprice competition;

oligopoly: few sellers, identical or differentiated products, interdependent behavior; monopoly: single seller
5. Answers will vary but should include the fact that the designer's name cannot be copied but the consumer may switch products if the designer charges too high of a price or falls out of fashion.
6. Sometimes monopolies can achieve economies of scale; they are natural monopolies, which the government regulates. There can also be geographic

monopolies, where a firm is the only seller within a large geographic area, and there can be technological monopolies on new inventions. These are protected by patents and exist to make sure that innovators reap the rewards of their efforts.
7. More firms result in little influence over price; one firm, however, results in extensive influence over price.
8. Answers will vary but should reflect analysis of the advertisements.

Profiles in Economics

Teach

C Critical Thinking

Formulating Questions
Have students come up with three questions that they would like to ask Bill Gates if he visited their school. Call on students at random to read one of their questions. Then discuss as a class how Gates might answer the questions. **OL**

Examining the Profile

Answers:

1. Gates understands the needs of average computer users and makes sure his products are user-friendly. He is thorough and committed and expects employees to be the same.

2. Students will likely say that Microsoft would have had more competition, with other PC companies developing their own systems rather than licensing MS-DOS from Microsoft.

Additional Support

Teacher Tip

Choosing a Book Suggest that students make a list of possible titles and then conduct an Internet search to find reviews of the books. Students can then quickly learn what the books are about and decide on one to read.

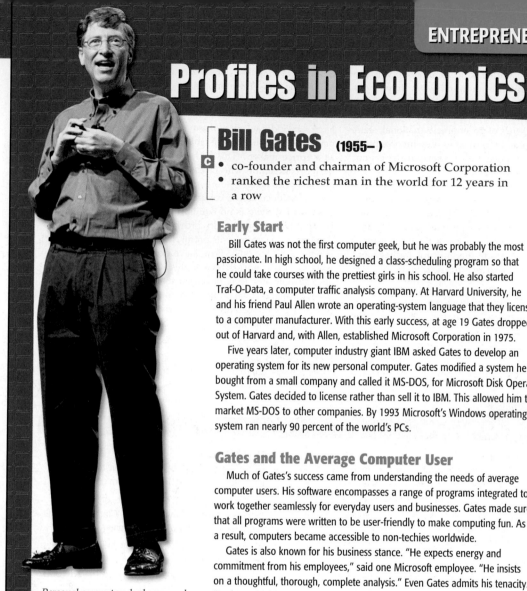

Personal computers had appeared in the marketplace by 1975, but they were still a novelty. Many people saw them as science fiction gadgets from the set of Star Trek. But Seattle teenagers Bill Gates and Paul Allen had a vision to "put a computer on every desktop and in every home."

Profiles in Economics

Bill Gates (1955–)

C
- co-founder and chairman of Microsoft Corporation
- ranked the richest man in the world for 12 years in a row

Early Start

Bill Gates was not the first computer geek, but he was probably the most passionate. In high school, he designed a class-scheduling program so that he could take courses with the prettiest girls in his school. He also started Traf-O-Data, a computer traffic analysis company. At Harvard University, he and his friend Paul Allen wrote an operating-system language that they licensed to a computer manufacturer. With this early success, at age 19 Gates dropped out of Harvard and, with Allen, established Microsoft Corporation in 1975.

Five years later, computer industry giant IBM asked Gates to develop an operating system for its new personal computer. Gates modified a system he had bought from a small company and called it MS-DOS, for Microsoft Disk Operating System. Gates decided to license rather than sell it to IBM. This allowed him to market MS-DOS to other companies. By 1993 Microsoft's Windows operating system ran nearly 90 percent of the world's PCs.

Gates and the Average Computer User

Much of Gates's success came from understanding the needs of average computer users. His software encompasses a range of programs integrated to work together seamlessly for everyday users and businesses. Gates made sure that all programs were written to be user-friendly to make computing fun. As a result, computers became accessible to non-techies worldwide.

Gates is also known for his business stance. "He expects energy and commitment from his employees," said one Microsoft employee. "He insists on a thoughtful, thorough, complete analysis." Even Gates admits his tenacity. "In the early days, I liked to review every line of code, to interview every job applicant," he said. "I've had to lighten up in both of those areas."

Examining the Profile

1. **Analyzing** What characteristics made Gates a successful entrepreneur?
2. **Predicting Consequences** How might the Microsoft story have been different if Gates had sold MS-DOS to IBM rather than licensing it?

Activity: Interdisciplinary Connection

Literature Have students choose and then read a book written by or about Bill Gates or a book about Microsoft. Ask students to write a three-page report on the book they selected. In their reports, students should answer the following questions: What made Bill Gates a successful entrepreneur? How did America's economic system contribute to Gates's success?

Remind students that a book report should identify the subject of the book and summarize its main points. Students should also include their opinions on the book, including what they found most interesting and how well they thought the author presented the material. **AL**

SECTION 2 Market Failures

GUIDE TO READING

Section Preview

In this section, you will find out that inadequate competition, inadequate information, immobile resources, public goods, and externalities can lead to market failures.

Content Vocabulary

- market failure *(p. 180)*
- public goods *(p. 181)*
- externality *(p. 181)*
- negative externality *(p. 182)*
- positive externality *(p. 182)*

Academic Vocabulary

- collude *(p. 180)*
- sustain *(p. 181)*

Reading Strategy

Listing As you read the section, think about why maintaining adequate competition is a worthwhile goal. Use a graphic organizer like the one below to list some of the effects of competition.

| If markets are competitive . . . | → | Effects |

COMPANIES IN THE NEWS

—USA Today

Enron

1400 Smith Street

A federal judge in Houston sentenced Richard Causey, former chief accounting officer of Enron, to 5 1/2 years in prison Wednesday, bringing an end to the government's prosecution of top managers at what was once the nation's seventh-largest company. . . .

Enron collapsed into bankruptcy five years ago after acknowledging that [Andrew] Fastow, the CFO, had entered into numerous business deals with the company that helped prop up Enron's earnings. Fastow later admitted that he embezzled close to $30 million from the company. Enron's market capitalization, which at one point exceeded $60 billion, was wiped out in the ensuing sell-off of stock.

In January 2002, the Department of Justice formed the Enron Task Force. Since then, prosecutors induced 16 former executives to plead guilty to related crimes, while several others were convicted at trial. . . . [W]ith Causey's sentencing, the last of the big Enron cases has been disposed of. ∎

The story about Enron reminds us of a serious fact of economic life—that markets sometimes fail. In fact, the Enron scandal was not the only accounting scandal dominating the news in the early 2000s. WorldCom, a telecommunications company, had to declare bankruptcy in 2002 amid charges of breaking the law.

These news stories showed clearly that a competitive free enterprise economy works best when several conditions, including adequate information, are met. If we want to avoid problems like this in the future, we need to be able to identify and then deal with different types of market failures.

CHAPTER 7   Market Structures   179

Teach

R Reading Strategy

Activating Prior Knowledge
Ask: What are the conditions necessary for perfect competition? *(many buyers and sellers acting independently; identical products; good information; freedom of entry into industry)* **OL**

D Differentiated Instruction

Logical/Mathematical Have students use the Internet to find the interest rates being offered on five different credit cards. Based on a bill of $1,000, have students identify the rate that is best for the borrower and the rate that is most profitable for the lender. Have students report to the class on why the information is important and how difficult it was to find. Suggest that students use a visual to display the information during the presentation. **OL**

Differentiated Instruction

---

market failure condition that causes a competitive market to fail

Types of Market Failures

MAIN Idea Markets can sometimes fail because of inadequate competition, inadequate information, resource immobility, public goods, and externalities.

Economics & You Have you ever been affected by something that somebody did to another person? Read on to learn how this can also happen in the economy.

R Unfortunately markets sometimes fail. A **market failure** occurs whenever one of the conditions necessary for competitive markets does not exist. As you will learn, five main causes of market failures exist.

Inadequate Competition

Over time, mergers and acquisitions result in larger and fewer firms dominating various industries. The decrease in competition tends to reduce the efficient use of scarce resources—resources that could be put to other, more productive uses if they were available. For example, why would a firm with few or no competitors have the incentive to use its resources carefully?

Inadequate competition can occur on both the demand and supply sides of the market. If we consider the supply side of the market, there is no competition when a monopolist dominates. In an oligopolistic market, the temptation to **collude** is strong.

Did You Know?

▶ **Expensive Memories** The first law to fight monopolies, the Sherman Antitrust Act, was enacted in 1890 as a response to growing concern over the power of trusts. Enforcement was left to the courts, and judges considered the language of the act too vague to make big companies change the way they did business. As a result, the number of trusts increased following passage of the act. It took another 14 years before the first major lawsuit, *Northern Securities* v. *the United States,* was filed.

Laws have become stronger since then, but price collusion still is a problem. In May 2006 three computer memory chip manufacturers were accused of fixing prices over a three-year period. This increased the price of chips for computer manufacturers, and thus the price of computers for consumers. The chipmakers agreed to pay $160 million to settle the case.

180   UNIT 2   Microeconomics: Prices and Markets

If we look at the demand side of the market, there is little or no competition if the government is the only buyer for space shuttles, hydroelectric dams, super computers, M-1 tanks, or high-technology fighter jets.

A firm that does not face adequate competition could easily spend its profits on huge salaries and bonuses, executive jets, country club memberships, and generous retirement plans. This is one of the reasons that public utilities such as electricity are regulated by the government—to make sure that the firms do not use their monopoly status to waste or abuse resources.

Inadequate competition also may enable a business to influence politicians in order to get special treatment that enriches its managers and owners. In fact, some of the players in the huge Enron energy scandal were accused of doing just that—lobbying administration and Energy Department officials for favorable treatment on policy issues that benefited Enron executives.

Inadequate Information

If resources are to be allocated efficiently, everyone—consumers, businesspeople, and government officials—must have adequate information about market conditions. A secretary or an accountant may receive a competitive wage in the automobile industry, but wages for the same skills might be higher in the insurance or banking industry.

D Some information is easy to find in the classified ads in the newspaper or on the Internet. Other information is more difficult to find. If this knowledge is important to buyers and sellers but is difficult to obtain, then it is an example of a market failure.

The consequences of inadequate information may not always be immediately visible, but in the long run it will put a slow drain on the economy, lowering the rate of growth and the overall standard of living.

Resource Immobility

A difficult problem in any economy is that of resource immobility. This means that land, capital, labor, and entrepreneurs

---

Public Goods

Objective: Understand public goods and current issues pertaining to them.

Focus/Teach: Discuss how students personally benefit from the public goods described in the activity. Then have pairs complete the activity.

Assess: Check students' articles against their sources.

Close: Create an oral class "blog," where one student comments on an article and then others build on each previous statement.

Differentiated Instruction Strategies

BL Have students write down two ideas or facts that they learned from the activity.

AL Ask students to suggest solutions for the problem at the center of their assigned topic.

ELL Have students create a visual of public goods and their characteristics.

Public Goods
Funding floodwalls is expensive, but failing to keep up with maintenance can have catastrophic results, as the photo of New Orleans after Hurricane Katrina shows. *Why does the market not provide more public goods?*

D Differentiated Instruction

Special Education For students who have problems with reading, practice a focused reading exercise. Have students read the subsection on public goods. When they have finished, have them write in their notebooks what they remember of the subsection. Then have them reread the subsection to look for answers to the following questions: What is a public good? Why doesn't the market supply public goods? **BL**

S Skill Practice
Drawing Conclusions
Ask: Why do you think that politicians might want to avoid higher taxes? *(Possible answer: Higher taxes are unpopular and may hurt a politician's chances of reelection.)* **OL**

Caption Answer: because they are not profitable

do not move to markets where returns are the highest. Instead they tend to stay put and sometimes remain unemployed.

What happens, for example, when a large auto assembly plant, steel mill, or mine closes, leaving hundreds of workers without employment? Certainly some workers can find jobs in other industries, but not all can. Some of the newly unemployed may not be able to sell their homes. Others may not want to move away from friends and relatives to find new jobs in other cities.

Public Goods
Another form of market failure shows up in the form of public goods. **Public goods** are products that are collectively consumed by everyone. Their use by one individual does not diminish the satisfaction or value available to others. Examples of public goods are uncrowded highways, flood-control measures, national defense, and police and fire protection.

When left to itself, the market either does not supply these items at all, or it supplies them inadequately. This is because a market economy produces only those items that can be withheld if people refuse to pay for them. It would be difficult, for example, to deny one person the benefits of national defense while supplying it to others. Because it is so difficult to have all individuals pay for their fair share of a public good, private markets produce too few of them.

In the aftermath of Hurricane Katrina, it was evident that the floodwalls in New Orleans could not **sustain** the onslaught of the hurricane. Floodwalls are public goods that are normally funded out of government expenditures; they are not built by the private sector because there is little profit to be gained by building them. A related problem is that government does not always see the need to spend tax dollars on public goods. In the case of the floodwalls, it was all too easy to postpone the necessary expenditures because they would have resulted in higher taxes or in not building other public goods.

Externalities
Many activities generate some kind of **externality,** or unintended side effect that either benefits or harms a third party not involved in the activity that caused it.

public goods
goods or services whose benefits are available to everyone and are paid for collectively

externality
economic side effect that affects an uninvolved third party

CHAPTER 7 Market Structures **181**

Leveled Activities

BL Guided Reading Activities, p. 20   **OL** Economic Cartoons, p. 26   **AL** Economic Concepts Transparencies, Strategies, and Activities, p. 21

Externalities Air pollution is a negative externality that affects those who did not cause it. *How can government action lead to the cleanup of pollution?*

negative externality
harmful side effect that affects an uninvolved third party

positive externality
beneficial side effect that affects an uninvolved third party

A **negative externality** is the harm, cost, or inconvenience suffered by a third party because of actions by others. The classic case of a negative externality is the noise and inconvenience some people suffer when an airport expands.

A **positive externality** is a benefit someone receives who was not involved in the activity that generated the benefit. For example, people living on the other side of town may benefit from the additional jobs generated by the airport expansion, or a nearby restaurant may sell more meals and hire more workers. Both the restaurant owners and the new workers gain from the airport expansion even though they had nothing to do with the expansion in the first place.

Externalities are market failures because their costs and benefits are not reflected in the market prices that buyers and sellers pay. For example, airlines do not compensate homeowners for the diminished value of properties located near a new runway extension. Nor does a restaurant owner share any additional profits with the airport. As a result, the prices that travelers pay for air travel will not reflect the external costs and benefits that an airport expansion generates.

✓ Reading Check Analyzing What type of market failure do you think is most harmful to the economy?

Dealing with Externalities

MAIN Idea Externalities indicate a market failure and can be corrected with government action.

Economics & You Have you ever been affected by someone else's pollution? Read on to learn how this can be remedied.

The problem with externalities is that they distort the decisions made by consumers and producers. Overall this makes the economy less efficient.

Correcting Negative Externalities

A classic example of pollution sheds some light on the distortions caused by negative externalities. Firms historically located near rivers because transportation was convenient. However, the firms also used the rivers as a giant waste disposal system, which helped keep their production cost low. This led to lower market prices for the final product, and consumers were able to buy more.

The negative externality of pollution generated several problems. Firms had the incentive to pollute because it was the most profitable way to produce. The low prices also encouraged more sales, and hence

182 UNIT 2 **Microeconomics: Prices and Markets**

Analyzing American Market Structures

Step 2: Doing Business in Different Market Structures. Students will survey local businesses to find out how they operate under different market structures.

Directions: Have students reassemble into the groups that were formed in Step 1. Have each group choose one of the four market structures on which they made posters. Make sure that all market structures are chosen by at least one group. Have groups identify local businesses

that exhibit characteristics of their chosen market structure. Have groups prepare a list of questions and then survey managers by phone or e-mail regarding product differentiation, ease of entry into the market, number of competitors, ability of firms to influence price, successful advertising strategies, and so on.

Comparing Have groups summarize their results and present them to the class. After all the presentations, have the class compare one another's businesses. **OL**

(Chapter Project continued in Section 3.)

more pollution. Finally, people living downstream from the polluting firms were, in effect, paying for some of the production costs even if they did not necessarily buy the products.

Suppose the government decided to force the firms to clean up their pollution by putting a $1 "pollution tax" on every unit of output sold. The firms, of course, would try to pass some of this expense on to the consumer in the form of higher prices. While higher prices might at first seem to be a problem, they would force the people who bought the products to pay for the increase in production costs.

The tax would help alleviate pollution problems. First, all firms would have less incentive to pollute because the tax drives up the price of their products. Second, higher prices would reduce the quantity demanded, so firms would produce less and therefore generate less pollution. Third, the people living downstream of the affected rivers would face less pollution.

Correcting Positive Externalities

Externalities can be positive as well as negative. You have learned that negative externalities lead to distortions. Yet even when externalities are positive, so that uninvolved third parties experience beneficial side effects, distortions can occur.

A classic example is education. We know that people generally earn more when they have more education. In addition, a community with a well-educated workforce will attract more industry, have more economic development, and enjoy a higher standard of living. For these and other reasons, it makes sense for the government to subsidize the cost of public education.

This is exactly what happens when local governments pay for the cost of primary and secondary public education. When it comes to the higher education offered by state universities, however, state governments only pay for part of the cost, leaving students to pick up the rest in the form of tuition payments.

Given education's value to the community, many experts feel that the government subsidies should be larger than they are. This is expensive, however, so government tends to underfund higher education even though more subsidies are warranted.

✓**Reading Check** **Explaining** If externalities are positive, why should they be corrected?

W **Writing Support**
Narrative Writing Have students write a short story about two teenagers living in a community where education is available only to those who can pay for it. One teenager's family should be able to pay and the other's should not. Students can choose to have the characters defeated by the situation or triumphant over it. **OL**

✓**Reading Check** **Answer:** As long as there are externalities, the market is not providing the amount of the good that consumers would want if all benefits and costs were reflected in the price.

Assess

💿 Use the Interactive Tutor Self-Assessment CD-ROM to review Section 2, and then assign the Section 2 Review as homework or as an in-class activity.

Close

Summarizing Have students list the types of market failures and an example of each. **OL**

Review **SECTION 2**

SECTION 2 Review

Vocabulary
1. **Explain** the significance of market failure, public goods, externality, negative externality, and positive externality.

Main Ideas
2. **Explaining** Why do markets need both adequate competition and adequate information?

3. **Identifying** Use a graphic organizer like the one below to identify and describe both types of externalities.

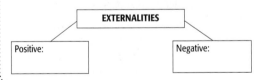

EXTERNALITIES

Positive: | Negative:

Critical Thinking
4. **The BIG Idea** List and explain the reasons why markets fail.

5. **Understanding Cause and Effect** Describe some of the positive and negative externalities that could result from the closing of a military base.

6. **Making Inferences** Under what circumstances would a private firm be willing to build private toll roads?

Applying Economics
7. **Negative Externality** Identify a situation in your community that resulted in a negative externality. How would you advise the government to reduce these negative effects? Write a short paper outlining your suggestions.

CHAPTER 7 Market Structures 183

Answers

1. All definitions can be found in the section and the Glossary.
2. Without adequate competition, producers have no incentive to use resources efficiently or to innovate. Without adequate information, consumers and workers cannot make informed decisions about what is best to buy or where it is best to work.
3. **Positive:** have benefits that uninvolved third parties receive, such as education. **Negative:** have costs that are not born by the seller or buyer, such as pollution.

4. Inadequate competition removes incentives for firms to be efficient or innovative; consumers or workers lack information necessary to make buying and working decisions; resources are immobile and cannot or will not move to their best uses; public goods are not provided by the market; externalities distort consumer decisions.
5. Answers will vary, but positive externalities might be a reduction in crowding and noise and negative externalities might be losses

to local businesses from the decrease in population.
6. Since a toll road is a good that can be withheld from people who don't pay for it, a private firm would be willing to build it if there were enough potential users to make the business profitable.
7. Answers will vary but should indicate an understanding of negative externalities and what might be done to deal with them.

BusinessWeek NEWSCLIP

In 1984 concerns over a telecommunications monopoly led to the breakup of AT&T into eight different companies. Just a little over 20 years later, AT&T mergers seem to recreate the former corporation. When such mergers result in larger and fewer firms dominating an industry, some economists worry.

Lord of the Rings

Competition in communications seems cutthroat. Companies are invading each other's turf, and prices are falling. You can make a video-phone call to Australia via the Internet, chat for three hours, and never pay a penny. Citing all this hubbub, AT&T Inc. argues that there's no threat of re-monopolization even as it bids to reunite five of the eight companies that emerged from the 1984 breakup of the Bell System.

Look out, though. The competition we're seeing is just a phase, and an unstable one at that. The key thing about communications networks is that they're very costly to build, but once they're built, it's cheap to add customers to them. This industry structure has special economic properties. At times it produces price wars. At other times it leads to merger waves, resulting in a small number of competitors with the ability to raise prices and garner big profits. . . .

In this delicate situation, [communications companies] have used two main strategies over the years. One has been to cut prices to fill up their networks. Remember, additional customers are cheap to serve, so there's room to cut. . . .

The alternative strategy, which [the CEO of AT&T] and others have also pursued, is consolidation. As long as regulators permit, the strong buy the weak and extinguish the excess capacity. As competition eases, the survivors can raise prices and restore their profitability. (Good for shareholders; bad for customers.)

—Reprinted from *BusinessWeek*

Fragile Competition

Communications companies may be shifting strategies from battling to consolidating.	
Strategy 1	**Strategy 2**
Price War Companies need lots of traffic to cover the costs of their expensive networks, so they cut prices. That forces other companies to reciprocate. Eventually profits vanish.	**Merger Wave** Companies merge, with the strong buying the weak. As competition diminishes, profits rise. This strategy is more desirable to the companies, but may be banned by regulators.

Examining the Newsclip

1. **Summarizing** What two strategies has AT&T used in recent years to gain new business, and why?
2. **Determining Cause and Effect** How does lack of competition increase prices for the consumer?

184 UNIT 2 Microeconomics: Prices and Markets

Extending the Content

The Merger of AT&T and Cingular
Mergers in the communications industry require more than approvals and contracts. Because companies develop their technologies separately, blending them together is also a technological process. AT&T's purchase of Cingular was approved by the federal government in 2004, but it was not until 2007 that the two brands were publicly combined. Both billing systems and support platforms

for services such as voice mail had to be integrated. Thousands of cell sites had to be integrated, and new sites had to be built. The integration cost hundreds of millions of dollars in 2006 alone. However, as fewer calls were dropped and connections improved, usage by consumers rose significantly.

SECTION

3 The Role of Government

GUIDE TO READING

Section Preview
In this section, you will learn that one of the economic functions of government in a market economy is to maintain competition.

Content Vocabulary
- trust *(p. 186)*
- price discrimination *(p. 186)*
- cease and desist order *(p. 186)*
- public disclosure *(p. 188)*

Academic Vocabulary
- restrained *(p. 186)*
- intervention *(p. 189)*

Reading Strategy
Describing As you read the section, complete a graphic organizer like the one below by describing how governments try to avoid market failures.

Government in Economic Affairs

PRODUCTS IN THE NEWS
—www.cpsc.gov

Electric Bass Recalled

The U.S. Consumer Product Safety Commission, in cooperation with Hoshino USA Inc., of Bensalem, Pa., and Chesbro Music Company, of Idaho Falls, Idaho, today announced a voluntary recall of about 700 Ibanez basses. If the battery is improperly installed, the bass can overheat, causing internal damage and a fire hazard. The firm has received three reports of the bass not working due to improper battery installation. There have been no reports of injuries or property damage.

This recall involves 2005 and 2006 Ibanez Soundgear, Roadgear and Gary Willis series basses. Model numbers are located on the back of the headstock. Consumers should stop using the basses immediately and contact their local Ibanez dealer for a free inspection and repair. Dealers will remedy the hazard by having affected basses updated with a new battery snap connector. ■

We know that resources are scarce, and because of scarce resources we have to make careful choices if we are to satisfy our many wants and needs. We also know that competitive markets are one of the best ways to make this happen. At the same time, markets can fail. When they do, the government can step in and fix the problem.

One way in which the federal government acts is by protecting the public from unreasonable risks of serious injury or death. For that task, it created the U.S. Consumer Product Safety Commission (CPSC), which oversees the safety of more than 15,000 types of consumer products. When necessary, the CPSC orders a recall of products for repair or replacement, as in the news story.

CHAPTER 7   Market Structures   185

Focus

Bellringer
Daily Focus Transparency 22

FOCUS ACTIVITIES
Transparency 22

GOVERNMENT REGULATION OF THE MARKET

GUIDE TO READING

Answers to Graphic:
maintaining competition; regulating monopolies; promoting transparency; providing public goods

Resource Manager

R Reading Strategies	C Critical Thinking	D Differentiated Instruction	W Writing Support	S Skill Practice
Teacher Edition • Act. Prior Know., p. 186 • Taking Notes, p. 187	**Teacher Edition** • Analyzing Visuals, p. 186	**Teacher Edition** • Interpersonal, p. 189 • Visual/Spatial, p. 190	**Teacher Edition** • Expository Writing, p. 188	**Teacher Edition** • Drawing Con., p. 187 • Interpreting Political Cartoons, p. 188 • Using Tables and Charts, p. 190
Additional Resources • Guid. Read. Act., p. 21 • Read. Ess. & Note-Taking Guide, p. 61	**Additional Resources** • Econ. Cartoons, pp. 2, 4 • Econ. Concepts Trans., Strat. and Act., p. 23	**Additional Resources** • Pri./Sec. Source Read., pp. 37, 39 • Free Ent. Act., p. 2	**Additional Resources** • High School Reading in the Content Area Strat. and Act.	**Additional Resources** • Reteaching Act., p. 7

Teach

R Reading Strategy

Activating Prior Knowledge
Tell students: The late nineteenth century was a time when giant corporations dominated much of the American economy. **Ask:** Aside from Standard Oil, what were two other industrial giants in the late 1800s? *(Possible answers: Carnegie Steel; American Tobacco Company; Union Pacific)* **AL**

C Critical Thinking

Analyzing Visuals Have students create a web diagram to express the information in the visual. The inner circle should say "Anti-Monopoly Legislation." Bubbles from the inner circle should list the four acts, and then each of those bubbles should have a connecting bubble explaining the act. **BL**

Economic Analysis

Answer: to regulate unfair methods of competition in interstate commerce

---

Differentiated Instruction

Economic Cartoons, p. 2

---

trust illegal combination of corporations or companies organized to hinder competition

price discrimination practice of selling the same product at different prices to different buyers

cease and desist order ruling requiring a company to stop an unfair business practice that reduces or limits competition

Maintain Competition

MAIN Idea The government exercises its power to maintain competition within markets.

Economics & You When you play sports, a referee regulates the game to make sure both sides are playing fairly. Read on to learn how the government can regulate the economy to do the same thing.

There are two ways that government can maintain competitive markets. One is by prohibiting market structures that are not competitive. The other is by regulating markets where full competition is not possible.

Antitrust Legislation

In the late 1800s, the United States passed laws to restrict monopolies and **trusts**—combinations of firms designed to restrict competition or control prices in a particular

Figure 7.3 ▶ Anti-Monopoly Legislation

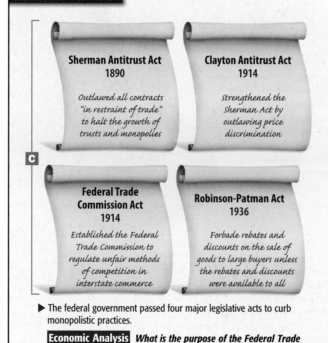

Sherman Antitrust Act 1890
Outlawed all contracts "in restraint of trade" to halt the growth of trusts and monopolies

Clayton Antitrust Act 1914
strengthened the Sherman Act by outlawing price discrimination

Federal Trade Commission Act 1914
Established the Federal Trade Commission to regulate unfair methods of competition in interstate commerce

Robinson-Patman Act 1936
Forbade rebates and discounts on the sale of goods to large buyers unless the rebates and discounts were available to all

▶ The federal government passed four major legislative acts to curb monopolistic practices.

Economic Analysis *What is the purpose of the Federal Trade Commission?*

---

industry. Since then, several laws have been passed that allow the government to either prevent or break up monopolies and trusts, thus preventing market failures due to inadequate competition.

In 1890 Congress passed the Sherman Antitrust Act "to protect trade and commerce against unlawful restraint and monopoly." The Sherman Act, described in **Figure 7.3**, was the nation's first significant law against monopolies. It sought to do away with monopolies and restraints that hindered competition. By the early 1900s, a number of businesses, including the Standard Oil Company, had been convicted of restraint of trade under the Sherman Act.

The Sherman Act laid down broad foundations for maintaining competition. However, the act was not specific enough to stop many other practices that **restrained** competition. As a result, Congress passed the Clayton Antitrust Act in 1914 to give the government more power over monopolies. This outlawed **price discrimination**—the practice of selling the same product to different consumers at different prices if it substantially lessens competition.

The Federal Trade Commission Act was passed in the same year to enforce the Clayton Antitrust Act. The act set up the Federal Trade Commission (FTC) and gave it the authority to issue cease and desist orders. A **cease and desist order** is an FTC ruling requiring a company to stop an unfair business practice, such as price-fixing, that reduces or limits competition among firms.

In 1936 Congress passed the Robinson-Patman Act in an effort to strengthen the Clayton Act, particularly the provisions that dealt with price discrimination. Under this act, companies could no longer offer special discounts to some customers while denying them to others.

Government Regulation

Not all monopolies are bad, and for that reason not all should be broken up. In the case of a natural monopoly, it makes sense to let the firm expand to take advantage of

---

Who Gets the Credit? Who Takes the Blame?

Objective: Understand how the government may seek to deflect blame for economic problems.

Focus/Teach: Discuss with students ways that the current presidential administration responds to criticism about the economy. Then have students study the cartoon and answer the questions.

Assess: Review the answers as a class.

Close: Have students evaluate how well the cartoon portrayed its message.

Differentiated Instruction Strategies

BL Have students research to identify the presidents shown in the cartoon.

AL Ask students to write a brief essay explaining how a mixed economy might create conflict between government and business.

ELL Have students draw a cartoon that conveys a similar message.

lower production costs, and then regulate its activities so that it cannot take advantage of the consumer.

Local and state governments regulate many monopolies, such as cable television companies, and water and electric utilities. For example, if a public utility wants to raise rates, it must argue its case before a public utility commission or other government agency.

Agencies of the federal government, such as those listed in **Figure 7.4**, regulate many different kinds of businesses. However, as you can see from the dates in the figure, in recent years the government has been less inclined to set up new regulatory bodies. Instead, the emphasis has shifted to promoting efficiency.

Skills Handbook
See page **R37** to learn about **Making Generalizations.**

[S]

✓Reading Check **Describing** Why are some government regulations beneficial for consumers?

Figure 7.4 ▶ Federal Regulatory Agencies

Agency	Tasks
Food and Drug Administration (FDA), 1906	Enforces laws to ensure purity, effectiveness, and truthful labeling of food, drugs, and cosmetics; inspects production and shipment of these products
Federal Trade Commission (FTC), 1914	Administers antitrust laws forbidding unfair competition, price fixing, and other deceptive practices
Federal Communications Commission (FCC), 1934	Licenses and regulates radio and television stations and regulates interstate telephone and telegraph rates and services
Securities and Exchange Commission (SEC), 1934	Regulates and supervises the sale of listed and unlisted securities and the brokers, dealers, and bankers who sell them
National Labor Relations Board (NLRB), 1935	Administers federal labor-management relations laws; settles labor disputes; prevents unfair labor practices
Federal Aviation Administration (FAA), 1958	Oversees the airline industry
Equal Employment Opportunity Commission (EEOC), 1964	Investigates and rules on charges of discrimination by employers and labor unions
Environmental Protection Agency (EPA), 1970	Protects and enhances the environment
Occupational Safety and Health Administration (OSHA), 1970	Investigates accidents in the workplace; enforces regulations to protect employees at work
Consumer Product Safety Commission (CPSC), 1972	Develops standards of safety for consumer goods
Nuclear Regulatory Commission (NRC), 1974	Regulates civilian use of nuclear materials and facilities
Federal Energy Regulatory Commission (FERC), 1977	Supervises transmission of various forms of energy

[R]

▶ The government has created a number of federal regulatory agencies to oversee the economy. Because of government's involvement in the economy, we have a modified free enterprise system.

Economic Analysis *Which agencies listed in the table are familiar to you? Which affect you directly? Why?*

[S] Skill Practice
Drawing Conclusions
Ask: Why do you think that the government has recently set up fewer agencies and spent more time promoting efficiency? *(Possible answer: The majority of taxpayers probably support making the current agencies more efficient before they support the creation of new agencies.)* **OL**

[R] Reading Strategy
Taking Notes Have students write the name of each federal agency on a separate note card. Next, ask students to take notes about the functions of the agencies on the back of the note cards. Have students find a partner and use their note cards to quiz each other about the functioning of the agencies. **BL**

✓Reading Check **Answer:** They result in lower prices, better quality, and improved safety for the consumer.

Economic Analysis
Answer: Students will likely be most affected by the FDA, FCC, and CPSC.

Leveled Activities

BL Reteaching Activities, p. 7

OL Economic Concepts Transparencies, Strategies, and Activities, p. 23

AL Primary and Secondary Source Readings, p. 37

public disclosure requirement that a business reveal information about its products or its operations to the public

$ Personal Finance Handbook
See page **R14–R15** for more information on loans.

Improve Economic Efficiency

MAIN Idea Providing public goods and promoting transparency can improve economic efficiency.

Economics & You Can you name some public goods in your community? Read on to learn why public goods must be provided by the public sector.

Fortunately, the government has the ability to correct two market failures that interfere with competitive markets: inadequate information and public goods.

Promote Transparency

Efficient and competitive markets need adequate information. *Transparency* is a term used to indicate that information and actions are not hidden and instead are easily available for review.

Public disclosure, the requirement that businesses reveal certain information to the public, is an important way to do this. For example, all corporations that sell stock

to the public must disclose financial and operating information on a regular basis to both their shareholders and the Securities and Exchange Commission (SEC). This data is stored in a free database that can be accessed by anyone on the Internet.

Disclosure requirements also exist for consumer lending. If you obtain a credit card or borrow money to buy a car, the lender will explain in writing the method for computing the monthly interest, the length of the loan, the size of the payments, and other lending terms. This is not an act of kindness on the lender's part because federal law requires these disclosures. Finally, "truth-in-advertising" laws prevent sellers from making false claims about their products.

Most government documents, studies, and reports are available on the Internet. This includes the annual budget of the U.S. government, the *Statistical Abstract of the United States,* Census Bureau reports, and nearly every other publication that you can find in the government documents section of your local public library.

Provide Public Goods

A free enterprise economy does not produce public goods in sufficient quantity because such efforts usually do not result in direct financial gain. This means that many of the things society values—good roads and highways, museums and libraries, and education—must be provided by government.

Public goods are important because they make the economy more productive. For example, businesses need reliable transportation so that they can move their raw materials and final products. In addition, their employees need to be able to easily commute to and from work. Firms also need an educated workforce that is both productive and able to purchase the products that are produced.

✓**Reading Check** **Interpreting** What negative things could happen in a market without disclosure?

Transparency Governments require disclosure to prevent companies from providing misleading information. ***What requirements protect you as a borrower?***

"This isn't rocket science, folks. One, we substitute code words for substantive ideology. Two, we create misleading advertising. Three, we issue bold pronouncements on phony profit margins. It's all right here in the corporate training manual."

188 UNIT 2 **Microeconomics: Prices and Markets**

Modified Free Enterprise

MAIN Idea Because the government is involved in certain aspects of our economy, it is a modified version of free enterprise.

Economics & You What role does government play in your life? Read on to learn why some government regulation is desirable.

The U.S. economy has changed dramatically over the years. One of the outcomes of this evolution is the rise of the modified free enterprise economy.

In the late 1800s, the freedom to pursue self-interests led some people to seek economic gain at the expense of others. Under the label of competition, many larger firms used their power to take advantage of smaller ones. In some markets, less competitive market structures such as monopoly replaced competition, and the economy became less efficient.

Because of these developments, Congress passed laws to prevent "evil monopolies" and to protect the rights of workers. It also passed food and drug laws to protect people from false claims and harmful products. Even public utilities faced significant government regulation to prevent the price gouging of

consumers. Collectively, these actions have resulted in a modification of free enterprise.

More recently, concern has shifted to economic efficiency and the role of the government in promoting it. Markets have become increasingly important, and we recognize that markets can fail in several different ways. When this happens, the government can take steps to remedy the situation.

In addition to occasional interventions to keep markets reasonably competitive, the government can make the economy more efficient by supplying public goods and promoting transparency. People will continue to debate the proper role of government, but it turns out that markets alone cannot provide all of our wants and needs.

Over the years, government's role in the economy has slowly evolved from concern over consumer protection to the promotion of economic competition and efficiency. As a result of this government **intervention,** we now have a modified private enterprise economy, or an economy based on markets with varying degrees of government regulation.

✓**Reading Check** **Summarizing** Why do we use the term *modified* to describe the American free enterprise economy?

Economics ONLINE
Student Web Activity Visit the *Economics: Principles and Practices* Web site at glencoe.com and click on *Chapter 7–Student Web Activities* for an activity on the government's role in promoting fair business practices.

Skills Handbook
See page **R45** to learn about **Synthesizing Information.**

D

SECTION 3 Review

Vocabulary
1. **Explain** the significance of trust, price discrimination, cease and desist order, and public disclosure.

Main Ideas
2. **Identifying** Use a graphic organizer similar to the one below to identify how the federal government can maintain competition and improve economic efficiency.

Action	Purpose
Antitrust legislation	

3. **Explaining** Why is the United States considered to have a modified free enterprise economy?

Critical Thinking
4. **The BIG Idea** Why is the government involved in economic affairs?

5. **Making Inferences** Why do governments regulate monopolistic cable companies and not prohibit them?

6. **Synthesizing Information** Identify at least two instances where you have personally benefited from government regulations. Explain the benefits.

Applying Economics
7. **Public Disclosure** Obtain literature describing the computation of interest and conditions for withdrawal on various savings accounts from a local bank. Summarize the information in a short paragraph. Why do you think the bank is so forthcoming with this information?

D Differentiated Instruction

Interpersonal Select teams of students to debate the following proposition: *The government is too involved in regulating our economy.* Have teams develop their stances using information in Section 3 and research that they do in the library or on the Internet. **AL**

✓**Reading Check** **Answer:** We have made changes, or modifications, to the free enterprise system.

Assess

Use the Interactive Tutor Self-Assessment CD-ROM to review Section 3, and then assign the Section 3 Review as homework or as an in-class activity.

Close

Summarizing Have students write a paragraph summarizing the U.S. government's policies, both historical and current, toward economic competition. **OL**

Review **SECTION 3**

Answers

1. All definitions can be found in the section and the Glossary.
2. **Antitrust legislation:** maintain competition. **Regulatory agencies:** promote consumer welfare, correct externalities. **Public disclosure laws:** promote transparency. **Provide public goods:** correct market failure.
3. because the government has an active, though limited, role in the U.S. economy
4. The government is involved in economic affairs to correct market failures such as lack of competition, lack of information, externalities, or lack of public goods.
5. **Possible answer:** Cable companies are natural monopolies and can deliver lower costs to consumers if regulated.
6. Answers will vary but should demonstrate knowledge of some of the ways that the government regulates business.
7. Answers will vary but should reference government regulations that require banks to fully disclose their financial terms.

Focus

D Differentiated Instruction

Visual/Spatial Ask students to describe traditional Disney movies as a class. Students should address the style of animation and type of story line. Then ask students who have seen *Toy Story* to describe how the movie was a departure from typical Disney animation. **OL**

Teach

S Skill Practice

Using Tables and Charts

Ask: Which Pixar movie earned the most money? (Finding Nemo) Which movie's receipts were not all counted when the chart was written? (Cars) **BL**

Analyzing the Impact

Answers:

1. Disney hoped to solidify its relationship with Pixar and raise its stock price.
2. It could reduce competition in the movie industry.

Additional Support

CASE STUDY

Pixar and Disney D

Birth of Pixar

The short, happy tale of Pixar began when John Lasseter left Walt Disney studios in 1984 to join Lucasfilm, Ltd. Two years later, Steve Jobs, CEO of Apple Computer Inc., bought the computer graphics division of Lucasfilm for $10 million and renamed it Pixar.

After winning numerous awards for short films and commercials, Pixar, with just 44 employees, teamed up with mega-studio Disney in 1991 to co-produce major films.

Box Office Magic, Stock Ticker Woes

Toy Story, the first collaboration by Disney and Pixar, was a box office home run, earning $358 million in box office receipts around the world as the highest-grossing film of 1995.

The dynamic duo produced six more commercial hits, but Disney's other work did not please moviegoers. Nor did its stock price satisfy stockholders.

BOX OFFICE RECEIPTS	
Toy Story	$358.1 million
A Bug's Life	$357.9 million
Toy Story 2	$485.7 million
Monster's Inc.	$528.9 million
Finding Nemo	$865.0 million
The Incredibles	$624.0 million
Cars	$367.6 million (and counting)

DISNEY STOCK PRICES, 1995–2006

Disney's management hoped to boost its stock price and remedy the sometimes tumultuous relationship between Disney and Pixar by entering into merger negotiations.

Animation Merger

By that time, Pixar had grown to a company of hundreds of employees, and federal regulatory authorities reviewed the merger for possible antitrust problems. The two companies finally merged in 2006 when Disney paid $7.5 billion for Pixar.

As hoped, the price of Disney stock started to increase. A few months later, *Cars* zoomed into theaters, bringing in more than $60 million its first weekend. If you think stock prices follow ticket sales, though, think again. Despite that impressive showing, Disney's stock fell slightly when the movie missed its $70 million goal.

Analyzing the Impact

1. **Summarizing** How did Disney expect to gain from the merger with Pixar?
2. **Drawing Conclusions** Why might federal regulators be concerned about the merger of these two movie companies?

Extending the Content

Pixar: Making Art a Team Sport

Unlike paintings or novels, which are usually produced by single artists, a movie requires an entire team to produce it. As a company, Pixar works to make all employees contributors. It hires outsiders, even if they might not fit in. It runs Pixar University, which offers employees four- to sixteen-week classes on subjects such as sculpture and improvisational comedy. Each Pixar film reveals an advance in photorealism, but all movies are built around the story, not technology. The company has imitated Disney's work process for animated films, but it refuses to rest on its laurels. When *Toy Story 2* was proclaimed "terrible" just eight months before it was due at the distributor, the company strained itself to overhaul the movie. Pixar's corporate culture demands that they produce only high-quality movies. So far, the company has won 17 Oscars and picked up 42 patents.

Visual Summary

▶ **Market Structures** We can differentiate among four different market structures. One is called perfect competition; the other three are different kinds of imperfect competition.

PERFECT COMPETITION	IMPERFECT COMPETITION		
Perfect Competition	Monopolistic Competition	Oligopoly	Monopoly
Large number of well-informed independent buyers and sellers who freely exchange identical products	Has all characteristics of perfect competition except product differentiation	A few very large sellers dominate the industry	Only one seller for a particular product

▶ **Market Failures** When one of the conditions necessary for competitive markets does not exist, market failures can occur. Markets usually fail because of five factors.

Inadequate information

Inadequate competition

Resource immobility

Market Failures

Need for public goods

Externalities

▶ **Government Roles** In order to carry out its legal and social obligations, the government can encourage competition and regulate monopolies.

Government Roles

Restrict monopolies that hinder competition

Regulate monopolies that provide services

Provide public disclosure to prevent market failures

Simulating Divide the class into four groups (or eight groups if the class is large). Assign each (or two) of the groups one of the four basic market structures. Tell groups that their task is to write a 45-second to 1-minute radio advertisement that explains the benefits of their assigned market structure. Suggest that groups listen to examples of radio ads before undertaking the task. Call on groups to "broadcast" their advertisements to the class. **OL**

Surveying Have students conduct an informal survey of family members, friends, students, and teachers on government's role in the economy. Suggest that they ask such questions as the following: Is there too much or not enough government regulation? Which regulatory agencies, if any, should be curtailed, expanded, or abolished? Have students share their survey results with the class. **BL**

Hands-On Chapter Project

Step 4: Wrap Up

Analyzing American Market Structures

Step 4: Complete the Analysis. Student teams will summarize what they learned in Steps 1–3.

Directions: Have the students on each team write papers summarizing what they learned about the market system they represented in Steps 2 and 3. Students will work alone on this activity—each student will write a summary paper. Students should describe the strengths and weaknesses of their market system, including an assessment of what the system's proper role in the American economy should be. Encourage students to use the example of the business they explored in Step 2 to support their positions. Have students representing each of the three different market systems read their summary papers to the class. Finally, discuss as a class the strengths, weaknesses, and possible proper role of the fourth market system—perfect competition. **OL**

Assessment & Activities

ExamView®
Assessment Suite

This easy-to-use software includes extensive question banks and allows you to create fully customized tests that can be administered in print or online.

Review Content Vocabulary

1.–10. Students' paragraphs will vary but should demonstrate understanding of each term's meaning in an economic context.

Review Academic Vocabulary

11.–16. Students' sentences will vary but should demonstrate understanding of each term's meaning in an economic context.

Review the Main Ideas

17. because its conditions are virtually never met in real life

18. Natural monopoly: can provide goods or services more cheaply than competing firms.
Geographic monopoly: no competitors within a certain geographic area.
Technological monopoly: the government grants a patent to new inventions.
Government monopoly: single sellers owned and run by the government.

19. inefficient use of resources, misuse of profits, and higher prices

20. benefits or costs that go to third parties who are not participants in a transaction

21. because they cannot be withheld from those who do not pay for them and therefore are not profitable

---

Review Content Vocabulary

Use all of the terms below to write a paragraph about each of the four types of markets. Underline the terms within your paragraphs.

1. market failure
2. geographic monopoly
3. imperfect competition
4. monopolistic competition
5. natural monopoly
6. oligopoly
7. product differentiation
8. trust
9. price-fixing
10. nonprice competition

Review Academic Vocabulary

Use each of these terms in a sentence that reflects the term's meaning in the chapter.

11. theoretically
12. equate
13. collude
14. sustain
15. restrained
16. intervention

Review the Main Ideas

Section 1 (pages 169–177)

17. Explain why perfect competition is a theoretical situation.

18. Describe the four types of monopolies by using a graphic organizer similar to the one below.

Type of Monopoly	Description

Section 2 (pages 179–183)

19. Explain what happens when markets do not have enough competition.

20. Describe what is meant by *externalities*.

21. Explain why the private sector is reluctant to produce public goods.

Section 3 (pages 185–189)

22. Identify the purpose of antitrust legislation.

23. Explain how public disclosure is used as a tool to prevent market failures.

24. Describe the characteristics that make the U.S. economy a "modified free enterprise" economy.

Critical Thinking

25. The BIG Idea Why does the federal government attempt to preserve competition among business enterprises? What different methods does the government have available for this task?

26. Making Inferences Do you think there would be any advantages to making monopolies or near monopolies break up into smaller, competing firms? Explain your answer.

27. Comparing and Contrasting Why are monopolies faced with more government regulations than other market structures?

28. Making Generalizations To what extent do you think government should be involved in the free enterprise economy? Defend your answer.

Analyzing Visuals

29. Look at Figure 7.2 on page 175. Analyze the columns labeled "Influence over price" and "Entry into market." How do the various types of market structures influence the results, and why? Present your answer and reasons in a short paragraph.

---

22. to maintain competition
23. Public disclosure increases the flow of information and therefore increases consumer and market welfare.
24. It relies on free enterprise, markets, prices, and the profit motive, with some government intervention.

Critical Thinking

25. because competition is the police force in a capitalist economy; antitrust legislation laws

26. Students should realize that the advantages depend on the type of monopoly.
27. Unlike other market structures, monopolies are not policed by competition.
28. Answers will vary but should discuss government involvement in the economy.

Analyzing Visuals

29. Answers should note that ease of entry will result in more firms and more competition. This reduces influence on price.

Economics ONLINE Self-Check Quiz Visit the
Economics: Principles and Practices Web site at glencoe.com and click
on Chapter 7–Self-Check Quizzes to prepare for the chapter test.

Assessment
and Activities CHAPTER

7

Math Practice

30. The table below shows the price, market demand, market supply, and the surplus and shortage for a firm providing a product under perfect competition. Study the information in the table, and then answer the questions below.

Price	Market demand	Market supply	Surplus/ Shortage
10	600	1550	950
9	----	1500	780
8	850	1450	----
7	990	1400	----
6	----	1350	210
5	1300	----	0
4	1470	----	−220
3	1650	1200	----
2	1840	1150	−690

a. Some of the information is missing from the table. Calculate the correct information.

b. What is the equilibrium price? How can you tell?

c. What price(s) will produce a surplus?

d. What price(s) will produce a shortage?

Applying Economic Concepts

31. **Product Differentiation** Choose a product offered by several producers that is advertised in newspapers or magazines. Then follow the steps below:

a. Clip and save at least three different advertisements.

b. In a journal, evaluate each advertisement and write why you would or would not buy a particular brand.

c. Based on the evaluations, develop an advertisement for a product of your choice.

d. Present your ad to the class and have other students evaluate how effectively you were able to differentiate your product from that of "competitors."

Thinking Like an Economist

32. **Profit Maximization** Economists like to analyze decisions incrementally, taking small steps and analyzing the costs and benefits of the steps as they are made. How is this way of thinking similar to the profit maximization logic illustrated in Figure 7.1 on page 171?

Writing About Economics

33. **Expository Writing** Select any five of the regulatory agencies described in Figure 7.4 on page 187 that relate directly to you. Write a short essay that discusses these agencies and evaluates whether they have a positive or negative effect on your life.

Interpreting Cartoons

34. **Critical Thinking** Look at the cartoon below. What does the cartoon imply about monopolies? What can the government do to prevent such business practices?

www.CartoonStock.com

' "Freddie, the Little Merger Mogul, didn't expect to have a monopoly right away. He planned to start small by rigging markets, restraining trade, and suppressing competition—then..." '

CHAPTER 7 Market Structures 193

Applying Economic Concepts

31. Answers will vary but should indicate that students understand the concept of product differentiation and how it might affect marketing strategy.

Thinking Like an Economist

32. The profit maximization logic compares the costs and returns from each increment of output. This is thinking at the margin, which is what economists do.

Writing About Economics

33. Answers will vary but should demonstrate an understanding of how government regulation impacts the lives of consumers.

Interpreting Cartoons

34. Answers will vary but should demonstrate an understanding of what can happen in the absence of competition.

Math Practice

30. a.

Quantity Demanded	Quantity Supplied
price = 9	demand = 720
price = 8	surplus = 600
price = 7	surplus = 410
price = 6	demand = 1140
price = 5	supply = 1300
price = 4	supply = 1250
price = 3	shortage = −450

b. The equilibrium price is 5, as that is where quantity demanded equals quantity supplied. There is no surplus or shortage.

c. Prices from 6 through 9 will produce a surplus. Prices below 4 will produce a shortage.

d. Answers will vary, but students should illustrate their decisions in a decision-making grid.

Planning Guide

Economic Institutions and Issues

UNIT PACING CHART				
	Chapter 8	**Chapter 9**	**Chapter 10**	**Chapter 11**
Day 1	Unit Opener Chapter Opener Section 1	Chapter Opener Section 1	Chapter Opener Section 1	Chapter Opener Section 1
Day 2	Profiles in Economics Section 2 Case Study	Profiles in Economics Section 2 Case Study	BusinessWeek Newsclip Section 2 Case Study	Profiles in Economics Section 2 Case Study
Day 3	Section 3 BusinessWeek Newsclip	Section 3 BusinessWeek Newsclip	Section 3 Profiles in Economics	Section 3 BusinessWeek Newsclip
Day 4	Review Chapter Assessment	Review Chapter Assessment	Review Chapter Assessment	Review Chapter Assessment
Day 5	The Global Economy & You	Debates in Economics		

Teacher to Teacher

Lisa Ellison
Kokomo High
School
Kokomo, Indiana

A Peek Into the Future Give each student an index card. On the top line, have students write a career title they are considering. Below the title, draw a vertical line down the center of the card. Have students visit the Bureau of Labor Statistics (http://stats.bls.gov/oes/current/oes_nat.htm) and click on the selected career. Have students label the left side of the card "National" and write the number of American workers in the occupation and the mean annual wage for the occupation.

Students can also find state information at the Bureau of Labor Statistics (http://stats.bls.gov/oes/current/oessrcst.htm). Students select their state, and then the occupation. Have students label the right column of their card as "State" and write the number of state workers in the occupation and the mean annual wage.

Have students compare the national and state average wages for the career. At the bottom of the card, have students explain in one sentence why they think wages in their state are higher or lower than the national average wages. Post the cards on a bulletin board for students to review.

Author Note

Dear Economics Teacher:

Government is one of the most frustrating topics for an economist to write about. On one hand, government is fascinating because it can do so many things well. For example, the U.S. system of laws, highways, and public education sets us apart from many other nations. Without government expenditures to improve and maintain our infrastructure, and without the support of government to keep the economy competitive, our world would be much different.

On the other hand, the government can also do many things poorly—as when leaders succumb to corruption or commit us to courses of action we may not agree with. How many times, for example, have you heard of massive budget overruns or a government expenditure that you think is unnecessary? All of these things are done with our money—yours, your students', and mine!

Because of problems like these, the "proper" role of government is often hotly debated, with some people wanting less government and others wanting more. In all honesty, even economists don't know exactly how much government is necessary, let alone optimal.

So how do I write about something that can be both satisfying and frustrating? The short answer is to be as descriptive as possible, provide the facts, weigh the costs and benefits of different government activities separately—and then let people make up their own minds. Evaluating the role of government isn't rocket science, although many people try to simplify the process by committing to an ideology of having either more or less government. As teachers, we must challenge our students to evaluate every situation on its own merits. We're not trying to think for our students, but we must give them the background and facts to analyze problems, and the tools to help make the correct decision!

Gary E. Clayton

Gary Clayton, Ph.D.
Author

UNIT 3
Economic Institutions and Issues

Unit Objectives

After studying this unit, students will be able to:

- **Trace** the development and influence of labor unions.
- **Explain** how government raises revenues.
- **Explain** how government allocates expenditures.
- **Describe** the organization and role of financial markets.

Unit Overview

Unit 3 discusses the role of labor, government, and financial markets in the American economy.

Chapter 8 describes organized labor in the United States and examines its influence on employment and wages.

Chapter 9 focuses on how government raises revenue and discusses the nature of taxation.

Chapter 10 details how government spends revenues.

Chapter 11 explains the importance of savings to the economy and describes investments in financial assets, equities, and markets.

Congress approves the ▶ federal budget, while the executive branch administers revenue collection and spending.

Activity: Launching the Unit

Economic Controversies Have each student list what he or she thinks are the three most controversial topics in economics today. Call on volunteers to share their lists with the class, noting new issues on the board as they are offered. Circle topics such as labor unions, taxes, government spending, deficit, national debt, social security, and so on. Then point out that the circled issues will be discussed at some length in Unit 3. **OL**

Making It Relevant

Ask: What are some positive uses of tax money? *(Students might mention education and public safety improvements.)* Tell students that local, state, and federal taxes pay for items that are public goods and services. Ask students to list public goods and services that they use, such as road maintenance and police protection. Ask students to look at deductions from their paychecks or a generic paycheck to see how much money is deducted by each level of government. Tell students that in Unit 3 they will learn more about the ways that the government makes and spends money. **OL**

BusinessWeek ONLINE

To find up-to-date news and analysis on the economy, business, technology, markets, entrepreneurs, investments, and finance, have students search feature articles and special reports on the BusinessWeek Web site, www.businessweek.com.

Extra Credit Project

Have students work in groups of five to prepare a two- or three-minute television newscast on labor in the United States. Some students might act as reporters, others might play experts or "people on the street," and still others might take the role of news anchors. Suggest that students incorporate charts and graphs to illustrate topics such as changes in the labor force, average wages over the years, union membership, and so on. Then allow time in class for groups to "broadcast" their news programs. **AL**

Key to Ability Levels

BL Below level **AL** Above level
OL On level **ELL** English Language Learners

Key to Teaching Resources

📁 Print Material 💿 DVD
💿 CD-Rom 🖨 Transparency

Levels					Resources	Chapter Opener	Section 1	Section 2	Section 3	Chapter Assess
BL	OL	AL	ELL							
					FOCUS					
BL	OL	AL	ELL	🖨	**Daily Focus Skills Transparencies**		39	38, 40	39, 41	
					TEACH					
BL	OL		ELL	📁	**Guided Reading Activities***		p. 22	p. 23	p. 24	
BL	OL	AL	ELL	📁	**Economic Content Vocabulary Activities***		p. 8	p. 8	p. 8	
	OL	AL		📁	**Critical Thinking Activities**		p. 13		p. 8	
BL	OL		ELL	📁	**Reading Essentials and Note-Taking Guide***		p. 64	p. 67	p. 70	
		AL		📁	**Enrichment Activities**				p. 8	
	OL	AL		📁	**Free Enterprise Activities**			p. 13		
BL	OL	AL	ELL	📁	**Primary and Secondary Source Readings**				pp. 3, 25	
BL	OL	AL	ELL	📁	**Economic Cartoons**			p. 1		
BL	OL	AL	ELL	📁	**Hands-On Economics**			p. 14	p. 14	
BL	OL	AL	ELL	🖨	**Economic Concepts Transparencies, Strategies, and Activities**		p. 9		p. 19	
BL	OL	AL	ELL	🖨	**Economics Forms and Financial Pages Transparencies, Strategies, and Activities**			p. 7		
BL	OL	AL	ELL	📁	**Personal Finance Activities**				p. 13	
BL	OL	AL	ELL	📁	**Reinforcing Economic Skills**		p. 10		p. 5	
BL	OL		ELL	📁	**High School Reading in the Content Area Strategies and Activities**	✓	✓	✓	✓	✓
BL	OL	AL	ELL	🖨	**High School Writing Process Transparencies**	✓	✓	✓	✓	✓
BL	OL	AL	ELL	📁	**Writer's Guidebook**	✓	✓	✓	✓	✓
BL	OL	AL	ELL	💿	**StudentWorks Plus CD-ROM**	✓	✓	✓	✓	✓
BL	OL	AL	ELL	💿	**Vocabulary PuzzleMaker CD-ROM**	✓	✓	✓	✓	✓

*Also available in Spanish

TeacherWorks *Plus*
All-In-One Planner and Resource Center

- Interactive Lesson Planner
- Interactive Teacher Edition
- Fully editable blackline masters
- Economics & You videos

- Differentiated Lesson Plans
- Printable reports of daily assignments
- Standards tracking system

Levels					Resources	Chapter Opener	Section 1	Section 2	Section 3	Chapter Assess
BL	OL	AL	ELL							
TEACH *(continued)*										
BL	OL	AL	ELL		Economics & You Video Program DVD— *The American Labor Force*	✓	✓	✓	✓	✓
BL	OL	AL	ELL		Graph Coach CD-ROM	✓	✓	✓	✓	✓
Teacher Resources					Differentiated Instruction Strategies	✓	✓	✓	✓	✓
					Success with English Learners	✓	✓	✓	✓	✓
					Presentation Plus! CD-ROM	✓	✓	✓	✓	✓
ASSESS										
BL	OL	AL	ELL		Section Quizzes and Chapter Tests		p. 97	p. 98	p. 99	pp. 101, 105
BL	OL	AL	ELL		Authentic Assessment Strategies and Activities		p. 13			
BL	OL	AL	ELL		*ExamView® Assessment Suite* CD-ROM		8-1	8-2	8-3	Ch. 8
BL	OL	AL	ELL		Interactive Tutor Self-Assessment CD-ROM		8-1	8-2	8-3	
CLOSE										
BL			ELL		Reteaching Activities*		p. 8	p. 8	p. 8	
BL	OL		ELL		Reading and Study Skills Foldables		p. 55	p. 55	p. 55	

*Also available in Spanish

Activity
Using Interactive Tutor Self-Assessment

Electronic Quiz

Technology Product

Glencoe's Interactive Tutor Self-Assessment software allows students to assess their mastery of chapter content, taking as much time as they need to review each section of a chapter. The Interactive Tutor Self-Assessment

- contains quizzes for individual section of chapters, with section overviews covering important concepts and keywords;
- allows students to read overviews based on sections, chapters, or units before starting quizzes;
- lets students check their answers, receive feedback and hints, and identify content areas for review;
- permits student to move back and forth among the questions during a quiz;
- generates performance reports and graphs to monitor student progress section by section.

Objectives

Using the Interactive Tutor Self-Assessment allows students to

- assess their mastery of chapter content;
- identify chapter content they need to review.

Steps

- Install Interactive Tutor Self-Assessment.
- Register yourself and create classes.
- Register new students/users in the database, organized by classes. Assign individual passwords to students.
- Save student records to a location easily accessible to students.
- Assign section quizzes to students.
- Generate performance reports and graphs for individual students and classes.

Economics ONLINE

	Student	Teacher	Parent
Beyond the Textbook	●	●	●
Chapter Overviews	●	●	●
ePuzzles and Games	●		●
Concepts in Motion	●		●
Multi-Language Glossaries	●		●
Online Student Edition	●	●	●
Self-Check Quizzes	●		●
Student Web Activities	●		●
Study Central™	●		●
Time Current Events	●	●	●
Teaching Today		●	
Vocabulary eFlashcards	●		●
Web Activity Lesson Plans		●	

Glencoe Media Center

❯ glencoe.com

Study-To-Go
- Vocabulary eFlashcards
- Self-Check Quizzes

❯ **Audio/Video**
- Student Edition Audio
- Spanish Summaries
- Economics & You Videos

READING SUPPORT FROM JAMESTOWN EDUCATION

- **Timed Readings Plus in Social Studies** helps students increase their reading rate and fluency while maintaining comprehension. The 400-word passages are similar to those found on state and national assessments.

- **Reading in the Content Area: Social Studies** concentrates on six essential reading skills that help students better comprehend what they read. The book includes 75 high-interest nonfiction passages written at increasing levels of difficulty.

- **Reading Social Studies** includes strategic reading instruction and vocabulary support in Social Studies content for both ELLs and native speakers of English. www.jamestowneducation.com

Reading List Generator CD-ROM — GLENCOE BOOKLINK 3

Use this database to search more than 30,000 titles to create a customized reading list for your students.

- Reading lists can be organized by students' reading level, author, genre, theme, or area of interest.
- The database provides Degrees of Reading Power™ (DRP) and Lexile™ readability scores for all selections.
- A brief summary of each selection is included.

Leveled reading suggestions for this chapter:

For students at a Grade 10 reading level:
- *The Rise of Industry: 1860–1900,* by Christopher Collier & James Lincoln Collier

For students at a Grade 11 reading level:
- *The Great Depression,* by Jacqueline Farrell

For students at a Grade 12 reading level:
- *The Great Depression and the New Deal: America's Economic Collapse and Recovery,* by Anne E. Schraff

* Review suggested books before assigning them.

NCEE

National Council on Economic Education

Voluntary Standards Emphasized in Chapter 8

Content Standard 10 Institutions evolve in market economies to help individuals and groups accomplish their goals. Banks, labor unions, corporations, legal systems, and not-for-profit organizations are examples of important institutions. A different kind of institution, clearly defined and enforced property rights, is essential to a market economy.

Content Standard 13 Income for most people is determined by the market value of the productive resources they sell. What workers earn depends, primarily, on the market value of what they produce and how productive they are.

Resources Available from NCEE
- Virtual Economics®: An Interactive Center for Economic Education Version 3.0
- Focus: Understanding Economics in U.S. History
- Advanced Placement Economics: Teacher Resource Manual, Third Edition
- Focus: Institutions and Markets

To order these materials, or to contact your State Council on Economic Education about workshops and programs, call 1-800-338-1192 or visit the NCEE Web site at store.ncee.net.

The BIG Idea

As students study the chapter, remind them to consider the chapter-based Big Idea. The **Essential Question** in the chapter launch activity below ties in to the Big Idea and helps students think about and understand important chapter concepts. In addition, the Hands-On Chapter Project relates the content from each section to the Big Idea. The steps in each section build on each other and culminate in the Wrap-Up Activity on the Visual Summary page.

 To generate student interest and provide a springboard for class discussion, access the Economics & You Topic 13 video, **The American Labor Force,** at glencoe.com or on the video DVD.

Dinah Zike's Foldables are three-dimensional, interactive graphic organizers that help students practice basic writing skills, review key vocabulary terms, and identify main ideas. Have students complete this chapter's Foldable activity or activities in *Dinah Zike's Reading and Study Skills Foldables* booklet. **OL**

Economics ONLINE

Introduce students to chapter content and key terms by having them access *Chapter 8—Chapter Overviews* at glencoe.com.

CHAPTER
8 Employment, Labor, and Wages

The more skills workers ▶ such as these construction workers have, the more they can expect to be paid.

Why It Matters

Yesterday you found out that your first college choice has accepted you and offered you a scholarship to cover your tuition and books. You will still have to pay for your room and board. Today, your best friend announced that she has received a "full ride" basketball scholarship to the same college—all her expenses will be covered. Why do you think she received a larger scholarship even though your grades are much better than hers? Read Chapter 8 to find out more about labor and wages.

The BIG Idea

The labor market, like other markets, is determined by supply and demand.

Economics ONLINE Chapter Overview Visit the *Economics: Principles and Practices* Web site at glencoe.com and click on *Chapter 8–Chapter Overviews* to preview chapter information.

Activity: Launching the Chapter

Problem-Solving Have students imagine that negotiations about pay and working conditions are about to take place at a fast-food restaurant. Ask one group to represent the workers and consider what they might ask for. Have another group represent the manager of the restaurant and consider what he or she might be willing to give. Ask students how workers and management might be able to bring what is being asked for and what is being offered closer together. Guide students toward the idea of compromise. **Essential Question:** How are work relationships governed by the law of supply and demand? *(The supply comes from the workers who offer their services to employers, while the demand comes from employers who require workers.)* **OL**

The Labor Movement

GUIDE TO READING

Section Preview

In this section, you will find out that labor unions are organizations that attempt to improve the working conditions of their members.

Content Vocabulary

- craft union *(p. 199)*
- trade union *(p. 199)*
- industrial union *(p. 199)*
- strike *(p. 199)*
- picket *(p. 199)*
- boycott *(p. 199)*
- lockout *(p. 199)*
- company union *(p. 199)*
- Great Depression *(p. 201)*
- right-to-work law *(p. 202)*
- independent union *(p. 203)*
- closed shop *(p. 203)*
- union shop *(p. 204)*
- modified union shop *(p. 204)*
- agency shop *(p. 204)*
- civilian labor force *(p. 204)*

Academic Vocabulary

- legislation *(p. 198)*
- prohibited *(p. 201)*

Reading Strategy

Sequencing As you read this section, note major events in the history of the U.S. labor movement by creating a time line similar to the one below.

↱ **1788** New York City Printers join to demand higher pay—first attempt to organize labor

1750　1800　1850　1900　1950　2000

Focus

ISSUES IN THE NEWS

—The Associated Press

Restaurant Fined over Youth Program

Alex Ray, owner of the Common Man restaurants, has been fined by the government for a program that helped a dozen teenagers start and run their own business last summer.

Ray paid a $2,000 fine after the Labor Department said the program violated child-labor laws. The teenagers, ages 13 to 15, worked at the Common Man Restaurant in Plymouth [New Hampshire], where they designed a business model, managed the business, scheduled fellow students to staff breakfast and made bank deposits.

Ray said the project through a program called Communities for Alcohol- and Drug-Free Youth was a huge success, but the Labor Department sent a violation notice, because kids under 16 worked before 7 A.M. ■

The restaurant owner in the news article did not intend to violate the Fair Labor Standards Act of 1938, but good intentions sometimes have unforeseen consequences. Even so, working is one of the single most important things we do. After all, how well we do, as measured by the satisfaction we get or the income we receive, affects virtually every aspect of our lives. Thus, in our study of economics it is important to examine the way the "labor" factor of production earns its income.

We also want to study the labor movement because the United States has a rich and colorful labor history. The historical struggle between workers and employers has shaped today's working environment, and the evolution is still continuing.

CHAPTER 8 Employment, Labor, and Wages **197**

Resource Manager

R Reading Strategies	**C** Critical Thinking	**D** Differentiated Instruction	**W** Writing Support	**S** Skill Practice
Teacher Edition • Outlining, p. 199 • Inferring, p. 201 • Sequencing Info., p. 203 • Summarizing, p. 204	**Teacher Edition** • Det. Cause/Effect, p. 198 • Defending, p. 200 • Ident. POV, p. 203 • Form. Quest., p. 205	**Teacher Edition** • Visual/Spatial, p. 200 • Adv. Learners, p. 201 • Interpersonal, p. 204	**Teacher Edition** • Expository Writing, p. 198 • Personal Writing, p. 202	**Teacher Edition** • Using Tables and Charts, p. 199 • Drawing Con., p. 202 • Analyzing Info., p. 206
Additional Resources • Guid. Read. Act., p. 22 • Read. Ess. & Note-Taking Guide, p. 64	**Additional Resources** • Authentic Assess., p. 13	**Additional Resources** • Reteach. Act., p. 8 • Reinforcing Econ. Skills, p. 10	**Additional Resources** • High School Reading in the Content Area Strat. and Act.	**Additional Resources** • Reading and Study Skills Fold., p. 55 • Econ. Concepts Trans., Strat. & Act., p. 9

Teach

W Writing Support

Expository Writing Have students research how the U.S. job market has changed since the Industrial Revolution. Have them report on their findings in a short paper. At the end of the paper, have them predict how the job market will change by the year 2050. **OL**

C Critical Thinking

Determining Cause and Effect Ask: Why did unions have strong bargaining power even though only a small fraction of workers belonged to them? *(Possible answer: The service the workers provided was specialized, so the unions were in a strong bargaining position.)* **OL**

Economic Analysis

Answer: Trade unions represent workers who perform the same kind of work; industrial unions represent all workers in the same industry.

Additional Support

Skills Handbook
See page R52 to learn about Sequencing Events.

Colonial Times to the 1930s

MAIN Idea Early unions formed to negotiate terms for their members, but employers and courts opposed them.

Economics & You Do you or any members of your family belong to a union? Read on to learn about the early years of the American union movement.

Today, only one out of every eight working Americans is a member of a labor union. Even so, unions are important because they played a major historical role in helping to create the **legislation** that affects our pay and working conditions today.

Early Union Development

In 1778 printers in New York City joined together to demand higher pay. This was the first attempt to organize labor in America. Before long, unions of shoemakers, carpenters, and tailors developed, each hoping to negotiate agreements that covered hours, pay, and working conditions. While only a small fraction of all workers belonged to unions, most unions were comprised of skilled workers and possessed strong bargaining power.

Until about 1820, most of America's workforce was made up of farmers, small business owners, and the self-employed.

Soon immigrants began to arrive in great numbers. Because they provided a supply of cheap, unskilled labor, they posed a threat to the unions that were working to preserve existing wage and labor standards.

In addition, public opinion was largely against union activity, and some parts of the country even banned labor unions. Labor organizers often were viewed as troublemakers, and many workers believed they could better negotiate with their employers on a one-to-one basis.

Civil War to the 1930s

The Civil War led to higher prices and a greater demand for goods and services. Manufacturing expanded, and the farm population declined. Hourly workers in industrial jobs made up about one-fourth of the country's working population.

Working conditions in some industries were difficult, and hostile attitudes toward unions slowly began to soften. Many of the cultural and linguistic differences between immigrants and American-born workers began to fade, and the labor force became more unified.

Types of Unions

In the industrial post–Civil War period, the two main types of labor unions shown in **Figure 8.1** dominated. The first was the

Figure 8.1 ▶ Trade (Craft) and Industrial Unions

TRADE (CRAFT) UNIONS

Printers' union | Electricians' union | Machinists' union | Carpenters' union | Plumbers' union

INDUSTRIAL UNIONS

All belong to the same union

▶ Labor unions can be categorized as either trade or industrial unions.

Economic Analysis *How do trade unions differ from industrial unions?*

Extending the Content

A Union for Everyone While almost all early unions represented only white men, the Noble Order of the Knights of Labor had a goal of bringing "men and women of every craft, creed, and color" into one big union. Founded in 1869, the Knights not only welcomed women workers but also gave them leadership roles. For example, Elizabeth Rodgers led a Chicago division of the Knights that represented about 50,000 male and

female workers. Married with a family, Rodgers listed her occupation as "housewife." To emphasize its commitment to representing all workers, the organization held its 1886 meeting in Richmond, Virginia—which had served as the former capital of the Confederacy—and gave prominent roles to African Americans in the proceedings.

Labor Strikes
This woodcut shows workers and firefighters during the Baltimore and Ohio Railroad strike of 1877. *What did unions try to accomplish with strikes?*

S Skill Practice

Using Tables and Charts On the board, create a two-column table with the headings "Craft Unions" and "Industrial Unions." Then have students call out the names of unions that they find through print and online research, identifying them as either craft or industrial. Write each union's name in the appropriate column. **OL**

R Reading Strategy

Outlining Students may have difficulty understanding the types of labor unions that developed and how unions are organized. They may find it easier to comprehend the material if they outline the section. Suggest that they list the different types of unions, the levels of union operations, and the major characteristics of each. **BL**

---

craft union or **trade union,** an association of skilled workers who perform the same kind of work. The Cigar Makers' Union, begun by union leader Samuel Gompers, is an example of this type of union.

The second type of union was the **industrial union**—an association of all workers in the same industry, regardless of the job each individual worker performs. The development of basic mass-production industries such as steel and textiles provided the opportunity to organize this kind of union. Because many of the workers in these industries were unskilled and could not join trade unions, they organized as industrial unions instead.

Union Activities

Unions tried to help workers by negotiating for higher pay, job security, and better hours and working conditions. If an agreement could not be reached, workers would **strike,** or refuse to work until certain demands were met. Unions also pressured employers by having the striking workers **picket,** or parade in front of the employer's business carrying signs about the dispute. The signs might ask other workers not to seek jobs with the company, or they might

ask customers and suppliers to show union support by taking their business elsewhere.

If striking and picketing did not force a settlement of the dispute, a union could organize a **boycott**—a mass refusal to buy products from targeted employers or companies. When a boycott was effective, it hurt the company's business.

Employer Resistance

Employers resented the strikes, pickets, and boycotts, so they fought unions in a number of ways. Sometimes the owners called for a **lockout,** a refusal to let employees work until they agreed to management demands.

At other times, management responded to a strike, or the threat of a strike, by hiring all new workers. Some owners even set up **company unions**—unions organized, supported, or run by employers—to head off efforts by others to organize workers.

The Ludlow Massacre

Perhaps nothing typified such struggles more than a strike in Colorado. The United Mine Workers of America had organized a strike against a mining company owned by

craft union or trade union labor union whose members perform the same kind of work

industrial union labor union whose members perform different kinds of work in the same industry

strike union-organized work stoppage designed to make an employer meet union demands

picket demonstrate or march before a place of business to protest a company's actions

boycott refusal to buy products from an employer or company

lockout management refusal to let employees work until demands are met

company union union organized, supported, or run by an employer

Caption Answer: to pressure employers to meet their demands on pay, job security, hours, and working conditions

Additional Support

CHAPTER 8 Employment, Labor, and Wages **199**

Activity: Collaborative Learning

Illustrating Organize students into several groups, and have groups create collages that illustrate the U.S. labor force. Have group members collect pictures of people at work from magazines, newspapers, and other media. Inform groups that jobs should range from blue-collar to white-collar and should include service workers. Have groups use

these pictures to create their collages. Point out that collages should show diversity in terms of occupations, types of employees, and types of locations. Have groups display their finished collages around the classroom. **BL**

Teacher Tip

Visual Learning Use the collages to help students learn the content. You might ask students to categorize the types of work shown in the collages or speculate on the likelihood of jobs shown being outsourced or offshored.

C Critical Thinking

Defending Write the following question on the board: *Were better working conditions and wages for American workers the result of labor union activity or the increased demand for skilled labor?* Call on volunteers to offer evidence supporting either side of the question. **AL**

D Differentiated Instruction

Visual/Spatial **Ask:** How would you describe the Haymarket riots based on the illustration? *(Students may describe a violent and chaotic scene based on the flames, the men shooting, the large police force, the impassioned speaker, and the injured men.)* **BL**

Caption Answer: unfavorably

✓**Reading Check** **Answer:** They developed in response to increased industrial activity following the Civil War. Workers banded together to pressure employers for more favorable pay, job security, working conditions, and hours.

Hands-On Chapter Project

Step 1

Going to Work

In this project, students will simulate the process of finding a new job, including applying, interviewing, and negotiating pay and benefits.

Step 1: Applying for a Job. Students will go through job listings and learn how to apply for a job.

Directions: Bring in job listings from local newspapers, online job-posting sites, or other sources. Tell students to imagine that

---

John D. Rockefeller to demand better pay and working conditions. When the company forced workers out of company-owned homes, the miners and their families moved into tents set up by the union.

The strike, expected to end after a few days, instead lasted 14 months. At times, fights broke out between striking miners and company guards. The mining company also hired a private detective agency and received assistance from the Colorado National Guard.

One fight in spring 1914 turned into an all-day battle and a devastating fire. In the end, dozens of people were killed, including 2 women and 11 children. The violence, quickly called the Ludlow massacre, sparked rioting in other coal mining communities. The resulting conflict eventually claimed nearly 200 lives.

Attitude of the Courts

Throughout this period, the courts had an unfavorable attitude toward unions. Under English common law, unions were considered conspiracies against business and were prosecuted in the United States. Even the Sherman Antitrust Act of 1890, aimed mainly at curbing monopolies, was used to keep labor in line.

For example, in 1902 the United Hatters Union called a strike against a Danbury, Connecticut, hat manufacturer that had rejected a union demand. The union decided to apply pressure on stores to not stock hats made by the Danbury firm. The hat manufacturer, charging a conspiracy in restraint of trade under the Sherman Act, filed a damage suit that went all the way to the Supreme Court. The Supreme Court ruled that the union had organized an illegal boycott in restraint of trade, thereby dealing a severe blow to organized labor.

C The Danbury Hatters case and several subsequent antiunion decisions pushed organized labor to call for relief. The passage of the Clayton Antitrust Act of 1914 helped to remedy the threat to unions by expressly exempting labor unions from prosecution under the Sherman Act.

✓**Reading Check** **Recalling** How did trade unions and industrial unions develop?

Antiunion Attitudes A nationwide strike on May 3, 1886, turned violent in Chicago's Haymarket Square when strikers and police clashed. *How did the Supreme Court view union activity?*

D

---

they have finished their schooling and are looking for a job. Have them go through the job listings to find a suitable job to apply for. Have students make copies of the job advertisements they are using.

Then tell students to proceed as if they are applying for the job. If the job requires an application, have them use the form on *Economic Forms and Financial Pages Transparencies, Strategies, and Activities*, p. 8, or give them another sample application to fill out. If the job requires a résumé, have

them put one together and write a cover letter. Suggest that they use the Internet or other references to help them write their cover letters and résumés.

Evaluating Have student pairs exchange job advertisements and applications (or cover letters and résumés) and then return them with a brief written or oral critique. Finally, have students make any changes they think are necessary. **OL**

(Chapter Project continued in Section 2.)

Unemployment
During the Great Depression, the unemployed lined up for food and other assistance. **What was the impact of the Great Depression on the labor movement?**

Labor Since the 1930s

MAIN Idea Most of the significant labor laws in effect today were passed in the 1930s, 1940s, and 1950s.

Economics & You Did you try to find a job before you turned 16 but were turned down? Read to learn how early labor legislation affects you today.

During the 1930s, times were especially hard for working people who lacked unemployment insurance. In response, Congress passed a series of laws that supported organized labor. Although a backlash against labor followed, these laws provided the most important labor protections that are still in effect today.

Labor in the Great Depression

The **Great Depression**—the worst period of economic decline and stagnation in the history of the United States—began with the collapse of the stock market in October 1929. Economic output reached bottom in 1933 and did not recover to its 1929 level until 1939. At times, as many as one in four workers was without a job. Others kept their jobs but saw pay cuts. In 1929 the average hourly manufacturing wage was 55 cents. By 1933 it plummeted to 5 cents.

The Great Depression brought misery to millions, but it also changed attitudes toward the labor movement. Common problems united factory workers, and union promoters renewed their efforts to organize workers.

Great Depression worst period of economic decline in U.S. history, lasting from 1929 to approximately 1939

Pro-Union Legislation

New legislation soon aided labor. The Norris-LaGuardia Act of 1932 prevented federal courts from issuing rulings against unions engaged in peaceful strikes, picketing, or boycotts. This forced companies to negotiate directly with their unions during labor disputes.

The National Labor Relations Act, or Wagner Act, of 1935 established the right of unions to collective bargaining. The act also created the National Labor Relations Board (NLRB), giving it the power to police unfair labor practices. The NLRB also could oversee and certify union election results. If a fair election resulted in a union as the employees' bargaining agent, employers had to recognize and negotiate with it.

The Fair Labor Standards Act of 1938 applied to businesses that engage in interstate commerce and set the first minimum wage. It established time-and-a-half pay for overtime, which was defined as more than 40 hours per week. The act also **prohibited**

CHAPTER 8 Employment, Labor, and Wages **201**

D Differentiated Instruction

Advanced Learners Tell students that labor and union songs make up a significant part of American folk music. Have volunteers prepare a presentation about the role of music in the struggles to unionize workers over the last 100 years or so. Encourage musically talented students to perform selections from the labor songbook. **AL**

R Reading Strategy

Inferring Ask: In what way did the Great Depression change attitudes toward union activities? Why do you think this change occurred? *(Possible answer: Common problems united factory workers, and many people may have sympathized with out-of-work laborers. Economic hardships were widespread and shared.)* **OL**

Caption Answer: Attitudes toward unions became more favorable, and new laws protected union activities.

Additional Support

Activity: Interdisciplinary Connection

Daily Life Have pairs of students interview seniors in the community about life and the economic situation during the Great Depression. Have students prepare a list of questions, identify potential interviewees, arrange the interview, and be prepared, if suitable and prearranged, to tape-record or videotape the interview. (You may want to prescreen questions for suitability or prepare a written handout for students to present to potential interview subjects, describing the project.) Have pairs share the results of their interviews with the class. If possible, prepare a class archive of Great Depression interviews. **OL**

S Skill Practice

Drawing Conclusions

Ask: Based on the map, what conclusions can you draw about the strength of unions in different states and regions of the country? *(Students should conclude that unions possessed enough political strength in the Northeast, Midwest, and West Coast states to prevent the passage of right-to-work laws in state legislatures.)* **OL**

W Writing Support

Personal Writing Have students conduct research to find out whether your state is a right-to-work state. Then have them write a journal entry explaining whether they agree or disagree with right-to-work laws. Remind them to give reasons for their feelings. **OL**

Economic Analysis

Answer: the Northeast, Midwest, and West Coast

Differentiated Instruction

Critical Thinking Activities, p. 13

Figure 8.2 ▶ Right-to-Work, State by State

▶ Today, 22 states have right-to-work laws that limit the power of unions. If a state has such a law, unions cannot force workers to join the union as a condition of continued employment.

Economic Analysis *Which regions have the fewest states with right-to-work laws?*

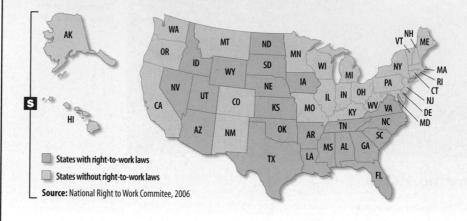

- States with right-to-work laws
- States without right-to-work laws

Source: National Right to Work Commitee, 2006

right-to-work law state law making it illegal to require a worker to join a union

oppressive child labor, which includes any labor for a child under 16 and work that is hazardous to the health of a child under 18.

Antiunion Backlash

The union movement had grown strong by the end of World War II, but then public opinion shifted again. Some people feared that Communists had secretly entered the unions. Others were concerned over production losses due to the increased number of strikes. People began to think that management, not labor, was the victim.

Growing antiunion feelings led to the Labor-Management Relations Act, or Taft-Hartley Act, of 1947. The act had a tough antiunion provision known as Section 14(b) that allows individual states to pass right-to-work laws. A **right-to-work law** is a state law making it illegal to force workers to join a union as a condition of employment, even though a union may already exist.

If a state does not have a right-to-work law, new workers may be required to join an existing union as a condition for employment shortly after being hired. If a state has a right-to-work law, then new hires can decide for themselves whether or not they want to join the union—even if the overwhelming majority of workers at the company support the union. Today, the 22 states shown in **Figure 8.2** have taken advantage of Section 14(b) to pass right-to-work laws.

Other legislation was aimed at stopping criminal influences that had begun to emerge in the labor movement. The most important law was the Labor-Management Reporting and Disclosure Act, or Landrum-Griffin Act, of 1959. This act required unions to file regular financial reports with the government and limited the amount of money union officials could borrow from the union.

The AFL-CIO

The American Federation of Labor (AFL) began in 1886 as an organization of craft or trade unions. It later added several industrial

---

Making Inferences

Objective: Make inferences to form ideas.

Focus/Teach: Brainstorm ways in which students make inferences every day. Then have them complete the activity.

Assess: Go over students' answers as a class, discussing any on which there is disagreement.

Close: Ask students to analyze how they were able to make inferences from the information provided.

Differentiated Instruction Strategies

BL Ask students to name examples of skilled labor and unskilled labor.

AL Ask: Is Gompers's story a "typical" American success story? Explain.

ELL Have students discuss the similarities and differences between immigrants in Gompers's time and those of today.

unions. The craft and industrial unions, however, did not always agree over the future of the union movement. As a result, eight of the AFL industrial unions formed a separate group headed by John L. Lewis, the president of the United Mine Workers of America.

The AFL and Lewis did not get along, so Lewis and his industrial unions were expelled in 1937 and formed the Congress of Industrial Organizations (CIO). The CIO quickly set up unions in industries that had not been unionized before, such as the steel and automobile industries. By the 1940s, the CIO had nearly 7 million members.

As the CIO grew stronger, it began to challenge the dominance of the AFL. In 1955 the AFL and the CIO joined to form the **R** American Federation of Labor and Congress of Industrial Organizations (AFL-CIO).

In 2005, a disagreement over the best way to spend union funds resulted in a breakup of the AFL-CIO. Initially, the Service Employees International Union (SEIU), the largest union in the federation, left with several other large unions to form the rival Change to Win Coalition. Other unions soon followed, leaving the labor movement split for the first time since 1955.

It is still too early to tell how this split will affect the power of organized labor. The remaining AFL-CIO unions want to focus their efforts on lobbying politicians. The Change to Win Coalition wants to focus its efforts on recruiting new union members.

Independent Unions

Although the AFL-CIO is still a major force, other unions are also important in the labor movement. Many of these are **independent unions**—unions that do not belong to the AFL-CIO or the Change to Win Coalition—such as the Brotherhood of Locomotive Engineers. Other examples of independent unions are the United Campus Workers at the University of Tennessee and the Virginia Public Service Workers Union.

✓Reading Check **Analyzing** Why did the Great Depression have such a strong and lasting impact on the labor movement?

Organized Labor Today

MAIN Idea Unionized workers can participate in several types of union arrangements.

Economics & You Have you ever noticed "Union Made" labels on clothing or other items? Read on to learn more about the different kinds of unions that make these products.

Unionized workers participate in several kinds of union arrangements. In addition, union participation in the labor force varies widely from one industry to another.

Kinds of Union Arrangements

The most restrictive kind of union arrangement is the **closed shop,** in which an employer agrees to hire only union members. In effect, this allows the union to determine who is hired by giving or denying a person union membership. In some cases, union members could get family members and friends hired as long as the union controlled membership access, which most employers strongly opposed.

This kind of union arrangement was common in the 1930s and early 1940s. However, the Taft-Hartley Act of 1947 made the closed shop illegal for all companies involved in interstate commerce.

YOU KNOW, IF IT WEREN'T FOR THE UNION, IN THIS ECONOMY, WE'D BE IN REAL TROUBLE.

YEAH, THANKS TO THE BARGAINING POWER WE HAVE AS A GROUP, WE CAN ALL TAKE PAY CUTS AND GET FIRED TOGETHER.

11-30   WISE/ALDRICH

REAL LIFE ADVENTURES © 2005 GarLanco. Reprinted with permission of UNIVERSAL PRESS SYNDICATE. All rights reserved.

CHAPTER 8 Employment, Labor, and Wages **203**

Economics ONLINE

Student Web Activity Visit the *Economics: Principles and Practices* Web site at glencoe.com and click on *Chapter 8– Student Web Activities* for an activity on labor unions.

independent union labor union not affiliated with the AFL-CIO or the Change to Win Coalition

closed shop arrangement under which workers must join a union before they are hired

Power of Unions
While unions remain a strong force, their bargaining power often is limited by economic conditions. *What recent event may change the power of unions?*

C

R Reading Strategy
Sequencing Information
Have students make a time line of key events in the relationship of the AFL and the CIO. Events should include the formation of the groups, their merger, and their split. **OL**

C Critical Thinking
Identifying Points of View
Ask: What point of view do you think the cartoonist is expressing about the power of unions? (*He or she seems to think that unions have little power against changes in the economy.*) Then ask whether students agree with this point of view. Have them explain their answers. **OL**

Caption Answer: the split between the AFL-CIO

✓Reading Check **Answer:** It helped bring about new laws that empowered unions and improved people's opinions of union activities.

Leveled Activities

BL Reinforcing Economic Skills, p. 10

OL Economic Concepts Transparencies, Strategies, and Activities, p. 9

AL Authentic Assessment Strategies and Activities, p. 13

R Reading Strategy

Summarizing Have students review the information about closed shops, union shops, modified union shops, and agency shops. Then have them make a T-chart listing characteristics of each arrangement. **BL**

D Differentiated Instruction

Interpersonal Organize students into several groups. Have groups investigate the roles that women and minority groups played in the development of the American labor movement. Then have them use their findings to create a brochure or poster that might accompany a museum exhibit on minorities and organized labor in the United States. Suggest that brochures or posters include an overview of the exhibit and several exhibit items—for example, paintings, photographs, charts, or graphs—accompanied by explanatory captions. Have groups present their brochures or posters to the class. **OL**

Additional Support

The Global Economy & YOU

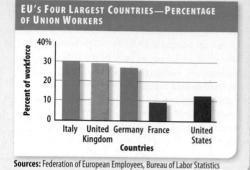

The Union Safety Net Unravels

If you have a part-time job, you are part of the reason that unions have declined. But don't blame yourself—other factors are causing this trend as well. In fact, union membership has declined both in the United States and around the globe. In 2005, 12.5 percent of American wage and salary workers were union members, down from the most recent peak of 20.1 percent in 1983. Although union membership is higher in Europe— 26.3 percent—experts predict the downward trend to continue there as well, with union membership falling under 20 percent by 2010.

Many factors have contributed to the decline of unions, including the increase in part-time workers, the rise in the number of women in the workforce, the growth in the number of white-collar workers, and the expansion of service industries. In addition, the trend toward smaller workplaces has hurt unionization.

EU's Four Largest Countries—Percentage of Union Workers

Sources: Federation of European Employees, Bureau of Labor Statistics

---

union shop arrangement under which workers must join a union after being hired

R

modified union shop arrangement under which workers have the option to join a union after being hired

agency shop arrangement under which nonunion workers must pay union dues

civilian labor force noninstitutionalized part of the population, aged 16 and over, either working or looking for a job

Because most firms in the United States today are directly or indirectly engaged in interstate commerce, few, if any, closed shops exist.

The second union arrangement is the **union shop,** where workers do not have to belong to the union to be hired, but must join soon after and remain a member for as long as they keep their jobs.

Another union arrangement is the **modified union shop.** Under this arrangement, workers do not have to belong to a union to be hired and cannot be made to join one to keep their jobs. If workers voluntarily join the union, however, they must remain members for as long as they hold their jobs.

Finally, **agency shop** is an agreement that does *not* require a worker to join a union as a condition to get or keep a job. It *does* require the worker to pay union dues to help pay for collective bargaining costs. Nonunion workers also are subject to the contract terms negotiated by the union, whether or not they agree with the terms.

An agency shop is also known as "fair share." Unions like to use this term to remind everyone that the dues the non-

members pay to the union are used on behalf of all the workers, whether they are union members or not.

Unionized Workers in the Labor Force

Today, the United States has a population of about 300 million people. Approximately half of the people belong to the **civilian labor force**—men and women 16 years old and over who are either working or actively looking for a job. The civilian classification excludes the prison population, other institutionalized persons, and members of the armed forces.

Approximately 12.5 percent of working Americans are union members. An additional 1.2 percent of working people are represented by unions in the form of the agency shop discussed above.

D Union membership is uneven among the different demographic groups in the United States. Men are more likely than women to be union members, although the gap has narrowed considerably in the last 20 years. Older workers, especially those over the age of 45, are more likely to be organized

---

Extending the Content

The AFL-CIO The merger of the AFL with the CIO in 1955 brought together some 16 million workers—more than 85 percent of all union members. Some major unions, however, did not affiliate with the AFL-CIO. The United Mine Workers of America (UMW) was one of the most prominent unions choosing to remain independent. This decision was due in large part to disagreements UMW president

John L. Lewis had with the leadership of the AFL. Even so, the UMW remained unaffiliated long after Lewis resigned his leadership. The miners' union did not join the AFL-CIO until 1989. Another large union, the United Auto Workers (UAW), left the federation for 13 years, beginning in 1968, over disagreements about civil rights and social welfare programs.

than younger workers. African Americans are more likely than others to belong to unions, while Asian Americans and Hispanic Americans are least likely to join. Finally, the rate of union memberships among full-time workers is more than twice as high as the rate for part-time workers.

Union membership also differs considerably by state. Five states—Alaska, Hawaii, Michigan, New Jersey, and New York—all have union membership rates above 20 percent, which means that one in five workers is unionized. Five other states—Arkansas, North Carolina, South Carolina, Virginia, and Utah—all have membership rates of less than five percent.

As shown in **Figure 8.3,** local, state, and federal governments have the highest rate of unionization. In fact, the rate of union membership in all levels of government is nearly three times that of workers in manufacturing. The food services industry, where most teenagers work, is the least likely to be unionized.

<u>✓Reading Check</u> **Contrasting** How do the types of union arrangements differ?

Figure 8.3 ▶

Union Membership and Representation by Industry

Industry	Percentage of employed workers who are:	
	Members of unions	Represented by unions
Local government	41.9	45.8
State government	31.3	35.0
Federal government	27.8	33.1
Utilities	27.4	28.6
Transportation and warehousing	23.4	24.4
Telecommunications	21.4	22.6
Motion pictures and sound recording	15.0	15.5
Construction	13.1	13.8
Manufacturing	13.0	13.7
Education and health services	8.3	9.4
Mining	8.0	9.5
Retail trade	5.2	5.8
Agriculture and related	2.7	3.0
Finance and insurance	1.6	2.1
Food services and drinking places	1.3	1.5

Source: Bureau of Labor Statistics, 2006

▶ Labor unions are most influential in the service industries, which include government, communications, public utilities, and transportation.

Economic Analysis *Which industries have few union members?*

C **Critical Thinking**

Formulating Questions Have students write five questions based on the information in the table. Then have them exchange work with a partner and answer each other's questions. Tell them to discuss the answers together afterward. **OL**

Economic Analysis

Answer: agriculture, finance and insurance, food service

<u>✓Reading Check</u> **Answer:** They differ in their degree of restrictiveness.

Assess

⊙ Use the Interactive Tutor Self-Assessment CD-ROM to review Section 1, and then assign the Section 1 Review as homework or as an in-class activity.

Close

Summarizing Have students use the Content Vocabulary to write a summary of Section 1. **OL**

Review **SECTION 1**

SECTION 1 Review

Vocabulary
1. **Explain** the significance of craft union, trade union, industrial union, strike, picket, boycott, lockout, company union, Great Depression, right-to-work law, independent union, closed shop, union shop, modified union shop, agency shop, and civilian labor force.

Main Ideas
2. **Stating** What is the purpose of labor unions?
3. **Explaining** Why did the AFL-CIO break up?
4. **Describing** Use a graphic organizer like the one below to describe the different types of union arrangements.

Labor Arrangements

Critical Thinking
5. **The BIG Idea** How do the major legislative acts discussed in the section reflect the rise and decline of the labor movement?
6. **Making Inferences** Why has union support in the United States gone through cycles of resistance and strong support? Write a short essay explaining your opinion.
7. **Comparing and Contrasting** Which of the four kinds of union arrangements would you prefer, and why?
8. **Analyzing Visuals** Look at Figure 8.2 on page 202. What does the pattern of right-to-work and non–right-to-work states imply about the strength of labor unions?

Applying Economics
9. **Civilian Labor Force** How would joining the armed services affect your participation in the civilian labor force?

Answers

1. All definitions can be found in the section and the Glossary.
2. to improve the working conditions, wages, and benefits of their members
3. Some members wanted to emphasize lobbying politicians, while others wanted to focus on recruiting new members.
4. closed shop: workers must join a union before they are hired; union shop: workers must join a union after they are hired; modified union shop: workers can join the union after they are hired;

agency shop: nonunion workers must pay union dues
5. At the turn of the century, unions were struggling; the Sherman Antitrust Act led to unions being prosecuted for interfering with trade. By the 1930s, unions were growing stronger and federal legislation protected them. After World War II, union support declined and the Taft-Hartley Act allowed unions to be sued and states to pass right-to-work laws.

6. Students' essays should assess union support throughout history.
7. Answers will vary but should reflect an understanding of the different types of union arrangements.
8. Possible answer: States in the south are generally right-to-work states. The unions in these areas are much weaker than unions in the northeast, which has no right-to-work laws.
9. You would no longer be part of the civilian labor force.

Teach

S Skill Practice

Analyzing Information

As a class, brainstorm characteristics that leaders often have. Write students' ideas on the board. **Ask:** Which of these characteristics did César Chávez possess? As students identify each characteristic, have them explain why they think it applied to Chávez, and then place a check mark beside it. **Ask:** What obstacles do you think Chávez faced? *(grueling work as a child; dropping out of school in eighth grade)* OL

Examining the Profile

Answers:

1. He formed the NFWA and traveled around California discussing problems and goals with farm workers.
2. It would reduce demand.

Additional Support

Profiles in Economics

César Chávez (1927–1993)

- led the only successful union to organize farmworkers S
- posthumously awarded the Presidential Medal of Freedom in 1994, the highest honor given to civilians

To Chávez and the farm workers he represented, La Causa (The Cause) was about something much bigger than themselves. According to Chávez, "The consumer boycott is . . . a gate of hope through which [farm workers] expect to find the sunlight of a better life for themselves and their families."

¡Sí, se puede!

César Chávez was born in Yuma, Arizona. Like that of many farmworkers, his life was grueling and impoverished. As a boy, he and his family worked all day in the fields picking fruits or vegetables. They moved from place to place throughout the year, forcing César to drop out of school in eighth grade.

Farmworkers who tried to organize for safer working conditions, better pay, and benefits were often harassed by farm owners and police. Some were even sprayed with agricultural poisons. With farms spread so far apart, it was difficult to organize strikes by migrant workers. But Chávez believed "it can be done."

Chávez joined the Community Service Organization (CSO) and began helping people with everyday tax, immigration, and education concerns. In 1962 he set up the National Farm Workers Association (NFWA). For three years, Chávez traveled all over California, discussing problems and goals with farm workers.

The Grape Boycott

When the Agricultural Workers Organizing Committee (AWOC), another farmworkers group, orchestrated a strike against the Delano table grape growers in 1965, Chávez and the NFWA decided to join their efforts. A year later, the two groups became the United Farm Workers (UFW). Chávez mobilized thousands of churches and student activists across the country to boycott grapes. At the peak of the boycott, table grape shipments were down by 24 percent in the top 10 North American markets, and more than 14 million people had participated.

The boycott's astounding success led to historic contracts between the UFW and the Delano growers in 1969. Chávez and his team had won union recognition, higher wages, a health plan, and other concessions. Yet for all of his labor struggles for others, Chávez never made more than $5,000 a year.

Examining the Profile

1. **Summarizing** How did Chávez initially try to approach farmworkers?
2. **Applying Information** How would a successful boycott impact the demand for grapes?

Extending the Content

Fighting for Rights for Farm Workers

Throughout much of the campaign to unionize farm workers, Chávez's second-in-command was Dolores Huerta. Born in 1930 in New Mexico, Huerta was inspired to fight for the rights of Hispanic workers by her father, a New Mexico state legislator. After working as a teacher, Huerta turned to community activism. She met César Chávez and together they formed the NFWA. Huerta's special talent for getting different groups to work together helped strengthen the union.

SECTION 2 — Wages and Labor Disputes

GUIDE TO READING

Section Preview

In this section, you will learn that unions and management negotiate contracts through a process known as collective bargaining.

Content Vocabulary

- wage rate (p. 208)
- unskilled labor (p. 208)
- semiskilled labor (p. 208)
- skilled labor (p. 208)
- professional labor (p. 208)
- market theory of wage determination (p. 209)
- equilibrium wage rate (p. 209)
- theory of negotiated wages (p. 210)
- seniority (p. 210)
- signaling theory (p. 210)
- collective bargaining (p. 211)
- grievance procedure (p. 211)
- mediation (p. 212)
- arbitration (p. 212)
- binding arbitration (p. 212)
- fact-finding (p. 212)
- injunction (p. 212)
- seizure (p. 212)

Academic Vocabulary

- anticipate (p. 211)
- distorted (p. 212)

Reading Strategy

Describing As you read the section, complete a graphic organizer similar to the one below that describes the different ways labor disputes are resolved.

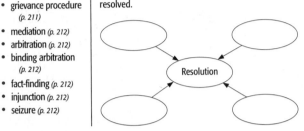

Resolution

ISSUES IN THE NEWS

—National Public Radio

NHL Shakes Off Lockout, Long Layoff

[The] NHL owners took a very hard line with the Player's Association and in the end the players accepted a big salary cut and a per team salary cap. Now the NHL has reduced its spending on players' salaries to about 54 percent of revenue, down from about 75 percent.

[The NHL] says it's going to save up to 400 million dollars. Twice as many teams are going to be in the black. Fans are returning to the rinks, but there's still some operating issues for teams in smaller markets. They're sort of facing a choice, do we lose five or $10 million or do we spend up to the salary cap and compete? ∎

Over the years, many disputes have occurred between labor and management. Sometimes employees take action against their employer, as during the 2005 transit worker strike in New York City that shut down buses and subways. Sometimes the employer takes action against its employees, as during the 2004 National Hockey League (NHL) player lockout that cancelled the professional hockey season for a full year.

Most labor disputes occur over pay and working conditions. If a dispute results in an actual work stoppage, both sides stand to lose enormous sums of money. As a result, and regardless of the reason for the dispute, the deliberations to end it are usually intense. While the NHL was finally able to settle its labor dispute through negotiation, there are other ways to resolve a deadlock.

CHAPTER 8 Employment, Labor, and Wages **207**

Teach

D1 Differentiated Instruction

English Language Learners
List the four categories of labor on the board. Have student pairs write a brief newspaper advertisement for a job in each category. If necessary, brainstorm with students several types of jobs in each skill category. Then have students read and compare their advertisements. **ELL**

D2 Differentiated Instruction

Interpersonal Organize the class into two groups to debate the following: *Should professional athletes, rock singers, and movie stars command high salaries for their labors?* Suggest that students analyze societal values in the debate. **OL**

Economic Analysis

Answer: Because they are highly skilled and low in number, managerial workers can demand higher wages whether or not they belong to a union.

Differentiated Instruction

---

wage rate prevailing pay scale for work performed in an occupation

unskilled labor workers not trained to operate specialized machines and equipment

semiskilled labor workers who operate machines that require a minimum amount of training

skilled labor workers who are trained to operate complex equipment and require little supervision

professional labor workers with a high level of training, education, and managerial skills

📊 Skills Handbook

See page R53 to learn about Comparing Data.

Wage Determination

MAIN Idea Different occupations and levels of training are rewarded with different wages.

Economics & You When you choose an occupation, do you want to earn as much income as possible? Read on to learn how your choices can result in a higher wage.

Most occupations have a **wage rate**, a standard amount of pay given for work performed. Wage rates usually differ from one occupation to the next, and sometimes even within the same occupation. There are four explanations as to why this happens.

Noncompeting Categories of Labor

One explanation recognizes four broad categories of labor that have different levels of knowledge and skills. The highest pay goes to people in jobs that require the most skills and training. Because workers in one category do not compete with those in other categories, wages differ.

The first category is **unskilled labor** and consists of workers in jobs that do not require people with special training and skills. People in these jobs work primarily with their hands at tasks such as picking fruit or mopping floors.

The second category comprises **semiskilled labor**—workers in jobs that require enough mechanical skills to operate machines for which they need a minimum amount of training. These workers may operate basic equipment such as electric floor polishers, cleaning equipment, lawnmowers, and other machines that call for a modest amount of training.

The third category is **skilled labor** and consists of workers who operate complex equipment and perform most of their tasks with little supervision. These workers have a higher investment in education, knowledge, and training. Examples include carpenters, electricians, tool and die makers, computer technicians, and computer programmers.

The final category is **professional labor**, or those individuals that have the highest level of knowledge-based education and managerial skills. Examples include teachers, doctors, scientists, lawyers, and top managers such as corporate executives.

If you examine the occupations shown in **Figure 8.4**, you will see that the income each occupation earns is closely associated with these four categories of labor. For example, semiskilled workers, such as transportation and material movers, generally receive more than unskilled workers in the food-service occupations. Likewise, the professional workers in legal and managerial occupations earn more than any of the other occupations in the figure.

Figure 8.4 ▶ Median Weekly Earnings by Occupation and Union Affiliation

▶ Weekly earnings are significantly higher for workers in highly skilled occupations or with union representation.

Economic Analysis *Why is the earnings gap between union and nonunion workers smaller in managerial occupations than in other occupations?*

Occupation	Represented by unions	Nonunion workers
Legal occupations	$1,147	$1,042
Management occupations	1,137	1,076
Computer and mathematical	1,009	1,141
Education, training, and library	913	710
Protective service occupations	896	568
Transportation and material moving	721	508
Office and administrative support	689	528
Sales and related occupations	623	622
Building and grounds, cleaning, maintenance	528	378
Food preparation and serving related	439	350

Source: Bureau of Labor Statistics, 2006

FREE ENTERPRISE ACTIVITY 13

USING ARBITRATION

Free Enterprise Activities, p. 13

Using Arbitration

Objective: Understand how two parties can use arbitration to arrive at a fair compromise.

Focus: Brainstorm compromises that students have had to make in their everyday lives.

Teach: Have students fill out the activity chart based on the information on the dispute.

Assess: Have students review their answers in pairs.

Close: Ask students how arbitration differs from mediation and from collective bargaining.

Differentiated Instruction Strategies

BL Ask: Which union demands would you be most willing to sacrifice?

AL Have student pairs negotiate demands and offers, with one student as the union and the other as management.

ELL Have students make a graphic organizer showing the steps in labor-management negotiations.

Figure 8.5 ▶ Market Theory of Wage Determination

Graphs In MOtion
See StudentWorks™ Plus or glencoe.com.

▶ The market theory of wage determination explains how the market forces of supply and demand determine the equilibrium wage rate. Panel A shows what happens when a relatively large supply of roofers is coupled with a relatively low level of demand. Panel B shows what happens when a relatively small supply of professional athletes is paired with a relatively high level of demand.

Economic Analysis *How does this theory differ from the theory of negotiated wages?*

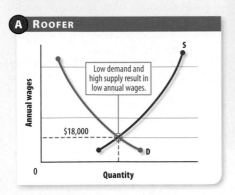

A ROOFER

Low demand and high supply result in low annual wages.

$18,000

B PROFESSIONAL ATHLETES

$1,000,000

High demand and low supply result in high annual wages.

C Critical Thinking

Classifying Call on students to identify different types of jobs, and list their responses on the board. Then ask students to make a three-column chart in their notebooks, using "Jobs," "Labor Category," and "Factors Affecting Supply and Demand" as column headings. Direct students to select 10 jobs from the list and enter them in the first column. In the second column, have them note whether the jobs are unskilled, semiskilled, skilled, or professional. In the third column, have them note what factors might affect how supply and demand determine wages. **OL**

S Skill Practice

Using Line Graphs Have students draw two line graphs showing (1) how the labor supply would change in a highly remote location if very high wages were offered to prospective employees, and (2) how the demand for labor would change in an industrial firm that just invested in robotics. **AL**

Market Theory of Wage Determination

Another explanation for the differences in pay many people receive is based on the **market theory of wage determination.** This theory states that the supply and demand for a worker's skills and services determine the wage or salary.

For example, if there is a low demand for roofers but a relatively large supply, the result would be relatively low wages for roofers. If conditions are reversed, so that the demand is high and supply is low, then wages would be much higher. This describes the market for the services of professional athletes. In this market, a small supply of talent combined with relatively high demand results in higher wages.

You can see this interaction of supply and demand in **Figure 8.5.** In each market, the intersection of supply and demand

determines the **equilibrium wage rate**—the wage rate that leaves neither a surplus nor a shortage in the labor market.

Exceptions to the market theory may appear to exist at certain times. Some unproductive workers may receive high wages because of family ties or political influence. Highly skilled workers may receive low wages because of discrimination based on their race or gender.

market theory of wage determination explanation of wage rates relying on theory of supply and demand

equilibrium wage rate wage rate leaving neither a surplus nor a shortage in the market

Did You Know?

▶ **Million-Dollar Paychecks** The pay for top CEOs reflects the high demand for the best business leaders in the nation. Their base salary actually may not be all that high. Yet CEOs usually pocket a variety of extras, such as retirement benefits, bonuses, stock options, and–for some–tax reimbursements. Add all this together, and total compensation can easily reach into the millions of dollars.

Economic Analysis

Answer: Only a few athletes are good enough to play in professional leagues.

CHAPTER 8 Employment, Labor, and Wages **209**

Leveled Activities

BL Guided Reading Activities, p. 23

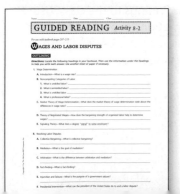

OL Economic Forms and Financial Pages Trans., Strat. and Act., p. 7

AL Economic Cartoons, p. 1

C Critical Thinking

Evaluating Ask: Do you think job seniority should be rewarded with higher wages? Explain. *(Students answering "yes" may cite the greater experience of workers with seniority, while those saying "no" may say that seniority alone does not indicate better job performance.)* **OL**

W Writing Support

Personal Writing Have students write an essay about their career expectations. What role does further education play in their plans? **OL**

Caption Answer: that the person is highly skilled

Caption Answer: a strong union

✓ Reading Check Answer:
market theory: wages set by supply and demand; theory of negotiated wages: set by union negotiations

Additional Support

Teacher Tip

Researching Jobs You might suggest that students visit the Occupational Outlook Handbook at the Bureau of Labor Statistics Web site (www.bls.gov/oco). The handbook provides in-depth information about jobs in the nation.

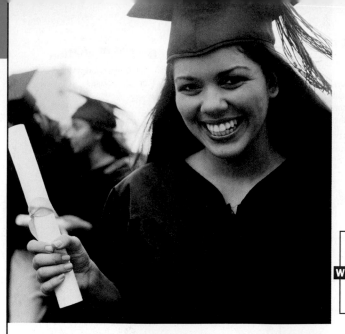

Signaling Theory People who enter the workforce with a college degree can expect higher pay. *What signal does a degree send to a potential employer?*

theory of negotiated wages explanation of wage rates based on the bargaining strength of organized labor

seniority length of time a person has been on a job

signaling theory theory that employers are willing to pay more for people with certificates, diplomas, and other indicators of superior ability

$ Personal Finance Handbook

See pages R16–R19 for more information on education.

Theory of Negotiated Wages

The third approach to wage rate determination recognizes the power of unions. The **theory of negotiated wages** states that the bargaining strength of organized labor is a factor that helps to determine wages. A strong union, for example, may have the power to force higher wages on some firms because the firms would not be able to afford work interruptions in case of a threatened strike.

Figure 8.4 on page 208 helps validate the theory of negotiated wages. With only one exception, the figure shows that workers who are represented by unions receive weekly salaries that are higher than those of nonunion workers.

One important factor for unions is **seniority**—the length of time a person has been on the job. Because of their seniority, some workers receive higher wages than others who perform similar tasks, even if they do not have better skills.

Signaling Theory

The fourth explanation for differences in wage rates is based on **signaling theory**. This theory states that employers are willing to pay more to people with certificates, degrees, and other indicators that "signal" superior knowledge or ability. For example, a sales firm might prefer to hire a college graduate with a major in history than a high school graduate who excelled in business courses. While this may seem odd, some firms view the degree as a signal that the individual possesses the intelligence, perseverance, and maturity to succeed.

You might hear from friends that they did not need their college degree to do the job they currently have—as if their education was not important. They overlook the signaling theory, which helps explain *why* they got the job in the first place.

✓ Reading Check Explaining What is the difference between the market theory of wage determination and the theory of negotiated wages?

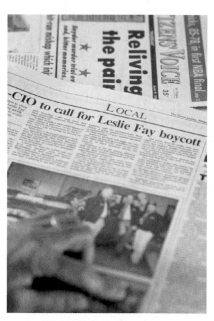

Theory of Negotiated Wages Unions sometimes threaten with a boycott to get wage concessions. *What factor is necessary for effective bargaining?*

Activity: Hands-On Economics

Job Opportunities in the United States Have students work in small groups to investigate job opportunities in the United States. Encourage groups to note the education and training required for each position, starting wage or salary, chances for advancement, and so on, for each position they list. Have groups present their findings to the class. Use these presentations as a starting point for a discussion on the kinds of positions that students might seek in the future. **OL**

Resolving Labor Disputes

MAIN Idea There are a number of different ways to resolve a labor dispute if collective bargaining fails.

Economics & You Have you ever bargained with someone to get something you wanted? Read on to find out how unions do the same thing to get the wages and benefits they want for their workers.

When organized labor negotiates with management, disputes are bound to happen. Both sides can use collective bargaining to minimize such disputes. If this fails, they can turn to mediation, arbitration, fact-finding, injunction and seizure or, in extreme cases, presidential intervention.

Collective Bargaining

Labor-management relations usually require **collective bargaining**—negotiations that take place between labor and management over issues such as pay, working hours, health care coverage, and other job-related matters. During collective bargaining, elected union officials represent workers, and company officials in charge of labor relations represent management. Collective bargaining requires compromise from both parties, and the discussions over issues may go on for months.

If the negotiations are successful, both parties agree on basic issues such as pay, working conditions, and benefits. Because it is difficult to **anticipate** future problems, a **grievance procedure**—a provision for resolving issues that may come up later—may also be included in the final contract.

Normally, union and management are able to reach an agreement because the costs of failure are so high. Workers, for example, still have to make regular payments on car loans and mortgages, and companies don't want to lose customers to other businesses. In short, everyone has a big stake in resolving labor issues.

collective bargaining process of negotiation between union and management representatives over pay, benefits, and job-related matters

grievance procedure provision in a labor contract that outlines how future disputes and disagreements will be resolved

---

CAREERS

Labor Relations Specialist

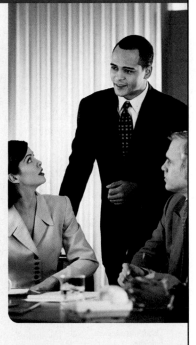

The Work
* Formulate labor policy, oversee industrial labor relations, and negotiate collective bargaining agreements
* Coordinate grievance procedures between unions, workers, and management
* Handle complaints that result from contract disputes

Qualifications
* Knowledge of fair wages and salaries, benefits, pensions, labor law, collective bargaining trends, and union and management practices

* Ability to be patient, fair-minded, and persuasive, and to function under pressure
* College courses in labor law, collective bargaining, labor economics, labor history, and industrial psychology
* Many positions require graduate studies in industrial or labor relations

Earnings
* Median annual earnings: $93,895

Job Growth Outlook
* Faster than average

Source: *Occupational Outlook Handbook, 2006–2007 Edition*

CHAPTER 8   Employment, Labor, and Wages   211

CHAPTER 8, SECTION 2

D Differentiated Instruction

Verbal/Linguistic Have students research a recent strike in your state. Have them note the reasons for the work stoppage, the procedures used to end the dispute, and the resolution. Have students present their findings in the form of a radio news report that lasts two to three minutes. Invite volunteers to "broadcast" their reports to the class. **OL**

R Reading Strategy

Visualizing Review the text on collective bargaining with students. Ensure that students understand that when conflicts arise between labor and management, mediation and arbitration may be used to find compromises. Then ask students to create a flowchart showing the collective bargaining process. Call on volunteers to display and explain their flowcharts. **OL**

Hands-On Chapter Project
Step 2

Going to Work

Step 2: Interviewing for a Job.
Students will role-play a job interview situation.

Directions: Have students organize in pairs, but not the same pairs as in Step 1. Within each pair, have students exchange job advertisements. Then have each student write a series of ten to twenty general questions based on the job advertisement that would help them in interviewing applicants.

Next, have students exchange job applications (or cover letters and résumés). Give them an opportunity to read through the applications and compare them with the advertisement. Then have them revise or add to the general questions they have already written.

Finally, have each pair take turns playing "employer" and "applicant." As "employer," each student will interview his or her partner, using the questions they have

previously prepared. Tell students that they are not limited to their prepared questions but may ask other questions based on what they learn during the interview process. Have "employers" take notes on the interview to use in making their hiring decisions.

Summarizing Have each student write a short paragraph explaining what he or she learned about the interviewing process. **OL**

(Chapter Project continued in Section 3.)

211

R Reading Strategy

Making Connections

Ask: What personal qualities to you think a good labor mediator needs? *(Possible qualities might include honesty, ability to see all sides of an issue, ability to reserve judgment, humor, patience, firmness, ability to communicate clearly, intelligence, ability to meet deadlines and work well under pressure, and flexibility.)* **OL**

W Writing Support

Narrative Writing Have students write two journal entries about a fictional local strike that is about to be settled by binding arbitration. One entry should be from the perspective of a union member. The other entry should be written from the point of view of management. **OL**

Caption Answer: Students will likely say that having a third party mediate the dispute might create better chances for compromise.

Additional Support

"A good negotiator can stand back and gain perspective."

Mediation Mediators need to objectively consider the viewpoints of all involved parties in their decisions **Why would unions and management agree to mediation?**

---

mediation process of resolving a dispute by bringing in a neutral third party

arbitration or binding arbitration agreement by two parties to place a dispute before a third party for a binding settlement

fact-finding agreement between union and management to have a neutral third party collect facts about a dispute and present nonbinding recommendations

injunction court order issued to prevent a company or union from taking action during a labor dispute

seizure temporary government takeover of a company to keep it running during a labor-management dispute

Mediation

One way to resolve differences is through **mediation,** the process of bringing in a neutral third person or persons to help settle a dispute. The mediator's primary goal is to find a solution that both parties will accept. A mediator must be unbiased so that neither party benefits at the expense of the other. If the mediator has the confidence and trust of both parties, he or she will be able to learn what concessions each side is willing to make.

In the end, the mediator recommends a compromise to both sides. Neither side has to accept a mediator's decision, although it often helps break the deadlock.

Arbitration

Another popular way to resolve differences is through **arbitration,** a process in which both sides agree to place their differences before a third party whose decision will be accepted as final. Because both sides must agree to any final decision the arbitrator makes, this type of negotiation is also called **binding arbitration.**

Arbitration is finding its way into areas beyond labor-management relations. Today, for example, most credit card companies require disputes with cardholders to be solved by an arbitrator rather than in the courts. This means that a credit card holder can no longer sue the credit card company in the event of a dispute because the matter goes to arbitration instead.

Fact-Finding

A third way to resolve a dispute is through **fact-finding,** an agreement between union and management to have a neutral third party collect facts about a dispute and present nonbinding recommendations. This process can be especially useful in situations where each side has deliberately **distorted** the issues to win public support, or when one side simply does not believe the claims made by the other side. Neither labor nor management has to accept the recommendations of the fact-finding committee.

Injunction and Seizure

A fourth way to settle labor-management disputes is through injunction or seizure. During a dispute, one of the parties may request an **injunction**—a court order not to act. If issued against a union, the injunction may direct the union not to strike. If issued against a company, it may direct the company not to lock out its workers. In 1995, after professional baseball players ended their strike and went back to work, the owners promptly called a lockout. The players then got an injunction against the owners, and the 1995 baseball season began—but without a labor agreement.

Under extreme circumstances, the government may resort to **seizure**—a temporary takeover of operations—while the government negotiates with the union. This occurred in 1946 when the government seized the bituminous coal industry. While operating the mines, government officials worked out a settlement with the miners' union.

Activity: Collaborative Learning

Role-Playing a Mediation Have students role-play a labor-management dispute that must be mediated. Select three students to act as mediators, and have them research conflict resolution methods used in mediation. Then select six students—three to act as union representatives and three to act as management representatives—and have them draw up opposing positions regarding wages, working conditions, and health benefits. Have the mediators implement a solution acceptable to both labor and management. Have the rest of the class evaluate the effectiveness of the solution, noting what each side lost and gained. **OL**

Presidential Intervention

The president of the United States may enter a labor-management dispute by publicly appealing to both parties to resolve their differences. While rarely used, this can be effective if the appeal has broad public support. The president also can fire federal workers. In 1981 President Ronald Reagan fired striking air traffic controllers because they were federal employees who had gone on strike despite having taken an oath not to do so.

The president also has emergency powers that can be used to end some strikes. When pilots from American Airlines went on strike in 1997 during a peak travel weekend, President Clinton used a 1926 federal law, the Railway Labor Relations Act, to order an end to the strike less than 30 minutes after it began.

✓Reading Check **Summarizing** In what ways can labor and management resolve disputes?

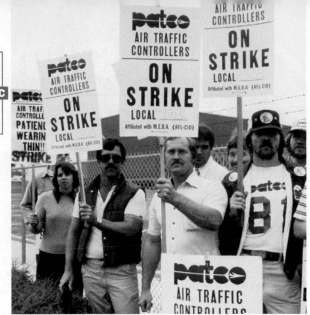

Intervention In 1981 President Reagan replaced striking air traffic controllers. *Why did the president think this step was necessary?*

C **Critical Thinking**

Assessing Have students write a list of criteria that a U.S. president should follow in deciding whether to intervene in a labor-management dispute. **OL**

Caption Answer: because they were federal employees who had taken an oath not to strike

✓Reading Check **Answer:** collective bargaining, mediation, arbitration, fact-finding, injunction and seizure, presidential intervention

Assess

Use the Interactive Tutor Self-Assessment CD-ROM to review Section 2, and then assign the Section 2 Review as homework or as an in-class activity.

Close

Evaluating Ask: Which method of resolving labor disputes is most effective? Why? **OL**

SECTION 2 Review

Vocabulary

1. **Explain** the significance of wage rate, unskilled labor, semiskilled labor, skilled labor, professional labor, market theory of wage determination, equilibrium wage rate, theory of negotiated wages, seniority, signaling theory, collective bargaining, grievance procedure, mediation, arbitration, binding arbitration, fact-finding, injunction, and seizure.

Main Ideas

2. **Describing** Use a graphic organizer like the one below to describe the four approaches to wage determination.

Method	Characteristics
Skill level	
Market theory	
Negotiated theory	
Signaling theory	

3. **Discussing** How do mediation, arbitration, and fact-finding differ from other ways to resolve labor disputes?

Critical Thinking

4. **The BIG Idea** How does the market theory of wage determination reflect the forces of supply and demand?

5. **Sequencing Information** If you represented a company during a collective bargaining session, and if negotiations were deadlocked, what course of action would you recommend? Why?

6. **Interpreting** If you were a semiskilled worker, what could you do to move into a higher category of noncompeting labor?

7. **Analyzing Visuals** Look at Figure 8.5 on page 209. The graphs show wage determination based on demand and supply. What might the demand and supply curves look like for a lawyer or for a person working in a fast-food restaurant?

Applying Economics

8. **Signaling Theory** Look at some help-wanted ads in your local paper. What criteria do they often specify, and how do these criteria relate to signaling theory?

CHAPTER 8 Employment, Labor, and Wages 213

Review SECTION 2

Answers

1. All definitions can be found in the section and the Glossary.
2. **Skill level:** lowest to highest pay: unskilled, semiskilled, skilled, professional.
   Traditional: supply and demand for worker's skills determine wages.
   Negotiated: organized labor's bargaining strength helps determine wages.
   Signaling: employers pay more for workers with certificates, diplomas, degrees, and other indicators that signal superior ability.

3. The parties are aided by a third party who helps them reach a compromise; in injunction and seizure and presidential intervention, a solution is imposed from outside.
4. The higher the demand and the lower the supply of labor, the higher the wages.
5. Answers will vary but should discuss negotiation and compromise.
6. **Possible answer:** Complete additional training and/or education.

7. The curve for a lawyer would likely resemble the one for the professional athlete, with high demand and lower supply, while the curve for a fast-food worker would resemble the one for the roofer, with low demand and high supply.
8. Answers will vary but may include such criteria as high school diplomas, associate's or bachelor's degrees, or other forms of technical certification and credentialing.

Focus

C Critical Thinking

Evaluating Ask: Do you think satisfied workers are more productive than those who are unhappy? Explain. *(Possible answer: Yes; they are more motivated to do well.)* **OL**

Teach

W Writing Support

Personal Writing

Have students write an essay explaining what policies and factors they think would make a company a good place to work. **OL**

Analyzing the Impact

Answers:

1. The company called on employees to provide leadership, take responsibility, and use their ingenuity to produce a better product.
2. Answers will vary but should be supported with logic.

Additional Support

CASE STUDY
Harley-Davidson

Revving It Up

Since its founding in 1903, Harley-Davidson Motor Company has survived wartime economies, the Great Depression, overseas competition from Japanese manufacturers, and in 1985 the threat of bankruptcy. When it went public in 1986, a new era began. Harley tackled problems of global competition and the need for U.S. expansion. More importantly, it broke away from the adversarial model of management versus union by creating a "circle organization based around the core processes at Harley—create demand, produce product, and provide support."

Partners in Business

C Harley-Davidson's unique partnership style of management allied with labor was labeled the High Performance Work Organization (HPWO). The strategy minimizes red tape and calls on employees for leadership, responsibility, and ingenuity. Workers provide input at every stage of the manufacturing process.

The absence of the "us against them" mentality so often found in labor relations—coupled with a true sense of ownership by unionized workers—has motivated Harley employees to work toward a common goal. In addition, the process has lowered the company's costs, allowing it to create new jobs and expand operations.

Happy Workers, Humming Hogs

W The HPWO is paying off for the motorcycle manufacturer, which in 2004 was named one of America's "100 Best Places to Work" by *Fortune* magazine. Employees and shareholders alike have cause for celebration. Since its turnaround in 1986, the company has experienced tremendous growth and reaped impressive profits. Harley-Davidson now sells motorcycles in over 60 countries. In 2006 it opened its first retail store in China. Now Chinese bikers donned in leather can buy a true American icon. Bandana sold separately.

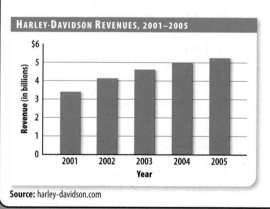

HARLEY-DAVIDSON REVENUES, 2001–2005

Revenue (in billions), by Year:
- 2001: ~3.4
- 2002: ~4.1
- 2003: ~4.6
- 2004: ~5.0
- 2005: ~5.2

Source: harley-davidson.com

Analyzing the Impact

1. **Summarizing** What change in business practices helped Harley-Davidson boost production and profits?
2. **Drawing Conclusions** Harley-Davidson also made a commitment to using only U.S. workers and parts suppliers. How might this commitment help or hinder the company? Explain.

Extending the Content

Bumps in the Road at Harley-Davidson

In spite of Harley-Davidson's HPWO management strategy, economic tensions can still lead to occasional rough rides for the "Hog" manufacturer. A strike at the company's York, Pennsylvania, plant idled production for three weeks in February 2007. The agreement that settled the strike called for a two-tiered wage system, in which new employees will be paid less than long-term employees, reaching parity after a few years. Employees will also pay more toward their own pension plans, with the company paying less. These changes are balanced by higher wages. Said a union spokesperson, "There is a time for sharing sacrifices and a time for sharing success." Over four years of record-breaking profitability at Harley-Davidson led union workers to check their watches.

SECTION 3
Employment Trends and Issues

GUIDE TO READING

Section Preview

In this section, you will learn that important employment issues include union decline, unequal pay, and the minimum wage.

Content Vocabulary

- giveback (p. 217)
- two-tier wage system (p. 217)
- glass ceiling (p. 219)
- set-aside contract (p. 219)
- minimum wage (p. 219)
- current dollars (p. 219)
- constant dollars (p. 221)
- real dollars (p. 221)
- base year (p. 221)

Academic Vocabulary

- trend (p. 216)
- equivalent (p. 219)

Reading Strategy

Explaining As you read the section, complete a graphic organizer similar to the one below to explain why women face an income gap.

```
            Lower pay for
               women
   ( )           ( )           ( )
               ( )
```

Focus

Bellringer
Daily Focus Transparency 41

GUIDE TO READING

Answers to Graphic: differences in skills and experiences; fewer women in higher-paying jobs and more in low-paying jobs; discrimination and the glass ceiling

ISSUES IN THE NEWS
—The Oregonian

Foreign Exchange at Minimum Wage

Four decades ago . . . Congress created a student exchange program intended to burnish America's worldwide reputation. The idea was simple: College students would visit for a few months, take a job, and return to their native lands imbued with affection for the red, white and blue.

Today, that initiative [is] a source of cheap labor for hotels, ski resorts and restaurants. Mt. Bachelor hired 30 exchange students from Peru for the winter, paying them $7.50 an hour. Timberline Lodge, at Mount Hood, employed 20 students from Chile and also paid them the Oregon minimum wage.

The tourism industry says it needs the cheap work force to keep prices down. In [such a] tight labor market, . . . the lures of a free ski pass and minimum wage are no longer enough for local ski bums, who can find longer-term jobs for better wages in town. ■

Important issues abound in today's labor market. While some workers are faced with layoffs when factories close, other industries have problems filling all their available jobs. This is especially true for those positions that pay only federal or state minimum wages, such as some of the resort jobs in the news story.

Difficulties in finding enough qualified workers to fill temporary jobs at the minimum wage is just one issue facing the national economy. Workers have seen a decline of unions, which limits their ability to influence wages, while women have to deal with differences in pay in the labor market.

CHAPTER 8 Employment, Labor, and Wages **215**

Resource Manager

R Reading Strategies	**C** Critical Thinking	**D** Differentiated Instruction	**W** Writing Support	**S** Skill Practice
Teacher Edition • Predicting, p. 217 • Making Connections, p. 221 **Additional Resources** • Guid. Read. Act., p. 24 • Read. Ess. & Note-Taking Guide, p. 70 • Pri./Sec. Source Read., pp. 3, 25	**Teacher Edition** • Designing, p. 218 • Evaluating, pp. 219, 227 **Additional Resources** • Econ. Concepts Trans., Strat. & Act., p. 19	**Teacher Edition** • ELL, p. 216 • Visual/Spatial, p. 222 **Additional Resources** • Enrichment Act., p. 8 • Crit. Think. Act., p. 8 • Reinforcing Econ. Skills, p. 5	**Teacher Edition** • Narrative Writing, p. 217 • Personal Writing, p. 218 • Persuasive Writing, p. 219 • Expository Writing, p. 226 **Additional Resources** • Writer's Guidebook • Reading and Study Skills Fold., p. 55	**Teacher Edition** • Using Line Graphs, p. 216 • Using Bar and Circle Graphs, p. 220 **Additional Resources** • Daily Focus Trans. 39, 41 • Personal Finance Act., p. 13

Teach

D Differentiated Instruction

English Language Learners

Have students create a cause-and-effect graphic organizer that explains the reasons for the decline in union membership. *(Causes that explain the effect—falling union influence—should include antiunion activities by management, more women and teenagers in the labor force, and rising prices of union-made goods.)* **ELL**

S Skill Practice

Using Line Graphs Ask: What other kinds of graphs could illustrate information about union membership? *(Possible answers: Circle graphs could show percentages of total workers who are unionized at different times. A bar graph could show total union membership over time or in different fields.)* **OL**

Economic Analysis

Answer: It has continued to fall.

Additional Support

Skills Handbook

See page **R36** to learn about determining **Cause and Effect.**

Decline of Union Influence

MAIN Idea Labor unions have been losing their influence and power ever since the 1940s.

Economics & You You learned earlier about the rise of unions. Read on to learn about the decline of unions today.

A significant **trend** in today's economy is the decline in union membership and influence. As **Figure 8.6** shows, 35.5 percent of nonfarm workers were union members in 1945. This number has dropped since then to about 12.5 percent by 2006.

D Reasons for Decline

Several reasons account for this decline. The first is that many employers have made a determined effort to keep unions out of their businesses. Some companies hire consultants to map out legal strategies to fight unions. Others try to head off the formation of a union by making workers part of the management team, adding employees to the board of directors, or setting up profit-sharing plans to reward employees.

A second reason for union decline is that new additions to the labor force—especially women and teenagers—traditionally have had little loyalty to organized labor. In addition, more Americans are working in part-time jobs to help make ends meet. People who work a second job have less time to join or even support a union.

Perhaps the most important reason is that unions are the victims of their own success. When union wages are higher than those of nonunion workers, union-made products become more expensive than those of foreign and nonunion producers.

Renegotiating Union Wages

Because unions have generally kept their wages above those of nonunion workers, union wages have been under pressure to come down. In fact, in recent years, there have been almost as many news reports of

Figure 8.6 ▶ Union Membership

Source: Bureau of Labor Statistics, 2005

▶ Union membership grew rapidly after 1933 and peaked at 35.5 percent in 1945.

Economic Analysis *How would you describe the trend of union membership during the last decade?*

Activity: Collaborative Learning

Union Recruiting Inform students that in recent years, the AFL-CIO and its affiliated unions have made great efforts to recruit new members. Organize students into several groups, and have groups research how union recruiting methods have changed recently. Suggest that groups consider such questions as the following:

- Have unions increased spending on recruiting? If so, by how much?
- Do unions use different recruiting tactics than they did in the past?
- Are unions aiming recruiting drives at different segments of the working population than they did in the past?

Direct groups to use library resources and the Internet in their research. If possible, they might also interview union representatives. Have groups present their findings in oral reports. **OL**

Figure 8.7 ► Gender and Income

► Over the years, the income earned by females has been only a fraction of that earned by males.

Economic Analysis *When did median female income first reach 70 percent of male median income?*

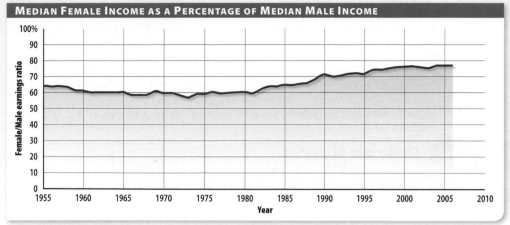

MEDIAN FEMALE INCOME AS A PERCENTAGE OF MEDIAN MALE INCOME

Source: Bureau of Labor Statistics, 2006

unions fighting to maintain wage levels as there were reports of union wages rising.

One way employers have been able to reduce union wages is by asking for give-backs from union workers. A **giveback** is a wage, fringe benefit, or work rule given up when a labor contract is renegotiated.

Some companies were able to get rid of labor contracts by claiming bankruptcy. If a company can show that wages and fringe benefits contributed significantly to its problems, federal bankruptcy courts usually allow management to terminate union contracts and establish lower wage scales.

Another way to reduce union salary scales is with a **two-tier wage system**—a system that keeps high wages for current workers, but has a lower wage for newly hired workers. This practice is becoming widespread and often has union approval.

✓ Reading Check **Identifying** Why do successful unions create problems for themselves?

Lower Pay for Women

MAIN Idea Men are generally paid more than women because of differences in skills, the types of jobs they choose, and discrimination.

Economics & You Are you or anyone in your family concerned about a job for which men are paid more than women? Read to find out about laws that will help correct the situation.

Overall, women face a substantial gap between their income and the income received by men. As **Figure 8.7** shows, female income has been only a fraction of male income over a 50-year period.

Human Capital Differences

About one-third of the male-female income gap is due to differences in the skills and experience that women bring to the labor market. For example, women tend to drop out of the labor force to raise families more often than men. Working women also

giveback wage, fringe benefit, or work rule given up when renegotiating a contract

two-tier wage system wage scale paying newer workers a lower wage than others already on the job

W

R

CHAPTER 8 **Employment, Labor, and Wages** 217

W Writing Support

Narrative Writing Instruct students to write and then perform for the class a dialogue between two unionized workers. The workers might be discussing a proposed giveback, a company bankruptcy, or a two-tier wage system. Have students research their topic, consider how two workers might feel about it, and then write and perform their dialogues. **AL**

R Reading Strategy

Predicting Ask: What do you think are some reasons why women have received lower pay than men? *(Possible answers: because they have children; some have less education or experience; discrimination)* Have students look for more reasons as they read the subsection. **OL**

Economic Analysis
Answer: 1990

✓ Reading Check Answer: by making the goods they produce more expensive than nonunion goods

Additional Support

Activity: Technology Connection

Jobs for Women Have students use an Internet search engine to create a report on jobs that experts feel will offer good advancement prospects for women over the coming years. Point out that reliable sites will include those sponsored by government agencies, colleges and universities, foundations, and professional and educational organizations. Have students share their reports and discuss issues that arise. Conclude the activity by asking students why these particular jobs are considered promising for women and whether they agree with the experts on their choices. **OL**

C Critical Thinking

Designing **Ask:** How could companies raise the number of women in higher-paying occupations such as construction and engineering? *(Possible answer: provide day care and family leave opportunities)* **OL**

W Writing Support

Personal Writing Share with students this quotation from Congresswoman Shirley Chisholm, the first African American woman in Congress and the first woman to run for president: "I've always met more discrimination being a woman than being black." Have students write a paragraph responding to this quotation. Then have them write which form of discrimination they feel is closer to being eliminated from our society and why. **AL**

Economic Analysis

Answer: personal care and service; office and administrative support; education, training, and library; health care practitioner and technical; community and social services

tend to have lower levels of education than their male counterparts. If these two factors—experience and education—were the same for men and women, about one-third of the wage gap would disappear.

Gender and Occupation

Slightly less than one-third of the wage gap is due to the uneven distribution of men and women among various occupations. For example, more men work in higher-paying construction and engineering trades than women. Likewise, more women work in lower-paying household service and office occupations than men.

The distribution of men and women in various occupations as reported by the Bureau of Labor Statistics is shown in **Figure 8.8.** As long as construction and engineering wages are higher than personal care and office worker wages, on average, men will earn more than women.

Discrimination

Finally, slightly more than one-third of the gap cannot be explained by specific reasons. Economists attribute this portion of differences in income to discrimination that women face in the labor market. In fact, women and minorities often encounter difficulties in getting raises and promotions

Figure 8.8 ▶ **Gender and Occupation**

DISTRIBUTION OF WOMEN AND MEN BY OCCUPATION

Source: Bureau of Labor Statistics, 2006

▶ One of the reasons for the difference in pay between men and women is their uneven distribution among occupations.

Economic Analysis *In which occupations do women make up between 60 and 80 percent of the workforce?*

Differentiated Instruction

ACTIVITY 4

PROFILING YOUR COMMUNITY'S LABOR FORCE

Hands-On Economics, p. 14

Profiling Your Community's Labor Force

Objective: Understand the composition of the community's labor force.

Focus/Teach: Ask students to name broad categories of labor (such as education or health care) that employ large numbers of local workers. Then have students complete the activity.

Assess: Discuss any discrepancies between students' surveys and the national and local profiles.

Close: Have students share their conclusions.

Differentiated Instruction Strategies

BL Have students produce a written summary of their completed graphs.

AL Ask students to write a paragraph explaining how entrepreneurs might benefit from knowing their community's labor profile.

ELL Have students write and practice a script for interviewing residents.

that are like reaching a **glass ceiling**—an invisible barrier that obstructs their advancement up the corporate ladder.

Legal Remedies

Two federal laws are designed to fight wage and salary discrimination. The first is the Equal Pay Act of 1963, which prohibits wage and salary discrimination for jobs that require **equivalent** skills and responsibilities. This act applies only to men and women who work at the same job in the same business establishment.

The second law is the Civil Rights Act of 1964. Title VII of this act prohibits discrimination in all areas of employment on the basis of gender, race, color, religion, and national origin. The law applies to employers with 15 or more workers.

The Civil Rights Act also set up the Equal Employment Opportunity Commission (EEOC). The EEOC investigates charges of discrimination, issues guidelines and regulations, conducts hearings, and collects statistics. The government can sue companies that show patterns of discrimination.

Market Remedies

Another way to overcome unfair hiring practices is by reserving some market activity for minority groups. One example is the government **set-aside contract,** a guaranteed contract reserved for a targeted group. The federal government, for example, requires that a certain percentage of defense contracts be reserved exclusively for minority-owned businesses. Some state governments do the same for state contracts. **C**

Many set-aside programs include a "graduation" clause that "promotes" minority-owned businesses out of the program once they reach a certain size or have received set-aside contracts for a certain number of years. Such limits are set because the program is intended to give these firms an initial boost, not a permanent subsidy.

✓**Reading Check** Synthesizing What are similarities between the Equal Pay Act and set-aside contracts?

The Minimum Wage

MAIN Idea The minimum wage has lost purchasing power over time because it was fixed at $5.15 while prices were rising.

Economics and You Have you or any of your friends ever had a job that paid exactly $5.15 an hour? Read on to learn why this wage does not buy as much as it did in the past.

The **minimum wage**—the lowest wage that can be paid by law to most workers—was intended to prevent the exploitation of workers and to provide some degree of equity and security to those who lacked the skills needed to earn a decent income. First set at $.25 per hour in 1939, the minimum wage increased to $5.15 by 1997.

Debate Over the Minimum Wage

The minimum wage has always been controversial. Supporters of the minimum wage argue that the objectives of equity and security are consistent with U.S. economic goals. Besides, the wage is not very high in the first place. Opponents object to it on the grounds of economic freedom, another economic goal. This group also believes that the wage discriminates against young people and is one of the reasons that many teenagers cannot find jobs.

Some parts of the country have instituted their own equivalent of a minimum wage. For example, the "living wage" of Los Angeles is substantially higher than the federal minimum wage. Any company doing business with the city is required to pay its workers at least that amount. **W**

Current Dollars

Panel A in **Figure 8.9** on the following page illustrates the minimum wage in **current dollars,** or dollars not adjusted for inflation, from 1939 to 2006. In this view the minimum wage appears to have increased dramatically over time. However, the figure does not account for inflation, which erodes the purchasing power of the minimum wage.

glass ceiling seemingly invisible barrier hindering advancement of women and minorities in a male-dominated organization

set-aside contract guaranteed contract or portion of a contract reserved for a targeted group, usually a minority

minimum wage lowest legal wage that can be paid to most workers (*also see page 58*)

current dollars dollar amounts or prices that are not adjusted for inflation

CHAPTER 8 Employment, Labor, and Wages 219

C Critical Thinking

Evaluating Have students write a response to this question: *Do you think it is right for a minority-owned business to receive a contract to do business, even if a non-minority-owned company could do the same work for less money?* Have students justify their answers. *(Answers will vary but should be well supported.)* **OL**

W Writing Support

Persuasive Writing Have students write a letter to a city official on the subject of a "living wage." Have them take and support a position on whether or not your community should adopt one. Have volunteers read their letters to the class. **OL**

✓**Reading Check** **Answer:** Both are designed to favor underrepresented groups in the economy, and both are enforced by government.

Leveled Activities

S Skill Practice

Using Bar and Circle Graphs

Ask: Why has the minimum wage adjusted for inflation dropped since 1997, even though the minimum wage has remained at $5.15 an hour? *(Because prices have risen over this time period, the purchasing power of the minimum wage has declined.)* In what year would you have wanted to be earning the minimum wage? Why? *(Most students will choose 1968 because the minimum wage adjusted for inflation and as a percentage of average manufacturing wage was at its highest level.)* OL

Economic Analysis

Answer: It ranges between 30 and 50 percent of the average manufacturing wage and is currently at about 30 percent.

Figure 8.9 ▶ **The Minimum Wage**

Graphs In MOtion
See StudentWorks™ Plus or glencoe.com.

▶ The minimum wage is expressed in current dollars in Panel A, adjusted for inflation in Panel B, and as a percentage of the average wage for workers in manufacturing in Panel C. The minimum wage has been fixed at $5.15 since 1997.

Economic Analysis *How does the minimum wage compare to average manufacturing wages?*

A THE MINIMUM WAGE IN CURRENT DOLLARS

B THE MINIMUM WAGE ADJUSTED FOR INFLATION

C THE MINIMUM WAGE AS A PERCENTAGE OF THE AVERAGE MANUFACTURING WAGE

Sources: *Statistical Abstract of the United States; Economic Report of the President,* various issues

220   UNIT 3   Economic Institutions and Issues

Hands-On Chapter Project

Step 3

Going to Work

Step 3: Negotiating and Hiring. Students will role-play the negotiating and hiring process.

Directions: Using the notes they took on the interviews they conducted in Step 2, have each student write a letter as an "employer" to the person he or she interviewed. Students' letters should indicate whether they would hire the students who applied for the jobs. If they are hiring, they should offer terms of employment. If they do not think that the applicant would make a suitable employee, they should state why, but list conditions under which they would be prepared to hire the "applicant" for a probationary period of six months. Have them give the letters to the "applicants" they interviewed in Step 2.

Then have each student "applicant" respond to the letter from the prospective "employers." They may either agree to the terms, turn down the offer, or counter with terms of their own. OL

(Chapter Project continued in Visual Summary.)

Inflation

To compensate for inflation, economists like to use **real** or **constant dollars**—dollars that are adjusted in a way that removes the distortion of inflation. This involves the use of a **base year**—a year that serves as a comparison for all other years.

Although the computations are complex, the results are not. **Panel B,** using constant base-year prices, shows that the minimum wage had relatively more purchasing power in 1968 than in any other year. As long as the base year serves as a common denominator for comparison purposes, the results would be the same regardless of the base year used.

Panel B also shows that the purchasing power of the minimum wage goes up whenever the wage increases faster than inflation. This was the case in 1997, when the wage was increased to $5.15. However, the minimum wage remained the same through 2006 while prices went up during the same time period. This means that the wage actually purchased a little less each year. As long as the minimum wage remains unchanged and inflation continues, the purchasing power of the wage will continue to decline.

Manufacturing Wages

Panel C shows the minimum wage as a percentage of the average manufacturing wage. In 1968, for example, the minimum wage was $1.60 and the average manufacturing wage $3.01, or 53.2 percent of the manufacturing wage for that year. The ratio peaked in 1968 and then slowly declined. As long as the minimum wage stays fixed and manufacturing wages go up, this ratio will continue to decline.

The minimum wage will certainly be raised again. What is not certain is when this will happen. When the minimum wage becomes unacceptably low to voters and their elected officials, Congress will increase it. Some people even want to link the minimum wage to inflation, so that the wage will automatically rise when prices rise.

✓**Reading Check** **Summarizing** What is the difference between current dollars and real dollars?

real dollars or constant dollars dollar amounts or prices that have been adjusted for inflation

base year year serving as point of comparison for other years in a price index or other statistical measure

R Reading Strategy
Making Connections Point out that wages often include fringe benefits, such as paid vacation time. Organize students into groups, and have each group write to the human resources department of a local company to discover what fringe benefits it offers. As a class, compare students' findings. **OL**

✓**Reading Check** **Answer:**
Current dollars are not adjusted for inflation; real dollars are adjusted in a way that removes the distortion of inflation.

Assess

🔘 Use the Interactive Tutor Self-Assessment CD-ROM to review Section 3, and then assign the Section 3 Review as homework or as an in-class activity.

Close

Predicting Ask students to predict the major employment trends of the next 25 years and their effects. **OL**

Review **SECTION 3**

SECTION 3 Review

Vocabulary

1. **Explain** the significance of giveback, two-tier wage system, glass ceiling, set-aside contract, minimum wage, current dollars, real or constant dollars, and base year.

Main Ideas

2. **Listing** List three ways firms renegotiate union contracts by using a graphic organizer like the one below.

Renegotiating Union Contracts	
Givebacks	

3. **Identifying** What are the reasons for the income gap between men and women?

4. **Explaining** Why is it necessary to consider inflation when examining the minimum wage?

Critical Thinking

5. **The BIG Idea** Have labor unions outlived their usefulness? Why or why not?

6. **Synthesizing Information** A number of arguments exist both in favor of and against having a minimum wage. With which side do you agree? Why? Explain your answer in a brief paragraph.

7. **Analyzing Visuals** Look at Figure 8.9 on page 220. When was the purchasing power of the minimum wage highest? When was it lowest?

Applying Economics

8. **Minimum Wage** Search the employment ads in your local or regional newspaper and list at least five jobs for which you qualify. Include the advertised salary for each job. Explain why each wage is higher, lower, or the same as the current federal minimum wage.

CHAPTER 8   Employment, Labor, and Wages   **221**

Answers

1. All definitions can be found in the section and the Glossary.
2. **Givebacks:** to protect jobs, unions give up a wage, fringe benefits, or work rule. **Two-tier wage system:** pays newly hired workers a lower wage than others already on the job. **Claiming bankruptcy:** courts allow management to terminate union contracts and establish lower wage scales.

3. differences in human capital (skills and experience); prevalence of women in lower-paying jobs and lack of them in higher-paying jobs; discrimination
4. It is necessary to consider inflation because of the loss of purchasing power.
5. Answers will vary but should be supported by logic and sound economic reasoning.

6. Answers will vary but should reflect an understanding of the minimum wage.
7. 1968; 1944
8. Answers will vary but should demonstrate an understanding of the minimum wage and factors that affect pay rates.

Teach

D Differentiated Instruction

Visual/Spatial Point out that the U.S. labor force has undergone many changes, including "what it takes" to compete in a world economy. Have students research and write an illustrated paper on how new technologies have impacted manufacturing's skilled labor force, such as that represented by the UAW. **OL**

BusinessWeek *ONLINE*

To find up-to-date news and analysis on the economy, business, technology, markets, entrepreneurs, investments, and finance, have students search feature articles and special reports on the BusinessWeek Web site, www.businessweek.com.

Examining the Newsclip

Answers:
1. wages and benefits for workers and retirees
2. Cars can be produced for less in other countries.

Additional Support

BusinessWeek NEWSCLIP

For more than a century, unions have fought hard for benefits many workers today take for granted—an 8-hour workday, paid vacations, and health care insurance. Unions, however, have now declined in both membership and influence.

Twilight of the UAW

For more than two decades, the United Auto Workers (UAW) has grudgingly allowed Detroit carmakers to slash jobs as they have struggled to keep pace with the onslaught from foreign rivals. That's what UAW President Ron Gettelfinger agreed to when he signed off on General Motors Corp.'s buyout of more than 40,000 jobs at the No. 1 carmaker and its former parts unit, bankrupt Delphi Corp. Where the union has always drawn the line is on bedrock issues: wages and benefits for workers and retirees.

This time, though, that line won't hold. GM's buyouts are the beginning, not the end, of the concessions the union will have to make over the next few years. . . .

What's going on is nothing less than the slow death of what was once the country's most powerful industrial union. Despite years of relentless global pressure, the UAW has been able to maintain some of the best blue-collar posts in the U.S.

D But like lumbering GM itself, the union failed to realize what it would take to compete in a world

economy. In the 1980s and 1990s, it fought concessions that would have helped U.S. carmakers fend off imports. . . . Like GM and Ford, it's paying the price today. . . .

The UAW's setbacks highlight a broader challenge faced by blue-collar America. Just as union bargaining muscle helped make the middle class, so too does its weakening signal the stiffer barriers less-skilled workers face in today's globalized economy. . . .

There's another buzzsaw coming: cars from China. Every big automaker is expanding production in the Chinese market, and analysts expect most to start exporting vehicles to the U.S. in a few years.

—Reprinted from *BusinessWeek*

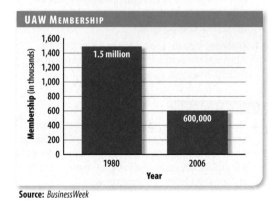

UAW MEMBERSHIP

Membership (in thousands)

- 1980: 1.5 million
- 2006: 600,000

Year

Source: *BusinessWeek*

222   UNIT 3   Economic Institutions and Issues

Examining the Newsclip

1. **Summarizing** On what two issues did the UAW refuse to negotiate in the past?
2. **Determining Cause and Effect** How has globalization led to the decline of the UAW?

Activity: Hands-On Economics

Unions in the Community Have students find out what local unions are active in your community. Have them conduct research to find out what national (or international) unions and federation(s) the local unions are affiliated with, and then make organizational charts for

them. Students should list the federation(s) at the top, the national (or international) unions in the middle, and the locals at the bottom. Have students compare their charts and then draw conclusions about labor in your community. **OL**

Visual Summary

▶ **Wage Determination** Wage rates can be explained in three ways. The market theory of wage determination relies on the tools of supply and demand. The theory of negotiated wages recognizes the influence of unions in bargaining for higher wages. The signaling theory states that employers are willing to pay higher wages to people with diplomas and other signals of ability.

MARKET THEORY OF WAGE DETERMINATION

Low demand and high supply result in low annual wages.

$18,000

Annual wages

Quantity

▶ **Labor Dispute Resolution** Union and management representatives can use several strategies to resolve deadlocks when collective bargaining fails.

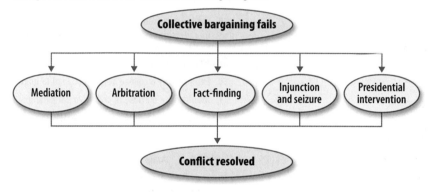

Collective bargaining fails

Mediation | Arbitration | Fact-finding | Injunction and seizure | Presidential intervention

Conflict resolved

▶ **Employment Issues** Current labor issues include the loss of influence and power since the 1940s, the wage gap between women and men, and the minimum wage and its purchasing power.

Employment Trends and Issues

Decline of unions since the 1940s | Wage gap and glass ceiling for women and minorities | Decline in purchasing power of the minimum wage

Interpersonal Organize the class into small groups. Tell them to imagine that they are union organizers trying to increase membership. Have each group come up with a campaign to attract new members. Their campaigns may consist of television advertisements (for which students should write scripts and create story boards), brochures, posters, and editorials. Have each group present its campaign to the class. **OL**

Analyzing Visuals Have students look at the cartoon on page 18 of *Economic Cartoons* and answer the questions below it. **Ask:** Why do you think women typically make less money for doing the same work as men? Write students' answers on the board. Then have them conduct research to find out in which lines of work men's and women's wages are most equal and in which lines of work they are most unequal. Guide students in a discussion of the possible reasons and what can be done to ensure that people are paid equally for equal work, regardless of gender. **OL**

Hands-On Chapter Project

Step 4: Wrap Up

Going to Work

Step 4: Putting It Together. Students will synthesize what they learned in Steps 1–3.

Directions: Tell students that upon being hired, one of the first things they will have to do is fill out paperwork such as a W-4 form for taxes. They may also have to fill out forms for health and life insurance, as well as forms for a retirement plan—either a pension system or 401(k) plan. Obtain copies of W-4 forms and walk students through the process of filling them out.

Summarizing Have each student write a brief essay telling what he or she learned about the process of applying for a job—from the point of view of the applicant and from the point of view of the employer. Then have students reunite with their partners from Step 2 and put together a folder of their job application materials and letters, with both students' names on the folders. **OL**

Assessment & Activities

ExamView®
Assessment Suite

This easy-to-use software includes extensive question banks and allows you to create fully customized tests that can be administered in print or online.

Review Content Vocabulary

1. pro-union	2. pro-union
3. antiunion	4. pro-union
5. neither	6. antiunion
7. neither	8. antiunion
9. neither	10. antiunion
11. antiunion	12. pro-union
13. antiunion	14. pro-union
15. pro-union	16. neither
17. neither	18. neither
19. pro-union	20. neither

Review Academic Vocabulary

21.–26. Students' sentences will vary but should demonstrate understanding of each term's meaning in an economic context.

Review the Main Ideas

27. **Possible answers:** organized to demand higher pay for skilled workers; growth in number of workers at manufacturing facilities where working conditions were difficult; change in public attitudes toward unions

28. **Employers:** fought unions by calling lockouts, hiring new workers to replace strikers, setting up company unions, or ending strikes with violence. **Supreme Court:** showed unfavorable attitude toward unions through antilabor decisions.

29. Membership is low and uneven by demographic group, state, and place of work.

Review Content Vocabulary

Classify each of the terms below as pro-union, antiunion, or neither.

1. boycott
2. closed shop
3. company union
4. seniority
5. fact-finding
6. giveback
7. grievance procedure
8. lockout
9. modified union shop
10. seizure
11. injunction
12. picket
13. right-to-work law
14. agency shop
15. strike
16. two-tier wage system
17. arbitration
18. mediation
19. theory of negotiated wages
20. signaling theory

Review Academic Vocabulary

Use each of these words in a sentence that reflects the word's meaning in the chapter. Then create a word search puzzle using the sentences—without the word—as clues.

21. legislation	24. distort
22. prohibit	25. trend
23. anticipate	26. equivalent

Review the Main Ideas

Section 1 *(pages 197–205)*

27. **Describe** several reasons for the rise of unions prior to 1930.

28. **Identify** the effects of union activities during the post–Civil War period by using a graphic organizer similar to the one below.

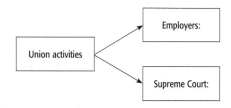

29. **Describe** current union influence in terms of membership and workers represented by unions.

Section 2 *(pages 207–213)*

30. **Explain** why a college degree can lead to higher wages.

31. **Identify** the purpose of collective bargaining.

32. **List** the approaches to resolving a deadlock between a union and a company's management.

Section 3 *(pages 215–221)*

33. **Explain** why men and women are said to have "human capital" differences.

34. **Describe** two corrective measures being taken to close the income gap between men and women workers.

35. **Identify** the original intent of the minimum wage.

Critical Thinking

36. **The BIG Idea** Unions generally argue that the best interests of workers can be served when employees are members of a union. Do you agree or disagree with this statement? Defend your answer.

30. Companies look at it as a signal of intelligence and maturity.

31. to negotiate with management over pay, benefits, and other job-related matters

32. collective bargaining, arbitration, mediation, fact-finding, injunction and seizure, and presidential intervention

33. Women tend to drop out of the labor force to raise families and tend to have lower levels of education.

34. The legal remedy outlaws wage and salary discrimination for jobs requiring equivalent skills and responsibilities. The market remedy reserves some hiring and contracts for minority groups.

35. to prevent the outright exploitation of workers and to provide some degree of equity and security to those who lacked the skills needed to earn a decent income

Critical Thinking

36. Answers will vary but should demonstrate knowledge of union goals.

Economics ONLINE Self-Check Quiz Visit the *Economics: Principles and Practices* Web site at glencoe.com and click on *Chapter 8—Self-Check Quizzes* to prepare for the chapter test.

Assessment and Activities

CHAPTER 8

37. Contrasting Identify the differences between mediation and arbitration. Which method do you think is more effective? Write a paragraph explaining your answer.

38. Analyzing Information Some people believe that in today's economy, the market theory of wage determination is more useful than the theory of negotiated wages. Explain why you agree or disagree.

39. Analyzing Visuals Look at Figure 8.2 on page 202. How does your state's position on this issue affect you? Why do you think your state supports or opposes right-to-work laws?

40. Inferring Why are workers in the food service industry least likely to be unionized?

Analyzing Visuals

41. Critical Thinking Explain how a supporter of raising the minimum wage would use the information from the graph below.

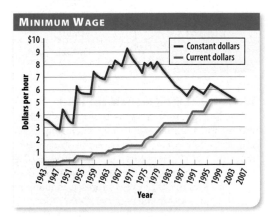

MINIMUM WAGE

- Constant dollars
- Current dollars

Dollars per hour vs *Year* (1943–2007)

Writing About Economics

42. Persuasive Writing Based on what you have learned about wage determination, write a short essay persuading a friend to continue his or her education after graduating from high school.

Applying Economic Concepts

43. Civilian Labor Force As you go to and from school, take note of the various occupations around you. List at least 10 occupations, and then classify them according to the four major categories of labor. Which category is represented most? Is a category not represented at all? Why do you think that might be?

44. Minimum Wage Poll at least 10 people of various ages, asking for their opinions on the following statement: There should be no minimum wage. Compile the responses and present your findings to the class.

Interpreting Cartoons

45. Critical Thinking Look at the cartoon below. What goal of the labor union movement does the cartoonist illustrate? What labor action are the beanie babies utilizing to achieve their goal?

www.offthemark.com

BEANIE BABIES AGAINST FORCED RETIREMENT

Analyzing Visuals

41. A supporter of raising the minimum wage would argue that the buying power (real dollar value) of the minimum has declined sharply since the current rate was established in 1997.

Writing About Economics

42. Answers will vary but should demonstrate an understanding of the economic benefits of a post-secondary education.

Applying Economic Concepts

43. Answers will vary but should demonstrate an understanding of the four categories of labor.

44. Answers will vary but should demonstrate the student's ability to acquire and analyze data.

Interpreting Cartoons

45. In the cartoon, the Beanie Babies are picketing the company that makes the toys. The issue is forced "retirement," or requiring someone to stop working at a mandatory age.

37. In mediation, a neutral third person recommends a compromise to both sides, which they are not bound to accept. In arbitration, a neutral third person studies the differences between the two sides and gives a decision, which the parties must accept as final. Students should support their opinions of which method is the most effective.

38. Answers will vary but should demonstrate an understanding of negotiated and market theories of wage determination.

39. Answers will vary but should demonstrate an understanding of the impact of right-to-work laws.

40. They often work for minimum wage, work part-time, are unskilled, and are teenagers.

The Global Economy
&YOU

Focus

Have students describe their experiences with offshore customer service. Discuss whether they were satisfied with the assistance they received, what problems may have arisen, and what advantages and disadvantages they see with the arrangement. **Ask:** Do you expect the offshoring of customer-service jobs to continue? Why or why not? *(Students will likely say it will continue because of the growing global economy.)*

Teach

W Writing Support

Expository Writing Have students review the table. Then have them write a paragraph discussing some kinds of jobs that they expect will *not* be outsourced and why. Have volunteers share their paragraphs. As a class, discuss the issues raised by students' work.
OL

Additional Support

"Offshoring" American Jobs to India

Have you called a customer service center recently? If so, you may have talked to a person with an American name and an unfamiliar accent. Many U.S. companies have decided to outsource a portion of their business, such as customer support, to companies located in the United States. Others send these jobs abroad, a practice called "offshoring." India is a favorite location.

Job Exodus

Customer service positions are not the only jobs headed for India. Work moving offshore also includes processing mortgages, overseeing payrolls, balancing business accounts, and handling insurance claims. When you surf the Internet, you're using search terms and archives keyed in or scanned mostly by Indian technicians.

India is attractive for several reasons. The country provides a large pool of educated people who speak English. In addition, India's day begins when ours ends, which means that U.S. companies can work all day and increase productivity by offshoring overnight work to India. With fiber-optic cables wrapped around the world, it is cheap to transmit data from North America to South Asia. Perhaps the most important reason for looking overseas is cheap labor. A software programmer in India earns about $10,000 compared to an American programmer's salary of roughly $60,000.

Projected Number of U.S. Jobs to Move Overseas by 2015	
Art, design	29,654
Life sciences	36,770
Legal	76,642
Architecture	184,347
Sales	226,564
Management	288,281
Business	348,028
Computer	472,632
Office	1,659,310

Source: Forrester Research, Inc.

White-Collar Workers Feel the Pinch

Previously reserved for low-wage jobs such as those in textile manufacturing, offshoring today impacts white-collar workers. Some studies estimate that offshoring cost U.S. workers 400,000 jobs in 2004 and predict that it will cost more than 3 million jobs by 2015. Others foresee as many as 4 million jobs lost in the services sector alone.

The ranks of high-profile American companies moving parts of their operations to India include Charles Schwab, AOL, American Express, GE, and Microsoft. And the list continues to grow. More than half of Fortune 500 companies have shipped jobs overseas, including Oracle, Dell, Delta Air Lines, J.P. Morgan Chase, British Airways, and Hewlett-Packard.

Salary Comparisons		
Job	United States	India
Software programmer	$66,100	$10,000
Mechanical engineer	$55,600	$5,900
IT manager	$55,000	$8,500
Accountant	$41,000	$5,000
Financial operations	$37,625	$5,500

Sources: Paàras Group; International Labour Organization

226   UNIT 3   Economic Institutions and Issues

Activity: Collaborative Learning

A Debate On Offshoring Organize students into two teams to debate this proposition: *The government should take steps to prevent the offshoring of American jobs.* Have teams research and prepare their position. Hold the debate, with some members of the class serving as judges/evaluators. At the conclusion of the debate, have the judges decide which team presented and supported its position better. Then discuss issues that arose from the debate. **OL**

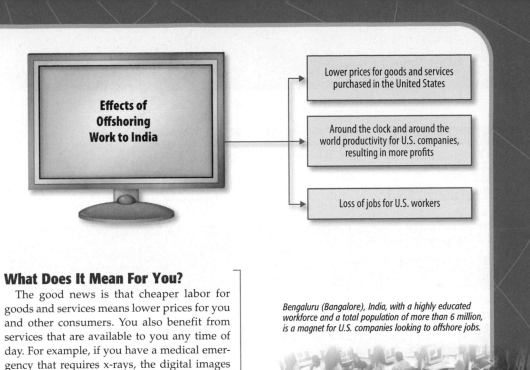

Effects of Offshoring Work to India

- Lower prices for goods and services purchased in the United States
- Around the clock and around the world productivity for U.S. companies, resulting in more profits
- Loss of jobs for U.S. workers

What Does It Mean For You?

The good news is that cheaper labor for goods and services means lower prices for you and other consumers. You also benefit from services that are available to you any time of day. For example, if you have a medical emergency that requires x-rays, the digital images can be interpreted by an Indian radiologist overnight, with results reported back to your doctor by the next morning.

The bad news is that many Americans may lose their jobs. Offshoring can even change your likelihood of future success. A college degree—even an M.D. or Ph.D.—may not be enough to compete with India's growing employment pool of cheap, educated labor.

Bengaluru (Bangalore), India, with a highly educated workforce and a total population of more than 6 million, is a magnet for U.S. companies looking to offshore jobs.

Analyzing the Issue

1. **Identifying** How can using workers in India increase an American company's productivity?
2. **Determining Cause and Effect** What are the main reasons why American jobs are sent overseas?
3. **Applying** Check your local newspaper or Internet news sources for recent reports about companies in your community or state that have sent jobs overseas. On a separate piece of paper, summarize the issues discussed in these articles and describe how they affect you and your community.

Assess/ Close

C Critical Thinking

Evaluating Have students decide whether the trend toward offshoring customer service and other tasks is positive or negative for the following groups: U.S. companies, American consumers, American workers, and Indians. Have students explain the reasoning behind their evaluations. **OL**

Analyzing the Impact

Answers:
1. They can vastly reduce their costs while obtaining the same amount of work.
2. Companies can save money spent on labor costs and get work done faster due to time shifts.
3. Answers will vary but should describe the personal or local effects of offshoring.

Additional Support

Activity: Interdisciplinary Connection

International Studies Tell students that for several decades, skilled workers from developing countries, including India, have had difficulty finding suitable work in their own countries and have emigrated to developed countries in search of jobs. Almost every student will have had contact with a doctor, engineer, or other skilled professional from another country. Explain that this flight of skilled workers from the developing to the developed world has been called the "brain drain." It seriously affects the economic potential of developing nations. Some countries are trying to prevent the brain drain; for example, Thailand has initiated a program called Reverse Brain Drain to create and attract more high-tech industries in order to retain its skilled workers. Ask students to discuss how the development of industries like India's customer-service industry may help prevent the brain drain from occurring in developing nations. Encourage students to consider how that might affect the U.S. economy.

Key to Ability Levels

BL Below level	**AL** Above level
OL On level	**ELL** English Language Learners

Key to Teaching Resources

Print Material	DVD
CD-Rom	Transparency

Levels					Resources	Chapter Opener	Section 1	Section 2	Section 3	Chapter Assess
BL	OL	AL	ELL							
FOCUS										
BL	OL	AL	ELL	📠	**Daily Focus Skills Transparencies**		74	64	66	
TEACH										
BL	OL		ELL	📁	**Guided Reading Activities***		p. 25	p. 26	p. 27	
BL	OL	AL	ELL	📁	**Economic Content Vocabulary Activities***		p. 9	p. 9	p. 9	
	OL	AL		📁	**Critical Thinking Activities**		p. 14	p. 14		
BL	OL		ELL	📁	**Reading Essentials and Note-Taking Guide***		p. 73	p. 76	p. 79	
		AL		📁	**Enrichment Activities**			p. 9		
	OL	AL		📁	**Free Enterprise Activities**			p. 14		
BL	OL	AL	ELL	📁	**Primary and Secondary Source Readings**				pp. 14, 27	
BL	OL	AL	ELL	📁	**Economic Cartoons**				p. 19	
BL	OL	AL	ELL	📁	**Hands-On Economics**			p. 19		
BL	OL	AL	ELL	📁	**Math Practice for Economics**			pp. 13, 14	p. 13	
BL	OL	AL	ELL	📠	**Economics Forms and Financial Pages Transparencies, Strategies, and Activities**			pp. 1, 3		
BL	OL	AL	ELL	📁	**Personal Finance Activities**				p. 15	
BL	OL	AL	ELL	📁	**Reinforcing Economic Skills**			pp. 4, 24	pp. 17, 18	
BL	OL		ELL	📁	**High School Reading in the Content Area Strategies and Activities**	✓	✓	✓	✓	✓
BL	OL	AL	ELL	📠	**High School Writing Process Transparencies**	✓	✓	✓	✓	✓
BL	OL	AL	ELL	📁	**Writer's Guidebook**	✓	✓	✓	✓	✓
BL	OL	AL	ELL	💿	**StudentWorks Plus CD-ROM**	✓	✓	✓	✓	✓
BL	OL	AL	ELL	💿	**Vocabulary PuzzleMaker CD-ROM**	✓	✓	✓	✓	✓

*Also available in Spanish

TeacherWorks Plus
All-In-One Planner and Resource Center

- Interactive Lesson Planner
- Interactive Teacher Edition
- Fully editable blackline masters
- Economics & You videos

- Differentiated Lesson Plans
- Printable reports of daily assignments
- Standards tracking system

Levels					Resources	Chapter Opener	Section 1	Section 2	Section 3	Chapter Assess
BL	OL	AL	ELL							
TEACH *(continued)*										
BL	OL	AL	ELL	🔒	Economics & You Video Program DVD— *How the Government Spends, Collects and Owes*	✓	✓	✓	✓	✓
BL	OL	AL	ELL	💿	Graph Coach CD-ROM	✓	✓	✓	✓	✓
Teacher Resources				📁	Differentiated Instruction Strategies	✓	✓	✓	✓	✓
				📁	Success with English Learners	✓	✓	✓	✓	✓
				💿	Presentation Plus! CD-ROM	✓	✓	✓	✓	✓
ASSESS										
BL	OL	AL	ELL	📁	Section Quizzes and Chapter Tests		p. 109	p. 110	p. 111	pp. 113, 117
BL	OL	AL	ELL	📁	Authentic Assessment Strategies and Activities		p. 14			
BL	OL	AL	ELL	💿	*ExamView® Assessment Suite* CD-ROM		9-1	9-2	9-3	Ch. 9
BL	OL	AL	ELL	💿	Interactive Tutor Self-Assessment CD-ROM		9-1	9-2	9-3	
CLOSE										
BL			ELL	📁	Reteaching Activities*		p. 9	p. 9	p. 9	
BL	OL		ELL	📁	Reading and Study Skills Foldables		p. 56			

*Also available in Spanish

Chapter Overviews

Technology Product

The Glencoe Web site offers in-depth overviews that summarize the content of each chapter. The overviews consist of brief chapter summaries and separate overviews for each section. The chapter overviews
- summarize and reinforce chapter content;
- provide discussion points to use in class.

Objectives

The overviews help students
- prepare for better understanding of chapter content;
- practice reading and comprehension skills.

Steps

Provide students with the following steps to complete the activities:
- Locate the Web page for the textbook being studied on the Glencoe Web site glencoe.com.
- Click on **Student Center** under the textbook title.
- Once you are in the Student Center, select a unit from the Unit Resources menu and a chapter from the Chapter Activities menu using the drop-down arrows.
- Click on the **Chapter Overviews** link.

Have students read the chapter overview in preparation for a reading assignment or activity.

Economics ONLINE

	Student	Teacher	Parent
Beyond the Textbook	●	●	●
Chapter Overviews	●	●	●
ePuzzles and Games	●		●
Concepts in Motion	●		●
Multi-Language Glossaries	●		●
Online Student Edition	●	●	●
Self-Check Quizzes	●		●
Student Web Activities	●		●
Study Central™	●		●
Time Current Events	●	●	●
Teaching Today		●	
Vocabulary eFlashcards	●		●
Web Activity Lesson Plans		●	

Glencoe Media Center

❯ glencoe.com

Study-To-Go
- Vocabulary eFlashcards
- Self-Check Quizzes

❯ **Audio/Video**
- Student Edition Audio
- Spanish Summaries
- Economics & You Videos

- **Timed Readings Plus in Social Studies** helps students increase their reading rate and fluency while maintaining comprehension. The 400-word passages are similar to those found on state and national assessments.

- **Reading in the Content Area: Social Studies** concentrates on six essential reading skills that help students better comprehend what they read. The book includes 75 high-interest nonfiction passages written at increasing levels of difficulty.

- **Reading Social Studies** includes strategic reading instruction and vocabulary support in Social Studies content for both ELLs and native speakers of English. www.jamestowneducation.com

Reading List Generator CD-ROM

Use this database to search more than 30,000 titles to create a customized reading list for your students.

- Reading lists can be organized by students' reading level, author, genre, theme, or area of interest.

- The database provides Degrees of Reading Power™ (DRP) and Lexile™ readability scores for all selections.

- A brief summary of each selection is included.

Leveled reading suggestions for this chapter:
For students at a Grade 10 reading level:
- *Your Money at Work: Taxes,* by Ernestine Giesecke

For students at a Grade 11 reading level:
- *Other Revenue Sources Should Be Pursued,* by William Straus

For students at a Grade 12 reading level:
- *Careers Inside the World of the Government,* by Sue Hurwitz

* Review suggested books before assigning them.

NCEE

National Council on Economic Education

Voluntary Standards Emphasized in Chapter 9

Content Standard 16 There is an economic role for government in a market economy whenever the benefits of a government policy outweigh its costs. Governments often provide for national defense, address environmental concerns, define and protect property rights, and attempt to make markets more competitive. Most government policies also redistribute income.

Content Standard 20 Federal government budgetary policy and the Federal Reserve System's monetary policy influence the overall levels of employment, output, and prices.

Resources Available from NCEE
- Virtual Economics®: An Interactive Center for Economic Education Version 3.0
- Civics and Government: Focus on Economics, Second Edition
- Capstone: The Nation's High School Economics Course
- Focus: Institutions and Markets

To order these materials, or to contact your State Council on Economic Education about workshops and programs, call 1-800-338-1192 or visit the NCEE Web site at store.ncee.net.

The **BIG** Idea

As students study the chapter, remind them to consider the chapter-based Big Idea. The **Essential Question** in the chapter launch activity below ties in to the Big Idea and helps students think about and understand important chapter concepts. In addition, the Hands-On Chapter Project relates the content from each section to the Big Idea. The steps in each section build on each other and culminate in the Wrap-Up Activity on the Visual Summary page.

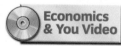
Economics & You Video
To generate student interest and provide a springboard for class discussion, access the Economics & You Topic 14 video, **How the Government Spends, Collects and Owes,** at glencoe.com or on the video DVD.

FOLDABLES
Study Organizer
Dinah Zike's Foldables are three-dimensional, interactive graphic organizers that help students practice basic writing skills, review key vocabulary terms, and identify main ideas. Have students complete this chapter's Foldable activity or activities in *Dinah Zike's Reading and Study Skills Foldables* booklet. **OL**

Economics ONLINE
Introduce students to chapter content and key terms by having them access *Chapter 9 —Chapter Overviews* at glencoe.com.

CHAPTER
9 Sources of Government Revenue

Why It Matters

You have just received your first paycheck and are looking forward to being paid $8 per hour for the 20 hours you worked. You look at your check and . . . "What? This check isn't for $160! Where's the rest of my money?" Make a list of the deductions that might be subtracted from your earnings. Read Chapter 9 to learn more about how governments raise revenue.

The **BIG** Idea

All levels of government use tax revenue to provide essential goods and services.

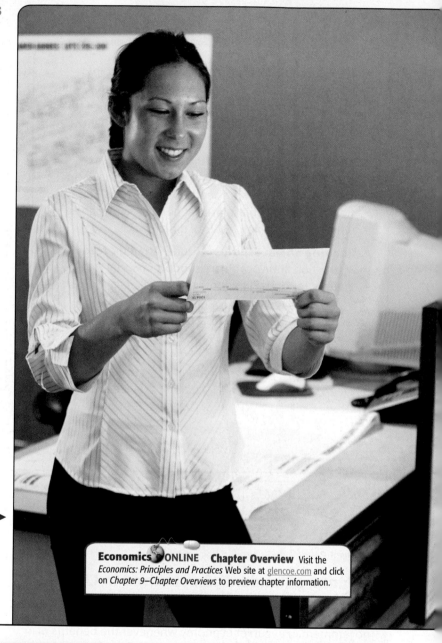

► When we receive paychecks for our work, a portion of our earnings goes to the government for taxes.

Economics ONLINE **Chapter Overview** Visit the *Economics: Principles and Practices* Web site at glencoe.com and click on *Chapter 9–Chapter Overviews* to preview chapter information.

228 UNIT 3

Activity: Launching the Chapter

Identifying Have students identify at least two sources of revenue for the federal, state, and local (county or city) levels of government. Next have students identify at least two goods or services provided by each of those levels of government. Ask students to create a chart presenting the information they identified.

Essential Question: What is one source of revenue collected by each level of government? *(taxes)* Have students write a paragraph explaining how they think each of the levels of government spends the tax money it collects. **OL**

The Economics of Taxation

GUIDE TO READING

Section Preview

In this section, you will learn that taxes are the most important way of raising revenue for the government.

Content Vocabulary

- sin tax (p. 230)
- incidence of a tax (p. 231)
- tax loophole (p. 232)
- individual income tax (p. 232)
- sales tax (p. 233)
- tax return (p. 233)
- benefit principle of taxation (p. 234)
- ability-to-pay principle of taxation (p. 234)
- proportional tax (p. 235)
- average tax rate (p. 235)
- Medicare (p. 235)
- progressive tax (p. 235)
- marginal tax rate (p. 235)
- regressive tax (p. 236)

Academic Vocabulary

- validity (p. 230)
- evolved (p. 234)

Reading Strategy

Defining As you read the section, complete a graphic organizer similar to the one below by listing the criteria for taxes to be effective. Then define each of the criteria in your own words.

Focus

Bellringer
Daily Focus Transparency 74

1. What was the major source of federal income in 1863? In the recent year depicted?
2. What are some generalizations you can make when comparing federal income in 1863 with federal income today?

GUIDE TO READING

Answers to Graphic:

Equity: should be fair and just

Simplicity: should be simple enough for taxpayers and tax collectors to understand

Efficiency: should be easy to administer and successful at generating revenue

PEOPLE IN THE NEWS

—Atlanta Journal-Constitution

Teenage Tax Preparers

Since the tax season got under way . . . [Oakwood High School's business management students] have prepared 44 returns for community members, fellow students and faculty members, so far netting more than $50,000 in refunds for their clients. The only high school-based Volunteer Income Tax Assistance program in [Georgia], Oakwood provide[s] free tax services for lower-income residents, nonspeakers of English and the disabled.

The student volunteers are saving taxpayers money. "Since we're targeting the low-income, many are not in a position to pay $200 or $300," [said Gloria Carithers, a senior tax specialist in the IRS Atlanta office]. "That could make the difference in paying a bill or buying something for the family." ■

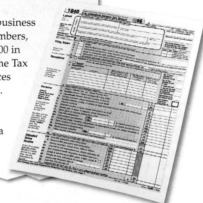

An enormous amount of money is required to run all levels of government—and the need seems to be growing every year. Taxes are the primary way to do this, and taxes affect the things we do in more ways than you think.

Governments levy a variety of taxes, from sales taxes on items we purchase in stores to the income tax we have to pay on our wages. One way in which we try to minimize taxes is by finding all the exemptions and deductions we are allowed to claim when we file our income tax returns. That is what the students in the news story were doing: helping their clients get the largest refund possible.

Resource Manager

R Reading Strategies	C Critical Thinking	D Differentiated Instruction	W Writing Support	S Skill Practice
Teacher Edition • Setting a Purpose, p. 230 • Predicting, p. 230 • Previewing, p. 232 • Identifying, p. 234 **Additional Resources** • Guid. Read. Act., p. 25 • Read. Ess. & Note-Taking Guide, p. 73	**Teacher Edition** • Analyzing Visuals, p. 234 • Contrasting, p. 235 • Analyzing, p. 237 **Additional Resources** • Authentic Assess., p. 14	**Teacher Edition** • Logical/Math., p. 231 • ELL, p. 233 **Additional Resources** • Reteach. Act., p. 9 • Quizzes and Tests, p. 109	**Teacher Edition** • Expository Writing, p. 232 • Persuasive Writing, p. 236 **Additional Resources** • High School Writing Process Trans.	**Teacher Edition** • Visual Literacy, p. 233 • Using Tables and Charts, p. 235 **Additional Resources** • Reading and Study Skills Fold., p. 56 • Economic Content Vocab. Act., p. 9

Teach

R1 Reading Strategy

Setting a Purpose Remind students that they read for different reasons. Ask students to set a purpose for reading the chapter by thinking about what they want to gain from the text. Explain that setting a purpose will help students focus on important information as they read. **BL**

R2 Reading Strategy

Predicting Ask: How might interest deductions affect a person's decision to buy a home? Explain. *(Students will likely predict that interest deductions encourage people to buy homes because they can deduct the interest on their mortgages; this lowers the total amount of taxes that people owe.)* **OL**

Caption Answer: Deductions lower the total amount of taxes that people pay.

---

sin tax relatively high tax designed to raise revenue and discourage consumption of a socially undesirable product

R1 Economic Impact of Taxes

MAIN Idea Taxes affect the decisions we make in a variety of ways.

Economics & You Have you ever not bought something because you could not afford the tax on it? Read on to find out how taxes affect our behavior.

Taxes and other governmental revenues influence the economy by affecting resource allocation, consumer behavior, and the nation's productivity and growth. In addition, the burden of a tax does not always fall on the party being taxed.

Resource Allocation

The factors of production are affected whenever a tax is levied. A tax placed on a good or service at the factory raises the cost of production and the price of the product.

People react to the higher price in a predictable manner—they buy less. When sales fall, some firms cut back on production, which means that some resources—land, capital, and labor—will have to go to other industries to be employed.

Behavior Adjustment

Taxes are sometimes used to encourage or discourage certain types of activities. For example, homeowners can use interest

payments on mortgages as tax deductions—a practice that encourages home ownership. Interest payments on other consumer debt, such as credit cards, are not deductible—a practice that makes credit card use less attractive.

A so-called **sin tax**—a relatively high tax designed to raise revenue while reducing consumption of a socially undesirable product such as liquor or tobacco—is another example of how a tax can change behavior. For the tax to be effective, however, it has to be reasonably uniform from one city or state to the next so that consumers do not have alternative sales outlets that allow them to avoid the tax.

Productivity and Growth

Taxes can affect productivity and economic growth by changing the incentives to save, invest, and work. For example, some people think that taxes are already quite high. Why, they argue, should they work to earn additional income if they have to pay much of it out in taxes?

While these arguments have **validity,** it is difficult to tell if we have reached the point where taxes are too high. For example, even the wealthiest individuals pay less than half of their taxable income to state and local governments in the form of income taxes. Are these taxes so high that people do not have the incentive to earn

Home Ownership People who purchase homes can deduct the interest on their mortgages. *How do deductions affect the total amount of taxes people owe?*

Differentiated Instruction

Critical Thinking Activities, p. 14

Synthesizing Figures for Change in Government Revenues

Objective: Learn how the government's revenues changed between 1995 and 1998.

Focus/Teach: Have students list what they believe are the three largest sources of government revenue. Write their ideas on the board. Then have students complete the activity.

Assess: Call on students to reveal their answers.

Close: Have students write a paragraph expanding upon their answer for question 6.

Differentiated Instruction Strategies

BL Ask: What does the table reveal about changes in the income tax rates between 1995 and 1998? *(They Increased.)*

AL Have students use the 2001 U.S. budget receipts to complete the activity again.

ELL Have students create a bar graph with the data from the completed table.

Figure 9.1 ▶ **Shifting the Incidence of a Tax**

Graphs In MOtion
See StudentWorks™ Plus
or glencoe.com.

▶ A tax on the producer increases the cost of production and causes a change in supply. Less of the tax can be shifted back to the taxpayer if demand is elastic, as in panel A. More of the tax can be shifted to the taxpayer if demand is inelastic, as in Panel B.

Economic Analysis *If a tax is placed on medicine, who is likely to bear the greater burden—the producer or the consumer?*

A ELASTIC DEMAND

Buyer pays 60 cents more because of elastic demand.

$1 tax on producer

$15.60
$15.00

Price

0   5 6
Quantity

B INELASTIC DEMAND

Buyer pays 90 cents more because of inelastic demand.

$1 tax on producer

$15.90
$15.00

Price

0   5.8 6
Quantity

D

D **Differentiated Instruction**

Logical/Mathematical
Ask: What is the difference in curve D from Panel A to Panel B? *(Curve D in Panel B is at a sharper vertical angle than curve D in Panel A.)* How do the shapes of the curves illustrate the concepts of elastic and inelastic demand? *(In Panel A, the curve is more relaxed or flexible and is described as elastic. In Panel B, the curve is at a sharper angle and is more rigid; it is described as inelastic.)* **OL**

Economic Analysis
Answer: the buyer

✓**Reading Check** **Answer:** When businesses are taxed, they may decrease production, raise prices, or both. Consumers then may have access to fewer products and may pay higher prices.

an additional $10 million because they can only keep half of it? Would they work any harder if income taxes took only 30 percent of their income? While we do not have exact answers to these questions, we do know that there must be some level of taxes at which productivity and growth would suffer.

Incidence of a Tax

Finally, there is the matter of who actually pays the tax. This is known as the **incidence of a tax**—or the final burden of the tax.

Suppose a city wants to tax a local electric utility to raise revenue. If the utility is able to raise its rates, consumers will likely bear the burden of the tax in the form of higher utility bills. However, if the company's rates are regulated, and if the company's profits are not large enough to absorb the tax increase, then shareholders may get smaller dividends—placing the tax burden on the owners. The company

also might delay a pay raise—shifting the burden to its workers.

Supply and demand analysis can help us analyze the incidence of a tax. To illustrate, **Figure 9.1** shows an *elastic* demand curve in **Panel A** and an *inelastic* demand curve in **Panel B.** Both panels have identical supply curves labeled S. Now, suppose that the government levies a $1 tax on the producer, thereby shifting the supply curve up by the amount of the tax.

In Panel A, the product's market price increases by 60 cents, which means that the producer must have absorbed the other 40 cents of the tax. In Panel B, however, the same tax on the producer results in a 90-cent increase in price, which means that the producer absorbed only 10 cents of the tax. The figure clearly shows that it is much easier for a producer to shift the incidence of a tax to the consumer if the consumer's demand curve is relatively inelastic.

✓**Reading Check** **Summarizing** How do taxes affect businesses and consumers?

incidence of a tax final burden of a tax

Skills Handbook
See page R39 to learn about Formulating Questions.

CHAPTER 9 Sources of Government Revenue **231**

Leveled Activities

BL **Reading Essentials and Note-Taking Guide, p. 73**

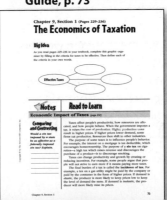

OL **Reading and Study Skills Foldables, p. 56**

AL **Authentic Assessment Strategies and Activities, p. 14**

231

R Reading Strategy

Previewing Have students preview the subsection by scanning the main idea, headings, and images.
Ask: What do you think you will learn about in this subsection? Have students share their answers with another classmate. **BL**

W Writing Support

Expository Writing Encourage students to imagine that they are writers for a current affairs magazine whose readers are middle school students. Ask them to write an article titled "The Economics of Taxation" that would be suitable for reading by that age group. **OL**

Did You Know?

In the United States, the idea of taxing income goes back to the 1640s when the colony of Massachusetts Bay taxed the "faculties" (earning power) of individuals and the "returns and gains" of tradespeople and craftpersons.

Additional Support

Economics ONLINE

Student Web Activity Visit the *Economics: Principles and Practices* Web site at glencoe.com and click on *Chapter 9–Student Web Activities* for an activity on the individual income tax.

tax loophole exception or oversight in the tax law allowing a taxpayer to avoid paying certain taxes

individual income tax federal tax levied on the wages, salaries, and other income of individuals

Criteria for Effective Taxes

MAIN Idea To be effective, taxes must be equitable, easy to understand, and efficient.

Economics & You Do you look forward to preparing your personal income tax returns? Read on to learn why you may be apprehensive about tax time.

Some taxes will always be needed, so we want to make them as fair and as effective as possible. To do so, taxes must meet three criteria: equity, simplicity, and efficiency.

Equity

The first criterion is equity, or fairness, which means that taxes should be impartial and just. Problems arise when we ask, *what is fair?* You might believe that everyone should pay the same amount. Your friend may think that wealthier people should pay more than those earning less.

There is no overriding guide to make taxes completely equitable. However, it does make sense to avoid **tax loopholes**—exceptions or oversights in the tax law that allow some people and businesses to avoid paying taxes. Loopholes are fairness issues, and most people oppose them based on equity. As a result, taxes generally are viewed as being fairer if they have fewer exceptions, deductions, and exemptions.

Simplicity

A second criterion is simplicity. Tax laws should be written so that both taxpayers and tax collectors can understand them. People seem more willing to tolerate taxes when they understand them.

The **individual income tax**—the federal tax on people's earnings—is a prime example of a complex tax. The entire federal code is thousands of pages long, and even the simplified instructions from the Internal

---

CAREERS

Certified Public Accountant

The Work

* Prepare, analyze, and verify financial reports that inform the general public and business firms
* Provide clients with sound advice on tax advantages and disadvantages, and repare their income tax statements
* Establish an accounting system and manage cash resources

Qualifications

* Strong mathematical skills and ability to analyze and interpret numbers and facts
* Ability to communicate results of analyses to clients and managers, both verbally and in writing
* Bachelor's degree in accounting, with many positions requiring an additional 30 hours beyond the usual 4-year bachelor's degree
* Successful completion of Uniform CPA Examination

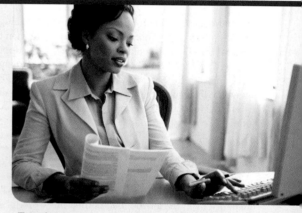

Earnings
* Median annual earnings: $50,770

Job Growth Outlook
* Faster than average

Source: *Occupational Outlook Handbook, 2006–2007 Edition*

Activity: Hands-On Economics

Distinguishing Fact From Opinion
Tell students that failure to distinguish fact from opinion can complicate the debate over fairness and taxes. Remind students that facts can be proven but opinions are based on people's differing values and beliefs. Read aloud the following statements and ask students to identify which is a fact and which is an opinion.

a. The fairest tax is the one that everybody pays. *(opinion)*
b. The luxury tax on private aircraft led to higher unemployment among workers in that industry. *(fact)*

Have students search for editorials dealing with taxes in newspapers or magazines and identify other examples of facts and opinions in the writing. **OL**

1-800-333-TOLL
E-ZPASS APPLICATIONS
ASK AT TOLL BOOTHS

Highway Taxes
In many states, you have to pay a toll to use certain roads. ***What does this photo imply about the efficiency of tolls?***

Revenue Service (IRS) are lengthy and difficult to understand. As a result, many people dislike the individual income tax code.

A **sales tax**—a general tax levied on most consumer purchases—is much simpler. The sales tax is paid at the time of purchase, and the amount of the tax is computed and collected by the merchant. Some goods such as food and medicine may be exempt, but if a product is taxed, then everyone who buys the product pays the tax.

Efficiency

A third criterion for an effective tax is efficiency. A tax should be relatively easy to administer and reasonably successful at generating revenue.

The individual income tax satisfies this requirement fairly well. An employer usually withholds a portion of an employee's pay and sends it to the IRS. At the end of the year, the employer notifies each employee of the amount of tax withheld so that the employee can settle any under- or overpayment with the IRS. Because of computerized payroll records, this withholding system is relatively easy.

After the close of the tax year on December 31 and before April 15 of the next year, employees file a **tax return**—an annual report to the IRS summarizing total income, deductions, and taxes withheld. Any difference between the amount already paid and the amount actually owed is settled at that time. Most differences are due to deductions and expenses that lower the amount of taxes owed, as well as additional income not subject to tax withholding. State and local governments usually require tax returns to be filed at the same time.

Other taxes, especially those collected in toll booths on state highways, are considerably less efficient. The state has to invest millions of dollars in heavily reinforced booths that span the highway. The cost to commuters, besides the toll, is the wear and tear on their automobiles as they brake for toll booths along the road.

Efficiency also means that a tax should raise enough revenue to be worthwhile while not harming the economy. One example is the federal luxury tax on small private aircraft in the early 1990s. The IRS collected only $53,000 in revenues during the first year of this tax because few planes were sold. This turned out to be less than the unemployment benefits paid to workers who lost jobs in that industry, so Congress quickly repealed that luxury tax.

sales tax general state or city tax levied on a product at the time of sale

tax return annual report by a taxpayer filed with the local, state, or federal government detailing income earned and taxes owed

✓**Reading Check** **Stating** Why is equity important?

CHAPTER 9   Sources of Government Revenue   233

C Critical Thinking

Analyzing Visuals Have students speculate about the condition of the road in the image. *(It has been repaired.)* **Ask:** What might have caused the road to deteriorate? *(Possible answer: Heavy traffic and weather probably created wear and tear over time.)* Invite students to give their opinions on the equity of gasoline and tire taxes. **OL**

R Reading Strategy

Identifying Ask: How is the amount each person has to pay determined under the ability-to-pay principle? *(The amount each pays depends on how much income each earns.)* **OL**

Caption Answer: People who drive often may be the ones who can least afford to pay the taxes. In addition, benefits from the tax are hard to measure.

✓**Reading Check Answer:** Answers will vary but should reflect an understanding of the principles of taxation.

Additional Support

---

benefit principle of taxation belief that taxes should be paid according to benefits received regardless of income

ability-to-pay principle of taxation belief that taxes should be paid according to level of income, regardless of benefits received

Benefit Principle Gasoline and tire taxes are used to pay for the upkeep of roads. *What are the limitations of gasoline taxes?*

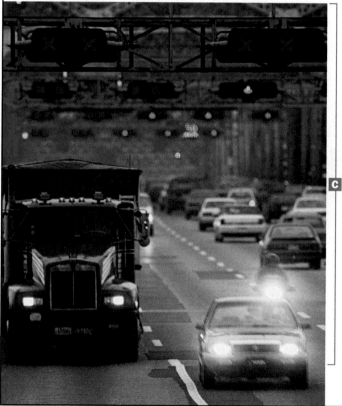

Two Principles of Taxation

MAIN Idea Taxes can be levied on the basis of benefits received or the ability to pay.

Economics & You Do you think the taxes you pay are fair? Read on to see if you prefer one principle of taxation over another.

Taxes in the United States are based on two principles that have **evolved** over the years. These principles are the benefit principle and the ability-to-pay principle.

Benefit Principle

The **benefit principle of taxation** states that those who benefit from government goods and services should pay in proportion to the amount of benefits they receive.

Gasoline taxes are a good example of this principle. Because the gas tax is built into the price of gasoline, people who drive more than others pay more gas taxes—and therefore pay for more of the upkeep of our nation's highways. Taxes on truck tires operate on the same principle. Since heavy vehicles like trucks are likely to put the most wear and tear on roads, a tire tax links the cost of highway upkeep to the user.

Despite its attractive features, the benefit principle has two limitations. The first is that those who receive government services may be the ones who can least afford to pay for them. Recipients of welfare payments or people who live in subsidized housing, for example, usually have the lowest incomes. Even if they could pay something, they would not be able to pay in proportion to the benefits they receive.

The second limitation is that benefits are often hard to measure. After all, the people who buy the gas are not the only ones who benefit from the roads built with gas taxes. Owners of property, hotels, and restaurants along the way are also likely to benefit from the roads that the gas tax helps provide.

Ability-to-Pay Principle

The belief that people should be taxed according to their ability to pay, regardless of the benefits they receive, is called the **ability-to-pay principle of taxation.** An example is the individual income tax, which requires people with higher incomes to pay more than those who earn less.

This principle is based on two factors. First, we cannot always measure the benefits derived from government spending. Second, it assumes that people with higher incomes suffer less discomfort paying taxes than people with lower incomes.

For example, a family of four with an annual taxable income of $20,000 needs every cent to pay for necessities. At a tax rate of about 13 percent, this family pays $2,623—a huge amount for them. A family of four with taxable income of $100,000 can afford to pay a higher average tax rate with much less discomfort.

✓**Reading Check Explaining** Which principle of taxation do you prefer, and why?

Extending the Content

Tax Equity Although the tax system has been modified to make it more equitable, it is impossible to have a system that is fair for everyone and that is seen by everyone as fair. An analysis of the benefit and ability-to-pay principles of taxation illustrates this point. As noted in the text on this page, it is often hard to measure exactly who benefits from a particular government service and even harder to assess how much benefit each person receives. In addition, although two families may have equal incomes, because of different circumstances they may not have the same ability to pay. This difficulty in determining equity is one reason why there are several different kinds of taxes at the federal, state, and local levels.

Figure 9.2 ▶ **Three Types of Taxes**

▶ Progressive, proportional, and regressive are the three main types of taxes.

Economic Analysis *Under which type of tax do individuals with lower incomes pay a smaller percentage than do those with higher incomes?*

Type of tax	Income of $10,000	Income of $100,000	Summary
Proportional (City income tax)	$97.50 or 0.975% of income	$975.00 or 0.975% of income	As income goes up, the percentage of income paid in taxes *stays the same*.
Progressive (Federal income tax)	$1,000 paid in taxes, or 10% of total income	$25,000 paid in taxes, or 25% of total income	As income goes up, the percentage of income paid in taxes *goes up*.
Regressive (State sales tax)	$5,000 in food and clothing purchases, taxed at 4% for a total tax of $200 or 2% of income	$20,000 in food and clothing purchases, taxed at 4% for a total tax of $800 or 0.8% of income	As income goes up, the percentage of income paid in taxes *goes down*.

Three Types of Taxes

MAIN Idea All taxes can be broken down into three categories—proportional, progressive, and regressive.

Economics & You You just learned about two principles of taxation. Find out how the principles apply to different types of taxes.

Three general types of taxes exist in the United States today—proportional, progressive, and regressive. As **Figure 9.2** shows, each type of tax is classified according to the way in which the tax burden changes as income changes. To calculate the tax burden, we divide the amount that someone pays in taxes by their taxable income. If a person pays $100 in taxes on a $10,000 income, then the tax burden is 0.01, or 1 percent.

Proportional Tax

A **proportional tax** imposes the same percentage rate of taxation on everyone, regardless of income. If the income tax rate is 20 percent, an individual with $10,000 in taxable income pays $2,000 in taxes. A person with $100,000 in taxable income pays $20,000.

If the percentage tax rate is constant, the **average tax rate**—total tax paid divided by the total taxable income—also is constant, regardless of income. If a person's income goes up, the *percentage* of total income paid in taxes does not change.

Few proportional taxes are used in the United States. One example is the 15 percent tax rate on corporate dividends. Regardless of overall income and how much someone receives in corporate dividends, individuals only pay 15 percent of that amount in personal income taxes.

Another example is the tax that funds **Medicare**—a federal health-care program available to all senior citizens, regardless of income. The Medicare tax is 1.45 percent of income, with no limit on the amount of income taxed. As a result, everyone who receives a paycheck pays exactly the same rate, regardless of the size of the paycheck.

Progressive Tax

A **progressive tax** is a tax that imposes a higher percentage rate of taxation on higher incomes than on lower ones. This tax uses a progressively higher **marginal tax rate,** the tax rate that applies to the next dollar of taxable income.

proportional tax tax in which the percentage of income paid in tax is the same regardless of the level of income

average tax rate total taxes paid divided by the total taxable income

Medicare federal health-care program for senior citizens

progressive tax tax in which the percentage of income paid in tax rises as the level of income rises

marginal tax rate tax rate that applies to the next dollar of taxable income

Using Tables and Charts
Ask: What would happen if a state sales tax became progressive? *(People who made more money would have to pay higher sales taxes than people who made less money.)* **OL**

C **Critical Thinking**

Contrasting Have students make a chart listing the three types of taxes and the characteristics of each. *(Proportional tax: imposes the same percentage rate of taxation on everyone, regardless of income. Progressive tax: imposes a higher percentage rate of taxation on higher incomes than on lower ones. Regressive tax: imposes a higher percentage rate of taxation on low incomes than on high incomes.)* As students read the subsection, have them record examples of each type of tax. **OL**

Economic Analysis

Answer: progressive tax

Hands-On Chapter Project

Step 1

Explaining Taxation and Revenue Systems

In this project, students will explore the taxation and revenue systems of all levels of government in the United States.

Step 1: Principles of Taxation and Types of Taxes. Students will identify and explain two principles of taxation and three types of taxes.

Directions: Organize the class into groups of three. Have them imagine that their group has been hired by the U.S. Treasury Department to create visual presentations to help taxpayers understand the taxation and revenue system of the United States.

Tell students that their group will create a pamphlet for taxpayers explaining the two principles of taxation and the three types of taxes. The pamphlet should focus on the attractive features of each principle of taxation and clearly explain each type of taxes. The text used in the pamphlet should be correctly spelled and

punctuated. Use of illustrations should enhance the topics of the pamphlet.

Summarizing Ask students to write a brief report, identifying and explaining two principles of taxation and three types of taxes. **OL**

(Chapter Project continued in Section 2.)

W Writing Support

Persuasive Writing Ask each student to take a position on the individual income tax: Does it work best as a progressive tax, or would it work better as a regressive or proportional tax? Have students write a persuasive essay arguing their position. Remind them to anticipate and address possible counterpoints made by people with opposing views. **AL**

✓Reading Check **Answer:**
Answers will vary but should demonstrate knowledge of the three types of taxes.

Assess

💿 Use the Interactive Tutor Self-Assessment CD-ROM to review Section 1, and then assign the Section 1 Review as homework or as an in-class activity.

Close

Evaluating Write the following on the board: *The only fair tax is a tax on someone else.* Then have students discuss how equity can be achieved in the tax system. **OL**

SECTION 1 Review

---

regressive tax
tax in which the percentage of income paid in tax goes down as income rises

For example, suppose the law required everyone to pay a rate of 10 percent on all taxable income up to $7,500, and then a rate of 15 percent on all income after that. If someone had taxable income of $5,000, this person would have to pay 10 percent on the 5,001st dollar earned. In this case, the marginal tax rate on the 5,001st dollar would be 10 percent.

However, if the same person had taxable income of $7,500, then the marginal tax rate would be 15 percent on the 7,501st dollar earned. In either case, the marginal tax is always the tax that is paid on the very next dollar of taxable income.

W The individual income tax code used in the United States today is structured just this way. It currently starts at 10 percent and then jumps to 15 percent, 25 percent, 28 percent, 33 percent, and 35 percent, depending on the amount of taxable income. One important outcome of this structure is that progressively higher marginal brackets also cause the average tax rate to go up as taxable income goes up.

Regressive Tax

A **regressive tax** is a tax that imposes a *higher* percentage rate of taxation on low incomes than on high incomes. For example, a person in a state with a 4 percent sales tax and an annual income of $10,000 may spend $5,000 on food and clothing and pay sales taxes of $200 (or .04 times $5,000). A person with an annual income of $100,000 may spend $20,000 on food and clothing and pay state sales taxes of $800 (or .04 times $20,000).

On a percentage basis, the person with the lower income pays 2 percent (or $200 divided by $10,000) of income in sales taxes, while the person with the higher income pays 0.8 percent (or $800 divided by $100,000). As a result, the 4 percent sales tax is regressive because the individual with the higher income pays a smaller percentage of income in sales taxes than does the individual with the lower income.

✓Reading Check **Synthesizing** Which of the types of taxes should be used for income taxes? Why?

SECTION 1 Review

Vocabulary

1. **Explain** the significance of sin tax, incidence of a tax, tax loophole, individual income tax, sales tax, tax return, benefit principle of taxation, ability-to-pay principle of taxation, proportional tax, average tax rate, Medicare, progressive tax, marginal tax rate, and regressive tax.

Main Ideas

2. **Describing** Use a graphic organizer like the one below to describe the economic impact of taxes.

Impact of Taxes

3. **Identifying** What are the criteria for effective taxes?

4. **Summarizing** What are the main points of the two principles of taxation?

Critical Thinking

5. **The BIG Idea** Compare and contrast the characteristics of proportional, progressive, and regressive taxes.

6. **Evaluating** Using the criteria described in this chapter, how would you evaluate the effectiveness of the personal income tax?

7. **Analyzing Visuals** School districts often are supported by property taxes. These taxes are based on a percentage of the value of a house or other real estate. Look at Figure 9.2 on page 235. In which category of taxes does the property tax fall?

Applying Economics

8. **Equity** Which of the two principles of taxation—the benefit principle or the ability-to-pay principle—do you think is more equitable? Explain your answer. Be sure to include in your answer how the two principles differ from one another.

Answers

1. All definitions can be found in the section and the Glossary.
2. resource allocation (factors of production are affected whenever a tax is levied); behavior adjustment (taxes can encourage or discourage certain activities); productivity and growth (taxes can change incentives to save, invest, and work); incidence of a tax (the final burden of a tax is determined by supply and demand)
3. equity, simplicity, and efficiency

4. The benefit principle states that those who benefit from government goods and services should pay in proportion to the amount of benefits they receive. The ability-to-pay principle states that people should be taxed according to their ability to pay, regardless of the benefits they receive.
5. A proportional tax applies the same tax rate. A progressive tax imposes a higher percentage rate of taxation on higher incomes than on lower ones, whereas a

regressive tax imposes a higher percentage rate of taxation on low incomes than on high incomes. All three types generate revenue that helps run the government.
6. Answers will vary, but students should evaluate whether the personal income tax is fair, efficient, and easy to understand.
7. proportional
8. Answers will vary but should demonstrate an understanding of the principles of taxation.

Profiles in Economics

Profiles in Economics

Monica Garcia Pleiman (1964–)

- president and CEO of OMS, a technology consulting firm
- publisher of Hispanic lifestyles magazine *Latino SUAVE*
- cofounder of the Latina Chamber of Commerce

Small Start

Denver-based businesswoman Monica Garcia Pleiman knew early what she wanted to do with her life. As the daughter of a small business owner, she learned that "hard work and entrepreneurial skills" could bring financial success. She also took her high school's only computer class—and loved it. In 1987 Pleiman earned a degree in Information Science, a 95 percent male program. After working for both large corporations and small companies, she formed the consulting firm Optimum Management Systems (OMS).

Small Business

Pleiman uses several successful strategies. Her practice of sharing the credit and allowing employees to grow in their jobs has resulted in a loyal OMS workforce—unusual in today's highly competitive, ever-changing technology sector. She tries to maintain a small-business environment while providing large-company benefits. She also focuses on serving small and minority businesses. Finally, she has taken advantage of assistance by the federal government's Small Business Administration, including attending the Minority Business Executive Program sponsored by the SBA.

These strategies have paid off. OMS grew 910 percent from its start in 1998 to 2003. Revenues over $7 million per year make it one of the country's most successful minority-owned businesses. This success allowed Pleiman to branch out and publish a new bilingual lifestyle magazine, *Latino SUAVE*.

Pleiman descends from a long line of hard workers. Her Spanish ancestors settled Colorado 200 years ago. With six brothers, "I learned how to compete against men, to prove I could make it as a woman and as a minority."

Examining the Profile

1. **Summarizing** What strategies helped Pleiman become a successful entrepreneur?
2. **For Further Research** What types of assistance does the Small Business Administration offer to entrepreneurs?

Teach

C Critical Thinking

Analyzing Ask: What contributed to Pleiman's success as an adult? *(Possible answers: She learned about running a small business from her family. She earned a degree in a male-dominated field. With six brothers, she learned how to compete with men.)* **OL**

Examining the Profile

Answers:
1. She created a loyal workforce by sharing credit with employees and allowing them to grow in their jobs, she maintained a small-business environment while providing large-company benefits, she focused on serving small and minority businesses, and she took advantage of assistance by the SBA.
2. Students should research and report on the types of assistance offered by the SBA.

Additional Support

Activity: Collaborative Learning

Designing Have students work together in small groups to design a poster celebrating the life and achievements of a famous minority entrepreneur. Students might choose Monica Garcia Pleiman; other examples might include Mary Kay Ash, John Johnson, Anita Roddick, Oprah Winfrey, and Wilson Wong. Students should research the life of their chosen figure and decide how to convey the information in a visually appealing way. Encourage students to include quotes from or about the entrepreneur or personal anecdotes that will help bring the figure alive for viewers. Display students' posters in the classroom. **OL**

Teacher Tip

Managing Time After dividing students into groups, ask them to begin by writing a plan of action that outlines who will do what and when. Such a plan encourages efficient use of time as students proceed through the various steps of the assignment.

Focus

Bellringer
Daily Focus Transparency 64

GUIDE TO READING

Answers to Graphic:

Federal: individual income taxes, FICA taxes, borrowing, corporate income taxes, excise taxes, estate and gift taxes, customs duties, miscellaneous fees

State: intergovernmental revenues, sales taxes, individual income taxes, other revenues

Local: intergovernmental revenues, property taxes, utility revenues, sales taxes, other revenue sources

Resource Manager

SECTION 2

Federal, State, and Local Revenue Systems

GUIDE TO READING

Section Preview

In this section, you will learn that federal, state, and local governments rely on different revenue sources.

Content Vocabulary

- Internal Revenue Service (IRS) (p. 238)
- payroll withholding system (p. 239)
- indexing (p. 239)
- FICA (p. 239)
- payroll tax (p. 239)
- corporate income tax (p. 240)
- excise tax (p. 240)
- estate tax (p. 241)
- gift tax (p. 241)
- customs duty (p. 241)
- user fee (p. 241)
- intergovernmental revenue (p. 242)
- property tax (p. 244)
- tax assessor (p. 244)
- natural monopoly (p. 244)

Academic Vocabulary

- implemented (p. 242)
- considerably (p. 243)

Reading Strategy

Describing As you read the section, complete a graphic organizer like the one below to identify and describe the revenue sources for federal, state, and local governments.

Revenue sources
— Federal
— State
— Local

ISSUES IN THE NEWS
—The Columbus Dispatch

Taxing Tycoons

Come to Newport, Rhode Island, and see what America was like before the income tax. The Elms is a Gilded Age mansion graced by a Louis XV ballroom and tapestries from Imperial Russia. Its owner made his tax-free fortune off the coal mines of Pennsylvania and West Virginia.

[B]ut by the dawn of the 20th century, American farmers, miners, and factory workers started thinking that the Vanderbilts and their ilk should contribute more to the country. And so on October 3, 1913, President Wilson signed the bill that created an income tax. It touched only the wealthiest 4 percent of Americans. ■

Internal Revenue Service (IRS) branch of the U.S. Treasury Department that collects taxes

The first federal income tax was enacted by the Union government in 1861 to help finance the Civil War. It was repealed in 1872. A later income tax was found unconstitutional in 1893, but it had the potential to be a major source of revenue.

It was not until the ratification of the Sixteenth Amendment in 1913 that Congress could enact the current individual income tax. Since then, the top marginal tax rate has varied widely, from 1 percent for incomes over $3,000 in 1913 to 94 percent for the highest incomes during World War II. The **Internal Revenue Service (IRS)** is the branch of the U.S. Treasury Department in charge of collecting taxes today.

R Reading Strategies	**C** Critical Thinking	**D** Differentiated Instruction	**W** Writing Support	**S** Skill Practice
Teacher Edition • Monitoring, p. 241 • Making Connections, p. 243 • Summarizing, p. 245 • Act. Prior Know., p. 246 **Additional Resources** • Guid. Read. Act., p. 26 • Read. Ess. & Note-Taking Guide, p. 76	**Teacher Edition** • Det. Cause/Effect, p. 240 • Speculating, p. 242 • Problem-Solving, p. 244 **Additional Resources** • Reinforcing Econ. Skills, pp. 4, 24	**Teacher Edition** • Adv. Learners, p. 239 • Logical/Math., p. 240 • Visual/Spatial, p. 242 **Additional Resources** • Hands-On Econ., p. 19 • Math Prac. for Econ., pp. 13, 14 • Free Enterprise Act., p. 14	**Teacher Edition** • Expository Writing, pp. 239, 246 • Personal Writing, p. 241 **Additional Resources** • Writer's Guidebook • Crit. Think. Act., p. 14	**Teacher Edition** • Analyzing Graphs, pp. 240, 244 • Interpreting Political Cartoons, p. 243 **Additional Resources** • Econ. Forms and Fin. Pages Trans., Strat. & Act., pp. 1, 3 • Enrichment Act., p. 9

Federal Government Revenue Sources

MAIN Idea Individual income taxes, FICA, and borrowing constitute the main sources of government revenue.

Economics & You Have you ever wondered what "FICA" on your pay stub means? Read on to find out about one of the main federal revenue sources.

The federal government gets its revenue from a number of sources. Taxes are the primary source of revenue, but borrowing also plays a big part. As shown in **Figure 9.3,** the four largest sources of government revenue are individual income taxes, Social Security taxes, borrowing, and corporate income taxes.

Individual Income Taxes **D**

The main source of federal government revenue is the individual income tax. In most cases, the tax is collected with a **payroll withholding system,** a system that requires an employer to automatically deduct income taxes from a worker's paycheck and send them directly to the IRS.

Because inflation can push a worker into a higher tax bracket, the tax code is also indexed. **Indexing** is an upward revision of the tax brackets to keep workers from paying more in taxes just because of inflation. Workers might otherwise move into a higher tax bracket when they receive a pay raise that makes up for inflation.

FICA Taxes

The second most important federal revenue source is FICA. **FICA** is the Federal Insurance Contributions Act tax, which is levied on employers and employees equally to pay for Social Security and Medicare. These two taxes are sometimes called **payroll taxes** because they are deducted from paychecks.

In 2007 the Social Security component of FICA was 6.2 percent of wages and salaries up to $97,500. Above that amount, Social **W** Security taxes are not collected, regardless of income. This means that a person with

payroll withholding system system that automatically deducts income taxes from paychecks on a regular basis

indexing adjustment of the tax brackets to offset the impact of inflation

FICA Federal Insurance Contributions Act; tax levied on employers and employees to support Social Security and Medicare

payroll tax tax on wages and salaries deducted from paychecks to finance Social Security and Medicare

---

Figure 9.3 ► Federal Government Revenue Sources

	2001		2007
Social security taxes	34.9%		31.9%
Corporate income taxes	7.6%		9.4%
Excise taxes	3.3%		2.7%
Customs duties	1.0%		1.0%
Estate and gift taxes	1.4%		0.9%
Borrowing	0%		12.8%
Miscellaneous	1.9%		1.7%
Individual income taxes	49.9%		39.6%

Source: *Economic Report of the President, 2006*

► In 2001 the federal government saved 1.7¢ of every dollar it spent. By 2007, the government was borrowing 12.8¢ for every dollar spent. The federal government now borrows more from investors than it collects from corporations in taxes.

Economic Analysis *What is the percentage of total revenue for the first four items?*

Activity: Hands-On Economics

Comparing and Contrasting Ask students to compare the Social Security tax and the Medicare tax. Have them make a chart stating the purpose of each tax and the similarities and differences between the two taxes. *(The taxes are both payroll deductions. However, Social Security is a proportional tax up to a $72,600 income and regressive thereafter. Medicare tax is proportional because the individual pays the same percentage regardless of the amount of income.)* Students may also wish to provide several examples of incomes and the taxes levied on those amounts. Finally, ask students to hypothesize why the government handles the two taxes differently. **OL**

S Skill Practice

Analyzing Graphs Ask: Which two countries have the lowest ratio of tax revenues to GDP? *(the United States and Japan)* **BL**

D Differentiated Instruction

Logical/Mathematical Have students determine what would be withheld for Social Security and Medicare from the paycheck of an individual who worked 40 hours at $6.50 per hour. *(40 × $6.50 = $260 total pay; 6.2% of $260 = $16.12 for Social Security tax; 1.45% of $260 = $3.77 for Medicare)* Invite students to write similar word problems for other classmates to solve. **OL**

C Critical Thinking

Determining Cause and Effect Ask: Why has the federal government become more reliant on borrowing as a source of revenue? *(because since 2001 it has spent more than it has collected)* **OL**

Differentiated Instruction

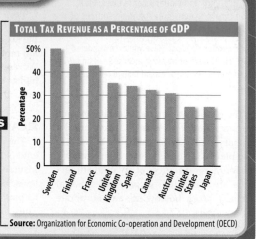

The Global Economy & YOU

High Taxes—Are You Sure?

You examine your paycheck and are dismayed to see how much money has been taken out for taxes. Before you get too outraged, however, do the math. What percentage of the total amount has been withheld for taxes? Ten percent? Twenty percent? This is a far cry less than would be withheld in many other countries.

One measure of a country's tax burden is the ratio of its tax revenues to gross domestic product (GDP). Despite the criticism over high taxes in the United States, our federal government's revenues as a percentage of GDP are much lower than people realize. Sweden is usually ranked first as the country with the world's highest taxes, whereas the United States boasts one of the lowest tax revenue-to-GDP ratios in the industrial world. **S**

TOTAL TAX REVENUE AS A PERCENTAGE OF GDP

Source: Organization for Economic Co-operation and Development (OECD)

---

corporate income tax tax on corporate profits

excise tax general revenue tax levied on the manufacture or sale of selected items

taxable income of $97,500 pays the same Social Security tax—$6,045—as does someone who earns $1,000,000,000.

In 1965 Congress added Medicare to the **D** Social Security program. The Medicare component of FICA is taxed at a flat rate of 1.45 percent. Unlike Social Security, there is no cap on the amount of income taxed, which makes it a proportional tax.

Borrowing

Borrowing by the federal government is the third-largest source of federal revenue. Because tax revenues fluctuate, the government never knows exactly how much it will need to borrow. Therefore, it continues with its spending as allocated in the budget. If it does not collect enough money in **C** taxes and user fees, it simply borrows the rest by selling bonds to investors.

Figure 9.3 shows that the federal government has become dependent on this source of funds, with the amount of money borrowed exceeding the total amount of taxes collected from corporations. The increased

borrowing has been mainly due to the increased levels of government spending since 2001 that have outpaced federal revenue collection.

Corporate Income Taxes

The fourth-largest source of federal revenue is the **corporate income tax**—the tax a corporation pays on its profits. The corporation is taxed separately from individuals because the corporation is recognized as a separate legal entity.

Several marginal tax brackets, which are slightly progressive, apply to corporations. The first is at 15 percent on all income under $50,000. The marginal brackets then rise slightly after that, and eventually a 35 percent marginal tax applies to all profits in excess of $18.3 million.

Excise Taxes

The **excise tax**—a tax on the manufacture or sale of selected items such as gasoline and liquor—is the fifth-largest source of federal government revenue. Some early

240   UNIT 3   Economic Institutions and Issues

Math Practice for Economics, p. 13

Analyzing a Paycheck

Objective: Understand the importance of analyzing a paycheck.

Focus: Ask how many students have received a paycheck. Have them share their understanding of the deductions listed on it.

Teach: Have students answer the activity questions.

Assess: Review the answers as a class.

Close: Ask students to explain what they might achieve by analyzing a paycheck.

Differentiated Instruction Strategies

BL Fill in the paycheck stub and have students complete the questions about it.

AL Have students create three different paycheck stubs, each for 40-hour weeks but at differing pay rates.

ELL Have students create a chart that lists and defines *gross pay*, *FICA*, *federal taxes*, *state taxes*, *retirement*, and *net pay*.

excise taxes were on carriages, snuff, and liquor. Today federal excise taxes are levied on telephone services, tires, legal betting, and coal. Because low-income families spend larger portions of their incomes on these goods than do high-income families, excise taxes tend to be regressive.

Estate and Gift Taxes

The **estate tax** is the tax on the transfer of property when a person dies. Estate taxes can range from 18 to 50 percent of the value of the estate, although estates worth less than $2,000,000 are exempt. The exemption will be raised to $3,500,000 by 2009, but because these amounts are so high, fewer than 2 percent of all estates pay any tax at all.

The **gift tax** is a tax on the transfer of money or wealth and is paid by the person who makes the gift. The gift tax is used to make sure that wealthy people do not try to avoid taxes by giving away their estates before they die. Figure 9.3 shows that estate and gift taxes account for only a small fraction of total federal government revenues.

Customs Duties

A **customs duty** is a charge levied on goods brought into the United States from other countries. The Constitution gives Congress the authority to levy customs duties. Congress then can decide which foreign imports will be taxed and at what rate. Many types of goods are covered, ranging from automobiles to silver ore. The duties are relatively low and produce little federal revenue today. Before the enactment of the income tax amendment, however, they were the largest income source for the federal government.

Miscellaneous Fees

Finally, only a fraction of federal revenue is collected through various miscellaneous fees. One example of a miscellaneous fee is a **user fee**—a charge levied for the use of a good or service. User fees were widely promoted by President Ronald Reagan, who wanted to find revenue sources that did not involve taxes.

User fees include entrance charges at national parks, as well as the fees ranchers pay when their animals graze on federal land. These fees are essentially taxes based on the benefit principle, because only the individuals who use the services pay them. People also seem more comfortable with them since they are not called "taxes."

✓**Reading Check** **Explaining** Why are corporations taxed separately from individuals?

estate tax tax on the transfer of property when a person dies

gift tax tax paid by the donor on transfer of money or wealth

customs duty tax on imported products

user fee fee paid for the use of a good or service

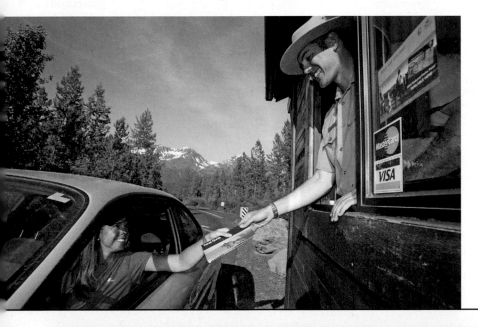

User Fees Visitors to national parks such as Kenai Fjords National Park in Alaska have to pay an entrance fee. *How are user fees assessed?*

Leveled Activities

BL Reinforcing Economic Skills, p. 24   **OL** Hands-On Economics, p. 19   **AL** Free Enterprise Activities, p. 14

C Critical Thinking

Speculating Ask: What might happen to state services such as welfare, education, and hospitals if the federal government didn't help fund them? *(Students will likely say that some state services would be nonexistent or would provide substandard service.)* **OL**

D Differentiated Instruction

Visual/Spatial Have students keep a record of the total amount of sales taxes that they pay during a week. **Ask:** Did sales taxes play a role in your purchasing decisions? How would your spending behavior have differed if there were no sales tax? *(Answers will vary but should reflect the personal impact of sales taxes.)* **OL**

Economic Analysis

Answer: The two largest sources of revenue for state governments are intergovernmental revenue and sales taxes. The two largest sources of revenue for local governments are intergovernmental revenue and property taxes.

Additional Support

---

intergovernmental revenue funds that one level of government receives from another level of government

Skills Handbook
See page **R50** to learn about *Using Bar and Circle Graphs.*

State Government Revenue Sources

MAIN Idea States rely on funds from the federal government in addition to income taxes and sales taxes.

Economics & You Do you ever wonder why you pay a tax on items you purchase in a store? Read on to learn about sales taxes.

State governments collect their revenues from several sources. **Figure 9.4** shows the relative proportions of these sources, the largest of which are examined below.

Intergovernmental Revenues

The largest source of state revenue consists of **intergovernmental revenue**—funds collected by one level of government that are distributed to another level of government for expenditures. States receive the majority of these funds from the federal government to help fund the state's expenditures for welfare, education, highways, health, and hospitals. **C**

Sales Taxes

Most states also have **implemented** sales taxes to add to their revenue. A sales tax is a general tax levied on consumer purchases of nearly all products. The tax is a percentage of the purchase price, which is added to the final price the consumer pays. Merchants collect the tax at the time of sale. The taxes are then turned over to the proper state government agency on a monthly or other periodic basis. Most states allow merchants to keep a small portion of what they collect to compensate for their time and bookkeeping costs. The sales tax is the second largest source of revenue for states, although five states—Alaska, Delaware, Montana, New Hampshire, and Oregon—do not have a general sales tax. **D**

Figure 9.4 ▶ State and Local Government Revenue Sources

Graphs In Motion
See StudentWorks™ Plus or glencoe.com.

▶ State and local governments have their own sources of revenue. While many have an individual income tax, this is not a major source of funding.

Economic Analysis
What are the two largest sources of state and local revenues?

	State governments		Local governments
Intergovernmental revenue	26.6%		34.9%
Sales taxes	20.1%		5.4%
Individual income tax	13.4%		1.5%
Employee retirement and insurance	12.2%		0.8%
Borrowing	4.7%		4.5%
Higher education fees	4.4%		0.6%
Interest earnings	2.2%		2.4%
Corporate income tax	2.1%		0.2%
Hospital fees	1.8%		3.7%
Utility revenue	0.9%		7.6%
Property taxes	0.8%		24.0%
Other	10.8%		14.4%

Activity: Collaborative Learning

Behavior and Taxes To learn more about how taxes affect the behavior of taxpayers, divide students into groups of three to interview a variety of taxpayers in your community, including small-business owners, high school students with part-time jobs, large-business managers, and retired persons. Instruct students to ask their subjects to name federal, state, and local taxes that they pay. Students should then ask their subjects to describe how paying taxes affects their economic behavior—hiring new workers, expanding the business, buying products, saving, and so on. Have each pair of students compile and summarize their findings, making special note of any differences among the four groups of taxpayers interviewed. Invite a volunteer from each group to share their findings with the class. **OL**

Harley Schwadron/www.CartoonStock.com

"DON'T WORRY! SINCE 28% OF MY SALARY GOES TO THE GOVERNMENT, I'VE DECIDED TO WORK 72% OF THE TIME."

Taxes Most people have to pay taxes to all levels of government. *What does the cartoon imply about the impact of taxes on people?*

S

Individual Income Taxes

All but seven states—Alaska, Florida, Nevada, South Dakota, Texas, Washington, and Wyoming—rely on the individual income tax for revenue. The tax brackets in each state vary **considerably**, and taxes can be progressive in some states and proportional in others.

Other Revenues

States rely on a variety of other revenue sources, including interest earnings on surplus funds; tuition and fees collected from state-owned colleges, universities, and technical schools; corporate income taxes; and hospital fees.

While the percentages for revenue sources in Figure 9.4 are representative of most states, wide variations among states exist. For example, Alaska is the only state without either a general sales tax or an income tax, so it has to rely on other taxes and fees for its operating revenue.

✓**Reading Check** **Contrasting** How do states without individual income taxes find sources of revenue?

Local Government Revenue Sources

MAIN Idea Local governments rely mostly on intergovernmental revenue and property taxes.

Economics & You Do you hope to own a house some day? Read on to learn how this will add another tax to those you are already paying.

Like state governments, local governments have a variety of revenue sources, as shown in Figure 9.4. These sources include taxes and funds from state and federal governments. The main categories are discussed below.

R

Intergovernmental Revenues

Local governments receive the largest part of their revenues—slightly more than one-third—in the form of intergovernmental transfers from state governments. These funds are generally intended for education and public welfare. A much smaller amount comes directly from the federal government, mostly for urban renewal.

CHAPTER 9 Sources of Government Revenue **243**

Activity: Interdisciplinary Connection

History Before the Civil War, the federal government collected most of its revenues from tariffs, or taxes on imports, and from the sale of public lands. During the war, a variety of taxes, including a 5 percent income tax, were imposed to pay for the costs of fighting. After the war, many of these taxes were dropped, but others, including increased property taxes, were added. However, the typical homeowner paid only about $90 in annual property taxes and only about 1 percent of the population ever paid income tax. By 1872, no one was paying income tax because the tax had been repealed. Have students identify which parts of the U.S. Constitution deal with taxation. **OL**

S Skill Practice

Analyzing Graphs Have students identify their states' level of taxes and then compare and contrast the level with that of neighboring states. *(Answers will vary according to students' location.)* **OL**

C Critical Thinking

Problem-Solving Ask: What is the main disadvantage of property taxes? *(It is difficult to assign value to personal property.)* How do most communities solve this problem? *(They hire one or more individuals to assess the value of a few big-ticket items such as buildings and motor vehicles. Other property taxes are seldom collected.)* **OL**

Economic Analysis

Answer: Highest level of taxes: Maine, Washington D.C., New York, Hawaii, Rhode Island. Lowest level of taxes: Alaska, New Hampshire, Delaware, Tennessee, Alabama

Hands-On Chapter Project

Step 2

Explaining Taxation and Revenue Systems

Step 2: Revenue Systems at the Federal, State, and Local Levels. Students will examine the federal, state, and local government's revenue systems, and provide examples of at least three revenue sources at each level.

Figure 9.5 ▶ State and Local Taxes as a Percentage of State Income

▶ State income is the sum of all income earned by all people in the state. State and local governments receive a percentage of that income as tax revenue from a number of sources. The five states without sales taxes—Alaska, Delaware, Montana, New Hampshire, and Oregon—rely on other taxes to provide state revenues.

Economic Analysis *Which states have the highest level of taxes? The lowest level?*

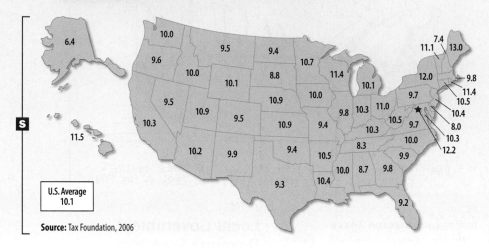

U.S. Average 10.1

Source: Tax Foundation, 2006

property tax tax on tangible and intangible possessions such as real estate, buildings, furniture, stocks, bonds, and bank accounts

tax assessor person who examines and assesses property values for tax purposes

natural monopoly market structure in which average costs of production are lowest when a single firm exists *(also see page 176)*

Property Taxes

The second-largest source of revenue for local governments is the **property tax**—a tax on tangible and intangible possessions. Such possessions usually include real estate, buildings, furniture, farm animals, stocks, bonds, and bank accounts. Most states also assess a property tax on automobiles.

The property tax that raises the most revenue is the tax on real estate. Taxes on other personal property, with the exception of automobiles, are seldom collected because of the problem of valuation. For example, how would the **tax assessor**—the person who assigns value to property for tax purposes—know the reasonable value of everyone's wedding silver, furniture, clothing, or other tangible property? Instead, most communities find it more efficient to hire one or more individuals to assess the value of a few big-ticket items such as buildings and motor vehicles.

Utility Revenues

The third-largest source of local revenue is the income from public utilities that supply water, electricity, sewerage, and even telecommunications. Because of economies of scale, many of of these companies are **natural monopolies**.

A community needs only one set of electrical power lines or underground water pipes, for example, so one company usually supplies all of the services. When people pay their utility bills, the payments are counted as a source of revenue for local governments.

Sales Taxes

Many cities have their own sales taxes. Merchants collect these taxes along with the state sales taxes at the point of sale. While these taxes typically are much lower than state sales taxes, they are the fourth most important source of local government revenues.

244 UNIT 3 Economic Institutions and Issues

Directions: Ask student groups to work together to complete Step 2. One group member should examine federal revenue sources, another group member should examine state revenue sources, and the third group member should examine local government revenue sources. After gathering information, the group members will come back together to

create a booklet, using illustrations and correct grammar and punctuation, to report their findings.

Identifying Have students give an example of a source of revenue at the federal, state, and local levels. **OL**

(Chapter Project continued in Section 3.)

Other Revenue Sources

Figure 9.4 on page 242 shows a variety of ways in which local governments collect their remaining revenues. Some local governments receive a portion of their funds from hospital fees. Others may collect income taxes from individuals and profit taxes from corporations. Still another revenue source for local governments is the interest on invested funds.

If local governments spend more than they collect in revenues, they can borrow from investors. While borrowed funds are small compared to those of the federal government, they form an important source of local government funding.

Local governments look for revenues in a number of ways. Still, the revenue sources available in general are much more limited than those available to the state and federal levels of government.

✓**Reading Check** **Recalling** Which property tax earns the most revenue for local governments?

Tax Assessments Tax assessors determine the value of property for tax purposes. ***Why are property taxes important for local communities?***

R **Reading Strategy**

Summarizing Ask students to list examples of other revenue sources for local government. *(hospital fees, income taxes, profit taxes from corporations, interest on invested funds, borrowed funds)* **BL**

Caption Answer: They provide a significant revenue source.

✓**Reading Check** **Answer:** real estate

Assess

💿 Use the Interactive Tutor Self-Assessment CD-ROM to review Section 2, and then assign the Section 2 Review as homework or as an in-class activity.

Close

Categorizing Have students create a three-column chart with the headings "Federal," "State," and "Local" and then list revenue sources for each. **OL**

SECTION 2 Review

Vocabulary

1. **Explain** the significance of Internal Revenue Service (IRS), payroll withholding system, indexing, FICA, payroll tax, corporate income tax, excise tax, estate tax, gift tax, customs duty, user fee, intergovernmental revenue, property tax, tax assessor, and natural monopoly.

Main Ideas

2. **Listing** Use a graphic organizer like the one below to list the federal government's major revenue sources.

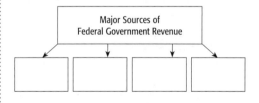

3. **Describing** How do the major revenue sources for state and local governments differ?

Critical Thinking

4. **The BIG Idea** Federal, state, and local governments receive revenue from various sources. Which source do you think best satisfies the tax criteria discussed in Section 1? Defend your answer in a written paragraph.

5. **Drawing Conclusions** Why do you think sales taxes are generally applied to food and beverages purchased in restaurants, but not to those purchased in stores?

6. **Analyzing Visuals** Look at Figure 9.4 on page 242. Why do you think the revenue from income taxes and property taxes differ so much between state and local governments?

7. **Synthesizing** How do excise taxes differ from other taxes such as sales taxes or estate taxes?

Applying Economics

8. **User Fees** User fees have been compared to taxes based on the benefit principle of taxation. Define user fees in your own words. What are the pros and cons of user fees for national parks?

CHAPTER 9 Sources of Government Revenue **245**

Review **SECTION 2**

Answers

1. All definitions can be found in the section and the Glossary.
2. individual income taxes, Social Security taxes, borrowing, corporate income taxes
3. States rely on funds from the federal government in addition to income taxes and sales taxes. Local governments rely mostly on intergovernmental revenue and property taxes.
4. Answers will vary but should demonstrate knowledge of revenue sources and tax evaluation criteria.

5. **Possible answer:** Food and beverages at grocery stores are necessities, whereas dining out is more of a luxury.
6. Property taxes are a major source of funding for local governments, but they are not for state governments. Income taxes are more important for state governments than for local governments.

7. An excise tax is a tax on the manufacture or sale of selected items. Other taxes such as sales taxes and estate taxes cover a broader range.
8. Answers will vary but should demonstrate an understanding of user fees.

Focus

Activating Prior Knowledge
Call students' attention to the title of the feature. **Ask:** Why might people dread tax returns? *(Possible answer: It is a complicated, time-consuming process.)* **OL**

Teach

W Writing Support

Expository Writing Have students write four questions about the information in the paragraph. Then have them choose one of the questions and research to find the answer. **OL**

Analyzing the Impact

Answers:
1. It contains almost 17,000 pages of tax code and more than 600 forms.
2. Answers will vary but should reflect an understanding of a flat tax.

Additional Support

CASE STUDY
Dreaded Tax Returns **R**

Buried in Paper

Every spring, you can tell it's close to the April 15 tax deadline by the anxious faces of frustrated taxpayers and exhausted accountants. The U.S. tax system is one of the most complicated in the world, with almost 17,000 pages of tax code and more than 600 forms. Record keeping, education, and compliance cost the nation $265 billion annually. In 2005 it took about 115,000 Internal Revenue Service (IRS) employees and almost $10.7 billion to collect about $1 trillion from 125 million taxpayers and 7 million businesses.

PERCENTAGE OF TAXPAYERS USING PROFESSIONAL HELP

Source: Internet Revenue Service

Time is Money

Because the tax code has become so complex, more and more Americans hire tax preparers to help them with their returns. On top of that, about 2.2 million taxpayers overpay—by an average of $438—because they either don't itemize deductions or don't include all deductions or exemptions they could claim. Although many Americans file their tax returns online, they still spend an average of 17 hours completing the forms. The complexity of the system has caused many people to long for a simpler flat-tax system.

The European Solution

Several eastern European countries have adopted a flat tax, where everyone pays the same percentage above an exempt amount, regardless of income. The first was the Baltic republic of Estonia, which adopted a flat tax rate of 26 percent in 1994. Most Estonians take only 5 to 20 minutes to complete and electronically file an "e-postcard." The country's tax department spends one penny for every dollar of income tax collected, compared to 25 cents the IRS spends in the United States.

NEWS FLASH

The Longest Return General Electric's 2006 tax return was 24,000 pages long. Had they filed a paper return, it would have been a stack 8 feet high; instead, they filed a 237-megabyte electronic return.

Analyzing the Impact

1. **Summarizing** Why is the U.S. income tax system so complicated?
2. **Drawing Conclusions** Do you think it is easier for a small country like Estonia to implement a flat tax than it would be for the United States? Explain.

Extending the Content

April 15: The Real Due Date?

On February 3, 1913, Congress adopted the 16th Amendment and instituted the income tax. They originally set March 1 as the deadline for filing taxes. Five years later, with the Revenue Act of 1918, they moved the date to March 15. That date was the deadline for the next 37 years. In 1955 it was changed to April 15, which is the present due date—for most years, that is. By law, filing and payment deadlines that fall on Saturday, Sunday, or legal holidays are set for the next business day. Therefore, in certain years, the deadline date might be April 17 or April 18. In those years, taxpayers may have an extra day or two to file their returns.

SECTION 3
Current Tax Issues and Reforms

GUIDE TO READING

Section Preview

In this section, you will learn that one consequence of tax reform was to make the individual tax code more complex than ever.

Content Vocabulary

• payroll withholding statement *(p. 248)*
• accelerated depreciation *(p. 249)*
• investment tax credit *(p. 249)*
• alternative minimum tax *(p. 249)*
• capital gains *(p. 250)*
• flat tax *(p. 251)*
• value-added tax (VAT) *(p. 252)*

Academic Vocabulary

• concept *(p. 251)*
• controversial *(p. 252)*

Reading Strategy

Listing As you read the section, complete a graphic organizer like the one below by listing the advantages and disadvantages of the flat tax. Include a definition of *flat tax* in your own words.

	Advantages	Disadvantages
Flat tax		
Value-added tax		

ISSUES IN THE NEWS
—The San Francisco Chronicle

A Trophy Loophole

One of the looniest tax loopholes imaginable . . . [is] . . . a tax break for big-game hunters who can deduct the cost of an expensive safari when they donate the stuffed trophy to a museum. By using tax-code provisions designed to encourage charitable donations, a hunter can give away a trophy specimen.

This gives a fat tax break to the hunter. It's also created a system of tax dodging and shady dealing. Little-known museums exist largely to take in the trophies and sign tax receipts.

Senator Charles Grassley . . . wants to end such hunting deductions [but] a similar proviso is missing from a tax overhaul in the House. . . . ■

The individual tax code is incredibly complex. The complete code is about 17,000 pages long and contains approximately 9 million words. It has been estimated that Americans spend more than *7 billion* hours every year filling out their federal tax returns for the IRS.

Every year, magazines like *Money* ask professional tax preparers to fill out tax returns for a hypothetical family—only to find out that no two returns are the same. If experts can't get it right, then the rest of us will obviously have a difficult time. Also, it is all too easy for lawmakers to insert special-interest provisions in the tax code, such as the one in the news story above.

It is no wonder that the tax code has been amended about 14,000 times in the last 20 years—and Congress is still not done with changes!

Teach

D Differentiated Instruction

Intrapersonal Ask students who work to bring paycheck stubs to class. Then review Figure 9.6 with them. Point out that while paycheck stubs may differ in appearance, most contain similar information. Have students locate where the federal, state, city, and Social Security tax amounts are noted on the paycheck stub in their textbook. **Ask: Which of these taxes are federal taxes?** *(federal income, FICA)* Then have students locate the various categories on their own paycheck stubs. **OL**

✓**Reading Check** **Answer:** The federal and state governments supply withholding tables for employers to use in determining deductions.

Economic Analysis

Answer: about 27 percent

---

payroll withholding statement document attached to a paycheck summarizing pay and deductions

S Personal Finance Handbook

See pages R24–R27 for more information on paying taxes.

Examining Your Paycheck

D

MAIN Idea The income taxes you pay are summarized on the stub that is attached to your paycheck.

Economics & You Do you have a job where your taxes are taken out before you are paid? Read on to learn how these taxes are deducted from your paycheck.

Most of the federal, state, and local taxes are deducted directly from your paycheck. Employers list these deductions on the **payroll withholding statement**—the stub attached to a paycheck that summarizes income, tax withholdings, and other deductions, as shown in **Figure 9.6.**

The worker to whom the check belongs makes $10 an hour and receives a check every two weeks. If the length of the workweek is 40 hours, the worker's gross pay amounts to $800. The worker is single, has no deductions, and lives and works in Kentucky.

According to withholding tables the federal government supplied for that year, biweekly workers making at least $800, but less than $820, have $104.70 withheld from their paychecks every pay period. Similar tables for the state of Kentucky specify that $40.01 is withheld for state income taxes. Because these are both estimates, and because even minor differences between the amounts withheld and the amount actually owed can grow, the worker will file state and federal tax returns between January 1 and April 15 of the following year to settle the differences.

Another deduction is the half-percent city income tax that amounts to $4. Because the amount is relatively small, most cities do not require taxpayers to file separate year-end tax forms.

The FICA tax amounts to 7.65 percent (6.20 percent for Social Security and 1.45 percent for Medicare) of $800, or $61.20. The FICA is deducted from the gross pay, along with $3.20 in miscellaneous deductions, which leaves a net pay of $586.89.

If the worker has insurance payments or retirement contributions, or puts money into a credit union, more deductions will appear on the pay stub.

✓**Reading Check** **Summarizing** How are payroll deductions calculated?

Figure 9.6 ▶ **Biweekly Paycheck and Withholding Statement**

▶ The withholding statement attached to your paycheck summarizes the federal and state tax deductions from your pay. Other withholdings may include city income taxes and voluntary deductions, such as health insurance payments and savings plans.

Economic Analysis *What percentage of this individual's pay has been deducted from the paycheck?*

Weaver & Higginson Attorneys at Law

21-2 / 000 Number 2,195,903

Date June 29 20 07

Pay to the order of _____ Sara Pěna _____ $ 586.89

Five Hundred Eighty-Six Dollars and 89/100 _____ Dollars

◆ THE CENTRAL BANK

Memo _____

5:5555555: 555:55555 Treasurer

PLEASE DETACH AND RETAIN THIS PORTION
AS YOUR RECORD OF EARNINGS AND DEDUCTIONS

Date	Pay End	Vo. No.	Emp. No.	Hrs.	Misc.	Cr. Un.	Ins.	Gross
6/29/07	6/23/07		1376	80	3.20			800 00
104 70	40 01	4 00	61 20					586 89
Federal	State	City	FICA	Ret.	Bonds	Other		Net

ECONOMIC CARTOON 14

FLIGHT OF THE IRS

Economic Cartoons, p. 19

Flight of the IRS

Objective: Understand the message of an economic cartoon.

Focus/Teach: Have students share their impressions of the IRS. Then have them study the cartoon and answer the questions that follow.

Assess: Review the answers to questions 1 through 4 as a class.

Close: Ask students whether they think most people have a positive or negative opinion of the IRS.

Differentiated Instruction Strategies

BL Ask students to summarize the cartoonist's message in one sentence.

AL Have students draw a cartoon about the IRS or taxes that alludes to a different movie.

ELL Explain to students the plot of *The Wizard of Oz.* If possible, show them pictures of similar scenes in the movie.

Differentiated Instruction

Figure 9.7 ▶ **Tax Table for Single Individuals, 2006**

If taxable income is over . . .	But not over . . .	The tax is:
$0	$7,550	10% of the amount over $0
$7,550	$30,650	$755 plus 15% of the amount over $7,550
$30,650	$74,200	$4,220 plus 25% of the amount over $30,650
$74,200	$154,800	$15,107.50 plus 28% of the amount over $74,200
$154,800	$336,550	$37,675.50 plus 33% of the amount over $154,800
$336,550	no limit	$97,653.00 plus 35% of the amount over $336,550

Source: IRS Schedule X

▶ According to the individual income tax table, a single individual with $6,000 of taxable income would pay $6,000 x .10, or $600 in taxes.

Economic Analysis

How much in taxes would an individual with $40,000 of taxable income pay? **S**

Tax Reform

MAIN Idea Numerous changes have been made to the federal income tax code since 1981.

Economics and You Do you or your family pay federal income taxes? Read on to learn why keeping up with the tax code is so difficult.

Tax reform has received considerable attention recently. Since 1981, there have been more changes in the tax code than at any other time in our nation's history.

Tax Reform in 1981

When Ronald Reagan was elected president in 1980, he believed that high taxes were the main stumbling block to economic growth. In 1981 he signed the Economic Recovery Tax Act, which included large tax reductions for individuals and businesses.

Before the Recovery Act, the individual tax code had 16 marginal tax brackets ranging from 14 to 70 percent. The act lowered the marginal rates in all brackets, capping the highest marginal tax at 50 percent. In comparison, today's tax code, shown in **Figure 9.7,** has six marginal brackets ranging from 10 to 35 percent.

Businesses also got tax relief in the form of **accelerated depreciation**—earlier and larger depreciation charges—which allowed firms to reduce federal income

R tax payments. Another section of the act introduced the **investment tax credit**—a reduction in business taxes that are tied to investment in new plants and equipment. For example, a company might purchase a $50,000 machine that qualified for a 10 percent, or $5,000, tax credit. If the firm owed $12,000 in taxes, the credit reduced the tax owed to $7,000.

Tax Reform: 1986, 1993

By the mid-1980s, the idea that the tax code favored the rich and powerful was gaining momentum. In 1983 more than 3,000 millionaires paid no income taxes.

In 1986 Congress passed sweeping tax reform that made it difficult for the very rich to avoid taxes altogether. The **alternative minimum tax**—the personal income tax rate that applies whenever the amount of taxes paid falls below a designated level—was strengthened. Under this provision, people had to pay a minimum tax of 20 percent, regardless of other circumstances or loopholes in the tax code.

As the United States entered the 1990s, the impact of 10 years of tax cuts was beginning to show. Government spending was growing faster than revenues, and the government had to borrow more. The resulting tax reform of 1993 was driven more by the need for the government to balance its

accelerated depreciation schedule that spreads depreciation over fewer years to generate larger tax reductions

investment tax credit tax credit given for purchase of equipment

alternative minimum tax personal income tax rate that applies to cases in which taxes would otherwise fall below a certain level

Skills Handbook

See page **R54** to learn about **Understanding Percentages.**

CHAPTER 9 Sources of Government Revenue 249

S Skill Practice

Using Tables and Charts Have students study the Tax Table for Single Individuals, 2006. Call their attention to the percentage increases in the column marked "The tax is." **Then ask:** What conclusion can you draw from the information in the column? *(Students will likely conclude that the higher an individual's income, the higher percentage of taxes he or she will pay.)* **OL**

R Reading Strategy

Questioning Before students read about tax reform, have them write three questions that they think will be answered in the text. As they read the passage, encourage them to look for the answers to their questions, and write them down. **OL**

Economic Analysis

Answer: $6,557.50 (tax of $4,220 plus 25% of the amount over $30,650, which is $2,337.50, equals $6,557.50)

Leveled Activities

BL Guided Reading Activities, p. 27

OL Personal Finance Activities, p. 15

AL Primary and Secondary Source Readings, p. 14

C Critical Thinking

Analyzing Ask: What were the two forces that created the tax reform in 1997? Explain. *(One force was economic; the government had unexpectedly high tax revenues in 1997. The other force was political; the Republicans had gained a majority in Congress. They reduced the tax on capital gains and lowered inheritance taxes.)* **OL**

W Writing Support

Persuasive Writing Ask students to take a position on whether the tax cuts of 1997 favored the wealthy. Allow them to conduct additional research if necessary. Then have students write a newspaper editorial presenting their opinion. **OL**

Economic Analysis

Answer: After 1981, revenue collections increased dramatically.

Hands-On Chapter Project

Step 3

Figure 9.8 ▶ **Total Government Receipts per Capita, Adjusted for Inflation**

▶ Although a recession in 2001 reduced revenues from 2002 to 2003, total revenue collections by all levels of government have grown dramatically over the years.

Economic Analysis *How does the graph reflect the tax reforms since 1981?*

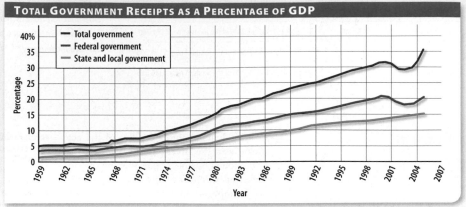

TOTAL GOVERNMENT RECEIPTS AS A PERCENTAGE OF GDP

- — Total government
- — Federal government
- — State and local government

Source: *Economic Report of the President, 2006*

---

capital gains profits from the sale of an asset held for 12 months or longer

budget than to overhaul the tax brackets. As a result, two top marginal tax brackets of 36 and 39.6 percent were added.

Tax Reform in 1997

The next significant reform followed four years later with the Taxpayer Relief Act of 1997. The forces that created it were both economic and political.

On the economic side, the government found itself with unexpectedly high tax revenues in 1997. The two new marginal tax brackets of 36 and 39.6 percent that had been added in 1993, along with the closure of some tax loopholes, meant that most people paid more taxes than before.

On the political side, the Republicans had gained a firm majority in Congress and now saw a need to fulfill a commitment to their supporters. They reduced the tax on **capital gains**—profits from the sale of an asset held for 12 months or longer—from 28 to 20 percent. The new law also lowered inheritance taxes.

Some people thought that the tax cuts favored the wealthy, and even the government agreed. An analysis by the United States Treasury Department determined that nearly half of the benefits went to the top 20 percent of wage and income earners. The lowest 20 percent received less than 1 percent of the tax reductions. With all its changes, the 1997 federal tax law became the most complicated ever.

Tax Reform in 2001

By 2001 politicians faced a new issue: the federal government was actually collecting more taxes than it was spending. These surpluses were projected to continue to the year 2010. Surpluses could have been used to repay some of the money the government borrowed in the 1980s or to fund new federal spending. The government also could cut taxes to "give the money back to the people." In the end, President Bush backed a massive $1.35 billion, "temporary" 10-year tax cut due to expire in 2011.

250   UNIT 3   Economic Institutions and Issues

Explaining Taxation and Revenue Systems

Step 3: The Present U.S. Tax System and Alternative Tax Approaches. Students will explain our present tax system and alternative tax approaches.

Directions: Have students meet in their groups of three. They will research our present tax system, the flat tax, and the value-added tax. They will then present their findings in a multimedia report.

Analyzing Visuals Have students decide on at least one visual they would like to use in their multimedia presentation to increase understanding. They can then assign a group member to create it. **OL**

(Chapter Project will continue in Visual Summary.)

The main feature of the 2001 tax reform was to reduce the top four marginal tax brackets of 27, 30, 35, and 38.6 percent to 25, 28, 33, and 35 percent by 2006. The law also introduced a 10 percent tax bracket and eliminated the estate tax on the wealthiest 2 percent of taxpayers by 2010.

Tax Reform in 2003

Slow economic growth in 2002 convinced the Bush administration and Congress to accelerate many of the 2001 tax reforms. Specifically, the top four marginal tax brackets were reduced immediately rather than in 2006.

For lower income taxpayers, the top end of the 10 percent bracket was increased modestly. The child tax credit was also expanded from $600 to $1,000. Finally, the 20 percent capital gains tax bracket was reduced from 20 to 15 percent.

The 2003 tax cuts put the federal government back in the same situation as in 1993. A series of tax cuts reduced taxes in upper income brackets, and government was still spending more than it collected in taxes.

Permanent Tax Cuts by 2011?

The tax cuts of 2001 and 2003 were "temporary" in the sense that they were due to expire in 2011. Whether that happens or not will depend on several things.

One complicating factor is that the rate of economic growth in the six years following the 2001 tax cuts was slightly lower than the rate of growth in the six years following the 1993 tax increase. This makes it difficult to argue that lower taxes are needed for higher rates of growth.

However, the biggest factor will be the extent to which the federal government continues to spend more than it collects in taxes. If the present trend continues, it will be difficult to preserve the tax cuts because the government will need so much additional revenue.

✓Reading Check **Inferring** Why have tax reforms occurred so frequently in recent years?

Alternative Tax Approaches

MAIN Idea The need for new federal revenues will influence future tax reform.

Economics and You You learned earlier about state sales taxes. Read on to find out how another tax is similar to the sales tax.

Some people want to change the personal income tax; others want to replace it with something else. Because of this, we hear a lot about two alternatives: the flat tax and the value-added tax.

The Flat Tax

The **concept** of a **flat tax**—a proportional tax on individual income after a specified threshold has been reached—did not receive much attention until Republican candidate Steve Forbes and others raised the issue in the 1996 presidential elections.

The primary advantage of the flat tax is the simplicity it offers to the taxpayer. A person would still have to fill out an income tax return every year but could skip many current steps, such as itemizing deductions. A second advantage is that a flat tax would close most tax loopholes if it did away with most deductions and exemptions. Finally, a flat tax reduces the need for tax accountants, tax preparers, and even a large portion of the IRS. As a result, Americans would no longer have to spend 7 billion hours every year preparing tax returns.

However, a flat tax also has disadvantages because it would remove many of the incentives built into the current tax code.

flat tax proportional tax on individual income after a specified threshold has been reached

DiD You KNow?

➤ **Tax Exempt?** Each year taxpayers take advantage of a long list of deductions and tax credits to reduce their tax burden. In the year 2006, the Tax Foundation reported that a record 43.4 million tax returns from 91 million individuals showed no taxes due. Combined with the 15 million Americans who don't file returns at all, about 41 percent of the U.S. population did not contribute to the federal treasury.

CHAPTER 9   Sources of Government Revenue   251

R Reading Strategy

Identifying Ask: What are two factors that might prevent the tax cuts in 2001 and 2003 from becoming permanent? *(First, the rate of economic growth in the years following the 2001 tax cuts was lower than the rate of growth in the years following the 1992 tax increase. This makes it difficult to argue that lower taxes are needed for economic growth. Second, if the federal government continues to spend more than it collects in taxes, it will be difficult to preserve the tax cuts.)* **OL**

D Differentiated Instruction

English Language Learners Have students use a dictionary to find the definition of the word *flat. (smooth, level, even)* Then have them explain how *flat* could apply to taxes. *(It would mean taxes would be smooth and even, without increases or decreases.)* **ELL**

✓Reading Check **Answer:** to increase and decrease government revenues

Additional Support

Extending the Content

Support of the Flat Tax Steve Forbes is a newspaper and magazine publisher who sought the Republican presidential nomination in 1996 and 2000. His grandfather founded *Forbes,* the business magazine which is still owned by the Forbes family. Steve Forbes was born in Morristown, New Jersey, in 1947 and graduated from Princeton University in 1970. While still in college, Forbes started *Business*

Today, a magazine that came out three times a year. In 1993 Forbes became chairman of Empower America, a research center dedicated to conservative principles. He supports a flat tax and an end to the federal government's progressive income tax.

C Critical Thinking

Predicting Consequences
Ask students if they have ever shopped at a factory outlet mall. Discuss the concept of outlet malls—manufacturers selling directly to the public through their own store. **Ask:** How do you think a federal value-added tax would affect the trend of factory outlet malls? Would the number of malls increase, decrease, or remain the same? On what do you base your prediction? *(Students may note that a value-added tax could increase the number of factory outlet malls. Outlet malls could sell products more cheaply because they could circumvent the retailers' tax that increases prices.)* **OL**

Economic Analysis

Answer: proportional; everyone pays the same percentage rate regardless of income

Additional Support

Figure 9.9 ▶ The Value-Added Tax

▶ The VAT is like a national sales tax added to each stage of production. As a result, it is built into the final price of a product and is less visible to consumers. The third and fifth columns show the value added at each stage, and the fourth and sixth columns show the cumulative values.

Economic Analysis *Is a VAT regressive, proportional, or progressive? Why?*

		No taxes		With a 10% value-added tax	
		Value added	Cumulative value	Value added with a 10% VAT	Cumulative with VAT
Step 1	Loggers fell trees and sell the timber to the mills for processing.	$1	$1	$1 + $.10 = $1.10	$1.10
Step 2	Mills cut the timber into blanks that will be used to make bats.	$1	$2	$1 + $.10 = $1.10	$2.20
Step 3	Bat manufacturers shape and paint or varnish the bats and sell them to wholesalers.	$5	$7	$5 + $.50 = $5.50	$7.70
Step 4	Wholesalers sell the bats to retail outlets where consumers can buy them.	$1	$8	$1 + $.10 = $1.10	$8.80
Step 5	Retailers put the bats on the shelves and wait for consumers.	$2	$10	$2 + $.20 = $2.20	$11.00
Step 6	Consumers buy the bats for:		$10		$11.00

value-added tax (VAT) tax on the value added at every stage of the production process

For example, the tax code now allows homeowners to deduct interest payments on home mortgages. Other incentives include deductions for education, training, and child care.

Another problem is that no one knows exactly what rate is needed to replace the revenues collected under the current tax system. Supporters of the flat tax argue that a 15 percent rate would work. Other estimates by the U.S. Treasury put the tax closer to 23 percent—which represents more of a burden on low-income earners because their taxes would increase compared to current rates.

Finally, there is no clear answer as to whether a flat tax would further stimulate economic growth. After all, the extraordinary growth of the American economy in the 1990s, the longest period of peacetime prosperity in our history, took place when taxes were much higher.

The Value-Added Tax

Another **controversial** proposal is to adopt the equivalent of a national sales tax by taxing consumption rather than income. This could be done with a **C value-added tax (VAT)**—a tax placed on the value that manufacturers add at each stage of production. The United States currently does not have a VAT, although it is widely used in Europe.

To see how the VAT works, consider how the tax impacts the manufacturing and selling of wooden baseball bats. First, loggers cut the trees and sell the timber to lumber mills. The mills process the logs for sale to bat manufacturers. The manufacturers then shape the wood into baseball bats.

After the bats are painted or varnished, they are sold to a wholesaler. The wholesaler sells them to retailers, who sell them to consumers. As **Figure 9.9** shows, a VAT tax is levied at each stage of production.

Activity: Interdisciplinary Connection

History Show students that the fairness of income taxes has been debated for thousands of years by reading the following quote from Plato (circa 428–348 B.C.): "When there is an income tax, the just man will pay more and the unjust less on the same amount of income." **Ask:** Based on this quote, do you think Plato would prefer a flat tax on income or the current progressive income tax system?

(Students should mention that, under the present system, taxpayers can use loopholes to pay less than others with the same income. As a result, Plato would probably prefer the flat tax.)

Invite students to find additional tax-related quotes from historical figures. Discuss the quotes as a class and speculate on how the figures might feel about the current U.S. tax system. **OL**

The VAT has several advantages. First, it is hard to avoid because it is built into the price of the product being taxed. Second, the tax incidence is widely spread, which makes it harder for a single firm to shift the burden of the tax to another group.

Third, the VAT is easy to collect, because firms make their VAT payments directly to the government. Consequently, even a relatively small VAT can raise a tremendous amount of revenue, especially when it is applied to a broad range of goods and services.

Finally, some supporters claim that the VAT would encourage people to save more than they do now. After all, if none of your money is taxed until it is spent, you might think more carefully about purchases, decide to spend less—and save more.

The main disadvantage of the VAT is that it tends to be virtually invisible. In the baseball bat example, consumers may be aware that bat prices went from $10 to $11, but they might attribute this to a shortage of good wood, higher wages, or some other factor. In other words, it is difficult for taxpayers to be vigilant about higher taxes if they cannot see them.

Inevitability of Future Reforms

The tax code is more complex now than at any time since 1981—a fact that virtually guarantees future attempts to simplify it. The recent flat tax movement provides just one such example. While simplification is desirable, unexpected events often require new expenditures—which in turn may require changes in the tax code. The unexpected cost of the war in Iraq, along with the enormous damage inflicted by hurricane Katrina in 2005, are two examples of such unexpected costs.

Reform also can result from political change, which tends to be abrupt as one party leaves office and another enters. New administrations often display a sense of urgency to finally do things the "right" way, or to clean up the presumed excesses of their predecessors.

Finally, it is difficult for politicians to give up the power to modify behavior, influence resource allocation, support pet projects, or grant concessions to special interest groups by changing the tax code.

✓Reading Check **Describing** How does a value-added tax work? Why is it useful?

W **Writing Support**

Personal Writing Have students write a letter to one of their congressional representatives explaining why they support or oppose tax reform. Tell students to keep their letters brief and to the point. **AL**

✓Reading Check **Answer:**
A VAT refers to taxes placed on the value that manufacturers add during production. It is easy to collect, hard to avoid, and may encourage people to save more.

Assess

💿 Use the Interactive Tutor Self-Assessment CD-ROM to review Section 3, and then assign the Section 3 Review as homework or as an in-class activity.

Close

Making Decisions Ask: If there is one thing you could change in the tax laws, what would it be? Why? Discuss answers as a class. **OL**

SECTION 3 Review

Vocabulary

1. **Explain** the significance of payroll withholding statement, accelerated depreciation, investment tax credit, alternative minimum tax, capital gains, flat tax, and value-added tax (VAT).

Main Ideas

2. **Identifying** What are the major types of federal, state, and local taxes on the payroll withholding statement?

3. **Listing** Use a graphic organizer like the one below to list the advantages and disadvantages of the value-added tax.

Value-Added Tax	
Advantages	Disadvantages

Critical Thinking

4. **The BIG Idea** What factors led to the tax reform measures passed in 1981, 1986, 1997, and 2001?

5. **Summarizing** What changes would you recommend if you were in charge of revising the federal tax code? Explain your answer in a written paragraph.

6. **Analyzing Visuals** Look at Figure 9.7 on page 249. How can you tell whether this tax is progressive, regressive, or proportional?

7. **Cause and Effect** Describe the factors that are likely to cause future revisions of the tax code.

Applying Economics

8. **Flat Tax** Use examples to explain what might happen to donations for charitable organizations under a flat tax.

CHAPTER 9 Sources of Government Revenue **253**

Review SECTION 3

Answers

1. All definitions can be found in the section and the Glossary.
2. federal income tax, state income tax, FICA (Social Security and Medicare), and possibly local income tax
3. **Advantages:** hard to avoid, tax incidence widely spread, easy to collect, might encourage more saving. **Disadvantages:** difficult for taxpayers to be vigilant since VAT is "invisible," competes with state sales taxes.

4. There were high taxes blocking economic growth, Congress felt that too many of the rich were able to completely avoid paying taxes, there was high tax revenue, Republicans were commited to reducing inheritance taxes and providing tax breaks for people with long-term investments, and the federal government was collecting more taxes than it was spending.
5. Answers will vary but should reflect knowledge of the current federal tax code.

6. The tax is progressive, based on a percentage of taxable income.
7. Factors likely to cause future revisions include the desire to simplify the tax code, the appearance of unexpected costs, political change, and the reluctance of politicians to give up their power to change the tax code.
8. Answers will vary but should demonstrate an understanding of the flat tax.

Teach

R Reading Strategy

Inferring Have students explain why Kia built a plant in Slovakia. *(Slovakia had low taxes.)* **Ask:** If more countries in Europe enact flat taxes, what might happen to manufacturing companies? *(They may build plants in countries with flat tax systems.)* **OL**

BusinessWeek ONLINE

To find up-to-date news and analysis on the economy, business, technology, markets, entrepreneurs, investments, and finance, have students search feature articles and special reports on the BusinessWeek Web site, www.businessweek.com.

Examining the Newsclip

Answers:

1. One low income tax rate is paid by all, there are no loopholes or graduated rates, and there is no need to enforce complex laws.

2. They were not in the former Soviet bloc.

Additional Support

BusinessWeek NEWSCLIP

A flat tax has often been debated in the United States. Today Russia and several countries in Eastern Europe utilize it as a way to keep taxes simple and avoid tax loopholes. This has spurred Western Europe to take a closer look.

Europe Circles the Flat Tax

The flat tax. In the eyes of many fiscal conservatives, it's the Holy Grail of public policy: One low income tax rate paid by all but the poorest wage-earners, who are exempt. No loopholes for the rich to exploit. No graduated rates that take a higher percentage of income from people who work hard to earn more. No need for a huge bureaucracy to police fiendishly complex tax laws. U.S. conservatives have been pushing the idea for decades. But it has gotten its first real road test in the former Soviet bloc, where at least eight countries, from minuscule Estonia to giant Russia, have enacted flat taxes since the mid-1990s.

Most of these countries' economies are growing at a far-healthier clip than those of their neighbors to the west. So it's no surprise that calls for a flat tax are now being heard in Western Europe, the most heavily taxed zone on the planet. . . . Even without pressure from the East, many Western European governments face growing complaints about the complexity of their tax regimes. . . .

Drawn by low taxes, Kia built a manufacturing plant in Slovakia.

There's no guarantee, of course, that flat taxes would work as well in Western Europe as they have in the countries to the east. In the former Soviet bloc, most of the countries that enacted flat taxes gained revenue as people who had worked in the shadow economy began reporting their income and paying taxes. The former tax dodgers figured that with rates so low, it was no longer worth running the risk of breaking the law. Moscow, which introduced a flat tax in 2001, saw its income tax revenues more than double in real terms from 2000 to 2004.

—Reprinted from *BusinessWeek*

FLAT TAXES		
Country	Year	Rate
Estonia	1994	23%
Latvia	1995	25%
Russia	2001	13%
Serbia	2003	14%
Slovakia	2003	19%
Ukraine	2003	13%
Georgia	2004	12%
Romania	2005	16%

Source: Hoover Institution

Examining the Newsclip

1. **Analyzing** According to the article, why do fiscal conservatives promote a flat tax?

2. **Determining Cause and Effect** Why might Western European countries not see similar revenue increases?

254 UNIT 3 Economic Institutions and Issues

Extending the Content

Is Flat Really Flat? Many Eastern European nations that were former members of the Soviet bloc have introduced a statutory flat personal rate as part of their reform packages in the hopes of generating sufficient revenue for government expenses. The results have been positive, but experts point out that many of these countries are using variations of a flat income tax rather than implementing the original concept. In these situations, Social Security contributions make much larger contributions to the total tax revenue than personal income tax. The combination of a flat income tax, high Social Security contributions, and indirect taxation means that there is a tax burden on individuals that is often higher than suggested by the original concept of a flat tax.

CHAPTER 9

Visual Summary

STUDY TO GO

Study anywhere, anytime!
Download quizzes and flash cards to your PDA from glencoe.com.

Visual Summary

CHAPTER 9

▶ **Types of Taxes** All taxes in the United States can be broken down into three categories: proportional, progressive, and regressive.

Proportional	Progressive	Regressive
• Percentage of income paid in taxes stays the same regardless of income • Example: Medicare	• Percentage of income paid in taxes goes up as income goes up • Example: individual income tax	• Percentage of income paid in taxes goes down as income goes up • Example: sales tax

▶ **Government Revenue Sources** Federal, state, and local revenue sources differ. Much of the federal revenue is sent on to state and local governments.

Federal Government
• Individual income taxes
• FICA
• Borrowing
• Corporate income taxes
• Excise taxes
• Estate and gift taxes
• Customs duties
• Miscellaneous fees

State Governments
• Intergovernmental revenue
• Sales taxes
• Individual income taxes
• Tuition and fees from colleges and universities
• Corporate income taxes
• Hospital fees
• Other

Local Governments
• Intergovernmental revenue
• Property taxes
• Public utilities
• Sales taxes
• Individual income taxes
• Hospital fees
• Other

▶ **Alternative Tax Approaches** Because the federal tax code has become so large and cumbersome, people have discussed the flat tax and the value-added tax as two alternatives.

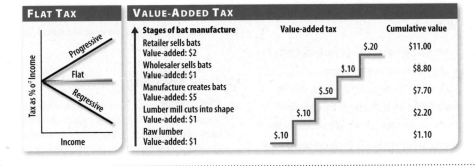

FLAT TAX	VALUE-ADDED TAX		
	Stages of bat manufacture	Value-added tax	Cumulative value
Tax as % of Income — Progressive / Flat / Regressive (Income)	Retailer sells bats Value-added: $2	$.20	$11.00
	Wholesaler sells bats Value-added: $1	$.10	$8.80
	Manufacture creates bats Value-added: $5	$.50	$7.70
	Lumber mill cuts into shape Value-added: $1	$.10	$2.20
	Raw lumber Value-added: $1	$.10	$1.10

Drawing Conclusions Have students review the types of taxes in the table. **Ask:** Why might the U.S. tax system be considered cumbersome? *(Possible answer: The tax code for a system with three categories is large, complicated, and difficult to understand. It requires the services of tax preparers, tax accountants, and an enormous government agency.)* **OL**

Analyzing Visuals Have students describe the graphic representation of a flat tax. *(Possible answer: a straight, horizontal line)* Next, have them describe the graphic representation of a value-added tax. *(Possible answer: stairsteps, with a percentage of value-added tax on each step, leading up to a cumulative value)* Ask students to share how the representations help them understand both tax alternatives. **BL**

Hands-On Chapter Project

Step 4: Wrap Up

Explaining Taxation and Revenue Systems

Step 4: Bringing It All Together.
Students will synthesize what they learned in previous steps.

Directions: Instruct each group to collect the work they've completed throughout the chapter. Collections should include the pamphlet and summary report from Step 1, the booklet from Step 2, and the multimedia presentation from Step 3. Then, review the

Big Idea with students by asking volunteers to explain how all levels of the government use tax revenue to provide essential goods and services. Have students compose their thoughts into a paragraph in their journals. **OL**

CHAPTER 9

Assessment & Activities

ExamView®
Assessment Suite

This easy-to-use software includes extensive question banks and allows you to create fully customized tests that can be administered in print or online.

Review Content Vocabulary

1. b	**2.** h
3. j	**4.** d
5. g	**6.** i
7. f	**8.** e
9. c	**10.** a

Review Academic Vocabulary

11. evolved
12. concept
13. implement
14. validity
15. considerably
16. controversial

Review the Main Ideas

17. to promote or discourage consumer buying
18. It may impact the poor, and its benefits are uncertain.
19. because those with higher incomes pay a smaller percentage of income in taxes than those with lower incomes
20. equity: should be impartial and just; simplicity: laws should be written clearly; efficiency: should be easy to collect and cost-effective
21. Social Security and Medicare
22. excise: on certain manu-factured items; estate: on transfer of property at death; gift: applied to transfer of wealth; customs: on imported goods
23. **State:** other governments; sales taxes, income taxes; interest earnings. **Local:** intergovernmental revenue; property taxes

Review Content Vocabulary

On a separate sheet of paper, choose the letter of the term identified by each phrase below.

a. ability-to-pay	**f.** VAT
b. payroll tax	**g.** tax return
c. estate tax	**h.** regressive tax
d. excise tax	**i.** sales tax
e. FICA	**j.** capital gains

1. tax on wages and salaries withheld from paycheck
2. average tax per dollar decreases as taxable income increases
3. profits from an asset held 12 months or longer
4. tax on the manufacture or sale of certain items
5. annual report to the government detailing income earned and taxes owed
6. large source of revenue for state governments
7. national sales tax on value added at each stage of production
8. Social Security and Medicare taxes
9. tax on the transfer of property when a person dies
10. tax paid by those who can most afford to pay

Review Academic Vocabulary

Replace the underlined word in each sentence below with the appropriate synonym from the following list: *validity, evolved, implement, considerably, concept,* and *controversial.*

11. The tax code has <u>developed</u> into a complicated system.
12. The <u>idea</u> of a flat tax has been debated for a long time.
13. The government needs tax revenue to <u>fulfill</u> its goals.
14. The IRS questioned the <u>legitimacy</u> of the deduction.
15. The tax code has changed <u>substantially</u> since its origin.
16. Abolishing tax deductions would be an <u>unpopular</u> move by the government.

Review the Main Ideas

Section 1 (pages 229–236)

17. **Describe** how taxes can be used to affect people's behavior.
18. **Describe** the limitations of the benefit principle of taxation.
19. **Explain** why a sales tax is considered to be a regressive tax.
20. **Explain** the three criteria used to evaluate taxes.

Section 2 (pages 238–245)

21. **Identify** the two components of FICA.
22. **Distinguish** between excise taxes, estate and gift taxes, and customs duties.
23. **List** the main sources of revenue for state and local governments by using a graphic organizer like the one below.

Sources of Revenue	
State	Local

Section 3 (pages 247–253)

24. **Discuss** the deductions that are withheld from paychecks.
25. **Describe** the major tax reform bills enacted since 1981.
26. **Explain** why Congress enacted the alternative minimum tax.
27. **Identify** the advantages and disadvantages of a flat tax.

Critical Thinking

28. **The BIG Idea** If you were an elected official who wanted to increase tax revenues, which of the following taxes would you prefer to use: individual income, sales, property, corporate income, user fees, VAT, or flat? Provide reasons for your decision.

24. taxes (Federal, state, FICA, city), insurance payments, retirement contributions, credit union contributions
25. The Economic Recovery Tax Act reduced marginal tax rates. The Taxpayer Relief Act reduced capital gains and inheritance taxes, and added education deductions. Reforms strengthened alternative minimum tax, added some tax brackets and reduced others, reduced estate tax and capital gains tax, and increased the child tax credit.
26. to ensure that the rich would pay some taxes
27. Advantages: simplicity, closes tax loopholes. Disadvantages: questionable rate needed to place current revenues, uncertainty over stimulation of economic growth.

Critical Thinking

28. Answers will vary but should indicate an understanding of the different types of taxes.

Economics ONLINE Self-Check Quiz Visit the
Economics: Principles and Practices Web site at glencoe.com and click
on *Chapter 9–Self-Check Quizzes* to prepare for the chapter test.

**Assessment
and Activities** **CHAPTER
9**

29. Inferring Why do you think Alaska has no sales tax or personal income tax?

30. Comparing and Contrasting What were the goals of the Economic Recovery Tax Act of 1981, the 1986 tax reform, and 2001 tax changes?

31. Synthesizing For one week, keep a list of all taxes you hear or read about in the news media or pay in your community. Classify your journal entries into three categories: federal, state, and local taxes. Then draw a matrix like the one below and classify each in the appropriate place. Which taxes appeared in the news most frequently?

	Ability-to-pay principle	Benefit principle
Regressive		
Proportional		
Progressive		

32. Analyzing What provisions of tax measures enacted in the last 20 years benefit taxpayers with higher incomes?

Applying Economic Concepts

33. User Fees In your own words, write a rationale for a user fee that you think should be enacted.

34. Taxes Some people object to state and local governments imposing sales and property taxes. What would you say to these people in defense of the two taxes?

Thinking Like an Economist

35. Critical Thinking Describe how an economist might go about analyzing the consequences of shifting from the individual income tax to a consumption tax like the VAT.

Writing About Economics

36. Expository Writing Does the concept of a flat income tax meet the three criteria for effective taxes? Write a brief summary of your findings and use it to either support or oppose such a proposal.

Math Practice

37. After deductions and exemptions, Mindy's unmarried brother had taxable income of $98,000 in 2006. According to the tax table in Figure 9.7 on page 249, what will he owe in federal income taxes? What did he pay in Social Security taxes? What did he pay in Medicare taxes?

Analyzing Visuals

38. Look at Figure 9.3 on page 239 and compare the revenue from the various sources for the years 2001 and 2007. In which categories did revenues decrease? How did the federal government make up these decreases?

Interpreting Cartoons

39. Critical Thinking Look at the cartoon below. Who are the people seated in the chairs? Whom do the figures in the bottom left corner represent? What statement is the cartoonist trying to make?

CHAPTER 9 Sources of Government Revenue **257**

Thinking Like an Economist

35. Answers will vary but should show an understanding of the advantages and disadvantages of a consumption tax.

Writing About Economics

36. Answers will vary but should include students' opinions on whether a flat income tax meets the criteria for effective taxes.

Math Practice

37. Mindy's brother will owe $21,771.50 in federal income taxes. He paid $6,076 in Social Security taxes and $1,421 in Medicare taxes.

Analyzing Visuals

38. Revenues decreased for Social Security taxes, excise taxes, estate and gift taxes, miscellaneous taxes, and individual income taxes. The federal government made up these decreases by increasing corporate income taxes and borrowing.

Interpreting Cartoons

39. Answers will vary but might reflect the view that the Reagan tax cuts greatly reduced taxes on the wealthy and on businesses while doing little to help the average taxpayer.

---

29. Possible answer: Alaska has alternative sources of revenue (oil royalties).

30. The Economic Recovery Tax Act of 1981 reduced taxes, while the 1986 measure made it difficult for the very rich to avoid taxes altogether. The 2001 tax change eliminated the estate tax on the wealthiest 2 percent of taxpayers.

31. Answers will vary but should demonstrate understanding of the tax types and principles.

32. Economic Recovery Tax Act of 1981, Taxpayer Relief Act of 1997, and the reforms in 2001 and 2003

Applying Economic Concepts

33. Answers will vary but should reflect knowledge of user fees.

34. Answers will vary but should reference sales and property taxes.

DEBATES IN ECONOMICS

Focus

Have students read the opening two paragraphs of the feature. Ask if they were aware that buying and selling on the Internet is not subject to taxation. Then have students discuss how this relates to the equality criterion for taxes.

Teach

S Skill Practice

Analyzing Information Divide students into pairs. Then draw students' attention to the column of Internet sales and taxes. Have them pay close attention to the state and local revenue loss section. **Ask:** How could state and local governments use an estimated $25 billion that are lost in revenue to benefit its citizens? *(Answers will vary, but students should be able to tell how state agencies and services could benefit from that much lost revenue.)* Have a volunteer from each pair share their ideas with the class. **OL**

Additional Support

DEBATES IN ECONOMICS

Should E-Commerce Be Taxed?

A lot of buying and selling occurs on the Internet—so much, in fact, that rumblings of an e-commerce sales tax have become a roar. In 2005 more than 700,000 people in the United States earned either full- or part-time income on eBay. This statistic alone ensures that a tax showdown between the IRS and e-commerce retailers is on the horizon.

Can you sift through the debate to determine whether or not buying and selling online should be subject to taxation? As you read the selections, ask yourself: "Should e-commerce be taxed?"

PRO SALES TAX REVENUE LOSSES

Inability to collect the [e-commerce sales] tax potentially has a number of important implications. Firms have an incentive to locate production and sales activity to avoid tax collection responsibility, thereby imposing economic efficiency losses on the overall economy. The sales tax becomes more regressive as those who are least able to purchase online are more likely to pay sales taxes than those who purchase online more frequently.

Internet sales in 2003
$1.27 trillion

Taxable internet sales in 2003
$751 billion

Sales on which taxes were not collected
$236.3 billion in 2003 **$329.2 billion in 2008***

State and local revenue loss
$15.5 billion in 2003 **$21.5–33.7 billion in 2008***

* 2008 figures are estimated

Further, state and local government tax revenues are reduced. . . . [T]he Census Bureau reports a combined $1.16 trillion in . . . e-commerce transactions by manufacturers, whole salers, service providers, and retailers, and Forrester Research, Inc.'s expectations continue to be for strong growth in e-commerce in coming years. Thus, the revenue erosion continues to represent a significant loss to state and local government.

—Dr. Donald Bruce and Dr. William F. Fox, Professors, Center for Business and Economic Research, University of Tennessee

258   UNIT 3   Economic Institutions and Issues

Extending the Content

Possible Options for Internet Sales In 1999 the Graziadio Business Report published by the Graziadio School of Business and Management proposed three options for collecting tax revenues from Internet sales. The National Sales Tax Option (NST) proposed that the federal government impose a uniform tax on all domestic e-commerce, collect the tax electronically, and then remit the proceeds to the states. The Freedom of States (FS) option proposed that all states be free to impose whatever tax they wished. The Internet Tax Equality Option (ITE) proposed that the federal government would create some uniform regulations but would give states freedom to determine their own tax rates and exemptions.

258

CON ONLINE TAX PROPOSAL MISGUIDED

The Direct Marketing Association (DMA) is cautioning legislators about bills introduced . . . that would allow states to force online sellers to collect sales taxes for all state and local taxing jurisdictions. . . . The failure of . . . these bills to address a reduction in the number of tax jurisdictions is a key flaw, and remains a critical obstacle to a workable streamlined sales tax program. There are currently approximately 7,600 different sales tax jurisdictions in this country, including states, counties and municipalities, and even block-by-block areas that collect additional sales taxes, such as sewer districts, sports arena districts or library districts. Currently, only businesses with a physical presence or "nexus" within a state are required to collect taxes for the jurisdictions within that state. . . .

The bills would also create a barrier to entry for small entrepreneurs, who rely on the Internet to help create markets, and a barrier to growth for medium-sized businesses seeking to grow

operations or expand a customer base. Many would not be able to afford the effort and expense it would take to collect and remit sales taxes for each of the thousands of jurisdictions, much less the cost of a possible audit at any time by 46 different state revenue departments. **W**

–Direct Marketing Association,
www.the-dma.org

Analyzing the Issue

1. **Identifying** What is the main argument in support of an e-commerce sales tax?
2. **Summarizing** Why does the DMA think it is not possible for online merchants to implement sales taxes?
3. **Deciding** With which opinion do you agree? Explain your reasoning.

CHAPTER 9   Sources of Government Revenue   **259**

Assess/ Close

W Writing Support

Persuasive Writing Have students imagine that they are entrepreneurs who have a small business that relies on the Internet. Have them write a newspaper editorial expressing their opinions about online tax proposals. Students should use information from the text to support their point of view. **OL**

Analyzing the Impact

Answers:
1. State and local government tax revenues are reduced.
2. There are thousands of different sales tax jurisdictions (states, counties, and cities). Collecting and remitting sales taxes for each of these would be costly.
3. Answers will vary but should demonstrate an understanding of the controversy.

Additional Support

Activity: Technology Connection

Identifying Points of View Point out to students that e-commerce and taxation will continue to be debated until the IRS and e-commerce retailers reach resolution. Organize students into groups, and have them use the Internet to research the major arguments for and against taxing e-commerce businesses. Encourage them to use their findings to create a Web site designed to inform people about the debate. Call on groups to display and discuss their Web site designs. **OL**

Teacher Tip

Arranging Student Groups Students in the class most likely have varying Web-design skills. Suggest that students divide the responsibilities so that those who are less involved in the Web site creation have a greater role in other parts of the project.

Levels					Resources	Chapter Opener	Section 1	Section 2	Section 3	Chapter Assess
BL	OL	AL	ELL							
					FOCUS					
BL	OL	AL	ELL	🖼	**Daily Focus Skills Transparencies**		69	67, 75	68, 76	
					TEACH					
BL	OL		ELL	📁	**Guided Reading Activities***		p. 28	p. 29	p. 30	
BL	OL	AL	ELL	📁	**Economic Content Vocabulary Activities***		p. 10	p. 10	p. 10	
	OL	AL		📁	**Critical Thinking Activities**		p. 15			
BL	OL		ELL	📁	**Reading Essentials and Note-Taking Guide***		p. 82	p. 85	p. 88	
		AL		📁	**Enrichment Activities**		p. 10			
	OL	AL		📁	**Free Enterprise Activities**			p. 15		
BL	OL	AL	ELL	📁	**Primary and Secondary Source Readings**				p. 29	
BL	OL	AL	ELL	📁	**Economic Cartoons**	pp. 15, 20				
BL	OL	AL	ELL	📁	**Math Practice for Economics**		p. 15			
BL	OL	AL	ELL	🖼	**Economics Forms and Financial Pages Transparencies, Strategies, and Activities**			p. 9		
BL	OL	AL	ELL	📁	**Reinforcing Economic Skills**			p. 19		
BL	OL		ELL	📁	**High School Reading in the Content Area Strategies and Activities**	✓	✓	✓	✓	✓
BL	OL	AL	ELL	🖼	**High School Writing Process Transparencies**	✓	✓	✓	✓	✓
BL	OL	AL	ELL	📁	**Writer's Guidebook**	✓	✓	✓	✓	✓
BL	OL	AL	ELL	💿	**StudentWorks Plus CD-ROM**	✓	✓	✓	✓	✓
BL	OL	AL	ELL	💿	**Vocabulary PuzzleMaker CD-ROM**	✓	✓	✓	✓	✓

*Also available in Spanish

TeacherWorks *Plus*
All-In-One Planner and Resource Center

- Interactive Lesson Planner
- Interactive Teacher Edition
- Fully editable blackline masters
- Economics & You videos

- Differentiated Lesson Plans
- Printable reports of daily assignments
- Standards tracking system

Levels					Resources	Chapter Opener	Section 1	Section 2	Section 3	Chapter Assess
BL	OL	AL	ELL							
TEACH *(continued)*										
BL	OL	AL	ELL		Economics & You Video Program DVD—*Government Spending*	✓	✓	✓	✓	✓
BL	OL	AL	ELL		Graph Coach CD-ROM	✓	✓	✓	✓	✓
Teacher Resources					Differentiated Instruction Strategies	✓	✓	✓	✓	✓
					Success with English Learners	✓	✓	✓	✓	✓
					Presentation Plus! CD-ROM	✓	✓	✓	✓	✓
ASSESS										
BL	OL	AL	ELL		Section Quizzes and Chapter Tests		p. 121	p. 122	p. 123	pp. 125, 129
BL	OL	AL	ELL		Authentic Assessment Strategies and Activities			p. 15		
BL	OL	AL	ELL		*ExamView®* Assessment Suite CD-ROM		10-1	10-2	10-3	Ch. 10
BL	OL	AL	ELL		Interactive Tutor Self-Assessment CD-ROM		10-1	10-2	10-3	
CLOSE										
BL			ELL		Reteaching Activities*		p. 10	p. 10	p. 10	
BL	OL		ELL		Reading and Study Skills Foldables		p. 57		p. 57	
BL	OL	AL	ELL		Graphic Organizer Transparencies			p. 7	p. 7	

*Also available in Spanish

Activity
Using Skillbuilder
Interactive Workbook
CD-ROM

Interpreting Maps

Technology Product

Glencoe's *Skillbuilder Interactive Workbook CD-ROM* provides self-paced instruction, practice, and assessment of key skills your students need in social studies, including interpreting maps. The *Skillbuilder Interactive Workbook*

- lets students learn, practice, and assess their knowledge of social studies skills;
- lists key terms and a glossary where appropriate;
- includes a **Management System** to create class rosters and monitor student progress.

Objectives

The *Skillbuilder Interactive Workbook* help students
- learn and practice reading maps;
- identify areas for reinforcement.

Steps

Provide students with the following information:
- Select **Interpreting Maps** from the Main Menu page. Then select one of the options.
- The **Instruction** option on the Activities page provides a step-by-step tutorial to learn the skill being taught, along with an audio component.
- The **Guided Practice** section presents comprehension questions to review the material covered in the Instruction section. Questions include multiple choice, true/false, fill-in-the-blank, and drag-and-drop types.
- The **Assessment** section includes 10 questions that test student mastery of the skill.

Have students complete the activity and use the Management System to monitor their progress.

Economics ONLINE	Student	Teacher	Parent
Beyond the Textbook	●	●	●
Chapter Overviews	●	●	●
ePuzzles and Games	●		●
Concepts in Motion	●		●
Multi-Language Glossaries	●		●
Online Student Edition	●	●	●
Self-Check Quizzes	●		●
Student Web Activities	●		●
Study Central™	●		●
Time Current Events	●	●	●
Teaching Today		●	
Vocabulary eFlashcards	●		●
Web Activity Lesson Plans		●	

Glencoe Media Center

❯ glencoe.com
Study-To-Go
- Vocabulary eFlashcards
- Self-Check Quizzes

❯ **Audio/Video**
- Student Edition Audio
- Spanish Summaries
- Economics & You Videos

READING SUPPORT FROM JAMESTOWN EDUCATION

- **Timed Readings Plus in Social Studies** helps students increase their reading rate and fluency while maintaining comprehension. The 400-word passages are similar to those found on state and national assessments.

- **Reading in the Content Area: Social Studies** concentrates on six essential reading skills that help students better comprehend what they read. The book includes 75 high-interest nonfiction passages written at increasing levels of difficulty.

- **Reading Social Studies** includes strategic reading instruction and vocabulary support in Social Studies content for both ELLs and native speakers of English.
  www.jamestowneducation.com

Reading List Generator CD-ROM

GLENCOE BOOKLINK 3

Use this database to search more than 30,000 titles to create a customized reading list for your students.

- Reading lists can be organized by students' reading level, author, genre, theme, or area of interest.
- The database provides Degrees of Reading Power™ (DRP) and Lexile™ readability scores for all selections.
- A brief summary of each selection is included.

Leveled reading suggestions for this chapter:
For students at a Grade 10 reading level:
- *National Defense,* by James Fallows

For students at a Grade 11 reading level:
- *Child Welfare: Opposing Viewpoints,* by Carol Wekesser

For students at a Grade 12 reading level:
- *Education,* by Mary E. Williams

* Review suggested books before assigning them.

NCEE

National Council on Economic Education

Voluntary Standards Emphasized in Chapter 10

Content Standard 16 There is an economic role for government in a market economy whenever the benefits of a government policy outweigh its costs. Governments often provide for national defense, address environmental concerns, define and protect property rights, and attempt to make markets more competitive. Most government policies also redistribute income.

Content Standard 20 Federal government budgetary policy and the Federal Reserve System's monetary policy influence the overall levels of employment, output, and prices.

Resources Available from NCEE
- Virtual Economics®: An Interactive Center for Economic Education Version 3.0
- Civics and Government: Focus on Economics, Second Edition
- Capstone: The Nation's High School Economics Course
- Focus: Institutions and Markets

To order these materials, or to contact your State Council on Economic Education about workshops and programs, call 1-800-338-1192 or visit the NCEE Web site at store.ncee.net.

CHAPTER

10 Government Spending

The BIG Idea

As students study the chapter, remind them to consider the chapter-based Big Idea. The **Essential Question** in the chapter launch activity below ties in to the Big Idea and helps students think about and understand important chapter concepts. In addition, the Hands-On Chapter Project relates the content from each section to the Big Idea. The steps in each section build on each other and culminate in the Wrap-Up Activity on the Visual Summary page.

Economics & You Video To generate student interest and provide a springboard for class discussion, access the Economics & You Topic 15 video, **Government Spending,** at glencoe.com or on the video DVD.

FOLDABLES Study Organizer **Dinah Zike's Foldables** are three-dimensional, interactive graphic organizers that help students practice basic writing skills, review key vocabulary terms, and identify main ideas. Have students complete this chapter's Foldable activity or activities in *Dinah Zike's Reading and Study Skills Foldables* booklet. **OL**

Economics ONLINE

Introduce students to chapter content and key terms by having them access *Chapter 10 —Chapter Overviews* at glencoe.com.

Why It Matters

Have you ever wondered what the government does with the money withheld from your paycheck? As you travel from home to school over the next three days, list all the examples you see of goods and services provided by federal, state, or local government. Try to determine which level of government funded them and who benefits from them the most. Share your list with the class.

The BIG Idea

All levels of government use tax revenue to provide essential goods and services.

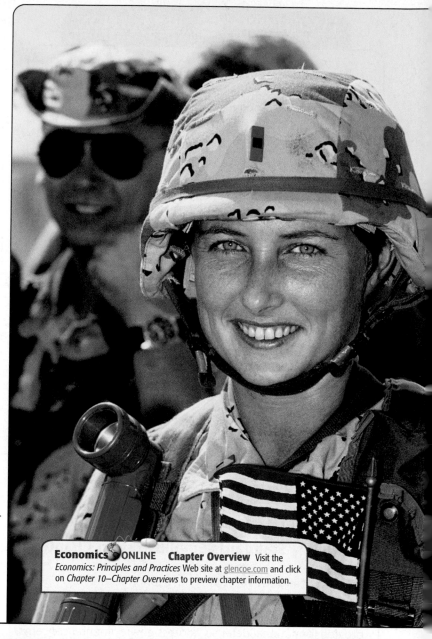

Spending for ▶ national defense is a responsibility of the federal government.

Economics ONLINE **Chapter Overview** Visit the *Economics: Principles and Practices* Web site at glencoe.com and click on *Chapter 10–Chapter Overviews* to preview chapter information.

260 UNIT 3

Activity: Launching the Chapter

Identifying Have students brainstorm a list of the goods and services provided by the federal, state, and local (county or city) levels of government. Write their ideas on the board in three separate columns—one for each governmental level. **Essential Question:** What are two spending categories that are common to each level of government?

(Possible answer: law enforcement and education) Have students write a paragraph explaining what they think are the top spending priorities of each of the three levels of government. **OL**

The Economics of Government Spending

GUIDE TO READING

Section Preview

In this section, you will learn that the role of the federal government has grown, making it a vital player in the economy.

Content Vocabulary

• pork *(p. 261)*
• public sector *(p. 262)*
• private sector *(p. 263)*
• transfer payment *(p. 263)*
• grant-in-aid *(p. 263)*
• subsidy *(p. 264)*
• distribution of income *(p. 264)*

Academic Vocabulary

• constituents *(p. 261)*   • reluctant *(p. 265)*

Reading Strategy

Listing As you read the section, complete a graphic organizer similar to the one below by listing reasons for the increase in government spending since the 1940s.

```
                          Reasons
                      ┌─────────────┐
    ┌──────────┐      │             │
    │ Rise in  │──────└─────────────┘
    │government│
    │ spending │──────┌─────────────┐
    └──────────┘      │             │
                      └─────────────┘
```

Focus

Bellringer
Daily Focus Transparency 69

FOCUS ACTIVITIES
Transparency 69

GOVERNMENT SPENDING DECISIONS

GUIDE TO READING

Answers to Graphic:

Reasons: increased size of government; larger government role in the economy; more goods and services provided; growth of population; greater accep-tance of government involve-ment in the economy; increasing transfer payments

ISSUES IN THE NEWS

—George Will, *Washington Post*

Grand Old Spenders

Conservatives have won seven of 10 presidential elections, yet . . . per-household federal spending [is] more than $22,000 per year, the highest in inflation-adjusted terms since World War II. Federal spending . . . has grown twice as fast under President Bush as under President Bill Clinton, 65 percent of it unrelated to national security.

In 1991, the 546 pork projects . . . cost $3.1 billion. In 2005, the 13,997 pork projects cost $27.3 billion, for things such as improving the National Packard Museum in Warren, Ohio (Packard, an automobile brand, died in 1958).

Washington subsidizes the cost of water to encourage farmers to produce surpluses that trigger a gusher of government spending to support prices . . . [and] . . . almost $2 billion is spent each year paying farmers *not* to produce. ■

The amount of net spending by all levels of government—federal, state, and local—amounts to an ever-increasing portion of our GDP, the dollar measure of all final goods and services produced in a country in a year. It wasn't always this way, but sometimes politicians have a hard time saying "no" when it comes to taking care of their **constituents** and the interests of their home districts.

A recent political trend, as discussed in the news article above, is the increasingly popular use of pork in the federal budget. **Pork** is a term used by some to describe a line-item budget expenditure that circumvents normal budget-building procedures. Because most pork projects provide generous benefits to a small number of individuals or businesses, taxpayers generally would not otherwise approve the projects.

pork a line-item budget expenditure that circumvents normal budget procedures and benefits a small number of people or businesses

Resource Manager

R — Reading Strategies	C — Critical Thinking	D — Differentiated Instruction	W — Writing Support	S — Skill Practice
Teacher Edition • Act. Prior Know., p. 264 • Academic Vocab., p. 265 **Additional Resources** • Guid. Read. Act., p. 28 • Read. Ess. & Note-Taking Guide, p. 82	**Teacher Edition** • Speculating, p. 263 **Additional Resources** • Math Prac. for Econ., p. 15 • Quizzes and Tests, p. 121	**Teacher Edition** • Adv. Learners, p. 262 **Additional Resources** • Reteach. Act., p. 10 • Econ. Cartoons, p. 20 • Enrichment Act., p. 10	**Teacher Edition** • Expository Writing, p. 263 • Personal Writing, p. 264 **Additional Resources** • Writer's Guidebook	**Teacher Edition** • Analyzing Graphs, p. 262 • Compare/Contrast, p. 266 **Additional Resources** • Reading and Study Skills Fold., p. 57 • Econ. Content Vocab. Act., p. 10

Teach

D Differentiated Instruction

Advanced Learners Have students select an economic program started by the government in the 1930s. Ask students to research and prepare a multimedia report on the program. Students should address the program's purpose, costs, and overall impact. **AL**

S Skill Practice

Analyzing Graphs Have students use a history textbook to make a list of U.S. presidents, including their dates in office, since 1960. **Ask:** *Government spending as a percentage of GDP declined by the greatest amount during the administration of which president?* (Bill Clinton) **OL**

Economic Analysis

Answer: Yes, in the late 1970s and the 1990s.

---

public sector that part of the economy made up of local, state, and federal governments

Government Spending in Perspective

MAIN Idea The government spends its revenues on goods, services, and transfer payments.

Economics & You Do you wonder how the taxes you pay are spent? Read on to learn about government expenditures.

Spending by the **public sector**—the part of the economy consisting of federal, state, and local governments—was relatively low prior to the Great Depression. Since then, attitudes have shifted and spending has increased sharply.

Spending Since the 1930s

The growth in government spending since the 1930s had two main causes. First, a major change in public opinion gave government a larger role in everyday economic affairs. This change, in turn, was a response to President Franklin D. Roosevelt's New Deal, which used large-scale government projects to fight the Great Depression. The Tennessee Valley Authority (TVA), for example, brought low-cost electricity to millions of people in the rural South during the mid-1930s.

Second, massive government spending funded the United States involvement in World War II. This resulted in more people working, as factories converted to war production. Most people, some of whom faced unemployment during the 1930s, seemed to become more comfortable with the government's larger role in the domestic economy.

As shown in **Figure 10.1**, expenditures by all levels of government—federal, state, and local—have grown ever since. From about 23 percent of GDP in 1960, they have increased to over 31 percent today. In fact, public-sector spending has grown so large that all levels of government combined now spend more than all of the privately owned businesses in the United States.

Figure 10.1 ▶ Government Spending

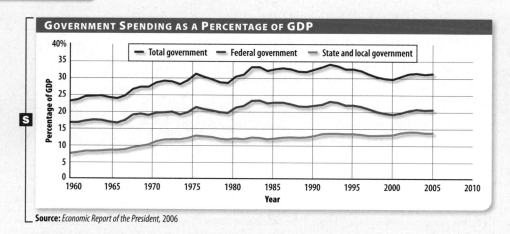

Source: *Economic Report of the President, 2006*

▶ Spending by all levels of government has grown considerably since 1959. Between 2000 and 2005 alone, government expenditures have consumed an additional 5.4 percent of GDP, a $674 billion increase.

Economic Analysis *Does the graph show any period of decreased government spending?*

Graphs In MOtion
See StudentWorks™ Plus or glencoe.com.

Differentiated Instruction

CRITICAL THINKING 15

Critical Thinking Activities, p. 15

Bias and Government Spending

Objective: Identify signs of bias in letters about government spending.

Focus/Teach: Ask students to list reasons why a local government might buy a parcel of land. Write their ideas on the board. Then have students complete the activity.

Assess: Discuss the answers as a class.

Close: Ask students to revise each letter so that the content appears less biased.

Differentiated Instruction Strategies

BL Ask: Which letter is the most persuasive? Why?

AL Direct students to write a letter to the newspaper suggesting a compromise to the Raccoon Lake issue.

ELL Help students list biased language that people commonly use (for example, "nobody likes that kind of food").

Some people question how many goods and services government should provide and, therefore, what level of revenue collection is required to support these expenditures. Others question which services the government should provide and which services the **private sector**—the part of the economy made up of private individuals and privately owned businesses—should provide.

Two Types of Spending

In general, government makes two broad kinds of expenditures. The first is in the form of goods and services. The government buys many goods, such as tanks, planes, ships, and even space shuttles. It needs office buildings, land for parks, and capital goods for schools and laboratories. The government also needs to purchase supplies and pay for utilities. Finally, it must hire people to work in its agencies and staff the military. Payments for these services include the wages and salaries for these workers. State and local governments have similar expenditures.

The second type of government expenditure is a **transfer payment**—a payment for which the government receives neither goods nor services in return. Transfer payments can be made to individuals and include Social Security, unemployment compensation, welfare, and aid for people with disabilities. With the exception of Social Security, people normally receive these payments solely because they need assistance.

A transfer payment that one level of government makes to another is known as a **grant-in-aid.** The receiving government counts this payment as intergovernmental revenue. Interstate highway construction programs are examples of grants-in-aid. The federal government grants money to cover the major part of the cost, while the states in which the highways will be built pay the rest. The construction of new public schools also can be financed through grants-in-aid.

✓ **Reading Check** Contrasting What is the difference between transfer payments and government spending on goods and services?

Grants-in-Aid
States usually receive federal funds to pay for the majority of highway construction projects. *Why do states rely on federal funds for such projects?*

private sector
that part of the economy made up of private individuals and businesses

transfer payment
payment for which the government receives neither goods nor services in return

grant-in-aid
transfer payment from one level of government to another that does not involve compensation

CHAPTER 10 Government Spending **263**

C Critical Thinking

Speculating Ask: Why do you think that some people object to the government providing certain goods and services? *(Answers will vary but may include a concern about higher taxes and a belief that the private sector can provide certain goods and services more efficiently.)* **OL**

W Writing Support

Expository Writing Have students select an example of federal grant-in-aid that their state has recently received. Tell them to use local newspapers or news Web sites to research the grant. Instruct students to write a short report explaining it. **OL**

Caption Answer: States generally do not have the funds to finance such large projects by themselves.

✓ **Reading Check** **Answer:** The government receives goods and services when it makes payments for those items. With transfer payments, the government receives neither goods nor services in return.

Leveled Activities

BL Reading Essentials and Note-Taking Guide, p. 82

OL Economic Content Vocabulary Activities, p. 10

AL Economic Cartoons, p. 15

Allocation of Resources States require students to take graduation exams because of federal legislation. ***How can such laws affect the economy?***

subsidy government payment to encourage or protect a certain economic activity *(also see page 122)*

distribution of income way in which the nation's income is divided among families, individuals, or other designated groups

Impact of Government Spending

MAIN Idea Government spending has a direct impact on our economy.

Economics & You Have you considered attending a public college because a private one seems out of reach? Read on to find out how government spending affects your life.

The enormous size of the public sector gives it the potential to affect people's daily lives in many ways. It can affect resource allocation, the distribution of income, production in the private sector, and the tax burden on people.

Affecting Resource Allocation

Government spending decisions directly affect how resources are allocated. If the government spends its revenues on missile systems in rural areas, for example, rather than on social welfare programs in urban areas, the shift of resources stimulates economic activity in rural areas.

R Public sector spending can indirectly affect allocation of resources. In agriculture, the decision to support the prices of cotton, milk, grains, or peanuts keeps the factors of production working in those industries.

If the government withdraws the **subsidies** for these crops, farmers would produce less of each and resources would be released for employment in other industries.

W Government is so involved in the economy that even seemingly modest decisions can have an enormous impact on the things we produce. For example, because of the No Child Left Behind legislation, the government now requires schools to conduct extensive testing in reading and math.

As a result, some schools have increased the amount of time they spend on these subjects and therefore have decreased the amount of time spent on other subjects. The decision to downgrade or even drop other subjects diminishes the demand and eventually the production of textbooks and educational supplies used in those areas, while increasing the demand for resources needed for reading and math.

Redistributing Income

Government spending also influences the **distribution of income,** or the way in which income is allocated among families, individuals, or other groups. Increasing or decreasing transfer payments, for example, can directly affect the incomes of needy families who receive financial support from the government.

Government decisions about where to make expenditures indirectly affect many people's incomes. The decision to buy fighter planes from one factory rather than another has an impact on the communities near both factories. The decision to spend billions on rebuilding Iraq and Afghanistan increased the incomes of those working in the national defense industries but not those who work in inner cities or other areas that lack such factories.

Competing With the Private Sector

When the government produces goods and services, it often competes with the private sector. In higher education, many public colleges and universities compete with more expensive private ones. The cost difference often is due to the subsidies public institutions receive from their states.

In the area of health care, the government runs a system of hospitals for military veterans, which are funded with taxpayer dollars. At the same time, these facilities compete with hospitals in the private sector that offer similar services.

Increasing the Tax Burden

Finally, the growth of government spending has not gone unnoticed by the average American. The increased tax burden that is needed to support the expenditures has attracted enormous attention in recent years. Most people would like to reduce their taxes, but most people are also **reluctant** to give up the many benefits that government provides. **R**

In short, spending by all levels of government, which amounts to about one-third of our GDP, has a large and often controversial impact on the American economy. Finding the money to pay for these expenditures is a difficult task. Yet many people seem to want even more of these goods, services, and transfer payments.

Skills Handbook
See page **R44** to learn about **Detecting Bias.**

✓**Reading Check** **Explaining** How does government spending affect the distribution of income?

R **Reading Strategy**

Academic Vocabulary Have students use a dictionary or thesaurus to find words that have similar meanings as *reluctant*. Have students reword the bracketed sentence in the text, substituting one of the synonyms that they identified. **OL**

✓**Reading Check** **Answer:**
Increasing or decreasing transfer payments affect the incomes of needy families. Government spending decisions may increase the incomes of people in certain industries while decreasing others.

Assess

💿 Use the Interactive Tutor Self-Assessment CD-ROM to review Section 1, and then assign the Section 1 Review as homework or as an in-class activity.

Close

Identifying Central Issues
Have students write a paragraph describing the central issues discussed in this section. **OL**

Review **SECTION 1**

SECTION 1 Review

Vocabulary
1. **Explain** the significance of pork, public sector, private sector, transfer payment, grant-in-aid, subsidy, and distribution of income.

Main Ideas
2. **Identifying** In which three ways might government spending impact the economy?

3. **Listing** Use a graphic organizer like the one below to list two kinds of government spending and provide three examples of each.

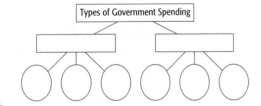

Types of Government Spending

Critical Thinking
4. **The BIG Idea** Describe two reasons for the growth of government spending since the 1930s.

5. **Analyzing Visuals** Look at Figure 10.1 on page 262. How does the spending by state and local governments compare to federal spending? What might explain any differences?

6. **Explaining** Why are people often reluctant to support a reduction in government spending?

7. **Detecting Bias** How does the "pork" spending described by the columnist on page 261 illustrate a conflict between political and economic goals?

Applying Economics
8. **Transfer Payments** Do you think that transfer payments, such as unemployment compensation, are a successful or unsuccessful way to accomplish the goal of economic security? Explain your answer.

CHAPTER 10 Government Spending **265**

Answers

1. All definitions can be found in the section and the Glossary.
2. **Possible answer:** affecting resource allocation, redistributing income, increasing the tax burden
3. **Goods and services:** ships; parks; staff salaries. **Transfer payments:** Social Security; unemployment compensation; aid for people with disabilities.

4. greater public acceptance of government involvement in everyday economic affairs; large-scale increase in defense spending for World War II and later military commitments
5. Federal government spending is consistently higher than state and local government spending. The federal government provides more goods and services and operates larger transfer payment programs.

6. People do not want to lose the benefits provided by the government.
7. Spending on "pork" projects wins support for elected officials but is an inefficient use of government resources.
8. Answers will vary but should be supported with logical arguments and facts about specific programs.

Teach

S Skill Practice

Comparing and Contrasting

Ask: How do you think a mathematician's work with the NSA 30 years ago was similar to and different from a mathematician's work with the NSA today? *(Possible difference: Communists were the primary concern while today terrorists are. Possible similarity: At both times they worked to strengthen national security.)* **OL**

BusinessWeek ONLINE

To find up-to-date news and analysis on the economy, business, technology, markets, entrepreneurs, investments, and finance, have students search feature articles and special reports on the BusinessWeek Web site, www.businessweek.com.

Examining the Newsclip

Answers:

1. protecting U.S.; breaking enemies' secret codes
2. Internet giants may offer higher salaries.

Additional Support

In the United States, the government sector competes with the private sector for scarce resources. This does not just mean the resources to build interstate highways or ensure food safety. In fact, there is a particularly scarce resource the government is trying to lure from the private sector—brains.

The NSA: Security in Numbers

The job offers arrived in plain envelopes. For decades, the mathematicians who accepted them stole off to Washington and the hush-hush National Security Agency, the nation's top techno-spy center. Through the cold war, NSA math whizzes matched wits with the Soviets. Each side protected its own secret codes while trying to break the other's.

Math is more important than ever at the NSA. Chances are, the world's growing rivers of data contain terrorist secrets, and it's up to the agency's math teams to find them. But to land the best brains, the NSA must compete with free-spending Web giants such as Google and Yahoo! This is leading the agency to open up its recruiting process.

"We have to look at new and innovative ways to find talent," says Cynthia Miller-Wentt, chief of the NSA's recruitment office. . . . There's a second hitch: Unlike the tech companies it must compete with, the NSA can hire only U.S. citizens. This is a severe constraint. About half of the estimated 20,000 math graduate students at U.S. universities are foreigners. They're off bounds, as are the bountiful math brains in India, China, Eastern Europe, and elsewhere.

The NSA's pitch? First the agency appeals to the recruits' patriotism. But there's also a lifestyle lure. NSA officials say a good number of mathematicians prefer a suburban Maryland life and a government job with predictable hours to the more frantic pace and market gyrations of an Internet company. . . .

—Reprinted from *BusinessWeek*

HOW MATH TRANSFORMS INDUSTRIES
Marketing
Umbria: The Colorado startup assigns numeric values to "picks" and "pans" of products that pop up on blogs and podcasts.
Consulting
IBM: Big Blue is building math profiles of 50,000 consultants so that computers can pick the perfect team for every assignment. Other tools eventually will be able to track their progress, hour by hour, and rate their performance.
Advertising
Efficient Frontier: The Silicon Valley startup calculates response rates and return on investment for every advertisement of online ad campaigns. It provides a broad shift from hunch-based campaigns to mathematical targeting.

Source: *BusinessWeek*

Examining the Newsclip

1. **Summarizing** What work do mathematicians perform for the NSA?
2. **Analyzing** Why is it difficult for the NSA to compete with the Internet giants in hiring mathematicians?

266   UNIT 3   Economic Institutions and Issues

Activity: Technology Connection

Working for the NSA Have students visit the National Security Agency's Web site (http://www.nsa.gov/). Instruct students to use the site to investigate a specific job available with NSA. Ask students to research the responsibilities of an NSA employee in the position they selected and find out how a high school student would go about preparing for that particular career path. Students might include information on the following:

- salary and benefits
- education requirements
- opportunities for students, such as internships or scholarships
- application and hiring process

Have students present their findings in a multimedia presentation. Encourage students to include in their presentations the reasons why the career path they researched would or would not appeal to them. **OL**

SECTION 2 — Federal, State, and Local Government Expenditures

GUIDE TO READING

Section Preview

In this section, you will learn that governments provide money for many services and programs.

Content Vocabulary

- federal budget *(p. 267)*
- fiscal year *(p. 268)*
- appropriations bill *(p. 268)*
- budget deficit *(p. 269)*
- budget surplus *(p. 269)*
- mandatory spending *(p. 269)*
- discretionary spending *(p. 270)*
- Medicare *(p. 270)*
- Medicaid *(p. 271)*
- balanced budget amendment *(p. 271)*
- intergovernmental expenditures *(p. 272)*

Academic Vocabulary

- ambiguity *(p. 267)*
- coincide *(p. 268)*

Reading Strategy

Describing As you read the section, complete a graphic organizer similar to the one below by describing the different types of government spending.

Government Spending

ISSUES IN THE NEWS

—Los Angeles Times

The President's Budget Plan

President Bush on Monday sent Congress a proposed $2.77 trillion budget for 2007 that would boost Defense and Homeland Security while trimming the growth of Medicare and other social service programs . . . [and] . . . leave a deficit of $354 billion next year—the fourth-largest ever in dollar terms—which would settle down to around $200 billion for the subsequent four years. . . . .

Departments that would gain the most under Bush's budget include the Pentagon, which would see spending rise 7%, and the Department of Homeland Security, where a 6% increase would go largely to immigration enforcement, air travel security and the Federal Emergency Management Agency. ■

When it comes to the numbers presented in the **federal budget**—the annual plan outlining proposed revenues and expenditures for the coming year—there is often a fair amount of **ambiguity**. As the news article above shows, the federal budget offers only a rough estimate of the actual revenues and expenditures.

For example, the economy could suddenly slow down or speed up, affecting the amount of tax revenues collected. In addition, events might occur that require unanticipated spending. This was the case after the terrorist attacks on September 11, 2001, and the subsequent wars in Afghanistan and Iraq.

federal budget
annual plan outlining proposed expenditures and anticipated revenues

CHAPTER 10 Government Spending **267**

Focus

GUIDE TO READING

Answers to Graphic:

Federal: Social Security, defense, income security, Medicare, health, interest on debt

State and Local:
intergovernmental expenditures, public welfare, insurance trust and retirement, education, utilities, public safety and health

Resource Manager

R Reading Strategies	**C** Critical Thinking	**D** Differentiated Instruction	**W** Writing Support	**S** Skill Practice
Teacher Edition • Making Connections, p. 269 • Reading Charts, p. 273 • Organizing, p. 275 • Act. Prior Know., p. 276 **Additional Resources** • Guid. Read. Act., p. 29 • Read. Ess. & Note-Taking Guide, p. 85	**Teacher Edition** • Compare/Contrast p. 268 • Predicting, p. 270 • Speculating, p. 274 **Additional Resources** • Econ. Forms and Fin. Pages Trans., Strat. and Act., p. 9	**Teacher Edition** • Visual/Spatial, p. 272 • Logical/Math., p. 273 **Additional Resources** • Free Enterprise Act., p. 15 • Daily Focus Trans. 67, 75 • Reinforcing Econ. Skills, p. 19	**Teacher Edition** • Expository Writing, p. 270 • Persuasive Writing, p. 271 • Personal Writing, p. 274 **Additional Resources** • High School Writing Process Trans.	**Teacher Edition** • Using Circle and Bar Graphs, p. 269 • Making Gen., p. 272 • Ident. Main Idea, p. 274 • Making Inferences, p. 276 **Additional Resources** • Graph. Org. Trans., p. 4 • Authentic Assess., p. 15

Teach

C Critical Thinking

Comparing and Contrasting
Have students make a list of how their family's purchasing decisions are similar to and different than the government's budget-making process. *(Possible similarities: both spend money on a variety of different items; both try to base spending decisions on projected income. Possible differences: the federal government receives income from a variety of different sources as opposed to one or two incomes; many people are involved in the federal budget-making process whereas one or two people usually make a family's budget decisions.)* **OL**

Caption Answer:
subcommittees of the House of Representatives

Additional Support

Economics ONLINE
Student Web Activity Visit the *Economics: Principles and Practices* Web site at glencoe.com and click on *Chapter 10–Student Web Activity* for an activity on the federal budget.

fiscal year 12-month financial planning period that may not coincide with the calendar year

appropriations bill legislation authorizing spending for certain purposes

Federal Government Expenditures

MAIN Idea The federal government establishes a budget and allocates funds accordingly.

Economics and You Has your family created a budget to control income and expenses? Read on to learn how the federal government makes its budget decisions.

The federal budget spans a **fiscal year**—a 12-month financial planning period that may or may not **coincide** with the calendar year. The government's fiscal year starts on October 1 and expires on September 30 of the following calendar year.

Establishing the Federal Budget

The president's Office of Management and Budget (OMB), part of the executive branch, is responsible for preparing the federal budget. However, the president's budget is only a request, and Congress can approve, modify, or disapprove it. By law, the budget must be sent to both houses of Congress by the first Monday in February.

Once the House of Representatives receives the president's budget request, it breaks down the budget into 13 major expenditure categories and assigns each to a separate House subcommittee. Each of the subcommittees then prepares an **appropriations bill,** an act of Congress that allows federal agencies to spend money for a specific purpose. Subcommittees hold hearings, debate, and vote on each bill. An approved bill is sent to the full House Appropriations Committee. If it passes there, the bill is sent to the entire House for a vote.

The Senate acts on the budget after the House has approved it. The Senate may approve the bill as sent by the House, or it may draft its own version. If differences exist between the House and the Senate versions, a joint House-Senate conference committee tries to work out a compromise bill. During this process, the House and the Senate often seek advice from the Congressional Budget Office (CBO). The CBO is a nonpartisan congressional agency that evaluates the impact of legislation and projects future revenues and expenditures that will result from the legislation.

If the House and Senate both approve the compromise bill, they send it to the president for signature. Because Congress literally took apart, rewrote, and put back together the president's budget, the final

Public Hearings Secretary of State Condoleezza Rice discusses the State Department's budget with an appropriations committee. *Which part of Congress holds hearings?*

Activity: Collaborative Learning

Assessing Organize the class into five groups and explain that each group should pretend to be a congressional subcommittee reviewing budget priorities. Ask subcommittees to discuss and rank the following programs in descending order, with the highest priority first. Have subcommittee members try to reach consensus, although it is not absolutely necessary. After discussion is completed, ask representatives from each subcommittee to share their lists with the class and explain their reasoning.

- national defense
- health care
- food for starving people in a nation involved in a civil war

- research on the environment
- space explorations
- housing for the homeless in the United States
- food stamps
- scholarships for needy students to attend college **OL**

Figure 10.2 ► The Federal Budget for Fiscal Year 2007

Graphs In MOtion
See StudentWorks™ Plus
or glencoe.com.

► In its budget, the federal government projected revenues of $2,416 billion and planned on spending $2,770 billion in fiscal year 2007. The difference of $354 billion, or 12.8 cents of every dollar spent, would be borrowed from investors.

Economic Analysis *What is the largest mandatory spending item in the budget? The largest discretionary item?*

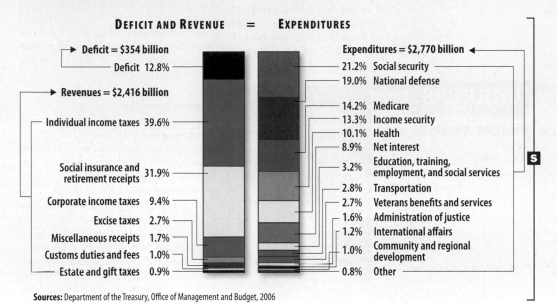

DEFICIT AND REVENUE = EXPENDITURES

→ Deficit = $354 billion
— Deficit 12.8%

► Revenues = $2,416 billion

Individual income taxes 39.6%

Social insurance and retirement receipts 31.9%

Corporate income taxes 9.4%

Excise taxes 2.7%

Miscellaneous receipts 1.7%

Customs duties and fees 1.0%

Estate and gift taxes 0.9%

Expenditures = $2,770 billion ◄
21.2% Social security
19.0% National defense
14.2% Medicare
13.3% Income security
10.1% Health
8.9% Net interest
3.2% Education, training, employment, and social services
2.8% Transportation
2.7% Veterans benefits and services
1.6% Administration of justice
1.2% International affairs
1.0% Community and regional development
0.8% Other

Sources: Department of the Treasury, Office of Management and Budget, 2006

version may not resemble the original proposal. In many cases, a bill may have changed considerably, with items added to the president's original budget.

If the budget was altered too much, the president can veto the bill and force Congress to come up with a budget closer to the original version. However, once signed by the president, the budget becomes the official document for the next fiscal year that starts on October 1.

The federal budget shown in **Figure 10.2** is called the fiscal year 2007 budget because 9 of the 12 calendar months fall within the year 2007. The figure shows $2,416 billion (over $2 trillion) of revenues and $2,770 billion of spending, leaving a **budget deficit**—an excess of expenditures

over revenues—of $354 billion. If expenditures were less than revenues, the result would be a **budget surplus.**

Social Security

The individual expenditures in the federal budget can be grouped into broad categories. The largest is for payments to aged and disabled Americans through the Social Security program. Retired persons receive benefits from the Old-Age and Survivors Insurance (OASI) program. Those unable to work receive payments from disability insurance (DI) programs.

Spending for Social Security is sometimes called **mandatory spending,** or spending authorized by law that continues

budget deficit
a negative balance after expenditures are subtracted from revenues

budget surplus
a positive balance after expenditures are subtracted from revenues

mandatory spending federal spending authorized by law that continues without the need for annual approvals by Congress

CHAPTER 10 Government Spending **269**

Skill Practice

Using Circle and Bar Graphs
Ask students to use the information in Figure 10.2 to create two circle graphs. Have students compare the original figure with the graphs they created and then write a paragraph explaining which format they believe presents the data most effectively, and why. **OL**

Reading Strategy

Making Connections
Ask: Aside from mandatory spending, how else can Social Security be classified? *(transfer payment)* If students have trouble answering the question, have them review Section 1. **BL**

Economic Analysis
Answer: Social Security; national defense

Additional Support

Extending the Content

The National Debt Hefty budget deficits in recent years have pushed the national debt of the United States to record levels. In 2006 the total federal debt topped the staggering figure of $8.5 trillion. That amount averages out to $28,504 per American. Some observers, however, maintain that the debt's effects on the economy are not as bad as a decade earlier. They point out that the percentage of the federal spending allocated to debt

financing has declined in recent years. For example, in 2005 interest paid on the debt represented 15 percent of federal outlays. In contrast, financing the debt represented more than 20 percent of federal spending each year of the 1990s. The peak year was 1997, when interest payments accounted for 22.2 percent of U.S. government outlays.

C Critical Thinking

Predicting Ask: What is an example of a future event that could increase defense expenditures? *(Possible answers: United States invades Iran; North Korea accelerates its nuclear weapons program.)* What is an example of a future event that could decrease defense expenditures? *(Possible answers: United States withdraws troops from Iraq; North Korea dismantles its nuclear weapons program.)* **BL**

W Writing Support

Expository Writing Have students research the origins of one of the programs listed on this page. Ask them to write a paper explaining when, why, and how the program began. **AL**

Did You Know?

In 2004 there were 57,586 budget analyst jobs in the United States. Anticipating a 10-year job growth rate, *Money Magazine* and Salary.com forecast that there will be 65,340 budget analyst jobs in 2014.

Differentiated Instruction

Free Enterprise Activities, p. 15

---

discretionary spending spending for federal programs that must receive annual authorization

Medicare federal health-care program for senior citizens, regardless of income

without the need for annual approvals by Congress. This is because the total Social Security payments in any given year are dependent on the number of people eligible for Social Security and the level of benefits already approved by Congress.

National Defense

For much of the late 1900s, national defense comprised the largest category of spending, although it is now second to Social Security. National defense includes

CAREERS

Budget Analyst

The Work

* Research, analyze, develop, and execute annual budgets or financial plans

* Seek new ways to improve a company's efficiency and increase profits

* Review financial requests, examine past and current budgets, and research developments that can affect spending

Qualifications

* Keen analytical skills and knowledge of mathematics, statistics, accounting, and computer science

* Strong oral and written communication skills to present—and defend—budget proposals

* Ability to work well under deadlines

* Bachelor's degree, with most firms and government employers requiring a master's degree

Earnings

* Median annual earnings: $56,040

Job Growth Outlook

* Average

Source: *Occupational Outlook Handbook, 2006–2007 Edition*

---

military spending by the Department of Defense and defense-related atomic energy activities, such as the development of nuclear weapons and the disposal of nuclear wastes.

Defense expenditures are called **discretionary spending**—spending that must be approved by Congress in the annual budgetary process. Unlike Social Security payments, which normally go up as the population gets older, annual defense expenditures can go up, down, or remain the same, depending on the will of the president and Congress.

Income Security

Income security consists of a wide range of programs that includes retirement benefits for both federal civilian employees and retired military. Other programs are designed to support people unable to fully care for themselves.

Federal programs pay for child care, foster care, and adoption assistance. Those unable to support themselves receive Supplemental Security Income (SSI), subsidized housing, federal child support, Temporary Assistance for Needy Families (TANF), and food stamps. Most income security expenditures are mandatory and therefore not authorized annually.

Medicare

Medicare, a health-care program available to all senior citizens regardless of income, began in 1966 and is another mandatory program. It provides an insurance plan that covers major hospital costs. Medicare also offers optional insurance that provides additional coverage for doctor and laboratory fees, outpatient services, and some equipment costs.

In recent years, Medicare expenditures have risen dramatically as the population has aged and the cost of caring for the elderly has gone up. Given the increasing cost of medicine and current population trends, increases in this category of expenditure are expected to continue.

The Federal Budget

Objective: Understand the factors that influence budget-making decisions.

Focus/Teach: Ask students to list the different programs that require government funding and then rank them according to importance. Then have students complete the activity.

Assess: Go over the answers as a class.

Close: Ask students to write a paragraph describing the difficulties of preparing the annual budget.

Differentiated Instruction Strategies

BL Have students select four programs in the table and then write a sentence that explains each program's purposes.

AL Ask students to create a fictional fourth representative (Representative D), and then describe his or her district.

ELL Ask students which programs representatives may want to expand.

Health

Health-care services for low-income people, disease prevention, and consumer safety account for a significant part of the federal budget. **Medicaid,** for example, is a joint federal-state medical insurance program for low-income persons. Because the payments have already been determined by Congress, this is one of the mandatory expenditure programs. Other mandatory programs include health-care services for working and retired federal employees.

Some programs in this category are discretionary. The Occupational Safety and Health Administration (OSHA), which monitors occupational safety and health in the workplace, is one such program. Other discretionary programs include AIDS and breast cancer research, substance abuse treatment, and mental health services.

Net Interest on Debt

When the federal government spends more than it collects in taxes and other revenues, it borrows money to make up the difference. The government has to pay interest on this debt, and the interest currently makes up the sixth-largest category of federal spending.

The amount of interest paid is a mandatory expenditure that varies with changes in interest rates and the size of the federal debt. The federal government is still running deficits and therefore adding to its total debt. If interest rates rise, then this will become an increasingly larger category in the federal budget.

Other Expenditure Categories

Other broad categories of the federal budget include education, training, employment, and social services; transportation; veterans' benefits; administration of justice; and natural resources and the environment. They include both mandatory and discretionary spending.

✓ **Reading Check** **Summarizing** What steps are involved in establishing the federal budget?

State Government Expenditures

MAIN Idea At the state level, expenditures include public welfare and higher education.

Economics and You If you want to attend college, have you found money available for financial aid? Read on to learn where these funds come from.

Individual states, like the federal government, also have expenditures. Like the federal government, states must approve spending before distributing funds.

The Budget Process

At the state level, the process of creating a budget and getting approval for spending can take many forms. For example, some states such as Kentucky have bi-annual budgets, or budgets that cover two years at a time. In most states, the process is loosely modeled after that of the federal government. Unlike the federal government, however, some states have a **balanced budget amendment**—a constitutional provision requiring that annual spending not exceed revenues.

Medicaid People with disabilities are among those eligible for Medicaid if they cannot afford health care. **Why is Medicaid a mandatory expenditure?**

Medicaid joint federal-state medical insurance program for low-income people

balanced budget amendment constitutional amendment requiring **W** government to spend no more than it collects in taxes and other revenues, excluding borrowing

CHAPTER 10 Government Spending **271**

W **Writing Support**

Persuasive Writing Ask students to research the arguments for and against a balanced budget amendment in their state. Instruct them to write a speech arguing why their state should or should not adopt such an amendment. If their state already has a balanced budget amendment, direct students to write a speech about why their state should keep or repeal the amendment. Have students deliver their speeches to the class. **OL**

Caption Answer: Payments have already been determined by Congress.

✓**Reading Check** **Answer:**
The president's OMB prepares a federal budget request. House subcommittees debate and vote on different expenditure categories. The House Appropriations Committee and then the full House approve a budget bill. The Senate then approves or drafts its own version of the bill. After both the House and Senate agree on a version of the bill, they send it to the president to sign.

Leveled Activities

BL Reinforcing Economic Skills, p. 19

OL Authentic Assessment Strategies and Activities, p. 15

AL Economic Forms and Financial Pages Trans., Strat. and Act., p. 9

D **Differentiated Instruction**

Visual/Spatial Have students create a collage-type poster illustrating the different categories of spending by their state government. Tell students that they may use pictures clipped from magazines, their own drawings, or a combination of both. **OL**

S **Skill Practice**

Making Generalizations

Ask: How do you think state governments benefit from supporting higher education? *(Possible answer: A well-educated population is better able to support itself.)* **OL**

Caption Answer:
intergovernmental expenditures, public welfare, insurance trust, retirement

✓ Reading Check **Answer:** It makes states keep annual spending from exceeding annual revenues. If revenue drops, states must cut expenses accordingly.

Hands-On Chapter Project

Step 2

Analyzing Government Spending

Step 2: Describing the Major Categories of Government Spending. Students will create brochures describing the goods and services provided by government.

Directions: Have students reassemble into the six groups that were formed in Step 1. Ask each group to research the major categories of expenditures made by their assigned level of government. Next have

---

intergovernmental expenditures funds that one level of government transfers to another level for spending

Under this provision, states often must cut spending when revenues drop. A reduction in revenues may occur if sales taxes or state income taxes fall because of a decline in the general level of economic activity.

Intergovernmental Expenditures
As **Figure 10.3** on the opposite page shows, the largest category of state spending is **intergovernmental expenditures**—funds that one level of government transfers to another level for spending. These funds come from state revenue sources such as sales taxes, and they are distributed to counties, cities, and other local communities to cover a variety of educational and other municipal expenditures.

D **Public Welfare**
The second largest category of state expenditures is public welfare. These payments take the form of cash assistance, payments for medical care, spending to maintain welfare institutions, and other welfare expenditures.

Insurance Trust and Retirement
Many states have their own insurance and retirement funds for state employees. The money in these funds is invested until

Higher Education
States usually fund part of the expenses for state colleges and universities. ***What are other large categories of state expenditures?***

272

employees retire, become unemployed, or are injured on the job. Contributions to these funds make this category a significant expenditure. Their main beneficiaries are teachers, legislators, highway workers, police, and other state employees.

Higher Education
State governments have traditionally taken responsibility for the large task of funding state colleges and universities. In most states, the tuition that students pay **S** covers only a portion of higher education expenses. States usually budget funds to pay the remainder of the cost. On average, higher education is the fifth-largest state expenditure.

Other Expenditures
The expenditures in the remaining state budget categories are relatively small. As Figure 10.3 shows, states spend money on a wide range of activities including corrections; utilities such as electricity, gas, and water; hospitals; and parks and recreation. Highways and road improvements are possible exceptions because they may require larger amounts of state money.

✓ Reading Check **Explaining** How does a balanced budget amendment work?

---

students create a brochure explaining the goods and services provided by their government. Brochures should advertise the merits of their government's programs with a positive and engaging tone. Encourage students to include graphics and statistical charts in their brochures.

Have students provide one brochure to each of the other groups. Encourage students to ask questions about the information provided in the other groups' brochures.

Making Decisions Have students write a short paper ranking the importance of the different goods and services provided by their assigned level of government. **OL**

(Chapter Project continued in Section 3.)

Figure 10.3 ▶ **State and Local Expenditures**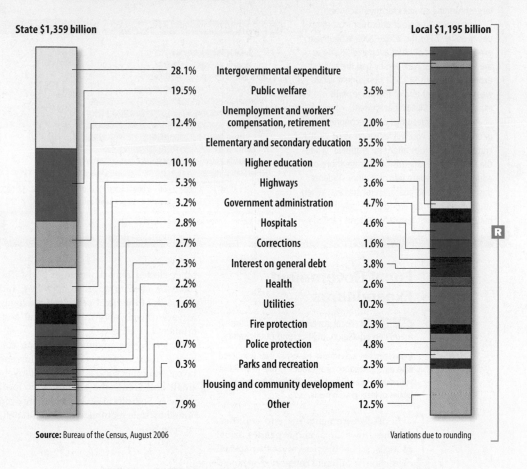

Graphs In MOtion
See StudentWorks™ Plus
or glencoe.com.

▶ Both state and local expenditures consist of a myriad of categories. Intergovernmental expenditures and public welfare use up almost half of state budgets, while education is the main expenditure for local governments.

Economic Analysis *How do expenditures for public welfare, education, and utilities compare between state and local governments?*

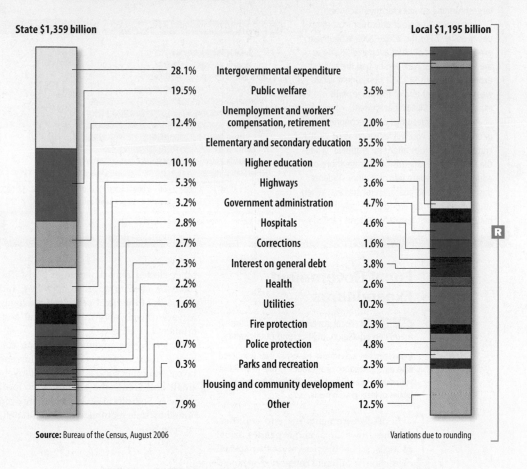

State $1,359 billion		Local $1,195 billion
28.1%	Intergovernmental expenditure	
19.5%	Public welfare	3.5%
12.4%	Unemployment and workers' compensation, retirement	2.0%
	Elementary and secondary education	35.5%
10.1%	Higher education	2.2%
5.3%	Highways	3.6%
3.2%	Government administration	4.7%
2.8%	Hospitals	4.6%
2.7%	Corrections	1.6%
2.3%	Interest on general debt	3.8%
2.2%	Health	2.6%
1.6%	Utilities	10.2%
	Fire protection	2.3%
0.7%	Police protection	4.8%
0.3%	Parks and recreation	2.3%
	Housing and community development	2.6%
7.9%	Other	12.5%

Source: Bureau of the Census, August 2006

Variations due to rounding

D Differentiated Instruction

Logical/Mathematical Have students use the chart to calculate the dollar amounts that state and local governments spend on education (all levels) and police protection. *(state: $137.26 billion, $9.51 billion; local: $450.52 billion, $57.36 billion)* **OL**

R Reading Strategy

Reading Charts Ask: What is the largest state government expense category that is not an expenditure of local government? *(intergovernmental expenditure)* What is the largest local government expense category that is not an expenditure of state government? *(elementary and secondary education)* **BL**

Economic Analysis

Answer: State governments spend more on public welfare, less on education, and less on utilities than local governments.

Additional Support

Activity: Hands-On Economics

Considering Budgetary Issues

Organize the class into groups of five to seven students each. Tell groups that they each will be performing a skit depicting a city council meeting that addresses some type of budgetary issue (for example, considering ways to cut expenditures to match a drop in revenues, or reviewing a proposal to grant tax breaks and other concessions to a business considering

locating a factory in town). Inform students that to research this topic they may wish to observe council meetings in person or via cable television (if a local access station provides such coverage). Have students perform their skits for the class. **AL**

Teacher Tip

Gathering Information
You might suggest that students prepare for their skits by interviewing council members and reviewing council meeting minutes. Copies of minutes are available at city hall or the city's Web site.

Teach

C Critical Thinking

Speculating Ask: Considering how much the United States spends on education, why do you think the math scores of U.S. students rank below the scores of students in other nations? *(Possible answers: other subjects receive greater emphasis in American schools; other nations place more importance on learning math.)* **OL**

S Skill Practice

Identifying the Main Idea
Ask: On what does your local government spend money? *(Answers will vary but will likely include education, utilities, and law enforcement.)* **BL**

W Writing Support

Personal Writing Ask students to write an essay describing their opinions about local government spending on their own education. Students might consider how and where the money is allocated. Tell students to include specific examples in their essays. **OL**

Additional Support

The Global Economy & YOU

Footing the Bill for Public Education

Nearly 50 million students are enrolled in public elementary and secondary schools in the United States. Property taxes and intergovernmental revenues are the largest funding sources for these schools.

How much does your education cost in tax-payer dollars? For the 2002–2003 school year, expenditures per student averaged $8,044 in the Unites States. New Jersey had the highest expenditures with $12,568 per student. Utah was at the lowest end of the range, with expenditures at $4,838 per student.

As the world becomes more economically interdependent, you will face increasing global competition for jobs after you graduate. While the United States spends on average more on education to prepare you and other students, this spending is no guarantee of success. When students all over the world participated in a math achievement test, U.S. students ranked

lower in the test than did those of other countries. Perhaps money can buy schools, but it cannot buy student learning.

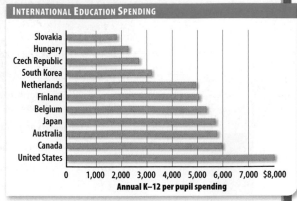

INTERNATIONAL EDUCATION SPENDING

Annual K–12 per pupil spending

Source: National Center for Education Statistics

Local Government Expenditures

....

MAIN Idea Local governments spend money mainly on education, utilities, and public safety.

....

Economics and You Have you ever wondered who pays for textbooks or extracurricular activities at your school? Read on to find out about the responsibilities of local governments.

....

S Local governments include counties, parishes, townships, municipalities, tribal councils, school districts, and other special districts. The different categories of expenditures made by these local governments are illustrated in Figure 10.3 on the previous page.

The Budget Process

At the local level, power to approve spending often rests with the mayor, the city council, the county judge, or some

other elected representative or body. The methods used to approve spending and the dates of the fiscal year itself are likely to vary considerably from one local government to the next.

Generally, the amount of revenues collected from property taxes, city income taxes, and other local sources is relatively small and limits the spending of local agencies. Some local governments are even bound by state requirements to avoid deficit spending.

Elementary and Secondary Education

W Local governments have primary responsibility for elementary and secondary education. Expenditures budgeted in this category include administrators' and teachers' salaries, wages for maintenance and cafeteria workers, textbooks, and other supplies. School districts also pay

---

Activity: Interdisciplinary Connection

Civics Instruct students to select a city, town, or county in another state. Have students use print or online resources to research the local government of the city, town, or county that they selected. Ask students to write a paper comparing their own local government with the one they researched. Instruct students to include statistics as part of their comparisons (for example, money spent on education, annual revenue collected, number of students

in public schools, number of government employees, and so on). In a class discussion, have volunteers share opinions on how their local government compared. What major differences and similarities did students find? **OL** for the construction and upkeep of all school buildings. Schools account for more than one-third of all local government spending, making it the largest item in most local budgets.

Utilities

Public utilities serve communities by providing services such as sewerage, electricity, natural gas, and water. For most local governments, spending on these utilities amounts to the second-largest expenditure and consumes about 10 percent of local spending.

In the typical community, the majority of expenditures on utilities are for schools, libraries, civic centers, and administrative buildings. Street lighting and traffic lights account for other expenditures.

Public Safety and Health

Most communities maintain a full-time, paid police force. Many have fire departments with paid, full-time firefighters as

well. However, some communities, especially those with smaller populations and limited budgets, maintain volunteer fire departments to keep the cost down. On the other hand, some communities, especially larger cities, own and staff their own hospitals.

Spending for health and safety in general tends to be about equal for each local government. However, the spending on these categories varies greatly from one state to another.

Other Expenditures

Highways, roads, and street repairs absorb most of the remaining spending. This category includes the repair of potholes, the installation and repair of street signs, snow removal, and other street-related items that are not covered by state budgets.

✓**Reading Check** Synthesizing Which local expenditures would you categorize as mandatory spending, and why?

🗎 **Skills Handbook**
See page R47 to learn about Making Predictions.

R **Reading Strategy**

Organizing Have students create a graphic organizer showing the major local government spending categories, including a section for "other expenditures." Ask students to include an example for each category. **OL**

✓**Reading Check** **Possible Answer:** elementary and secondary education and utilities; local governments have primary responsibility for these services, which are necessities in every community

Assess

💿 Use the Interactive Tutor Self-Assessment CD-ROM to review Section 2, and then assign the Section 2 Review as homework or as an in-class activity.

Close

Questioning Have students write a fifteen-question quiz covering the main ideas of this section. Ask students to exchange quizzes and answer the questions written by their partners. **OL**

Review **SECTION 2**

SECTION 2 Review

Vocabulary
1. **Explain** the significance of federal budget, fiscal year, appropriations bill, budget deficit, budget surplus, mandatory spending, discretionary spending, Medicare, Medicaid, balanced budget amendment, and intergovernmental expenditures.

Main Ideas
2. **Listing** Use a graphic organizer like the one below to list the five largest federal government expenditures.

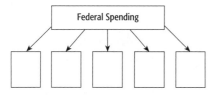

Federal Spending

3. **Discussing** What is the focus of state budgets?
4. **Describing** How do local governments spend their funds?

Critical Thinking
5. **The BIG Idea** Describe the difference between mandatory and discretionary spending.
6. **Making Predictions** People are living longer, and families have fewer members. How will the combination of these two factors affect future transfer payments such as Social Security?
7. **Making Generalizations** If you were to argue for reduced spending at the state and local levels, which categories would you choose?
8. **Analyzing Visuals** Look at Figure 10.3 on page 273. Why do state expenditures not include elementary and secondary education? Do they not pay for it? Explain.

Applying Economics
9. **Local Government Spending** Conduct research on the budget procedures for your local city or county government. Write an essay describing how the budget is created and who has spending authority.

Answers

1. All definitions can be found in the section and the Glossary.
2. Social Security; national defense; income security; Medicare; health
3. intergovernmental expenditures and public welfare
4. Local governments spend their funds on elementary and secondary education, utilities, public safety and health, and other expenditures such as highways, roads, and street repairs.

5. Mandatory spending includes funding for programs authorized by law and those that do not need annual approvals by Congress. Discretionary spending requires annual congressional approval.
6. Answers will vary, but students should recognize that more recipients and fewer workers paying into the system could drain the resources of Social Security and other transfer payment programs in future years.

7. Answers will vary but will likely include categories that are not considered to be necessities, such as parks and recreation.
8. Local governments have primary responsibility for elementary and secondary education. States do pay for these levels of education indirectly, through intergovernmental expenditures.
9. Answers will vary but should reflect an understanding of the budget-making process of students' local government.

CASE STUDY
Boeing Going Strong

Wide Range of Products

The United States government spends billions of dollars for defense every year; in 2005 alone, that amount exceeded $500 billion. One of the companies the government has turned to for its defense needs is aircraft manufacturer Boeing. **S** Employees at Boeing have built helicopters and passenger planes, fighter planes and missiles, satellites and spacecraft. They have sent astronauts to the moon and brought countries together aboard the International Space Station.

NEWS FLASH
Fighting Terrorism
In 2002, Boeing was awarded a contract by the U.S. Department of Transportation to provide explosive detection systems in 438 U.S. airports.

Boeing's Defense Link

William Boeing, founder and owner, started the company in 1916 with the incorporation of the Pacific Aero Products Company. That same year, Boeing produced its first airplane, the B&W

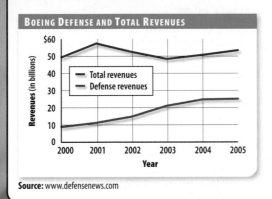

BOEING DEFENSE AND TOTAL REVENUES

Revenues (in billions)

— Total revenues
— Defense revenues

Years: 2000, 2001, 2002, 2003, 2004, 2005

Source: www.defensenews.com

Seaplane. Just a year later the company began its relationship with the government through test flights for the U.S. Navy. The Navy responded by ordering 50 seaplane trainers for a total of $116,000. Almost 90 years later in 2003, the Navy purchased 210 Super Hornets for a staggering $8.6 billion.

Ahead of the Pack

Over time, Boeing has become the world's leading aerospace producer and the largest manufacturer of commercial jetliners and military aircrafts combined. From its small beginnings, the company now has customers in nearly 150 countries, with 150,000 workers in 48 states and 67 countries. While Boeing sells its products to both governments and private customers, defense revenues make up more than half of total revenues—and help Boeing to be the second-largest defense company in the United States.

Analyzing the Impact

1. **Summarizing** Why is defense spending important to Boeing?
2. **Drawing Conclusions** What world events may have contributed to the increase in defense revenues from 2000 to 2005?

Extending the Content

Lockheed Martin The top five U.S. aerospace businesses in the United States are Boeing, United Technologies, Lockheed Martin, Northrop Grumman, and Honeywell International. These companies, along with several others, frequently compete for large U.S. government contracts. Despite its number three ranking on the previous list, Lockheed Martin is currently the largest defense company in the United States. In 2006, the company beat out Boeing and Northrop Grumman for a multibillion-dollar NASA project to build a new spacecraft to replace the space shuttles. Lockheed Martin will receive $3.9 billion through 2013 to develop the Orion crew exploration vehicle and build two spacecrafts for space station deliveries. The company could receive an additional $4 billion through 2019 for follow-up purchases and services.

SECTION 3 Deficits, Surpluses, and the National Debt

GUIDE TO READING

Section Preview

In this section, you will learn that deficit spending has helped create a national debt.

Content Vocabulary

- deficit spending (p. 278)
- national debt (p. 278)
- balanced budget (p. 278)
- trust funds (p. 278)
- per capita (p. 279)
- crowding-out effect (p. 281)
- "pay-as-you-go" provision (p. 282)
- line-item veto (p. 282)
- spending cap (p. 282)
- entitlement (p. 283)

Academic Vocabulary

- mandate (p. 282)
- instituted (p. 282)

Reading Strategy

Discussing As you read the section, list the various attempts by government to reduce the federal deficit and the national debt, then discuss the results.

Attempt	Result

ISSUES IN THE NEWS
—The Kentucky Post

Expensing Our Wars

[T]he chairman of the Senate Budget Committee, Judd Gregg, a Republican from New Hampshire, is considering treating the cost of the wars in Iraq and Afghanistan as a regular budget item.

The Bush administration has spent $440 billion so far on those wars, $120 billion of it this fiscal year, and the meter is running at the rate of $4.5 billion a month in Iraq and $800 million a month in Afghanistan.

The wars have been funded in a series of five emergency spending measures [that] are intended to deal with sudden, unexpected and short-term emergencies like [hurricane] Katrina. The bills are passed outside the regular appropriations process and are carried off budget, [which] tends to minimize the apparent cost. ∎

In the past 45 years, the federal budget has shown a surplus only five times. The first was in 1969, and the last four occurred in the years 1998 to 2001. Federal budget deficits in most years have added to the total amount of debt that the government owes. Since 2001 more than $2 trillion in debt has been added, bringing the total national debt to about $8.5 trillion.

Deficits occur for a number of reasons. For one, tax reductions are politically popular. For another, most people are in favor of the government spending more money on them. Finally, expenses such as wars and natural disasters are difficult to predict. However, as we read in the news article, expenditures don't go away simply because they are not recorded in the budget.

CHAPTER 10 Government Spending **277**

Focus

GUIDE TO READING

Possible Answers to Graphic:

Attempt: legislation. **Result:** weaker economy, unpopular program cuts, failure

Attempt: tax increases. **Result:** four years of budget surpluses until Congress cut taxes and increased spending

Attempt: reduced spending. **Result:** tax cuts and unplanned defense spending led to large deficits

Resource Manager

R Reading Strategies	C Critical Thinking	D Differentiated Instruction	W Writing Support	S Skill Practice
Teacher Edition • Previewing, p. 278 • Reading Graphs, p. 280 • Inferring, p. 282 **Additional Resources** • Guid. Read. Act., p. 30 • Read. Ess. & Note-Taking Guide, p. 88	**Teacher Edition** • Detecting, p. 278 • Analyzing, p. 280 • Predicting, p. 283 • Sequencing, p. 284 **Additional Resources** • Econ. Content Vocab. Act., p. 10	**Teacher Edition** • Visual/Spatial, p. 279 • Verbal/Linguistic, p. 282 **Additional Resources** • Reading and Study Skills Fold., p. 57 • Reteach. Act., p. 10	**Teacher Edition** • Narrative Writing, p. 278 • Persuasive Writing, p. 281 **Additional Resources** • High School Reading in the Content Area Strat. and Act.	**Teacher Edition** • Reading Graphs, p. 279 **Additional Resources** • Daily Focus Trans. 68, 76 • Graph. Org. Trans., p. 7

Teach

R Reading Strategy

Previewing Have students preview the headings in this chapter and then write a paragraph describing what they think they will learn from reading the text. **OL**

C Critical Thinking

Detecting Ask: Why do you think the wars in Iraq and Afghanistan have been financed through "supplemental requests"? (*Possible answer: Not including the war expenses in the budget helps mask the costs of these conflicts from the public.*) **OL**

W Writing Support

Narrative Writing Have students write a short story describing what the country might be like in the year 2100 if the trend of federal deficits is not reversed. **OL**

Differentiated Instruction

deficit spending annual government spending in excess of taxes and other revenues

national debt total amount borrowed from investors to finance the government's deficit spending

balanced budget annual budget in which expenditures equal revenues

trust fund special account used to hold revenues designated for a specific expenditure such as Social Security, Medicare, or highways

R From Deficits to Debt

MAIN Idea Because of deficit spending, the national debt has increased dramatically.

Economics and You Do you recall news stories about the nation's budget deficit? Read on to learn how deficits are created.

Historically, a remarkable amount of **deficit spending**—or spending in excess of revenues collected—has characterized the federal budget. Sometimes the government plans deficit spending. At other times, the government is forced to spend more than it collects because unexpected developments cause a drop in revenues or a rise in expenditures.

Predicting the Deficit

The government projected a $354 billion deficit for fiscal year 2007. Whether this is the actual amount at the end of the fiscal year, however, depends on the way expenditures are reported and the state of the economy.

C For example, no money was budgeted for the wars in Afghanistan and Iraq in the fiscal year 2007 budget. Instead, the president and Congress made nearly $100 billion of "supplemental requests" to cover the anticipated war costs. These war expenditures will ultimately be reflected in the amount of money the government spends, but they did not appear in the budget when it was first released.

Second, changes in the economy affect budget projections. Strong economic growth could cause the deficit to shrink because of

Did You Know?

➤ **Deficits Anyone?** European countries that want to become members of the European Union (EU) and adopt the euro as their currency have to take their deficits seriously. To be eligible, they must be able to control their economies—and that includes their budgets. In order to be accepted into the "euro zone," a nation is expected to keep its budget deficit at less than 3 percent of its GDP and its public debt at less than 60 percent of its GDP.

higher tax collections and lower unemployment claims. Likewise, a downturn in the economy could result in lower tax collections and higher unemployment insurance payments.

Deficits Add to the Debt

Panel A of **Figure 10.4** on the opposite page shows the history of the federal budget deficit since 1965. When the federal government runs a deficit, it must finance the revenue shortage by borrowing. It does this by selling U.S. Treasury notes and other securities to the public. If we add up all outstanding federal notes, bonds, and other debt obligations, we have a measure of the **national debt**—the total amount borrowed from investors to finance the government's deficit spending.

As **Panel B** in Figure 10.4 shows, the national debt grows whenever the government runs a deficit by spending more than it collects in revenues. If the federal budget runs a surplus, then some of the borrowed money is repaid and the amount of total debt goes down, as it did from 1998 to 2001. If the federal government achieves a **balanced budget**—an annual budget in which expenditures equal revenues—the national debt will not change.

A Growing Public Debt

The national debt has grown almost continuously since 1900, when the debt was $1.3 billion. By 1929 it had reached $16.9 billion, and by 1940 it was $50.7 billion. By mid-2006 the total national debt had reached about $8.5 trillion.

Some of this debt is money that the gov-**W** ernment owes itself. For example, approximately $3.5 trillion of this debt is in government **trust funds**—special accounts used to fund specific types of expenditures such as Social Security and Medicare. When the government collects the FICA or payroll tax, it puts the revenues in these trust accounts. The money is then invested in government securities until it is paid out.

Primary and Secondary Source Readings, p. 29

The Best of Legislation, The Worst of Legislation

Objective: Understand the potential consequences of budget deficits.

Focus: Ask students to rank on a scale of 1 to 10 how concerned they are about the national debt.

Teach: Instruct students to read the passage and then answer the questions that follow.

Assess: Discuss students' answers as a class.

Close: Ask students to expand their response to question 5 into a speech to be delivered to the class.

Differentiated Instruction Strategies

BL Have students write a paragraph explaining the difference between budget deficits and the federal debt.

AL Ask students to list additional information that they would like to know to help them evaluate the reading.

ELL Have students use a dictionary to look up any unfamiliar words.

Figure 10.4 ▶ The Federal Deficit and the National Debt

▶ Panel A shows the annual budget deficit since 1962. Panel B shows the national debt during the same time period. The government ran a surplus from 1998 to 2001 which allowed it to pay off some of the national debt.

Economic Analysis *Why has the deficit increased so rapidly since 2002?*

A ANNUAL BUDGET DEFICIT

B NATIONAL DEBT

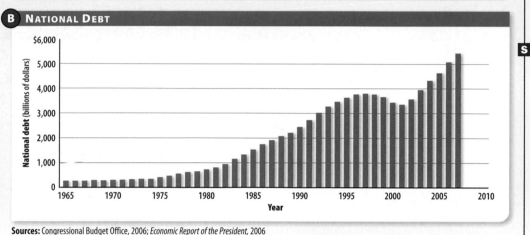

Sources: Congressional Budget Office, 2006; *Economic Report of the President*, 2006

Because trust fund balances represent money the government owes to itself, most economists tend to disregard this portion of the debt. Instead, they view the public portion of the debt—which amounted to nearly $5 trillion in mid-2006—as the economically relevant part of the debt.

Figure 10.5 on the next page presents two alternative views of the total national debt held by the public. **Panel A** shows the debt as a percentage of GDP. In **Panel B,** the national debt is computed on a **per capita,** or per person, basis.

Public vs. Private Debt

Despite the size of the public debt, several important differences between public and private debt mean that the country can never go bankrupt. One is that we owe most of the national debt to ourselves—whereas private debt is owed to others.

Another difference is repayment. When private citizens borrow, they usually make plans to repay the debt by a specific date. When the government borrows, it gives little thought to repayment and simply issues new bonds to pay off the old bonds.

per capita
per person basis; total divided by population

CHAPTER 10 Government Spending **279**

S Skill Practice

Reading Graphs **Ask:** How is the information in the two graphs related? *(The amounts in Panel A add to or subtract from the amounts in Panel B.)* **BL**

D Differentiated Instruction

Visual/Spatial Have students draw a picture or cartoon illustrating the concepts of public debt and private debt. Instruct students to trade their cartoons with a partner. Ask students to then interpret the images in their partners' drawings. **OL**

Economic Analysis

Answer: tax rates decreased while expenditures on homeland security and the wars in Iraq and Afghanistan caused federal spending to increase

---

Leveled Activities

BL **Guided Reading Activities, p. 30**

OL **Reteaching Activities, p. 10**

AL **Graphic Organizer Transparencies, p. 7**

R Reading Strategy

Reading Graphs Ask: How is the debt situation today better than it was in the mid-1990s? *(The debt today is a lower percentage of the GDP.)* How is it worse? *(The per-capita debt is higher.)* **BL**

C Critical Thinking

Analyzing Instruct students to use reliable print or online resources to analyze the public debt owed to foreigners. Ask students to prepare a statistical summary of this portion of the debt. Students should include the different companies and nations, along with the corresponding amounts, to which the government owes money. **OL**

Economic Analysis

Answer: It has increased.

✓Reading Check Answer:
Public debt is debt that the government owes to itself. Private debt is debt that the government owes to others.

Additional Support

Figure 10.5 ▶ Two Views of the National Debt

▶ The national debt as a percent of GDP has ranged from about 34 to almost 50 percent since 1965. The amount owed per person increased most years during the same period.

Economic Analysis *What has happened to the size of the national debt since 2001?*

A **AS A PERCENTAGE OF GDP**

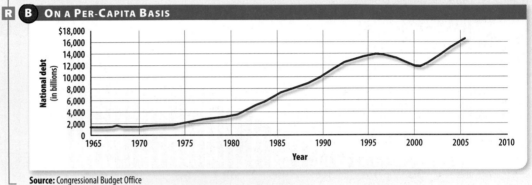

R **B** **ON A PER-CAPITA BASIS**

Source: Congressional Budget Office

A third difference has to do with purchasing power. When private individuals repay debts, they give up purchasing power because they have less money to buy goods and services. The federal government does not give up purchasing power, because the taxes collected from some groups are simply transferred to other groups. The exception is the 15 to 20 percent of the public **C** debt owned by foreigners. When payments are made to investors outside the United States, some purchasing power is temporarily diverted from the U.S. economy.

✓Reading Check **Contrasting** What are the differences between public and private debt?

280 UNIT 3 Economic Institutions and Issues

Impact of the National Debt

MAIN Idea The national debt affects the distribution of income and transfers purchasing power from the private to the public sector.

Economics and You Do you hear your parents talk about interest rates? Read on to learn how the national debt affects interest rates.

Even though we owe most of the national debt to ourselves, it affects the economy by transferring purchasing power, reducing economic incentives, causing a crowding-out effect, and redistributing income.

Extending the Content

Budget Deficits Around the World The United States is not the only country facing the issue of increasing national debt. Several other nations face budget deficits that have a greater impact on their economies than the U.S. deficit has on the American economy. In 2005, the U.S. budget deficit as a percent of GDP was 3.8%. That same year, Hungary (6.1%), Portugal (6.0%), Japan (5.2%), Greece (4.4%), and Italy (4.3%) ran deficits that were a greater percentage of their GDPs. On the other hand, Norway and New Zealand had surpluses in 2005 that totaled 15.8% and 5.8% of their respective GDPs.

John Cole / Scranton Times-Tribune

National Debt
The more the government borrows today, the more future generations will have to repay. *What other effects does the national debt have on the nation?*

Transferring Purchasing Power

The national debt can cause a transfer of purchasing power from the private sector to the public sector. In general, when the public debt increases, taxes increase and people have less money for themselves.

Purchasing power can also be transferred from one generation to another. If the government borrows today and leaves the repayment to future taxpayers, then today's adults will consume more and their children less. The accumulation of debt by one generation can thus reduce the economic well-being of the next.

Reducing Economic Incentives

Government can reduce economic incentives if it appears to spend money in a careless manner. A community, for example, may use a federal grant to purchase expensive equipment that its citizens would not want to pay for themselves. If the taxpayers that benefit from a project would not fund it themselves, other taxpayers would not want their taxes to go to such projects.

Crowding Out

When the federal government uses deficit spending, it must borrow money in financial markets. This borrowing can drive interest rates up, forcing all borrowers to pay more for the temporary use of funds.

Because the government borrows so much, it competes with businesses and individuals such as potential home buyers for available money. This competition can cause a **crowding-out effect**—the higher-than-normal interest rates caused by heavy government borrowing. If private borrowers cannot afford the higher interest rates, they are squeezed out of the market.

crowding-out effect
higher-than-normal interest rates and diminished access to financial capital faced by private borrowers when they compete with government borrowing in financial markets

Redistributing Income

Finally, the national debt and the tax structure can impact the distribution of income. Suppose that the government taxes upper-income individuals and spends the money on the poor. This would redistribute income from the rich to the poor. The opposite would happen if the poor were taxed and the money spent on the rich. In either case, the people paying less in taxes would benefit from the tax policy. **W**

This is not a purely hypothetical situation. The individual income tax cuts made since 2001 have made income taxes *less* progressive, shifting some of the tax burden from higher- to lower-income groups.

✓**Reading Check** Analyzing How does the transfer of purchasing power between generations affect you?

CHAPTER 10 Government Spending 281

Activity: Interdisciplinary Connection

History Point out to students that the federal government has been paying off a debt since 1789. Most years, just the interest on the debt has been in the millions. Have volunteers consult an almanac to find out how much the federal government paid in interest on the debt for every tenth year between 1800 and 1900. Then have them use the information to create a time line to display in the classroom. *(1800: $3 million, 1810: $3 million, 1820: $5 million, 1830: $2 million, 1840 [information unavailable], 1850: $4 million, 1860: $3 million, 1870: $129 million, 1880: $96 million, 1890: $36 million, 1900: $40 million)* Also ask students to hypothesize about why the interest on the debt increased by 4300 percent between 1860 and 1870. *(Students will likely answer that the debt increased by that amount because of the costs of the Civil War and Reconstruction.)* **OL**

D Differentiated Instruction

Verbal/Linguistic Have students use print or online resources to find out more information about one of the legislative efforts described on this page. Ask students to use their findings to write a report expanding upon the text's description of their selected topic. **AL**

R Reading Strategy

Inferring Ask: What can you infer about how American voters felt about the federal debt in 1985? *(Students will likely point out that many Americans were concerned about the debt, leading Congress to pass the GRH legislation.)* **OL**

Economic Analysis

Possible Answers: tax increases and program cuts generally spark voter opposition; politicians find ways around spending limitations

Figure 10.6 ▶ The Size of the National Debt

▶ The publicly held portion of the national debt reached $5 trillion in 2006 and continues to rise. Attempts to reduce the debt by legislation alone have failed. The only other ways to reduce it are by raising taxes or reducing federal spending.

Economic Analysis *Why is it difficult for legislators to increase revenues or reduce spending?*

WILL WE EVER SHRINK THE NATIONAL DEBT?

A $1 bill is about 6 inches (15.2 cm) long. If 5 trillion of these bills were laid end to end, they would form a chain 474 million miles (764 km) long—more than enough to stretch from the surface of the earth to the surface of the sun and back—two and a half times!

"pay-as-you-go" provision requirement that new spending proposals or tax cuts must be offset by reductions elsewhere

line-item veto power to cancel specific budget items without rejecting the entire budget

spending cap limits on annual discretionary spending

Skills Handbook

See page **R35** to learn about **Identifying the Main Idea.**

D Reducing Deficits and the Debt

MAIN Idea Congress has tried a number of measures to reduce deficits and the national debt.

Economics and You Did your parents teach you how to avoid overspending? Read on to learn about attempts to limit the nation's debt.

In order to control the size of the national debt, we have to first address the federal budget deficit. Concern over deficit spending since the 1980s has led to a number of attempts to control it.

R Legislative Failures

One of the first significant attempts to control the federal deficit took place when Congress tried to **mandate** a balanced budget. The legislation was formally called the Balanced Budget and Emergency Deficit Control Act of 1985, or Gramm-Rudman-Hollings (GRH) after its sponsors.

Despite high hopes, GRH failed for two reasons. First, Congress discovered that it could get around the law by passing spending bills that took effect two or three years later. Second, the economy started to decline in 1990, triggering a suspension of budget cuts when the economy was weak.

Ir 1990 Congress passed the Budget Enforcement Act (BEA). The BEA's main feature was a **"pay-as-you-go" provision**—a requirement that new spending proposals or tax cuts must be offset by reductions elsewhere in the budget. If no agreement on the reductions could be reached, then automatic, across-the-board spending cuts would be **instituted.** Congress soon discovered that cutting spending was more difficult than it thought, so it suspended the provision in order to increase spending.

In 1996 Congress gave the president a **line-item veto**—the power to cancel specific budget items without rejecting the entire budget—but the Supreme Court declared it unconstitutional. This was followed by the Balanced Budget Agreement of 1997, which featured rigid **spending caps**—legal limits on annual discretionary spending—to assure that Congress balanced the budget by 2002. However, the caps required politically unpopular cuts in many programs such as health, science, and education, so the caps were also abandoned.

Hands-On Chapter Project

Step 3

Analyzing Government Spending

Step 3: Analyzing Government Budgets. Students groups will analyze the recent budgets of their assigned level of government.

Directions: Have students return to their project groups. Ask each group to research the annual budgets of their assigned government over the past 10 years. Instruct students to prepare a graph illustrating their government's budget

surpluses and/or deficits in the past decade. Next, have groups prepare a report explaining the reasons for the budget figures (for example, increased federal spending on defense, state balanced budget amendment, state requirement prohibiting deficit spending, and so on).

Have each group present its findings to the class using visual aids such as a poster-sized chart or multimedia presentation. After the presentations, discuss the major

trends that have shaped federal, state, and local spending in recent years.

Making Connections Ask students to write a short paper discussing how recent budget trends at the federal, state, and local level have impacted people in their community. **OL**

(Chapter Project continued in Visual Summary.)

Raising Revenues

President Clinton's Omnibus Budget Reconciliation Act of 1993 was an attempt to trim $500 billion from the deficit over a five-year period. The act featured a combination of spending reductions and tax increases that made the individual income tax more progressive—especially for the wealthiest 1.2 percent of taxpayers.

Higher tax rates, along with strong economic growth, combined to produce four consecutive years of federal budget surpluses. By 2001 Congress expected annual surpluses for another 10 years. Rather than pay down the debt, however, Congress cut tax rates while also increasing spending.

Reducing Spending

Another way to control the deficit is by reducing federal spending. This can be more difficult than it sounds because spending is subject to unexpected change.

For example, the 2001 terrorist attacks led to unplanned government spending on homeland security and wars in Afghanistan and Iraq. Because this was also the first year of President Bush's tax cuts, and because economic activity was low, the federal government had fewer tax revenues to spend. As a result, record federal budget deficits returned in 2002.

In addition, spending was difficult to reduce because the federal budget had so many **entitlements**—broad social programs with established eligibility requirements to provide health, nutritional, or income supplements to individuals. People are entitled to draw benefits if they meet the eligibility requirements. Although most entitlements are classified as mandatory spending, Congress can revise them. Still, this is difficult to do for members of Congress because the programs are so popular.

In the end, Congress has a difficult task ahead. Any action to reduce budget deficits and the national debt will depend on the willpower of Congress to make unpopular and difficult choices.

✓Reading Check Describing What events in 2001 have added to the national debt?

entitlement
program or benefit using established eligibility requirements to provide health, nutritional, or income supplements to individuals

C Critical Thinking

Predicting Ask: Do you think that the federal government will reduce the national debt in the next 15 years? Explain. *(Students answering yes may say that different leadership may make that possible. Students answering no may say that efforts to decrease spending will be controversial.)* **OL**

✓Reading Check **Possible Answer:** terrorist attacks on the U.S., invasion of Afghanistan

Assess

Use the Interactive Tutor Self-Assessment CD-ROM to review Section 3, and then assign the Section 3 Review as homework or as an in-class activity.

Close

Making Connections

Ask students to find a recent newspaper article about the federal budget, and write a short essay explaining how the article relates to this section. **OL**

SECTION 3 Review

Vocabulary

1. **Explain** the significance of deficit spending, national debt, balanced budget, trust fund, per capita, crowding-out effect, pay-as-you-go provision, line-item veto, spending cap, and entitlement.

Main Ideas

2. **Describing** What is the difference between the national debt and the federal deficit?

3. **Listing** Use a graphic organizer like the one below to list five ways the national debt can affect the economy.

National Debt: Possible Effects on the Economy
1.
2.
∿∿∿∿∿∿∿∿∿

4. **Identifying** What were the results of government efforts to reduce deficits?

Critical Thinking

5. **The BIG Idea** Why is it so difficult to rein in the national debt? Use examples to explain your answer.

6. **Analyzing Visuals** Look at Figure 10.5 on page 280. Why do you think the national debt as a percentage of GDP has not risen at the same rate as the debt per capita?

7. **Determining Cause and Effect** How can the federal debt affect worker incentives?

8. **Drawing Conclusions** Which do you think is a better way to reduce budget deficits: pay-as-you-go provisions or line-item vetoes? Explain your answer in a brief paragraph.

Applying Economics

9. **Deficit Spending** If you were given the task of reducing entitlement programs to limit deficit spending, which ones would you select to reduce or alter? Write a short essay that includes the reasons for your choices.

Answers

1. All definitions can be found in the section and the Glossary.
2. The national debt is the cumulative amount of funds borrowed by the federal government. The deficit is the amount of government spending that exceeds government revenue in a given year.
3. transfer purchasing power; reduce economic incentives; increase interest rates; crowd private borrowers out of financial markets; redistribute income

4. Aside from the brief success of Clinton's Omnibus Budget Reconciliation Act, government efforts to reduce deficits have failed.
5. **Possible answer:** Voters generally do not like tax increases. Cuts to entitlement programs, such as Medicare, are also unpopular. Global events, such as the rise of the terrorist threat, create new spending priorities.
6. GDP growth has limited the increase of the debt's percentage of the GDP.

7. Workers who believe that larger portions of their income will go to taxes to pay the interest on the debt will be less likely to work harder to earn more money.
8. Answers will vary but should reflect knowledge of pay-as-you-go provisions and line-item vetoes.
9. Answers will vary, but students should demonstrate an understanding of entitlement programs.

Teach

C Critical Thinking

Sequencing Have students consult a reliable Web site containing biographical information about Alice Rivlin. Ask students to create a time line that includes important dates in her life (for example, birth, publication of books, appointment to White House OMB). Instruct students to include at least ten dates in their time lines. **OL**

Examining the Profile

Answers:
1. balanced federal budgets and a low national debt
2. Rivlin believes that to attract business, states should engage in an aggressive effort to improve their infrastructure and their education systems.

Additional Support

Teacher Tip

Ordering Books Some of Alice Rivlin's books may not be available at libraries in your area. You may wish to use interlibrary loan to order one or more of her books several weeks before assigning this activity.

Profiles in Economics

Alice Rivlin is an outspoken critic of budget deficits. She argues that spending cannot be brought under control until Congress is willing to take action. While the problems are large, Rivlin believes that "we will find ways to solve them."

Alice Rivlin (1931–) C

- founding director of the Congressional Budget Office
- director of the White House Office of Management and Budget
- vice chair of the Federal Reserve Board

Ms. Economics

At a time when few women had full-time jobs, fewer went to college, and almost none pursued economics, Alice Rivlin discovered the subject and found her niche. Rivlin is well known for her insistence on solid analysis, innovative thinking, and a steadfast insistence on "fiscal sanity"–balanced federal budgets and a low national debt. These traits served her well as the founding director of the Congressional Budget Office. Rivlin likened the job to an entrepreneurship, because she had to find ways to provide Congress with nonpartisan projections on the impact of proposed legislation on the nation's budget and debt.

Balancing the Federal Checkbook

Rivlin believed that Reaganomics had a negative effect on the U.S. economy. In 1992 she published *Reviving the American Dream: The Economy, the States, and the Federal Government,* which outlined her plan for "fiscal sanity" and the responsibilities of national and state governments. She believes that competition between states to attract corporations leads to too many tax breaks, resulting in too few tax dollars to implement needed–and often federally mandated–social programs. Instead states should engage "in an aggressive effort to improve their infrastructure and improve their education systems in order to attract business."

The book influenced then-presidential candidate Bill Clinton, for whom she became Director of the White House Office of Management and Budget. In this position she oversaw a transition from federal debt to surplus in just two years. This success led her to membership on the Federal Reserve Board. Today Rivlin looks for ways to fight budget deficits as a Senior Fellow at the Brookings Institution, an economics and policy think tank located in Washington, D.C.

Examining the Profile

1. **Summarizing** How does Rivlin define "fiscal sanity"?
2. **Determining Cause and Effect** According to Rivlin, what is the best way for states to attract business?

284 UNIT 3 Economic Institutions and Issues

Activity: Collaborative Learning

Identifying Central Issues Organize the class into small groups. Assign a different book that Alice Rivlin wrote or co-wrote to each of the groups (for example: *Reviving the American Dream, Restoring Fiscal Sanity, Caring for the Disabled Elderly, Systematic Thinking for Social Action*, and *The Role of the Federal Government in Financing Higher Education*). Instruct each group to prepare an oral report highlighting the main arguments of its assigned book. Students should include a visual component, such as a chart or graphic organizer, in their reports. Have each group present its report to the class. After the presentations, discuss as a class Alice Rivlin's economic and political philosophy. **AL**

Visual Summary

▶ **Federal Budget Process** Each year, the president sends a federal budget to Congress. The budget undergoes a lengthy approval process until it is signed into law.

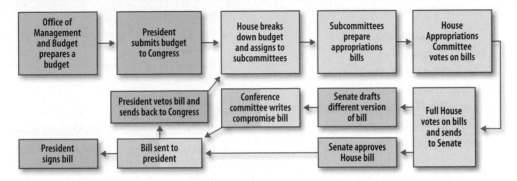

▶ **Major Budget Categories** The major budget categories vary for federal, state, and local governments. The focus of the federal government is on nationwide programs and expenditures. States pass on much of their budget to local governments and spend the rest on state-level programs. Local governments focus their expenditures on local needs.

Federal government
- Social Security
- National defense
- Income security
- Health care

State governments
- Intergovernmental expenditure
- Public welfare
- Insurance trust and retirement
- Higher education

Local governments
- Elementary and secondary education
- Utilities
- Public safety and health

▶ **Surpluses, Deficits, and Debt** When revenues exceed expenditures, governments enjoy a budget surplus. If revenues are less than expenditures, governments are faced with a budget deficit. They then have to borrow money to meet expenditures and incur debt.

CHAPTER 10 Government Spending **285**

Analyzing Review with students the constitutional principle of checks and balances. Then have students reread the flowchart of the federal budget process on this page. **Ask:** How does the federal budget process demonstrate the principle of checks and balances? *(OMB works with the president to prepare a budget; committees in both the House and Senate review the president's proposed budget and then draft versions; Congress sends compromise bill to the president, who vetoes or signs the bill.)* **OL**

Identifying Direct students to travel around their area and identify examples of federal, state, and local spending (at least five examples for each). Possible ideas include an interstate highway, a state park, and an elementary school. Instruct students to create a collage illustrating their findings. Students may use photographs they have taken or their own drawings. **OL**

Hands-On Chapter Project

Step 4: Wrap Up

Analyzing Government Spending

Step 4: Complete the Analysis. Students will summarize what they learned in the previous steps.

Directions: Have students write a paper summarizing how spending by their group's assigned level of government affects them personally. Students will work alone on this activity—each student will write a summary paper. Students should include in their papers concepts they learned in each of the previous steps. Ideas that could possibly appear in a paper include tests that a student took to measure No Child Left Behind progress, a state-funded highway that a student frequently uses, and textbooks supplied by their local government. Students should conclude their reports with an evaluation, based in part on personal experience, of the overall effectiveness of their assigned level of government in using tax revenue to provide goods and services. **OL**

Assessment & Activities

ExamView® Assessment Suite

This easy-to-use software includes extensive question banks and allows you to create fully customized tests that can be administered in print or online.

Review Content Vocabulary

1.–10. Students' sentences will vary but should demonstrate understanding of how the terms are related.

Review Academic Vocabulary

11. e	**12.** d
13. b	**14.** c
15. a	**16.** f

Review the Main Ideas

17. One type of government spending is for goods and services, such as aircraft, ships, and staff salaries. The other type of spending is transfer payments, such as welfare, for which the government receives neither goods nor services in return.

18. Government-subsidized colleges compete with private institutions for students. Government hospitals compete with private facilities for patients.

19. to insure that projects benefiting their own constituents receive funding

20. to prevent a budget deficit by requiring that annual spending not exceed revenues

21. **Federal:** national defense, Social Security, Medicare, income security, health, interest on the debt. **State:** intergovernmental expenditures, public welfare, higher education.

Review Content Vocabulary

Write a sentence about each pair of terms below. The sentences should show how the terms are related.

1. public sector, private sector
2. transfer payment, grant-in-aid
3. distribution of income, deficit spending
4. federal budget, fiscal year
5. appropriations bill, balanced budget amendment
6. deficit spending, national debt
7. deficit spending, crowding-out effect
8. entitlement, balanced budget
9. mandatory spending, discretionary spending
10. spending cap, budget deficit

Review Academic Vocabulary

Each of the sentences below contains a synonym for one of the following terms. Match the sentence to the term.

a. constituents
b. reluctant
c. coincide
d. ambiguity
e. mandate
f. instituted

11. States have a requirement to provide public schools.
12. The federal budget leaves some uncertainty about actual expenditures.
13. The state legislature was hesitant when it came to reducing spending for roads.
14. The fiscal year often does not correspond with the calendar year.
15. The representative was concerned about maintaining the support of the voters in his district.
16. Some states have passed balanced budget amendments.

Review the Main Ideas

Section 1 *(pages 261–265)*

17. **Explain** the two kinds of government spending.
18. **Describe** the way the government competes with the private sector.
19. **Explain** why politicians insert "pork" items into other legislation.

Section 2 *(pages 267–275)*

20. **Identify** the purpose of a balanced budget amendment.
21. **Identify** the categories of federal, state, and local spending by using a graphic organizer like the one below.

Categories of Spending		
Federal	State	Local

22. **List** the three major categories of spending by local governments.

Section 3 *(pages 277–283)*

23. **Discuss** the relationship of the federal deficit to the federal debt.
24. **List** four legislative attempts to deal with the problem of federal budget deficits.
25. **Explain** why entitlements are so named.

Critical Thinking

26. **The BIG Idea** Why is it more difficult for politicians to reduce mandatory spending than discretionary spending?
27. **Comparing and Contrasting** What is the difference between transfer payments and government spending on goods and services?

Local: elementary and secondary education, utilities, highways, roads, street repairs.

22. education, utilities, and public safety and health

23. The deficit amount in the federal budget is added to the national debt each year.

24. Gramm-Rudman-Hollings, Budget Enforcement Act, line-item veto, Balanced Budget Agreement of 1997

25. because recipients have the right to the benefits if they meet the eligibility requirements

Critical Thinking

26. It is authorized by law and does not require annual approval from Congress. Such spending includes many benefits that people do not want to lose. Discretionary spending must be approved by Congress and can be more easily reduced.

27. The government receives goods and services when it spends money for those items. It receives no goods and services in exchange for transfer payments.

Economics ONLINE Self-Check Quiz Visit the *Economics: Principles and Practices* Web site at glencoe.com and click on *Chapter 10–Self-Check Quizzes* to prepare for the chapter test.

Assessment and Activities CHAPTER **10**

28. **Drawing Conclusions** Review the discussion on attempts to reduce the deficit on pages 282 and 283. Use a chart similar to the one below to outline the main features and weaknesses of these legislative attempts. Can you find a common reason why these attempts have failed? What do you think would need to be done to avoid future failures?

Legislation	Features	Weaknesses

29. **Determining Cause and Effect** How does a balanced budget amendment affect the budget process?

30. **Making Inferences** Do you think transfer payments are the best way to distribute tax revenue? How would the tax collection system have to change if the government levels that actually spend the money had to collect the taxes themselves?

Applying Economic Concepts

31. **Human Capital** Which of the categories in Figure 10.3 on page 273 reflect an investment in human capital?

32. **Government Spending** Make a list of ways you and your family benefit from government expenditures. Provide at least one example each for the federal, state, and local government.

Math Practice

33. A neighbor spent $25,000 a year for 10 years and had an annual income of $20,000 during this period. What is the neighbor's total debt?

Analyzing Visuals

34. **Classifying Information** Examine the major types of federal expenditures in Figure 10.2 on page 269. Classify each as to whether they are entitlement or nonentitlement programs.

Thinking Like an Economist

35. **Critical Thinking** An economist likes to think in terms of trade-offs and opportunity costs. If you wanted to make changes to a balanced state budget in any given year, what would be the opportunity cost of lowering taxes? Of increasing discretionary spending?

Writing About Economics

36. **Persuasive Writing** Which of the two types of government spending has the most impact on the economy? Explain your answer in a two-page paper.

Interpreting Cartoons

37. **Critical Thinking** What is the topic of the cartoon below? What point is the cartoonist making about the topic? How does he do it? Do you think the cartoon is effective?

Paul Combs, Editorial Cartoonist / The Tampa Tribune.

CHAPTER 10 Government Spending **287**

32. Answers will vary but should demonstrate an understanding of how citizens benefit from such spending.

Math Practice

33. $50,000

Analyzing Visuals

34. Entitlement: Social Security; Medicare; income security; health; education, training, employment, and social services; veterans' benefits. Nonentitlement: national defense, net interest, transportation, justice administration, international affairs, community development.

Thinking Like an Economist

35. Answers will vary but should mention opportunity costs and trade-offs.

Writing About Economics

36. Answers will vary but should show sound reasoning.

Interpreting Cartoons

37. The topic is government spending. The cartoonist is saying that out-of-control government spending is wasting taxpayer dollars. The government is portrayed as a fat pig demanding more taxes to devour.

28. **Gramm-Rudman-Hollings:** mandated a balanced budget; Congress avoided the law with later spending bills
Budget Enforcement Act: new spending must be offset by reductions elsewhere in the budget
line-item veto passed: president can cancel specific budget items; Supreme Court declares it unconstitutional
Balanced Budget Agreement of 1997: rigid spending caps; caps required cuts that were not enacted

29. Balanced budget amendments may require states to amend their budgets to reduce spending to match revenues.

30. Answers will vary but should demonstrate an understanding of transfer payments and tax collection.

Applying Economic Concepts

31. intergovernmental expenditure, public welfare, unemployment and workers' compensation, retirement, education, hospitals, corrections, health

Key to Ability Levels
BL Below level   **AL** Above level
OL On level   **ELL** English Language Learners

Key to Teaching Resources
Print Material   DVD
CD-Rom   Transparency

Levels					Resources	Chapter Opener	Section 1	Section 2	Section 3	Chapter Assess
BL	OL	AL	ELL							
FOCUS										
BL	OL	AL	ELL		Daily Focus Skills Transparencies		42, 45	44, 46	43	
TEACH										
BL	OL		ELL		Guided Reading Activities*		p. 31	p. 32	p. 33	
BL	OL	AL	ELL		Economic Content Vocabulary Activities*		p. 11	p. 11	p. 11	
	OL	AL			Critical Thinking Activities				p. 17	
BL	OL		ELL		Reading Essentials and Note-Taking Guide*		p. 91	p. 94	p. 97	
		AL			Enrichment Activities		p. 11			
	OL	AL			Free Enterprise Activities		pp. 16, 17	p. 17	pp. 8, 12	
BL	OL	AL	ELL		Primary and Secondary Source Readings			p. 23		
BL	OL	AL	ELL		Economic Cartoons		p. 21		pp. 17, 22	
BL	OL	AL	ELL		Hand-On Economics		p. 10			
BL	OL	AL	ELL		Math Practice for Economics		pp. 12, 18	pp. 18, 20		
BL	OL	AL	ELL		Economics Forms and Financial Pages Transparencies, Strategies, and Activities			p. 24	pp. 19, 22	
BL	OL	AL	ELL		Personal Finance Activities		p. 21			
BL	OL	AL	ELL		Reinforcing Economic Skills		p. 7	p. 29	pp. 8, 12	
BL	OL		ELL		High School Reading in the Content Area Strategies and Activities	✓	✓	✓	✓	✓
BL	OL	AL	ELL		High School Writing Process Transparencies	✓	✓	✓	✓	✓
BL	OL	AL	ELL		Writer's Guidebook	✓	✓	✓	✓	✓
BL	OL	AL	ELL		StudentWorks Plus CD-ROM	✓	✓	✓	✓	✓
BL	OL	AL	ELL		Vocabulary PuzzleMaker CD-ROM	✓	✓	✓	✓	✓

CHAPTER 11

- Interactive Lesson Planner
- Interactive Teacher Edition
- Fully editable blackline masters
- Economics & You videos

- Differentiated Lesson Plans
- Printable reports of daily assignments
- Standards tracking system

Levels					Resources	Chapter Opener	Section 1	Section 2	Section 3	Chapter Assess
BL	OL	AL	ELL							
					TEACH (continued)					
BL	OL	AL	ELL		Economics & You Video Program DVD—*Saving and Investing*	✓	✓	✓	✓	✓
BL	OL	AL	ELL		Graph Coach CD-ROM	✓	✓	✓	✓	✓
Teacher Resources					Differentiated Instruction Strategies	✓	✓	✓	✓	✓
					Success with English Learners	✓	✓	✓	✓	✓
					Presentation Plus! CD-ROM	✓	✓	✓	✓	✓
					ASSESS					
BL	OL	AL	ELL		Section Quizzes and Chapter Tests		p. 133	p. 134	p. 135	pp. 137, 141
BL	OL	AL	ELL		Authentic Assessment Strategies and Activities				p. 17	
BL	OL	AL	ELL		*ExamView® Assessment Suite* CD-ROM		11-1	11-2	11-3	Ch. 11
BL	OL	AL	ELL		Interactive Tutor Self-Assessment CD-ROM		11-1	11-2	11-3	
					CLOSE					
BL			ELL		Reteaching Activities*		p. 11	p. 11	p. 11	

*Also available in Spanish

Research Using Famous Person

Technology Product

CyberScout is a convenient and dynamic search engine that provides several easy ways to locate information outside the McGraw-Hill Learning Network. CyberScout only searches Web sites that have been reviewed by teachers, so the information students find is always appropriate and accurate.

Objectives

After students learn using CyberScout, they will be able to

- research information on famous people in economics;
- exercise research and study skills;
- practice writing skills.

Steps

- From the McGraw-Hill Learning Network home page (www.mhln.com), click on **For Students.**
- Choose **CyberScout** below **Homework Help.**
- Enter a name (last, or first and last) in the **Famous Person** field and click **Go.**
- The CyberScout page will display a set of results.
- Select the Famous Person's name from the results.
- Click the link to a Web site of interest.
- Students will be redirected to the Web site in a new window.
- Students navigate through the chosen Web site to gain information on their topic and take notes.

Economics ONLINE

	Student	Teacher	Parent
Beyond the Textbook	●	●	●
Chapter Overviews	●	●	●
ePuzzles and Games	●		●
Concepts in Motion	●		●
Multi-Language Glossaries	●		●
Online Student Edition	●	●	●
Self-Check Quizzes	●		●
Student Web Activities	●		●
Study Central™	●		●
Time Current Events	●	●	●
Teaching Today		●	
Vocabulary eFlashcards	●		●
Web Activity Lesson Plans		●	

Glencoe Media Center

❯ glencoe.com

Study-To-Go
- Vocabulary eFlashcards
- Self-Check Quizzes

❯ **Audio/Video**
- Student Edition Audio
- Spanish Summaries
- Economics & You Videos

READING SUPPORT FROM JAMESTOWN EDUCATION

- **Timed Readings Plus in Social Studies** helps students increase their reading rate and fluency while maintaining comprehension. The 400-word passages are similar to those found on state and national assessments.

- **Reading in the Content Area: Social Studies** concentrates on six essential reading skills that help students better comprehend what they read. The book includes 75 high-interest nonfiction passages written at increasing levels of difficulty.

- **Reading Social Studies** includes strategic reading instruction and vocabulary support in Social Studies content for both ELLs and native speakers of English.
  www.jamestowneducation.com

Reading List Generator CD-ROM — GLENCOE BOOKLINK 3

Use this database to search more than 30,000 titles to create a customized reading list for your students.

- Reading lists can be organized by students' reading level, author, genre, theme, or area of interest.

- The database provides Degrees of Reading Power™ (DRP) and Lexile™ readability scores for all selections.

- A brief summary of each selection is included.

Leveled reading suggestions for this chapter:

For students at a Grade 10 reading level:
- *Everyday Banking: Consumer Banking,* by Ernestine Giesecke

For students at a Grade 11 reading level:
- *Taxpayers Will Get a Return on Investment,* by John Harrington

For students at a Grade 12 reading level:
- *Business Builders in Real Estate,* by Nathan Aaseng

* Review suggested books before assigning them.

NCEE

National Council on Economic Education

Voluntary Standards Emphasized in Chapter 11

Content Standard 10 Institutions evolve in market economies to help individuals and groups accomplish their goals. Banks, labor unions, corporations, legal systems, and not-for-profit organizations are examples of important institutions. A different kind of institution, clearly defined and enforced property rights, is essential to a market economy.

Content Standard 15 Investment in factories, machinery, new technology, and in the health, education, and training of people can raise future standards of living.

Resources Available from NCEE
- Virtual Economics®: An Interactive Center for Economic Education Version 3.0
- Capstone: The Nation's High School Economics Course
- Focus: High School Economics, Second Edition
- Focus: Institutions and Markets

To order these materials, or to contact your State Council on Economic Education about workshops and programs, call 1-800-338-1192 or visit the NCEE Web site at store.ncee.net.

The BIG Idea

As students study the chapter, remind them to consider the chapter-based Big Idea. The **Essential Question** in the chapter launch activity below ties in to the Big Idea and helps students think about and understand important chapter concepts. In addition, the Hands-On Chapter Project relates the content from each section to the Big Idea. The steps in each section build on each other and culminate in the Wrap-Up Activity on the Visual Summary page.

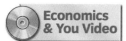
Economics & You Video To generate student interest and provide a springboard for class discussion, access the Economics & You Topic 12 video, **Saving and Investing,** at glencoe.com or on the video DVD.

FOLDABLES
Study Organizer
Dinah Zike's Foldables are three-dimensional, interactive graphic organizers that help students practice basic writing skills, review key vocabulary terms, and identify main ideas. Have students complete this chapter's Foldable activity or activities in *Dinah Zike's Reading and Study Skills Foldables* booklet. **OL**

Economics ONLINE
Introduce students to chapter content and key terms by having them access *Chapter 11 —Chapter Overviews* at glencoe.com.

CHAPTER 11 Financial Markets

Why It Matters

You have just been hired as a financial planner to provide advice on how to invest wisely and effectively. Miguel, your client, is a widower raising two young children. He wants to be sure that (1) he will have enough money to send his children to college, and (2) he will be financially secure in his retirement. What advice would you give Miguel? Read Chapter 11 to learn more about how people can accomplish their financial goals.

The BIG Idea

Governments and institutions help participants in a market economy accomplish their financial goals.

► Traders on the Chicago Mercantile Exchange talk to one another with hand signals.

288 UNIT 3

Economics ONLINE **Chapter Overview** Visit the *Economics: Principles and Practices* Web site at glencoe.com and click on *Chapter 11—Chapter Overviews* to preview chapter information.

Activity: Launching the Chapter

Making Connections Have students identify and describe methods of investing and savings with which they are familiar. Have students work in pairs or small groups to create tables listing these methods and briefly describing how they work. **Essential Question:** Why do you think governments and institutions would want participants in a market to save and invest their money?

(Answers will vary, but students may suggest that governments and institutions benefit when individuals invest in them and that everyone— individuals, government, and institutions— benefits from economic conditions in which people accumulate savings rather than debt.) **OL**

SECTION 1

Savings and the Financial System

GUIDE TO READING

Section Preview

In this section, you will learn how the components of a financial system work together to transfer savings to investors.

Content Vocabulary

- saving (p .289)
- savings (p. 289)
- certificate of deposit (p. 290)
- financial asset (p. 290)
- financial system (p. 290)
- financial intermediary (p. 290)
- nonbank financial institution (p. 292)
- finance company (p. 292)
- premium (p. 292)
- pension (p. 292)
- pension fund (p. 292)
- risk (p. 293)

Academic Vocabulary

- sector (p. 291)
- compensation (p. 294)

Reading Strategy

Describing As you read the section, complete a graphic organizer like the one below by describing how financial intermediaries channel money.

Financial intermediary	Way to channel money

ISSUES IN THE NEWS
—www.businessweek.com

Follow My Money

Jonathan Ping is not a financial guru. And he's not a millionaire (yet). He's simply a 27-year-old engineer living with his wife and dog in a rented house in Portland, Oregon. Within the next 18 months he hopes to scrape up $100,000 for a down payment on a home, and he wants to build a net worth of $1 million by age 45. So far he's at $88,953.

How do I know this? It's in bold type in the top right-hand corner of his Web log, where Ping keeps a daily tally of his progress. He's one of more than 150 bloggers, mostly 22 to 35, who have adopted an open-source approach to personal finance. In stark contrast to their parents' generation, for whom comparing incomes can be awkward, if not downright taboo, bloggers list financial information down to the dollar in retirement, brokerage, and savings accounts. They recommend investments, decry credit-card debt, and wallow together over high taxes. ■

For an economic system to grow, it must produce capital—the equipment, tools, and machinery used in production. In order for this to happen, saving must take place. To the economist, **saving** means the absence of spending, while **savings** refers to the dollars that become available when people abstain from consumption.

Our financial system continually evolves to meet the needs of both savers and investors. If you decide to save your income, as Jonathan Ping in the news story and other bloggers are doing, you should learn about some important investment considerations. You also will see that you can choose from a wide variety of options.

saving absence of spending that frees resources for use in other activities or investments

savings the dollars that become available for investors to use when others save

CHAPTER 11 Financial Markets 289

Focus

Bellringer
Daily Focus Transparency 45

GUIDE TO READING

Answers to Graphic:

Banks: obtain funds by accepting deposits; lend money to borrowers

Finance companies: make loans to consumers and buy installment contracts from merchants who sell goods on credit

Life insurance companies: collect cash for insurance premiums; loan surplus funds to others

Resource Manager

R Reading Strategies	**C** Critical Thinking	**D** Differentiated Instruction	**W** Writing Support	**S** Skill Practice
Teacher Edition • Summarizing, p. 290 • Inferring, p. 294 **Additional Resources** • Guid. Read. Act., p. 31 • Read. Ess. & Note-Taking Guide, p. 91 • Free Ent. Act., pp. 16, 17	**Teacher Edition** • Ident. Cent. Issues, p. 291 • Evaluating, p. 292 • Compare/Contrast, p. 293 **Additional Resources** • Econ. Content Vocab. Act., p. 11 • Hands-on Econ., p. 10	**Teacher Edition** • ELL, p. 290 • Visual/Spatial, p. 292 **Additional Resources** • Daily Focus Trans. 42, 45 • Enrichment Act., p. 11 • Reinforcing Econ. Skills, p. 7	**Teacher Edition** • Expository Writing, p. 291 **Additional Resources** • High School Reading in the Content Area Strat. and Act.	**Teacher Edition** • Analyzing Tables, p. 293 • Drawing Con., p. 295 **Additional Resources** • Econ. Cartoons, p. 21 • Math Prac. for Econ., pp. 12, 18

Teach

R Reading Strategy

Summarizing Ask: What are the three parts of the financial system? *(The first part is made up of the funds that a saver transfers to a borrower. The second part is the financial assets that certify the condition of the loan. The third part includes the organizations that bring the surplus funds and financial assets together.)* **BL**

D Differentiated Instruction

English Language Learners

Help students interpret the meaning of the word *intermediaries*. Explain that the prefix *inter-* means "between or among" and the word *mediate* means "to work between two parties." **ELL**

Caption Answer: through financial intermediaries

Additional Support

---

certificate of deposit document showing that an investor has made an interest-bearing loan to a financial institution

financial asset a stock or other document that represents a claim on the income and property of a borrower, such as a CD, bond, Treasury bill, or mortgage

financial system network of savers, investors, and financial institutions working together to transfer savings for investment uses

financial intermediary institution that channels savings to investors

$ **Personal Finance Handbook**

See pages **R6–R9** for more information on saving and investing.

Saving When you open a savings account, you make money available for business investments. ***How does money from savers reach investors?***

290

Saving and Economic Growth

MAIN Idea The financial system brings savers and borrowers together and helps the economy grow.

Economics & You Do you have a personal savings account? Read on to learn how your savings are used to help the economy.

When people save, they make funds available for others to use. Businesses can borrow these savings to produce new goods and services, build new plants and equipment, and create more jobs. Saving thus makes economic growth possible.

Savers and Financial Assets

People can save in a number of ways. They can open a savings account, buy a bond, or purchase a **certificate of deposit**—a document showing that an investor has made an interest-bearing loan to a bank. In each case, savers obtain a receipt for the funds they save.

Economists call these documents **financial assets**—claims on the property and the income of the borrower. The documents are assets because they are property that has value. They represent claims on the borrower because they specify the amount loaned and the terms at which the loan was made.

Stocks, or ownership claims on a corporation, are another type of financial asset. However, because stocks have some unique features that require additional consideration, we will discuss them separately in the last section of this chapter. Collectively, investors have a full range of financial assets from which to choose.

The Circular Flow of Finance

In order for people to use the savings of others, the economy must have a **financial system**—a network of savers, investors, and financial institutions that work together to transfer savings to investors.

R The financial system has three parts. The first part is made up of the funds that a saver transfers to a borrower. The second consists of the financial assets that certify conditions of the loan. The third comprises the organizations that bring the surplus funds and financial assets together.

Financial intermediaries are the institutions that lend the funds that savers provide. Financial intermediaries include depository institutions such as banks and credit unions, life insurance companies, pension funds, and other institutions that channel savings to borrowers. These institutions are especially helpful to small savers, who have only limited funds available to deposit.

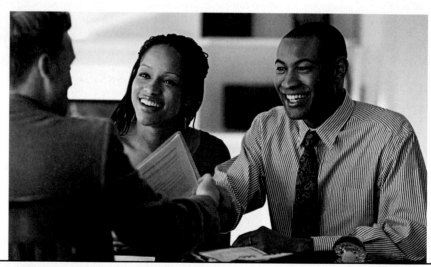

Activity: Collaborative Learning

Researching Methods of Saving

Organize students into small groups. Direct each group member to conduct an informal poll among his or her family members, neighbors, and friends to discover how many people save and for what reasons. Then instruct students to combine their results with other group members and work together to produce a wall chart or graph that displays their findings. Invite each group to present their finished visuals to the class and discuss the results of their research. **AL**

Teacher Tip

Survey Details If possible, encourage students to survey people of both genders who represent a range of ages, ethnic groups, and income levels.

Figure 11.1 ► Overview of the Financial System

▶ Financial intermediaries help channel surplus funds from savers to borrowers, who put the money to work. Savers also lend directly to governments and businesses, who issue bonds or other financial assets for the money they borrow.

Charts In MOtion
See StudentWorks™ Plus or glencoe.com.

Economic Analysis *What do lenders receive in return for their funds?*

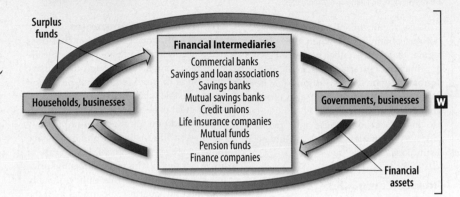

Figure 11.1 shows the circular flow that takes place when funds are transferred from savers to borrowers. Savers can provide their funds directly to the borrower. They also can do so indirectly through the many financial intermediaries in the economy, such as banks, life insurance companies, and credit unions. The documents that certify the ownership of the funds—the certificates of deposit, savings and other bank accounts, as well as bonds—are the financial assets that return to the lender.

Financing Capital Formation

Any **sector** of the economy can borrow, but governments and businesses are the largest borrowers. If a corporation borrows directly from savers—or indirectly from savers through financial intermediaries—the corporation will issue a bond or other financial asset to the lender. When the government borrows, it issues government bonds or other financial assets to the lender.

Any sector of the economy can supply savings, but households and businesses are the biggest sources of funds. Savers can provide some funds directly to borrowers, as when households or businesses purchase bonds directly from government or businesses.

Capital formation depends on saving and borrowing. When households borrow, they invest some of the funds in homes. When businesses borrow, they invest some of the funds in tools, equipment, and machinery. When governments borrow, they invest some of the funds in highways, hospitals, universities, and other public goods.

In the end, everyone benefits from the financial system. The smooth flow of funds through the system helps ensure that savers will have an outlet for their savings. Borrowers, in turn, will have a source of financial capital that can be invested in capital goods to benefit future economic growth.

✓Reading Check **Summarizing** How does the financial system bring savers and borrowers together?

CHAPTER 11 Financial Markets **291**

W **Writing Support**

Expository Writing Have students write a brief paragraph summarizing the information in the visual. Tell students to write for readers who are unfamiliar with the financial system. **OL**

C **Critical Thinking**

Identifying Central Issues
Ask: How does the financial system benefit both borrowers and savers? *(It ensures that savers will have outlets in which to invest their savings. It also provides a source of financial capital that borrowers can draw from to benefit future economic growth.)* **OL**

Economic Analysis
Answer: financial assets in the form of documents that certify ownership of the funds

✓Reading Check **Answer:**
allowing borrowers to borrow funds directly from savers or by borrowing funds that savers have invested in financial intermediaries

Hands-On Chapter Project

Step 1

Designing an Investment Portfolio

In this project, students will design and assemble an investment portfolio.

Step 1: Choosing a Savings Plan.
Student pairs or groups will evaluate and then choose a savings plan.

Directions: Tell each pair or group that they will have $10,000 to invest. Students can invest some, but not all, of their money in one of these savings accounts:

- a savings account that pays 0.6% interest compounded monthly, with no minimum deposit and no limitations on availability of funds
- a pension plan requiring annual deposits of $1,000, collecting simple interest at 0.9% monthly, in which funds cannot be withdrawn until retirement
- a certificate of deposit that pays 3.5% annually, with a minimum deposit of $1,500 and a maturity of one year

Have students create a fact sheet that identifies the plan they selected, how much they invested, and the reasoning for their choices. Students should also calculate and show in a graph or table the value of their investment after 6 months.

Assessing Have students write a short paragraph assessing the strengths and weaknessess of their portfolio. **OL**

(Chapter Project continued in Section 2.)

D Differentiated Instruction

Visual/Spatial Ask pairs to create a graphic organizer that compares and contrasts finance companies, life insurance companies, and pension funds. **OL**

C Critical Thinking

Evaluating Ask: Why do you think life insurance companies are likely to collect a great deal of cash? *(These companies collect regular premiums from individuals who purchase life insurance policies and only pay for benefits when an individual dies. As a result, they are able to collect a great deal of cash during the length of the policy.)* **BL**

✓**Reading Check** **Answer:**
Finance companies lend directly to consumers and purchase installment contracts. Life insurance companies lend surplus funds they collect to others. Pension funds disburse regular payments to eligible participants.

Differentiated Instruction

Personal Finance Activities, p. 21

292

---

nonbank financial institution nondepository institution that channels savings to investors

finance company firm that makes loans directly to consumers and specializes in buying installment contracts from merchants who sell on credit

premium price paid at regular intervals for an insurance policy

pension regular payment to someone who has worked a certain number of years, reached a certain age, or has suffered an injury

pension fund fund that collects and invests income until payments are made to eligible recipients

---

Nonbank Financial Intermediaries

MAIN Idea Organizations other than banks can transfer money from savers to borrowers.

Economics & You Have you ever heard your parents discuss pensions? Read on to learn why these are called nonbank financial intermediaries.

Banks, credit unions, and savings associations obtain funds when they accept regular deposits. Another important group of financial intermediaries is called **nonbank financial institutions**—or nondepository institutions that also channel savings to borrowers. Finance companies, life insurance companies, and pension funds are examples of nonbank financial institutions.

Finance Companies

A **finance company** is a firm that specializes in making loans directly to consumers. It also buys installment contracts from merchants who sell goods on credit.

Many merchants, for example, cannot afford to wait years for their customers to pay off high-cost items purchased on an installment plan. Instead, a merchant will sell a customer's installment contract to a finance company for a lump sum. This allows the merchant to advertise easy credit terms without actually accepting the full risks of the loan. The finance company then carries the loan full term, absorbing losses for an unpaid account or taking customers to court if they do not pay.

Did You Know?

► **Tough Payoff** Finance companies charge much higher interest rates than banks or credit unions, which makes their loans much more expensive. Let's assume you want a 60-month car loan for $6,000. A bank loan with an 8-percent interest rate would cost you $1,300 in interest over the life of the loan. Interest on the same loan at a finance company charging 12 percent interest would total $2,008, or at 16 percent, $2,755. A few percentage points make a big difference!

Some finance companies make loans directly to consumers. These companies generally check a consumer's credit rating and will make a loan only if the individual qualifies. Because they make some risky loans and pay more for the funds they borrow, finance companies charge more than commercial banks for loans.

Life Insurance Companies

Another financial institution that does not get its funds through deposits is the life insurance company. Although its primary purpose is to provide financial protection for the people who are insured, it also collects a great deal of cash.

The head of a family, for example, may purchase a life insurance policy to leave money for a spouse and children in case of his or her death. The **premium** is the price the insured pays for this policy, usually paid monthly, quarterly, or annually for the length of the protection. Because insurance companies collect cash for these premiums on a regular basis, they often lend surplus funds to others.

Pension Funds

The pension fund is another nondepository financial institution. A **pension** is a regular payment intended to provide income security to someone who has worked a certain number of years, reached a specified age, or suffered a particular kind of injury. A **pension fund** is a fund set up to collect income and disburse payments to those persons eligible for retirement, old-age, or disability benefits.

In the case of private pension funds, employers regularly withhold a percentage of workers' salaries to deposit in the fund. During the 30- to 40-year lag between the time the savings are deposited and the time the workers generally use them, the money is usually invested in high-quality corporate stocks and bonds.

✓**Reading Check** **Comparing and Contrasting** How do finance companies, life insurance companies, and pension funds channel savings to borrowers?

The Penalty for Early Withdrawal

Objective: Examine why banks apply penalties for early withdrawal of CDs.

Focus/Teach: Ask students to consider why CDs would prove particularly valuable to lenders. Then have students complete the activity.

Assess: Review responses with students.

Close: Direct students to identify an investment that would not be subject to the same types of penalties as CDs.

Differentiated Instruction Strategies

BL Have students draw a cartoon about the benefits of investing in CDs.

AL Ask students to explain why a bank could offer a higher interest rate on a CD than it could on a savings account.

ELL Direct student pairs to orally explain the meaning of the cartoon to each other.

Figure 11.2 ▶ The Power of Compound Interest

Tables In MOtion
See StudentWorks™ Plus
or glencoe.com.

▶ This table shows the balance in an account if monthly deposits of $10 were compounded monthly. The higher the interest rate and the longer money is invested, the larger the final balance will be.

Economic Analysis *How much interest is earned after the first 10 years at 6 percent?*

COMPOUND INTEREST

Annual interest (in percent)	Value at end of year					
	5	10	15	20	25	30
0	$600	$1,200	$1,800	$2,000	$2,500	$3,600
2	$630	$1,327	$2,097	$2,948	$3,888	$4,927
4	$663	$1,472	$2,461	$3,668	$5,141	$6,940
6	$698	$1,639	$2,908	$4,620	$6,930	$10,045
8	$735	$1,829	$3,460	$5,890	$9,510	$14,904
10	$774	$2,048	$4,145	$7,594	$13,268	$22,605
12	$817	$2,300	$4,996	$9,893	$18,788	$34,950

S

Basic Investment Considerations

MAIN Idea Investors should consider several factors before investing their money.

Economics & You Have you thought about investing some of your savings? Read on to learn what factors to consider.

You may want to participate in the financial system by investing in stocks, bonds, and other financial assets. Before you do so, you should be aware of four basic investment considerations.

Consistency

Most successful investors invest consistently over long periods of time. In many cases, the amount invested is not as important as investing on a regular basis.

Figure 11.2 shows how a monthly deposit of $10 would grow over a 5- to 30-year period at various interest rates. Even at modest rates, the balance in the account accumulates fairly quickly. Because $10 is a small amount, imagine how the account

would grow with a larger deposit! That is why many investment advisers tell people to save something every month.

Simplicity

Most analysts advise investors to stay with what they know. Thousands of investments are available, and many are quite complicated. Knowing a few fundamental principles can help you make good choices among these options.

One rule that many investors follow is to ignore any investment that seems too complicated. Another often-cited rule is that an investment that seems too good to be true probably is. A few investors do get lucky, but most build wealth because they invest regularly, and they avoid the investments that seem too far out of the ordinary.

The Risk-Return Relationship

Another important factor is the relationship between risk and return. **Risk** is the degree to which the outcome is uncertain but a probable outcome can be estimated. Investors realize that some investments are riskier than others, so they normally

risk situation in which the outcome is not certain, but the probabilities can be estimated

Skills Handbook
See page **R57** to learn about **Interest Rates.**

C

CHAPTER 11 Financial Markets **293**

S Skill Practice

Analyzing Tables Ask: At what annual interest rate would the account balance reach $1,829 after 10 years? *(8 percent)* What would the value of the account be after 20 years, with an interest rate of 10 percent? *($7,594)* **OL**

C Critical Thinking

Comparing and Contrasting Lead students in a brief discussion of the similarities and differences between *consistency* and *simplicity*. Guide students to understand that both concepts are basic considerations that can help protect investors. Have students create Venn diagrams summarizing how these ideas are alike and different. **BL**

Economic Analysis
Answer: $1,639

Leveled Activities

BL Reinforcing Economic Skills, p. 7   **OL** Hands-On Economics, p. 10   **AL** Enrichment Activities, p. 11

R Reading Strategy

Inferring Ask: In what type of situation might an investor seek an investment with a high level of risk? *(Possible answer: when he or she has plenty of money to risk and wants to take a chance on getting a high return)* **OL**

Economic Analysis

Answer: because some investments require a higher level of risk

✓Reading Check Possible

Answer: saving money for education or retirement

Assess

Use the Interactive Tutor Self-Assessment CD-ROM to review Section 1, and then assign the Section 1 Review as homework or as an in-class activity.

Close

Summarizing Have students explain why savings must occur to grow the economy. **OL**

SECTION 1 Review

Figure 11.3 ▶ Risk and Return

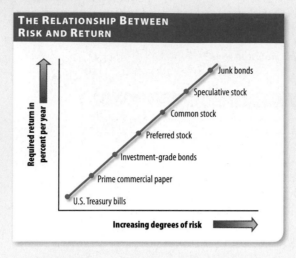

THE RELATIONSHIP BETWEEN RISK AND RETURN

▶ The level of risk for investments can vary considerably. U.S. Treasury bills are regarded as the safest investments, while speculative stock and junk bonds are considered among the riskiest.

Economic Analysis *Why do investors require higher returns for some investments?* ▶

---

demand higher returns as **compensation.** This relationship between increasing risks and returns is illustrated in **Figure 11.3.**

As an investor, you must consider the level of risk that you can tolerate. If you are comfortable with high levels of risk, then you may want to purchase risky investments that promise high returns. Otherwise consider lower-risk investments instead.

Investment Objectives

Finally, you need to consider your reason for investing. For example, if you want to cover living expenses during periods of unemployment, you might want to accumulate assets that can easily be converted into cash. If you want to save for retirement, you might want to purchase common stocks that generate dividend income and appreciate in value over time.

Investors have a large number of stocks, financial assets, and other investments from which to choose. The investor's knowledge of his or her own needs is important in making these decisions.

✓Reading Check Identifying If you were to invest your money, what would your objectives be?

SECTION 1 Review

Vocabulary

1. **Explain** the significance of saving, savings, certificate of deposit, financial asset, financial system, financial intermediary, nonbank financial institution, finance company, premium, pension, pension fund, and risk.

Main Ideas

2. **Describing** How does saving compare to savings?

3. **Identifying** Use a graphic organizer like the one below to describe the nonbank financial intermediaries.

Nonbank Financial Intermediaries

4. **Explaining** Why is consistency important when saving?

Critical Thinking

5. **The BIG Idea** What is the relationship between the financial system and the economy?

6. **Comparing and Contrasting** How do life insurance companies and pension funds differ in the way they serve their clients?

7. **Analyzing Visuals** Look at Figure 11.2 on page 293. If you invested $10 a month for 20 years at an annual interest rate of 6 percent, what would be your ending balance? How much of that would be your initial investment? How much would be the interest earned?

Applying Economics

8. **Financial Assets** Why is an I.O.U. that you write and give to a friend in payment of a debt considered an example of a financial asset?

Answers

1. All definitions can be found in the section and the Glossary.
2. Saving means the absence of spending that frees resources for use in other activities or investments. Savings refers to the dollars that are available when people abstain from consumption.
3. finance companies: specialize in making loans directly to consumers; life insurance companies: provide financial protection for the people who are insured; pension funds: collect income and disburse payments to eligible members

4. because consistent deposits made over a long period of time, even at modest interest rates, will accumulate quickly
5. The financial system is a network through which savers, investors, and financial institutions transfer savings to investors. This savings is necessary for the production of capital, which then causes the economy to grow.

6. Life insurance companies provide financial protection to their clients. Pension funds offer regular payments intended to provide income security to their clients.
7. The ending balance would be $4,620. Of that total, $2,400 would be the initial investment, while $2,220 would be the interest earned.
8. because it represents a claim on one's property and income

Profiles in Economics

Sallie Krawcheck (1965–)

- chief financial officer for Citigroup Inc., the world's largest financial institution
- ranked number 6 on *Forbes*'s top 100 of "The World's Most Powerful Women" for 2006

Indirect Road to Success

While Sallie Krawcheck came to her current position at a fast pace, it was not on a straight path. Armed with a journalism degree, she became an investment banker but did not enjoy it. Instead she decided to pursue an MBA at Columbia University, only to return to investment banking when she could not find other job opportunities. Then, in a quick series of events, Krawcheck got married, had a baby, quit her job, and discovered within just two weeks of quitting that she enjoyed working too much to give it up. She decided to try her hand as a research analyst, but was rejected by every firm except the one—Sanford C. Bernstein—that would eventually help launch her fast-track career.

Rising Star

As a research analyst, Krawcheck evaluated the stock of financial institutions. She looks back on this time as the best possible training for her future roles. Krawcheck learned to be persistent, work hard, be willing to learn from mistakes and, perhaps most importantly, stand by her decisions: "As an analyst, I was very comfortable being uncomfortable, and as a CFO I have to be comfortable being uncomfortable. I have to be fine with delivering bad news."

Krawcheck's reputation grew along with her success. Called "Mrs. Clean" because of her unwavering insistence on ethics and honesty, she was hired as the CEO of Smith Barney, the research and brokerage division of Citigroup which had gone through a period of ethical turmoil. Two years later, she found herself in the position of CFO at Citigroup, with an annual salary of $500,000 in 2005. Bonuses and other benefits pushed the total up to nearly $10 million.

Sallie Krawcheck thinks that nothing prepared her better for Wall Street than feeling like an outcast in seventh grade. Ready to take contrarian stands today, she believes that one of the best lessons she learned then was to "zig when everyone else is zagging."

Examining the Profile

1. **Identifying** What skills helped Krawcheck most in being promoted and becoming a successful CFO?
2. **Making Inferences** What lessons do you think Krawcheck learned from her early career?

CHAPTER 11   Financial Markets   **295**

Teach

S Skill Practice

Drawing Conclusions
Have students brainstorm the qualifications that a person might need to become the CEO of a large financial institution. **Ask:** How do you think Sallie Krawcheck's unconventional career path helped her become a successful executive? *(Answers will vary, but students might suggest that Krawcheck's career path would have likely helped her develop unique skills that would set her apart from other executives. For instance, her journalism background would have helped her be an effective communicator.)* **OL**

Examining the Profile

Answers:
1. persistence, hard work, a willingness to learn from mistakes, and a willingness to stand by her decisions
2. **Possible answer:** Krawcheck learned to pursue a career that she genuinely enjoyed and to not be discouraged by rejection.

Additional Support

Activity: Hands-On Economics

Formulating Questions Invite to class two or more community business leaders who work in fields related to finance and investing. Guide students in formulating questions for these individuals. Students' questions may focus on topics from the chapter about which they would like to learn more, as well as the practical aspects of working with financial markets on a daily basis. When the visitors come to the classroom, invite student volunteers to ask their questions. Encourage students to take notes on the answers the visitors provide. Following the question-and-answer session, direct students to compose a response paper detailing what they learned from the experience. Have them include any additional questions that were sparked during their writing. Address these questions in a class discussion. **OL**

Focus

Bellringer
Daily Focus Transparency 44

GUIDE TO READING

Possible Answers to Graphic:

Bonds: contract to repay borrowed money and interest on the borrowed money at regular future intervals

Certificates of deposit (CDs): loans that investors make to financial institutions

Individual retirement accounts (IRAs): in the form of a long-term deposit; annual contributions not taxed until withdrawn during retirement

Resource Manager

SECTION 2

Financial Assets and Their Markets

GUIDE TO READING

Section Preview
In this section, you will learn about the characteristics of various investments to help with your investments.

Content Vocabulary
- bond (p. 297)
- coupon rate (p. 297)
- maturity (p. 297)
- par value (p. 297)
- current yield (p. 297)
- junk bond (p. 299)
- municipal bond (p. 299)
- tax-exempt (p. 300)
- savings bond (p. 300)
- beneficiary (p. 301)
- Treasury note (p. 301)
- Treasury bond (p. 301)
- Treasury bill (p. 301)
- Individual Retirement Account (IRA) (p. 302)
- capital market (p. 302)
- money market (p. 302)
- primary market (p. 303)
- secondary market (p. 303)

Academic Vocabulary
- offset (p. 298)
- presumed (p. 300)

Reading Strategy
Identifying As you read the section, use a graphic organizer similar to the one below to identify and describe at least four financial assets.

Financial Assets

ISSUES IN THE NEWS
—www.usatoday.com

Want More Interest? Meet Bond, Junk Bond

Let's think about a little number: 4.59%. It's not the percentage of Americans who understand Olympic curling rules. It's the amount of interest you can earn annually on a 10-year Treasury note. That would be $45.90 a year on a $1,000 investment. Ah, good times. Good times.

You might be wondering, "Is there any way I can get a bit more interest?" Well, yes. You could invest some of your portfolio in a junk-bond fund. Bonds are long-term, interest-bearing IOUs . . . [and] . . . bonds issued by corporations tend to pay higher interest. That's because they can go bankrupt and default on their bonds. Bonds issued by companies with poor credit ratings pay the highest interest of all. The only problem: When you buy junk bonds at high prices, you run the risk of nastiness if the economy gets smacked. ■

When you decide to invest your money, you will have a variety of investment options. As you read in the news story, not all options are alike. Some investments carry only a small risk, but they also offer a smaller return. Other investments may offer the possibility of larger returns, but the higher risk means you may never see that money if the company defaults on its promise to pay.

Many financial assets are available in the market. Before you invest in any of these, it helps to know the risks involved in each.

R Reading Strategies	C Critical Thinking	D Differentiated Instruction	W Writing Support	S Skill Practice
Teacher Edition • Skimming, p. 299 • Reading Charts, p. 302 • Identifying, p. 303 **Additional Resources** • Guid. Read. Act., p. 32 • Read. Ess. & Note-Taking Guide, p. 94	**Teacher Edition** • Making Inferences, p. 298 • Synthesizing, p. 300 • Det. Cause/Effect, p. 301 **Additional Resources** • Econ. Forms and Fin. Pages Trans., Strat. & Act., p. 24	**Teacher Edition** • Visual/Spatial, p. 297 • Adv. Learners, p. 300 • Verbal/Linguistic, p. 302 **Additional Resources** • Daily Focus Trans. 44, 46 • Quizzes and Tests, p. 134	**Teacher Edition** • Expository Writing, pp. 298, 301 **Additional Resources** • High School Writing Process Trans. • Reinforcing Econ. Skills, p. 29 • Reteaching Act., p. 11	**Teacher Edition** • Interpreting Political Cartoons, p. 297 • Visual Literacy, p. 299 • Using Charts and Tables, p. 304 **Additional Resources** • Free Enterprise Act., p. 17 • Math Prac. for Econ., p. 20

Bonds as Financial Assets

MAIN Idea A bond is a long-term investment, with the price determined by supply, demand, and the buyer's assessment of repayment risk.

Economics and You Have you ever received a government bond as a birthday present? Read on to learn how the value of a bond is determined.

Governments and businesses issue bonds when they need to borrow funds for long periods. A **bond** is a formal long-term contract that requires repayment of borrowed money and interest on the borrowed funds at regular intervals over time.

Increasingly bonds are taking on an international flavor, with companies in one country issuing bonds in another. While this may seem complex, the main components of a bond are relatively simple.

Bond Components

A bond has three main components: the **coupon rate**, or the stated interest on the debt; the **maturity**, or the life of the bond; and the **par value**, the principal or the total amount initially borrowed that must be repaid to the lender at maturity.

Suppose, for example, that a corporation sells a 6 percent, 20-year, $1,000 par value bond that pays interest semiannually. The coupon payment to the holder is $30 semiannually (.06 times $1,000, divided by 2). When the bond reaches maturity after 20 years, the company retires the debt by paying the holder the par value of $1,000.

Bond Prices

The investor views the bond as a financial asset that will pay $30 twice a year for 20 years, plus a final par value payment of $1,000. Investors can offer $950, $1,000, $1,100, or any other amount for this future payment stream. Investors consider changes in future interest rates, the risk that the company will default, and other factors before they decide what to offer. Supply and demand among buyers and sellers will then establish the final price of the bonds.

Bond Yields

In order to compare bonds, investors usually compute the bond's **current yield**, the annual interest divided by the purchase price. If an investor paid $950 for the bond described above, the current yield would be $60 divided by $950, or 6.32 percent. If the investor paid $1,100 for the bond, the current yield would be $60 divided by $1,100, or 5.45 percent.

It may appear as if the issuer fixes the return on a bond when the bond is first issued. However, the interest received and the price paid determine the actual current yield of each bond. The result is that the bond yield, like the bond price, is determined by supply and demand.

---

bond contract to repay borrowed money and interest on the borrowed money at regular future intervals

coupon rate stated interest on a corporate, municipal, or government bond

maturity life of a bond or length of time funds are borrowed

par value principal of a bond or total amount borrowed

current yield bond's annual coupon interest divided by purchase price; measure of a bond's return

---

Farcus

by David Waisglass
Gordon Coulthart

© 1994 Farcus Cartoons

WAISGLASS/COULTHART

www.farcus.com

David Waisglass/Laughingstock

"Money isn't everything, son ... there's also stocks, bonds and real estate."

Bonds Corporate and government bonds are attractive because they can be safe and may be tax-exempt. ***How is the actual return of a bond determined?***

Teach

D Differentiated Instruction

Visual/Spatial Organize students into groups of four. Assign each group member one of the following categories: bond components, bond prices, bond yields, and bond ratings. Have members create flash cards with questions about their category. Then have group members quiz one another with the flash cards. **BL**

S Skill Practice

Interpreting Political Cartoons Ask: What familiar idea does the cartoonist play upon in this illustration? *(There is more to life than just money.)* What does the father suggest to his son instead? *(Money is only one type of financial asset.)* **OL**

Caption Answer: The actual return of a bond is determined by calculating the current yield (taking the annual coupon interest divided by the purchase price).

Additional Support

Activity: Hands-On Economics

Researching Types of Bonds Organize students into four groups to undertake further study of bonds. Ask one group to interview the school superintendent or another administrator to learn about bonds for schools. The second group could interview a finance official in the city, county, or state government to ask about municipal bonds. The third group could interview the controller or president of a local corporation to find out about corporate bonds. The fourth group might interview a member of Congress or a staff employee of a member of Congress to learn about U.S. Treasury bonds. Have each group present its interview results to the class. Then have students discuss the similarities and differences among the various bonds. **OL**

C Critical Thinking

Making Inferences Ask: Why would an investor want to find bond ratings? *(Possible answer: to make sure that the issuing agency has a good credit rating)* **OL**

W Writing Support

Expository Writing Direct students to research a bond that they might consider purchasing. Have them find the Standard & Poor's and Moody's ratings for the bonds and research how these corporations evaluated the bonds. Students should write a brief essay about their findings. **AL**

✓**Reading Check** **Answer:** the basic financial health of the issuer, the expected ability to make future coupon and principal payments, the issuer's past credit history

---

Economic Analysis

Answer: Bond prices increase and decrease along with bond ratings.

Additional Support

Bond Ratings

Because the credit-worthiness, or financial health, of corporations and governments differ, all 6 percent, 20-year, $1,000 bonds will not cost the same. There are no guarantees that the issuer will be around in 20 years to redeem the bond. Therefore, investors will pay more for bonds issued by an agency with an impeccable credit rating. However, investors will pay less for a similar bond if it is issued by a corporation with a low credit rating.

Fortunately, investors have a way to check the quality of bonds. Two major corporations, Standard & Poor's and Moody's, publish bond ratings. They rate bonds on a number of factors, including the basic financial health of the issuer, the expected ability to make the future coupon and principal payments, and the issuer's past credit history.

Bond ratings, shown in **Figure 11.4**, use letters scaled from AAA, which represents the highest investment grade, to D, which generally stands for default. If a bond is in default, the issuer has not kept up with the interest or other required payments. These ratings are widely publicized, and investors can find the rating of any bond they plan to purchase.

Bonds with high ratings sell at higher prices than do bonds with lower ratings. A 6 percent, 20-year, $1,000 par value bond with an AAA-grade rating may sell for $1,100 and have a current yield of 5.45 percent. Another 6 percent, 20-year, $1,000 par value bond issued by a different company may have a BBB rating, and may therefore only sell for $950 because of the higher risk. The second bond, however, has a higher current yield of 6.32 percent. This is consistent with the basic risk-return relationship, which states that investors require higher returns to **offset** increased levels of risk.

Bonds issued by the U.S. government are considered to be the safest of all financial assets because they have almost no risk of ever being in default. Because of this, these bonds also have the lowest yields.

✓**Reading Check** **Describing** What factors determine a bond's value?

Figure 11.4 ▶ Bond Ratings

Standard & Poor's			Moody's
Highest investment grade	AAA	Aaa	Best quality
High grade	AA	Aa	High quality
Upper medium grade	A	a	Upper medium grade
Medium grade	BBB	Baa	Medium grade
Lower medium grade	BB	Ba	Possesses speculative elements
Speculative	B	B	Generally not desirable
Vulnerable to default	CCC	Caa	Poor, possibly in default
Subordinated to other debt rated CCC	CC	Ca	Highly speculative, often in default
Subordinated to CC debt	C	C	Income bonds not paying income
Bond in default	D	D	Interest and principal payments in default

Sources: Standard & Poor's; Moody's.

▶ Both Standard & Poor's and Moody's publish bond ratings. Junk bonds, those with ratings of BB or Ba and lower, are generally the riskiest types of bonds.

Economic Analysis *How do bond ratings affect the price of bonds?*

Activity: Collaborative Learning

Making Comparisons Have students work in groups of three or four to select three investment options and compare their levels of safety and returns. Students can develop their own rating systems in order to evaluate these investment options. They may wish to include corresponding visual symbols with their ratings and prepare presentations to compare information. They may consider any of the following: government or corporate bonds, equities, certificates of deposit, and Treasury bills. Discuss group findings in class. **OL**

Panel 1: WHEN I WAS YOUR AGE, I USED TO SAVE MONEY IN THIS PIGGY BANK

Panel 2: THAT'S REALLY NICE, MR. B.

Panel 3: I PUT MY MONEY IN LONG-TERM CDs AT 5% PER ANNUM

Financial Assets and Their Characteristics

MAIN Idea Investments include CDs, bonds, bills, and IRAs, all of which vary in cost, maturity, and risk.

Economics and You Have you seen bank advertisements for CDs? Read to find out how these compare to other investments.

The modern investor has a wide range of financial assets from which to choose. These include certificates of deposit, bonds, and Treasury notes and bills. They vary in cost, maturity, and risk.

Certificates of Deposit

Certificates of deposit (CDs) are one of the most common forms of investments available. Many people think of them as just another type of account with a bank, but they are really loans investors make to financial institutions. Because banks and other borrowers count on the use of these funds for a certain time period, they usually impose a penalty if people try to cash in their CDs early.

CDs are attractive to small investors because they can cost as little as $500 or $1,000. Investors can also select the length of maturity, giving them an opportunity to tailor the expiration date to future expenditures such as college tuition, a vacation, or some other expense.

Finally, the CDs issued by commercial banks, savings banks, and savings associations are included in the $100,000 FDIC

R insurance limit. The National Credit Union Association insures most CDs issued by credit unions.

Corporate Bonds

Corporate bonds are an important source of corporate funds. Some individual corporate bonds have par values as low as $1,000, but par values of $10,000 are more common. The actual prices of the bonds are usually different from the par values.

Investors generally decide on the highest level of risk they are willing to accept. They then try to find a bond that has the best current yield. **Junk bonds**—exceptionally risky bonds with a Standard & Poor's rating of BB or lower, or a Moody's rating of Ba or lower—carry a high rate of return as compensation for the higher possibility of default.

Investors usually purchase corporate bonds as long-term investments, but these bonds can be quickly sold if investors need cash for other purposes. The Internal Revenue Service considers the interest, or coupon, payments on corporate bonds as taxable income, a fact investors must consider when they invest in bonds.

Municipal Bonds

Municipal bonds, or "munis," are bonds issued by state and local governments. States issue bonds to finance highways, state buildings, and some public works. Cities issue bonds to pay for baseball parks and football stadiums, or to fund libraries, parks, and other civic improvements.

Certificates of Deposit CDs can vary in cost and length of maturity. *What are other characteristics of Certificates of Deposit?*

junk bond
bond that carries an exceptionally high risk of nonpayment and a low rating

municipal bond
bond, often tax exempt, issued by state and local governments

📊 **Skills Handbook**
See page R58 to learn about Interpreting Cartoons.

CHAPTER 11 Financial Markets **299**

S Skill Practice

Visual Literacy Ask: What does the cartoon suggest about young people and investing today? *(Young people are more informed about finances and investing today than they were in previous generations.)* **OL**

R Reading Strategy

Skimming Remind students that skimming involves pre-reading a text's titles and subtitles. Students should also look for main ideas at the beginnings and ends of paragraphs, and they should not stop skimming if they come across information that they don't understand. Ask students to skim the text on this page to find the definitions for certificates of deposit, corporate bonds, and municipal bonds. **OL**

Caption Answer: borrowers usually face a penalty for trying to cash in CDs early; attractive to small investors; most insured by FDIC or National Credit Union Association

Additional Support

Activity: Interdisciplinary Connection

Mathematics The interest rate on certificates of deposit (CDs) is usually expressed in two ways—the actual interest rate and the annual percentage yield. The interest rate differs among banks and at different times. Ask students to figure out the annual yield on $500 for a CD at an annual yield of 3.92 percent and a CD at an annual yield of 4.86 percent. *($19.60; $24.30)* Then have students write their own word problems about CDs and exchange them with a partner. Have students solve each other's word problems. **OL**

C Critical Thinking

Synthesizing Ask: What are some of the factors that make municipal bonds attractive investments? *(Possible answers: regarded as safe investments; presumed that governments will be able to pay interest and principal because of power to tax; municipal bonds are tax-exempt; states at times exempt the interest payments from state taxes)* **OL**

D Differentiated Instruction

Advanced Learners Tell students that after the attack on Pearl Harbor, the government introduced savings bonds called war bonds to increase public funding for the war effort. Public figures urged citizens to buy war bonds, and department stores encouraged customers to accept war stamps in place of change. Have students use print or online resources to research advertisements for war bonds. Then have them create a poster urging people to buy war bonds. Students should follow the style of World War II ads but include their own text and images. **AL**

Differentiated Instruction

Math Practice for Economics, p. 18

---

tax-exempt not subject to tax by federal or state governments

savings bond low-denomination, non-transferable bond issued by the federal government

Municipal bonds are attractive investments for several reasons. First, they are generally regarded as safe investments. Unlike companies, state and local governments do not go out of business and therefore rarely default. In addition, because governments have the power to tax, it is generally **presumed** that in the future they will be able to pay interest and principal for any bonds they have issued.

More importantly, municipal bonds are generally **tax-exempt**, meaning that the federal government does not tax the interest paid to investors. In some cases, the states issuing the bonds also exempt the **C** interest payments from state taxes, which makes them very attractive to investors. The tax-exempt feature also allows the government agencies to pay a lower rate of interest on the bonds, thereby lowering the government's cost of borrowing.

CAREERS

Stockbroker

The Work

* Supply the latest price quotations on stocks and keep informed about the financial activities of corporations issuing stock

* Provide clients with financial counseling and advice on the purchase or sale of particular securities

* May design an individual client's financial portfolio, which could include securities, life insurance, corporate and municipal bonds, mutual funds, certificates of deposit, annuities, and other investments

Qualifications

* Excellent sales skills and communication skills

* Ability to act quickly is helpful in building and keeping a strong customer base

* College degree in business administration, economics, or finance

* Must pass licensing exam

Earnings

* Median annual earnings: $69,200

Job Growth Outlook

* Average

Source: *Occupational Outlook Handbook, 2006–2007 Edition*

D Government Savings Bonds

The federal government generates financial assets when it sells savings bonds. **Savings bonds** are low-denomination, nontransferable bonds issued by the U.S. government that are also called EE savings bonds. Investors can purchase them through banks and financial intermediaries, obtain them through payroll-savings plans, or buy them directly from the U.S. Treasury over the Internet. Regardless of how they are purchased, there are two kinds of savings bonds; one is paper-based, and the other is paperless.

The paper bonds are available in denominations ranging from $50 to $10,000, and they are purchased at a 50 percent discount from their redemption value. For example, you might obtain a new $50 savings bond today for $25, or a $10,000 bond for $5,000. You may then have to hold the bond for up to 30 years before you can redeem it for the full face value, depending on the purchase date and the interest rate. The government pays interest on these bonds, but it builds the interest into the redemption price rather than sending checks to millions of investors on a regular basis.

Paperless bonds are purchased directly from the Treasury over the Internet. All an investor has to do is open an account, and the bonds will be issued electronically to the investor's account. The electronic bonds sell at face value, so you pay $50 for a $50 bond, or $10,000 for a $10,000 bond. Interest is added monthly and compounded semiannually, but to take some of the

---

Planning for the Future

Objective: Understand the benefits of diversifying investments for future planning.

Focus/Teach: Ask students to list possible pros and cons of saving money in a variety of investments. Then have them complete the activity.

Assess: Verify that students have correctly completed each of the steps.

Close: Discuss with students whether the example given proved to be effective.

Differentiated Instruction Strategies

BL Ask students to identify two additional investments that could be included in this plan.

AL Have students create a brochure that explains how to develop an investment plan like the one in the activity.

ELL Review with students the terms *assets*, *liabilities*, and *net worth*.

uncertainty out of the investment, the U.S. Treasury guarantees that the bond will at least double in value every 20 years.

Savings bonds are popular because they are easy to obtain and there is virtually no risk of default. They cannot be sold to someone else if the investor needs cash, but they can be redeemed early, with some loss of interest, if the investor must raise cash for other purposes. Most investors who purchase long-term savings bonds treat them as a form of automatic savings.

Other investors buy the bonds for their heirs by designating a **beneficiary,** or someone who inherits the ownership of the financial asset if the purchaser dies. A grandmother, for example, may buy EE saving bonds in her name and designate a grandchild as the beneficiary. When the grandmother dies, the beneficiary automatically takes ownership of the savings bond without having to pay any inheritance taxes.

Treasury Notes and Bonds

When the federal government borrows funds for periods lasting longer than one year, it issues Treasury notes and bonds. **Treasury notes** are United States government obligations with maturities of 2 to 10 years, while **Treasury bonds** have maturity dates ranging from more than 10 to as many as 30 years. The only collateral that secures both is the faith and credit of the United States government.

Treasury notes and bonds come in denominations of $1,000, which means that small investors can afford to buy them. The notes and bonds are issued electronically, and investors purchase them directly from the U.S. Treasury. Since the investors' accounts are computerized, the Treasury adds the periodic interest payments directly to these accounts rather than mailing checks to the investors.

Although these financial assets have no collateral or backing, they are popular because they are generally regarded as the safest of all financial assets. Due to the trade-off between risk and return, however, these assets also have the lowest returns of all financial assets.

Treasury Bills

Federal government borrowing generates other financial assets known as **Treasury bills.** A Treasury bill, also called a T-bill, is a short-term obligation with a maturity of 4, 13, or 26 weeks and a minimum denomination of $1,000.

T-bills do not pay interest directly but instead are sold on a discount basis, much like government savings bonds. For example, an investor may pay the auction price of $960 for a 26-week bill that matures at $1,000. The $30 difference between the amount paid and the amount received

beneficiary
person designated to take ownership of an asset if the owner of the asset dies

Treasury note
U.S. government obligation with a maturity of 2 to 10 years

Treasury bond
U.S. government bond with a maturity of 10 to 30 years

Treasury bill
short-term United States government obligation with a maturity of one year or less in denominations of $1,000

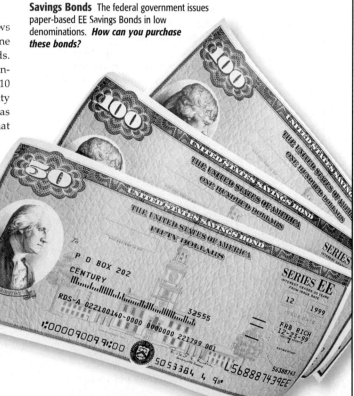
Savings Bonds The federal government issues paper-based EE Savings Bonds in low denominations. *How can you purchase these bonds?*

CHAPTER 11, SECTION 2

C Critical Thinking

Determining Cause and Effect Ask: What would cause a person to designate a beneficiary for a government savings bond that he or she owns? *(to allow the beneficiary to take ownership of the savings bond after the person's death, without having to pay inheritance taxes)* **OL**

W Writing Support

Expository Writing Have students write a comparison-and-contrast essay about the ways in which investors receive returns on their investments in Treasury notes and Treasury bills. Students' paragraphs should explain that periodic interest is directly added to Treasury note accounts, while Treasury bills are sold on a discount basis. **OL**

Caption Answer: through banks and financial intermediaries, payroll-savings plans, or the U.S. Treasury

Leveled Activities

BL Reading Essentials and Note-Taking Guide, p. 94

OL Economic Forms and Financial Pages Trans., Strat. and Act., p. 24

AL Primary and Secondary Source Readings, p. 23

Figure 11.5 ▶ **Financial Assets and Their Markets**

▶ Assets in the money or capital market differ in the length of maturity. The ability to sell the asset to someone other than the original issuer determines whether that asset is part of the primary or the secondary market.

Economic Analysis Why do some financial assets, such as CDs, appear in more than one market? R

	Money market (less than 1 year)	Capital market (more than 1 year)
Primary market	Money market mutual funds Small CDs	Government savings bonds IRAs Money market mutual funds Small CDs
Secondary market	Jumbo CDs Treasury bills	Corporate bonds International bonds Jumbo CDs Municipal bonds Treasury bonds Treasury notes

Individual Retirement Account (IRA) retirement account in the form of a long-term time deposit, with annual contributions not taxed until withdrawn during retirement

capital market market in which financial capital is loaned and/or borrowed for more than one year

money market market in which financial capital is loaned and/or borrowed for one year or less

is the investor's return. The investor receives $30 on a $960 investment, for a semiannual return of $30 divided by $960, or 3.1 percent.

Individual Retirement Accounts

Many employees invest money in **Individual Retirement Accounts (IRAs)**, long-term, tax-sheltered time deposits that can be set up as part of an individual retirement plan. For example, a worker may decide to deposit $4,000 annually in such an account. If the worker's spouse does not work outside the home, the spouse also can deposit $4,000 per year in a separate account.

D   The worker deducts these deposits from the taxable income, thereby sheltering up to $8,000 from the individual income tax. Taxes on the interest and the principal will eventually have to be paid. However, the tax-deferment feature gives the worker an incentive to save today, postponing the taxes until the worker is retired and in a lower tax bracket. IRAs cannot be transferred, and penalties exist if they are liquidated early. In addition, the government sets annual contribution limits.

✓**Reading Check** **Analyzing** What features of a government bond appeal most to you?

Markets for Financial Assets

MAIN Idea Financial assets are grouped into different markets depending on their maturity and liquidity.

Economics and You Would you be willing to invest your money for a 20-year term? Read to learn in which market you would be involved.

Investors often refer to markets according to the characteristics of the financial assets traded in them. These markets overlap to a considerable degree.

Capital Markets

Investors speak of the **capital market** when they mean a market in which money is loaned for more than one year. Long-term CDs and corporate and government bonds that take more than a year to mature belong in this category. Capital market assets are shown in the right-hand column of **Figure 11.5.**

Money Markets

Investors refer to the **money market** when they mean a market in which money is loaned for periods of less than one year.

The financial assets that belong to the money market are shown in the left-hand column of Figure 11.5.

Note that a person who owns a CD with a maturity of one year or less is involved in the money market. If the CD has a maturity of more than one year, the person is involved in the capital market as a supplier of funds.

Many investors purchase money market mutual funds. These funds are created when stockbrokers or other financial managers pool the deposits of their customers **R** to purchase stocks or bonds. Money market mutual funds usually pay slightly higher interest rates than banks.

Primary Markets

Another way to view financial markets is to focus on the liquidity of a newly created financial asset. One market for financial assets is the **primary market**, a market where only the original issuer can sell or repurchase a financial asset. Government savings bonds and IRAs are in this market because neither of them can be transferred. Small CDs are also in the primary market because investors tend to cash them in early if they need cash, rather than trying to sell them to someone else.

Secondary Markets

If a financial asset can be sold to someone other than the original issuer, it then becomes part of the **secondary market,** where existing financial assets can be resold to new owners.

The major difference between the primary and secondary markets is the liquidity the secondary market provides to investors. If a strong secondary market exists for a financial asset, investors know that the asset can be liquidated fairly quickly and without penalty, other than the fees for handling the transaction.

✔**Reading Check** Contrasting How are capital and money markets different? How do primary and secondary markets differ?

primary market market in which only the original issuer can sell or repurchase a financial asset

secondary market market in which financial assets can be sold to someone other than the original issuer

R **Reading Strategy**

Identifying Ask: How are money market mutual funds created? *(when financial managers pool the deposits of their customers to purchase stocks or bond)* OL

✔**Reading Check** **Answer:** The capital market involves money that is loaned for more than a year, while the money market involves loans of one year or less. The primary market features assets that only the original issuer can sell or repurchase. The secondary market includes assets that can be sold to others.

Assess

Use the Interactive Tutor Self-Assessment CD-ROM to review Section 2, and then assign the Section 2 Review as homework or as an in-class activity.

Close

Making Connections Ask students why a strong secondary market for an asset proves advantageous for an investor. OL

SECTION 2 Review

Vocabulary

1. **Explain** the significance of bond, coupon rate, maturity, par value, current yield, junk bond, municipal bond, tax-exempt, savings bond, beneficiary, Treasury note, Treasury bond, Treasury bill, Individual Retirement Account, capital market, money market, primary market, and secondary market.

Main Ideas

2. **Explaining** What is the relationship between a bond rating and the price of the bond?

3. **Identifying** Use a graphic organizer like the one below to identify the characteristics of financial assets.

Financial Asset	Characteristics
Certificate of deposit	

4. **Stating** What are markets for financial assets?

Critical Thinking

5. **The BIG Idea** Why would an investor want to choose a certificate of deposit over a corporate bond?

6. **Comparing and Contrasting** What do corporate bonds, municipal bonds, and government savings bonds have in common? How do they differ?

7. **Drawing Conclusions** Why would someone be willing to invest in "junk" bonds?

8. **Analyzing Visuals** Look at Figure 11.5 on page 302. If you wanted to invest your money for retirement, in which market would you most likely invest? In which market would you invest to save for a vacation? Explain your answer using specific examples of financial assets.

Applying Economics

9. **Risk-Return Relationship** If you had money to invest, which financial asset or assets, if any, would you choose? Explain your answer in a brief paragraph.

CHAPTER 11 Financial Markets **303**

Review SECTION 2

Answers

1. All definitions can be found in the section and the Glossary.
2. The price of a bond will increase and decrease along with the bond rating.
3. Answers will vary, but students should identify characteristics of the financial assets discussed in the section.
4. capital markets, money markets, primary markets, and secondary markets
5. A certificate of deposit is a less risky investment than a corporate bond and may require a smaller amount of money for the initial investment.
6. Corporate bonds represent loans to the business, municipal bonds represent loans to state/local governments, and savings bonds are loans to the federal government. Savings and municipal bonds are considered safe; corporate bonds have widely varying levels of risk. Municipal bonds are usually tax-exempt, while corporate and savings bonds are taxable.
7. **Possible answer:** Some people are willing to deal with the high risks associated with junk bonds in order to get the high returns.
8. Answers will vary, but students may suggest that they would invest in money market assets such as small CDs in order to save for a vacation. When saving for retirement, they may choose capital market assets such as IRAs.
9. Answers will vary but should demonstrate an understanding of the risks and returns associated with different financial assets.

CASE STUDY

Teach

S Skill Practice

Using Charts and Tables
Ask: What was the market capitalization of NYSE-listed companies in 2004? What percentage of all market capitalization did this represent? *($12.6 trillion; 33 percent)* What was the market capitalization of Euronext-listed companies in 1998? How did this figure compare to that of the NYSE in the same year? *($1.8 trillion; represented about 17 percent of the market capitalization of NYSE companies)* **OL**

Analyzing the Impact

Answers:
1. to expand into new markets and avoid the strict regulations of the Sarbanes-Oxley Act
2. It has gradually decreased.

Additional Support

CASE STUDY
The NYSE

Starting Small . . .
On a warm May afternoon in 1792, 24 New York City stockbrokers and merchants met beneath a buttonwood tree to sign an agreement. This deal—the Buttonwood Agreement—marked the creation of the New York Stock Exchange (NYSE).

. . . and Growing Big
Today the 37,000-square-foot floor of the New York Stock Exchange is where the action is. Although some shares are traded electronically, traders on the floor of the exchange match buyers and sellers of listed stocks in a daily high-stakes dance. Companies pay an initial fee of up to $250,000 just to be listed on the NYSE, and yearly listing fees can reach $500,000.

The NYSE, also called the "Big Board," serves as auctioneer for about 2,600 U.S. and foreign companies. It also works to earn a profit for its own shareholders. After nearly 214 years as a not-for-profit exchange, the NYSE went public on March 8, 2006, selling shares in itself. It also merged with Archipelago Holdings Inc. and the Pacific Exchange to become the NYSE Group, the largest stock exchange ever.

Competition From Abroad
After corporate accounting scandals such as Enron were made public in the early 2000s, Congress and the Securities and Exchange Commission instituted the Sarbanes-Oxley Act in 2002. SarbOx created reams of new rules and regulations aimed at eliminating corporate corruption. The fallout from SarbOx has led many investors, companies, and even the NYSE Group itself to look to overseas exchanges, where regulations are less strict. In May 2006, the NYSE announced its $10 billion intention to merge with Euronext, which runs the Amsterdam, Brussels, Paris, and Lisbon exchanges. By merging with Euronext, the NYSE can bypass the red tape created by SarbOx and tap into new markets.

Market Capitalization* of Listed Companies (in trillions)			
NYSE	NYSE	NYSE % of all	Euronext
2005	$13.3	33%	$2.70
2004	$12.6	34%	$2.40
2003	$11.4	36%	$2.10
2002	$9.0	39%	$1.60
2001	$11.0	41%	$1.80
2000	$11.5	37%	$2.30
1999	$11.4	32%	$2.40
1998	$10.3	39%	$1.80
1997	$8.9	40%	$1.30
1996	$6.8	34%	$1.10
1995	$5.7	33%	$0.90
1990	$2.7	28%	$0.50

* Number of common shares multiplied by current price of those shares
Source: 2006 NYSE Group, Inc.

Analyzing the Impact
1. **Summarizing** Why did the NYSE decide to expand into overseas markets?
2. **Analyzing Visuals** Look at the market capitalization table. What has happened to NYSE's share of market capitalization since the enactment of SarbOx?

Extending the Content

More About the New York Stock Exchange After growing from the Buttonwood Agreement of 24 stockbrokers and merchants in 1792, this group was officially organized in 1817 as the New York Stock and Exchange Board. It became known as the New York Stock Exchange in 1863. Since 1953, membership on the exchange has been limited to 1,366 members. Today, if a company wants to join the exchange, it must purchase a membership from a current member. The highest price ever paid for such a membership was $4,000,000 in 2005. Other current membership requirements include a minimum of 1,100,00 shares of outstanding stock and aggregate pretax earnings of at least $6,500,000 for the past three years. Corporations listed on the exchange must also grant voting rights to shareholders in the corporation and provide regular financial statements.

SECTION 3 Investing in Equities and Options

COMPANIES IN THE NEWS
—www.cme.com

Snowfall Futures

The Chicago Mercantile Exchange (CME), the world's largest and most diverse financial exchange, announced today that it will begin listing and trading snowfall futures and options. Snowfall futures will be based on a CME Snowfall Index and will be offered initially on two U.S. cities—Boston and New York. These contracts will trade on a monthly basis from October through April.

"CME weather futures provide the safety and soundness investors are seeking to manage their weather-related risk," said CME's Rick Redding. "From municipal snow removal budgets to holiday retail sales, snowfall, or lack thereof, can have a major impact on local and regional economies." ■

While government bonds rank among the safest financial assets, equities and futures, such as the snowfall futures in the news story, are at the opposite end of the risk spectrum. They offer the lure of large returns—or a complete loss.

Purchasing stock used to be complicated and required professional help. With computers and the Internet, though, today anyone can easily invest in stocks, mutual funds or, as you read in the news story, the snowfall depth futures for New York.

CHAPTER 11 Financial Markets **305**

Teach

D Differentiated Instruction

Special Education Help students understand the concept of equities by relating the classroom to a corporation. Explain that all of the equities would be divided among the members of the class. Suggest that some class members might own more shares than others. Ask students to consider how trading of these shares among class members, as well as with outside individuals, might affect the price of these shares. **BL**

S Skill Practice

Using Charts and Tables

Ask: What was the closing price of Exxon Mobil stock on this day? *($60.18)* How had this changed from the previous day? *(It represented a decrease of $1.78.)* **OL**

Economic Analysis

Answer: Fedex Corp

Additional Support

---

equities stocks that represent ownership shares in corporations

stockbroker person who buys or sells securities for investors

Skills Handbook

*See page **R59** to learn about Reading the **Stock Market Report**.*

Stocks and Efficient Markets

MAIN Idea Investors can purchase stock through stockbrokers on exchanges, through mutual funds, or through 401(k) plans.

Economics and You Does anyone in your family save for retirement through a 401(k)? Read on to learn how this is a way to invest in the stock market.

Equities, or shares of common stocks that represent ownership of corporations, form another type of financial asset that is available to investors.

Share Values

There are different ways to buy equities. An investor may want to use a **stockbroker**—a person who buys or sells equities for clients. The investor can also open an Internet account with a discount brokerage firm. This allows the investor to buy, sell, and monitor his or her stock portfolio from a personal computer.

The value of a single share of stock depends on several things. Both the number of outstanding shares to be traded and a company's profitability influence the price. Expectations are especially important, because demand for a company's

stock increases when the **prospects** for its growth improve.

Common to almost all stocks is that their value goes up and down daily, sometimes gaining or losing a few cents a share and at other times gaining or losing much more. This is due to a change in either the supply or the demand for a share of stock.

Figure 11.6 shows a typical listing of several stocks. During the last 12 months, Exxon stock sold for as much as $65.96 and as little as $53.08 a share. Its annual dividend (DIV) is $1.28, paid in four equal installments. The yield (Yld%) is the dividend divided by the closing price. The PE, or price-earnings ratio, is a stock's closing price divided by annual earnings of each share of common stock outstanding. Finally, Exxon closed at $60.18, which is $1.78 lower than the day before, as indicated by the Net Change (NET CHG) column.

Stock Market Efficiency

Most large equity markets are reasonably competitive, especially if they have a large number of buyers and sellers. When these conditions exist, stocks can be easily bought and sold, so any news that affects the supply or demand for stocks can affect stock prices on a daily basis.

Figure 11.6 ▶ **A New York Stock Exchange Listing**

52 weeks		Stock (SYM)	DIV	Yld%	PE	100S	LAST	NET CHG
Hi	Lo							
42.01	29.98	Estee Lauder (EL)	0.40	1.00	34.02	691	41.16	0.26
65.96	53.08	ExxonMobil (XOM)	1.28	2.10	10.25	25,966	60.18	−1.78
120.01	76.81	Fedex Corp (FDX)	0.32	0.30	20.11	3,175	109.92	−5.51
11.48	6.75	Ford Motor (F)	0.40	5.60	N/A	19,606	6.91	−0.11

▶ A typical New York Stock Exchange newspaper listing might include the highest and lowest prices for a 52-week period, the annual dividend payment, yield, price-earnings ratio, number of shares traded in 100s, closing price, and price change from the previous day. Other listings on the Internet show even more information.

Economic Analysis *Which of the stocks had the largest variation in a year?*

Activity: Technology Connection

Researching Stock Purchases
Organize students into small groups. Have groups conduct Internet research to find three companies that produce products or services that students use. Groups should then continue researching to find the current stock price of these companies, as well as the high and low stock price during the past year.

Have each group present its three companies to the class (you might suggest that students display the information in a visual, such as a chart or graph). Ask the class as a whole to identify the two companies that would have been the best investments for the year. **OL**

There is no sure way to invest in stocks in order to always make a profit. Stock prices can vary considerably from one company to the next, and the price of any stock can change dramatically from one day to the next. Because of this variability, investors are always looking at stocks to find the best ones to buy or sell and those to avoid. All of this attention makes the market more competitive.

Many stock market experts subscribe to a theory called the **Efficient Market Hypothesis (EMH)**—the argument that stocks are usually priced correctly and that bargains are hard to find because stocks are followed closely by so many investors. The theory states that each stock is constantly analyzed by many different professional analysts in a large number of stock investment companies. If the analysts observe anything that might affect the fortunes of the companies they watch, they buy or sell the stocks immediately. This in turn causes stock prices to adjust almost immediately to new market information.

The main **implication** for the investor is that if all stocks are priced correctly, it does not matter which ones you purchase. You might be lucky and pick a stock about to go up, or you might get unlucky and pick a stock about to go down. Because **W** of this, **portfolio diversification**—the practice of holding a large number of different stocks so that increases in some stocks can offset declines in others—is a popular strategy.

Mutual Funds

Because of the advantages of diversification, many investors buy shares in a mutual fund. A **mutual fund** is a company that sells stock in itself to individual investors. It then invests the money it receives in stocks and sometimes bonds issued

BALDWIN
www.CartoonStock.com
© Mike Baldwin/ Cornered

Diversification
Many investors put their money into a variety of stocks. *Why is it a good idea to diversify?*

"This next song's about spreading risk in a volatile market by diversification."

by other corporations. Mutual fund stockholders receive dividends earned from the mutual fund's investments.

Stockholders can also sell their mutual fund shares for a profit, just like other stocks. The market value of a mutual fund share is called the **net asset value (NAV)**—the net value of the mutual fund divided by the number of shares issued by the mutual fund.

Mutual funds allow people to invest in the market without risking all they have in one or a few companies. The large size of the typical mutual fund makes it possible **C** to hire a staff of experts to monitor market conditions and to analyze many different stocks and bonds before deciding which ones to buy or sell.

401(k) Plans

Portfolio diversification and the need for retirement planning have also increased the popularity of the **401(k) plan**—a tax-deferred investment and savings plan that acts as a personal pension fund for employees. To contribute to the plan, employees of a company authorize regular payroll deductions. The money from all employees

Efficient Market Hypothesis (EMH) argument that stocks are always priced about right because they are closely watched

portfolio diversification strategy of holding different investments to protect against risk

mutual fund company that sells stock in itself and uses the proceeds to buy stocks and bonds issued by other companies

net asset value (NAV) the market value of a mutual fund share found by dividing the net value of the fund by the number of shares issued

401(k) plan tax-deferred investment and savings plan that acts as a personal pension fund for employees

CHAPTER 11   Financial Markets   **307**

W **Writing Support**

Persuasive Writing
Ask students to write a persuasive essay in which they attempt to convince a potential investor in the stock market to practice portfolio diversification. Encourage students to highlight the benefits of diversification and propose a general strategy through which an investor might assemble a diverse stock portfolio. **AL**

C **Critical Thinking**

Assessing Ask: How does the large size of a typical mutual fund benefit potential investors? *(The large size allows these funds to hire a staff of experts to monitor market conditions and analyze many stocks and bonds before deciding which ones to buy or sell. This offers investors the benefit of contributing funds to a number of carefully chosen investments.)* **OL**

Caption Answer: so that increases in some stocks can offset declines in others

Additional Support

Activity: Interdisciplinary Connection

Language Arts Have students select a major corporation and investigate the goods or services it produces, how many employees it has, where it is located, and what its prospects are for future growth. Instruct students to consult Standard and Poor's, Moody's, or Value Line, or to contact a stockbroker for information. After students have studied the corporation and followed the stock, have them write a letter to a friend describing the stock from the viewpoint of a prospective investor interested in buying shares of the corporation. Call on students to read their letters to the class. **OL**

R Reading Strategy

Sequencing Information

Ask students to use sequence graphic organizers to show the steps of investing in a 401(k) plan. Tell students to construct their organizers under the assumption that the company will match employees' contributions to the plan. **BL**

C Critical Thinking

Drawing Conclusions

Ask: What is one trade-off involved with investing in a 401(k) plan? What is one risk that might be associated with the plan? *(Possible trade-off: giving up part of one's income to invest in the plan. Possible risk: investments approved by the company could lose money.)* **OL**

✓Reading Check **Answer:** the number of outstanding shares to be traded, a company's profitability, and expectations for the company's growth

---

Economic Analysis

Answer: about $40,000

Differentiated Instruction

Economic Cartoons, p. 17

---

stock exchange or securities exchange physical place where buyers and sellers meet to exchange securities

is then pooled and invested in mutual funds or other investments approved by the company.

Contributing to a plan lowers your taxable income because you don't have to pay income taxes on the money you contribute until you withdraw it. An added benefit of a 401(k) plan is that most employers typically match a portion of an employee's **R** contributions.

For example, if your employer matches your contribution at 50 cents on the dollar, you have an immediate 50 percent return on the investment—even before the funds are invested. **Figure 11.7** illustrates that an annual contribution of $2,000 with an employer match of 25 percent can provide a substantial retirement fund in 30 years.

The 401(k) is popular because it provides a simple, consistent, and relatively safe **C** way for employees to save—and you can take the 401(k) with you if you change jobs.

✓Reading Check **Explaining** What determines the value of a stock?

Figure 11.7 ▶ **How Much Money Will You Have at Retirement?**

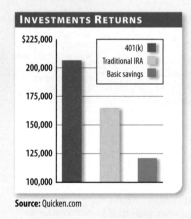

INVESTMENTS RETURNS

- 401(k)
- Traditional IRA
- Basic savings

$225,000
200,000
175,000
150,000
125,000
100,000

DATA BASED ON:

- $2,000 in income invested each year for 30 years
- 8% return on investment
- Company matching 25% of employee contributions
- 28% income tax; 20% capital gains tax (paid yearly for basic savings)

Source: Quicken.com

Charts In MOtion

See StudentWorks™ Plus or glencoe.com.

▶ Returns from retirement investment plans vary.

Economic Analysis *How much more would a traditional IRA earn than a basic savings plan?*

Stock Markets and Their Performance

MAIN Idea Several different stock markets exist, and each is organized in a different way.

Economics and You Have you ever heard the closing bell of the New York Stock Exchange on the news? Read on to learn about different stock markets.

Stocks, like almost everything else, are traded in markets. Investors follow these markets daily because the performance of the market is likely to affect their stocks.

Stock Exchanges

Historically, investors would gather at an organized **stock** or **securities exchange**, a place where buyers and sellers meet to trade stocks. An organized exchange gets its name from the way it conducts business. Members pay a fee to join, and trades can only take place on the floor of the exchange.

The oldest, largest, and most prestigious of the organized stock exchanges in the United States is the New York

---

It's a Wild Ride

Objective: Interpret the economic cartoon to learn more about the stock market.

Focus/Teach: Ask students to describe the nature of the stock market, in terms of risks and returns. Then have them complete the activity.

Assess: Review the correct answers as a class. Discuss different interpretations that students might have.

Close: Ask students to describe other images that might be used to represent the stock market.

Differentiated Instruction Strategies

BL Have students draw an economic cartoon that refers to the potential high returns of the stock market.

AL Ask students to write a paragraph describing other investments that might be characterized as a roller coaster.

ELL Have students define *Dow Jones averages*, *indexes*, and *stock market*.

The Global Economy & YOU

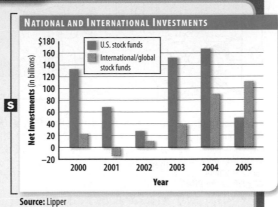

Sell, надувательство, Verkaufen

After you have saved some money, you may decide to become part-owner of a company by purchasing its stock. Your investment options are not limited to those companies listed on the NYSE, however. The United States is home to an additional nine stock exchanges.

You can also buy stocks in international companies. At last count, nearly 100 world stock exchanges spanned the globe. In 2005 investors spent more on international and global markets than on U.S. stocks.

Where does this global trading take place? Among others, investors can buy and sell on the Bolsa de Comercio de Buenos Aires in Argentina, the Moscow Stock Exchange, or the Tokyo Stock Exchange.

NATIONAL AND INTERNATIONAL INVESTMENTS

Net Investments (in billions)

- U.S. stock funds
- International/global stock funds

Years: 2000, 2001, 2002, 2003, 2004, 2005

Source: Lipper

Stock Exchange (NYSE), located on Wall Street in New York City. The NYSE lists stocks from about 2,700 companies. The firms have to pay a membership fee. They also must meet profitability and size requirements, which virtually guarantees that they are among the largest and most profitable publicly held companies.

Another national exchange is the American Stock Exchange (AMEX), which also is located in New York City. It features companies that are smaller and more speculative than those listed on the NYSE. Many regional exchanges are located in other cities such as Chicago, Philadelphia, and Memphis. They list corporations that are either too small or too new to be listed on the NYSE or the AMEX.

Organized stock exchanges are found in major cities all over the world, including in developing countries such as Ghana, Pakistan, and China. Developments in computer technology and electronic trading have linked the biggest markets. This means that today you can trade in most major stocks around the clock, somewhere in the world.

Over-the-Counter Markets

Despite the importance of the organized exchanges, the majority of stocks in the United States are not traded on these exchanges. Instead, they are traded in an **over-the-counter market (OTC)**—an electronic marketplace for securities that are not traded on an organized exchange such as the NYSE.

The most important OTC market is the National Association of Securities Dealers Automated Quotation (NASDAQ), the world's largest electronic stock market. Rather than being limited to a single trading location, NASDAQ trading is executed with a sophisticated telecommunications and computer network that connects investors in more than 80 countries. The total number of stocks listed on NASDAQ exceeds the combined total of the NYSE and AMEX.

The organized exchanges and the OTC markets may differ, but this means little to individual investors. An investor who opens an Internet account with a brokerage firm may buy and sell stocks in both markets. When the investor places an order to buy shares, the broker forwards the order

Economics ONLINE

Student Web Activity Visit the *Economics: Principles and Practices* Web site at glencoe.com and click on *Chapter 11–Student Web Activity* for an activity on the stock market.

over-the-counter market (OTC) electronic marketplace for securities not listed on organized exchanges such as the NYSE

S Skill Practice

Reading a Graph Ask: Between which two years did investments in international/global stock funds experience the greatest increase? *(between 2003 and 2004)* When were investments in U.S. stock funds the lowest? The highest? *(2002; 2004)* Invite students to share their opinions on why international investments may have increased since 2003. *(Possible answer: We are living in an increasingly global market. People might feel more comfortable making international investments.)* **BL**

D Differentiated Instruction

Visual/Spatial Have each student choose a publicly traded company to research. Ask students to use print and library sources to identify the exchanges on which the company's stock is traded. Then instruct students to track the prices of these stocks over the course of a business week. When this period has concluded, tell students to depict in a line graph the changes in value for the stock. **AL**

CHAPTER 11 Financial Markets 309

Leveled Activities

BL Reteaching Activities, p. 11   **OL** Critical Thinking Activities, p. 17   **AL** Free Enterprise Activities, p. 12

OUR INVESTMENTS ARE NOT GOING STRAIGHT UP, DEAR.

HUMOR ME. PLEASE.

W Writing Support

Personal Writing Have students review the information in the text about measures of stock performance. Then have them choose one of the measures and write a response detailing why they think their chosen measure would be the most reliable. Remind students to support their responses with facts from the text. **OL**

Caption Answer: the average closing price of a sample of 30 active stocks

✓Reading Check **Answer:** An over-the-counter market is an electronic marketplace for securities that are not traded on an organized exchange. The NYSE is an organized exchange that lists stock from companies that pay a membership fee and meet requirements for size and profitability.

Hands-On Chapter Project

Step 3

Designing an Investment Portfolio

Step 3: Selecting Stocks for the Portfolio. Students will revisit the investments they made in Steps 1 and 2 and choose stocks to complement these investments.

Directions: Ask groups to review the investments made in Steps 1 and 2 of the project. Direct students to use this review to "purchase" a number of stocks, mutual

310

Performance of Stocks Investors use several indicators to help with their investments. *What does the DJIA measure?*

Dow Jones Industrial Average (DJIA) measure of stock market performance based on 30 representative stocks

Standard & Poor's 500 (S&P 500) measure of stock market performance based on 500 stocks traded on the NYSE, AMEX, and OTC market

bull market period during which stock market prices move up for several months or years in a row

bear market period during which stock market prices move down for several months or years in a row

to the exchange where the stock is traded—whether it is on the NYSE, AMEX, or NASDAQ—and the purchase is made there.

Measures of Performance

Because they are concerned about the performance of their stocks, most investors consult one of two popular indicators. When these indicators go up, stocks in general also go up. When they go down, stocks in general go down.

The first of these indicators is the **Dow Jones Industrial Average (DJIA)**, the most popular and widely publicized measure of stock market performance. The DJIA began in 1884, when the Dow Jones Corporation published the average closing price of 11 active stocks. Coverage expanded to 30 stocks in 1928. Since then, some stocks have been added and others deleted, but the sample remains at 30.

Because of these changes, the DJIA is no longer a mathematical average of stock prices. Also, the evolution of the DJIA has obscured the meaning of a "point" change in the index. At one time, a one-point change in the DJIA meant that an average share of stock changed by $1. Since this is no longer true, it is better to focus on the percentage change of the index rather than the number of points.

Investors also use another popular benchmark of stock performance, the **Standard & Poor's 500 (S&P 500)**. It uses the price changes of 500 representative stocks as an indicator of overall market

performance. Because the sum of 500 stock prices would be very large, it is reduced to an index number. Unlike the Dow Jones, which focuses primarily on the NYSE, the Standard & Poor's 500 reports on stocks listed on the NYSE, AMEX, and OTC markets.

The NASDAQ also computes several measures of market performance for investors. The most popular is the NASDAQ composite. In addition, there are more than 20 sub-indices that focus on everything from the size of the firms traded on the NASDAQ to the performance of individual industries.

Bull vs. Bear Markets

Investors often use colorful terms to describe which way the market is moving. For example, a **bull market** is a "strong" market with the prices moving up for several months or years in a row. One of the strongest bull markets in history began in 1995, when the DJIA broke 4,000—and then reached 12,000 five years later.

A **bear market** is a "mean" or "nasty" market, with the prices of equities falling sharply for several months or years in a row. The most spectacular bear market since the 1930s was in 2001–2003, when the DJIA lost more than one-third of its value. These two terms take their names from the characteristics people associate with the animals for which they are named.

✓Reading Check **Contrasting** What is the difference between an over-the-counter market and the NYSE?

---

funds, and futures contracts with some of the remaining funds in their account. Groups may also want to consider investing money into a 401(k) plan. Investments should include at least one stock purchase. Have students use the Internet or current newspapers to research the stocks they wish to purchase and to monitor the price of the stock(s) they select.

Organizing Have students continue to monitor the price of the stocks in their

portfolios over a given period, such as 5 or 10 days. Have each group organize this information in a line graph or bar graph and then explain the reasons for any significant increases or decreases in value. **OL**

(Chapter Project continued in Visual Summary.)

Trading in the Future

MAIN Idea Financial assets can be bought and sold in the future as well as the present.

Economics and You Have you ever bought something that later went on sale? Read on to learn how an investor can protect against future price changes.

Most buying and selling takes place in the present, or in a **spot market.** In this market, a transaction is made immediately at the prevailing price. The spot price of gold in London, for example, is the price as it exists in that city at that moment.

Sometimes the exchange takes place later, rather than right away. This occurs with a **futures contract**—an agreement to buy or sell at a specific future date at a predetermined price. For example, you may agree to buy gold at $580 an ounce in six months, hoping that the actual price will be higher when the date arrives.

A futures contract can be written on almost anything, including the size of the S&P 500 or the level of future interest rates. In most cases, the profit or loss on the contract is settled with a cash payment rather than the buyer taking delivery.

An **option** is a special type of futures contract that gives the buyer the right to cancel the contract. For example, you may pay $5 today for a **call option**—the right to *buy* something at a specific future price. If the call option gives you the right to purchase 100 shares of stock at $70 a share, and if the price drops to $30, you tear up the option and buy the stock elsewhere for $30. If the price rises to $100, you execute the option, buy the stock for $70, and resell it for $100—or take a cash settlement.

You could also buy a **put option**—the right to *sell* something at a specific future price. The put option, like the call option, gives the buyer the right to tear up the contract if the actual future price is not advantageous to the buyer.

✓Reading Check **Explaining** Why might a contract that takes place in the future be an advantage to the buyer or seller?

spot market market in which a transaction is made immediately at the prevailing price

futures contract an agreement to buy or sell at a specific date in the future at a predetermined price

R **option** futures contract giving a buyer the right to cancel the contract

call option futures contract giving a buyer the right to cancel a contract to buy something

put option futures contract giving a buyer the right to cancel a contract to sell something

R **Reading Strategy**

Summarizing Ask: How does a call option protect a buyer? Explain. *(It protects a buyer from having to pay too high a price for a futures contract. It does this by allowing the buyer to cancel the contract if the price drops below the contract price.)* **OL**

✓Reading Check **Answer:** The price of the item may be higher or lower than the price agreed upon in the contract. This will offer an advantage to the buyer or seller, respectively.

Assess

Use the Interactive Tutor Self-Assessment CD-ROM to review Section 3, and then assign the Section 3 Review as homework or as an in-class activity.

Close

Making Decisions Ask students whether they would invest in a futures contract and why. Remind students to consider the risk-reward relationship. **OL**

Review **SECTION 3**

SECTION 3 Review

Vocabulary
1. **Explain** the significance of equities, stockbroker, Efficient Market Hypothesis, portfolio diversification, mutual fund, net asset value, 401(k) plan, stock or securities exchange, over-the-counter market, Dow Jones Industrial Average, Standard & Poor's 500, bull market, bear market, spot market, futures contract, option, call option, and put option.

Main Ideas
2. **Describing** What are the stock performance measures?

3. **Evaluating** Use a graphic organizer like the one below to evaluate the risks and rewards of investments.

Investment	Major Advantage	Risk Level
Stocks		

4. **Defining** What is a futures contract?

Critical Thinking
5. **The BIG Idea** What options are available to individuals who wish to invest in stocks?

6. **Analyzing** Would you ever invest in a futures contract? Why or why not?

7. **Determining Cause and Effect** If the price of a share of stock goes up, what does this suggest about the quantity demanded and quantity supplied for that stock?

8. **Analyzing Visuals** Look at Figure 11.6 on page 306. If you wanted to buy stock that paid large dividends, which stock would you choose?

Applying Economics
9. **Market Efficiency** What does the Efficient Market Hypothesis mean to you as a potential investor as you investigate your future stock portfolio?

CHAPTER 11 Financial Markets **311**

Answers

1. All definitions can be found in the section and the Glossary.
2. the Dow-Jones Industrial Average and the Standard & Poor's 500
3. Students should accurately characterize the risks and rewards of stocks, mutual funds, 401(k) plans, and futures contracts.

4. an agreement to buy or sell at a specific future date at a predetermined price
5. They can open an Internet account with a discount brokerage firm, buy stock through stockbrokers on exchanges, or invest in mutual funds or 401(k) plans.
6. Answers will vary but should reflect knowledge of futures contracts.

7. This suggests that the quantity demanded has increased, while the quantity supplied has decreased.
8. Exxon Mobil
9. Students may suggest that the Efficient Market Hypothesis may prompt them to choose stocks based on the potential for stable, long-term growth, rather than rapid, short-term growth.

Teach

BusinessWeek NEWSCLIP

C Critical Thinking

Determining Cause and Effect Ask: What factors have caused many companies to refrain from listing their stock on a U.S. stock exchange? *(Possible answer: the expense and difficulty of facing the Sarbanes-Oxley Act)* **OL**

BusinessWeek ONLINE

To find up-to-date news and analysis on the economy, business, technology, markets, entrepreneurs, investments, and finance, have students search feature articles and special reports on the BusinessWeek Web site, www.businessweek.com.

Examining the Newsclip

Answers:
1. globalization and electronic trading
2. It created additional expense and difficulty for companies seeking to list their stock on American exchanges.

Additional Support

W all Street in New York City has long been synonymous with wealth and corporate power. This is no longer true. Home to the New York Stock Exchange, Wall Street is losing some of its prestige to Paternoster Square in London, site of the London Stock Exchange.

Taking Their Business Elsewhere

If the state-owned Russian giant OAO Rosneft Oil Co. had been going public a decade ago, it would have jumped through hoops to list its shares on a U.S. stock exchange. Back then a U.S. listing was viewed as a rite of passage for up-and-coming global companies, offering not only direct access to the world's largest capital market but also a certain cachet.

This is 2006, though, and Rosneft plans to list its shares on the London Stock Exchange. . . . Rosneft isn't alone. Companies are increasingly forsaking the U.S. for friendlier overseas environs.

The New York Stock Exchange and NASDAQ pin much of the blame on the Sarbanes-Oxley Act (SarbOx), the controversial 2002 corporate governance rules, for their recent woes in attracting new listings. . . .

The exchanges say the expense and difficulty of dealing with SarbOx could transform the U.S. from one of the most attractive markets in the world to one of the least. But beyond SarbOx lies a troubling trend that's far less easily remedied—companies

simply don't need to list in New York anymore. Globalization and electronic trading have made U.S. investors mobile as never before. While some argue that the higher governance standards in the U.S. boost investor confidence, lead to higher valuations, and could prevent fraud, many companies no longer want to put up with the regulatory nuisances given the availability of money abroad. . . .

Europe's three main exchanges—the London Stock Exchange, the Deutsche Börse, and Euronext, which runs the Paris, Amsterdam, and Brussels exchanges—are ready for the business. . . .

—Reprinted from BusinessWeek

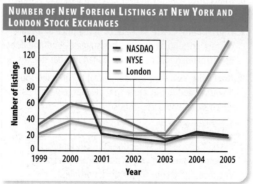

NUMBER OF NEW FOREIGN LISTINGS AT NEW YORK AND LONDON STOCK EXCHANGES

Legend: NASDAQ, NYSE, London

Y-axis: Number of listings (0–140); X-axis: Year (1999–2005)

Sources: NASDAQ, NYSE, London Stock Exchange

Examining the Newsclip

1. **Determining Cause and Effect** What has enabled investors to buy shares on overseas exchanges?
2. **Drawing Conclusions** Why did SarbOx have a negative impact on American stock exchanges?

312   UNIT 3   Economic Institutions and Issues

Extending the Content

Investing Globally Many people think that there are too many uncertainties associated with investing in overseas markets. Governments can be unstable and economic information about the region may be sketchy. Countries can devalue their currencies or maintain poor accounting standards. Economists, however, believe that investing a portion of one's money in Latin American, Asian, or European companies is a wise strategy, and many mutual funds exist today for that purpose. Even though the U.S. market has been prosperous, shifting some assets overseas can serve as a safety net if the U.S. market plunges. Stock markets around the world generally do not experience simultaneous highs and lows, so maintaining a level of profit making can be steady. Many overseas companies are restructuring to become more efficient, creating healthy investment opportunities for American investors.

CHAPTER 11

Visual Summary

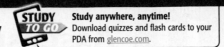

Study anywhere, anytime! Download quizzes and flash cards to your PDA from glencoe.com.

Visual Summary

CHAPTER 11

▶ **Financial System** Households and businesses invest their surplus funds to earn interest. Governments and businesses invest this money for economic growth.

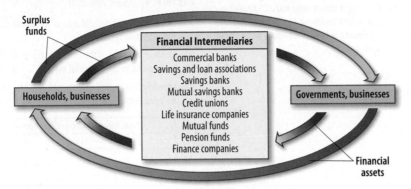

▶ **Investment Risk and Return** Investors must weigh the risks of their investments against the returns they expect. Generally, the higher the risk of an investment, the higher the return investors require.

THE RELATIONSHIP BETWEEN RISK AND RETURN

▶ **Equities and Futures** The riskiest investments consist of equities and futures. Equities can be purchased as individual stocks, or as part of a mutual fund or 401(k) plan. Futures allow investors to speculate on future prices of commodities.

Evaluating Ask students to review the graphic showing the financial system and the flow of funds throughout this system. Instruct them to consider how this system works to meet the needs of both borrowers and lenders. **Ask:** How might a transaction involving a life insurance company progress throughout the financial system? *(Possible answer: The people in a household would pay a life insurance company cash premiums for the protection the company offers. The life insurance company could then take these surplus funds and lend them to a business that needed funding for growth.)* **OL**

Personal Writing Have students write a personal essay in which they reflect on the potential risks involved in each type of equity and future shown in the graphic organizer at the bottom of the page. Students should identify which types of investments would be most appealing to them and discuss the reduction in risk offered by investments such as mutual funds and call options. **OL**

Hands-On Chapter Project

Step 4: Wrap Up

Designing an Investment Portfolio

Step 4: Organize the Portfolio.
Students will put together the information from each of the previous three steps, and present a completed portfolio with all of their investments.

Directions: Have students gather the materials they produced in each step of the Chapter Project to assemble their

completed portfolios. Students should include a detailed list of their investments. They should also identify the amount of money they allotted to each investment and any relevant information about the investments' changes in value, profits made, and losses suffered. Along with this information, students should compose a short paragraph that gives an overview of their portfolio holdings, how well it met their investment goals, and their reasoning

for the investment decisions they made. Students' paragraphs should also assess the potential of their portfolios for immediate and long-term growth. **OL**

ExamView® Assessment Suite

This easy-to-use software includes extensive question banks and allows you to create fully customized tests that can be administered in print or online.

Review Content Vocabulary

1.–15. Students' reports should demonstrate an understanding of how the terms relate to the investment process.

Review Academic Vocabulary

16. b	**17.** d
18. e	**19.** c
20. a	**21.** f

Review the Main Ideas

22. Financial assets are created when a lender/investor receives a receipt like a CD showing he has a claim on the borrower for an amount loaned under specific terms.

23. Finance companies lend directly to consumers and buy up installment contracts. Life insurance companies lend surplus funds. Pension funds invest money until payments are made to eligible recipients.

24. goals, consistency, simplicity, risk-return relationship

25. by dividing its annual coupon interest by the purchase price

26. Small CDs are in the primary market because investors tend to cash them in early. Long-term CDs belong in the capital market. A CD with maturity of less than one year belongs in the money market. If the CD can be sold to someone else, it would be found in the secondary market.

Review Content Vocabulary

Assume that you are an investment adviser who has to advise a 30-year-old, single client who earns $35,000 a year and has saved $10,000 to invest for retirement. Use the terms below to prepare a report advising your client of the best investment course.

1. financial asset
2. financial system
3. risk
4. capital market
5. money market
6. bond
7. Treasury note
8. IRA
9. 401(k) plan
10. mutual fund
11. pension fund
12. certificate of deposit
13. portfolio diversification
14. stock exchange
15. over-the-counter market

Review Academic Vocabulary

Match each term with its synonyms in the list below.

a. sector	**d.** presumed
b. compensation	**e.** prospects
c. offset	**f.** implication

16. payment, reparation, payback
17. supposed, expected, believed
18. likelihood, possibilities, expectations
19. counterbalance, neutralize, cancel out
20. section, part, segment
21. association, meaning, consequence

Review the Main Ideas

Section 1 *(pages 289–294)*

22. Describe how financial assets are created in a free enterprise system.

23. Explain the role of the major nondepository financial institutions in the financial system.

24. Identify the factors one should consider when investing by completing a graphic organizer like the one below.

Basic Investment Considerations
1.
2.
3.
4.

Section 2 *(pages 296–303)*

25. Explain what determines a bond's current yield.

26. Explain how CDs can appear in multiple markets.

27. Identify the characteristics of Treasury notes, bonds, and bills.

Section 3 *(pages 305–311)*

28. Describe how options contracts are different from futures contracts.

29. Explain why equity markets are reasonably competitive.

30. Explain how the NASDAQ differs from the NYSE.

Critical Thinking

31. **The BIG Idea** How might the four basic investment considerations vary for people in different age groups? Write a paragraph explaining your answer.

32. Making Generalizations Why might an individual choose to borrow money from a finance company that charges higher interest rates rather than from a commercial bank with lower interest rates?

---

27. Treasury notes: maturities of 2–10 years; bonds: maturities from 10–30 years; bills: maturities of 4, 13, or 26 weeks

28. Options give one of the parties the opportunity to back out of the agreement.

29. They have a large number of buyers and sellers, investors possess reasonably good information, and any news that affects the supply or demand for stocks can affect prices daily.

30. NYSE: trading done on the floor of the exchange on Wall Street. NASDAQ: trading done over a computer network that connects investors in many countries.

Critical Thinking

31. Answers will vary but should address factors that vary with age.

32. It may be the only option because other financial institutions consider the individual to be too great of a risk.

Economics ONLINE Self-Check Quiz Visit the
Economics: Principles and Practices Web site at glencoe.com and click
on *Chapter 11–Self-Check Quizzes* to prepare for the chapter test.

Assessment
and Activities

CHAPTER
11

33. Determining Cause and Effect How does each of the following affect saving?

a. A decrease in the federal personal income tax is implemented.

b. The United States undergoes a prolonged period of inflation.

34. Drawing Conclusions Interest rates on CDs usually vary only slightly from one institution to another. What do you think causes these similarities?

35. Drawing Conclusions Which investments are the safest and which are the riskiest? Why would investors choose either of those investments? Explain.

Math Practice

36. Determine income, consumption, and saving in each row by completing the following table.

Total Income	Consumption	Saving
a. $2,000	$1,800	
b.	$2,500	$1,000
c. $7,000		−$500
d. $10,000	$10,000	
e. $12,500		$400

Applying Economic Concepts

37. Investing in Stocks Assume that you have saved $10,000 and have decided to invest in stocks. Research the performance of 2 to 3 stocks listed on the NYSE, AMEX, or NASDAQ. Then write a short paper that includes the following:

a. Reasons you chose the stocks

b. Stock performance

c. Factors influencing the gain/loss in value

d. Analysis of why you would hold your stocks for either the short term or the long term

Analyzing Visuals

38. Look at Figure 11.1 on page 291. In a brief paragraph, describe the financial assets savers would receive from financial intermediaries. Then describe those that savers would receive directly from governments and businesses.

39. Look at Figure 11.7 on page 308 and compare the returns for investments in traditional IRAs and 401(k) plans. If the annual investment amounts and interest rates are the same, what accounts for the large difference in returns for these investment options?

Writing About Economics

40. Expository Writing Return to the activity in the chapter opener on page 288. Based on what you have learned in the chapter, devise a general investment plan for Miguel. In your planning, keep in mind the mid-term goals of college cost and long-term goals of retirement.

Interpreting Cartoons

41. Critical Thinking What do the figures of bulls and bears in the cartoons depict? What point is the cartoonist trying to make about the stock market?

I DON'T LIKE THE LOOKS OF THIS MARV.

John S. Pritchett/www.pritchettcartoons.com

CHAPTER 11 Financial Markets **315**

Applying Economic Concepts

37. Students should analyze the stock performance and provide valid reasons for purchasing the stock on the short- or long-term basis.

Analyzing Visuals

38. Students' paragraphs should identify the financial assets that savers receive from financial intermediaries as documents that certify the ownership of funds, such as CDs. They should further explain that the financial assets that savers receive from governments and businesses are bonds.

39. the employee's company matching 25 percent of the contributions

Writing About Economics

40. Answers will vary, but students' recommendations should be consistent with the mid-term and long-term goals identified.

Interpreting Cartoons

41. The bulls in the cartoon represent a "strong" stock market, while the bears represent a "mean" or "nasty" stock market. The cartoonist is making the point that many signs point to the stock market taking a turn for the worse.

33. a. Saving will decline if income taxes increase. People will have less take-home pay and therefore will save less.

b. Saving will decline during a prolonged period of inflation because people will have to spend more of their income to purchase goods and services. This assumes that wage increases do not offset inflation.

34. Answers will vary but should demonstrate sound economic reasoning.

35. Answers will vary but should demonstrate knowledge of the risks associated with different types of investments.

Math Practice

36. a. $200
b. $3,500
c. $7,500
d. $0
e. $12,100

Macroeconomics: Performance and Stabilization

UNIT PACING CHART				
	Chapter 12	**Chapter 13**	**Chapter 14**	**Chapter 15**
Day 1	Unit Opener Chapter Opener Section 1	Chapter Opener Section 1	Chapter Opener Section 1	Chapter Opener Section 1
Day 2	Profiles in Economics Section 2 Case Study	BusinessWeek Newsclip Section 2 Profiles in Economics	Case Study Section 2 Profiles in Economics	BusinessWeek Newsclip Section 2 Profiles in Economics
Day 3	Section 3 BusinessWeek Newsclip	Section 3 Case Study	Section 3 BusinessWeek Newsclip	Section 3 Case Study
Day 4	Review Chapter Assessment	Review Chapter Assessment	Review Chapter Assessment	Review Chapter Assessment
Day 5	The Global Economy & You	Debates in Economics		

Teacher to Teacher

**Ken Olson
Bremen High
School
Bremen, Indiana**

Penny Supply and Fractional Reserves Start by giving a volunteer 10 pennies. The student (Student One) deposits the pennies in a bank (Bank A). (The "bank" is another student volunteer.) Set the reserve requirement at "1 penny" of each new deposit. **Ask:** How many pennies can be loaned out? *(9 pennies)* Then have Bank A loan the pennies to another student (Student Two). **Ask the class:** How many pennies are in the money supply now? *(There are now 19 pennies in the money supply—10 deposited in* Bank A and 9 on loan to Student Two.) Have Student Two "make a purchase at the cost of 9 pennies" from a third student, who then deposits the money in a second bank (Bank B). **Ask:** How many pennies are in the money supply now? *(28 pennies)* Then have Bank B loan out 8 pennies. Again take a count of the money supply. *(36 pennies are in the money supply: 10 in Bank A, 9 loaned out from Bank A, 9 deposited in Bank B, and 8 loaned out)* Continue until students grasp the concept.

Author Note

Dear Economics Teacher:

With an economy as large as ours, there is a lot at stake for everyone. For example, we need to do more than make sure that the basic WHAT, HOW, and FOR WHOM to produce questions are addressed in a suitable way. We also want to make sure that the economy functions smoothly and does not suffer unnecessary and harmful setbacks. Accordingly, we need to know how to measure economic performance as well as fix problems if something should go wrong. Fortunately, as your students have already learned in the first unit, our market economy generally requires little coordination and supervision. This means that we don't have to waste a lot of scarce resources on an administrative bureaucracy.

Still, market economies are not perfect. They do not benefit everyone equally, which is why I discuss poverty in this unit. In addition, the historical record of market economies is replete with periods of recession, inflation, and unemployment. Fortunately, though, our economic expansions are considerably longer than our brief periods of recessions.

This means that there is a role and a place for stabilization policies, although such policies have changed over time. Political gridlock has largely resulted in the demise of fiscal policy in favor of monetary policy, but that may change in the future as new ideas come and go. Our challenge is to learn about and teach our students these ideas so that we all can decide for ourselves whether these economic theories and ideas actually solve problems without introducing new ones.

There are no shortcuts or easy ways out. We simply can't be vigilant about the state of the economy without understanding how it works. No pain, no gain, we might say—but the gains we get from understanding how our economy works are definitely worth the pain of finding out.

Gary E. Clayton

Gary Clayton, Ph.D.
Author

UNIT 4

Macroeconomics:
Performance and Stabilization

Unit Objectives

After studying this unit, students will be able to:

- **Discuss** the different methods of measuring economic performance.

- **Describe** the phases of the business cycle and its possible causes.

- **Describe** the evolution of money, the banking system, and the role of the Federal Reserve System.

- **Understand** the purpose of monetary and fiscal policies.

Unit Overview

Unit 4 explains the measurement of the U.S. economy and policies designed to achieve economic growth and stability.

Chapter 12 focuses on the nation's economic performance and its Gross Domestic Product (GDP). It also discusses the distribution of poverty and income.

Chapter 13 discusses the business cycle, inflation, and unemployment.

Chapter 14 discusses the development of the banking system and the role of the Federal Reserve System as manager of the country's money supply.

Chapter 15 focuses on the goal of economic stability and the policies needed to achieve it.

Economists like to monitor all ▶ economic activity, including the productivity of the workers and the output of this aircraft engine plant.

316   UNIT 4

Activity: Launching the Unit

Stimulating the Economy Organize students into several groups, and ask them to imagine they are panels of economic advisers reporting to the president. Then provide the following hypothetical situation: Recently, the national economy has been in a recession, with unemployment at 7 percent and rising, inflation at 4 percent, investment at low levels, and economic growth close to 1.5 percent. The president has asked for recommendations on how to stimulate the economy.

Have groups investigate the different methods that might be used to stimulate the economy, starting with the information in this unit. Ask groups to prepare a written report listing their recommendations. **OL**

Making It Relevant

Ask: What issues help us measure the performance of the national economy? *(Possible answers: unemployment rate, inflation, number of people living in poverty, housing market)* Call on volunteers to share their ideas with the rest of the class. On the board, list the issues that students mentioned. Ask students to explain what they think these issues indicate about the performance of the American economy. Conclude by mentioning that many of these issues will be discussed in this unit. **OL**

BusinessWeek ONLINE

To find up-to-date news and analysis on the economy, business, technology, markets, entrepreneurs, investments, and finance, have students search feature articles and special reports on the BusinessWeek Web site, www.businessweek.com.

Extra Credit Project

Ask each student to select a country and look up macroeconomic statistics about it. Have them find real GDP, the population, the unemployment rate, and the inflation rate. On a long sheet of paper, draw a scale of per capita real GDP. Have students mark on the scale where their countries lie. On another large sheet of paper, draw a scaled graph with the inflation rate on the vertical axis and the unemployment rate on the horizontal axis. Have students mark the positions of their countries on that graph. Discuss the differences among the countries' statistics. **OL**

Levels					Resources	Chapter Opener	Section 1	Section 2	Section 3	Chapter Assess
BL	OL	AL	ELL							
FOCUS										
BL	OL	AL	ELL	📠	Daily Focus Skills Transparencies		27, 65	53	71	
TEACH										
BL	OL		ELL	📁	Guided Reading Activities*		p. 34	p. 35	p. 36	
BL	OL	AL	ELL	📁	Economic Content Vocabulary Activities*		p. 12	p. 12	p. 12	
	OL	AL		📁	Critical Thinking Activities		p. 18			
BL	OL		ELL	📁	Reading Essentials and Note-Taking Guide*		p. 100	p. 103	p. 106	
		AL		📁	Enrichment Activities			p. 12		
BL	OL	AL	ELL	📁	Primary and Secondary Source Readings		p. 35			
BL	OL	AL	ELL	📠	Economic Concepts Transparencies, Strategies, and Activities		p. 25			
BL	OL	AL	ELL	📁	Math Practice for Economics		p. 24			
BL	OL	AL	ELL	📁	Reinforcing Economic Skills		pp. 1, 2, 13			
BL	OL		ELL	📁	High School Reading in the Content Area Strategies and Activities	✓	✓	✓	✓	✓
BL	OL	AL	ELL	📠	High School Writing Process Transparencies	✓	✓	✓	✓	✓
BL	OL	AL	ELL	📁	Writer's Guidebook	✓	✓	✓	✓	✓
BL	OL	AL	ELL	💿	StudentWorks Plus CD-ROM	✓	✓	✓	✓	✓
BL	OL	AL	ELL	💿	Vocabulary PuzzleMaker CD-ROM	✓	✓	✓	✓	✓

*Also available in Spanish

TeacherWorks Plus
All-In-One Planner and Resource Center

- Interactive Lesson Planner
- Interactive Teacher Edition
- Fully editable blackline masters
- Economics & You videos

- Differentiated Lesson Plans
- Printable reports of daily assignments
- Standards tracking system

Levels					Resources	Chapter Opener	Section 1	Section 2	Section 3	Chapter Assess
BL	OL	AL	ELL							
TEACH *(continued)*										
BL	OL	AL	ELL		**Economics & You Video Program DVD— *Fighting Unemployment, Inflation and Poverty***	✓	✓	✓	✓	✓
BL	OL	AL	ELL		**Graph Coach CD-ROM**	✓	✓	✓	✓	✓
Teacher Resources					**Differentiated Instruction Strategies**	✓	✓	✓	✓	✓
					Success with English Learners	✓	✓	✓	✓	✓
					Presentation Plus! CD-ROM	✓	✓	✓	✓	✓
ASSESS										
BL	OL	AL	ELL		**Section Quizzes and Chapter Tests**		p. 149	p. 150	p. 151	pp. 153, 157
BL	OL	AL	ELL		**Authentic Assessment Strategies and Activities**				p. 23	
BL	OL	AL	ELL		***ExamView® Assessment Suite* CD-ROM**		12-1	12-2	12-3	Ch. 12
BL	OL	AL	ELL		**Interactive Tutor Self-Assessment CD-ROM**		12-1	12-2	12-3	
CLOSE										
BL			ELL		**Reteaching Activities***		p. 12	p. 12	p. 12	
BL	OL		ELL		**Reading and Study Skills Foldables**		p. 59			
BL	OL	AL	ELL		**Graphic Organizer Transparencies**				pp. 21, 23	

*Also available in Spanish

Self-Check Quizzes

Technology Product
Students can assess their comprehension of chapter content with Self-Check Quizzes on the Glencoe Web site. The Web site provides a 10-question quiz for each chapter.

Objectives
The Self-Check Quizzes help students
- assess their comprehension and recall of chapter content;
- build study skills;
- identify areas for additional study and reinforcement.

Steps
Provide students with the following steps to complete the activities:
- Locate the Web page for the textbook being studied on the Glencoe Web site glencoe.com.
- Click on **Student Center** under the textbook title.
- In the Student Center, select a unit from the Unit Resources menu and a chapter from the Chapter Activities menu using the drop-down arrows.
- Click on the **Self-Check Quizzes** link.
- Have students answer the questions in the chapter quiz and review feedback on incorrect answers.

Provide students with an e-mail address to submit their quiz results for analysis and recording.

Economics ONLINE

	Student	Teacher	Parent
Beyond the Textbook	●	●	●
Chapter Overviews	●	●	●
ePuzzles and Games	●		●
Concepts in Motion	●		●
Multi-Language Glossaries	●		●
Online Student Edition	●	●	●
Self-Check Quizzes	●		●
Student Web Activities	●		●
Study Central™	●		●
Time Current Events	●	●	●
Teaching Today		●	
Vocabulary eFlashcards	●		●
Web Activity Lesson Plans		●	

Glencoe Media Center

> glencoe.com

Study-To-Go
- Vocabulary eFlashcards
- Self-Check Quizzes

> **Audio/Video**
- Student Edition Audio
- Spanish Summaries
- Economics & You Videos

READING SUPPORT FROM JAMESTOWN EDUCATION

- **Timed Readings Plus in Social Studies** helps students increase their reading rate and fluency while maintaining comprehension. The 400-word passages are similar to those found on state and national assessments.

- **Reading in the Content Area: Social Studies** concentrates on six essential reading skills that help students better comprehend what they read. The book includes 75 high-interest nonfiction passages written at increasing levels of difficulty.

- **Reading Social Studies** includes strategic reading instruction and vocabulary support in Social Studies content for both ELLs and native speakers of English.
www.jamestowneducation.com

Reading List Generator CD-ROM

GLENCOE BOOKLINK 3

Use this database to search more than 30,000 titles to create a customized reading list for your students.

- Reading lists can be organized by students' reading level, author, genre, theme, or area of interest.

- The database provides Degrees of Reading Power™ (DRP) and Lexile™ readability scores for all selections.

- A brief summary of each selection is included.

Leveled reading suggestions for this chapter:

For students at a Grade 10 reading level:
- *Poverty in America,* by Milton Meltzer

For students at a Grade 11 reading level:
- *Population: Opposing Viewpoints,* by Charles F. Hohm & Lori Justine Jones

For students at a Grade 12 reading level:
- *Poverty: Opposing Viewpoints,* by Karen Balkin

* Review suggested books before assigning them.

NCEE

National Council on Economic Education

Voluntary Standards Emphasized in Chapter 12

Content Standard 15 Investment in factories, machinery, new technology, and in the health, education, and training of people can raise future standards of living.

Content Standard 13 Income for most people is determined by the market value of the productive resources they sell. What workers earn depends, primarily, on the market value of what they produce and how productive they are.

Content Standard 18 A nation's overall levels of income, employment, and prices are determined by the interaction of spending and production decisions made by all households, firms, government agencies, and others in the economy.

Resources Available from NCEE
- Virtual Economics®: An Interactive Center for Economic Education Version 3.0
- Financing Your Future
- Learning, Earning and Investing, High School
- Focus: Institutions and Markets

To order these materials, or to contact your State Council on Economic Education about workshops and programs, call 1-800-338-1192 or visit the NCEE Web site at store.ncee.net**.**

The **BIG** Idea

As students study the chapter, remind them to consider the chapter-based Big Idea. The **Essential Question** in the chapter launch activity below ties in to the Big Idea and helps students think about and understand important chapter concepts. In addition, the Hands-On Chapter Project relates the content from each section to the Big Idea. The steps in each section build on each other and culminate in the Wrap-Up Activity on the Visual Summary page.

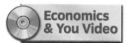 To generate student interest and provide a springboard for class discussion, access the Economics & You Topic 20 video, **Fighting Unemployment, Inflation and Poverty,** at glencoe.com or on the video DVD.

 Dinah Zike's Foldables are three-dimensional, interactive graphic organizers that help students practice basic writing skills, review key vocabulary terms, and identify main ideas. Have students complete this chapter's Foldable activity or activities in *Dinah Zike's Reading and Study Skills Foldables* booklet. **OL**

Economics ONLINE

Introduce students to chapter content and key terms by having them access *Chapter 12 —Chapter Overviews* at glencoe.com.

CHAPTER 12 Macroeconomic Performance

Why It Matters

Have you ever thought about what it means when someone is described as "successful"? Is the person wealthy, happy, or well known? Work with a partner and develop a list of the qualities or characteristics for your definition of *successful*. Share your list with the class and listen carefully to what the other students think. Is there a consensus among your classmates? Read Chapter 12 to learn more about how economists assess the success of a nation's economy by measuring its growth and performance.

The **BIG** Idea

Economists look at a variety of factors to assess the growth and performance of a nation's economy.

 Busy factories such as this car manufacturing plant are indicators of economic growth.

Economics ONLINE **Chapter Overview** Visit the *Economics: Principles and Practices* Web site at glencoe.com and click on *Chapter 12–Chapter Overviews* to preview chapter information.

318   UNIT 4

Activity: Launching the Chapter

Assessing Have students imagine they are economic forecasters who must determine the total supply and demand in the U.S. economy for a particular month. Discuss what information to gather and how this information might be obtained. Then, ask the **Essential Question:** Is the total supply and demand in the U.S. economy over the past five years an accurate indicator of the nation's economy? Why or why not?

What other things might we look at to gauge the nation's economic health? *(Students may note that supply and demand only focuses on goods and services, not on debt, employment rates, foreign trade, or the outcome of investments, each of which is important when analyzing the national economy; suggestions might include total production, income, exports, or tax revenues.)* **OL**

Measuring the Nation's Output and Income

GUIDE TO READING

Section Preview

In this section, you will learn how we measure the output and income of a nation.

Content Vocabulary

- macroeconomics *(p. 319)*
- gross domestic product (GDP) *(p. 320)*
- intermediate products *(p. 321)*
- secondhand sales *(p. 321)*
- nonmarket transactions *(p. 321)*
- underground economy *(p. 321)*
- base year *(p. 321)*
- real GDP *(p. 322)*
- current GDP *(p. 322)*
- GDP per capita *(p. 322)*
- gross national product (GNP) *(p. 324)*
- net national product (NNP) *(p. 324)*
- national income (NI) *(p. 324)*
- personal income (PI) *(p. 324)*
- disposable personal income (DPI) *(p. 324)*

- household *(p. 325)*
- unrelated individual *(p. 326)*
- family *(p. 326)*
- output-expenditure model *(p. 327)*
- net exports of goods and services *(p. 327)*

Academic Vocabulary

- excluded *(p. 321)*
- components *(p. 325)*

Reading Strategy

Describing As you read the section, complete a graphic organizer like the one below by describing how the different economic sectors contribute to the nation's economic activity.

Economic Sectors

| Consumer sector | Investment sector | Government sector | Foreign sector |

ISSUES IN THE NEWS

—CNNMoney.com

GDP posts smallest gain in 3 years

The nation's economy grew at its slowest pace in three years in the fourth quarter, according to the government's gross domestic product report Friday, which came in far weaker than economists' forecasts.

The broad measure of the nation's economic activity showed an annual growth rate of 1.1 percent in the fourth quarter, down from the 4.1 percent growth rate in the final reading of third-quarter growth. ∎

The report in the news story above may be of little interest to many people, but it was worrisome for economists. When the nation's economic growth rate drops to a meager 1.1 percent, the news is not good. Welcome to **macroeconomics,** the branch of economics that deals with the economy as a whole, using aggregate measures of output, income, prices, and employment.

Gross Domestic Product is one of our most important macro measures and the most important statistic in the National Income and Product Accounts (NIPA). The NIPA keeps track of the nation's production, consumption, saving, and investment. Other key measures exist, and collectively they tell us a great deal about the economic health and performance of our country.

> **macroeconomics** part of economics that deals with the economy as a whole and uses aggregate measures of output, income, prices, and employment

CHAPTER 12   Macroeconomic Performance   319

Bellringer
Daily Focus Transparency 27

GUIDE TO READING

Answers to Graphic:

Consumer sector: income in the form of disposable personal income

Investment sector: income in the form of retained earnings

Government sector: income in the form of taxes

Foreign sector: represents the difference in dollar value of goods sent abroad and goods purchased from abroad

Resource Manager

R Reading Strategies	**C** Critical Thinking	**D** Differentiated Instruction	**W** Writing Support	**S** Skill Practice
Teacher Edition • Making Connections, pp. 324, 325 • Summarizing, p. 326 **Additional Resources** • Guid. Read. Act., p. 34 • Read. Ess. & Note-Taking Guide, p. 100 • Pri./Sec. Source Read., p. 35	**Teacher Edition** • Form. Quest., p. 321 • Synthesizing, p. 322 • Speculating, p. 323 • Evaluating, p. 328 **Additional Resources** • Econ. Concepts Trans., Strat. & Act., p. 25 • Crit. Think. Act., p. 18	**Teacher Edition** • ELL, p. 320 • Logical/Math., p. 320 **Additional Resources** • Daily Focus Trans. 27, 65 • Reinforcing Econ. Skills, pp. 1, 2, 13	**Teacher Edition** • Expository Writing, p. 323 • Narrative Writing, p. 326 **Additional Resources** • High School Writing Process Trans.	**Teacher Edition** • Making Pred., p. 321 • Using Tables and Charts, pp. 322, 327 • Analyzing Info., p. 324 • Visual Literacy, p. 325 **Additional Resources** • Reading and Study Skills Fold., p. 59

Teach

Differentiated Instruction

English Language Learners
Have each student, without using the textbook or a dictionary, write definitions of *gross*, *domestic*, and *comprehensive*. Then have students explain the meanings to partners. Finally, have pairs check their definitions in a dictionary. **BL**

D2 Differentiated Instruction

Logical/Mathematical
Ask: Why do scientific sampling techniques give an accurate picture of the economy, even though economists do not record every single good and service produced? *(Sampling techniques are created to draw out an exact representative picture of the nation's economic activity, which includes some estimation.)* **AL**

Economic Analysis

Answer: quantity multiplied by price per unit

Additional Support

---

gross domestic product (GDP) the dollar value of all final goods, services, and structures produced within a country's national borders during a one-year period *(also see page 9)*

GDP—The Measure of National Output

MAIN Idea GDP measures national output.

Economics and You Did you know that your work may be counted in our GDP? Read on to find out how we measure output.

Gross domestic product (GDP) is our most comprehensive measure of national output. This means that Japanese automobiles produced in Kentucky, Ohio, and Indiana count in GDP even if the owners of the plants live outside the United States. On the other hand, production in U.S.-owned plants located in Mexico, Canada, or other countries is not counted in GDP.

Measuring Current GDP

The measurement of GDP is fairly easy to understand. Conceptually, all we have to do is to multiply all of the final goods and services produced in a 12-month period by their prices, and then add them up to get the total dollar value of production.

Figure 12.1 provides an example. The first column contains three product categories—goods, services, and structures—used in the NIPA. The third of these categories, structures, includes residential housing, apartments, and buildings for commercial purposes. The total number of final goods and services produced in the year is in the quantity column, and the price column shows the average price of each product. To get GDP, we simply multiply the quantity of each good by its price and then add the results, as is done in the last column of the table.

Of course it is not possible to record every single good and service produced during the year, so government statisticians instead use scientific sampling techniques to estimate the quantities and prices

Figure 12.1 ▶ Estimating Total Annual Output

ESTIMATING GROSS DOMESTIC PRODUCT		Quantity (millions)	Price (per 1 unit)	Dollar value (millions)
Product				
Goods	Automobiles	6	$25,000	$150,000
	Replacement tires	10	$60	$600
	Shoes	55	$50	$2,700
	...*	...*	...*	...*
Services	Haircuts	150	$8	$1,200
	Income tax filings	30	$150	$4,500
	Legal advice	45	$200	$9,000
	...*	...*	...*	...*
Structures	Single family	3	$175,600	$525,000
	Multifamily	5	$300,000	$1,500,000
	Commercial	1	$1,000,000	$1,000,000
	...*	...*	...*	...*

Note: *...other goods, services, and structures

Total GDP = $13.5 trillion

▶ Gross domestic product is the total dollar value of production within a country's borders in a 12-month period. It can be found by multiplying all of the goods and services produced by their prices, and then adding them up.

Economic Analysis *How is the dollar value for each of the products on the table calculated?*

Activity: Hands-On Economics

A Community GDP Have students make a rough estimate of the GDP for your community using a chart like the one in Figure 12.1. (Students may wish to consult local government offices, business development offices, colleges, or the chamber of commerce when researching your community's statistics.) They should list the items, services, and structures produced by the community in the first column, the approximate quantity in the second column, and the approximate price per unit in the third column. Students should then multiply the quantity by the price to get the dollar value, which they should record in the fourth column. Have them calculate the community's GDP by adding the dollar value of each item, as in the chart on this page. **AL**

of the individual products. To keep the report as current as possible, they estimate GDP quarterly, or every three months, and then revise the numbers for months after that. As a result, it takes several months to discover how the economy actually performed.

Some Things Are Excluded

C GDP is a measure of final output. This means that **intermediate products**—goods used to make other products already counted in GDP—are **excluded**. If you buy new replacement tires for your automobile, for example, the tires are counted in GDP because they were intended for final use by the customer and not combined with other parts to make a new product. However, tires on a new car are *not* counted separately because their value is already built into the price of the vehicle. Other goods such as flour and sugar are part of GDP if they are bought for final use by the consumer. However, if a baker buys them to make bread for sale, only the value of the bread is counted.

Secondhand sales—the sales of used goods—are also excluded from GDP because no new production is created when products already in existence are transferred from one owner to another. Although the sale of a used car, house, or compact disc player may give others cash that they can use on new purchases, only the original sale is included in GDP.

Nonmarket transactions—economic activities that do not generate expenditures in the market—also are excluded. For example, GDP does not take into account the value of your services when you mow your own lawn or do your own home repairs. Instead, these activities are counted only when they are done for pay outside the home. For this reason, services that homemakers provide are excluded from GDP even though they would amount to billions of dollars annually if actually purchased in the market.

Finally, transactions that occur in the **underground economy**—economic activities that are not reported for legal or tax collection purposes—are not counted in GDP. Some of these activities are illegal, such as those found in gambling, smuggling, prostitution, and the drug trade. Other activities are legal, such as those in flea markets, farmers' markets, garage sales, or bake sales, but they involve cash payments, which are difficult to trace.

Current GDP vs. Real GDP

Because of the way it is computed, GDP can appear to increase whenever prices go up. For example, if the number of automobiles, replacement tires, and other products in Figure 12.1 stays the same from one year to the next while prices go up, GDP will go up every year. Therefore, in order to make accurate comparisons over time, GDP must be adjusted for inflation.

To do so, economists use a set of constant prices in a **base year**—a year that serves as the basis of comparison for all

"Sure, I'll buy a watch. You take plastic?"

Underground Economy
Although there is no consensus on the size of the underground economy, estimates suggest that it is between 5 and 15 percent of the recorded GDP. *What activities make up the underground economy?*

---

intermediate products products that are components of other final products included in GDP

secondhand sales sales of used goods not included in GDP

nonmarket transaction economic activity not taking place in the market and, therefore, not included in GDP

underground economy unreported legal and illegal activities that do not show up in GDP statistics

base year year serving as point of comparison for other years in a price index or other statistical measure

CHAPTER 12 Macroeconomic Performance **321**

C Critical Thinking

Formulating Questions Have students create a 5-question quiz about gross domestic product based on the text on this page. Questions should cover the main points about GDP. Have students exchange quizzes with a partner. With textbooks closed, each student should then take the quiz his or her partner created. **OL**

S Skill Practice

Making Predictions Ask: What would happen if a nation counted the sales of used items in its GDP? Of nonmarket transactions? *(GDP totals would be artificially inflated; the inaccurate information would prevent the nation from effectively addressing its economic concerns.)* **OL**

Caption Answer: illegal activities such as gambling, smuggling, and other crimes; some legal activities, such as garage sales, bake sales, or farmers' markets, which involve cash payments that are hard to trace

Additional Support

Activity: Hands-On Economics

Examining the Underground Economy
Remind students that the GDP might be larger by 5 to 15 percent if underground transactions were tracked and included. Ask students to analyze ways to decrease the amount of activity in the underground economy. Note suggestions on the board. *(Suggestions may include lower taxes, increased policing of underground economic activities, or harsher penalties for those taking part in* underground economic activities.*)* Have students also address the issue of what kinds of responses those taking part in underground economic activities might make to these suggested policy changes. Have students use the information discussed to write a letter to their member of Congress on ways to address the problem of the underground economy. **OL**

C Critical Thinking

Synthesizing Ask: Why is per capita GDP a better measure of a country's prosperity than total GDP? *(Per capita GDP describes the average prosperity of each person, while total GDP says nothing about the share of the prosperity of an individual person; larger countries may have higher total GDPs, but if the individual's per capita GDP is lower than that of an individual in a smaller country, that person has a lower standard of living.)* **OL**

S Skill Practice

Using Tables and Charts
Have students explain what would happen to the line showing current GDP if the economy experienced a period of deflation, or falling prices. *(The line would be artificially flattened.)* **OL**

Economic Analysis

Answer: current GDP

---

real GDP gross domestic product after adjustments for inflation

current GDP gross domestic product measured in current prices, unadjusted for inflation

GDP per capita gross domestic product on a per person basis; can be expressed in current or constant dollars

Skills Handbook
See page **R56** to learn about *Understanding Nominal and Real Values.*

other years. For example, if we compute GDP over a period of time using only prices that existed in 2000, then any increases in GDP must be due to changes in the quantity column and cannot be caused by changes in the price column.

This measure is called **real GDP**, or GDP measured with a set of constant base year prices. In contrast, the terms *GDP, current dollar GDP, nominal GDP,* and **current GDP** all mean that the output in any given year was measured using the prices that existed in those years. Because these prices change from one year to the next, nominal or current GDP is not adjusted for inflation.

When the two series are plotted together, as in **Figure 12.2**, you can see that real GDP grows more slowly than current GDP. The difference in growth rates occurs because current GDP reflects the distortions of inflation. The U.S. Department of Commerce uses 2000 as the base year, so the two series are equal in that year. The U.S. Department of

Commerce updates the base year in four-year increments and will eventually switch to 2004, but only after a substantial lag. Any other year would work just as well.

GDP per Capita

There may be times when we want to adjust GDP for population. For example, we may want to see how the economy of a country is growing over time, or how the output of one country compares to that of another. If so, we use **GDP per capita**, or GDP divided by the population, to get the amount of output on a per person basis. Per capita GDP can be computed on a current or constant basis.

Limitations of GDP

Despite GDP's advantages, there are several limitations to keep in mind. First, by itself GDP tells us nothing about the composition of output. If GDP increases

Figure 12.2 ▶ **Current GDP and Real GDP**

Source: Bureau of Economic Analysis, U.S. Department of Commerce

▶ Because prices tend to rise over time, current GDP rises faster than real GDP, which uses a constant set of prices to value the output in every year.

Economic Analysis *Which series is distorted by inflation?*

Differentiated Instruction

Math Practice for Economics, p. 24

Computing Per Capita Gross Domestic Product (GDP)

Objective: Compute a nation's per capita GDP.

Focus/Teach: Explain that the definition of *per capita* is "per person." Discuss why per capita calculations are significant. Have students fill in the table and answer the questions in the activity.

Assess: Go over the correct answers with the class.

Close: Have each student write a paragraph explaining how per capita GDP and life expectancy are related.

Differentiated Instruction Strategies

BL Have students rank all 12 nations based on their per capita GDP.

AL Have students complete the activity again with data for 10 other nations.

ELL Ask: In which other areas would per capita measurements be of interest to economists? *(income, food, and so on)*

The Global Economy & YOU

World GDP

Why should you be concerned about the size of the U.S. economy or that of other countries? A healthy U.S. economy means manufacturing and employment increase, tax revenues go up, and the standard of living improves. When the economies of other countries also do well, they are better able to purchase products that American firms export, which further improves the U.S. economy.

How big is the U.S. economy, and how big is the world economy? One way to find out is to look at GDP. According to economists at the Central Intelligence Agency (CIA), the United States accounted for one out of every five dollars of output produced worldwide in 2005. The 25 countries in the European Union had a GDP only slightly lower. China, the world's third-largest economy, produced 13.7 percent, or more than one-eighth, of total

Country	GDP (in billions)	Percentage of World GDP
United States	$12,410	20.8%
China	$8,182	13.7%
Japan	$3,914	6.6%
India	$3,699	6.2%
Germany	$2,454	4.1%
United Kingdom	$1,869	3.1%
France	$1,822	3.0%
Italy	$1,651	2.8%
Brazil	$1,568	2.6%
European Union	$12,180	20.4%
World	$59,590	100.0%

Source: www.cia.gov/cia/publication/factbook/rankorder

world output. This means that GDP for the remaining countries in the world was less than half of world GDP.

---

by $10 billion, for example, we know that production is growing and that jobs and income are generated, so we are likely to view the growth as a good thing. However, we might feel differently if we discovered that the extra output consisted of military nerve gas stockpiles rather than new libraries and parks.

Second, GDP also tells little about the impact of production on the quality of life. The construction of 10,000 new homes may appear to be good for the economy. However, if the homes threaten a wildlife refuge, the value of the homes may be viewed differently. In practice, GDP does not take into account quality of life issues, so it is helpful to be aware of such matters to gain a better understanding of GDP.

Finally, some GDP is produced to control activities that give us little utility or satisfaction, thus making GDP even larger. The money spent to fight crime is one example. If we had less crime, our GDP might actually be smaller because of lower government spending to control it—leaving us better off as well.

W

A Measure of Economic Performance and Well-Being

Even with these minor limitations, GDP is still our best measure of overall economic performance and well-being, because it is a measure of the voluntary transactions that take place in the market. Voluntary transactions occur only when both parties in a transaction think they are better off after they have made it than before. This is one reason why GDP is considered an indicator of our overall economic health.

Changes in GDP even influence national elections. Whenever the economy is growing slowly or contracting, the political party in power usually does not fare as well as it would have during a time of economic growth. Economic growth, as measured by increases in real GDP, means that jobs are plentiful and that incomes are rising. Such economic trends often influence the decisions of voters. As a result, GDP is the single most important economic statistic compiled today.

C

✓ **Reading Check** **Explaining** What does GDP measure, and why is it important?

CHAPTER 12 Macroeconomic Performance **323**

W **Writing Support**

Expository Writing Have students write a short essay, intended for younger students, that explains the weaknesses of GDP as a measure of the nation's economic health. Remind them to provide a general background of the subject and use language and examples that younger people would readily understand. Have volunteers read their explanations to the class. **OL**

C **Critical Thinking**

Speculating **Ask:** How do you think the current economic situation will affect the next election? Why? *(Answers will vary depending on the current economy but should note that economic issues and people's perceptions about them influence voting patterns.)* **OL**

✓ **Reading Check** **Answer:** It represents the dollar value of all final goods, services, and structures produced in a country during a year; it is the most accurate gauge we have of a country's economic health.

Leveled Activities

BL **Reinforcing Economic Skills, p. 2**

OL **Economic Concepts Transparencies, Strategies, and Activities, p. 25**

AL **Primary and Secondary Source Readings, p. 35**

R Reading Strategy

Making Connections Ask:
How do you and your family affect the measurements that economists use to evaluate the U.S. economy? *(Wages that students, siblings, parents, and other family members earn are counted as personal income. This total is then added to the national income for the United States.)* **OL**

S Skill Practice

Analyzing Information Have students compute their weekly or monthly disposable personal income. Have them review how to find it. Then have them estimate how they dispose of this amount. **OL**

✓Reading Check **Answer:**
gross national product, net national product, national income, personal income, and disposable personal income

Additional Support

---

gross national product (GNP) total dollar value of all final goods, services, and structures produced in one year with labor and property supplied by a country's residents, regardless of where the production takes place

net national product (NNP) GNP less depreciation charges for wear and tear on capital equipment

national income (NI) net national product less indirect business taxes

personal income (PI) total amount of income going to the consumer sector before individual income taxes are paid

disposable personal income (DPI) personal income less individual income taxes

---

GNP—The Measure of National Income

MAIN Idea National income can be measured in a number of different ways

Economics and You Have you ever wondered about the deductions on your pay stub? Read on to find out how your net pay is part of an economic measure.

Whenever business activity creates output, it generates jobs and income for someone. GDP, then, is like a two-sided coin, where one side represents output and the other side an equal amount of income. If we want to see how much output is produced, we look at one side of the coin. If we want to see how much income is generated, we look at the other side of the coin. Economists recognize one major category and several subcategories of national income.

Gross National Product

When economists focus on total income rather than output, they measure it with **gross national product (GNP)**—the dollar value of all final goods, services, and structures produced in one year with labor and property owned by a country's residents. While GDP measures the value of all the final goods and services produced within U.S. borders, GNP measures the income of all Americans, whether the goods and services are produced in the United States or in other countries.

To go from GDP to GNP, we add all payments that Americans receive from outside the United States, then subtract the payments made to all foreign-owned businesses located in the United States. The result, GNP, is the most comprehensive measure of our nation's income.

Net National Product

The second measure of national income is **net national product (NNP)**, or GNP less depreciation. Depreciation is also called

capital consumption allowances. It represents the capital equipment that wore out or became obsolete during the year.

National Income

The third measure in the NIPA is **national income (NI)**. National income is the income that is left after all taxes except the corporate profits tax are subtracted from NNP. Examples of these taxes, also known as indirect business taxes, are excise taxes, property taxes, licensing fees, customs duties, and general sales taxes.

Personal Income

The fourth measure of the nation's total income is **personal income (PI)**—the total amount of income going to consumers before individual income taxes are subtracted. To go from national to personal income, several adjustments must be made. For example, personal income would not include payments into the Social Security fund that working people make. It would include Social Security checks that retired individuals receive.

Disposable Personal Income

The fifth measure of income in the NIPA is **disposable personal income (DPI)**—the total income the consumer sector has at its disposal after personal income taxes. Although it is the smallest measure of income, it is important because it reflects the actual amount of money consumers are able to spend.

At the individual level, a person's disposable income is equal to the amount of money received from an employer after taxes and Social Security have been taken out. When you look at the pay stub that is illustrated in Figure 9.6 on page 248, the disposable personal income consists of the $586.89 net pay on the check plus the $3.20 of deductions which the individual chose to make.

✓Reading Check **Summarizing** What are the different measures of national income?

Activity: Collaborative Learning

Graphing Information Tell students:
The Census Bureau collects information on personal income groups for large metropolitan areas in the United States. Then organize students into several groups, and have them use the most recent print edition or Web site edition of the *Statistical Abstract of the United States* to find the top 10 metropolitan areas in terms of personal income. Have them note how personal income has changed for these metropolitan areas over time. Then have groups present their findings in annotated graph form. Encourage groups to display and discuss their graphs. **OL**

Economic Sectors and Circular Flows

MAIN Idea The production of output generates income which flows though different sectors of the economy.

Economics and You Have you ever thought about your role as a consumer? Read on to find out how consumers are part of an economic model.

It helps to think of the economy as consisting of several different parts, or sectors. These sectors receive various **components** of the national income, which they then use

to purchase the total output. These sectors are part of the circular flow of economic activity illustrated in **Figure 12.3**.

Income generated by production flows to the business, government, and consumer sectors. These sectors then use the income to purchase the nation's output.

Consumer Sector

The largest sector in the economy is the consumer, or household, sector. Its basic unit, the **household**, consists of all persons who occupy a house, apartment, or room that constitutes separate living quarters. **R**

> **household** basic unit of consumer sector consisting of all persons who occupy a house, apartment, or separate living quarters

Figure 12.3 ▶ Circular Flow of Economic Activity

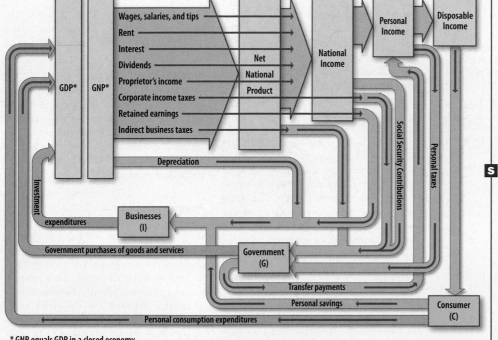

* GNP equals GDP in a closed economy.

▶ Income generated by production flows to the business, government, and consumer sectors. These sectors then use the income to purchase the nation's output.

Economic Analysis *What is the difference between national income and personal income?*

Charts In MOtion
See StudentWorks™ Plus or glencoe.com.

R **Reading Strategy**

Making Connections

Ask students to suggest ways that consumers as a whole can affect the nation's economy. *(buying decisions, savings patterns, living arrangements, and so on)* Have them explain their answers. Also ask them to identify the section of the circular flow chart where these activities are located. *(the bottom of the chart)* **OL**

S **Skill Practice**

Visual Literacy Ask: What expenditures make up gross domestic product? *(personal consumption expenditures, government purchases of goods and services, and investment expenditures)* **OL**

Economic Analysis

Answer: National income is the income that is left after all taxes except corporate profits tax are subtracted from the net national product; personal income is the total amount of income going to consumers before individual income taxes are subtracted.

Additional Support

Extending the Content

Three Kinds of Consumption National income accounting records three classifications of consumption in the consumer sector. Durable goods are goods with an average life of more than three years; examples are automobiles, furniture, and appliances. Nondurable goods are goods that have an average life of less than three years: shampoo, food products, gasoline, and clothing, for example. Services, such as financial or legal advice, health care, and

haircuts, make up the final classification of consumption. In some cases the classifications seem arbitrary. A well-made coat may last for five to ten years, and a large bottle of hot pepper sauce could sit in some refrigerators for more than three years. Nevertheless, an item of clothing and a kind of food are both regarded as nondurable goods.

W Writing Support

Narrative Writing Have students write a story describing an item they or their family owned that experienced depreciation. Stories should explain the rate of the depreciation and approximate estimates of the value of the item before and after depreciation. **OL**

R Reading Strategy

Summarizing Ask: Why might the foreign sector appear to be insignificant when, in fact, large numbers of goods and services may be traded? *(If imports and exports are about equal, the foreign sector [the difference between the two] of the economy will appear small.)* **OL**

Caption Answer: consumer, government, foreign

✓Reading Check Answer: A household consists of all persons who occupy a living place, while a family is a group of two or more persons related by blood, marriage, or adoption living in the same place.

Hands-On Chapter Project

Step 1

Evaluating an Economy

In this project, students will create a fictional nation with figures on national income, population, economic growth, and poverty. Students will create an economic status report using these statistics.

Step 1: Measuring National Income. Students will create statistics that indicate the national income of a fictional country.

Directions: Organize the class into five different groups, each representing a

Investment Sector Businesses such as this auto manu-facturer that produce the nation's output are included in the investment sector. *What other sectors are part of the circular flow of economic activity?*

unrelated individual person living alone even though that person may have relatives living elsewhere

family two or more persons living together who are related by blood, marriage, or adoption

Households include related family members and all others—such as lodgers, foster children, and employees—who share the living quarters.

A household also can consist of an **unrelated individual**—a person who lives alone even though he or she may have family living elsewhere. Finally, we have the **family**—a group of two or more persons related by blood, marriage, or adoption who are living together in a household.

The consumer sector, shown as **C** in Figure 12.3, receives its income in the form of disposable personal income. This is the income that is left over after all of the depreciation, business and income taxes, and FICA payments are taken out, and after any income received in transfer payments is added back in.

Investment Sector

The next sector of the macro economy is the business, or investment, sector, which is labeled **I** in Figure 12.3. This sector is made up of proprietorships, partnerships, and corporations that are responsible for producing the nation's output. The income of this sector comes from the retained earnings—the profits not paid out to owners—

that are subtracted from NI and the **W** depreciation or capital consumption allowances that are subtracted from GNP.

Government Sector

The third sector is the public sector, which includes all local, state, and federal levels of government. Shown as **G** in Figure 12.3, this sector receives its income from indirect business taxes, corporate income taxes, Social Security contributions, and individual income taxes.

Foreign Sector

The fourth sector of the macro economy is the foreign sector. Although not shown in Figure 12.3, it includes all consumers and producers outside the United States.

R This sector does not have a specific source of income. Instead, it represents the difference between the dollar value of goods sent abroad and that of goods purchased from abroad, identified as **(X – M)**. If the two are reasonably close, the foreign sector appears to be small, even when large numbers of goods and services are traded.

✓Reading Check Contrasting How do households and families differ?

326   UNIT 4   Macroeconomics: Performance and Stabilization

fictional country. Assign each of the groups a letter: A, B, C, D, F. The letter assigned to them represents the "grade" of their nation's economy (for example, the nation of the "A" group could be a thriving industrial powerhouse; the nation of the "F" group could be an impoverished single-crop country). Have students come up with a name for their fictional nation and numbers for the five major statistical categories described in this section. Statistics should reflect an understanding of the concepts of this section, as well as the grade assigned

to the nation (for example, the "D" country should have a relatively low GDP). Encourage groups to come up with brief creative explanations for their figures (for example, labor unrest weakened GDP; lower taxes increased PI). Ask each student group to use the numbers they generated to create graphics like the ones on pages 320 and 322.

Summarizing Have students write a short essay summarizing how economists measure the performance of a nation's economy. **OL**

(Chapter Project continued in Section 2.)

The Output-Expenditure Model

MAIN Idea The output-expenditure model is used to explain aggregate economic activity.

Economics and You Have you learned in math class how to write a problem as an equation? Read on to learn how this can be done in economics.

The circular flow can be represented by the **output-expenditure model.** This macroeconomic model shows how GDP is equal to the sum of aggregate demand by the consumer, investment, government, and foreign sectors. When written as

$$GDP = C + I + G + (X - M)$$

the equation becomes a formal output-expenditure model used to explain and analyze the economy's performance.

According to this model, the consumer sector spends its income on the goods and services used by households. These personal consumption expenditures include groceries, rent, and almost anything else people buy. Income that is not spent appears as personal saving, which is borrowed by the business and government sectors.

The investment, or business, sector spends its income on labor, factories, equipment, inventories, and other investment goods. These expenditures include the total value of capital goods created in the economy during the year.

The government sector spends its income on many categories, including national defense, income security, interest on the national debt, health care, and roads. The only major government expenditure not included in total output is transfer payments, because this money is diverted for use by others to buy goods and services.

The foreign sector also buys many U.S. goods—such as tractors, airplanes, and agricultural products—and services—such as insurance—that make up our GDP. In return, it supplies products—such as Japanese cars, Korean steel, and Brazilian shoes—to U.S. consumers. For this reason, the foreign sector's purchases are called **net exports of goods and services**. They are abbreviated as (X – M) to reflect the difference between exports and imports.

✓**Reading Check** **Describing** How does the foreign sector fit into the output-expenditure model?

output-expenditure model macroeconomic model describing aggregate demand by the consumer, investment, government, and foreign sectors

net exports of goods and services net expenditures by the foreign sector; equal to total exports less total imports

S **Skill Practice**

Using Tables and Charts
Have students construct a table describing the four sectors that make up GDP, using the information on this page and elsewhere in the section. **OL**

✓**Reading Check** **Answer:** It represents the difference in dollar values between goods and services imported and exported, or *(X – M)*, and includes all consumers and producers in a country.

Assess

Use the Interactive Tutor Self-Assessment CD-ROM to review Section 1, and then assign the Section 1 Review as homework or as an in-class activity.

Close

Outlining Have students create an outline for this section. Suggest that they use the headings as the main entries for their outline and the main ideas within the entries as supporting details. **OL**

SECTION 1 Review

Vocabulary
1. **Explain** the significance of macroeconomics, gross domestic product, intermediate products, secondhand sales, nonmarket transactions, underground economy, base year, real GDP, current GDP, GDP per capita, gross national product, net national product, national income, personal income, disposable personal income, household, unrelated individual, family, output-expenditure model, and net exports of goods and services.

Main Ideas
2. **Comparing** Use a graphic organizer like the one below to compare GDP and GNP.

| GDP | → | plus:
less:
GNP |

3. **Stating** What is the circular flow of economic activity?

Critical Thinking
4. **The BIG Ideas** Explain why GDP is important to economists.
5. **Synthesizing Information** Describe the limitations of GDP.
6. **Analyzing Visuals** Use Figure 12.3 on page 325 to describe how your personal spending and saving contribute to the circular flow of economic activity.
7. **Drawing Conclusions** What would be the effects of a decline in GDP?

Applying Economics
8. **Gross Domestic Product** What effect do you think the computer industry has had on GDP? Use examples.

CHAPTER 12 Macroeconomic Performance **327**

Review SECTION 1

Answers

1. All definitions can be found in the section and the Glossary.
2. Both GDP and GNP measure the value of final goods and services produced in a single year. GDP measures goods and services produced inside the United States, while GNP measures all products made with labor and property supplied by U.S. residents, no matter where the production takes place.
3. the constant circulation of money that flows to the business, government, and consumer sectors; these sectors then use the income to purchase the nation's output
4. Because it represents the dollar value of all final goods, services, and structures produced in a country during a year, it is the most accurate gauge we have of a country's economic health.
5. GDP does not identify the composition of the output, it tells little about the impact of the production on the quality of life, and it excludes some economic activity.
6. Consumers' disposable income becomes personal expenditures, which is counted as a part of GDP.
7. A decline in GDP would mean that fewer transactions are taking place, so people and firms do not feel better off. If severe enough, this could lead to a change in political leadership.
8. Most students will recognize that computer companies, such as Microsoft, Intel, and Cisco, contribute huge amounts to the GDP.

327

Teach

C Critical Thinking

Evaluating Guide a class discussion by asking students the following questions: *Is it the role of government to shape people's values? Would Galbraith's plan work? Who would decide which values the government would endorse? Is individual wealth wrong? Does it necessarily lead to a neglect of public projects?* Conclude by having students decide whether Galbraith's ideas are in general favor today, and in what ways. **OL**

Examining the Profile

Answers:

1. He favored public projects over individual wealth and believed that corporations convinced people to buy goods they really didn't need.

2. **Possible answer:** A person might view positively the results of government intervention to right the nation's economy.

Additional Support

Galbraith attended college during the early years of the Great Depression. His experiences taught him to question accepted theories and challenge what he called "conventional wisdom."

John Kenneth Galbraith (1908–2006)

- advocated public works funding in *The Affluent Society*
- served as economic adviser to five presidents

Iconoclast Economist

Shaped by his experiences during the Great Depression, John Kenneth Galbraith believed in the government's ability to solve problems. Early in his career, he also developed a love of writing and an engaging, witty style. This turned the Harvard professor of economics into the most widely read American economist of his generation and turned his books into bestsellers.

Galbraith developed a reputation as an iconoclast—a person willing to challenge accepted belief. Other economists objected to the liberal ideas Galbraith promoted. For example, in his classic *The Affluent Society,* Galbraith argued that Americans needed to reconsider their values. The U.S. economy had resulted in individual wealth, while public projects such as education and highways were neglected or underfunded. According to Galbraith, Americans were "artificially affluent" because corporations convinced people to buy goods they did not want or need. Government regulation of prices on certain goods would steer Americans away from spending and help them refocus on more important matters, such as attaining an education or appreciating culture.

Presidential Influence

Unlike most other economists, Galbraith was able to apply his economic theories in the social and political arenas. As an adviser to presidents Franklin Roosevelt, Harry Truman, John Kennedy, Lyndon Johnson, and Bill Clinton, Galbraith was a major force in directing the Democratic Party's economic platform. Under President Roosevelt, he administered wage and price controls in the Office of Price Administration. His most direct influence, though, is reflected in President Johnson's "war on poverty," which incorporated many of Galbraith's ideas, and increased funding for public works projects.

Examining the Profile

1. **Making Inferences** Which viewpoint made Galbraith an iconoclast to other economists?
2. **Drawing Conclusions** How might living through the Great Depression lead to liberal economic thought?

Extending the Content

A Gift for Words It wasn't only his height of six feet eight inches that made John Kenneth Galbraith the most famous economist of his generation. His wit and gift for expressing ideas in colorful language also made him well known. Among his witticisms are these:

- Economics is extremely useful as a form of employment for economists.

- It is a far, far better thing to have a firm anchor in nonsense than to put out on the troubled sea of thought.
- Under capitalism man exploits man. Under communism, it's just the opposite.
- If all else fails, immortality can always be assured by spectacular error.
- The only function of economic forecasting is to make astrology look respectable.

2 Population and Economic Growth

GUIDE TO READING

Section Preview
We are interested in population because it makes up the economy's largest sector, the consumer sector, and affects the economic performance of a nation.

Content Vocabulary
- census *(p. 329)*
- urban population *(p. 330)*
- rural population *(p. 330)*
- center of population *(p. 331)*
- infrastructure *(p. 332)*
- baby boom *(p. 332)*
- population pyramid *(p. 333)*
- dependency ratio *(p. 333)*
- demographers *(p. 334)*
- fertility rate *(p. 334)*
- life expectancy *(p. 334)*
- net immigration *(p. 334)*

Academic Vocabulary
- residence *(p. 329)*
- projected *(p. 334)*

Reading Strategy
Identifying As you read the section, complete a graphic organizer like the one below by identifying changes in the United States in the listed categories.

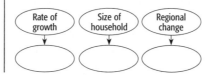

Rate of growth → ⬭   Size of household → ⬭   Regional change → ⬭

ISSUES IN THE NEWS
—U.S. Census Bureau

Census Bureau Selects Sites for Census Dress Rehearsal

San Joaquin County, Calif., and the city of Fayetteville, N.C., and surrounding area . . . have been selected by the U.S. Census Bureau to serve in 2008 as the dress rehearsal sites for the 2010 Census. . . .

San Joaquin County [is] an urban location with a multilingual population and an assortment of group quarters housing such as hospitals, college residence halls, nursing homes, prisons and facilities for the homeless. . . .

The Fayetteville site [has] a mix of . . . urban, suburban and rural areas and has two military bases (Fort Bragg and Pope Air Force Base). ■

Population is important for a number of reasons. First, a country's population is the source of its labor, one of the four factors of production. Second, the population is the primary consumer of the nation's output and has a direct effect on how much is produced. Because of this, the size, composition, and rate of growth of a country's population has an impact on macroeconomic performance.

The Constitution of the United States requires the government to periodically take a **census,** an official count of all people living in the United States, including their place of **residence.** Because the official census occurs every 10 years, it is called the decennial census. As you can see in the news story, the U.S. Census Bureau begins making plans for the decennial census several years ahead of time.

census complete count of population, including place of residence

CHAPTER 12 Macroeconomic Performance **329**

Focus

Bellringer
Daily Focus Transparency 53

GUIDE TO READING

Answers to Graphic:

Rate of growth: has slowed

Size of household: has shrunk

Regional change: center of population has moved to the Southwest

Resource Manager

R Reading Strategies	C Critical Thinking	D Differentiated Instruction	W Writing Support	S Skill Practice
Teacher Edition • Skimming, p. 330 • Making Connections, p. 332 • Monitoring, p. 334 **Additional Resources** • Guid. Read. Act., p. 35 • Read. Ess. & Note-Taking Guide, p. 103	**Teacher Edition** • Speculating, p. 331 • Compare/Contrast, p. 334 • Predicting, p. 335 • Evaluating, p. 336 **Additional Resources** • Econ. Cont. Vocab. Act., p. 12	**Teacher Edition** • ELL, p. 330 • Intrapersonal, p. 333 **Additional Resources** • Enrichment Act., p. 12 • Quizzes and Tests, p. 150	**Teacher Edition** • Personal Writing, p. 332 • Expository Writing, p. 336 **Additional Resources** • Writer's Guidebook	**Teacher Edition** • Synthesizing Info., p. 331 • Using Bar and Circle Graphs, p. 333 **Additional Resources** • Reteach. Act., p. 12

Teach

D Differentiated Instruction

English Language Learners
Have students write a business letter or e-mail to the U.S. Census Bureau requesting information on how census information is gathered and analyzed. Have volunteers share their letters. **ELL**

R Reading Strategy

Skimming Students who have trouble reading a passage may benefit from skimming it before reading to develop a timeframe for the events or ideas that are presented. Have students skim the subsection "Historical Growth" for time markers such as "between 1790 and 1960" and "from the beginning of the Civil War until 1900." Ask students to point out other similar markers in other subsections. **BL**

Caption Answer: track population growth, identify trends, predict future developments

Additional Support

---

urban population those persons living in incorporated cities, towns, and villages with 2,500 or more inhabitants

rural population those persons not living in urban areas

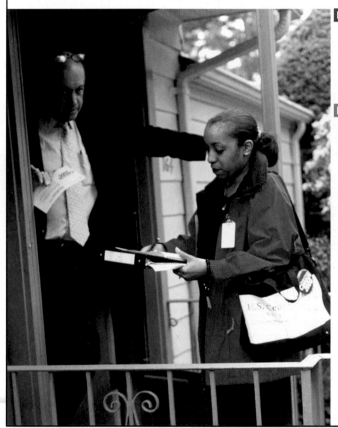

Census Some census workers interview a select group of people in person. *How are census data used?*

Population in the United States

MAIN Idea The country's population has shifted from a fast-growing, mostly rural population to a slower-growing, mostly urban one.

Economics and You Have you ever wondered how we know the size of the U.S. population? Read on to learn how it is measured.

One of the original uses of the census was to apportion the number of representatives that each state elects to Congress. Ever since, the census has given us a wealth of data about our nation, and we even use it to make projections into the future.

Counting the Population

The federal government conducted the first census in 1790. Throughout the 1800s, it created temporary agencies each decade to do the counting. In 1902, Congress permanently established the U.S. Census Bureau. Today, the Bureau works year-round, conducting monthly surveys relating to the size and other characteristics of the population.

When the Census Bureau conducted the last decennial census, it used the household as its primary survey unit. In this census, about five in every six households received a "short form," which took just a few minutes to fill out. The remaining households received a "long form," which included more questions and served to generate a more detailed profile of the population. Bureau employees also used different methods to count special groups, such as homeless persons, who do not normally conform to the household survey unit.

The Census Bureau tabulates and presents its data in a number of ways. One such classification considers the size of the **urban population**—people living in incorporated cities, villages, or towns with 2,500 or more inhabitants. The **rural population** makes up the remainder of the total, including those persons who live in sparsely populated areas along the fringes of cities.

R Historical Growth

The population of the United States has grown considerably since colonial times. The rate of growth, however, has slowly declined. Between 1790 and 1860, the population grew at a compounded rate of about 3.0 percent a year. From the beginning of the Civil War until 1900, the average fell to 2.2 percent. From 1900 to the beginning of World War II, the rate dropped to 1.4 percent. The rate of increase declined slowly but steadily after that, and today the rate of population growth is less than 1.0 percent annually.

The census also shows a steady trend toward smaller households. During colonial times, household size averaged about 5.8 people. By 1960, the average had fallen to 3.3 and today is about 2.6 people. The figures reflect a worldwide trend toward

---

Activity: Hands-On Economics

Analyzing Census and Other Government Economic Data Census information can be valuable to the small, private businesses that are so important to the growth and success of the American free enterprise economy. Ask students to choose a particular small business, such as a restaurant, lawn-care service, or movie-rental store. Then have students consult the print edition or Web site edition of the *Statistical Abstract of the United States* or census data publications and look for trends in your region. You may want to have students brainstorm a suitable list of relevant questions to research, such as: *Is the population increasing? By how much? In what age groups and other categories? Is the number of businesses increasing? What kinds of businesses? Is any kind of business decreasing? Is disposable personal income increasing? Is sales volume increasing?* Have students write a paragraph, based on the data they find, explaining why they would or would not recommend that a friend enter the selected business. **OL**

Figure 12.4 ▶ Center of Population, 1790–2000

Maps In Motion
See StudentWorks™ Plus
or glencoe.com.

▶ The center of population is the point where the country would balance if the map were flat and every person weighed the same.

Economic Analysis *Why has the center moved since the first census was conducted in 1790?*

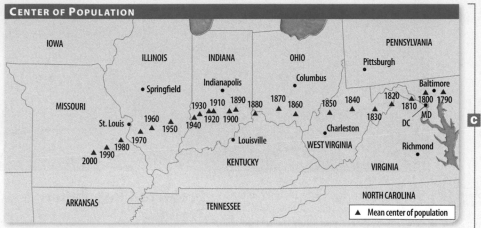

CENTER OF POPULATION

▲ Mean center of population

Source: U.S. Census Bureau

smaller families in industrialized countries. The figures also show that more individuals are living alone today than ever before.

Regional Change

An important population shift began in the 1970s with a migration to the western and southern parts of the United States. These regions have grown quite rapidly, while most of the older industrial areas in the North and East have grown more slowly or even lost population. As people have left the crowded, industrial Northeast for warmer, more spacious parts of the country, the population in states such as Nevada, Arizona, Colorado, Utah, Idaho, Georgia, and Florida has been increasing steadily.

Another indicator of population shift is the **center of population**—the point where the country would balance if it could be laid flat and everyone weighed the same.

In 1790, the center was 23 miles east of Baltimore, Maryland. Since then, as you can see in **Figure 12.4,** it has moved farther west. By the 2000 decennial census, the center of population had reached a point about 2.8 miles east of Edgar Springs, Missouri.

Consequences of Growth

Changes in population can distort some macroeconomic measures like GDP and GNP. As a result, both measures are often expressed on a per capita, or per person, basis. One result is GDP per capita, which is determined by dividing GDP by the population. GDP per capita is especially useful when making comparisons between countries.

Population growth can have several consequences. If a nation's population grows faster than its output, per capita output grows more slowly, and the country could

center of population point where the country would balance if it were flat and everyone weighed the same

CHAPTER 12 Macroeconomic Performance **331**

C Critical Thinking

Speculating Ask students to speculate on how the center of population is found. *(Many students will recognize that the area of the country is compared mathematically with the population and the population's location to find the theoretical center.)* **AL**

S Skill Practice

Synthesizing Information

Ask: What are some reasons Americans are moving to the Sun Belt, the name for the western and southern parts of the United States? Have students discuss suggested reasons. Then ask them to rank the reasons in importance for (1) most people, and (2) themselves. *(Possible reasons may include climate, job opportunities, or desire to be near relatives. Students' rankings will vary.)* **OL**

Economic Analysis

Answer: The places where Americans live, along with the nation's boundaries, have changed, moving westward and southward.

Additional Support

Activity: Interdisciplinary Connection

Music Play for students a recording of Bruce Springsteen's song about Sun Belt migration, "My Hometown," from his 1984 album *Born in the USA* (or ask a musical student to perform the song). Tell students that Bruce Springsteen is from New Jersey and is known for his songs about working-class life. Have students read the lyrics and discuss the issues the song raises in the context of migration to western and southern parts of the country from the North and East. **Ask:** What might "Rust Belt" states do to prevent workers from leaving for more promising employment opportunities in the Sun Belt? *(Answers will vary, but students may suggest tax breaks for residents and tax incentives for new businesses.)* **OL**

W Writing Support

Personal Writing Have students write a letter to the editor of a local newspaper taking and supporting a position, pro or con, on this statement: *If our society does not significantly increase its spending on infrastructure, our economic well-being will be threatened.* **OL**

R Reading Strategy

Making Connections Have students list three ways in which population trends are used. Then have them give examples of each trend from history or current events, either locally or nationally. **OL**

Caption Answer: resources such as fresh water can become scarcer; infrastructure is stressed

✓Reading Check Answer: population has grown enormously, households have become smaller, the center of population has shifted to the West and South

Urban Sprawl When the population grows, it results in heavier traffic. *What are other effects of population growth?*

Economics ONLINE

Student Web Activity Visit the *Economics: Principles and Practices* Web site at glencoe.com and click on *Chapter 12–Student Web Activities* for an activity about population trends.

infrastructure the highways, mass transit, communications, power, water, sewerage, and other public goods needed to support a population

baby boom historically high birthrate years in the United States from 1946 to 1964

end up with more mouths than it can feed. On the other hand, if a nation's population grows too slowly, there may not be enough workers to sustain economic growth. In addition, a growing population puts more demand on resources.

When a growing population shifts toward certain areas, such as cities or suburbs, it puts different pressures on existing resources. In Atlanta, Georgia, for example, urban sprawl and traffic congestion have become major problems. In heavily populated areas of Arizona, Nevada, and southern California, adequate supplies of fresh water have become concerns.

W Because it takes a long time to plan and construct a country's **infrastructure**—the highways, levees, mass transit, communications systems, electricity, water, sewer, and other public goods needed to support a population—we need to pay attention to future population trends. If we neglect them, even modest shifts in the population can cause enormous problems in the future.

✓Reading Check Explaining What have been the major population changes since the first census in 1790?

Projected Population Trends

MAIN Idea Fertility, life expectancy, and net immigration influence population trends.

Economics and You Have you considered how immigration affects population growth? Read on to learn how the U.S. population is expected to change.

R Population trends are important to many groups. Political leaders watch population shifts to see how voting patterns may change. Community leaders are interested because changes in local population affect services such as sanitation, education, and fire protection. Businesses use census data to help determine markets for products and sales territories.

Age and Gender

When making its projections, the Census Bureau assumes that the aging generation of baby boomers will drive many characteristics of the population. People born during the **baby boom**, the high birthrate years from 1946 to 1964, make up a sizable portion of the current population. As

Differentiated Instruction

ENRICHMENT Chapter 12

THE POPULATION-ECONOMY CONNECTION

Enrichment Activities, p. 12

The Population-Economy Connection

Objective: Understand the relationship between population and economics.

Focus/Teach: Have students list some ways that an aging population will affect them in the future. Then have students complete the activity.

Assess: Go over students' answers as a class, pausing to discuss any on which there is disagreement.

Close: Ask students how the federal government could prepare for each demographic change.

Differentiated Instruction Strategies

BL Ask: Which of the expected changes will affect you the most? Why?

AL Have students list three businesses they would start, based on the chart answers, and three they would avoid.

ELL Have students make a graph that represents one piece of demographic information in the left-hand column.

shown in **Figure 12.5,** people born during this time span created a significant bulge in the **population pyramid**, a type of bar graph that shows the breakdown of population by age and gender.

The bulge in the middle of the pyramid represents the baby boomers. A second, minor bulge represents the children born to the baby boom generation. As years pass, more births add to the bottom of the pyramid and push earlier groups upward into higher age brackets.

Eventually, the baby boomers will reach their retirement years and want to collect pensions, Social Security, and Medicare benefits. Because most of these payments are transfer payments, they will place a heavy burden on the younger and **D** relatively smaller working population. The burden becomes evident with changes in the **dependency ratio**—the number of children and elderly people in the population for every 100 persons in the working-

age bracket of ages 18 through 64. The dependency ratio was 63.9 in 1998, but according to Census Bureau projections, it will rise to 67.5 by 2020, to 77.5 by 2030, and to 78.0 by 2040.

Finally, if you compare the left side of the population pyramid with the right, you will see that women tend to outlive men. Separate population pyramids can also be created for any racial or ethnic group.

Race and Ethnicity

The Census Bureau also makes projections for racial and ethnic groups. In 2000, whites were the largest component of the total population. The numbers of African Americans, Hispanic Americans, Asian Americans, and Native Americans followed in that order.

Differences in fertility rates, life expectancies, and immigration rates will change the racial statistics dramatically in the future. By 2050, the Asian and Hispanic

population pyramid diagram showing the breakdown of population by age and gender

dependency ratio number of children and elderly people in the population for every 100 persons in the 18 to 64 working-age bracket

D **Differentiated Instruction**

Intrapersonal Have students review the information on the effects of age on the population. Then have them write a few paragraphs on how these population changes will affect them personally. Have students share their ideas with the class. **OL**

S **Skill Practice**

Using Bar and Circle Graphs
Ask: How do you think this bar graph will look in the year 2030? Give reasons to support your predictions. *(Likely changes include the baby boom "bulge" moving higher on the graph, another minor bulge to represent the children of the large baby boomer cadre, and more people living longer due to advances in health care.)* **OL**

Economic Analysis
Answer: 45–49; 45–49

Figure 12.5 ▶ **Projected Distribution of the Population by Age and Gender, 2010**

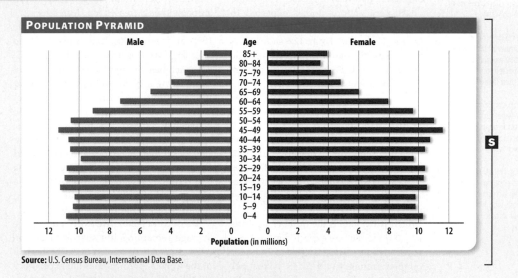

Source: U.S. Census Bureau, International Data Base.

▶ Population pyramids are one way to show the distribution of population. In this pyramid, the population is divided by age and gender.

Economic Analysis *To which age bracket do most males belong? Most females?*

Leveled Activities

BL Reteaching Activities, p. 12

OL Economic Content Vocabulary Activities, p. 12

ELL Guided Reading Activities, p. 35

C Critical Thinking

Comparing and Contrasting

Ask: How would a graph about your own community be similar to or different from the one in the book? Have students explain their reasons for the differences they cite. **OL**

R Reading Strategy

Monitoring To help students understand the material in the subsection on population growth, have them create word webs for each of the three factors that affect population growth: *fertility*, *life expectancy*, and *net immigration levels*. Have students contribute their ideas to webs on the board. **BL**

Economic Analysis

Answer: Asians and Hispanics; whites

Figure 12.6 ▶ Projected Change in U.S. Population by Race and Ethnic Origin, 2000–2050

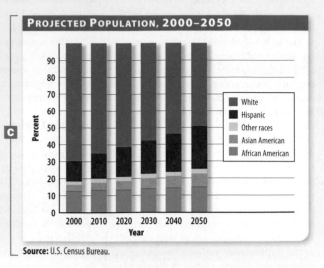

PROJECTED POPULATION, 2000–2050

Legend:
- White
- Hispanic
- Other races
- Asian American
- African American

Source: U.S. Census Bureau.

▶ The distribution of population by race is projected to change dramatically by the year 2050.

Economic Analysis *Which ethnic groups are expected to increase the most? Which will decrease in proportion to the total population?*

---

demographer
person who studies growth, density, and other characteristics of the population

fertility rate
number of births that 1,000 women are expected to undergo in their lifetime

life expectancy
average remaining life span in years for persons who attain a given age

net immigration
net population change after accounting for those who leave as well as enter a country

portions of the population are expected to nearly double. The number of African Americans will also increase. The white non-Hispanic population is expected to remain a majority of the total population at just over 50 percent. **Figure 12.6** shows how the Census Bureau projects the ethnic makeup of the U.S. population to change over the next few decades.

Population Growth

According to **demographers**—people who study the growth, density, and other characteristics of population—three major factors affect population growth. These factors are fertility, life expectancy, and net immigration levels.

The **fertility rate** is the number of births that 1,000 women are expected to undergo in their lifetime. A fertility rate of 2,119, for example, translates to 2.119 births per woman. According to the Bureau of the Census, this rate is **projected** as the most likely fertility rate for the United States. That rate is barely above the replacement

population rate—the rate at which the number of births in a population offsets the number of deaths and the size of the population neither increases nor decreases.

This was not always the case. In the late 1800s and early 1900s, Americans tended to have large families. In the days before modern machines and appliances, the work of maintaining a home and family and earning a living was difficult and time-consuming. Children were needed to do household chores, work on family farms, and bring in additional money from outside jobs. Later, as life became mechanized and fewer people lived on farms, having large families became less important. As a result, the nation's birthrate dropped steadily throughout the last century.

The second factor, **life expectancy,** is the average remaining life span of a person who has reached a given age. The Bureau of the Census predicts that life expectancy at birth will go from about 75.9 years today to 82.1 years by 2050.

The third factor is **net immigration**—the overall change in population caused by

334 **UNIT 4 Macroeconomics: Performance and Stabilization**

Hands-On Chapter Project

Step 2

Evaluating an Economy

Step 2: Examining Population and Economic Growth. Student groups will create statistics that reflect the population and economic growth of a fictional country.

Directions: Have students reassemble into the groups formed in Step 1. For this step, have student groups create a graph like the one on page 333 showing population distribution for the present and for

20 years in the future for their fictional nation. Then have the group produce a press release from the nation's economic ministry about its plans for future economic development, based on the population data and other relevant facts about the economy. The press release should answer the questions *who, what, where, when,* and *how.*

Contrasting Have a few students in the group produce a "dissenting report" that

proposes the nation develop in a different way. Remind students to support their alternative recommendations with economic data. **OL**

(Chapter Project continued in Section 3.)

people moving into and out of the country. The Census Bureau recently estimated a constant net immigration of about 880,000 per year. This figure is based on 1,040,000 immigrants—those entering the country—and 160,000 emigrants—those leaving the country—in the future.

Taking into account these three factors, analysts expect the rate of population growth in the United States to continue to decline. The growth rate, already below 1 percent today, is likely to decrease further until the year 2050. At that time, the resident United States population is expected to be about 420 million people.

Future Population Growth

Most of the demographic factors examined in this section point to a population that is likely to grow more slowly in the future. While this may seem like a matter for concern, it is important to note that increases in productivity can easily offset the negative effects of declining population growth. If slightly fewer people produce significantly more on average, then total output will continue to grow.

The larger concern is the age composition of the future population. As the population matures, a greater percentage of people reach retirement age. This will cause an increase in the demand for medicines, medical facilities, retirement homes, and other products that are needed for the retired and the elderly. At the same time, there may be a declining need for schools, playgrounds, and other facilities as the young become a smaller percentage of the population.

These changes tend to be gradual, and their impact on the economy can be anticipated with some degree of certainty. As you learned in Chapter 2, one of the major advantages of a market economy is that it accommodates change with the least amount of disruption of daily life. **C**

⬛ Skills Handbook
See page **R47** to learn about *Making Predictions*.

✓**Reading Check** **Summarizing** Why is the rate of population growth declining?

C Critical Thinking

Predicting Have students predict and explain possible factors that would change the expected low population growth of the United States over the next 50 years. (*Possible answer: a higher immigration rate due to ecological, economic, or social chaos in other countries*) **OL**

✓**Reading Check** **Answer:** Life expectancy is increasing, and net immigration is not as high as at some periods in the past.

Assess

💿 Use the Interactive Tutor Self-Assessment CD-ROM to review Section 2, and then assign the Section 2 Review as homework or as an in-class activity.

Close

Evaluating Have students identify the population trend that they feel will have the greatest effect on the nation and on your community over the next 25 years. **OL**

SECTION 2 Review

Vocabulary
1. **Explain** the significance of census, urban population, rural population, center of population, infrastructure, baby boom, population pyramid, dependency ratio, demographers, fertility rate, life expectancy, and net immigration.

Main Ideas
2. **Explaining** How does the rate of population growth affect economic growth?

3. **Listing** Use a graphic organizer like the one below to list the three most important factors that determine future population.

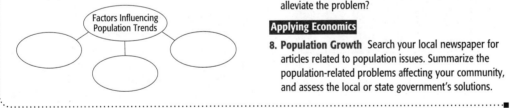

Factors Influencing Population Trends

Critical Thinking
4. **The BIG Idea** How can the projection of population trends help determine the direction of economic development?

5. **Drawing Conclusions** How will the retirement of baby boomers affect your generation? How do you think the baby boomers will feel about this?

6. **Determining Cause and Effect** What special demands does a high birthrate put on a nation's economy?

7. **Analyzing Visuals** Look at the photograph of traffic congestion on page 332. What effect does urban sprawl have on the city of Atlanta? What could the city do to alleviate the problem?

Applying Economics
8. **Population Growth** Search your local newspaper for articles related to population issues. Summarize the population-related problems affecting your community, and assess the local or state government's solutions.

CHAPTER 12 Macroeconomic Performance 335

Review SECTION 2

Answers

1. All definitions can be found in the section and the Glossary.
2. A growing population means more available labor and consumers, resulting in increased economic growth. A declining population means a decrease in consumers and available workers, leading to reduced production and slower economic growth.
3. fertility rate, life expectancy, and net immigration

4. It helps businesses determine the best locations for future plants, where they can find enough workers, and the best types of products to advertise and sell in particular areas. Governments might use the information to determine where new roads, schools, and other infrastructure will be needed in the future.
5. Answers will vary but may include the increasing costs of providing Social Security payments and Medicare.

6. A high birthrate may mean that population is growing faster than output, which could mean the nation cannot feed its population.
7. freeways are congested, more must be spent on roads, the air quality drops; improve public transportation to decrease congestion, or encourage businesses to stagger working hours or locate in less-busy areas
8. Answers will vary but should include your local government's response to population issues.

Focus

C Critical Thinking

Evaluating Ask: What kind of shopping do you prefer: one big store with everything or smaller specialty stores? Why? *(Answers will vary.)* **OL**

Teach

W Writing Support

Expository Writing Have students write a business memo to the manager of a store in your community proposing several ideas about incentives that would encourage students to shop there. List suggestions on the board. **OL**

Analyzing the Impact

Answers:

1. travel services, insurance, home improvement, super stores, a bank, a credit card
2. **Possible answers:** met customers' needs better; provided one-stop convenience

Additional Support

CASE STUDY
Falabella Flourishes

Chilean Retail Giant

Latin American countries have experienced tremendous population growth. Yet this alone does not guarantee business success, because it is hard to get people to buy your products when they have very little money to spend. Big-name foreign companies, such as Sears and J.C. Penney, have called it quits in Chile because of this roadblock. A domestic retail company, however, has found a highly successful way around it.

Tailored to Consumers

Chile's S.A.C.I. Falabella began in 1889 as a small tailor shop and has since grown to become the largest department store chain in Chile and one of the largest in South America. Falabella's strategy for growth is simple: find a way to satisfy consumers' needs. In 1980, Falabella created CMR—its own credit card. Today, the CMR card, issued to more than 4 million people in Chile, Peru, Argentina, and Colombia, is the most widely used credit card in Chile. As an added incentive for frequent CMR users, Falabella offers rewards in the form of cellular phone minutes. Customers can even charge a cellular account directly to their card.

REVENUE COMPOSITION

- 27% Falabella Chile
- 34% Sodimac Chile
- 8% Tottus Chile
- 9% CMR Chile
- 5% Argentina
- 15% Peru
- 2% Others

Source: Falabella

Diversify, Diversify

Despite great success with the CMR card, the department store did not realize its potential for growth until it expanded and diversified. Falabella opened stores in neighboring Argentina and Peru, acquired a large share of ownership in The Home Depot Chile, and purchased the home improvement chain Sodimac. Building on these successes, it created a travel agency and an insurance brokerage, then built a chain of Tottus super stores called hypermarkets.

To help all financial aspects of the company work together smoothly, the company added a financial division with the new Banco Falabella (Falabella Bank) . This explosive growth has nearly tripled the number of Falabella-owned stores, and they all accept the CMR card.

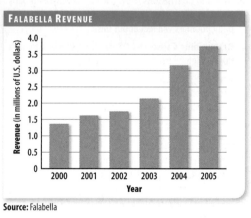

FALABELLA REVENUE

Revenue (in millions of U.S. dollars) by Year

Source: Falabella

Analyzing the Impact

1. **Summarizing** What services does Falabella provide?
2. **Making Inferences** Why has Falabella succeeded where others have failed?

336 UNIT 4 Macroeconomics: Performance and Stabilization

Activity: Technology Connection

Hunting for a Bargain Point out that many "big box" stores such as Target, Kohl's, Wal-Mart, Best Buy, and Home Depot now offer extensive Internet shopping possibilities. Services include rapid inventory information, delivery or pick-up at a specific store, and sometimes better prices for online shoppers. Point out that comparing prices at Web sites saves time and energy—and often money— for shoppers. Have students choose a durable good, such as a TV, music player, appliance, or other product and research its price and availability at three different "big box" stores. Have students share the results of their searches. Discuss their impressions of Internet shopping at super stores. **OL**

Poverty and the Distribution of Income

GUIDE TO READING

Section Preview

In this section, you will learn about the factors that contribute to income inequality and the programs that have been implemented to reduce poverty.

Content Vocabulary

- poverty threshold *(p. 338)*
- poverty guidelines *(p. 338)*
- Lorenz curve *(p. 339)*
- welfare *(p. 342)*
- food stamps *(p. 342)*
- Medicaid *(p. 343)*
- Earned Income Tax Credit (EITC) *(p. 343)*
- enterprise zone *(p. 344)*
- workfare *(p. 344)*
- negative income tax *(p. 344)*

Academic Vocabulary

- impact *(p. 340)*
- uniform *(p. 342)*

Reading Strategy

Outlining As you read the section, complete a graphic organizer similar to the one below by outlining three explanations for a growing income gap.

Income Gap

ISSUES IN THE NEWS

—Toledo Blade

Need for Food Help Is Growing

Once believed to affect only the homeless or unemployed, hunger in America has taken on a new face: the working poor. According to a new nationwide study, more than 25 million Americans seek emergency food assistance each year. In the Toledo area, nearly 297,000 visits were made by people seeking help from a local food distribution agency last year. Nearly 26 percent of those local clients had at least one adult working in the family.

The study, called "Hunger in America 2006," shows hunger has become an issue for even those with jobs. "What is really telling about this study is that such a large number of clients we're serving have at least one adult working," said Maura Daly, director of the study. "It's difficult to imagine that people who have a job are coming home at the end of the day and have to make choices between food and other basic necessities like rent, utilities, or medicine." ∎

In the world today, poverty can be viewed as an indicator of macroeconomic performance. Unfortunately, about one person in eight in the United States lives in poverty despite several years of solid economic growth. As you can read in the news story, this number includes people who hold jobs but do not earn enough money to fully support their families.

Governments on all levels have initiated programs to reduce poverty. Before we discuss these programs, however, we must first understand how poverty is defined and measured.

CHAPTER 12 **Macroeconomic Performance** 337

Focus

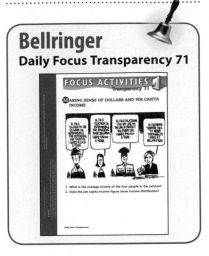

GUIDE TO READING

Possible Answers to Graphic: growing gap between well-educated and poorly educated workers; service jobs that pay poorly are increasing; changing structure of families

Resource Manager

R **Reading Strategies**	C **Critical Thinking**	D **Differentiated Instruction**	W **Writing Support**	S **Skill Practice**
Teacher Edition • Analyzing Text Structure, p. 338 • Summarizing, p. 339 **Additional Resources** • Guid. Read. Act., p. 36 • Read. Ess. & Note-Taking Guide, p. 106	**Teacher Edition** • Problem-Solving, p. 341 • Drawing Con., p. 342 • Evaluating, p. 343 • Analyzing, p. 345 • Predicting, p. 346 **Additional Resources** • Graph. Org. Trans., p. 23	**Teacher Edition** • Visual/Spatial, p. 340 • Interpersonal, p. 344 • Verbal/Linguistic, p. 350 **Additional Resources** • Econ. Content Vocab. Act., p. 12	**Teacher Edition** • Expository Writing, pp. 340, 343 • Descriptive Writing, p. 341 • Persuasive Writing, p. 342 **Additional Resources** • High School Reading in the Content Area Strat. and Act.	**Teacher Edition** • Using Bar and Circle Graphs, p. 339 • Problems and Solutions, p. 344 • Using Tables and Charts, p. 351 **Additional Resources** • Reteach. Act., p. 12

Teach

R Reading Strategy

Analyzing Text Structure

Refer students to the first paragraph in the text on this page. Point out the word *relative* in the first sentence. Then "think out loud" in this way to demonstrate how the text first uses a term and then explains its meaning: "The text says poverty is a relative measure. I'm not sure what that means, but as I continue reading, I find out. *Relative* means something like 'different things to different people.' The text is saying that a certain amount of money could make someone well off in one country, but leave him or her poor in another." Have students look for more examples of this text structure as they read this subsection. **BL**

Economic Analysis

Answer: to determine eligibility for federal programs like food stamps and Head Start

Additional Support

poverty threshold
annual dollar income used to determine the number of people in poverty

poverty guidelines
administrative guidelines used to determine eligibility for certain federal programs

Poverty

MAIN Idea A portion of the U.S. population lives in poverty, and the gap in the distribution of income is widening every year.

Economics and You Have you ever thought about what it would be like to be either very rich or very poor? Read on to find out how income is distributed in the United States.

R Poverty is a relative measure that depends on prices, the standard of living, and the incomes that others earn. What may seem like poverty to one person may seem like riches to another, so we first need to understand how poverty is defined.

Defining Poverty

People are classified as living in poverty if their incomes fall below a predetermined level, or threshold. The **poverty threshold** is the benchmark used to evaluate the income that people receive. If they have incomes below the threshold, they are considered to be in poverty even if they have supplements such as food stamps, subsidized housing, and Medicaid.

The Social Security Administration developed the thresholds in 1964 using two studies done by the U.S. Department of Agriculture in the 1950s. The first study developed four alternative but nutritionally adequate food plans for individuals and families of different sizes. The least expensive food plan was then selected as the food budget that would keep people out of poverty.

The second study found that families typically spend one-third of their total income on food. To obtain the threshold, the Social Security Administration simply took the least expensive food budget of the four food plans and multiplied it by three. Today the thresholds are adjusted upward every year by an amount just enough to offset increases in inflation.

For administrative purposes, the poverty threshholds are then simplified to appear as **poverty guidelines**, or administrative guides used to determine eligibility for certain federal programs such as the Food Stamps Program and Head Start. **Figure 12.7** shows the guidelines that had been established for two recent years.

Figure 12.7 ▶ Poverty Guidelines

▶ The table lists the poverty guidelines for families of different sizes for two recent years. Families and households with incomes below the official poverty guidelines are eligible for certain federal programs.

Economic Analysis *How are the poverty guidelines used today?*

Persons in Family or Household	2005	2006
1	$9,570	$9,800
2	12,830	13,200
3	16,090	16,600
4	19,350	20,000
5	22,610	23,400
6	25,870	26,800
7	29,130	30,200
8	32,390	33,600
For each additional person, add	3,260	3,400

Source: *Federal Register*

Activity: Collaborative Learning

Making a Budget Organize students into groups of four. Explain that each group represents a family of four living on the 2006 poverty threshold—an annual income of $20,000, or about $385 a week. Have each group develop a detailed family budget, making certain that their budget is balanced.

After several groups have shared their budgets, have students discuss what they felt were difficult choices, how much discretionary income they had left, and other issues related to the difficulty of living at the poverty threshold. **OL**

Figure 12.8 ▶ **The Distribution of Income**

CHAPTER 12, SECTION 3

▶ Panel A shows the rankings of all household income for two separate years. When the 2004 data are plotted in Panel B, the curve shows the cumulative income from the lowest to the highest quintiles. Because incomes are not distributed evenly among households, the Lorenz curve is not a diagonal line.

Graphs In MOtion
See StudentWorks™ Plus
or glencoe.com.

Economic Analysis *What percentage of income is received by the richest quintile in 1980? In 2004?*

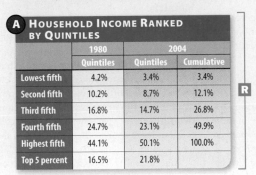

A **HOUSEHOLD INCOME RANKED BY QUINTILES**

	1980	2004	
	Quintiles	Quintiles	Cumulative
Lowest fifth	4.2%	3.4%	3.4%
Second fifth	10.2%	8.7%	12.1%
Third fifth	16.8%	14.7%	26.8%
Fourth fifth	24.7%	23.1%	49.9%
Highest fifth	44.1%	50.1%	100.0%
Top 5 percent	16.5%	21.8%	

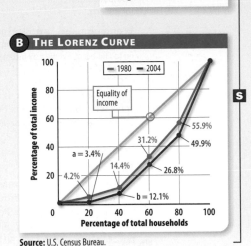

B **THE LORENZ CURVE**

Source: U.S. Census Bureau.

Distribution of Income

In addition to determining the actual number of people in poverty, economists are interested in finding out how income is distributed among households. To do so, the incomes of all households are ranked from highest to lowest, and the ranking is then divided into quintiles, or fifths, for examination. Then the total amount of the nation's income earned by each quintile is calculated.

The table in **Panel A** of **Figure 12.8** shows household income quintiles for two different years. As before, only money income is counted, while other aid such as Medicaid, food stamps, or subsidized housing is excluded. Using the most recent year in the figure as our example, the percentage of income earned by each quintile is added to the other quintiles. These incomes are plotted as a Lorenz curve. The **Lorenz curve**, which shows how the actual distribution of income varies from an equal distribution, appears in **Panel B.**

To illustrate, in 2004 the 3.4 percent of total income received by the lowest quintile is plotted in Panel B as point **a.** This amount is added to the 8.7 percent the next quintile earns and plotted as point **b.** This process continues until the cumulative amounts of all quintiles are plotted.

If all households received exactly the same income—so that 40 percent of the households earn 40 percent of the total income and so on—the Lorenz curve would appear as a diagonal line running from one corner of the graph to the other. Because all households do not receive the same income, however, the Lorenz curve is not a diagonal. As you can see in the figure, the distribution of income recently has become more unequal than it was in 1980.

A Lorenz curve can also be shown for groups other than households. These would include Lorenz curves for individuals, families, or occupations.

✓ Reading Check **Describing** How were poverty thresholds developed?

Lorenz curve
graph showing how the actual distribution of income differs from an equal distribution

R **Reading Strategy**

Summarizing Have students write a paragraph summarizing the information in Figure 12.8, Panel A. Then ask them why the information was presented in a table, rather than as text. *(A graphic presentation saves space and is easier to read.)* **BL**

S **Skill Practice**

Using Bar and Circle Graphs Have students analyze the graphs in Figure 12.8 and use the data to formulate statements. *(Possible statement: The income gap between the richest and poorest citizens of the United States is widening.)* **OL**

Economic Analysis
Answer: 44.1%; 50.1%

✓ Reading Check **Answer:** by determining the cost of the least expensive nutritionally adequate food plan and multiplying it by three

Additional Support

Activity: Technology Connection

Using Graphing Software Have students use a computer software graphing program like Microsoft Excel to present the information in Panel A of Figure 12.8 in graph form. Have them analyze the information in the table, choose the most suitable format for a graph, and input the data. Then have volunteers present their graphs to the class, as well as offer tips on choosing and using the graphing software. *(Students could create line graphs for each quintile, pie charts for each year, or bar graphs that show both years' quintile information.)* **OL**

Teacher Tip

Creating Graphs One popular spreadsheet program, Microsoft Excel, can create line, bar, and circle graphs from data entered into spreadsheet cells. You may want to ask computer-savvy students to help others create graphs with the program.

W **Writing Support**

Expository Writing Have students write an essay addressing the problem of a lack of education among many poor people and proposing a solution the government could take to address the problem. Have volunteers share their solutions. **OL**

D **Differentiated Instruction**

Visual/Spatial Have students create a cause-and-effect chart about the influence of wealth on life choices. Ask volunteers to re-create their charts on the board. *(Charts should illustrate that wealth, as distinct from income, allows people to send children to expensive schools, start businesses for children, choose not to work, and live off investments.)* **OL**

Caption Answer: education, wealth, tax law changes, decline of unions, more service jobs, monopoly power, discrimination, changing family structure

Hands-On Chapter Project

Step 3

$ **Personal Finance Handbook**
See pages R16–R19 for information on getting an education.

Reasons for Income Inequality

MAIN Idea Lack of education and uneven distribution of wealth are among the reasons for poverty.

Economics and You Have you ever considered how your education could affect your income? Read on to find out about the way income is distributed in the United States.

There are at least eight, if not more, reasons why incomes vary. Education and wealth are among the most important of these reasons.

Education

One of the most important reasons for income inequality is the difference in individuals' educational levels. People's income normally goes up as they get more education. However, in the last 30 years, the gap between well-educated and poorly educated workers has widened. This has caused wages for highly skilled workers to soar, while wages for the less skilled have remained about the same.

You saw proof of the importance of education earlier in Figure 1.4 on page 16. This figure shows that someone who has earned a college degree makes about three times more on average than someone without a high school diploma. Likewise, someone with a college degree makes nearly twice as much as someone with a high school diploma.

Wealth

Income also varies because some people hold more wealth than others, and the distribution of wealth is even more unequal than the distribution of income. When wealth holders are ranked from highest to lowest, the top fifth holds about 75 percent of all the wealth in the country. The bottom two-fifths, or 40 percent of the people in the country, have less than 2 percent of the total wealth.

This inequality has a dramatic **impact** on people's ability to earn income. Wealthy families can send their children to expensive colleges and universities. The wealthy also can afford to set their children up in businesses where they can earn a better

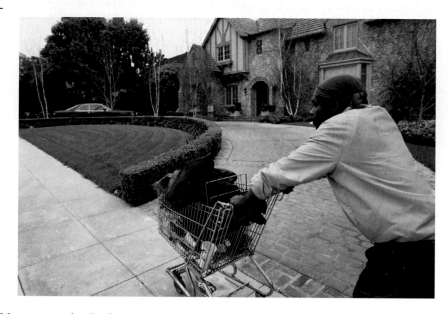

Inequality of Income Some Americans live in mansions, while others cannot afford to pay rent and are homeless. *What are the major reasons for varying incomes?*

Evaluating an Economy

Step 3: Analyzing Poverty. Student groups will create a United Nations report that describes poverty in their fictional nation.

Directions: Have students return to the groups established for the first two steps of this project. Ask each student group to create a short report, including statistics and graphs like those on pages 339 and 342, on the problem of poverty in their nation. Point out that the statistics for the A and, to a lesser extent, B nations will

resemble those for the United States, while those for the C, D, and F nations will be significantly different. The UN report should include several recommendations on how the nation should address poverty. Remind students to review and use the information in the section on the causes of poverty and types of programs available to alleviate it. **OL**

(Chapter Project continued in Visual Summary.)

income. Even if the very wealthy choose not to work, they can make investments that will earn additional income.

Tax Law Changes

In recent years, Congress has changed many tax laws, reducing taxes for almost all Americans. Marginal tax rates on high incomes, however, have been reduced more than rates on lower incomes, thereby adding to the growing inequality of income.

The 15 percent tax rate that applies to corporate dividend payments and capital gains, for example, is the same as the second-lowest rates that apply to the poorest Americans. This means that a millionaire who receives tens of thousands of dollars in corporate dividends pays the same percentage rate on those dividends as someone who only earns $20,000 a year.

Decline of Unions

As heavy manufacturing has declined in the United States, union membership has fallen, especially among less-skilled workers, adding to the growing income gap. High school graduates who once followed their parents into high-paying factory jobs can no longer do so. This leaves them to find other work, often for much less pay.

More Service Jobs

A structural change in the U.S. economy saw industry convert from goods production to service production. This event widened the income differential. Because wages are typically lower in service industries such as restaurants, movie theaters, and clothing stores, annual incomes also tend to be lower.

Monopoly Power

Another factor is the degree of monopoly power that some groups have. You learned in Chapter 8 that unions have been able to obtain higher wages for their members. Some white-collar workers—clerical,

Did You Know?

▶ **Income Gap** The rising inequality of income is a worldwide phenomenon, especially for the developing countries of Asia. A major reason for this trend is the lack of jobs for the growing population. The widening income gaps have troubling results. More and more countries experience public complaints, protests, and political crises. In one year alone, China was faced with tens of thousands of protests, often in rural areas where people's earnings are a small fraction of the average income their fellow citizens in cities and coastal regions receive.

business, or professional workers who generally are salaried—also hold a degree of monopoly power. The American Medical Association, for example, has successfully limited the number of people entering the profession by restricting medical school certifications. This has been a major factor in driving up the incomes of doctors.

C

Discrimination

Discrimination also affects the distribution of income. Women may not be promoted to executive positions because male executives simply are not accustomed to women in roles of power. Some unions may deny membership to immigrants or ethnic minorities.

Although workplace discrimination is illegal, it still occurs. When it does, it causes women and minority groups to be crowded into other labor markets where oversupply drives wages down.

Changing Family Structure

A final reason for the growing income gap concerns the changing structure of the American family. The shift from two-parent families to single-parent families and other household living arrangements tends to decrease the average family income. This and the other factors mentioned above contribute to the trend of the rich getting richer and the poor getting poorer.

✓**Reading Check** **Synthesizing** Which factors are most important in unequal income distribution? Why?

C Critical Thinking

Problem-Solving Ask: Do you think having more doctors might slow the rise in health care costs? Why or why not? *(Answers will vary. Students saying "yes" may cite the law of supply and demand, arguing that raising the supply of doctors would lower their cost; students saying "no" might claim that most of the expense in health care is not due to a lack of doctors but to expensive drugs, equipment, and other factors.)* **AL**

W Writing Support

Descriptive Writing Have students write a short story about the effect of one of these eight factors (education, wealth, tax law changes, decline of unions, more service jobs, monopoly power, discrimination, and changing family structure) on a family living in poverty. **OL**

✓**Reading Check** **Answer:**
Answers will vary, although many students will probably choose education or wealth; these factors give children a head start over their peers.

Additional Support

Activity: Interdisciplinary Connection

Art Have a group of students create a mural about the income gap and rising economic inequality, either in the United States or in the world. Suggest they begin by brainstorming visual ideas that represent the gap between rich and poor. Then have them paint their murals and show them to the class. Ask groups to be prepared to answer questions about their ideas and their work. **OL**

Teacher Tip

Finding Inspiration To help students get started, you might show them images of artwork that portrays social issues, such as the work of Jack Levine, Diego Rivera, and Jacob Lawrence.

W Writing Support

Persuasive Writing Have students write a persuasive essay taking and supporting a position on this statement: *The government has a responsibility to help needy people through activities such as income and general assistance, and social service programs.* Have volunteers read their essays. When a variety of opinions have been presented, discuss issues raised. **OL**

C Critical Thinking

Drawing Conclusions

Ask: Why do you think it has been so difficult to eliminate poverty? Have students discuss their opinions on this question. Remind them to review the eight reasons for income variation explained on the previous pages. **OL**

Economic Analysis

Answer: mid-1970s; early 1960s

Differentiated Instruction

welfare
government or private agency programs that provide general economic and social assistance to needy individuals

food stamps
government-issued coupons that can be exchanged for food

Skills Handbook

See page **R48** to learn about *Problems and Solutions.*

Antipoverty Programs

MAIN Idea Since the 1960s, the government has experienced modest success with a number of anti-poverty programs.

Economics and You Did you know there are programs designed to help people escape or avoid poverty? Read on to find out about these programs.

Over the years, the federal government has tried a number of programs to help the needy. Most come under the general heading of **welfare**—economic and social assistance from the government or private agencies because of need.

Reducing poverty has been difficult. As **Figure 12.9** shows, even the record economic expansions of the 1980s and 1990s failed to make a significant dent in the percentage of Americans living in poverty. In fact, the proportion of the population living in poverty today is about the same as it was in the 1970s—and it might have been worse without some of the following programs.

Income Assistance

Programs that provide direct cash assistance to those in need fall into the category of income assistance. One such program is the Temporary Assistance for Needy Families (TANF), which began in 1997. Although provisions and benefits vary from state to state, many families qualify for modest cash payments because of the death, continuous absence, or permanent disability of a parent. More recently, Congress voted to tighten provisions of the law and toughen work standards for two-parent households.

Another income assistance program is the Supplemental Security Income (SSI), which makes cash payments to blind or disabled persons or to people age 65 and older. Originally, the states administered the program, but because benefits varied so much from state to state, the federal government took it over to assure more **uniform** coverage.

General Assistance

Programs that assist poor people but do not provide direct cash assistance fall into the category of general assistance. One example is the food stamp program that serves millions of Americans. **Food stamps** are government-issued coupons that can be redeemed for food. They may be given or sold to eligible low-income persons.

Figure 12.9 ▶ Poverty in the United States: Total Number and Rate

▶ Since the mid-1960s, the poverty rate has hovered between 10 and 15 percent of the population. In that same time span, the number of people in poverty has increased.

Economic Analysis *When was the poverty rate lowest? When did it reach the highest numbers?*

Graphs In Motion
See StudentWorks™ Plus or glencoe.com.

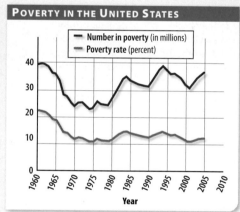

POVERTY IN THE UNITED STATES

— Number in poverty (in millions)
— Poverty rate (percent)

Source: U.S. Census Bureau

Poverty in America

Authentic Assessment Strategies and Activities, p. 23

Objective: Understand the causes of poverty and the variety of government responses to it.

Focus/Teach: Ask students to describe Congressional committee meetings they have seen or read about. Then have students complete the activity.

Assess: Use the rubrics at the back of the booklet.

Close: Have students discuss what they learned from the skits.

Differentiated Instruction Strategies

BL Have students review relevant sections of the text before choosing a cause and writing their stories.

AL Have students write a newspaper account or create a video film report of the hearing.

ELL Have students write and practice their stories together.

Job Training
Many states have introduced job training, such as this computer class, to help people out of poverty. **How are such programs usually funded?**

C **Critical Thinking**

Evaluating Have students discuss this statement: *Welfare programs such as Medicaid and food stamps would be administered more effectively and cheaply by private companies.* Have students offer support for their responses.
AL

W **Writing Support**

Expository Writing Have students identify one social service program available in your state. Then have them research it using your state's official Web site to write a short report on the program. Have them explain the goal of the program, its cost and history, and some of its activities. Have students share their reports with the class. Conclude with a discussion of other programs students think the state should offer to alleviate poverty. **OL**

Caption Answer: States pay for some of the cost and receive matching funds from the federal government.

For example, if a person pays 40 cents for a $1 food stamp, that person can get a dollar's worth of food for a fraction of its cost. The program, which became law in 1964, is different from other programs because eligibility is based solely on income.

Another general assistance program is **Medicaid**—a joint federal-state medical **C** insurance program for low-income people. Under the program, the federal government pays a majority of health-care costs, and the state governments cover the rest of the cost. Medicaid serves millions of Americans, including children, the visually impaired, and the disabled.

Social Service Programs

Over the years, individual states have developed a variety of social service programs to help the needy. These include such areas as child abuse prevention, foster **W** care, family planning, job training, child welfare, and day care.

Although states control the kinds of services the programs provide, the federal government may match part of the cost. To be eligible for matching funds, a state must file an annual service plan with the federal government. If the plan is approved, the state is free to select social issues it wishes to address, set the eligibility requirements for the programs, and decide how the programs are to be carried out. As a result, the range of services and the level of support may vary from state to state.

Tax Credits

Many working Americans qualify for special tax credits. The most popular is the **Earned Income Tax Credit (EITC)** which provides federal tax credits and even cash to low-income workers. The credit was created to partially offset the payroll tax burden on working families. The credit is applied first to federal income taxes. Low-income workers can take the remainder of the credit in cash if the credit is larger than the taxes owed. The credit has proved to be popular, with millions of working families receiving benefits annually.

Medicaid joint federal-state medical insurance program for low-income people *(also see page 271)*

Earned Income Tax Credit (EITC) federal tax credits and cash payments for low-income workers

CHAPTER 12 Macroeconomic Performance 343

Leveled Activities

BL Guided Reading Activities, p. 36

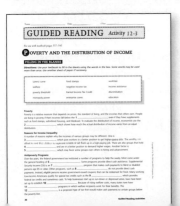

OL Reading Essentials and Note-Taking Guide, p. 106

AL Graphic Organizer Transparencies, p. 23

D Differentiated Instruction

Interpersonal Have small groups of students review the discussion of workfare programs. Then have them suggest underlying assumptions that support the idea. You may want to spur discussion by suggesting one: *People who receive welfare from the government should earn it by performing work that benefits society.* Write each group's suggestions on the board and discuss them. **OL**

S Skill Practice

Problems and Solutions
Ask students to identify a possible objection to the idea of the negative income tax. *(Possible answer: Giving poor people cash means there is no government control over how they spend it; some might spend their cash payment on nonessentials while ignoring needs for food, health care, or other necessities.)* Then have them suggest solutions to this problem. **OL**

Additional Support

enterprise zone area free of tax laws and other operating restrictions

workfare program requiring welfare recipients to work in exchange for benefits

negative income tax tax system that would make cash payments to individuals with incomes below certain levels

Enterprise Zones

Special **enterprise zones** are areas where companies can locate free of some local, state, and federal tax laws and other operating restrictions. Many enterprise zones are established in run-down or depressed areas. This benefits area residents because they can find work without worrying about transportation. Enterprise zones thus help depressed areas to grow again in several different ways.

Nearly everyone agrees that a healthy and growing economy helps alleviate poverty.

CAREERS

Actuary

The Work
* Help businesses assess risks and formulate policies
* Gather and analyze statistics on death, sickness, injury, disability, retirement, and property loss
* Design insurance and pension plans and calculate premium rates that are high enough to cover any claims and expenses

Qualifications
* Strong background in mathematics, statistics, probability, finance, and business
* Knowledge of economic, social, health, and legislative trends
* Ability to develop and use spreadsheets, databases, and statistical analysis software
* Bachelor's degree in mathematics or statistics
* Must pass a series of actuarial examinations

Earnings
* Median annual earnings: $76,340

Job Growth Outlook
* Faster than average

Source: *Occupational Outlook Handbook, 2006–2007 Edition*

The enterprise zone concept is an attempt to focus some of that growth directly in the areas that need it most by making more employment opportunities available.

Workfare Programs

Because of rising welfare costs, many state and local governments require individuals who receive welfare to provide labor in exchange for benefits. **Workfare** is a program in which welfare recipients work for their benefits. People on workfare often assist law enforcement officials or sanitation and highway crews, work in schools or hospitals, or perform other types of community service work.

Most states that have workfare programs require almost everyone except for the disabled, the elderly, and those with very young children to work. If the workfare assignments are well designed, then recipients have a valuable opportunity to learn new skills that will eventually help them get other jobs.

Many welfare-to-work programs have had promising results. In some cases, companies can even earn federal tax credits when they hire workers directly from the welfare rolls. Under these circumstances, the employment is a win-win situation for both employer and employee.

Negative Income Tax

The **negative income tax** is a proposed type of tax that would make cash payments to certain groups below the poverty line. While the program is not in use today, the proposal is attractive because cash payments would take the place of existing welfare programs rather than supplementing them. Also, everyone would qualify for the program, not just working people as with the EITC.

Under the negative income tax, the federal government would set an income level below which people would not have to pay taxes. Then the government would pay a certain amount of money to anyone who earned less than that amount.

Activity: Interdisciplinary Connection

Geography Poverty is not evenly distributed across the United States. Share the following information with students. In 2005 these states and the District of Columbia had the highest per capita personal income:

District of Columbia	$54,985
Connecticut	$47,819
Massachusetts	$44,289
New Jersey	$43,771
Maryland	$41,760
New York	$40,507

In contrast, the lowest per capita personal incomes were in these states:

Louisiana	$24,820
Mississippi	$25,318
Arkansas	$26,874
West Virginia	$27,215
New Mexico	$27,644
Utah	$28,061

Ask students to make generalizations about this set of poverty data. *(The richest states are in the Northeast and East; the poorest ones are in the South and West, except for West Virginia.)* **OL**

For example, suppose that an individual's tax liability was computed using the following formula:

$$\text{taxes} = (25\% \text{ of income}) - \$8,000$$

Under this formula, a person with no income would have a tax of minus $8,000—which is another way of saying that the person will receive $8,000 from the government. If the person earned exactly $12,000, then the taxes would be $3,000 minus $8,000, so they would receive $5,000 for a total of $17,000 (or $5,000 from the tax formula plus the $12,000 in earned income). Under this formula, a person would have to make $32,000 before he or she actually paid any taxes.

The negative income tax differs from other antipoverty programs in two respects. First, it is a market-based program designed to encourage people to work. The objective is to make the minimum payment large enough to be of some assistance, yet small enough so that people are better off working. Then, when people do go to work, the taxes they pay need to be low enough to not discourage them from working.

Second, the negative income tax would be cost-effective because it would take the place of other, more costly, welfare programs. In addition, government would save on administrative costs.

A Difficult Problem

We might ask how the U.S. economy has done as a result of all these programs with the strong economic growth since the 1980s. The answer, unfortunately, is that poverty has been a remarkably difficult problem to solve. Economic growth is important, of course, but by itself it is not sufficient to reduce poverty.

Even so, there are sound reasons to try to improve the problem of poverty. Not only would millions of Americans be better off, but everyone else in the economy would be better off as well. After all, if too many people find themselves without the capacity to earn and spend, there will be fewer people to purchase the products that our economy produces.

✓ **Reading Check** Summarizing What are the benefits of the EITC to a working person?

C Critical Thinking

Analyzing Have students review the last paragraph in the section. **Ask:** Do you agree that everyone would be better off if the United States could improve the problem of poverty? Why or why not? **OL**

✓ Reading Check **Answer:** It provides benefits to the working poor and sets a limit below which people would not have to pay taxes.

Assess

Use the Interactive Tutor Self-Assessment CD-ROM to review Section 3, and then assign the Section 3 Review as homework or as an in-class activity.

Close

Making Decisions Tell students that they are deciding what to include in a time capsule, to be opened in the year 2100. Have them select 10 items that would tell people about U.S. poverty in the early twenty-first century. **OL**

SECTION 3 Review

Vocabulary
1. **Explain** the significance of poverty threshold, poverty guidelines, Lorenz curve, welfare, food stamps, Medicaid, Earned Income Tax Credit (EITC), enterprise zone, workfare, and negative income tax.

Main Ideas
2. **Defining** How is poverty defined?
3. **Describing** What are reasons for income inequality?
4. **Identifying** Use a graphic organizer like the one below to identify the major programs and proposals designed to alleviate the problem of poverty

Alleviating the problem of poverty
1.
2.

Critical Thinking
5. **The BIG Idea** Which of the factors that contribute to income inequality do you feel has the most impact? Explain your answer.
6. **Drawing Conclusions** Do you think that a workfare program is the best way to address income inequalities within our economy? Explain your answers.
7. **Analyzing Visuals** Look at Figure 12.9 on page 342. How do the lines for the number of people in poverty and the poverty rate compare? Why are the lines not more similar?

Applying Economics
8. **Distribution of Income** What would happen to the Lorenz curve if nonfinancial aid such as food stamps and Medicaid were treated as income? Explain why this would occur.

Review SECTION 3

CHAPTER 12 Macroeconomic Performance 345

Answers

1. All definitions can be found in the section and the Glossary.
2. People are living in poverty if their incomes fall below a certain threshold.
3. education, wealth, monopoly power, decline of unions, increase in service jobs, discrimination, changes in tax laws and changing family structures
4. federal programs: Temporary Assistance for Needy Families, Supplemental Security Income, food stamps, Medicaid; state/local programs: foster care, family planning, job training, child welfare, child abuse prevention, and day care
5. The factors are education, wealth, monopoly power, decline of unions, increase in service jobs, discrimination, changes in tax laws, and changing family structures. The student may select any one of these, but the explanation should demonstrate a clear understanding of the factors and sound economic reasoning.
6. Answers will vary but should demonstrate understanding of the effects of the workfare program.
7. They are similar in that they generally go up and down at the same time; they are not more similar because of the effects of inflation, unemployment, number of workers, wage levels, and other factors.
8. The Lorenz curve would move closer to the "equal distribution" curve if nonfinancial aid was counted as income since this would increase income figures.

C Critical Thinking

Predicting Have students contribute to a class list of predictions about (1) whether the income gap will continue to grow, stay the same, or lessen, and (2) how a continuing or growing gap between rich and poor will affect the U.S. society and economy. **OL**

BusinessWeek *ONLINE*

To find up-to-date news and analysis on the economy, business, technology, markets, entrepreneurs, investments, and finance, have students search feature articles and special reports on the BusinessWeek Web site, www.businessweek.com.

Examining the Newsclip

Answers:

1. Possible answers include *shame on us, chimera, chasm, Great Depression, sorry situation, sadly,* and *gulf.*

2. Both; most students will detect disapproval of income inequality.

Additional Support

BusinessWeek NEWSCLIP

A gap in income between high- and low-paid workers has always existed. Some people argue that income inequality today is as high as before the Great Depression.

The Rich Get (Much) Richer

Shame on . . . us, passive witnesses to the emergence of a second Gilded Age, another Roaring Twenties, in which the fruits of economic success have gone not to the broad populace but to a slim sliver at the top. For this handful, life is a sweet mélange [mix] of megafortunes, grand houses, and massive yachts. Meanwhile, the bottom 80% endures economic stagnation. . . .

Much of the recent commentary has focused on class mobility, the opportunity for individuals to move up the ladder. But trumpeting mobility as a reason for ignoring growing income inequality is a chimera [illusion]. Even if mobility is high— a questionable assertion—it is hardly a consolation for those who remain at the bottom, gazing across a growing distance at the more successful.

C We can debate a lot of economic data but not income inequality. Every serious study shows that the U.S. income gap has become a chasm [gulf]. Over the past 30 years, the share of income going to the highest-earning Americans has risen steadily to levels not seen since shortly before the Great Depression. . . .

What's to blame for this sorry situation? Certainly globalization has taken its toll. Cheaper labor in emerging markets means relentless wage pressure on U.S. workers. Meanwhile, the fruits of American success in fast-growing services and technology remain available only to the slice of our workforce with the necessary skills. Other factors, such as an increasingly regressive tax code, have also played a role.

Growing inequality helps explain why so many Americans feel so vulnerable even as the overall economy continues to expand. Moods understandably darken when many have to take second jobs and go into debt to improve their living standards. . . .

Sadly, there is no magic bullet. We need to provide more education and training to fix our problem of too many low-skilled workers. We don't need to become tax-code Robin Hoods, but we can be vigilant about tax plans . . . that widen the gulf between haves and have-nots. Finally, we can provide more protection for those at risk, such as better wage insurance to cushion the effects of globalization.

—Reprinted from *BusinessWeek*

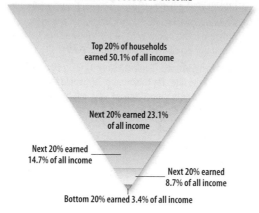

SHARE OF HOUSEHOLD INCOME

Top 20% of households earned 50.1% of all income

Next 20% earned 23.1% of all income

Next 20% earned 14.7% of all income

Next 20% earned 8.7% of all income

Bottom 20% earned 3.4% of all income

Examining the Newsclip

1. **Identifying Points of View** What words and phrases can you identify in the article that help reveal the author's point of view?

2. **Detecting Bias** Does the author state opinions or facts? What bias might be evident in these statements?

346   UNIT 4   Macroeconomics: Performance and Stabilization

Extending the Content

The Income Gap in Other Countries
The income gap varies considerably in countries around the world. These statistics show the percentage of the national average income that is earned by people in the lowest 10 percent (decile) of the population. Data is from the year 2000, unless otherwise noted.

Country	Percentage
Luxembourg	66%
Sweden	57%
Germany	54%
Poland (1999)	52%
Canada	48%
Italy	44%
United States	39%
Russia	33%
Mexico (1998)	28%

Study anywhere, anytime! Download quizzes and flash cards to your PDA from glencoe.com.

▶ **National Output and Income** Gross domestic product (GDP) measures the nation's output, while gross national product (GNP) measures the nation's income.

GDP	GNP
• Market value of all final goods, services, and structures produced within a country's national borders in a year • Indicator of the condition of the nation's economy • Includes output of foreign-owned firms located in the United States • Includes only final products	• Market value of all final goods, services, and structures produced in one year with labor and property supplied by a country's residents • Includes all payments to citizens, regardless of where the production takes place • Excludes income earned by foreign-owned resources in the country

▶ **Population** Governments count the population and project population trends to plan the use of resources and to prepare infrastructure.

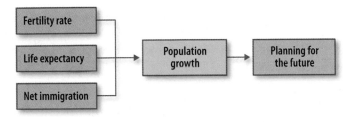

▶ **Poverty** People are described as living in poverty if they live below an income level called the poverty threshold. Poverty has a number of causes, and governments have established some programs to reduce it.

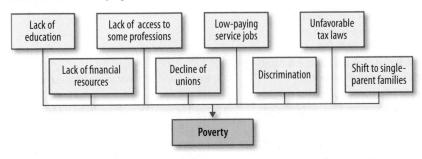

Designing Refer students to the middle chart on this page. Review the three factors that influence population growth. Then have students write a paragraph describing a business they could start, based on one of the factors as it affects today's society and the future. Have volunteers share their business descriptions and explain why they made their particular choice. You may also want to have students discuss businesses they expect would not be successful, based on current trends in fertility, life expectancy, and immigration. **OL**

Categorizing Refer students to the chart at the bottom of this page and review each cause, if necessary. **Ask:** Which of the causes of poverty do you feel could best be solved by government? By the private sector? By a government-private sector combination? Explain your answers. *(Answers will vary but should be logical and well supported.)* **OL**

Hands-On Chapter Project

Step 4: Wrap Up

Evaluating an Economy

Step 4: Complete the Analysis. Student teams will summarize what they learned in Steps 1–3.

Directions: Have the students on each team collaborate to write an "economic status report" of their assigned nation. Students should include concepts learned at each of the previous steps in describing the current status of their nation's economy.

Encourage students to also provide a history section that explains how their country's economy came to be in its current state. Have students make a copy of their report for the four other groups. As the students review the different reports, direct them to consider the effectiveness of the methods economists use to measure an economy's performance. Finally, discuss each report as a class. **OL**

ExamView®
Assessment Suite

This easy-to-use software includes extensive question banks and allows you to create fully customized tests that can be administered in print or online.

Review Content Vocabulary

1–9. Students' sentences will vary but should demonstrate understanding of the relationship between the terms.

Review Academic Vocabulary

10. d	**11.** a
12. f	**13.** e
14. b	**15.** c

Review the Main Ideas

16. all the final goods, services, and structures produced within a country's borders during one year

17. GDP: add payments to Americans from overseas; subtract payments to foreign-owned resources in the United States. GNP: subtract depreciation. NNP: subtract all taxes except corporate profits tax. NI: add Social Security retirement checks; subtract Social Security withholding taxes. PI: subtract income taxes paid.

18. consumer sector: disposable personal income; investment sector: retained earnings; government sector: indirect business taxes, corporate income taxes, Social Security contributions, and personal income taxes from the consumer sector; foreign sector: does not have a source of income specific to it

Review Content Vocabulary

Examine the pairs of words below. Then write a sentence explaining what each pair has in common.

1. food stamps, Medicaid
2. gross national product, net national product
3. household, unrelated individuals
4. intermediate products, secondhand sales
5. underground economy, nonmarket transactions
6. workfare, welfare
7. life expectancy, dependency ratio
8. demographer, center of population
9. baby boom, population pyramid

Review Academic Vocabulary

Identify which of the following terms correctly complete the sentences below.

a. excluded	**d.** projected
b. components	**e.** impact
c. residence	**f.** uniform

10. The Census Bureau has _____ the most likely U.S. fertility rate as 2.119 births per woman.

11. Nonmarket transactions are _____ from GDP.

12. The federal government now administers the Supplemental Security Income program to assure more _____ coverage across the nation.

13. The unequal distribution of wealth has an enormous _____ on people's ability to earn income.

14. The sectors of our economy receive various _____ of the national income, which they then use to purchase the total output.

15. Every ten years the U.S. government takes an official count of all people, including their place of _____.

Review the Main Ideas

Section 1 *(pages 319–327)*

16. Describe what goods and services are included in the GDP.

17. Explain the connections between the various measures of income using a graphic organizer like the one below.

Begin with . . .	Add	Subtract	Equals
GDP			GNP
GNP			NDP
NDP			NI
NI			PI
PI			DPI

18. Identify the source of income for the four sectors of the economy.

19. Identify the components of GDP by decoding the formula GDP = C + I + G + (X – M).

Section 2 *(pages 329–335)*

20. Describe the historical growth of population in the United States.

21. Identify the political and economic importance of the census.

22. Explain how the age composition of the future population might impact our economy.

Section 3 *(pages 337–345)*

23. Explain what is meant by the term *distribution of income*.

24. Identify the major reasons for inequality in the distribution of income.

25. Explain how enterprise zones benefit residents of run-down or depressed areas.

19. C for consumers, I for investments, G for government or public sector, and (X–M) for the foreign sector or net exports

20. 1790–1860: 3.0 percent a year; Civil War–1900: 2.2 percent; 1900–World War II: 1.4 percent; post World War II: slow decline; today: less than 1.0 percent annually

21. political: basis for determining the number of representatives allotted to each state; economic: for predicting population trends

22. Possible answer: Younger workers will carry a heavy burden as "baby boomers" begin to collect pensions, Social Security, and Medicare benefits.

23. how income is distributed among a country's households

24. education, wealth, monopoly power, decline of unions, increase in service jobs, discrimination, changes in tax laws and changing family structures

25. Residents can find work without worrying about transportation, thereby helping depressed areas to grow again.

Economics ONLINE Self-Check Quiz Visit the *Economics: Principles and Practices* Web site at glencoe.com and click on *Chapter 12–Self-Check Quizzes* to prepare for the chapter test.

Assessment and Activities CHAPTER 12

Critical Thinking

26. **The BIG Idea** How do the different measures of output and income allow us to assess the economy of a nation?

27. **Comparing and Contrasting** Which program do you think is more effective, workfare or welfare? Why?

28. **Determining Cause and Effect** Which of the factors affecting population growth will have the greatest impact on the United States in the next 50 years? Why?

29. **Synthesizing** Under what circumstances might you prefer economic security to a better standard of living?

30. **Synthesizing** Suppose you were told that you would earn $95,000 in 2020. Explain why this information would say little about the standard of living you might enjoy. What other information would you need before you could evaluate how well you could live in 2020?

Applying Economic Concepts

31. **Economic Sectors** Imagine you must teach a younger class the differences among the four sectors that make up our economy. Then take the following steps:

   a. For one week, clip articles from newspapers that refer to expenditures by one or more of the economic sectors. Log the expenditures in a graphic organizer similar to the one below.

   b. Prepare a poster or computer presentation that explains how the sectors work together.

Consumer sector	Investment sector	Government sector	Foreign sector

Analyzing Visuals

32. **Critical Thinking** Look at Figure 12.5 on page 333. How can you use this figure to help you plan expenditures for education?

Math Practice

33. Based on the information in the table below, determine the percentage of total expenditures that consumers spend on durable goods, nondurable goods, and services.

Personal Consumption Expenditures	Amount (in billions)	Percentage
Total expenditures	$9,081.7	100%
Durable goods	1,047.6	
Motor vehicles and parts	432.3	
Furniture and household equipment	397.7	
Other	217.6	
Nondurable goods	2,687.7	
Food	1,282.4	
Clothing and shoes	358.4	
Gasoline and other energy goods	327.4	
Other	719.5	
Services	$5,346.4	
Housing	1,318.9	
Household operation	495.2	
Transportation	337.1	
Medical care	1,578.9	
Recreation	365.2	
Other	1,251.2	

Thinking Like an Economist

34. In your own words, explain why greater life expectancies and declining birthrates make some entitlements like Social Security and Medicare more difficult to fund.

Writing About Economics

35. **Expository Writing** Research the following topic: Is there an income gap between men's and women's wages? If so, is the income gap narrowing or widening? Prepare a three-page written report. Be sure to include a list of the references you used in your report.

CHAPTER 12 Macroeconomic Performance 349

30. Students should take into account inflation, cost of living, income distribution, tax burden, and other factors that influence standard of living.

Applying Economic Concepts

31. Students should place expenditures in the correct column of the graphic organizer.

Analyzing Visuals

32. The chart tells how many people are in those ages that will require education expenditures.

Math Practice

33. Durable goods: 11.53%; Nondurable goods: 29.59%; Services: 58.87%

Thinking Like an Economist

34. Both of these programs are for older people and are paid for by the contributions of younger workers; if older people live longer and fewer workers are born to support them, these programs will become more difficult to fund.

Writing About Economics

35. Answers will vary but should demonstrate an understanding of the income gap.

Critical Thinking

26. **Possible answer:** Economists use a variety of factors because no single measurement captures the entire picture of the growth and performance of a nation's economy.

27. Both workfare and welfare are programs designed to aid those living in poverty. Workfare requires welfare recipients to exchange some of their labor for benefits. People on workfare perform types of community service work.

Welfare includes government or private agency programs that provide general economic and social assistance to needy individuals. Student assessment of effectiveness will vary.

28. Answers will vary but should demonstrate an understanding of the factors influencing population growth.

29. Answers will vary but should demonstrate an understanding of the trade-off between increased economic security and standard of living.

Focus

Have students describe foreign fruits and vegetables that they have bought or seen at the grocery store. Where did they come from? What time of year was it? How did the price compare with domestic produce? Was the produce of high quality? How did other shoppers seem to react to the imported produce?

Teach

D Differentiated Instruction

Verbal/Linguistic Have students write (and perform, if appropriate) a dialogue between a fruit grower in the United States and a fruit grower in a Latin American country. You may want to first brainstorm a list of issues the two might disagree about and address in the dialogue. **OL**

Additional Support

Global Fruit

Take a stroll through the produce department of your local supermarket, and you will discover an amazing variety of fresh fruits. Americans are eating more fruit—in both quantity and variety—and these fresh fruits are available not only during the summer months. Produce that was once deemed "seasonal" can now be found year-round.

Global Goodness

Fresh fruit choices at any grocery store in the United States include the standard fare of apples, oranges, and grapes. But you also find more exotic items, such as star fruit and papaya. How do tropical fruits find their way to grocery shelves in the dead of winter? And why can we purchase a gallon of orange juice when Florida and California farmers have been hit with an early frost? We have the global economy to thank for turning the produce aisle into a perpetual smorgasbord, continuously delivering fruits from around the world.

From There to Here

For many fruits, the trip from field to market involves a specific process of packing and shipping. For example, bananas leave Costa Rica and other Central and South American countries

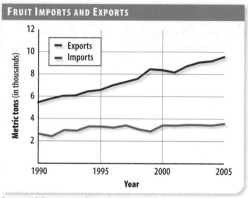

FRUIT IMPORTS AND EXPORTS

- Exports
- Imports

Metric tons (in thousands) — vertical axis: 2, 4, 6, 8, 10, 12
Year — horizontal axis: 1990, 1995, 2000, 2005

Source: U.S. Department of Agriculture

packed in boxes weighing about 40 pounds each. Roughly 970 boxes fit into a refrigerated cargo container, which is then placed aboard a ship. The bananas must remain at a temperature of around 57°F to keep them from ripening while in transit.

Bananas take two to seven days to reach U.S. ports. There the cargo containers full of not-yet-ripe bananas are taken to different warehouse locations around the country. Before the bananas can be sent to your local supermarket, however, they must spend some time in special "ripening rooms." Considering this lengthy journey, bananas seem like quite a bargain at less than fifty cents per pound.

From Here to There

D Americans not only buy fruits—we sell them, too. The United States is the world's fifth-largest fruit producer and the largest exporter of fresh fruit. Canada is our biggest customer, importing

Activity: Hands-On Economics

Imported Produce—How Common?
Have student teams visit at least two local grocery stores and research the availability of imported fruits and vegetables. Have them find out the following:

- About what percentage of items seems to be imported?
- What items are most frequently imported?

- How does the quality of imported items compare with that of U.S. produce?
- How do shoppers feel about imported produce? How do managers feel?

Have teams report to the class about their findings. Discuss issues that arise. Conclude by having students decide if the availability of imported produce is an overall positive or negative for the U.S. economy. **OL**

SOURCES OF FRESH FRUIT

Fruit	U.S. Producers	Foreign Producers
Apples	Washington, New York, California, Michigan, Pennsylvania, Virginia	Canada, New Zealand
Bananas		Colombia, Costa Rica, Ecuador, Guatemala, Honduras, Panama, Mexico, Nicaragua
Kiwi	California	New Zealand, Chile
Mangoes	Florida	India, South America
Papaya	Florida	Jamaica, Central America
Peaches	California, South Carolina, Georgia, Michigan, Pennsylvania, New Jersey, Washington	Chile, Canada, Mexico
Pears	Washington, Oregon, California, Michigan, Pennsylvania, New York	Chile, New Zealand, Australia, Argentina, Canada
Strawberries	California, Oregon, Florida	New Zealand, Mexico

Source: Food and Agriculture Organization of the United Nations

S

47 percent of all U.S. fresh fruit exports. U.S. producers also export to Japan, Hong Kong, the European Union, and South Korea, among others. Yet the United States faces new competitors in the fruit trade. Mexico, China, Chile, and South Africa all impact the marketplace as they expand their reach.

What Does It Mean For You?

Global trade provides you with your favorite fruits throughout the year. While most U.S. fields and orchards lie dormant during winter, countries in the Southern Hemisphere are harvesting and shipping their summer crops. The worldwide competition also means lower prices for you and other fruit lovers. In addition, you now have more choices. The global exchange allows new and unusual fruits to make their way to U.S. stores for curious palates.

photo: unloading containers in U.S. port

Analyzing the Issue

1. **Identifying** What country is the largest buyer of U.S. fruit?
2. **Analyzing** What are concerns about shipping fresh fruit from other countries?
3. **Applying** Check out the fruit section of your local grocery store. What fruit is available because of global trade?

Assess/Close

S Skill Practice

Using Tables and Charts
Have students analyze the table on page 351. **Ask:** What states might have the most to fear from imported fruits? Why? *(California, Florida, Michigan, Oregon, and Washington; these states are leading fruit producers and might fear a loss of business.)* **BL**

Analyzing the Issue

Answers:
1. Canada
2. competition with U.S.-produced fruit; possible uncertainty about food safety
3. Answers will vary but should display an understanding of global trade.

Additional Support

Extending the Content

Behind the Scenes The import and export of fruits and vegetables is affected by more than just different growing seasons. One key element in the business of trading produce is tariffs. According to a newsletter of the U.S. Department of Agriculture, tariff levels strongly influence whom we buy from and sell to. Mexico and Canada, for example, are among the largest sources and destinations of produce because of low or no tariff barriers. The North American Free Trade Agreement, or NAFTA, made our continent a free-trade zone. In other parts of the world, however, it is a different story. The global average tariff on fruits and vegetables is over 50 percent. Most Japanese and European tariffs on fruit range from 5 to 25 percent. High tariffs discourage the importation of U.S. produce. In contrast, U.S. tariffs on imported produce tend to be low; most are under 5 percent. The winners are American consumers, who can buy imported produce for less; the losers may be U.S. farmers, who find it harder and harder to compete with foreign produce.

Key to Ability Levels

BL Below level	**AL** Above level
OL On level	**ELL** English Language Learners

Key to Teaching Resources

📁 Print Material	🔒 DVD
💿 CD-Rom	📠 Transparency

Levels					Resources	Chapter Opener	Section 1	Section 2	Section 3	Chapter Assess
BL	OL	AL	ELL							
FOCUS										
BL	OL	AL	ELL	📠	**Daily Focus Skills Transparencies**		56	54	70	
TEACH										
BL	OL		ELL	📁	**Guided Reading Activities***		p. 37	p. 38	p. 39	
BL	OL	AL	ELL	📁	**Economic Content Vocabulary Activities***		p. 13	p. 13	p. 39	
	OL	AL		📁	**Critical Thinking Activities**			p. 19		
BL	OL		ELL	📁	**Reading Essentials and Note-Taking Guide***		p. 109	p. 112	p. 115	
		AL		📁	**Enrichment Activities**			p. 13		
	OL	AL		📁	**Free Enterprise Activities**		p. 18		p. 19	
BL	OL	AL	ELL	📁	**Primary and Secondary Source Readings**			p. 41		
BL	OL	AL	ELL	📁	**Economic Cartoons**		p. 23		p. 24	
BL	OL	AL	ELL	📠	**Economic Concepts Transparencies, Strategies, and Activities**				p. 31	
BL	OL	AL	ELL	📁	**Math Practice for Economics**			p. 19		
BL	OL	AL	ELL	📠	**Economic Forms and Financial Pages Transparencies, Strategies, and Activities**				p. 13	
BL	OL	AL	ELL	📁	**Reinforcing Economic Skills**		p. 1	p. 6	p. 14	
BL	OL		ELL	📁	**High School Reading in the Content Area Strategies and Activities**	✓	✓	✓	✓	✓
BL	OL	AL	ELL	📠	**High School Writing Process Transparencies**	✓	✓	✓	✓	✓
BL	OL	AL	ELL	📁	**Writer's Guidebook**	✓	✓	✓	✓	✓
BL	OL	AL	ELL	💿	**StudentWorks Plus CD-ROM**	✓	✓	✓	✓	✓
BL	OL	AL	ELL	💿	**Vocabulary PuzzleMaker CD-ROM**	✓	✓	✓	✓	✓

*Also available in Spanish

- Interactive Lesson Planner
- Interactive Teacher Edition
- Fully editable blackline masters
- Economics & You videos

- Differentiated Lesson Plans
- Printable reports of daily assignments
- Standards tracking system

Levels					Resources	Chapter Opener	Section 1	Section 2	Section 3	Chapter Assess
BL	OL	AL	ELL							
TEACH *(continued)*										
BL	OL	AL	ELL	🔒	**Economics & You Video Program DVD—** *Fighting Unemployment, Inflation and Poverty*	✓	✓	✓	✓	✓
BL	OL	AL	ELL	💿	**Graph Coach CD-ROM**	✓	✓	✓	✓	✓
Teacher Resources				📁	**Differentiated Instruction Strategies**	✓	✓	✓	✓	✓
				📁	**Success with English Learners**	✓	✓	✓	✓	✓
				💿	**Presentation Plus! CD-ROM**	✓	✓	✓	✓	✓
ASSESS										
BL	OL	AL	ELL	📁	**Section Quizzes and Chapter Tests**		p. 161	p. 162	p. 163	pp. 165, 169
BL	OL	AL	ELL	📁	**Authentic Assessment Strategies and Activities**		p. 18	p. 19		
BL	OL	AL	ELL	💿	*ExamView® Assessment Suite* **CD-ROM**		13-1	13-2	13-3	Ch. 13
BL	OL	AL	ELL	💿	**Interactive Tutor Self-Assessment CD-ROM**		13-1	13-2	13-3	
CLOSE										
BL			ELL	📁	**Reteaching Activities***		p. 13	p. 13	p. 13	
BL	OL		ELL	📁	**Reading and Study Skills Foldables**		p. 60			

*Also available in Spanish

Activity
Using the McGraw-Hill Learning Network

Web Site Builder

Technology Product

The Web Site Builder is a convenient and dynamic McGraw-Hill Learning Network tool that helps you build Web sites quickly. The site allows you to include your own images, videos, and text to customize it to your needs. The Web site builder also provides you with a variety of tools to make your Web site inviting. Use the Web Site Builder to

- provide assignments and important dates to your students;
- keep students and parents informed of events in your classroom;
- publish your contact information.

Steps

- On the McGraw-Hill Learning Network home page (www.mhln.com), log in as a member.
- Choose **Web Site Builder** under **Resources**.
- Choose a template from the **Create a new site** pull-down options, and follow the prompts on the screen to select a design, insert text, and select fonts, colors, and sizes.
- Create the content students will need to study for a chapter text or post homework assignments.
- Use the navigation buttons on the bottom of the screen to edit, add, and delete information, images, and videos.
- Publish the site and provide the URL to your students.

Economics ONLINE

	Student	Teacher	Parent
Beyond the Textbook	●	●	●
Chapter Overviews	●	●	●
ePuzzles and Games	●		●
Concepts in Motion	●		●
Multi-Language Glossaries	●		●
Online Student Edition	●	●	●
Self-Check Quizzes	●		●
Student Web Activities	●		●
Study Central™	●		●
Time Current Events	●	●	●
Teaching Today		●	
Vocabulary eFlashcards	●		●
Web Activity Lesson Plans		●	

Glencoe Media Center

> glencoe.com

Study-To-Go
- Vocabulary eFlashcards
- Self-Check Quizzes

> **Audio/Video**
- Student Edition Audio
- Spanish Summaries
- Economics & You Videos

READING SUPPORT FROM JAMESTOWN EDUCATION

- **Timed Readings Plus in Social Studies** helps students increase their reading rate and fluency while maintaining comprehension. The 400-word passages are similar to those found on state and national assessments.

- **Reading in the Content Area: Social Studies** concentrates on six essential reading skills that help students better comprehend what they read. The book includes 75 high-interest nonfiction passages written at increasing levels of difficulty.

- **Reading Social Studies** includes strategic reading instruction and vocabulary support in Social Studies content for both ELLs and native speakers of English. www.jamestowneducation.com

Reading List Generator CD-ROM

GLENCOE BOOKLINK 3

Use this database to search more than 30,000 titles to create a customized reading list for your students.

- Reading lists can be organized by students' reading level, author, genre, theme, or area of interest.
- The database provides Degrees of Reading Power™ (DRP) and Lexile™ readability scores for all selections.
- A brief summary of each selection is included.

Leveled reading suggestions for this chapter:

For students at a Grade 10 reading level:
- *The New Deal and the Great Depression in American History,* by Lisa A. Wroble

For students at a Grade 11 reading level:
- *Free to Choose: A Personal Statement,* by Milton Friedman & Rose Friedman

For students at a Grade 12 reading level:
- *Voices of Protest: Huey Long, Father Coughlin and the Great Depression,* by Alan Brinkley

* Review suggested books before assigning them.

NCEE

National Council on Economic Education

Voluntary Standards Emphasized in Chapter 13

Content Standard 18 A nation's overall levels of income, employment, and prices are determined by the interaction of spending and production decisions made by all households, firms, government agencies, and others in the economy.

Content Standard 19 Unemployment imposes costs on individuals and nations. Unexpected inflation imposes costs on many people and benefits some others because it arbitrarily redistributes purchasing power. Inflation can reduce the rate of growth of national living standards because individuals and organizations use resources to protect themselves against the uncertainty of future prices.

Resources Available from NCEE
- Virtual Economics®: An Interactive Center for Economic Education Version 3.0
- Capstone: The Nation's High School Economics Course
- Focus: High School Economics, Second Edition
- Civics and Government: Focus on Economics, Second Edition

To order these materials, or to contact your State Council on Economic Education about workshops and programs, call 1-800-338-1192 or visit the NCEE Web site at store.ncee.net.

The BIG Ideas

As students study the chapter, remind them to consider the chapter-based Big Ideas. The **Essential Question** in the chapter launch activity below ties in to the Big Ideas and helps students think about and understand important chapter concepts. In addition, the Hands-On Chapter Project relates the content from each section to the Big Ideas. The steps in each section build on each other and culminate in the Wrap-Up Activity on the Visual Summary page.

Economics & You Video To generate student interest and provide a springboard for class discussion, access the Economics & You Topic 20 video, **Fighting Unemployment, Inflation and Poverty,** at glencoe.com or on the video DVD.

FOLDABLES Study Organizer **Dinah Zike's Foldables** are three-dimensional, interactive graphic organizers that help students practice basic writing skills, review key vocabulary terms, and identify main ideas. Have students complete this chapter's Foldable activity or activities in *Dinah Zike's Reading and Study Skills Foldables* booklet. **OL**

Economics ONLINE

Introduce students to chapter content and key terms by having them access *Chapter 13 —Chapter Overviews* at glencoe.com.

CHAPTER
13 Economic Instability

Why It Matters

Do your grandparents talk about the "good old days" when gas was 25 cents per gallon and a loaf of bread cost 10 cents? Compile a list of things that you have been purchasing for several years. Note the prices you paid in the past and those you are currently paying. What do you think accounts for the price differences? Read Chapter 13 to find out what factors can lead to economic instability.

The BIG Ideas

1. Economists look at a variety of factors to assess the growth and performance of a nation's economy.

2. The labor market, like other markets, is determined by supply and demand.

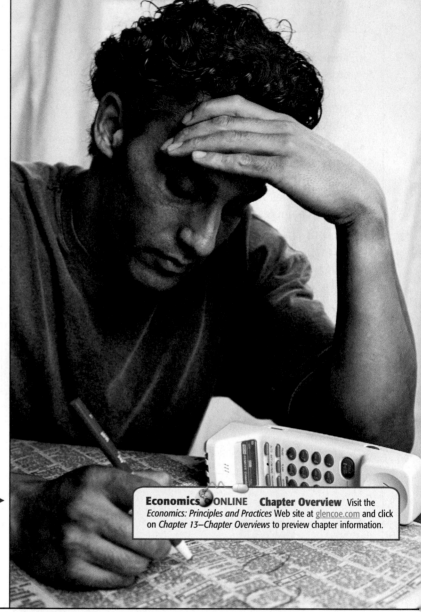

◀ During times of economic instability, people may lose their jobs and have problems finding new ones.

352 UNIT 4

Economics ONLINE **Chapter Overview** Visit the *Economics: Principles and Practices* Web site at glencoe.com and click on *Chapter 13–Chapter Overviews* to preview chapter information.

Activity: Launching the Chapter

Visualizing Write the latest U.S. unemployment and Consumer Price Index figures on the board. This information is available at www.bls.gov. Using the given percentages, have students figure out how many of their classmates would be unemployed if the class represented the total labor force. Then have students calculate the future price of a product they recently bought if the current monthly CPI continues at the same rate for three months.

Essential Question: What causes instability in the U.S. economy? Why is it a problem? *(Instability is caused by changes in spending, innovations, external shocks, and changes in government policy. Instability can lower economic productivity, reduce consumer spending, weaken the government, and increase crime and poverty.)* **OL**

SECTION 1 — Business Cycles and Fluctuations

CHAPTER 13, SECTION 1

GUIDE TO READING

Section Preview
In this section, you will learn that business cycles are the alternating increases and decreases in the level of economic activity.

Content Vocabulary
- business cycles (p. 353)
- business fluctuation (p. 353)
- recession (p. 354)
- peak (p. 354)
- trough (p. 354)
- expansion (p. 354)
- trend line (p. 354)
- depression (p. 354)
- depression scrip (p. 356)
- leading economic indicator (p. 358)
- composite index of leading economic indicators (p. 359)
- econometric model (p. 359)

Academic Vocabulary
- innovation (p. 355)
- series (p. 358)

Reading Strategy
Identifying As you read the section, complete a graphic organizer like the one below by identifying factors that can cause changes in the business cycle.

Changes in the Business Cycle

Focus

Bellringer
Daily Focus Transparency 56

GUIDE TO READING

Answers to Graphic:

changes in investment spending; innovation; imitation; monetary policy decisions; external shocks

ISSUES IN THE NEWS
—Associated Press

Economic Growth Totters

The economy has slowed to a snail's pace, growing . . . at the slowest rate in more than three years and stirring fresh debate about the country's financial health heading into the elections. The Commerce Department reported Friday that economic growth during the July-to-September period [of 2006] clocked in at an annual rate of just 1.6 percent, a subpar performance. . . .

The fresh reading. . . disappointed economists, rattled investors and gave Republicans and Democrats plenty to argue about. Economic matters are expected to influence voters' choices when they go to the polls Nov. 7.

On Wall Street, stocks sagged. The Dow Jones industrials, which had hit new highs in recent sessions, lost 73.40 points. . . . The third quarter's performance was the weakest since a 1.2 percent growth rate eked out in the first quarter of 2003, when a nervous nation hunkered down for the start of the Iraq war. ■

Economic growth is something that is beneficial to almost everyone. However, we cannot take economic growth for granted. Sometimes **business cycles**—regular ups and downs of real GDP—interrupt economic growth. **Business fluctuations**—the rise and fall of real GDP over time in an irregular manner—interrupt growth at other times.

Slower economic growth, as you read in the news story, is always a matter of concern. Businesses lose sales, voters become unhappy, investors get nervous—and even the stock market shows its disapproval. Because of this, economists have developed elaborate forecasting models and statistical tools. After all, we all want to know where we are headed.

> **business cycles** regular increases and decreases in real GDP
>
> **business fluctuations** irregular increases and decreases in real GDP

Resource Manager

CHAPTER 13 Economic Instability **353**

R Reading Strategies

Teacher Edition
- Identifying, p. 355
- Summarizing, p. 357
- Act. Prior Know., p. 359

Additional Resources
- Guid. Read. Act., p. 37
- Read. Ess. & Note-Taking Guide, p. 109

C Critical Thinking

Teacher Edition
- Assessing, p. 354
- Making Connections, pp. 355, 357

Additional Resources
- Authentic Assess., p. 18
- Reading and Study Skills Fold., p. 60

D Differentiated Instruction

Teacher Edition
- Visual/Spatial, p. 355
- Logical/Math., pp. 356, 360
- Adv. Learners, p. 357

Additional Resources
- Econ. Cartoons, p. 23
- Reteach. Act., p. 13

W Writing Support

Teacher Edition
- Descriptive Writing, p. 354
- Narrative Writing, p. 356
- Expository Writing, p. 358

Additional Resources
- High School Writing Process Trans.

S Skill Practice

Teacher Edition
- Using Line Graphs, pp. 354, 358

Additional Resources
- Free Ent. Act., p. 18
- Reinforcing Econ. Skills, p. 1
- Econ. Content Vocab. Act., p. 13

Teach

C Critical Thinking

Assessing Ask: What are the positives and negatives for people when the economy hits a trough? *(negatives: the economy has reached a low point, people experience hard times; positives: the GDP has stopped falling, recovery will soon follow)* **OL**

W Writing Support

Descriptive Writing Ask students to write a one-page description of the events that might occur in a small town after a factory there must lay off half of its workforce. **OL**

S Skill Practice

Using Line Graphs Ask: Where is Real GDP in relation to the trend line after a recession? *(below the trend line)* What is the name of the phase when GDP is rising? *(expansion)* **BL**

Economic Analysis

Answer: The GDP has stopped declining, and expansion will follow.

Differentiated Instruction

---

recession decline in real GDP lasting at least two quarters

peak point in time when real GDP stops expanding and begins to decline

trough point in time when real GDP stops declining and begins to expand

expansion period of uninterrupted growth of real GDP

trend line growth path the economy would follow if it were not interrupted by alternating periods of recession and recovery

depression state of the economy with large numbers of unemployed people, declining real incomes, overcapacity in manufacturing plants, and general economic hardship

---

Business Cycles: Characteristics and Causes

MAIN Idea Business cycles are marked by alternating periods of expansion and recession.

Economics and You Has a slow economy ever shut down a factory in your community? Read on to learn about some possible causes.

We can describe the basic features of an expansion or a recession, or the *phases* of the business cycle as they are sometimes called. When it comes to identifying the actual causes, though, no one theory seems to explain all past events or predict future ones because each seems to be a little different from the last.

Phases of the Business Cycle

The two phases of the business cycle are illustrated in **Figure 13.1.** The first phase is **recession,** a period during which real GDP—GDP measured in constant prices—declines for at least two quarters in a row, or six consecutive months. The recession begins when the economy reaches a **peak**—the point where real GDP stops going up. It ends when the economy reaches a **trough**—the turnaround point where real GDP stops going down.

As soon as the declining real GDP bottoms out, the economy moves into the second phase, **expansion**—a period of recovery from a recession. Expansion continues until the economy reaches a new peak. When it does, the current business cycle ends and a new one begins.

If periods of recession and expansion did not occur, the economy would follow a steady growth path called a **trend line.** As Figure 13.1 shows, the economy departs from, and then returns to, its trend line as it passes through phases of recession and expansion. To make it easier to read, recessions in figures such as this are usually shaded to separate them from periods of expansion.

If a recession becomes very severe, it may turn into a **depression**—a state of the economy with large numbers of people out of work, acute shortages, and excess capacity in manufacturing plants. Most experts agree that the Great Depression of the 1930s was the only depression the United States experienced during the twentieth century.

Changes in Investment Spending

Changes in capital expenditures are thought to be one cause of business cycles. When the economy is expanding, businesses expect future sales to be high, so

---

Figure 13.1 ► Business Cycles

Graphs In MOtion
See StudentWorks™ Plus or glencoe.com.

▶ A business cycle is normally measured from peak to peak so that it includes one recession and one expansion.

Economic Analysis *What does a trough indicate?*

PHASES OF THE BUSINESS CYCLE

What Economic Indicators Really Indicate

Objective: Understand the limitations of the Consumer Price Index.

Focus: Have students review the CPI and other indices in the textbook.

Teach: Ask students to study the cartoon and answer the questions.

Assess: Discuss students' answers to question 3 as a class.

Close: Poll the class on their responses to question 4. Call on students to explain their answers.

Differentiated Instruction Strategies

BL Have each student explain the meaning of the cartoon to a partner.

AL Direct students to write two paragraphs explaining how inflation rates impact Social Security payments and the setting of income tax brackets.

ELL Have small groups brainstorm other examples of "creative exaggeration."

they invest heavily in capital goods. Companies may build new plants or buy new equipment to replace older equipment. At first this generates jobs and income, but after a while businesses may decide they have expanded enough. If they then cut back on their capital investments, layoffs and eventually recession may result.

Innovation and Imitation

Another possible cause of business cycles is an **innovation** that may be a new product or a new way of performing a task. When a business innovates, it often gains an edge on its competitors because costs go down or sales go up. In either case, profits increase and the business grows.

If other businesses in the same industry want to remain competitive, they must copy what the innovator has done or develop something even better. The imitating companies must invest heavily to do this, and an investment boom follows. After the innovation takes hold in the industry, further investments are unnecessary, and economic activity may slow down.

Monetary Policy Decisions

Another possible cause of business cycles is the Federal Reserve System's policy on interest rates. When "easy money" policies are in effect, interest rates are low and loans easy to get. Easy money encourages the private sector to borrow and invest, which stimulates the economy for a short time.

Eventually the increased demand for loans causes interest rates to rise, which in turn discourages new borrowers. As borrowing and spending slow down, the level of economic activity may decline.

External Shocks

Another potential cause of business cycles is external shocks, such as increases in oil prices, wars, and international conflict. Some shocks drive the economy up, as when Great Britain discovered North Sea oil in the 1970s. Other shocks can be negative, as when high oil prices hit the United States in mid-2005.

Finally, in many cases, several factors seem to work together to create a cycle. In these situations, a disturbance in one part of the economy seems to have an impact somewhere else, causing an expansion to begin or a recession to end.

✓ Reading Check **Summarizing** What are thought to be the causes of business cycles?

CAREERS

Statistician

The Work

* Scientifically apply mathematical principles to the collection, analysis, and presentation of numerical data

* Gather and interpret data pertaining to a variety of fields, including biology, finance, economics, engineering, insurance, medicine, public health, psychology, marketing, education, scientific research, and sports

* Gauge the public's feelings on certain topics by taking samples of opinions

Qualifications

* Aptitude for and an interest in mathematics and computers

* Knowledge in subject matter of chosen field

* Strong communication skills

* Bachelor's degree in mathematics or statistics, with many private sector jobs requiring a master's degree

Earnings

* Median annual earnings: $58,620 (private sector), $81,262 (government sector)

Job Growth Outlook

* Average

Source: *Occupational Outlook Handbook, 2006–2007 Edition*

R Reading Strategy

Identifying Ask: What are five innovations that have helped the U.S. economy expand? *(Possible answer: computers, the Internet, cell phones, cars, TV)* BL

D Differentiated Instruction

Visual/Spatial Have students create a collage about the effects of OPEC's oil price increases in the 1970s. *(Collage items might include pictures of lines at gas stations, "out of gas" signs, and newspaper headlines about wage-price controls.)* OL

C Critical Thinking

Making Connections Have students write a paragraph explaining how statistics impact their lives. For example, students might write about an athlete's sports statistics, a calculation of car insurance rates based on age statistics, or the cancellation of a favorite TV show because of poor ratings. AL

✓ Reading Check **Answer:** changes in investment spending, innovations and imitation, monetary policy decisions, external shocks

CHAPTER 13 Economic Instability 355

Leveled Activities

BL Reteaching Activities, p. 13

OL Free Enterprise Activities, p. 18

AL Authentic Assessment Strategies and Activities, p. 18

W Writing Support

Narrative Writing Have students consult historical sources to research how the stock market crash affected individuals. Ask students to then create a character who would have experienced or observed the events of "Black Tuesday." *(Possible characters include a broker, a stockholder, the manager of a publicly held firm, or a hot dog vendor on Wall Street.)* Instruct students to write a story about what the character saw, heard, and felt on that day. **AL**

D Differentiated Instruction

Logical/Mathematical Have students calculate how their weekly income (from allowance or work) would change if it fell by the same rate that manufacturing wages dropped between 1929 to 1933. **Ask:** How would you economize if this happened to you? *(Possible answers: cut back on entertainment expenses; ride a bicycle instead of drive)* **OL**

Caption Answer: 12.8 million

Additional Support

---

depression scrip currency issued by towns, chambers of commerce, and other civic bodies during the Great Depression of the 1930s

---

Great Depression During the height of the depression, the unemployed lined up **W** in employment offices. *How many people were unemployed during the Great Depression?*

Business Cycles in the United States

MAIN Idea Business cycles have become much more moderate since the Great Depression of the 1930s.

Economics and You Do you have a savings account at a bank? Read on to learn why the money in your account is insured.

Economic activity in the United States followed an irregular course throughout the twentieth century. The worst downturn was the Great Depression of the 1930s. The years since World War II have taken on a special pattern of their own.

The Great Depression

The stock market crash on October 29, 1929, known as "Black Tuesday," marked the beginning of the Great Depression, one of the darkest periods in American history. Between 1929 and 1933, real GDP declined nearly 50 percent, from approximately $103 billion to $55 billion. At the same time, the number of people out of work rose nearly 800 percent—from 1.6 million to 12.8 million. During the worst years of the Depression, one out of every four workers was unemployed. Even workers who had **D** jobs suffered. The average manufacturing wage, which was 55 cents an hour in 1929, plunged to 5 cents an hour by 1933.

Many banks across the country failed. Federal bank deposit insurance did not exist at the time, so depositors were not protected. To prevent panic withdrawals, the federal government declared a "bank holiday" in March 1933 and closed every bank in the country. The closure lasted for only a few days, but about one-quarter of the banks never reopened.

The size of the money supply fell by one-third. Official paper currency was in such short supply that people began using **depression scrip**—unofficial currency that towns, counties, chambers of commerce, and other civic bodies issued. Billions of dollars of scrip were used to pay salaries for teachers, firefighters, police officers, and other municipal employees.

Causes of the Great Depression

An enormous gap in the distribution of income was one important cause. Poverty prevented workers from stimulating the economy by spending. The rich had the income but often used it for such nonproductive activities as stock market speculation.

Easy credit also played a role. Many people borrowed heavily in the late 1920s to buy stocks. Then, as interest rates rose, it was difficult for them to repay their loans. When the crunch came, heavily indebted people had nothing to fall back on.

Global economic conditions also played a part. During the 1920s, the United States had made many loans to foreign countries to help support international trade. When these loans suddenly

---

Activity: Interdisciplinary Connection

Mathematics Easy credit played a role in causing the Depression, and some economists are worried that it could contribute to a future recession. For example, in 2007 the mortgage securities market fell into crisis. The housing market slumped. Combined with loan delinquencies from borrowers with poor credit ratings, this slump caused more than two dozen mortgage lenders to go bankrupt. These bankruptcies in turn dragged the housing market down further, which slowed the overall economy. Have students calculate monthly mortgage payments on a $100,000 30-year loan at 6.125 percent interest. *($607.61)* Next have students calculate monthly mortgage payments on a $100,000 15-year loan at 5.5 percent interest. *($817.08)* **Ask:** What are the advantages and disadvantages of each type of loan? *(The monthly payments on the 30-year loan are lower, but the total financing costs will be greater over the duration of the loan. The monthly payments on the 15-year loan are higher, but the total financing charge will be lower because the loan will be paid off much faster.)* **OL**

Recovery Wartime production during the 1940s provided an additional stimulus in the post-Depression era. *What other efforts led to economic recovery?*

C

C **Critical Thinking**

Making Connections

Ask: What U.S. social change that took place during World War II does this image show? *(Large numbers of women took jobs outside the home.)* **BL**

R **Reading Strategy**

Summarizing Have students write a summary of the Social Security program. **BL**

D **Differentiated Instruction**

Advanced Learners Have students visit www.fdic.gov to find out the basic insurance coverage on deposits provided by the FDIC. Ask students to speculate on whether the amount is enough for today and whether it would have made a difference in the 1930s. **Ask:** How does the FDIC reduce the possibility of runs on banks? *(People know that even if their bank fails, the government will give them a certain amount of their money back.)* **AL**

Caption Answer: government legislation and agencies

Additional Support

were harder to get, foreign buyers purchased fewer American goods, and U.S. exports fell sharply.

At the same time, high U.S. tariffs kept many countries from selling goods to the United States, leading to economic crises abroad. As world trade declined, American exports dropped even further.

Recovery and Legislation

The Great Depression finally ended ten years after it started, when real GDP returned to its 1929 high. The economy recovered partly because of increased government spending and partly on its own. The massive spending during World War II added another huge stimulant that further propelled the economy.

The country was so shaken by the Great Depression that a number of laws were passed and agencies established from 1933 to 1940 both to protect people and to prevent another such disaster. The Social Security Act of 1935 was one of the most important and significant pieces of legislation passed during this time. To protect people during their working years, the minimum wage was established at about

the same time. New unemployment programs gave some relief to people who were temporarily out of work.

Because so many public stock companies went out of business, the Securities and Exchange Commission (SEC) was created to put requirements on the disclosure of financial statements by public corporations. The resulting federal regulation made stock ownership by the public much safer.

Finally, the newly established Federal Deposit Insurance Corporation (FDIC) provided modest bank insurance for depositors. Such safeguards were not available earlier, when nearly one-third of the banks had failed. In all, the period from 1933 to 1940 saw the establishment of many federal institutions to make working, banking, investing, and retirement safer. **D**

The reforms of the 1930s seemed to help, and most economists today think that it would be unlikely, if not impossible, for another Great Depression to occur.

R **Cycles After World War II**

Business cycles became much more moderate after World War II, with shorter recessions and longer periods of expansion.

CHAPTER 13 Economic Instability 357

Extending the Content

Monetary Policy and the Great Depression Monetarists view the Great Depression differently from Keynesian economists. Monetarists do not deny that a lack of business investment in the early 1930s reduced aggregate demand. However, they feel that the fall in aggregate demand resulted from the reduced amount of money in circulation. According to monetarists, the

Fed should have greatly increased the amount of money in the economy. Instead, the steps taken by the Fed cut the money supply by one-third between 1929 and 1933. By its actions, the monetarists claim, the Fed turned what would have been just another recession into an economic disaster.

Figure 13.2 ▶ **The Index of Leading Economic Indicators**

Graphs In Motion
See StudentWorks™ Plus
or glencoe.com.

S Skill Practice

Using Line Graphs Ask: What happened to the index in 2001–2002? *(decreased)* What happened to it from 1985–1988? *(increased)*
BL

W Writing Support

Expository Writing Have students research other statistics that predict changes in GDP. Then have them write a one-page paper explaining why economists consider those statistics to be important factors in determining the future state of the economy.
AL

Economic Analysis

Answer: Economists watch how the index moves; it usually turns down nine months before a recession begins.

✓ Reading Check **Answer:** lower GDP, high unemployment, lower wages, bank failures, smaller money supply

▶ The index of leading economic indicators is one of the tools used to predict future economic activity.

Economic Analysis *How do economists use this index to predict recession?*

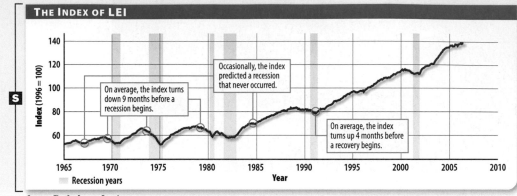

THE INDEX OF LEI

On average, the index turns down 9 months before a recession begins.

Occasionally, the index predicted a recession that never occurred.

On average, the index turns up 4 months before a recovery begins.

Index (1996 = 100)

□ Recession years   Year

Source: The Conference Board

---

leading economic indicator statistical series that turns down before the economy turns down, or up before the economy turns up

During this time, the average length of recessions was about 10 months, while expansions averaged about 54 months. With the possible exception of the Vietnam War period, most recessions from 1965 to 1980 occurred on a fairly regular basis.

After the early 1980s, recessions occurred less frequently. A record-setting peacetime expansion during the Reagan administration began in November 1982 and lasted for almost eight years. This was followed by a longer, and even more prosperous, expansion during the Clinton years from 1991 to 2001. In fact, this 10-year period of uninterrupted economic growth is the longest peacetime expansion in U.S. history.

Although the Clinton expansion ended in March 2001, a new one began again in November of that year, shortly after the 9/11 terrorist attacks. Whether the latest expansion can set another record is yet to be seen, but it has already exceeded the historical 54-month average.

✓ Reading Check **Inferring** What impact did the Great Depression have on the United States?

Forecasting Business Cycles

MAIN Idea Economists use statistics and models to predict business cycles.

Economics and You Would you change your post-graduation plans if you knew a recession was coming? Read on to find out how economists try to predict future recessions and expansions.

Economists use several methods to predict business cycles. One uses the statistical **series** shown in **Figure 13.2.** Another makes use of macroeconomic modeling.

Using Everyday Economic Statistics

A change in a single statistic often indicates a change in future GDP. For example, **W** the length of the average workweek may change just before a recession begins if people work fewer hours. This makes the measure a **leading economic indicator**—a statistical series that normally turns down

---

Hands-On Chapter Project

Step 1

Economic Indicators and the U.S. Economy

In this project, students will research economic indicators and problems and then prepare and present a TV talk show focusing on the U.S. economy.

Step 1: Explaining Economic Indicators. Students will identify and explain economic indicators, and predict what will happen to the economy based on current indicators.

Directions: Organize the class into groups of five. Instruct group members to take on the roles of talk show host, an economic indicators "expert," an inflation "expert," an unemployment "expert," and a summarizer/questioner. Then have students work together within their groups to consult Web sites such as www.nber.org (National Bureau of Economic Research), www.bls.gov (Bureau of Labor Statistics), www.bea.gov (Bureau of Economic Analysis) and any other reliable sites needed to find current figures for

leading economic indicators and explanations of what the indicators show.

Summarizing Direct students in each group to use their research to write the portion of the talk-show script that will include the host and questioner discussing economic indicators with the indicators "expert." Students should then work together within their groups to construct a forecast for the economy, based on current indicators, to be included in the script. **OL**

before the economy turns down or turns up before the economy turns up.

However, no single series has proven completely reliable, so several individual series are combined into an overall index. This is the approach used by the **composite index of leading economic indicators (LEI)**, a monthly statistical series that uses a combination of 10 individual indicators to forecast changes in real GDP.

The composite index is shown in Figure 13.2, where the shaded areas represent recessions. The average time between a dip in the index and the onset of a recession is about nine months. The average time between a rise in the index and the start of an expansion is about four months.

Using Econometric Models

An **econometric model** is a mathematical model that uses algebraic equations to describe how the economy behaves. Most models start with the output-expenditure model we examined on page 327:

$$GDP = C + I + G + (X - M)$$

To see how we use it, suppose that a survey of consumers revealed that households annually spend a fixed amount of money called 'a', along with 95 percent of their disposable personal income, or DPI. We could express this as **C = a + .95(DPI)** and then substitute this equation into the output-expenditure model to get:

$$GDP = a + .95(DPI) + I + G + (X - M)$$

This process is repeated until each of the terms in the model is expanded and the equation is broken down into smaller and smaller components. To find GDP, forecasters put in the latest values for the variables on the right side of the equation and solve for GDP.

Over time, actual changes in the economy are compared to the model's predictions. The model is then updated by changing some of the equations. In the end, some models give reasonably good forecasts for up to nine months into the future.

R ✓ **Reading Check** Analyzing Why are short-term econometric models more accurate than long-term models?

composite index of leading economic indicators (LEI) composite index of 10 economic series that move up and down in advance of changes in the overall economy; statistical series used to predict turning points in the business cycle

econometric model mathematical expression used to describe how the economy is expected to perform in the future

CHAPTER 13, SECTION 1

R **Reading Strategy**

Activating Prior Knowledge
Ask: What are the components of the output-expenditure model? *(GDP = gross domestic product; C = consumption expenditures; I = investment spending; G = government expenditures; X = exports; M = imports; X — M = net exports)* **OL**

✓**Reading Check** **Answer:** Long-term models include more factors that can change over time and require updating.

Assess

● Use the Interactive Tutor Self-Assessment CD-ROM to review Section 1, and then assign the Section 1 Review as homework or as an in-class activity.

Close

Organizing Have students create a chart with the columns "Recession" and "Expansion," and list section terms and concepts in each column. Some terms will be used in both columns. **OL**

SECTION 1 Review

Vocabulary
1. **Explain** the significance of business cycles, business fluctuation, recession, peak, trough, expansion, trend line, depression, depression scrip, leading economic indicator, composite index of leading economic indicators, and econometric model.

Main Ideas
2. **Explaining** How are business cycles forecast?
3. **Describing** What are the two main phases of a business cycle?
4. **Identifying** Use a graphic organizer like the one below to identify the causes and effects of the Great Depression.

Critical Thinking
5. **The BIG Idea** Why is it difficult to explain the causes of business cycles?
6. **Analyzing Visuals** Use Figure 13.1 on page 354 to explain how a business cycle can be compared to a roller coaster.
7. **Determining Cause and Effect** Assume that business inventories are falling, the average number of hours worked per week is going up, and there is an increase in the number of new building permits. What would these indicators say about the economy, and why?

Applying Economics
8. **Economic Security** Suppose you were the head of a household. How would you plan spending for your family if you had an accurate prediction of future business cycles? Include examples in your response.

Review **SECTION 1**

Answers

1. All definitions can be found in the section and the Glossary.
2. Economists use models and statistical tools to forecast business cycles.
3. The two main phases of a business cycle are recession and expansion.
4. **Causes:** unequal distribution of income, easy credit, global economic conditions. **Effects:** GDP fell almost 50 percent, unemployment rose nearly 800 percent, average manufacturing wage fell from 55 cents an hour to 5 cents an hour, banks failed, money supply contracted.
5. It is hard to pinpoint the cause of business cycles because many different factors are impacting the economy at the same time, and disturbances spread quickly through the economy.
6. A business cycle can be compared to a roller coaster because both have ups and downs.
7. These indicators say that the economy is expanding. Goods, including houses, are being rapidly bought. Meanwhile, people are working more and increasing overall production.
8. Answers will vary, but students should demonstrate the understanding that spending levels should be adjusted to match fluctuations in the economy.

Teach

D Differentiated Instruction

Logical/Mathematical Ask students to visit the American Research Group Web site (www.americanresearchgroup.com) to find the most current opinions of Americans regarding the future of the economy. Have students write a report that describes the polling figures, sample size, and margin of error. **OL**

BusinessWeek *ONLINE*

To find up-to-date news and analysis on the economy, business, technology, markets, entrepreneurs, investments, and finance, have students search feature articles and special reports on the BusinessWeek Web site, www.businessweek.com.

Examining the Newsclip

Answers:
1. The National Bureau of Economic Research
2. adjust expectations and reduce spending

Additional Support

Teacher Tip

Choosing Businesses Ideas for businesses to survey can be found in the Yellow Pages of the phone directory. Have groups turn in their business lists before calling so you can prevent multiple surveys of the same business.

BusinessWeek NEWSCLIP

Economists have developed a variety of tools and indicators to spot the beginnings of a recession or expansion. They also might want to take a look at one restaurant in New York that has an indicator all its own.

Dog Days: A Frank Look at the Economy

Corporate chiefs and economists don't toss around the word "recession" lightly—bad for morale. But New York hot dog chain Gray's Papaya, the 24-hour eatery frequented by bag ladies and bankers alike, isn't bashful.

Word is that the highly visible outpost on New York's Upper West Side is about to plaster a sign for its "recession special" in its huge front windows. The last time it did that was March 2001, just as the economy was dipping into recession. The National Bureau of Economic Research, which officially calls business cycle turns, reported that March onset eight months later.

Already, perhaps seeing economic clouds (and an interior "recession special" sign left over from past downturns), more Gray's customers are asking for the dog deal ($2.75 for two franks and a drink, including tax).

"People are getting more realistic and adjusting their expectations and budgets," says Jackie Schwimmer, a senior vice-president at one of the city's largest real estate brokers, in between chomps. She doesn't see an imminent full-blown recession but concedes a pinch in the housing market.

Then there's the Wall Street guy who'd ventured uptown for his frank fix. Times are good in his neck of the woods, he admits, but he's feeling less inclined to drop $11 on a Financial District designer salad more than twice a week. And he'd gladly trade the savory bliss of Gray's recession special for added job security. "I love the dogs, and I love the deal," he says, "but I hope [Gray's Papaya is] wrong."

—Reprinted from *BusinessWeek*

Anxious Times for Americans

Americans are growing increasingly uneasy about the economy

THE NATIONAL ECONOMY A YEAR FROM TODAY WILL BE:

BETTER:	6%
THE SAME:	25%
WORSE:	67%

Source: American Research Group, Inc.

Examining the Newsclip

1. **Identifying** Which organization is responsible for calling turns in the business cycle?
2. **Determining Cause and Effect** According to the article, what do people do when they expect a recession?

Activity: Hands-On Economics

Adjusting to Recession Have students work in groups of five or six to conduct phone surveys of businesses in your community to find out how the businesses adjust to recession. Students within each group should first brainstorm a list of questions to ask such as: Are prices adjusted? Is the workforce reduced?

Have groups develop a script to use for their phone calls, including opening and closing comments. Next, each student should survey one of the businesses using the list of questions created by his or her group. Groups should then present their findings to the class in an oral report. Discuss as a class the similarities and differences among students' findings. **OL**

SECTION 2 Inflation

GUIDE TO READING

Section Preview

In this section, you will find out that inflation is a rise in the general level of prices that disrupts the economy.

Content Vocabulary

- inflation (p. 361)
- deflation (p. 361)
- price index (p. 362)
- consumer price index (CPI) (p. 362)
- market basket (p. 362)
- base year (p. 362)
- creeping inflation (p. 364)
- hyperinflation (p. 364)
- stagflation (p. 364)
- producer price index (PPI) (p. 364)
- implicit GDP price deflator (p. 364)

- demand-pull inflation (p. 365)
- cost-push inflation (p. 365)
- creditor (p. 367)
- debtor (p. 367)

Academic Vocabulary

- construction (p. 362)
- recover (p. 365)

Reading Strategy

Illustrating As you read the section, complete a graphic organizer similar to the one below by illustrating the steps in a wage-price spiral.

Step 1 → Step 2 → Higher Prices

ISSUES IN THE NEWS

—The New York Times

Hyperinflation in Zimbabwe

How bad is inflation in Zimbabwe? Well, consider this: at a supermarket near the center of the capital, Harare, toilet paper costs $417. No, not per roll. Four hundred seventeen Zimbabwean dollars is the value of a single two-ply sheet. A roll costs $145,750—in American currency, about 69 cents.

For untold numbers of Zimbabweans, toilet paper—and bread, margarine, meat, even the once ubiquitous morning cup of tea—have become unimaginable luxuries. All are casualties of the hyperinflation that is roaring toward 1,000 percent a year, a rate usually seen only in war zones. ■

Macroeconomic instability is not limited to fluctuations in the level of national output (GDP) or national income (GNP). Changes in prices can be equally disruptive to the economy. When the general level of prices rises, the economy is experiencing **inflation.** A decline in the general level of prices is called **deflation.** Both situations are harmful to the economy and should be avoided whenever possible.

Inflation in the United States has varied over the years. We may grumble when the price of gas goes up by a few cents. As you can see in the news story, though, price increases can go to extremes and turn everyday products into luxury items.

inflation increase in the general level of prices of goods and services

deflation decrease in the general level of prices for goods and services

CHAPTER 13 Economic Instability 361

Teach

D Differentiated Instruction

Logical/Mathematical Have students suppose that the BLS decided to change the base year for the Consumer Price Index to 1992–1994. **Ask:** How would that change in the base year affect the CPI rating for 2007? *(It would lower the rating.)* Why would that change occur? *(The prices during the new base year were higher than those in 1982–1984, so the price difference between the base and 2007 would not be as great.)* **OL**

S Skill Practice

Using Circle and Bar Graphs

Have students use the data in Figure 13.3 to create three different bar graphs: one for the individual product prices, one for the total market basket costs, and one for the Index Number. **OL**

Economic Analysis

Answer: A CPI of 163.2 means that prices have risen 63.2 percent since the base year.

Additional Support

---

price index statistical series used to measure changes in the price level over time

consumer price index (CPI) series used to measure price changes for a representative sample of frequently used consumer items

market basket representative selection of goods and services used to compile a price index

base year year serving as point of comparison for other years in a price index or other statistical measure *(also see page 221)*

Measuring Prices and Inflation

MAIN Idea Several price indexes are used to measure inflation.

Economics and You Have you noticed that prices for some items go up while others go down? Read on to learn how this affects the rate of inflation.

To understand inflation, we must first examine how it is measured. This involves the **construction** of a **price index**—a statistical series used to measure changes in the level of prices over time. A price index can be compiled for a range of items. We will focus on the **consumer price index (CPI)**, a statistical series that tracks monthly changes in the prices paid by urban consumers for a representative "basket" of goods and services.

The Market Basket

The first step we have to take is to select a **market basket**—a representative selection of commonly purchased goods and services. The CPI uses the prices of approximately 364 goods and services, such as those shown in **Figure 13.3**. While this may seem like a small number, these items are scientifically selected to represent the types of purchases that most consumers make.

The next step is to find the average price of each item in the market basket. To do so, every month employees of the U.S. Census Bureau sample prices on nearly 80,000 items in stores across the country. They then add up the prices to find the total cost of the market basket. The hypothetical results of such a monthly activity are shown in Figure 13.3 for three separate periods.

A **base year**—a year that serves as the basis of comparison for all other years, is then selected. While almost any year will do, the Bureau of Labor Statistics (BLS) in the U.S. Department of Commerce currently uses average prices as they existed from 1982 to 1984. While this is likely to be updated in the future, it is still the most popular base year used for prices today.

Figure 13.3 ▶ Constructing the Consumer Price Index

Item	Description	Price Base Period (1982–1984)	Price Second Period (1998)	Price Third Period (January 2006)
1	Toothpaste (7 oz.)	$1.40	$1.49	$2.25
2	Milk (1 gal.)	1.29	1.29	1.79
3	Peanut butter (2-lb. jar)	2.50	2.65	3.73
4	Lightbulb (60 watt)	.45	.48	.65
.....	.....	.....	.....	.....
364	Automobile engine tune-up	40.00	42.00	84.75
	Total cost of market basket	$1,792.00	$2,925.00	$3,582.00
	Current market basket cost / Base market basket cost	$\frac{\$1,792}{\$1,792} = 1.000$	$\frac{\$2,925}{\$1,792} = 1.632$	$\frac{\$3,582}{\$1,792} = 1.999$
	Index Number (%):	100 (%)	163.2 (%)	199.9 (%)

▶ Every month the Bureau of Labor Statistics reprices its market basket of commonly used consumer items and reports the results as a percentage of the cost for the base period.

Economic Analysis *How do we interpret a CPI of 163.2?*

Activity: Collaborative Learning

Calculating CPI Have students work together in groups of five or six. Ask students to create a market basket for their group. Each basket should include 20 items that students typically buy. Totaling the prices of the items, students should figure the current cost of their group's market basket. Ask students to then calculate the total cost of the basket for the next three years if prices rise by 4 percent each year. Have students determine the CPI for the third year using the current market basket cost as the base year. Make copies of each group's basket list and distribute them to the other groups. Have students compare baskets and, as a class, create a composite market basket. **OL**

Figure 13.4 ► **Measuring Prices and Inflation**

CHAPTER 13, SECTION 2

► Consumer prices have risen steadily since the mid-1960s. Inflation peaked in the early 1980s and then declined.

Economic Analysis *How is the CPI used to compute inflation?*

THE RATE OF INFLATION AND THE CONSUMER PRICE INDEX, 1965–2006

Source: Bureau of Labor Statistics

The Price Index

The last step in the process is to make the numbers in the table easier to interpret by converting the dollar cost of a market basket to an index value. This is done by dividing the cost of every market basket by the base-year market basket cost. For example, the $3,582 cost for January 2006 is divided by the $1,792 base-period cost to get 1.999, or 199.9 percent. The index number for January—199.9—represents the level of prices in comparison to the base-period prices.

In practice, all of the conversions are understood to be a percentage of the base-period cost even though the % sign or the word *percent* is not used. For example, prices in January 2006 are 199.9 percent of those in the base period, which is another way of saying that prices have nearly doubled. A different base year would give a different index number. However, to avoid confusion, the base year is changed only infrequently.

Because so many prices are sampled all over the country, the BLS publishes specific consumer price indexes for selected cities and large urban areas, as well as one for the economy as a whole.

Skills Handbook
See page R54 to learn about ***Understanding Percentages.***

Measuring Inflation

Now that we have the price index, we can find the percentage change in the monthly price level, which is how inflation is measured. To illustrate, suppose that the CPI in January of one year is 199.9, and it was 190.4 exactly one year earlier. To find the *percentage* change, we would divide the change in the CPI by the beginning value of the CPI in the following manner:

$$\frac{(199.9-190.4)}{190.4} = \frac{9.5}{190.4} = 0.05 = 5\%$$

In other words, the rate of inflation was 5 percent for the 12-month period.

Figure 13.4 shows what the level of prices and the resulting inflation look like over a much longer period. The two lines are

CHAPTER 13 Economic Instability 363

S Skill Practice

Using Line Graphs Ask:
According to the graph, what was the annual rate of inflation in 2005? *(about 3.5 percent)* What was the CPI in 2000? *(about 160 percent)* In which years were there two separate recessions? *(between 1980 and 1985)* **BL**

R Reading Strategy

Determining Importance
Have students visit the Bureau of Labor Statistics Web site (www.bls.gov) and locate the Frequently Asked Questions for the CPI. Ask students to select a question and then write a paragraph explaining why it is important for economists and/or consumers to know the answer. **OL**

Economic Analysis

Answer: The CPI computes changes in price levels. Dividing the CPI difference from one period to the next by the beginning value of the CPI gives the inflation rate between those two periods.

Hands-On Chapter Project
Step 2

Economic Indicators and the U.S. Economy

Step 2: Explaining Inflation. Students will research and write the portion of the talk show script that covers inflation.

Directions: Have students return to their previously established groups. Ask them to use the textbook and the Web sites they consulted for Step 1 to research inflation, its current levels and effects, and possible future inflationary trends. Suggest that students visit a Web site such as

www.minneapolisfed.org to find an inflation calculator to help them construct examples of the effects of inflation. Remind students that as they conduct their research, they should keep in mind that TV talk shows aim to inform but in an interesting way.

Summarizing Direct students in each group to use their research to write the portion of the talk-show script that will include the host and questioner discussing inflation with the inflation

"expert." Groups should include in this section of their scripts a forecast of future inflationary trends. **OL**

(Chapter Project continued in Section 3.)

C Critical Thinking

Making Connections Explain that the CPI compares prices in the same stores over time. If, when prices rise, consumers switch to stores that charge lower prices, the CPI will exaggerate what shoppers are paying. **Ask:** Why are some people concerned that the CPI might be overestimating inflation? *(Inflation impacts Social Security payments and other cost-of-living adjustments.)* **OL**

D Differentiated Instruction

Intrapersonal Have students write a paragraph explaining why they should care about the producer price index. **OL**

Caption Answer: inflation in excess of 500 percent a year

✔**Reading Check** **Answer:** The government monitors changes in the prices of its contents to measure changes in general price levels.

Hyperinflation
During the 1920s, inflation in Germany reached such levels that banknotes in denominations of "100 Billionen Reichsmark" (the equivalent of 100 trillion) circulated. *How is hyperinflation defined?*

creeping inflation relatively low rate of inflation, usually 1 to 3 percent annually

hyperinflation inflation in excess of 500 percent per year

stagflation period of slow economic growth coupled with inflation

producer price index (PPI) index used to measure prices received by domestic producers

implicit GDP price deflator index used to measure price changes in GDP

C shown together because the level of prices is sometimes confused with the rate of inflation, when in fact the level of prices is used to compute the inflation rate.

The rate of inflation tends to change over long periods of time. In the last 20 years, the United States could be described as having **creeping inflation**—inflation in the range of 1 to 3 percent per year. When inflation is this low, it is generally not seen as much of a problem. However, inflation can rise to the point where it gets out of control. **Hyperinflation**—inflation in the range of 500 percent a year and above—does not happen very often. When it does, it is generally the last stage before a total monetary collapse.

The record for hyperinflation was set in Hungary during Word War II. At that time, huge amounts of currency were printed to pay the government's bills. By the end of the war, it was claimed that 828 *octillion* (828,000,000,000,000,000,000,000,000,000) pengös equaled 1 prewar pengö.

An economy also may experience **stagflation**, a period of stagnant economic growth coupled with inflation. Stagflation was a concern in the 1970s, a time of rising prices coupled with high unemployment. Even today, some people worry that the high price of oil could cause prices to go up and economic growth to slow down.

Other Price Indexes

A price index can be constructed for any segment of the economy in exactly the same way. The agricultural sector, for example, constructs a separate price index for the products it buys (diesel fuel, fertilizer, and herbicides), and then compares it to the prices it gets for its products.

The **producer price index (PPI)** is a monthly series that reports prices received by domestic producers. Prices in this series are recorded when a producer sells its output to the very first buyer. This sample D consists of about 100,000 commodities, using 1982 as the base year. Although it is compiled for all commodities, it is broken down into various subcategories, including farm products, fuels, chemicals, rubber, pulp and paper, and processed foods.

The **implicit GDP price deflator,** used to measure changes in GDP, is another series. This series is used less frequently because the figures for real GDP, or GDP already adjusted for price increases, are provided when GDP is announced.

Finally, these are just a few of the many price indexes that the government maintains. Even so, the CPI is by far the most popular and the one we watch most often.

✔**Reading Check** **Analyzing** How is a market basket used to measure the price level?

364 UNIT 4 **Macroeconomics: Performance and Stabilization**

Differentiated Instruction

Math Practice for Economics, p. 19

Figuring Inflation's Effects

Objective: Understand how inflation affects purchasing power.

Focus/Teach: Have students review the text's definitions of *inflation*, *purchasing power*, and *consumer price index*. Then have them complete the activity.

Assess: Review the answers. Go over the calculations for any problematic questions.

Close: Have students write a paragraph summarizing what they learned in the activity.

Differentiated Instruction Strategies

BL **Ask:** Which increased the most between 2000 and 2005: housing, food, or medical expenses? *(medical)*

AL Have students redo the activity with new amounts for the expenses in the third paragraph.

ELL Have students create a bar graph illustrating the information in the table.

Causes of Inflation

MAIN Idea Causes of inflation include strong demand, rising costs, and wage-price spirals, along with a growing supply of money.

Economics and You Have you ever wanted something so much you did not care about the price? Read on to learn how such behavior can fuel inflation.

Economists have offered several explanations for the causes of inflation. Nearly every period of inflation is due to one or more of the following causes: demand-pull inflation, cost-push inflation, wage-price spiral, or excessive monetary growth.

Demand-Pull

According to the explanation called **demand-pull inflation**, all sectors in the economy try to buy more goods and services than the economy can produce. As consumers, businesses, and governments converge on stores, they cause shortages, which drives up prices. Thus prices are "pulled" up by excessive demand. This could happen, for example, if consumers decided to use their credit cards and go into debt to buy things they otherwise could not afford.

A similar explanation blames inflation on excessive spending by the federal government. After all, the government borrows and then spends billions of dollars, thus putting upward pressure on prices. Unlike the demand-pull explanation, however, which cites the excess demand on all sectors of the economy, this explanation holds only the federal government's deficit spending responsible for inflation.

Cost-Push

The **cost-push inflation** explanation claims that rising input costs, especially energy and organized labor, drive up the cost of products for manufacturers and thus cause inflation. This situation might occur, for example, when a strong national union wins a large wage contract, forcing manufacturers to raise prices to **recover** the increase in labor costs.

Another cause of cost-push inflation could be a sudden rise in the international price of oil, which can raise the price of everything from plastics and gasoline to shipping costs and airline fares. Such an increase in prices occurred during the 1970s, when prices for crude oil went from $5 to $35 a barrel. It happened again in 2006, when the price of oil surged to over $75 a barrel.

Wage-Price Spiral

A more neutral explanation does not blame any particular group or event for rising prices. According to this view, a self-perpetuating spiral of wages and prices becomes difficult to stop.

The spiral might begin when higher prices force workers to ask for higher wages. If they get the higher wages, producers try to recover that cost with higher

demand-pull inflation explanation that prices rise because all sectors of the economy try to buy more goods and services than the economy can produce

cost-push inflation explanation that rising input costs, especially energy and organized labor, drive up the prices of products

Inflation Several causes of inflation exist, but an increase in allowance would probably not have a large impact. *Which explanation does the father in the cartoon use?*

"... but if daddy raised your allowance he'd be hurting the economy by stimulating inflation. You wouldn't want him to do that would you?"

© KAZ –Larry Katzman

C Critical Thinking

Making Inferences Ask: Which type of inflation might be accompanied by unemployment? Explain. *(Cost-push inflation. With demand-pull inflation, there is a higher level of spending and therefore no reason to lay people off. With cost-push inflation, a rise in prices can reduce the amount being bought, which would cause production, and therefore employment, to be cut back.)* **OL**

W Writing Support

Persuasive Writing Have students imagine that they have worked at the same part-time job for the past three years. During that time, their wages have remained the same. Have students write a letter to their boss asking for a raise. Students should use information about inflation to justify their request. **OL**

Caption Answer: The father is using either the wage-price spiral or the cost-push explanation, since an allowance increase could be interpreted as a rising labor cost.

CHAPTER 13 Economic Instability **365**

Leveled Activities

BL Guided Reading Activities, p. 38

OL Critical Thinking Activities, p. 19

AL Primary and Secondary Source Readings, p. 41

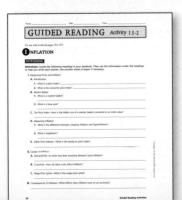

S Skill Practice

Using Line Graphs Ask: In what year was the purchasing power of the dollar equal to 10 percent of its value in 1947? *(2005)* In which decade did the purchasing power of the dollar decline by the greatest amount? *(1970s)* **OL**

D Differentiated Instruction

Logical/Mathematical Have students use the Internet to find out the current maximum monthly Social Security payment. Then have students calculate how much purchasing power (in dollars) the payment would lose in one year if the inflation rate was 3 percent, 4 percent, and 6 percent. **AL**

Economic Analysis

Answer: It declines.

✓Reading Check Answer:
Answers will vary but should address the possible causes of inflation.

Additional Support

Figure 13.5 ▶ The Purchasing Power of the Dollar

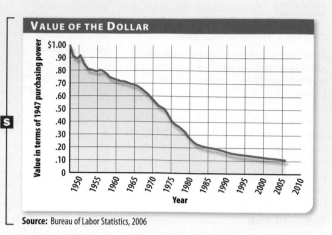

VALUE OF THE DOLLAR

Source: Bureau of Labor Statistics, 2006

▶ When the price level goes up, the purchasing power of the dollar goes down. When the price level rises more slowly, as it did after 1980, the value of the dollar does not decline as fast.

Economic Analysis *What happens to the purchasing power of the dollar during a period of inflation?* **S**

Economics ONLINE

Student Web Activity Visit the *Economics: Principles and Practices* Web site at glencoe.com and click on *Chapter 13– Student Web Activities* for an activity on working with economic statistics.

---

prices. As each side tries to improve its relative position with a larger increase than before, the rate of inflation keeps rising.

Excessive Monetary Growth

The most popular explanation for inflation is excessive monetary growth. This occurs when the money supply grows faster than real GDP. According to this view, any extra money or additional credit created by the Federal Reserve System will increase someone's purchasing power. When people spend this additional money, they cause a demand-pull effect that drives up prices.

Advocates of this explanation point out that inflation cannot be maintained without a growing money supply. For example, if the price of gas goes up sharply, but the amount of money people have remains the same, then consumers will simply have to buy less of something else. While the price of gas may rise, the prices of other things will fall, leaving the overall price level unchanged.

✓Reading Check Explaining Which explanation do you think gives the most reasonable cause of inflation? Why?

Consequences of Inflation

MAIN Idea Inflation can reduce purchasing power, distort spending, and affect the distribution of income.

Economics and You What would you do if the price of your favorite food became too high? Read on to learn how inflation changes people's buying habits.

While low levels of inflation may not be a problem, inflation can have a disruptive effect on an economy if it gets too high.

Reduced Purchasing Power

The most obvious effect of inflation is that the dollar buys less as prices rise, and thus it loses value over time. **Figure 13.5** shows the declining value of the dollar since 1947 as inflation has eroded its purchasing power.

This may not be a problem for everyone, but decreasing purchasing power can be especially hard on retired people or those with fixed incomes because their money buys a little less each month. Those not on fixed incomes are better able to cope. They can increase their fees or wages to keep up with inflation. **D**

Extending the Content

The Gold Standard In the late nineteenth and the early twentieth centuries, the United States, like most industrialized nations, was committed to the gold standard. During this period, the U.S. money supply was linked to its supply of gold. Banks issued paper money that people could redeem for a fixed amount of gold. Because the money supply was

so linked to the gold supply, price levels usually did not vary much. Inflation was not a persistent economic problem during the nation's gold standard years. Major gold discoveries, however, could abruptly increase the money supply and price levels. When gold was discovered in California in the mid-1800s, a monetary shock jolted the U.S. economy. Because

the gold standard left economies vulnerable to such instability and was costly to maintain, most nations abandoned it in the twentieth century. Today, governments use monetary policies to regulate the money supplies.

Distorted Spending Patterns

Inflation has a tendency to make people change their spending habits. For example, when prices went up in the early 1980s, interest rates—the cost of borrowed money—also went up. This caused spending on durable goods, especially housing and automobiles, to fall dramatically.

To illustrate, suppose that a couple wanted to borrow $100,000 over 20 years to buy a house. At a 7 percent interest rate, their monthly mortgage payments would be $660.12. At 14 percent, their payments would be $1,197.41. In 1981 some mortgage rates reached 18 percent, which meant a monthly payment of $1,517.32 for the same size loan! As a result of the high interest rates in that period, the homebuilding industry almost collapsed.

Encouraged Speculation

Inflation tempts some people to speculate heavily in an attempt to take advantage of rising prices. People who ordinarily put their money in reasonably safe investments begin buying luxury condominiums, diamonds, and other exotic items that might be expected to increase in price.

Some people actually make money on speculative ventures like this, but even speculators lose money on deals from time to time. For the average consumer, a large loss could have devastating consequences.

Distorted Distribution of Income

Inflation can alter the distribution of income. During long inflationary periods, **creditors,** or people who lend money, are generally hurt more than **debtors,** or borrowers, because earlier loans are repaid later with dollars that buy less.

Suppose, for example, that you borrow $100 to buy bread that costs $1 a loaf. You could buy 100 loaves of bread today. If inflation set in, and if the price level doubled by the time you paid back the loan, the lender would be able to buy only 50 loaves of bread because each loaf now would cost $2.

creditor person or institution to whom money is owed

debtor person who borrows and therefore owes money

✓Reading Check Identifying Why is inflation especially hard on people with fixed incomes?

SECTION 2 Review

Vocabulary

1. **Explain** the significance of inflation, deflation, price index, consumer price index, market basket, base year, creeping inflation, hyperinflation, producer price index, stagflation, implicit GDP price deflator, demand-pull inflation, cost-push inflation, creditor, and debtor.

Main Ideas

2. **Listing** What are the main causes and consequences of inflation?

3. **Identifying** Use a graphic organizer like the one below to identify the steps in measuring inflation.

Steps	Details
1.	
2.	

Critical Thinking

4. **The BIG Idea** How can inflation destabilize a nation's economy?

5. **Understanding Cause and Effect** In 2005 and 2006, the price of crude oil suddenly increased. What type of inflation might this development cause? Why?

6. **Categorizing Information** What kind of inflation might be described as "too many dollars chasing too few goods"? Why?

7. **Analyzing Visuals** Look at Figure 13.4 on page 363. How does the rate of inflation change during times of recessions? What might explain these changes?

Applying Economics

8. **Market Basket** Construct a market basket of goods and services that high school students typically consume. Would it be a useful economic indicator? Explain.

Answers

1. All definitions can be found in the section and the Glossary.
2. Inflation can be caused by overspending by all sectors or just the government, rising input costs, a wage-price spiral, or excessive monetary growth. Consequences include reduced purchasing power, distorted spending patterns, distorted distribution of income, and increased speculation.
3. **Step 1:** Measure prices. **Detail:** Determine the average prices of items in a market basket.

Step 2: Construct a price index. **Detail:** Convert the dollar cost of a market basket to an index value.
Step 3: Compare the indices of two time periods. **Detail:** Divide the change in the CPI by the beginning value of the CPI.

4. Inflation can destabilize a nation's economy because the reduced spending it creates may cause industries to weaken or collapse.
5. cost-push inflation; higher oil prices increase input costs for much of the economy

6. demand-pull inflation; excess spending pulls up prices
7. The rate of inflation tends to fall during a recession. This is because unemployment often causes a decline in consumer spending, which causes prices to stop rising.
8. Answers will vary but should show that students understand the market basket concept.

Teach

C Critical Thinking

Analyzing Primary Sources
Remind students that the federal budget deficit is currently very large. This means that annual government expenditures far exceed tax revenues. **Ask:** What do you think Freidman meant when he said that taxes should be cut "whenever it's possible"? How "possible" would it be now? *(Friedman was not in favor of fiscal irresponsibility; he would want reductions in spending to accompany tax cuts. Today, reducing taxes is less advisable since it would increase an already large deficit.)* **AL**

Examining the Profile

Answers:
1. At a time when most economists favored fiscal policy, Friedman argued that controlling the money supply was the key to achieving economic stability.
2. Answers will vary but should address how free market principles would apply to education.

Additional Support

A popular column in Newsweek *helped Milton Friedman become one of the best-known economists. His views appealed to people:* "I am in favor of cutting taxes under any **C** circumstances and for any excuse, for any reason, whenever it's possible."

Profiles in Economics

Milton Friedman (1912–2006)

- received the Nobel Prize for economics for his theories on economic stabilization policy
- strong proponent of monetary policy

It's About the Money Supply

As a founder of the Chicago school of economic thought, Milton Friedman has largely defined modern monetary policy. In an era when most economists believed in fiscal policy, or government spending on public projects, Friedman disagreed. He argued that monetary policy, or controlling the supply of money in circulation, was the key to economic health and stability.

Friedman's research fundamentally changed U.S. economic policy on inflation, unemployment, and business cycles. His findings, for example, rejected the idea that high inflation helped to limit unemployment. His influential books and articles in *Newsweek* promoted the steadying role of the Federal Reserve in monitoring the amount of money available to individuals, households, and businesses in order to maintain the value of the dollar.

Stay Off Our Backs

A fervent believer in individual freedom, Friedman advocated free markets with minimal government involvement. In his book *Capitalism and Freedom,* he argued for a flat tax rate and the elimination of deductions, such as those for mortgage interest. Friedman also voiced opposition to such popular policies as agricultural subsidies, price controls, and the minimum wage.

Friedman also wanted parents to be free to choose their children's schools. Together with his wife Rose Director Friedman, he established the Friedman Foundation to promote the use of school vouchers in the United States. Vouchers, he thought, would improve education by forcing schools, through free market competition, to either excel or shut down. While many of Friedman's ideas were once considered radical, some have become widely accepted.

Examining the Profile

1. **Contrasting** How did Friedman disagree with other economists about achieving economic stability?
2. **Predicting Consequences** How do you think the quality of education would be affected if free market principles were applied to schools?

368 UNIT 4 Macroeconomics: Performance and Stabilization

Extending the Content

Friedman's Influence After his death in November 2006 at the age of 94, Milton Friedman was remembered as one of the most important economic thinkers of all time. Friedman has been called a modern Adam Smith because of his support for free market competition and his opposition to government intervention in the economy. He was the chief promoter of supply-side economics, the economic policy adopted by President Ronald Reagan and British Prime Minister Margaret Thatcher in the 1980s. While his ideas were praised by many business leaders, they sparked controversy by exposing ordinary citizens to economic forces beyond their control.

GUIDE TO READING

Section Preview

In this section, you will find out how unemployment is measured as well as what causes it.

Content Vocabulary

- civilian labor force *(p. 370)*
- labor force *(p. 370)*
- unemployed *(p. 370)*
- unemployment rate *(p. 370)*
- frictional unemployment *(p. 372)*
- structural unemployment *(p. 372)*
- outsourcing *(p. 372)*
- technological unemployment *(p. 372)*
- cyclical unemployment *(p. 373)*
- seasonal unemployment *(p. 373)*
- GDP gap *(p. 374)*
- misery index *(p. 374)*
- discomfort index *(p. 374)*

Academic Vocabulary

- confined *(p. 370)*
- fundamental *(p. 372)*
- unfounded *(p. 374)*

Reading Strategy

Describing As you read the section, complete a graphic organizer similar to the one below by describing the different sources of unemployment.

Sources of Unemployment

PEOPLE IN THE NEWS

—The Atlanta Journal-Constitution

Opting Out

Louis Myer is one of the uncounted. . . . [He volunteers at] a Stone Mountain-based nonprofit that refurbishes donated medical equipment and gives it to those who need it.

Laid off in 2001 from a job as an engineer, the Atlanta native struggled in vain to catch another employer's interest.

He volunteered for a while at Habitat for Humanity. In October, he started helping out at the Stone Mountain nonprofit. It is good work, but it is not paid work. Even so, he is not counted as unemployed. . . . [T]he unemployment rate . . . does not include people who have abandoned the job search, for whatever reason. ■

Approximately half of the people in the United States belong to the labor force, and at any given time millions are without jobs. Sometimes this is because they choose not to work, as when they have quit one job to look for another. In most cases, however, people are out of work for reasons largely out of their control.

Most Americans identify strongly with their work. If you were to ask someone to describe themselves, most likely they would tell you their occupation, such as a cook, a teacher, or a sales associate. Some people, such as Louis Myer in the news article, work for no pay when they cannot find another job.

Focus

Bellringer
Daily Focus Transparency 70

GUIDE TO READING

Answers to Graphic:
frictional—workers between jobs; structural—economic progress or changing preferences; technological—workers replaced by machines; cyclical—swings in the business cycle; seasonal—seasonal changes in weather or demand

Resource Manager

R Reading Strategies	C Critical Thinking	D Differentiated Instruction	W Writing Support	S Skill Practice
Teacher Edition • Act. Prior Know., p. 370 • Questioning, p. 373 **Additional Resources** • Guid. Read. Act., p. 39 • Read. Ess. & Note-Taking Guide, p. 115 • Quizzes and Tests, p. 163	**Teacher Edition** • Dist. Fact/Opinion, p. 372 • Differentiating, p. 373 • Theorizing, p. 375 • Making Connections, p. 380 **Additional Resources** • Free Ent. Act., p. 19 • Econ. Concepts Trans., Strat. & Act., p. 31	**Teacher Edition** • Special Ed., p. 372 • Logical/Math., p. 374 **Additional Resources** • Econ. Forms and Fin. Pages Trans., Strat. and Act., p. 13	**Teacher Edition** • Personal Writing, p. 370 • Descriptive Writing, p. 371 • Expository Writing, p. 376 • Persuasive Writing, p. 381 **Additional Resources** • Writer's Guidebook	**Teacher Edition** • Using Line Graphs, pp. 371, 374 • Using Tables and Charts, p. 376 **Additional Resources** • Econ. Cartoons, p. 24 • Reinforcing Econ. Skills, p. 14

Teach

W Writing Support

Personal Writing Have students think of a job that interests them. Ask students to suppose that they were hired for this job and were pleased with the position. Explain that after five years, however, the company had to lay them off. Ask students to write a journal entry describing the feelings they would have after losing their jobs. **OL**

R Reading Strategy

Activating Prior Knowledge Tell students that before the women's liberation movement of the 1960s and 1970s, many people believed that women should not work outside the home. **Ask:** What happened to the labor force after the 1960s? *(Possible answer: It increased in size and diversity.)* **BL**

Caption Answer: age, ability to work, military service

Additional Support

---

civilian labor force or labor force non-institutionalized part of the population, aged 16 and over, either working or looking for a job *(also see page 204)*

unemployed working for less than one hour per week for pay or profit in a non-family-owned business, while being available and having made an effort to find a job during the past month

unemployment rate percentage of people in the civilian labor force who are classified as unemployed

---

Measuring Unemployment People are considered unemployed if they are out of work and actively seeking a job. *What other factors are considered?*

Measuring Unemployment

MAIN Idea The government takes monthly surveys to measure the unemployment rate.

Economics and You Have you ever wanted a job but couldn't find one? Read on to learn how the government measures such unemployment.

To understand the severity of joblessness, we need to know how it is measured and what is overlooked. The measure of joblessness is the unemployment rate, one of the most closely watched and politically charged statistics in the economy.

Civilian Labor Force

The Bureau of Labor Statistics defines the **civilian labor force,** more commonly called the **labor force,** as the sum of all persons age 16 and above who are either employed or actively seeking employment. This measure excludes members of the military. Since only people able to work are included in the labor force, those persons who are **confined** in jail or reside in mental health facilities are also excluded.

Unemployed Persons

The process of deciding if someone is able to work, willing to work, or even at work is more complicated than most people

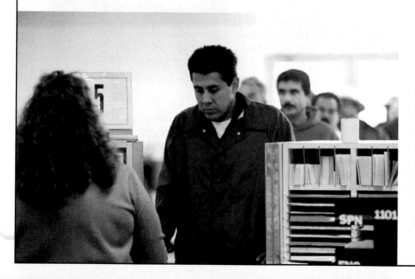

realize. In the middle of any given month, about 1,500 specialists from the Bureau of the Census begin their monthly survey of about 60,000 households in nearly 2,000 counties, covering all 50 states. Census workers are looking for the **unemployed**—people available for work who made a specific effort to find a job during the past month and who, during the most recent survey week, worked less than one hour for pay or profit. People are also classified as unemployed if they worked in a family business without pay for less than 15 hours a week.

After the census workers collect their data, they turn it over to the Bureau of Labor Statistics for analysis and publication. This data is then released to the American public on a monthly basis.

Unemployment Rate

Unemployment is normally expressed in terms of the **unemployment rate,** or the number of unemployed individuals divided by the total number of persons in the civilian labor force.

For example, in May 2006 the unemployment rate was calculated as follows:

$$\frac{\text{Number of unemployed persons}}{\text{Civilian Labor Force}} =$$

$$\frac{7,015,000}{150,991,000} = 0.046 = 4.6\%$$

The monthly unemployment rate is expressed as a percentage of the entire labor force. Monthly changes in the unemployment rate, often as small as one-tenth of 1 percent, may seem minor even though they have a huge impact on the economy. With a civilian labor force of approximately 151 million people, a one-tenth of 1 percent rise in unemployment would mean that nearly 150,000 people had lost their jobs. This number is more than

---

Extending the Content

Working in the New Economy A great source for information on employment trends is the *Occupational Handbook* printed by the Bureau of Labor Statistics. According to the handbook, in 1998 the ten industries with the most workers were education, public and private; self-employed workers; eating and drinking establishments; hospitals; local

government except education and hospitals; wholesale trade; personnel supply services; grocery stores; department stores; and state government, except education and hospitals. The outlook for 2008 is a little different. Computer and data processing services are expected to replace grocery stores as the eighth largest employer in the nation. Also, hospitals will

have more employees than local governments, and the need for doctors will increase more than the need for workers in state government. This is likely to happen because the population will be aging as well as becoming more technologically proficient.

Figure 13.6 ▶ The Unemployment Rate

▶ The unemployment rate goes up sharply during a recession and then comes down slowly afterward. When the rate moves as little as 0.1 percent, approximately 151,000 workers are affected.

Economic Analysis *How would you characterize the unemployment rate during the period from 1990 to 2007?*

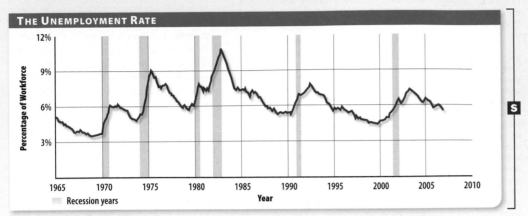

THE UNEMPLOYMENT RATE

Source: Bureau of Labor Statistics, 2006

the current population of cities such as Kansas City, Kansas; Syracuse, New York; Bridgeport, Connecticut; or Savannah, Georgia.

Figure 13.6 shows how much the unemployment rate can vary over time. In general, it tends to rise just before a recession begins and then continues to rise sharply during the recession. Sometimes the unemployment rate continues to rise well after the recession ends, as it did in 2003. When the rate finally starts to go back down, it may take from five to seven years for it to reach its previous low.

Underemployment

It might seem that a measure as comprehensive as the unemployment rate would include all of the people who are without a job. If anything, however, the unemployment rate understates employment conditions for two reasons.

First, the unemployment rate does not count those too frustrated or discouraged to look for work. During recessionary periods, these labor force "dropouts" may include nearly a million people. Although they are not working and probably would like to find work, these people are not classified as unemployed because they did not actively seek a job within the previous four-week period.

Second, people are considered employed even when they only hold part-time jobs. For example, suppose a worker lost a high-paying job requiring 40 hours a week and replaced it with a minimum-wage job requiring one hour a week. Although that worker would work and earn less, he or she would still be considered employed. In other words, being employed is not the same as being fully employed.

> **Personal Finance Handbook**
> See pages **R20–R23** for more information on getting a job.

W

✓**Reading Check** **Summarizing** How do we calculate the monthly unemployment rate?

CHAPTER 13 Economic Instability 371

Activity: Interdisciplinary Connection

Health Studies have linked unemployment to increasing rates of suicide, depression, substance abuse, and several other minor and serious illnesses. Organize students into groups of five to research these connections. Have each group make a collage-type poster illustrating the link between unemployment and an illness or substance abuse issue. To avoid overlap, you may wish to assign topics to each

group before they begin work. Then, after the groups are completed with their individual posters, have students combine their work into one large display illustrating the connection between unemployment and health issues. **OL**

C Critical Thinking

Distinguishing Fact from Opinion Ask: Which type of unemployment do you think is most common in your community? Explain. *(Answers will vary.)* Have students conduct research to find out which type of unemployment is *actually* most common in their community. Discuss their findings as a class. **OL**

D Differentiated Instruction

Special Education Students who have difficulty categorizing information may find it useful to use a framework for comparing the different types of unemployment discussed in this section. Have students look for the answers to the following questions:

- What is the nature of this type of unemployment?
- What are the causes of this type of unemployment?
- How does this type of unemployment differ from other types?
- How is it similar?
- Who does this type of unemployment affect? **BL**

Differentiated Instruction

Free Enterprise Activities, p. 19

---

frictional unemployment unemployment involving workers changing jobs or waiting to go to new ones

structural unemployment unemployment caused by a fundamental change in the economy that reduces the demand for some workers **C**

outsourcing hiring outside firms to perform non-core operations to lower operating costs

technological unemployment unemployment caused by technological developments or automation that makes some workers' skills obsolete

---

Sources of Unemployment

MAIN Idea Unemployment is often caused by circumstances outside an individual's control and is therefore very difficult to remedy.

Economics and You Did you ever have a job and then lose it for no fault of your own? Read on to learn about the different causes of unemployment.

D Economists have identified several kinds of unemployment. The nature and cause of each kind affects how much the unemployment rate can be reduced.

Frictional Unemployment

A common type of unemployment is **frictional unemployment**—the situation where workers are between jobs for one reason or another. This is usually a short-term condition, and workers suffer little economic hardship.

As long as workers have the freedom to choose or change occupations, some people will always be leaving their old jobs to look for better ones. Because there are always some workers doing this, the economy will always have some frictional unemployment.

Structural Unemployment

A more serious type of unemployment is **structural unemployment**—when economic progress, a change in consumer tastes and preferences, or a **fundamental** change in the operations of the economy reduces the demand for workers and their skills. In the early 1900s, for example, technological and economic progress resulted in the

Did You Know?

► **Measuring Unemployment** Some countries measure unemployment by counting the number of persons filing unemployment claims. Others count only those receiving unemployment insurance payments. This makes for relatively low unemployment rates, because some people may not be eligible for unemployment insurance.

---

development of the automobile, which soon replaced horses and buggies and left highly skilled buggy whip makers out of work. Later, consumer tastes changed away from American-made automobiles in favor of foreign-made cars, causing considerable unemployment in Michigan, Ohio, and the industrial Northeast.

More recently, **outsourcing**—the hiring of outside firms to perform non-core operations to lower operating costs—has become popular. Outsourcing was first used when firms found that they could have other companies perform some routine internal operations, such as the preparation of weekly paychecks. Later, improvements in technology and communications made it possible for companies to move some of their customer service operations abroad where wages are much lower. For example, if you call your telephone company or a computer software maker for customer assistance, your call is likely to be routed to an English-speaking worker in China or India rather than a U.S. office.

Sometimes the government contributes to structural unemployment. Congress's decision to close military bases in the 1990s is a prime example. Military bases are much larger than most private companies, and the impact of the base closings was concentrated in selected regions and communities. A few areas were able to attract new industry that hired some of the unemployed workers, but most workers either developed new skills or moved to other locations to find jobs.

Technological Unemployment

A third kind of unemployment is **technological unemployment**—unemployment that occurs when workers are replaced by machines or automated systems that make their skills obsolete. Technological unemployment is closely related to structural unemployment, although the technological changes are not always as broad in scale or as influential on society as cars replacing buggies.

Types of Unemployment

Objective: Be able to differentiate between the four types of unemployment.

Focus: Ask students to brainstorm examples of each type of unemployment.

Teach: Have students read the scenarios and identify the type of unemployment that each illustrates.

Assess: Review students' answers as a class.

Close: Ask students to list jobs that they think would be least likely affected by large-scale unemployment.

Differentiated Instruction Strategies

BL Ask students to brainstorm services that would be helpful to people who are unemployed.

AL Have students write a paragraph explaining how a specific occurrence of unemployment can be reduced.

ELL Have students design a poster showing the types of unemployment.

The Global Economy & YOU

Finding Work Overseas

Unemployment can be the first step toward expanding your horizons. Can't find a job in your area? Then look abroad. U.S. businesses are becoming increasingly global, and companies are scrambling to expand overseas. As many as 400,000 Americans relocate internationally each year.

Some human resource specialists encourage people to travel and work abroad. This will increase the chances of being hired for management positions in the future.

Many books and Web sites offer advice to Americans who want to work in other countries. Here are some tips: **R**

- Find the nearest consulate of the country in which you wish to work. The consulate is your ticket to learning about all the entry or residency requirements you'll need to work in another country.

- A nation's main presence in a foreign country is the embassy. Embassy workers can provide information and help you find a nearby consulate office.
- Different countries require different documentation for a visa or work permit. These often include a valid passport, a statewide criminal history record check, and a medical certificate.

R **Reading Strategy**

Questioning Encourage students to think about working abroad. Have them construct a list of questions to ask about a country that interests them as a potential place of employment. Possible questions might be: What kind of work is available there? How much income could I make? What language would I need to learn? What is the climate like? If time allows, extend the activity by having students answer their questions through Internet research. **OL**

C **Critical Thinking**

Differentiating Ask: A jobless trend that lasts three years is an example of which type of unemployment? *(cyclical unemployment)* A sales clerk losing his or her job in early January is most likely an example of which type of unemployment? *(seasonal)* **OL**

✓**Reading Check** **Possible Answer:** structural and technological; they require workers to learn new skills and find new occupations

One example is the reduced need for bank tellers by commercial banks because of the increased use of automated teller machines. Another example would be the introduction of word processing programs whose spell-checking, formatting, and text manipulation functions have greatly reduced the demand for typists.

Cyclical Unemployment

A fourth kind of unemployment is **cyclical unemployment**—unemployment directly related to swings in the business cycle. During a recession, for example, many people put off buying durable goods such as automobiles and refrigerators. As a result, some industries must lay off workers until the economy recovers.

If we look at Figure 13.6 on page 371, we can see that the unemployment rate rose dramatically whenever the economy was in recession. During the 2001 recession, more than 2 million jobs were lost. Laid-off workers may eventually get their jobs back when the economy improves, but it usually takes several years of economic growth before the unemployment rate returns to where it was before the recession. In the meantime, the pain of unemployment is a fact of life for those who are out of work.

Seasonal Unemployment

Finally, a fifth kind of unemployment is **seasonal unemployment**—unemployment resulting from seasonal changes in the weather or in the demand for certain products or jobs. Many carpenters and builders, for example, have less work in the winter because some tasks, such as replacing a roof or digging a foundation, are harder to do during cold weather. Department store sales clerks often lose their jobs after the December holiday season is over.

The difference between seasonal and cyclical unemployment relates to the period of measurement. Cyclical unemployment takes place over the course of the business cycle, which may last three to five years. Seasonal unemployment takes place every year, regardless of the general health of the economy. **C**

✓**Reading Check** **Interpreting** Which categories of unemployment do you think are the most troublesome for the U.S. economy? Why?

cyclical unemployment unemployment directly related to swings in the business cycle

seasonal unemployment unemployment caused by annual changes in the weather or other conditions that reduce the demand for jobs

CHAPTER 13 Economic Instability 373

Leveled Activities

BL **Economic Cartoons, p. 24**

OL **Economic Forms and Fin. Pages Trans., Strat. and Act., p. 13**

AL **Reinforcing Economic Skills, p. 14**

S Skill Practice

Using Line Graphs **Ask:** During which decade did the misery index drop by the greatest amount? *(1980s)* What is being measured on the vertical axis? *(the combined percentage rate of inflation and unemployment)* **BL**

D Differentiated Instruction

Logical/Mathematical Have students visit the U.S. Bureau of Economic Analysis Web site (www.bea.gov). Ask them to select one or more tables that include information about the GDP gap. Instruct students to write a paragraph that describes what the data in their tables reveals about the GDP gap. Students should also explain why economists would be interested in that information. **AL**

Economic Analysis

Answer: 1980–1981

Hands-On Chapter Project

Step 3

Economic Indicators and the U.S. Economy

Step 3: Explaining Unemployment. Students will research and write the portion of the talk show script that covers unemployment.

Directions: Have students reassemble into their project groups. Instruct students to use their textbooks and the Web sites they consulted for the previous steps to research unemployment, its current levels and effects, and possible future trends. For

---

Figure 13.7 ▶ **Measuring Consumer Discomfort**

Graphs In MOtion
See StudentWorks™ Plus or glencoe.com.

▶ The misery index is an unofficial measure of consumer discomfort that is compiled by adding the monthly inflation and unemployment rates.

Economic Analysis *When did the misery index reach its highest point?*

THE MISERY INDEX

Recession years — Year

Source: Bureau of Labor Statistics, 2006

GDP gap
difference between what the economy can and does produce

misery index or discomfort index
unofficial statistic that is the sum of the monthly inflation and unemployment rates

Costs of Instability

MAIN Idea Unemployment can cause uncertainty, political instability, and social problems.

Economics and You What would you do if you wanted a job but could not find one? Read on to learn about the costs of unemployment.

Recession, inflation, and unemployment are all forms of instability that hinder economic growth. These problems can occur separately or at the same time. Fears about these conditions are not **unfounded,** because economic instability carries enormous costs that can be measured in economic as well as human terms.

GDP Gap

One measure of the economic cost of unemployment is the **GDP gap**—the difference between the actual GDP and the potential GDP that could be produced if all resources were fully employed. In other words, the gap is a type of opportunity

cost—a measure of output not produced because of unemployed resources.

If we were to illustrate the gap with a production possibilities curve, the amount that could be produced would be any point on the frontier. The amount actually produced would be represented by a point inside the frontier. The distance between the two would be the GDP gap.

In a more dynamic sense, the business cycle may cause the size of this gap to vary over time. The scale of GDP is such that if GDP declines even a fraction of a percentage point, the amount of lost production and income could be enormous. For example, suppose that an economy with a $13.5-trillion-dollar GDP declines by just one-tenth of one percent. This translates into $13.5 billion in lost output.

Misery Index

Figure 13.7 shows the **misery index,** sometimes called the **discomfort index**—the sum of the monthly inflation and

374 UNIT 4 Macroeconomics: Performance and Stabilization

---

more information, suggest that students visit www.whitehouse.gov, click on "Federal Statistics," and visit the Economic Statistics Briefing Room. Students might search under "unemployment products" to find gift and T-shirt ideas to add humor to their scripts.

Summarizing Direct each group to use their research to write the portion of the talk show script that will include the host and questioner discussing unemployment with the unemployment "expert." Groups

should include in this section of their scripts a forecast of future unemployment trends. **OL**

(Chapter Project continued in Visual Summary.)

unemployment rates. As the figure shows, the index usually reaches a peak either during or immediately following a recession.

Although it is not an official government statistic, the misery index provides a reasonable measurement of consumer suffering during periods of high inflation and high unemployment.

Uncertainty

When the economy is unstable, a great deal of uncertainty exists. Workers may not buy something because of concern over their jobs. This uncertainty translates into many consumer purchases that are not made, causing unemployment to rise as jobs are lost.

Workers are not the only ones affected **C** by uncertainty. The owner of a business that is producing at capacity may decide against an expansion even though new orders are arriving daily. Instead, the producer may try to raise prices, which increases inflation. Even the government may decide to spend less on schools and roads if it is not sure of its revenues.

Political Instability

Politicians also suffer the consequences of economic instability. When times are hard, voters are dissatisfied and incumbents often voted out of office. For example, many experts agree that Bill Clinton's victory over President George Bush in 1992 was due in part to the 1991 recession.

If too much economic instability exists, as during the Great Depression of the 1930s, some voters are willing to vote for radical change. As a result, economic stability adds to the political stability of our nation.

Crime, Poverty, and Family Instability

Recession, inflation, and unemployment can also lead to higher rates of crime and poverty. They can contribute to problems such as fights and divorce when individuals and families face uncertainty because lost jobs and income make it difficult to pay the bills. Thus all of us have a stake in reducing economic instability.

✓**Reading Check** Identifying What makes the GDP gap a type of opportunity cost?

C Critical Thinking

Theorizing Ask: How might the wars in Iraq and Afghanistan contribute to both inflation and unemployment? *(Government wartime spending increases could contribute to inflation; the rising costs of the wars could cause a rise in uncertainty, which would reduce consumer spending and increase unemployment.)* **OL**

✓**Reading Check** **Answer:** The GDP gap represents output not produced because of unemployed resources.

Assess

🖥 Use the Interactive Tutor Self-Assessment CD-ROM to review Section 3, and then assign the Section 3 Review as homework or as an in-class activity.

Close

Summarizing Have students write a paragraph summarizing the information presented in Section 3. Remind students to include the section's main points in their summaries. **OL**

SECTION 3 Review

Vocabulary
1. **Explain** the significance of civilian labor force, unemployed, unemployment rate, frictional unemployment, structural unemployment, outsourcing, technological unemployment, cyclical unemployment, seasonal unemployment, GDP gap, misery index, and discomfort index.

Main Ideas
2. **Explaining** How do economists measure the economic cost of instability?

3. **Defining** What is frictional unemployment?

4. **Identifying** Use a graphic organizer like the one below to identify the people who are considered unemployed and those excluded from the civilian labor force.

Unemployed:	Excluded from the labor force:

Critical Thinking
5. **The BIG Idea** Why is structural unemployment a more difficult problem for the economy and for individual workers than other types of unemployment?

6. **Drawing Inferences** What factors make it difficult to determine the unemployment rate?

7. **Categorizing Information** List three reasons why a person may become discouraged from finding a job.

8. **Analyzing Visuals** Look at Figure 13.6 on page 371 and Figure 13.7 on page 374. How do the line graphs compare?

Applying Economics
9. **Employment** Give examples of individuals caught in each of the five types of unemployment. Find new examples.

CHAPTER 13 Economic Instability **375**

Review SECTION **3**

Answers

1. All definitions can be found in the section and the Glossary.
2. by calculating the GDP gap and the misery index
3. unemployment involving workers changing jobs or waiting to go to new ones
4. **Unemployed:** people available for work who made an effort to find a job during the past month and who worked less than one hour for pay or profit during the most recent survey week; people who worked in a family business without pay for less than

15 hours a week. **Excluded from the labor force:** members of the military; people in jail or in mental health facilities
5. It involves fundamental changes in the economy that are hard for workers to adjust to.
6. Calculating the unemployment rate involves deciding whether someone is able to work, willing to work, or at work. Also, during their surveys Census workers must find unemployed people.

7. People might become discouraged if their skills are out of date, if their job skills are no longer commercially profitable, or if the competition for jobs is too fierce.
8. The lines on the two graphs follow a similar pattern.
9. Answers will vary but should identify the types of unemployment as frictional, structural, technological, cyclical, and seasonal.

Focus

W Writing Support

Expository Writing Ask students to visit and write a report on a local thrift store covering items sold, prices and source of stock. **OL**

Teach

S Skill Practice

Using Tables and Charts
Ask: What were Winmark's total revenues in 2005? *($26.42 million)* How much profit per employee did the company average that year? *($24,607.84)* **OL**

Analyzing the Impact

Answers:
1. Winmark receives a share of the profits from its franchises and provides profitable services to its entrepreneurs.
2. **Possible answer:** Unemployment and inflation reduce purchasing power, making the cheaper prices at resale shops more attractive.

Additional Support

CASE STUDY
Resale Universe

Winmark Wins Customers

Everyone loves a bargain, especially during times of economic instability. That's what Winmark counted on when it incorporated its business model in 1988. Winmark Corp. is the parent company of four buy-sell-trade franchises: Play It Again Sports, Plato's Closet, Music Go Round, and Once Upon A Child. In 2006 these franchises numbered more than 800.

Bargain Hunter's Paradise

If purchased new at a mall, clothing from such top brands as Abercrombie & Fitch, Juicy Couture, Seven for All Mankind, and Baby Phat come with hefty price tags. But astute customers who comb the racks and shelves of Winmark's resale universe find the same high-end brands at nearly 70 percent off retail price. The average clothing price at Plato's Closet, for example, is about $10.

The resale concept has turned many teens into consignment gurus. They sell their old threads, buy new ones at the lower prices, and count their savings, because they beat even mall sales by a wide margin. Plato's Closet buys and sells only "gently used" merchandise, meaning it must be in style and in great condition. The same holds true for Play It Again Sports and Music Go Round,

where customers can find new and almost-new sports and music equipment, from hockey skates and treadmills to amplifiers and saxophones.

Footing the Bill

Winmark receives a percentage of the profits from its franchises, but the corporation makes most of its money by providing services to the entrepreneurs who run the individual resale stores. It helps owners set up shop, advertise, and gather inventory. Winmark also leases technology to small businesses. On top of that, in 2005 the company launched a new division called Wirth Business Credit, which provides financing to small businesses. With just over 100 employees, the parent company posted profits of roughly $2.5 million in 2005.

S

WINMARK CORP* 2005	
Total Revenues:	$26.42 million
Profits:	2.51 million
Employees:	102

Source: finapps.forbes.com
* Figures for Winmark corporate headquarters

Analyzing the Impact

1. **Summarizing** How does Winmark Corporation's business model enable it to profit from its franchises?
2. **Drawing Conclusions** How do you think economic instability impacts resale shops?

Activity: Hands-On Economics

Donating Versus Reselling
Have students consider why some people donate items to charity rather than sell them to stores like Plato's Closet. Instruct students to choose five articles of clothing or household items that they would consider donating to charity. Have students use the Salvation Army's valuation guide (found at www.satruck.com/ValueGuide.aspx)

to estimate the values of their items. Tell students they could deduct that amount as a charitable contribution when figuring their income tax. Ask students to assume that income tax brackets are as follows:

- 0 to $7,550 = 10%
- $7,550 to $30,650 = 15%
- $30,650 to $61,850 = 25%
- $61,850 to $94,225 = 28%

- $94,225 to $168,275 = 33%
- $168,275 and above = 35%

Have students figure how much their donation would save them on their taxes if their income was: $6,500; $23,000; $47,800; $79,850; $113,000; and $212,000.
Ask: In which bracket do taxpayers save the most money from charitable donations? *(the highest bracket)* **OL**

CHAPTER 13 Visual Summary

STUDY TO GO Study anywhere, anytime! Download quizzes and flash cards to your PDA from glencoe.com.

▶ **Business Cycles** Economic growth is typically marked by periods of recession followed by periods of expansion. A business cycle is the period from the beginning of one recession to the beginning of the next.

BUSINESS CYCLES

▶ **Inflation** The economy faces inflation when the general level of prices increases. If excessive, inflation can have a disruptive effect on the economy.

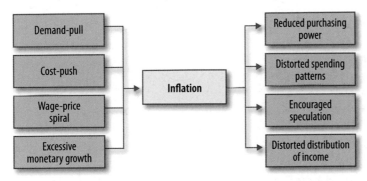

▶ **Unemployment** The unemployment rate includes those individuals who are actively looking for a job but work less than one hour a week for pay or profit. It does not include people who are underemployed, working part-time, or have given up the job search.

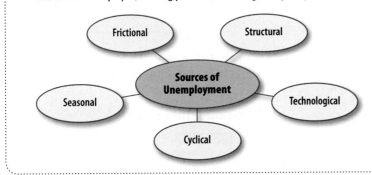

Visual Literacy Have students create a poster representing the different types of inflation. An example of an item for the poster could be a photo of customers in a store frantically trying to buy a popular toy before supplies run out. Ask students to include captions identifying each type of inflation. **BL**

Personal Writing Ask: Which type of unemployment do you think is most likely to affect you in the coming year? Explain. *(Answers may include seasonal and frictional unemployment, because most employed students have part-time jobs and because most of them are learning up-to-date technological skills.)* Have students write an essay expressing their concerns about unemployment and how they think the different types of unemployment could affect them in the future. Encourage students to include ideas on how their concerns could be alleviated. **OL**

CHAPTER 13   Economic Instability   377

Hands-On Chapter Project
Step 4: Wrap Up

Economic Indicators and the U.S. Economy

Step 4: Bringing It All Together.
Students will present what they learned in previous steps.

Directions: Have students reassemble into their project groups. Ask each group to use its script to present its talk show on the U.S. economy to the class. Have a volunteer record each group's forecast figures on the board. Lead the class in a discussion comparing the different groups' figures after all presentations are completed. Students should then vote on which group's forecast they believe is best supported and most likely to occur. Save the groups' forecasts and review them with students at the end of the year to assess which one was most accurate. **OL**

ExamView®
Assessment Suite

This easy-to-use software includes extensive question banks and allows you to create fully customized tests that can be administered in print or online.

Review Content Vocabulary

1. f	2. i
3. d	4. k
5. b	6. j
7. a	8. h
9. g	10. c
11. l	12. e

Review Academic Vocabulary

13.–19. Students' sentences will vary but should demonstrate understanding of each term's meaning in an economic context.

Review the Main Ideas

20. Recession: real GDP declines for at least two quarters in a row. Depression: very severe recession; has high unemployment, acute shortages, excess capacity in manufacturing plants.

21. real GDP declined almost 50 percent, number of people out of work rose nearly 800 percent, average manufacturing wage dropped, banks failed, money supply fell by one-third

22. Econometric models use algebraic equations to represent the relationships between economic variables.

23. Price level: agglomeration of the prices that consumers pay for goods and services. Inflation: increase in price level from one time period to another.

Review Content Vocabulary

Write the letter of the key term that best matches each definition below.

- a. trend line
- b. cyclical unemployment
- c. unemployed
- d. base year
- e. civilian labor force
- f. peak
- g. trough
- h. inflation
- i. market basket
- j. consumer price index
- k. structural unemployment
- l. recession

1. marks the beginning of a recession
2. representative selection of commonly purchased goods
3. point of comparison for other years in statistical measures
4. caused by a shift in demand or a change in the way the economy operates
5. caused by periodic swings in business activity
6. used to measure price changes for a market basket of consumer items
7. growth path in absence of recession or expansion
8. measured by changes in the CPI
9. lowest point of the business cycle
10. works less than one hour per week for pay or profit
11. real GDP declines for two consecutive quarters
12. all persons aged 16 or older who are working or actively seeking a job

Review Academic Vocabulary

Use each of the following terms in a sentence that relates to either inflation or unemployment.

- 13. innovation
- 14. series
- 15. construction
- 16. recover
- 17. confined
- 18. fundamental
- 19. unfounded

Review the Main Ideas

Section 1 (pages 353–359)

20. **Explain** the difference between a depression and a recession.
21. **Describe** the effects of the Great Depression.
22. **Discuss** how econometric models describe the behavior of the economy.

Section 2 (pages 361–367)

23. **Explain** the difference between the price level and the rate of inflation.
24. **Identify** three major price indexes.
25. **Identify** four ways inflation destabilizes the economy using a graphic organizer like the one below.

Section 3 (pages 369–375)

26. **Describe** the five major kinds of unemployment by using a graphic organizer like the one below.

UNEMPLOYMENT		
Type	**Description**	**Example**
Frictional		
Structural		
Cyclical		
Technological		
Seasonal		

27. **Describe** the costs and benefits of outsourcing.
28. **Identify** the political costs of economic instability.

Critical Thinking

29. **The BIG Idea** Why do leading economic indicators and econometric models not provide long-term predictions of economic behavior?

---

24. Consumer Price Index, Producer Price Index, implicit GDP price deflator
25. reduces purchasing power; distorts spending patterns; encourages speculation; distorts income distribution
26. **Frictional:** workers between jobs. **Structural:** due to a structural change in the economy. **Technological:** due to changes in technology. **Cyclical:** due to a downturn in the business cycle. **Seasonal:** due to business needs that change with the seasons. Students' examples will vary.

27. benefits: reduction in production costs and retail prices; costs: unemployment
28. If times are hard, voters become dissatisfied and vote politicians out of office. If instability persists, voters may support radical change.

Critical Thinking

29. Too many factors can change over a long period, and sometimes the factors change at the same time, making it impossible to isolate cause and effect.

Economics ONLINE Self-Check Quiz Visit the *Economics: Principles and Practices* Web site at glencoe.com and click on *Chapter 13—Self-Check Quizzes* to prepare for the chapter test.

Assessment and Activities CHAPTER 13

30. Determining Cause and Effect How would a 10 percent inflation rate affect both lenders and borrowers? Why?

31. Drawing Conclusions Which type of unemployment do you think is the most troublesome for the U.S. economy? Why?

32. Comparing and Contrasting What are the similarities and differences between the CPI and the PPI?

33. Synthesizing Information Describe structural and technological unemployment and give an example of each. Why are these kinds of unemployment serious problems for an economy?

Applying Economic Concepts

34. Inflation Go to the Minneapolis Fed's site at http://www.minneapolisfed.org/ and click on "Inflation Calculator." Follow the directions to find the adjusted prices for the items listed in the chart below. Then use the Internet or other sources to find the current price for each item. Write a paragraph on the topic: "Were the 'good old days' really all that good?"

Item	Year and Price	Price Adjusted for Inflation	Today's Price
Teacher's starting salary (Richmond, VA)	1969 $6,500		
2-bdrm apartment with den; gas for heating/cooking included (Richmond, VA)	1969 $147.50		
Gallon of gas	1969 $0.25		
Minimum wage	1978 $2.65		
Tuition/room and board at Longwood Univ. (VA)	1968 $550 per semester		

35. Recession If we were to enter a period of recession, what would likely happen to the unemployment rate? The inflation rate? The poverty rate? Explain your answers.

36. Inflation Explain why inflation cannot take place without an expansion of the money supply.

37. Misery Index How might the psychological strains that many people feel during difficult economic times help prolong an economic downturn? Provide at least one example with your answer.

Math Practice

38. Look at Figure 13.3 on page 362. Then find current prices for the first four items on the list. Use the equation on page 363 to determine the percentage change in prices since 1998.

Analyzing Visuals

39. Look at Figure 13.6 on page 371. What was the lowest unempoyment rate immediately before the 1991 recession, and when was it recorded? How long did it take for the unemployment rate to reach this previous low?

Interpreting Cartoons

40. Critical Thinking How does the cartoon below relate to what you have learned in this chapter?

CHAPTER 13 Economic Instability 379

Applying Economic Concepts

34. Prices Adjusted for Inflation to 2007: $36,396.46, $825.92, $1.40, $8.35, $3,247.84 Today's prices will vary.

35. In a recession, the unemployment rate rises, inflation usually holds steady or falls, and the poverty rate rises. This is due to lost output and lost income.

36. If the price of an item rises without an increase in the money supply, consumers have no choice but to decrease the amount they buy. Other prices then fall to offset the rise in price of the first item.

37. Psychological strains lead to uncertainty, which could cause businesses to forgo expansion and consumers to cut back purchases. Both trends would prolong the economic downturn.

Math Practice

38. Answers will vary according to current prices.

Analyzing Visuals

39. 5 percent in 1990; about 7 years

Interpreting Cartoons

40. Possible answer: The flower represents growth, which the stampeding bulls, representing higher prices and expenses, are about to trample.

30. Inflation benefits borrowers at the expense of lenders. With 10 percent inflation, a debtor paying back a loan would be paying 10 percent less in purchasing power than originally borrowed.

31. Answers will vary but should be logical.

32. Both are price indices, but the CPI measures the prices that consumers pay for final goods and services, while the PPI measures prices received by domestic producers.

33. Structural unemployment results from a fundamental change in the economy, such as a change in demand. Technological unemployment, the result of workers being replaced by machines, is a type of structural unemployment. Both types are serious because they can place many people out of jobs, and they require workers to be retrained.

DEBATES IN ECONOMICS

Should the Trade Embargo on Cuba Be Lifted?

Three years after Fidel Castro took power in Cuba and installed a Communist regime, the U.S. government initiated a trade embargo against the nation. The embargo was intended to put economic pressure on the Cuban government. Today the embargo is still in effect— one of the longest trade embargos in modern history. Opponents on each side of the issue debate its effectiveness.

Who is right? As you read the selections, ask yourself: Should the trade embargo on Cuba be lifted or remain in place?

PRO A HALF-CENTURY OF FAILURE

For almost half a century, the U.S. government has tried to isolate Cuba economically in an effort to undermine the [Communist] regime [of Fidel Castro] and deprive it of resources. Since 1960, Americans have been barred from trading with, investing in, or traveling to Cuba. . . .

As a foreign policy tool, the embargo actually enhances Castro's standing by giving him a handy excuse for the failures of his homegrown Caribbean socialism. . . . If the embargo were lifted, the Cuban people would be a bit less deprived and Castro would have no one else to blame for the shortages and stagnation that will persist without real market reforms. . . .

Many of the dollars Cubans could earn from U.S. tourists would come back to the United States to buy American products, especially farm goods. In 2000, Congress approved a modest opening of the embargo. The Trade Sanctions Reform and Export Enhancement Act of 2000 allows cash-only sales to Cuba of U.S. farm products and medical supplies. The results of this opening have been quite amazing. Since 2000, total sales of farm products to Cuba have increased from virtually zero to $380 million. . . .

—Daniel Griswold, Professor of Law and Economics, Columbia University

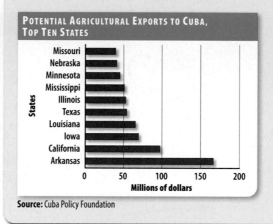

POTENTIAL AGRICULTURAL EXPORTS TO CUBA, TOP TEN STATES

States (top to bottom): Missouri, Nebraska, Minnesota, Mississippi, Illinois, Texas, Louisiana, Iowa, California, Arkansas

x-axis: Millions of dollars (0, 50, 100, 150, 200)

Source: Cuba Policy Foundation

380   UNIT 4   Macroeconomics: Performance and Stabilization

Focus

Display a map of the United States that includes the Caribbean Sea. Point out how close Cuba is to the United States. Have a volunteer use the map scale to determine Cuba's distance from the coast of Florida. *(about 90 miles)*

Teach

C Critical Thinking

Making Connections Lead a class discussion on how contacts with the United States may have promoted the growth of free markets in Russia and China. **Ask:** Is it possible that Cuba might follow the same pattern as Russia and China? Explain. *(Possible answer: Yes; the experience of Russia and China demonstrates that it is possible for communist nations to embrace free market capitalism.)* **OL**

Additional Support

Extending the Content

Tourism Apartheid in Cuba In the early 1990s, the loss of Soviet aid and declining sugar exports plunged the Cuban economy into a near depression. Cuba's government embraced tourism as the solution to the nation's economic woes. More than new 22,000 hotel rooms have been built on the island since 1990. However, while beautiful beaches and luxurious hotels have become increasingly available to foreign tourists, they have become less available to the Cuban people. By law, Cubans and tourists are only allowed to mix in public places if the tourist initiates contact. Cubans are furthermore not allowed to listen to music in the same nightclubs or drink in the same bars as tourists. Moreover, some of Havana's most beautiful plazas are now reserved for tourists. Ironically, the Cuban Revolution promised equal access to the island's resources and facilities. In the twenty-first century, however, Cubans must live with a government-imposed discrimination.

CON SUBSIDIZE COMMUNIST CUBA?

At the end of July [2002], the U.S. House of Representatives voted on two amendments, each approved by 95 vote margins, to end restrictions on travel and lift restrictions on financing exports to Cuba. . . . While the White House has threatened to veto any legislation that would "bolster the Cuban dictatorship," the anti-Embargo lobby argues that U.S. tourism will benefit Cubans without strengthening Castro, and that trade with Havana will mean substantial American profits. These arguments are misguided at best and disingenuous at worst.

Fidel Castro is broke, and at issue is not trade, but extending American export credit and export insurance to his regime, both of which are funded by American taxpayers. Since [2006], American companies are allowed to 'trade' with Castro's government on a cash and carry basis. But when Castro defaults on his purchases, under the proposed policy American taxpayers will have the burden of picking up his tab. . . .

France, Spain, Italy and Venezuela have suspended official credits to Castro's Cuba—not because of the Cuban communities in those nations—but because Cuba has failed to make payments on its debt, including debt incurred on agricultural purchases. . . . Havana owes billions of dollars to western banks and former socialist countries.

—Frank Calzon, executive director of Center for a Free Cuba

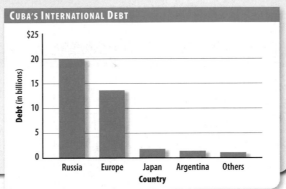

CUBA'S INTERNATIONAL DEBT

Debt (in billions): Russia 20, Europe ~14, Japan ~2, Argentina ~1.5, Others ~1

Source: U.S. Department of State

Analyzing the Issue

1. **Summarizing** What argument does Griswold use to support his argument that the embargo should be lifted?
2. **Analyzing** Review Calzon's argument. Do you agree with him that trade with Cuba would be a misguided policy?
3. **Deciding** With which opinion do you agree? Explain your reasoning.

CHAPTER 13   Economic Instability   381

Assess/ Close

W Writing Support

Persuasive Writing Direct students to write a letter to their congressional representative or senator expressing their views on the trade embargo against Cuba. **OL**

Analyzing the Issue

Answers:
1. Griswold maintains that the embargo provides Castro with an excuse for Cuba's economic failures. He states that if it were lifted, the money Cubans would earn from U.S. tourists would return to the United States in payment for American goods.
2. Answers will vary but should analyze Calzon's argument.
3. Answers will vary but should be logical and well supported.

Additional Support

Activity: Interdisciplinary Connection

Literature Tell students that one of America's greatest writers, Ernest Hemingway, lived for a time in Cuba. The island was the setting for one of his best-known novels, *The Old Man and the Sea*. The book tells the story of a poor Cuban fisherman who, after a long, bitter struggle, hooks and boats a very large fish, only to have it eaten by sharks on the way home. The theme of the novel clearly states Hemingway's esteem for the character trait he called "grace under pressure." *The Old Man and the Sea* contributed to Hemingway's Nobel Prize for Literature. Cubans today still deeply admire the author's work. Have students read *The Old Man and the Sea* and write book reports on it. Instruct students to include in their reports a comparison of the poverty depicted in the book with the poverty experienced by Cubans today. **AL**

<table>
<tr><th colspan="5">Key to Ability Levels</th></tr>
</table>

Key to Ability Levels	
BL Below level	**AL** Above level
OL On level	**ELL** English Language Learners

Key to Teaching Resources	
Print Material	DVD
CD-Rom	Transparency

BL	OL	AL	ELL		Resources	Chapter Opener	Section 1	Section 2	Section 3	Chapter Assess
	FOCUS
BL	OL	AL	ELL	📊	**Daily Focus Skills Transparencies**		58, 60, 61	31, 59	62, 63, 79	
	TEACH
BL	OL		ELL	📁	**Guided Reading Activities***		p. 40	p. 41	p. 42	
BL	OL	AL	ELL	📁	**Economic Content Vocabulary Activities***		p. 14	p. 14	p. 14	
	OL	AL		📁	**Critical Thinking Activities**		p. 16		p. 20	
BL	OL		ELL	📁	**Reading Essentials and Note-Taking Guide***		p. 118	p. 121	p. 124	
		AL		📁	**Enrichment Activities**			p. 14		
	OL	AL		📁	**Free Enterprise Activities**				pp. 20, 21	
BL	OL	AL	ELL	📁	**Primary and Secondary Source Readings**		p. 16	p. 31		
BL	OL	AL	ELL	📁	**Economic Cartoons**			p. 20	p. 25	
BL	OL	AL	ELL	📊	**Economic Concepts Transparencies, Strategies, and Activities**		p. 11	p. 9	p. 35	
BL	OL	AL	ELL	📁	**Math Practice for Economics**			p. 9		
BL	OL	AL	ELL	📊	**Economic Forms and Financial Pages Transparencies, Strategies, and Activities**		pp. 5, 24	p. 5		
BL	OL	AL	ELL	📁	**Personal Finance Activities**		p. 1			
BL	OL	AL	ELL	📁	**Reinforcing Economic Skills**			p. 3		
BL	OL		ELL	📁	**High School Reading in the Content Area Strategies and Activities**	✓	✓	✓	✓	✓
BL	OL	AL	ELL	📊	**High School Writing Process Transparencies**	✓	✓	✓	✓	✓
BL	OL	AL	ELL	📁	**Writer's Guidebook**	✓	✓	✓	✓	✓
BL	OL	AL	ELL	💿	**StudentWorks Plus CD-ROM**	✓	✓	✓	✓	✓
BL	OL	AL	ELL	💿	**Vocabulary PuzzleMaker CD-ROM**	✓	✓	✓	✓	✓

*Also available in Spanish

TeacherWorks *Plus*
All-In-One Planner and Resource Center

- Interactive Lesson Planner
- Interactive Teacher Edition
- Fully editable blackline masters
- Economics & You videos

- Differentiated Lesson Plans
- Printable reports of daily assignments
- Standards tracking system

Levels					Resources	Chapter Opener	Section 1	Section 2	Section 3	Chapter Assess
BL	OL	AL	ELL							
TEACH *(continued)*										
BL	OL	AL	ELL		Economics & You Video Program DVD—*Money and Banking*	✓	✓	✓	✓	✓
BL	OL	AL	ELL		Graph Coach CD-ROM	✓	✓	✓	✓	✓
Teacher Resources					Differentiated Instruction Strategies	✓	✓	✓	✓	✓
					Success with English Learners	✓	✓	✓	✓	✓
					Presentation Plus! CD-ROM	✓	✓	✓	✓	✓
ASSESS										
BL	OL	AL	ELL		Section Quizzes and Chapter Tests		p. 173	p. 174	p. 175	pp. 177, 181
BL	OL	AL	ELL		Authentic Assessment Strategies and Activities		p. 16			
BL	OL	AL	ELL		*ExamView®* Assessment Suite CD-ROM		14-1	14-2	14-3	Ch. 14
BL	OL	AL	ELL		Interactive Tutor Self-Assessment CD-ROM		14-1	14-2	14-3	
CLOSE										
BL			ELL		Reteaching Activities*		p. 14	p. 14	p. 14	
BL	OL		ELL		Reading and Study Skills Foldables		p. 58	p. 58	p. 62	
BL	OL	AL	ELL		Graphic Organizer Transparencies		p. 11		p. 33	

*Also available in Spanish

Vocabulary eFlashcards

Technology Product
The Vocabulary eFlashcards on the Glencoe Web site enable students to review vocabulary and their definitions for each chapter. The Vocabulary eFlashcards provide separate card sets for content vocabulary and academic vocabulary, and a separate set for people, places, and events, along with textbook page references. The final set combines all words and terms. Students can print sets of card to review vocabulary away from the computer.

Objectives
The Vocabulary eFlashcards help students
- practice and reinforce their comprehension of vocabulary and key terms in each chapter;
- identify areas for additional study and reinforcement.

Steps
Provide students with the following steps to work with the Vocabulary eFlashcards:
- Locate the Web page for the textbook being studied on the Glencoe Web site glencoe.com.
- Click on **Student Center** under the textbook title.
- In the Student Center, select a unit from the Unit Resources menu and a chapter from the Chapter Activities menu using the drop-down arrows.
- Click on the **Vocabulary eFlashcards** link.
- Select and review one of the vocabulary lists for the chapter: Academic; Content; People, Places, Events; or Combined. A new window will open.
- Review vocabulary in one of the three viewing modes: View Terms and Definitions, View Terms, and View Definitions. Click on **Flip Card** to read the relevant term or definition.

Economics ONLINE

	Student	Teacher	Parent
Beyond the Textbook	●	●	●
Chapter Overviews	●	●	●
ePuzzles and Games	●		●
Concepts in Motion	●		●
Multi-Language Glossaries	●		●
Online Student Edition	●	●	●
Self-Check Quizzes	●		●
Student Web Activities	●		●
Study Central™	●		●
Time Current Events	●	●	●
Teaching Today		●	
Vocabulary eFlashcards	●		●
Web Activity Lesson Plans		●	

Glencoe Media Center

❯ glencoe.com
Study-To-Go
- Vocabulary eFlashcards
- Self-Check Quizzes

❯ **Audio/Video**
- Student Edition Audio
- Spanish Summaries
- Economics & You Videos

- **Timed Readings Plus in Social Studies** helps students increase their reading rate and fluency while maintaining comprehension. The 400-word passages are similar to those found on state and national assessments.

- **Reading in the Content Area: Social Studies** concentrates on six essential reading skills that help students better comprehend what they read. The book includes 75 high-interest nonfiction passages written at increasing levels of difficulty.

- **Reading Social Studies** includes strategic reading instruction and vocabulary support in Social Studies content for both ELLs and native speakers of English. www.jamestowneducation.com

Reading List Generator CD-ROM

Use this database to search more than 30,000 titles to create a customized reading list for your students.

- Reading lists can be organized by students' reading level, author, genre, theme, or area of interest.

- The database provides Degrees of Reading Power™ (DRP) and Lexile™ readability scores for all selections.

- A brief summary of each selection is included.

Leveled reading suggestions for this chapter:
For students at a Grade 10 reading level:
- *From Seashells to Smart Cards: Money and Currency,* by Ernestine Giesecke

For students at a Grade 11 reading level:
- *Money Business: Banks and Banking,* by Ernestine Giesecke

For students at a Grade 12 reading level:
- *The House of Morgan: An American Banking Dynasty and the Rise of Finance,* by Ron Chernow

* Review suggested books before assigning them.

National Council on Economic Education

Voluntary Standards Emphasized in Chapter 14

Content Standard 11 Money makes it easier to trade, borrow, save, invest, and compare the value of goods and services.

Content Standard 12 Interest rates, adjusted for inflation, rise and fall to balance the amount saved with the amount borrowed, which affects the allocation of scarce resources between present and future uses.

Content Standard 20 Federal government budgetary policy and the Federal Reserve System's monetary policy influences the overall levels of employment, output, and prices.

Resources Available from NCEE
- Virtual Economics®: An Interactive Center for Economic Education Version 3.0
- Civics and Government: Focus on Economics, Second Edition
- Focus: High School Economics, Second Edition
- Advanced Placement Economics: Teacher Resource Manual, Third Edition
- Focus: Understanding Economics in U.S. History

To order these materials, or to contact your State Council on Economic Education about workshops and programs, call 1-800-338-1192 or visit the NCEE Web site at store.ncee.net.

The **BIG** Idea

As students study the chapter, remind them to consider the chapter-based Big Idea. The **Essential Question** in the chapter launch activity below ties in to the Big Idea and helps students think about and understand important chapter concepts. In addition, the Hands-On Chapter Project relates the content from each section to the Big Idea. The steps in each section build on each other and culminate in the Wrap-Up Activity on the Visual Summary page.

 To generate student interest and provide a springboard for class discussion, access the Economics & You Topic 17 video, **Money and Banking,** at glencoe.com or on the video DVD.

 Dinah Zike's Foldables are three-dimensional, interactive graphic organizers that help students practice basic writing skills, review key vocabulary terms, and identify main ideas. Have students complete this chapter's Foldable activity or activities in *Dinah Zike's Reading and Study Skills Foldables* booklet. **OL**

Economics ONLINE

Introduce students to chapter content and key terms by having them access *Chapter 14 —Chapter Overviews* at glencoe.com.

CHAPTER

14 Money, Banking, and the Fed

Why It Matters

Congratulations, you have just been hired by the federal government to completely redesign our money. Before getting started on your design, think about how we use money. Working with a partner, create a design for the new bills and coins. Share your finished product with the class and explain why your money will serve the same purpose(s) as our existing money. Read Chapter 14 to learn more about our monetary system and how the government works to promote economic stability and growth.

The **BIG** Idea

Governments strive for a balance between the costs and benefits of their economic policies to promote economic stability and growth.

▶ **Our modern banking system allows you to access your money anywhere in the world.**

382 UNIT 4

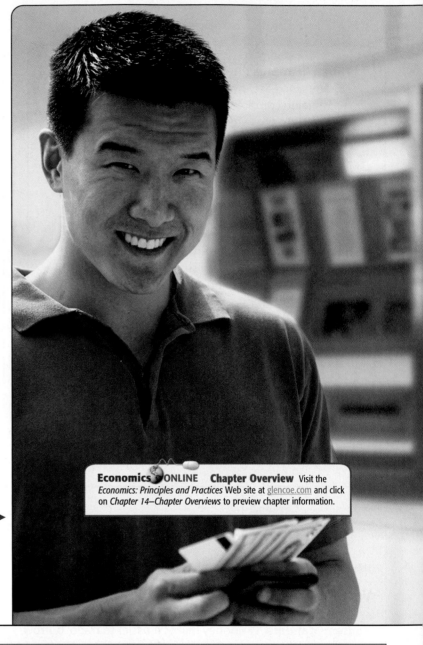

Economics ONLINE Chapter Overview Visit the *Economics: Principles and Practices* Web site at glencoe.com and click on *Chapter 14—Chapter Overviews* to preview chapter information.

Activity: Launching the Chapter

Speculating Have a volunteer read aloud the Big Idea. **Essential Question:** What are some ways that the government can influence economic stability and growth? *(Possible answers: raising or lowering taxes; buying goods and services; encouraging saving or spending by influencing inflation rates; passing laws to favor certain activities over others)* As they read this chapter, encourage students to look for examples of government intervention in the U.S. economy. **OL**

SECTION 1
The Evolution, Functions, and Characteristics of Money

GUIDE TO READING

Section Preview
In this section, you will learn that money functions as a medium of exchange, a measure of value, and a store of value.

Content Vocabulary
- Federal Reserve System (Fed) (p. 383)
- Federal Reserve notes (p. 383)
- barter economy (p. 384)
- commodity money (p. 384)
- fiat money (p. 384)
- specie (p. 385)
- monetary unit (p. 386)
- medium of exchange (p. 387)
- measure of value (p. 387)
- store of value (p. 387)
- demand deposit accounts (DDAs) (p. 388)
- M1 (p. 388)
- M2 (p. 388)

Academic Vocabulary
- revolution (p. 385)
- converted (p. 387)

Reading Strategy
Describing As you read the section, complete a graphic organizer similar to the one below that describes the characteristics of money.

Characteristics of money

PRODUCTS IN THE NEWS
—www.ptma.org

Early Money

Before there was money as we know it, there was barter. People in early societies developed forms of proto-money—the use of commodities that everyone agreed to accept in trade. Aztecs used cacao beans. Norwegians once used butter. The early U.S. colonists used tobacco leaves and animal hides (settlers traded deer hides—the origin of our modern word for money: "bucks").

Some items, such as arrowheads, salt, and animal hides, were useful in and of themselves. Gradually, however, people began exchanging items that had no intrinsic value, but which had only agreed-upon or symbolic value. An example is the cowrie shell. Cowrie shells are found on an island off the coast of India. They have been widely used as currency in China, India, Thailand, and in West Africa. ■

It may seem odd that people once used tobacco or shells as a form of money. Frequently, people used things that were easily available and valued by others as a form of money. As a result money came in a variety of forms, shapes, and sizes.

The use of money developed because it makes life easier for people and serves everyone's best interests. In fact, over time money has become a social convention, much like the general acceptance of laws and government.

Today most of our money is issued by the **Federal Reserve System (Fed),** the privately owned, publicly controlled central bank of the United States. It issues paper currency known as **Federal Reserve notes,** a key part of our money supply.

Federal Reserve System (Fed) privately owned, publicly controlled central bank of the United States

Federal Reserve note paper currency issued by the Fed in use today

Resource Manager

R Reading Strategies	C Critical Thinking	D Differentiated Instruction	W Writing Support	S Skill Practice
Teacher Edition • Identifying, p. 385 • Questioning, p. 386 • Making Connections, p. 309 **Additional Resources** • Guid. Read. Act., p. 40 • Read. Ess. & Note-Taking Guide, p. 118	**Teacher Edition** • Evaluating, p. 384 • Det. Cause/Effect, p. 385 • Contrasting, p. 389 **Additional Resources** • Econ. Concepts Trans., Strat. & Act., p. 11 • Econ. Forms and Fin. Pages Trans., Strat. and Act., pp. 5, 24	**Teacher Edition** • Special Ed., p. 384 • ELL, p. 386 • Interpersonal, p. 387 **Additional Resources** • Daily Focus Trans. 58, 60, 61 • Reteach. Act., p. 14 • Personal Finance Act., p. 1	**Teacher Edition** • Expository Writing, p. 388 **Additional Resources** • High School Reading in the Content Area Strat. and Act. • Crit. Think. Act., p. 16	**Teacher Edition** • Analyzing Graphs, p. 387 **Additional Resources** • Graph. Org. Trans., p. 11 • Reading and Study Skills Fold., p. 58 • Math Prac. for Econ., p. 9

Teach

D Differentiated Instruction

Special Education Show students with learning disorders the importance of headings and subheadings for understanding the framework of each section. Illustrate the method by asking students what they would do if they wanted to discover what Section 1 was about. Read aloud the section's headings and subheadings. Ask students to rephrase each one into a complete sentence. **BL**

C Critical Thinking

Evaluating Ask: How effective would a bartering system be in today's economy? Explain. *(Answers will vary, but students should point out that it would likely be ineffective. Bartering typically works only in small societies with fairly simple economic systems.)*

Caption Answer: It is exchanged for goods and services provided.

Differentiated Instruction

barter economy moneyless economy that relies on trade or barter

commodity money money that has an alternative use as an economic good

fiat money money by government decree

D The Evolution of Money

MAIN Idea People invented money to make life easier.

Economics and You Have you ever tried to trade for something with your friends? Read on to learn how societies began using money to make exchange easier.

Take a moment to think what life would be like in a **barter economy**, a moneyless economy that relies on trade. Without money, the exchange of goods and services would be more difficult because the products some people have to offer are not always acceptable or easy to divide for payment. For example, how could a farmer with a pail of milk obtain a pair of shoes if the cobbler wanted a basket of fish? Unless there is a "mutual coincidence of wants"—where two people want exactly what the other has and are willing to trade what they have for it—it is difficult for trade to take place.

Life is simpler in an economy with money. The farmer sells the milk for cash and then exchanges the cash for shoes. The cobbler takes the cash and looks for some-one selling fish. Money, as it turns out, makes life easier for everybody in ways we may have never considered.

Money in Primitive Societies

Tea leaves compressed into "bricks" comprised money in ancient China, and compressed cheese was used in early Russian trade. In early colonial America, corn and even animal pelts were used as a form of money.

Today, this money would be classified as **commodity money**—money that has an alternative use as an economic good, or commodity. For example, the compressed tea leaves could be used to make tea when not needed for trade. Other items became **fiat money**—money by government decree—such as tiny metallic coins used in Asia Minor in the seventh century B.C. These coins served as money because the government said they were money.

Money in Colonial America

The money used by early settlers in the American colonies was similar to that found in early societies. Some of it consisted of commodity money, and some was fiat money.

Many products—including corn, hemp, gunpowder, and musket balls—served as commodity money. They could be used to settle debts and make purchases. At the same time, colonists could consume these products if necessary.

A commonly accepted commodity money was tobacco, for which the governor of colonial Virginia set a value of three English shillings per pound in 1618. Two years later, colonists used some of this money to bring wives to the colonies.

Other colonies established fiat monies. For example, in

Barter Economy As the cartoon shows, trading in a barter economy can be difficult for those wanting to exchange goods for products they may use. *How does money function as a medium of exchange?*

www.CartoonStock.com

All fixed Ma'am: You owe me two hay-bales, four sugar cubes and three apples...

384 UNIT 4 Macroeconomics: Performance and Stabilization

Authentic Assessment Strategies and Activities, p. 16

The Functions and Characteristics of Money

Objective: Determine the functions and characteristics of money.

Focus: Have students discuss bartering, including its limitations as a medium of exchange.

Teach: Guide students through the steps of the activity, and have them complete the assessment items.

Assess: Lead students in a discussion of their responses.

Close: Ask students how they have personally witnessed the functions and characteristics of money.

Differentiated Instruction Strategies

BL Ask students to explain why businesses cannot pay employees with goods such as those shown in the activity.

AL Have students write a short story about life without money.

ELL Have students create an illustration for each of the four characteristics.

Specie Immigrants brought coins made of gold and silver, such as the Austrian taler on the left and the Spanish peso on the right. These coins were used throughout the colonies. *Why were such coins desirable?*

1637 Massachusetts established a monetary value for wampum—a form of currency the Wampanoag Native Americans made out of white and purple mussel shells. The Wampanoag and the settlers used these shells in trade. White shells were more plentiful than purple ones, so one English penny was made equal to six white or three purple shells.

Early Paper Currency

As time passed, Americans used other forms of money. In some cases, state laws allowed individuals to print their own paper currency. Usually backed by gold and silver deposits in banks, it served as currency for the immediate area. States even printed money in the form of tax-anticipation notes and used them to pay salaries, buy supplies, and meet other expenditures until they received taxes and redeemed the notes.

The Continental Congress issued paper money to finance the Revolutionary War. In 1775 it printed Continental dollars, a form of fiat paper currency with no gold or silver backing. By the end of the war, nearly one-quarter billion Continental dollars had been printed—a volume so large that it was virtually worthless by the end of the **revolution.**

Specie in the Colonies

Colonists also used modest amounts of **specie**—or money in the form of silver or gold coins. These included English shillings, Austrian talers, and various European coins that immigrants had brought to the colonies. Coins were the most desirable form of money, not only because of their mineral content, but because they were in limited supply. By 1776 only $12 million in specie circulated in the colonies, compared to nearly $500 million in paper currency.

The most popular coin in the colonies was the Spanish peso that came to America through trade and piracy. Long before the American Revolution had begun, the Spanish were mining silver in Mexico. They melted the silver into bullion—ingots or bars of precious metals—or minted it into coins for shipment to Spain. When the Spanish treasure ships stopped in the West Indies to buy fresh provisions, however, they often became victims of Caribbean pirates who spent their stolen treasure in America's southern colonies.

The "triangular trade" between the colonies, Africa, and the Caribbean brought more pesos to America. Traders took molasses and pesos from the Caribbean to the colonies. There they sold the molasses to be made into rum and spent their pesos on other goods. The rum was shipped to

specie money in the form of gold or silver coins

CHAPTER 14 Money, Banking, and the Fed **385**

C Critical Thinking

Determining Cause and Effect Ask: Why were the Continental dollars virtually worthless at the end of the Revolutionary War? *(They were not backed by gold or silver, and there were too many in circulation.)* **OL**

R Reading Strategy

Identifying Have students create a two-column chart with the headings "Name of Coin" and "Country of Origin." Students should complete their charts by identifying coins that the colonists used and the countries those coins represented. *(shillings from England, talers from Australia, pesos from Spain)* **Then ask:** Why were so many foreign coins in circulation in the colonies? *(Answers may vary but should include the concept that the colonies were populated with people from various countries.)* **BL**

Caption Answer: They were made of gold or silver and were in limited supply.

Leveled Activities

BL Personal Finance Activities, p. 1

OL Graphic Organizer Transparencies, p. 11

AL Primary and Secondary Source Readings, p. 16

monetary unit
standard unit of
currency in a country's
money supply

Africa, where it was traded for enslaved Africans. The enslaved Africans were taken to the Caribbean to be sold for pesos and more molasses. The trade cycle started anew when molasses and pesos were taken to the colonies.

R Reading Strategy

Questioning Have student pairs read the subsection and then write three questions that can be answered by the text. Ask pairs to exchange work with partners and answer each other's questions. **BL**

D Differentiated Instruction

English Language Learners
Call on students to name objects that might be used as money today if there were no dollar bills or coins. List at least 10 responses on the board. Then organize students into small groups and direct each group to apply the characteristics of money to the listed objects. Have groups select the object that would best serve as money based on their analysis. **ELL**

Caption Answer: to make it easier to understand

✓**Reading Check** **Answer:**
commodity money, fiat money, paper currency, and specie or coins

From "Talers" to "Dollars"

Pesos were known as "pieces of eight," because they were divided into eight subparts known as "bits." Because the pesos resembled the Austrian talers, they were nicknamed "talers," which sounds similar to the word *dollars*. This term became so popular that the dollar became the basic **monetary unit**, or standard unit of currency, in the U.S. money system.

Rather than divide the dollar into eighths as the Spanish had done with the peso, it was decided to divide it into tenths, which was easier to understand. Still, some of the terminology associated with the Spanish peso remains, as when people sometimes call a 25-cent coin—one quarter of a dollar—"two bits."

Dollars Today's money is available in both bills and coins. *Why was the dollar divided into tenths?*

✓**Reading Check** **Describing** What kind of money was used in colonial America?

R Characteristics and Functions of Money

MAIN Idea Anything can be used as money as long as it is portable, durable, divisible, and limited in supply.

Economics and You When you go shopping, you carry your money with you. Read on to learn how this feature of money is helpful to us.

The study of early money is useful because it helps us understand the characteristics that give money its value. In fact, any substance can serve as money if it possesses four main characteristics.

Characteristics of Money

First, money must be *portable*, or easily transferred from one person to another, to make the exchange of money for products easier. Most money in early societies was very portable—including shells, wampum, tobacco, and compressed blocks of tea.

Second, money must also be reasonably *durable* so it does not deteriorate when it is handled. Most colonial money was quite durable, especially monies like musket balls and wampum. Even the fiat paper money of the colonial period was durable in the sense that it could be easily replaced by new bills when old ones became worn.

D Third, money should be easily *divisible* into smaller units so that people can use only as much as they need for a transaction. Most early money was highly divisible. The blocks of tea or cheese were cut with a knife. Bundles of tobacco leaves could easily be broken apart. Even Spanish pesos were cut with a knife into eights to make "bits" for payment.

Finally, if something is to serve as money, it must be available, but only in *limited supply*. Stones used as money on the Yap Islands, for example, were carried in open canoes from other islands 400 miles away. Because navigation was uncertain and the weather was unpredictable, only one canoe in 20 completed the round-trip, resulting in a limited supply of stone money.

Hands-On Chapter Project

Step 1

Creating a U.S. Currency Time Line

In this project, students will research and evaluate the types of currency used throughout U.S. history.

Step 1: Researching Forms of Money.
Students will break into small groups to research the types of currency used throughout U.S. history.

Directions: Organize the class into small groups. Explain to students that they will be learning about the history of currency in the United States and evaluating the changes to it over time. Assign each group a particular time period in U.S. history. Instruct each group to use library resources and the Internet to research the various types of currency found in the United States during their assigned period. Encourage students to use simple outlines or graphic organizers to record their findings.

Organizing When students have completed their research, ask them to review their findings and determine what information they would choose to include on a class time line depicting the history of currency in the United States. Direct them to prepare a list of the types of currency they researched and the dates each type was used. **OL**

(Chapter Project continued in Section 2.)

The Global Economy &YOU

The Euro

Go to any U.S. coin shop, and you can buy German marks, French francs, Italian lira, and Greek drachmas–often a whole bag of coins–for just a few bucks. Why so cheap? Because those coins have been replaced by the euro, they are now virtually worthless.

In January 2002, most European Union (EU) nations replaced their own money with the euro. A historic milestone in the process of European integration, the euro has created a new monetary reality for 300 million Europeans. A generation ago, few would have believed this possible. People take their money personally. It usually includes national symbols, heroic figures, or government leaders. So how did the EU countries agree on a single type of currency? The fact is, they didn't.

The euro bills depict stylized buildings from different architectural periods. The coins, however, are unique for

each country. While one side of the coins is the same, the other side reflects the country from which it originated.

Money, like almost everything else, loses its value whenever there is too much of it. **S** This was a major problem for most types of commodity money. In Virginia, the price of tobacco went from 36 pennies a pound to 1 penny a pound after every-one started growing their own money. Wampum even lost its value when settlers used industrial dyes to turn white shells into purple—thereby doubling their value.

Functions of Money

Any substance that is portable, durable, divisible, and limited in supply can serve **D** as money. If it does, it will serve three roles in the economy.

Money is a **medium of exchange**—something accepted by all parties as payment for goods and services. Throughout history, societies have used many materials as a medium of exchange, including gold, silver, and even salt. In ancient Rome, salt was so valuable that each soldier received an annual salt payment called a "salarium."

The modern term for an annual income—*salary*—is based on this Latin term.

The second function of money is to serve as a **measure of value**—a common measuring stick that can be used to express worth in terms that most individuals understand. This is what we observe whenever we see a price tag on something—a value that we can use to make comparisons with other products. In the United States, our measure of value is expressed in dollars and cents.

Third, money serves as a **store of value**—the quality that allows purchasing power to be saved until needed. For example, goods or services can be **converted** into money, which is easily stored until needed. This feature of money allows a period of time to pass between earning and spending an income.

Modern Money

Today we have several different types of money. Some of it is in the form of Federal Reserve notes and some in the form of

medium of exchange money or other substance generally accepted as payment for goods and services

measure of value a function of money that allows it to serve as a common way to express value

store of value a function of money that allows people to preserve value for future use

CHAPTER 14   Money, Banking, and the Fed   **387**

Extending the Content

The First Central Bank The Bank of Amsterdam was established in Holland in 1609. At that time, Amsterdam was a center of world trade. More than 340 kinds of silver coins and about 500 types of gold coins circulated throughout the city. Dutch merchants had little idea how much these coins were worth, so the Bank of Amsterdam was set up under a charter from the city to standardize the currency. The Bank of Amsterdam operated as Holland's

central bank for more than 200 years. After making a series of bad loans, however, it failed and went out of business in 1819 — almost 100 years before America's central bank was founded.

W Writing Support

Expository Writing Have each student write a paragraph explaining the different types of money and the definitions the federal government uses for the money supply. **OL**

✓ Reading Check **Answer:** It is lightweight and convenient, and it can be easily transferred from one person to another. It is reasonably durable, is divisible, and has limited availability.

Assess

💿 Use the Interactive Tutor Self-Assessment CD-ROM to review Section 1, and then assign the Section 1 Review as homework or as an in-class activity.

Close

Inferring Ask: What changes can be made to money that do not affect its functions and characteristics? *(Possible answer: Different illustrations or designs can be used.)* **OL**

SECTION 1 Review

---

demand deposit account (DDA) account from which funds can be removed by writing a check and without having to gain prior approval from the depository institution

M1 component of the money supply relating to money's role as a medium of exchange

M2 component of the money supply relating to money's role as a store of value

---

📖 Skills Handbook

See page R46 to learn about Drawing Conclusions.

---

metallic coins issued by the U.S. Bureau of the Mint. Other forms of money include **demand deposit accounts (DDAs)**, or funds deposited in a bank that can be accessed by writing a check and without having to secure prior approval of the institution.

Because of this, the Fed uses different definitions for the money supply. The first **W** is **M1,** which includes coins and currency, traveler's checks, DDAs, and checking accounts held at other depository institutions. This definition of the money supply relates to money's function as a medium of exchange. A broader definition is **M2,** which includes M1 along with savings deposits, time deposits, and money market funds—all of which relate to money's function as a store of value.

While our modern money may seem to be quite different from earlier forms of money, it shares the fundamental characteristics and functions of money. Modern money is *portable*. Our currency is lightweight, convenient, and can be easily transferred from one person to another. The same applies to the use of checks.

Modern money is reasonably *durable*. Metallic coins last about 20 years under normal use. Paper currency is also reasonably durable, with a $1 bill lasting about 18 months in circulation. The introduction of the Sacagawea dollar coin was part of an attempt to make the money supply even more durable by replacing the $1 bill, a low-denomination currency, with longer-lasting coins.

Modern money is *divisible*. The penny, which is the smallest denomination of coin, is small enough for almost any purchase. In addition, people can write checks for the exact amount of a purchase.

If anything, modern money has an uneven track record when it comes to *limited availability* and stability in value. The money supply often grew at a rate of 10 to 12 percent a year in the 1970s, which contributed greatly to the inflation of the early 1980s. It has slowed considerably since then, which has led to a period of price stability.

✓ Reading Check **Explaining** How does modern money reflect the functions and characteristics of money?

SECTION 1 Review

Vocabulary

1. **Explain** the significance of Federal Reserve System (Fed), Federal Reserve note, barter economy, commodity money, fiat money, specie, monetary unit, medium of exchange, measure of value, store of value, demand deposit account (DDA), M1, and M2.

Main Ideas

2. **Explaining** Why was the "dollar" adopted as the basic monetary unit of the United States?

3. **Identifying** Use a graphic organizer like the one below to identify the functions of money.

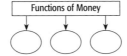

Functions of Money

Critical Thinking

4. **The BIG Idea** How does money advance the exchange of goods and services?

5. **Inferring** Why would some people be more willing to accept commodity money rather than fiat money?

6. **Drawing Conclusions** Why did the use of money replace the barter system?

7. **Analyzing Visuals** Study the cartoon on page 384. How does this cartoon spotlight the basic problem of a barter economy?

Applying Economics

8. **Functions of Money** Create a list of the ways you have used money during the last week. Write the actions on a piece of paper. Next to each, identify which of the functions of money your actions illustrated.

Answers

1. All definitions can be found in the section and the Glossary.
2. Spanish pesos, the most popular coin in the colonies, were nicknamed talers, which sounds like "dollars." This term became so popular that it was made the basic monetary unit in the U.S. money system.
3. medium of exchange; measure of value; store of value
4. The use of money advances the exchange of goods and services because it helps buyers and sellers complete a trade.

Without money, buyers would have to want exactly what the sellers have and the sellers would have to be willing to accept exactly what the buyers have to trade.

5. If individuals have no faith in the government that issues the fiat money, they might prefer commodity money. Commodity money has an alternate economic use and consequently has value even when not used as money.
6. Money replaced the barter system because people found it difficult to trade what they

had for what they wanted. Unless there is a "mutual coincidence of wants," it is difficult for trade to take place.

7. The problem with a barter economy is finding someone who will exchange what they have for what you have.
8. Answers will vary but should demonstrate a clear understanding of the functions of money.

CASE STUDY
Keep the Change

Thinking Outside the Bank

When you think of banks, you probably see an unimaginative, conservative industry. Most banks offer very similar services and interest rates on loans, savings accounts, and certificates of deposit. So how can a bank differentiate itself to attract new customers?

"Keep the Change"

Bank of America came up with a plan and in 2005 launched a new program called "Keep the Change." The bank tallies each purchase its customers make with their debit cards and rounds it up to the next higher dollar. The bank then transfers the difference, or "change," into the Bank of America savings accounts of customers. To sweeten the pot, the bank matches the first three months of savings at 100 percent and each month

HOW IT WORKS

Go into a store, buy a cup of coffee for $1.50

↓

Pay for it with your Keep the Change debit card, B of A rounds it off to $2

↓

B of A transfers $.50 from your checking to your savings account, matching 5% of the annual total up to $250

thereafter at 5 percent, up to a yearly total of $250. The bank's contributions are made annually, but customers can still watch their money grow with interest on a daily basis.

IT ADDS UP!		
Daily Purchases	Purchase Price	Amount Transferred to Savings
CD:	$9.63	$.37
Latte:	$3.80	$.20
Burger:	$2.29	$.71
Total:	$15.72	$1.28

Don't Even *Think* About Saving

How did Bank of America come up with such a new idea in an industry not known for innovation? In early 2004, the bank hired researchers to study people's banking and spending habits. They found that some people rounded up their payments to make balancing their checkbooks easier and quicker. They also saw purchasing behaviors that reinforced the stereotype that Americans are big spenders but not big savers.

The "Keep the Change" program takes the responsibility for saving out of customers' hands while it rewards spending. Even so, it's still money in the bank. Instead of tossing change into a jar each night, 2.5 million new Bank of America customers allow the bank to slip their change into an interest-bearing savings account.

Analyzing the Impact

1. **Summarizing** Why did Bank of America introduce its "Keep the Change" program?
2. **Drawing Conclusions** How much money would a person save per month and per year if making a weekly purchase of the items in the table?

Focus

Making Connections Lead a discussion about saving money. Ask students why people might find it difficult to save money. *(Possible answer: It takes time, planning, and organization.)* **OL**

Teach

C Critical Thinking

Contrasting Ask: What is the difference between saving by putting change into a jar each night and saving by putting change into an interest-bearing savings account? *(Putting change into a jar does not earn interest as it would if you put it into an interest-bearing savings account.)* **OL**

Analyzing the Impact

Answers:
1. to reward customers for using debit cards and encourage savings contributions
2. per month: $35.84; per year: $553.73

Additional Support

Activity: Technology Connection

Comparing and Contrasting

Organize students into groups of three, and have groups use Internet resources to investigate the services of different banks located in your area. Have groups compare and contrast services offered on checking and savings accounts, online banking, and other incentives offered by the banks to attract future customers. Ask each group to present their findings to the

class in a multimedia presentation. After all groups have presented, have the class discuss which bank they think offers the most lucrative services, which services they feel are most important, and what incentives banks could use to secure students' business. Take a class poll to determine students' preferences. **OL**

Teacher Tip

Ensuring Variety Make sure that each group is researching different banks so that students' presentations cover a wide range of banks in your area. You might also suggest that at least one group research an online bank.

Focus

Bellringer
Daily Focus Transparency 31

FOCUS ACTIVITIES
Transparency 31

FINANCIAL INSTITUTIONS

Financial Institutions in the United States, 2004
(selected types)

Type	Number of Establishments	Assets (billions of dollars)
Commercial banks	7,630	8,412.8
Savings institutions	1,345	1,691.8
Credit unions	9,514	647.0

Source: Statistical Abstract of the United States: 2006

1. What is the most common type of financial institution listed in the table?
2. What conclusions can you draw from the table?

Daily Focus Transparencies

GUIDE TO READING

Answers to Graphic:

1861: Congress authorizes legal tender

1863: Congress creates a national banking system

1878: U.S. government introduces silver certificates

1913: Congress creates the Federal Reserve

1934: 10,000 banks close or merge

Resource Manager

The Development of Modern Banking

GUIDE TO READING

Section Preview
In this section, you will learn that many different types of money have been used throughout American history, and fiat money is used today.

Content Vocabulary

- state bank (p. 391)
- legal tender (p. 392)
- national bank (p. 392)
- national currency (p. 392)
- gold certificate (p. 393)
- silver certificate (p. 393)
- central bank (p. 394)
- bank run (p. 395)
- bank holiday (p. 395)
- fractional reserve system (p. 396)
- legal reserves (p. 396)
- reserve requirement (p. 396)
- member bank reserve (MBR) (p. 396)
- excess reserves (p. 396)

Academic Vocabulary

- clauses (p. 391)
- initially (p. 395)

Reading Strategy

Listing As you read the section, complete a time line similar to the one below by listing major events in U.S. monetary history in the appropriate spaces.

1860	1880	1900	1920	1940

1862
1861
1886
1900
1934

Gold certificates issues

PRODUCTS IN THE NEWS
—Bureau of Engraving and Printing

New $10 Bills

On March 2, 2006, the Federal Reserve banks issued a redesigned Series 2004 $10 note to the public through commercial banks. The notes will begin circulating immediately in the United States, and will then be introduced in other countries. . . .

New money designs are being issued as part of an ongoing effort to stay ahead of counterfeiting, and to protect the economy and the hard-earned money of U.S. currency users. The new series began with the introduction of the $20 note on October 9, 2003, and continued with the $50 note issued on September 28, 2004. ■

Creating and maintaining a dependable money supply is more difficult than most people think. Over the years, the United States has experimented with different kinds of money with varying success.

Early attempts included coins made of gold and silver, as well as paper currency backed by gold and silver. Today some of our money circulates as paper currency, but most of it exists in the form of electronic bookkeeping entries. Neither is backed by gold or silver. Instead, we have a managed money supply that is accepted by everyone simply because people have faith in it.

Managing this money supply takes an enormous amount of work. As you read in the news story, we even have to make it difficult for others to copy money so that it stays in limited supply—lest it go the way of the Continental dollar.

R Reading Strategies	**C** Critical Thinking	**D** Differentiated Instruction	**W** Writing Support	**S** Skill Practice
Teacher Edition • Skimming, p. 391 • Identifying, p. 392 • Sequencing, p. 393 **Additional Resources** • Guid. Read. Act., p. 41 • Read. Ess. & Note-Taking Guide, p. 121 • Econ. Cont. Vocab. Act., p. 14	**Teacher Edition** • Contrasting, p. 393 • Evaluating, p. 397 **Additional Resources** • Econ. Concepts Trans., Strat. & Act., p. 9 • Quizzes and Tests, p. 174 • Enrichment Act., p. 14	**Teacher Edition** • Adv. Learners, p. 391 • ELL, p. 392 • Special Ed., p. 394 • Auditory/Musical, p. 395 **Additional Resources** • Daily Focus Trans. 59, 31 • Math Prac. for Econ., p. 9	**Teacher Edition** • Persuasive Writing, p. 396 • Expository Writing, p. 398 **Additional Resources** • High School Writing Process Trans. • Pri./Sec. Source Read., p. 31	**Teacher Edition** • Making Predictions, p. 394 • Visual Literacy, p. 395 • Using Tables and Charts, p. 396 **Additional Resources** • Reading and Study Skills Fold., p. 58 • Reinforcing Econ. Skills, p. 3

The Development of Banking in America

MAIN Idea The United States experimented with many different kinds of money before it created the Federal Reserve System.

Economics and You Have you ever wondered why the dollar bill is green? Read on to learn why the government decided to print our money this way.

Banking in the United States has gone through many changes. At one time, banking was virtually unregulated. This led to abuses, and problems with the money supply eventually required the intervention of government.

Privately Issued Bank Notes

During the Revolutionary War, nearly 250 million Continental dollars were printed. By the end of the Revolution, Continental currency had become worthless, and people did not trust the government to issue anything except coins. Accordingly, Article 1, Section 8, of the United States Constitution states:

The Congress shall have the power
To coin money, regulate the value thereof, and of foreign coin, and fix the standard of weights and measures;
To provide for the punishment of counterfeiting the securities and current coin of the United States; . . .
To make all laws which shall be necessary and proper for carrying into execution the foregoing powers, and all other powers vested by this Constitution in the government of the United States, or in any department or officer thereof.

Article 1, Section 10, further states:

No State shall . . . coin money; emit bills of credit; make anything but gold and silver coin a tender in payment of debts. . . .

Because of these **clauses**, the federal government did not print paper currency until the Civil War. Instead, the printing, distribution, and regulation of the paper money supply were left to the discretion of privately owned banks.

Growth of State Banking

Banking became popular after the Revolution because the new Constitution allowed private banks to issue paper currency. By 1811 the country had about 100 state banks. A **state bank** is a bank that receives its operating charter from a state government.

Banks issued their own currency by printing their notes at local printing shops. The banks then put these notes in circulation with the assurance that people could exchange them for gold or silver if they ever lost faith in the bank or its currency.

At first, most banks printed only the amount of currency they could reasonably back with their gold and silver reserves. Others, however, were not as honest and printed large amounts of currency in remote areas to make it difficult for people to redeem their currency.

Problems With Currency

Even when banks were honest, problems with their currency arose. First, each bank issued its own currency in different sizes,

state bank bank that receives its charter from the state in which it operates

Money Paper currency such as this Continental dollar helped finance the Revolutionary War. ***Why did the federal government stop printing paper currency?***

CHAPTER 14 Money, Banking, and the Fed **391**

Teach

R Reading Strategy

Skimming Have students skim the page to find the answer to this question: What happened to currency at the end of the Revolutionary War? *(It had become worthless.)* **BL**

D Differentiated Instruction

Advanced Learners Have students redesign forms of U.S. currency. Ask students to brainstorm a list of national leaders, prestigious citizens, or well-known places that they think should be honored on currency. You might suggest that they research foreign currencies for design ideas. Post students' designs in the classroom. **AL**

Caption Answer: Clauses in the Constitution gave Congress the power to coin money. States and the federal government did not have that power.

Additional Support

Extending the Content

Have You Got a Buck? In the frontier areas during the colonial period, hunters often left their deerskins at trading posts until they could pick them up at a later date. As proof of ownership, the hunters would obtain a receipt, which they could exchange among themselves or use at the trading post for supplies. The receipts, worth about a dollar because of the value of the hides, were called "bucks"—hence, the common name for the dollar.

R Reading Strategy

Identifying Ask: What major event in U.S. history changed commercial banking forever? (the Civil War) **BL**

D Differentiated Instruction

English Language Learners
To help students understand the term *legal tender*, tell them that there are several different meanings for the word *tender*. In the case of money, it means "the thing offered." Money is the thing offered in payment of a debt, and it must be accepted as payment. Ask students to write a sentence using the term *legal tender*. Then have student pairs check the accuracy of each other's sentences. **ELL**

Caption Answer: There were hundreds of different kinds of notes, too many notes issued, and problems with counterfeiting.

Economic Cartoons, p. 20

392

Private Bank Notes After the Revolutionary War, private banks issued their own currencies. *What were the major problems with such currencies?*

legal tender fiat currency that must be accepted for payment by decree of the government

national bank commercial bank chartered by the National Banking System

national currency currency backed by government bonds and issued by commercial banks in the National Banking System

colors, and denominations. As a result, hundreds of different kinds of notes could be in circulation in any given city.

Second, banks were tempted to issue too many notes because they could print more money whenever they wanted. Third, counterfeiting became a major problem. With so many different types of notes in circulation, many counterfeiters did not even bother to copy other notes. Instead, they just made up new ones.

By the time of the Civil War, more than 1,600 banks were issuing more than 10,000 different kinds of paper currency. Each bank was supposed to have backing for its notes in the form of gold or silver, but this was seldom the case. As a result, when people tried to buy something, merchants would often check their notes against the latest listing of good and bad currencies before deciding which ones they would accept in payment.

R The paper currency component of the nation's money supply was badly in need of an overhaul. Politically powerful local bankers, however, resisted change until an event came along that would change commercial banking in the United States forever—the Civil War.

Greenbacks

When the Civil War erupted, both the Union and the Confederacy needed to raise enormous sums to finance the war. Congress tried to borrow money by selling

bonds, but this did not raise as much money as the federal government needed. As a result, Congress decided to print paper currency for the first time since the Constitution was adopted.

In 1861 Congress authorized the printing of $60 million in the new currency. **D** Although this currency had no gold or silver backing, it was declared **legal tender**—fiat currency that must be accepted in payment for debts. These new notes were soon dubbed "greenbacks" because the reverse sides of the notes were printed with green ink. The green backs distinguished the new notes from the state notes already in circulation, because these were usually blank on the back.

The National Banking System

As the war dragged on, people feared that the greenbacks—like the Continental dollars used almost a century earlier to finance the Revolutionary War—might become worthless. When the greenbacks did lose some of their value, people avoided using them, forcing Congress to find another way to pay for the war.

In 1863 Congress enacted the National Currency Act, which created a National Banking System (NBS) made up of national banks. A **national bank** is a privately owned bank that receives its operating charter from the federal government. These banks issued their own notes called **national currency** that were backed with

---

The Shirt Off Lincoln's Back

Objective: Interpret a cartoon to learn more about the history of banking in the United States.

Focus/Teach: Ask students to describe Abraham Lincoln and the ideals that he represents. Then have students complete the activity.

Assess: Discuss students' interpretations of the cartoon.

Close: Discuss with students how events such as the bailout of the savings and loan industry have affected American banking.

Differentiated Instruction Strategies

BL Ask students to identify clues to the cartoonist's perspective.

AL Have students draw a cartoon about another U.S. banking event.

ELL Have students create a table identifying the bailout's effects on the upper and lower/middle classes.

Differentiated Instruction

bonds that the banks bought from the federal government. The government hoped that rigorous bank inspections and other high standards would give people confidence in the new banking system and its currency. The new system also would help the government because banks that joined the NBS would buy the bonds that helped supply the government with funds needed to finance the Civil War.

Initially, only a few state-chartered banks joined the system because it was easier for them to print their money at local printers. Finally, in 1865 the federal government forced state banks to become part of the National Banking System by placing a 10 percent tax on all privately issued bank notes. Because state-chartered banks could not afford the tax, they withdrew their notes, leaving only the greenbacks and currency issued by the NBS in circulation.

As a result of the need to finance the Civil War, the makeup of the paper component of the money supply shifted from being entirely privately issued to being entirely publicly issued.

Other Federal Currencies

The 10 percent tax greatly simplified the money supply by causing the removal of more than 10,000 different sizes and denominations of state bank notes. Before long, however, new types of federal currency appeared.

In the same year the NBS was created, the government issued **gold certificates**—paper currency backed by gold placed on deposit with the United States Treasury. At first, these certificates were printed in large denominations for use exclusively by banks, but by 1882 they were also issued in smaller denominations for use by the general public.

In 1878 the government introduced **silver certificates**—paper currency backed by silver dollars and bullion placed on reserve with the Treasury. The government was already minting silver dollar coins, but their bulky size made them inconvenient.

When silver dollars were used as backing, the certificates became more popular and increased the demand for silver. This appeased both the silver miners and the public who wanted an alternative to the bulky silver dollars.

✓**Reading Check** **Explaining** Why did the government issue greenbacks in 1861?

gold certificate
paper currency backed by gold and issued between 1863 and 1934

silver certificate
paper currency backed by, and redeemable for, silver from 1878 to 1968

CAREERS

Bank Teller

The Work

* Handle a wide range of banking transactions, including cashing checks, accepting deposits and loan payments, and processing withdrawals

* Sell savings bonds and traveler's checks, and handle foreign currencies or commercial accounts

* Explain to customers the various types of accounts and financial services the bank offers

Qualifications

* Solid computer, numerical, clerical, and communication skills

* Consistent attention to detail

* Must enjoy public contact, feel comfortable handling large amounts of money, and should be discreet and trustworthy

* High school diploma

Earnings

* Median annual earnings: $21,120

Job Growth Outlook

* Slower than average

Source: *Occupational Outlook Handbook, 2006–2007 Edition*

CHAPTER 14   Money, Banking, and the Fed   **393**

Teach

R Reading Strategy

Sequencing Ask: What steps did the National Bank take to create a new banking system and establish its currency? *(issued their own notes called national currency; implemented bank inspections; set high standards for the industry; placed a 10 percent tax on privately owned bank notes)* **OL**

C Critical Thinking

Contrasting Have students use a graphic organizer to list the differences between gold certificates and silver certificates. *(Gold certificates were issued in 1863, backed by gold, placed on deposit with the U.S. Treasury, and printed in large denominations used by banks and small denominations used by the general public. Silver certificates were issued in 1878, backed by silver, placed on reserve with the Treasury, and used by the public.)* **OL**

✓**Reading Check** **Answer:** to finance the Civil War

Leveled Activities

BL Reinforcing Economic Skills, p. 3 | **OL** Economic Forms and Financial Pages Trans., Strat. and Act., p. 5 | **AL** Enrichment Activities, p. 14

Teach

D Differentiated Instruction

Special Education Ask students to read the first sentence of the bracketed paragraph. Then set a purpose for reading the rest of the paragraph by having students look for ways that the banking system was showing signs of strain. *(The National Banking System was having trouble providing enough currency for the growing nation, it was not designed to deal with checking accounts, and minor recessions were causing major problems for banks.)* **BL**

S Skill Practice

Making Predictions Ask: How do you think that the Great Depression impacted banking? *(Students will likely predict that the Depression devastated the banking industry.)* Have students continue reading to check the accuracy of their predictions. **OL**

Caption Answer: Depositors were concerned about the safety of their money and wanted to withdraw it before the bank failed.

Additional Support

---

central bank
bank that can lend money to other banks in times of need

The Great Depression
When depositors became concerned about the safety of their money, they often started bank runs, such as this on on the Federal American Bank. *Why did bank runs occur?*

The Creation of the Fed

MAIN Idea The Federal Reserve System is the nation's central bank.

Economics and You Have you ever wondered where the money you might borrow to buy a car comes from? Read on to learn how banks generate these funds.

D By the turn of the twentieth century, the banking system was showing signs of strain. First, the National Banking System, designed primarily to help the federal government finance the Civil War, was having difficulty providing enough currency for the growing nation. Second, checking accounts were becoming more popular, and the banking system was not designed to deal with this new method of payment. Third, even minor recessions were causing major problems for banks and other lending institutions.

The Federal Reserve System

Reform came in 1913 when Congress created the Federal Reserve System, or Fed, as the nation's central bank. A **central bank** is a bank that can lend to other banks in times of need.

To ensure membership in the Fed, all national banks were required, and all state-chartered banks were eligible, to become "members"—or part owners—of the Fed. Because the Fed was organized as a corporation, any bank that joined had to purchase shares of stock in the system, just as a private individual purchases shares in a regular corporation. As a result, privately owned banks, not the government, own the Federal Reserve System.

The Fed issued its own currency, called Federal Reserve notes, which eventually replaced all other types of federal currency. Because the Fed had the resources to lend to other banks during periods of difficulty, the Fed became the nation's first true central bank.

S Banking in the Great Depression

Despite the creation of the Fed, many banks were only marginally sound during the 1920s. Part of the reason was an overexpansion of banking between the Civil War and 1921, when the total number of banks exceeded 31,000. Although some consolidation occurred between 1921 and 1929, the banking industry was overextended when the Great Depression began in 1929.

Activity: Interdisciplinary Connection

Literature Have students research the Internet or visit the library to find personal memoirs of people who lived through the Great Depression. (One example of such a book is *Hard Times: An Oral History of the Great Depression* by Studs Terkel. Some of the personal histories in the book are about people who lost all their savings during the Depression.) Have students prepare reports on their findings. Then organize students into groups of three or four, and allow time for them to share their reports with the group. Ask groups to identify common characteristics found in the various pieces they read. Then invite groups to compare their results in a class discussion. **OL**

Figure 14.1 ▶ State and National Banks

CHAPTER 14, SECTION 2

▶ The number of banks in the United States grew rapidly after 1880 and peaked in 1921. A period of mergers and consolidations took place from 1921 to 1929, after which the Great Depression took its toll. The number of banks remained relatively constant from 1933 to 1985, when another wave of mergers took place.

Graphs In Motion
See StudentWorks™ Plus or glencoe.com.

Economic Analysis *What can you infer about the ratio of state banks to national banks?*

NUMBER OF STATE AND NATIONAL BANKS

- State charter
- National charter
- All banks

1921 More than 31,000 state and national banks exist in the country

1929 About 25,500 banks exist when the depression starts

1934 Five years after the Depression begins, aproximately 14,100 banks remain

Number of banks

Source: Federal Deposit Insurance Corporation; *Historical Statistics of the United States, Colonial Times to 1970*; Office of the Comptroller of the Currency

Teach

S Skill Practice

Visual Literacy Ask: What statement would summarize the graph content? *(Possible answer: The number of state and national banks has decreased since 1921.)* **OL**

D Differentiated Instruction

Auditory/Musical Have students listen to songs from the Great Depression that touch upon the poverty and misery of the era. Examples include "Brother, Can You Spare a Dime?" (performed by Bing Crosby), "I Ain't Got No Home" (by Woody Guthrie), and "Eleven Cent Cotton, Forty Cent Meat" (by Bob Miller). Discuss the subject matter in the songs, especially whom the singers seem to blame for their poor conditions. Have each student write a paragraph responding to the songs. **OL**

Economic Analysis

Answer: From 1890 until the present, state banks have outnumbered national banks.

Additional Support

As **Figure 14.1** shows, a staggering number of bank failures occurred during the 1930s. At the start of the Depression, about 25,500 banks existed—none of which had deposit insurance for their customers. As a result, concern about the safety of bank deposits often caused a **bank run**—a rush by depositors to withdraw their funds from a bank before it failed. This made the situation worse, causing more banks to fail.

On March 5, 1933, President Roosevelt announced a **bank holiday**—a brief period during which every bank in the country was required to close. Several days later, after Congress passed legislation to strengthen the banking industry, most banks were allowed to reopen. Still, the

Great Depression took its toll, and by 1934 more than 10,000 banks had closed or merged with stronger banks.

Federal Deposit Insurance

When banks failed during the Great Depression, depositors lost all their savings. The Banking Act of 1933, also known as the Glass-Steagall Act, was passed to strengthen the banking industry. The act also created the Federal Deposit Insurance Corporation (FDIC), which **initially** insured customer deposits to a maximum of $2,500 in the event of a bank failure.

The insurance did little for those who lost their savings before 1934, but it has provided a sense of security in banking

bank run sudden rush by depositors to withdraw all deposited funds, generally in anticipation of bank failure or closure

bank holiday brief period during which all banks or depository institutions are closed to prevent bank runs

CHAPTER 14 Money, Banking, and the Fed **395**

Extending the Content

Confidence in Banks Returns The importance of people's confidence in banks became apparent on March 1, 1933. Six states declared a "bank holiday" to prevent depositors from making a run on the banks to withdraw their money. Widespread panic peaked a few days later. By March 13, banks around the country began to reopen, and by the end of March, three-fourths of the nation's banks were operating. In June, Congress

passed the Banking Act of 1933, which established the Federal Deposit Insurance Corporation (FDIC). The U.S. Treasury and the twelve Federal Reserve Banks provided the capital necessary to establish the FDIC, and steps were taken to form the organization. With the success of deposit insurance in 1934, public sentiment toward the banking industry began to change and the public's confidence in banks returned.

Teach

S Skill Practice

Using Tables and Charts

Ask: What conclusion can you draw from the information in the graph? *(Possible answer: Banks gain a large amount of money with the 20 percent reserve requirement.)* What would be the eventual size of the money supply if there was a 25 percent reserve requirement? *($4,000)* A 15 percent reserve requirement? *($6,666.67)* **OL**

W Writing Support

Persuasive Writing Have students write a paragraph stating their opinion of the fractional reserve system. Is it a fair or an unfair practice from the point of view of depositors? Invite volunteers to share their opinions in a class discussion. **OL**

Economic Analysis
Answer: $10,000

Hands-On Chapter Project
Step 2

Creating a U.S. Currency Time Line

Step 2: Assembling the Time Line. Students will use the information they learned in Step 1 to construct and illustrate a class time line.

Directions: Students will return to the groups they formed in Step 1. Ask them to review the information they selected for inclusion in the time line. Instruct groups to choose an image for each item that they plan to include on the class time line.

Figure 14.2 ► **Fractional Reserves and the Money Supply**

▶ With a 20 percent reserve requirement, a $1,000 cash deposit will result in a fivefold expansion of the money supply.

Economic Analysis *If the initial reserves were $2,000, how large could the money supply get?*

---

fractional reserve system
system requiring financial institutions to set aside a fraction of their deposits in the form of reserves

legal reserves
currency and deposits used to meet the reserve requirement

reserve requirement
formula used to compute the amount of a depository institution's required reserves

member bank reserve (MBR)
reserves kept by member banks at the Fed to satisfy reserve requirements

excess reserves
financial institution's cash, currency, and reserves not needed for reserve requirements

ever since. After the FDIC was created, people worried less about the safety of their deposits, reducing the number of runs on banks. If a bank is in danger of collapse today, the FDIC can seize the bank and either sell it to a stronger one or liquidate it and pay off the depositors. If it is sold, the sale is done in secrecy to prevent panic withdrawals or to keep shareholders from selling their worthless stock to unsuspecting investors.

Either way, depositors today have little to fear because they are now covered up to the current $100,000 FDIC insurance limit per customer per bank. If an account holds more than this amount, the depositor may go to court and sue the bank's owners to recover the rest.

Fractional Reserves and Deposit Expansion

The growing popularity of checking accounts in the last century led to the refinement of another important banking practice, the use of fractional bank reserves. Under a **fractional reserve system**, banks are required to keep only a portion of their total deposits in the form of legal reserves. **Legal reserves** consist of coins and currency that banks hold in their vaults, plus deposits at the Fed. The size of the reserves

are determined by a **reserve requirement**, the percentage of every deposit that must be set aside as legal reserves. The result is a money supply that is several times larger than the total reserves of the banking system.

To see how this works, let us assume that on Monday, a depositor named Kim opens a demand deposit account (DDA) by depositing $1,000 in a bank that is subject to a 20 percent reserve requirement. We will also assume that no one else has any money, so the size of the entire money supply is also $1,000. **Figure 14.2** illustrates the monetary expansion process that takes place under these conditions.

Because of the 20 percent reserve requirement, $200 of Kim's deposit must be set aside as a reserve in the form of vault cash or in a **member bank reserve (MBR)**—a deposit a member bank keeps at the Fed to satisfy reserve requirements. The remaining $800 of **excess reserves**—legal reserves beyond the reserve requirement—represents the bank's lending power and can be loaned out. At the end of Monday the total money supply in the hands of the public amounts to Kim's $1,000 checking account.

On Tuesday, the bank lends its $800 excess reserves to Bill. Bill decides to take the loan in the form of a DDA so that the

---

Explain that these images could depict the types of currency or people using the currency during the historical period in which they were found. Then, as a class, have students determine the dates that their class time line should span and the intervals at which the time line should be divided. When these decisions have been made, have the groups work together to draw a blank time line on a large piece of paper.

Sequencing Direct each group to find the section of time line that corresponds to the historical period they researched. Then have them add their information and illustrations to the time line. **OL**

(Chapter Project continued in Section 3.)

cash never leaves the bank. Even so, the bank treats the new DDA as a new deposit, so 20 percent, or $160, must be set aside as a reserve. This leaves $640 of excess reserves to be lent to someone else. By the end of Tuesday, the total money supply in the hands of the public amounts to $1,800—the sum of Kim's and Bill's DDAs.

On Wednesday, Maria enters the bank and borrows the $640 excess reserves. If she takes the loan in the form of a DDA, the bank treats it as a new $640 deposit, 20 percent of which must be set aside as a required reserve, leaving $512 of excess reserves. By the end of the day, the money supply in the hands of the public (DDAs and cash) has grown to $2,440—the sum of the DDAs owned by Kim, Bill, and Maria. **C**

The $2,440 result would be exactly the same if Maria had borrowed the bank's $640 excess reserves in cash. Had she done so, the money supply in the hands of the public would have consisted of the $1,800 in Kim's and Bill's checking accounts, plus Maria's $640.

However, the money expansion process will now come to a temporary halt until the $640 cash returns to the bank as a deposit. If Maria spends the money, and if the person who receives it opens a new deposit account so that additional excess reserves are created, the expansion process can resume.

This expansion will continue as long as the bank has excess reserves to lend and as long as lenders deposit part or all of that money. In fact, as long as every dollar of DDAs is backed by 20 cents of legal reserves, the total amount of DDAs would be:

$$\frac{\text{Total MBRs}}{\text{Reserve Requirement}} = \frac{\$1,000}{.20} = \$5,000$$

Some people will use cash, of course, so the DDA component of the money supply may never reach $5,000. Even so, it is clear that fractional reserve banking allows the DDA component of the money supply to grow several times larger than the total amount of member bank reserves.

✓Reading Check **Describing** What is the purpose of the FDIC?

$ Personal Finance Handbook
See pages **R14–R15** to learn more about loans.

C Critical Thinking

Evaluating Have students explain in their own words how the Fed's policy of fractional reserve banking (set at 20%) can increase the amount of money in the economy by 500%. *(Answers will vary but should note that banks must keep 20% of each deposit and then can to lend out the rest. As borrowers pay back loans, or banks get additional deposits, banks can continue to lend out money.)* **OL**

✓Reading Check **Answer:**
The FDIC protects deposits up to $100,000 per customer per bank.

Assess

💿 Use the Interactive Tutor Self-Assessment CD-ROM to review Section 2, and then assign the Section 2 Review as homework or as an in-class activity.

Close

Speculating Have students speculate on what might happen to the U.S. banking system if the government ordered the Fed to stop all its operations. **OL**

SECTION 2 Review

Vocabulary

1. **Explain** the significance of state bank, legal tender, national bank, national currency, gold certificate, silver certificate, central bank, bank run, bank holiday, fractional reserve system, legal reserves, reserve requirement, member bank reserve (MBR), and excess reserves.

Main Ideas

2. **Describing** How did experiences during and after the Revolutionary War affect banking in the United States?

3. **Listing** Use a graphic organizer like the one below to list the reasons for creating the Federal Reserve System.

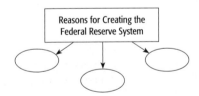

Reasons for Creating the Federal Reserve System

Critical Thinking

4. **The BIG Idea** Why did the United States move to a single national currency in the 1860s?

5. **Synthesizing** How does the system of fractional reserves "create" money?

6. **Making Comparisons** How do the operations of a central bank like the Fed compare to the operations of a normal bank?

7. **Analyzing Visuals** Examine the photo on page 394. What weaknesses in the banking system led to the actions pictured in this photo?

Applying Economics

8. **National and State Banks** Interview the branch managers of different banks in your locality. Ask whether the bank is a national bank or a state bank and how that designation affects the bank's operation and relationship with the Fed.

Review SECTION 2

Answers

1. All definitions can be found in the section and the Glossary.
2. People lost confidence in the banking system.
3. The National Banking System was having trouble providing enough currency for the growing nation; checking accounts were becoming more popular, and the banking system was not designed to deal with them; even minor recessions were causing major problems for lending institutions.
4. It needed to finance the Civil War.

5. Banks are required to keep only a portion of their deposits in the form of legal reserves. They may lend any excess reserves. Whether these loan proceeds are immediately deposited or spent on goods and services, they will eventually end up being deposited in a bank. The initial deposit will continue to generate "new" money as long as a bank has excess reserves to lend.
6. Central banks like the Fed are organized as corporations and are owned by national banks and some privately owned banks.

They have more resources than other banks and can make loans to other banks.
7. **Possible answers:** unsound banking practices; loan proceeds used to speculate on the stock market or in real estate; lack of deposit insurance; fear of losing money in bank accounts
8. Answers will vary but should discuss the effects of the bank's designation.

Teach

W Writing Support

Expository Writing Share this statement by Fed chairman Ben Bernanke about the Great Depression: " . . . the whole experience of the 1930s clearly shows some of the threats associated with large-scale . . . bank failures, including collapse of the money supply, disruptions of credit extension and other banking services, and blows to confidence." Then have students write a paragraph analyzing how that statement relates to Bernanke's policy of promoting transparency and straightforward communication. **OL**

Examining the Profile

Answers:

1. He promotes transparency and direct communication and views inflation differently.
2. It would build public confidence in the system, which would have a positive affect on financial markets.

Additional Support

Profiles in Economics

Ben S. Bernanke (1953–)

- distinguished academic career as an economics professor
- sworn in as chairman of the Federal Reserve Board in 2006

When his high school did not offer calculus, Ben Bernanke taught it to himself—not an unusual feat for the student with the highest SAT score in his state that year. Bernanke went on to major in economics at Harvard and MIT because he thought it combined math and people.

Maestro of the Economy

Before becoming the second most powerful man in America (after the president), Ben S. Bernanke was professor of Economics and Public Affairs at Princeton University. As chair of the Fed, Bernanke now is responsible for U.S. monetary policy. His tenure follows that of Alan Greenspan, Fed chair from 1987 to 2006, who is credited with presiding over the period of greatest economic growth in U.S. history. These are large shoes to fill. Bernanke's academic career, with a focus on monetary policy, prepared him well for the task.

Clear Talk, Clear Target

W

Unlike Greenspan, who was known to be vague when reporting his monetary decisions to Congress, Bernanke promotes transparency and straightforward communication. He believes that "as public servants whose policy actions affect the lives of every citizen, central bankers have a basic responsibility" to clearly state reasons for any Fed action. "Fedspeak," as U.S. media and financial markets called earlier central bank talk, was out. Even so, Bernanke learned to be careful about what he says in public. When he mentioned offhand at a dinner party that rising inflation concerned him, the stock market dropped 250 points in two days. Such is the power of the Fed chair's words.

Besides his transparency, Bernanke differs from Greenspan in how he looks at inflation. Rather than relying on hunches, Bernanke wants to base Fed policy on analysis of economic data and predetermined inflation targets. The Fed can then adjust monetary policy to meet those targets. It is a strategy he advocated several years before his appointment, when he wrote that "the Fed needs an approach that consolidates the gains of the Greenspan years and ensures that those successful policies will continue."

Examining the Profile

1. **Contrasting** How does Bernanke differ from his predecessor Greenspan?
2. **Making Inferences** What effect would a more transparent monetary policy have on financial markets?

Extending the Content

Big Shoes to Fill Fed chairman Ben Bernanke was selected to follow a legend as the nation's chief banker. His predecessor was Alan Greenspan, who led the Federal Reserve for 18 years. Greenspan, appointed by President Ronald Reagan, took the wheel of the American economy shortly before the stock market crash of 1987. He led the country back to financial health and guided it through the high-flying days of the 1990s. His aggressive anti-inflation policies earned him harsh criticism from many economists. However, for most of his tenure, the nation experienced a period of sustained economic growth and low inflation.

SECTION 3
The Federal Reserve System and Monetary Policy

GUIDE TO READING

Section Preview

In this section, you will learn how the Federal Reserve System is organized and conducts monetary policy.

Content Vocabulary

- member bank *(p. 400)*
- monetary policy *(p. 402)*
- interest rate *(p. 402)*
- easy money policy *(p. 402)*
- tight money policy *(p. 402)*
- open market operations *(p. 403)*
- discount rate *(p. 404)*
- prime rate *(p. 404)*
- quantity theory of money *(p. 405)*
- currency *(p. 406)*
- coins *(p. 406)*
- bank holding companies *(p. 407)*
- Regulation Z *(p. 407)*

Academic Vocabulary

- aspects *(p. 401)*
- functions *(p. 401)*

Reading Strategy

Describing As you read this section, complete a graphic organizer similar to the one below by describing the features of the Federal Reserve System.

The Federal Reserve System

Focus

Bellringer
Daily Focus Transparency 63

GUIDE TO READING

Answers to Graphic: is privately owned; directed by a board of governors; served by district banks; has a policy-making body; has advisory committees

---

PEOPLE IN THE NEWS
−Associated Press

Fed Raises Rates

The Federal Reserve, in the last major piece of business for retiring chairman Alan Greenspan, pushed borrowing costs to the highest point in nearly five years Tuesday and hinted that another rate increase was possible.

Shortly after the Fed's rate announcement, the Senate [approved] Ben Bernanke's nomination to be the 14th chairman of the central bank. Bernanke, 52, will be sworn in as Fed chief Wednesday morning in a private ceremony at the Fed's marble headquarters.

At Greenspan's final meeting, the Fed boosted the federal funds rate . . . to 4.50 percent. . . . In response, commercial banks raised their prime lending rates . . . by a corresponding amount to 7.50 percent. ■

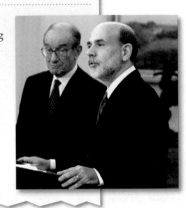

The U.S. economy reached a milestone in early 2006 when Alan Greenspan ended his tenure of over 18 years as Chairman of the Federal Reserve System's Board of Governors. This position is important because the Fed Chair has immense influence over the economy.

The new chairman is Ben Bernanke. As the head of the Fed, he has an unusual degree of independence. Along with other Fed officials and without the approval of elected officials, he can change interest rates to try to speed up the economy when it is growing too slowly, or try to slow it down when it is growing too fast. Like his predecessor, the new chairman will be especially concerned about economic instability, recessions, and inflation.

Resource Manager

R Reading Strategies	C Critical Thinking	D Differentiated Instruction	W Writing Support	S Skill Practice
Teacher Edition • Monitoring, p. 400 • Inferring, p. 401 • Using Context Clues, p. 404	**Teacher Edition** • Drawing Conclusions, p. 401 • Theorizing, p. 403 • Synthesizing, p. 408	**Teacher Edition** • ELL, p. 402 • Visual/Spatial, p. 404 • Kinesthetic, p. 405 • Adv. Learners, p. 406	**Teacher Edition** • Persuasive Writing, p. 403 • Personal Writing, p. 407	**Teacher Edition** • Analyzing Charts, p. 400 • Det. Cause/Effect, p. 402
Additional Resources • Guid. Read. Act., p. 42 • Read. Ess. & Note-Taking Guide, p. 124	**Additional Resources** • Free Enterprise Act., pp. 20, 21 • Econ. Concepts Trans., Strat. & Act., p. 35	**Additional Resources** • Reading and Study Skills Fold., p. 62 • Econ. Cartoons, p. 25	**Additional Resources** • Writer's Guidebook	**Additional Resources** • Daily Focus Trans. 62, 63, 79 • Graph. Org. Trans., p. 17

Teach

R Reading Strategy

Monitoring Make flash cards that detail some aspect of the Federal Reserve System that is described in the section. After students read the section, hold up the flash cards, one at a time, and call on students to identify what aspect of the Fed is being described. If students struggle, direct them to review the text to find the answer. **OL**

S Skill Practice

Analyzing Charts Ask: What are two functions that member banks perform? *(contribute funds to the 12 district banks and receive stock)* Who is in charge of deciding monetary policy? *(the Federal Open Market Committee)* **OL**

Economic Analysis

Answer: It supervises and regulates the Fed.

Additional Support

---

member bank
bank belonging to the Federal Reserve System

Skills Handbook
See page **R51** to learn about *Using Tables and Charts.*

R Structure of the Fed

MAIN Idea The Fed is organized as a corporation, owned by its member banks, and directed by a government-appointed board.

Economics and You Does your local school board have advisory committees to help with board decisions? Read on to find out about similar advisory committees for the Fed.

The main components of the Fed, shown in **Figure 14.3**, have remained practically unchanged since the Great Depression.

Private Ownership

One of the unique features of the Fed is that it is privately owned by its member banks. A **member bank** is a commercial bank that is a member of, and holds shares of stock in, the Fed. National banks—those chartered by the national government—must belong to the Fed. State banks—those receiving their charters from state governments—have the choice to belong or not.

The original decision to make the Fed a stock corporation was a matter of necessity because the government did not have enough money to set up a new banking system. Instead, banks were required to purchase shares when they joined. This made the banks part-owners of the Fed, just as someone might own shares in IBM or Ford Motor Company. Private individuals are not allowed to buy shares in the Fed, although they become indirect owners by buying shares of stock in a Fed-member bank.

Board of Governors

The Fed is directed by a seven-member Board of Governors. Each member is appointed by the president of the United

---

Figure 14.3 ▶ Structure of the Federal Reserve System

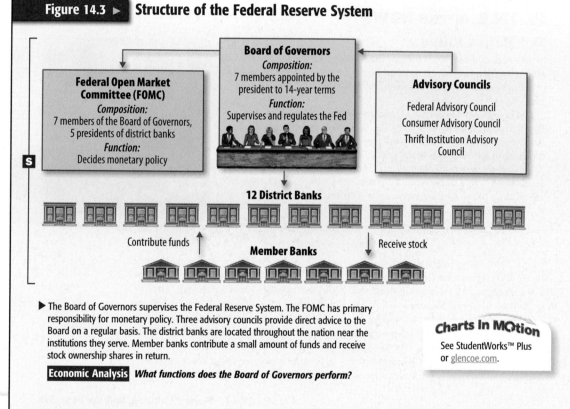

▶ The Board of Governors supervises the Federal Reserve System. The FOMC has primary responsibility for monetary policy. Three advisory councils provide direct advice to the Board on a regular basis. The district banks are located throughout the nation near the institutions they serve. Member banks contribute a small amount of funds and receive stock ownership shares in return.

Charts In MOtion
See StudentWorks™ Plus or glencoe.com.

Economic Analysis *What functions does the Board of Governors perform?*

Activity: Interdisciplinary Connection

Geography Remind students that legislation establishing the Federal Reserve System with its 12 Federal Reserve District Banks was passed in 1913. Have students work in groups of three to conduct Internet research on the location of the 12 district banks. Then have them create a map illustrating those locations. Next, have students decide how they would change the 12 districts and in which cities they would recommend locating the Federal Reserve District Banks today. Ask each group to write a brief explanation for their recommendations, and create a second map illustrating the changes. Invite volunteers from each group to present their explanation and map to the class. **OL**

States and approved by the Senate to serve a 14-year term of office. The appointments are staggered, so that one appointment becomes vacant every two years. In addition, care is taken to appoint people who will govern the Fed in the public interest. Because of this, it is often said that the Fed is "privately owned, but publicly controlled."

The Board is primarily a regulatory and supervisory agency. It sets general policies for its member banks to follow and regulates certain **aspects** of state-chartered member banks' operations. It helps make policies that affect the level of interest rates and the general availability of credit. Finally, it reports annually to Congress and puts out a monthly bulletin that covers national and international monetary matters.

District Banks

The Fed was originally intended to operate as a system of 12 independent and equally powerful banks. Each reserve bank was responsible for a district, and some Federal Reserve notes today still have the district bank's name in the seal to the left of the portrait. More recently, advances in technology have minimized the need for a regional structure, so the new Fed seal on our currency does not incorporate any mention of the district banks.

Today the 12 Federal Reserve district banks and their branches are strategically located to be near the institutions they serve. The district banks provide many of the same **functions** for banks and depository institutions that banks provide for us. For example, the district banks accept deposits from, and make loans to, privately owned banks and thrift institutions.

Federal Open Market Committee

The Federal Open Market Committee (FOMC) makes decisions about the level of interest rates. It has 12 voting members: seven members from the Board of Governors, the president of the New York

district Fed, and four district Federal Reserve bank presidents who serve one-year rotating terms.

The FOMC meets eight times a year to review the economy and to evaluate factors such as trends in construction, wages, prices, employment, production, and consumer spending. Its decisions have a direct impact on the cost and availability of credit. While decisions are made in private, they are announced almost immediately. The FOMC is the Fed's primary monetary policy-making body.

Advisory Committees

Three advisory committees advise the Board of Governors. The Federal Advisory Council consists of one representative from each of the 12 district banks. It provides advice to the Federal Reserve on matters concerning the overall health of the economy.

The Consumer Advisory Council's 30 members meet with the Board three times a year to advise on consumer credit laws. Members include educators, consumer legal specialists, and representatives from consumer and financial industry groups.

The third advisory group is the Thrift Institutions Advisory Council, with representatives from savings and loan associations, savings banks, and credit unions. It meets with the Board three times a year to advise on matters pertaining to the Savings and Loan industry.

✔Reading Check **Explaining** What is the purpose of the Federal Open Market Committee?

CHAPTER 14 Money, Banking, and the Fed **401**

R **Reading Strategy**

Inferring Ask: Why is it said that the Fed is "publicly controlled"? *(Members are appointed by the president and approved by the Senate, they serve for 14 years, have staggered appointments, and exhibit characteristics of governing the Fed in the public interest.)* **OL**

C **Critical Thinking**

Drawing Conclusions

Ask: Why is it important that members of the Federal Advisory Council be from each member bank? *(Possible answers: They provide insight into the economy of their district. They offer different perspectives on the overall health of the economy.)* **AL**

✔Reading Check **Answer:** It is the Fed's primary monetary policy-making body. It reviews the economy, evaluates factors in economic trends, and makes decisions about the level of interest rates.

Hands-On Chapter Project

Step 3

Creating a U.S. Currency Time Line

Step 3: Evaluating Time Line Entries.
Students will work with their groups to evaluate each type of currency identified on the class time line.

Directions: Ask students to resume work in their groups. Have them review the types of currency listed on the class time line according to the characteristics of money discussed in the chapter. After the evaluation is completed, have the groups organize the information on a table according to the type of currency and the characteristics by which the currency was evaluated.

Assessing Ask each group to select one or two representatives to present their finished tables to the class. If groups differ in their assessments of the various types of currency, lead the members of these groups in a discussion until a consensus can be reached. **OL**

(Chapter Project continued in Visual Summary.)

D Differentiated Instruction

English Language Learners

For students who have difficulty understanding the concept of an *interest rate*, explain that interest is the price for a service—the right to use the money. Explain that low interest rates often encourage people to borrow money. **ELL**

S Skill Practice

Determining Cause and Effect **Ask:** Under what conditions might the Fed want to institute an easy money policy? Why? *(if economic growth is slow; it expands the money supply to increase business activity)* Under what conditions might the Fed want to institute a tight money policy? Why? *(if inflation is rising; it restricts the money supply to slow economic growth)* **OL**

Economic Analysis

Answer: The supply of money is fixed at any given time.

Differentiated Instruction

Critical Thinking Activities, p. 20

---

monetary policy actions by the Federal Reserve System to expand or contract the money supply in order to affect the cost and availability of credit

interest rate the price of credit to a borrower

easy money policy monetary policy that results in lower interest rates and greater access to credit

tight money policy monetary policy that results in higher interest rates and restricted access to credit

Conducting Monetary Policy

MAIN Idea Monetary policy involves expanding and contracting the money supply to change the level of interest rates.

Economics and You Have you noticed that prices for some items go up faster than those for others? Read on to learn that inflation is one of the Fed's main concerns.

One of the most important functions of the Fed is to conduct **monetary policy**—changes in the money supply in order to affect the availability and cost of credit. This in turn influences economic activity.

How Monetary Policy Works

Monetary policy is based on the mechanism of supply and demand. **Figure 14.4** shows that the demand curve for money has the usual shape, which illustrates that more money will be demanded when the **interest rate**, or the price of credit to a borrower, is low. However, the supply curve does not have its usual shape. Instead, its vertical slope indicates that the supply of money is fixed at any given time.

When the Fed conducts its monetary policy, it changes interest rates by changing the size of the money supply. Under an **easy money policy**, the Fed expands the money supply, causing interest rates to fall. Such a policy stimulates the economy because people borrow more at lower interest rates. This is illustrated in **Panel A,** where a larger money supply lowers the rate from 10 to 8 percent.

Under a **tight money policy**, the Fed restricts the size of the money supply. This is shown in **Panel B,** where a contraction of the money supply drives the cost of borrowing up from 10 to 12 percent. This tends to slow economic growth because higher interest rates normally encourage everyone to borrow and spend less.

The Fed can use three major tools to conduct monetary policy. Each tool works in a different way to change the amount of excess reserves—the amount of money a bank can lend to others.

Figure 14.4 ▶ Short-Run Impact of Monetary Policy

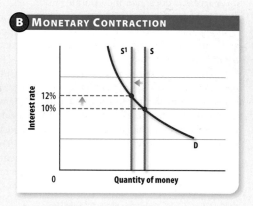

▶ In the short run, monetary policy impacts interest rates, or the price of credit. When the money supply expands, the price of credit goes down. When the money supply contracts, the price of credit goes up.

Economic Analysis *Why is the supply curve of money shown as a vertical line?*

Facts and Opinions About the Federal Reserve System

Objective: Identify facts and opinions about the Federal Reserve System.

Focus/Teach: Have volunteers explain the difference between a fact and an opinion, and give examples of each. Then have students complete the activity.

Assess: Go over the answers, explaining why each item is a fact or an opinion.

Close: Have students give a fact and an opinion about the U.S. economy.

Differentiated Instruction Strategies

BL Have students work in groups to find examples of facts and opinions in a newspaper article.

AL Have students rewrite each fact statement as an opinion.

ELL Have one student write a statement. Ask a partner to explain orally why it is a fact or an opinion.

▶ The Fed can control the size of the money supply by changing the reserve requirement. A low requirement, such as 10 percent, can be used to expand the money supply. A higher requirement, such as 40 percent, has the opposite effect.

Charts In MOtion
See StudentWorks™ Plus or glencoe.com.

Economic Analysis *What would be the size of the money supply if the Fed set the reserve requirement at 25 percent?*

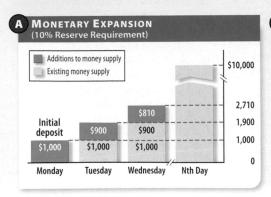

A MONETARY EXPANSION (10% Reserve Requirement)

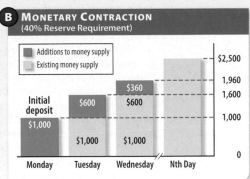

B MONETARY CONTRACTION (40% Reserve Requirement)

Writing Support

Persuasive Writing Have students write a letter to the editor of the local newspaper arguing for a rise or a drop in the Fed's reserve requirement. If necessary, give students an editorial letter to follow as a model. Remind them to support their opinions with facts. **OL**

C Critical Thinking

Theorizing Ask: Why do you think that other monetary policy tools work better than the reserve requirement? *(Possible answer: It may be difficult to predict the amount of change to make, and it takes time for the changes to take effect.)* **AL**

Economic Analysis
Answer: $4,000

Reserve Requirement

The first tool of monetary policy is the reserve requirement. Within limits that Congress sets, the Fed can change this requirement for all checking, time, and savings accounts.

For instance, in Figure 14.2 on page 396 we assumed that a 20 percent reserve requirement applied to the DDAs held by Bill, Maria, and other depositors. In the figure, an initial deposit of $1,000 could expand to as much as $5,000 in total bank deposits. However, the Fed could also lower the reserve requirement to 10 percent or increase it to 40 percent.

Figure 14.5 shows the results of such changes with the same initial deposit of $1,000. In **Panel A,** the 10 percent reserve requirement means that $900 of excess reserves could be lent out on the second day, $810 on the third day, and so on. Excess reserves are available until the DDAs reach a maximum of:

$$\frac{\text{Total MBRs}}{\text{Reserve Requirement}} = \frac{\$1,000}{.10} = \$10,000$$

In **Panel B,** the reserve requirement increases to 40 percent. The result is that $600 of excess reserves are available for the first loan, $360 of excess reserves are available for the second loan, and so on until $2,500 of DDAs are generated.

Historically, the Fed has been reluctant to use the reserve requirement as a policy tool, in part because other monetary policy tools work better. Even so, the reserve requirement can be powerful should the Fed decide to use it.

Open Market Operations

The second tool of monetary policy is **open market operations**—the buying and selling of government securities in financial markets. This method is the Fed's most popular tool and allows the Fed to influence short-term interest rates.

Suppose the Fed wants to expand the money supply. All it has to do is buy a bond from an investor and pay for it with a check drawn on itself or an equivalent amount of cash. When the money is put in a bank, the

open market operations sales or purchases of U.S. government securities by the Fed

CHAPTER 14 Money, Banking, and the Fed **403**

Leveled Activities

BL Reading Essentials and Note-Taking Guide, p. 124

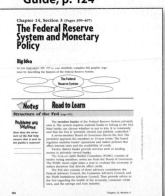

OL Economic Cartoons, p. 25

AL Free Enterprise Activities, p. 20

Teach

D Differentiated Instruction

Visual/Spatial Have students use computer software to make a table, chart, or other graphic aid that explains how the Fed increases or decreases the money supply using open market operations. Ask students to share their graphic aids in a class discussion. **OL**

R Reading Strategy

Using Context Clues

Ask: What does *prime* mean in the term *prime rate*? Why is it used in this context? *(Prime means "first in importance." Banks' best customers, in terms of their ability to repay the loan, are given the prime rate.)* **OL**

Caption Answer: The discount rate is set by the Fed, and any changes directly affect the prime rate, which in turn affects other interest rates.

Additional Support

discount rate interest rate that the Federal Reserve System charges on loans to the nation's financial institutions

prime rate lowest rate of interest rate that banks charge their best customers

bank will have additional excess reserves and the loan expansion process can begin. The result is that whenever the Fed *buys* government securities, excess reserves are created and the money supply *expands*.

Suppose the Fed were to sell some of its government securities. When a buyer takes money out of the banking system to pay for the securities, member bank reserves go down, forcing the money supply to contract. A smaller money supply, as we saw in Panel B of Figure 14.4, raises the interest rate. In the end, whenever the Fed *sells* government securities, excess reserves contract and the money supply *contracts*.

In practice, every day the Fed buys and sells billions of dollars of government securities through dealers. The Fed pays for the securities by writing checks drawn on itself. The dealers deposit the checks in their banks—thereby creating excess reserves. If the Fed sells securities, it accepts checks from the dealers, which reduces both dealers' bank deposits and member banks' reserves.

The Federal Open Market Committee (FOMC) is the part of the Fed that conducts open-market operations. Normally the

Discount Rate
The Fed monitors consumer behavior so it knows when to adjust the money supply with tools such as the discount rate and open market operations. *Why do changes in the discount rate affect the prime rate and most other interest rates?*

The leading economic indicator the Fed watches to know when to raise interest rates is you.

FOMC decides whether interest rates are too high, too low, or just right. After the committee votes to set targets, officials at the trading desk take over. The trading desk at the Fed's New York district bank is the physical location where the daily buying and selling actually occurs. It is permanently located in New York to be close to the nation's major financial markets.

Discount Rate

As a central bank, the Fed makes loans to other depository institutions. The **discount rate**—the interest the Fed charges on loans to financial institutions—is the third major tool of monetary policy. Only financial institutions can borrow from the Fed; private individuals and companies are not allowed to do so.

The discount rate is the price of credit for an institution that borrows from the Fed. If the discount rate goes up, fewer banks will want to borrow from the Fed, and banks will have fewer excess reserves available to loan out. If the Fed wants to expand the money supply, it might lower the rate to encourage additional borrowing, thus increasing excess reserves.

A bank may want to borrow from the Fed if it has an unexpected drop in its required reserves. A bank could also have high seasonal demands for loans. For example, a bank in an agricultural area might face a heavy loan demand during the planting season. In either case, a short-term loan from the Fed could restore its reserves.

Effects on Other Interest Rates

While the Fed directly sets only one interest rate—the discount rate—its monetary policy actions influence other interest rates. For example, changes can directly affect the **prime rate**—the lowest rate of interest commercial banks charge their best customers. At many large banks, the prime rate is linked to other interest rates, so the banks usually adjust

---

Activity: Hands-On Economics

Simulating Conduct the following simulation of open market operations. Organize students into two groups to represent the public and the Fed. Give 10 slips of paper, each representing $1,000, to each member of the public. Count the money and record the total amount in circulation on the board. Next, give 10 whole sheets of paper, each one depicting a $1,000 bond, to each person representing the Fed. Announce that a new issue of bonds is available for purchase at a good interest rate from the Fed. Have the public buy some. Count and record the money in circulation. Ask the class what happened to the money supply. *(decreased)* Next, have the Fed buy back some of the bonds. Count and record the money now in circulation among buyers. Ask students what has happened to the money supply. *(increased)* Have students explain open market operations in their own words. **OL**

Figure 14.6 ▶ Monetary Policy Tools

▶ The key to understanding monetary policy is to see how the excess reserves in the system are affected.

Economic Analysis *How does the Fed use the reserve requirement to affect the money supply?*

SUMMARY OF MONETARY POLICY TOOLS

Tool	Fed Action	Effect on Excess Reserves	Money Supply
Reserve requirement	Lower	Frees excess reserves because fewer are needed to back existing deposits in the system.	Expands
	Raise	More reserves are required to back existing deposits. Excess reserves contract.	Contracts
Open market operations	Buy securities	Checks written by the Fed add to reserves in the banking system.	Expands
	Sell securities	Checks written by buyers are subtracted from bank reserves. Excess reserves in the system contract.	Contracts
Discount rate	Lower	Additional reserves can be obtained at lower cost. Excess reserves expand.	Expands
	Raise	Additional reserves through borrowing are now more expensive. Excess reserves are not added.	Contracts

D

their prime rate up or down whenever the Fed changes the discount rate.

Changes in monetary policy spill over to almost all other interest rates as well. Any tightening of the money supply will affect the interest rate on home mortgages, savings bonds, certificates of deposits, and even Treasury bills and bonds.

Monetary Policy Dilemmas

The impact of monetary policy on the economy is complex. The problem is that we never know for sure how long it will take for a particular policy to take effect. As a result, it is often difficult for the Fed to please everyone.

For example, some people blamed the 2001 recession on the Fed's tight money policy of 2000. The Fed was worried about inflation and raised interest rates to slow the economy. When the economy went into recession in 2001, the Fed acted quickly to reverse itself and lower interest rates to stimulate GDP. The economy responded slowly, though, and the unemployment rate took unusually long to recover.

In the long run, the money supply also affects the general price level. If the money supply were to expand for a prolonged period of time, we would have too many dollars chasing too few goods, and demand-pull inflation would result. This is the basis for the **quantity theory of money,** and it often has been observed in history.

When the Spanish brought gold and silver back to Spain from the Americas in the 1700s, the increase in the money supply started an inflation that lasted for 100 years. During the Revolutionary War, the economy suffered severe inflation when the Continental Congress issued $250 million of currency. The country saw similar effects during the Civil War when the Union printed nearly $500 million of greenbacks. As a result, the Fed normally proceeds with a great deal of caution.

quantity theory of money hypothesis that the supply of money directly affects the price level over the long run

✓**Reading Check** **Examining** Why does the Fed use open market operations?

CHAPTER 14 Money, Banking, and the Fed **405**

Teach

D Differentiated Instruction

Kinesthetic Organize students into several groups to role-play members of the Federal Reserve Board of Governors. Tell half the groups that they must decide on a policy to expand the money supply and the other half to develop a policy to restrict the growth of the money supply. Have groups consider the following: *What tools of monetary policy should be used? How should they be used? Why should they be used?* Call on group representatives to explain their plans to the class. **OL**

Economic Analysis

Answer: They lower the reserve requirement to expand the money supply and raise it to contract the money supply.

✓**Reading Check** **Answer:** It is a quick, relatively easy way to expand or contract the money supply.

Additional Support

Activity: Collaborative Learning

Predicting Consequences Tell students that at the end of 1999, some people feared that the Y2K problem would affect depositors' ability to withdraw money from their banks. The Y2K problem affected older computer systems, which used just the last two digits of the year ('99) instead of the full four digits (1999). Some people worried that bank computers would think the year 2000 was the year 1900. Some people planned to withdraw their money before the end of 1999. However, most banks fixed their computers by the end of 1999 and reassured the public, so few people withdrew their money. Ask students to predict what would have happened if most people had withdrawn their money from banks. Have students present radio news reports about the consequences of widespread withdrawals of money from most banks. **OL**

Teach

D Differentiated Instruction

Advanced Learners Tell students that most Fed district banks shred old money when they take it out of circulation. It is sometimes used for bookmarks, filler for paperweights, and so on. Have students agree on a class project or fund-raiser that would utilize free shredded currency. Then have volunteers call their local Fed bank and ask if their class can have shredded money for their specific class project. **AL**

Caption Answer: They work with agencies in the payment system, establish specific guidelines governing banking behavior, implement consumer legislation, and provide financial services to the federal government and its agencies.

Additional Support

---

currency paper component of the money supply, today consisting of Federal Reserve notes

coins metallic forms of money such as pennies, nickels, dimes, and quarters

---

Money Today's bills are printed on large sheets of paper. They undergo extensive inspection before being cut up for circulation. *What are other Fed responsibilities?*

Other Fed Responsibilities

MAIN Idea As the nation's central bank, the Fed is responsible for most aspects of banking and the payments system.

Economics and You Have you ever bought anything on credit and seen the loan information disclosed to you by the merchant? Read to learn how the Fed helped provide this information.

The Federal Reserve has other responsibilities as well. These include maintaining the money supply and the payments system, regulating and supervising banks, preparing consumer legislation, and serving as the federal government's bank.

Maintaining the Money Supply

Today's **currency**, the paper component of the money supply, is made up of Federal Reserve notes that are printed by the U.S. Bureau of Engraving and Printing. This currency, issued in amounts of $1, $2, $5, $10, $20, $50, and $100, is distributed to the Fed's district banks for storage until it is needed by the public.

The Bureau of the Mint produces **coins**—metallic forms of money—such as pennies, nickels, dimes, quarters, and the new presidential dollar coin. After the coins are minted, they are shipped to the Fed district banks for storage. When member banks need additional coins or currency, they contact the Fed to fulfill their needs.

D When banks come across coins or currency that are mutilated or cannot be used for other reasons, they return them to the Fed for replacement. The Fed then destroys the old money so that it cannot be put back into circulation.

Maintaining the Payments System

The payments system involves more than the money supply. It also covers the electronic transfer of funds between businesses, state and local governments, financial institutions, and foreign central banks. In addition, specialized operations called clearinghouses process the billions of checks that are written every year. The Fed works with all of these agencies to ensure the payments system operates smoothly.

Next to cash, checks are the most popular form of payment in the United States. A 2003 law, however, has changed the way checks are processed. Whereas checks used to be returned to the person who originally wrote them, now only electronic images of the checks are returned to the issuer.

Online banking is another major innovation in the banking system. Now that people can open an account anywhere in the country using the Internet, the Fed is designing new procedures to make sure that no abuses occur.

Regulating and Supervising Banks

The Fed is responsible for establishing specific guidelines that govern banking behavior. It also has the responsibility for monitoring, inspecting, and examining various banking agencies to verify that they comply with existing banking laws.

Activity: Collaborative Learning

Evaluating On the board, write the following responsibilities of the Fed: *Conducting Monetary Policy*, *Maintaining the Money Supply*, *Maintaining the Payments System*, *Regulating and Supervising Banks*, *Preparing Consumer Legislation*, and *Acting as the Government's Bank*. Ask students to give an example of each Fed responsibility, and note their responses on the board under the appropriate heading. Then organize the

class into groups of equal size. Have group members discuss which of the Fed's responsibilities they believe is most important to the U.S. economy and why. Call on group representatives to report and explain their group's decision. **OL**

As a result, the Fed is charged with watching over foreign branches of its own member banks, as well as U.S. branches of foreign-owned banks. The Fed also has jurisdiction over many activities of state banks. This includes the operations of **bank holding companies**—firms that own and control one or more banks.

Preparing Consumer Legislation

The Fed is responsible for implementing some consumer legislation, such as the federal Truth in Lending Act, which requires sellers to make complete and accurate disclosures to people who buy on credit. Under **Regulation Z,** the Fed has the authority to extend truth-in-lending disclosures to millions of individuals who borrow from retail stores, automobile dealers, banks, and lending institutions.

If you buy furniture or a car on credit, for example, you will discover that the seller must explain several items before you make the purchase. These items include the size of the down payment, the number and size of the monthly payments, and the total amount of interest over the life of the loan. All of the disclosures that the seller makes were determined by the Fed.

Acting as the Government's Bank

A final Fed function is the range of financial services it provides to the federal government and its agencies. For example, the Fed conducts nationwide auctions of Treasury securities. It also issues, services, and redeems these securities on behalf of the Treasury. In the process, it maintains numerous demand deposit accounts for the Treasury.

The Fed also maintains accounts for the government. In fact, any check written to the U.S. Treasury is deposited in the Fed. Any federal agency check, such as a monthly Social Security payment, comes from accounts held at the Fed. In essence, the Fed serves as the government's bank.

W

✓ Reading Check **Summarizing** How does the Fed regulate banks?

bank holding company company that owns and controls one or more banks

Regulation Z provision extending truth-in-lending disclosures to consumers

W **Writing Support**

Personal Writing Have students write a paragraph describing one way that they have been affected personally by the activities of the Federal Reserve. Refer them to the discussion of consumer legislation on this page. **OL**

✓ Reading Check **Possible Answer:** They establish specific guidelines that govern banking behavior, examine banking agencies to verify their compliance with banking laws, and oversee foreign branches of member banks and activities of state banks.

Assess

Use the Interactive Tutor Self-Assessment CD-ROM to review Section 3, and then assign the Section 3 Review as homework or as an in-class activity.

Close

Describing Have students name and describe the three major tools that the Fed uses to conduct monetary policy. **OL**

Review **SECTION 3**

SECTION 3 Review

Vocabulary

1. **Explain** the significance of member bank, monetary policy, interest rate, easy money policy, tight money policy, open market operations, discount rate, prime rate, quantity theory of money, currency, coins, bank holding companies, and Regulation Z.

Main Ideas

2. **Listing** What are the components of the Federal Reserve System?

3. **Describing** What are the additional responsibilities the Fed has beyond monetary policy?

4. **Identifying** Use a graphic organizer like the one below to identify the tools of monetary policy.

Critical Thinking

5. **The BIG Idea** Why and how does the Fed conduct monetary policy?

6. **Contrasting** How do "tight money" and "easy money" impact the economy?

7. **Drawing Conclusions** What are the advantages of having the Fed oversee the U.S. banking system?

8. **Analyzing Visuals** Look at Figure 14.4 on page 402. What would happen if supply shifted to the right? To the left? Why?

Applying Economics

9. **Truth-in-Lending Laws** Visit any local store that sells goods on credit, such as appliances, cars, or furniture. Ask the owner or manager about the type of information that the store is required to disclose when the sale is made. Obtain copies of the disclosure forms and share the disclosure details with your classmates.

CHAPTER 14 Money, Banking, and the Fed **407**

Answers

1. All definitions can be found in the section and the Glossary.
2. 12 district banks, Board of Governors, FOMC, Federal Advisory Council, Consumer Advisory Council, Thrift Institutions Advisory Council
3. maintaining the money supply and the payments system, regulating and supervising banks, preparing consumer legislation, and serving as the federal government's bank
4. reserve requirement; open market operations; discount rate
5. By lowering the reserve requirement or discount rate and buying government securities, the Fed increases the money supply, which stimulates the economy. By raising the reserve requirement or discount rate and selling government securities, the Fed decreases the money supply, which slows the economy.
6. Tight money contracts the money supply and increases the cost of credit. Most people/businesses react by borrowing less, so the economy slows. Easy money expands the money supply, reducing the cost of credit. Most people/businesses react by borrowing more, so the economy grows.
7. Answers may vary but should recognize that the application and enforcement of rules and regulations benefits the nation.
8. If the curve shifts right, interest rates will decrease. If the curve shifts left, interest rates will increase.
9. Answers will vary but should include disclosure information from a local store.

Teach

C Critical Thinking

Synthesizing Why might using inflation expectations to determine monetary policy be problematic? *(Possible answer: Consumers may not be truthful with pollsters.)* **AL**

BusinessWeek *ONLINE*

To find up-to-date news and analysis on the economy, business, technology, markets, entrepreneurs, investments, and finance, have students search feature articles and special reports on the BusinessWeek Web site, www.businessweek.com.

Examining the Newsclip

Answers:
1. the beliefs about how fast prices will rise in the future
2. If people believe that inflation will stay low, the Fed plans to relax monetary policy and vice versa.

Additional Support

BusinessWeek NEWSCLIP

As head of the Federal Open Market Committee (FOMC), the Fed chair monitors a number of economic indicators to help him make decisions on monetary policy. One of these indicators is the rate of inflation. The chairman also likes to watch something new these days: inflation expectations.

Inflation: What You Foresee Is What You Get

What . . . are inflation expectations, anyway? You won't find the term in any of the major economic data releases put out by the government. Yet whether inflation expectations are rising or falling may turn out to be a critical factor in determining how far and how fast the Federal Reserve raises interest rates.

That, at least, is the new line coming out of the Fed these days. Inflation expectations—a bit of a touchy-feely concept—represent the beliefs of consumers, investors, corporate execs, and economists about how fast prices will rise in the future. To new Fed Chairman Ben S. Bernanke, inflation expectations are a key indicator. If people believe inflation will stay low, the Fed can afford to relax a bit. But if the masses start anticipating faster inflation, the odds are greater that the Fed will need to hit them with higher rates even if actual price hikes **C** remain moderate. . . .

How are beliefs about future inflation measured? One way is to ask economists what they think is

going to happen. According to the Philadelphia Fed's Survey of Professional Forecasters, economists expect consumer inflation to average 2.5% over the next 10 years, only a tad above their 2.45% forecast of a year earlier. That's not very worrisome.

Another way to judge expectations is to look at the behavior of investors—in particular, the people who buy [s]ecurities . . . which are indexed to inflation to give investors a fixed real return. . . .

The danger, of course, is that expectations about future prices might jump, forcing the Fed to raise rates sharply to maintain its credibility as an inflation fighter. That's what happened in the 1970s, when the public's lack of faith in the Fed's inflation-fighting resolve sent prices—and expectations of future inflation—spiraling out of control after the oil shock.

Contrast that with [the situation] today. The Fed has built credibility by both aggressively fighting inflation and communicating its commitment to price stability. As a result, even as energy prices skyrocketed in recent years, inflation expectations hardly budged, and non-energy inflation stayed relatively low.

—*Reprinted from BusinessWeek*

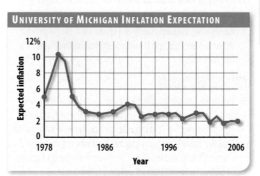

UNIVERSITY OF MICHIGAN INFLATION EXPECTATION

Source: Survey Research Center: University of Michigan

Examining the Newsclip

1. **Defining** How does the author of the article define inflation expectations?
2. **Analyzing** Why are inflation expectations important to the Fed?

408   UNIT 4   Macroeconomics: Performance and Stabilization

Activity: Hands-On Economics

Identifying Central Issues What are the inflation expectations of people in your community? Have the class write an opinion poll designed to gauge the inflation expectations of teens and adults in the community. Then organize the class into groups of three, and have them ask people to participate in the opinion poll. After groups have gathered the data, have them create a visual to illustrate the results of their poll. Ask

each group to explain their visual to the class. Then have students discuss this question as a class: *What recommendations would you make to the Fed chairman based on these results?* **OL**

Study anywhere, anytime! Download quizzes and flash cards to your PDA from glencoe.com.

▶ **Money** People began using money because it made buying and selling easier than barter.

▶ **Development of Modern Banking** Problems with the money supply before 1914 led to the creation of the Federal Reserve System.

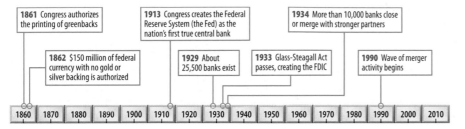

1861 Congress authorizes the printing of greenbacks

1862 $150 million of federal currency with no gold or silver backing is authorized

1913 Congress creates the Federal Reserve System (the Fed) as the nation's first true central bank

1929 About 25,500 banks exist

1933 Glass-Steagall Act passes, creating the FDIC

1934 More than 10,000 banks close or merge with stronger partners

1990 Wave of merger activity begins

1860 1870 1880 1890 1900 1910 1920 1930 1940 1950 1960 1970 1980 1990 2000 2010

▶ **Monetary Policy** The Federal Reserve System has three main policy tools at its disposal. It uses these tools to affect the money supply and interest rates.

SUMMARY OF MONETARY POLICY TOOLS			
Tool	**Fed Action**	**Effect on Excess Reserves**	**Money Supply**
Reserve requirement	Lower	Frees excess reserves because fewer are needed to back existing deposits in the system.	Expands
	Raise	More reserves are required to back existing deposits. Excess reserves contract.	Contracts
Open market operations	Buy securities	Checks written by the Fed add to reserves in the banking system.	Expands
	Sell securities	Checks written by buyers are subtracted from bank reserves. Excess reserves in the system contract.	Contracts
Discount rate	Lower	Additional reserves can be obtained at lower cost. Excess reserves expand.	Expands
	Raise	Additional reserves through borrowing are now more expensive. Excess reserves are not added.	Contracts

Identifying Call students' attention to the portion of the web diagram listing characteristics of money. Discuss with students the meaning of each characteristic listed in the green ovals. Then ask students to write a paragraph in which they explain how the money used in the United States meets each of these characteristics. **OL**

Determining Cause and Effect Ask students to speculate on when most borrowing is done. *(Students should recognize that most borrowing occurs when interest rates are low.)* Then lead a class discussion on how consumer borrowing affects the Fed's decisions to use a policy tool. **Ask:** What tools might the Fed use to slow consumer borrowing? *(Possible answer: open market operations to lower bank reserves or the discount rate to raise the interest rate)* **Ask:** What tools might the Fed use to encourage consumer borrowing? *(Possible answer: open market operations to add to bank reserves or the discount rate to lower the interest rate)* **OL**

Hands-On Chapter Project

Step 4: Wrap Up

Creating a U.S. Currency Time Line

Step 4: Putting It All Together. Students will synthesize what they learned in the previous steps.

Directions: Ask students to review the work they have completed throughout the chapter project. Encourage them to revisit their initial research, as well as the class time line and the tables they created in Step 3. After students review these materials, have each group discuss the ways in which currency has evolved throughout the history of the United States. Encourage them to give special consideration to ways in which the monetary system has improved.

Inferring Ask students to use their conclusions to write a brief paper in which they make inferences about how currency in the United States may continue to change in the near future. **OL**

ExamView®
Assessment Suite

This easy-to-use software includes extensive question banks and allows you to create fully customized tests that can be administered in print or online.

Review Content Vocabulary

1. b		**2.** d	
3. g		**4.** e	
5. h		**6.** a	
7. f		**8.** c	

Review Academic Vocabulary

9. e		**10.** c	
11. b		**12.** f	
13. d		**14.** a	

Review the Main Ideas

15. portable, reasonably durable, easily divisible, in limited supply
16. because the products were not always acceptable or easy to divide for payment
17. **Possible answer:** Colonial—commodity (tobacco, gunpowder, corn, hemp). Revolutionary—fiat (Continentals). Civil War—fiat (greenbacks). Post-Civil War—fiat (gold certificates, silver certificates).
18. M1 relates to money's function as a medium of exchange. M2 relates to money's function as a store of value.
19. hundreds of different kinds of notes circulated in any given area; merchants might not accept certain notes; no stability in money supply; easy to counterfeit
20. to finance the war and give people confidence in the banking system
21. to insure customer deposits in the event of a bank failure

Review Content Vocabulary

Write the key term that best completes the following sentences.

a. fiat money   e. excess reserves
b. central bank   f. M1
c. Regulation Z   g. barter economy
d. easy money policy   h. open market operations

1. The Fed serves as the _____ of the United States.
2. A(n) _____ would expand the money supply and tend to lower interest rates.
3. In a _____ people rely on trade to obtain goods and services.
4. If a bank has _____ , it is able to make additional loans to customers.
5. The most popular and effective tool of monetary policy is that of _____.
6. _____ is money that must be accepted by government decree.
7. _____ is the component of the money supply that acts as a medium of exchange.
8. _____ gives the Fed the authority to extend truth-in-lending disclosures to consumers.

Review Academic Vocabulary

Match the terms on the left with their synonyms on the right.

9. aspect
10. clause
11. converted
12. function
13. initially
14. revolution

a. major change, transformation
b. altered, revised
c. stipulation, provision
d. originally, in the beginning
e. situation, condition
f. purpose, duty

Review the Main Ideas

Section 1 (pages 383–388)
15. **Describe** the characteristics of money.
16. **Explain** why trade was difficult in a barter system.
17. **Identify** and provide examples of the types of money used in different periods of American history by using a graphic organizer like the one below.

History of American Money		
Time period	Type of money	Example(s)

18. **Compare** M1 and M2.

Section 2 (pages 390–397)
19. **Identify** the problems that existed with pre–Civil War currency.
20. **Explain** why the National Banking System was created during the Civil War.
21. **Explain** why the U.S. government created the Federal Deposit Insurance Corporation.

Section 3 (pages 399–407)
22. **Describe** the role of the Board of Governors of the Fed.
23. **Explain** why member banks borrow from the Fed.
24. **Describe** the three major tools of monetary policy available to the Fed.
25. **Discuss** how the reserve requirement allows the money supply to expand.

Critical Thinking

26. **The BIG Idea** How does regulating the U.S. banking system reflect our concern about balancing monetary policies with a free enterprise economy?
27. **Making Inferences** How did the popularity of checking accounts lead to the expansion of a fractional reserve system?

22. It sets general policies for the member banks, regulates certain operations of state-chartered member banks, conducts some aspects of monetary policy, and provides reports to Congress.
23. when they have unexpected drops in their required reserves and borrow to meet the requirement; when high seasonal demands for loans require additional excess reserves
24. Answers will vary, but students should describe reserve requirement, open market operations, and discount rate.

25. by freeing excess reserves (fewer are needed to back existing deposits in the system)

Critical Thinking

26. A free enterprise economy is founded on the principle of private ownership. The Fed is owned by its member banks, not by any part of the federal government.
27. It increased deposits, which expanded the fractional reserve system.

Economics ONLINE **Self-Check Quiz** Visit the
Economics: Principles and Practices Web site at glencoe.com and click
on *Chapter 14–Self-Check Quizzes* to prepare for the chapter test.

**Assessment
and Activities**

**CHAPTER
14**

28. Determining Cause and Effect At times, someone with a good credit rating may not be able to get a loan. When this happens, the potential customer may be told to try again in the near future. What does this tell you about the bank's reserves? How should the customer react to a situation like this?

29. Predicting Our money supply, as well as the different forms of money and ways to hold it, has changed considerably over the years. Describe one or two ways you think American money might change even more in the future.

30. Determining Cause and Effect Why do business cycles make it difficult to time monetary policy?

31. Drawing Conclusions Defend or refute the following statement: The independence of the Federal Reserve System is essential to the health of the economy.

32. Evaluating The FDIC insures deposits up to $100,000. What would you do if you had $400,000 you wanted to deposit and insure?

Thinking Like an Economist

33. You have been invited to speak to your school's PTA to explain how actions of the Federal Reserve impact the economy and individuals. Prepare a chart like the one below to illustrate your presentation.

Fed's Action	Impact on Money Supply	Impact on the Economy	Impact on You
Increase reserve requirement			
Sell securities			
Reduce discount rate			
Buy securities			
Lower reserve requirement			

Interpreting Cartoons

34. Critical Thinking What point is the cartoonist making about the relationship between the Chairman of the Board of Governors of the Federal Reserve and the performance of the stock market?

THAT'S HIGH ENOUGH.

Michael Ramirez/Copley News Service

Applying Economic Concepts

35. Fractional Bank Reserves Your local bank is required to keep its reserves in the form of vault cash and member deposits with the Fed. Why do you suppose that other assets, such as common stocks or real estate, are not suitable reserves?

36. Barter Assume that you live in a barter society. Compile a list of 10 items that you use frequently, and then identify alternative goods of comparable worth that you would be willing to trade for them.

Analyzing Visuals

37. Look at Figure 14.5 on page 403. How do the differences in the panels reflect the expansion or contraction of the money supply?

CHAPTER 14   Money, Banking, and the Fed   411

Buy securities: increase; stimulate; possibly more available jobs. Lower reserve requirement: increase; stimulate; easier/cheaper to get credit.

Interpreting Cartoons

34. The actions and comments of the Fed chairman can cause strong reactions on Wall Street.

Applying Economic Concepts

35. The value of common stocks and real estate are subject to unpredictable changes in value and therefore are not suitable as reserves.

36. Answers will vary but should indicate an understanding of the bartering system.

Analyzing Visuals

37. The expansion or contraction of the money supply is reflected in the differences in the reserve requirement. Panel A has a 10 percent reserve requirement and reflects greater contraction of the money supply. Panel B has a 40 percent reserve requirement and reflects greater expansion of the money supply.

28. Answers may vary but should include that a bank would deny loans to good customers only if it did not have sufficient reserves to cover the loan.

29. Answers will vary but should discuss the functions and characteristics of money.

30. Business cycles follow no set pattern.

31. Answers will vary but should reflect knowledge of the independence of the Fed.

32. Possible answers: divide the money between different banks; create joint accounts with spouse or children; set up trust or retirement accounts

Thinking Like an Economist

33. Possible answer: Increase reserve requirement: decrease; slow; possibly harder to get job. Sell securities: decrease; slow; more expensive to buy items on credit. Reduce discount rate: increase; stimulate; easier/cheaper to get credit.

Key to Ability Levels
BL Below level   **AL** Above level
OL On level   **ELL** English Language Learners

Key to Teaching Resources
📁 Print Material   💿 DVD
💿 CD-Rom   ⚡ Transparency

BL	OL	AL	ELL		Resources	Chapter Opener	Section 1	Section 2	Section 3	Chapter Assess
					FOCUS					
BL	OL	AL	ELL	⚡	**Daily Focus Skills Transparencies**		55	77	63, 78, 79	
					TEACH					
BL	OL		ELL	📁	**Guided Reading Activities***		p. 43	p. 44	p. 45	
BL	OL	AL	ELL	📁	**Economic Content Vocabulary Activities***		p. 15	p. 15	p. 15	
	OL	AL		📁	**Critical Thinking Activities**			pp. 21, 23	p. 23	
BL	OL		ELL	📁	**Reading Essentials and Note-Taking Guide***		p. 127	p. 130	p. 133	
		AL		📁	**Enrichment Activities**			p. 15		
	OL	AL		📁	**Free Enterprise Activities**			p. 21		
BL	OL	AL	ELL	⚡	**Economic Concepts Transparencies, Strategies, and Activities**		pp. 27, 29	p. 37	p. 35	
BL	OL		ELL	📁	**High School Reading in the Content Area Strategies and Activities**	✓	✓	✓	✓	✓
BL	OL	AL	ELL	⚡	**High School Writing Process Transparencies**	✓	✓	✓	✓	✓
BL	OL	AL	ELL	📁	**Writer's Guidebook**	✓	✓	✓	✓	✓
BL	OL	AL	ELL	💿	**StudentWorks Plus CD-ROM**	✓	✓	✓	✓	✓
BL	OL	AL	ELL	💿	**Vocabulary PuzzleMaker CD-ROM**	✓	✓	✓	✓	✓

*Also available in Spanish

- Interactive Lesson Planner
- Interactive Teacher Edition
- Fully editable blackline masters
- Economics & You videos

- Differentiated Lesson Plans
- Printable reports of daily assignments
- Standards tracking system

Levels					Resources	Chapter Opener	Section 1	Section 2	Section 3	Chapter Assess
BL	OL	AL	ELL							
TEACH *(continued)*										
BL	OL	AL	ELL	🔒	**Economics & You Video Program DVD—** *Economic Growth and Stability*	✓	✓	✓	✓	✓
BL	OL	AL	ELL	💿	**Graph Coach CD-ROM**	✓	✓	✓	✓	✓
Teacher Resources				📁	**Differentiated Instruction Strategies**	✓	✓	✓	✓	✓
				📁	**Success with English Learners**	✓	✓	✓	✓	✓
				💿	**Presentation Plus! CD-ROM**	✓	✓	✓	✓	✓
ASSESS										
BL	OL	AL	ELL	📁	**Section Quizzes and Chapter Tests**		p. 185	p. 186	p. 187	pp. 189, 193
BL	OL	AL	ELL	📁	**Authentic Assessment Strategies and Activities**			pp. 20, 21	p. 20	
BL	OL	AL	ELL	💿	*ExamView® Assessment Suite* **CD-ROM**		15-1	15-2	15-3	Ch. 15
BL	OL	AL	ELL	💿	**Interactive Tutor Self-Assessment CD-ROM**		15-1	15-2	15-3	
CLOSE										
BL			ELL	📁	**Reteaching Activities***		p. 15	p. 15	p. 15	
BL	OL		ELL	📁	**Reading and Study Skills Foldables**		p. 61	p. 61	pp. 61, 62	

*Also available in Spanish

Online Jumble Puzzles

Technology Product

Glencoe's Vocabulary PuzzleMaker™ 3.1 CD-ROM is an easy-to-use program that lets you create your own puzzles based on the glossary for classroom use. The PuzzleMaker allows you to

- create jumble puzzles based on content vocabulary and academic vocabulary that is specific to what is taught in the classroom;
- create online (LAN-based, or local area network) or paper jumble puzzles.

Objectives

After students complete the jumble puzzles, they will be able to

- recall and identify scrambled terms with the help of clues;
- reinforce their understanding of the vocabulary.

Steps

- Run PuzzleMaker™ 3.1. On the main menu, click on **Create a New Puzzle.**
- From the list of *Puzzle Databases*, select the appropriate database for the vocabulary.
- The *PuzzleMaker Wizard* will take you through selecting a puzzle type and grid type.
- Then select one or more chapters from the list. Indicate whether you want the words selected randomly or manually.
- Select the language and words you wish to use within the maximum for the puzzle. Click **Finish.**
- Save your jumble puzzle to a location that is easily accessible by your students with PuzzlePlayer™ 3.1, or print copies for your students to complete.
- Use PuzzlePlayer™ 3.1 to review the puzzles after your students have worked on and saved them.

Economics ONLINE

	Student	Teacher	Parent
Beyond the Textbook	●	●	●
Chapter Overviews	●	●	●
ePuzzles and Games	●		●
Concepts in Motion	●		●
Multi-Language Glossaries	●		●
Online Student Edition	●	●	●
Self-Check Quizzes	●		●
Student Web Activities	●		●
Study Central™	●		●
Time Current Events	●	●	●
Teaching Today		●	
Vocabulary eFlashcards	●		●
Web Activity Lesson Plans		●	

Glencoe Media Center

❯ glencoe.com

Study-To-Go
- Vocabulary eFlashcards
- Self-Check Quizzes

❯ **Audio/Video**
- Student Edition Audio
- Spanish Summaries
- Economics & You Videos

READING SUPPORT FROM
JAMESTOWN EDUCATION

- **Timed Readings Plus in Social Studies** helps students increase their reading rate and fluency while maintaining comprehension. The 400-word passages are similar to those found on state and national assessments.

- **Reading in the Content Area: Social Studies** concentrates on six essential reading skills that help students better comprehend what they read. The book includes 75 high-interest nonfiction passages written at increasing levels of difficulty.

- **Reading Social Studies** includes strategic reading instruction and vocabulary support in Social Studies content for both ELLs and native speakers of English.
www.jamestowneducation.com

Reading List Generator CD-ROM

GLENCOE BOOKLINK 3

Use this database to search more than 30,000 titles to create a customized reading list for your students.

- Reading lists can be organized by students' reading level, author, genre, theme, or area of interest.
- The database provides Degrees of Reading Power™ (DRP) and Lexile™ readability scores for all selections.
- A brief summary of each selection is included.

Leveled reading suggestions for this chapter:
For students at a Grade 10 reading level:
- *Considering a Job Offer,* by Stuart Schwartz & Craig Conley

For students at a Grade 11 reading level:
- *In Search of Excellence: Lessons From America's Best-Run Companies,* by Thomas J. Peters & Robert H. Waterman

For students at a Grade 12 reading level:
- *Presidential Leadership: Rating the Best and Worst in the White House,* by James Taranto

* Review suggested books before assigning them.

NCEE

National Council on Economic Education

Voluntary Standards Emphasized in Chapter 15

Content Standard 12 Interest rates, adjusted for inflation, rise and fall to balance the amount saved with the amount borrowed, which affects the allocation of scarce resources between present and future uses.

Content Standard 17 Costs of government policies sometimes exceed benefits. This may occur because of incentives facing voters, government officials, and government employees, because of actions by special interest groups that can impose costs on the general public, or because social goals other than economic efficiency are being pursued.

Content Standard 20 Federal government budgetary policy and the Federal Reserve System's monetary policy influence the overall levels of employment, output, and prices.

Resources Available from NCEE
- Virtual Economics®: An Interactive Center for Economic Education Version 3.0
- Capstone: The Nation's High School Economics Course
- Focus: High School Economics, Second Edition
- Focus: Institutions and Markets

To order these materials, or to contact your State Council on Economic Education about workshops and programs, call 1-800-338-1192 or visit the NCEE Web site at store.ncee.net.

The **BIG** Idea

As students study the chapter, remind them to consider the chapter-based Big Idea. The **Essential Question** in the chapter launch activity below ties in to the Big Idea and helps students think about and understand important chapter concepts. In addition, the Hands-On Chapter Project relates the content from each section to the Big Idea. The steps in each section build on each other and culminate in the Wrap-Up Activity on the Visual Summary page.

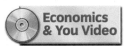
Economics & You Video To generate student interest and provide a springboard for class discussion, access the Economics & You Topic 22, **Economic Growth and Stability,** at glencoe.com or on the video DVD.

FOLDABLES Study Organizer **Dinah Zike's Foldables** are three-dimensional, interactive graphic organizers that help students practice basic writing skills, review key vocabulary terms, and identify main ideas. Have students complete this chapter's Foldable activity or activities in *Dinah Zike's Reading and Study Skills Foldables* booklet. **OL**

Economics ONLINE Introduce students to chapter content and key terms by having them access *Chapter 15 —Chapter Overviews* at glencoe.com.

CHAPTER
15 Economic Stabilization Policies

Why It Matters

Do you remember Hurricane Katrina or the invasion of Iraq and the subsequent war? How did these events—along with growing demand—affect gasoline prices? Did the higher gasoline prices change the spending habits of you and your friends? How and why? Conduct a simple survey of your friends and family to find out how higher prices impacted their lives. Present the survey to your class. Read Chapter 15 to learn what the government might do to stabilize the economy.

The **BIG** Idea

Governments strive for a balance between the costs and benefits of their economic policies to promote economic stability and growth.

◀ A busy lunch hour at Times Square in New York City indicates a stable, growing economy.

412 UNIT 4

Economics ONLINE Chapter Overview Visit the *Economics: Principles and Practices* Web site at glencoe.com and click on *Chapter 15–Chapter Overviews* to preview chapter information.

Activity: Launching the Chapter

Speculating Remind students that they studied the concepts of supply and demand in Chapters 4 and 5. Have students brainstorm a list of factors that they believe can affect the total supply and total demand in the U.S. economy. Write their ideas on the board. Ask for volunteers to briefly explain how a certain factor might affect supply and demand in the nation. **Essential Question:** What are different ways that the government can impact total supply and demand in the U.S. economy? *(Answers may include raising or lowering taxes, increasing spending, and adjusting interest rates.)* Have students write a paragraph predicting what they think they will learn about in this chapter. **OL**

Macroeconomic Equilibrium

GUIDE TO READING

Section Preview

In this section, you will learn that macroeconomic equilibrium takes place at the intersection of aggregate demand and aggregate supply.

Content Vocabulary

- macroeconomics *(p. 413)*
- equilibrium price *(p. 414)*
- aggregate supply *(p. 414)*
- aggregate supply curve *(p. 414)*
- aggregate demand *(p. 415)*
- aggregate demand curve *(p. 415)*
- macroeconomic equilibrium *(p. 416)*

Academic Vocabulary

- framework *(p. 416)*
- unduly *(p. 417)*

Reading Strategy

Listing As you read the section, complete a graphic organizer similar to the one below by listing at least three factors that could lower production costs and lead to an increase in aggregate supply.

```
┌─────────────┐
└─────────────┘ ─┐
┌─────────────┐  │──► Effect: Increase
└─────────────┘ ─┤    in aggregate
┌─────────────┐  │    supply
└─────────────┘ ─┘
```

ISSUES IN THE NEWS
—BusinessWeek

This Porridge Looks a Little Too Warm

Goldilocks lives. The economic scenario, that is. Those who believe in her think the economy this year will be not too hot, not too cold, but just right. Currently, it's the view most widely held by economists, investors, and Wall Street pros. So, the tale goes, after the unusually warm winter heated up the economy in the first quarter, growth will cool down to a pace of about 3%. . . .

[T]wo things are happening right now that are affecting both manufacturing and the economy. One, businesses are rushing to expand their operations in the face of strong demand and insufficient production capacity. And two, because factory output is growing . . . manufacturing operating rates have risen sharply during the past year. The only way to know for sure . . . is to watch the economy and the data. ∎

"Not too hot, not too cold, but just right." According to the news story above, the concept of equilibrium seems to be alive and well. In literature as well as in life, we seem to like things best when they can achieve a reasonable balance. The economy is no exception.

When we deal with **macroeconomics,** the part of economics concerned with the economy as a whole and decision making by large units, we also seek a balance. To do so, we can use a set of "tools" already familiar to us—supply and demand—to find out just where the balance is.

> **macroeconomics**
> part of economics that deals with the economy as a whole *(also see page 197)*

Focus

Bellringer
Daily Focus Transparency 55

GUIDE TO READING

Answers to Graphic: decline in price of energy; lower interest rates; higher labor productivity

Resource Manager

R Reading Strategies	C Critical Thinking	D Differentiated Instruction	W Writing Support	S Skill Practice
Teacher Edition • Questioning, p. 415 • Academic Vocab., p. 417 **Additional Resources** • Guid. Read. Act., p. 43 • Read. Ess. & Note-Taking Guide, p. 127	**Teacher Edition** • Assessing, p. 415 • Drawing Con., p. 416 **Additional Resources** • Econ. Concepts Trans., Strat. & Act., p. 27 • Econ. Content Vocab. Act., p. 15	**Teacher Edition** • ELL, p. 414 • Visual/Spatial, p. 418 **Additional Resources** • Reteach. Act., p. 15 • Quizzes and Tests, p. 185	**Teacher Edition** • Expository Writing, p. 416 **Additional Resources** • High School Reading in the Content Area Strat. and Act.	**Teacher Edition** • Analyzing Graphs, p. 414 **Additional Resources** • Reading and Study Skills Fold., p. 61

Teach

D Differentiated Instruction

English Language Learners
Instruct students to write a definition of the word *aggregate* based on how it is used in the text. Next, have students look up the dictionary definition of the word and compare it with their own definitions. Finally, ask students to write a sentence using the word *aggregate* to refer to something other than supply or demand. (*Possible sentence: The company's aggregate profits this quarter exceeded expectations.*) **ELL**

S Skill Practice

Analyzing Graphs Ask: Which of the two curves in Figure 15.1 would consumers prefer? Explain. (*AS¹; that curve represents an increased supply, which would lower the price level*) **OL**

Economic Analysis
Answer: increased production costs

Differentiated Instruction

equilibrium price price where quantity supplied equals quantity demanded (also see page 149)

aggregate supply the total value of all goods and services that all firms would produce in a specific period of time at various price levels

aggregate supply curve hypothetical curve showing different levels of real GDP that would be produced at various price levels

Aggregate Supply and Demand

MAIN Idea Aggregate supply and demand help us study supply and demand for the economy as a whole.

Economics and You In your English classes, you might study a part of a novel in depth to understand the whole book better. Read on to learn about a similar approach in economics.

When we study markets, we often use the tools of supply and demand to show how the **equilibrium price** and quantity of output are determined. When we study the economy as a whole, we can use these tools in much the same way.

Aggregate Supply
You learned in Chapter 5 that supply is the amount of a particular product offered for sale at all possible prices. When it comes to the economy as a whole, economists like to look at **aggregate supply,** the total value of goods and services that all firms would produce in a specific period of time at various price levels. If the period was exactly one year, and if all production took place within a country's borders, then aggregate supply would be the same as GDP.

Figure 15.1 ► The Aggregate Supply Curve

► The aggregate supply curve shows the amount of real GDP that would be produced at various price levels. An increase in aggregate supply occurs when production costs decrease for all individual producers. When economists use 2 curves to show changes in aggregate supply, they label the first curve **AS⁰** and the second **AS¹**.

S Economic Analysis *What causes a decrease in aggregate supply?*

Graphs In Motion
See StudentWorks™ Plus or glencoe.com.

CHANGE IN AGGREGATE SUPPLY

The concept of aggregate supply assumes that the money supply is fixed and that a given price level prevails. If prices should change, however, then individual firms would respond by adjusting their output to produce a slightly different level of GDP. If it were somehow possible to keep adjusting the price level to observe how total output changed, we could then construct an **aggregate supply curve,** which shows the amount of real GDP that would be produced at various price levels.

Figure 15.1 shows how an aggregate supply curve for the whole economy might look. Like the supply curve of an individual firm or the market supply curve, it is shown as upward sloping as you move from left to right. To distinguish the aggregate supply curve from other supply curves, it is labeled **AS.**

In Figure 15.1, note that the vertical axis of the graph is labeled 'Price level' rather than just 'Price', as you have seen in earlier chapters. The price level includes the price of everything produced in the economy. In contrast, the word *price* would indicate the cost of only a single good or service. Economists often use an aggregate measure like the price level rather than a single price. Aggregate measures help them better explain changes in the economy.

Aggregate Demand

Economic Concepts Trans., Strat. and Act., p. 29

Objective: Understand the concept of aggregate demand.

Focus/Teach: Ask students to list the different components that comprise aggregate demand. Write their responses on the board. Then have students answer the activity questions.

Assess: Review the students' answers as a class.

Close: Ask students to write a paragraph describing any new insights about aggregate demand that they learned from this activity.

Differentiated Instruction Strategies
BL Have students describe other goods and services that could have been shown to teach the same lesson.

AL Have students answer the "Suggested Activities" questions that appear on page 30 of the booklet.

ELL Have students illustrate the concept of aggregate demand.

Figure 15.2 ► **The Aggregate Demand Curve**

CHAPTER 15, SECTION 1

CHANGE IN AGGREGATE DEMAND

Graphs In MOtion

See StudentWorks™ Plus or glencoe.com.

► The aggregate demand curve shows the amount of real GDP the economy would demand at all possible price levels. Aggregate demand, like aggregate supply, can either increase or decrease. When economists use two curves to show changes in aggregate demand, they label the first curve **AD⁰** and the second **AD¹**.

Economic Analysis *What causes the aggregate demand curve to shift?*

R Reading Strategy

Questioning Instruct students to write a five-question multiple-choice quiz about the important ideas presented on this page. After they finish writing their quizzes, ask students to write an explanation for why they chose to ask each question. **OL**

C Critical Thinking

Assessing Ask: Why is the aggregate demand curve a hypothetical curve? *(because desire, ability, and willingness to purchase a product are abstract concepts that are not easily quantified, especially across an entire population)* **OL**

Economic Analysis

Answer: changes in taxes, transfer payments, and consumer spending preferences

Finally, note that the horizontal axis is labeled 'Real GDP'. This is because we want to know the value of all goods and services produced, not just the output of a single product. While there are some other differences between the supply curve of a single product and aggregate supply, the two curves are otherwise fairly similar.

Changes in Aggregate Supply

Aggregate supply, like the supply of an individual firm, can increase or decrease. Many increases in aggregate supply are tied to the cost of production for an individual firm. For example, if the price of energy should suddenly go down, most if not all firms will be able to produce a little more output, and real GDP will go up. Since this increase in output would happen at all price levels, the increase shows as a shift of the original aggregate supply curve **AS⁰** to the right, and the new aggregate supply curve **AS¹**.

Factors that increase the cost of production for individual firms tend to decrease aggregate supply. These factors include higher oil prices, higher interest rates, and lower labor productivity. Any increase in cost that causes individual firms to offer fewer goods and services for sale at each and every price would shift the aggregate supply curve to the left.

Aggregate Demand

In Chapter 4 you learned that demand is the desire, ability, and willingness to purchase a product. If it were possible to add up everyone's demand for every good and service in the economy, we would have a measure of aggregate, or total, demand. Accordingly, economists call this concept **aggregate demand,** the total value of all goods and services demanded at different price levels. Aggregate demand is labeled **AD** to keep it separate from other demand curves. It is a summary measure of all demand in the economy. Like aggregate supply, it can be represented as a graph, and it can either increase or decrease.

The **aggregate demand curve** appears in **Figure 15.2** and shows the amount of total output, measured in terms of real GDP, that would be purchased at every possible price level. This curve is labeled **AD** and represents the sum of all consumer, business, government, and net foreign demands

aggregate demand the total value of goods and services demanded at all different price levels

aggregate demand curve hypothetical curve showing different levels of real GDP that would be purchased at various price levels

CHAPTER 15 Economic Stabilization Policies 415

Leveled Activities

BL Guided Reading Activities, p. 43

OL Economic Content Vocabulary Activities, p. 15

AL Economic Concepts Transparencies, Strategies, and Activities, p. 27

W Writing Support

Expository Writing Have students use reliable online and print resources to investigate the subject of American saving and spending habits. Ask students to write a paper explaining why the personal savings rate is so low among people in the United States. Students should support their points with facts from articles and books. **AL**

C Critical Thinking

Drawing Conclusions

Ask: How would increased competition in the economy likely affect aggregate demand? *(Increased competition would lower prices and thus increase aggregate demand.)* **OL**

✓Reading Check **Answer:**
Rather than using the price or output of a single product, economists use aggregates, like price level and real GDP, to measure AS and AD. Nonetheless, the slopes of those curves are similar to the slopes of curves measuring individual supply and demand.

Hands-On Chapter Project

Step 1

Effects of Government Stabilization Policies

In this project, students will assess how government economic policies and other factors impact the economy.

Step 1: Assessing Aggregate Supply and Demand. Student groups will use graphs to show how various factors impact aggregate supply and aggregate demand.

Directions: Organize the class into small groups. Ask each group to create a

---

The Global Economy & YOU

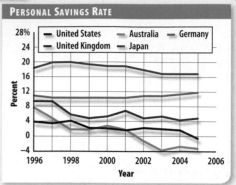

Banking on the Future

When consumers save less and spend more, the aggregate demand curve shifts to the right. This has been the case recently in the United States, where seemingly tireless consumers shop online, in the mall, and at every stop in between. In a country where the minimum wage is $5.15 per hour—compared to Mexico's $4.36 per day—one would think Americans could afford to sock away substantial savings. Instead, we are spending our money at an astonishing rate.

Why are Americans not saving more? Given the dismal outlook for Social Security, shaky pension plans, and rising interest rates, they should be more concerned than ever about their economic future. Despite these issues, the U.S. personal savings rate dipped lower in 2005 than it has since 1933, during the Great Depression. That year it reached negative 0.4 percent.

PERSONAL SAVINGS RATE

(Legend: United States, United Kingdom, Australia, Japan, Germany; Percent axis 28%, 24, 20, 16, 12, 8, 4, 0, −4; Year axis 1996, 1998, 2000, 2002, 2004, 2006)

Source: St. Louis Federal Reserve

Compared with personal savings rates from around the globe, those of Americans are well below the international average.

---

macroeconomic equilibrium level of real GDP consistent with a given price level and marked by the intersection of aggregate supply and aggregate demand

at various price levels. It slopes downward and to the right like the individual and the market demand curves.

Changes in Aggregate Demand

Aggregate demand can increase or decrease depending on certain factors. For example, if consumers decide to spend more and save less, the increase in consumer spending also increases aggregate demand, shifting the original aggregate demand curve AD^0 to the right to form the new aggregate demand curve AD^1.

A decrease in aggregate demand can occur if the same factors act in an opposite manner. If people were to save more and spend less, the aggregate demand curve would shift to the left. Higher taxes and lower transfer payments could also reduce aggregate spending. Such decisions shift the aggregate demand curve to the left because all sectors of the economy collectively buy less GDP at all price levels.

✓Reading Check **Comparing** How do AS and AD compare to individual supply and demand?

Macroeconomic Equilibrium

MAIN Idea Macroeconomic equilibrium is reached when the level of real GDP is consistent with a given price level.

Economics and You You learned earlier about the equilibrium price. Read on to learn how this concept applies to the economy as a whole.

Aggregate supply and demand curves are useful concepts because they provide a **framework** to help us analyze the impact of economic policy proposals on economic growth and price stability. They also can give us an idea of the way and direction in which things will change. They do not provide us with exact predictions, however. Even so, they are useful when we analyze macroeconomic issues.

Macroeconomic equilibrium, for example, is the point at which the level of real GDP is consistent with a given price level. It is determined by the intersection of the aggregate supply and demand curves.

---

poster-sized graph illustrating the condition of macroeconomic equilibrium. Instruct each group to use actual price level figures for the vertical axis and actual GDP figures for the horizontal axis. Next, assign a different hypothetical economic situation to each group (for example, growing underemployment, sharp cuts to Social Security, OPEC oil embargo, increase in minimum wage, rise in consumer confidence, and so on). Ask each group to prepare a second graph demonstrating

how its assigned event affected the equilibrium it depicted on its first graph. Have groups present their two graphs to the class.

Summarizing Choose two or more of the economic situations you assigned to the groups. Have students write a short paper explaining how these multiple factors, if they occurred at the same time, would impact the macroeconomic equilibrium. **OL**

(Chapter Project continued in Section 2.)

This equilibrium is shown in **Figure 15.3**. In this figure, quantity **Q** is the level of real GDP that is consistent with price level **P**, or where the aggregate supply curve **AS** and the aggregate demand curve **AD** intersect. This equilibrium represents a specific situation at a particular point in time and could change if either **AS** or **AD** changes.

For example, if a new government policy caused the aggregate demand curve **AD** to shift to the right, the new equilibrium would take place at a higher level of real GDP and a higher price level. This is one of the dilemmas facing economic policy makers—how to make real GDP grow without **R** **unduly** increasing the price level and thereby the rate of inflation.

As you will see in the next section, we can use aggregate supply and demand to analyze the impact of fiscal and monetary policies, two of the major ways of affecting the level of output and real GDP.

✔**Reading Check** **Explaining** How does the macro-economic equilibrium work? How is it used?

Figure 15.3 ▶ **The Economy in Equilibrium**

▶ The economy is at equilibrium when the quantity of real GDP demanded is equal to the real GDP supplied.

Economic Analysis *What happens to the price level when output increases?*

MACROECONOMIC EQUILIBRIUM

SECTION 1 Review

Vocabulary
1. **Explain** the significance of macroeconomics, equilibrium price, aggregate supply, aggregate supply curve, aggregate demand, aggregate demand curve, and macroeconomic equilibrium.

Main Ideas
2. **Identifying** Use a graphic organizer like the one below to identify the factors that might cause aggregate supply to increase and aggregate demand to decrease.

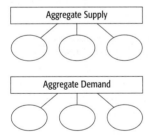

Aggregate Supply

Aggregate Demand

3. **Explaining** Why is macroeconomic equilibrium important?

Critical Thinking
4. **The BIG Idea** How do aggregate supply and aggregate demand help economic policy makers?
5. **Drawing Conclusions** How is it possible for an economy to grow without a general increase in price levels?
6. **Analyzing Information** What kind of effect would higher taxes have on aggregate supply? Explain.
7. **Analyzing Visuals** Look at Figure 15.3 on this page. What would happen to the price level if AD decreased?

Applying Economics
8. **Aggregate Supply and Demand** Search your local newspaper for articles relating to the impact of changing gasoline prices. Summarize the articles and answer the following question: "How do changing gasoline prices impact AS and AD?" Explain your answer.

CHAPTER 15 Economic Stabilization Policies **417**

R **Reading Strategy**

Academic Vocabulary Have students write three different sentences related to economics that use the word *unduly*. **OL**

Economic Analysis
Answer: It decreases.

✔**Reading Check** **Answer:**
By marking the intersection of aggregate supply and aggregate demand, the macroeconomic equilibrium indicates the level of real GDP consistent with a given price level. Economists use it to analyze economic policies.

Assess

🔘 Use the Interactive Tutor Self-Assessment CD-ROM to review Section 1, and then assign the Section 1 Review as homework or as an in-class activity.

Close

Summarizing Have students summarize the main points of the section. **OL**

Review SECTION 1

Answers

1. All definitions can be found in the section and the Glossary.
2. **Aggregate Supply:** price of energy drops; lower interest rates; higher labor productivity. **Aggregate Demand:** decline in consumer spending; higher taxes; lower transfer payments
3. Economists can use it to assess the impact of factors that affect the economy.
4. They provide a framework for analyzing equilibrium, economic growth, and price stability.
5. Students will likely realize that it is possible if lower productivity costs increase aggregate supply.
6. Higher taxes on businesses increase production costs, which in turn causes the AS curve to shift to the left.
7. The price level would increase.
8. Answers will vary but should demonstrate an understanding that increasing gasoline production costs reduces AS and that higher gas prices at the pump reduce AD.

BusinessWeek

Teach

BusinessWeek ONLINE

To find up-to-date news and analysis on the economy, business, technology, markets, entrepreneurs, investments, and finance, have students search feature articles and special reports on the BusinessWeek Web site, www.businessweek.com.

Examining the Newsclip

Answers:

1. Asian automobile products are in tune with American customer preferences.
2. The Japanese economy declined in recent years, and an aging population will continue to limit demand.

Additional Support

BusinessWeek NEWSCLIP

Aggregate demand and aggregate supply are becoming global concepts. When demand for a product drops in one country, producers often look for markets in other countries to take up the slack. Asian automakers did just that when demand for Japanese cars decreased in Japan.

Asia's Automakers Think Globally

The global market may be becoming increasingly competitive, but Japan's and Korea's top automakers are hitting new production records and expanding outside their domestic markets at a rapid pace. Faced with stagnant demand in their home countries and a need to reduce foreign exchange risks, the big automakers in both countries are rapidly expanding production overseas and shearing off market shares from the foreign incumbents.

So far, the big three Japanese companies—Toyota Motor Corp., Honda Motor Co. Ltd., and **D** Nissan Motor Co. Ltd.—are enjoying successes as their tight controls on costs and mostly competitive product lineups enable them to take market share from overseas rivals. . . .

Over the past decade, Japanese automakers have been setting up and expanding production facilities overseas. . . . In comparison, Hyundai and its

subsidiary Kia are late starters in their localization plans in the U.S. and Europe. But . . . all five automakers' prospects for further expansion in North America look promising. In the current high gasoline price environment, their product mixes look to be in tune with customer shifts, with more fuel-efficient cars becoming popular. . . .

Success in the U.S. carries some risks. . . . The impact of a sudden change in purchasing habits by American auto buyers on these companies' earnings and cash flow could be amplified because of this heavy dependence. . . .

The Japanese domestic market remains flat, however. Although the economy is recovering, weak demand is unlikely to be reversed. With a rapidly aging population, long-term growth prospects in Japan are very limited.

—Reprinted from *BusinessWeek*

WORLD AUTOMOBILE SALES

4.3% 1%
6.5%
32.2%
56.9%

○ Japanese automakers
● U.S. automakers
● European automakers
● Korean automakers
● Others

Source: Autodata Corp.

Examining the Newsclip

1. **Determining Cause and Effect** According to the article, what is causing demand for Japanese and other Asian autos to increase in the United States?
2. **Analyzing** Why is demand for Japanese cars decreasing in Japan?

Extending the Content

Imported Car Sales in the United States In 2005 Japanese manufacturers produced the five top-selling passenger cars in the United States:

1. Toyota Camry
2. Honda Accord
3. Toyota Corolla/Matrix
4. Honda Civic
5. Nissan Altima

Nonetheless, the Japanese share of the total U.S. car sales that year was little more than half of what it was two decades earlier. In 1980 Japanese-made automobiles accounted for 21.2 percent of retail car sales in the United States. In 2005 this figure was 12 percent. German manufacturers, on the other hand, have claimed a larger portion of the American car market. In 1980 cars made in Germany

represented 3.3 percent of automobiles sold in the United States. Twenty-five years later, the German share of car sales in American had more than doubled to 7.0 percent.

SECTION 2
Stabilization Policies

GUIDE TO READING

Section Preview
In this section, you will learn how government can promote economic growth through economic policies.

Content Vocabulary
- Medicare (p. 419)
- fiscal policy (p. 420)
- Keynesian economics (p. 420)
- multiplier (p. 420)
- accelerator (p. 420)
- automatic stabilizer (p. 422)
- entitlements (p. 422)
- unemployment insurance (p. 422)
- supply-side policies (p. 423)
- deregulation (p. 424)
- monetarism (p. 426)
- wage-price controls (p. 427)

Academic Vocabulary
- unstable (p. 420)
- explicit (p. 427)

Reading Strategy
Describing As you read the section, complete graphic organizers similar to the ones below by describing the role of government under demand-side and supply-side policies.

Demand-side policies →

Supply-side policies →

ISSUES IN THE NEWS
—www.cato.org

Time for "Wise and Frugal"

Federal spending has increased 45 percent in the past five years; the government has run deficits in thirty-three of the past thirty-seven years; the costs of programs for the elderly are set to balloon and impose huge burdens on coming generations of young workers.

Clearly, policymakers are failing to run a "wise and frugal government," as Thomas Jefferson advised in his first inaugural address. A key problem is that federal budget rules stack the deck in favor of continual program expansion. The costly Medicare drug bill and the explosion in pork spending illustrate how a lack of structural controls leads to an undisciplined scramble to spend, spend, spend. ■

Whenever the government spends money on **Medicare,** the federal program that provides health-care expenditures for the elderly, it shifts the aggregate demand curve to the right. As you read in the news story above, it costs the government more money—and it puts an upward pressure on the price level.

Medicare expenditures are important to those who benefit from them, since economic security is one of the seven major economic goals. Still, policy makers must often choose among a number of competing economic policies. Finding the proper balance between them is an important part of stabilization policy.

Medicare federal health-care program for senior citizens, regardless of income (also see page 235)

R Reading Strategies	C Critical Thinking	D Differentiated Instruction	W Writing Support	S Skill Practice
Teacher Edition • Act. Prior Know., p. 420 • Reading Charts, p. 424 • Predicting, p. 427 **Additional Resources** • Guid. Read. Act., p. 44 • Read. Ess. & Note-Taking Guide, p. 130	**Teacher Edition** • Contrasting, p. 420 • Ident. POV, p. 422 • Theorizing, p. 425 **Additional Resources** • Crit. Think. Act., pp. 21, 23 • Econ. Concepts Trans., Strat. & Act., p. 37	**Teacher Edition** • Auditory/Musical, p. 421 • Visual/Spatial, p. 423 • Intrapersonal, p. 426 **Additional Resources** • Enrichment Act., p. 15 • Authentic Assess., pp. 20, 21	**Teacher Edition** • Persuasive Writing, p. 422 • Expository Writing, p. 424 • Narrative Writing, p. 428 **Additional Resources** • High School Writing Process Trans.	**Teacher Edition** • Ident. the Main Idea, p. 421 • Using Tables and Charts, p. 423 • Making Gen., p. 426 **Additional Resources** • Reading and Study Skills Fold., p. 61

Teach

R Reading Strategy

Activating Prior Knowledge
Ask: Why do you think Keynes's theories were so well-received at the time he posited them? *(Possible answer: In 1936 the economy was still mired in the Great Depression, so people were more open to trying new economic ideas.)* **OL**

C Critical Thinking

Contrasting Have students consult books or Web sites to identify and research the economic theory that prevailed in the United States prior to the Great Depression. Ask students to write a report contrasting the main points of that economic theory with Keynesian economics. **AL**

Caption Answer:
John Maynard Keynes

Additional Support

---

fiscal policy
use of government spending and revenue collection measures to influence the economy

Keynesian economics
government spending and taxation policies suggested by John Maynard Keynes to stimulate the economy

multiplier
magnified change in overall spending caused by a change in investment spending

---

Demand-Side Policies

MAIN Idea Demand-side policies are designed to affect total demand through taxing, government spending, and automatic stabilizers.

Economics and You You learned earlier that government implements policies to help people. Read on to learn how it uses policies to affect the economy.

Demand-side policies are designed to increase or decrease total demand in the economy. These policies try to shift the aggregate demand curve to the right or the left. One approach to changing demand is known as **fiscal policy**—the federal government's attempt to influence or stabilize the economy through taxing and government spending.

Government Spending During the Great Depression, the government funded public works, such as the construction of Hoover Dam shown below, to stabilize the economy. *Which economist made fiscal policy popular?*

Fiscal policies are derived from **Keynesian economics,** an economic policy approach designed to lower unemployment by stimulating aggregate demand. John Maynard Keynes put forth these theories in 1936, and they dominated the thinking of economists until the 1970s.

Keynesian Economics

Keynes provided the basic framework by using the output-expenditure model, $GDP = C + I + G + F$. According to this model, any change in GDP on the left side of the equation could be traced to changes on the right side of the equation. The question was: which of the four components caused the instability?

According to Keynes, the net impact of the foreign sector (F) was so small that it could be ignored. The government sector (G) was not the problem either, because its expenditures were normally stable over time. According to Keynes, spending by the consumer sector (C), was the most stable of all. It appeared that the business, or investment, sector (I) was to blame for the instability.

In Keynes's theory, spending by the investment sector was not only **unstable** but had a magnified effect on other spending. If investment spending declined by $50 billion, for example, many workers would lose their jobs. These workers in turn would spend less and pay fewer taxes. Soon, the amount of spending by all sectors in the economy would be down by more than the initial decline in investment.

This effect is called the **multiplier.** It says that a change in investment spending will have a magnified effect on total spending. The multiplier is believed to be about 2 in today's economy. Thus, if investment spending goes down by $50 billion, the decline in overall spending could reach $100 billion. The multiplier also works in the other direction. An increase in spending by $50 billion would increase overall spending by twice that amount.

Extending the Content

Demand-Side Policies During a recession, demand-side economics calls for an expansionary fiscal policy. This involves increased government spending, or tax cuts, or a combination of both. This approach would tend to move the government's budget toward a deficit. In times of high inflation, demand-side economics calls for a contractionary fiscal policy. This would mean government spending cuts, or tax increases, or a mix of the two. This approach would move the government's budget toward a surplus.

Public Works The federal government continues to fund large-scale public works projects, such as the Hyperion water treatment facility in Los Angeles. *How does public spending offset the loss of business spending?*

D Differentiated Instruction

Auditory/Musical Ask students to write a song, rap, or jingle that explains Keynes's theory of the output expenditure model (GDP = C + I + G + F). Encourage students to provide catchy, memorable lyrics that will help their classmates learn this topic. Ask for volunteers to perform their songs, raps, or jingles for the class. **OL**

Conditions are likely to be made even worse by the **accelerator**—the change in investment spending caused by a change in total spending. After a decline in overall spending begins, investors tend to become cautious, causing investment spending to be reduced even further. Before long, the economy is trapped in a downward spiral. The combined multiplier-accelerator effect is important because it contributes to the instability of GDP.

Role of Government

Keynes argued that only the government was big enough to step in and offset changes in investment-sector spending. The government could take a direct role in the economy and undertake its own spending to offset the decline in spending by businesses. The government could also play an indirect role by lowering taxes and enacting other measures to encourage businesses and consumers to spend more.

Suppose the government wanted to take direct steps quickly to offset a $50 billion decline in business spending. To do this, it could spend $10 billion to build a dam, give $20 billion in grants to cities to fix up poor neighborhoods, and spend another $20 billion in other ways. By adding up individual programs, government spending would replace the $50 billion that businesses do not spend. Thus, the overall sum of C + I + G + F would remain unchanged.

Instead of spending the $50 billion, the government could affect the economy indirectly by reducing tax rates to give investors and consumers more purchasing power. If they spent the $50 billion not collected in taxes, investors and consumers would offset the initial decline in investment spending. Again, there would be no change in the sum of C + I + G + F.

Either way, the government would run the risk of a short-term federal deficit. In Keynes's view, the deficit was unfortunate but necessary to stop further declines in economic activity. When the economy recovered, tax collections would rise, the government would run a surplus, and the debt could be paid back. The justification for *temporary* federal deficits was one of the lasting contributions of Keynesian economics and a major departure from the economic thinking of the time.

accelerator change in investment spending caused by a change in overall spending

CHAPTER 15 Economic Stabilization Policies **421**

S Skill Practice

Identifying the Main Idea
Ask: Does the federal government's recent pattern of deficit spending match Keynes's ideas about the topic? Why or why not? *(No; Keynes advocated temporary federal deficits, whereas the federal government's current deficits are ongoing.)* **OL**

Caption Answer: More public spending would increase the value of G, which would offset the decrease in I (business spending), leaving the overall sum of C + I + G + F unchanged.

Additional Support

Activity: Technology Connection

Building a Web Site Organize the class into small groups. Ask students to research the major principles of Keynesian economics. Instruct each group to construct a Web site that explains Keynes's economic theories in an engaging manner. Possible topics that could be discussed on these Web sites include output-expenditure model, government spending, short-term deficits, and the Great Depression. Students may also wish to include graphs that demonstrate Keynesian theories, as well as quotes from Keynes's writings. Have students present their Web sites to the class. **AL**

Teacher Tip

Sharing the Workload
Suggest that students divide the responsibilities so that those who play a smaller role in the creation of the Web site have a larger role in researching information, and so forth.

C Critical Thinking

Identifying Points of View
Ask: Why might some people criticize the entitlement programs of the United States? *(Answers may include higher taxes, reduced incentives to work, or fear of creating a permanent welfare class.)* **OL**

W Writing Support

Persuasive Writing Direct students to write and then perform a speech arguing for or against a greater application of Keynesian principles in the U.S. economy. Instruct students to use the information in the text as well as reliable Internet or library resources that provide factual material to strengthen their arguments. **OL**

Economic Analysis

Answer: point a

✓**Reading Check** **Answer:** Keynes's ideas dominated the thinking of economics from the 1930s to the 1970s. Elements of this fiscal policy are still practiced today.

Differentiated Instruction

Free Enterprise Activities, p. 21

Figure 15.4 ▶ **Fiscal Policy and Aggregate Demand**

▶ Fiscal policies are designed to affect aggregate demand. Increases in government spending or tax reductions increase aggregate demand. As a result, the economy moves from **a** to **b**.

Economic Analysis *Which point on the graph represents the lowest aggregate demand?*

THE AGGREGATE DEMAND CURVE

---

automatic stabilizer program that automatically provides benefits to offset a change in people's incomes

entitlement broad social program that uses established eligibility requirements to provide health, nutritional, or income supplements to individuals *(also see page 283)*

unemployment insurance government program providing payments to unemployed workers

Automatic Stabilizers

Another key component of fiscal policy is the role of **automatic stabilizers**, programs that automatically trigger benefits if changes in the economy threaten income. The benefits are automatic because they were approved in prior legislation.

Most **entitlements**—broad social programs that use established eligibility requirements to provide health, nutritional, or income supplements—function as automatic stabilizers. These progams provide some financial assistance to people who lose a job, are injured on the job and receive medical benefits, or are forced to retire because of age or health. **C**

One such entitlement program is **unemployment insurance**—insurance that workers who lose their jobs through no fault of their own can collect from individual states for a limited amount of time. This insurance cannot be collected by people who are fired because of misconduct or who quit their jobs without good reason.

Another important automatic stabilizer is the progressive income tax. For example, if someone loses his or her job or ends up working fewer hours because of cutbacks, that person will earn less. If the reduction in income is significant, that person is likely to fall into a lower tax bracket, which cushions the decline in income.

Fiscal Policy and Aggregate Demand

We can illustrate the impact of such fiscal policies with the aggregate demand curve AD. **Figure 15.4** shows a single aggregate supply curve and two aggregate demand curves. When aggregate demand is weak, the economy would be at point **a**, where AD^0 intersects AS. Increases in government spending or tax reductions could shift aggregate demand to AD^1 and move the economy to point **b**, where both real GDP and the price level are higher.

Because aggregate demand basically is the sum of C + I + G + F, it makes little difference which sector provides the stimulus. As long as government policies cause the spending of one sector to expand, AD will shift to the right.

Limitations of Fiscal Policy

Keynes envisioned the role of government spending as a counterbalance to changes in investment spending. Ideally, the government would increase its spending to offset declines in business spending, and conversely government would decrease spending whenever business spending recovered. In practice, however, the federal government generally has not been able to limit or reduce spending. **W**

As a result, the most effective fiscal policies to counter business cycles are the automatic stabilizers. The advantage of the stabilizers is the speed at which they can be implemented because the legislation is already approved.

✓**Reading Check** **Analyzing** Why are Keynes's ideas important in the study of economics?

Policies for Growth

Objective: Understand how a reduction in interest rates can trigger economic growth.

Focus: Ask students to speculate about why the Federal Reserve Board would cut interest rates.

Teach: Have students complete the activity.

Assess: Call on students to share their answers.

Close: Ask students to write a paragraph summarizing how cuts in interest rates can impact the economy as a whole.

Differentiated Instruction Strategies

BL Have students write a brief article to accompany one of the headlines.

AL Ask students to write about the negative effects that excessive interest rate reductions could cause.

ELL Instruct students to write a definition for the term *interest rate*. Allow them to use a dictionary, if necessary.

Supply-Side Policies

MAIN Idea Supply-side economics focuses on policies that increase production through less government and lower taxes.

Economics and You If you and your family had to pay less in taxes, would you spend or save the extra money? Read on to find out what supply-siders think.

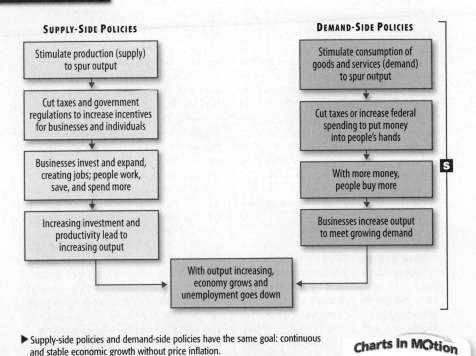

Supply-side policies are policies designed to stimulate output and lower unemployment by increasing production rather than by stimulating demand. The supply-side view gained support in the late 1970s because demand-side policies did not seem to be controlling the nation's growing unemployment and inflation. In the 1980s, supply-side policies became the hallmark of President Ronald Reagan's administration.

The differences between supply-side policies and demand-side policies are smaller than most people realize. Both policies, which are summarized in **Figure 15.5,** have the same goal: increasing production and decreasing unemployment without increasing inflation.

Smaller Role for Government

A key goal for supply-siders is reducing government's role in the economy. One way to do this is to reduce the number of federal agencies. Another way is to spend less at the federal level. Yet another way is to lessen the government's role by relaxing

supply-side policies economic policies designed to stimulate the economy by increasing production

Figure 15.5 ► Comparing Supply-Side and Demand-Side Policies

SUPPLY-SIDE POLICIES

Stimulate production (supply) to spur output
↓
Cut taxes and government regulations to increase incentives for businesses and individuals
↓
Businesses invest and expand, creating jobs; people work, save, and spend more
↓
Increasing investment and productivity lead to increasing output

DEMAND-SIDE POLICIES

Stimulate consumption of goods and services (demand) to spur output
↓
Cut taxes or increase federal spending to put money into people's hands
↓
With more money, people buy more
↓
Businesses increase output to meet growing demand

With output increasing, economy grows and unemployment goes down

▶ Supply-side policies and demand-side policies have the same goal: continuous and stable economic growth without price inflation.

Economic Analysis *How does the role of the government differ under supply-side and demand-side policies?*

Charts In MOtion
See StudentWorks™ Plus or glencoe.com.

D Differentiated Instruction

Visual/Spatial Have students draw a cartoon illustrating one or more of the concepts related to supply-side economics. Inform students that they may include relevant people (Reagan, for example) or events (savings and loan deregulation, for example) in their cartoons. **OL**

S Skill Practice

Using Tables and Charts
Ask: How are supply-side policies and demand-side policies similar? *(Both may use tax cuts, both intend for people to spend more money, and both have the goal of higher output and lower unemployment.)* **OL**

Economic Analysis

Answer: Under supply-side economics, the government's role in the economy is limited. With demand-side economics, the role of the government in the economy is expanded.

Leveled Activities

BL Reading Essentials and Note-Taking Guide, p. 130

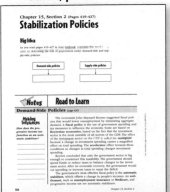

OL Authentic Assessment Strategies and Activities, p. 21

AL Enrichment Activities, p. 15

Figure 15.6 ▶ **Tax Rates and Tax Receipts**

▶ The Laffer curve is a hypothetical relationship between federal income tax rates and tax revenues. Panel A illustrates the argument that lower individual income tax rates would generate higher tax collections, as shown in the movement from **a** to **b**. Panel B shows that federal tax revenues declined after individual income tax rates were reduced in 2001.

Economic Analysis *How does personal income in 2000 and 2005 compare to individual income tax receipts during the same years?*

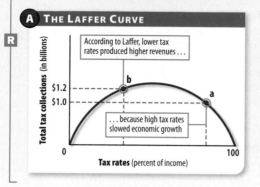

A THE LAFFER CURVE

According to Laffer, lower tax rates produced higher revenues . . .

. . . because high tax rates slowed economic growth

Total tax collections (in billions)
$1.2
$1.0
0
Tax rates (percent of income)
100

B TAX RECEIPTS

Year	Personal income (in billions)	Individual income tax receipts (in billions)
2000	$8,430	$1,004
2001	8,724	994
2002	8,882	858
2003	9,164	794
2004	9,731	809
2005	10,239	927

Source: *Economic Report of the President*

deregulation relaxation or removal of government regulations on business activities

or removing government regulations that restrict the activities of firms in certain industries—a process called **deregulation**.

Deregulation is a major objective of supply-siders. The policy has been popular among politicians ever since President Reagan deregulated the savings and loan industry in the 1980s. Since then, the American economy has seen a flood of deregulation ranging from airlines and banking to telecommunications and interstate trucking.

Lower Federal Taxes

Supply-siders also target the federal tax burden on individuals and businesses. They believe that if taxes are too high, people will not want to work as much, and businesses will therefore produce less. Lower tax rates, they argue, allow individuals to keep more of the money they earn, which encourages them to work harder. This would give workers more money to

spend in the long run. Government revenues would also increase, as additional business activity leads to greater production, resulting in greater tax collections.

During the 1980s, somewhat optimistic supply-siders argued that lower individual income tax rates would stimulate the economy so much that the government could collect even more taxes than before. This idea of increased tax revenue was formalized in the Laffer curve—a hypothetical relationship between federal income tax rates and tax revenues.

The Laffer curve shown in **Panel A** of **Figure 15.6** illustrates the expected gain in tax revenues when taxes were reduced from point **a** to point **b**. This proposition was the basis for President Reagan's 1981 tax cut, which reduced the tax rates for individual income taxes 25 percent over a three-year period. The Laffer curve was popular at the time because it gave people a seemingly sound reason to have lower marginal tax brackets.

When President George W. Bush was elected in 2000, he also made individual income tax cuts one of his highest priorities. The first round of his proposed tax cuts was passed in 2001, and several extensions followed in subsequent years.

However, as **Panel B** in Figure 15.6 shows, individual income tax receipts generally declined from 2000 to 2004, even though personal income rose in each of those years. Unfortunately, the increased tax revenue collections predicted by the Laffer curve never materialized, although it is highly likely that the increase in personal income worked to stimulate economic growth.

Impact of Supply-Side Policies

The aggregate supply and demand curves can illustrate the impact of supply-side policies. As **Figure 15.7** shows, when aggregate supply is low, the economy is at point **a**. This is the point where the original aggregate demand curve AS^0 intersects with the aggregate demand curve **AD**.

If supply-side policies were successful, more would be produced at every price level. The aggregate supply curve would then shift to AS^1, and the point of macroeconomic equilibrium would move to **b**. As long as there was no corresponding change in aggregate demand, real output would grow, and the price level would come down.

Limitations of Supply-Side Policies

One limitation of supply-side policies is a lack of enough experience with them to know how they affect the economy. Even aggregate supply and aggregate demand are largely conceptual, making it difficult to predict the exact consequence of any particular supply-side policy.

In the case of the Laffer curve, total personal income tax collections, when adjusted for inflation, actually declined after the implementation of President Reagan's 1981 tax reductions. They declined again after the Bush tax cuts of 2001. The result was

that one of the main foundations of the supply-side school—that tax cuts would lead to higher tax revenues—proved to be false. Even so, policies that promote productivity, reduce unnecessary paperwork, or otherwise stimulate the economy to grow to its maximum potential are certainly worthwhile. Almost everyone, including demand-siders, favors these policies.

Finally, we should note that supply-side economic policies are designed to promote economic growth rather than to remedy economic instability. Many economists believe that supply-side policies during both the Reagan and the Bush presidencies weakened the automatic stabilizers by making the federal tax structure less progressive and by reducing many "safety net" programs. Both actions may have stimulated growth. However, neither was designed to add to short-term economic stability.

✓Reading Check Interpreting What are the main goals of supply-side economists?

Figure 15.7 ▶ **Supply-Side Policies and Aggregate Supply**

THE AGGREGATE SUPPLY CURVE

▶ Supply-side policies are designed to increase aggregate supply through decreased government spending and involvement as well as lower taxes.

Economic Analysis *What happens to the price level when the aggregate supply curve shifts to the right?*

C Critical Thinking

Theorizing Tell students: In the 1980s, supply-side economics were sometimes referred to as "trickle-down economics." **Ask:** Why do you think supply-side polices were called this? *(The tax cuts and relaxed regulations were designed to increase the productivity of manufacturers and the wealthy, who in turn would create more jobs for the middle- and lower-classes. The benefits of supply-side policies were thus intended to "trickle down" to all elements of society.)* **OL**

✓Reading Check **Answer:** lower taxes and less government regulation, increased investing and business expansion, more jobs and more consumer spending, increased economic productivity and economic growth, less unemployment

Economic Analysis **Answer:** It drops.

Additional Support

Extending the Content

Impact of Reaganomics The impact of President Reagan's economic policies remains the subject of intense debate, just as it was in the 1980s. Supporters point out that Reagan's tax cuts and deregulation efforts sparked a full recovery for the U.S. economy, which was mired in a severe downturn when he took office in 1981. Inflation, interest rates, and unemployment fell during the Reagan years, and the economy entered the longest period of continual expansion in American history. On the other hand, Reagan's supply-side policies created record budget deficits and a staggering national debt. Detractors also maintain that real wages declined during the Reagan years and that the growth of other leading world economies outpaced that of the United States in the 1980s.

D Differentiated Instruction

Intrapersonal Have students review the main ideas of demand-side, supply-side, and monetary policies. Ask students to write an essay describing their opinions about each of the three policies. Instruct students to include in their essays which policy they believe is best for the United States and the reasons for their selection. **OL**

S Skill Practice

Making Generalizations

Ask: Based on the text, what usually happened to the U.S. economy during wartime? *(expansive monetary policy and inflation)* Why do you think this happened? *(Students may note that the government needed money to fight the war, so it allowed excessive monetary growth, which brought about inflation.)* **OL**

Caption Answer:
more borrowing and increased demand

Hands-On Chapter Project

Step 2

Effects of Government Stabilization Policies

Step 2: Assessing Government Policies. Students will create graphs showing the effects of different government economic policies.

Directions: Have students return to the groups formed in Step 1. Ask groups to research examples from U.S. history when each of the three types of policies described in this section were implemented (for example, demand-side policies during

426

Money Supply and Interest Rates
When the Fed decreases interest rates, more money becomes available to grow the economy. *What is the short-run impact of lower interest rates?*

MCCOY © 2001 Glen McCoy. Reprinted with permission of UNIVERSAL PRESS SYNDICATE. All rights reserved.

Monetary Policies

MAIN Idea Monetarist policies seek steady economic growth by controlling the money supply.

Economics and You Neither demand-siders nor supply-siders consider the money supply. Read on to learn why monetarists disagree with both.

Both demand-side policies and supply-side policies are concerned with stimulating production and employment. Neither assigns much importance to the money supply. An approach called **monetarism**, however, places primary importance on the role of money in the economy.

Monetarists believe that fluctuations in the money supply can be a destabilizing element that leads to unemployment and inflation. Therefore, they favor policies that lead to stable, long-term monetary growth at levels low enough to control inflation.

monetarism school of thought stressing the importance of stable monetary growth to control inflation and stimulate long-term economic growth

Skills Handbook
See page **R52** to learn about **Sequencing Events.**

Short-Run Impacts

A monetary policy in which the money supply is tightened is called a contractionary monetary policy. In the short run, this

426 UNIT 4 Macroeconomics: Performance and Stabilization

---

policy can raise interest rates. Higher interest rates might be desirable if the economy is growing too fast and prices are rising. The higher interest rates would slow consumer and business borrowing, leading to a decrease in aggregate demand. As a result, the aggregate demand curve would shift to the left, lowering both the price level and real GDP.

If the economy is growing too slowly, an expansionary policy can increase the money supply and lower interest rates. This would reduce the cost of consumer and business borrowing and increase aggregate demand. The aggregate demand curve would then shift to the right, causing real GDP and the price level to increase.

In the short run, monetary policy affects interest rates. Changes in the level of interest rates can have a significant impact on the demand for real GDP. In the longer run, however, monetary policy can have very different results.

Long Run Impacts

Expansionary monetary policy, with a larger money supply, can lower interest rates. At the same time, it could also increase the possibility of future inflation, as past events have shown. During the Revolutionary War, so much money was printed that prices rose dramatically, and the Continental dollar soon became worthless. Prices also increased significantly during the Civil War when too many greenbacks were printed. Finally, excessive monetary growth allowed by the Fed to help the government finance the Vietnam War resulted in the inflation of the 1970s.

The money supply can grow over time, but how fast should it be allowed to grow? According to the monetarists, it should grow at a slow but steady rate. Specifically, the rates of growth of real GDP and productivity would determine the rate at which the money supply grows.

For example, with real GDP growing by 3 percent and productivity growing by 1 percent, the money supply could be allowed

---

the Great Depression, supply-side policies during the 1980s, the Fed lowering interest rates in 2001). Have each group create three sets of graphs showing the effects of the policies they researched. Students, for example, may draw a line graph showing how federal spending increased in the 1930s, or they may create a bar graph showing how unemployment rates changed after interest rates were lowered in 2001. Have students present their three sets of graphs to the class.

Summarizing Instruct students to work together within their groups to write a short summary report assessing the economic impact of the three policies they researched. **OL**

(Chapter Project continued in Section 3.)

to grow at about 4 percent without causing inflation. At this rate, there would be just enough extra money each year to buy the additional goods and services the economy produces.

This approach to inflation control is in sharp contrast to approaches that other administrations tried earlier. In the early 1970s, for example, President Richard Nixon attempted to stop inflation by imposing **wage-price controls**—regulations that make it illegal for businesses to give workers raises or to raise prices without the **explicit** permission of the government. Most monetarists at the time said the controls would not work. Events soon proved them correct, as prices rose despite the legislated controls.

Use of Monetary Policy

Economists have discovered that timing can be difficult when it comes to implementing monetary policy. An expansionary monetary policy may affect the economy right away—or several years later. The same thing is true for a contractionary monetary policy. In either case, the desired changes may happen immediately or only after a lag. For this reason, monetarists argue that changes in the money supply should be gradual so that they do not destabilize the economy.

Because of these lags, monetary policy does not seem to be very effective in reducing short-term unemployment. For example, when the Fed aggressively lowered interest rates in 2001 to move the economy out of the recession, it took several years for the unemployment rate to come down. In the end, most monetarists argue that monetary policy can be used to maintain long-term price stability. However, it must be used with caution because its short-run impacts are uncertain.

wage-price controls policies and regulations making it illegal for firms to give raises or raise prices without government permission

R

✓ Reading Check **Summarizing** What problems are associated with expansionist monetary policy?

R **Reading Strategy**

Predicting Have students write a paragraph predicting the type of monetary policy, if any, the Fed is likely to pursue in the next few months. *(Answers will vary based on the current economic climate. If inflation is high, then the Fed may pursue a tight monetary policy. If unemployment is high, the Fed may promote an expansionary monetary policy.)* **OL**

✓ Reading Check **Answer:** high inflation, devalued currency

Assess

Use the Interactive Tutor Self-Assessment CD-ROM to review Section 2, and then assign the Section 2 Review as homework or as an in-class activity.

Close

Organizing Ask students to create a graphic organizer that includes the main points of the three economic policies described in this section. **OL**

SECTION 2 Review

Vocabulary

1. **Explain** the significance of Medicare, fiscal policy, Keynesian economics, multiplier, accelerator, automatic stabilizer, entitlements, unemployment insurance, supply-side policies, deregulation, monetarism, and wage-price controls.

Main Ideas

2. **Listing** What are the assumptions of supply-siders?

3. **Explaining** What problems exist for monetary policy?

4. **Identifying** Use a graphic organizer like the one below to identify the tools of demand-side policies.

Tools of demand-side policies

Critical Thinking

5. **The BIG Idea** How do supply-side economists and demand-side economists differ with regard to the role of government in the economy?

6. **Drawing Conclusions** Do you agree with the opinion that fiscal policy is ineffective? Explain your reasons for agreeing or disagreeing.

7. **Analyzing Information** According to monetarists, how do fluctuations in the money supply affect the economy?

8. **Analyzing Visuals** Look at the photo on page 420. How does it reflect the views of John Maynard Keynes on the role of government in the economy?

Applying Economics

9. **Deregulation** Identify an industry in your state that has been or is being deregulated. Why did legislators make the decision to deregulate the industry? Did deregulation have the expected benefits? Were there any unanticipated costs? Explain.

CHAPTER 15 Economic Stabilization Policies **427**

Review **SECTION 2**

Answers

1. All definitions can be found in the section and the Glossary.
2. deregulation and lower taxes will increase aggregate supply
3. uncertain short-term impacts; possible future inflation with an expansive monetary policy; high interest rates and a decline in borrowing with a tight monetary policy
4. taxing; spending; automatic stabilizers
5. Supply-side economists believe the government's role in the economy should be reduced through cutting federal

agencies and deregulating business. Demand-side economists believe the government should take a greater role in the economy through increased spending and possibly by lowering taxes and enacting other measures to encourage business and consumer spending.
6. Answers will vary, but students should demonstrate a clear understanding of the limits of fiscal policy.
7. If the money supply grows too fast, then inflation will result; if the money supply

contracts too much, then productivity will fall.
8. The government-funded Hoover Dam is an example of the government spending money to offset the decline in investment-sector spending that occurred during the Great Depression.
9. Answers will vary, but students should explain why legislators decided to deregulate the industry (to increase competition, for example) and the effects of this deregulation.

Teach

Narrative Writing Direct students to review the main economic ideas of John Maynard Keynes. Ask students to then write a story in which Keynes uses a time machine to travel to the United States today. Instruct students to include in their stories Keynes's likely reactions to, and opinions about, the current economic situation in this country. **OL**

Examining the Profile

Answers:

1. Such a policy broke with longstanding governmental practice, and leaders in the 1930s generally believed that laissez-faire policies would allow the market to correct itself in the long run.

2. A government should spend money, taking on debt if necessary, to help lift a country out of a recession or depression; the government should save money during prosperous times to prevent inflation.

Additional Support

Profiles in Economics

John Maynard Keynes (1883–1946)

- his "Keynesian economics" caused governments to implement fiscal policy
- instrumental in the planning of the World Bank

The Long Run

During the Great Depression of the 1930s, government leaders desperately sought solutions to widespread unemployment and poverty. Yet they remained reluctant to "unbalance" the budget by using federal money to help the nation's people directly. Instead, they believed that laissez-faire policies would allow the market to correct itself in the long run.

Enter Keynes

A brilliant intellectual, John Maynard Keynes established a reputation for straight talking and insightful critique early in his career. He served as an adviser to the British Treasury and as a British representative at the World War I peace conference at Versailles. He correctly predicted that the high reparations imposed on Germany after World War I would lead to another war.

As an economist, Keynes was not impressed with perfectly balanced budgets. In fact, he considered balanced budgets—when that meant government inaction—to be disastrous if a nation's consumer and business sectors had no money to spend or invest to create jobs. In his masterpiece, *The General Theory of Employment, Interest, and Money* (1936), Keynes argued that governments should spend money—and even take on debt—to help correct an economic recession or depression. They should then save money during an overly successful period to prevent inflation.

To Keynes, it did not help anyone to wait for the long run because "in the long run we are all dead." His theories were revolutionary, and they provided much needed insight into the workings of a depression-era economy. Soon, the label *Keynesian economics* stood for any government spending or taxing policies designed to stimulate the private sector.

John Maynard Keynes is widely regarded as the most influential economist of the twentieth century. His theories led the U.S. government to take an active role in preventing economic instability that could lead to widespread joblessness.

Examining the Profile

1. **Analyzing Information** Why were government leaders reluctant to help people during the Great Depression?
2. **Summarizing Information** What is the basic premise of Keynesian economics?

Activity: Collaborative Learning

Preparing an Exhibit Divide the class into small groups. Instruct students to use reliable online or print resources to research the implementation of Keynesian economics during the Great Depression. Ask groups to then prepare an exhibit based on their findings. Encourage students to be creative when thinking of ideas for their exhibits. Possible ideas include photos of Keynes from 1930s newspapers; a model of the

Hoover Dam or other government-funded projects during the Depression; a copy of *The General Theory of Employment, Interest, and Money*; logos of New Deal agencies; a graph of government spending in the 1930s; and so on. Have groups display their exhibits in the class. Ask students to explain the various components as you review their exhibits. **AL**

Economics and Politics

GUIDE TO READING

Section Preview

In this section, you will learn that economic policies change as time and circumstances change.

Content Vocabulary

- monetary policy (p. 431)
- baby boomers (p. 432)
- Council of Economic Advisers (p. 433)

Academic Vocabulary

- ideology (p. 431)
- advocates (p. 433)

Reading Strategy

Identifying As you read the section, complete a graphic organizer similar to the one below by identifying the different kinds of fiscal policy.

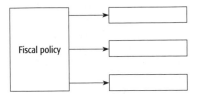

Fiscal policy →

Focus

Bellringer
Daily Focus Transparency 63

GUIDE TO READING

Answers to Graphic:
discretionary fiscal policy; passive fiscal policy; structural fiscal policy

ISSUES IN THE NEWS —TIME

Enthusiastic Capitalism

American culture is today, as ever, uniquely suited for growth, innovation, and advancement.

The most obvious bedrock of success is entrepreneurial spirit. The U.S. has the most risk-taking, most laissez-faire, least regulated economy in the advanced Western world. America is heartily disdained by its coddled and controlled European cousins for its cowboy capitalism. But it is precisely America's tolerance for creative destruction—industries failing, others rising, workers changing jobs and cities and skills with an [enthusiasm] and [casualness] that Europeans find astonishing—that keeps its economy churning and advancing. . . . The mistake of the Soviets, Japanese, and so many others was to assume that creativity could be achieved with enough government planning and funding. . . . ■

As we look at the economic history of the United States, it is clear that times are better than ever. Inflation is largely under control, and the economy is larger and more productive than ever. Recessions still occur, of course, but business cycles have generally turned into fluctuations, and economic expansions are longer than ever.

Major domestic or even international events can temporarily interrupt the economy, but capitalistic market economies have a remarkable ability to cope with adversity. If anything, the task before us is to manage our prosperity in a way that both improves our economic health and benefits everyone.

CHAPTER 15   Economic Stabilization Policies   429

Resource Manager

R Reading Strategies	**C** Critical Thinking	**D** Differentiated Instruction	**W** Writing Support	**S** Skill Practice
Teacher Edition • Using Context Clues, p. 430 **Additional Resources** • Guid. Read. Act., p. 45 • Read. Ess. & Note-Taking Guide, p. 133	**Teacher Edition** • Speculating, p. 431 • Making Predictions, p. 432 **Additional Resources** • Econ. Concepts Trans., Strat. & Act., p. 35	**Teacher Edition** • Adv. Learners, p. 430 • Visual/Spatial, p. 432 **Additional Resources** • Authentic Assess., p. 20 • Reteach. Act., p. 15	**Teacher Edition** • Persuasive Writing, p. 431 **Additional Resources** • Writer's Guidebook • Reading and Study Skills Fold., pp. 61, 62	**Teacher Edition** • Making Inferences, p. 430 • Problems and Solutions, p. 433 • Drawing Con., p. 434 **Additional Resources** • Daily Focus Trans. 63, 78, 79

Teach

D Differentiated Instruction

Advanced Learners To help build discussion skills for gifted students, appoint two or three students to plan and lead a class or panel discussion on the different approaches of fiscal policy. **AL**

S Skill Practice

Making Inferences Ask: Based on this information, what can you infer about Congress after Roosevelt took office? *(Possible answer: Congress was controlled by the Democrats and was supportive of Roosevelt's ambitious agenda.)* **OL**

R Reading Strategy

Using Context Clues Have students write a definition of *lag* based on how the word is used in this paragraph. *(Possible answers: delay; holdup)* **Ask:** What context clues helped reveal the meaning of the word? *(Students should point out references to the passing of time, such as "takes several months" and "a year or more.")* **OL**

Differentiated Instruction

Critical Thinking Activities, p. 23

Changing Nature of Economic Policy

> **MAIN Idea** The government can influence the economy with discretionary, passive, or structural fiscal policies.

Economics and You Today, major recessions are rare in the United States. Read on to learn how this has affected government policies.

Fiscal policies are government attempts to influence the economy through taxing and spending actions. This may involve ways to speed up the economy with tax cuts or with additional federal spending. It may also include government efforts to slow the economy down by either increasing taxes or reducing spending.

D Types of Fiscal Policy

Several different kinds of spending and taxing policies exist. These fiscal policies can be either discretionary, passive, or structural.

Discretionary fiscal policy is policy that someone must choose to implement. It requires an action by Congress, the president, or an agency of government to take effect. One example is a federal expenditure to build a highway or renovate a downtown area in order to offset a decline in business spending. As you read in Chapter 10, about one-third of all federal spending is discretionary rather than mandatory.

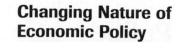

> ▶ **Early Practitioner** While John Maynard Keynes was widely credited as the first person to advocate fiscal policy to stimulate the economy in the mid-1930s, President Franklin D. Roosevelt preceded him by several years. When Roosevelt took office on March 4, 1933, the U.S. economy was suffering from its worst depression. With little economic theory to guide him, Roosevelt introduced 15 new bills during his first 100 days in office, some of which poured billions of dollars into state-run welfare and public-works programs. Roosevelt's aggressive use of discretionary fiscal policy was instrumental in helping the economy out of the Great Depression.

Passive fiscal policies do not require new or special action to go into effect. Instead, the policies react automatically when the economy changes. Examples of passive fiscal policies include unemployment insurance and Social Security benefits. In fact, most of the automatic stabilizers you learned about earlier are examples of passive fiscal policies.

Finally, *structural* fiscal policies are policies designed to strengthen the economy over a longer period of time. Examples include reforms of popular programs such as Social Security and welfare in order to make the programs financially secure and more effective in the long run. Most of the supply-side policies, which advocate a smaller role for government and lower taxes, are structural fiscal policies.

Decline of Discretionary Fiscal Policy

At one time, discretionary fiscal policies were the most popular economic policies. In the 1940s, massive government spending for World War II helped pull the economy out of the Great Depression. Both President Kennedy, in the early 1960s, and later President Reagan, in the early 1980s, used large tax cuts to get a sluggish economy moving again.

However, for several reasons discretionary fiscal policy is used less today. The first reason relates to the various lags that inevitably occur between recognizing that there is a problem and actually doing something about it. Suppose, for example, that the problem is a potential recession, and that the ideal remedy would be to spend $50 billion on roads and highways.

Policy makers first face a recognition lag because it normally takes several months to confirm that a recession is actually taking place. A legislative lag would follow because it may take a year or more for Congress to pass laws authorizing expenditures. This would be followed by an implementation lag because it often takes several more years to build the highways

---

Drawing Inferences and Making Conclusions

Objective: Categorize stabilization policies by drawing inferences based on available information.

Focus: Ask students to share instances in which they have made inferences.

Teach: Ask students whether each statement is an example of demand-side or supply-side economics.

Assess: Go over students' answers as a class.

Close: Ask students to think of other examples of supply-side or demand-side policies.

Differentiated Instruction Strategies

BL Explain reasons why each statement would be made by a supply-sider or a demand-sider.

AL Have students create a script for a debate between a supply-sider and a demand-sider.

ELL Ask students to explain *demand-side economics* in their own words.

and pump the money into the economy. In the end, the recession—which historically lasts for less than a year—will be over by the time the spending begins to stimulate the economy.

The second reason for the decline of discretionary fiscal policy is the gridlock that can occur when the political parties in Congress oppose each other's views on the budget. In both 1995 and 1996, for example, Congress shut down the federal government when Republicans and Democrats could not agree on the federal budget.

Ideology is the third reason. President Bush's tax cuts, for example, were based on the belief the American economy needed a structural change. As a result, in 2001 Bush proposed tax cuts that would extend to the year 2010 and beyond. Thus, the preference for structural policies has displaced the use of discretionary ones.

Rise of Monetary Policy

The declining use of discretionary fiscal policy left a void filled by the Federal Reserve System, which has the responsibility for conducting monetary policy. As you learned earlier, **monetary policy** involves changing the amount and availability of credit in order to influence interest rates.

Such a situation occurred during the recession of 2001. That recession was so mild and so short—lasting about eight months—that policymakers altogether ignored discretionary fiscal policy. In addition, Congress was preoccupied with a response to the terrorist attacks on September 11.

On the other hand, the Fed was actively lowering the discount rate on an almost monthly basis in order to stimulate the economy. The policy worked, and the Fed took much of the credit for the short duration and mild impact of the recession.

Of course, even the Fed is not above criticism. For example, the Fed's efforts to prevent inflation by raising interest rates in 2000 may have contributed to the 2001 slowdown. Even so, most members of

Congress believe that the power to create money and to manage the money supply should remain with an independent agency rather than with elected officials.

✓**Reading Check** **Summarizing** Why is discretionary fiscal policy used less and less frequently?

monetary policy actions by the Federal Reserve System to expand or contract the money supply in order to affect the cost and availability of credit *(also see page 400)*

CAREERS

Credit Manager

The Work

* Manage the preparation of financial reports

* Oversee a firm's granting of credit by establishing credit-rating criteria, determining credit ceilings, and monitoring the collections of past-due accounts

* Solicit business, authorize loans, and direct the investment of funds

Qualifications

* Ability to analyze detailed information and draw conclusions

* Excellent communication skills to explain complex financial data

* Expertise on government appropriations, budgeting, tax laws, and regulations

* Knowledge about global trade, changes in federal and state laws, and new financial instruments

* Bachelor's degree in business, finance, accounting, or a related field, with many positions requiring a master's degree in business administration, economics, finance, or risk management

Earnings

* Median annual earnings: $81,880

Job Growth Outlook

* Average

Source: *Occupational Outlook Handbook, 2006–2007 Edition*

C Critical Thinking

Speculating **Ask:** Why might President Bush's proposed tax cuts not extend to the year 2010 and beyond? *(Possible answer: Bush's term in office cannot extend past January 2009; the next president, as well as the Congress in 2009–2010, may not support Bush's tax cuts.)* **BL**

W Writing Support

Persuasive Writing Instruct students to search for recent news articles about the Fed in magazines, newspapers, and news Web sites. Ask students to write a letter to the editor expressing their opinions about the Fed's recent policies. Tell students to support their points with facts and convincing arguments. **OL**

✓**Reading Check** **Answer:** Reasons include lags that occur after recognition of a problem, gridlock in Congress, and ideological preferences of politicians for structural policies.

CHAPTER 15 Economic Stabilization Policies **431**

Leveled Activities

BL Reteaching Activities, p. 15

OL Reading and Study Skills Foldables, p. 62

AL Economic Concepts Transparencies, Strategies, and Activities, p. 35

D Differentiated Instruction

Visual/Spatial Have students draw a cartoon depicting how the views of an economist or economists can change. For example, a student may draw an economist sitting at a desk reading a book titled "supply-side economics." In a garbage can next to the desk is a book titled "demand-side economics." **OL**

C Critical Thinking

Making Predictions

Review with students the general concerns related to the issue of retiring baby boomers. **Ask: What economic problems do you think economists will focus on in the 2010s?** *(Answers may include bankruptcy of Social Security, massive national debt, and large trade deficits.)* **OL**

Caption Answer: Economists prioritize problems differently, they embrace theories based on the prevailing concerns of their times, and they have different ideologies.

Hands-On Chapter Project

Step 3

Effects of Government Stabilization Policies

Step 3: The Changing Nature of Economic Policy. Student groups will identify and categorize the differing views of economists over time.

Directions: Have students return to their project groups. Instruct each group to use library or reliable Internet resources to identify 10 different economists—one to represent each decade from the 1920s

---

Differing Opinions Economists have different ideas about economic policies, although they don't come to blows as in the cartoon. **Why do economists differ?**

Hang In There!

"ECONOMISTS. ONE'S A KEYNESIAN...THE OTHER ISN'T."

baby boomers people born in the United States during the historically high birthrate years from 1946 to 1964

Skills Handbook

See page **R41** to learn about *Evaluating Information.*

Economics and Politics Today

MAIN Idea Current conditions shape the views of economists and policy makers.

Economics and You Have you ever perceived an issue to be a certain way and then found out later that it was completely different? Read on to learn why economists' views change as well.

Choosing which economic policies will work best is difficult. When economists offer proposals that sometimes seem contradictory, it makes choosing even more difficult. These differences of opinions among economists, however, are smaller than most people realize.

Economic Politics

In the 1800s, the science of economics was known as "political economics." After a while, economists broke away from the political theorists and tried to establish economics as a science in its own right.

In recent years, the two fields have merged again. This time, however, they have done so in a way better described as "economic politics." Today, politicians are

concerned largely with the economic consequences of what they do. Most of the major debates in Congress are over spending, taxes, and other budgetary matters.

Why Economists Differ

Economists who choose one policy over another normally do so because they think that some problems are more critical than others. For example, one economist might think that unemployment is the crucial issue, while another believes that inflation is. Yet if we surveyed all economists on the best way to deal with one specific problem, their recommendations would be much more consistent.

Another reason economists differ is that most economic theories are a product of the times. The unemployment and other problems that occurred during the Great Depression influenced a generation of demand-side economists. Because the government sector was so small during the 1930s, supply-side policies designed to make government's role even smaller probably would not have helped much then.

Later, from the 1960s through 1980s, the monetarists gained influence because of the slow decline of discretionary fiscal policy. Then, by the 1980s, the ideological rejection of "big government" created a generation of supply-siders who thought that the key to economic growth was a smaller government.

By 2010 and beyond, the large population of retired **baby boomers,** who were born between 1946 and 1964, will have its own unique problems. The problems facing this group may well prompt another generation of economists to focus on a whole new set of issues. In the end, then, the views of economists are very much affected by the problems of the current moment.

Council of Economic Advisers

Generally, economists and politicians work together fairly closely. To help keep track of the economy, the president has a

---

through the current decade. Inform students that each of their selected economists must have published a major economic work in the decade that he or she represents. For example, John Kenneth Galbraith with *The Affluent Society* (1958) and *The New Industrial State* (1967) could represent either the 1950s or 1960s. Ask each group to create a database for their 10 economists. Categories for these databases should include name, decade, major publications, economic

theory (can be summarized into a paragraph), and major events that likely influenced the economists' views.

Describing Ask students to write a short paper discussing how economic theories change over time. **OL**

(Chapter Project continued in Visual Summary.)

Council of Economic Advisers, a three-member group that reports on economic developments and proposes strategies. The economists are the advisers, while the politicians direct or implement the policies. In its role as "the president's intelligence arm in the war against the business cycle," the council gathers information and makes recommendations.

The president listens to the economists' advice but may not be willing or able to follow it. For example, if the president **advocates** a balanced budget, the economic advisers may recommend raising taxes to achieve this goal. If one of the president's campaign pledges was not to raise taxes, however, the president might reject the advisers' suggestion and let a deficit develop.

Increased Public Understanding

Despite disagreeing on some points, economists have had considerable success with the description, analysis, and explanation of economic activity. They have developed many statistical measures of the economy's performance. Economists also have constructed models that are helpful with economic analysis and explanation. All of these tools are necessary if we are to understand the opportunity costs of the trade-offs we must make when we select one policy over another.

In the process, economists have helped the American people become more aware of the workings of the economy. This awareness has benefited everyone, from the student just starting out to the politician who must answer to the voters.

Today economists know enough about the economy to prevent a depression like the one in the 1930s. It is doubtful that economists know enough—or can persuade others that they know enough—to avoid minor recessions. Even so, they can devise policies to stimulate growth, help disadvantaged groups when unemployment rises or inflation strikes, and generally make the American economy more successful.

✓Reading Check **Interpreting** What is the role of the Council of Economic Advisers?

Economics ONLINE

Student Web Activity
Visit the *Economics: Principles and Practices* Web site at glencoe.com and click on *Chapter 15– Student Web Activities* for an activity on the Council of Economic Advisers.

Council of Economic Advisers three-member group that devises strategies and advises the president of the United States on economic matters

---

S Skill Practice

Problems and Solutions
Ask: Do you think the United States could enter another Great Depression today? Why or why not? *(Students answering "no" may point out that economists now have a better understanding of how the economy works. Students answering "yes" may suggest that events overseas could trigger a depression.)* **OL**

✓Reading Check **Answer:** It gathers information, reports on economic developments, and proposes strategies to the president.

Assess

 Use the Interactive Tutor Self-Assessment CD-ROM to review Section 3, and then assign the Section 3 Review as homework or as an in-class activity.

Close

Identifying Central Issues
Ask students to write a short paper explaining the central issues in this section. **OL**

Review **SECTION 3**

SECTION 3 Review

Vocabulary
1. **Explain** the significance of monetary policy, baby boomers, and Council of Economic Advisers.

Main Ideas
2. **Explaining** Why have structural fiscal policies replaced discretionary fiscal policies?

3. **Describing** What actions did the Fed take in response to the recession of 2001?

4. **Describing** Use a graphic organizer like the one below to describe the different types of fiscal policy.

Types of Fiscal Policy		
Type	Description	Example
Discretionary		
Passive		
Structural		

Critical Thinking
5. **The BIG Idea** Why do economists have differing views over which policy is most effective in producing stability and economic growth?

6. **Drawing Conclusions** Why do some people blame the Fed for the recession of 2001?

7. **Analyzing Information** Why might monetary and fiscal policy conflict during an election year?

8. **Analyzing Visuals** Look at the cartoon on the previous page. Why do you think economists care so strongly about their views?

Applying Economics
9. **Fiscal and Monetary Policy** Suppose that Congress passes a massive tax cut during an election year even though inflation is very high. What actions might the Fed take in response? Explain your answer.

Answers

1. All definitions can be found in the section and the Glossary.
2. time lag between recognizing a problem and acting on it; Congressional gridlock; economic legislation is now often driven by ideology
3. lowered interest rates on a monthly basis to stimulate the economy
4. **Discretionary:** description—must be implemented by Congress, the president, or a governmental agency; example—federal expenditures to build a highway. **Passive:** description—occurs automatically when economy changes; example—unemployment insurance. **Structural:** description—designed to strengthen the economy over a period of time; example—Social Security
5. They have differing views on the most pressing economic problems.
6. Some believe that the Fed contributed to the 2001 recession by raising interest rates too much in 2000.
7. Politicians may implement certain economic policies to win votes, while at the same time the Fed may implement a contradictory policy that addresses another economic concern.
8. Answers will vary, but students should recognize that economists believe that economic policies affect millions of people.
9. The Fed would likely contract the money supply to reduce inflation.

Teach

S Skill Practice

Drawing Conclusions Ask:
What does the success of the Geek Squad suggest about Best Buy's product line? *(Possible answer: The products Best Buy sells are complicated; when they break or do not function properly, the average person is not able to solve the problem without help.)* **OL**

Analyzing the Impact

Answers:

1. It is a business model that determined the lifestyle of Best Buy's most profitable customers. It helped Best Buy target the customer groups that would maximize company revenues.

2. by employing a tech support team (the Geek Squad) that provides emergency service and support for Best Buy customers

---

Additional Support

CASE STUDY
Best Buy Gets Better

Too Big, Too Fast

In 1996 Best Buy found itself in a predicament. Despite astounding growth over a three-year period, the company had not changed the way it did business. As a result, its stock tumbled and profits dwindled. The company switched gears, opting for a smaller array of products, a new pricing strategy, and new store layouts.

Customer Focus

In addition, Best Buy turned to a business model called Customer Insight that determined the lifestyles of its most profitable customers. The five segments Best Buy identified include wealthy professionals desiring the best technology products, young males seeking the latest technology and accessories, fathers looking for technology to improve entertainment, mothers on the lookout for gadgets to enrich their children, and small-business owners who use technology to increase their profits. Best Buy began targeting these groups, increasing revenues from $7.8 million in 1997 to more than $30 million in 2006.

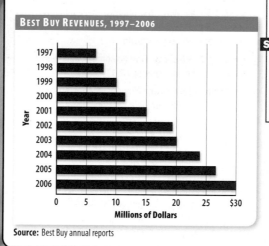

BEST BUY REVENUES, 1997–2006

Year	Millions of Dollars
1997	~7
1998	~8
1999	~10
2000	~11
2001	~15
2002	~19
2003	~20
2004	~23
2005	~26
2006	~30

(Scale: 0, 5, 10, 15, 20, 25, $30 — Millions of Dollars)

Source: Best Buy annual reports

Geek Squad

Best Buy still faced strong competition from other technology retailers such as Circuit City. Enter, the Geek Squad. This army of 2,500 "agents" provides emergency services 24 hours a day, seven days a week, 525,600 minutes a year to fix computers, printers, and networks for individual customers and businesses alike. The ability to provide full technology service and support for the products sold in stores helped Best Buy win back customers and shareholders.

Analyzing the Impact

1. **Summarizing** What is Customer Insight, and how did it help change the way Best Buy does business?

2. **Drawing Conclusions** How did Best Buy differentiate itself from other technology retailers?

---

434   UNIT 4   Macroeconomics: Performance and Stabilization

Activity: Interdisciplinary Connection

Daily Life Have students find a Best Buy advertisement, such as the ones commonly inserted into newspapers. Ask students to identify at least three products in the advertisement that a customer from each of the five target segments listed in this feature might buy (for example, a notebook computer might appeal to a wealthy professional desiring the best technology products; a high-definition TV might appeal to a young male seeking the latest technology). Instruct students to cut out the pictures of the products and create a collage that illustrates buying preferences of the five customer segments targeted by Best Buy. **OL**

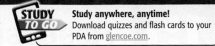

Study anywhere, anytime! Download quizzes and flash cards to your PDA from glencoe.com.

Visual Summary

CHAPTER
15

▶ **Aggregate Supply and Demand** In order to understand the economy as a whole, we need to study aggregate supply and demand. The economy reaches macroeconomic equilibrium when aggregate supply and demand are equal at a given price level.

MACROECONOMIC EQUILIBRIUM

▶ **Stabilization Policies** The government can pursue three different policies to stabilize and grow the economy.

Demand-Side Policies	Supply-Side Policies	Monetary Policies
• Stimulate consumption of goods and services (demand) • Introduced by John Maynard Keynes • Government's role is to offset changes in investment-sector spending • Includes automatic stabilizers	• Stimulate production of goods and services (supply) • Smaller role for government • Lower taxes • Difficult to predict results	• Focuses on money supply • Money supply to grow at a steady rate to match growth of real GDP and production • Difficult to time policy

▶ **Influences on Economic Policies** Several factors influence economic policies.

CHAPTER 15 Economic Stabilization Policies **435**

Analyzing Remind students that both supply-side policies and demand-side policies can impact the macroeconomic equilibrium. **Ask:** Which direction would the macroequilibrium point move on the graph if supply-side policies were successful? *(down and to the right)* Which direction would the macroequilibrium point move on the graph if demand-side policies were successful? *(up and to the right)* **OL**

Simulating Provide students with the following scenario: *The United States is experiencing a severe recession. Nationwide unemployment is at 10 percent, but in some regions it stands at 25 percent. Inflation, however, is running at an annual rate of 3 percent. Consumer and business spending are down. GDP has fallen 5 percent over the last 3 quarters, and government revenues have declined.* Have students select an economic policy—demand-side, supply-side, or monetarism— to bring the United States out of the recession. Direct students to write a brief report detailing and justifying the actions they would take. **AL**

Hands-On Chapter Project
Step 4: Wrap Up

Effects of Government Stabilization Policies

Step 4: Complete the Assessment. Students will synthesize what they learned in the first three steps.

Directions: Have students reassemble into their previously established project groups. Have students in each group compile the data they have gathered in the previous steps into a three-ring binder. Ask groups to write a short paper explaining how their findings in this project relate to the Big Idea. Instruct groups to next write an essay predicting which economic policy will likely prevail in the United States over the next decade. Students should explain the reasons for their selection. Have groups add their Big Idea papers and prediction essays to their binders before turning in their work. **OL**

ExamView®
Assessment Suite

This easy-to-use software includes extensive question banks and allows you to create fully customized tests that can be administered in print or online.

Review Content Vocabulary

1.–12. Students' paragraphs will vary but should demonstrate understanding of economic stabilization policies.

Review Academic Vocabulary

13.–18. Students' sentences should reflect a clear understanding of the terms and the goals of the three economic policies.

Review the Main Ideas

19. the quantity of real GDP demanded is equal to the real GDP supplied

20. Supply curve: what a firm is willing to produce at various price levels. Aggregate supply curve: output of economy at various price levels; includes prices of everything produced.

21. how to increase real GDP without unduly increasing the price level

22. Increase AS: anything that decreases production costs. Decrease AS: the reverse. Increase AD: anything that increases consumer spending. Decrease AD: the reverse.

23. business investment sector

24. Multiplier: magnified effects of a change in investment spending. Accelerator: change in investment

Review Content Vocabulary

Use all of the terms below to write a paragraph about government policies to stabilize the economy.

1. aggregate supply
2. supply-side policies
3. fiscal policy
4. aggregate demand
5. monetarism
6. automatic stabilizer
7. deregulation
8. accelerator
9. macroeconomic equilibrium
10. monetary policy
11. wage-price controls
12. Keynesian economics

Review Academic Vocabulary

Use the words below to construct three sentences that summarize the goals of demand-side, supply-side, and monetarist economic policies.

13. unduly
14. framework
15. unstable
16. explicit
17. ideology
18. advocates

Review the Main Ideas

Section 1 *(pages 413–417)*

19. Describe the circumstances under which prices are consistent with a given level of real GDP.

20. Explain the difference between the supply curve of a firm and the aggregate supply curve.

21. State the major dilemma that faces economic policy makers.

22. Identify the factors influencing the increase or decrease of aggregate supply and aggregate demand by using a graphic organizer like the one below.

Aggregate Supply (AS) and Aggregate Demand (AD)	
Factors that increase AS	
Factors that decrease AS	
Factors that increase AD	
Factors that decrease AD	

Section 2 *(pages 419–427)*

23. Identify which component of GDP Keynes labeled as the cause of instability.

24. Discuss the effects of the multiplier and the accelerator.

25. Describe how monetarists determine the proper growth rate for the money supply.

26. Explain how supply-siders would reduce the government's role in the economy.

Section 3 *(pages 429–433)*

27. Discuss the difficulty of using discretionary fiscal policy.

28. Explain why new problems will arise in the economy, even as old ones are solved.

29. State an example of how politics sometimes overrides economic policies.

30. Describe how economists sometimes differ in their views about the economy.

Critical Thinking

31. **The BIG Idea** Why and how could monetary policy be destabilizing?

32. Contrasting How do aggregate supply and demand differ from simple supply and demand?

33. Comparing What are the limitations of demand-side, supply-side, and monetarist economic policies?

---

spending caused by a change in total spending.

25. by studying the growth rates of real GDP and productivity

26. deregulate business, cut spending and lower taxes, reduce federal agencies

27. recognition and implementation time lags, gridlock in Congress, and ideological differences among politicians

28. Business fluctuations are continually occurring.

29. Answers should show sound economic reasoning.

30. They disagree about the most severe problem plaguing the economy.

Critical Thinking

31. Expansive could cause inflation. Restrictive could cause a recession.

32. Aggregate refers to whole economy. Simple refers to single good or service.

33. Students may note that demand-side delays policies, supply-side lacks experience, and monetarist may not reduce unemployment.

Economics ONLINE **Self-Check Quiz** Visit the *Economics: Principles and Practices* Web site at glencoe.com and click on *Chapter 15–Self-Check Quizzes* to prepare for the chapter test.

Assessment and Activities

CHAPTER 15

34. **Analyzing Information** How do the events of the 1980s and the early 2000s support or disprove the central supply-side position about the relationship between taxes, economic growth, and tax revenues? Provide examples in your answer.

35. **Drawing Conclusions** Why are the automatic stabilizers effective fiscal policies that counter business cycles?

36. **Contrasting** Compare the use of discretionary fiscal policy and monetary policy to offset the effects of a short recession. Which policy would you choose? Include reasons to support your choice.

Analyzing Visuals

37. **Synthesizing** Look at Figure 15.4 on page 422. Use what you have learned to explain what policies might make the demand curve shift. What effect does this have on aggregate supply?

Applying Economic Concepts

38. **Monetary Policy** At one time or another, some presidents have complained about the independence that the Fed enjoys when it conducts monetary policy. Do you think this independence is beneficial and should be maintained, or would you prefer that elected officials have more control over monetary policy? Support your answer.

39. **Fiscal Policy** Which fiscal policy do you think the government would use in each of the scenarios described in the table below? Explain your answers.

Scenario	Fiscal Policy	Explanation
Inflation is rising and real GDP is growing strongly		
GDP is down and the unemployment rate has increased by 10 percent		

Interpreting Cartoons

40. Look at the cartoon below. What is the topic of the cartoon? What point is the cartoonist making about the impact of tax cuts and the war in Iraq? How does the cartoonist illustrate this point?

" LOOK, KIDS! THEY'RE DIGGING YOUR SHARE OF THE NATIONAL DEBT!"

Thinking Like an Economist

41. Like demand-side and supply-side policies, monetary policies are designed to promote stable economic growth. The three approaches differ on what should be done to achieve this goal. Assume that real GDP growth was negative during the last quarter. Using Figure 15.5 as an example, construct a similar chart listing the policies that monetarists would follow to help the economy.

Writing About Economics

42. **Expository Writing** Some economists favor policies that stimulate demand, while others favor those that stimulate the supply of goods and services. Still other economists prefer policies based on the growth of the money supply. With which group of economists do you agree? Write a two-page paper outlining the policies and the reason for your choice.

CHAPTER 15 Economic Stabilization Policies **437**

Applying Economic Concepts

38. Answers will vary, but students should demonstrate understanding of the Fed and monetary policy.

39. Row 1: increase taxes; the government will gain a surplus and be able to pay down its debt.
Row 2: increase spending; this will increase economic activity, creating jobs and GDP growth.

Interpreting Cartoons

40. the national debt; tax cuts and the war in Iraq are increasing the national debt; by showing the Iraq war as blasting a larger hole in an already vast canyon that represents the national debt

Thinking Like an Economist

41. Students' charts should demonstrate a clear understanding of monetarist policies.

Writing About Economics

42. Answers will vary, but students should support their preference with sound economic reasoning.

---

34. Answers will vary, but students should use specific examples about tax revenues and economic growth in the 1980s and 2000s to support their answers.

35. They do not require any government action to take effect; thus, no time lags or political differences limit their effectiveness.

36. With discretionary fiscal policy, the government would increase spending to try to deal with the recession. With monetary policy, the Fed would increase the money supply to spur economic activity. Student policy preferences will vary but should be supported by sound economic reasoning.

Analyzing Visuals

37. Changes in taxes, transfer payments, and consumer saving could cause the demand curve to shift. Such changes would cause the aggregate demand curve to intersect with the aggregate supply curve at a different point.

Planning Guide

The Global Economy

UNIT PACING CHART			
	Chapter 16	**Chapter 17**	**Chapter 18**
Day 1	Unit Opener Chapter Opener Section 1	Chapter Opener Section 1	Chapter Opener Section 1
Day 2	Case Study Section 2 BusinessWeek Newsclip	Case Study Section 2 BusinessWeek Newsclip	BusinessWeek Newsclip Section 2 Case Study
Day 3	Section 3 Profiles in Economics	Section 3 Profiles in Economics	Section 3 Profiles in Economics
Day 4	Review Chapter Assessment	Review Chapter Assessment	Review Chapter Assessment
Day 5	Debates in Economics		The Global Economy & You

Teacher to Teacher

Jay Grenawalt
George
Washington High
School
Denver, Colorado

Foreign Investment Increasingly, new factories are being constructed outside of national boundaries. In such an environment, nations will have to compete for foreign companies just as U.S. cities and states do today. **Ask:** What factors might lead a firm to build a factory in Country A instead of Country B? *(Some factors that might provide incentives/ disincentives include wages, skilled labor, political stability, transportation and communication systems, import-export restrictions, government regulations, cultural and linguistics factors, and the size of the foreign country's market.)*

Present students with a hypothetical situation. Suppose a company wants to build an automobile plant. Organize students into groups and ask each group to pick five nations that represent a diversity of development and regions. Using current encyclopedias, the *World Development Report*, *The Index of Economic Freedom*, and magazine and newspaper articles, have groups compile brief overviews of each economy using the previous criteria. The students in each group should discuss and reach a consensus about which country would be their choice for the plant. As a class, tabulate the votes of the groups and lead a discussion about the choices.

Author Note

Dear Economics Teacher:

Just a few years ago, any textbook that wanted to talk about the global economy would only have to mention the opening of a new McDonald's in Moscow or speculate about the impact of the rising number of low-cost Japanese cars that were beginning to compete with the so-called "big three" automakers in Detroit. Some of the big issues of today, such as offshoring, globalization, and global warming, were not even part of our everyday vocabulary. How things have changed!

On balance, they have changed for the better. Consumers have more choices than ever, and the flood of low-priced products from abroad has helped to keep prices down. While some jobs have gone abroad, economists generally agree that we are better off now than we were 20 years ago.

When I think about the global economic changes in the last 20 years, I am reminded of our earlier discussion of voluntary exchange, exchange that takes place only because each party feels better off after the transaction than before. A lot of exchanges occurred on the way to globalization, and so a lot of people must have felt that the changes were beneficial to them. In short, globalization is happening because we want it and allow it to happen!

The rapid globalization dramatically validates our economic theories—in particular specialization, competition, comparative advantage, and the gains from trade. People sometimes wonder about the usefulness of abstract economic theories, but the current global economic changes show that the economist's view of why and how things happen is right on target! In fact, it is the global economy where real-world developments fall most neatly into the theoretical and methodological framework we covered in this text.

Making accurate predictions about the future is part of why economics is so useful and fun. It's also been fun authoring this book. I hope that using it has been fun for you and your students as well!

Gary Clayton, Ph.D.
Author

UNIT 5

The Global Economy

Unit Objectives

After studying this unit, students will be able to:

- **Recognize** the importance of international trade, foreign exchange, and the inter-dependence among nations.

- **Anlayze** the problems of economically developing countries.

- **Describe** significant global challenges.

Unit Overview

Unit 5 examines economics from a global perspective.

Chapter 16 examines absolute and comparative advantage, barriers to international trade, and foreign exchange and trade deficits.

Chapter 17 discusses the problems faced by developing countries, including countries moving toward more capitalistic economic systems.

Chapter 18 reviews the economic challenges that the world faces and the use of economics in analyzing choices and making decisions.

This Japanese-owned ► Honda manufacturing plant in Marysville, Ohio, reflects increasingly global markets and production.

438 UNIT 5

Activity: Launching the Unit

International Trade Have the class role-play a congressional subcommittee meeting on a plan to raise tariffs on imported products—athletic shoes, for example. Select several students to act as subcommittee members and four or five others to act as witnesses—consumer advocates, workers in the shoe-making industry, executives from American shoe manufacturers, and executives from foreign shoe manufacturers. Encourage expert witnesses to make presentations to the subcommittee for or against the raise in tariffs, and have subcommittee members ask them questions. Have the rest of the class act as reporters and write summaries of the procedures. **OL**

HONDA

ES ASSEMBLED IN NORTH AMERICA!

Making It Relevant

Provide students with copies of newspapers and current affairs magazines. Direct them to skim through these periodicals to locate advertisements for foreign goods. Encourage students to ask themselves the following questions about the advertisements: What good is advertised? Where is it made? How was it transported to the United States? Do American companies make this good? If so, why do you think we buy it from other countries? Have students discuss their answers. Conclude by pointing out that the chapters in this unit deal with such topics as international trade and the growing interconnectedness of the world's economies. **OL**

BusinessWeek ONLINE

To find up-to-date news and analysis on the economy, business, technology, markets, entrepreneurs, investments, and finance, have students search feature articles and special reports on the BusinessWeek Web site, www.businessweek.com.

Extra Credit Project

Have students research organizations such as the Ford Foundation, the International Finance Corporation (IFC), and agencies of the United Nations (UN) that offer loans or grants to economically developing nations. Have students write short reports with graphs showing trends in assistance offered. Suggest that students combine their reports into a pamphlet titled *International Organizations and Economic Development*. **AL**

CHAPTER 16 Planning Guide

Key to Ability Levels

BL	Below level	AL	Above level
OL	On level	ELL	English Language Learners

Key to Teaching Resources

Print Material — DVD — CD-Rom — Transparency

Levels					Resources	Chapter Opener	Section 1	Section 2	Section 3	Chapter Assess
BL	OL	AL	ELL							
FOCUS										
BL	OL	AL	ELL	📽	Daily Focus Skills Transparencies		80	82	81	
TEACH										
BL	OL		ELL	📁	Guided Reading Activities*		p. 46	p. 47	p. 48	
BL	OL	AL	ELL	📁	Economic Content Vocabulary Activities*		p. 16	p. 16	p. 16	
	OL	AL		📁	Critical Thinking Activities		p. 22	p. 22	p. 22	
BL	OL		ELL	📁	Reading Essentials and Note-Taking Guide*		p. 136	p. 139	p. 142	
		AL		📁	Enrichment Activities		p. 16			
	OL	AL		📁	Free Enterprise Activities			p. 22		
BL	OL	AL	ELL	📁	Primary and Secondary Source Readings			p. 43		
BL	OL	AL	ELL	📁	Hands-On Economics				p. 24	
BL	OL	AL	ELL	📽	Economic Concepts Transparencies, Strategies, and Activities		p. 39		p. 41	
BL	OL	AL	ELL	📁	Math Practice for Economics				p. 22	
BL	OL	AL	ELL	📽	Economics Forms and Financial Pages Transparencies, Strategies, and Activities		p. 11		p. 26	
	OL	AL		📁	BusinessWeek Focus on the Global Economy			pp. 2, 10, 17	p. 25	
BL	OL	AL	ELL	📁	Reinforcing Economic Skills		p. 26		p. 20	
BL	OL		ELL	📁	High School Reading in the Content Area Strategies and Activities	✓	✓	✓	✓	✓
BL	OL	AL	ELL	📽	High School Writing Process Transparencies	✓	✓	✓	✓	✓
BL	OL	AL	ELL	📁	Writer's Guidebook	✓	✓	✓	✓	✓
BL	OL	AL	ELL	💿	StudentWorks Plus CD-ROM	✓	✓	✓	✓	✓
BL	OL	AL	ELL	💿	Vocabulary PuzzleMaker CD-ROM	✓	✓	✓	✓	✓

*Also available in Spanish

TeacherWorks *Plus*
All-In-One Planner and Resource Center

- Interactive Lesson Planner
- Interactive Teacher Edition
- Fully editable blackline masters
- Economics & You videos

- Differentiated Lesson Plans
- Printable reports of daily assignments
- Standards tracking system

Levels					Resources	Chapter Opener	Section 1	Section 2	Section 3	Chapter Assess
BL	OL	AL	ELL							
TEACH *(continued)*										
BL	OL	AL	ELL		Economics & You Video Program DVD— *International Trade*	✓	✓	✓	✓	✓
BL	OL	AL	ELL		**Graph Coach CD-ROM**	✓	✓	✓	✓	✓
Teacher Resources					**Differentiated Instruction Strategies**	✓	✓	✓	✓	✓
					Success with English Learners	✓	✓	✓	✓	✓
					Presentation Plus! CD-ROM	✓	✓	✓	✓	✓
ASSESS										
BL	OL	AL	ELL		**Section Quizzes and Chapter Tests**		p. 201	p. 202	p. 203	pp. 205, 209
BL	OL	AL	ELL		**Authentic Assessment Strategies and Activities**		p. 22	p. 8	p. 25	
BL	OL	AL	ELL		*ExamView*® *Assessment Suite* **CD-ROM**		16-1	16-2	16-3	Ch. 16
BL	OL	AL	ELL		**Interactive Tutor Self-Assessment CD-ROM**		16-1	16-2	16-3	
CLOSE										
BL			ELL		**Reteaching Activities***		p. 16	p. 16	p. 16	
BL	OL		ELL		**Reading and Study Skills Foldables**		pp. 63, 64	pp. 63, 64	pp. 63, 64	

*Also available in Spanish

Daily Assignments and Grade Log

Technology Product

Glencoe's *StudentWorks™ Plus* CD-ROM contains everything your students need, including the complete Student Edition and access to all student workbooks. *StudentWorks™ Plus* also includes a Daily Assignment and Activity Log that allows students to

- record and track progress on their daily assignments and responsibilities;
- log results achieved, including their grades;
- sort assignments alphabetically or by category;
- view and print the assignment and grade log in a table or calendar format.

Objectives

Using *StudentWorks™ Plus* will help your students

- take responsibility for their individual tasks;
- improve independent study skills.

Steps

Provide students with the following information:

- Launch *StudentWorks™ Plus*.
- Select the **Daily Assignments and Grade Log** button at the bottom of the launch screen.
- Create a new file or open an existing one. The log is organized as a table, with a row of information for each assignment.
- Add information for each assignment, including the date of the assignment, the name, additional comments, the due date, and the grade.
- Edit rows as assignment information is provided or changed. Add a new row to the log for each new assignment.

Economics ONLINE

	Student	Teacher	Parent
Beyond the Textbook	●	●	●
Chapter Overviews	●	●	●
ePuzzles and Games	●		●
Concepts in Motion	●		●
Multi-Language Glossaries	●		●
Online Student Edition	●	●	●
Self-Check Quizzes	●		●
Student Web Activities	●		●
Study Central™	●		●
Time Current Events	●	●	●
Teaching Today		●	
Vocabulary eFlashcards	●		●
Web Activity Lesson Plans		●	

Glencoe Media Center

❯ glencoe.com

Study-To-Go
- Vocabulary eFlashcards
- Self-Check Quizzes

❯ **Audio/Video**
- Student Edition Audio
- Spanish Summaries
- Economics & You Videos

READING SUPPORT FROM
JAMESTOWN EDUCATION

- **Timed Readings Plus in Social Studies** helps students increase their reading rate and fluency while maintaining comprehension. The 400-word passages are similar to those found on state and national assessments.

- **Reading in the Content Area: Social Studies** concentrates on six essential reading skills that help students better comprehend what they read. The book includes 75 high-interest nonfiction passages written at increasing levels of difficulty.

- **Reading Social Studies** includes strategic reading instruction and vocabulary support in Social Studies content for both ELLs and native speakers of English.
  www.jamestowneducation.com

Reading List Generator CD-ROM

GLENCOE
BookLink 3

Use this database to search more than 30,000 titles to create a customized reading list for your students.

- Reading lists can be organized by students' reading level, author, genre, theme, or area of interest.

- The database provides Degrees of Reading Power™ (DRP) and Lexile™ readability scores for all selections.

- A brief summary of each selection is included.

Leveled reading suggestions for this chapter:

For students at a Grade 10 reading level:
- *India: A Study of an Economically Developing Country,* by David Cumming

For students at a Grade 11 reading level:
- *Voyaging to Cathay: Americans in the China Trade,* by Alfred Tamarin & Shirely Glubok

For students at a Grade 12 reading level:
- *Ghana: A Study of an Economically Developing Country,* by Steve Brace

* Review suggested books before assigning them.

NCEE

National Council on Economic Education

Voluntary Standards Emphasized in Chapter 16

Content Standard 6 When individuals, regions, and nations specialize in what they can produce at the lowest cost and then trade with others, both production and consumption increase.

Content Standard 17 Costs of government policies sometimes exceed benefits. This may occur because of incentives facing voters, government officials, and government employees, because of actions by special interest groups that can impose costs on the general public, or because social goals other than economic efficiency are being pursued.

Resources Available from NCEE
- Virtual Economics®: An Interactive Center for Economic Education Version 3.0
- Civics and Government: Focus on Economics, Second Edition
- Advanced Placement Economics: Teacher Resource Manual, Third Edition
- Focus: Understanding Economics in U.S. History
- Focus: High School Economics, Second Edition
- Capstone: The Nation's High School Economics Course
- Focus: Institutions and Markets

To order these materials, or to contact your State Council on Economic Education about workshops and programs, call 1-800-338-1192 or visit the NCEE Web site at store.ncee.net**.**

CHAPTER 16 International Trade

The BIG Idea

As students study the chapter, remind them to consider the chapter-based Big Idea. The **Essential Question** in the chapter launch activity below ties in to the Big Idea and helps students think about and understand important chapter concepts. In addition, the Hands-On Chapter Project relates the content from each section to the Big Idea. The steps in each section build on each other and culminate in the Wrap-Up Activity on the Visual Summary page.

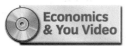 **Economics & You Video** To generate student interest and provide a springboard for class discussion, access the Economics & You Topic 23 video, **International Trade,** at glencoe.com or on the video DVD.

FOLDABLES **Study Organizer** **Dinah Zike's Foldables** are three-dimensional, interactive graphic organizers that help students practice basic writing skills, review key vocabulary terms, and identify main ideas. Have students complete this chapter's Foldable activity or activities in *Dinah Zike's Reading and Study Skills Foldables* booklet. **OL**

Economics ONLINE

Introduce students to chapter content and key terms by having them access *Chapter 16 —Chapter Overviews* at glencoe.com.

Why It Matters

You and a classmate are planning to open a lawn-service business. You will each contribute $200 toward the purchase of a mower, gas can, trimmer, and other materials for the business. Now it is time to get organized. Work with a classmate and make a list of the different "jobs" associated with your lawn-service business. What criteria will you use to divide up these jobs? Why? Read Chapter 16 to find out how nations make decisions about what to produce and trade with other nations.

The BIG Idea

Trade and specialization lead to economic growth for individuals, regions, and nations.

International trade allows us to ▶ purchase items produced in any country, such as the items from Africa and the Caribbean in a store in Syracuse, New York.

Economics ONLINE **Chapter Overview** Visit the *Economics: Principles and Practices* Web site at glencoe.com and click on *Chapter 16–Chapter Overviews* to preview chapter information.

440 UNIT 5

Activity: Launching the Chapter

Identifying Have students imagine that they are owners of a small manufacturing company. Tell them that they have an opportunity to increase sales of their products by exporting them. Ask students to identify the laws, customs, consumer preferences, and other types of information they would need to know about the countries to which they intend to export. Discuss their responses as a class. **Essential Question:** Why do governments encourage the businesses in their country to trade with other nations? *(World trade strengthens a nation's economy by allowing a country to acquire needed goods and services while making efficient use of its own resources.)* **OL**

SECTION 1 Absolute and Comparative Advantage

GUIDE TO READING

Section Preview

In this section, you will learn that comparative advantage is the basis for international trade.

Content Vocabulary

- exports (p. 442)
- imports (p. 442)
- absolute advantage (p. 443)
- production possibilities frontier (p. 444)
- comparative advantage (p. 444)
- opportunity cost (p. 444)

Academic Vocabulary

- volume (p. 443)
- enabled (p. 444)

Reading Strategy

Defining As you read the section, complete graphic organizers similar to the ones below by defining each term and providing an example of each.

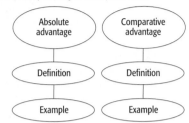

Focus

Bellringer
Daily Focus Transparency 80

GUIDE TO READING

Answers to Graphic:

Absolute advantage: country's ability to produce more of a given product than another country can produce. Examples will vary.

Comparative advantage: country's ability to produce a given product relatively more efficiently than another country by doing it at a lower opportunity cost. Examples will vary.

ISSUES IN THE NEWS

—*BusinessWeek*

Russia: Shoppers Gone Wild

It's midday on Saturday, and the Mega-1 mall in southern Moscow is packed. Shoppers have come to stock up on groceries at the mall's French-owned Auchan hypermarket, buy furniture at Swedish retailer IKEA, and browse dozens of boutiques selling everything from Yves Rocher cosmetics to Calvin Klein underwear. Although crammed with expensive Western merchandise, Mega has been a hit since it opened its doors in December, 2002. Last year it was the world's most frequented shopping center, with 52 million visitors.

Down the road at the Rolf car dealership, Oxana Starostina is filling in registration forms for her new Mitsubishi Lancer, purchased with $20,000 in cash. She and her husband, Maxim, saved the money from their small construction supply business.

. . . [F]or many multinationals from the U.S., Europe, and Asia, the consumer boom, not oil and gas, is the investment story to watch. ∎

Nations trade for the same reasons that individuals do—because they believe that the products they receive are worth more than the products they give up. International trade is partially responsible for the incredible variety of goods and services both we and the shoppers in the news story consume.

For example, we purchase clothing made in China, oil from the Middle East, bananas from Honduras, and coffee beans from Colombia and Brazil. We consume a service when we vacation in the Caribbean or in Europe. The shoppers in Moscow are doing the same thing: enjoying the goods produced in France, Sweden, and Japan.

Resource Manager

R Reading Strategies	C Critical Thinking	D Differentiated Instruction	W Writing Support	S Skill Practice
Teacher Edition • Reading Graphs, p. 444 • Det. Importance, p. 445 **Additional Resources** • Guid. Read. Act., p. 46 • Read. Ess. & Note-Taking Guide, p. 136	**Teacher Edition** • Analyzing, pp. 442, 446 **Additional Resources** • Crit. Think. Act., p. 22 • Econ. Concepts Trans., Strat. and Act., p. 39 • Enrichment Act., p. 16	**Teacher Edition** • ELL, p. 443 **Additional Resources** • Bus. Focus on the Global Economy, p. 2 • Econ. Forms and Fin. Pages Trans., Strat. and Act., p. 11	**Teacher Edition** • Expository Writing, p. 444 **Additional Resources** • Writer's Guidebook • Reading and Study Skills Fold., p. 63	**Teacher Edition** • Using Charts and Tables, p. 442 • Visual Literacy, p. 443 **Additional Resources** • Reinforcing Econ. Skills, p. 26 • Reteach. Act., p. 16

Teach

C Critical Thinking

Analyzing Ask: What is the relationship between a state or nation's exports and its specialization? *(A state or nation's main exports show what the place produces and sells to other countries; this indicates that the state or nation has specialized in these goods.)* Invite students to research exports produced in their state and then analyze why the state might specialize in these items. **AL**

S Skill Practice

Using Charts and Tables

Ask: From which countries does the United States import tin? *(Peru, China, Bolivia, Indonesia)* What percent of U.S. tin consumption do these imports represent? *(88 percent)* **BL**

Economic Analysis

Answer: They must become interdependent with one another in order to acquire the raw materials they need.

---

exports the goods and services that a nation sells to other nations

imports the goods and services that a nation buys from other nations

Why Nations Trade

MAIN Idea Trade allows nations to specialize in some products and then trade them for goods and services that are more expensive to produce.

Economics and You When you were young, did you ever trade toys, cards, or candy with your friends? Read on to learn about international trade.

Some trade takes place because countries lack goods at home. **Figure 16.1** shows some essential raw materials used in the United States that come from abroad.

Specialization

A more important reason for trade—whether among people, states, or countries—is specialization. When people specialize, they produce the things they do best and exchange those products for the things that other people do best.

States also specialize. For example, New York is a financial center for stocks and bonds, while automobiles are a major industry in Michigan. Texas is known for oil and cattle, while Florida and California are famous for citrus fruit. Countries specialize in different goods and services in much the same way.

If you want to find out what a country specializes in, look at its **exports**—the goods and services that it produces and sells to other nations. If you want to see what a country would like to have but does not produce as efficiently, look at its **imports**—the goods and services that one country buys from other countries.

Extent of Trade

International trade is important to all nations, even a country as large as the United States. Most of the products that

Figure 16.1 ▶ American Dependence on Trade

Raw Material	Imports as a Percent of Consumption	Primary Foreign Sources	Use of Raw Materials
Industrial diamonds	100	South Africa, Australia, Democratic Republic of the Congo, Botswana	Industrial cutting tools, oil well drills
Bauxite	100	Jamaica, Guinea, Brazil, Guyana	Anything made of aluminum
Columbium	100	Brazil, Canada, Thailand	Rocket structures and heat radiation shields
Mica (sheet)	100	India, Belgium, France	Electrical insulation, ceramics
Strontium	100	Mexico, Spain	Flares, fireworks
Tin	88	Peru, China, Bolivia, Indonesia	Cans and containers, electrical components
Tantalum	80	Thailand, Germany, Brazil	Surgical instruments, missile parts
Barite	79	China, India	Filler for gas and oil well drilling fluids, paint, plastics
Cobalt	76	Democratic Republic of the Congo, Zambia, Canada	High-temperature jet fighter engines
Chromium	72	South Africa, Zimbabwe, Turkey	Chrome, ball bearings, trim on appliances and cars

Sources: *Statistical Abstract of the United States*; U.S. Geological Survey

▶ International trade is the primary means by which nations, including the United States, obtain many essential materials.

Economic Analysis *How does the lack of certain raw materials force nations to become more interdependent?*

Differentiated Instruction

Authentic Assessment Strategies and Activities, p. 22

Trade and Interdependence

Objective: Define interdependence and understand how scarcity promotes trade.

Focus/Teach: Ask students why nations might trade with one another. Then have students complete the activity.

Assess: Have students use their charts and papers to make a presentation about interdependence.

Close: Have students explain which trade commodities the items used in the activity could represent.

Differentiated Instruction Strategies

BL Rearrange each group's materials, and have them complete the activity again.

AL Have students redesign the activity using different materials.

ELL Have students create a poster depicting major items imported and exported by the United States.

Figure 16.2 ► **U.S. Merchandise Trade by Area**

► The United States exports merchandise (goods) all over the world. The biggest trade imbalance is with China, followed by the OPEC members.

Economic Analysis *Which single area of the world trades the most with the United States?*

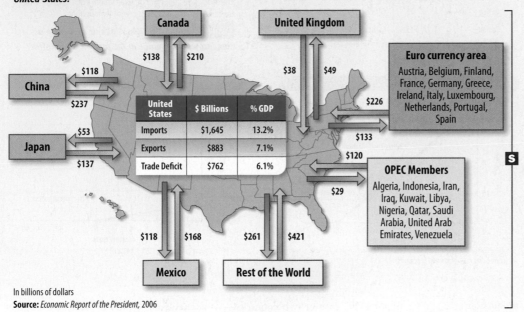

United States	$ Billions	% GDP
Imports	$1,645	13.2%
Exports	$883	7.1%
Trade Deficit	$762	6.1%

Canada — $138 $210
China — $118 / $237
Japan — $53 / $137
Mexico — $118 $168
Rest of the World — $261 $421
United Kingdom — $38 $49
Euro currency area — Austria, Belgium, Finland, France, Germany, Greece, Ireland, Italy, Luxembourg, Netherlands, Portugal, Spain — $226 / $133
$120
OPEC Members — Algeria, Indonesia, Iran, Iraq, Kuwait, Libya, Nigeria, Qatar, Saudi Arabia, United Arab Emirates, Venezuela — $29

In billions of dollars
Source: *Economic Report of the President, 2006*

[S]

countries exchange are goods. However, trade in services such as banking and insurance is increasing.

Figure 16.2 shows the patterns of merchandise trade for the United States with the rest of the world. The import of goods alone amounts to $1,645 billion, or about $5,500 per person. The numbers in the figure would be even larger if we included the value of services.

In the end, international trade is much more than a way to obtain exotic products. The sheer **volume** of trade between nations with such different geographic, political, and religious characteristics is proof that trade is beneficial.

✓**Reading Check** **Explaining** Why is specialization a good idea in trade?

The Basis for Trade

MAIN Idea Trade works best when countries focus on those products they can produce best.

Economics and You Have you ever bought anything, such as clothing or a meal, that you could have made yourself? Read on to learn how this action relates to international trade.

It may be cheaper for a country to import a product than to manufacture it. The difference between absolute and comparative advantage makes this clear. **[D]**

Absolute Advantage

A country has an **absolute advantage** when it can produce more of a product than another country. For example, assume

absolute advantage country's ability to produce more of a given product than another country can produce

S **Skill Practice**

Visual Literacy Ask: What percentage of the U.S. GDP do exports represent? *(7.1 percent)* What is the difference in value between the United States' imports and exports with Mexico? *(The United States imports $50 billion more from Mexico than it exports to Mexico.)* **OL**

D **Differentiated Instruction**

English Language Learners Explain that *absolute* means "ultimate or unquestionable," while *comparative* means "related to a comparison between things." Model the use of these terms in sentences for students, and then ask students to explain the meanings in their own words. **ELL**

Economic Analysis

Answer: Euro currency area

✓**Reading Check** **Answer:** because it allows people to produce the things they do best and exchange those products for the things that other people do best

Leveled Activities

BL Reinforcing Economic Skills, p. 26

OL Economic Concepts Transparencies, Strategies, and Activities, p. 39

AL Enrichment Activities, p. 16

443

Figure 16.3 ► The Gains From Trade

Graphs In Motion
See StudentWorks™ Plus
or glencoe.com.

Reading Graphs Ask: How many pounds of cashew nuts could Alpha produce if it produced 30 million pounds of coffee? *(2 million pounds)* How many pounds of coffee could Beta produce if it produced 6 pounds of cashew nuts? *(zero; it wouldn't produce any coffee)* **BL**

W **Writing Support**

Expository Writing Have students review the information about production possibilities frontiers. Then ask them to write a paragraph that identifies the information contained in the graphics and explains how to interpret them. Remind students to include brief descriptions of how these visuals can be used to pinpoint opportunity cost. **OL**

Economic Analysis

Answer: Alpha

A	Total Output Before Specializing			Total Output After Specializing		
	Alpha	Beta		Alpha	Beta	
Coffee	20 +	5 =	25	Coffee	40 + 0 = 40	
Cashews	4 +	1 =	5	Cashews	0 + 6 = 6	

► If Alpha and Beta each specializes in the product it can produce relatively more efficiently, total output for both countries goes up. After specialization, each country would trade its surplus production with its neighbor.

Economic Analysis *Does Alpha or Beta have a comparative advantage in the production of coffee?*

B ALPHA

After specialization — a'
Before specialization — a
Alpha's opportunity cost of production: 8 cashews = 40 coffee, or 1 cashew = 5 coffee

(Coffee and nuts measured in pounds)

C BETA

Beta's opportunity cost of production: 6 cashews = 6 coffee, or 1 cashew = 1 coffee
Before specialization — b
After specialization — b'

production possibilities frontier diagram showing the maximum combinations of goods and/or services an economy can produce when all resources are fully employed *(also see page 21)*

comparative advantage country's ability to produce a given product relatively more efficiently than another country by doing it at a lower opportunity cost

opportunity cost cost of the next-best alternative use of money, time, or resources when making a choice *(also see page 20)*

the hypothetical case of two countries—Alpha and Beta—which are the same size in terms of area, population, and capital stock. Only their climate and soil fertilities differ. In each country, only two crops can be grown—coffee and cashew nuts.

In **Figure 16.3** you see an illustration of the **production possibilities frontiers** for Alpha and Beta. Note that if both countries devote all of their efforts to producing coffee, Alpha could produce 40 million pounds and Beta six million—giving Alpha an absolute advantage in the coffee production. If both countries concentrate on producing cashew nuts, Alpha could produce eight million pounds and Beta six million. Alpha, then, also has an absolute advantage in the production of cashew nuts because it can produce more than Beta.

For years, people thought that absolute advantage was the basis for trade because

it **enabled** a country to produce enough of a good to consume domestically while leaving some for export. However, the concept of absolute advantage did not explain how two countries could benefit from an exchange in which a country with a large output like Alpha traded with a country with a smaller output like Beta.

Comparative Advantage

Even when one country enjoys an absolute advantage in the production of all goods, as in the case of Alpha above, trade between it and another country is still beneficial. This happens whenever a country has a **comparative advantage**—the ability to produce a product relatively more efficiently, or at a lower opportunity cost.

To illustrate, because Alpha can produce either 40 pounds of coffee or 8 pounds of cashew nuts, the **opportunity cost** of

Hands-On Chapter Project

Step 1

Analyzing World Trade

In this project, student groups will profile one country's international trade, exchange rates, balance of trade, and trade restrictions.

Step 1: Studying the Importance of Trade to a Nation. Student groups will study the international trade of a specific nation.

Directions: Organize the class into five different groups. Assign each of the groups one of the following continents: North America, South America, Europe, Africa, and Asia. Student groups should then select a nation located on their assigned continent to profile. The North America group should choose a nation other than the United States. Have students research the major imports, exports, absolute advantages, and

comparative advantages of their nation. Ask students to present their findings on a large poster, featuring images, statistical graphs, and text.

Display each group's completed poster in the classroom. Have members discuss their posters with the class.

Describing Ask students to write a short paper describing the importance of trade to the nation that they researched. **OL**

(Chapter Project continued in Section 2.)

producing 1 pound of cashew nuts is 5 pounds of coffee (40 pounds of coffee divided by 8). At the same time, Beta's opportunity cost of producing 1 pound of cashew nuts is 1 pound of coffee (6 pounds of coffee divided by 6). Beta is the lower-cost producer of cashew nuts because its opportunity cost of producing 1 pound of nuts is 1 pound of coffee—whereas Alpha would have to give up 5 pounds of coffee to produce the same amount of cashews.

If Beta has a comparative advantage in producing cashews, then Alpha must have a comparative advantage in coffee production. Indeed, if we try to find each country's opportunity cost of producing coffee, we would see that Alpha's opportunity cost of producing 1 pound of coffee is 1/5 of a pound of cashews (8 pounds of cashews divided by 40). Using the same computations, Beta's opportunity cost is 1 pound of cashews (6 pounds of cashews divided by 6). Alpha, then, has a comparative advantage in coffee production, because its opportunity cost of production is lower than Beta's.

The Gains from Trade

R The concept of comparative advantage is based on the assumption that everyone will be better off specializing in the products they produce best. This applies to individuals, companies, states, and regions as well as to nations.

If we look at the final result of trade between Alpha and Beta, we can see that specialization and trade increased the total world output. Without trade, both countries together produced 25 coffee and 5 cashews. After trade, total world output grew to 40 coffee and 6 cashews.

This explains why countries such as the United States and Colombia trade. The United States has the necessary resources to produce farm equipment efficiently, while Colombia has the resources to produce coffee efficiently. Because each country has a comparative advantage in a product the other country wants, trade will be beneficial to both.

✓**Reading Check** **Summarizing** Why is it beneficial for a country to trade with another when it has comparative advantage?

Economics ONLINE
Student Web Activity Visit the *Economics: Principles and Practices* Web site at glencoe.com and click on *Chapter 16—Student Web Activities* for an activity on international trade agreements.

Skills Handbook
See page R43 to learn about **Comparing and Contrasting.**

CHAPTER 16, SECTION 1

R **Reading Strategy**

Determining Importance
Ask: What is the assumption on which the concept of comparative advantage is based? *(The concept is based on the assumption that everyone will be better off specializing in the products they produce best.)* **OL**

✓**Reading Check** **Answer:**
because it can trade a product it produces best in exchange for a product it wants that another country produces best

Assess

💿 Use the Interactive Tutor Self-Assessment CD-ROM to review Section 1, and then assign the Section 1 Review as homework or as an in-class activity.

Close

Comparing and Contrasting
Have students draw a Venn diagram comparing and contrasting absolute and comparative advantage. **OL**

SECTION 1 Review

Vocabulary
1. **Explain** the significance of exports, imports, absolute advantage, and comparative advantage.

Main Ideas
2. **Listing** Use a graphic organizer like the one below to list the reasons that nations trade with one another.

Why Nations Trade

3. **Describing** How do specialization and trade benefit both trading partners?

4. **Explaining** Why does total world output increase as countries specialize to engage in trade?

Critical Thinking
5. **The BIG Idea** What does the theory of comparative advantage suggest that countries should do?

6. **Contrasting** How do comparative advantage and absolute advantage differ? Use examples to support your comparison.

7. **Predicting** Suppose a nation has a great deal of human capital but few natural resources. In what kinds of products might the nation specialize?

8. **Analyzing Visuals** Look at Figure 16.3 on page 444. What would happen to total output if Alpha preferred growing cashew nuts and Beta specialized in coffee?

Applying Economics
9. **Comparative Advantage** Do you know of a product for which your state has a comparative advantage? Explain how this might affect trade with another state.

Review SECTION 1

Answers

1. All definitions can be found in the section and the Glossary.
2. lack of goods at home; need for raw materials; specialization; exotic products; profit
3. They allow both trading partners to produce the things they do best and exchange those products for the things that other people do best.
4. because specialization allows countries to specialize in the things that they produce most efficiently

5. specialize in the products that they produce best
6. Absolute advantage is a country's ability to produce more of a given product than another country can produce. For instance, if country A could produce more cars than country B, country A would have an absolute advantage. Comparative advantage is a country's ability to produce a given product more efficiently than another country by doing it at a lower opportunity cost. If country B could

produce cars at a lower opportunity cost than country A, it would hold the comparative advantage.
7. **Possible answer:** services such as financial consulting
8. The production of both coffee and cashew nuts, as well as total production, would decrease.
9. Students should realize that a comparative advantage might allow the state to trade for products another state produces more efficiently.

445

CASE STUDY

Teach

C Critical Thinking

Analyzing Ask: Why do you think the Virgin Group was likely to have a comparative advantage in the markets it expanded into? *(Branson chose markets that were either under-served or lacked competition. With the significant resources of the Virgin Group, it was likely to hold a comparative advantage in these markets.)* **OL**

Analyzing the Impact

Answers:

1. It includes many individual companies united under the Virgin brand, whereas other companies are organized as a single corporation with many divisions.

2. Establishing many smaller companies that target specific markets allowed those companies to gain a comparative advantage in each market.

Additional Support

Teacher Tip

Visual Learners If you have extra time, you might suggest that students illustrate their time lines (for example, they might show a logo or product for each new company). They can create drawings or print images from the Internet showing the actual events described.

CASE STUDY
Virgin Group

Unlimited Advantage

The theory of comparative advantage has led many companies to narrow their product lines. Richard Branson, founder of Virgin Group, did just the opposite. He decided to expand into a wide range of products in an even wider geographic area. Rather than building one large corporation with many divisions, though, Branson decided to create many individual companies united under the Virgin brand. The result: companies located on most continents, selling everything from train rides and low-cost flights to music, mobile phones, and luxury vacations.

Virgin's Success	
1968	Company begins
1970	Start of mail order record sales
1971	Opens first record shop
1973	Virgin record label launched
1984	Virgin Atlantic Airways opens
1987	Virgin Records America founded
1991	Virgin Publishing Company founded
1993	Virgin Radio begins
1999	Virgin Mobile launched
2000	Virgin Cars Produced
2002	Virgin Credit Card established

Source: www.virgin.com

Finding Niche Markets

Virgin traces its origins back to 1968, when Branson published the first issue of Student Magazine for his university. Shortly after, he expanded into mail-order record sales and record shops. He also launched his own record label, signing such artists as Phil Collins and Boy George.

For over a decade, Branson limited his business ventures to those related to music. During the 1980s, Branson decided to begin his expansion into other products and worldwide markets. His business plan was to find markets that are either underserved or lack competition. First steps included Virgin Atlantic Air Cargo and a luxury hotel in Spain.

Success Story

Today, Virgin Group has about 200 companies on most continents. Some provide their everyday customers with affordable vacations. Others cater to a more exclusive crowd, such as a luxury game resort in Africa and a motorcycle limousine service that can skirt London traffic jams. His latest venture will take vacationers into space. Branson's formula for success is apparently working. In 2005 the Virgin Group reported revenues of about $8 billion.

Analyzing the Impact

1. **Recalling** How does the organization of Virgin Group differ from that of most other corporations?

2. **Drawing Conclusions** How did Branson's business plan allow him to use comparative advantage?

Activity: Collaborative Learning

Make a Time Line Direct students to review the information presented in the chart on page 446. Then, have students work with partners to present this information on a time line. Instruct student pairs to conduct research to learn more about the Virgin Group and to then place additional entries on their time lines. Tell students to organize their time lines logically and to include any necessary benchmark labels that will help readers better read and understand the time lines. Remind students to also include detailed labels for each time line entry. Invite volunteers to present their time lines to the class. **OL**

SECTION 2
Barriers to International Trade

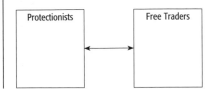
Focus

Bellringer
Daily Focus Transparency 82

ISSUES IN THE NEWS
—www.usinfo.state.gov

China Economic Ties Under Scrutiny

U.S. Commerce Secretary Carlos Gutierrez warns that the United States might be forced to reassess its economic relationship with China if Beijing fails to address economic frictions between the two countries quickly and effectively. . . . He said that China maintains a range of non-tariff barriers that, in combination with other policies, prevent the United States from achieving balanced trade with that country. . . .

He said that "with a stroke of a pen" China could open critical closed sectors to competition from abroad. "Progress would greatly strengthen those of us who oppose protectionist policies," Gutierrez said. But if the Chinese government refuses or fails to act quickly, the U.S. Congress might "go down a path that none of us want," that is "build protectionist barriers around the U.S. market," he said. ■

While free markets and international trade can bring many benefits, some people still object, because trade can displace selected industries and groups of workers. When these people object to trade, they look for ways to prevent it, or to at least slow the rate of growth.

Because of the wealth that a market economy can generate, China has decided to join the community of nations committed to markets and trade. China is still new at this, however, and as you read in the news story, it is trying to protect some sectors of the economy while opening up to trade.

Resource Manager

R Reading Strategies	C Critical Thinking	D Differentiated Instruction	W Writing Support	S Skill Practice
Teacher Edition • Summarizing, p. 448 • Outlining, p. 451 • Identifying, p. 454 **Additional Resources** • Guid. Read. Act., p. 47 • Read. Ess. & Note-Taking Guide, p. 139	**Teacher Edition** • Interpreting, p. 449 • Analyzing Visuals, p. 450 • Drawing Con., p. 453 **Additional Resources** • Authentic Assess., p. 8 • Bus. Focus on the Global Economy, pp. 2, 10, 17	**Teacher Edition** • Verbal/Linguistic, p. 449 • Visual/Spatial, p. 452 • Adv. Learners, p. 453 **Additional Resources** • Pri./Sec. Source Readings, p. 43 • Quizzes and Tests, p. 202	**Teacher Edition** • Expository Writing, p. 448 • Persuasive Writing, p. 452 **Additional Resources** • High School Writing Process Trans. • Crit. Think. Act., p. 22	**Teacher Edition** • Using Geo. Skills, p. 450 • Visual Literacy, pp. 451, 455 **Additional Resources** • Econ. Content Vocab. Act., p. 16 • Reading and Study Skills Fold., pp. 63, 64

Teach

R Reading Strategy

Summarizing Ask: What are the goals of a government when levying a protective tariff and a revenue tariff? *(A government levies a protective tariff with the goal of raising the costs of imports so that domestic industries are protected from being undersold. A revenue tariff generates government revenue without prohibiting imports.)* **OL**

W Writing Support

Expository Writing Have students research a time in which the U.S. government used tariffs prior to 1913. Tell students to write a short essay evaluating the government's use of the tariffs they researched. Instruct them to categorize the tariffs as either protective or revenue tariffs, and discuss whether the tariffs were successful in achieving the government's goals. **AL**

Caption Answer: protective tariff

Additional Support

---

tariff tax placed on an imported product

quota limit on the amount of a good that is allowed into a country

R **protective tariff** tax on an imported product designed to protect less-efficient domestic producers

revenue tariff tax placed on imported goods to raise revenue

Tariffs In 2002 a temporary tariff on steel imports protected the jobs of steelworkers such as this one. *What is the name of this kind of tariff?*

448   UNIT 5   The Global Economy

Restricting International Trade

MAIN Idea Tariffs and quotas are the main ways to restrict international trade.

Economics and You Have you noticed where your clothes, electronics, or home appliances are made? Read on to find out about ways to restrict imports of such goods.

Historically, trade has been restricted in two major ways. One is through a **tariff**—a tax placed on imports to increase their price in the domestic market. The other is with a **quota**—a limit placed on the quantities of a product that can be imported.

Tariffs

Governments generally levy two kinds of tariffs—protective tariffs and revenue tariffs. A **protective tariff** is a tariff that is high enough to protect less-efficient domestic industries. Suppose, for example, that it costs $1 to produce a mechanical pencil in the United States, while the same product can be imported for 35 cents from another country. If a tariff of 95 cents is placed on each imported pencil, the cost for these imports climbs to $1.30 per pencil—more than the cost of the American-made one.

The result of the tariff is that a domestic industry is protected from being undersold by a foreign one.

The **revenue tariff** is a tariff that is high enough to generate revenue for the government without actually prohibiting imports. If the tariff on imported mechanical pencils were 40 cents, the price of the imports would be 75 cents, or 25 cents less than the American-made ones. As long as the two products are identical, consumers would prefer the imported one because it is less expensive, so the tariff would raise revenue rather than protect domestic producers from foreign competition.

W Traditionally, tariffs were used more for revenues than for protection. Before the Civil War, tariffs were the chief source of revenue for the federal government. From the Civil War to 1913, tariffs provided about one-half of the government's total revenue. After the federal income tax became law in 1913, the government had a new and more lucrative source of revenue. Since then tariffs—also called customs duties—have accounted for only a small portion of total government revenue, as shown in Figure 9.3 on page 239.

In practice, a tariff achieves a little bit of both goals—it gives some protection and it raises some revenue. In 2002, for example, the Bush administration **imposed** a 30 percent temporary tariff on foreign steel imports to protect the domestic steel industry. The tariff raised some revenue and preserved some jobs during an election year, but it also raised the price of domestic steel by 20 to 30 percent—and hence the cost of goods to U.S. consumers.

Quotas

Foreign goods sometimes cost so little that even a high tariff on them might not protect the domestic market. In

---

Activity: Collaborative Learning

Predicting One way to motivate students to read is to have them make predictions about the content beforehand and then evaluate their predictions after they read. Remind students that to make predictions, they should use what they already know combined with information from the text. Ask students to predict what might happen if harsh trade restrictions were erected between all nations of the world. Then have students read the section, helping them as necessary. After students have finished reading, have them work in small groups to review the accuracy of their predictions. Direct students to discuss their predictions in their groups. Encourage group members to identify the pieces of information that helped them make accurate predictions, as well as the missing information that might have made their incorrect predictions more accurate. **BL**

such cases, the government can use a quota to keep foreign goods out of the country. Quotas can even be set as low as zero to keep a product from ever entering the country. More typically, quotas are used to reduce the total supply of a product to keep prices high for domestic producers.

In 1981, for example, domestic automobile producers faced intense competition from lower-priced Japanese imports. Rather than lower their own prices, domestic manufacturers wanted President Ronald Reagan to establish import quotas on Japanese cars. The Reagan administration agreed. As a result, Americans had fewer cars from which to choose, and the prices of all cars were higher than they otherwise would have been.

More recently, the threat of a quota has been used as a way to persuade other nations to change their trade policies. For example, the United States became concerned when the low prices China charged for its exports of textiles created problems for the domestic textile industry. In order to make China raise prices, in 2005 the government threatened China with quotas on these textiles. While it may seem odd to have the U.S. government pursue policies that would raise the cost of products to American citizens, the real purpose of a quota is to protect domestic industries and the jobs in those industries.

Other Barriers

Tariffs and quotas are not the only barriers to trade. Many imported foods are subject to health inspections that are far more rigorous than those given to domestic foods. For years this tactic was used to keep beef from Argentina out of the United States. Another method is to require a license to import. If the government is slow to grant the license, or if the license fees are too high, international trade is restricted. Other nations also use health issues to restrict trade. Several European countries, for example, refuse to import genetically altered crops grown in the United States.

Nationalism and culture often play a role in these debates. Europeans frequently claim that they prefer regional and traditional foods to genetically altered ones. While these may or may not be legitimate arguments, they do restrict trade.

✓ Reading Check Comparing How do tariffs and quotas differ?

CAREERS

Customs Inspector D

The Work

* Inspect cargo, baggage, and articles worn or carried by people, vessels, vehicles, trains, and aircraft entering or leaving the United States

* Examine, count, measure, weigh, gauge, and sample commercial and noncommercial cargoes entering and leaving the United States

* Seize prohibited or smuggled articles and intercept contraband

* Apprehend, search, detain, and arrest violators of U.S. laws

Qualifications

* Must be a U.S. citizen between 21 and 36 years of age when hired

* Possess a valid driver's license and pass a civil service exam

* Must pass a background investigation, meet certain health requirements, and undergo a drug screening test

* Bachelor's degree and one year of related work experience

Earnings

* Starting annual salary: $35,100

Job Growth Outlook

* Average

Source: *Occupational Outlook Handbook, 2006–2007 Edition*

CHAPTER 16 International Trade 449

C Critical Thinking

Interpreting Ask: Why might the U.S. government pursue a trade policy that would raise the costs of products for American consumers? *(to protect domestic industries and the jobs of workers in those industries)* OL

D Differentiated Instruction

Verbal/Linguistic Direct students to use the content in the feature to compose a short job listing for a customs inspector. Students should summarize the position's responsibilities, qualifications, and salary. Encourage students to review job listings in the classified section of a newspaper or online help-wanted ads for guidance when writing their listings. OL

✓ Reading Check **Answer:** A tariff is a tax placed on an imported product. A quota is a limit on the amount of a good that is allowed into the country.

Additional Support

Activity: Interdisciplinary Connection

Speech Tell students: You are the president of a nation with a relatively healthy economy. However, one of your major industries—computer parts—is in decline, largely because of foreign competition. Members of your political party who represent districts where computer parts are the main industry want a high tariff on imported computer parts. In addition, workers in the computer parts industry have launched a huge publicity campaign in support of a tariff increase. At the same time, many people are calling for no tariff because they want to be able to buy inexpensive computer parts.

Have students explain what they, as leaders, intend to do and why. Have them write their decision in the form of a speech to be made to the nation. Invite students to give their speeches to the class. AL

Teacher Tip

Public Speaking Before students make their speeches, review several public speaking strategies. For example, remind students to make eye contact with every listener, speak slowly and clearly, and practice their speeches beforehand.

449

S Skill Practice

Using Geography Skills Have students use library and Internet resources to locate resource maps of the United States. Direct them to study the maps and evaluate how the nation's resources might allow it to prepare for war. Then have students use the maps to explain why the United States might seek to institute trade protection for the purpose of national defense. **AL**

C Critical Thinking

Analyzing Visuals Ask: How might trade protection help a company such as Harley-Davidson become a worldwide competitor? *(Possible answer: Trade protection might allow such a company to improve its production process. This might help it make its products more inexpensively or improve its products' quality.)* **OL**

Caption Answer: because they think that new industries need to gain strength and experience before they can compete against established industries

Additional Support

protectionist person who wants to protect domestic producers against foreign competition with tariffs, quotas, and other trade barriers

free trader person who favors fewer or even no trade restrictions

infant industries argument argument that new and emerging industries should be protected from foreign competition until they are strong enough to compete

Protecting Industries While Harley-Davidson was not a new industry at the time, trade protection in the 1980s helped it to retool and become a worldwide competitor. *Why do protectionists believe that new industries need protection?*

Arguments for Protection

MAIN Idea Protectionists disagree with free traders over the best way to protect a country's independence, industries, and workers.

Economics and You What might you be willing to do to ensure the well-being of your family? Read on to learn why protectionists want to limit international trade.

Freer international trade has been a subject of debate for many years. **Protectionists** are people who favor trade barriers to protect domestic industries. Other people, known as **free traders,** prefer fewer or even no trade restrictions. The debate between the two groups usually centers on the six arguments for protection discussed below.

Aiding National Defense

S The first argument for trade barriers centers on national defense. Protectionists argue that without trade barriers, a country could become so specialized that it would end up becoming too dependent on other countries.

During wartime, protectionists argue, a country might not be able to get critical supplies such as oil and weapons. As a

result, some smaller countries such as Israel and South Africa have developed large armaments industries to prepare for such crises. They want to be sure they will have a domestic supply should hostilities break out or other countries impose economic sanctions such as boycotts.

Free traders admit that national security is a compelling argument for trade barriers. They believe, however, that the advantages of having a reliable source of domestic supply must be weighed against the disadvantages that the supply will be smaller and possibly less efficient than it would be with free trade.

The political problem of deciding which industries are critical to national defense and which are not must also be considered. At one time, the steel, automobile, ceramic, and electronics industries all have argued that they are critical to national defense and so should receive some protection.

Promoting Infant Industries

The **infant industries argument**—that new or emerging industries should be protected from foreign competition—is also used to **justify** trade barriers. Protectionists claim that some industries need to gain

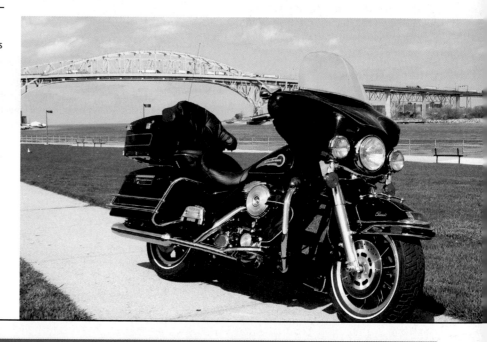

Activity: Hands-On Economics

Hold a Classroom Debate Organize students into three groups. Assign two groups the pro or con position on the following proposition: *U.S. industries should be protected from foreign competition.* Instruct the two groups to review the relevant content from the text regarding their assigned positions. Encourage group members to conduct additional research to strengthen their arguments in preparation

for the debate. Have the third group act as moderators for the debate. Tell these students to study the important issues related to trade protection and prepare a series of debate questions that address these topics. When students have completed their preparations, carry out the debate by having the group of moderators take turns asking questions of the other two groups. Assign specific

amounts of time for groups to respond to these questions, as well as to offer rebuttals to the opposing teams' responses.

After the debate, discuss as a class students' opinions about the strengths and weaknesses of the experience. Have the moderators declare a winner and explain how they arrived at their decision. **OL** strength and experience before they can compete against established industries in other countries. Trade barriers, they argue, would give them the time they need to develop.

Many people are willing to accept the infant industries argument, but only if protection will eventually be removed so that the industry is forced to compete on its own. The problem is that industries that become accustomed to having protection are often unwilling to give it up, making for difficult political decisions later on.

To illustrate, some Latin American countries have used tariffs to protect their own infant automobile industries, with tariffs as high as several hundred percent. In some cases, the tariff raised the price of used American-made cars to more than double the cost of new ones in the United States. In spite of this protection, no country in Latin America has been able to produce a globally competitive automobile on its own. To make matters worse, governments have come to rely on the revenue supplied by tariffs, so prices for automobiles remain high for their citizens.

Protecting Domestic Jobs

A third argument—and the one used most often—is that tariffs and quotas protect domestic jobs from cheap foreign labor. Workers in the shoe industry, for example, have protested the import of lower-cost Italian, Spanish, and Brazilian shoes. Garment workers have opposed the import of lower-cost Korean, Chinese, and Indian clothing. Some steelworkers have even blocked foreign-made cars of coworkers from company parking lots to show their displeasure with the foreign-made steel components in the cars.

In the short run, protectionist measures provide temporary protection for domestic jobs. This is especially attractive to people who want to work in the communities where they grew up. In the long run, however, industries that find it difficult to compete today will find it even more difficult

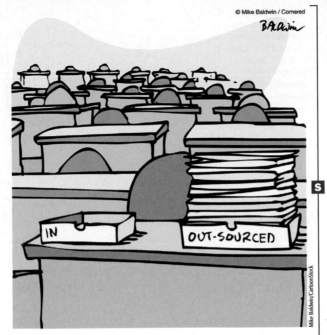

© Mike Baldwin / Cornered

BALDWIN

Outsourcing Protectionists fear that U.S. jobs might move to other countries and Americans will become unemployed. *Why do free traders disagree with this reasoning?*

to compete in the future unless they change the way they operate. As a result, most free traders believe that it is best not to interfere, thereby keeping the pressure on threatened industries to modernize and improve.

When inefficient industries are protected, the economy produces less and the standard of living goes down. Because of artificially high prices, people buy less of everything, including those goods produced by the protected industries. If the prices of protected products get too high, people look for substitute products, and the jobs that were supposed to be protected will still be lost. Free traders argue that the profit-and-loss system is one of the major features of the American economy and should be allowed to work. Profits reward the efficient and hard working, while losses eliminate the inefficient and weak.

CHAPTER 16 International Trade 451

R Reading Strategy

Outlining Direct students to reread the information in the subsection. Ask them to produce an outline that organizes the main ideas and important details from this text. Remind students that their outlines should be written in their own words and should not include complete sentences. Have students compare their completed outlines with partners, making revisions if necessary. **BL**

S Skill Practice

Visual Literacy Ask: What point does the cartoonist make about the jobs of workers at the company pictured? *(The cartoonist points out that because the company has outsourced all of its work, there are no longer jobs available to domestic workers.)* **OL**

Caption Answer: Free traders disagree because they believe it is best to keep pressure on threatened industries to modernize and improve.

Hands-On Chapter Project

Step 2

Analyzing World Trade

Step 2: Examining Trade Restrictions. Student groups will create scenarios describing the effects of a trade restriction against a specific product.

Directions: Have students reassemble into their groups. Tell students to "create" a product that could be manufactured in one or more of the countries on their assigned continent. Groups should provide a written or visual description of their

product. Next, have groups devise a scenario in which people in the United States want to restrict the importation of the product. Students may use any plausible reason for this agenda (for example, domestic producers of the item are losing business to foreign competition or human rights groups oppose the foreign government's domestic policies). Ask groups to include in their scenarios a description of the implementation of a trade restriction against the product, and the subsequent

impact—both home and abroad—of this trade barrier.

Have each group present its scenario to the class in a multimedia format or a skit. After each group has presented, discuss the immediate and long-term effects of trade barriers.

Personal Writing Have students write a short paper expressing their opinions about free trade. **OL**

(Chapter Project continued in Section 3.)

451

D Differentiated Instruction

Visual/Spatial Direct students to draw a cartoon of their own that focuses on an important issue surrounding trade protection. Remind students to include labels and captions to help convey their message. **OL**

W Writing Support

Persuasive Writing Ask students to write a brief persuasive essay in which they argue either for or against protection on the basis of national pride. Direct them to support their arguments using evidence from the text or other reference materials. **OL**

Caption Answer: Domestic companies can sell more of their products to consumers.

✓ Reading Check Answer: Answers will vary, but students should provide valid reasons for their position.

Limiting Imports
With fewer imports, domestic companies can sell more of their products. *What happens when imports are limited?*

"I move we go on record for fewer imports here and more imports there!"

Tom Prisk/Cartoonstock

balance of payments difference between money paid to, and received from, other nations in trade

Keeping the Money at Home

Another argument for trade barriers claims that limiting imports will keep American money in the United States instead of allowing it to go abroad. Free traders, however, point out that the American dollars that go abroad generally come back again. The Japanese, for example, use the dollars they receive for their automobiles to buy American cotton, soybeans, and airplanes. These purchases benefit American workers in those industries.

The same is true of the dollars used to buy oil from the Middle East. The money comes back to the United States when oil-wealthy foreigners buy American-made oil technology. Keeping the money at home also hurts those American industries that depend on exports for their jobs.

Helping the Balance of Payments

Another argument in the free trade debate involves the **balance of payments**— the difference between the money a country pays out to, and receives from, other

nations when it engages in international trade. Protectionists argue that restrictions on imports reduce trade deficits and thus help the balance of payments.

Protectionists overlook the dollars that return to the United States to stimulate employment in other industries. As a result, most economists do not believe that interfering with free trade can be justified on the grounds of helping the balance of payments.

National Pride

A final argument for protection is national pride. France, for example, is proud of its wines and cheeses and protects those industries for nationalistic reasons. In the 1980s, the United States gave temporary protection to Harley-Davidson, an American icon. Whether this is a good idea depends on how long the protection lasts. If it is permanent, then the government is simply protecting inefficient producers.

✓ Reading Check Synthesizing Do you agree with the protectionists' arguments or those of the free traders? Why?

452   UNIT 5   The Global Economy

Free Enterprise Activities, p. 22

Free Trade and Jobs

Objective: Understand how free trade has affected U.S. jobs.

Focus/Teach: Ask students how free trade has impacted the U.S. labor force. Then have students complete the activity.

Assess: Review the answers as a class, discussing any that give students difficulty.

Close: Ask students to write a paragraph explaining their opinions on NAFTA.

Differentiated Instruction Strategies

BL Ask: In which two states did workers suffer the greatest loss in pay? *(New York, Kansas)*

AL Have students research and then write a short report on the TAA program.

ELL Ask students to use the data in the table to create a bar graph for each region.

The Free Trade Movement

MAIN Idea Because tariffs hurt more than they helped during the Great Depression, the United States has found ways to reduce trade restrictions.

Economics and You You learned about the Great Depression in your history courses. Read on to find out how tariffs during that time have affected international trade today.

The use of trade barriers to protect domestic industries and jobs works only if other countries do not retaliate with their own trade barriers. If they do, all countries suffer, because they have neither the benefits of efficient production nor access to less costly products and raw materials from other nations.

Tariffs During the Great Depression

In 1930 the United States passed the Smoot-Hawley Tariff Act, one of the most restrictive tariffs in history. It set import duties so high that the prices of many imported goods rose nearly 70 percent. When other countries did the same, international trade nearly came to a halt.

Before long, most countries realized that high tariffs hurt more than they helped. As a result, in 1934 the United States passed the Reciprocal Trade Agreements Act, which allowed it to reduce tariffs up to 50 percent if other countries agreed to do the same. The act also contained a **most favored nation clause**—a provision allowing a country to receive the same tariff reduction that the United States gives to any third country.

Suppose, for example, that the United States and China have a trade agreement with a most favored nation clause. If the United States then negotiates a tariff reduction with a third country

such as Canada, the reduction would also apply to China. This clause is very important to China, because its goods will then sell at an even lower price in the American market.

The World Trade Organization

In 1947, 23 countries signed the General Agreement on Tariffs and Trade (GATT). The GATT extended tariff concessions and worked to eliminate import quotas. Later, the Trade Expansion Act of 1962 gave the president of the United States the power to negotiate further tariff reductions. As a result of this legislation, more than 100 countries agreed to reduce the average level of tariffs by the early 1990s.

More recently, GATT was replaced by the **World Trade Organization (WTO)**, an international agency that administers trade agreements signed under GATT. The WTO also settles trade disputes between nations, organizes trade negotiations, and provides technical assistance and training for developing countries.

Because so many countries have been willing to reduce tariffs and quotas under GATT and the WTO, international trade is flourishing. Tariffs that in the past nearly doubled the price of many goods now increase prices by only a small percentage. Other tariffs have been dropped altogether.

most favored nation clause trade law allowing another country to enjoy the same tariff reductions the United States negotiates with any third country

World Trade Organization (WTO) international agency that administers trade agreements, settles trade disputes between governments, organizes trade negotiations, and provides technical assistance and training for developing countries

D World Trade Organization Regular meetings of the WTO assist in smoothing out or eliminating trade disagreements. *Why do countries enter trade agreements?*

CHAPTER 16, SECTION 2

C Critical Thinking

Drawing Conclusions
Ask: What do you think might prompt a country like the United States to offer a most favored nation clause to another nation? *(Possible answer: The United States would likely offer the clause because the nation is a major trading partner and the United States wants to preserve a beneficial trading relationship with the nation.)* **OL**

D Differentiated Instruction

Advanced Learners Ask students to research the World Trade Organization, including its members, structure, and key responsibilities. Ask students to use their findings to produce a report on the WTO and its role in international trade. Encourage students to include charts, graphs, or other visuals that they feel may enhance their essays. **AL**

Caption Answer: to maintain conditions for international trading that benefit all of the nations involved

---

Leveled Activities

BL Reading Essentials and Note-Taking Guide, p. 139

OL Primary and Secondary Source Readings, p. 43

AL BusinessWeek Focus on the Global Economy, p. 10

R Reading Strategy

Identifying Ask: What three major trading partners created NAFTA in 1993? *(the United States, Canada, and Mexico)* **BL**

✓**Reading Check** **Answer:** The WTO helped countries reduce tariffs and quotas, which has allowed international trade to flourish. Stores can now offer a wide variety of industrial and consumer goods from all over the world.

Assess

💿 Use the Interactive Tutor Self-Assessment CD-ROM to review Section 2, and then assign the Section 2 Review as homework or as an in-class activity.

Close

Sequencing Information
Have students work in pairs to make a simple time line showing important developments in the free trade movement. **OL**

SECTION
2 **Review**

North American Free Trade Agreement (NAFTA) agreement signed in 1993 to reduce tariffs and increase trade among the United States, Canada, and Mexico

📊 **Skills Handbook**
See page **R55** to learn about **Determining Averages.**

As a result, stores are able to offer a wide variety of industrial and consumer goods from all over the world.

NAFTA

R The **North American Free Trade Agreement (NAFTA)** is an agreement to liberalize free trade by reducing tariffs among three major trading partners: Canada, Mexico, and the United States. It was a bipartisan agreement proposed by President George Bush and concluded by the Clinton administration in 1993.

Before NAFTA, U.S. goods entering Mexico faced tariffs averaging 10 percent. At the same time, approximately half of the goods entering the United States from Mexico were duty free, while the other half faced taxes averaging only 4 percent. NAFTA terms outlined a phase-out of tariffs among the three countries over a 15-year period.

Free trade is beneficial in general, but it is not painless. NAFTA was controversial specifically because some workers would be displaced when trade barriers were lowered. Opponents predicted that some high-paying American jobs would be lost to Mexico. Proponents predicted that trade among all three nations would increase dramatically, stimulating growth and bringing a wider variety of lower-cost goods to everyone.

Some of the costs and benefits identified during the NAFTA debate actually occurred, but not to the extent originally predicted. Trade among the three countries has grown steadily since NAFTA was created. In the end, freer trade has allowed the NAFTA partners to capitalize on their comparative advantages for everyone's benefit.

✓**Reading Check** **Recalling** How did the WTO help international trade?

SECTION
2 **Review**

Vocabulary
1. **Explain** the significance of tariff, quota, protective tariff, revenue tariff, protectionists, free traders, infant industries argument, balance of payments, most favored nation clause, World Trade Organization (WTO), and North American Free Trade Agreement (NAFTA).

Main Ideas
2. **Describing** Use a graphic organizer like the one below to describe three barriers to international trade.

Barriers to Trade

3. **Listing** What six arguments are commonly used to support the protectionists' views on trade?

4. **Describing** What happened to tariffs during the Great Depression?

Critical Thinking
5. **The BIG Idea** How do the views of protectionists and free traders differ?

6. **Drawing Conclusions** If you, as a member of Congress, were approached by a delegation of autoworkers seeking additional tariff or quota protection, how would you respond? Defend your response.

7. **Synthesizing** How would a high tariff on sugar affect U.S. sugar producers, manufacturers of products containing sugar, consumers, workers in the sugar industry, and workers in other related businesses?

8. **Analyzing Visuals** Look at the cartoon on page 452. Explain the meaning of "fewer imports here and more imports there" as it relates to the balance of payments.

Applying Economics
9. **Quotas and Tariffs** Suppose you were in charge of trade policy for the United States. Would you recommend that we increase or decrease trade barriers on athletic shoes? Explain your answer.

Answers

1. All definitions can be found in the section and the Glossary.
2. **Possible answers:** tariffs, quotas, health inspections, licenses, health issues
3. aiding national defense, promoting infant industries, protecting domestic jobs, keeping money at home, helping the balance of payments, national pride
4. A restrictive tariff known as the Smoot-Hawley Tariff Act raised the prices of imports and caused other countries to do the same. International trade nearly stopped.

5. In general, protectionists favor trade barriers to protect domestic industries; free traders prefer fewer trade barriers.
6. Answers will vary, but students should offer evidence to support their position.
7. U.S. sugar producers will benefit from reduced competition; manufacturers of products containing sugar will pay higher prices for sugar; workers in the sugar industry will keep their jobs, while workers in related industries could see job

layoffs; U.S. consumers will pay more for sugar and products containing sugar.
8. The balance of payments is the difference between the money a country pays out to, and receives from, other nations when trading. "Fewer imports here and more imports there" suggests that by importing less and exporting more, the country can improve its balance of payments.
9. Answers will vary but should demonstrate an understanding of trade barriers.

Barriers to international trade include tariffs, quotas, and . . . censorship? Before Yahoo!, Google, and other U.S. tech companies enter the Chinese search engine market, they must censor themselves. With more than 110 million Chinese using the Internet, censoring online content is evidently worth the profits generated.

The Great Firewall of China

It's no secret that Western Internet companies have to hew to the party line if they want to do business in China. Google, Yahoo!, and scores of other outfits, both domestic and foreign, have made concessions to China's censors. . . .

Getting a phone call from the government is one part of the picture. What few Westerners know is the size and scope of China's censorship machine and the process by which multinationals, however reluctantly, censor themselves. Few also know that China's censors have kept up with changing technologies, from cell phone text messaging to blogs.

How do the Chinese do it? Beijing has a vast infrastructure of technology to keep an eye on any potential online dissent. It also applies lots of human eyeballs to monitoring. The agencies that watch over the Net employ more than 30,000 people to prowl Web sites, blogs, and chat rooms on the lookout for offensive content as well as scammers. In the U.S., by contrast, the entire CIA employs an estimated 16,000 people.

Companies, both foreign and domestic, also abet the government's efforts. Virtually all Net outfits on the mainland are given a confidential list of hundreds of banned terms they have to watch for. . . .

The restrictions have led many companies to make both subtle and substantial changes to their operations. . . . IDG Venture Technology Investment . . . has invested in a Chinese company that operates online bulletin boards on real estate, entertainment, technology, autos, and more. But "we don't touch politics at all," says Quan Zhou, managing director of the group's Chinese arm. . . . Not that such policies deter investors.

—Reprinted from *BusinessWeek*

SEARCH ENGINE MARKET SHARE IN CHINA

- 10.4%
- 7.4%
- 15.7%
- 50.3%
- 16.2%

- ● Baidu
- ○ Yahoo! China
- ● Google
- ● Sohu
- ● Other

Examining the Newsclip

1. **Summarizing** How does China censor Internet traffic?
2. **Making Connections** Why is censorship a form of trade barrier?

BusinessWeek

Teach

S Skill Practice

Visual Literacy Ask: What percent of the search engine market does Yahoo! China hold? *(16.2%)* Which company holds the largest share of this market? *(Baidu)* The smallest? *(Sohu)* **BL**

BusinessWeek *ONLINE*

To find up-to-date news and analysis on the economy, business, technology, markets, entrepreneurs, investments, and finance, have students search feature articles and special reports on the BusinessWeek Web site, www.businessweek.com.

Examining the Newsclip

Answers:
1. through human monitors and a vast infrastructure of technology
2. because it limits the ability of Western Internet companies to offer their products in China

Additional Support

Activity: Hand-On Economics

Complying With Censorship Ask students to use library and Internet resources to learn more about the ways in which Western Internet companies comply with Chinese censorship regulations for search engine content. Have students organize the findings from their research and produce a report summarizing what they learned. Encourage students to include any charts, graphs, or fact sheets that may enhance the content of their reports. When students have completed their reports, lead the class in a discussion of whether companies such as those discussed in the feature should agree to censor their content in order to receive the profits generated. Tell students that they should support their arguments using evidence they found through their research. **AL**

Focus

Foreign Exchange and Trade Deficits

Bellringer
Daily Focus Transparency 81

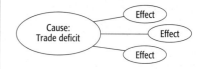

FOCUS ACTIVITIES
Transparency 81

WHO BENEFITS FROM A CHEAP DOLLAR?

1. If the exchange rate causes the U.S. dollar to drop in value, will the American tourists in the first photograph be able to buy more goods and services or fewer goods and services in the country they are visiting?

2. When the U.S. dollar is weak, foreign goods become more expensive and American exports less costly for the rest of the world. How will American workers, such as factory workers producing goods for export, benefit from a weak dollar?

Daily Focus Transparencies

GUIDE TO READING

Possible Answers to Graphic:

Effect: The foreign exchange market is flooded with dollars.

Effect: The dollar loses some of its value.

Effect: Imports become more expensive for Americans.

Effect: Exports become less expensive for foreigners.

Resource Manager

GUIDE TO READING

Section Preview

In this section, you will learn that a long-lasting trade deficit affects the value of a nation's currency as well as the value and volume of its exports and imports.

Content Vocabulary

- foreign exchange (p. 457)
- foreign exchange rate (p. 457)
- fixed exchange rates (p. 457)
- flexible exchange rates (p. 458)
- floating exchange rates (p. 458)
- trade deficit (p. 460)
- trade surplus (p. 460)
- trade-weighted value of the dollar (p. 460)

Academic Vocabulary

- secure (p. 457)
- persistent (p. 460)

Reading Strategy

Describing As you read this section, complete a graphic organizer similar to the one below by describing the effects of a long-lasting trade deficit.

Cause: Trade deficit → Effect / Effect / Effect

ISSUES IN THE NEWS
—BusinessWeek

A Ray of Hope for the Trade Gap

In recent years the U.S. trade deficit has been the No. 1 blight on an otherwise robust economy. Its persistent widening has fueled trade tensions around the world, outsourcing worries among workers, and protectionist sentiment in Washington. Is there a chance for improvement in the trade gap anytime soon?

Well, don't look for outright shrinkage, but the emerging strength in exports is the best sign yet that the rate of deterioration is slowing and that the deficit may even level off later this year.

. . . Overseas demand is picking up as economies from Japan to Europe shake off the blahs of recent years. . . . The other big plus in the export outlook is the dollar's renewed decline, which will give U.S. goods an extra bit of competitiveness in many global markets. ■

 Skills Handbook

See page **R38** to learn about **Distinguishing Fact From Opinion.**

The decline in the value of the American dollar, as you read in the news story above, helped exports by making goods made in the United States cheaper for the rest of the world to buy.

It turns out that this is simply a matter of supply and demand. Whenever people in other countries sell their American dollars, the worldwide supply of dollars increases, and the value of the dollar declines. If people in other countries decide to buy more American dollars, then the decrease in supply of dollars on world markets drives up the value of the dollar.

As a result, the value of the dollar, euro, yen, and most other international currencies tends to fluctuate daily with changes in supply and demand.

R Reading Strategies	C Critical Thinking	D Differentiated Instruction	W Writing Support	S Skill Practice
Teacher Edition • Reading Charts, pp. 457, 466 • Reading Graphs, p. 460 **Additional Resources** • Guid. Read. Act., p. 48 • Read. Ess. & Note-Taking Guide, p. 142	**Teacher Edition** • Det. Cause/Effect, p. 459 • Synthesizing, p. 461 **Additional Resources** • Econ. Concepts Trans., Strat. and Act., p. 41 • Econ. Forms and Fin. Pages Trans., Strat. and Act., p. 26	**Teacher Edition** • ELL, p. 457 • Verbal/Linguistic, p. 460 **Additional Resources** • Authentic Assess., p. 25 • Bus. Focus on the Global Economy, p. 25	**Teacher Edition** • Expository Writing, pp. 458, 467 • Personal Writing, p. 462 **Additional Resources** • High School Reading in the Content Area Strat. and Act.	**Teacher Edition** • Using Line Graphs, p. 458 • Visual Literacy, p. 459 **Additional Resources** • Hands-On Economics, p. 24 • Reinforcing Econ. Skills, p. 20

Financing International Trade

MAIN Idea International trade relies on the ability to exchange foreign currencies.

Economics and You Have you ever seen a coin or bill from another country? Read on to learn how the exchange rates for currencies are determined.

Scenarios like the following occur every day around the globe. A clothing firm in the United States wants to import business suits from a company in Great Britain. Because the British firm pays its bills in the British currency, called "pound sterling," it also wants to receive all of its payments in pound sterling. Therefore, the American firm must sell its American dollars to buy British pounds.

Foreign Exchange

In the field of international finance, **foreign exchange**—different currencies used to facilitate international trade—are bought and sold in the foreign exchange market. This market includes banks that help **secure** foreign currencies for importers, as well as banks that accept foreign currencies from exporters.

Suppose that one pound sterling, or £1, is equal to $1.89. If the business suits are valued at £1,000 in London, the American importer can go to a U.S. bank and buy a £1,000 check for $1,890 plus a small service charge. The American firm then pays the British merchant in pounds, and the suits are shipped.

American exporters sometimes accept foreign currency or checks written on foreign banks in exchange for their goods. They deposit the payments in their own banks, which helps the U.S. banking system build a supply of foreign currency. This currency can then be sold to American firms that want to import goods from other countries. As a result, both the importer and the exporter end up with the currency they need.

The **foreign exchange rate** is the price of one country's currency in terms of another country's currency. The rate can be quoted in terms of the United States dollar equivalent, as in $1.89 = £1, or in terms of foreign currency units per United States dollar, as in £0.5291 = $1. The rate is reported both ways, as shown in the foreign currency listings in **Figure 16.4**.

Fixed Exchange Rates

Today, two major kinds of exchange rates exist—fixed and flexible. For most of the 1900s, the world depended on the use of **fixed exchange rates**—a system under

foreign exchange various currencies used to conduct international trade

foreign exchange rate price of one country's currency in terms of another country's currency

fixed exchange rate system under which the values of currencies are fixed in relation to one another

Figure 16.4 ► **Foreign Exchange Rates**

Exchange Rates, May 12, 2006		
Country	U.S. $ Equivalent	Currency per U.S. $
Australia (dollar)	0.7728	1.2940
Brazil (real)	0.4686	2.1340
Britain (pound)	1.8900	0.5291
Canada (dollar)	0.9021	1.1085
China (yuan)	0.1249	8.0056
Denmark (krone)	0.1729	5.7841
EU (euro)	1.2888	0.7759
Hong Kong (dollar)	0.1290	7.7532
India (rupee)	0.0223	44.8900
Japan (yen)	0.0091	110.4900
Malaysia (ringgit)	0.2791	3.5825
Mexico (peso)	0.0905	11.0525
South Africa (rand)	0.1603	6.2375
South Korea (won)	0.0011	932.7662
Sri Lanka (rupee)	0.0097	102.6500
Sweden (krona)	0.1377	7.2632
Switzerland (franc)	0.8319	1.2020
Thailand (bhat)	0.0264	37.900

Source: finance.yahoo.com

► Exchange rates change constantly according to the supply and demand for different national currencies.

Economic Analysis *About how many Japanese yen equal one U.S. dollar?*

Teach

D Differentiated Instruction

English Language Learners
Guide English language learners in understanding the term *fixed exchange rates*. Point out that in addition to meaning "repaired or mended," the term *fixed* also means "to set absolutely or definitely." Invite volunteers to repeat this definition and apply it to the concept of fixed exchange rates. **ELL**

R Reading Strategy

Reading Charts Have students study the chart showing foreign exchange rates. **Ask:** Which foreign currency has a value most similar to that of the U.S. dollar? *(Canadian dollar)* Which type of foreign currency has the lowest value? *(South Korean won)* The highest value? *(British pound)* **OL**

Economic Analysis
Answer: about 933 Japanese yen

Additional Support

Activity: Interdisciplinary Connection

Mathematics Write the following exchange rate problems on the board, and have students solve them:
1. A television set sells for ¥52,500 in Tokyo. How much would it cost in U.S. dollars if the exchange rate was ¥110 = $1.00? (52,500 ÷ 110 = $477.27)
2. A clock in London sells for £200. How much would it cost in U.S. dollars if the exchange rate was £1 = $1.62? (200 × 1.62 = $324)

3. A pair of blue jeans costs $29.99 in Los Angeles. How much would this item cost in Canadian dollars if the exchange rate was $1.00 Canadian = $0.76 U.S.? (29.99 ÷ .076 = $39.46 Canadian) **OL**

The Global Economy & YOU

The Big Mac Index

Exchange rates should adjust to even out the cost of a market basket of goods and services, wherever it is bought around the world. For example, if you use Canadian dollars to buy a sandwich at a Tim Horton's restaurant in Canada, it should cost the same as if you bought the same sandwich using U.S. dollars at a Tim Horton's in the United States.

One way to see whether a currency is devalued or overvalued against the U.S. dollar is to use the "Big Mac Index" developed by *The Economist* magazine. Economists compare the price of a Big Mac hamburger in the United States to what it costs in another country's local currency. Converting the foreign price to U.S. dollars shows whether the price of a Big Mac is undervalued or overvalued against the U.S. dollar. The cheapest burger in the chart here is in China,

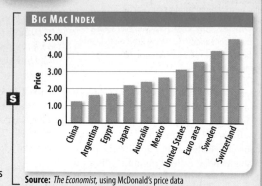

BIG MAC INDEX

Source: *The Economist,* using McDonald's price data

where it costs $1.30, compared with an average American price of $3.15. This implies that China's currency, the yuan, is 59 percent undervalued.

---

flexible exchange rates or floating exchange rates system that relies on supply and demand to determine the value of one currency in terms of another

which the price of one currency is fixed in terms of another currency so that the rate does not change.

Fixed exchange rates were popular when the world was on a gold standard. Gold served as the common denominator that allowed comparisons of currencies, and it kept exchange rates in line. For example, suppose that a country allowed its money supply to grow too fast and that some of the money was spent on imports. Under a gold standard, the countries receiving the currency had the right to demand that it be converted into gold. Because no country **W** wanted to lose its gold, each country worked to keep its money supply from growing too fast.

This practice worked until the early 1960s when the United States developed a huge appetite for imports. During that time, American consumers bought large quantities of foreign goods with dollars. At first, foreign countries willingly held U.S. dollars because the dollars were acceptable throughout the world as an international currency. This meant that only a portion of

these dollars came back when other countries bought American exports.

As dollars began to pile up in the rest of the world, many countries wondered if the United States could honor its promise that the dollar was "as good as gold." Eventually several countries started redeeming their dollars, which drained U.S. gold reserves. As a result, President Richard Nixon announced in 1971 that the United States would no longer redeem foreign-held dollars for gold. This action saved the gold stock, but it also angered many foreign governments that had been planning on cashing their American dollars into gold.

Flexible Exchange Rates

As soon as the United States stopped redeeming foreign-held dollars for gold, the world monetary system shifted to a floating, or flexible, rate system. Under **flexible exchange rates**, also known as **floating exchange rates**, the forces of supply and demand establish the value of one country's currency in terms of another country's currency.

458   UNIT 5   The Global Economy

Working With Foreign Exchange Rates

Figure 16.5 shows how flexible exchange rates work. For example, in 2006 the price of the dollar was 8 yuan, as shown in **Panel A.** Alternatively, we could say that the price of one yuan was $0.125 as shown in **Panel B,** because the two numbers are reciprocals of each other.

Suppose now that an American importer wanted to purchase sandals that could be bought for 40 yuan in China. The American importer would have to sell $5 in the foreign exchange market to obtain the 40 yuan needed to buy the sandals. If this continued over a long period of time, the increased supply of dollars shown in Panel A would drive the price of the dollar down to 6 yuan. The dollar is now cheaper because one dollar costs only 6 yuan rather than 8. At the same time, the increased demand for yuan, shown in Panel B, would raise the price of a single yuan to $0.167 from $0.125. The yuan is now more expensive because it costs more in terms of U.S. currency.

When the yuan reaches $0.167, the price of a pair of sandals is less competitive. This is because the importer now has to pay $6.68 (or 40 times $0.167) to obtain enough yuan to purchase a pair of sandals. Excessive imports thus can cause the value of the dollar to decline, making imports cost more.

This is bad news for U.S. firms that import products from China, but it is good news for exporters. A Chinese firm that bought American soybeans at $6 a bushel before the fall in the dollar, for example, would have paid 48 yuan (or $6/0.125) per bushel. Afterward, it had to pay only 36 yuan (or $6/0.167) per bushel. Soybeans became cheaper, and U.S. farmers could sell more abroad. Whenever the dollar falls, exports tend to go up and imports down. If the dollar rises, the reverse will occur.

The system of flexible exchange rates has worked relatively well. More importantly, the switch to flexible rates did not interrupt the growth in international trade as many people had feared. China is not yet on a system of flexible rates, but it is selling so many products abroad that the yuan is under intense pressure to revalue upward, thus becoming more expensive as in the example above.

✓Reading Check Summarizing How do U.S. banks build a supply of foreign currency?

Figure 16.5 ▶ Flexible Exchange Rates

A THE FOREIGN EXCHANGE MARKET FOR DOLLARS

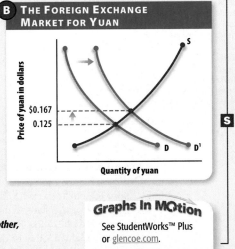

B THE FOREIGN EXCHANGE MARKET FOR YUAN

▶ The value of foreign exchange is determined by supply and demand.

Economic Analysis *When investors sell one currency to buy another, what happens to the value of the currency that is sold?*

Graphs In MOtion
See StudentWorks™ Plus or glencoe.com.

C Critical Thinking

Determining Cause and Effect Have students draw a series of cause-and-effect graphic organizers that trace the effects of flexible exchange rates on the values of currencies for two trading partners over a long period of time. Remind students to consider how supply and demand cause the value of items, such as currency, to change. Tell students to clearly label their organizers so that they can be easily understood. **AL**

S Skill Practice

Visual Literacy Ask: Which type of currency shown in the graphs experienced an increase in demand? How did this influence the supply of that currency? *(The yuan experienced an increase in demand. This caused the supply of that currency to increase.)* **BL**

✓Reading Check **Answer:** by purchasing these currencies on the foreign exchange market

Economic Analysis
Answer: It eventually decreases.

Leveled Activities

BL Guided Reading Activities, p. 48

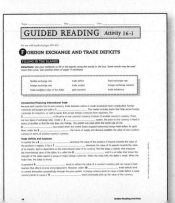

OL Economic Forms and Financial Pages Trans., Strat. and Act., p. 26

AL Hands-On Economics, p. 24

R Reading Strategy

Reading Graphs Ask: In what year did the trade-weighted value of the dollar peak? *(1985)* How would you describe the change of this value over the time period shown on the graph? *(Possible answer: The trade-weighted value of the dollar generally seems to gradually rise and fall over the course of several years throughout the time period shown on the graph.)* **BL**

D Differentiated Instruction

Verbal/Linguistic Request that verbal/linguistic learners practice explaining to the class the definitions of important concepts such as *trade deficit* and *trade surplus*. Further, invite these learners to describe in their own words the relationship between these concepts and the international value of a nation's currency. **OL**

Economic Analysis

Answer: Imports become more expensive for Americans.

Hands-On Chapter Project

Step 3

Analyzing World Trade

Step 3: Studying Exchange Rates and Balance of Trade. Student groups will identify currency exchange rates and the U.S. trade balance with specific nations.

Directions: Organize the class into the same five groups that were formed for Step 1. Tell groups to imagine that they run "international" stores that take many different currencies. Tell groups to assign

---

Figure 16.6 ▶ **International Value of the Dollar**

▶ The forces of supply and demand help set the international value of the dollar. Because the United States now imports more than it exports, the international value of the dollar has fallen.

Economic Analysis *What happens to the cost of imports when the dollar falls?*

Source: Federal Reserve System

trade deficit balance of payments outcome when spending on imports exceeds revenues received from exports

trade surplus balance of payments outcome when revenues received from exports exceed spending on imports

trade-weighted value of the dollar index showing strength of the U.S. dollar against a group of major foreign currencies

Trade Deficits and Surpluses

MAIN Idea The strength of the dollar affects trade and therefore trade deficits and surpluses.

Economics and You Have you ever bought an imported product because it was cheaper than the domestic alternative? Read on to find out how the changing value of the dollar affects the cost of goods.

A country has a **trade deficit** whenever the value of the products it imports exceeds the value of the products it exports. It has a **trade surplus** whenever the value of its exports exceeds the value of its imports. Each is dependent on the international value of its currency.

International Value of the Dollar

Since the dollar started to float in 1971, the Fed has kept a statistic that measures the strength of the dollar. **Figure 16.6** shows the **trade-weighted value of the dollar**, an index displaying the strength of the dollar against a group of major foreign currencies. When the index falls, the dollar is weak in relation to other currencies. When the index rises, the dollar is strong.

When the dollar is strong, as it was in 1985 and 2002, foreign goods become less costly and American exports become more costly for the rest of the world. As a result, imports rise, exports fall, and trade deficits result. With more dollars going abroad, the value of the dollar then goes down.

Effect of a Trade Deficit

A **persistent** trade imbalance can cause a chain reaction that affects income and employment. To illustrate, the large U.S. trade deficit in 2005 and 2006 flooded the foreign exchange markets with dollars. The increase in the supply of dollars on world markets caused the dollar to lose some of its value, making imports more expensive for Americans and exports less expensive for foreigners.

---

one retailing area (for example, clothing, groceries, electrical appliances, and so on) to each of its students. Students should then investigate the prices charged at local stores for five items in their assigned retailing area. Then have students use the exchange rate table in a newspaper business section to find equivalent prices in the currencies of at least three nations on the continent assigned to their group in Step 1. Students may select the same nations as other members of their group.

Direct groups to combine their findings to create price billboards showing items, countries, and prices.

Assessing Have groups research the current U.S. balance of trade with the nations they studied. Then ask each group to write a short paper assessing how exchange rates may have affected the nation's trade with the United States. **OL**

(Chapter Project continued in Visual Summary.)

The recent trade imbalance provided some relief to the U.S. automobile industry. A weaker dollar drives up the price of Japanese-built cars relative to American-built ones. As a result, imported automobiles becomes less attractive to American buyers. If the dollar continues to weaken, other domestic industries will be affected in a similar manner.

When the value of the dollar gets low enough, the process will reverse. Foreigners will sell their currency so that they can buy more American products. This will drive the value of the dollar up, making it more difficult for American export industries and easier for import industries.

A Strong vs. a Weak Dollar

Changes in the international supply and demand for dollars cause the value of the dollar to change daily. What is best—a strong dollar or a weak dollar?

The answer is: neither. Under flexible exchange rates, trade deficits tend to correct themselves automatically through the price system. A strong currency generally

leads to a deficit in the balance of goods and services and a subsequent decline in the value of the currency. A weak currency tends to cause a trade surplus, which eventually pulls up the value of the currency.

Because one sector of the economy is hurt while another is helped, there is no net gain in having either a strong or a weak dollar. As a result, the United States and many other countries no longer design economic policies just to improve the strength of their currency on international markets.

✓**Reading Check** Describing Why did the value of the dollar fall in 2005 and 2006?

C Critical Thinking

Synthesizing Ask: Why might many countries have decided against designing economic policies in order to improve the international strength of their currencies? *(These countries may have decided against this practice because doing so often benefits one sector of a nation's economy, while having a negative impact on other sectors of the economy.)* **OL**

✓**Reading Check** **Answer:** because a large U.S. trade deficit flooded the foreign exchange markets with dollars

Assess

💿 Use the Interactive Tutor Self-Assessment CD-ROM to review Section 3, and then assign the Section 3 Review as homework or as an in-class activity.

Close

Making Connections Have students write a short response detailing how a change in the value of the dollar might affect their daily lives. **OL**

SECTION 3 Review

Vocabulary
1. **Explain** the significance of foreign exchange, foreign exchange rate, fixed exchange rates, flexible exchange rates, floating exchange rates, trade deficit, trade surplus, and trade-weighted value of the dollar.

Main Ideas
2. **Identifying** What are the factors involved in determining exchange rates?

3. **Describing** Use a graphic organizer like the one below to describe what is meant by a strong or weak dollar, and how each affects the prices of imports and exports.

	Description	Effect on imports	Effect on exports
Strong dollar			
Weak dollar			

Critical Thinking
4. **The BIG Idea** What is the relationship between foreign trade and the international value of the dollar?

5. **Making Generalizations** What would happen if the United States lost its comparative advantage in producing soybeans?

6. **Analyzing Visuals** Use the information from Figure 16.4 on page 457 to compare the price of a pair of $100 tennis shoes in the United States with the same brand sold (a) in South Korea at 11,000 ₩ (won) and (b) in France for 100€ (euros).

Applying Economics
7. **Exchange Rates** You are planning to travel to Canada in the next week and have just learned that the Canadian dollar has weakened. Is this good news or bad news? Explain your answer.

CHAPTER 16 International Trade **461**

Review SECTION 3

Answers

1. All definitions can be found in the section and the Glossary.
2. supply and demand for a nation's currency in relation to another nation's currency
3. **Strong dollar:** dollar has increased in value in relation to other currencies; Effect on imports—less expensive for U.S. buyers, imports increase; Effect on exports—more expensive for foreign buyers, exports decrease. **Weak dollar:** dollar has decreased in value in relation to other currencies; Effect on imports—

more expensive for U.S. buyers, imports decrease; Effect on exports—less expensive for foreign buyers, exports increase
4. When the value of the dollar increases, imports increase because they are relatively cheaper and exports decrease because they are more expensive. When the value of the dollar decreases, the reverse occurs.
5. If the dollar rises, U.S. farmers will be less able to sell their products abroad because soybeans from other sources would be relatively cheaper to produce.

6. In South Korea, the shoes would sell for the equivalent of $11.79. In France, the shoes would sell for the equivalent of $128.88.
7. Students should recognize that this is good news because U.S. dollars will now have an increased value in Canada, meaning that the purchasing power has increased.

461

Teach

W Writing Support

Personal Writing Tell students to suppose that a business planner from a company such as Yahoo! has asked them to share their ideas about ways that they would like to see Internet technologies improve in the future. Direct students to write a brief personal essay in which they share their views on this subject. Remind students that in a personal essay they may choose to support their opinions with facts and observations from their own experience. **OL**

Examining the Profile

Answers:

1. Yang began partly to do research for his doctoral thesis and partly to find information about his fantasy basketball league.

2. by finding new ways to build the audience for Yahoo! and by seeking input from current users

Additional Support

Jerry Yang, along with his partner David Filo, built a search engine in a trailer at Stanford University to help with their research—and to have some fun. Soon "people from all over the world were using this database that we created."

Profiles in Economics

Jerry Yang (1968–)

- cofounder of the Internet Web portal Yahoo!
- became a billionaire three years after starting the company
- ranked on *Forbes*'s list of the world's richest people

Yahoo! . . . and Having Fun

When 10-year-old Jerry Yang immigrated to the United States from Taiwan, getting an advanced degree was a distant dream. But in 1994, he found himself working on his Ph.D. at Stanford University. Along with his friend David Filo, he began searching sites on the Internet, partly to do research for their doctoral theses . . . and partly to find information about their fantasy basketball leagues.

Frustrated by the chaos of information on the Web, the two students began to organize sites into subject-based categories. Soon the online traffic flocking to "Jerry's Guide to the World Wide Web" caught the attention of venture capitalists, who provided funds for the start-up company in 1995. Yang and Filo renamed their site Yahoo!, short for "Yet Another Hierarchical Officious Oracle," and called themselves "Chief Yahoos."

The Face of Business

Yang has become the public face and business mind of Yahoo!, but he does not direct the day-to-day operations of the company. Instead, he helps develop business strategy and future business direction. Constant travel brings him to all parts of the world, where he can see firsthand how people use his search engine. This helps him with ideas for growing and expanding Yahoo!.

W Yang wants to stay on the cutting edge of Web development, and he wants "to continue to get audience." He knows his site is a hub for online groups worldwide. One way he plans to expand his audience is by tapping into these user groups to find out what they want. Yang also does not hesitate to move away from the Web and develop information delivery on cell phones and other tools.

Despite all this success, Yang has not quite given up on his educational dream. Even today, the Yahoo media relations site lists him as "currently on a leave of absence from Stanford's electrical engineering Ph.D. program."

Examining the Profile

1. **Summarizing** Why did Yang begin organizing Internet sites?
2. **Analyzing** How does Yang hope to stay ahead of the competition?

Extending the Content

About Yahoo! Founded in 1994, Yahoo! has become one of the most popular search engines on the World Wide Web. The site now offers a variety of specialized search options that allow users to locate sites related to news, shopping, video, and images. In addition to its utility as a search engine, Yahoo! also provides e-mail, instant messaging, and other communication services to users. Further, Yahoo! has partnered with numerous media providers to offer users access to content in a variety of fields, such as entertainment, sports, and finance. Yahoo! is based in Sunnyvale, California, but now has offices around the world.

Study anywhere, anytime! Download quizzes and flash cards to your PDA from glencoe.com.

▶ **Absolute and Comparative Advantage** A country has absolute advantage when it can produce more of a product than can another country. It has comparative advantage when it can produce a product at a lower opportunity cost than another country. When countries focus on those products for which they have comparative advantage, world production increases.

▶ **Free Trade Movement** After strict tariffs severely limited world trade during the early years of the Great Depression, the United States and other countries worked to open trade.

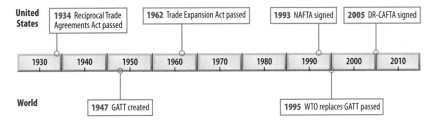

United States

| 1934 Reciprocal Trade Agreements Act passed | 1962 Trade Expansion Act passed | 1993 NAFTA signed | 2005 DR-CAFTA signed |

| 1930 | 1940 | 1950 | 1960 | 1970 | 1980 | 1990 | 2000 | 2010 |

World

1947 GATT created

1995 WTO replaces GATT passed

▶ **Trade Deficits and Surpluses** The strength of the dollar affects the balance of trade of the United States.

Strong Dollar

Exports low → Imports high } Trade deficit → Dollar decreases in value

Weak Dollar

Exports high → Imports low } Trade Surplus → Dollar increases in value

Assessing Ask students to think about the factors that might give one country an absolute advantage over another country. Then have them contrast these factors with those that might give a country a comparative advantage. **Ask:** What process has taken place between the graphs labeled "Before" and "After"? Which country holds a comparative advantage in which product? *(Specialization has taken place between the "Before" and "After" graphs. Country Alpha holds a comparative advantage in coffee, while Country Beta holds a comparative advantage in cashews.)* **BL**

Speculating Direct students to review the information presented in the time line. Then ask them to write a brief essay in which they speculate on the reasons for the increasing openness of international trade throughout the twentieth century and into the present. Students should use information from the time line, as well as the chapter text, to support their speculations. Invite students to share their responses with the class. **OL**

Hands-On Chapter Project

Step 4: Wrap Up

Analyzing World Trade

Step 4: Complete the Analysis. Student teams will summarize what they learned in Steps 1–3.

Directions: Write the Big Idea for this chapter on the board. Have students write an essay elaborating on how trade and specialization have promoted economic growth in the nations on the continent assigned to their group. Students will work alone on this activity—each student will write his or her own essay. Students should integrate into their essays concepts that they learned from each of the previous steps of this chapter project. Ask volunteers to read their essays to the class. Discuss as a class the ideas brought up by students' essays. **OL**

CHAPTER
16 Assessment & Activities

ExamView®
Assessment Suite

This easy-to-use software includes extensive question banks and allows you to create fully customized tests that can be administered in print or online.

Review Content Vocabulary

1.–12. Clues should demonstrate a clear understanding of the terms in an economic context.

Review Academic Vocabulary

13. f
14. a
15. b
16. c
17. e
18. d

Review the Main Ideas

19. Everyone will be better off producing the products they produce relatively best.
20. It allows countries to trade the things that they produce best in exchange for the resources they otherwise lack.
21. It raises the total world output and standard of living.
22. Protective tariff: places a high tax on imports in order to protect less-efficient domestic industries. Revenue tariff: high enough to generate revenue for a government without prohibiting imports.
23. by preventing American industries from being undersold by foreign companies
24. **Possible answer:** WTO: international agency that administers trade agreements signed under GATT; settles trade disputes, organizes trade negotiations;

Review Content Vocabulary

Write crossword puzzle clues for the terms below. All clues should relate to the content of this chapter and should differ from the definitions in the textbook. Create a puzzle grid as an additional challenge.

1. absolute advantage
2. balance of payments
3. comparative advantage
4. foreign exchange rate
5. exports
6. trade surplus
7. imports
8. protectionism
9. quota
10. tariff
11. trade deficit
12. flexible exchange rate

Review Academic Vocabulary

Match each term below with its synonym.

a. enable
b. imposed
c. justify
d. persistent
e. secure
f. volume

13. capacity, amount, quantity
14. facilitate, permit, make possible
15. forced, established, ordered
16. defend, excuse, rationalize
17. gain, acquire, access
18. tenacious, enduring, constant

Review the Main Ideas

Section 1 (pages 441–445)

19. **Identify** the basic assumption supporting the theory of comparative advantage.
20. **Explain** how comparative advantage helps nations acquire goods, services, and the resources they otherwise lack.
21. **Explain** why international trade is important in today's economy.

Section 2 (pages 447–454)

22. **Describe** the different types of tariffs.
23. **Explain** how tariffs and quotas protect American jobs.
24. **Describe** two attempts to facilitate the growth of international trade by using a graphic organizer like the one below.

Agreement or Organization	Description	Encourages trade by…

Section 3 (pages 456–461)

25. **Describe** how the value of the dollar is established using a flexible exchange rate.
26. **Describe** the meaning and effect of a trade deficit.
27. **Identify** the reason why the United States switched to a flexible exchange-rate system in the early 1970s.

Critical Thinking

28. **The BIG Idea** Why is a nation with abundant resources better off trading than being self-sufficient?
29. **Synthesizing** How does comparative advantage make trade between countries of different sizes possible?
30. **Drawing Conclusions** Do you favor protectionism as a national trade policy? Why or why not?

assists and trains developing countries. NAFTA: agreement to liberalize free trade among the United States, Canada, and Mexico; plans to phase out trade restrictions among the members

25. Supply and demand establishes the value in terms of another country's currency.
26. Meaning: a country's spending on imports exceeds revenues received from its exports. Effect: the dollar loses some of its value, making imports more expensive and exports less expensive.

27. because nations tried to redeem dollars for gold, which drained the gold supply

Critical Thinking

28. Being self-sufficient will result in a lower standard of living than would be possible with specialization and trade.
29. Students should note that the efficient use of resources is most important.
30. Answers will vary but should demonstrate an understanding of protectionism.

Economics ONLINE Self-Check Quiz Visit the
Economics: Principles and Practices Web site at glencoe.com and click
on Chapter 16—Self-Check Quizzes to prepare for the chapter test.

Assessment
and Activities

CHAPTER
16

31. **Making Inferences** How might the issue of protectionism differ for a worker and a consumer? Use examples to support your argument.

32. **Analyzing Information** Some people think the United States should return to a system of fixed exchange rates. Defend or oppose this view. Cite examples to support your position.

33. **Drawing Conclusions** How do trade deficits correct themselves under a system of flexible exchange rates?

34. **Synthesizing Information** Why do you need to know the exchange rate when you plan a trip to a foreign country?

Math Practice

35. **Imagine** that you are traveling through South America and staying in budget hotels. Based on the average room rates and exchange rates in the table below, establish the room rates in dollars for each country.

Country	Cost of room in foreign currency	Currency per U.S. $	Cost of room in U.S. $
Argentina (peso)	70	0.3247	
Bolivia (boliviano)	96	0.1251	
Brazil (real)	71	0.4561	
Chile (peso)	80	0.001853	
Paraguay (guarani)	41,100	0.0001826	
Peru (neuvo sol)	49	0.3086	
Uruguay (new peso)	299	0.04185	
Venezuela (bolivar)	35,000	0.0003818	

Thinking Like an Economist

36. Assume that the United States is running a large trade deficit. What predictions would you make about future changes in the value of the dollar in foreign exchange markets? Would these developments be a matter of concern? Explain your answer.

Writing About Economics

37. **Persuasive Writing** During the course of one day, make a list of at least 10 manufactured items that you handle, such as your clothing and the cafeteria trays used in your school. Find out where each item is produced, and make a log of the items, noting whether each is domestic- or foreign-made. Based on your log and the information in this chapter, write a persuasive essay supporting or opposing international trade.

Applying Economic Concepts

38. **Foreign Exchange** How does a weak U.S. dollar affect you as a consumer? How does a strong dollar affect you? Explain.

39. **Comparative Advantage** Think of a project you recently completed with a friend. Apply the principle of comparative advantage to the way you and your friend worked. How could you have completed the project more efficiently? Explain.

Interpreting Cartoons

40. **Critical Thinking** What aspect of foreign trade does the cartoonist illustrate in this cartoon? Do you think the cartoon is effective? Explain.

CHAPTER 16   International Trade   465

Math Practice

35. Argentina—$22.73
    Bolivia—$12.01
    Brazil—$32.38
    Chile—$0.15
    Paraguay—$7.50
    Peru—$15.12
    Uruguay—$12.51
    Venezuela—$13.36

Thinking Like an Economist

36. Answers should demonstrate understanding of foreign exchange markets and be supported by sound economic reasoning.

Writing About Economics

37. Answers will vary but should address the issue of international trade.

Applying Economic Concepts

38. A weak dollar means that consumers will pay more for any imported good or for products made with imported parts/resources. With a strong dollar, consumers will pay less for the imported items.

39. Answers will vary but should demonstrate an understanding of comparative advantage.

Interpreting Cartoons

40. The cartoonist points out that one of the potential costs of international trade is the loss of domestic jobs. Students' assessments of the cartoon will vary.

31. Workers in a threatened industry will likely support protectionists because they do not want to lose their jobs. Consumers tend to oppose protectionism because trade barriers generally lead to higher prices. Examples will vary.

32. Students should present their arguments using supporting details from the text.

33. A persistent trade deficit tends to reduce the value of a country's currency. In other words, supply of currency exceeds demand. This, in turn, makes imports cost more and exports cost less. Over time,

foreigners will sell their currency to acquire U.S. dollars so they can buy the cheaper U.S. goods. Supply and demand move toward equilibrium, and the trade deficit declines.

34. Since other countries do not use the U.S. dollar as their currency, you need to know how much your dollars are worth and what your spending power will be. You can plan your trip more effectively and stay within your trip budget if you are aware of the exchange rates.

465

DEBATES IN ECONOMICS
Will CAFTA Be Beneficial to the U.S.?

As you learned in Chapter 1, the United States has a remarkable degree of economic interdependence with other nations. On August 2, 2005, President George W. Bush expanded this interdependence by signing into law DR-CAFTA——the Dominican Republic-Central America Free Trade Agreement. This agreement among the United States and Costa Rica, the Dominican Republic, El Salvador, Guatemala, Honduras, and Nicaragua takes effect as soon as all countries involved ratify it. Still, it was hotly debated. Some believe the agreement, sometimes called CAFTA, will help the U.S. economy. Others fear it will be harmful.

Who is right? As you read the selections, ask yourself: Will DR-CAFTA help or harm the U.S. economy?

PRO CAFTA: A WIN-WIN CASE

The economic case for CAFTA is compelling. First, the level playing field created by the pact would benefit U.S. consumers and businesses. Currently about 80% of Central American products enter the U.S. duty-free. CAFTA would provide some balance with reciprocal treatment for U.S. goods and agricultural exports, and all tariffs on U.S. goods would be eliminated over time. CAFTA would also require increased transparency in corporate governance, legal systems, and due process in the region, strengthening the local economies. For U.S. business, the newly expanded access to the region would benefit companies in financial services, telecommunications, entertainment, and computer services. CAFTA, moreover, would create jobs in Central America and make the region's economies more competitive with Asian nations.

CAFTA-DR eliminates these tariffs:

- El Salvador's 30% auto tariff
- Guatemala's 23% tariff on certain footwear
- Plastics and cosmetics tariff of up to 15%
- Air conditioning and refrigeration equipment tariffs of up to 15%
- Building products and home construction accessories, including fixtures, sinks, and doors, 15% tariffs

Current Tariffs on Central America and Dominican Republic Imports from the U.S.	
Motor vehicles/parts	11.0%
Wood products	10.0%
Textile/apparel/leather products	10.0%
Chemicals/petroleum/coal/rubber	5.0%
Ferrous metals	6.3%
Other metals/metal products	3.5%
Transport equipment	3.5%
Electronic equipment	1.4%
Other machinery/equipment	4.0%
Other manufactures	7.1%

Source: www.export.gov

... There are foreign policy reasons to favor the CAFTA accord. Since the 1970s, CAFTA nations have moved toward market economies and democracy, becoming commercial and political allies of the U.S. CAFTA's boost to economic growth and incomes in Central America would further bolster support for free markets and democratic institutions.

—Glenn Hubbard, Dean of the Columbia University Business School

Extending the Content

About CAFTA The U.S. Congress approved the Dominican Republic-Central America Free Trade Agreement, or CAFTA, in July of 2005. President George W. Bush signed the agreement into law on August 2, 2005. The legislature of the Dominican Republic, as well as those of El Salvador, Guatemala, Honduras, and Nicaragua, has ratified CAFTA. Such ratification is currently pending in Costa Rica. Because different countries have approved the agreement at different times, the United States has chosen to enact the legislation in each country as the nation takes the necessary steps to comply with CAFTA. The first country to do so was El Salvador, in March of 2006. The nations of CAFTA have become an increasingly important destination for U.S. exports in recent years. These countries represent the tenth largest U.S. export market in the world, ahead of nations such as Russia and India.

CON CAFTA COULD LEAD TO FURTHER U.S. JOB DISPLACEMENT

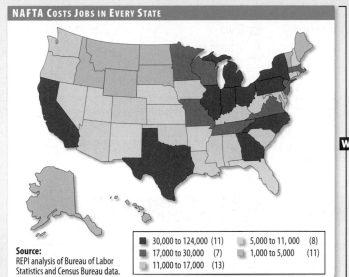

NAFTA Costs Jobs in Every State

■ 30,000 to 124,000 (11)	▨ 5,000 to 11,000 (8)
■ 17,000 to 30,000 (7)	▨ 1,000 to 5,000 (11)
▨ 11,000 to 17,000 (13)	

Source:
REPI analysis of Bureau of Labor
Statistics and Census Bureau data.

No protections were contained in [NAFTA] to maintain labor or environmental standards. As a result, NAFTA tilted the economic playing field in favor of investors and against workers and the environment, causing a hemispheric "race to the bottom" in wages and environmental quality.

. . . These experiences raise serious questions about the likely economic impact **W** of the . . . DR-CAFTA agreement on the economies of the United States, and equally important, its neighbors in the Dominican Republic and Central America.

—Robert E. Scott, Director of International Programs, Economic Policy Institute, and David Ratner, research assistant at the Economic Policy Institute

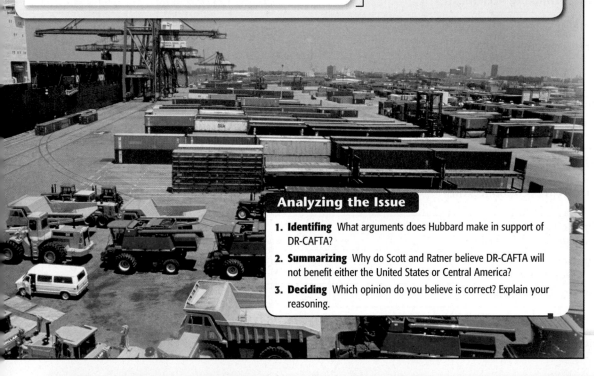

Analyzing the Issue

1. **Identifying** What arguments does Hubbard make in support of DR-CAFTA?
2. **Summarizing** Why do Scott and Ratner believe DR-CAFTA will not benefit either the United States or Central America?
3. **Deciding** Which opinion do you believe is correct? Explain your reasoning.

Assess/ Close

W Writing Support

Expository Writing Direct students to use library and Internet resources to research the impact of NAFTA on employment in their home state. Then have students write a brief essay describing their findings. **AL**

Analyzing the Issue

Answers:
1. would provide a more balanced treatment of U.S. goods and agricultural exports; would lead to better corporate governance; would give U.S. businesses greater access to these countries, while strengthening each nation
2. They believe that CAFTA will not institute labor or environmental standards.
3. Answers will vary but should be logical and well supported.

Additional Support

Activity: Technology Connection

Plan a Web Site Organize the class into small groups. Instruct students in each group to conduct Internet research to find Web sites that both support and oppose the Dominican Republic-Central America Free Trade Agreement. Ask students to study these Web sites and identify the components that the designers have

included, such as text, graphics, photos, and so on.

After students have studied several of these Web sites, direct each group to choose one side of the debate and then plan their own Web site for this position. Remind groups to consider which elements they found most

compelling and convincing during their study of the other CAFTA Web sites. Have group members work together to select what elements they will include and then sketch out a plan for the design of the Web site and its contents. Invite each group to present their Web site plans to the class. **OL**

CHAPTER 17 Planning Guide

Key to Ability Levels
- **BL** Below level
- **OL** On level
- **AL** Above level
- **ELL** English Language Learners

Key to Teaching Resources
- Print Material
- CD-Rom
- DVD
- Transparency

Levels					Resources	Chapter Opener	Section 1	Section 2	Section 3	Chapter Assess
BL	OL	AL	ELL							
FOCUS										
BL	OL	AL	ELL	🖋	**Daily Focus Skills Transparencies**		83, 84, 87	86, 88	83, 84	
TEACH										
BL	OL		ELL	📁	**Guided Reading Activities***		p. 49	p. 50	p. 51	
BL	OL	AL	ELL	📁	**Economic Content Vocabulary Activities***		p. 17	p. 17	p. 17	
	OL	AL		📁	**Critical Thinking Activities**		p. 24	p. 12		
BL	OL		ELL	📁	**Reading Essentials and Note-Taking Guide***		p. 145	p. 148	p. 151	
		AL		📁	**Enrichment Activities**			p. 17		
	OL	AL		📁	**Free Enterprise Activities**		p. 24	pp. 23, 24	p. 24	
BL	OL	AL	ELL	📁	**Economic Cartoons**		p. 27	p. 28	p. 27	
BL	OL	AL	ELL	📁	**Math Practice for Economics**		p. 23	pp. 17, 21	p. 23	
	OL	AL		📁	**BusinessWeek Focus on the Global Economy**			pp. 2, 10		
BL	OL	AL	ELL	📁	**Reinforcing Economic Skills**			pp. 9, 25	p. 27	
BL	OL		ELL	📁	**High School Reading in the Content Area Strategies and Activities**	✓	✓	✓	✓	✓
BL	OL	AL	ELL	🖋	**High School Writing Process Transparencies**	✓	✓	✓	✓	✓
BL	OL	AL	ELL	📁	**Writer's Guidebook**	✓	✓	✓	✓	✓
BL	OL	AL	ELL	💿	**StudentWorks Plus CD-ROM**	✓	✓	✓	✓	✓
BL	OL	AL	ELL	💿	**Vocabulary PuzzleMaker CD-ROM**	✓	✓	✓	✓	✓

*Also available in Spanish

All-In-One Planner and Resource Center

- Interactive Lesson Planner
- Interactive Teacher Edition
- Fully editable blackline masters
- Economics & You videos

- Differentiated Lesson Plans
- Printable reports of daily assignments
- Standards tracking system

Levels					Resources	Chapter Opener	Section 1	Section 2	Section 3	Chapter Assess
BL	OL	AL	ELL		**TEACH** *(continued)*					
BL	OL	AL	ELL		**Economics & You Video Program DVD—** *Developing Countries*	✓	✓	✓	✓	✓
BL	OL	AL	ELL		**Graph Coach CD-ROM**	✓	✓	✓	✓	✓
Teacher Resources					**Differentiated Instruction Strategies**	✓	✓	✓	✓	✓
					Success with English Learners	✓	✓	✓	✓	✓
					Presentation Plus! CD-ROM	✓	✓	✓	✓	✓
					ASSESS					
BL	OL	AL	ELL		**Section Quizzes and Chapter Tests**		p. 213	p. 214	p. 215	pp. 217, 221
BL	OL	AL	ELL		**Authentic Assessment Strategies and Activities**		p. 24			
BL	OL	AL	ELL		*ExamView® Assessment Suite* **CD-ROM**		17-1	17-2	17-3	Ch. 17
BL	OL	AL	ELL		**Interactive Tutor Self-Assessment CD-ROM**		17-1	17-2	17-3	
					CLOSE					
BL			ELL		**Reteaching Activities***		p. 17	p. 17	p. 17	
BL	OL		ELL		**Reading and Study Skills Foldables**		p. 65		p. 65	
BL	OL	AL	ELL		**Graphic Organizer Transparencies**			p. 5		

*Also available in Spanish

Activity
Using the Glencoe Web Site

ePuzzles and Games

Technology Product
The Glencoe Web site offers activities that students can perform as they study the chapter content. The activities consist of a variety of puzzles and games that help students test their comprehension and recall and reinforce vocabulary and facts in each chapter.

Objectives
The Student Web Activities help students
- assess their comprehension of chapter content;
- build study skills;
- identify areas for additional study and reinforcement.

Steps
Provide students with the following steps to complete the activities:
- Locate the Web page for the textbook being studied on the Glencoe Web site glencoe.com.
- Click on **Student Center** under the textbook title.
- In the Student Center, select a unit from the Unit Resources menu and a chapter from the Chapter Activities menu using the drop-down arrows.
- Click on the **ePuzzles and Games** link.
- Click on and complete the featured puzzle or game for the chapter selected.

Economics ONLINE

	Student	Teacher	Parent
Beyond the Textbook	●	●	●
Chapter Overviews	●	●	●
ePuzzles and Games	●		●
Concepts in Motion	●		●
Multi-Language Glossaries	●		●
Online Student Edition	●	●	●
Self-Check Quizzes	●		●
Student Web Activities	●		●
Study Central™	●		●
Time Current Events	●	●	●
Teaching Today		●	
Vocabulary eFlashcards	●		●
Web Activity Lesson Plans		●	

Glencoe Media Center

❯ glencoe.com

Study-To-Go
- Vocabulary eFlashcards
- Self-Check Quizzes

❯ **Audio/Video**
- Student Edition Audio
- Spanish Summaries
- Economics & You Videos

READING SUPPORT FROM
JAMESTOWN EDUCATION

- **Timed Readings Plus in Social Studies** helps students increase their reading rate and fluency while maintaining comprehension. The 400-word passages are similar to those found on state and national assessments.

- **Reading in the Content Area: Social Studies** concentrates on six essential reading skills that help students better comprehend what they read. The book includes 75 high-interest nonfiction passages written at increasing levels of difficulty.

- **Reading Social Studies** includes strategic reading instruction and vocabulary support in Social Studies content for both ELLs and native speakers of English. www.jamestowneducation.com

Reading List Generator CD-ROM

GLENCOE
BOOKLINK 3

Use this database to search more than 30,000 titles to create a customized reading list for your students.

- Reading lists can be organized by students' reading level, author, genre, theme, or area of interest.

- The database provides Degrees of Reading Power™ (DRP) and Lexile™ readability scores for all selections.

- A brief summary of each selection is included.

Leveled reading suggestions for this chapter:
For students at a Grade 10 reading level:
- *China: A Study of an Economically Developing Country,* by Julia Waterlow

For students at a Grade 11 reading level:
- *The Arms Trade,* by Richard Bingley

For students at a Grade 12 reading level:
- *Poverty: Opposing Viewpoints,* by David L. Bender & Bruno Leone

* Review suggested books before assigning them.

NCEE

National Council on Economic Education

Voluntary Standards Emphasized in Chapter 17

Content Standard 3 Different methods can be used to allocate goods and services. People acting individually or collectively through government, must choose which methods to use to allocate different kinds of goods and services.

Content Standard 15 Investment in factories, machinery, new technology, and in the health, education, and training of people can raise future standards of living.

Content Standard 16 There is an economic role for government in a market economy whenever the benefits of a government policy outweigh its costs. Governments often provide for national defense, address environmental concerns, define and protect property rights, and attempt to make markets more competitive. Most government policies also redistribute income.

Resources Available from NCEE
- Virtual Economics®: An Interactive Center for Economic Education Version 3.0
- Capstone: The Nation's High School Economics Course
- Focus: International Economics
- Focus: Globalization

To order these materials, or to contact your State Council on Economic Education about workshops and programs, call 1-800-338-1192 or visit the NCEE Web site at store.ncee.net**.**

The **BIG** Ideas

As students study the chapter, remind them to consider the chapter-based Big Ideas. The **Essential Question** in the chapter launch activity below ties in to the Big Ideas and helps students think about and understand important chapter concepts. In addition, the Hands-On Chapter Project relates the content from each section to the Big Ideas. The steps in each section build on each other and culminate in the Wrap-Up Activity on the Visual Summary page.

 To generate student interest and provide a springboard for class discussion, access the Economics & You Topic 25 video, **Developing Countries,** at glencoe.com or on the video DVD.

 Dinah Zike's Foldables are three-dimensional, interactive graphic organizers that help students practice basic writing skills, review key vocabulary terms, and identify main ideas. Have students complete this chapter's Foldable activity or activities in *Dinah Zike's Reading and Study Skills Foldables* booklet. **OL**

Economics ONLINE

Introduce students to chapter content and key terms by having them access *Chapter 17 —Chapter Overviews* at glencoe.com.

CHAPTER
17 Developing Countries

Why It Matters

Your pen pal from abroad has asked for your school's help on a project to improve the quality of life for the students in his school and community. As a member of the planning committee, your task is to suggest ideas. Create a list of ways to help students and the neighborhood as a whole. Present your proposals to the class. Read Chapter 17 to learn about the ways that developing nations can improve the quality of life for their citizens.

The **BIG** Ideas

1. Every society has an economic system to allocate goods and services.

2. The study of economics helps us deal with global economic issues and global demand on resources.

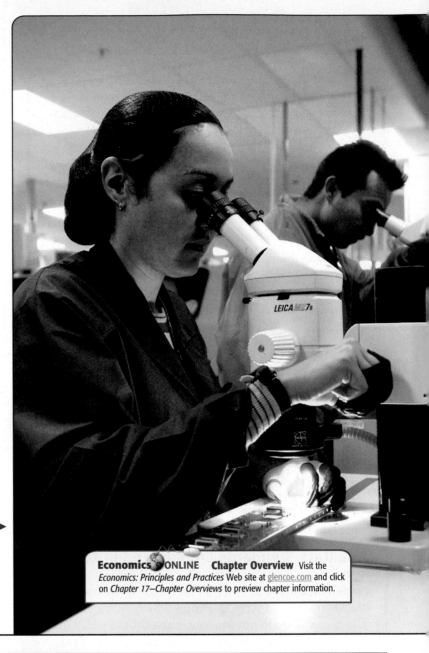

▶ Foreign investments help developing countries by bringing jobs and technology, such as in this optical chip factory in Mexico.

Economics ONLINE Chapter Overview Visit the *Economics: Principles and Practices* Web site at glencoe.com and click on *Chapter 17–Chapter Overviews* to preview chapter information.

468 UNIT 5

Activity: Launching the Chapter

Differentiating Have students, without using a map, globe, or textbook, brainstorm a list of different countries in the world. Ask a volunteer to write the country names on the board. Stop when the class has listed 20 nations. Have students then try to describe the economic system or major economic issues that exist in each country listed on the board. **Essential Question:** What are the different factors that can influence the economic development of nations? *(Answers may include natural resources, population, disease, education, political system, foreign aid, and foreign investment.)* As they read this chapter, ask students to take note of the different ways that nations impact the economic development of other nations. **OL**

SECTION 1
Economic Development

GUIDE TO READING

Section Preview

In this section, you will learn that developing countries face a number of obstacles that make economic growth difficult.

Content Vocabulary

- developing country (p. 469)
- primitive equilibrium (p. 472)
- takeoff (p. 473)
- crude birthrate (p. 474)
- life expectancy (p. 474)
- zero population growth (ZPG) (p. 474)
- external debt (p. 475)
- default (p. 476)
- capital flight (p. 477)

Academic Vocabulary

- proportion (p. 472)
- primary (p. 475)

Reading Strategy

Identifying As you read the section, complete a graphic organizer similar to the one below by identifying at least two reasons why it would probably be more difficult to bring about change in a traditional economic system than in a market economy.

The difficulty of change in a traditional economy

PEOPLE IN THE NEWS

—www.cbsnews.com

Bono's War On Poverty

Actor Brad Pitt is among the celebrities featured in new public service announcements for a war on poverty and AIDS led by U2 singer Bono.

The Irish rock star and political activist says that instead of being focused on donations, the ads for "ONE: The Campaign to Make Poverty History" are aimed at increasing public awareness of the problem and recruiting new advocates for the goals of the campaign.

Pitt, who visited Africa after being inspired by Bono's advocacy, said he was struck by how extreme poverty there has made it difficult for the sick to gain access to drugs to minimize the effects of AIDS. "I've seen it, I've been there, and to walk away from it and turn my back makes me culpable," Pitt said. "I can't do that." ∎

Most of the people in the world today live in **developing countries**—countries whose average per capita GNP is a fraction of that in more industrialized countries. Poverty is rampant in most of these countries, with about 1 billion people worldwide now living on the equivalent of less than $1 per day.

There are many ways to deal with poverty, including direct government aid and voluntary civic organizations. As we read in the news story above, assistance sometimes comes from unexpected sources. Even so, the best way to improve the lot of impoverished people in all nations is with economic growth and development.

developing country country with relatively low average per capita income and less developed infrastructure, education, and health care system

CHAPTER 17 Developing Countries **469**

Focus

Bellringer
Daily Focus Transparency 87

GUIDE TO READING

Answers to Graphic: cultural values discourage change; less access to technology

Resource Manager

R Reading Strategies	**C** Critical Thinking	**D** Differentiated Instruction	**W** Writing Support	**S** Skill Practice
Teacher Edition • Reading Maps, p. 471 • Academic Vocab., p. 472 • Using Word Parts, p. 477 **Additional Resources** • Guid. Read. Act., p. 49 • Read. Ess. & Note-Taking Guide, p. 145	**Teacher Edition** • Ident. POV, p. 472 • Det. Cause/Effect., p. 473 • Assessing, p. 475 • Predicting, p. 478 **Additional Resources** • Econ. Cartoons, p. 27 • Quizzes and Tests, p. 213	**Teacher Edition** • Logical/Math., p. 470 • Intrapersonal, p. 474 • ELL, p. 476 **Additional Resources** • Free Ent. Act., p. 24 • Math Prac. for Econ., p. 23	**Teacher Edition** • Persuasive Writing, p. 470 • Narrative Writing, p. 476 **Additional Resources** • High School Reading in the Content Area Strat. and Act. • Reading and Study Skills Fold., p. 65	**Teacher Edition** • Using Geo. Skills, p. 471 • Visual Literacy, p. 474 • Det. Averages, p. 475 **Additional Resources** • Econ. Content Vocab. Act., p. 17 • Daily Focus Trans. 83, 84

Teach

W Writing Support

Persuasive Writing

Have students write an essay explaining why it is important for people in all nations, including those that are wealthy, to work together to try to end poverty around the world. **OL**

D Differentiated Instruction

Logical/Mathematical

Ask: Which nation in the Americas is in the third highest GNI per capita category? *(Canada)* **BL**

Did You Know?

The United States, though it has the highest GDP in the world, is surpassed by four other nations in GDP per capita. In 2005 the five countries with the highest per capita GDP were **1)** Luxembourg; **2)** Equatorial Guinea; **3)** United Arab Emirates; **4)** Norway; **5)** United States.

Additional Support

Skills Handbook

See page R43 to learn about Comparing and Contrasting.

The Importance of Economic Development

MAIN Idea In a global economy, the economic health of all nations is important.

Economics & You Do you remember reading about poverty in the United States? Read on to learn how this compares to poverty in the rest of the world.

Poverty, whether domestic or global, is more than an economic problem—it is also the source of social discontent and political unrest. It can even threaten the very stability of a country.

In order to make comparisons between countries, economists convert all currencies to a common unit such as the U.S. dollar. Then, to compensate for populations of different sizes, they express all income on a per capita basis.

International Comparisons

The map in **Figure 17.1** shows the total national income for most countries in the world. The United States, which has the largest total income, is the largest area on the map. Countries with smaller incomes are scaled accordingly.

The map is also color coded to show countries with similar national incomes on a per capita basis. Viewed this way, the map clearly shows the contrast between the industrialized economies of North America, Western Europe, and Japan and the developing countries of South America, the Caribbean, Africa, and Asia.

Impact of Economic Growth

W Even though about 1 billion people live in poverty today, there has been considerable improvement in recent years. In 1981, for example, 1.5 billion people, or 40 percent of the world population, lived on less than $1 per day. This figure dropped to 1.2 billion in 1990, or about 28 percent of the world population. By 2001, the number had declined to 1.1 billion, accounting for about 21 percent of the world population.

Figure 17.1 ▶

Maps In Motion
See StudentWorks™ Plus
or glencoe.com.

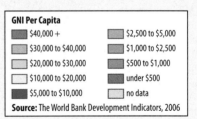

GNI Per Capita

- $40,000 +
- $30,000 to $40,000
- $20,000 to $30,000
- $10,000 to $20,000
- $5,000 to $10,000
- $2,500 to $5,000
- $1,000 to $2,500
- $500 to $1,000
- under $500
- no data

Source: The World Bank Development Indicators, 2006

Activity: Interdisciplinary Connection

Geography Assign one nation from Figure 17.1 to each of the students in your class. Instruct students to use print resources (such as an almanac) or reliable Web sites to research their assigned country's geography and natural resources. Ask students to write a short paper explaining how the factors of geography and natural resources impacted their nation's economy and thus contributed to its per capita GNI. In their papers, students should speculate about the future of their country. Will it continue to stay in the same GNI per capita range, or will their GNI per capita rise or decline? When finished, have students present their papers to the class. **OL**

Gross National Income and Gross National Income Per Capita

▶ If every nation's gross national income were proportional to its total land area, a political map of the world would look like the cartogram in this figure. The colors indicate different levels of national income on a per capita basis and provide another view of a nation's prosperity.

Economic Analysis *Which nations have a per capita gross national income similar to that of the United States?*

The size of every country is proportional to its gross national income (**GNI**). The colors indicate the **GNI** per capita.

S Skill Practice

Using Geography Skills
Ask: What are three nations that have a larger area on this map than their actual geographical sizes on a globe? *(Answers may include Japan, United Kingdom, and Germany.)* What are three nations that have a smaller area on this map than their actual geographical sizes on a globe? *(Answers may include Russian Federation, Sudan, China, Mongolia, and Australia.)* OL

R Reading Strategy

Reading Maps Have students examine the map and take note of any trends that stand out to them. Instruct students to write a short paper summarizing what this map reveals about each of the six inhabited continents. OL

Economic Analysis

Answer: Norway, Denmark, Switzerland, Luxembourg

Additional Support

Activity: Collaborative Learning

Comparing GDP Organize the class into five groups. Assign a continent to each of the groups: North and Central America (group together for the purposes of this activity), South America, Europe, Africa, and Asia. Have groups use an almanac or trustworthy Internet sources to research Gross Domestic Product figures for the nations on their assigned continent. Ask groups to then create a map similar to the one in Figure 17.1, in which each nation's land area is proportional to its GDP. Instruct students to use colors to categorize countries according to their per capita GDP (assign colors and per capita groupings so that the groups' maps will match). Have groups combine their continent maps to form a world map based on GDP and GDP per capita. **AL**

R Reading Strategy

Academic Vocabulary Direct students to study the sentence containing the word *proportion*. Ask students to draw a picture or diagram illustrating the concept described in the sentence. **OL**

C Critical Thinking

Identifying Points of View

Ask: Why might people in a primitive equilibrium society prefer to remain in that stage?

(Answers may include fear among elites that economic change will threaten their position, fear of violating tradition or religious beliefs, lack of understanding about the effects of technology, or contentment with current system.) **OL**

✓Reading Check **Answer:**
It allows economists to compensate for population size when assessing the economic health of nations.

Differentiated Instruction

Critical Thinking Activities, p. 24

Did You Know?

▶ **Economic Development** Economic growth is often uneven. As a result, some countries may be in several stages of development at the same time. For example, many developing nations in Asia went from having no telephones to widespread use of cell phones. At the same time, their populations continue to base other parts of their daily lives on customs and traditions.

primitive equilibrium
first stage of economic development during which the economy is stagnant

Concern for Developing Countries

The international community shares humanitarian as well as economic concern for the developing countries. For example, many people in the more developed countries believe that it is their moral responsibility to help those who have less income and wealth than they do.

The concern for the welfare of developing countries is also rooted in self-interest. After all, the developed industrial nations **C** need a steady supply of critical raw materials from the developing nations. In turn, developing countries provide markets for the products of industrial nations.

Political considerations also play a role. Despite the dramatic failure of communism in most countries, various political ideologies wage a continuing struggle for the allegiance of developing countries. Countries that develop strong market economies will not only grow faster, they will also find it both necessary and easier to cooperate with developed countries in world markets. Global economic cooperation, in turn, leads to a more stable political climate.

✓Reading Check **Interpreting** Why is an understanding of per capita national income important to assess the economic health of nations?

This progress is due largely to the economic growth that has occurred since 1981. In fact, economists found out that a 1 percent increase in the per capita income of developing countries reduces the **R** **proportion** of people in those countries living on less than $1 a day by about 2 percent. Economic growth thus is the most effective way of dealing with global poverty.

Stages of Economic Development

MAIN Idea Thinking about economic growth as occurring in stages helps us understand economic development.

Economics & You You learned earlier about traditional economies. Read on to find out how this relates to economic development.

Some economists have suggested that developing countries normally pass through several stages of economic development. Others argue that the process is not uniform for all countries. Even if the boundaries between these stages are not always clear-cut, it is helpful to think of economic development as occurring in stages.

Primitive Equilibrium

Economic development starts with a stage called **primitive equilibrium.** It is "primitive" in the sense that the society has no formal economic organization. One example would be the Inuit of the past century you studied in Chapter 2, who shared the spoils of the hunt with other families in the village.

A people—or a country—in primitive equilibrium often has no monetary system and may not be economically motivated toward growth. No capital investment takes place, and the society is in equilibrium because nothing measurable changes. Rules are handed down from one generation to the next, while culture and tradition direct economic decision making.

Transition

The second stage of economic development is a period of transition. It involves breaking away from the primitive equilibrium that exists in a society and moving toward economic and cultural changes. The break may be brief and sudden, or it may take years. A country does not grow economically in this transitional stage, but

---

Comparing Fish Consumption

Objective: Compare an important food source in developing countries.

Focus/Teach: Have volunteers describe different kinds of graphs. *(bar, circle, line)* Then have students complete the activity.

Assess: Have a volunteer re-create a graph on the board. Then review the answers as a class.

Close: Discuss as many of students' opinions as time allows.

Differentiated Instruction Strategies

BL Have pairs list the important data from the quoted paragraphs.

AL **Ask:** Why is fish more important in the diet of people in developing nations than elsewhere?

ELL Have students scan the chapter text to find examples of developed and developing nations.

old customs begin to crumble. Societies that enter this stage begin to question their traditions and try new patterns of living.

Takeoff

The third stage of development is **takeoff.** This stage is not reached until the barriers of primitive equilibrium have been overcome. A country in the takeoff stage begins to grow more rapidly than before. One reason is that people put customs aside as they seek new and better ways of doing things. In this stage, people also begin to imitate the new or different techniques that outsiders have brought to their country. Still another reason is that an industrialized nation might be providing financial, educational, or military aid. Such assistance helps pay for the things needed to further economic development.

During the takeoff stage, a country starts to save and invest more of its national income. New industries begin to grow rapidly. Industries use new production techniques, and agricultural productivity improves as well.

Semidevelopment

The fourth stage is semidevelopment. During this stage, the makeup of the country's economy changes. National income grows faster than population, which leads to higher per capita income. At the same time, the country builds its core industries, spends more heavily on capital investment, and makes technological advances.

High Development

The final stage is high development, where efforts to obtain food, shelter, and clothing are more than successful. Because most people have their basic needs and wants met, they turn their attention to services and consumer goods such as washing machines, refrigerators, cell phones, and video equipment.

The nation no longer emphasizes industrial production. Instead, it increases services and provides more public goods. Mature service and manufacturing sectors are signs of a highly developed economy.

✓ **Reading Check** **Summarizing** What happens at each stage of economic development?

takeoff third stage of economic development when barriers of primitive equilibrium have been overcome

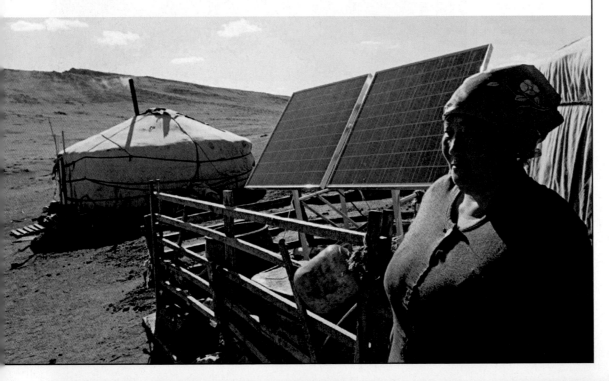

Stages of Development
Countries may experience several stages of development at the same time. This Mongolian nomad uses solar panels to power the television in her *ger*, or tent.
What stages of development do the solar panels and tent represent?

C **Critical Thinking**

Determining Cause and Effect **Ask:** What is an example of a national trend or achievement that could help a country advance from the semidevelopment to the high development stage? *(Answers may include mass production of profitable export goods, implementation of a fair tax system, or adoption of more advanced machinery for factories.)* **OL**

Caption Answer: The solar panels represent high development; the tent represents primitive development.

✓**Reading Check** **Answer:** primitive equilibrium: economy is stagnant; transition: society breaks with tradition and moves toward economic and cultural changes; takeoff: barriers of primitive equilibrium are overcome; semidevelopment: per capita income grows, core industries expand, and new technology is adopted; high development: basic needs of the population are met, and mature service and manufacturing sectors grow

Leveled Activities

BL **Reading Essentials and Note-Taking Guide, p. 145**

OL **Economic Cartoons, p. 27**

AL **Free Enterprise Activities, p. 24**

D Differentiated Instruction

Intrapersonal Ask students to consider and write down their thoughts about the issue of population growth. Direct students to write a poem, parable, or proverb based on their reflections. Ask for volunteers to share their writings with the class. **OL**

S Skill Practice

Visual Literacy Ask: What does this photograph suggest about Brazil's stage of development? *(Possible answer: The tall modern buildings, streetlights, contemporary clothing, and the paved city street suggest that the country has advanced past takeoff and is in one of the final two stages of development.)* **OL**

Caption Answer: high birthrates and increasing life expectancy

crude birthrate number of live births per 1,000 people

life expectancy average remaining life span in years for persons who attain a given age

zero population growth condition in which the average number of births and deaths balance so that the population size is unchanged

Obstacles to Development

MAIN Idea Numerous obstacles make economic growth in developing countries more difficult than in developed countries.

Economics & You You take graduating from high school for granted. Read on to learn why children in other countries may not be able to attend school at all.

Several possible solutions exist to alleviate the plight of developing countries. However, we first need to take a closer look at some common problems and challenges they face.

Population Growth

D One obstacle to economic development is population growth. The populations of most developing countries grow at a rate much faster than the populations of industrialized countries. When a population grows rapidly, there are more people to feed, and a greater demand for services such as education and health care exists.

One reason for this growth is the high **crude birthrate**—the number of live births per 1,000 people. People in many developing countries are also experiencing an increase in **life expectancy**—the average remaining lifetime in years for persons who reach a certain age. Longer life expectancies, coupled with a high crude birthrate, make it difficult for developing countries to increase per capita GNP.

As a result of the problems posed by population pressures, some countries, such as China, have encouraged lower birth rates and smaller families. Some people even feel that societies should work for **zero population growth (ZPG)**—the condition in which the average number of births and deaths balance.

It is not always possible to restrict population growth, however. In some cultures large families are valued for economic and

S

Population Growth
This busy street in Sao Paulo, Brazil, reflects the rapid population growth many developing countries experience. *Why does population growth occur?*

474

Hands-On Chapter Project

Step 1

International Economic Development Conference

In this project, students will research, plan, organize, and role play a mock international development conference.

Step 1: Introducing the Conference. Students will discuss the aims of an international development conference and decide on their roles.

Directions: Tell the class that they will be holding a mock international development conference. Have students make a class list of poor nations, developed nations, the media, and international organizations who might attend and what each might want to achieve.

Next, have students choose whom they will portray. The conference should include major developed nations; several more-industrialized developing nations; commodity-rich nations; and several very poor, debt-ridden countries from different continents. International organizations should include the World Bank and IMF, and media organizations should be represented. After all roles are filled, have students meet to talk about how they will organize their research.

Organizing Have each group make an outline of what they need to do to prepare for the conference. **OL**

(Chapter Project continued in Section 2.)

personal reasons. In other cultures efforts to disrupt population growth are considered morally wrong for religious reasons.

Natural Resources and Geography

Limited natural resources, such as unproductive land, harsh climates, and scarce energy needed for industry, also can hinder economic growth. Even a limited supply of land becomes critical if a country faces a growing population.

In some cases, countries with limited natural resources can make up for the deficiency by engaging in international trade, as Japan has done. However, if a country is landlocked, such as Paraguay, Nepal, or Chad, trade is more difficult. It is no accident that all of the major economic powers today have long had coastal cities with access to major trade routes.

Disease and Substance Abuse

For many developing nations, health has become a major problem. The HIV/AIDS epidemic has been especially devastating in Africa, with some countries experiencing infection rates as high as 20 percent. Because AIDS generally affects young adults, many families have lost their parents and their **primary** income providers, leaving grandparents and neighbors to raise the children.

In parts of Asia, infectious diseases such as bird flu are a constant concern. When even a minor infestation of this disease occurs, entire stocks of poultry have to be destroyed to prevent its spread. In the areas of Asian and South American nations where illegal drugs are grown and produced, high rates of drug addiction among the local population severely impede the prospects for growth.

Education and Technology

Still another obstacle is a lack of appropriate education and technology. Many developing countries lack the literacy and

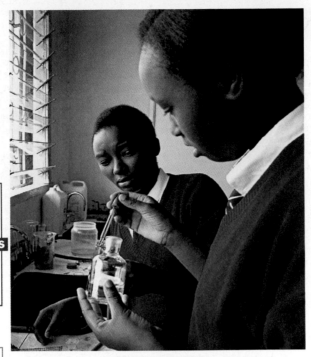

Education Science classes, such as this one in a school in Nairobi, Kenya, help countries develop technology skills. *Why is technology important?*

the high level of technical skills needed to build an industrial society.

Many developing countries also cannot afford free public education for children. In those that can, not everyone is able to take advantage of it because children must work to help feed their families.

External Debt

Another major problem facing the developing nations today is the size of their **external debt**—money borrowed from foreign banks and governments. Some nations have borrowed so much that they may never be able to repay these loans.

Today, some developing countries such as the Democratic Republic of the Congo have external debts significantly larger than their GDP. Burundi's external debt is more than twice its GDP, and Liberia's is more than five times larger.

external debt borrowed money that a country owes to foreign countries and banks

CHAPTER 17 Developing Countries 475

S Skill Practice

Determining Averages

Direct students to make a list of 10 landlocked countries and a list of 10 countries with an ocean coastline. Have students use an almanac to record the total value of imports and exports for each nation (using the most recent data available). Ask students to then calculate the average value of imports and exports for each group. Discuss how the averages differ. **OL**

C Critical Thinking

Assessing Ask: What are some of the ways that an HIV/AIDS epidemic could impact a nation's economy? *(Possible answers: deaths and illnesses of workers reduce productivity; money spent on healthcare lowers consumer spending; deaths and illnesses slow the transfer of job skills and technical knowledge from one generation to the next.)* **OL**

Caption Answer: Students will likely say that it speeds the economic development of a nation.

Additional Support

Extending the Content

Avian Flu The avian flu has sparked grave concerns around the globe since the first case of a human fatality from the illness was reported in Hong Kong in 1997. Also called the bird flu, the virus has since killed 60 percent of humans infected. The World Health Organization predicted that if the mutating avian flu merged with a common human influenza virus,

the resulting outbreak could claim between 5 million and 150 million lives worldwide. Governments and health officials have gone to great lengths to contain the threat. Millions of birds, including chickens, ducks, and geese, have been exterminated. In 2006 the WHO estimated that the bird flu had cost $10 billion in lost agricultural

revenues, a setback affecting 300 million farmers. Having received more than a billion dollars in funding from the U.S. government, American drug companies continue to work toward developing more effective vaccines for the avian flu.

Figure 17.2 ▶ **The Corruption Perception Index**

Writing Support

Narrative Writing Have students select one of the 20 nations currently perceived as having the most corruption. Direct students to use reliable library or Internet resources to investigate examples of corruption that have occurred in their chosen country. Ask students to write a short story illustrating this corruption. Though works of fiction, students' stories should be based on factual events. **AL**

D Differentiated Instruction

English Language Learners
Inform students that they may use a dictionary and thesaurus for this activity. **Ask:** What are four words that, like *default*, relate to the issue of a nation being unable to repay a large external debt? *(Possible answers: overspend, non-payment, bankrupt, failure)* Ask students to then write a paragraph using the words they listed, as well as *default*. **ELL**

Economic Analysis

Answer: They are developed.

Additional Support

▶ The corruption perception index shows the degree to which people think corruption exists among their public officials and politicians. The highest score for Iceland indicates that people there think their country has the least corrupt leaders. Chad, with the lowest number, is perceived to have the most corruption.

Economic Analysis *What generalization can you make about economic conditions in the countries with the highest scores?*

Rankings of countries perceived to have the least corruption		Rankings of countries perceived to have the most corruption	
1. Iceland (9.7)	11. Netherlands (8.6)	140. Indonesia (2.2)	150. Tajikistan (2.0)
2. Finland (9.6)	12. United Kingdom (8.6)	141. Iraq (2.2)	151. Angola (1.9)
3. New Zealand (9.6)	13. Luxembourg (8.5)	142. Liberia (2.2)	152. Cote d'Ivoire (1.9)
4. Denmark (9.5)	14. Canada (8.4)	143. Uzbekistan (2.2)	153. Equatorial Guinea (1.9)
5. Singapore (9.4)	15. Hong Kong (8.3)	144. Congo, Dem. Rep. (2.1)	154. Nigeria (1.9)
6. Sweden (9.2)	16. Germany (8.2)	145. Kenya (2.1)	155. Haiti (1.8)
7. Switzerland (9.1)	17. United States (7.6)	146. Pakistan (2.1)	156. Myanmar (1.8)
8. Norway (8.9)	18. France (7.5)	147. Paraguay (2.1)	157. Turkmenistan (1.8)
9. Australia (8.8)	19. Belgium (7.4)	148. Somalia (2.1)	158. Bangladesh (1.7)
10. Austria (8.7)	20. Ireland (7.4)	149. Sudan (2.1)	159. Chad (1.7)

Source: www.transparency.org

default act of not repaying borrowed money

When debts get this large, countries have trouble just paying interest on the loans. As a result, some developing nations have teetered on the brink of **default,** or not repaying borrowed money. Even this outcome is dangerous, however, because a country that defaults on its loans may not be able to borrow again.

Corruption

Government corruption can be an obstacle to economic progress. Corruption can occur on a massive scale, or it can take the form of minor officials requiring modest bribes to get small things done.

Figure 17.2 shows the 20 countries in the world that are perceived to be the least corrupt, along with the 20 considered most corrupt. A casual look at the list reveals

that the countries with the least corruption are more developed than those with the most corruption. Corruption is harmful because it redirects resources into less productive uses. It also makes a few people rich while robbing everyone else.

For example, Nigeria has enormous oil reserves and is one of the 11 members of the Organization of Petroleum Exporting Countries (OPEC). Despite its vast natural wealth, decades of corruption and mismanagement by government officials have left it relatively poor.

War and Its Aftermath

Unfortunately, many of the developing nations of the world—Angola, Afghanistan, Ethiopia, Cambodia, Somalia, and Vietnam, to name just a few—suffered through

Activity: Technology Connection

Mapping the Corruption Perception Index Organize the class into five groups. Assign a continent to each of the groups: North and Central America (group together for the purposes of this activity), South America, Europe, Africa, and Asia. Instruct students to visit the www.transparency.org Web site to access the corruption

perception index for all the nations of the world. Next have groups use a map maker program (or, if unavailable, distribute line drawing of each continent) to create a map that illustrates the corruption rankings for the countries on their continent. Suggest that students use a color coding system (similar to that of Figure 17.1) to differentiate the

different levels of perceived corruption. For example, countries ranked 1–20 could be blue, countries ranked 21–40 could be green, and so on. Have students display their maps to the class. When finished, combine the continents to create a global map. **OL** bloody civil wars. The immediate impact of war is the devastating loss of lives and property, not to mention the damage to the country's infrastructure.

The aftermath of war can linger for decades. Poland lost virtually all of its *intelligentsia*—its scientists, engineers, and most of its merchant class—to the gas **R** chambers and concentration camps in World War II. The loss of this talent contributed to the slow recovery of the Polish economy after the war, and even hindered its economic development after the fall of communism.

The widespread use of chemical weapons and land mines makes simple activities like farming extremely difficult in many areas. Moreover, many of the people injured by toxic residue and unexploded weapons, such as children playing in fields, were not participants in the war in the first place. The result is that the weapons of war often impede economic development long after the war is over.

Capital Flight

Finally, developing nations also face the problem of **capital flight**—the legal or illegal export of a nation's currency and foreign exchange. Capital flight occurs because people lose faith in their government or in the future of their economy. When capital flight occurs, businesses and even the government often face a cash shortage. At a minimum, capital flight limits the funds available for domestic capital investment.

Private citizens can contribute to capital flight. Suppose that someone in Moscow wants to turn rubles into dollars. The person would first purchase traveler's checks in rubles. Next, the individual would destroy the checks and fly to New York. There the person would declare the checks lost or stolen and get replacement checks in dollars, thereby completing the conversion of rubles into dollars.

✓ **Reading Check** **Recalling** What are the major obstacles to economic growth in developing countries?

> **capital flight** legal or illegal export of a nation's currency and foreign exchange

R **Reading Strategy**

Using Word Parts **Ask:** What adjective is contained in the word *intelligentsia*? *(intelligent)* How does that adjective relate to the noun *intelligentsia*? *(The noun* intelligentsia *refers to a group of people who are intelligent.)* **OL**

✓ **Reading Check** **Answer:** population growth, limited natural resources, disease, substance abuse, lack of education and technology, external debt, corruption, war, capital flight

Assess

💿 Use the Interactive Tutor Self-Assessment CD-ROM to review Section 1, and then assign the Section 1 Review as homework or as an in-class activity.

Close

Outlining Have students work in pairs to write an outline that includes the important ideas included in this section. **OL**

Vocabulary

1. **Explain** the significance of developing country, primitive equilibrium, takeoff, crude birthrate, life expectancy, zero population growth (ZPG), external debt, default, and capital flight.

Main Ideas

2. **Explaining** Why is economic development important?

3. **Describing** Use a graphic organizer like the one below to describe the stages of economic development that many nations experience.

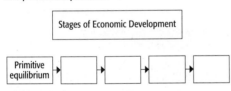

Stages of Economic Development

Primitive equilibrium → ☐ → ☐ → ☐ → ☐

4. **Listing** What factors can be obstacles to economic development?

Critical Thinking

5. **The BIG Idea** Suppose you are an official in charge of economic development in a developing country. Choose two obstacles to economic development that you would address and explain why you would tackle them first.

6. **Drawing Conclusions** Why is aiding developing countries in the self-interest of the United States?

7. **Predicting** Imagine that a society is in primitive equilibrium. Provide an example of an event that could bring about change and explain why this might be so.

8. **Analyzing Visuals** Examine Figure 17.1 on pages 470 and 471. Compare the per capita income of countries in northern Africa with those in Africa south of the Sahara. What do you think accounts for this, and why?

Applying Economics

9. **External Debt** Many people have suggested debt relief for the poorest of the developing countries. Research debt relief and discuss how it would be applied.

Answers

1. All definitions can be found in the section and the Glossary.
2. Economic development influences the economic health of a nation. Underdeveloped nations face more problems related to poverty.
3. Transition; Takeoff; Semidevelopment; High development
4. population growth, limited natural resources, disease, substance abuse, lack of education and technology, external debt, corruption, war, capital flight

5. Answers will vary but should demonstrate an understanding of the obstacles to economic development and explain the importance of addressing the two obstacles students selected.
6. By aiding developing nations, the United States gains new sources of raw materials and new markets for its products.
7. Students should describe an event that could cause a society to question its old traditions (for example, conquest by a more technologically advanced society).

8. Students should recognize that per capita income is generally higher in the northern African nations. To account for this, students may note the presence of oil in the northern African countries and the larger obstacles to development (AIDS and external debt, for example) in the countries south of the Sahara.
9. Students should demonstrate a clear understanding of how debt relief would be applied in developing nations.

Teach

C Critical Thinking

Predicting Ask: Based on the information in this feature, what do you think are Celtel's goals for the next decade? *(Possible answers: expand service area to more African countries; establish a continental network; double the number of its subscribers; invest more money in African communities.)*
OL

Analyzing the Impact

Answers:

1. They can now use their phones to easily communicate with people in other villages, access medical information, and make banking transactions. Communication no longer requires miles of walking.

2. Much of that region is impoverished and ravaged by war.

Additional Support

CASE STUDY
Celtel

Can't Live Without It

In the United States today, many people cannot imagine life without cell phones. The same goes for people living in Africa south of the Sahara, where cell phones often play a high-stakes role. In some areas, such as war-torn Congo, users rely on phones as their only means to keep in touch with family members and friends. Under such dangerous conditions as war, cell phones can truly mean the difference between life and death.

Celtel Boosts African Economy

Throughout most of the 1990s, cell phone service was either nonexistent or very expensive and hard to come by throughout most of central Africa. Then, in 1998, the South African company Celtel launched a mobile communications network in the region. Today it operates in 15 countries and provides more than one-third of the African continent with cell phone service. It has also invested more than $1.3 billion in African communities.

C Celtel had to clear some initial hurdles. Building a communications network is expensive, and many Africans cannot afford to buy the phones, which they usually have to pay for in full. Still, the number of cell phone users has grown from 2 million in 1998 to 117 million in 2005, making Africa the world's fastest-growing cell phone market.

Making a Difference

Access to cell phone service has changed the lives of many people in central Africa. They no longer need to walk miles to talk to a doctor and can more easily communicate with relatives. Celtel's "Celpay" allows people to make banking transactions through their cell phones and to transfer phone minutes to others living in remote villages, where the valuable air time has become a hot commodity. So has battery power. Entrepreneurs provide cell phones for customers to make calls and use car batteries to recharge phones.

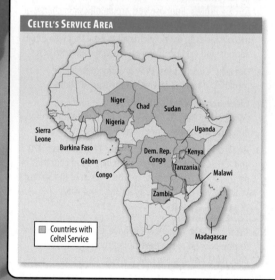

CELTEL'S SERVICE AREA

Niger
Chad
Sudan
Nigeria
Sierra Leone
Uganda
Burkina Faso
Gabon
Dem. Rep. Congo
Kenya
Congo
Tanzania
Malawi
Zambia
Madagascar

☐ Countries with Celtel Service

Analyzing the Impact

1. **Summarizing** How has cell phone service changed the lives of many people in remote African villages?

2. **Inferring** Why would it be difficult to build a cell phone network in Africa south of the Sahara?

Extending the Content

Celtel's Africa Challenge Celtel has remained visible and built goodwill across Africa with a multifaceted strategy of community involvement. In 2007 the telecommunications giant sponsored a 15-week televised game show. Modeled after the popular British program *University Challenge*, Celtel's game show matched university teams from Kenya, Tanzania, and Uganda against each other in a quiz show

contest. Questions were drawn from a variety of categories, including science, history, African culture, literature, music, and current events. Students on the winning team received $1,000 each, plus laptops with Internet access, and Nokia phones. The university represented by the winning team received $50,000 in grants. In addition, the other teams and universities received scholarship monies based on how high they finished in the contest.

Achieving Economic Development

GUIDE TO READING

Section Preview

In this section, you will learn that developing countries can progress in economic development by finding domestic and international funding and by encouraging regional cooperation.

Content Vocabulary

- micro loan (p. 480)
- International Monetary Fund (IMF) (p. 481)
- World Bank (p. 481)
- soft loan (p. 482)
- expropriation (p. 482)
- free-trade area (p. 483)
- customs union (p. 483)
- European Union (EU) (p. 483)
- euro (p. 484)
- ASEAN (p. 484)
- cartel (p. 484)

Academic Vocabulary

- ethic (p. 480)
- duration (p. 481)

Reading Strategy

Describing As you read the section, complete a graphic organizer similar to the one below by describing the ways developing countries can finance economic development.

Funding Economic Development

Focus

Bellringer
Daily Focus Transparency 86

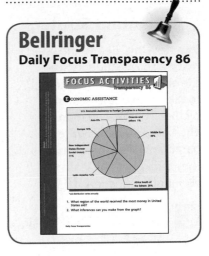

GUIDE TO READING

Answers to Graphic:
increase savings; micro loans; IMF loans; aid grants from other governments; private foreign investment

ISSUES IN THE NEWS
—www.dailytimes.com.pk

Mitsubishi Investments in Pakistan

Hajime Katsumura, CEO [of] Mitsubishi Corporation, Japan, has said that his company is keen to invest in the agriculture sector of Pakistan as a joint venture and would like to provide modern technology in the dairy sector. . . . "Pakistan is open for investment in all sectors without any discrimination or restrictions on bringing in or taking out capital," said Zahid Hamid, Minister for Privatization & Investment.

The minister said that the government was ready to facilitate investors to promote both foreign and domestic investment activity in the country. Investors were free to form joint ventures or establish their own businesses with 100% equity. More than 600 multinational companies were successfully operating and making profits in Pakistan, which had become an attractive location for investors. . . . ■

Economic development is important to most countries, but economic development normally requires some type of financing. Sometimes the funding can be generated internally, and sometimes it can be secured from external sources such as foreign governments and foreign investors.

If a developing country has a market economy and the government is politically stable, the country has an even better chance of attracting foreign investment. The search for profits, as you read in the news article above, is a global one that crosses national boundaries.

Resource Manager

R Reading Strategies	**C** Critical Thinking	**D** Differentiated Instruction	**W** Writing Support	**S** Skill Practice
Teacher Edition • Previewing, p. 480 • Act. Prior Know., p. 481 **Additional Resources** • Guid. Read. Act., p. 50 • Read. Ess. & Note-Taking Guide, p. 148 • Enrichment Act., p. 17	**Teacher Edition** • Speculating, p. 480 • Contrasting, p. 483 **Additional Resources** • Bus. Focus on the Global Economy, pp. 2, 10 • Crit. Think. Act., p. 12 • Graphic Org. Trans., p. 3	**Teacher Edition** • Visual/Spatial, p. 482 • Adv. Learners, p. 483 **Additional Resources** • Free Enterprise Act., p. 24 • Reteaching Act., p. 17 • Math Prac. for Econ., pp. 17, 21	**Teacher Edition** • Expository Writing, p. 481 • Persuasive Writing, p. 485 **Additional Resources** • Writer's Guidebook • Econ. Cartoons, p. 28	**Teacher Edition** • Using Circle and Bar Graphs, p. 482 • Ident. the Main Idea, p. 484 **Additional Resources** • Daily Focus Trans. 86, 88 • Reinforcing Econ. Skills, pp. 9, 25

Teach

R Reading Strategy

Previewing Before they start reading, have students scan the entire section. Ask them to take note of the headings, pictures, graph, and map. Then have students write a paragraph describing what they think they will learn about in this section. **BL**

C Critical Thinking

Speculating Ask: What is another example of how a micro loan might help someone start a small business in Africa today? *(Possible answers: a woman receives a small loan to buy a cart from which she will sell vegetables; a woman receives a small loan to purchase materials needed to make wind chimes that she will sell.)* **OL**

Caption Answer: because two-thirds of the GDP in developing countries is produced in activities that are not serviced by banks

Differentiated Instruction

Free Enterprise Activities, p. 23

---

micro loan small, unsecured loan made primarily to women to help them undertake an income-generating project in a developing country

Micro Loans
These three Ugandan sisters used a micro loan to purchase serving trays so that they could start a catering business. *Why are micro loans important to developing countries?*

R Funding Economic Development

MAIN Idea Developing countries can fund economic development through savings, international aid and loan programs, and foreign investment.

Economics & You You learned earlier that capital is needed to start or expand a business. Read on to learn how the same principle applies to the developing countries.

The funding for economic development can come from a number of sources. Some sources are internal, while other sources are external, but all are important.

Importance of Savings

Internally generated funds in many cases are the only source of capital for a developing country. To generate these internal funds, an economy must produce more than it consumes.

If a developing country has a market economy, the incentive to save stems from the profit motive. Firms often try to borrow funds for various projects. Banks in turn pay interest rates on savings that are set by the forces of supply and demand. If the demand for money is high, the interest rate will rise, encouraging savings that can be used for investments by firms.

If a developing country has a command economy, its government may still be able to force saving by requiring people to work on farms, roads, or other projects. However, most command economies do not always mobilize resources to promote economic growth. All too often, resources instead are used for political reasons or personal gain. In addition, forced mobilizations fail to instill long-term incentives or work **ethic** in people.

Microfinance

One of the more successful approaches to economic development in developing countries is the use of **micro loans.** A micro loan is a small unsecured loan, often as small as $50, made primarily to women who want to undertake an income-generating project. Because more than two-thirds of the GDP in a developing country is produced in activities that are not serviced by banks, the loans provide a way to extend the features of capitalism to the poorest of the poor.

For example, in Africa today, a woman might get the equivalent of a $50 loan to buy a hybrid goat that produces a higher milk yield. Since the borrower would be too poor to supply collateral, she would get several other women to co-sign the loan in case she defaulted. The loan would have a

---

Funding Economic Growth in Developing Nations

Objective: Learn about the needs of different developing countries and practice reading tables.

Focus: Have students think about developing countries. **Ask:** What kinds of needs do poor countries have?

Teach: Have students complete the activity.

Assess: Go over the answers with the class.

Close: **Ask:** What generalizations can you make about the relationship of per capita GDP to the other data in the table?

Differentiated Instruction Strategies

BL Ask: Does the adult literacy rate affect a country's response to problems like HIV/AIDS? Explain.

AL Ask: Do figures like these measure the quality of life in a country? Explain.

ELL Have students find the countries on a world map and write a paragraph describing their locations.

International Aid
World Bank loans funded this metal rolling plant in Mombasa, Kenya. *What other agencies provide assistance to developing countries?*

R Reading Strategy

Activating Prior Knowledge
Ask: What was happening in 1944 when the World Bank was founded? How might this have influenced the desire for an organization like the World Bank? *(World War II was coming to an end; the soon-to-be-victorious Allies might have wanted an organization in place that could help newly independent nations develop.)* **OL**

W Writing Support

Expository Writing
Have students use online or print resources to research a current project financed by the International Bank for Reconstruction and Development. Ask students to write a paper describing the project and the benefits it will create. **OL**

Caption Answer: International Monetary Fund, International Bank for Reconstruction and Development, International Finance Corporation, International Development Association

three-month **duration** and require small weekly payments on the principal. To make the payments, the woman would charge a small fee to other villagers to breed her goat with other goats and thus improve the stock of the whole village. Such loans have been enormously popular, and repayment rates in some areas have been as high as 98 percent.

International Agencies

The problems of the developing countries have not gone unnoticed by the developed countries of the world. Two agencies established by the developed nations work directly with developing nations to help solve their problems.

The **International Monetary Fund (IMF)** is an international organization that offers advice to all countries on monetary and fiscal policies. The IMF also helps support currencies so that the countries can compete in an open market and attract foreign investors.

For example, after the Berlin Wall came down and the Soviet Union collapsed, a number of former Soviet-bloc countries wanted to trade their currencies on global exchanges. The IMF provided loans to help with the conversion. This is important because investors must be able to purchase the currencies of these countries to conduct international trade with them.

The second important international agency is the World Bank Group, more commonly known as the World Bank. The **World Bank** is an international corporation that makes loans and provides financial assistance and advice to developing countries. The World Bank is owned by IMF member nations, but it operates as a separate organization.

The World Bank has undertaken projects to control the desert locust in East Africa. It also has funded projects to develop inland water transportation in Bangladesh, rural transportation systems in Vietnam, and even tax modernization in Kazakhstan.

The International Bank for Reconstruction and Development—part of the World Bank Group—helps developing countries with loans and guarantees of loans from private sources. Many of these loans paid for projects such as dams, roads, and factories. Loans are also made to encourage developing nations to change or improve their economic policies.

Another part of the World Bank Group is the International Finance Corporation (IFC), an agency that invests in private businesses and other enterprises. Finally, the International Development Association

Economics ONLINE

Student Web Activity Visit the *Economics: Principles and Practices* Web site at glencoe.com and click on *Chapter 15–Student Web Activity* for an activity on the International Monetary Fund.

International Monetary Fund (IMF) international organization that offers advice, financial assistance, and currency support to all nations

World Bank international agency that makes loans and provides financial assistance and advice to developing countries

CHAPTER 17 Developing Countries **481**

Leveled Activities

BL Reteaching Activities, p. 17

OL BusinessWeek Focus on the Global Economy, p. 10

AL Enrichment Activities, p. 17

S Skill Practice

Using Circle and Bar Graphs
Ask: Out of every 10 Peace Corps volunteers, how many are married? (1) What do you think accounts for this ratio? (Possible answer: Many people in the Peace Corps are young and not yet ready to settle down.) **OL**

D Differentiated Instruction

Visual/Spatial Have students draw a political cartoon based on an example of one nation granting aid to another. Inform students that they may choose an example from the past (for example, Soviet aid to Cuba) or the present (for example, U.S. aid to Pakistan). Instruct students to incorporate the granting nation's motives into their cartoons. **OL**

✓Reading Check **Answer:**
Private foreign investors are seeking to make profits from their investments. International agencies grant aid to help developing nations solve problems and strengthen their economies.

Hands-On Chapter Project

Step 2

International Economic Development Conference

Step 2: Planning the Development Conference. Students will research their roles at the development conference.

Directions: Have each group review its notes on how to research roles at the conference. Then have students use the time for research (Note: You may want to extend the research period or assign the research as homework.)

The Global Economy &YOU

High-Tech Peace Corps

Are you thinking about joining the Peace Corps? If you sign up, don't be surprised to find that you may need some computer skills. The Peace Corps has entered the twenty-first century. In the past, this organization—which provides aid to 183 countries—was mostly about helping farmers, improving infrastructure, and teaching English. Just like the rest of the world, however, the Peace Corp has gone high-tech, thanks in part to the dot-com bust of the late 1990s.

As techies fled Silicon Valley and the failed Internet start-ups in the early 2000s, many of them turned to the Peace Corps for peace of mind. In doing so, they brought new skills to the organization. A new generation of Peace Corps volunteers is now helping developing countries establish computer learning centers and providing support for small business development.

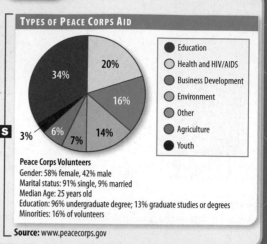

TYPES OF PEACE CORPS AID

- Education — 34%
- Health and HIV/AIDS — 20%
- Business Development — 16%
- Environment — 14%
- Other — 7%
- Agriculture — 6%
- Youth — 3%

Peace Corps Volunteers
Gender: 58% female, 42% male
Marital status: 91% single, 9% married
Median Age: 25 years old
Education: 96% undergraduate degree; 13% graduate studies or degrees
Minorities: 16% of volunteers

Source: www.peacecorps.gov

---

soft loan loan that might never be paid back

expropriation government confiscation of private- or foreign-owned goods without compensation

(IDA) makes **soft loans**—loans that might never be paid back—to the neediest countries. IDA loans are interest-free and may be for periods of 35 or 40 years.

Government Aid Grants

Developing countries can also obtain external funds by borrowing from foreign governments. The United States, Canada, and several countries in Western Europe provide this type of aid.

Political considerations usually play a large role in these grants, so the neediest nations do not always receive the funds. For example, the largest recipient of U.S. government aid is Israel. Pakistan receives financial help from the United States because of its assistance in the war on terrorism.

The former Soviet bloc also gave economic assistance to developing countries. More than half of its aid, however, went to allies such as Cuba, Ethiopia, and Iraq. Like most other foreign aid, it was given to promote political, rather than economic, ends.

Private Foreign Investment

Another way to obtain funds is to attract private funds from foreign investors who might be interested in a country's natural resources. For example, vast oil reserves drew the interest of investors to the Middle East, while copper attracted them to Chile, and mahogany and teakwood to Southeast Asia. In each case, foreign investors supplied the financial capital needed to develop those industries.

If foreign investments are to work, the arrangement must be beneficial to both the investor and the host country. Many investors are unwilling to take major financial risks unless they are sure that the country is politically stable. Developing countries that follow a policy of **expropriation**—the taking over of foreign property without some sort of payment in return—make it harder for all developing nations to attract foreign capital.

✓Reading Check **Contrasting** How do private foreign investments differ from aid through international agencies?

Remind students that the goal of their research is to be able to act their role at the mock development conference. Suggest that they try to answer these and other questions you may add:

- If I am a country, what are my major concerns? What do I want to happen? What can my country do to further its goals? What is my history in the world economy? What role do I play today?
- If I am an international organization, what are my goals for the conference?

What have I done in the past to further these goals? What problems have I encountered?

- If I am a media organization, what kinds of information would I like to obtain at the conference? What do my readers or viewers want to know about world economic development?

Have students add more questions as appropriate. **OL**

(Chapter Project continued in Section 3.)

Regional Economic Cooperation

MAIN Idea Regional economic agreements foster trade and economic growth among member nations.

Economics & You When you have to complete a large project, do you ask others for help? Read on to find out how economic cooperation helps countries.

One way to promote regional economic cooperation is to form a **free-trade area**—an agreement in which two or more countries reduce trade barriers and tariffs among themselves. The free-trade area does not set uniform tariffs for nonmembers.

Several countries could also establish a **customs union**—an agreement in which two or more countries abolish tariffs and trade restrictions among themselves and adopt uniform tariffs for nonmember countries. The customs union has more uniformity than a free-trade area, so it represents a higher level of economic integration.

The European Union

The most successful example of regional cooperation in the world today is the **European Union (EU)**. The EU started out as a customs union and consists of the member nations shown in **Figure 17.3**.

In January 1993, the EU became the largest single unified market in the world in terms of population and output, although the United States has since surpassed the EU in terms of GDP. The EU is a single market because there are no internal barriers regulating the flow of workers, financial capital, or goods and services. Citizens

free-trade area group of countries that have agreed to reduce trade barriers among themselves but lack a common tariff barrier for nonmembers

customs union group of countries that have agreed to reduce trade barriers among themselves and have uniform tariffs for nonmembers

European Union economic, political, and social union established in 1993 by the Maastricht Treaty as the successor of the European Community

C **Critical Thinking**

Contrasting Ask: What is the primary difference between a *free-trade area* and a *customs union*? *(A customs union sets a common tariff barrier for nonmembers, while a free-trade area does not.)* **BL**

D **Differentiated Instruction**

Advanced Learners
Have students select a member nation of the EU. Instruct students to research the value of the nation's total exports and imports for the five years before it joined the EU and the five years after it joined the EU (or as many years are available if the nation joined fewer than five years ago). Ask students to then write a report assessing how EU membership affected the trade of their nation. **AL**

Economic Analysis

Answer: no internal barriers to the movement of goods, services, capital, and workers among member nations; tariff protection from imports from nonmembers; common currency

Figure 17.3 ▶ The European Union

THE EUROPEAN UNION

27 existing members and year they joined:
Austria	1955
Belgium	1952
Bulgaria	2007
Cyprus	2004
Czech Republic	2004
Denmark	1973
Estonia	2004
Finland	1995
France	1952
Germany	1952
Greece	1981
Hungary	2004
Ireland	1973
Italy	1952
Latvia	2004
Lithuania	2004
Luxembourg	1952
Malta	2004
Netherlands	1952
Poland	2004
Portugal	1986
Romania	2007
Slovakia	2004
Slovenia	2004
Spain	1986
Sweden	1995
United Kingdom	1973

Candidate Countries:
Croatia
Macedonia
Turkey

▶ The 27 members of the European Union, with almost 500 million people, currently make up the largest single market in the world.

Economic Analysis *What are the benefits of membership in the EU?*

Graphs In MOtion
See StudentWorks™ Plus or glencoe.com.

Additional Support

Activity: Technology Connection

Making a Documentary Organize the class into small groups. Instruct groups to use reliable print and online sources to research the operations of the European Union. Ask groups to then prepare a 10-minute documentary (a video or slides with audio commentary) advertising the merits of the EU. The purpose of the documentary is to promote the organization to citizens of nonmember European nations.

Inform students that they can use existing EU-related footage/pictures, scenes they shoot themselves, or a combination of both for their documentaries. Have groups present their documentaries to the class. After each group's presentation, lead a discussion about which parts of the documentary would likely be most effective at convincing citizens of nonmember nations to support joining the EU. **AL**

S Skill Practice

Identifying the Main Idea
Ask: What must happen for a cartel to function effectively? *(All members must sell their products at the price set by the cartel.)* What could disrupt the functioning of a cartel? *(Possible answer: One member sells its product at a lower price to try to increase its own share of the market.)* **OL**

✓Reading Check **Answer:**
The reduction of trade barriers increases trade among member nations.

Assess

● Use the Interactive Tutor Self-Assessment CD-ROM to review Section 2, and then assign the Section 2 Review as homework or as an in-class activity.

Close

Determining Importance
Have students discuss as a class the different approaches that nations use to achieve economic development. **OL**

SECTION 2 Review

---

euro single currency of the EU introduced in January 2002 and adopted by many member nations

ASEAN group of 10 Southeast Asian nations working to promote regional cooperation, economic growth, and trade

cartel group of sellers or producers acting together to raise prices by restricting availability of a product

of EU member nations hold common passports and can travel anywhere in the EU to work, shop, save, and invest.

The last stage of European integration occurred in 2002 with the introduction of the **euro**—a single EU currency. About half of the member nations have adopted it to replace their national currencies.

ASEAN

The success of the EU has encouraged other countries to try regional cooperation. In 1967 five nations—Indonesia, Malaysia, Singapore, the Philippines, and Thailand—formed the Association for Southeast Asian Nations, or ASEAN. Today, **ASEAN** is a 10-nation group working to promote regional peace and stability, accelerate economic growth, and liberalize trade policies in order to become a free-trade area.

OPEC

In 1960, a number of oil-producing nations formed a **cartel**—a group of producers or sellers who agree to limit the production or sale of a product in order to control prices. The members of OPEC (Organization of Petroleum Exporting Countries) tried to create the equivalent of **S** a monopoly and push up world oil prices. Since it was organized, higher oil prices have transferred trillions of dollars from industrialized nations to OPEC member countries.

Even with all this financial capital, most OPEC nations have grown slowly by most standards. In Iran, revolution interrupted the development of the domestic economy. In Nigeria, corruption siphoned off most of the oil profits that could have been used for economic development.

High oil prices returned in 2006, but the price increases appeared to be driven more by a strong global demand than by artificially tight supplies caused by OPEC. As a result, OPEC has generally failed to turn the oil cartel into an engine of economic development.

✓Reading Check **Describing** How do agreements for regional cooperation help member nations?

SECTION 2 Review

Vocabulary
1. **Explain** the significance of micro loan, International Monetary Fund (IMF), World Bank, soft loan, expropriation, free-trade area, customs union, European Union (EU), euro, ASEAN, and cartel.

Main Ideas
2. **Identifying** What are two external sources of funds for economic development?
3. **Describing** What problem is associated with aid grants from foreign nations to developing countries?
4. **Listing** Use a graphic organizer like the one below to list three examples of regional economic cooperation.

Critical Thinking
5. **The BIG Idea** What can a country do to encourage economic development?
6. **Inferring** What are the costs and benefits of regional economic cooperation?
7. **Synthesizing Information** Why would developing nations be interested in obtaining funding from private sources rather than a government?
8. **Analyzing Visuals** Look at Figure 17.3 on page 483 and identify the countries that became members of the EU most recently. When did they join?

Applying Economics
9. **Growth and Development** Provide an example to support the following statement: Economic growth in developing nations is often slowed by the internal political problems and external political goals of industrialized nations.

Answers

1. All definitions can be found in the section and the Glossary.
2. international agencies, such as the World Bank, and aid grants from foreign governments
3. Political considerations often keep the neediest nations from receiving these funds.
4. free-trade area; customs union; cartel

5. encourage savings among its citizens, maintain political stability, join a regional economic agreement, seek advice and assistance from international agencies, protect property rights of foreign investors
6. Possible costs include loss of jobs to other nations, loss of control over aspects of the economy, and loss of certain economic traditions. Possible benefits include reduced foreign tariff barriers, increase in markets for exports, and improved access to needed resources.

7. Possible answers: fewer political strings attached with private investments; greater possibility of maximizing profit potential of natural resources with capitalist investors.
8. Bulgaria and Romania; 2007
9. Answers will vary but should demonstrate understanding of the internal and external political factors that can slow the economic growth of developing nations.

As the world's economies become more interdependent, regional cooperation has gained greater importance—even among the most unlikely of partners. In 2006 North Korea, one of the last bastions of communism, cracked open the door to its capitalist neighbor to the south.

Hands Across the DMZ

For decades, there has not been much traffic across the demilitarized zone dividing North and South Korea, where hundreds of thousands of soldiers are on constant alert. But these days, some 200 cars, trucks, and buses cross the border every day.

They're going to the Kaesong Industrial Complex, a dusty outpost that is North Korea's boldest economic initiative in decades. Just an hour north of Seoul, Kaesong is cordoned off from the rest of North Korea by seven-foot-high fences patrolled by squads of soldiers.

Just after 7:00 a.m., Monday through Saturday, dozens of buses from North Korea enter Kaesong, ferrying some 6,000 northern workers to 11 South Korean-owned factories to make shoes, clothing, pots, and other low-tech goods. . . .

The idea behind the effort is simple: North Korea is home to a huge, cheap, and underemployed workforce. South Korea needs a low-wage manufacturing base to compete with China. By 2012, Kaesong could be home to 725,000 jobs and generate $500 million in wages annually for the North Korean economy. . . .

North Korea's "Dear Leader," Kim Jong Il, has little choice but to experiment, given the dire condition of the North's economy. . . .

[S]ince 2002 he has embraced—however grudgingly—tentative economic reforms. . . .

For South Korean companies, Kaesong offers plenty of advantages. North Korean workers at Kaesong earn about $50 a month, around half the average wage for unskilled workers in China and less than 10% of what South Koreans earn. . . .

Outsourced work for South Korean capitalists may not be exactly what Marx and Engels—or Kim Il Sung (Kim Jong Il's father)—had in mind, but it could be the only hope for Pyongyang.

—Reprinted from *BusinessWeek*

Two Koreas
GDP per capita

South	$20,300
North	$1,800

Based on purchasing power parity

Source: *CIA World Factbook*

Examining the Newsclip

1. **Summarizing** How does the Kaesong Industrial Complex meet the needs of both North and South Koreans?

2. **Making Inferences** Why would North Korea's leadership be opposed to opening up its economy more quickly?

W Writing Support

Persuasive Writing Have students research current events relating to Korea. Ask them to write a speech on the subject of why the Kaesong Industrial Complex is or is not a step toward the unification of Korea. Have students give their speeches to the class. **OL**

BusinessWeek ONLINE

To find up-to-date news and analysis on the economy, business, technology, markets, entrepreneurs, investments, and finance, have students search feature articles and special reports on the BusinessWeek Web site, www.businessweek.com.

Examining the Newsclip

Answers:
1. The Complex provides jobs for North Koreans and helps South Korea develop a low-wage manufacturing base.
2. It might cause the government to face unrest.

Additional Support

Activity: Hands-On Economics

Promoting Economic Cooperation in Korea Have students suppose that they are an independent economic advisor assigned to promote economic cooperation between North and South Korea. Ask students to devise a program that, similar to the Kaesong Industrial Complex, would promote economic development

for both nations. Inform students that for this activity they will likely need to consult reliable print or online sources to learn more about the current economic situation in Korea. They will also want to learn about natural resources specific to the area and ongoing manufacturing and business efforts. Once students have done this,

have them meet to brainstorm possible businesses and uses of North Korean labor or resources. Students should then describe their proposed programs in a report that would be presented to representatives of both North and South Korea. **OL**

Focus

GUIDE TO READING

Possible Answers to Graphic:

Russia: perestroika (managers have more freedom to pursue profits and small business encouraged), privatization accelerated, stock market opens, vouchers issued to citizens to buy stocks

Resource Manager

SECTION

3 The Transition to Capitalism

GUIDE TO READING

Section Preview

In this section, you will learn that reforms in the former Soviet Union, China, and many Latin American and eastern European nations have moved these economies toward more capitalistic, market-oriented systems.

Content Vocabulary

- capitalism (p. 486)
- privatization (p. 487)
- vouchers (p. 488)
- Five-Year Plan (p. 489)
- Gosplan (p. 489)
- collectivization (p. 490)
- perestroika (p. 490)
- Great Leap Forward (p. 490)
- Solidarity (p. 491)
- black market (p. 491)
- capital-intensive (p. 492)
- keiretsu (p. 493)
- population density (p. 493)

Academic Vocabulary

- undertaking (p. 488)
- isolationism (p. 491)

Reading Strategy

Describing As you read the section, complete a graphic organizer similar to the one below by selecting a country and describing how it is making the transition to capitalism.

Country — Action / Action / Action / Action → Capitalism

ISSUES IN THE NEWS

—The Columbus Dispatch

South America—Following India or China?

Latin America's challenge can be described in a lot of ways. . . . But the big question facing Latin Americans is: Are they going to emulate India or get addicted to China?

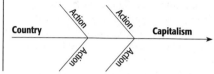

. . . Latin Americans may think that their big choice is between two models of Western capitalism: a European welfare state model and a hyper-competitive U.S. model. But . . . their most important choice is between an India example that focuses on developing human resources and a China syndrome that focuses on selling natural resources. . . . But countries that get addicted to selling their natural resources rarely develop their human resources and the educational institutions and innovative companies that go with that. So after the ore has been mined, the trees cut and the oil pumped, their people are actually even more behind. ■

---

capitalism
economic system in which private citizens own and use the factors of production in order to generate profits *(also see page 38)*

As countries develop their economies, **capitalism,** the economic system in which private citizens own and use the factors of production, is spreading around the globe. In fact, when an economy becomes large and complex, capitalism is the most efficient way to organize production and provide the necessary economic incentives.

As countries make the transition to capitalism, the final form of capitalism they adopt will reflect many of their own cultural and social values. As you read in the news story above, countries can follow several different models. That is why so many different faces of capitalism exist in the world today.

R Reading Strategies	C Critical Thinking	D Differentiated Instruction	W Writing Support	S Skill Practice
Teacher Edition • Det. Importance, p. 489 • Academic Vocab., p. 491 • Predicting, p. 492 • Act. Prior Know., p. 494 **Additional Resources** • Guid. Read. Act., p. 51 • Read. Ess. & Note-Taking Guide, p. 151	**Teacher Edition** • Theorizing, p. 487 • Comparing, p. 490 • Hypothesizing, p. 493 • Differentiating, p. 495 **Additional Resources** • Econ. Cartoons, p. 27 • Quizzes and Tests, p. 215 • Free Ent. Act., p. 24	**Teacher Edition** • ELL, p. 488 • Verbal/Linguistic, p. 490 • Intrapersonal, p. 491 • Visual/Spatial, p. 494 **Additional Resources** • Math Prac. for Econ., p. 23 • Reading and Study Skills Fold., p. 65	**Teacher Edition** • Narrative Writing, p. 488 • Expository Writing, p. 489 • Descriptive Writing, p. 493 **Additional Resources** • High School Reading in the Content Area Strat. and Act.	**Teacher Edition** • Visual Literacy, p. 487 • Reading a Time Line, p. 491 • Using Line Graphs, p. 492 • Evaluating Info., p. 496 **Additional Resources** • Econ. Content Vocab. Act., p. 17 • Daily Focus Trans. 83

Problems of Transition

MAIN Idea Countries in transition to capitalism must learn to abide by the rules of free market economies.

Economics & You Have you ever played a game without knowing the rules? Read on to learn why changing to capitalism can be difficult.

The dominant macroeconomic trend of our lifetime has been the transition of communist and socialist economic systems to capitalism. It has been a transition of epic proportions, and it shows few signs of slowing down.

Even so, the transition is difficult. For one thing, a country making the transition has to convert public property to private ownership. For another, a massive shift of political power takes place during transition. Finally, everyone has to learn to live with the discipline of markets and to abide by a new sets of economic incentives. **C**

Why Capitalism?

Simply put, capitalism is the most powerful engine for generating wealth the world has ever seen. Because of capitalism, countries as culturally diverse as Sweden, Japan, the United States, Singapore, Germany, South Korea, and Hong Kong have greatly increased their productivity and experienced exceptional economic growth.

This growth has improved nearly everyone's standard of living in these countries, and other countries have taken notice. In a world that is becoming increasingly connected by the media and the Internet, people everywhere are aware of—and then begin to want—some of the wealth that capitalism can generate.

In contrast, the collapse of the Soviet Union indicates that communism as an economic system has reached an evolutionary dead end. Pure capitalism can be harsh and may not be attractive to everyone, but in democratic nations, people can modify capitalism to meet more of their economic and social goals. However, there is no guarantee that countries attempting a transition to capitalism will be able to do it smoothly, or that they can do it at all.

Privatization

A key feature of capitalism is the ownership of private property. In order for the transition to capitalism to take place, **privatization,** or the conversion of state-owned factories and other property to private ownership, must be accomplished. Privatization is important because entrepreneurs want to receive rewards for

privatization
conversion of state-owned factories and other property to private ownership

Skills Handbook
See page R39 to learn about Formulating Questions.

S **Privatization**
The Dunai Vismu ironworks factory was privatized after the fall of communism and today is the largest of its kind in Hungary. *Why is privatization important?*

Teach

C Critical Thinking

Theorizing Ask: Why might nations resist making the transition to capitalism? *(Possible answers: governmental leaders fear a loss of political power and control over the population; fear of economic chaos during the transition; devotion to anti-capitalist ideology)* **OL**

S Skill Practice

Visual Literacy Have students write a paragraph describing what this photo reveals about the characteristics of capitalism. *(Students may write about pollution, working conditions, the vast productive capabilities of modern factories, and so on.)* **OL**

Caption Answer: Privatization allows entrepreneurs to make profits from business ventures in which they have invested money, giving them a personal stake in the success of their efforts.

Additional Support

Activity: Interdisciplinary Connection

Language Arts Have students find a quotation or passage written by Karl Marx that expresses some part of his philosophy about economic systems. Then have students write an essay that: 1) paraphrases the passage in their own words; 2) describes how the passage reflects Marx's larger economic philosophy; 3) offers an interpretation of why Marx's vision, as expressed in the passage, was unable to be implemented as a successful economic system. **AL**

Teacher Tip

Preparing Before Class If you have limited time allocated for students to complete this project, consider finding quotations or passages beforehand and allowing students to choose which ones to write their essays on.

Differentiated Instruction

D Differentiated Instruction

English Language Learners

Ask: What are two goods or services that vouchers are used for in the United States? *(Possible answers: food [food stamps] and housing)* **OL**

W Writing Support

Narrative Writing Have students use reliable print or Internet sources to research the story of an individual who lived in an Eastern European nation during the fall of communism. Ask students to write a paper telling the story of that individual and how he or she adjusted to the transition to a new economic system. Remind students to base their fictional story on facts about the time period. **OL**

Caption Answer: working for promotions and higher wages; investing money to make profits

voucher certificate that could be used to purchase government-owned property during privatization

undertaking business ventures involving risk. Private property is also important because people take better care of property they actually own.

D In Poland, Hungary, and the Czech Republic, this transition was accomplished by using vouchers. **Vouchers** were certificates that could be used to purchase government-owned property. In practice, vouchers were either given to the citizens of a country or sold at very low prices. State-owned companies could then be converted to corporations, and the corporate stock could be auctioned for vouchers. As vouchers were exchanged for shares, ownership of state-owned enterprises transferred to private hands.

Loss of Political Power

Under communism, the Communist Party was the ruling class. When countries changed to capitalism, the party lost much of its political power as a new class of entrepreneurs and capitalists took over.

In countries such as Czechoslovakia, Hungary, and Poland, the Communist Party leaders who were ousted from office lost their power before their country's industry was privatized. In these countries,

the voucher system worked reasonably well to redistribute wealth to new leaders.

W In other countries, Communist leaders grabbed a large share of vouchers and thus a large portion of ownership in many privatized companies. In the most blatant cases, some of which occurred in Russia following the collapse of the Soviet Union, the ownership of companies was directly transferred to politicians who were influential during the transition period.

As a result, former political leaders traded their political power for economic power in the form of resource ownership, and the old ruling group simply became the new ruling group. In almost every case of transition, the members of the ruling party had a difficult time actually giving up their power.

Underestimating the Costs

Many countries that want the advantages of capitalism have focused on its benefits, but they have not fully considered its costs. Yet the costs can hinder or even prevent a country's successful transition.

The costs of capitalism during the Great Depression, for example, included instability, unemployment, and social unrest. At

Transition Countries transitioning to capitalism have to adjust to new costs and incentives. *What are some new incentives?*

Hartley Schwadron/Cartoonstock

Reinforcing Economic Skills, p. 27

Using Library Resources

Objective: Identify library resources to use for different research goals.

Focus/Teach: Ask students to list different resources that they have used at a library. Have students answer the questions in the activity.

Assess: Go over the answers with the class.

Close: Ask students to write a paragraph explaining why it is important for them to understand how to use the different resources at a library.

Differentiated Instruction Strategies

BL Have students list five additional resources available at a library.

AL **Ask:** What library resources would you consult to write a report on the impact of EU membership on former communist nations?

ELL **Ask:** How can a library help a person learning English?

Russia Today's grocery shoppers in Ekaterinberg, Russia, enjoy a wide range of products in supermarkets. *How does this store compare to grocery stores in the United States?*

that time, the United States did not have the fiscal policies, automatic stabilizers, and social welfare nets needed to lessen the devastation of the Depression. Now that such assistance exists, most economists agree that another Great Depression will not occur in the United States.

The same cannot be said for the countries in transition. They have not yet developed the automatic stabilizers and the social welfare nets that cushion the instabilities of capitalism. During transition, nations will most likely experience the instabilities of early capitalism long before they experience the benefits.

Responding to New Incentives

Finally, people in countries that make the transition to capitalism have to adjust to a whole new set of incentives. They have to learn how to make decisions on their own, take the initiative, interpret prices, and fend for themselves in free markets. Many of these adjustments will be enormous, perhaps even prohibitive. Still, impatience for the end result can be a major obstacle to a successful transition.

✓Reading Check **Summarizing** What are the main problems for a nation transitioning to capitalism?

Countries and Regions in Transition

MAIN Idea Different countries have had varying success in their transitions to capitalism.

Economics & You Do you remember adjusting from middle school to high school? Read on to find out why adjusting to a new situation is also difficult for nations in transition.

Despite the transitional problems, nations and regions all over the globe are moving toward capitalism.

Russia

To see why the transition to capitalism has been so difficult for Russia, it helps to understand how the economy was managed during the Soviet era. During this period, the government controlled economic activity with five-year plans. The first **Five-Year Plan**—a comprehensive, centralized economic plan designed to achieve rapid industrialization—was introduced by Joseph Stalin in 1927.

The **Gosplan** was the central authority that devised the plans and directed overall economic activity. It tried to manage the economy by assigning production quotas

Five-Year Plan comprehensive, centralized economic plan used by the former Soviet Union to coordinate the development of industry and agriculture

Gosplan central authority in the former Soviet Union that devised and directed Five-Year Plans

CHAPTER 17 Developing Countries **489**

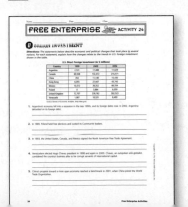

D Differentiated Instruction

Verbal/Linguistic Inform students that Gorbachev also introduced *glasnost* policy in the Soviet Union. Have students research the meaning of that word and write a paragraph explaining how *glasnost* influenced the economic changes that occurred during the final years of the U.S.S.R. **AL**

C Critical Thinking

Comparing **Ask:** How were Joseph Stalin's economic plans and Mao Zedong's economic plans similar? *(Both included five-year plans, both wanted to rapidly industrialize, both featured planning and common ownership, and both eventually failed.)* **OL**

Caption Answer: After the fall of communism in Russia, a rapid shift to privatization occurred. In communist China, the move toward capitalism has occurred at a slower pace.

Hands-On Chapter Project

Step 3

China The People's Republic of China boasts modern manufacturing plants, such as this silk factory in Hotan Xinjiang. *How do the economic developments of Russia and China differ?*

collectivization forced common ownership of all agricultural, industrial, and trading enterprises used in the former Soviet Union to boost output

perestroika fundamental restructuring of the Soviet economy introduced by Gorbachev

Great Leap Forward China's second five-year plan that began in 1958 and forced rapid industrialization and collectivization of agriculture

D

to all Soviet industries. Central planning also extended to agriculture with the introduction of **collectivization**—the forced common ownership of all agricultural, industrial, and trading enterprises. Planners then sought to ensure the growth of the economy simply by increasing the quotas given to the farms and factories.

Despite its efforts, central planning eventually failed. The Soviet economy had become too complex and large to be managed by a single planning bureaucracy. Shortages appeared everywhere, and people lacked the incentives to work.

After Mikhail Gorbachev assumed power in 1985, he introduced **perestroika,** the restructuring of the Soviet economy. Under the restructuring, plant managers had more freedom to pursue profits, and small business was encouraged.

Gorbachev's successor, Russian President Boris Yeltsin, accelerated privatization after the fall of the Soviet Union. The government distributed vouchers to citizens so that they could purchase shares of stock in companies being privatized. Eventually Russia opened a stock market, which made the ownership of capital by private individuals a reality in a country that once preached the evils of private property.

490   UNIT 5   The Global Economy

Under president Vladimir Putin, privatization began to slow. Under the guise of fighting corruption, Putin used his power to regain centralized control of key energy and mineral industries.

China

The People's Republic of China became a communist economy in 1949. That year the Chinese Communist Party, under the leadership of Mao Zedong, gained control of the country. Over the next few decades, China modeled itself after the Soviet Union, adopting a series of Five-Year Plans to manage its growth.

In 1958 Chinese leaders instituted the **Great Leap Forward,** an attempt to revolutionize industrial and agricultural production almost overnight. This ambitious and radical five-year plan forced farmers off their land to live and work on large, state-owned communal farms.

The Great Leap Forward was a disaster. The agricultural experiment failed, and the economy never came close to achieving the planned degree of industrialization. Other plans followed, but by the late 1970s China finally decided to abandon the Soviet model.

C

International Economic Development Conference

Step 3: Holding the Development Conference. Students will play their roles at the development conference.

Directions: Have students hold the development conference. You may want to give students an agenda/schedule, or they may set it themselves. Suggest that they include these or other elements:

- introductory remarks by the conference's sponsor (an international organization)
- list of discussion topics
- set of conference rules
- a concluding statement

Taking Notes Remind participants to take notes during the conference so that they will be prepared for a discussion of the conference in the activity wrap-up, which will take place in the next session. **OL**

(Chapter Project continued in Visual Summary.)

By the early 1980s, the influence of other successful market economies in Asia—especially Hong Kong—was too much for China to ignore. Guangdong Province, one of China's provinces just north of Hong Kong, copied many of the free-market practices of the region and was even allowed to officially experiment with capitalism.

Today China is privatizing industries, introducing market reforms, and otherwise acting in a capitalistic manner. China still has a long way to go, but the progress made so far is remarkable. China has become one of the world's major economic powers, a transition made possible because of its willingness to replace communist ideology and control with capitalistic practices.

Latin America

In the past, many Latin American countries followed a path of economic development that combined socialism and **isolationism.** Chile, however, took major steps to foster the growth of capitalism when it privatized airlines, telephone services, and utilities. The country even used the billions deposited in its pension funds to supply capital to new entrepreneurs. As a result, it now exports copper, paper and pulp, fruit, and chemicals.

Argentina has similarly embarked on a program to remove government from the everyday business of running the economy. The government has sold state-owned oil fields, petrochemical plants, and a number of other businesses to private companies.

Eastern Europe

The nations of Eastern Europe, especially those that were unwilling members of the former Soviet bloc, were eager to shed communism and embrace capitalism. By 2007 ten of these nations had joined the European Union as full-fledged members.

The struggle for freedom began in Poland with **Solidarity,** the independent and sometimes illegal labor union established in 1980. Solidarity was influential in securing a number of political freedoms

in Poland. Eventually, the Communist party lost power, and interest in capitalism grew. In 2004 Poland joined the EU.

Hungary also made a successful transition to a market economy. It was considered the most "Western" Communist bloc country, with a thriving **black market**—a market in which entrepreneurs and merchants sold goods illegally. Hungary's

Solidarity independent Polish labor union founded in 1980 by Lech Walesa

black market market in which economic products are sold illegally

CAREERS

Urban and Regional Planner

The Work

* Develop long- and short-term plans for the growth and revitalization of urban, suburban, and rural communities

* Help local officials make decisions concerning social, transportation, economic, and environmental problems

* Promote the best use of a community's land and resources for residential, commercial, institutional, and recreational purposes

* Ensure that developers follow zoning codes, building codes, and environmental regulations

Qualifications

* Strong analytical, spatial-relationship, and problem-solving skills

* Master's degree from an accredited program in urban or regional planning, urban design, or geography

* College courses in architecture, law, earth sciences, demography, economics, finance, health administration, geographic information systems, and management

* Experience with computer programming and statistics

Earnings

* Median annual earnings: $53,450

Job Growth Outlook

* Average

Source: *Occupational Outlook Handbook, 2006–2007 Edition*

R Reading Strategy

Academic Vocabulary
Ask: How might a policy of isolationism affect a nation's economic development? *(Answers may include limited foreign investment, fewer grants from other nations, and less trade with other nations.)* **BL**

S Skill Practice

Reading a Time Line Have students select a nation of Eastern Europe that was formerly part of the Soviet bloc. Ask students to create a time line that includes the major events in that nation's economic history since 1980. **OL**

D Differentiated Instruction

Intrapersonal Ask students to review the Careers feature and then write a paragraph explaining why they would or would not like to pursue a career as an urban and regional planner. **BL**

Additional Support

CHAPTER 17 Developing Countries 491

Extending the Content

Poland in the European Union Like other former Soviet bloc nations, Poland has faced challenges while making the transition to capitalism. Since joining the European Union in 2004, the Polish economy has become heavily reliant on subsidies from other member nations. Despite this assistance, Polish leaders, fearing possible limitations to economic growth, have resisted complying with the EU's environmental regulations. Droves of Polish workers, meanwhile, have seized the opportunity provided by EU membership to leave the nation. Since 2004 more than one million Poles have sought jobs in Britain, Ireland, and other Western European countries. While this exodus has reduced Poland's unemployment problem, the nation's 15 percent jobless rate remains the highest in the EU. To make matters worse, wages in Poland remain far below those of other European nations.

R Reading Strategy

Predicting Ask: What does this table suggest about the economic future of North Korea? *(Possible answer: The nation will soon begin making the transition to capitalism.)* **OL**

S Skill Practice

Using Line Graphs Instruct students to use reliable sources to find Japan's annual GDP figures since 1950. Ask students to create a line graph based on their findings. **OL**

Economic Analysis

Answer: Russia has a much larger population than Hungary and Poland.

✓**Reading Check** **Answer:**
Similarities: both made rapid transitions from communism to capitalism, both lacked experience with capitalism. Differences: some Eastern European nations have joined the EU, privatization in Russia slowed under Putin, Hungary's "Western" influences eased its transition to capitalism.

Additional Support

Figure 17.4 ▶ Economic Systems and Economic Success

▶ Countries that have had longer experience with capitalism also have higher per capita GDPs.

Economic Analysis *Why is Russia's per capita GDP lower than that of Hungary or Poland?*

ECONOMIC SYSTEMS AND PER CAPITA GDP

Country	Economic System	Per Capita GDP
United States	Capitalistic	$41,800
Hong Kong	Capitalistic	$32,900
Japan	Capitalistic	$31,500
Sweden	Capitalistic	$29,800
Singapore	Capitalistic	$28,100
Korea, South	Capitalistic	$20,400
Czech Republic	Capitalistic	$19,500
Estonia	Capitalistic	$16,700
Hungary	Capitalistic	$16,300
Slovakia	Capitalistic	$16,100
Lithuania	Capitalistic	$13,700
Poland	Capitalistic	$13,300
Latvia	Capitalistic	$13,200
Argentina	Transition	$13,100
Chile	Transition	$11,300
Russia	Transition	$11,100
Mexico	Capitalistic	$10,000
China	Transition	$6,800
Korea, North	Command	$1,700

Source: *CIA 2006 Factbook*
Note: Comparisons are on a Party Purchasing Power (PPP) basis.

capital-intensive production method requiring relatively large amounts of capital relative to labor

experience with these markets helped ease the transition to capitalism. It too became a full member of the EU in 2004.

Finally, the Czech and Slovak Republics, along with the Baltic states of Estonia, Latvia, and Lithuania, also made great strides toward capitalism following the collapse of the Soviet Union. These countries, along with Slovenia, were all granted admission to the European Union in 2004. All of these countries thus completed one of the more remarkable transitions of economic systems in history—going from communism to capitalism in a relatively short time.

✓**Reading Check** **Comparing** How were the transitions similar and different for Russia and the Eastern European countries?

Other Faces of Capitalism

MAIN Idea A number of nations have developed successful free market economies.

Economics & You You are familiar with capitalism in the United States. Read on to learn how it can differ in other countries.

Some former socialist or communist countries are still making the transition to capitalism. Other countries have had successful capitalist economic societies for some time. This is one reason that so many other countries are trying to make the transition. As **Figure 17.4** shows, capitalistic countries have much higher per capita incomes than other countries.

Japan

Japan, like the United States, has a capitalist economy based on markets, prices, and the private ownership of capital. There are several reason for Japan's success. One reason is that Japan has a loyal and dedicated work force. At many companies, employess even arrive early for work to take part in group calisthenics and meditation with the intent on making their day more productive.

Another reason is the ability and willingness of the Japanese to develop new technologies. Because of its small population, Japan has worked to boost productivity by developing methods that are **capital-intensive**—using a large amount of capital for every person employed—rather than labor-intensive. As a result, Japan is recognized as the world leader in the area of industrial robots.

The feature that sets Japan apart from the United States is the degree to which Japan's government is involved in the day-to-day activities of the private sector. The country's Ministry of International Trade and Industry (MITI), for example, is a government body that identifies promising export markets. The ministry then provides subsidies to industries to make them competitive in those areas.

Extending the Content

Lifetime Employment In Japan, "lifetime employment" means that a person will have a job with the same firm for the rest of his or her life. These jobs often go to graduates of the best universities. To gain admission to these institutions, it is necessary to score high on the comprehensive examinations given in high school. In other words, a person's job is directly related to success in education. With lifetime employment, an individual can move up or down within the same firm depending on his or her success at each level. For example, unproductive workers may be assigned to unimportant jobs. Even when corporations go through tough times, many have tried to avoid layoffs, preferring instead to reassign employees.

Despite Japan's successes, it experienced stagnation for most of the 1990s. Part of the reason is that most large Japanese firms belong to a *keiretsu* (kay • reht • soo), a tightly knit group of firms governed by an external board of directors. The role of the *keiretsu* is to ensure that competition does not threaten individual firms. This group also supervises potential competitors, which harms economic growth. A similar agreement in the United States among competing firms would be illegal under our antitrust laws.

Modest economic growth returned in 2004, but the close relationship between government and industry makes it difficult for incremental change, one of the features of capitalism, to take place. This is an ironic turn of events because the world looked to Japan as the very model of growth in the 1980s. Today Japan turns to the United States for guidance on restructuring so that it can resume its previous growth.

South Korea

One of the most successful nations in Asia is South Korea. In the mid-1950s, after it became divided from North Korea, South Korea was one of the poorest countries in Asia. It needed to rebuild an economy torn up by war. The country also had the highest **population density**—number of people per square mile of land area—in the world.

The South Korean government began by opening its markets to world trade. At first, the government focused on only a few industries. This allowed its people to gain experience producing and exporting for world markets. Businesses in the South Korean economy began to produce inexpensive toys and consumer goods. As they became skilled in production and exports, businesses next moved into textiles such as shirts, dresses, and sweaters. They then invested in heavy industry, such as shipbuilding and steel manufacturing.

keiretsu independently owned group of Japanese firms governed by an external board of directors in order to regulate competition

population density number of people per square mile of land area

South Korea Electronics manufacturing such as in this Samsung plant has helped South Korea become a highly developed country. *What were initial stumbling blocks for South Korea?*

W Writing Support

Descriptive Writing Have students select a Japanese company that interests them. Ask students to write a report describing the company's plants, workforce, products, and customer base. **OL**

C Critical Thinking

Hypothesizing Ask: How do you think Korea's economy would be different today if North Korea had won the Korean War? *(Possible answer: The entire peninsula would be struggling economically. The economic boom that took place in South Korea would not have occurred.)* How do you think Korea's economy would be different today if South Korea had won the Korean War? *(Possible answer: The entire peninsula would be thriving economically. The economic boom would have surpassed that which actually occurred in South Korea.)* **OL**

Caption Answer: poverty, wartime devastation, high population density

Additional Support

Activity: Collaborative Learning

Creating a Diorama Divide the class into small groups. Ask each group to create a diorama illustrating the economic growth of Japan or South Korea. Encourage students to be creative with this activity. Possible ideas for dioramas include a factory producing automobiles or electronic goods, workers exercising, executives at a board meeting, ships exporting goods to other nations, and so on. Display dioramas throughout the classroom. While reviewing dioramas, ask students questions about their content and interpretations. **OL**

Teacher Tip

Preparing Students Recommend that students first consult illustrated books on the Japanese or South Korean economy. Have students look through these books to find pictures that could be recreated in a diorama.

D Differentiated Instruction

Visual/Spatial Have students review the section in the text on Singapore. Ask students to draw a poster that advertises the country as a favorable location for multinational businesses. Before they start this project, encourage students to consult outside sources to learn more about the incentives Singapore offers to prospective companies. **OL**

R Reading Strategy

Activating Prior Knowledge
Ask: Why does Taiwan have a separate government from the People's Republic of China? *(During the Chinese Civil War, the defeated Nationalist regime fled to Taiwan and set up a separate government.)* **OL**

Caption Answer: excessive central planning; interference from the People's Republic of China

Additional Support

Taiwan Taipei, the capital of Taiwan, is home to this Ford Motor factory. *What issues might slow future growth for Taiwan?*

Today, South Korea is a major producer of consumer and electronic goods such as home appliances and televisions. The country also has become a leading producer of automobiles. The South Korean experience shows that capitalism can change a badly war-damaged economy into a well-developed, highly industrial one in just a few generations.

Singapore
D Singapore is a small island nation about 3.5 times larger than Washington, D.C. It has a per capita GNP slightly more than two-thirds of that of the United States. The lure of generous tax breaks, government subsidies, and government-sponsored training of employees has attracted thousands of multinational firms to Singapore. Efforts to develop its own technologies through spending on research and development account for a significant part of its strong economic growth.

The government of Singapore has focused on a few select industries, including telecommunications services, software, and biotechnology. The government has spent millions on laboratories, attracting

top scientists from all over the world. The biotechnology industry has scored some original successes, one of which is the transfer of firefly genes to orchids to make them glow in the dark.

Taiwan
The Republic of China, also known as Taiwan, is located off the coast of the **R** much larger People's Republic of China. The population of Taiwan is about 23 million, and the per capita GNP is almost two-thirds of that of the United States.

Planning has always been a feature of the Taiwanese economy, with the government trying to identify those industries most likely to grow in the future. Most of these plans target high-tech industries such as telecommunications, consumer electronics, semiconductors, precision machinery, aerospace, and pharmaceuticals.

Taiwan was one of the early economic powers in Asia, but some experts have warned that the centralized planning process will hamper future economic growth. Another concern is the looming presence of the People's Republic of China, which regards Taiwan as a "renegade province"

494   UNIT 5   The Global Economy

Activity: Interdisciplinary Connection

International Studies Have each student select one of the nations featured in this section. Direct students to gather either current or historical information about the economic system of their selected nation. Then have students investigate their chosen nation's cultural heritage. Finally, ask students to collate their findings in a report, showing direct relationships between the country's societal values and characteristics of its economic system. Call on students to present their reports to the class. **AL**

and vows eventual unification. Despite its early start, the per capita GNP in Taiwan has fallen behind those of Hong Kong and Singapore.

Sweden

Sweden, now a mature industrial nation, was once regarded as the "socialist state that works." The reputation was apt at the time, because Sweden provided a broader range of social welfare programs for its citizens than did any other noncommunist country. The Swedish economy—with its generous maternity, education, disability, and old-age benefits—was thought to be the model of European socialism.

Social benefits were expensive, however, and to pay for them tax receipts were about 50 percent of GDP in the mid-1970s. In addition, some marginal tax brackets reached 80 percent, meaning that a person who earned an additional $100 would keep only $20. Many individuals even left the country to avoid high taxes. When tennis star Bjorn Borg was at the peak of his career, for example, he resided outside of Sweden to avoid paying high taxes.

Eventually the heavy tax burden, the costs of the welfare state, and massive government deficits cut into Sweden's economic growth and led to the defeat of the Socialist Party. By 1991 a government committed to a free market economy was firmly in place. It reduced the role of the public sector, lowered taxes, and privatized many **C** government-owned businesses.

Today Sweden features a mix of high-tech capitalism and liberal welfare benefits. The generous welfare system is thought to be the reason why Swedish workers report in sick more often than other European workers. The taxes required to support the welfare system also have kept its GDP per capita below that of its closest neighbors, Denmark, Finland, and Norway.

✓Reading Check **Explaining** How did Japan, Singapore, and South Korea manage to become successful?

C **Critical Thinking**

Differentiating Ask: How does Sweden's recent economic history differ from that of the nations of Eastern Europe? *(Possible answer: In Sweden, citizens voted the socialists out of power; in Eastern Europe, people overthrew the communist governments.)* **OL**

✓Reading Check **Answer:** They embraced capitalism and developed industries that produced profitable exports.

Assess

🔘 Use the Interactive Tutor Self-Assessment CD-ROM to review Section 3, and then assign the Section 3 Review as homework or as an in-class activity.

Close

Identifying Have students identify and describe the problems faced by economies in transition. **OL**

Review **SECTION** **3**

SECTION 3 Review

Vocabulary
1. **Explain** the significance of capitalism, privatization, vouchers, Five-Year Plan, Gosplan, collectivization, perestroika, Great Leap Forward, Solidarity, black market, capital-intensive, *keiretsu,* and population density.

Main Ideas
2. **Listing** Use a graphic organizer like the one below to list four problems faced by economies in transition.

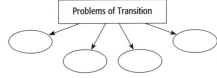

Problems of Transition

3. **Describing** How do economies in transition handle privatization?

4. **Explaining** What are the contrasting approaches to economic growth in Taiwan and China?

Critical Thinking
5. **The BIG Idea** Evaluate the progress of Poland, Russia, and South Korea in moving toward a market system.

6. **Drawing Conclusions** Why would a developing nation want to choose capitalism?

7. **Making Connections** Suppose you are visiting a nation in Central Asia. What questions would you ask local officials to determine whether they are successfully moving toward a market economy?

8. **Analyzing Visuals** Compare the photo of a Russian supermarket on 489 with that of a North Korean grocery story on page 37. How do the two stores reflect the differences in economic systems?

Applying Economics
9. **Economic Growth** Why would capital equipment and other property last longer when it is privatized rather than collectively owned?

CHAPTER 17 Developing Countries **495**

Answers

1. All definitions can be found in the section and the Glossary.
2. loss of political power; instability; unemployment; difficulty adjusting to new incentives
3. by issuing vouchers that people could use to purchase government-owned property
4. China used a communist model that included radical five-year plans to manage growth; when that failed China adopted free market and privatization practices. Taiwan adopted a capitalist system but

used government planning to try to identify industries with potential.
5. Poland's acceptance into the EU is evidence of its progress. Russia made rapid progress towards privatization in the 1990s, but under President Putin the government has regained control over key energy and mineral industries. South Korea successfully moved to a free market system by developing different export industries.

6. Capitalism is a powerful engine for generating wealth; it increases the standard of living in a nation.
7. Answers will vary but should discuss the transition to a market economy.
8. Answers will vary, but students will likely note that the Russian store is more prosperous.
9. People generally take better care of items that they own.

Teach

S Skill Practice

Evaluating Information
Ask: Why do you think that Marx's theories attracted such a large following in the 1900s? *(Possible answer: The workers really were exploited in many nations, just as Marx described. Marx's ideas inspired masses of people discontent with their treatment by the ruling classes.)* **OL**

Examining the Profile

Answers:

1. He believed that they were oppressed by the bourgeoisie and denied a fair compensation for their labor.
2. Student answers will vary but should reflect an awareness of class struggles in the modern world.

Additional Support

Profiles in Economics

Karl Marx (1818–1883)

- published *The Communist Manifesto* in 1848
- his ideas inspired communist revolutions

The Communist Manifesto

Karl Marx was an economic historian and social scientist who earned his degrees at the University of Berlin. Because of his radical views, however, he could not get a teaching position in Germany and eventually moved to the United Kingdom.

Marx is best known for *The Communist Manifesto,* published in 1848, and *Das Kapital,* the first volume of which was published in 1867. In these works, Marx asserted that "the history of all hitherto existing society is the history of class struggles," and in each era, one class was pitted against another. Marx believed that the oppressed of his day were the proletariat–people who must work for others because they have no means of production of their own. Their oppressors were the bourgeoisie, or capitalists–people who own the means of production.

Ideas to Spread the Wealth

Marx argued that labor was exploited in a capitalist society, and that capitalists unfairly kept surplus value–the difference between wages and market value of workers' output–as profits. To fight unequal wealth, the proletariat should violently overthrow the ruling class: "Working men of all countries, unite!"

During the transition from capitalism to communism, Marx thought that the proletariat would first have to depend on a strong government–a "Dictatorship of the Proletariat." Eventually this would be replaced by a classless or communal society, with no need for a government. People would produce to the best of their abilities and consume to the extent of their needs.

S The ideas of Marx served as the basis for communist revolutions around the world in the early to mid-1900s. Since then, most communist governments have collapsed, and today only a few communist countries remain.

Karl Marx's ideas were so radical during his time that he was persecuted by authorities. In 1849 he fled to London, where he began a life of exile and later died in poverty. Still, Marx was named the "Greatest Philosopher of All Time" in a BBC poll in 2005.

Examining the Profile

1. **Analyzing** Why did Marx believe that workers would be interested in staging a revolution and overthrowing the ruling class?
2. **Making Inferences** Do you believe class struggles are occurring in the world today? Explain your answer.

496   UNIT 5   The Global Economy

Activity: Collaborative Learning

Performing a Skit Organize the class into groups of four to six students. Instruct each group to conduct further research into Karl Marx's economic theories. Ask each group to then write a skit in which Karl Marx visits the modern age and comments about current economic developments. Have groups perform their skits for the class. Aside from Marx, roles that students could portray in their group's skits include world leaders, business owners, factory workers, and modern-day Marxist economists. **OL**

Study anywhere, anytime! Download quizzes and flash cards to your PDA from glencoe.com.

▶ **Stages of Economic Development** Countries usually go through several stages of economic development, although the boundaries between these stages may overlap.

Primitive Equilibrium → Transition → Takeoff → Semi-development → High Development

▶ **Funding Economic Development** Countries that need to develop their economies have a variety of funding sources available to them.

Internal Funding Sources		External Funding Sources		
Saving	**Microfinance**	**International Agencies**	**Government Aid Grants**	**Private Foreign Investments**
• Profit motive as incentive • Generates financial capital	• Small unsecured loans for new businesses • No bank loans required	• IMF: advice on fiscal policies and currency support • World Bank: financial assistance	• Grants and loans from foreign governments • Usually linked to political alliances	• Foreign investors develop specific industries • Must be beneficial to investor and host country

▶ **Problems of Transition** While capitalism provides a remarkable degree of economic growth, making a successful transition to capitalism can be difficult.

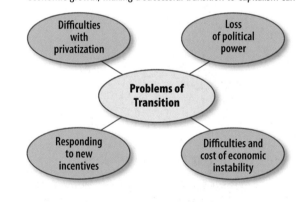

- Difficulties with privatization
- Loss of political power
- **Problems of Transition**
- Responding to new incentives
- Difficulties and cost of economic instability

Categorizing Have students search recent newspapers and news magazines for articles about developing countries. Ask students to clip at least one article describing an example of each type of funding listed in the graphic in the center of this page. **OL**

Problem-Solving Divide the class into four discussion groups. Assign each group one of the four problems of transition shown in the graphic at the bottom of the page. Have groups come up with a list of four specific examples related to their assigned problem. Then have them list possible solutions that people in a nation transitioning to capitalism could take to address each problem. Have each group report to the class on the problems and solutions it identified. Conclude by having the class write a paragraph that answers this question: *What would likely happen in a transitioning nation that did not address these problems? (Answers will vary, but students should recognize the specific issues that would arise.)* **OL**

Hands-On Chapter Project
Step 4: Wrap Up

International Economic Development Conference

Step 4: Processing the Development Conference. Students will discuss the development conference of the previous session.

Directions: At the conclusion of the conference, have the class discuss what they learned. Ask:

- What did you learn about world economic development that you did not know?

- Do you disagree with anything you heard in the conference? Why?
- Was there a topic that was not discussed that you feel is important?
- What would you do differently if you took part in another mock conference on this topic?

Synthesizing Have students discuss this question: *What are the most difficult challenges facing the world community in its efforts to promote economic development?* **OL**

ExamView®
Assessment Suite

This easy-to-use software includes extensive question banks and allows you to create fully customized tests that can be administered in print or online.

Review Content Vocabulary

1. c	2. h
3. e	4. d
5. g	6. j
7. a	8. f
9. i	10. b

Review Academic Vocabulary

11.–16. Students' sentences should reflect a clear understanding of the terms' meanings in an economic context.

Review the Main Ideas

17. developing nations provide critical raw materials and markets; countries with strong market economies are more cooperative and stable

18. primitive equilibrium: economy is stagnant; transition: society breaks with tradition and moves toward change; takeoff: barriers of primitive equilibrium are overcome; semidevelopment: per capita income grows, core industries expand, and new technology is adopted; high development: basic needs of the population are met, and mature service and manufacturing sectors grow

19. The increased demand for goods can strain a country's resources.

20. granting loans for projects and providing financial assistance and advice

Review Content Vocabulary

Write the key term that best completes the following sentences.

a. capital flight
b. capital-intensive
c. cartel
d. crude birthrate
e. customs union
f. expropriation
g. external debt
h. micro loan
i. population density
j. takeoff

1. A(n) _____ is a formal arrangement to limit the production of a product.

2. A _____ helps people in developing countries obtain minimal funding to start small businesses.

3. A(n) _____ is a cooperative arrangement among nations that sets uniform tariffs for nonmembers.

4. A developing country may have a very high _____ , contributing to rapid population growth.

5. When _____ becomes too large, countries have difficulty paying the interest.

6. The third stage of economic development is the _____ .

7. The problem of _____ occurs when corrupt officials take money out of the country and deposit it abroad.

8. When _____ takes place, it is more difficult for developing nations to attract foreign capital.

9. The number of people per square mile of land is a measure of _____ .

10. In _____ industries, a large amount of capital is used for every person employed in manufacturing.

Review Academic Vocabulary

Use each of the following terms in a sentence that reflects the term's meaning in the chapter.

11. proportion
12. primary
13. ethic
14. duration
15. undertaking
16. isolationism

498 UNIT 5 The Global Economy

Review the Main Ideas

Section 1 (pages 469–477)

17. **List** two reasons why there is concern for the plight of developing countries.

18. **Describe** the stages of economic development.

19. **Explain** why the size of the population can create a problem for a developing country.

Section 2 (pages 479–484)

20. **Describe** how the World Bank assists developing countries.

21. **Explain** how a developing country can attract foreign capital.

22. **Identify** the benefits of membership in the European Union.

Section 3 (pages 486–495)

23. **Explain** why countries would want to make a transition to capitalism.

24. **Describe** how Latin American countries have approached the transition to capitalism.

25. **Identify** the steps in South Korea's economic development by using a graphic organizer like the one below.

South Korea's Economic Development

Critical Thinking

26. **The BIG Ideas** What do you think would happen if industrialized nations and international agencies chose to withdraw their support from developing nations?

21. by demonstrating political stability and protecting investor rights

22. no internal barriers limiting the flow of workers, financial capital, or goods and services; common currency makes transactions easier and less expensive; uniform tariffs for nonmembers provide protection

23. It is the most effective way to generate wealth and raise the standard of living.

24. Many nations combined socialism and isolationism; Chile and Argentina have gradually adopted privatization.

25. open markets to world trade; gain experience by producing inexpensive toys and consumer goods; produce textiles; invest in heavy industry, like shipbuilding and steel manufacturing; produce consumer and electronic goods, and automobiles

Critical Thinking

26. **Possible answer:** The reduced funding would greatly hinder development.

Economics ONLINE **Self-Check Quiz** Visit the
Economics: Principles and Practices Web site at glencoe.com and click
on *Chapter 17–Self-Check Quizzes* to prepare for the chapter test.

**Assessment
and Activities**

**CHAPTER
17**

27. **Synthesizing** What actions can the United States take to help the developing countries of Latin America? Use a graphic organizer similar to the one below to describe the actions and the possible results.

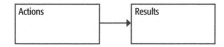

28. **Drawing Conclusions** What economic and political conditions in developing countries encourage foreign investment?

29. **Making Generalizations** Studies indicate that, in general, landlocked nations tend to have lower per capita income levels than surrounding nations that are bordered by oceans and seas. Why do you think this is the case?

30. **Predicting** How might continued economic growth in Asia affect the United States?

31. **Drawing Conclusions** Why do many U.S. companies think their Chinese competitors have an unfair advantage?

32. **Drawing Conclusions** The Communists promised people that their system would lead to workers' paradises throughout the world, but by the early 1990s, most communist systems and their command economies in Eastern Europe had collapsed. Why do you think communism failed?

33. **Drawing Conclusions** How has Sweden's transition from socialism to capitalism helped promote economic growth?

Analyzing Visuals

34. Look at the photo on page 474 of Tokyo, Japan. Describe the photo and explain how it reflects rapid population growth. Then consider if this photo reminds you of similar places. Now look at the photo of Times Square in New York City on page 412. How are the two images similar? How are they different?

Thinking Like an Economist

35. **Critical Thinking** What advice would you give a developing Latin American nation that was trying to decide whether to pattern its economic development strategy on India or China? Explain your answer.

Writing About Economics

36. **Expository Writing** News media often report on the economic problems of developing nations. For one week, keep a journal of all the news stories you see and read about. Then complete the following steps.

   a. Create a list with the countries in one column and their problems in a second column.

   b. Using the information you collected, write a plan detailing how the United States could assist in alleviating some of the economic problems of a specific country. Be sure to support your proposal with statistics, facts, quotes, and historical events.

   c. Present your conclusions to the class.

Applying Economic Concepts

37. **Growth and Development** How do you think the economic growth of developing countries will affect you and your family in the future?

38. **Economic Development** On their way to high development, many developing countries may go through several stages of economic development at the same time. Select three developing countries. In a table similar to the one below, identify the stages of economic development for each. Explain your reasons.

Country	Stages	Reason

CHAPTER 17 Developing Countries 499

33. Lower taxes and privatization increased incentives among Swedish entrepreneurs and workers to work harder and increase productivity.

Analyzing Visuals

34. Similarities: Both cities are busy and crowded with buildings. Differences: There are motor vehicles in New York City, and the advertising is more technologically advanced.

Thinking Like an Economist

35. Answers will vary, but students should demonstrate understanding of the different strategies India and China have used for economic development.

Writing About Economics

36. Students' journals, lists, plans, and conclusions will vary.

Applying Economic Concepts

37. Answers will vary, but students should demonstrate understanding of how issues relating to developing countries affect people in other nations.

38. Students' tables will vary based on countries selected.

---

27. **Possible answers:** Actions—increase aid grants; Results—greater economic development, stronger political ties

28. political stability and government protection of property rights

29. Answers will vary, but students should recognize that landlocked nations do not have access to oceanic trade routes, and thus have more difficulty generating trade revenue.

30. **Possible answers:** American exports would face greater competition from Asian goods in international markets; more Asian imports would enter U.S. markets; there would be an increased demand for American goods in Asian markets.

31. China's trade barriers make it difficult for American goods to compete there; low wages allow Chinese manufacturers to mass produce goods at a lower cost than American manufacturers.

32. Answers will vary, but students should recognize that worker incentives are generally reduced under central planning and collectivization.

Levels					Resources	Chapter Opener	Section 1	Section 2	Section 3	Chapter Assess
BL	OL	AL	ELL		**FOCUS**					
BL	OL	AL	ELL		**Daily Focus Skills Transparencies**		91, 93, 94, 95	90	92, 97	
					TEACH					
BL	OL		ELL		**Guided Reading Activities***		p. 52	p. 53	p. 54	
BL	OL	AL	ELL		**Economic Content Vocabulary Activities***		p. 18	p. 18	p. 18	
	OL	AL			**Critical Thinking Activities**		p. 26	p. 15		
BL	OL		ELL		**Reading Essentials and Note-Taking Guide***		p. 154	p. 157	p. 160	
		AL			**Enrichment Activities**			p. 18		
	OL	AL			**Free Enterprise Activities**		p. 25	p. 25		
BL	OL	AL	ELL		**Economic Cartoons**		p. 29			
BL	OL	AL	ELL		**Math Practice for Economics**			p. 25		
	OL	AL			**BusinessWeek Focus on the Global Economy**		pp. 2, 17	pp. 36, 38		
BL	OL		ELL		**High School Reading in the Content Area Strategies and Activities**	✓	✓	✓	✓	✓
BL	OL	AL	ELL		**High School Writing Process Transparencies**	✓	✓	✓	✓	✓
BL	OL	AL	ELL		**Writer's Guidebook**	✓	✓	✓	✓	✓
BL	OL	AL	ELL		**StudentWorks Plus CD-ROM**	✓	✓	✓	✓	✓
BL	OL	AL	ELL		**Vocabulary PuzzleMaker CD-ROM**	✓	✓	✓	✓	✓

*Also available in Spanish

TeacherWorks *Plus*
All-In-One Planner and Resource Center

- Interactive Lesson Planner
- Interactive Teacher Edition
- Fully editable blackline masters
- Economics & You videos

- Differentiated Lesson Plans
- Printable reports of daily assignments
- Standards tracking system

Levels					Resources	Chapter Opener	Section 1	Section 2	Section 3	Chapter Assess
BL	OL	AL	ELL							
TEACH *(continued)*										
BL	OL	AL	ELL		Economics & You Video Program DVD— *Global Economic Challenges*	✓	✓	✓	✓	✓
BL	OL	AL	ELL		Graph Coach CD-ROM	✓	✓	✓	✓	✓
Teacher Resources					Differentiated Instruction Strategies	✓	✓	✓	✓	✓
					Success with English Learners	✓	✓	✓	✓	✓
					Presentation Plus! CD-ROM	✓	✓	✓	✓	✓
ASSESS										
BL	OL	AL	ELL		Section Quizzes and Chapter Tests		p. 225	p. 226	p. 227	pp. 229, 233
BL	OL	AL	ELL		Authentic Assessment Strategies and Activities		p. 25			
BL	OL	AL	ELL		*ExamView®* Assessment Suite CD-ROM		18-1	18-2	18-3	Ch. 18
BL	OL	AL	ELL		Interactive Tutor Self-Assessment CD-ROM		18-1	18-2	18-3	
CLOSE										
BL			ELL		Reteaching Activities*		p. 18	p. 18	p. 18	
BL	OL		ELL		Reading and Study Skills Foldables		p. 66	p. 66	p. 66	
BL	OL	AL	ELL		Graphic Organizer Transparencies		p. 39			

*Also available in Spanish

Activity
Using the McGraw-Hill Learning Network

Presentation Builder

Technology Product

Presentation Builder is a convenient and dynamic McGraw-Hill Learning Network tool to create online presentations. Use the Presentation Builder to

- create your own presentation slides;
- insert graphics from your Glencoe textbook;
- distribute presentations to students using **Assignments** from the *Classroom Tools*.

Steps

- On the McGraw-Hill Learning Network home page (www.mhln.com), log in as a member.
- Choose **Presentation Builder** under **Resources.**
- Click the **New Presentation** button.
- Enter a title in the **Presentation Title** box, and then follow the prompts to select colors and fonts.
- Click the **Next** button and select a slide. Follow the prompts to insert information and complete the

slide. The text boxes automatically adjust in size to accommodate the length of each question.

- Click the **Add Slide** button if you have additional presentation information, and follow the prompts.
- Click **Review Presentation** when you are done.
- Click **View Presentation** to review the presentation in a pop-up window.
- Click on an underlined slide title to edit slides; use the drop-down keys to change the order of the slides; push the **Delete** button to delete a slide; and press **Insert Slide** to add a slide.
- Click the **Save** button when you are satisfied with your presentation. The presentation is saved to your **File Cabinet** and can be distributed to students through **Assignments.**

Economics ONLINE

	Student	Teacher	Parent
Beyond the Textbook	●	●	●
Chapter Overviews	●	●	●
ePuzzles and Games	●		●
Concepts in Motion	●		●
Multi-Language Glossaries	●		●
Online Student Edition	●	●	●
Self-Check Quizzes	●		●
Student Web Activities	●		●
Study Central™	●		●
Time Current Events	●	●	●
Teaching Today		●	
Vocabulary eFlashcards	●		●
Web Activity Lesson Plans		●	

Glencoe Media Center

❯ glencoe.com

Study-To-Go
- Vocabulary eFlashcards
- Self-Check Quizzes

❯ **Audio/Video**
- Student Edition Audio
- Spanish Summaries
- Economics & You Videos

- **Timed Readings Plus in Social Studies** helps students increase their reading rate and fluency while maintaining comprehension. The 400-word passages are similar to those found on state and national assessments.

- **Reading in the Content Area: Social Studies** concentrates on six essential reading skills that help students better comprehend what they read. The book includes 75 high-interest nonfiction passages written at increasing levels of difficulty.

- **Reading Social Studies** includes strategic reading instruction and vocabulary support in Social Studies content for both ELLs and native speakers of English. www.jamestowneducation.com

Reading List Generator CD-ROM

Use this database to search more than 30,000 titles to create a customized reading list for your students.

- Reading lists can be organized by students' reading level, author, genre, theme, or area of interest.
- The database provides Degrees of Reading Power™ (DRP) and Lexile™ readability scores for all selections.
- A brief summary of each selection is included.

Leveled reading suggestions for this chapter:
For students at a Grade 10 reading level:
- *Globalization,* by Adam Hibbert

For students at a Grade 11 reading level:
- *Globalize It!: The Stories of the IMF, the World Bank, and the WTO,* by Brendan January

For students at a Grade 12 reading level:
- *The Internet,* by Helen Cothran

* Review suggested books before assigning them.

NCEE

National Council on Economic Education

Voluntary Standards Emphasized in Chapter 18

Content Standard 4 People respond predictably to positive and negative incentives.

Content Standard 5 Voluntary exchange occurs only when all participating parties expect to gain. This is true for trade among individuals or organizations within a nation, and among individuals or organizations in different nations.

Resources Available from NCEE
- Virtual Economics®: An Interactive Center for Economic Education Version 3.0
- Civics and Government: Focus on Economics, Second Edition
- Economies in Transition: Command to Market
- From Plan to Market
- Focus: Economic Systems

To order these materials, or to contact your State Council on Economic Education about workshops and programs, call 1-800-338-1192 or visit the NCEE Web site at store.ncee.net.

The **BIG** Ideas

As students study the chapter, remind them to consider the chapter-based Big Ideas. The **Essential Question** in the chapter launch activity below ties in to the Big Ideas and helps students think about and understand important chapter concepts. In addition, the Hands-On Chapter Project relates the content from each section to the Big Ideas. The steps in each section build on each other and culminate in the Wrap-Up Activity on the Visual Summary page.

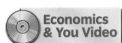
Economics & You Video To generate student interest and provide a springboard for class discussion, access the Economics & You Topic 26 video, **Global Economic Challenges,** at glencoe.com or on the video DVD.

FOLDABLES Study Organizer **Dinah Zike's Foldables** are three-dimensional, interactive graphic organizers that help students practice basic writing skills, review key vocabulary terms, and identify main ideas. Have students complete this chapter's Foldable activity or activities in *Dinah Zike's Reading and Study Skills Foldables* booklet. **OL**

Economics ONLINE

Introduce students to chapter content and key terms by having them access *Chapter 18 —Chapter Overviews* at glencoe.com.

CHAPTER 18 Global Economic Challenges

Why It Matters

Have you decided what you want to be "when you grow up"? What factors are you considering when making your plans for the future? Which career interests you the most? How will you decide? List the advantages and disadvantages of your top two career choices. Share your reasoning with other students in your class. Read Chapter 18 to find out how globalization affects your personal choices as well as those of businesses and nations.

The **BIG** Ideas

1. The study of economics helps us deal with global economic issues and global demand on resources.
2. Scarcity is the basic economic problem that requires people to make choices about how to use limited resources.

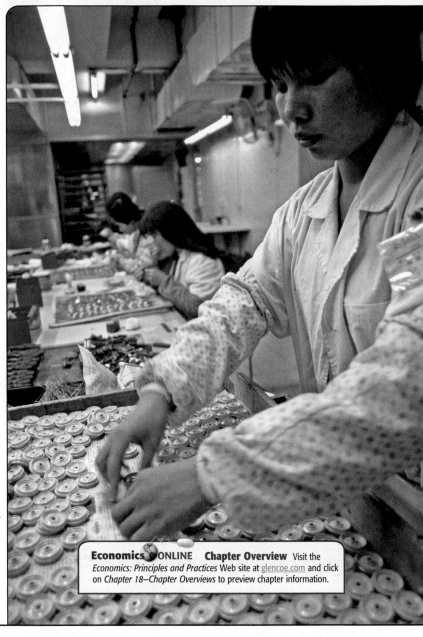

▶ Many U.S. manufacturers use components produced in overseas factories, such as this Deere parts manufacturing plant in Macau.

Economics ONLINE **Chapter Overview** Visit the *Economics: Principles and Practices* Web site at glencoe.com and click on *Chapter 18—Chapter Overviews* to preview chapter information.

500 UNIT 5

Activity: Launching the Chapter

Speculating Ask students to name ways in which they learn about events that happen in other countries. Most will mention cable TV and the Internet. **Essential Question:** How are we affected by our ability to learn, almost instantly, about an event that occurs anywhere in the world? *(Most students will say that this capability makes the world seem much smaller than it did a generation ago.)* **Ask:** What effect do you think this "smaller world" will have on the world economy? *(Many students will say that economic changes in one part of the world will inevitably and more readily cause changes in other parts of the world.)* Tell students that this chapter examines the ways a "smaller world" has influenced— and will continue to influence—the global economy. **OL**

SECTION
1

Globalization: Characteristics and Trends

GUIDE TO READING

Section Preview

In this section, you will learn that globalization leads to growing interaction among countries and the development of international organizations.

Content Vocabulary

• globalization (p. 501)
• multinational (p. 502)
• outsourcing (p. 503)
• General Agreement on Tariffs and Trade (GATT) (p. 504)
• division of labor (p. 504)
• comparative advantage (p. 504)
• European Coal and Steel Community (ECSC) (p. 505)
• Free Trade Area of the Americas (FTAA) (p. 506)

Academic Vocabulary

• strategy (p. 504)
• context (p. 504)

Reading Strategy

Explaining As you read the section, complete a graphic organizer similar to the one below by explaining how globalization affects products and countries.

```
        Globalization
        /          \
   Products      Countries
   / | \          / | \
```

COMPANIES IN THE NEWS
—The Motley Fool

Name That Company

Founded in 1868 and based in Camden, N.J., I'm a global maker of soups, snacks, vegetable-based beverages, premium chocolate and more. My brands include Godiva, Pace, Pepperidge Farm, Prego, Swanson, and V8. I invented condensed soup in 1897. I rake in more than $7 billion in annual sales. The colors on my soup cans were inspired by the Cornell football team's uniforms in 1898. Americans consume about 2.5 billion bowls of my top three soups each year. I sell watercress and duck gizzard soup in China. Who am I? ■
(Answer: Campbell Soup)

One of the most important trends in the world today is **globalization**—the movement toward a more integrated and interdependent world economy. Globalization, as the news story shows, means that people in any country can purchase products made anywhere else in the world.

Globalization is taking place because of the voluntary decisions we make as consumers. People today are buying more foreign products, and firms are extending their operations on a global scale. Both actions have important consequences for our future economic well-being.

globalization
the movement toward a more integrated and interdependent world economy

---

Teach

W Writing Support

Descriptive Writing Tell students that they have gone on a trip to a foreign country of their choice. Have students write a humorous post card home from that country describing familiar products they see people using and in stores, on signs, and in other places. **OL**

D Differentiated Instruction

English Language Learners Have a volunteer define the term *multinational. (a company that does business in many different countries)* Then ask students to speculate on what the prefix *multi-* means. *(many)* Have students list words with this prefix and explain their meanings. *(Possible answers: multiply, multitalented, multicultural, multilingual, multiple, multiple sclerosis, multiplex, multipurpose)* **ELL**

Caption Answer: Stores are filled with products made overseas or by multinational corporations.

Additional Support

---

multinational corporation producing and selling without regard to national boundaries and whose business activities are located in several different countries *(also see page 76)*

Skills Handbook
See page **R37** to learn about **Making Generalizations.**

Characteristics of Globalization

MAIN Idea Globalization involves the global spread of products, markets, and production, while international organizations aid trade.

Economics & You Do you ever check where the everyday products you use come from? Read on to learn how globalization brings the world to you.

There was a time when most markets were local. As transportation and communication improved and populations grew, markets expanded to nearby communities. Local markets expanded into regions, then the nation, and today the world.

As a result of this progress, many economists view globalization as a natural, almost inevitable, process. Globalization involves more than markets, however. We also see the globalization of production, institutions, and even culture.

Global Products and Markets

W Today you can find specific goods, such as products from McDonald's, KFC, Pizza Hut, Starbucks, or Pepsi, all over the globe.

This would have been news just a few years ago, but today the global presence of a product is the rule rather than the exception.

D Many of the products we use are made by **multinationals** that produce and sell without regard to national boundaries. Some of these giant corporations, such as British Petroleum (United Kingdom), Ford Motor Company (United States), and Shell Oil Company (United Kingdom and Netherlands) are well known to most people. Others, such as News Corporation (Australia), Kyocera (Japan), Schlumberger (Netherlands), and Vodaphone (United Kingdom) are less well known but make products that millions of Americans use every day.

As a result of globalization, stores are stocked with a wide variety of products from other countries. Switzerland's Nestle provides us with chocolate bars, coffee, and Stouffers frozen foods. Baskin-Robbins is owned by a firm in the United Kingdom. The Citgo gas station you might use is owned by a Venezuelan company, and the 7-Eleven store by a Japanese firm. The products these companies offer have the

Global Products The Nestlé Company is headquartered in Switzerland but sells its products worldwide. *How is globalization reflected in stores?*

502 UNIT 5 The Global Economy

Activity: Technology Connection

Foreign and Domestic Sales Have students go to a corporate Web site to find out information about a multinational's revenues. Have students choose one of the multinational corporations mentioned on this page or another that they are interested in. Then have them use their Internet searching skills to find out (1) the company's home country; (2) the percentage of the company's revenues that comes from domestic sales (that is, in the home country) and foreign sales (from all other countries); and (3) the foreign country that contributes the most to the company's foreign sales. Have students share their findings with the class. **OL**

The Global Economy & YOU

Global Anatomy of an American Rock Band

Rock 'n' roll music is as American as apple pie. To put together a band, however, you need instruments of global origin. A great example is the Steinway grand piano, which is truly a work of international proportion. Steinway manufactures its grand piano in both New York and Hamburg, Germany. The strings are made from Swedish steel, and the keys are crafted from Bavarian spruce.

Many other musical inventions, such as the guitar, steel drums, synthesizer, and the microphone, led to the American sound. Look at the table to see how global efforts have made American music possible.

Musical Instrument/Invention	Inventor	Country of Origin/Date
Hydraulic organ	Ctesibius of Alexandria	Egypt, 246 B.C.
Steel drums	Enslaved people from West Africa	Trinidad, 1500s
Pianoforte	Bartolomeo Cristofori	Italy, c. 1720
Harmonica	Friedrich Ludwig Buschmann	Germany, 1821
Saxophone	Adolphe Sax	Belgium, 1841
Microphone	Emile Berliner	Germany, 1876
Fender guitar	Leo Fender	United States, 1946
Synthesizer	Hugh Le Caine	Canada, 1970

same features regardless of the country in which they are sold. This similarity makes selling in a global market easy.

Global Production

Globalization means more than having standardized products all over the world, though. It extends to production as well. **C** In some cases, multinationals move their production facilities to be nearer to customers. For example, firms such as Toyota, Nissan, and Honda have opened manufacturing operations in the United States. Others, such as IBM, Boeing, and Intel, moved production facilities abroad to be closer to less expensive sources of labor and raw materials.

Most global manufacturing operations are highly sophisticated. For example, Dell uses the Internet to track production and shipping in its plants around the world. By **R** keeping close watch on its operations, Dell is able to keep a modest three-day inventory in its assembly plants. If conditions in one location should suddenly change, Dell can either speed up or slow down shipments of parts to keep production flowing smoothly.

One of the more controversial aspects of global production is **outsourcing**—hiring outside firms for non-core operations to lower operating costs. Many Americans consider outsourcing a controversial issue because they fear losing their jobs to overseas workers. While this is a concern to many workers, in the long run the lower costs of production, and the lower prices **W** that consumers pay, are benefits that more than offset the lost jobs.

This is little comfort to those who lose their jobs. Yet it is likely that these workers have benefited from and contributed to globalization by buying low-priced clothes made in Indonesia, TV sets from Korea, or other products made abroad.

Global Institutions

Another aspect of globalization is the growth of international organizations that promote trade between nations. One such

> **outsourcing**
> hiring outside firms to perform non-core operations to lower operating costs

C Critical Thinking

Evaluating Ask: What are some advantages and disadvantages that a multinational gains by being large and operating in many different countries? *(Possible advantages: ability to draw talent from many different countries, chance to spread risk. Possible disadvantages: risk of political and social unrest in other countries, difficulty in communicating and coordinating, language and social problems, unfamiliarity with other cultures.)* **OL**

R Reading Strategy

Inferring Ask: Do you think globalization would have been possible without computers? Why or why not? *(Most students will say no based on the speed with which modern telecommunications takes place.)* **BL**

W Writing Support

Personal Writing Have students write a paragraph on whether they agree or disagree that lower costs and prices more than offset jobs lost to outsourcing. Have volunteers read their paragraphs. **OL**

Additional Support

Activity: Collaborative Learning

Business in Far-Flung Places Have student groups research and compile a list of tips or "dos and don'ts" for doing business in another part of the world. You may want to assign groups countries such as Japan, China, Russia, Saudi Arabia, Korea, Nigeria, South Africa, and any Latin American or European country. Also, you may want to suggest that students focus their research on tips for several different types of manners or etiquette: appearance (including proper clothing and gestures), behavior (including body language and eating manners), and communication (including proper greetings). After students have shared their lists of tips, discuss this question: *Why should businesspeople take the time to learn about the customs of places where they are doing business?* **OL**

Teacher Tip

Drama Students might enjoy acting out some of their research findings. For example, have students present a skit about two businesspeople in a foreign country—one who is savvy about business etiquette, manners, and appearance, and one who is not.

C Critical Thinking

Defending Tell students that the United States is a major financial contributor to international aid organizations like the IMF and World Bank. Then ask students to argue for or against this statement: *U.S. foreign aid to developing countries is a waste of money and would be better spent fighting problems at home.* Have students debate the topic, citing evidence from the text and current events. **OL**

R Reading Strategy

Previewing Have students preview the subsection by looking at headings and graphics. Then have them write a sentence describing what they expect to learn in the subsection. **BL**

Caption Answer: the International Monetary Fund, the World Trade Organization, the United Nations

✓ **Reading Check** **Answer:** They produce and sell items around the world.

General Agreement on Tariffs and Trade (GATT) international agreement to extend tariff concessions and reduce import quotas

division of labor separation of work into a number of individual tasks to be performed by different workers *(also see page 17)*

comparative advantage a country's ability to produce a given product at a lower opportunity cost than another country *(also see page 444)*

example is the **General Agreement on Tariffs and Trade (GATT).** The GATT is an international agreement signed in 1947 between 23 countries to extend tariff concessions and do away with import quotas. The success of the GATT led to its successor, the World Trade Organization (WTO). Today nearly 150 countries belong to the WTO and turn to it whenever conflicts arise between member countries.

The International Monetary Fund (IMF) offers advice and financial assistance to nations so that their currencies can compete in open markets. Without the IMF, many countries would be unable to engage in international trade because their money would not be accepted by other nations.

The World Bank is another global agency that helps developing countries join global markets as part of their economic development **strategy.** It provides technical assistance, financial support, and grants for infrastructure to help even the poorest of nations join the growing globalization movement. Finally, the United Nations has a role to play in preserving peace through international cooperation.

✓ **Reading Check** **Analyzing** How do multinational firms contribute to globalization?

Project Funding The World Bank has approved funding to improve the rail and road transport system in Mumbai (Bombay), India, where 6.4 million people commute every day. *What other organizations provide assistance to developing countries?*

504

Globalization Trends

MAIN Idea Growing economic interdependence has led to increased regional integration.

Economics & You Do you remember learning about the European Union? Read on to find out how this organization has spurred integration in other regions. **R**

With continued globalization, two trends stand out. The first is the growing economic interdependence among nations. The second is growing regional economic integration around the world.

Growing Interdependence

As markets develop, producers become more specialized in their activities. Specialization and the **division of labor** lead to higher levels of productivity. If producers who perform a specialized task have a **comparative advantage,** or the ability to do something at a relatively lower opportunity cost than someone else, they will be able to compete more effectively in the market.

In the **context** of the family, this usually means that the strongest person handles those tasks that require the most strength.

Differentiated Instruction

Economic Cartoons, p. 29

504

The Global Economy: Hanging Together

Objective: Analyze a political cartoon about the global economy.

Focus: Have students describe examples of how humor can be used to get across a serious message.

Teach: Have students complete the activity questions.

Assess: Go over the answers with the class. Have students share their answers to question 5.

Close: Ask students to list one pro and one con of globalization.

Differentiated Instruction Strategies

BL **Ask:** Why doesn't the cartoon show poor countries from Africa or Latin America?

AL Have students create a political cartoon on the subject of misguided aid to a developing country.

ELL Have students explain the meaning of the cartoon in their own words.

Global Interdependence Because of trade and the uneven distribution of resources, the global economy is interdependent. *How does the cartoon illustrate this interdependence?*

cagliecartoons.com

In a global context, the countries most effective at using capital and technology are the ones manufacturing products such as automobiles, which they then exchange for the raw materials of other nations.

The result is an incredible amount of interdependence. This means that we depend on others, and others depend on us, for almost everything we do. On a global scale, it allows a country such as Japan, which has almost no domestic energy resources, to become an advanced industrial nation. It also allows other countries with little manufacturing capacity, such as Saudi Arabia, to exchange their energy resources for a wide range of consumer and other manufactured goods.

The weakness of interdependence is the possibility that a breakdown anywhere in the global system could affect everyone. For example, if oil exports from the Persian Gulf should be halted as a result of terrorism or war, industrial output and standards of living all over the globe will suffer.

Regional Economic Integration

In a global economy, the culture, currency, or laws of an individual country can interfere with the increase in economic integration. As a result, a number of countries have pursued various degrees of integrating their economies within regions.

Economic integration is furthest along in the 27-nation European Union (EU), which had its roots in the **European Coal and Steel Community (ECSC).** The ECSC consisted of Belgium, France, Germany, Italy, Luxembourg, and the Netherlands. It was organized in 1951 to coordinate iron and steel production so that it would be difficult for the nations to ever again go to war with one another. The ECSC was enormously successful, and over the years the cooperation evolved into the EU.

Today, approximately half of the EU countries have given up their national currencies in favor of the euro. EU members also have removed most internal barriers to the movement of workers, financial capital, goods, and services. The European Union has not yet achieved complete economic integration because many differences remain; still, the EU is one of the largest unified markets in the world.

The economic success and political stability of the EU have given regional economic integration a huge boost around the world. One consequence is the creation of the Association for Southeast Asian

European Coal and Steel Community (ECSC) group of six European countries formed in 1951 to coordinate iron and steel production to ensure peace among member countries

Skills Handbook

See page **R58** to learn about *Interpreting Cartoons.*

CHAPTER 18 Global Economic Challenges 505

S **Skill Practice**

Using Tables and Charts
Have students create a graph that illustrates the interdependent nature of global trade involving industrialized countries like Japan and resource-rich countries like Saudi Arabia. **OL**

R **Reading Strategy**

Making Connections Ask:
What important event ended in Europe only six years before the founding of the ECSC? *(World War II)* Have students speculate on why nations like France, Italy, and West Germany might have wanted to encourage closer economic cooperation among nations. *(Possible answer: They probably felt that closer economic integration was a good way to prevent another catastrophic war.)* **OL**

Caption Answer: It shows different places on the globe "plugged in" to a worldwide network of telecommunications, such as computers, telephones, and other electronic devices.

Leveled Activities

BL **Graphic Organizer Transparencies, p. 39**

OL **Critical Thinking Activities, p. 26**

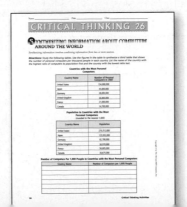

AL **BusinessWeek Focus on the Global Economy, p. 17**

D Differentiated Instruction

Special Education Students with various reading and organizational difficulties may have problems relating graphics and the main text. Have students identify what the map illustrates. Then direct students to read the section, restate what each graphic illustrates, and suggest reasons why the graphics were included in the section. **BL**

C Critical Thinking

Contrasting **Ask:** What challenges might the member countries of COMESA face that the EU nations in Europe did not face? *(Answers will vary depending on students' knowledge of Europe and Africa but may include extreme poverty, ethnic and tribal rivalries, different colonial histories, civil wars, and lack of resources and infrastructure.)* Then have students make and justify predictions about the future of COMESA. **OL**

Economic Analysis
Answer: the European Union (EU)

Hands-On Chapter Project

Step 1

Global Economy Factbook

In this project, students will create and present a global economy factbook.

Step 1: Planning the Factbook. Students will plan an information booklet about the global economy.

Directions: Tell the class that they will be dividing into six groups to create a four-page global economy factbook aimed at educating fellow students about the world

---

Free Trade Area of the Americas (FTAA) 34-nation group established in 1994 in order to set up a regional free trade area in the Americas with no internal barriers to trade

Nations (ASEAN), which seeks cooperation similar to that in the EU. Two other associations are less successful than either the EU or ASEAN. The Common Market for Eastern and Southern Africa (COMESA), shown below in **Figure 18.1**, consists of 20 countries. The other association is called the **Free Trade Area of the Americas (FTAA).** The FTAA includes 34 nations and was established in 1994 in order to set up a regional free-trade area in the Americas with no internal barriers to trade.

As globalization continues, different regional groups may merge into even larger global markets. This will have additional benefits, because economic cooperation among countries usually leads to increased political cooperation. Thus, globalization will likely enhance economic growth and political stability among all nations.

Figure 18.1 ▶ **The Common Market for Eastern and Southern Africa (COMESA)**

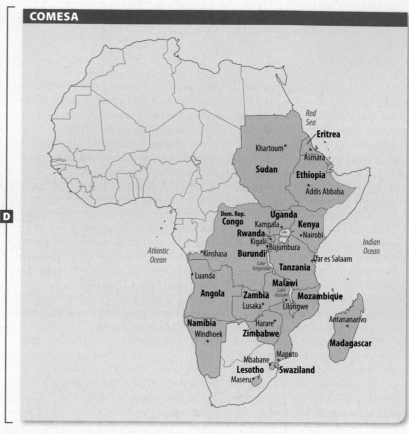

▶ COMESA is an emerging 20-country common market (customs union) for eastern and southern Africa. The organization was formed to remove all internal barriers to trade and to adopt uniform trade standards for nonmember countries.

Economic Analysis *What other regional group served as an example for COMESA?*

---

economy. Have students review the Big Ideas and skim the chapter, taking notes on what should be included in the factbook. Then have them compile a list on the board of suggested topics. The class list may include such items as:

- definitions for key terms
- the role of telecommunications
- changes in financial markets
- foreign investment and debt
- foreign aid
- multinationals

- effects of global integration on society (in general or on a local community)

Have students copy the list of suggestions and break up into groups. Have them begin planning their factbook, assigning roles for each group member.

Identifying Central Issues Have students list three objectives that they feel their factbooks should accomplish in presenting the global economy. **OL**

(Chapter Project continued in Section 2.)

Will Globalization Continue?

Despite the growth and support for globalization, progress has not always been smooth. Change can be threatening to established ways of doing business. Clashes erupt when people fear that not just their jobs but their way of life is at risk. Problems can arise on a small scale when McDonald's or KFC opens a store in a scenic European location. It also happens when Wal-Mart brings a new store to England, China, or any other country where it might force local "mom and pop" businesses to close.

These concerns apply to services as well. France has rules that protect domestic filmmakers by restricting the number of American movies that can be shown. Canada requires its radio stations to reserve a certain amount of air time for music performed by Canadian artists.

Politics can also play a role in helping or hindering globalization. When nations get along well with one another, they are more likely to cooperate by forming free-trade areas or customs unions. If nations do not get along well, or if an international conflict should erupt, then the opposite result could occur. For example, a dispute with the United States over the future of Taiwan could interrupt China's globalization process. If this happens, trade will likely fall off between the two nations, dealing a severe blow to globalization.

Finally, some radical political organizations oppose the capitalism that drives globalization. Before World War I broke out in 1914, Russian revolutionaries known as Bolsheviks fought against capitalism. Now fundamentalist extremists such as al-Qaeda oppose globalization.

In short, while globalization can lead to great economic gains, these gains may not be important to everyone. Even a perceived **D** threat to culture, politics, or religion can slow or halt the process of globalization.

✓**Reading Check** **Describing** What characteristics show that the European Union is successful at regional integration?

CHAPTER 18, SECTION 1

D **Differentiated Instruction**

Advanced Learners Have students choose an artistic medium to illuminate some aspect of the globalization debate. Examples include a monologue, dialogue, or play about the effects of globalization in a developing country; a poem or short story; or a mural, collage, video, or other visual. **AL**

✓**Reading Check** **Answer:** the common currency and movement of workers, capital, goods, and services

Assess

💿 Use the Interactive Tutor Self-Assessment CD-ROM to review Section 1, and then assign the Section 1 Review as homework or as an in-class activity.

Close

Problem-Solving Have students identify obstacles to world economic integration and suggest ways of resolving them. **OL**

SECTION 1 Review

Vocabulary
1. **Explain** the significance of globalization, multinational, outsourcing, General Agreement on Tariffs and Trade (GATT), division of labor, comparative advantage, European Coal and Steel Community (ECSC), and Free Trade Area of the Americas (FTAA).

Main Ideas
2. **Describing** Use a graphic organizer like the one below to describe the effects of globalization on markets, production, and institutions.

	Effects
Markets	
Production	
Institutions	

3. **Identifying** What trends result from continued globalization?

Critical Thinking
4. **The BIG Idea** What is the relationship between globalization and interdependence?

5. **Drawing Conclusions** Why might a company move its production facilities to another country? Why would it not move its headquarters in the same way?

6. **Analyzing Visuals** Look at the photo on page 504. How does this photo show you that the public transportation system of Mumbai needs to be improved?

Applying Economics
7. **Globalization** Visit your local grocery store and make a list of at least 10 products that reflect globalization. Create a poster illustrating these products and showing where each originates (or where the producer is based). Present your poster to the class and explain why you do or do not personally benefit from globalization. Be prepared to defend your position.

Review **SECTION 1**

CHAPTER 18 Global Economic Challenges 507

Answers

1. All definitions can be found in the section and the Glossary.
2. **Markets:** Goods from many countries now available in most markets. **Production:** Jobs are outsourced to countries with lower labor costs. **Institutions:** New organizations promote international trade.
3. growing interdependence, regional economic integration, opposition to globalization

4. Globalization leads to greater economic interdependence.
5. **Possible answer:** to lower labor costs or to be nearer customers; to not disrupt home-office operations or to take advantage of highly trained personnel in the developed country

6. It is very crowded; more trains, larger trains, or more stations are clearly needed.
7. Posters will vary but should show an understanding of issues surrounding globalization.

Teach

C Critical Thinking

Evaluating Discuss students' feelings about imported products. **Ask:** Would you prefer to buy an American-made product? How much more would you pay for a U.S.-made product over one from a developing country?
OL

BusinessWeek ONLINE

To find up-to-date news and analysis on the economy, business, technology, markets, entrepreneurs, investments, and finance, have students search feature articles and special reports on the BusinessWeek Web site, www.businessweek.com.

Examining the Newsclip

Answers:
1. Multinationals from developing countries are now competing with those from developed countries.
2. access to dynamic markets, lower costs, sound business and marketing practices

Additional Support

BusinessWeek NEWSCLIP

American companies have been selling their products in other countries for quite some time. With globalization, though, the tide is turning. Today businesses from other parts of the world are finding their way to the U.S. market.

Emerging Giants

Like other rural residents of southern Mississippi, Jamie Lucenberg, 35, faced a huge cleanup job . . . in the wake of Hurricane Katrina. He needed a tractor fast to clear debris and trees from his 17-acre family farm, just 16 miles north of devastated Biloxi. . . . But rather than buy an American-made John Deere or New Holland, brands he grew up with, Lucenberg chose a shiny red Mahindra 5500 made by India's Mahindra & Mahindra Ltd. . . .

Surprised that a company from India is penetrating a U.S. market long dominated by venerable names like Deere & Co.? Then it's time to take a look at how globalization has come full circle. A new breed of ambitious multinational is rising on the world scene, presenting both challenges and opportunities for established global players.

These new contenders hail from seemingly unlikely places, developing nations such as Brazil, China, India, Russia, and even Egypt and South Africa. They are shaking up entire industries, from farm equipment and refrigerators to aircraft and telecom services, and changing the rules of global competition. . . .

What makes these upstarts global contenders? Their key advantages are access to some of the world's most dynamic growth markets and immense pools of low-cost resources, be they production workers, engineers, land, petroleum, or iron ore. But these aspiring giants are about much more than low cost. The best of the pack are proving as innovative and expertly run as any in the business, astutely absorbing global consumer trends and technologies and getting new products to market faster than their rivals.

—Reprinted from *BusinessWeek*

GLOBAL STRATEGIES

TAKE BRANDS GLOBAL
Establish primacy at home, expand in neighboring nations, then move to the West.

TARGET A NICHE
Focus on an industry, build scale, and expand globally by acquiring smaller players.

ENGINEERING TO INNOVATE
Tap ample low-cost talent at home, then develop innovative products.

LEVERAGE NATURAL RESOURCES
Take advantage of domestic oil, mineral, or timber resources to attain a cost edge, then go global.

ACQUIRE OFFSHORE ASSETS
Becoming a global player by buying oil and mineral reserves or partnering with other developing-nation companies.

EXPORT BUSINESS MODEL
Hone a management system, then replicate it globally through acquisitions.

Examining the Newsclip

1. **Describing** How is globalization changing the presence of multinationals?
2. **Determining Cause and Effect** What helps multinationals from emerging markets compete globally?

Extending the Content

Multinationals in Developing Countries
While most of the largest multinational corporations are still located in the "Big 3" geographic regions of the United States, Japan, and Europe, the list of the largest companies is beginning to include some based in developing nations. A 2006 report by the United Nations found that, ranked by total foreign assets, one company from the developing world had cracked the top 25.

It is the Hong Kong diversified industrial company Hutchinson Whampoa, at number 17. That makes it larger than more familiar names such as Honda, Nestlé, Chevron, Texaco, and Daimler Chrysler. The next three largest multinationals from outside the United States, Japan, and Europe are Petronas, a Malaysian oil company; Singtel, a telecommunications company from Singapore; and Samsung, the South Korean electronics giant.

SECTION 2
Global Problems and Economic Incentives

GUIDE TO READING

Section Preview

In this section, you will learn that global economic challenges include overpopulation, resource depletion, and pollution.

Content Vocabulary

- scarcity (p. 509)
- subsistence (p. 510)
- renewable resource (p. 512)
- hydropower (p. 512)
- biomass (p. 512)
- gasohol (p. 513)
- nonrenewable resource (p. 513)
- glut (p. 515)
- pollution (p. 516)
- acid rain (p. 516)
- pollution permit (p. 517)

Academic Vocabulary

- compounded (p. 509)
- successive (p. 518)

Reading Strategy

Identifying As you read the section, complete a graphic organizer like the one below by identifying and describing the global problems that scarcity can bring.

Problem	Description

Focus

Bellringer
Daily Focus Transparency 90

GUIDE TO READING

Answers to Graphic:

scarcity of resources (fierce competition over them); rising prices for scarce resources (severe economic challenges for poor countries); need to exploit resources to develop economically (more pollution)

ISSUES IN THE NEWS

—*The New York Times*

Pollution From Chinese Coal Casts a Global Shadow

One of China's lesser-known exports is a dangerous brew of soot, toxic chemicals and climate-changing gases from the smokestacks of coal-burning power plants.

In early April [2006], a dense cloud of pollutants over Northern China sailed to nearby Seoul [Korea], sweeping along dust and desert sand before wafting across the Pacific. An American satellite spotted the cloud as it crossed the West Coast [of America].

. . . Coal is indeed China's double-edged sword—the new economy's black gold and the fragile environment's dark cloud.

Already, China uses more coal than the United States, the European Union and Japan combined. . . . To make matters worse, India is right behind China in stepping up its construction of coal-fired power plants—and has a population expected to outstrip China's by 2030. ■

The fundamental economic problem is **scarcity,** the condition that results from not having enough resources to produce all of the things people would like to have. We experience scarcity at the personal and national levels, even in relatively prosperous nations such as the United States. At the global level, scarcity reveals itself through food, energy, and other resource shortages, all of which are **compounded** as world population grows.

As countries increase their populations and grow their economies, they are faced with the problem of how to use scarce resources without harming another important resource—the environment.

> **scarcity**
> fundamental economic problem of meeting people's virtually unlimited wants with scarce resources (also see page 6)

CHAPTER 18   Global Economic Challenges   509

Resource Manager

R Reading Strategies	**C** Critical Thinking	**D** Differentiated Instruction	**W** Writing Support	**S** Skill Practice
Teacher Edition • Skimming, p. 510 • Predicting, p. 515 • Monitoring, p. 516 • Inferring, p. 517 • Making Connections, p. 519 **Additional Resources** • Guid. Read. Act., p. 53 • Read. Ess. & Note-Taking Guide, p. 157	**Teacher Edition** • Evaluating, p. 514 • Assessing, p. 514 • Making Inferences, p. 515 • Ident. Cent. Issues, p. 518 **Additional Resources** • Bus. Focus on the Global Economy, pp. 36, 38	**Teacher Edition** • Logical/Math., p. 510 • Visual/Spatial, p. 511 • ELL, p. 512 **Additional Resources** • Free Enterprise Act., p. 25 • Reteach. Act., p. 18 • Enrichment Act., p. 18	**Teacher Edition** • Expository Writing, p. 511 • Persuasive Writing, p. 513 • Personal Writing, pp. 516, 519 **Additional Resources** • High School Reading in the Content Area Strat. and Act.	**Teacher Edition** • Det. Cause/Effect, p. 512 • Interpreting Political Cartoons, p. 513 **Additional Resources** • Math Prac. for Econ., p. 25 • Reading and Study Skills Fold., p. 66

Teach

R Reading Strategy

Skimming Students who have trouble reading a passage may benefit from skimming it before reading to develop a time frame for the events or ideas that are presented. Have students skim the subsection "Global Population Growth" for time markers such as "1798" and "from 1950 to 2050." Have them point out similar markers in other subsections. **BL**

D Differentiated Instruction

Logical/Mathematical

Have students write a paragraph explaining the difference discussed in this section between *population* and *population growth rate*. Ask them to make clear how the latter can be falling while the former is rising. **OL**

Economic Analysis

Answer: growth rates in developed countries are low and falling; economic incentives push people away from having children

Additional Support

---

subsistence
state in which a society produces only enough to support itself

R Global Population Growth

MAIN Idea While the world's overall population growth rate is decreasing, population in developing countries still grows faster than in the developed ones.

Economics & You Do you or any of your friends have fewer brothers and sisters than either of your parents? Read on to see how an economist would explain this change.

Population growth has fascinated the world ever since Thomas Malthus published his *Essay on the Principle of Population* in 1798. His views, written over 200 years ago, are still relevant today because of the growing demand for resources.

Malthus: Views on Population

Thomas Malthus argued that a population would grow faster than its ability to feed itself. The problem, he stated, was that population tended to grow geometrically, as in the number sequence 1, 2, 4, 8, 16, 32, 64, and so on. The ability of the earth to feed people, however, would grow at a slower and more constant rate, such as 1, 2,

3, 4, 5, and so on. Eventually, according to Malthus, the masses of the world would be reduced to a condition of **subsistence**—the state in which a population produces only enough to support itself.

In many countries in the developing world, poverty is widespread. Whether in the African country of Somalia or the Indian city of Kolkata (Calcutta), thousands of street dwellers search for food in refuse piles by day and sleep in the streets at night. Similar conditions exist in other parts of the world. In these places, the Malthusian prediction of a subsistence standard of living is a cruel reality.

World Population Growth

D Despite the dire predictions, population growth appears to be slowing. **Figure 18.2** shows the rate of world population growth from 1950 to 2050. According to the figure, population grew the fastest in 1962 and 1963 but the rate of growth has declined, or is expected to decline, steadily thereafter.

According to the U.S. Census Bureau, the world population is currently growing at a rate of about 1.13 percent per year, but the growth rate is expected to fall below

---

Figure 18.2 ▶ **Projected Annual World Population Growth Rate, 1950–2050**

▶ The annual rate of world population growth peaked in 1962 and 1963 and has slowly declined ever since.

Economic Analysis *Why is a slower rate of population growth expected?*

WORLD POPULATION GROWTH

Source: U.S. Census Bureau

Extending the Content

Father of "the Dismal Science"

Thomas Malthus, the pioneer of modern population study, was born in England in 1766. He was a kind, gentle person who was devoted to his church and his father. At age 18, he became a student at Cambridge University and studied mathematics and classical languages. While away, he wrote letters to his father. One subject they discussed was the

optimistic view, then popular, that a future of peace, prosperity, and equality awaited the world. Malthus disagreed and wrote his father a 50,000-word letter arguing against this utopian vision. His father was so impressed with his son's reasoning that he encouraged him to publish his ideas. The book was *An Essay on the Principle of Population As It Affects the Future Improvement of Society*. This book

changed forever the way people would think about population. Its gloomy predictions led Malthus himself to call economics "the dismal science," a label it has retained ever since.

Figure 18.3 ▶ World Population Growth by Country

▶ The map shows the population growth rates of the countries of the world.

Economic Analysis *How does the annual growth rate in China compare with that of Brazil?*

Maps In Motion
See StudentWorks™ Plus
or glencoe.com.

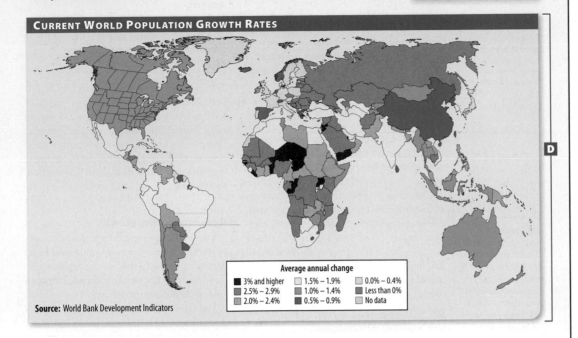

CURRENT WORLD POPULATION GROWTH RATES

Average annual change

- ■ 3% and higher
- ■ 2.5% – 2.9%
- ■ 2.0% – 2.4%
- □ 1.5% – 1.9%
- ■ 1.0% – 1.4%
- ■ 0.5% – 0.9%
- □ 0.0% – 0.4%
- ■ Less than 0%
- □ No data

Source: World Bank Development Indicators

one percent by 2017. If the world population keeps growing at the rates shown in Figure 18.2, it will reach about 8 billion in 2027, and then hit 9 billion by 2045.

Was Malthus Wrong?

Population is growing at different rates around the world. As **Figure 18.3** shows, industrialized nations have the lowest rates of population growth, while the poorer nations in the developing world tend to have the highest population growth rates.

Malthus did not foresee the enormous advances in productivity that allowed a rising standard of living to accompany a growing population. He also did not foresee that families might choose to have fewer children. This is especially true for a number of industrialized countries, including Japan, Russia, and Germany, that have shrinking populations.

Malthus's predictions may not have been entirely accurate for the industrialized countries, but they still have long-term consequences for all nations. Today, for example, population pressures in the developing world are causing problems for many industrialized countries, such as the United States, which is besieged by illegal immigrants from China, Mexico, and Haiti.

Economic Incentives

Economic incentives play a role in population growth. For example, children are relatively expensive to raise in an industrialized country. Medical costs at birth, health

CHAPTER 18 Global Economic Challenges **511**

D Differentiated Instruction

Visual/Spatial Have students compare the map with one in a world atlas to name five countries that are growing the fastest and five that are losing population. Then ask students to speculate on what each group of countries has in common. *(Students may note that the countries losing population are located in Europe and mostly developed nations, while those growing the fastest are in Africa or the Middle East, and include several Muslim countries.)* **AL**

W Writing Support

Expository Writing Have students write a paragraph explaining how population pressures are leading to increased emigration to developed countries. *(Explanations should note that rising populations in developing countries cause competition for resources, jobs, and so on and lead people to seek these resources in richer countries.)* **OL**

Economic Analysis
Answer: Brazil: 1.5%–1.9%; China: 0.5%–0.9%

Additional Support

Activity: Interdisciplinary Connection

Health Ask students to research important health statistics. Have them find the life expectancy, infant mortality, average daily calorie intake, and health care expenditures per capita for the following developed and developing countries: the United States, Japan, China, Mexico, Uganda, and Haiti. Suggest that students begin by brainstorming a list of key words to use as they search the Internet for health statistics. After students have completed their searches, ask: *What generalizations can you make about health care and other health-related issues in developed and developing countries?* **OL**

S Skill Practice

Determining Cause and Effect Have students draw charts that show the effects of incentives and disincentives on the decision to have children in developed and developing nations. **OL**

D Differentiated Instruction

English Language Learners Have students identify the prefix *(re-)* and suffix *(-able)* used in the term *renewable*. Have them give the meanings of each *(again; ability to be or do something)* and name other words they know that use *re-* or *-able*. **OL**

Caption Answer: dams, rivers, streams

✓**Reading Check** **Answer:** He did not foresee advances in productivity, and he did not expect families to choose to have fewer children.

Critical Thinking Activities, p. 25

renewable resource natural resource that can be replenished for future use

hydropower power or energy generated by moving water

biomass energy made from wood, peat, municipal solid waste, straw, corn, tires, landfill gases, fish oils, and other waste

Hydropower
Portugal is the site of the first wave farm to use Pelamis wave energy converters that were developed in Scotland. **What are other sources of hydropower?**

insurance, larger homes, cars, and college expenses add to the cost of raising children. In addition, one parent bears an opportunity cost if he or she forgoes a career while staying home to raise the children. If a family wants to minimize these costs, as they might other costs, part of the answer is to have fewer children.

The opposite happens in the developing world because children there are regarded as an asset. Medical expenses are minimal or nonexistent, insurance is rare, homes are often shared, and cars and college educations are seldom available. Even young children are likely to help with house work or farm work. Since developing countries do not have retirement programs like Social Security, parents tend to have many children in hopes that some of the children will care for them in their old age.

The result is predictable. If children are an asset to the family rather than a cost, then parents will try to have as many children as they can. This explains the high rate of population growth in developing countries and the declining—or negative—rate of population growth in the developed world.

✓**Reading Check** **Explaining** Why might Malthus have been wrong in his predictions?

The Demand for Resources

MAIN Idea Because of scarcity, societies need to conserve nonrenewable resources while finding efficient ways to harness renewable resources.

Economics & You Do changes in gas prices affect your daily activities? Read on to learn how changes in gas prices affect the demand for alternative energy sources.

Population pressures add to the depletion of many important resources. Some of these resources are in the form of raw materials, minerals, arable land, and energy. Energy is especially important because it is necessary for the production of the technological goods that make our lives more comfortable.

Renewable Resources

Economists recognize two general types of resources. One is a **renewable resource**, or natural resource that can be replenished for future use. Four main sources of renewable resources are used today.

The renewable resource that contributes the most to our energy needs today is **hydropower**, power or energy generated by moving water. In the 1800s, hydropower propelled the mills and factories of the Northeast. The power was reliable, and its source—water—was abundant and free. Later, generators at the Hoover Dam and the Tennessee Valley Authority were completed to generate power on a much larger scale. Today, many countries are trying to harness the power of moving water found in ocean waves and tides.

Another source is **biomass**, or energy made from wood and wood waste, peat, municipal solid waste, straw, corn, tires, landfill gases, fish oils, and other waste. While relatively new, this is the second most important form of renewable energy produced in the United States today. An example of biomass is ethanol, or grain alcohol that is made from corn or other

Sequencing Global Information in the News

Objective: Learn about pollution's effects and practice organizing events in correct sequence.

Focus/Teach: Point out the position of Kenya on a map of the continent of Africa. Have students complete the activity.

Assess: Go over students' answers as a class.

Close: **Ask:** Do you think all world events can be sequenced as clearly as this one? Why or why not? Discuss students' answers.

Differentiated Instruction Strategies

BL **Ask:** How did modern technology help pollution in Lake Victoria?

AL Have students write predictions of what might have happened to Lake Victoria without intervention.

ELL Have students make a list of clue words to help them sequence events.

W Writing Support

Persuasive Writing
Have students write a letter to the editor of your local newspaper supporting government funding for research in one of the renewable sources of energy discussed in this section. Have them do research as necessary to support their recommendations. Ask volunteers supporting several different energy sources to share their letters with the class. **OL**

S Skill Practice

Interpreting Political Cartoons Have students create a political cartoon on the subject of renewable and nonrenewable energy sources. You may want to begin by briefly brainstorming some ideas for cartoons. Display students' cartoons in the classroom and invite volunteers to interpret their meanings. **OL**

Caption Answer: nonrenewable

crops. Ethanol is used to make **gasohol**—a fuel that is a mixture of 90 percent unleaded gasoline and 10 percent ethanol. Since 1998, many American cars have also been designed to run on E85, a mixture of 85 percent ethanol and 15 percent gasoline.

The third-largest source of renewable energy is solar power, or energy that is harnessed from the sun. Solar power has never been effectively developed, however, and did not get much attention when the price of oil was low. While solar power holds much promise, it accounts for only a fraction of the renewable energy used today.

The fourth-largest category of renewable energy sources is wind-generated electricity. Since the early 1980s, many wind farms have been built, each producing enough electricity to power a medium-sized city. California is the largest producer of wind-generated energy, but wind farms can be found in many other states as well.

Nonrenewable Resources

Most of the energy we use today comes from **nonrenewable resources**—resources that cannot be replenished once they are used. The major nonrenewable resource

category—fossil fuels—is being consumed at an alarming rate and at current consumption levels may only last for a few more generations.

Oil is the biggest nonrenewable energy source in use today, primarily because it was so inexpensive during much of the 1900s. Oil also is much more convenient to use than natural gas or coal.

Natural gas and coal are tied for the second-largest nonrenewable energy source. Historically, natural gas was more difficult to transport and use than oil, so it did not become an important energy source until much later. Eventually inexpensive natural gas became popular as an industrial fuel, and many factories and industrial technologies were built around it.

Coal was the first nonrenewable fuel to be used on a large scale, but oil and natural gas soon displaced it because they are easier to use. Still, coal is both inexpensive and plentiful. Nearly two-thirds of the world's known coal deposits are in the United States, Russia, and China, with reserves estimated to last about 200 years.

Nuclear energy is the next-largest and newest source of nonrenewable energy, accounting for nearly 8 percent of all energy

Oil Refineries such as this one in France prepare oil for general use.
What type of resource is oil?

gasohol mixture of 90 percent unleaded gasoline and 10 percent grain alcohol, or ethanol

nonrenewable resource resource that cannot be replenished once it is used

CHAPTER 18 Global Economic Challenges 513

Leveled Activities

BL Reteaching Activities, p. 18

OL BusinessWeek Focus on the Global Economy, p. 38

AL Enrichment Activities, p. 18

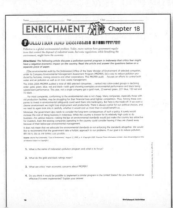

C1 Critical Thinking

Evaluating Point out that nuclear power has been much in the news lately as an alternative to fossil fuels, especially in the discussion of how to reduce greenhouse gases that contribute to global warming. **Ask: Do you think the risks of nuclear power should be reevaluated in light of the need to reduce emissions that cause climate change? Are these risks more manageable in light of what we know about the risks of continuing to burn fossil fuels?** *(Answers will vary but should be logical and supported by facts.)* **AL**

C2 Critical Thinking

Assessing Refer students to the right side of the chart in Figure 18.4 Then have students discuss this question: *In which of the four sectors do you think the United States could most easily reduce its energy use? Why?* **OL**

Economic Analysis
Answer: 38.5%

Additional Support

---

used in the United States. The future of nuclear power is uncertain, however, for a number of reasons.

Cost is one reason. Nuclear reactors are expensive to build and maintain. Second, nuclear energy produces highly hazardous by-products which are difficult to dispose of safely. Finally, there is always some chance that a nuclear plant will fail, or that another accident would happen like the 1979 near-meltdown at Three Mile Island in Pennsylvania. The 1986 meltdown of the Chernobyl reactor in Chernobyl, Ukraine, served as another reminder of the possible dangers of nuclear power. These and other reactor shutdowns are all daunting problems, but safety issues need to be addressed and dealt with before nuclear power becomes more widespread.

Energy Use in the United States

Figure 18.4 shows the sources and uses of energy in the United States. About two thirds, or 67.5 percent of our energy, comes from domestic production in the form of coal, natural gas, crude oil, nuclear power, and other sources. Slightly less than one third, or 31.7 percent, is imported from abroad. Most of this energy is in the form of petroleum.

The figure also shows that most of the energy we consume, or 82.2 percent of the total, is from fossil fuels such as coal, natural gas, and petroleum. Only a relatively small fraction comes from nuclear power and renewable energy resources.

Finally, the figure shows that nearly one-third of our total energy is used in industry. Only about one-fifth of the energy, or 20.3 percent, goes to residential use.

Nonmarket Conservation Efforts

With resources becoming increasingly scarce, efforts are underway to find the best ways to use and preserve them. One way is to appeal to everyone's sense of civic responsibility. For example, we can ask people to drive their automobiles less, to turn off the

Figure 18.4 ▶ Energy Flows in the United States

Charts In MOtion
See StudentWorks™ Plus or glencoe.com.

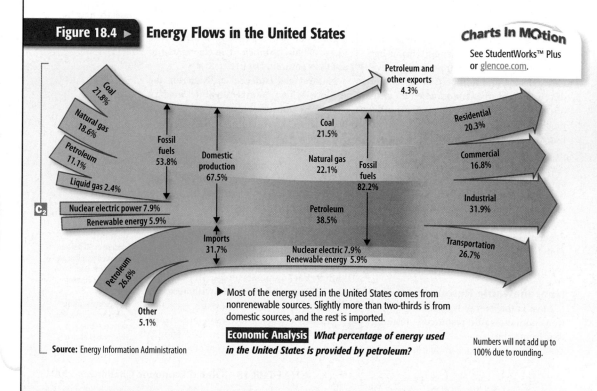

▶ Most of the energy used in the United States comes from nonrenewable sources. Slightly more than two-thirds is from domestic sources, and the rest is imported.

Economic Analysis *What percentage of energy used in the United States is provided by petroleum?*

Source: Energy Information Administration

Numbers will not add up to 100% due to rounding.

Activity: Hands-On Economics

Creating an Energy Poll Have students create a series of questions to gauge support in your community for different energy alternatives. Begin by brainstorming what students would like to know about how people in your community feel about energy. For example:

- Do you think energy availability is a growing problem?
- What sources should the nation investigate?
- Should energy policy be directed by the government or controlled by the free market?
- What is your opinion of biofuels? Nuclear power? Renewable energy sources? Conservation?

- How should the country balance its need for energy with environmental conservation?

After students have written their survey questions, have them find at least 25 people to take the survey. Have students tabulate their answers and share them with the class. Discuss the results of the poll. **OL** lights when they leave a room, or to adjust thermostats when they are not at home.

Such measures have been tried, but generally they fail to work. Even the 55-mile-per-hour speed limit, which was instituted to conserve gasoline, did not work. Not only did drivers routinely ignore the law, most individual states eventually repealed the lower speed limits.

Markets and Price Incentives

People seem to be much more responsive to changes in prices. When oil was cheaper before 1973, few countries were willing to devote large resources to retrieving it. In 1973, however, the OPEC oil embargo dramatically raised the price of oil. When the price increased sharply, many countries increased their production almost overnight. At the same time, interest in alternative energy sources soared, and countries poured billions into energy-research projects ranging from shale oil to solar power.

By 1981 oil prices had dropped considerably because of a worldwide **glut**—a substantial oversupply—of oil. At the same time, a worldwide recession and efforts at energy conservation further reduced the demand for oil. Oil prices were also kept **R** low after the first Gulf War in the early 1990s because some OPEC members increased production to replenish their financial reserves, which had been depleted during the war.

Lower oil prices had several consequences. First, the search for alternative energy sources began to wane. Second, the exploration for new oil reserves slowed dramatically. Third, consumers changed

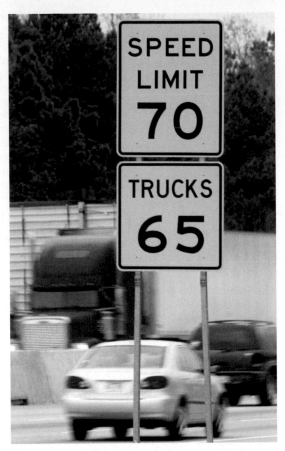

Speed Limits
When lower speed limits failed to reduce energy use, most states repealed them. *Why was the 55-miles-per-hour speed limit introduced?*

their spending habits again, buying more large houses and low-mileage SUVs instead of fuel-efficient cars. By 2006 increasing demand caught up with stable supply, and energy prices shot up again. This price hike, in turn, renewed interest in conserving energy and stimulated the global search **C** for alternative energy sources.

In the end, the price system that encourages people to conserve energy when oil prices are high does exactly the opposite when oil prices go down. High prices thus help conserve resources, while low prices tend to do the opposite.

glut substantial oversupply of a product

✓**Reading Check** **Analyzing** Why is the percentage of renewable energy sources in the United States relatively low?

⚞ Skills Handbook
See page **R40** to learn about **Analyzing Information.**

CHAPTER 18   Global Economic Challenges   **515**

R **Reading Strategy**

Predicting Ask: What do you think will happen on the energy front over the next ten years? Why? **OL**

C **Critical Thinking**

Making Inferences Have students explain how supply and demand have influenced the price of oil and the interest in developing energy alternatives. *(When oil prices have been high, production increases supply, but people use less and have more interest in finding alternatives; when prices are low, people use more, production and exploration fall, and there is less interest in finding alternatives.)* **OL**

Caption Answer: to conserve gasoline

✓**Reading Check** **Answer:** Many factories and cars are built to run on fossil fuels, we have large reserves of these fuels, and renewable sources tend to be expensive.

Hands-On Chapter Project
Step 2

Global Economy Factbook

Step 2: Researching the Factbook.
Students will begin researching their factbook and assembling data to use to write the text and create the graphics.

Directions: Have students join their groups from the previous session. In this session, students will research their factbooks, using the Internet,

school library, and other available resources. (Note: You may want to add an additional research session outside the classroom or assign the research as homework.) As students plan and research their factbooks, circulate around the room to check their ideas and offer suggestions.

Analyzing Visuals Have each group decide on several visuals, such as graphs, charts, tables, photographs, illustrations,

and cartoons to include in their factbooks. For example, you may want to suggest a graph that shows comparable levels of direct foreign investment in the U.S. and other economies. **OL**

(Chapter Project continued in Section 3.)

W Writing Support

Personal Writing Discuss instances of pollution that students have seen or read about, ideas they have for preventing or cleaning up pollution, and any other aspects of the topic that occur to you. Then have students write a journal entry that describes their feelings about pollution. **OL**

R Reading Strategy

Monitoring To help students understand the material in the subsection on pollution and economic incentives, have them create word webs for each of the three ways of controlling pollution: *legislated standards*, *pollution fees*, and *pollution permits*. Have students contribute their ideas to webs on the board. **BL**

Caption Answer: that the fresh produce has been exposed to toxic substances

Additional Support

---

pollution
contamination of air, water, or soil by the discharge of a poisonous or noxious substance

acid rain
pollution in the form of rainwater mixed with sulfur dioxide to create a mild form of sulfuric acid

Pollution and Economic Incentives

MAIN Idea Pollution is a problem for society that can be controlled through legislation, fees, and permits.

Economics & You Does your school have an environmental club? Read on to find what societies do to protect the environment.

W   Economic incentives can help solve the global problem of pollution. **Pollution** is the contamination of air, water, or soil by the discharge of a poisonous or noxious substance. Most economists argue that the best way to attack the problem is to attack the incentives that caused pollution in the first place.

The Incentive to Pollute

Pollution does not occur on its own: it occurs because people and firms have an incentive to pollute. If that incentive can be removed, pollution will be reduced.

For example, factories historically located along the banks of rivers so they could discharge their refuse into the moving waters. Factories that generated smoke and other air pollutants often were located

Pollution Toxic run-off and air pollution can affect agriculture. *What does the protective suit imply?*

FRESH FARM PRODUCE

www.CartoonStock.com

516   UNIT 5   The Global Economy

---

farther from the water, but their tall smokestacks still blew the pollutants long distances. Others tried to avoid the problem by digging pits on their property to bury their toxic wastes.

In all three situations, factory owners were trying to lower production costs by using the environment as a giant waste-disposal system. From a narrow viewpoint, the reasoning was sound. Firms increase their profits when they lower production costs. Those who produce the most at the least cost make the most profits.

The cost of pollution to society as a whole, however, is enormous. For example, **acid rain**—a mixture of water and sulfur dioxide that makes a mild form of sulfuric acid—falls over much of North America, damaging forests and rivers. Fertilizer buildup and raw sewage runoff poison **R** ecosystems in other areas. The damage caused by pollution is extensive, but it can be controlled. One way is through government standards passed by law. Another way is through economic incentives.

Legislated Standards

Legislated standards include laws that specify the minimum levels of purity for air, water, and auto emissions. These government standards can be effective, but they are generally inflexible. Once a standard is set, a firm has to meet it or cease production. Because of this, many firms lobby extensively to exempt their industry from pollution control standards.

Congress has declared that all automobiles sold in the United States cannot exceed certain maximum emission standards. Once these standards have been set, the Environmental Protection Agency (EPA) tests random vehicles in every model line of cars. It also samples random cars on the road to ensure that they adhere to the emission controls.

Another pollution-control program was the Superfund that Congress established in 1980 to identify and clean up some of the most hazardous waste sites in the country.

Activity: Hands-On Economics

Debating Pollution Control Select about 10 students and organize them into two teams. Have the teams take opposite sides and debate the following statement: *Limits on pollution should be established by market forces, not by government legislation.* Have students not directly involved in the debate act as judges and list the major arguments presented in the debate. At the conclusion of the debate, call on a number of judges to share their lists of arguments with the class. Then have students use this information to write a short paper supporting or opposing the statement. **OL**

The intent was to track down the original polluters and make them pay for the cleanup. When it was discovered that many of the original polluters had gone out of business and could not be forced to pay, the law was amended to force existing businesses to help with the cleanup costs. This was not popular with businesses because some firms were forced to pay for the cleanup of wastes that others left behind.

Pollution Fees

A more market-based approach is to charge firms in proportion to the amount of pollutants they release. Depending on the industry, the size of the tax would depend on the severity of the pollution and the quantity of toxic substances being released. A firm can then either pay the fees or take steps to reduce the pollution.

For example, suppose a community wants to reduce air pollution caused by four factories, each of which releases large quantities of coal dust. A $50 tax on every ton of coal dust released into the air might be applied to each factory. Devices attached to the top of the factory's smokestacks would measure the amount of dust released during a given period, and the factory would be billed accordingly.

Under these conditions, some firms might choose to pay the $50 tax. Others, however, might decide to spend $10, $20, or $30 to clean up a ton of pollution. As long as it is cheaper to clean up the pollution than to pay the tax, individual firms will have the incentive to clean up and stop polluting.

This tax approach does not try to remove all of the pollution, but it can remove a significant amount. In addition, it provides flexibility that legislated standards lack by giving individual firms freedom of choice.

Real-world examples of pollution fees are more complicated than this hypothetical example, but they all work the same way. In addition, firms that pay the tax also help defray some of the costs of the program, which is a relief to taxpayers.

Tradable Pollution Permits

An expanded version of pollution fees is the EPA's use of **pollution permits**—federal permits allowing public utilities to release specific amounts of emissions into the air—to reduce sulfur dioxide emissions at coal-burning electric utilities. Sulfur dioxide emissions from the

pollution permit
federal permit allowing a public utility to release pollutants into the air

CAREERS

Environmental Scientist

The Work

* Identify and eliminate sources of pollutants or hazards that affect people, wildlife, and their habitats

* Analyze measurements or observations of air, food, water, soil, and other resources and make recommendations on how best to clean and preserve the environment

* May design and monitor waste disposal sites, preserve water supplies, and reclaim contaminated land and water to comply with federal environmental regulations

Qualifications

* Master's degree with a specialization in environmental or biological science, plus several years of experience in the field

* Experience with computer modeling, data analysis and integration, digital mapping, remote sensing, and geographic information systems

* Strong oral and written communication skills

* Must pass a civil service examination

Earnings

* Median annual earnings: $51,080

Job Growth Outlook

* Average

Source: *Occupational Outlook Handbook, 2006–2007 Edition*

CHAPTER 18   Global Economic Challenges   517

R Reading Strategy

Inferring Have students infer answers to the following questions from the text:

* Why might a company want to pay a tax on some pollution it causes and clean up another kind of pollution? *(It would make cost and benefit calculations for each type and choose the more cost-effective solution for each.)*

* Why might a supporter of strong environmental regulation oppose pollution fees? *(He or she might feel that the fees do not eliminate pollution, but just reduce it. The fees could actually allow companies to continue to pollute if they are willing to pay money to do so.)* OL

Additional Support

Activity: Interdisciplinary Connection

Civics In 1999, a district court judge ordered the U.S. Environmental Protection Agency to set pollution limits on Louisiana's waters. The ruling judge said she was requiring the EPA's involvement because the state was slow to set its own water pollution limits. Over the next seven years, limits were to be set first in coastal waters, then in each basin across the state. Have students research the problem and solution on the Internet. Ask them to create a news report about the situation, including the most recent developments and the effects of Hurricane Katrina, if any, on the decision and its enforcement. News reports should clearly state details of the problem and solution. Remind students to explain the current state of enforcement and any predictions about the future of the decision. OL

C Critical Thinking

Identifying Central Issues

Ask: How do pollution permits limit pollution through supply and demand? (Because the supply of permits is limited, their price will rise as they become more scarce. When the price is higher than the cost of eliminating the pollution, companies will choose what's cheaper.) **OL**

✓ Reading Check **Answer:** legislative standards, pollution fees, tradable pollution permits

Assess

⊙ Use the Interactive Tutor Self-Assessment CD-ROM to review Section 2, and then assign the Section 2 Review as homework or as an in-class activity.

Close

Evaluating Have students discuss, from economic and environmental perspectives, the responsibilities people have toward the planet. **OL**

SECTION 2 Review

Did You Know?

▶ **Pollution Permits** In 2005 the European Union started to use tradable pollution control permits to control emissions. The supply of permits in the first year was large—resulting in values of a one-ton permit ranging from 9.5 to 13 euros ($10 to $15). As fewer permits are issued in successive years, their price will rise.

Economics ONLINE
Student Web Activity Visit the *Economics: Principles and Practices* Web site at glencoe.com and click on *Chapter 18– Student Web Activities* for an activity on the Environmental Protection Agency.

burning of coal and oil react with water and oxygen to form compounds that fall to the earth as acid rain.

Under this program, the EPA awards a limited number of permits to all utilities. If reducing or cleaning up one ton of emissions costs a utility $300, and if it can sell a permit for $350, the firm will decrease its own emissions and sell the unused permit to another utility whose cleanup or reduction costs are higher. If removing a ton of pollutants would cost the second utility $400, then that company would be better off to buy the permit for $350 from the first

utility. In either case, one of the utilities has the incentive to clean up a ton of pollutants.

The first set of pollution permits went on sale in March 1993 at the Chicago Board of Trade. The one-ton permits brought prices ranging from $122 to $450. The EPA issued additional permits in **successive** years, but it will issue fewer permits as time goes on, making them scarcer and more expensive. Ultimately, higher prices for the permits will give more utilities the incentive to spend larger amounts of money on antipollution devices.

The system also has advantages for environmentalists who want utilities to reduce pollution at even faster rates. Several environmental groups have purchased pollution permits with their own funds, making them scarcer and therefore more expensive for the utilities.

✓ Reading Check **Summarizing** In which ways can governments control pollution?

SECTION 2 Review

Vocabulary
1. **Explain** the significance of scarcity, subsistence, renewable resource, hydropower, biomass, gasohol, nonrenewable resource, glut, pollution, acid rain, and pollution permit.

Main Ideas
2. **Describing** How did Malthus believe population growth would affect the future of the planet?
3. **Identifying** Use a graphic organizer like the one below to identify four renewable and four nonrenewable resources.

Resources	
Renewable	Nonrenewable
1.	1.
2.	2.

4. **Describing** What legislative attempts have been undertaken to control pollution?

Critical Thinking
5. **The BIG Idea** How does population growth affect world resources? How does this relate to the fundamental economic problem of scarcity?
6. **Drawing Conclusions** Why does the United States continue to rely on oil as its primary energy source? Write a paragraph explaining your answer.
7. **Contrasting** How do legislated standards and economic incentives differ in regard to pollution control?
8. **Analyzing Visuals** Look at Figure 18.3 on page 511. Compare the population growth rates in the United States, Germany, Mexico, India, the Democratic Republic of the Congo, and Afghanistan. What conclusions can you draw from this information?

Applying Economics
9. **Scarcity** As the president's chief expert on energy issues, what would you suggest we do to conserve our nonrenewable resources? Why?

Answers

1. All definitions can be found in the section and the Glossary.
2. that it would grow geometrically while our ability to feed the people would eventually be reduced to a subsistence level
3. **Renewable:** hydropower, biomass, solar, wind. **Nonrenewable:** oil, natural gas, coal, nuclear.
4. minimum levels of purity for air, water, and auto emissions; the Superfund cleanup legislation

5. It puts stress on economies to deliver increasing amounts of goods and services utilizing scarce resources. This problem of scarcity requires everyone to make choices about the best way to use limited resources.
6. **Possible answer:** Much of the nation's industrial infrastructure runs on oil.
7. Legislated standards: can be effective but are generally inflexible; once a standard is set, a firm has to meet it or cease production. Economic incentives: size of the tax would depend on the severity and quantity of toxic

substances being released. Individual firms have the incentive to clean up pollution as much as they can or at least up to the point where it becomes more expensive to clean up the pollution than to pay the tax.
8. Answers will vary but should note that, as countries become more developed, their birth rates decline.
9. Answers will vary but should reflect an understanding of nonrenewable resources.

CASE STUDY

Toyota Leads in Hybrids

Ahead of the Competition

When Toyota began developing the Prius in 1995, gasoline averaged $1.24 a gallon. Skeptics stated that such low gas prices did not justify the expense of switching from an internal combustion engine (ICE) to a hybrid gasoline-and-battery-powered "greener" car. Toyota did not listen to the skeptics and instead invested heavily in hybrid technology. A decade later, gas prices had more than doubled, and sales of the Prius hit the half-million mark.

Engineering Green

The long road to the hybrid's success was riddled with problems—from touchy batteries and an "un-American" design to a trunk so small that it could not hold even a stroller. Yet top managers at Toyota were determined to create an environmentally friendly car that got great gas mileage. Toyota pushed its engineers—more than 1,000 of them—to work out the kinks, delivering the hybrid to the U.S. auto market in July 2000—5 years and $1 billion after the car's conception. Despite the Prius's "jerky ride" and its high sticker price, Toyota's new model was a success. Fans of the hybrid car overlook the less-than-smooth ride for the improved gas mileage they get and the money they save at the pump. They also like to do their part for a cleaner planet with the lower emissions produced by the Prius compared to ICE cars.

Setting a Trend

Since the Prius was introduced, many other automakers have jumped on the hybrid bandwagon. But Toyota keeps expanding its list of hybrid cars. Couple that with a strong demand for low-cost, fuel-efficient cars not just in the United States but in other parts of the world, especially Europe, and it's easy to understand why Toyota has become the market leader in the United States—and one of the world's biggest automakers.

COMPARING HYBRIDS			
2006 Autos	**Combined Gas Mileage (MPG)**	**Monthly Gas Savings**	**Sticker Price**
Honda Insight	63	$79.37	$19,330
Toyota Prius	55	$70.71	$21,275
Honda Civic Hybrid	50	$63.89	$21,850
Ford Escape 2WD	33	$25.25	$27,515
Mazda Tribute Hybrid 4WD	31	$17.92	$20,705
Mercury Mariner Hybrid 4WD	31	$17.92	$29,840
Toyota Highlander Hybrid 2WD	30	$13.89	$33,030
Lexus RX 400h 2WD	30	$13.89	$49,060

Source: omninerd.com

Analyzing the Impact

1. **Summarizing** Why did Toyota build the Prius?
2. **Drawing Conclusions** What problems with the Prius did Toyota have to overcome in order to be successful in the U.S. auto market?

Focus

R   Reading Strategy

Making Connections Have students who have driven or ridden in a hybrid car describe the experience. How was it different from riding in a car with an ICE? **OL**

Teach

W   Writing Support

Personal Writing Have students write a paragraph telling whether they would buy a hybrid car and why. Encourage them to consider, personal, environmental, and economic reasons. Have volunteers read their paragraphs to the class. **OL**

Analyzing the Impact

Answers:
1. The company wanted to make money and create an environmentally friendly car that got great gas mileage.
2. naysayers, touchy batteries, small trunk design

Additional Support

Activity: Hands-On Economics

Shopping for a Hybrid Have students visit a car dealer who sells one of the hybrid vehicles listed in the feature or another who sells a different type of hybrid vehicle. Have them obtain information about the vehicle, including its mileage estimates, recommended maintenance schedules, and other information they would need to make a buying decision about a hybrid vehicle. Have them also find the manufacturer's suggested retail price of the vehicle. Then have them use an online auto-buying information site, such as www.edmonds.com or www.AutoTrader.com, to find out what they are likely to pay for the specific hybrid vehicle they have researched. Conclude the activity by having students discuss whether they would buy the vehicle they have researched and at what price. **OL**

Focus

Bellringer
Daily Focus Transparency 92

FOCUS ACTIVITIES
Transparency 92

APPLYING ECONOMIC THINKING

Making an Economic Decision:
The Five Steps

1. State the problem or issue.

2. Determine the personal or broad social goals to be attained.

3. Consider the principal alternative means of achieving the goals.

4. Select the economic concepts needed to understand the problem and use them to appraise the merits of each alternative.

5. Decide which alternative best leads to the attainment of the most goals or the most important goals.

—National Council on Economic Education

1. How does the concept of opportunity costs relate to these steps?
2. How does cost-benefit analysis relate to these steps?

Daily Focus Transparencies

GUIDE TO READING

Possible Answers to Graphic:

provides a reasoned framework for decision making; cost-benefit analysis; opportunity costs; adaptable to changing needs of people; free market economy can adjust to change

Resource Manager

Applying the Economic Way of Thinking

GUIDE TO READING

Section Preview
Economics provides a foundation for analyzing choices and making decisions today and in the future.

Content Vocabulary
- cost-benefit analysis *(p. 522)*
- opportunity costs *(p. 522)*
- modified free enterprise economy *(p. 522)*

Academic Vocabulary
- equipped *(p. 521)*
- incapacitated *(p. 523)*

Reading Strategy
Describing As you read the section, complete a graphic organizer like the one below by describing how capitalism helps us with economic choices.

Capitalism

ISSUES IN THE NEWS

—*U.S. News & World Report*

Can America Keep Up?

. . . Over the past century, Americans have become accustomed to winning every global battle that mattered: two world wars, the space race, the Cold War, the Internet gold rush. Along the way, Americans have enjoyed unprecedented prosperity and lived lives that were the envy of the rest of the world.

Today, while unemployment remains low, home values continue to surge, and fearless American consumers keep spending beyond their means, the land of the free is slowly, but unmistakably, yielding advantages earned over decades to foreigners who work harder, expect less, and, often, are better educated. But business leaders, top academics, and other experts . . . increasingly see America as a nation that has pulled into the slow lane. . . . ■

The U.S. economy had a remarkable run in the last century, making it the world's largest economy. However, where will we be by the end of this century—or in the next few decades, for that matter?

Most economic measures put the U.S. economy on top, but there are no guarantees that it will always be that way. When teams compete in sports, staying on top is usually more difficult than getting to the top. The same holds true for our economy. How well we do, and how long we continue to do well, depends in large part on our understanding of how we got into this position—and what we need to do to stay there. As you read in the news story, some people have their doubts about how well we will be able to accomplish this feat.

R Reading Strategies	**C** Critical Thinking	**D** Differentiated Instruction	**W** Writing Support	**S** Skill Practice
Teacher Edition • Making Connections, p. 522 **Additional Resources** • Guid. Read. Act., p. 54 • Read. Ess. & Note-Taking Guide, p. 160	**Teacher Edition** • Analyzing Visuals, p. 521 • Evaluating, p. 524 **Additional Resources** • Quizzes and Tests, p. 227	**Teacher Edition** • Interpersonal, p. 523 • Visual/Spatial, p. 528 **Additional Resources** • Reading and Study Skills Fold., p. 66 • Reteach. Act., p. 18	**Teacher Edition** • Personal Writing, p. 521 • Persuasive Writing, p. 529 **Additional Resources** • High School Writing Process Trans.	**Teacher Edition** • Form. Quest., p. 522 **Additional Resources** • Econ. Content Vocab. Act., p. 18 • Daily Focus Trans. 92, 97

A Framework for Decision Making

MAIN Idea The study of economics and economic tools help us make the best economic choices.

Economics & You What tools do you use when you make a decision? Read on to learn how the study of economics can help us make choices for the future.

Through your study of economics, you have learned that scarcity requires us to make choices. This began when you discovered different ways to analyze a problem and evaluate alternative solutions for it. You also found out that the social science of economics has evolved to the point where it functions as a generalized theory of choice.

Economics provides a framework for decision making that helps people to become better decision makers. The future will be different from the past, or even the present for that matter. Yet one thing in economics is likely to remain the same—the way we think about problems.

A Reasoned Approach

Economic decision making requires a careful, reasoned approach to problem solving. The National Council on Economic Education, an organization dedicated to the improvement of economic literacy in the United States, recommends the following five steps to useful decision making:

1. State the problem or issue.
2. Determine the personal or broad social goals to be attained.
3. Consider the principal alternative means of achieving the goals.
4. Select the economic concepts needed to understand the problem and use them to appraise the merits of each alternative.
5. Decide which alternative best leads to the attainment of the most goals or the most important goals.

—*A Framework for Teaching the Basic Concepts*, 2005

Life is full of trade-offs, but you will be better **equipped** to deal with the future if you know how to analyze the problems you will encounter.

Decision Making These high school students discuss different solutions to problems with their project. *Why should you follow decision-making steps?*

521

Teach

W Writing Support

Personal Writing Have students write a paragraph about which of the five steps in the decision-making model they think is the most difficult for them to perform effectively. Have them give examples from their own lives and support their choice with other reasons. Ask volunteers to share their paragraphs. Conclude by asking for suggestions on how students can perform each step more effectively. **OL**

C Critical Thinking

Analyzing Visuals Ask: What evidence can you see in the photo that the students are using good decision-making skills? *(Answers will vary but may include listening carefully to each other and making notes about the discussion.)* **BL**

Caption Answer: to make better decisions; to learn how to use the process in all decision-making situations

Additional Support

Activity: Hands-On Economics

Gazing Into the Economic Crystal Ball
Have students break up into several groups and discuss this question: *What will the U.S. economy look like in the future?* Have students consider the impact of changes in technology, an aging population, foreign economic competition, the environment, and other factors that could affect the American economy. Tell groups to make predictions about 10 years, 25 years, and 50 years into the future. Call on group representatives to share their predictions with the class. Write on the board any similarities among groups' predictions. **OL**

R Reading Strategy

Making Connections Have students describe how they use cost-benefit analyses, including determining opportunity costs, in their everyday decision making. **OL**

S Skill Practice

Formulating Questions Have students review the subsection "Coping With the Future." Then have them write three questions based on the text, along with answers. Students might consider what they want to know about the topic or what information is critical. Have volunteers take turns asking the class their questions. **BL**

Caption Answer: It must change to meet the changing desires and needs of people in the future.

✓**Reading Check** **Answer:** The basic steps are the same in economic decision making as in any kind of decision making.

Adaptability
Capitalism adapts to the changing wants and needs of people. *Why is adaptability important for an economic system?*

cost-benefit analysis
way of thinking that compares the cost of an action to its benefits *(also see page 24)*

opportunity cost
cost of the next best alternative use of money, time, or resources when one choice is made rather than another *(also see page 20)*

modified free enterprise economy
free enterprise system with some government involvement *(also see page 53)*

Decision Making at the Margin

Economists use a number of tools to help them analyze problems and make decisions. Some of these tools include production possibilities curves, supply and demand curves, and production functions.

One of the most important decision-making tools is marginal analysis. For example, when a firm makes a decision to produce more output, it compares the extra cost of production with the extra benefits to be gained. If the benefits outweigh the costs, the firm decides to produce more. If the costs outweigh the benefits, the firm decides otherwise.

This process of **cost-benefit analysis** involves comparing the costs of an action to its benefits. Firms use such cost-benefit analyses for most of their production or purchase decisions. Government agencies apply it when they evaluate programs. Individuals use it when they have to make decisions about specific actions they need to take. Cost-benefit analysis is used in a similar way to make choices among economic goals because even if goals conflict, it helps to evaluate the costs and benefits of each choice.

R Finally, we must remember that economists use a very broad definition of costs—that of **opportunity costs.** This ensures that we account for all of the costs of a decision, not just the monetary ones.

✓**Reading Check** **Analyzing** How do the five steps to resolving problems relate to economic decision making?

Coping With the Future

S **MAIN Idea** The ability of capitalism to adapt to changes in the market helps economies address economic issues of the future.

Economics & You Do you remember learning how free market economies gradually adapt to change? Read on to find out how this adaptability will help in the future.

Everyone wants to know what will happen to the economy in the future. How will it adjust, and what course will it take? We can find part of the answer by examining the way we make incremental decisions and part of the answer by understanding how markets work.

The success of capitalism, the economic system in which private citizens own the factors of production and use them to generate a profit, will play a role. Capitalism has demonstrated an ability to generate wealth., and it also has shown that it can adapt to the changing desires and needs of people. If it continues to show this adaptability in the future, capitalism will play a dominant role in our lives.

The Success of Markets and Prices

A **modified free enterprise economy**— a free enterprise economy with some government involvement—allows buyers and sellers to freely make all the decisions that satisfy their wants and needs. In such an economy, the forces of supply and demand are allowed to interact to establish prices in a market. Prices, in turn, act as signals for producers and consumers to make or change their production and spending decisions.

A market economy has many advantages, including the ability to adjust to change gradually without the need for government intervention. As long as the forces of supply and demand are allowed to function, they will send producers and consumers the signals needed to reallocate resources.

Hands-On Chapter Project

Step 3

Global Economy Factbook

Step 3: Publishing the Factbook.
Students will finish writing and then publish their factbooks.

Directions: Have students write their text and complete their graphic aids. If members of the groups are proficient in creating computer graphics, suggest that they include computer-created graphs, diagrams, and charts and import photos and other illustrations into their factbooks.

As an alternative, students can cut illustrations from magazines and newspapers, or download them from Internet sources, and glue them into their booklets. Tell groups that they should have their factbooks completed by the next session, when they will present them.

Assessing Remind students that focusing on one example of something can often give insights into a general situation. Suggest that students think about and

include an example of one multinational company as a way of exemplifying the activities and organizations of all multinationals. **OL**

(Chapter Project continued in Visual Summary.)

The Triumph of Capitalism

During the 1930s, the forces of socialism and communism were sweeping the world, while capitalist countries were in economic depression. Communism in the Soviet Union had considerable impact upon the world, and socialist parties were on the rise in Europe and the European colonies in Africa and Asia.

Since then, communism in the former Soviet Union has collapsed under the weight of its own inefficiencies. Many socialist countries have embraced capitalism and the discipline of the market system.

Capitalism is now the dominant economic force in the world, but it is not the laissez-faire capitalism of the past. Capitalism has changed because people have addressed some of the weaknesses that Karl Marx and others identified many years ago.

The capitalism of the 1930s was ruthlessly efficient in providing only for those who produced or earned enough to buy the necessities of life. Early capitalism had little room or consideration for the elderly, the ill, or the **incapacitated.**

Most capitalistic economies today, including the United States, have modified their systems to make them more compatible with prevailing norms of what is right and wrong. The result is a free market economy based on capitalism, yet modified to satisfy the economic goals of freedom, efficiency, equity, security, full employment, price stability, and economic growth.

Capitalism has evolved over the years, and it shows every sign of continuing to do so in the future. In this respect, capitalism adjusts to changes the same way a market adjusts to small changes in supply and demand—incrementally, with adjustments **D** so small that they are hardly noticed in the short run. This ability to evolve, and to adjust to the demands placed on it, are strengths of capitalism that will continue to ensure its success in the future.

✓**Reading Check** **Summarizing** Why has capitalism been able to become the dominant economic system in the world?

D **Differentiated Instruction**

Interpersonal Have small groups describe three major challenges facing our free market capitalist economy. Then have them discuss ways to meet the challenges and propose one way as the most likely to succeed. Have the groups report the information to the class. **OL**

✓**Reading Check** **Possible Answer:** It has proven to be the most successful at adapting to changes.

Assess

💿 Use the Interactive Tutor Self-Assessment CD-ROM to review Section 3, and then assign the Section 3 Review as homework or as an in-class activity.

Close

Identifying Central Issues Have students develop a one-sentence description of economics. *(For example: Economics is the study of choices.)* **OL**

Review **SECTION 3**

SECTION 3 Review

Vocabulary
1. **Explain** the significance of cost-benefit analysis, opportunity costs, and modified free enterprise economy.

Main Ideas
2. **Identifying** Use a graphic organizer like the one below to identify the steps in the decision-making process.

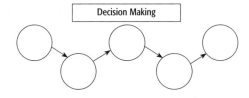

Decision Making

3. **Describing** How does today's capitalism in the United States differs from that of the 1930s?

Critical Thinking
4. **The BIG Idea** How is cost-benefit analysis useful in the decision-making process?

5. **Synthesizing** Why has capitalism developed into the most successful economic system? What might this imply about the future?

6. **Inferring** How does marginal analysis assist in decision making?

7. **Analyzing Visuals** Look at the photo on page 521. Are the students making their decisions as a group, or do they have a leader? Which approach is better, and why?

Applying Economics
8. **Cost-Benefit Analysis** Think of a decision you must make in the next few days. Write a paragraph about how you will use your estimates of the costs and benefits to make your decision.

CHAPTER 18   Global Economic Challenges   523

Answers

1. All definitions can be found in the section and the Glossary.
2. state problem; set goals; identify alternatives; evaluate alternatives; make a decision
3. The capitalism of the 1930s provided only for those who produced or earned enough to buy necessities and had little room for the needs of others. Today, most capitalist economies satisfy the economic goals of freedom, efficiency, equity, security, full employment, price stability, and growth.

4. It compares the extra cost of an action—the opportunity cost—with the extra benefits to be gained. If the benefits outweigh the costs, then the action should be taken. If the costs outweigh the benefits, then the action should not be taken.
5. its ability to adapt to changing circumstances and ideas of right and wrong; it is likely it will continue to adapt in the future

6. Answers may vary, but students should understand that marginal analysis looks at the cost and benefits of various alternatives.
7. Most students will say that the students are making decisions as a group; answers will vary as to which approach is better.
8. Answers will vary but should demonstrate an understanding of cost-benefit analysis.

Teach

C Critical Thinking

Evaluating Have students break into pairs and discuss the idea that encouraging more women to become economic participants will be positive for all of a society. Tell students to consider benefits as well as potential costs. Then call on volunteers to share their thoughts with the class. **OL**

Examining the Profile

Answers:

1. Answers may include better opportunities for education and health care and bringing more poor people into the economic life of their communities.
2. Most students will agree with Nancy Barry that women will benefit more from micro loans than from subsidies.

Additional Support

Profiles in Economics

Nancy Barry (1950–)

- president of Women's World Banking since 1990
- recipient of the Forbes Trailblazer Award for her efforts in opening doors for women in business

Nancy Barry has shown many people in the banking industry that it pays to provide money to the poor. In particular, she wants to "bring the poor woman into the center of our focus."

Banking on Women

Unlike her classmates at the Harvard Business School, Nancy Barry did not want to be an investment banker. She wanted to change the world. For 25 years, Barry has fulfilled that dream in her role as a member and president of Women's World Banking (WWB), a "global not-for-profit financial institution devoted to increasing poor women's economic access, participation and power."

Her early experience in the less developed countries of Peru and Tanzania convinced her that systematic change was necessary to encourage development. According to Barry, women need "access, not subsidies. They need opportunities, not paternalism." As a member of the UN Expert Group on Women and Finance, she has worked with governments in developing countries to ensure that their policies hinder neither business growth nor women's access to it.

Microfinance Provides the Push

Barry passionately believes that microfinance—the practice of lending very small amounts of capital to business upstarts—has the potential to revolutionize women's lives. For example, a micro loan might help a woman in Bangladesh to operate a fruit stand, which would allow her daughters to go to school and her family to have health insurance. The average micro loan from WWB is only $532—not much by American standards but a huge amount for someone used to surviving on less than $2 a day.

Unlike traditional bank loans, micro loans are almost always paid off. This has prompted other lenders to offer such loans. Under Barry's leadership, the WWB has grown to include more than 55 microfinance institutions that now serve about 18 million low-income women around the world.

Examining the Profile

1. **Determining Cause and Effect** What is the impact of financially successful women on families and communities?
2. **Drawing Conclusions** What form should financial aid to women take?

Extending the Content

A Nobel Prize The idea of microfinance received a huge shot in the arm in 2006. In that year, one of the pioneers in making small loans to poor people to encourage economic development was awarded the Nobel Peace Prize. He is Dr. Muhammad Yunnus of Bangladesh. Dr. Yunnus is the founder of the Grameen Bank, which, since 1974, has handed out small loans to farmers and others in the poor but populous (141 million people) South Asian nation of Bangladesh. *Grameen* means "rural" in the Bengali language. On awarding Yunnus their honor, the Nobel Prize committee made clear the link between economic development and peace and human rights: "Lasting peace cannot be achieved unless large population groups find ways in which to break out of poverty. Microcredit is one such means. Development from below also serves to advance democracy and human rights."

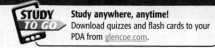

Study anywhere, anytime! Download quizzes and flash cards to your PDA from glencoe.com.

▶ **Globalization** With increasing globalization of products, markets, and production, global economic integration and interdependence are growing.

▶ **Global Problems** An increasing world population puts pressure on available resources, leads to the search for new and alternative energy sources, and requires ways to deal with pollution.

Global Problems

Population Growth	Resources	Pollution
• Malthus predicted condition of subsistence • Rate of world population growth decreasing • Rate of growth smaller in developed nations and higher in developing nations	• Limited use of renewable resources • Limited levels of non-renewable resources • Market and prices to spur search for new and alternative energy sources	• Lower production costs are incentive to pollute • EPA to enforce laws establishing pollution control standards • Pollution fees and permits provide incentives to limit pollution

▶ **Decision Making** Whenever we have to make an economic decision, we can use several tools and models to help with the decision.

Determine the choices and alternatives **+** Conduct a cost-benefit analysis **+** Identify the opportunity cost **➡** **Decision**

CHAPTER 18   Global Economic Challenges   525

Categorizing Refer students to the chart at the top of this page, and review each result of globalization, if necessary. **Ask:** What do you consider to be a positive about each factor? What is a negative about each factor? **OL**

Problem-Solving Divide the class into three discussion groups. Assign each group one of the three global problems shown in the center graphic. Have groups write a one-sentence statement summarizing the problem. Then have them list possible solutions that developed countries, international organizations, and developing countries could take to address each problem. Have each group report to the class on the problems and solutions it identified. After all the groups have reported, conclude by having the class discuss this question: *What is likely to happen if these problems are not solved?* **OL**

Hands-On Chapter Project
Step 4: Wrap Up

Global Economy Factbook

Step 4: Presenting the Factbook.
Students will present their factbooks and discuss issues they raise.

Directions: Have students present their factbooks to classmates, describing how they chose what to include and how to present their information. As an alternative, you may want to have groups exchange booklets and evaluate one another's work, giving it letter grades in various areas, such

as information, presentation, use of graphics, and so on.

Synthesizing Ask: What steps can our community take now to make sure that the growing global economy of the future is beneficial, rather than harmful, to our businesses, labor force, and way of life? *(Answers will vary but may include paying increased attention to tolerance and understanding others' customs or taking proactive measures now to avoid future problems.)* **OL**

CHAPTER
18 # Assessment & Activities

ExamView®
Assessment Suite

This easy-to-use software includes extensive question banks and allows you to create fully customized tests that can be administered in print or online.

Review Content Vocabulary

1. h	2. g
3. c	4. d
5. f	6. a
7. e	8. b

Review Academic Vocabulary

9. f	10. e
11. b	12. a
13. c	14. d

Review the Main Ideas

15. Markets expand beyond national boundaries; products from many different countries become available and standardized; production tends to migrate to be near customers and the cheapest resources.

16. EU, NAFTA, ASEAN, FTAA, COMESA

17. Economies of various countries are more closely linked and more dependent on each other than ever before.

18. Malthus did not foresee advances in productivity that allow an increasing standard of living to accompany a growing population. He also did not foresee that families might have fewer children.

19. production increased; interest in alternative energy sources soared, and countries poured billions into energy-research projects; consumers demanded more fuel-efficient cars

Review Content Vocabulary

Identify the term that best completes the following sentences.

a. acid rain	e. opportunity cost
b. division of labor	f. outsourcing
c. gasohol	g. pollution permits
d. globalization	h. subsistence

1. The state in which the population produces barely enough to support itself is _____.

2. By issuing fewer and fewer _____, the EPA hopes to reduce sulfur dioxide emissions.

3. _____ is a mixture of 90 percent unleaded gasoline and 10 percent grain alcohol, or ethanol.

4. _____ is the movement toward a more integrated and interdependent world economy.

5. Many U.S. companies use _____ to lower operating costs by shifting some operations to countries with lower wage rates.

6. _____ is a type of pollution in which rain mixes with sulfur dioxide emissions to create a form of sulfuric acid.

7. Economists use the term _____ to ensure that all the costs of a decision, not just the monetary ones, are included.

8. An example of _____ is the separate tasks performed by employees who work on an assembly line.

Review Academic Vocabulary

Match each of the terms with its synonyms.

a. compounded	d. incapacitated
b. context	e. strategy
c. equipped	f. successive

9. following, subsequent	12. intensified, worsened
10. design, tactic	13. outfitted, prepared
11. framework, situation	14. injured, disabled

Review the Main Ideas

Section 1 *(pages 501–507)*

15. **Describe** how markets, products, and production increase globalization.

16. **Identify** regional economic organizations by using a graphic organizer like the one below.

17. **Explain** the meaning of *global interdependence*.

Section 2 *(pages 509–518)*

18. **Describe** why, despite Malthus's predictions, certain parts of the world have enjoyed steadily increasing standards of living.

19. **Describe** how American consumers and the automobile industry reacted to the oil price increases of the 1970s.

20. **Explain** why incentives exist that cause pollution and how they work.

Section 3 *(pages 520–523)*

21. **Identify** the importance of cost-benefit analysis.

22. **Describe** why adapting to change is important for an economic system.

Critical Thinking

23. **The BIG Ideas** As both an environmentalist and an economist, which of the incentives to preserve scarce resources would you advise using? Why?

24. **Synthesizing** Select one of the resources discussed in Section 2. How can the price system help ensure that this resource is used wisely?

20. The incentive to pollute is that it costs less than to not pollute; companies will choose the lower-cost alternative.

21. It allows one to compare the potential costs and benefits of a decision.

22. The success of any economy depends on its ability to adapt to change. Examples of this are (1) the failure of communism in the former Soviet Union and Eastern Europe to provide for citizens, and (2) the success of modified free market capitalism.

Critical Thinking

23. Answers will vary but should take into account the viewpoints of both an environmentalist and an economist.

24. Answers will vary but should demonstrate an understanding of how the price system in a market economy influences the behavior of both consumers and producers.

526

Economics ONLINE **Self-Check Quiz** Visit the *Economics: Principles and Practices* Web site at glencoe.com and click on *Chapter 18–Self-Check Quizzes* to prepare for the chapter test.

Assessment and Activities

CHAPTER 18

25. **Making Comparisons** If you had to decide to use either legislated standards or a pollution tax to reduce pollution, which would you choose? In your reasoning, explain the pros and cons of each approach.

26. **Predicting** How might the world be different in 50 years if we do not use resources wisely today?

27. **Analyzing** Globalization has led to an increase in interdependence. In your opinion, is this a positive or negative trend? Explain your reasoning.

Thinking Like an Economist

28. **Critical Thinking** Renewable energy resources account for only a small portion of our total energy production. Explain the changes that would have to take place in order for people to make greater use of renewable energy resources.

Math Practice

29. The table below shows the average gross domestic product (GDP) for low-, middle-, and high-income countries for the years 1990 and 2004. Study the table, and then answer the following questions in short paragraphs.

   a. Determine the percentage change in GDP for low-, middle-, and high-income countries. How do these rates compare?

   b. What might explain the difference between the growth rates?

   c. How might growing globalization change the GDP for these countries?

GDP AND INCOME		
	1990	**2004**
Low income	$609,821	$1,239,169
Middle income	$3,238,587	$7,156,777
High income	$17,887,372	$32,900,093

Source: World Development Indicators, 2006, World Bank

Interpreting Cartoons

30. Examine the cartoon below. What issue is being addressed by this cartoon? Why is this a problem?

OY!... I DON'T THINK I CAN SUPPORT MUCH MORE, FOLKS...

Applying Economic Concepts

31. **Scarcity** Scarce natural resources are an issue that concerns citizens throughout the world. What can you personally do to help conserve resources?

32. **Modified Free Enterprise Economy** The United States has a modified free enterprise economy in which the government provides some regulation. Based on what you have learned about globalization and global problems, do you think the government should play a smaller or larger role in regulating the U.S. economy? Give reasons to support your answer.

Writing About Economics

33. **Expository Writing** Access to clean water and sanitation is important to maintaining health. Research the availability of clean water for a developing country. Determine what problems exist and how these problems affect economic development. Then identify steps the country is taking to deal with the problem. Also discuss aid the country might receive from outside sources to deal with the problem.

CHAPTER 18 Global Economic Challenges **527**

Economics ONLINE

Have students visit the Web site at glencoe.com to review Chapter 18 and take the **Self-Check Quiz.**

financial, to research and develop renewable energy resources, an infrastructure to support their uses, and public acceptance of these energy resources.

Math Practice

29. **a.** 96.8%; 120.9%; 83.9%
   b. Partly developed countries in the middle group, such as China and India, developed faster than very rich or very poor countries.
   c. It is likely to raise the GDP for poor and medium countries, as they gain more production facilities because of their lower labor costs.

Interpreting Cartoons

30. the growing global population; because there are limited resources

Applying Economic Concepts

31. Answers will vary but should be logical and well reasoned.
32. Answers will vary but should demonstrate sound economic reasoning.

Writing About Economics

33. Answers will vary but should demonstrate an understanding of the economic and environmental issues involved.

25. Answers will vary but should demonstrate an understanding of the pros and cons of each.
26. Answers will vary but should demonstrate an understanding of the consequences of depleting nonrenewable resources.
27. positive: greater variety of products, lower costs, standardized products, increased regional economic integration, may lead to greater international cooperation and peaceful solutions to world problems

negative: outsourcing, may be seen as threat to national security and national culture, possible job loss as developing countries produce items once produced in industrialized nations, threats to national economies when one "link" in the global economies weakens or collapses

Thinking Like an Economist

28. Answers will vary but may include government incentives, including

The Global Economy
&YOU

Focus

Ask for a show of hands to identify students whose families recycle. Have volunteers describe their family's recycling practices. **Ask:** What things would make it easier for your family to recycle even more waste? *(Students may mention economic incentives, closer proximity to recycling facilities, or companies using less packaging.)*

Teach

D Differentiated Instruction

Visual/Spatial Have groups of students create the story board for a television public service announcement (PSA) about recycling. Ask groups to share their story boards with the class. Alternatively, ask auditory/musical learners to create radio PSAs and present them to the class. **OL**

Additional Support

Recycling

D The average American generates about 4.5 pounds of waste each day. Thanks to the growing popularity of recycling, only about 3.1 pounds of that waste make it to the landfill. Americans concerned about the environment increasingly are willing to recycle. They have much to learn from their European counterparts.

Waste Not, Want Not

Many Europeans are avid recyclers. Much of this enthusiasm is due to widespread concern about space for landfills. Each country takes a different approach to recycling, though. Switzerland, for example, charges a hefty fee for each bag of waste, while recycling is free. In addition, recycling is extremely convenient, with bottle banks at every supermarket, paper collection in every town, and even a pick-up service for green waste.

In Germany, all apartment courtyards and most neighborhoods have color-coded sorting bins for separating packaging material, paper and cardboard, glass, and bio-waste such as fruit and vegetable

photo: recycling bins outside Cloth Hall in Krakow, Poland

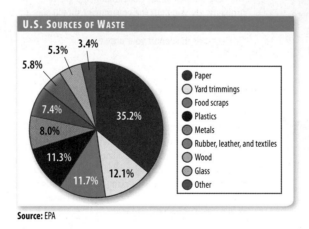

U.S. Sources of Waste

- 3.4%
- 5.3%
- 5.8%
- 7.4%
- 8.0%
- 11.3%
- 11.7%
- 12.1%
- 35.2%

- ● Paper
- ○ Yard trimmings
- ● Food scraps
- ● Plastics
- ● Metals
- ● Rubber, leather, and textiles
- ● Wood
- ● Glass
- ● Other

Source: EPA

528   UNIT 5   The Global Economy

peelings. The bins for "other" household trash often are the size of a regular kitchen trash can and may hold weekly trash for up to 3 families. With all the material that gets recycled, that's usually plenty of space.

While the Germans may call themselves the "world champions of recycling," the citizens of Copenhagen, Denmark's capital, may be the real thing. The city adopted regulations in 1991 to recycle 58 percent of household, commercial, and industrial waste, incinerate 24 percent, and deposit only 18 percent in landfills. Copenhagen has not quite reached its goals, but it reduced the number of landfills from 30 to 3.

Activity: Hands-On Economics

Recycling Dollars and Sense Have a student team contact a local recycling center to find out about the economics of recycling. Have them talk to a manager to find out information such as the following:

- Does our community's recycling program pay for itself?
- How have the prices you receive for various recyclables such as glass, newsprint, and aluminum varied over the years?

- Are prices now relatively high or low?
- What trends do you see in the recycling industry?
- What plans does your facility have for the future?
- How can students help your recycling efforts?

Have the team report to the class about their findings. **OL**

Take Back That Apple

Companies doing business in Europe have had to adapt to European attitudes and laws. In many countries, for example, stores are required to take back any unwanted packaging material. This has had a surprising side effect: packaging became simplified—and cheaper. Today, U.S. computer companies such as IBM, Apple, and Dell take back old computers and components when customers purchase new ones.

What Does It Mean for You?

While U.S. recycling efforts have been largely voluntary, the European example has had an impact on this side of the Atlantic. Today you can find trash cans that divide waste into recyclables and regular waste in many public places. In 2006 Maine became the first state to require makers of televisions and computer monitors to pay for recycling and safely disposing of their old products. U.S. companies have learned that customers appreciate their recycling efforts. Many European recycling programs are now in effect in the United States, Canada, and elsewhere in the world.

WASTE MANAGEMENT IN EUROPE AND THE UNITED STATES

Legend: Landfill | Recycled/composted | Incineration | Other

Countries (top to bottom): Greece, Ireland, United Kingdom, Italy, Portugal, Spain, Finland, France, Luxembourg, Belgium, Austria, Germany, Sweden, Netherlands, Denmark, United States

X-axis: Percentage of total waste (0 to 100)

Sources: Defra; National Energy Education Development Project, Museum of Solid Waste

photo: landfill in the United States

Analyzing the Issue

1. **Identifying** How do European countries make recycling easy for their citizens?

2. **Analyzing Visuals** Take a look at the graph titled "U.S. Sources of Waste." What are the three largest sources of waste? How could individuals and corporations help lower this percentage?

3. **Applying** Research recycling efforts in your community. Then use the examples from these pages to outline improvements to these efforts.

Assess/Close

W Writing Support

Persuasive Writing Have students use the information in the bar graph to write a letter to the local newspaper encouraging recycling in your community. Have volunteers share their letters. Discuss issues they raise as a class. **OL**

Analyzing the Issue

Answers:

1. They charge for trash disposal, while recycling is free; recycling bins are placed near homes and stores; and stores are required to take back packaging material.

2. plastic, fabric, paper; answers will vary about possible actions that might lower this percentage

3. Answers will vary but should demonstrate an understanding of issues raised in this feature.

Additional Support

Activity: Interdisciplinary Connection

Science Ask a science teacher or local recycling expert to speak to your class about the science of recycling. Have him or her prepare a short presentation on how certain common materials are recycled, costs associated with recycling, how much energy or raw material is saved when recycling is used, special scientific challenges the recycling industry faces, and other relevant topics. Have your students prepare questions for the guest speaker to address. **OL**

Reference Section

Financial Fitness: Money and Real Life

- Can you afford a cool car?
- How can you avoid the credit trap?
- Is college for you?
- Can you become a millionaire?

Only you can answer those questions—and thousands of others. Your life is ahead of you; it's up to you to decide how you'll live it. Whatever goals or dreams you may have, the way you live your life will be determined, at least in part, by your relationship to money: how you get it and how you use it.

The opportunities you create for yourself are greatly affected by the money habits you form when you're young. This handbook is designed to help you learn how to use money to meet your goals and to live the way you want to live. It can help you make intelligent decisions about money so you can get what you want and need— today and throughout your life.

R1

INTRODUCING THE PERSONAL FINANCE HANDBOOK

The Personal Finance Handbook addresses financial issues that nearly everybody encounters at some point during their lifetimes. The lessons in the 10 features teach skills that will help students make wise decisions with their money. As they study the Handbook, remind students that now is the time for them to start planning for their futures. Encourage students to be continually thinking of how the content of each feature can apply to their lives, both today and in the years to come.

Focus

R Reading Strategy

Identifying Have students make a list of at least five reasons why a person would want to open a checking account. Next, ask students to write a sentence next to each reason describing a disadvantage that a person without a checking account would face. *(For example, He could not pay bills with a check. She could not get cash from an ATM machine.)* **OL**

Teach

C Critical Thinking

Evaluating Tell students: Banks offer many different types of accounts.
Ask: What types of advantages does a checking account offer over other types of accounts? *(money is available for use by the account holder; no or fewer limits on number of withdrawals; lower minimum balance)* **OL**

Additional Resources

Your Checking Account:
Check into independence

Are all banks alike? What if you bounce a check? Where do checks go?
Knowing the smart way to open and manage a checking account can help you avoid hassles—and save money.

How It Works

A checking account gives you a safer place to keep cash than a cookie jar while making it easy to pay bills and buy things.

Opening an Account To open an account, you need identification and usually a deposit (money you put into the account). Some banks offer student accounts requiring no initial deposit. The amount in your account at any given time is the balance. Putting money in or taking it out is a transaction.

To deposit a check, endorse (sign) it on the back. If you're depositing the entire check rather than keeping some cash, write "for deposit only" and your account number below your signature. When you open an account, you'll get a receipt for your deposit and, soon, numbered checks printed with your name, address, and account number; a check register; and a debit card. A debit card acts like an electronic check: money is taken out of your account immediately (a withdrawal or debit).

Making Withdrawals There are five ways to make withdrawals:

1. Write a paper check, or pay by check over the phone.
2. Get cash from a teller at a bank branch.
3. Use a debit card at a store or automated teller machine (ATM).
4. Use your bank's Web site to pay a bill.
5. Authorize the bank to automatically pay recurring bills.

Keeping Good Records Record all transactions in your check register. You'll get a monthly statement showing activity for the previous month. Compare it with your check register for errors and keep both in a file.

Did You Know?

▶ Help! If your debit card is lost or stolen, your liability for an unauthorized withdrawal can vary. If you notify the financial institution within two business days after learning of the loss or theft, you're liable for only $50. If you don't report unauthorized use that appears on your statement within 60 days after its mailing date, you could lose all the money in your account.

R2 PERSONAL FINANCE HANDBOOK

Extending the Content

Check 21 The Check Clearing for the 21st Century Act (Check 21) went into effect on October 28, 2004. Congress passed this law to increase the efficiency of check payment processing. Check 21 allows banks to replace original cancelled checks with "substitute checks." A substitute check is a special paper copy, front and back, of an original check. Substitute checks are legal copies of checks and serve as the proof of payment in the same way that cancelled checks did before Check 21. In the past, a checking account holder generally received their cancelled checks with their statements. Most banks today destroy original checks. Bank customers instead receive substitute checks, reduced pictures of their checks printed on a page, a list of paid checks, or a combination of these items.

Which Bank, What Account?

Some banks offer better service or lower fees, or are conveniently located. Banks offer different types of accounts, some of which pay interest in exchange for having the use of your money. Before opening an account, savvy consumers ask if there's a minimum balance requirement, how many checks can be written per month, if there are fees for writing checks, and if the account will earn interest.

Choose a traditional bank that offers some services online or a bank that exists only on the Net. If you bank online, don't rely on the bank's system to protect you. Install a firewall and don't open suspicious e-mails or provide personal information to anyone who contacts you. Check your balance often to see if a thief has taken money from your account. You're liable for only the first $50 if you report it to the bank within two days. Find more tips at www.idtheftcenter.org.

Tip **Balancing Act** Be sure your balance is greater than the amount you withdraw. Otherwise, your check will bounce; that is, the recipient's bank will return it and you'll be charged a hefty fee by your bank—and usually theirs, too—for having an overdrawn account.

How To Write A Check

In this example, if you spelled out "Eleven fifty" instead of "Eleven hundred fifty," the bank would pay only $11.50—not $1,150.00. Be sure the numerals and longhand version are the same amount.

- Spell out the amount of the check, including cents (expressed as a fraction) beside "Dollars."
- Enter the payee's name.
- Enter the date you write the check.
- Enter the amount of the check in numerals.
- Note the purpose of the check as a handy reference.
- Sign the check.
- Fill in the blank with a line so no one can change the amount.

Bernadette C. Dabney
12 Vico Lane
Haddonfield, NJ 08033   Date _Today's date_ 20 ____   137

Pay to the order of _ABC Rental Company_ $ _1150.00_

Eleven hundred fifty and no/100 _____ Dollars ■

◌ FIRST NATIONAL BANK OF CHICAGO

Memo _April Rent_   _Bernadette C. Dabney_

5:5555555: 555 555555:0137

Test Your Financial Fitness

1. **Explaining** Why is it important to balance your checkbook?
2. **Determining Cause and Effect** List two reasons to avoid bouncing a check.
3. **Paraphrasing** Describe three ways to protect yourself from online theft.

PERSONAL FINANCE HANDBOOK   R3

Assess/Close

W Writing Support

Personal Writing Have students write an essay describing how their lives changed after they opened their own checking account. For those students who do not yet have an account, ask them to write about how they believe their lives will change after they open a checking account. Encourage students to include any lessons they have learned (or likely will learn) through having an account. **OL**

Test Your Financial Fitness

Answers:

1. to know how much money is currently in the account; to make sure no unauthorized withdrawals have occurred
2. the check will be returned with a hefty fee; the bill for which the check was intended may be past due by the time the bounced check is returned
3. install a firewall on the computer; frequently check account balance; don't open suspicious e-mails or give out personal information

---

Activity: Interdisciplinary Connection

Art Inform students that banks and independent companies offer many different check designs to checking account holders. Have students review bank Web sites or printed advertisements (often included as newspaper inserts) to see examples of the many different designs that are currently available. Ask students to create a brochure that offers at least 10 different check designs. Students should include the standard formatting of a check (space for name/address, box for amount, bank name, and so on) along with drawings of their original designs. Have students present their checks to the class and explain the target market for each design. **OL**

Teacher Tip

Informing Students You may want to go over features of checks that are not listed in the visual. For example, the check number, the bank routing number, the bank's name and address, and the account holder's name and address.

Focus

C Critical Thinking

Speculating **Tell students:** By the end of 2004, household debt in America had risen to 113 percent of personal disposable income, the amount of take-home cash consumers have to spend.
Ask: Why do you think so many American families spend more than they earn? *(possible answers: easily attainable credit, high standard of living in nation, aggressive advertising)* **OL**

Teach

W Writing Support

Descriptive Writing Have students write a short story about a teenager who falls into debt. Tell students to include the reasons for the main character's financial difficulties and what he or she does to try to make his or her situation better. **OL**

Additional Resources

Budgeting:
Take control of your cash

Did you really need that cashmere sweater or those $200 sneakers? How did you get $5,000 in debt? Getting control of what you spend—budgeting—is a skill you'll need throughout your life.

Where Does Your Money Go?

Many people have no idea what happens to their money. It just seems to "disappear." Here's how to find out how where yours goes:

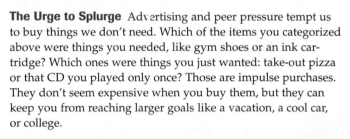

1. List the bills you pay every month.
2. For one month, jot down everything you buy and the price—no matter how little it costs.

At the end of the month, categorize the items you've listed: "Food," "Transportation," etc. Then break down each category; for example, "Food: School Lunches, Snacks, Restaurants." Now you know where your money goes.

The Urge to Splurge Advertising and peer pressure tempt us to buy things we don't need. Which of the items you categorized above were things you needed, like gym shoes or an ink cartridge? Which ones were things you just wanted: take-out pizza or that CD you played only once? Those are impulse purchases. They don't seem expensive when you buy them, but they can keep you from reaching larger goals like a vacation, a cool car, or college.

Think Before You Buy Before you buy an item, ask yourself whether the item is worth the time you'll have to work to pay for it. The better you get at saying "no" to unnecessary spending, the more money you'll have for what's important to you.

Creative Budgeting

Using the expenses you listed before, complete a chart like the one on the next page. Look at each expense in column 2 and think of ways to reduce it. Enter the lesser amount in column 3, your New Budget. Be sure to budget 10 to 30 percent of your income for "Savings." (To see why, go to Saving and Investing on page R6.) Total column 3 to see if your budget matches your income. If not, you'll need to keep trimming expenses until it does or find another source of income.

Extending the Content

Budgeting The vast majority of Americans seem to accept the theory that budgeting is important. Putting the theory of budgeting into practice, however, isn't quite as popular. A recent survey found that nearly 90 percent of Americans believe that a monthly budget is "very important" or "essential." Only 74 percent of respondents, however, reported actually having a budget. And of that group, one quarter said that they did not do a good job of sticking to their budgets. 60 percent of people making $25,000 per year or less reported that they do a good job of living within their budgets. That figure jumps to 78 percent of those making more than $25,000 per year. Also, 10 percent more women than men reported that they are staying within their budgets.

Building Your Budget

Part-time Job: $_____
Monthly allowance: $_____
Total income: $_____

Spending Category	Current Expenses	New Budget
Food:		
School lunches		
Restaurants & take-out		
Snacks		
Transportation:		
Car payment		
Insurance		
Gasoline		
Maintenance (estimate)		
Entertainment:		
Movies		
Music		
Games		
Sports and hobbies		
Personal care:		
Clothes		
Shoes		
Haircuts		
Accessories		
Cosmetics		
Savings (10–30% of income)		
Utilities:		
Phone		
Internet access		
Medical/dental		
Donations to charity		
Miscellaneous		
TOTAL		

Advertising executive Gary Dahl became a millionaire by convincing people to pay $3.95 each for "Pet Rocks" in 1975. The product was simply a beach stone that cost him a penny, packaged in a box with a "Care and Training of a Pet Rock" manual.

Test Your Financial Fitness

1. **Listing** List five ways you can start saving money. How much could you save in a year by cutting these costs?

2. **Defining** What is an impulse purchase? What was the last one you made?

3. **Explaining** Why is it important to live on a budget?

4. **Applying** Make a list of three ways you can re-use things you usually throw away.

Assess/Close

S Skill Practice

Using Tables and Charts After students have completed the Test Your Financial Fitness questions have them revisit their answers to question 1. Ask students to add a column to the budget chart they completed. Have students use the new column to list ways that they will cut expenses in each spending category. **OL**

Test Your Financial Fitness

Answers:

1. Answers may include buying less expensive clothes, going to matinees rather than evening movies, clipping coupons, eating out less frequently, and carpooling to school.

2. Buying an unneeded item on the spur of the moment. Student examples will vary.

3. Without a budget, a person can more easily fall into debt.

4. Answers may include returning cans and bottles to collect the deposit, printing rough drafts of school reports on the other side of used paper, and patching a punctured bicycle tire.

Activity: Technology Connection

Creating a Budget Spreadsheet Have students create a spreadsheet file based on the budget chart they complete on this page. Spreadsheets should include cell formulas that will make the calculations in each row. Ask students to add a fourth column to include the difference between the "Current Expenses" and "New Budget" figures. Ask for volunteers to demonstrate the workings of their spreadsheets. **OL**

Teacher Tip

Finishing Touches After students complete the activity, you may want to go over ways they can modify their spreadsheets to present the information more attractively. Possible modifications include changing the font type, adding borders, or adding colors.

Personal Finance Handbook

Focus

C Critical Thinking

Contrasting Point out to students that savings accounts are different from checking accounts, which they learned about earlier. Have them write a paragraph explaining why a person would want to open a savings account instead of a checking account. *(higher rate of interest, maximize the impact of compounding, desire to accumulate rather than spend money)* **OL**

Teach

D Differentiated Instruction

Logical/Mathematical Ask: If given the choice, would you rather have a savings account with interest compounded annually, quarterly, monthly, or daily? *(daily)* What is the reason for your answer? *(more frequent compounding yields more interest)* **BL**

Additional Resources

Saving and Investing:
Make your money grow

Want a faster computer or a great car? How about retiring at 40? You don't have to be old or rich to save and invest. People with ordinary jobs and moderate incomes can build wealth—and financial freedom—just by starting young.

Saving: The Frugal Habit

Frugality is the attempt to save money instead of spending it. Why save? Because saved money grows. Here's why it's worth it:

1. Savings are your only safety net in financial emergencies.
2. With an early start, you can amass huge amounts of money over time.
3. Having a savings account improves your credit rating (see Credit and You on page R10).

The Secret of Compounding Why save now? Because of a simple but very important concept: compounding. It's the process of interest earning interest. And it takes time to kick in. If a family saves $75 a month at 5 percent interest from the day a child is born, they'll have more than $24,000 by the time she's ready for college. More than $9,000 of it is interest—money their money earned. If they wait until the child is seven to start, they'll have to save almost $137 a month to get the same result. Two key concepts make compounding work: yield and time.

Yield: Different types of accounts offer different annual percentage rates (APR). That's the rate you'll get if the interest is compounded only once a year.

Example: You deposit $10,000 in an account with an APR of 5 percent. At the end of the year, your money has earned $500 ($10,000 × 5% × one year = $500). So you have $10,500.

Interest for some accounts is compounded more often: semi-annually, quarterly, monthly, daily, or even continuously. The more frequently it's compounded, the more interest you get. That's because interest is added to your deposit periodically and the entire amount earns, or yields, interest—the annual percentage yield (or APY).

In recent years, the average American family has earned about $40,000 per year but saved 0 percent of its income. The Chinese earn on average $1,500 per year—but save 23 percent of their incomes. The worldwide average is about 20 percent.

R6   PERSONAL FINANCE HANDBOOK

Extending the Content

Poor Savers A recent survey revealed that Americans are among the worst savers in the world. According to a Nielsen poll, nearly a quarter of U.S. citizens have no left over money after paying for living expenses and purchases. None of the other 42 countries included in the survey had a worse saving rate than the U.S.A. Only Portugal matched America's 22% rate of saving futility. Thailand, where only 3% of the population reported not saving money, topped the list as the world's best savers.

The History of Savings The earliest savings banks developed in Italy as a means of encouraging poor people to help themselves. The concept of savings banks spread from The Netherlands to Germany and England in the early 1800s. Savings banking in the United States developed at roughly the same time period. These charitable institutions were nonprofit and were located primarily in the northeastern portion of the United States.

Example: You deposit the same $10,000 at 5% APR, but interest is compounded twice a year. After six months, your money has earned half the annual interest ($10,000 × 5% × ½ year = $250). The bank adds that interest to your original deposit. Now the $250 also earns interest for six months. The APY is 5.0625%. So at the end of the year, you have $10,506.25 instead of $10,500. That may seem like a small change, but it can make a big difference as your balance grows over the years.

Time: The longer you leave your money in an account, the better compounding works—especially in an account with frequent compounding. If you left $10,000 in an account for 10 years, with interest compounded quarterly, you'd have almost $16,500—without ever adding another cent!

Ways to Save Your goals should determine which savings methods you choose. A savings account is ideal for "emergency funds," since you have fast access to cash. But it also pays low interest, so you'll want to find other ways—including investments—to get enough interest to offset the taxes you'll pay on the interest, plus inflation.

Did You Know?

▶ **Who Is Rich?**
Looking rich and being rich are not the same. Most millionaires drive used cars, live in modest houses, and don't wear expensive clothes. They save at least 15% of their earned income, and four out of five of them did not inherit their money.

SAVINGS VEHICLES AND RISKS

Savings account: Safe (FDIC-insured). Some student accounts offer no deposit requirement. Easy access to funds makes them good for emergencies, but interest is low.

Money market deposit account: Safe (FDIC-insured), with easy but infrequent withdrawals. These accounts pay slightly higher interest than savings accounts, with various deposit requirements.

Money market mutual fund: Relatively low risk because invested in a pool in short-term vehicles such as certificates of deposit and commercial paper. Terms are from 90 days to 13 months. Interest is comparable to money market deposit accounts.

Certificate of deposit (CD): FDIC-insured time deposit with slightly higher interest than savings accounts and opening requirements as low as $250. Terms are from 3 months to 5 years with varying interest and low penalties for early withdrawal.

U.S. savings bond: Safe (government-backed) and available for as little as $25. Terms vary, but after a waiting period bonds can be redeemed before maturity. Not taxed until redeemed. Most types offer interest higher than savings accounts.

Personal Finance Handbook

S Skill Practice

Understanding Interest Rates
Ask: What would the APY be if interest was compounded quarterly? *(5.0945%)* How much would you have at the end of the year if you originally deposited $10,000? *($10,509.45)* **AL**

R Reading Strategy

Making Connections Ask: What type of person would most likely be interested in opening a CD account? *(someone seeking to save money over a long period of time)* What type of person would NOT likely be interested in opening a CD account? *(someone who needs quick access to his or her money; for example, a person who will soon be buying a car or a house)* **OL**

PERSONAL FINANCE HANDBOOK   R7

Activity: Collaborative Learning

Comparing Organize students into small groups. Assign to each of the groups one of the following accounts: savings, money market deposit, money market mutual, and certificate of deposit. Have students call or visit at least four local banks to learn each institution's current interest rates for their group's assigned account. Ask groups to create a large chart comparing the bank's different rates. After each group has presented its chart to the class, discuss the importance of comparing banks when seeking to open an account. **OL**

Reference Section

C Critical Thinking

Evaluating Suppose you have a friend who asks you if he should invest money he recently inherited in the stock market. **Ask:** What factors should you consider before advising your friend? *(Possible answers: financial goals—the length of time he can leave the money in an investment; current market trends—is it a bull or bear market? and personal tolerance for risk—will he panic if stock prices drop?)* **OL**

W Writing Support

Expository Writing Have students research economic conditions in the United States in the 1920s. Ask students to write a paper explaining the major causes of the stock market crash of 1929. **AL**

Personal Finance Handbook

Common Investments		
Type of investment	**Advantages**	**Disadvantages**
Stocks	High earnings potential	High risk Need broker to buy and sell
Stock mutual funds	Some risk, but less than buying stocks individually Professional investment manager	Need fund company or broker to buy and sell Minimum investment usually $1,000 or more
Bonds	Good earnings potential **Federal:** no default risk (see **Ways to Save** on page R7) **Municipal:** low risk, no federal tax **Corporate:** moderate risk	Federal tax on federal and corporate bond interest
Bond mutual funds	Professional investment manager Less risk than individual bonds	Need broker to buy and sell

Investing: Not Just for the Rich

About 19 percent of students in grades 8–12 own stocks or bonds. If you think you don't have enough money to invest now, remember the compounding principle: time is on your side. Even the spare change you keep in a jar every week, invested consistently and well, can reap big rewards in time. Investment advice can be confusing and, let's face it, boring. A good way to learn is to join—or start—an investment club. Get information at www.better-investing.org/youth/youth.html.

All investments involve two unknowns: the possibility of making money (the return), and the risk of losing it. In choosing investments, you're always balancing those two realities. Common investments include the following:

Stocks A stock is a share of a company's assets. Say you want to start a company that sells jewelry but can't afford to buy the beads. So you ask three friends for money. Now each of you owns one fourth of the company—one share. When you sell the jewelry, you each get a fourth of the profits. If it doesn't sell, you all lose money. That's the stock market, simplified.

Most investment professionals consider stocks the best way to get a fairly dependable, high return—but only if you keep them for more than ten years. Individual stocks and the stock market itself shoot up and down like a roller coaster. But over the last 50 years, the average return for stocks has been 10 percent—higher than savings vehicles and most other types of investments. Patience is the key to success.

You can buy stocks online, through a stockbroker or mutual fund company, or directly from companies that offer "Drip"

The stock market crash of 1929 ushered in the Great Depression, which plunged one-third of Americans into poverty. By 1933, the market had lost 80% of its precrash value, and the unemployment rate had reached about 25%.

R8   PERSONAL FINANCE HANDBOOK

Activity: Hands-On Economics

Tracking Stock Prices Have students suppose that they have $1,000 to invest in a stock. Allow students three days to investigate the market before turning in the name of their stock selection. Have students use a newspaper or the Internet to track the progress of their stock's price over a period of time (for example, a month or the semester). At the end of the time period, have students turn in a line graph showing the price fluctuations of their stock. Ask students to include on their graphs a calculation of how much money they would have made or lost if they had actually bought $1,000 worth of the stock. **OL**

(direct reinvestment) funds in which earnings are automatically reinvested in more of their stock.

To reduce your risk, you can buy stocks through a mutual fund, a pool of money from many people invested in a variety of stocks or bonds by an investment manager.

There are two ways to make money with stocks. You can sell them when their value is high; the profit is called a capital gain and is taxed as income. Or you can keep them and receive regular payments (dividends), if the company pays dividends.

Bonds Governments (federal, state, and local) and corporations sell bonds to raise funds for projects like schools, bridges, or business expansion. They're borrowing your money. In return, you generally get periodic interest and a fixed amount of money at a specified time in the future (maturity date). Some types of federal bonds offer different payment plans. Maturity dates vary. Most bonds are considered less risky than stocks, and government bonds are less risky than corporate bonds, since companies sometimes lose money.

U.S. Treasury Instruments Treasury instruments are loans you make to the government. They include T-bills, T-notes, T-bonds, Treasury Inflation-Protected Securities (TIPS), and several series of savings bonds. (See the Savings Vehicles table on page R8). They offer various interest rates and maturity dates. Because they're issued by the government, treasury instruments offer low risk. They can be bought directly from the government online, or through banks or brokers. Minimum investments for most are $1,000–$10,000; some savings bond minimums are much lower.

Other Investments A home may be the largest investment you'll make. Real estate is considered a good investment because most properties increase in value—but *not all*. Other types of investments include precious metals (like gold and silver) and retirement plans.

Test Your Financial Fitness

1. **Explaining** Look at the budget you prepared on page R5, and see if you can increase the amount you're saving. If so, what type of savings vehicle or investment will you use, and why?
2. **Defining** What is the difference between APR and APY?
3. **Summarizing** How can you make buying stocks less risky?
4. **Applying** In the library or on the Internet, research an investment you think you'd like to make. Write down your reasons.

PERSONAL FINANCE HANDBOOK   R9

DID YOU KNOW?

▶ **Early Investing**
A 16-year-old who invests $2,000 a year at 10 percent APR will have more than $2 million at age 65. By waiting until you're 26 to begin, you'd have less than $803,000.

Personal Finance

Assess/Close

S Skill Practice

Making Predictions Have students consider what their lives will be like 10 years from now. Ask them to write a paragraph describing what types of savings accounts and investments they think they will have at that time. Then ask students to do the same thing for their lives 25 years and 50 years from now. After students have finished their paragraphs, discuss as a class how saving and investing goals change as a person grows older. **OL**

Test Your Financial Fitness

Answers:

1. Answers will vary. Students should support their choice with logical arguments.
2. APR is the annual return on a deposit if interest is compounded only once a year. APY is the annual return on a deposit if interest is compounded more than once a year.
3. buy stocks through a mutual fund
4. Answers will vary. Students should support their choices with logical arguments.

Activity: Interdisciplinary Connection

Civics Tell students: treasury instruments (or *money market statements*) refer to financial tools used by banks and financial institutions to transfer and represent funds. Examples include treasury bills, federal agency securities, municipal notes, and certificates of deposit.

Have students use reliable Internet or print resources to research U.S. treasury instruments. Tell students to find information such as types of instruments available, average yields over the past decade, and how the government uses the money generated. Ask students to create a collage-type poster

advertising the benefits of buying U.S. treasury instruments. Students may include text boxes and statistical graphs along with the images in their posters. Display posters in the classroom. **OL**

Personal Finance Handbook

Credit and You:
Use it, don't abuse it

How can you buy a hot new car if you don't have $25,000? Can you avoid the credit card trap? Whenever you buy something but don't have the cash, you're using credit. Mastering the wise use of credit gives you a head start on financial fitness.

Are You Creditworthy?

"Credit" means borrowing someone else's money. In exchange for the loan, you'll have to pay back more than you borrow. That's called interest. It's a percentage of the borrowed amount.

Who Decides? Lenders decide whether to lend you money and how much interest to charge by looking at three things:

1. **Can you pay them back?** Add your monthly income to your bank account balances to find your total assets. Then total your monthly expenses, including debts (obligations). Compare the two to see if you're able to take on more debt.

YOUR CAPACITY TO REPAY DEBT

Monthly income
+ Checking account
+ Savings account
= **Your assets**

Compared to

Monthly expenses
+ Total debt
= **Your obligations**

2. **Do you have a good credit rating?** Lenders want to know if you've repaid previous debts on time.

3. **Do you have collateral?** Collateral is used mostly to buy homes or cars. If you don't make the payments, the lender takes the property.

Your Credit Score Like your shadow, your credit score, or credit rating, follows you throughout your life. It's a number from 300 to 900 that shows how responsible you've been with your finances—recently and in the past. The higher your score is, the more likely you are to get credit and a low interest rate.

Credit scores are assigned by three credit bureaus—Equifax, Experion, and TransUnion—that track each person's financial history and create credit reports. Check yours at least once a year to be sure it contains no incorrect information.

Tip **Check Your Credit**
You can get one free report per year from each credit bureau. Call 877-322-8228; write to Annual Credit Report Request Service, P.O. Box 105281, Atlanta, GA 30348-5281; or go to www.annualcreditreport.com.

R10   PERSONAL FINANCE HANDBOOK

Extending the Content

Credit Score Killers A person's credit score is determined by a mixture of five elements. In order of importance, these elements are: payment history, debt, length of credit history, new credit, and types of credit used. A person's amount of income is not figured in to their credit score. For instance, if you have a large income, but never pay your bills, you will have a low credit score.

According to *FDIC Consumer News*, people commonly make seven simple mistakes that lower their credit scores: 1) paying bills after the due date; 2) not paying the minimum amount required; 3) keeping high credit card balances; 4) owning too many credit cards; 5) not regularly checking your credit report; 6) not using your full legal name in bank accounts and financial documents; 7) not alerting creditors when moving to a different address.

How Do You Score?

Paying on time raises your credit score; paying late lowers it. Here's how:

Good Credit!

You buy a DVD on credit, with payments due on the 1st of each month → You make payments on time → Store tells credit bureaus you made timely payments → Credit bureaus raise your credit score

You buy a DVD on credit, with payments due on the 1st of each month → You fail to make payments on time → Store tells credit bureaus your payments were late → Credit bureaus lower your credit score

Bad Credit!

Credit Cards

When you use a credit card, you're *borrowing* money that must be paid back—*plus interest*. Card issuers set a limit on the total amount you can spend. Smart borrowers avoid reaching that limit because it lowers their credit score.

Once you've established credit, you'll get offers for many cards. To avoid the temptation to rack up debt, keep no more than two or three. Choose those with the lowest annual percentage rates (APR)—not just low introductory rates that bounce up later. Be sure to read the fine print on the contracts—all of it.

The Price vs. the Real Cost The longer it takes you to pay off your credit card balance (the total amount you owe), the more the items you bought with the card actually cost. That's because card issuers make their profits by charging interest—from 1 to 25 percent or more—*on the amount still owed.*

Example: If you pay cash for a pair of $100 sneakers, they cost $100. If you use a credit card at an interest rate of 18.9% and take a year to pay it off, they cost $118.90 or more, depending on how the interest is calculated.

The Credit Card Trap Every month, you'll get a statement listing everything you bought in the previous month, payments you made, and the balance. You are usually allowed to pay less than the total balance as long as you make at least the "minimum payment due" listed on the statement. This is how many people fall into the credit trap: they make only the minimum payment, racking up more debt month after month.

Did You Know?

▶ **Endless Payments**
It will take you almost 22 years to pay off a $1,000 charge on an average credit card if you pay only a 2 percent minimum payment. The $1,000 purchase will wind up costing you $3,000—$2,000 of it in interest!

PERSONAL FINANCE HANDBOOK R11

Personal Finance

D Differentiated Instruction

Intrapersonal Have students reflect upon their recent shopping experiences. Ask them to draw from these recollections to write a short essay explaining how they think credit cards affect shoppers. *(Many students will write that credit cards influence a shopper to buy more because they are so easy to use.)* **OL**

C Critical Thinking

Speculating Ask: What would cause credit card companies to go out of business? *(if all of their card holders paid their entire balances on time)* Do you think the companies are worried about that occurring? Why or why not? *(no; American consumers have a long tradition of spending more than they can pay for)* **OL**

Activity: Collaborative Learning

Identifying Points of View Inform students that many people believe that credit is too easily accessible and restrictions should be enacted. Others believe that the problem of credit card debt has been exaggerated. Organize the class into several small groups. Have each group research the different arguments regarding credit and then create a multimedia presentation on the major points of both sides. Tell students not to take sides for this project. They should adopt the mindset of an impartial journalist seeking to fairly represent both sides of an issue. **OL**

Reference Section

S Skill Practice

Visual Literacy Have students suppose that the credit card statement shown on this page was sent to them. **Ask:** How much do you have to pay to avoid accruing additional interest charges for the next month? *($1,650)* By when must CreditCo National Bank receive this payment before additional charges will be added? *(July 15)* **BL**

R Reading Strategy

Visualizing Have students review the different forms of retail store credit described on this page. Ask them to draw a diagram with visual images depicting the three types of credit. Students may use any type of visual format they choose, including cartoons, pictures, or their own original art. **OL**

Additional Resources

Personal Finance Handbook

Sample Credit Card Statement

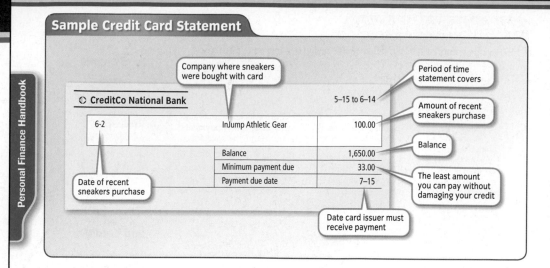

Company where sneakers were bought with card

Period of time statement covers

Amount of recent sneakers purchase

Balance

The least amount you can pay without damaging your credit

Date of recent sneakers purchase

Date card issuer must receive payment

◯ CreditCo National Bank		5–15 to 6–14
6-2	InJump Athletic Gear	100.00
	Balance	1,650.00
	Minimum payment due	33.00
	Payment due date	7–15

Other Sources of Credit

There are a number of ways to borrow money besides credit cards. These include relatives and friends, as well as retail stores and financial institutions, such as banks, credit unions, and savings and loan associations.

Retail Stores Most department stores and other retailers let customers with good credit buy merchandise from their stores with one of three types of credit:

- *Installment sales credit:* Major items like refrigerators are often bought by making equal payments, which include interest and service charges, over a set period of time.
- *Regular charge accounts:* You can buy goods or services within a set dollar limit by agreeing to pay off the balance in the future. Interest is charged only if the balance is not paid in 30 days.
- *Revolving credit:* You usually make no deposit but can buy items on credit on an ongoing basis, up to a certain dollar limit. If you repay the balance by a certain date, some stores charge no interest; most charge interest on each month's unpaid balance. Credit cards are also a type of revolving, or open-ended, credit.

Service providers Your agreements with providers of services (electricity, cell phone, Internet, etc.) are credit arrangements. The history of your payments to them often appears on credit reports—especially if you pay late.

Did You Know?

▶ **Revolving Debt** By 2005, Americans owed $750 billion in revolving debt—six times more than they did 20 years before.

Extending the Content

Early Credit Cards The concept of making purchases on credit dates back to ancient times. The credit card, however, is a more recent phenomenon. Diners Club issued the first "plastic money" in 1950. Holders of the Diners Club card could use it to charge meals at 27 restaurants in New York City. In 1958 Bank of America issued the first bank credit card: the BankAmericard (now Visa). The concept gradually gained popularity. By 1965 there were five million credit cards in use. Three decades later Americans owned nearly 1.4 billion credit cards. Technology is partly to blame for the increase in credit cards: computerized approvals make validating charges quick and easy, and online shops typically allow customers to utilize credit cards to purchase goods and services.

Financial Institutions Commercial banks, savings banks, credit unions, finance companies, and some insurance companies lend money, with varying interest rates and fees. Shop and compare costs before borrowing. Some loans require a single, lump-sum payment on a specific date; others accept monthly payments for either a set or indefinite period of time.

Comparing Costs

As with credit cards, the length of time it takes you to repay the balance of a loan from other creditors affects the total amount you pay. You can see in the table below that when you take longer to pay off a loan, you pay less each month, but your total cost is higher. That is because interest gets compounded over a longer period of time.

COSTS OF 3- AND 5-YEAR INSTALLMENT LOANS

$10,000 loan at 12% interest compounded annnually

	3-year loan	5-year loan
Number of monthly payments	36	60
Amount of each payment	$347	$231
Total interest paid	$2,492	$3,770

The annual percentage rate (APR) of the loan also affects the total amount you pay. Be sure to check it before signing any loan agreement.

APR COMPARISON
5-year Loan of $8,000

	Lender A	Lender B
APR	11%	13%
Monthly payment	$174	$180
Total interest to be paid	$2,436	$2,921
Total cost	$10,436	$10,921

HOW TO ESTABLISH CREDIT

Paying cash for everything does not make you a good credit risk. To prove you're responsible enough to get credit, you have to establish a credit history.

About 15% of a credit score is based on *how long you've had credit.* So it's important to establish credit as soon as possible.

1. Apply for a "secured credit card" at a bank. You'll have to make a deposit—usually about $300—and you'll get a credit card you can use to make purchases up to the amount you deposited. Buy something each month with the card and be sure to make monthly payments on time. After about a year, if you've paid off the balance, you can get your deposit back and switch your secured credit card to an unsecured one.

2. Open an account at a major retail store. (They will probably ask for your current bank credit card number and expiration date.) Buy something on credit and make the payments on time.

3. Have someone with good credit co-sign a credit application. A co-signer agrees to pay your debt if you don't.

Personal Finance

R Reading Strategy

Determining Importance Have students write a paragraph explaining why a "secured credit card" could be important to them someday. *(students should discuss how a secured credit card offers them the opportunity to build a positive credit rating)* **OL**

S Skill Practice

Analyzing Information Have students review information in the installment loan table to gain a thorough understanding of the concept it illustrates.
Ask: Suppose Homebuyer A took out a 30-year mortgage and Homebuyer B took out a 15-year mortgage. Which Homebuyer will end up paying more interest? *(Homebuyer A)* Given the additional interest expense, why would that person take out such a mortgage? *(lower monthly payments)* **OL**

Activity: Technology Connection

Loan Payments Organize students into pairs. Have each pair use a computer to create a file (such as a spreadsheet) that will calculate monthly payments and total loan cost based on varying APR rates. Students can model their work after the table at the bottom of page R13. Tell students that their files should be able to make calculations based on varying loan amounts and APR rates. After they have finished, test their work by entering different amounts and rates. **AL**

Teacher Tip

Technology Connection Some students may have difficulty understanding the concept of APR and how to make the necessary calculations. Try to assign partners with above average math skills to those students.

W Writing Support

Narrative Writing Ask students to write a cautionary tale about a person who became a victim of identity theft. Stories should describe mistakes the person made that increased his or her vulnerability, what the thief did after stealing the victim's identity, and the changes the victim made afterwards to prevent future thefts. **OL**

D Differentiated Instruction

Auditory/Musical Have students write a song, rap, or jingle about the tips on this page regarding identity theft. The goal of the song is to create a catchy way for people to remember the tips. Ask for volunteers to perform their songs, raps, or jingles for the class. **OL**

Shredding old financial documents helps guard against identity theft.

Identity Theft

Criminals could steal your name, social security number, date of birth, and other private information—and use it to run up debts in your name: credit cards, wireless phone accounts, or loans. Here are some tips to help protect your identity; find more at www.idtheftcenter.org.

- Be careful who sees your personal information. Never provide it on the Internet or by phone to anyone who contacts *you*. Banks don't request private information by e-mail.
- Thieves sort through people's trash and mailboxes. Shred statements that include account numbers and any unused offers of credit cards you receive in the mail.
- Always know where your cards are. When you buy something with a card, watch to see that it's not copied and get it back as quickly as possible.
- Check your credit report periodically for accuracy.
- Report lost or stolen credit cards immediately to the fraud department of a credit bureau. You're liable for only the first $50 after your report.
- Do business only with companies that will provide their name, street address, and phone number.
- Don't use the links in an e-mail to get to any Web page. Type the Web address in your browser window. A secure site begins with "https://" rather than "http://".

R14 **PERSONAL FINANCE HANDBOOK**

Activity: Interdisciplinary Connection

Daily Life Tell students: The U.S. Federal Trade Commission reports that 3.3 million Americans had their identities fraudulently used to open bank, credit card, or utility accounts, resulting in losses of $32.9 billion to businesses and $3.8 billion to individuals in 2002. The report also stated that account theft, such as use of stolen credit cards and automatic teller machine (ATM) cards, victimized 6.6 million Americans, resulting in losses of $14 billion to businesses and $1.1 billion to individuals.

Have students search the Internet, newspapers, or magazines for stories about people who were victims of identity theft. Ask students to research the effects of identity theft on the victims. Have students write a paper describing the experiences of the victims and the hardships they experienced while trying to restore their credit rating. Encourage students to close their reports with suggestions about what they believe lawmakers should do about identify theft. **OL**

CREDIT BASICS

Annual percentage rate (APR): The percentage of interest you are charged for every year you owe money. A fixed APR will stay the same; a variable APR will rise and fall with changes in national economic indicators.

Compounding: The process of charging interest on the amount of interest still owed. This interest is added to the stated interest rate because it's money you owe but have not yet paid.

EXAMPLE: If the stated APR on a $10,000 loan is 10%, you'd expect to pay $1,000 in interest per year (10% of $10,000). But since lenders compound interest, you may pay an extra $47 on the same $10,000 loan—for a total interest of $1,047. Some lenders compound interest more often—even daily. The more often interest is compounded, the more you will owe.

Delinquent payment: A payment that is 30 days or more past due. This is not the same as a late payment, which is one received after the due date but before it's 30 days past due. If a car payment due on the first of the month is received on the 20th, for example, it's late and you'll pay a late charge. But it's not delinquent and won't appear on your credit report.

Grace period: A period of time after you buy something on credit during which some creditors charge no interest if you pay the balance before the due date.

Finance charge: The total cost of credit. In addition to interest, some companies charge fees for annual membership, cash advances, services, transactions, and exceeding the credit limit.

Introductory rate: A lower rate of interest offered by some credit card companies to persuade consumers to apply for their card. After an initial period, the APR you're charged increases. It's important to read the fine print on the offer to find out when the APR increases and whether the low rate applies only to balances you transfer from another credit card, to new purchases, or to both. You also need to know how long you have to transfer balances; some cards feature a fixed APR on balance transfers for the life of the card; others for only 45 days to six months.

Did You Know?

▶ *A Big Difference*
Your credit score makes a big difference in the interest rates lenders charge. For example, a person with a credit score of 720 or above applying for a 3-year loan to buy an $18,000 car may pay 7.258% interest. The same dealer might charge a person with a credit score between 500 and 559 a rate of 15.294% for the same loan. At the end of the 3 years, the first applicant would have paid $2,085 in interest; the applicant with the low credit score would have paid $4,557.

Test Your Financial Fitness

1. **Summarizing** Why is a good credit score important?
2. **Identifying** What are two ways to establish good credit?
3. **Listing** List two ways to avoid paying interest when you buy something.
4. **Applying** Analyze three credit card offers your family has received in the mail or that you have seen advertised. Which one offers the best deal? Why?

PERSONAL FINANCE HANDBOOK   R15

Assess/Close

S Skill Practice

Using Practical Mathematics Have students review the bracketed feature about credit scores. Ask them to calculate interest on a 3-year loan to buy a car costing $21,500 at each of the credit scores listed. Direct students to an online loan calculator to make this calculation. (*at 7.258% interest, the total would be $2,491; at 15.294% interest, the total would be $5,441.*) **OL**

Test Your Financial Fitness

Answers:

1. Credit score determines the likelihood of receiving a loan and the interest rate charged if a loan is granted.
2. apply for a "secured credit card" and make monthly payments on time; pay off the entire balance of a credit card bill
3. pay with cash; pay the entire credit card balance before the due date
4. Answers will vary. Students should provide logical reasons for their selection of the offer they believe is the best deal.

Activity: Hands-On Economics

Viewing your Credit Report Have students enlist the assistance of a parent or guardian to visit www.annualcreditreport.com and access either their own free credit report or the free credit report of a family member from either Equifax, TransUnion, or Experian. Ask students, after they have completed the task, to write about their experience. They should describe how user-friendly the process was, if their report was accurate, and if they would recommend that others use the Web site to access their credit reports. Some parents may not want their children to access their credit report, while some students may not yet have a credit score. In such cases, have students review the www.annualcreditreport.com Web site and write a report about the information and services it provides. **OL**

Focus

C Critical Thinking

Making Decisions Have students consider what they will do after graduation. Ask them to write an essay describing their educational or career plans along with explanations for why they are favoring that course of action. After completing this feature, have students revisit their essays and write an addendum paragraph explaining if the textbook material caused them to reconsider or more firmly commit to their plans. **OL**

Teach

R Reading Strategy

Identifying Ask students to make a list of 10 colleges or vocational schools within a 50-mile (use a longer distance if necessary) radius of their house. For each school listed, have students write one reason why a high school graduate would want to attend that institution. **BL**

Additional Resources

Your Education:
Jump-start your future

Is college for you? Which one? How can you pay for it? Whether you plan to attend college or enroll in vocational training after high school, don't let rising costs keep you from realizing your dreams.

Why Go to College?

A college education enriches a life in ways that can't be measured in dollars. But there's a practical reason to continue your education beyond high school, too: what you learn usually determines what you earn. Compared to workers with only high-school educations, those with bachelor's degrees have greater lifelong earning power and are less likely to be unemployed.

College-degreed workers earn an average of 62 percent more than those with high-school educations—roughly $2 million more overall during their working years.

Unemployment and Earnings			
Full-Time Workers Age 25 and Over by Educational Level			
Education Level	Unemployment Rate	Median Annual Earnings	
		Males	Females
No high school diploma	8.8%	$19,802	$10,613
High school diploma/GED	5.5%	$27,526	$15,972
Bachelor's degree (4 years)	3.3%	$55,188	$34,292

Source: *Statistical Abstract of the United States*, 2006.

Did You Know?

➤ **How Much Is It?**
A bachelor's degree can cost between $48,000 and $116,000, depending on the school. That's for tuition, fees, room, and board—but not transportation or living expenses.

Choosing the Right School

Some schools are better at certain fields of study than others. Costs, too, vary widely from school to school. Consider these factors when choosing a college or vocational school:

- *Your goals:* Can you get the educational experience you want at a public school? If not, don't rule out a private school because of cost; some are generous with financial aid. Another option is to start out at an inexpensive community college and transfer to a four-year school.
- *Income potential:* If you choose a career with high income potential—like medicine or computer engineering—you can afford to take on a higher debt at an expensive school.
- *Location:* Out-of-state students pay a surcharge—usually thousands of dollars a year—to attend public universities. Costs also vary in different parts of the country.

R16   PERSONAL FINANCE HANDBOOK

Activity: Hands-On Economics

Determining Entrance Requirements Have students research the academic requirements of five colleges of their choosing. Ask students to create a chart comparing the requirements of the different schools. Students should include information such as minimum high school GPA, class rank, minimum ACT or SAT score, and any other academic requirements the chosen college may have. Students should also make a separate chart that lists due dates for admissions, financial aid, housing, and parking applications. Finally, students should obtain campus maps from the Web sites or catalogs of their five colleges. Students should circle or highlight the college administration offices on the maps. **Tell students:** Although applying for college includes many deadlines and applications, organizing the necessary information, and planning out beforehand where to file the applications will make the process much easier and less overwhelming. **OL**

Comparative Costs and Financial Aid

4-Year Public and Private Colleges, Academic Year 2005–2006

Type of Institution	Cost and tuition and fees	Total cost	Percentage of students qualifying for financial aid	Average aid amount (loans and grants)
Four-year private	$21,235	$29,026	76%	$11,600
Four-year public	$5,491	$12,127*	62%	$6,200

*Average annual costs at two-year public community colleges are about half those of four-year public colleges.

Personal Finance Handbook

Financial Aid Basics

Tuition is the amount a school charges for instruction. This does not include room, food, books, or other fees. In recent years, the cost of college tuition has risen faster than incomes or inflation. Few parents can afford the full cost of educating their children, and so most students need financial aid. The good news is that most students qualify for some type of financial aid. It takes research to find it, so the sooner you start looking, the better. How much aid you receive depends on these criteria:

- income—yours and your parents' or guardians'
- family assets and expenses
- number of college students in your family
- amount of aid available at the school
- number of students applying for aid and their financial need compared with yours

THE COST OF EDUCATION

Total Cost (tuition, board, books, fees, living expenses)
− **Total Aid** (loans, scholarships, grants, work-study)
= **What you owe**

Types of Aid Available Apply for all types of financial aid for which you may be qualified, including:

Scholarships and grants: Both are outright gifts you don't have to pay back. Most scholarships are based on academic, athletic, or artistic ability. Many companies offer them to employees' children, and some states provide them to residents; for example, Georgia guarantees free tuition to drug-free students with at least a B average.

Tip **Advanced Credit**
You can lower college costs by taking advanced placement courses in high school and by scoring high on the College-Level Examination Program (CLEP) test. You'll get college credits for what you already know.

PERSONAL FINANCE HANDBOOK   R17

S Skill Practice

Using Tables and Charts Have students use the information in the table to create a bar graph comparing the costs and the average aid amounts at private and public colleges. **Ask:** What is the difference in total cost between a four-year private and a four-year public school? *($16,899)*
OL

C Critical Thinking

Problem-Solving Ask: How can you get a start on paying for college before you graduate from high school?
(Answers may include: taking advanced level classes may count as college credit and may help assist students in passing CLEP tests; excelling at academics, art, or sports may result in a scholarship.) **OL**

Extending the Content

Rising Costs of Education The cost of higher education was not always quite so burdensome for American families. In 1970 the average in-state tuition at a public four-year college was $427. A decade later this figure had nearly doubled to $840. By 1990 tuition charges at four-year public colleges averaged $2,035. In 2005 the average tuition rate had reached $5,038, more than 10 times greater than it was only 35 years ear-

lier. Charges at private institutions rose at a similar rate. In 1970 the average tuition at a four-year private college was $1,809. By 2005 this figure had ballooned to $18,838.

One way of bringing the high cost of a college education down is by attending a community college. Tuition and fees at community colleges average just $2,076, less than half of the average tuition rate at four-year public colleges. Students can

attend a community college for two years, then transfer to a four-year college or university with substantial savings. University students can also save money by taking summer classes at community colleges. Many community colleges also offer their courses to high school juniors and seniors, allowing them to earn college credit before they graduate from high school.

D Differentiated Instruction

English Language Learners Have students reread the text on this page and make a list of three words that are unfamiliar to them. Ask students to then look up the words in a dictionary and write three new sentences using the words (one sentence for each word). **ELL**

S Skill Practice

Using Tables and Charts Have students study the FAFSA image on this page.

Ask: If you applied for state aid for the 2006–2007 academic year, by what date would you have needed to have submitted your application? *(Answers will vary based on the students' state.)* What are three pieces of information you would have needed to complete the FAFSA worksheet? *(Answers may include Social Security number, driver's license number, and federal income tax return for 2005.)* **OL**

Additional Resources

Personal Finance Handbook

Some grants, such as federal Pell grants and Supplemental Educational Opportunity grants, are awarded for "exceptional financial need." Others are given to students belonging to a certain ethnic group, club, or civic organization. The armed forces offer aid in return for military service after graduation.

Work-study programs: Many colleges offer federally funded, on-campus jobs to students receiving financial aid.

Loans: More than half of all financial aid is in the form of loans—which *must* be repaid. Regardless of your income, you probably qualify for one of these loans:

- *Government loans:* The U.S. Department of Education (DOE) offers low-interest loans to students and parents. Some are subsidized (the government pays the interest until you're out of school) and are based on need; others are unsubsidized (interest accrues while you're in school) and are not need based. In order of desirability, they are
  a. subsidized Perkins Loan
  b. subsidized Stafford or Direct Loan
  c. unsubsidized Stafford or Direct Loan
  d. unsubsidized Parent Loans for Undergraduate Students (PLUS)
- *Private and college-sponsored loans:* Private loans are available from banks and other financial institutions. Interest rates are generally higher than those of federal loans.

Aid Application 1-2-3 Once you've been accepted at several schools, follow this loan application process:

1. *Gather up documents.* You'll need proof of income, such as tax returns, W-2 forms, pay stubs; mortgage statements; and proof of any unusual financial hardships in the family, such as high medical expenses or unemployment.

2. *Find aid sources.* Use the Internet to find grants and scholarships, then loans. Be sure to check deadlines.

3. *Fill out and send in applications.* The first form to complete is the Free Application for Federal Student Aid (FAFSA), available from your high school, library, or DOE's Web site. It's needed for any type of government aid. DOE will send you a number called an *Expected Family Contribution* (EFC), which is an amount computed according to a formula established by law. Colleges use it to determine the amounts of grants, loans, and work-study awards.

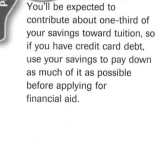

Maximizing Aid You'll be expected to contribute about one-third of your savings toward tuition, so if you have credit card debt, use your savings to pay down as much of it as possible before applying for financial aid.

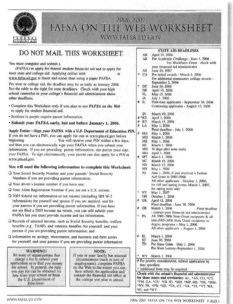

R18 PERSONAL FINANCE HANDBOOK

Activity: Technology Connection

The Department of Education Web site Have students visit the U.S. Department of Education financial aid Web site (http://www.ed.gov/finaid). Ask students to use the site to research one topic that is not discussed, or only briefly mentioned, on this page of the textbook. Examples may include student loan consolidation, checking your financial aid history, or finding information on what questions to ask if you are thinking about attending a career college or technical school. Have students write a report describing the topic they selected and how they might use the information they found at the Web site. **OL**

W **Writing Support**

Persuasive Writing Discuss as a class the information presented in this feature. Ask students to write a persuasive essay describing the accessibility of higher education in the United States today. Students should defend a position such as "through financial aid, a college education is still widely attainable today" or "spiraling costs have shut the door on too many young Americans seeking a college education." **OL**

Payback You don't begin repaying some government loans until after you're out of school. Other loans, such as PLUS loans, require you to begin making payments within 60 days after you receive the funds. Since unsubsidized loans accrue (accumulate) interest while you're still in school, you'll want to pay those off first. For some loans, you can repay just the interest for a period of time or start with smaller payments that increase as your income presumably increases. Some lenders even tie payment amounts to rises and drops in your income level.

Graduates who take teaching jobs in certain schools; who volunteer with the Peace Corps, Americorps, or VISTA; or who serve in the military may have their federal loans deferred, partially repaid, or even canceled.

It's important to repay your loan on schedule to avoid penalties and damage to your credit, as well as to reduce the amount of interest you pay. Some lenders lower the principal or the interest rate if you make on-time payments. Your lender or the school's financial aid office can help you establish a workable repayment plan.

Did You Know?

▶ *Payback* The average student graduates from a 4-year college with a debt of almost $19,000. About 60 percent of all students receive grants—averaging $3,300 at public, four-year schools in 2004–2005.

Test Your Financial Fitness

Answers:

1. males: $27,662; females: $18,320

2. Answers will vary according to student preferences, but should include things that will assist the student in choosing a college or vocational school.

3. Answers will vary according to schools selected.

Test Your Financial Fitness

1. **Stating** How much more money will the average college graduate earn per year than someone with only a high school diploma?

2. **Listing** List four things that are important to you in choosing a college or vocational school. Using the Internet or library resources, find three schools that meet your criteria.

3. **Applying** Choose one of the schools you identified above and calculate how much it would cost to attend that school for one year. Then find two types of financial aid for which you might qualify.

PERSONAL FINANCE HANDBOOK   R19

Activity: Collaborative Learning

Paying for College Divide the class into small groups. Have each group write and perform a skit depicting a high school student who hopes to attend college but does not know how he or she will be able to afford it. Skits should incorporate the information included in this textbook feature. Beyond that requirement, groups may use a wide range of ideas for their skits. For example, a group may wish to perform a dramatic piece in which a student has a difficult conversation with his parents about family finances. Or a group may perform a comedic skit featuring a costumed monster representing tuition costs and a knight in armor representing government loans. **OL**

R20

Focus

W Writing Support

Personal Writing Have students recall the work experiences they have had thus far in their lives. These experiences may include paid jobs such as paper routes and bagging groceries or unpaid chores done around the house. Ask students to write a short paper describing what their past work experiences have taught them about the type of job they would or would not like in the future. **OL**

Teach

C Critical Thinking

Making Connections Have students use the resources listed in the section to make a list of 5 actual jobs in their town that interests them. For each item on their list, ask students to write a sentence explaining why they might want to apply for that job at this point in their lives. **OL**

Additional Resources

Personal Finance Handbook

Getting a Job:
Make it work for you

Where are the jobs? What are your skills? Do you need a resume? Whether you're searching for a summer job or planning to enter the labor market right after high school, looking for work is hard work. Knowing where to look and how to present yourself can help you land a better job.

The Right Job

Besides earning money and learning good work habits, use your first few jobs to find out what tasks you like to do—and what you don't. Take the time to explore what interests you.

One good method is the "informational interview." Many businesspeople who may not have current job openings are willing to chat briefly with young job seekers. Call and ask if they have a few minutes to give you information about their field. Don't ask about job openings. Ask how they got their start in the field or what a typical day is like. Leave a resume and ask for names of others who might be helpful. You'll gain interviewing experience, contacts, and possibly a job lead. Always mail a handwritten thank-you note.

Eighty percent of jobs are never advertised in newspapers or online. Three-fourths of all employees find their jobs through networking.

Finding Openings

The best way to find a job is to ask family, friends, and acquaintances for leads. It's called networking. Everyone you meet is a potential source of information about a job—now or in the future. Other resources include:

- *"Help Wanted" Signs:* Walk around town or the mall and apply in person. Dress appropriately and be ready for an on-the-spot interview and application.
- *Newspapers and the Internet:* Your local newspaper carries help-wanted ads every day. On the Internet, you can find job postings and post your resume.
- *Placement Agencies:* Free state-run employment services match qualifications with available jobs. Private placement companies charge applicants or employers; ask who pays before signing up.
- *Start Your Own Business:* Teenagers start businesses every day. Not all teen businesses are financially successful, but they all provide invaluable experience that impresses college admissions officers and potential employers.

Tip **Be the Boss**
For ideas and advice for teen entrepreneurs (people who own their own businesses), check out the Web sites of the Small Business Administration (www.sba.org) and Junior Achievement (www.ja.org).

R20   PERSONAL FINANCE HANDBOOK

Activity: Collaborative Learning

Categorizing Job Sources Divide the class into several small groups. Have each group ask 20 people with jobs how they found their current position. The people a group interviews must have different job titles from each other—none of the 20 job titles should be a repeat. Ask student groups to create a two-column chart listing the job titles and the ways the people they interviewed found their jobs. Next, have all groups combine their results into one report and determine the percentages for each job source category (for example, networking, Internet, newspaper, and so on). Discuss the combined results as a class. **OL**

Getting in the Door

For some jobs, like retail sales, you'll see a sign in the window and can simply walk in and complete an application. But most employers expect you to send a resume and cover letter first.

Your Resume: A resume is a document that summarizes your experience, skills, and education. Its purpose is to present you in the best possible light so that employers will contact you for an interview. You'll need more than one resume, since an effective one focuses on skills related to a *specific job*. These tips can help you get started:

1. Make a list of everything you've accomplished in your life. You can use it to identify skills that relate to various jobs, now and in the future.

For every job opening, employers receive about 500 resumes and spend about 5 seconds glancing at each one.

Your Resume

White or off-white resume paper (with matching envelopes).

Name (bold type), address, phone number, e-mail address, if any.

Optional. If you list an objective, tailor it to the job you are applying for.

Your work and relevant volunteer experience (most recent first).

School graduation month and year. Revise when you have a diploma or job training.

Skill in other languages for a competitive edge. Also list all computer software programs and business equipment you can use.

Job-related activities, if possible. If your experience is minimal, a few unrelated ones show good citizenship.

John D. Smith
123 Main Street
Pasadena, CA 91101
(626) 555-7345
e-mail: jdsmith@myaddress.com

OBJECTIVE   A challenging part-time sales position in the auto industry.

EXPERIENCE

6/2007 to present   **Bagger, Star Market, Pasadena, CA**
Bag groceries after school, weekends and summers
Received employee of the month twice

1–5/2006   **Team Leader, Enterprise Project,
Pasadena High School, Pasadena, CA**
Working with three other students, manufactured
and sold $460 worth of plastic CD travel cases

9/2005–5/2006   **Office Assistant, Pasadena High School, Pasadena, CA**
Assisted secretary after school by correctly filing student
records, copying and distributing teaching materials

EDUCATION   Pasadena High School, will graduate in (month, year)

SKILLS   Speak Spanish fluently
Proficient in Microsoft Word, Excel and internet research
Cash register experience

ACTIVITIES   Oakdale Community Health Clinic, volunteer
National Honor Society

Personal Finance

D Differentiated Instruction

Verbal/Linguistic Tell students: You may wish to use a dictionary to answer the following questions. **Ask:** From which language does the word *resume* originate? *(French)* What are the three different ways to write the word *resume*? *(resume, résumé, or resumé)* **OL**

S Skill Practice

Making Inferences Ask: Why do you think more recent work experience should be listed first on a resume? *(Potential employers consider most recent work experiences most relevant in assessing the suitability of an applicant)* **OL**

A resume is sometimes called a vita, which means "a brief biographical sketch." The term vita is most commonly used in academic professions.

Activity: Hands-On Economics

Writing a Resume Have students suppose that they are 10 years older than they are now. Ask them to write a resume for this future version of themselves. They may wish to use the "John D. Smith" example on this page as a model. Encourage students to include an objective that reflects what they believe will be their future career interest.

Tell students to be optimistic, but realistic, in listing their achievements and experiences over the next decade. Have students exchange resumes with a partner. Students should provide feedback on the content and appearance of their partner's resume. **OL**

R Reading Strategy

Questioning Have students suppose that they are an employer seeking to fill a job opening (assign an appropriate position such as office assistant, salesperson, stocker, and so on). Ask students to write a list of at least five questions that they would like applicants' resumes and cover letters to answer. **OL**

C Critical Thinking

Identifying Points of View Ask: Why do you think cover letters should contain no more than three paragraphs after the opening? *(Employers receive a large number of cover letters and do not have time to read lengthy descriptions from each applicant.)* **OL**

Additional Resources

2. Get a description of the job you want from the company's Web site, ad, or human resources department. You can also check your local library for *The Dictionary of Occupational Titles* or the *Occupational Outlook Handbook* (also at http://stats.bls.gov/oco/oco1002.htm).

3. From your list of accomplishments, select those that match *this* job and list them in the "Experience" section of your resume (see the sample on the previous page for formatting). Be brief and use active verbs like *organized, developed,* or *implemented.* If you can truthfully claim results, do so: "raised $1,700" or "reduced filing errors by half."

4. Employers often toss resumes with typos or misspellings, so ask several people to proofread yours.

The Cover Letter: Your resume should be accompanied by a letter typed in a format similar to the sample below. First, state why you are interested in the company and where you heard about the opening. In the next two paragraphs (three at most), "sell" yourself: How will your skills be valuable to the employer? If an e-mailed resume was requested, type the cover letter in the e-mail itself.

Cover Letter

> John D. Smith
> 123 Main Street
> Pasadena, CA 91101
> (Date)
>
> Mrs. Helen Jones, Manager
> Sales and Marketing
> ABC Company
> 345 Central Avenue
> Pasadena, CA 91101
>
> Dear Mrs. Jones:
> I am an experienced sales person responding to your *Pasadena Press* ad for a part time sales assistant.
>
> ABC Company interests me because of its reputation as an aggressive marketer of high-quality auto parts. I also have a personal interest in cars and helped restore a 1957 Thunderbird last summer.
>
> I believe my skills could be useful to you in several areas:
> • Successful sales experience (CD travel cases)
> • Ability to track accurately (class treasurer for two years)
> • Excellent clerical skill: organizing, filing, photocopying
> I hope you will contact me at (626) 555-7345. I look forward to talking with you.
>
> Sincerely,
>
> *John Smith*
>
> John Smith
> Enclosure

Figure out what the employer needs and mention your skills that meet those needs.

Activity: Technology Connection

Learning to Write Cover Letters Have students use an Internet search engine to research techniques that can be used to write cover letters. Ask them to find at least three Web sites that contain useful information about how to write effective letters. Have students prepare an oral presentation that synthesizes the information they found at the sites they researched on how to write a cover letter. Then, have students compose sample cover letters for a position that the student may one day want to explore. Encourage students to use visual aids (such as sample cover letters or lists with bullet points) for their presentations to the class. **OL**

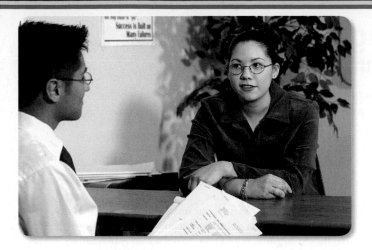

The Job Interview

Appearance is important, so dress appropriately for all interviews. Be prepared to answer questions like "Why do you want to work here?" Interviewers often ask this to see if you've researched the company's products, financial status, etc. You can request brochures from the company's human resource department or find this information on the Internet. Be ready to explain how your skills qualify you for the job.

Example: "Although I don't have professional sales experience, I believe the skills I demonstrated selling school raffle tickets will be useful to you. According to the product vendor, my aggressive selling efforts increased sales by 22 percent."

Before you leave, hand the interviewer a typed sheet listing three references: names, titles, companies, and phone numbers. Send a brief thank-you letter; summarize why you're right for the job and include your daytime phone number.

Test Your Financial Fitness

1. **Summarizing** What is the purpose of a resume?
2. **Listing** List ten of your accomplishments that you think demonstrate skills an employer might want.
3. **Applying** Write a resume applying for a job you would like to have. In the "Experience" section, incorporate some of the accomplishments you listed.
4. **Analyzing** List four questions an employer might ask you during an interview and the answers you would give.

Personal Finance

Assess/Close

R Reading Strategy

Summarizing Have students review the text in this feature, noting its main points. Ask students to write a pamphlet that summarizes the steps to getting a job. Students may include art in their pamphlets but should not overuse this option due to limited space. While reviewing the pamphlets, ask students to explain where they could be given out (job fairs, for example) and who they think would benefit the most from reading them. **OL**

Test Your Financial Fitness

Answers:

1. to summarize a jobseeker's experience, skills, and education in a way that encourages employers to call for an interview
2. Answers will vary according to student accomplishments.
3. Students should include some of the accomplishments they listed for Question 2.
4. Possible questions include: "What are your career goals?"; "Where do you see yourself in five years?"; "What assets will you bring to our company?"

Extending the Content

The Best Jobs in America In 2006 *Money Magazine* and Salary.com published a list of the 50 best jobs in America. Occupations were rated based such factors as salary, number of openings, stress level, and possibilities for advancement. In addition, each job required at least a bachelor's degree. The top 10 jobs and their average pay for 2006 were: 1) software engineer - $80,427; 2) college professor - $81,491; 3) financial advisor - $122,462; 4) human resources manager - $73,731; 5) physician assistant - $75,117; 6) market research analyst - $82,317; 7) computer/IT analyst - $83,427; 8) real estate appraiser - $66,216; 9) pharmacist - $91,998; and 10) psychologist - $66,359.

Personal Finance Handbook

Paying Taxes:
Simplify the annual event

Who pays taxes? How do you file a return? If you have an income or buy anything, you'll pay taxes, regardless of your age. Being organized can make the process easier and maybe save you some money.

What Taxes?

The largest chunk of tax money goes to the federal government to fund programs such as the military, retirement security, space exploration, aid to foreign countries, and disaster recovery. When you see news reports about arguments in Congress over the budget, they're arguing about how to spend your tax dollars. States, cities, and other entities also assess taxes for various purposes.

Federal Income Tax Money you earn is taxable, including wages, tips, interest earned by bank accounts, and profits from the sale of property, like cars or stocks. Every year, the Internal Revenue Service (IRS) sets a taxable minimum income. If you earn more than that, it's taxed—even income from self-employment like babysitting or mowing lawns.

The IRS is the agency within the U.S. Treasury Department that administers tax laws and provides forms and advice. The IRS also has the power to ensure that people pay what they owe. It can assess penalties; charge interest on unpaid tax; confiscate wages, bank accounts, or property; and even imprison debtors for nonpayment. It's to your advantage to learn how to be a responsible taxpayer.

Notorious mafia boss Al "Scarface" Capone was never convicted of most of the violent crimes he allegedly committed—but he spent eight years in prison for not paying his taxes.

Other Taxes States, cities, and some school districts assess income taxes to pay for schools, fire protection, police, highways, and similar services. You'll file tax forms (returns) for those at the same time as you file your federal return. In most states, sales tax is added to the price of products sold in the state, including items bought online. Some states also assess this tax for online purchases when the seller does not have a "brick and mortar" store in that state. Then there are use (excise) taxes on things like gasoline, guns, gambling, tobacco, alcohol, and airline tickets. Finally, property owners pay taxes based on the value of their house or other real estate.

R24   PERSONAL FINANCE HANDBOOK

Extending the Content

Using Taxation to Influence Economic Decisions Government uses taxation not only to raise revenue, but also to influence the economic decisions of businesses and individuals. Government can adjust taxes to encourage business. State and local governments, for example, may reduce or eliminate taxes for a company to persuade it to locate in a particular area. Taxes also can be used to discourage activities. High taxes on cigarettes and alcohol are designed, in part, to discourage smoking and drinking. Similarly, customs duties make imports more expensive and discourage American customers from buying foreign goods.

Withholding If you haven't received your first paycheck yet, it will be an eye-opener. Employers are required by law to deduct—or "withhold"—a certain percentage of wages for taxes and other payments. These are listed on your pay stubs and include:

- **Federal taxes:** Your employer will withhold a part of your pay based on a table from the IRS. The more you earn, the higher the amount withheld.

- **State and city taxes:** The amount varies from state to state and from city to city. If you live in one city and work in another, your employer will withhold the tax for the city where you work. You may have to pay a separate income tax to the city where you live.

- **Social Security:** The Social Security system provides a financial safety net for retirees and disabled citizens who contributed to the system throughout their working lives. Your employer matches your contribution.

- **Medicare:** Everyone who receives Social Security benefits automatically receives Medicare Part A benefits, which partially cover stays in hospitals and skilled nursing facilities. (Other Medicare benefits must be purchased after you reach age 65.) Your employer matches this contribution as well.

- **Optional withholdings:** You may decide to have your employer deduct more money. For example, you might get health insurance through your work. (See **Insurance Matters** on page R32.) Many employers also offer automatic savings plans and match a part of your contributions. (See **Saving and Investing** on page R6.)

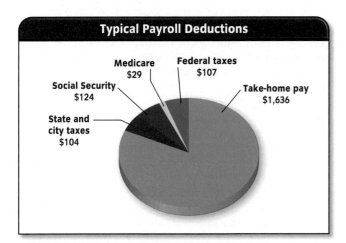

Typical Payroll Deductions

- Medicare $29
- Federal taxes $107
- Social Security $124
- Take-home pay $1,636
- State and city taxes $104

PERSONAL FINANCE HANDBOOK   R25

W Writing Support

Persuasive Writing Inform students that the future of Social Security has been a much-debated political issue in the past few years. Have students use reliable Internet or library resources to research several viewpoints on this topic. Ask students to write and deliver a speech supporting one of the major positions on what should be done to preserve the future of Social Security. **AL**

D Differentiated Instruction

Logical/Mathematical Have students suppose that this pie chart is based on their paycheck. **Ask:** What percentage of your gross earnings do you receive in take-home pay? *(81.8%)* **OL**

Activity: Collaborative Learning

Understanding Withholdings Organize the class into small groups. Have students research the types and purposes of each deduction withheld from a typical paycheck. Next, ask groups to perform a skit in which one of the students portrays a character who just received his or her first paycheck, but is confused by all the deductions. The other characters (a family member, boss, or friend, for example) will then explain the withholdings. Students may wish to create flashcards or visuals containing the correct terms for the withholding items to display to the class during their skits. **OL**

Personal Finance Handbook

C Critical Thinking

Contrasting Ask: What is the difference between a W-4 form and a W-2 form? *(A W-4 form is filled out at the time of employment indicating how much money an employee wants an employer to withhold; an employer sends a W-2 form in January listing wages and withholdings from the previous year.)* **OL**

S Skill Practice

Determining Cause and Effect
Ask: How did the Internet improve the taxpaying process for American citizens? *(taxpayers can now download forms rather than wait for them to be mailed; taxpayers can file their returns online and receive refunds sooner; taxpayers can use the IRS Web site to find answers to questions they may have)* **OL**

Additional Resources

Rock 'n' roll legend Jerry Lee Lewis's personal property was confiscated by the IRS twice for nonpayment of taxes. IRS agents took his cars, furniture, and piano and showed up at his concerts to collect gate receipts. Similar tax problems have sidetracked the finances of rapper M.C. Hammer and country singer Willie Nelson, among others.

Paperwork

Four kinds of paperwork are used in the tax process: a form you fill out when you're hired by a company (W-4), documentation of your income (W-2), your tax return, and records you'll need to complete the return.

W-4 Form When you start a job, you get a W-4 form on which you tell the employer how much money to withhold for federal income taxes. You choose the number of exemptions by asking yourself: Do I want to have the government keep the money for a year to make sure I don't spend it before tax time? Or, would I rather invest the money and make the payment in April? If more money is withheld than you owe, you'll get a refund, which makes tax season more pleasant. But your money is with the government instead of earning interest in a bank account or investment.

W-2 Form Every January, your employer(s) will send you a W-2 form listing your wages and withholdings for the previous year. If you don't receive yours by mid-February, call the employer. You'll attach this form to your tax return to prove your income.

Tax Return Every year, you'll complete a paper or online form telling the IRS how much tax you still owe or how much you believe should be refunded to you. If your income is below a certain level set annually by the IRS, you don't have to file a return, but you should anyway. It's the only way to get your refund. These guidelines may make it easier:

- *Forms:* The IRS will mail you a form and instructions. Free forms are also available at post offices, banks, libraries, and on the IRS Web site at www.irs.gov. Be sure your name and Social Security number are correct.
- *Deadline:* File any time between January 1 and April 15. If you file after April 15, you'll be charged a penalty and, if money is owed, interest on the amount owed.

INCOME TAX TERMS

Earned income: Wages, tips, and taxable scholarship and fellowship grants. You'll need to total these amounts to calculate your taxes.

Unearned income: Interest (from bank accounts, stocks, etc.) and dividends or capital gains from stocks.

Gross income: The total of earned and unearned income.

Adjusted gross income: Gross income minus deductions. This is the figure used to calculate the amount of your federal income tax.

R26 PERSONAL FINANCE HANDBOOK

Activity: Technology Connection

Comparing Tax Preparation Software Inform students that there are a variety of different computer programs designed to aid in the tax preparation process. Ask students to choose three different products and then compare them using manufacturers' Web sites as well as sites that review software products. Have students prepare a chart comparing the features, prices, and ratings for each tax preparation product. Ask students to select which product they would buy if they were currently in the market for a tax preparation program. **OL**

- *Deductions:* The amount you pay is a percentage of your income minus any eligible deductions. These are expenses that meet IRS guidelines, like donations to charity and interest on college loans.
- *Preparing your return:* Whether you're filing a paper or electronic return, you'll have to decide several things:
  1. What status to file under. For now, select "single."
  2. Whether you want to take the standard deduction or list (itemize) your eligible deductions separately. If you choose the standard deduction, you can use a simple 1040EZ form. Or, you can try to lower the amount you owe by itemizing deductions on a 1040 form. (More complicated taxes use other forms.) With this form, you may need help from a tax preparer, because tax regulations are complicated and change frequently. The IRS offers free advice by phone at 800-829-1040 or on its Web site. Some nonprofit organizations also offer free services to low-income taxpayers.

Your Records You have two choices for tax recordkeeping: you can wait until tax time and search for documentation, or start a file in January and keep handy the papers you'll need to file a return the next year. Here's what tax experts recommend keeping for four to seven years:

TAX RECORDS
- Pay stubs and W-2 forms
- Bank statements
- Receipts for major purchases and charitable donations
- Records of insurance and medical payments
- Proof of any theft losses: value, date missing, proof of ownership

Test Your Financial Fitness
1. **Stating** Who is responsible for paying income taxes?
2. **Explaining** Why do young workers have to contribute to the Social Security system?
3. **Defining** What is "adjusted gross income"?
4. **Locating** How can you find out how much money was withheld from your pay?
5. **Listing** List three forms you need to file your income tax.

PERSONAL FINANCE HANDBOOK   R27

Personal Finance

Assess/Close

C Critical Thinking

Defending Divide the class into two groups. Tell groups that they will be debating the following statement, "the tax preparation process is too complex." Assign one group the pro position and the other group the con position. Have students interview taxpayers, review IRS publications, and search the Internet for data to support their group's position. Ask groups to select several spokespeople for a multi-round classroom debate on this topic. Evaluate the effectiveness of the students' arguments. **OL**

Test Your Financial Fitness
Answers:
1. all citizens who earn more than the taxable minimum income
2. so the system can meet its current benefit payment requirements
3. gross income minus deductions
4. review a pay stub or, for the previous year, a W-2 form
5. 1040EZ or 1040 form for federal taxes, state income tax forms and W-2 form

Activity: Hands-On Economics

Filling out a Tax Return Have students suppose they earned $25,000 in wages and $500 in interest income last year. Tell them their employer withheld $1,500 in federal taxes and that they had no other sources of income. Ask students to fill out a 1040EZ tax return form (instructions and form are available at the www.irs.gov site) based on the above figures. Students may assume that they meet all other requirements for using the 1040EZ form. Have students who are able to quickly complete the form act as "tax preparation advisors" for those students having difficulty with this activity. **AL**

R27

Personal Finance Handbook

Focus

R Reading Strategy

Predicting Have students think about when they will be ready to rent their first apartment. **Ask:** How much do you think you will need to pay each month to live in an apartment? *(Answers will vary based on local rent rates. Students should also remember to consider the security deposit and the utilities that renters are responsible for paying.)* OL

Teach

W Writing Support

Personal Writing Have students write a short story describing what they think their first experience renting an apartment will be like. Tell students to include as many relevant details as possible, such as the town it will be in, possible roommates, size of the unit, appliances, parking, distance from school or work, and so on. OL

Additional Resources

Renting an Apartment:
Know what to look for

How much rent should you pay? How do you find the best deal? What if your roommate moves out? Moving to a new apartment can be exciting. Finding and renting one takes work. Making good decisions and meeting your responsibilities as a tenant can make it easier—and avoid money problems later on.

The Rental Process

Before you begin searching for an apartment, first consider how you'll pay for it. Rent is only the beginning. Tenants usually pay for heat, air conditioning, electricity, and sometimes water and garbage pick-up. Many landlords expect the first and last months' rent in advance, plus a security deposit they hold until tenants move. If you damage the property, your deposit pays for repairs. Any remainder should be returned to you, sometimes with interest, depending on local laws. If you own expensive items, you may want to add the cost of renter's insurance. Remember: rent plus utilities should generally equal no more than one-fourth of your monthly income.

Finding a Home Once you know how much you can afford, ask yourself:
- How close to school or a job do I want to live?
- Will I have roommates?
- How many rooms do I need?
- What else is important to me: Security? Noise level? Storage? Laundry facilities?

Begin your search with friends, newspaper ads, the Internet, bulletin boards, and/or rental agencies. Make appointments to view several apartments and be prepared to provide:
- identification
- social security number
- income amount and employer's name and phone number
- contact numbers for references (current or previous landlords, teachers, coaches, or employers) who can vouch for your character

R28   PERSONAL FINANCE HANDBOOK

Extending the Content

Renter's Insurance Many renters believe that their landlord's insurance policy would cover them if they lost their possessions due to fire or theft. This is not true. Landlords' policies cover their own property, not the possessions of their renters. Tenants need to take out their own policy—renter's insurance—to cover their possessions. People considering renter's insurance might be interested to learn that a recent U.S. Department of Justice report revealed that renters face a higher risk of theft than people who own their homes. According to the Department's Bureau of Justice Statistics, in 2005 renters experienced 192 property crimes per 1,000 households, while homeowners experienced 137 property crimes per 1,000 households.

Signing a Lease

You'll be required to sign a lease or a rental agreement. This is a binding legal contract, so read it—fine print and all—before signing. A lease requires the tenant to pay rent for the number of months listed—even if the tenant moves before the lease ends. Rental agreements are from month to month.

The Walk-Through Before signing anything, "walk through" the apartment with the landlord and note its condition. To safeguard your deposit, make sure any damages are listed on the lease. Take dated photos before you move in and when you move out.

The Right Roommates If you plan to share an apartment with roommates, be sure that they can afford the apartment and that they sign the lease to ensure equal legal responsibility. Make it clear that if they move before the lease ends, they're responsible for either paying their share of the rent until the lease ends or for finding replacement roommates. Agree on house rules up front: overnight guests, parties, chores, etc.

Rights and Responsibilities Your apartment is your home, but it belongs to the property owner. Landlords must keep it structurally safe and sanitary, and provide access to heat, water, and electricity. They can enter your apartment only to make repairs or show it to prospective tenants. In some states, they must give you advance notice. Prospective landlords can check references, employment, and credit, but it is against the law to discriminate on the basis of race, national origin, religion, gender, familial status, or disability. A local tenants' union can provide information and advice.

You're responsible for paying rent on time, keeping the apartment clean and in good condition, following the terms of the lease, and being considerate of neighbors. Remember: being a responsible tenant makes your new landlord a good reference for your next one.

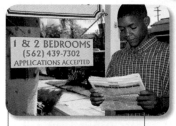

WALK-THROUGH CHECKLIST

❑ Sturdy door and window locks

❑ Working smoke and carbon monoxide detectors

❑ Fire exits in front and back

❑ Enough rooms, closets, and storage space

❑ Damages such as:
- _____ broken kitchen appliances or bathroom fixtures
- _____ stains, loose tiles, or large scratches on floors
- _____ cracks in windows or walls
- _____ stained or peeling wallpaper, or garish paint colors

Test Your Financial Fitness

1. **Explaining** What are two reasons for taking good care of a landlord's property?

2. **Listing** What costs are involved in renting an apartment?

3. **Applying** List four factors that would affect your choice of an apartment, in order of importance to you. Then explain why they're important.

Assess/Close

C Critical Thinking

Assessing Have students review the Walk-Through Checklist on this page. Ask them to expand upon it to include all the factors they should consider throughout the entire apartment-renting process (for example, roommates, location, landlord reputation, and so on). Have students exchange their lists with a partner and share advice about additional factors that could be added. **BL**

Test Your Financial Fitness

Answers:

1. to get the deposit back; to get a good reference

2. rent, security deposit, heat, air conditioning, electricity, water (sometimes), garbage pick-up (sometimes), and renter's insurance (optional)

3. Answers will vary. Students may list such factors as location, size, rent, noise level, and proximity of laundry facilities.

Activity: Interdisciplinary Connection

Art Organize the class into pairs. Inform the students in each pair that they are roommates renting their first apartment. Ask pairs to design a diorama of their two bedroom apartment. Students should personalize their own rooms and include a kitchen, living room, bathroom, and anything else that will be part of their living space. Students should attempt to create a realistic representation of an apartment they might rent in the next few years (no futuristic appliances, for example). Display completed dioramas around the classroom. **OL**

Focus

C Critical Thinking

Comparing Have students search the Internet and newspaper advertisements to select five different cars that they would consider buying, and that they could potentially afford in the next few years. To meet the latter requirement, encourage students to consider used automobiles. Ask students to use the Internet to gather information on the different cars and create a comparison chart that would help them decide which one to buy. Chart categories may include: price, mileage, warranty, safety rating, miles-per-gallon, and so on. **OL**

Teach

S Skill Practice

Drawing Conclusions Ask: From what do car dealers make most of their profits? *(loans)* Why do you think that is the case? *(finance charges and late fees make loans profitable ventures for lenders)* **OL**

Additional Resources

Personal Finance Handbook

Buying a Car:
Drive a good deal

Is a cool car in your future? Where will you get the money? Picture yourself in the car of your dreams. Wait: Now picture yourself under a mountain of debt. Before you rush to a Ferrari dealer, do the homework that can help you get a good deal on a vehicle that meets your needs now—and down the road.

Choosing Your Car

The most important step in the car-buying process is figuring out how much you can afford. Do this *before* deciding which car you want. In general, car payments should be less than 15 percent of your monthly income.

Do the Research Check the Internet or consumer publications for comparisons of:
- *Safety:* Is the car likely to protect you in a crash or poor road conditions, and avoid rolling over? Also find unbiased reviews at www.nhtsa.dot.gov.
- *Performance:* The number of miles per gallon of gasoline (fuel efficiency) and the impact a car makes on the environment (emissions) vary with the type of car. You can check both at www.fueleconomy.gov. High gas prices alone make it essential to check mileage. Hybrid cars are designed to use less gas and pollute less by running on a combination of gas and electricity, but they cost more up front than gasoline-powered cars.
- *Repairs:* Consumer publications list which vehicles require fewer repairs and cost less to fix.

Compare Financing Dealers make most of their profit on loans, not car sales. Before discussing financing with a dealer, research loans at banks and other financial institutions. Also check your credit score, since it determines whether you'll get a loan and how much interest you'll pay. (See **Credit and You** on page R10.) If you're applying for credit at more than one place, do it within a 14-day period. Otherwise, your credit rating will drop because of "too many inquiries."

Every car has a "pink slip," or title—a document that proves ownership. You won't get the pink slip until you've made all the payments. Meanwhile, the seller gives you a receipt you'll need to register your car and buy license tags.

R30   PERSONAL FINANCE HANDBOOK

Extending the Content

Car Advertising Selling cars is a big business in the United States. Automobile manufacturers invest billions of dollars in campaigns designed to entice buyers to select their product. In 2005, for example, nearly $21 billion was spent on automotive advertisements, making it the top ad spending category in the United States that year. Nearly half of that total ($9.9 billion) came in the form of television commercials. Car ads in newspapers and magazines totaled $6.3 billion and $2.4 billion, respectively. Car sellers also spent $1.6 billion on radio ads. Spending on car advertisements on the Internet totaled only $422 million in 2005.

Getting a Deal

A new car is exciting, offers warranties, and requires fewer repairs. But a new car depreciates (loses value) the minute you drive it off the lot. Used cars depreciate more slowly and cost a lot less to begin with. Some even offer limited warranties.

New Cars A cool head and a game plan can save you thousands of dollars. Here are some tips:

1. *Take your time.* Don't let "special offers" or high-pressure sales tactics rush you into buying on your first visit.

2. *Find the fair price.* On the Internet, find the factory invoice price, which is the price the dealer paid for the car. This is not the "sticker" price on the car's window (a higher Manufacturer's Suggested Retail Price, or MSRP). Offer to pay that price plus a fair profit, usually 3 to 5 percent.

3. *Get bids.* Ask five dealers for written bids. Those bids are your bargaining edge.

Used Cars Check the Internet or newspapers for ads. If you're buying from a dealer, ask for names and phone numbers of previous customers. Contact them or the Better Business Bureau for any complaints against the dealer. Weed out the "lemons" with these tips:

- Drive the car, noticing odd noises and how it handles.
- Look at the title to see if the car was "salvaged." That means an insurer declared it a "total loss"; it probably has structural damage that could affect safety and performance.
- Have a mechanic you trust or the American Automobile Association (AAA) test the car. If the seller won't allow testing, don't buy the car.
- Ask to see receipts for recent repairs. Also get the vehicle identification number (VIN) (usually on the dash). At the CARFAX Web site, check the car's history.

Test Your Financial Fitness

1. **Explaining** What is the most important thing to consider when choosing a car? List three other important factors.
2. **Listing** List three things you can do to avoid getting a "lemon" when you buy a used car.
3. **Describing** Describe the process a smart car buyer would use before visiting a car dealer.
4. **Defining** What is the difference between the retail price and the factory invoice price?

PERSONAL FINANCE HANDBOOK   R31

Did You Know?

> **High Cost of Driving**
> The average annual cost of driving a new car in the United States is more than 56 cents per mile, including gas, oil, maintenance, tires, insurance, licenses, registration, vehicle depreciation, and finance charges. That's $8,410 a year!

Assess/Close

W Writing Support

Persuasive Writing Have students review the information on this page about new and used cars. Ask students to use reliable Web sites and print materials to research the advantages and disadvantages of buying a new and a used automobile. Have students write and deliver a speech advocating one of those two options as the best choice for a young person's first car purchase. **OL**

Test Your Financial Fitness

Answers:

1. determine how much I can afford; safety, performance, and environmental impact
2. test drive the car, examine the title of the car, and have a mechanic examine the car
3. calculate how much he or she can afford, compare safety, performance, and repair ratings for different cars, research loans at banks, research a fair price, and contact the Better Business Bureau for any complaints against a dealer.
4. The factory invoice price is what the dealer paid for the car; the retail price is the price the dealer offers to consumers.

Activity: Collaborative Learning

Buying a Car Organize the class into groups of three. Ask each group to research the interactions that occur between salespeople and customers during the car buying process. Have each group perform a skit depicting this interaction. Students may choose which characters to include in their skits. For example, students could portray a customer, a salesperson, and a dealership owner; or they could portray two customers and a salesperson; or any other logical combination of roles. Groups should incorporate the lessons included in this feature into their skits. **OL**

Personal Finance Handbook

Insurance Matters:
Protect yourself

Is your car legal? Who pays if you get sick or robbed? Nobody enjoys thinking about—or paying for—insurance. If you have an emergency, you'll be glad you did.

How It Works

Insurance is like a life raft. You pay an insurance company monthly or quarterly premiums. Then, if something bad happens, such as a traffic accident, an illness, or an apartment fire, insurance helps you stay afloat financially. If nothing bad happens, the company keeps the money.

A document detailing what your insurance covers is a policy. Most policies require a deductible, an amount you have to pay before the insurance kicks in.

Example: You chose car insurance with a $1,000 deductible and you're involved in an accident. You'll have to pay the first $1,000 to fix the car. The insurance company will pay the rest, up to the amount you've purchased. If you had chosen a $500 deductible, you'd pay only the first $500, but your premiums would be higher.

TYPES OF CAR INSURANCE

Collision: Damage to your car, regardless of who caused the accident.

Comprehensive: Damage to your car not caused by an accident, such as theft, vandalism, and natural disasters.

Liability: Bodily injury and property damage to others, plus legal costs. State laws determine how much coverage you must have.

Medical: Medical expenses for everyone injured, regardless of fault.

Personal injury protection: Medical expenses for the insured driver, regardless of fault.

Uninsured motorist: Damage to your car in an accident caused by a driver with no liability insurance.

Underinsured motorist: Damage to your car in an accident caused by someone with insufficient liability insurance.

Rental reimbursement: Car rental if your vehicle cannot be driven after an accident.

R32   PERSONAL FINANCE HANDBOOK

Types of Insurance

Some types of insurance are useful to you now, but most can wait until you're out of school and have more responsibilities.

Auto It's illegal to drive in most states without basic liability insurance to cover property damage and injuries to others; some also require personal injury coverage for the driver. But you may want to buy more insurance than the law requires. Teenage drivers are involved in four times as many crashes as other age groups and are three times more likely to die in a traffic accident. Auto insurance helps pay the costs of injuries, car and property damage, and lawsuits.

Health Even if you're healthy, health insurance is a good idea at any age. It pays for hospitalization, surgery, exams, and other medical costs. Some employers pay part of the cost for employees and their families. Health insurance has deductibles and most plans require a small payment (co-payment, or "co-pay") whenever you visit a doctor's office.

Property What would it cost to replace everything you own: computer, TV, clothes, bicycle? If it's more than you could afford, it should be insured against theft, fire, and other dangers. *Renters insurance* covers the contents of rented property and injury to visitors. *Homeowners insurance* covers a house, its contents, and visitor injuries. Separate insurance is needed for flood or earthquake damage.

Other Insurance *Life insurance* provides financial support to loved ones when a person dies. Some types of life insurance offer lending or retirement income features. *Disability insurance* partially replaces income if you can't work because of illness or injury. *Long-term care insurance* pays for care in nursing homes, assisted living facilities, or private homes when an elderly or disabled person can't manage daily tasks.

Test Your Financial Fitness

1. **Stating** What type of insurance covers a stolen car?
2. **Determining Cause and Effect** Why do you think most states require drivers to have liability insurance, but not collision or comprehensive?
3. **Defining** What is a deductible?
4. **Listing** What two disasters are not covered by renters or homeowners insurance?
5. **Naming** Name three ways to cut the cost of car insurance.

INSURANCE TIPS

- Find out if the policy covers the amount it would cost you to replace the item (**replacement cost**), or only the amount the item was worth before it was damaged, lost, or stolen (**actual cash value**, or **ACV**).
- Read the fine print before signing a policy.
- Document your property with photos and keep receipts.
- To lower insurance costs:
  - Shop to get the lowest premium.
  - Maintain good credit.
  - Drive a low-profile car, not one that's flashy or expensive to repair.
  - Drive safely and ask about discounts for "good students," nonsmokers, nondrinkers, and good drivers.
  - Get an education: some insurers charge less to customers with higher educational levels.
  - If your car is worth less than $1,000, consider dropping collision and comprehensive coverage—but not liability.
  - Install safety and anti-theft devices (airbags, alarms).
  - Buy several types of insurance from the same company to qualify for a multiple-policy discount.

Assess/Close

D Differentiated Instruction

Logical/Mathematical Have students review the different types of insurance on this page. Ask students to create a chart with each of the insurance types as a column head. Tell students to include two rows with the labels "Insurance I have now" and "Insurance I plan to have someday." Ask students to fill in the chart, explaining for each type of insurance why they have it now, or why they think they will need it someday. **OL**

Test Your Financial Fitness

Answers:

1. comprehensive
2. Drivers should have the option whether they want to pay for insurance covering the repair of their own car, but, unless compelled by law, many would be tempted to not pay for insurance covering injury to other people or damage to their cars.
3. an amount a policy holder must pay before the insurance kicks in
4. floods and earthquakes
5. maintain good credit, drive a low-profile car, drop collision and comprehensive coverage if car is worth less than $1,000

Activity: Hands-On Economics

Learning about the Insurance Business Organize the class into pairs. Ask each pair to use a phone book, newspaper, or the Internet to select an insurance agent in their city. Have each pair inform you of which agent they have selected so that the same agent is not selected more than once. Ask each pair to write a set of interview questions to ask the agent to learn about his or her business. Topics students may wish to ask about include: how the agent got into the business, the most common type of policy written, how new customers are found, how natural disasters in other states affect rates, and so on. Have pairs present the results of their interviews to the class in an oral report. **AL**

Introducing the Skills Handbook

The Skills Handbook contains step-by-step instructions designed to develop students' critical thinking and economics skills. Each page also contains reasons why that particular skill is useful and an opportunity to practice applying that skill. As they study the Handbook, remind students that the skills they are learning can apply not only to economics, but to many different disciplines and areas of their lives.

Skills Handbook

CONTENTS

Critical Thinking Skills

$ Economics Skills

Identifying the Main Idea

Why Learn This Skill?

Finding the main idea in a reading passage will help you see the "big picture" by organizing information and assessing the most important concepts to remember.

Learning the Skill

Follow these steps when trying to identify the main idea:

- Determine the setting of the passage.
- As you read the material, ask: What is the purpose of this passage?
- Skim the material to identify its general subject. Look at headings and subheadings.
- Identify any details that support a larger idea or issue.
- Identify the central issue. Ask: What part of the selection conveys the main idea?

▼ Industrial robot

Practicing the Skill

Read the excerpt below and answer the questions that follow.

Industrial robots can't speak English or Chinese, but they can communicate very well with their controllers—something they do 24/7, with no vacations and no health care. They don't receive a pension after they're retired, either. Instead, they get recycled or remanufactured and go to work again.

The average wage for a U.S. warehouse or distribution worker is around $15 per hour (plus benefits). The average wage for this same work in China is about $3 per hour. The average wage for a skilled UAW U.S. automobile worker is $25 to $30 per hour, plus the staggering costs of health care coverage and retirement.

The average cost per hour to operate an industrial robot is 30 cents per hour according to Ron Potter, director of robotic technologies of Factory Automation Systems.

—www.forbes.com, January 3, 2006

1. Where did this article appear?
2. When was it written?
3. What is the main idea of this article?
4. What additional details support the main idea?

Applying the Skill

Bring to class an article from a newspaper, magazine, real-estate buying guide, or other publication. Identify the main idea, and explain why it is important.

Teach

D Differentiated Instruction

Special Education Help students understand the difference between a main idea and supporting details. Explain that the main idea is the most important thought or idea in a text; the details support and elaborate on the main idea. Have students use a main idea and supporting details graphic organizer as they read the excerpt. **BL**

Reinforcing Economic Skills, Activity 12: Finding the Main Idea

 Glencoe Skillbuilder Interactive Workbook CD-ROM, Level 2

Practicing the Skill

Practicing the Skill
Answers:

1. on the Internet (www.forbes.com)

2. January 3, 2006

3. Industrial robots are more cost-effective to employ than U.S. or Chinese workers.

4. Possible answer: Robots don't require health care, vacations, or retirement plans. After they're retired, robots are recycled or remanufactured. Robots cost about 30 cents an hour to operate; industrial workers in China make $3 per hour and workers in the United States make from $15 to $30 per hour.

Applying the Skill
Answer:
Answers will vary, but students should identify the main idea of an article and explain its importance.

Critical Thinking Skills

Teach

C Critical Thinking

Determining Cause and Effect Tell students that one cause can have many effects and that one effect can have many causes. Challenge students to list as many possible causes as they can for this one effect: Independent Music, a small CD company with two stores in Los Angeles, closed after more than 15 years in business. *(Possible answers: Company couldn't keep prices competitive with larger chains; company didn't plan for rise in digital music; more customers shop online.)* **AL**

Reinforcing Economic Skills, Activity 10:
Understanding Cause and Effect

Glencoe Skillbuilder Interactive Workbook CD-ROM, Level 2

Determining Cause and Effect

Why Learn This Skill?

Determining cause and effect involves considering *why* an event occurred. A *cause* is the action or situation that produces an event. What happens as a result of a cause is an *effect.*

Learning the Skill

To identify cause-and-effect relationships, follow these steps:
- Identify two or more events or developments.
- Decide whether one event caused the other. Look for "clue words" such as *because, led to, brought about, produced, as a result of, so that, since,* and *therefore.*
- Look for logical relationships between events, such as "She overslept, and then she missed her bus."
- Identify the outcomes of events. Remember that some effects have more than one cause, and some causes lead to more than one effect. Also, an effect can become the cause of yet another effect.

Practicing the Skill

The classic cause-and-effect relationship in economics is between price and quantity demanded/quantity supplied. As a price for a good rises, the quantity demanded goes down and the quantity supplied rises.

1. Look at the photo above. What might cause a store to have a big sale on plasma televisions? What is the effect on consumers?
2. Now look at the demand curve for plasma televisions below. If the price is $5,000, how many will be demanded per year? If the price drops to $1,000, how many will be demanded per year?

Demand Curve for Plasma Televisons

Applying the Skill

In your local newspaper, read an article describing a current event. Determine at least one cause and one effect of that event.

Practicing the Skill

Practicing the Skill
Answers:

1. Possible answer: The store might need to get rid of some of its stock; consumers might be encouraged to purchase a plasma television if they think they are saving money.

2. 1 million; 5 million

Applying the Skill
Answer:

Answers will vary, but students should determine at least one cause and one effect of a current event.

Making Generalizations

Why Learn This Skill?

Generalizations are judgments that are usually true, based on the facts at hand. If you say, "We have a great soccer team," you are making a generalization. If you also say that your team is undefeated, you are providing evidence to support your generalization. Generalizations are useful in the study of economics because they help economists see trends. Examples include the generalizations that men earn more than women and that prices go down when there is more competition. There are exceptions to both of these statements, but they are generally true.

Learning the Skill

To learn how to make a valid generalization, follow these steps:

- Identify the subject matter.
- Collect factual information and examples relevant to the topic.
- Identify similarities among these facts.
- Use these similarities to form some general ideas about the subject.

Practicing the Skill

Read the excerpt, then identify whether each generalization that follows is valid or invalid. Explain your answers.

Few times in a young person's life are as stressful as the first year out of college. If all goes well, you land a dream job in your chosen profession. But now everything hangs in the balance. Do well in your rookie job and it could put your career into overdrive. Your employer may shower you with promotions, pay raises, and increased responsibility, and you'll be able to leapfrog ahead of the competition in your next position. Do poorly, and you may be sent down to the minors.

The good news: Barring any serious infractions, relatively few people get completely sidetracked in their first year on the job, as most employers allow for a learning curve. The bad news is the reputation you make for yourself will be yours for a good long time—the corporate equivalent of your permanent academic record—coloring the way people see you for many years.

—*BusinessWeek Online,* September 18, 2006

1. The first year out of college is one of the most stressful times in a person's life.
2. All young workers who do well in their first year will have successful careers.
3. Most employers will tolerate a few rookie mistakes.
4. A young employee can never recover from a bad reputation.

Applying the Skill

Read at least three editorials in your local newspaper. Then make a generalization about each editorial.

Skills Handbook

Critical Thinking Skills

Teach

R Reading Strategy

Using Context Clues Have students use context clues to determine the meaning of *valid* and *invalid*. Point out the following sentences and phrases as clues: "generalizations are judgments that are usually true," "providing evidence to support your generalization," "based on the facts." Students should conclude that generalizations should be valid, or true. **Ask:** What is the opposite of valid, or true? *(invalid, or false)* **BL**

Reinforcing Economic Skills, Activity 14: Making Generalizations

Glencoe Skillbuilder Interactive Workbook CD-ROM, Level 2

Practicing the Skill

Practicing the Skill
Answers:

1. valid; supported by details in the excerpt

2. invalid; excerpt does not support that this is true for *all* young workers

3. valid; supported by details in the excerpt

4. invalid; excerpt does not support that this can *never* happen

Applying the Skill
Answer:

Answers will vary, but students should make generalizations about three editorials.

Teach

C Critical Thinking

Draw Conclusions Draw students' attention to the words listed in italics. **Ask:** Why might these words indicate opinions? *(Possible answer: because it is often impossible to prove that something is the best or greatest or that something is always true for all people)* **OL**

Reinforcing Economic Skills, Activity 18: Distinguishing Fact from Opinion

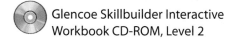

Glencoe Skillbuilder Interactive Workbook CD-ROM, Level 2

Distinguishing Fact from Opinion

Why Learn This Skill?

Distinguishing fact from opinion can help you make reasonable judgments about what others say and write. Facts can be proved by evidence such as records, documents, or historical sources. Opinions are based on people's differing values and beliefs.

Learning the Skill

To learn how to identify facts and opinions, follow these steps:

- Read or listen to the information carefully. Identify the facts. Ask: Can these statements be proved? Where would I find information to verify them?
- If a statement can be proved by information from a reliable source, it is factual.
- Identify opinions by looking for statements of feelings or beliefs. They may contain words like *should, would, could, best, greatest, all, every,* or *always.*

Practicing the Skill

Read the excerpt and answer the questions that follow.

> Office architects are envisioning improved cubicles—newbicles?—that feel private yet collegial, personal yet interchangeable, smaller yet somehow more spacious. Employing advanced materials, tomorrow's technology, and the fruits of sociological research, designers are fitting the future workplace to workers who are increasingly mobile and global. . . .

The father of the cubicle never meant to wreak such bleakness on the American office. We know this from the delightfully delusional name Robert Propst gave his invention: the Action Office. Back then, in 1968, most office workers toiled in open bull pens. Propst's pod offered at least as much privacy as they had in a toilet stall, albeit without the door. Corporate America, which is run by people whose offices have doors, has snapped up more than $5 billion worth of the units from maker Herman Miller. Today 70% of U.S. office workers sit in cubicles, which have long transcended mere office furniture to become a pop-cultural icon (thank you, Dilbert).

—*Time,* July 9, 2006

1. What are three factual statements in the passage?
2. Which statements are opinions? Explain.

Applying the Skill

Watch a television interview, and then list three facts and three opinions that you hear.

▼ A modern cubicle

Practicing the Skill

Practicing the Skill Answers:

1. Possible answer: Back then, in 1968, most office workers toiled in open bull pens. Corporate America…has snapped up more than $5 billion worth of the units from maker Herman Miller. Today 70% of U.S. office workers sit in cubicles.

2. Possible answer: The father of the cubicle never meant to wreak such bleakness on the American office (this cannot be proved from a reliable source). We know this from the delightfully delusional name Robert Propst gave his invention (it is an opinion that the name is "delightfully delusional"). Cubicles… [have] become a pop-cultural icon (this cannot be proved from a reliable source).

Applying the Skill Answer:

Answers will vary, but students should list three facts and three opinions from a television interview.

Formulating Questions

Why Learn This Skill?

Asking questions helps you to process information and understand what you read.

Learning the Skill

Follow these steps to formulate questions as you read:

- Think about questions you have. Often you can find the answers in the next paragraph or section.
- Ask *who, what, when, where, why,* and *how* about the main ideas, people, places, and events.
- Reread to find answers to your questions.

Read the following excerpt, and then study the sample questions below.

A global fashion icon and megabrand, Hello Kitty is one of the most bizarre stories in modern-day marketing. After all, we are talking about a minimalist graphic rendering of a cat, one with a moon-shaped head and no mouth. Yet this simplistic image brings in a half-billion dollars annually in franchise fees for Tokyo-based corporate parent Sanrio. Licensees in Japan, the U.S., and Europe have plastered the cutesy image on 20,000-plus products world-wide—everything from waffle makers to diamond-studded luxury watches.

- Who or what is Hello Kitty?
- Why is Hello Kitty an interesting marketing story?
- Where is Hello Kitty popular?

Practicing the Skill

Read the second excerpt about Hello Kitty. Then, using a chart like the one below, ask questions about the excerpt and reread the selection to find the answers.

	Question	Answer
Who?		
What?		
Where?		
When?		
Why?		
How?		

The business mind behind [Hello Kitty] is Shintaro Tsuji, the founder, president, and CEO of Sanrio. In Japan, Tsuji is considered the closest thing the country has to a Walt Disney. He turned Sanrio, founded in 1960 as a small trinket maker, into a nearly $1 billion character-goods purveyor and theme park operator. Hello Kitty came on the scene in 1974 and appealed primarily to Japanese girls age 5 to 15.

Today, the fabulous feline is embraced by Parisian fashion houses, U.S. pop divas such as Mariah Carey and Christina Aguilera, and legions of fashion-conscious women in rich world markets.

—*BusinessWeek,* June 23, 2006

Applying the Skill

Select any section of this textbook to read or reread. Make a questioning chart to help you ask and answer five or more questions about the section as you read.

Skills Handbook

Teach

R Reading Strategy

Activating Prior Knowledge Ask:
Where have you heard these questions before? *(Some students will recognize these questions from news writing.)*
Why might these be good questions to ask when writing a news article?
(Possible answer: They help a reporter find out the most important information about a topic.) **OL**

 Glencoe Skillbuilder Interactive Workbook CD-ROM, Level 2

Practicing the Skill

Practicing the Skill

Answers:

Who—Who is the founder of Hello Kitty? Shintaro Tsujl. Who did Hello Kitty merchandise appeal to in 1974? Japanese girls age 5 to 15.

What—What does Sanrio do? Originally a trinket maker, they are now a nearly $1 billion character-goods purveyor and theme park operator.

Where—Where is Sanrio located? Japan.

When—When was Sanrio founded? 1960. When did Hello Kitty merchandise first appear? 1974. When was this excerpt published? June 23, 2006.

Why—Why has Shintaro Tsujl been compared to Walt Disney? He is the founder of Sanrio, a small trinket maker that evolved into a nearly $1 billion character-goods purveyor and theme park operator.

How—How did Sanrio grow to a nearly $1 billion character-goods business? Through the efforts of its founder, Shintaro Tsujl.

Applying the Skill

Answer:

Answers will vary, but students should make a questioning chart to help them read a section of the textbook.

R39

Teach

C Critical Thinking

Contrasting Ask: How are main points and summaries different? *(Summaries look at the main points as a whole and then make a statement on that basis. Summaries are created from main points but do not use the exact words of the text. Main points quote from the text, while summaries use the reader's own words.)* **OL**

Reinforcing Economic Skills, Activity 13: Summarizing Information

Glencoe Skillbuilder Interactive Workbook CD-ROM, Level 2

Skills Handbook

Analyzing Information

Why Learn This Skill?

The ability to analyze information is important in deciding what you think about a subject. For example, you need to analyze the effects of international free trade versus the effects of trade restrictions to decide where you stand on the issue of U.S. trade policy.

Learning the Skill

To analyze information, use the following steps:

- Identify the topic that is being discussed.
- Examine how the information is organized. What are the main points?
- Summarize the information in your own words, and then make a statement of your own based on your understanding of the topic and on what you already know.

Practicing the Skill

Read the excerpt and answer the questions that follow.

In May, the U.S. Mint informed Congress that the cost of making a penny and a nickel will soon exceed the actual value of each coin. . . . The U.S. mint estimates that by the end of the fiscal year, the cost of producing one penny will come to around 1.23 cents. . . . The news revived efforts to take the penny out of circulation. On July 18, Representative Jim Kolbe (R., Ariz.) introduced the Currency Overhaul for an Industrious Nation

(COIN) Act that calls for the modernization of America's currency system. The bill includes implementing a rounding system for cash transactions that would eliminate the penny, increasing the production and circulation of the golden dollar while phasing out the dollar bill, and studying whether a change in the composition of coins to include less expensive metals would be worthwhile.

—*BusinessWeek,* July 19, 2006

1. What topic is being discussed?
2. What are the main points of this excerpt?
3. Summarize the information in this excerpt, and then provide your analysis based on this information and what you already know about the subject.

Applying the Skill

Select an issue in economics that is currently in the news, such as Social Security, oil prices, the national debt, or taxation. Read an article or watch a news segment about the issue. Analyze the information and make a brief statement of your own about the topic. Explain your thinking.

Practicing the Skill

Practicing the Skill
Answers:

1. modernizing the U.S. currency system

2. The cost of producing a penny and a nickel will soon exceed the actual value of each coin. The COIN Act in Congress calls for the modernization of the

currency system. This bill calls for the gradual elimination of the penny and dollar bill.

3. Summaries will vary but should mention the need to revamp the U.S. currency system to make it more cost-effective and reflective of current needs.

Applying the Skill
Answer:

Answers will vary, but students should analyze and then summarize a current economic event.

Evaluating Information

Why Learn This Skill?

We live in an information age. The amount of information available can be overwhelming, and it is sometimes difficult to know when information is true and useful. You need to evaluate what you read and hear to determine the reliability of the information presented.

Learning the Skill

When evaluating information to determine its reliability, ask yourself the following questions as you read:

- Is there bias? In other words, does the source unfairly present just one point of view, ignoring any arguments against it?
- Is the information published in a credible, reliable publication?
- Is the author or speaker identified? Is he or she an authority on the subject?
- Is the information up-to-date?
- Is the information backed up by facts and other sources? Does it seem to be accurate?
- Is it well-written and well-edited? Writing that has errors in spelling, grammar, and punctuation is likely to be careless in other ways as well.

Practicing the Skill

Look at the following statements about oil prices. Rank them in order of most reliable to least reliable, and then explain why you ranked them as you did.

> **"**Oil prices are so high, becuz big oil companys are tryng to goug us. Greedy oil executives, are driven up prices to get richer.**"**
>
> —published on an individual's blog on the Internet

> **"**It's certainly clear that high oil prices aren't dulling demand for energy products. According to the Energy Dept.'s Energy Information Administration (EIA), U.S. demand for gasoline in June was 9.5 million barrels per day, a record.**"**
>
> —*BusinessWeek,* July 7, 2006

> **"**The single biggest factor in the inflation rate last year was from one cause: the skyrocketing prices of OPEC oil. We must take whatever actions are necessary to reduce our dependence on foreign oil—and at the same time reduce inflation.**"**
>
> —President Jimmy Carter, January 23, 1980

Applying the Skill

Find an advertisement that contains text and bring it to class. In a brief oral presentation, tell the class whether the information in the advertisement is reliable or unreliable and why.

Skills Handbook

SKILLS HANDBOOK R41

Teach

W Writing Support

Personal Writing Ask: What does it mean to say that we live in an information age? *(Possible answer: Most people have quick and relatively easy access to all sorts of information like never before in history.)* Have students write a journal entry describing what they think are the pros and cons of living in an information age. After they finish, ask students to evaluate their overall feelings about having access to so much information. **OL**

 Glencoe Skillbuilder Interactive Workbook CD-ROM, Level 2

Practicing the Skill

Practicing the Skill
Answers:
Students should rank the statements in order of most reliable to least reliable: BusinessWeek, President Jimmy Carter, individual's blog. They should recognize that a newsmagazine is a reliable publication and that it gives a current statement support by a fact. President

Jimmy Carter expresses an opinion about what the country should do to fight inflation; his statement is not a fact, and it's from 1980. The individual's blog is the least reliable because the author is not identified, the statement contains grammatical errors, and the text is not backed up by facts or sources.

Applying the Skill
Answer:
Answers will vary, but students should evaluate the reliability of an advertisement based on the Learning the Skill questions in the text.

Teach

D Differentiated Instruction

English Language Learners Call students' attention to the phrase "read between the lines." Explain the analogy by saying that white space appears between lines of information. Readers need to fill in that "space" with their own observations, based on information they already know and information they learn from the text, or "lines." In this way, readers make inferences. **ELL**

Reinforcing Economic Skills, Activity 16: Drawing Inferences and Conclusions

Glencoe Skillbuilder Interactive Workbook CD-ROM, Level 2

Making Inferences

Why Learn This Skill?

To *infer* means to evaluate information and arrive at a conclusion. When you make inferences, you "read between the lines," or use clues to figure something out that is not stated directly in the text.

Learning the Skill

Follow these steps to make inferences:
- Read carefully for stated facts and ideas.
- Summarize the information and list important facts.
- Apply related information that you may already know.
- Use your knowledge and insight to develop some logical conclusions.

Practicing the Skill

Read the passage and answer the questions that follow.

> Texans know their barbecue. But lots of them apparently don't know their Chinese food. The top question at the 10 Panda Express stores opened in Texas this year is "What's orange chicken?"
>
> Andrew and Peggy Cherng, the husband-and-wife team who created Panda Express, know that answering that question and many others about their menu is part of the diner-education process that has turned a one-store eatery inside a California mall into an 820-store Chinese food empire. Orange chicken, a lightly sweetened fried chicken dish, is their best seller but not as familiar in Texas as fajitas and hamburgers.
>
> If they get their way, it will be. And not just on the coasts. The two are well on their way to cracking a frontier in fast food: creating a national Chinese fast-food chain.

—*USA Today,* September 11, 2006

1. What facts are presented in the passage?
2. What can you infer about the importance of educating Panda Express customers about Chinese food? Explain.
3. Can you also infer that there is currently no national Chinese fast-food chain? Explain.

Applying the Skill

Look over the headlines in today's Business and Finance section in your local newspaper. What can you infer about what economic issues are important in your community, the nation, and the world right now? Skim an article. Can you tell how the writer feels about the topic? How?

Practicing the Skill

Practicing the Skill
Answers:

1. Possible answer: Andrew and Penny Cherng are married and created Panda Express; they started with one eatery inside a California mall and grew the business into 820 stores; orange chicken is their best-selling menu item.

2. Possible answer: If people don't know what is in a dish or aren't sure how it will taste, most will not order it from a restaurant. Educating Panda Express customers is important so they will feel more comfortable ordering food.

3. Students should infer that there is currently no national chain because Panda Express is described as an "empire" that is on its way to "cracking a frontier" of creating a national Chinese fast-food chain. This is another way of saying that Panda Express is charting a new course.

Applying the Skill
Answer:

Answers will vary, but students should make inferences about important economic issues in the community on the basis of newspaper headlines. They should also try to determine the writer's feelings based on indicators such as word choice and tone.

Comparing and Contrasting

Why Learn This Skill?

When you make comparisons, you determine similarities among ideas, objects, or events. When you contrast, you are noting differences between ideas, objects, or events. Comparing and contrasting are important skills because they help you choose among several possible alternatives.

Learning the Skill

To learn how to compare and contrast, follow these steps:

- Identify or decide what two or more items will be compared and/or contrasted.
- To compare, determine a common area or areas in which comparisons can be drawn. Look for similarities within these areas.
- To contrast, look for areas that are different. These areas set the items apart from each other.

Practicing the Skill

Study the advertisements for two computers at the bottom of the page, and then answer the questions that follow.

1. How are these products similar?
2. How are they different?
3. Which of these two computers would you choose? Why?

Applying the Skill

Survey your classmates about an issue in the news. Summarize the opinions and write a paragraph or two comparing and contrasting the different opinions.

The BasicBox XL is a reliable and versatile entry-level computer system designed especially for students.

Priced at a tidy $550, the BasicBox XL features:

- 3.06 GHz processor
- 512 MB of memory
- 160 GB hard drive
- 16X CD/DVD burner
- multiple USB ports
- keyboard and mouse

BasicBox XL

You can add a 15-inch flat panel monitor for a small extra charge.

Introducing the CompuFun 2000LH, the perfect computer for modern teens:

Ideal for homework, gaming, emailing, and surfing the Internet, the CompuFun 2000LH is reasonably priced at just $999.

It has a speedy 3.06 GHz processor, 1 GB of memory, a 250GB hard drive, a 16X CD/DVD burner, and multiple USB ports.

The CompuFun 2000LH also has a high-end video card and multimedia speakers. A 19-inch flat panel monitor, keyboard, and mouse are always included with our desktop system at no extra charge.

SKILLS HANDBOOK   R43

Skills Handbook

Teach

D Differentiated Instruction

Interpersonal Have each student write a paragraph explaining why they think that studying economics is important. Then ask students to exchange paragraphs with a partner and compare and contrast their explanations. You might provide students with a Venn diagram to help them identify similarities and differences. **OL**

Reinforcing Economic Skills, Activity 11: Making Comparisons

 Glencoe Skillbuilder Interactive Workbook CD-ROM, Level 2

Practicing the Skill

Practicing the Skill
Answers:

1. The products are both computers with 3.06 GHz processors, 16x CD/DVD burners, multiple USB ports, keyboard and mouse.

2. The CompuFun is more expensive, has more memory, has a larger hard drive, and comes with a flat panel monitor. The BasicBox XL offers a smaller flat panel monitor for an extra charge.

3. Answers will vary, but students should choose a computer that best fits their needs and budget.

Applying the Skill
Answer:

Answers will vary, but students should survey the class about a news issue and then compare and contrast the results.

Teach

C Critical Thinking

Make Inferences Ask: Why might it be useful to examine the author's identity? *(Possible answer: The author might be more subjective or opinionated about topics in which he or she is involved or interested. It might be difficult for the author to see opposing views on an issue in which he or she strongly believes.)* **OL**

Reinforcing Economic Skills, Activity 19: Recognizing Bias

Glencoe Skillbuilder Interactive Workbook CD-ROM, Level 2

Skills Handbook

Detecting Bias

Why Learn This Skill?

Most people have a point of view, or bias. This bias influences the way they interpret and write about events. Recognizing bias helps you judge the accuracy of what you hear or read.

Learning the Skill

Follow these steps to learn how to recognize bias:

- Examine the author's identity, especially his or her views and particular interests.
- Identify statements of fact.
- Identify any expressions of opinion or emotion. Look for words that have positive or negative overtones for clues about the author's feelings on a topic.
- Determine the author's point of view.
- Determine how the author's point of view is reflected in the work.

Practicing the Skill

Read the passage and answer the questions that follow.

> Sometime in October the U.S. will join China and India in the very small club of countries with at least 300 million residents. This really is a big deal, like hitting 700 home runs in baseball. No other country is expected to reach the 300 million mark for at least 30 more years. . . .

But here are a couple of questions for you to ponder as the U.S. gets closer to the big 300: Is it coincidence that the three countries with the largest populations also have the most dynamic economies in the world? And is it coincidence that the most innovative major industrialized country, the U.S., also has the fastest growing population and the most young people?

No coincidence at all, as it turns out.

—*BusinessWeek*, September 5, 2006

1. What statements of fact are presented in this passage?
2. What opinions are stated?
3. What is the purpose of this passage?
4. What evidence of bias do you find? Does the author think it is a good thing or a bad thing that the United States is hitting this population milestone?

Applying the Skill

Find an editorial in the newspaper that deals with a topic of specific interest to you. Apply the steps for recognizing bias to the editorial. Write a paragraph summarizing your findings.

Practicing the Skill

Practicing the Skill
Answers:

1. U.S., China, and India will soon all have at least 300 million residents each. No other country is expected to reach that mark for at least 30 more years. The United States has the fastest-growing population and the most young people in the world.

2. The U.S. reaching a population of 300 million is "a big deal." All three countries have "the most dynamic economies in the world." The United States is the "most innovative major industrialized country" in the world.

3. Possible answer: to inform readers that the United States is soon joining China and India with a population of at least 300 million

4. Possible answer: The author describes the United States in very positive terms and seems to think the U.S.'s growing population is a good thing.

Applying the Skill
Answer:

Answers will vary, but students should apply the steps for recognizing bias to a newspaper editorial.

Synthesizing Information

Why Learn This Skill?

Synthesizing information involves combining information from two or more sources. Information gained from one source often sheds new light upon other information.

Learning the Skill

Follow these steps to learn how to synthesize information:

- Analyze each source separately to understand its meaning.
- Determine what information each source adds to the subject.
- Identify points of agreement and disagreement between the sources. Ask: Can Source A give me new information or new ways of thinking about Source B?
- Find relationships between the information in the sources.

Practicing the Skill

Read the passages and answer the questions that follow.

Source A "The flat tax. In the eyes of many fiscal conservatives, it's the Holy Grail of public policy: One low income tax rate paid by all but the poorest wage-earners, who are exempt. No loopholes for the rich to exploit. No graduated rates that take a higher percentage of income from people who work hard to earn more. No need for a huge bureaucracy to police fiendishly complex tax laws."

—*BusinessWeek,* September 26, 2005

Source B "Under Steve Forbes' plan the flat [income tax] rate would be 17%. All families would get generous personal exemptions, so that a family of four would not pay taxes until its income exceeded $46,000. To encourage growth, the Forbes plan exempts income that is saved and invested. Which means that the Forbes plan is really a consumption tax. It taxes people based on what they take out of the system, not on what they put in."

—*Forbes,* September 29, 2005

1. What is the main subject of each source?
2. Does Source B support or contradict Source A? Explain.
3. Summarize what you learned from both sources.

Applying the Skill

Find two sources of information on banking practices. What are the main ideas in each? How does each add to your understanding of the topic?

▼ Steve Forbes

SKILLS HANDBOOK   R45

Teach

D Differentiated Instruction

English Language Learners Explain to students that the "Holy Grail" is a reference to medieval legend, in which noble knights undertook journeys of great danger to find a cup, or Holy Grail, that was supposed to hold the key to magical healing. **Ask:** What does calling the flat tax a "Holy Grail" indicate about fiscal conservatives? *(Possible answer: Many fiscal conservatives have pushed for a flat tax for a long time, believing that it will solve many of today's problems.)* **ELL**

Reinforcing Economic Skills, Activity 20: Synthesizing Information

🔘 Glencoe Skillbuilder Interactive Workbook CD-ROM, Level 2

Practicing the Skill

Practicing the Skill Answers:

1. the flat tax
2. It supports it; the Forbes plan provides a flat tax rate and offers exemptions to the poorest wage-earning families.
3. Both sources discuss simplifying tax law through the institution of a flax income tax rate. The plan discussed in Source A exempts poor wage-earners and does not contain loopholes for the rich to exploit. Source B describes a similar plan, but one that also exempts from taxation any income that is saved and invested.

Applying the Skill Answer:

Answers will vary, but students should synthesize information provided in two sources on banking practices.

Teach

D Differentiated Instruction

Advanced Learners Invite students to read a Sherlock Holmes short story by Sir Arthur Conan Doyle, such as "The Red-Headed League" or "The Adventure of the Speckled Band." Ask students to find examples of how Sherlock Holmes draws conclusions and then write a one-page paper describing how drawing conclusions helps the detective solve the mystery. **AL**

Reinforcing Economic Skills, Activity 16: Drawing Inferences and Conclusions

Glencoe Skillbuilder Interactive Workbook CD-ROM, Level 2

Skills Handbook

Drawing Conclusions

Why Learn This Skill?

A conclusion is a logical understanding that you reach based on details or facts that you read or hear. When you draw conclusions, you use stated information to figure out ideas that are unstated.

Learning the Skill

Follow these steps to draw conclusions:
- Read carefully for stated facts and ideas.
- Summarize the information and list important facts.
- Apply related information that you may already know.
- Use your knowledge and insight to develop some logical conclusions.

Practicing the Skill

Read the passage and answer the questions that follow.

In the automotive business these days, big is out and small is in. Sales of large sport-utility vehicles are down 45%. Small-car sales have increased 70%. Of course, having suffered from $3-plus-a-gallon gasoline for longer, the rest of the world has been thinking small for years. And there is no production car smaller than the Smart Car from DaimlerChrysler.

But can a car that is just slightly more than 8 feet long and 5 feet high with 15-inch wheels co-exist with the mastodons that rule the American road? . . . Only time will tell.

—*BusinessWeek*, August 24, 2006

1. What topic is the writer describing?
2. What facts are given in the selection?
3. What do you already know about the subject?
4. What conclusion can you draw about why small-car sales are increasing while sales of large sport-utility vehicles are decreasing?

Applying the Skill

Read one of the "People & Perspectives" features about a prominent economist or entrepreneur in this text. Using the information in the profile, what can you figure out about the life of the person described? Draw three conclusions about this famous person's life and ideas.

▼ DaimlerChrysler's Smart Car

Practicing the Skill

Practicing the Skill
Answers:

1. the Smart Car

2. Sales of large sports-utility vehicles are down 45%. Small-car sales have increased 70%. The Smart Car is a little more than 8 feet long and 5 feet high, and it has 15-inch wheels.

3. Answers will vary, but many students will be familiar with vehicles that run on alternative fuels.

4. Possible answer: because gasoline is expensive and larger cars use more fuel

Applying the Skill
Answer:

Answers will vary, but students should draw three conclusions about a person highlighted in one of the "People and Perspectives" features in the textbook.

Making Predictions

Why Learn This Skill?

Predicting future events can be difficult and sometimes risky. The more information you have, however, the more accurate your predictions will be. Making good predictions will help you understand what you read.

Learning the Skill

To help you make predictions, follow these steps:

- Gather information about the decision or action.
- Use your knowledge of history and human behavior to identify what consequences could result.
- Analyze each of the consequences by asking: How likely is it that this will occur?

Practicing the Skill

Read the passage and answer the questions that follow.

Google and Yahoo! have been raking in the cash for years, as large advertisers shift more spending to online media. But judging by recent earnings figures from the Internet leaders, the trend is just hitting its stride. . . .

Driving this breakneck growth [in Internet advertising] is the companies' ability to draw advertising dollars onto the Internet—and away from other media. In 2002, 2.5% of U.S. ad dollars were spent online. The figure is expected to reach 4.6% this year [2005] and 7.5% by 2009, according to researcher eMarketer.

—*BusinessWeek*, October 21, 2005

1. What trend does the passage describe?
2. Do you think this trend is likely to continue?
3. On what do you base this prediction?
4. What are three possible consequences of this trend?

Applying the Skill

Analyze three articles in the business section of a newspaper. Predict three consequences of the actions in the articles. On what do you base your predictions?

Teach

C Critical Thinking

Theorizing Ask students to think of a scenario in which predicting a future event could be risky. Ask volunteers to share their scenarios with the class. (*Possible answer: Predicting that a stock will rise and investing money based on that prediction would be risky.*) **OL**

Reinforcing Economic Skills, Activity 15: Making Predictions

 Glencoe Skillbuilder Interactive Workbook CD-ROM, Level 2

Practicing the Skill

Practicing the Skill
Answers:

1. advertisers shifting more spending to online media

2. Possible answer: yes

3. Students will likely say yes because the trend is expected to continue, as more and more people use the Internet for everyday needs.

4. Possible answer: other forms of media will struggle to find advertising; people using the Internet will have to navigate through more ads; online media will need to increase staff to handle the additional interest in online advertising

Applying the Skill
Answer:
Answers will vary, but students should predict three consequences of an action described in a business newspaper article.

Teach

W Writing Support

Personal Writing Have students write a journal entry describing a problem in their lives and what they did to solve it. Tell students to address the possible solutions to their problem and how they decided which solution to try. Ask students to finish the entry by evaluating the effectiveness of the solution. **OL**

 Glencoe Skillbuilder Interactive Workbook CD-ROM, Level 2

Skills Handbook

Problems and Solutions

Why Learn This Skill?

Suppose you are not doing well in basketball. You wonder why you cannot do better since you always go to practice, try your best, and pay attention to the coach's instructions. In order to improve a situation such as this one, you need to identify a specific problem and then take actions to solve it.

Learning the Skill

Follow these steps to help you through the problem-solving process:

- Identify the problem.
- Gather information.
- List possible solutions.
- Consider the advantages and disadvantages of each solution.
- Choose the best solution to your problem and carry it out.
- Evaluate the effectiveness of the solution.

Practicing the Skill

Read the selection and answer the questions that follow.

> The soaring price of cement is having a disproportionate effect on lower-middle to middle-income families. Why? Because the denser housing that tends to get built for them uses lots of concrete, which is made from cement, sand, gravel, and water. Designs with lots of concrete are becoming so expensive to build that they're getting out of the potential buyers' price range, says Tim Sullivan, president of Sullivan Group Real Estate Advisors. . . .
>
> [Sullivan says] that because of the high price of cement and concrete products, builders are putting more of their efforts into homes that are built primarily of lumber. These are single-family homes or town homes that tend to be aimed at higher-income families. Tall condo and apartment buildings made of concrete are so expensive to build that these days they're aimed almost exclusively at wealthier buyers. . . .
>
> —*BusinessWeek Online*, June 9, 2006

1. What problem does the writer present in this selection?
2. What options are available to solve this problem? Can you think of any other options?
3. Explain the solution that was implemented according to the selection.
4. Evaluate the solution described in the passage. Was it successful? How do you determine this?

Applying the Skill

Select an economic problem that needs to be solved. The problem can be anything from how you plan to pay for an upcoming expense to how the United States might solve the problem of funding Social Security long-term. Create a simple presentation in which you identify the problem, list options with their advantages and disadvantages, choose a solution, and evaluate the chosen solution.

Practicing the Skill

Practicing the Skill
Answers:

1. The high price of cement is hurting lower-middle to middle-income families.

2. Possible answer: Provide low-income housing made from materials that are less expensive than concrete. Develop more cost-effective methods of producing and working with cement in the hopes of driving down prices.

3. Builders are focusing on creating homes that are built mostly of lumber.

4. Possible answer: It is not successful because those homes are aimed at higher-income families. Lower-middle to middle-income families cannot afford these other types of homes and so are still being hurt by the high cost of concrete.

Applying the Skill
Answer:

Answers will vary, but students should apply the steps of the problem-solving process to an economic problem.

$ Economics Skills

Using Line Graphs

Why Learn This Skill?

A graph, like a picture, may present information in a more concise way than words. Line graphs are drawings that compare numerical values. They often are used to compare changes over time or differences between places, groups of items, or other related events.

Learning the Skill

Follow these steps to learn how to understand and use line graphs. Then answer the questions below.

1. Read the title of the graph. This should tell you what to expect or look for.

2. Note the information on the left side of the graph—the vertical axis. The information being compared usually appears on this axis.

3. Note the information along the bottom of the graph—the horizontal axis. Time often appears along this axis.

4. Determine what the line(s) or curve(s) symbolizes.

5. Select a point on the line, then note the date below this point on the horizontal axis and the quantity measured on the vertical axis.

6. Analyze the movement of the line (whether increasing or decreasing over time) or compare lines (if more than one is on the graph) to determine the point being made.

Self-Employed Workers (in thousands)

— Professional   — Agriculture
— Wholesale and retail

Number of workers: 1,300 1,250 1,200 1,150 1,100 1,050 1,000 950 900

Year: 2000 2001 2002 2003 2004

Source: *Statistical Abstract of the United States, 2004*

Practicing the Skill

1. About how many people in wholesale and retail businesses were self-employed in 2003? In 2004?

2. How many more people were self-employed professionals in 2003 than in 2001?

Applying the Skill to Economics

1. What trends are shown on the graph?

2. What economic forces might have influenced the changes shown on the graph?

3. What kinds of jobs do you think are represented in each category shown?

SKILLS HANDBOOK   R49

Skills Handbook

Teach

D Differentiated Instruction

English Language Learners Assist English language learners as they familiarize themselves with the various components of a line graph. Name different parts of the graph, such as the title, key, axes, or source line. Then ask English language learners to locate these items on the graph shown. Once they have correctly located each item, invite them to explain what information it contains in relation to the graph as a whole. **ELL**

Reinforcing Economic Skills, Activity 1: Using Graphs

 Glencoe Skillbuilder Interactive Workbook CD-ROM, Level 2

Practicing the Skill

Practicing the Skill
Answers:

1. About 1,250,000 in the wholesale and retail business were self-employed in 2003. In 2004, about 1,150,000 people in the wholesale and retail business were self-employed.

2. About 50,000 more people were self-employed professionals in 2003 than in 2001.

Applying the Skill
Answers:

1. Trends in self-employment among workers in the professional, wholesale and retail, and agriculture industries are shown on the graph.

2. Answers will vary, but students may suggest that forces such as higher self-employment taxes or increasing costs of health insurance may have influenced

the decreases in the number of self-employed workers shown on the graph.

3. Answers will vary, but students should make reasonable suggestions about the types of jobs that would be represented in each category.

Critical Thinking Skills

Teach

S Skill Practice

Making a Bar and Circle Graph Have the class divide into small groups. Instruct each group to think of a topic on which to gather information about the members of the class. For instance, groups may choose to survey students about their favorite foods. When groups have finished gathering information from all members of the class, direct them to make a chart or table that organizes the data they have gathered. Then, ask students to create a bar graph showing the quantities found in their results, as well as a circle graph showing the relationship of the various responses to the class as a whole. **OL**

Reinforcing Economic Skills, Activity 1: Using Graphs

 Glencoe Skillbuilder Interactive Workbook CD-ROM, Level 2

Using Bar and Circle Graphs

Why Learn This Skill?

Bar graphs are often used to show changes over time or to compare quantities between similar categories of information. Circle graphs usually show the relationship of parts to a whole.

Learning the Skill

Follow these steps to learn how to understand and use bar graphs.

1. Read the title and labels. They tell you the topic, what is being compared, and how it is counted or measured.

3. Analyze the change over time or compare bars to determine the point being made.

2. Examine a bar on the graph. Note the date below the bar on the horizontal axis and the quantity measured on the vertical axis.

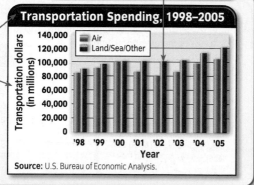

Transportation Spending, 1998–2005

Source: U.S. Bureau of Economic Analysis.

Learning the Skill

Follow these steps to learn how to understand and use circle graphs.

1. Examine the title to determine the subject.

3. Compare the relative sizes of the circle segments, thus analyzing the relationship of the parts to the whole.

2. Read the legend to see what each segment represents.

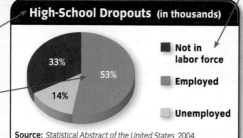

High-School Dropouts (in thousands)

Source: *Statistical Abstract of the United States*, 2004.

Practicing the Skill

1. In the bar graph, what year had the lowest spending on air travel?
2. According to the circle graph, what percentage of high school dropouts are employed?

Applying the Skill to Economics

1. Using the bar graph, what projection could you make about the future of air transportation?
2. Based on the circle graph, what can you tell about the employment chances of high-school dropouts?

Practicing the Skill

Practicing the Skill Answers:

1. According to the bar graph, the year 2002 had the lowest spending on air travel.

2. According to the circle graph, 53 percent of high school dropouts are employed.

Applying the Skill Answers:

1. Based on the bar graph, you could make the projection that air transportation will continue to grow in the future. After a decrease in spending from 2000 to 2002, the amount of money that people have spent on air travel has risen steadily since.

2. Based on the circle graph, you can tell that high-school dropouts have only about a fifty-fifty chance of gaining employment.

Using Tables and Charts

Why Learn This Skill?

Tables and charts are often used to show comparisons between similar categories of information. Tables usually compare statistical or numerical data. Tabular data is presented in columns and rows. Charts often show a wider variety of information than tables.

Learning the Skill

Follow these steps to learn how to understand and use tables. Then answer the questions below.

1. Read the title of the table to learn what content is being presented.

2. Read the headings in the top row. They define the groups or categories of information to be compared.

3. Examine the labels in the left-hand column. They describe ranges or subgroups and are often organized chronologically or alphabetically.

4. Note the source of the data. It may tell you about the reliability of the information in the table.

5. Compare the data presented in the other columns. This is the body of the table.

Number of Full-Time Workers by Age and Gender (in thousands)

Age	Total	%	Male	%	Female	%
16 to 19 years old	580,704	4.7	288,653	4.5	291,099	4.9
20 to 24 years old	1,334,383	10.8	699,181	10.9	635,666	10.7
25 to 34 years old	2,817,031	22.8	1,539,480	24.0	1,283,213	21.6
35 to 44 years old	3,051,784	24.7	1,603,625	25.0	1,443,614	24.3
45 to 54 years old	2,804,676	22.7	1,404,776	21.9	1,402,029	23.6
55 to 64 years old	1,420,871	11.5	712,010	11.1	712,896	12.0
65 years and older	345,951	2.8	173,192	2.7	178,224	3.0

Source: *Statistical Abstract of the United States, 2004.*

Skills Handbook

Practicing the Skill

1. What age group has the most workers?
2. What age group has the smallest percentage of female full-time workers?
3. Which age groups have a higher percentage of male than female full-time workers?

Applying the Skill to Economics

1. What age-related trends do you notice in this table?
2. What conclusions could you draw from this data about the peak working years for most U.S. workers?
3. At what age do people apparently begin to retire from full-time work?

SKILLS HANDBOOK   R51

Teach

R Reading Strategy

Reading Charts and Tables Ask: What information is contained in the headings in the top row of a table or chart? Why is it important to pay attention to the source of the data presented in a table or chart? *(The headings in the top row of a table or chart tell what information is presented for comparison in each of the columns included in the table or chart. It is important to pay attention to the source of the data presented because this can provide clues about the reliability of the information presented.)* OL

Reinforcing Economic Skills, Activity 2: Using Charts and Tables

 Glencoe Skillbuilder Interactive Workbook CD-ROM, Level 2

Practicing the Skill

Practicing the Skill
Answers:

1. The age group 35 to 44 years old has the most workers.

2. The age group 65 years and older has the smallest percentage of female full-time workers.

3. The following age groups have a higher percentage of male than female full-time workers: 20 to 24 years old, 25 to 34 years old, and 35 to 44 years old.

Applying the Skill
Answers:

1. Possible answer: Both male and female workers make up increasingly larger parts of the workforce until they reach the 35 to 44 years old age group. After that time, the percentage of the workforce represented by male and female workers steadily decreases.

2. Possible answer: One could draw the conclusion that the peak working years for most U.S. workers are from the ages of 35 to 44 years old.

3. Many people apparently begin to retire from full-time work around the age of 55.

R51

Teach

W Writing Support

Narrative Writing Direct students to think of a time in which they made an important economic decision, such as choosing to save money for an important purchase. Then ask them to write a brief narrative essay in which they recount the events that took place surrounding this decision. Instruct students to carefully sequence the information presented in their essays and use signal words to help readers understand the chronological order of this information. **OL**

Reinforcing Economic Skills, Activity 9: Sequencing and Categorizing Information

 Glencoe Skillbuilder Interactive Workbook CD-ROM, Level 2

Sequencing Events

Why Learn This Skill?

Sequencing involves placing facts in the order in which they occurred. Sequencing helps you deal with large quantities of information in an understandable way. In economics, sequencing can help economists understand cause-and-effect relationships between events. This in turn helps analysts to predict outcomes of various events or policies.

Learning the Skill

To sequence events, follow these steps:
- Look for dates or clue words that provide you with chronological order: *in 2007, the late 1990s, first, then, finally, after the Great Depression,* and so on.
- Arrange facts in the order in which they occurred.
- You might use an organizational tool such as a time line to sequence events so that it is easy to see a chronology as well as any cause-and-effect relationships that occur between events.

Practicing the Skill

Read the passage and answer the questions that follow.

At about eight in the morning on June 16, a young man named Remi Frazier from Fort Collins, Colo., sat down on a bench in Manhattan's Columbus Circle, glued a cell phone to his ear, and spread a New York City map across his lap. By early afternoon he had launched an unlikely entrepreneurial project—to make $1 million within one month, using only a cell phone, a digital video camera, and a $100 bill. His self-imposed set of rules also meant he had made no advance contact with anyone in the city.

To achieve his goal, Frazier, 27, planned to build a volunteer network of business consultants, conceptualize and design a product, conduct market research for that product, and finally manufacture and sell it on a wide scale. He would have 30 days to complete what a startup usually takes years to do.

—*BusinessWeek,* June 30, 2006

1. What dates or clue words in this passage can help you determine the sequence of events being described?
2. Fill in a time line such as the one below to show the sequence of events described in the selection.

First Event — — — — Final Event

Applying the Skill to Economics

Find a newspaper or magazine article about a local business. Sequence the information presented in the article in a time line or chart.

Practicing the Skill

Practicing the Skill
Answers:

1. Answers may include: eight in the morning, June 16, early afternoon, one month, 30 days, years

2. Students should accurately fill in a time line such as the one shown using events mentioned in the passage.

Applying the Skill
Answer:

Students should successfully locate a newspaper or magazine article about a local business. They should then correctly sequence the information presented in their articles using a time line or chart. Students' time lines and charts should be well-organized and easy to understand.

Comparing Data

Why Learn This Skill?

Economists compare data in order to identify economic trends, draw conclusions about the relationships of sets of economic information, analyze the effectiveness of economic programs, or perform other types of analysis. It is often easiest to compare data that is organized in charts, tables, or graphs.

Learning the Skill

Follow these steps to compare and contrast data:
- Look at each set of data separately to understand what each one means on its own.
- Look for relationships among the sets of data. Ask yourself: How are these sets of information connected to each other?
- Note similarities and differences among the sets of data.
- Draw conclusions about what the sets of data, taken together, might mean.

Practicing the Skill

Compare the data in the charts at the bottom of the page, and then answer the questions below.

1. Look at the left graph. What was the overall trend in manufacturing employment from 1996 to 2005?
2. Look at the right graph. What was the overall trend in professional and business employment during the same period?
3. How are the data in the two charts related?
4. What conclusions can you draw about the two areas of employment?

Applying the Skill to Economics

Look in a world almanac or on the Internet to find two sets of data about an economic topic of your choice. Compare the data and draw at least two conclusions based on your analysis. Share your conclusions with a partner.

Skills Handbook

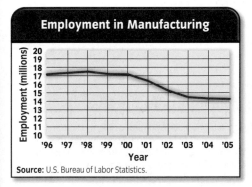

Employment in Manufacturing

Year

Source: U.S. Bureau of Labor Statistics.

Employment in Professional and Business Services

Year

Source: U.S. Bureau of Labor Statistics.

SKILLS HANDBOOK   R53

Teach

C Critical Thinking

Making Generalizations Ask: Why do you think it is often easiest to compare data when it has been organized in charts, tables, or graphs? *(Possible answer: It is often easiest to compare data when it is organized in charts, tables, or graphs because these visuals allow a person to visualize more easily the changes taking place among two or more sets of data. This can help with interpreting the individual sets of data, as well as with observing similarities and differences among the trends affecting each set.* **BL**

Reinforcing Economic Skills, Activity 11: Making Comparisons

 Glencoe Skillbuilder Interactive Workbook CD-ROM, Level 2

Practicing the Skill

Practicing the Skill
Answers:

1. The overall trend in manufacturing employment was a slight decrease in employment.

2. The overall trend in professional and business employment was an increase in employment.

3. The data are related because they measure the same time period.

4. Answers will vary. Students might suggest that while manufacturing jobs may have decreased due to increased automation and outsourcing, the demand for professional and business services continued to increase.

Applying the Skill
Answer:

Students should successfully locate two sets of data about a relevant economic topic. They should then draw at least two reasonable conclusions from the data, and discuss these conclusions with a partner.

Teach

D Differentiated Instruction

Logical/Mathematical Have students practice calculating and using percentages by asking questions of the class. For instance, you might ask the class how many of them have made a purchase in the past week. Then, instruct students to identify the number of class members who respond affirmatively, and calculate the percentage of the entire class this figure represents. **BL**

Reinforcing Economic Skills, Activity 4: Understanding Percentages

⊙ Glencoe Skillbuilder Interactive Workbook CD-ROM, Level 2

Skills Handbook

Understanding Percentages

Why Learn This Skill?

If you shop, you probably like seeing the word *percent*, as in "30 percent off." Stores often advertise sale prices as a percent of regular prices. *Percent* means "parts per hundred." So, 30 percent means the same thing as 30/100 or 0.30. Expressing change as a percentage allows you to analyze the relative size of the change.

Learning the Skill

Follow these steps to learn how to calculate and use percentages. Then answer the questions below.

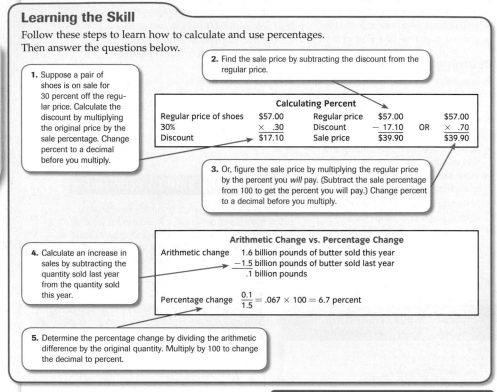

Practicing the Skill

1. A store advertises a shirt at 25 percent off the original price of $44. What is the sale price?
2. What is the percentage increase in high school enrollment from 1,165 students to 1,320?

Applying the Skill to Economics

The total number of digital single music tracks downloaded online or to mobile phones rose to 470 million units in 2005, up from 160 million in 2004. What was the percentage change of single-track downloads from 2004 to 2005?

Practicing the Skill

Practicing the Skill
Answers:

1. $33

2. 13.3 percent

Applying the Skill
Answer:

The percentage change of single-track downloads from 2004 to 2005 was 193.7 percent.

Determining Averages

Why Learn This Skill?

The most commonly used summary statistic is the average. There are two ways to compute the average: by using the mean or the median. The *mean* is the average of a series of items. When your teacher computes the class average, he or she is really computing the mean. Sometimes using the mean to interpret statistics is misleading, however. This is especially true if one or two numbers in the series are much higher or lower than the others. The median can be more accurate. The *median* is the midpoint in any series of numbers arranged in order.

Learning the Skill

Follow these steps to learn how to determine and use averages.

1. Suppose you want to find the mean weekly salary for a group of teenagers. First, add all the earnings together.

Students' Weekly Earnings From After-School Jobs

$ 20
32
34
41
53
65
175
―――
$420

$420 ÷ 7 = $60

2. Divide the sum by the number of students to find the mean.

3. Locate the median by finding the midpoint in the series ($41). Compare the mean with the median. Determine which is the more useful statistic.

Median Weekly Income of the Four Highest-Paid Students

$ 41 $ 53
53   + 65
65   ――――
175        $ 118

$118 ÷ 2 = $59

5. When an even number of figures is in the series, the median is the mean of the two middle numbers. Follow steps 1 and 2 to find the mean.

4. Suppose you want to calculate the median for the four highest-paid students. First, arrange the numbers in order, from least to greatest.

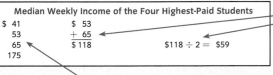

Practicing the Skill

1. What is the mean salary for the four lowest-paid students?
2. What is the median salary for the four lowest-paid students?

Applying the Skill to Economics

Average Monthly Rent: 2005

Miami, FL	$ 971	Dallas, TX	$ 709
Boston, MA	$1,216	Los Angeles, CA	$1,330

1. What is the mean monthly rent for these four cities?
2. What is the median monthly rent?

Skills Handbook

Teach

R Reading Strategy

Making Connections Ask students to think about instances in their daily lives in which they calculate or use averages. Invite volunteers to identify examples of these occasions, such as calculating one's average grade in a particular class or comparison shopping based on the average price of a potential purchase. Ask students to consider whether the median or mean would be more useful in each situation. **OL**

Reinforcing Economic Skills, Activity 5: Determining Averages: Mean and Median

 Glencoe Skillbuilder Interactive Workbook CD-ROM, Level 2

Practicing the Skill

Practicing the Skill
Answers:

1. The mean salary for the four lowest-paid students is $31.75.

2. The median salary for the four lowest paid students is $33.

Applying the Skill
Answers:

1. The mean monthly rent for these four cities is $1,056.50.

2. The median monthly rent for these four cities is $1,093.50.

Teach

C Critical Thinking

Evaluating Ask students to explain how inflation can make the use of nominal prices misleading for comparisons between the prices of things in the past and today. Students should recognize that inflation causes the prices of all goods to rise over time, so an increase in the nominal price of a good over a period of time does not necessarily reflect a change in its value compared to other items. **Ask:** How would two graphs—one showing the nominal price of an item over a period of ten years, and the other showing the real price of the item during the same period—likely differ? *(The graph showing the nominal price of the item would likely show a gradual increase over the period as inflation drove the price upward. However, the graph showing the real price of the item would likely show a less pronounced change, with the price only increasing or decreasing slightly.)* **AL**

 Glencoe Skillbuilder Interactive Workbook CD-ROM, Level 2

Understanding Nominal and Real Values

Why Learn This Skill?

The rise in the economy's average price level is called inflation. To make comparisons between the prices of things in the past and those of today, you have to make the distinction between *nominal*, or current, and *real*, or adjusted for inflation, values. You can use the consumer price index (CPI), an index of average prices for consumer goods, to calculate real values. Then you can accurately compare changes in income and prices over time.

Skills Handbook

Learning the Skill

Follow these steps to learn how to calculate nominal and approximate real values when price changes are small.

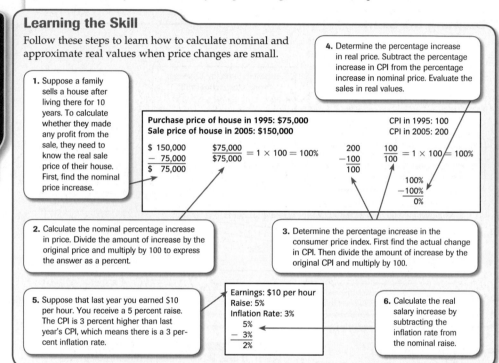

4. Determine the percentage increase in real price. Subtract the percentage increase in CPI from the percentage increase in nominal price. Evaluate the sales in real values.

1. Suppose a family sells a house after living there for 10 years. To calculate whether they made any profit from the sale, they need to know the real sale price of their house. First, find the nominal price increase.

Purchase price of house in 1995: $75,000
Sale price of house in 2005: $150,000

CPI in 1995: 100
CPI in 2005: 200

$$\begin{array}{r} \$\,150{,}000 \\ -\ 75{,}000 \\ \hline \$\,\ 75{,}000 \end{array}$$

$$\frac{\$75{,}000}{\$75{,}000} = 1 \times 100 = 100\%$$

$$\begin{array}{r} 200 \\ -100 \\ \hline 100 \end{array}$$

$$\frac{100}{100} = 1 \times 100 = 100\%$$

$$\begin{array}{r} 100\% \\ -100\% \\ \hline 0\% \end{array}$$

2. Calculate the nominal percentage increase in price. Divide the amount of increase by the original price and multiply by 100 to express the answer as a percent.

3. Determine the percentage increase in the consumer price index. First find the actual change in CPI. Then divide the amount of increase by the original CPI and multiply by 100.

5. Suppose that last year you earned $10 per hour. You receive a 5 percent raise. The CPI is 3 percent higher than last year's CPI, which means there is a 3 percent inflation rate.

Earnings: $10 per hour
Raise: 5%
Inflation Rate: 3%

$$\begin{array}{r} 5\% \\ -\ 3\% \\ \hline 2\% \end{array}$$

6. Calculate the real salary increase by subtracting the inflation rate from the nominal raise.

Practicing the Skill

1. What was the nominal price increase on the sale of the house?
2. How much money, in real dollars, was made on the house?
3. How much was the real value of the raise?

Applying the Skill to Economics

From 2004 to 2005, the cost of employer health insurance premiums increased by 9.2 percent—nearly three times the rate of inflation. Based on this information, what was the inflation rate that year? How could you adjust the cost of health insurance for inflation?

Practicing the Skill

Practicing the Skill
Answers:

1. The nominal price increase on the sale of the house was $75,000.

2. In real dollars, no money was made on the sale of the house.

3. The real value of the raise was $.20.

Applying the Skill
Answer:

The inflation rate for that year was around 3 percent. The cost of health insurance could be increased at a rate of approximately 6 percent to reflect the real value of the increase in employer health insurance premiums.

Understanding Interest Rates

Why Learn This Skill?

When you deposit money in a savings account, the bank pays you interest for the use of your money. The amount of interest is expressed as a percent, such as 6 percent, for a time period, such as per year. Two types of interest exist: simple and compound. *Simple interest* is figured only on the principal, or original deposit, not on any interest earned. *Compound interest* is paid on the principal plus any interest that has been earned.

Learning the Skill

Follow these steps to learn how to understand and calculate interest rates.

1. Suppose you deposit $100 in a savings account that earns 6 percent simple interest per year. Get ready to figure your earnings by converting 6 percent to a decimal.

2. To calculate the simple interest earned, multiply the principal by the interest rate.

3. Calculate the account balance for the first two years, assuming the bank pays the same interest rate each year. Add the principal, the first year's interest, and the second year's interest.

Simple Interest

6% = .06
```
 $ 100      $ 100
 × .06      +   6
 $6.00          6
            $ 112
```

4. Suppose you deposit $100 in a savings account that earns 6 percent compound interest per year. Calculate the interest earned the first year.

5. Find the bank balance for the end of the first year. Add the principal and first year's interest.

6. Determine the interest earned in the second year. Multiply the new balance by the interest rate.

7. Figure the total bank balance after two years. Add the second year's interest to the first year's balance.

Compound Interest
```
$ 100    $100    $ 106    $106.00
× .06    +  6    × .06    +  6.36
$6.00    $106    $6.36    $112.36
```

Practicing the Skill

1. What would be the difference in earnings between simple and compound interest if your initial balance was $1,000 rather than $100?

2. What would be the difference in earnings between simple and compound interest on your $100 savings after five years?

Applying the Skill to Economics

1. What would be the impact of compounding interest on a daily basis rather than an annual basis?

2. Banks often pay higher rates of interest on money you agree to keep in the bank for longer periods of time. Explain why this might be.

SKILLS HANDBOOK   R57

Teach

W Writing Support

Expository Writing Direct students to review the procedures for calculating simple and compound interest outlined in this lesson. Then, instruct them to write an expository paragraph that could guide a reader who is unfamiliar with these concepts through the steps necessary to carry out these calculations. When students have completed their paragraphs, have them exchange their work with partners and evaluate one another's work. Encourage students to make any suggested revisions to their paragraphs based on their partners' feedback. **OL**

Reinforcing Economic Skills, Activity 7: Understanding Interest Rates

 Glencoe Skillbuilder Interactive Workbook CD-ROM, Level 2

Practicing the Skill

Practicing the Skill Answers:

1. The difference in earnings would be $3.60.

2. The difference in earnings between compound and simple interest after five years would be $3.83.

Applying the Skill Answers:

1. The value of the account would increase more quickly because of the additional earnings from the more frequent compounding of interest.

2. Possible answer: Banks likely pay higher rates of interest on money that customers agree to keep in the bank because they can then lend the money to other customers with greater certainty, knowing that the money will not be removed until a certain time.

Teach

S Skill Practice

Visual Literacy Ask students to identify a political issue facing the community, state, or nation that holds special importance to them. Then direct them to conceptualize and draw a political cartoon that expresses their view about the issue. Encourage students to use elements like those shown in the cartoon on page R58, such as captions, conversation bubbles, symbols, and caricatures. When students have completed their work, display their finished cartoons for the class. Invite volunteers to offer interpretations of the various cartoons. **OL**

Glencoe Skillbuilder Interactive Workbook CD-ROM, Level 2

Skills Handbook

Interpreting Political Cartoons

Why Learn This Skill?

Political cartoonists use art to express opinions. Their work appears in newspapers, magazines, books, and on the Internet. Political cartoons usually focus on public figures, political events, or economic or social conditions. They can give you a summary of an event or circumstance and the artist's opinion in a quick, entertaining manner.

Learning the Skill

To interpret a political cartoon, follow these steps:

1. Read the title, caption, or conversation balloons. They help you identify the subject of the cartoon.

3. Identify any symbols shown. Symbols are things that stand for something else. Commonly recognized symbols may not be labeled. Unusual symbolism will be labeled.

5. Identify the cartoonist's purpose. What statement or idea is he or she trying to get across? Decide if the cartoonist wants to persuade, criticize, or just make people think.

2. Identify the characters or people shown. They may be caricatures, or unrealistic drawings that exaggerate the characters' physical features.

4. Examine the actions in the cartoon—what is happening and why?

Practicing the Skill

1. What is "cow tipping"? What does this imply about the U.S. economy as it is pictured in the cartoon?
2. What does the rhinoceros represent? Why might the cartoonist have chosen this particular symbol?
3. What overall message do you think the cartoonist is trying to send?

Applying the Skill to Economics

Bring a newspaper or business magazine to class. With a partner, analyze the message in each political cartoon that you find.

Practicing the Skill

Practicing the Skill
Answers:

1. Cow tipping is a prank in which people "tip" cows on to their sides so the cows cannot get back upright. The cartoon implies that the U.S. economy is stagnant and unaware of some of the serious threats it faces.

2. The rhinoceros represents inflation. The cartoonist may have chosen this symbol because the animal is known for its powerful, ferocious charges and might suggest that inflation is similarly powerful and difficult to stop.

3. Possible answer: The cartoonist is trying to send the message that inflation has the power to do serious, irreparable damage to the U.S. economy.

Applying the Skill
Answer:

Students should successfully locate political cartoons in newspaper and magazine sources. Each student pair should make reasonable interpretations of the messages contained in their selected political cartoons.

Reading Stock Market Reports

Why Learn This Skill?

A stock market report alphabetically lists stocks and provides information about stock prices and trades. Every business day, shares of stock are bought and sold. At the beginning of each trading day, stocks open at the same prices they closed at the day before. Prices generally go up and down throughout the day as the conditions of supply and demand change. At the end of the day, each stock's closing price is recorded.

Learning the Skill

Follow these steps to learn how to understand and use the financial page.

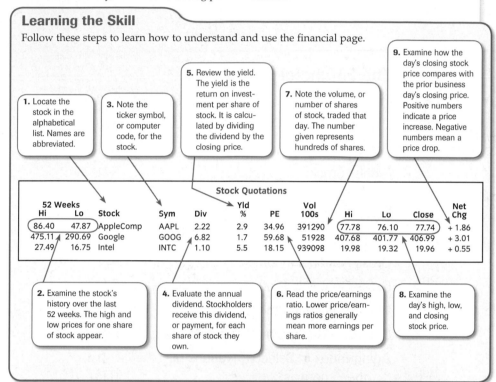

9. Examine how the day's closing stock price compares with the prior business day's closing price. Positive numbers indicate a price increase. Negative numbers mean a price drop.

5. Review the yield. The yield is the return on investment per share of stock. It is calculated by dividing the dividend by the closing price.

7. Note the volume, or number of shares of stock, traded that day. The number given represents hundreds of shares.

1. Locate the stock in the alphabetical list. Names are abbreviated.

3. Note the ticker symbol, or computer code, for the stock.

Stock Quotations

| 52 Weeks | | Stock | Sym | Div | Yld % | PE | Vol 100s | Hi | Lo | Close | Net Chg |
Hi	Lo										
86.40	47.87	AppleComp	AAPL	2.22	2.9	34.96	391290	77.78	76.10	77.74	+ 1.86
475.11	290.69	Google	GOOG	6.82	1.7	59.68	51928	407.68	401.77	406.99	+ 3.01
27.49	16.75	Intel	INTC	1.10	5.5	18.15	939098	19.98	19.32	19.96	+ 0.55

2. Examine the stock's history over the last 52 weeks. The high and low prices for one share of stock appear.

4. Evaluate the annual dividend. Stockholders receive this dividend, or payment, for each share of stock they own.

6. Read the price/earnings ratio. Lower price/earnings ratios generally mean more earnings per share.

8. Examine the day's high, low, and closing stock price.

Practicing the Skill

1. How many shares of Google stock were traded on the day shown?
2. What was the day's highest price for a share of Apple Computer stock?
3. Which stock had the greatest increase in closing price from the previous day?

Applying the Skill to Economics

If you had purchased 100 shares of Intel stock at its lowest 52-week price and sold it at this day's closing price, how much money would you have made?

SKILLS HANDBOOK   R59

Teach

C Critical Thinking

Drawing Conclusions Ask: Why might investors want to know the high and low prices for a stock over the last 52 weeks? What clues could the daily volume of a stock provide to investors? *(Investors might want to know the high and low prices for a stock over the last 52 weeks in order to gauge whether the stock has recently gained or lost a significant amount of value, as well as to predict how its value might change. The daily volume of a stock can tell investors whether or not many people are trading the stock. A high volume may help predict a change in value, as it could indicate that many people want to either purchase or sell the stock.)* **OL**

 Glencoe Skillbuilder Interactive Workbook CD-ROM, Level 2

Practicing the Skill

Practicing the Skill Answers:

1. 5,192,800 shares of Google stock were traded.

2. The days' highest price for a share of Apple Computer stock was $77.78.

3. Google stock had the greatest increase in closing price from the previous day.

Applying the Skill Answer:

$321

The data and forecasts for the graphs, tables, and charts in the Databank are based on information from Standard & Poor's.

U.S. Population Projections, 2000–2050

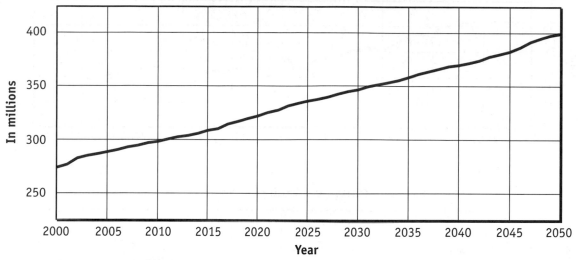

Source: U.S. Bureau of the Census

Civilian Labor Force, 1950–2010

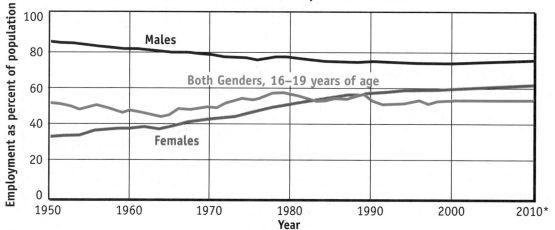

Source: Department of Labor, Bureau of Labor Statistics
*Estimate

Standard & Poor's Databank

Hours and Earnings in Private Industries, 1960–2006

A Average Weekly Hours of Production Workers

B Average Weekly Earnings of Production Workers, Current Dollars

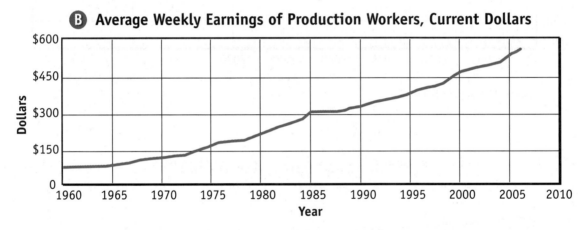

C Average Weekly Earnings, 1982 Dollars

Source: Bureau of Labor Statistics

Standard & Poor's Databank

Gross Domestic Product, 1950–2005

Source: U.S. Department of Commerce, Bureau of Economic Analysis

A Look at Stock Market History

Source: Standard & Poor's

Real Personal Consumption Expenditures, 1990–2005

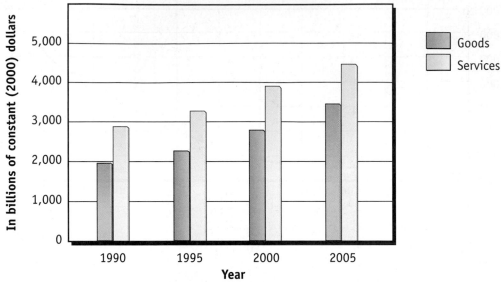

Source: Department of Commerce, Bureau of Economic Analysis

Personal Consumption Expenditures, 1960–2005

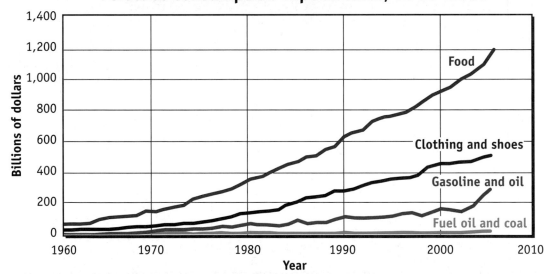

Source: Department of Commerce, Bureau of Economic Analysis

Average Prices of Selected Goods, 1990–2006

Electricity per 500 KWH

Utility natural gas, 40 therms
(1 therm = 100,000 British thermal units)

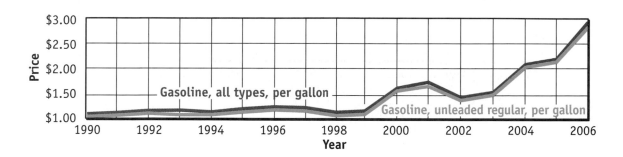

Gasoline, all types, per gallon

Gasoline, unleaded regular, per gallon

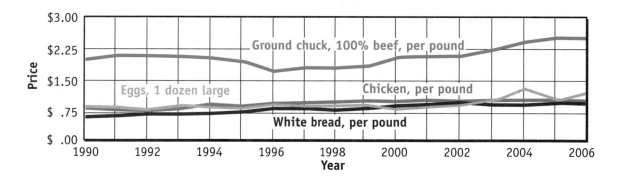

Ground chuck, 100% beef, per pound

Eggs, 1 dozen large

Chicken, per pound

White bread, per pound

Tomatoes, per lb.

Apples, red delicious, per lb.

Bananas, per lb.

Source: Bureau of Labor Statistics; U.S. city average prices for July

Standard & Poor's Databank

Annual Changes in Consumer Price Indexes, 1950–2006

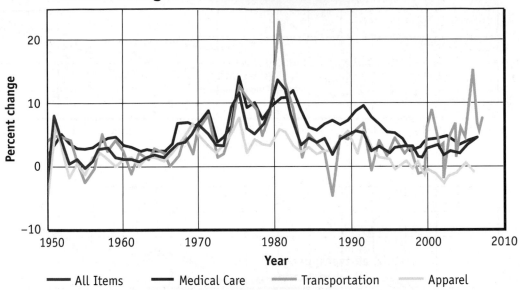

— All Items   — Medical Care   — Transportation   — Apparel

Inflation in Consumer Prices, 1950–2006

Source: Bureau of Labor Statistics

Standard & Poor's Databank

Federal Government Expenditures, 1950–2010

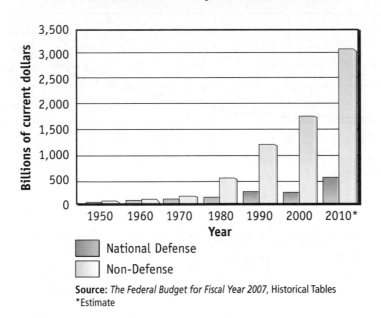

Source: *The Federal Budget for Fiscal Year 2007*, Historical Tables
*Estimate

Total Government Expenditures, 1965–2005

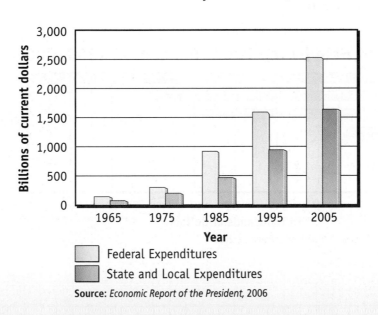

Source: *Economic Report of the President,* 2006

Standard & Poor's Databank

The Government Sector

Federal Government Total Receipts and Total Outlays, 1950–2007

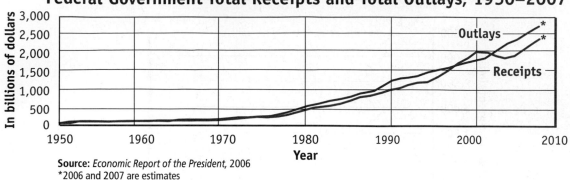

Source: *Economic Report of the President,* 2006
*2006 and 2007 are estimates

Federal Debt Held by the Public, 1950–2007

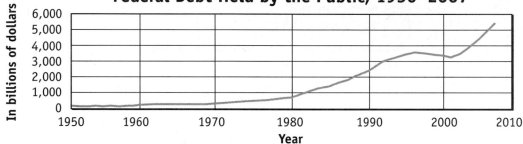

Source: *Economic Report of the President,* 2006
*2006 and 2007 are estimates

Federal Debt Held by the Public Per Capita, 1950–2007

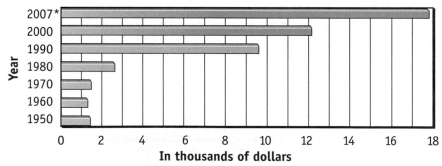

Source: *Economic Report of the President,* 2006
*Estimate

The Government Sector

Federal Budget Receipts, 1990–2010

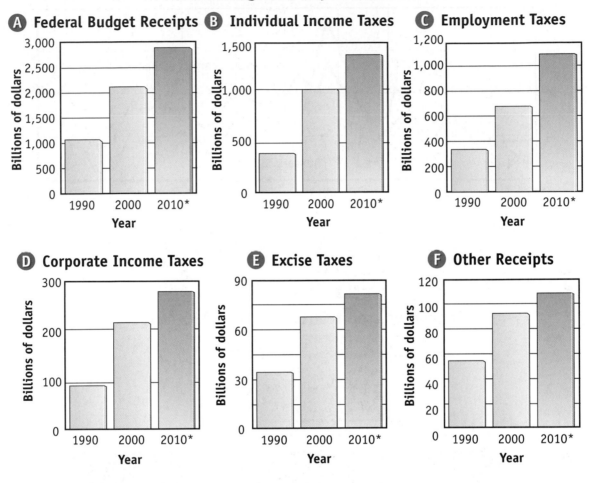

A Federal Budget Receipts

B Individual Income Taxes

C Employment Taxes

D Corporate Income Taxes

E Excise Taxes

F Other Receipts

Percentage of Total Receipts

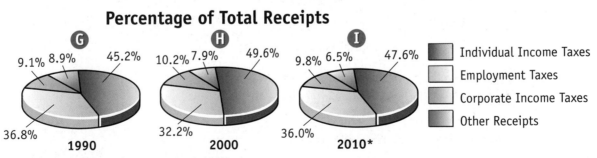

G 1990
- 45.2%
- 8.9%
- 9.1%
- 36.8%

H 2000
- 49.6%
- 7.9%
- 10.2%
- 32.2%

I 2010*
- 47.6%
- 6.5%
- 9.8%
- 36.0%

Legend:
- Individual Income Taxes
- Employment Taxes
- Corporate Income Taxes
- Other Receipts

Source: *Federal Budget for FY 2007,* Historical Tables
*Estimates

Interest Rates, 1960–2005

Prime rate charged by banks

Treasury Bill Rate

Consumer Credit Outstanding, 1985–2005

Total Consumer Credit	
1985	$599.7 billion
1995	$1,141.4 billion
2005	$2,147.9 billion

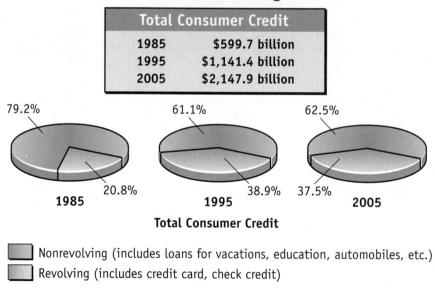

79.2%

20.8%

1985

61.1%

38.9%

1995

62.5%

37.5%

2005

Total Consumer Credit

Nonrevolving (includes loans for vacations, education, automobiles, etc.)

Revolving (includes credit card, check credit)

Source: Board of Governors of the Federal Reserve System

Personal Saving, 1960–2006

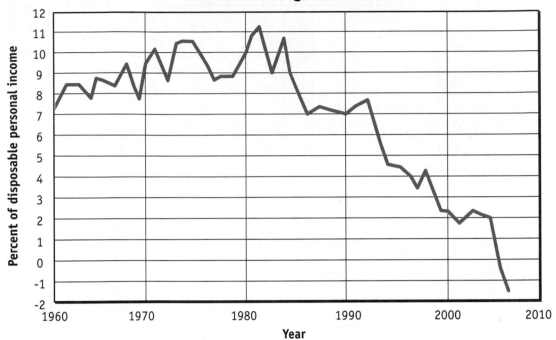

Source: U.S. Department of Commerce, Bureau of Economic Analysis

Money Stock, 1975–2005

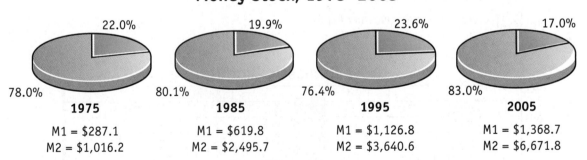

1975	1985	1995	2005
22.0%	19.9%	23.6%	17.0%
78.0%	80.1%	76.4%	83.0%
M1 = $287.1	M1 = $619.8	M1 = $1,126.8	M1 = $1,368.7
M2 = $1,016.2	M2 = $2,495.7	M2 = $3,640.6	M2 = $6,671.8

In billions of dollars

M1 consists of all currency and checkable deposits.

M2 consists of M1 plus noncheckable savings accounts, money market deposit accounts, time deposits, and money market mutual funds.

Source: Board of Governors of the Federal Reserve System

Standard & Poor's Databank

The Global Economy

Population

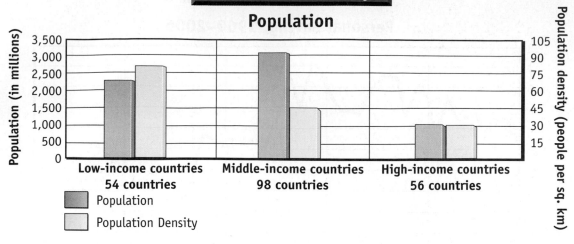

- Population
- Population Density

Low-income countries — 54 countries
Middle-income countries — 98 countries
High-income countries — 56 countries

Gross National Income

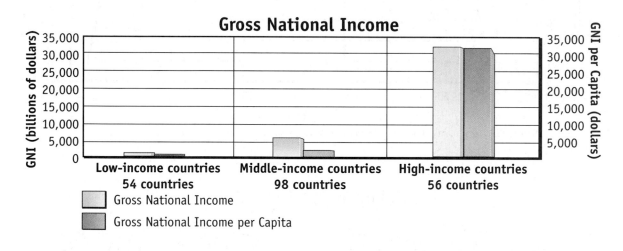

- Gross National Income
- Gross National Income per Capita

Low-income countries — 54 countries
Middle-income countries — 98 countries
High-income countries — 56 countries

Gross Domestic Product

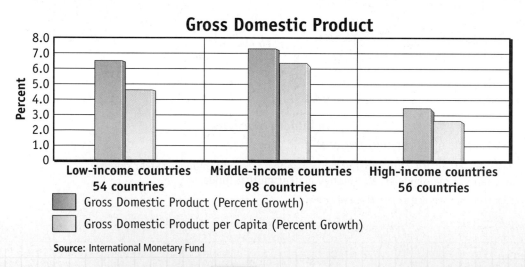

- Gross Domestic Product (Percent Growth)
- Gross Domestic Product per Capita (Percent Growth)

Low-income countries — 54 countries
Middle-income countries — 98 countries
High-income countries — 56 countries

Source: International Monetary Fund

The Global Economy

World Population by Age, 2000–2050

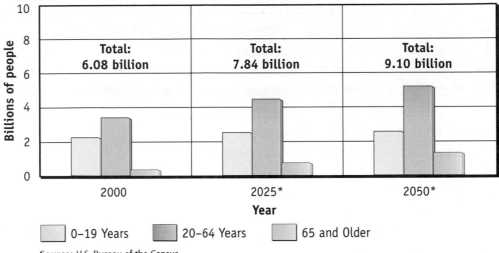

Source: U.S. Bureau of the Census
*Estimate

Countries Ranked by Population, 2000 and 2050

Country	Year 2000		Year 2050*	
	Population (in millions)	Rank	Population (in millions)	Rank
China	1,261	1	1,470	(2)
India	1,014	2	1,620	(1)
United States	276	3	404	(3)
Indonesia	224	4	338	(4)
Brazil	173	5	207	(7)
Russia	146	6	118	(14)
Pakistan	142	7	268	(6)
Bangladesh	129	8	205	(8)
Japan	127	9	101	(16)
Nigeria	123	10	304	(5)
Mexico	100	11	153	(12)

Source: U.S. Bureau of the Census
*Estimate

Aging Index in Selected Nations of the Americas, 2000 and 2025

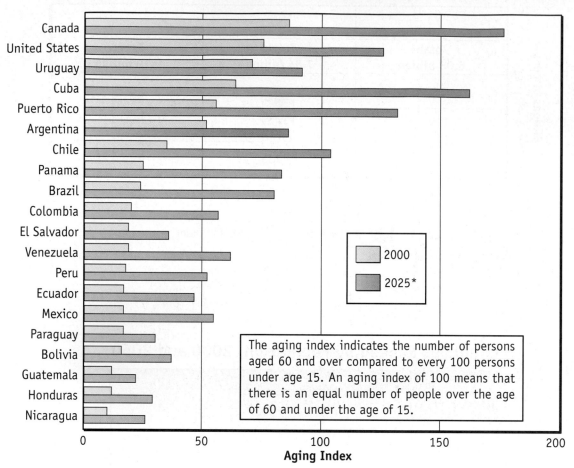

The aging index indicates the number of persons aged 60 and over compared to every 100 persons under age 15. An aging index of 100 means that there is an equal number of people over the age of 60 and under the age of 15.

Median Age, World, 1975–2025

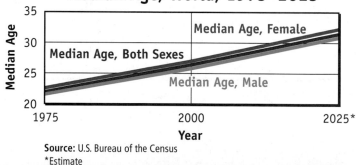

Source: U.S. Bureau of the Census
*Estimate

U.S. Exports and Imports, 1960–2005

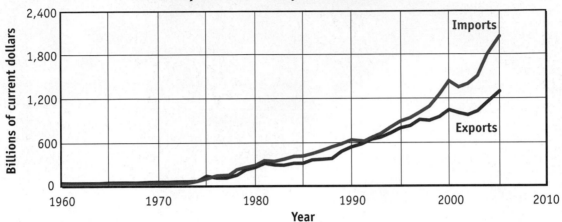

Inflation and Unemployment, Selected Economies 1990–2005

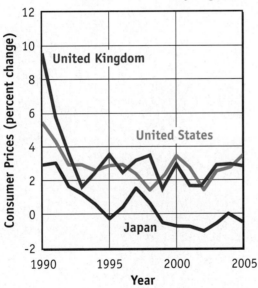

Source: *Economic Report of the President,* 2006

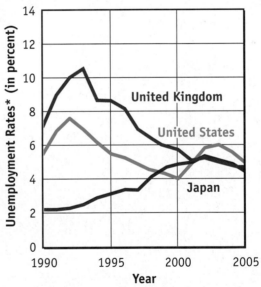

Source: International Monetary Fund
*Based on national definitions

REFERENCE ATLAS

NATIONAL GEOGRAPHIC

ATLAS KEY

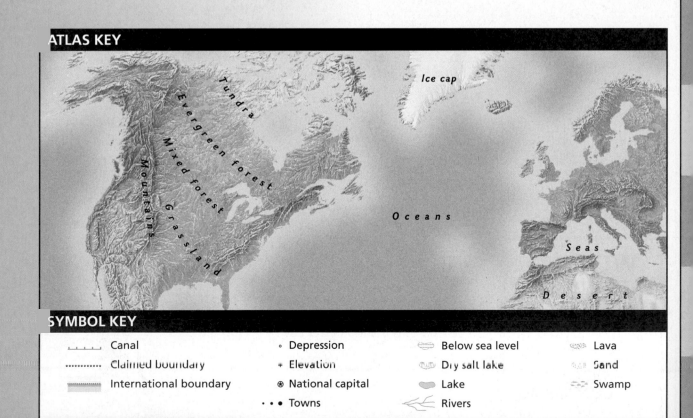

SYMBOL KEY

Canal	◦ Depression	Below sea level	Lava			
Claimed boundary	+ Elevation	Dry salt lake	Sand			
International boundary	⊛ National capital	Lake	Swamp			
	• • Towns	Rivers				

WORLD
POLITICAL

0 mi — 2000
0 km — 2000

WINKEL TRIPEL PROJECTION

NATIONAL GEOGRAPHIC

| 9 | 10 | 11 | 12 | 13 | 14 | 15 | 16 |

A

O C E A N
30°E   60°E   90°E   120°E   150°E

Franz Josef
Land
Svalbard
Nor.
Barents
Sea
Novaya
Zemlya
Severnaya
Zemlya
New Siberian
Islands
Laptev Sea
Kara
Sea
East
Siberian Sea

B

Norwegian
Sea
NORWAY
SWEDEN
FINLAND
Oslo
Yenisey
Ob
Lena
Yakutsk
60°N
Bering
Sea
Kamchatka
Peninsula

R U S S I A

Sea of
Okhotsk
Sakhalin
Hokkaido
Sapporo
Honshu

C

DENMARK
NETH.
GERMANY
BELG.
Paris
SWITZ.
FRANCE
ITALY
Rome
St. Petersburg
Volga
Moscow
Samara
Yekaterinburg
Omsk
Ural
Irtysh
Novosibirsk
Astana
Aral Sea
KAZAKHSTAN
Ulaanbaatar
MONGOLIA
Harbin
NORTH
KOREA
P'yŏngyang
Shenyang
Beijing
Tianjin
SOUTH
KOREA
Seoul
Osaka
JAPAN
Tokyo
Kyushu
30°N

N O R T H

P A C I F I C

O C E A N

EST.
LATVIA
LITH.
POLAND
BELARUS
CZECH
REP.
SLOVAKIA
AUST. HUNG.
SLOV.
CROAT.
B.&H. SERB.
MONT. ALBANIA MACED.
GREECE
BULGARIA
ROMANIA
MOLD.
Kyiv (Kiev)
UKRAINE
Baltic Sea
Black Sea
GEORGIA
ARMENIA
AZERBAIJAN
Tashkent
Almaty
Bishkek
KYRGYZSTAN
UZBEKISTAN
TAJIKISTAN
Dushanbe
Caspian Sea
TURKMENISTAN
Ashgabat
Ankara
TURKEY
CYPRUS
LEBANON
SYRIA
ISRAEL
JORDAN
Tehran
IRAN
Baghdad
IRAQ
KUWAIT
Islamabad
Lahore
C H I N A
Chengdu
Wuhan
Shanghai
Chung Jiang
(Yangtze)
Huang He
(Yellow)

D

Algiers
TUNISIA
Mediterranean Sea
Tripoli
Cairo
LIBYA
EGYPT
Riyadh
BAHRAIN
QATAR
U.A.E.
SAUDI
ARABIA
Masqat
OMAN
Red Sea
Karachi
PAKISTAN
Delhi
New
Delhi
NEPAL
BHUTAN
Brahmaputra
Indus
Dhaka
BANGLADESH
Kolkata
(Calcutta)
MYANMAR
(BURMA)
Yangon
(Rangoon)
Hanoi
Hong Kong
Guangzhou
Taipei
TAIWAN
Philippine
Sea
The People's Republic
of China claims Taiwan
as its 23rd province.
NORTHERN
MARIANA
ISLANDS
U.S.
30°N

E

ALGERIA
NIGER
CHAD
SUDAN
Khartoum
ERITREA
Sanaa
YEMEN
DJIBOUTI
Socotra
Yemen
Arabian
Sea
MALDIVES
Mumbai
(Bombay)
I N D I A
Hyderabad
Bengaluru
(Bangalore)
Chennai
(Madras)
Colombo
SRI
LANKA
Bay
of
Bengal
THAILAND
Bangkok
LAOS
Phnom
Penh
CAMBODIA
Ho Chi Minh
City
BRUNEI
VIETNAM
Hainan
South
China
Sea
Luzon
Manila
PHILIPPINES
MARSHALL
ISLANDS
PALAU
FEDERATED STATES
OF MICRONESIA
KIRIBATI
NAURU
Niamey
NIGERIA
Lagos
BENIN
TOGO
CAMEROON
CENTRAL
AFRICAN
REPUBLIC
Bangui
EQ.
GUINEA
N'Djamena
Addis Ababa
ETHIOPIA
SOMALIA
Mogadishu
UGANDA
KENYA
Nairobi
EQUATOR
SEYCHELLES
Kuala
Lumpur
MALAYSIA
SINGAPORE
Borneo
Celebes
Sumatra

F

GABON
CONGO
SAO TOME
& PRINCIPE
CABINDA
Ang.
Luanda
ANGOLA
DEM. REP.
OF THE
CONGO
Brazzaville
Kinshasa
RWANDA
BURUNDI
Dodoma
Dar es Salaam
TANZANIA
MALAWI
COMOROS
Jakarta
Java
Surabaya
I N D O N E S I A
New
Guinea
PAPUA
NEW GUINEA
Arafura Sea
Darwin
Port
Moresby
SOLOMON
ISLANDS
TUVALU

G

ZAMBIA
Lusaka
Harare
ZIMBABWE
NAMIBIA
Windhoek
BOTSWANA
Gaborone
Tshwane (Pretoria)
SOUTH
AFRICA
Bloemfontein
Cape Town
MOZAMBIQUE
Maputo
SWAZILAND
LESOTHO
Orange
Antananarivo
MADAGASCAR
MAURITIUS
Reunion
Fr.
I N D I A N
O C E A N
EAST TIMOR
(TIMOR-LESTE)
A U S T R A L I A
Perth
Darling
Murray
Brisbane
New Caledonia
Fr.
Coral VANUATU
Sea
FIJI
ISLANDS
S O U T H
P A C I F I C
O C E A N

H

Kerguelen Islands
Fr.
Sydney
Canberra
Melbourne
Tasman
Sea
Tasmania
NEW ZEALAND
Wellington
South
Island
Auckland
North
Island
60°S

ABBREVIATIONS

AUST.	AUSTRIA
B.&H.	BOSNIA & HERZEGOVINA
BELG.	BELGIUM
CROAT.	CROATIA
CZECH REP.	CZECH REPUBLIC
DEM. REP. OF THE CONGO	DEMOCRATIC REPUBLIC OF THE CONGO
EQ. GUINEA	EQUATORIAL GUINEA
EST.	ESTONIA
HUNG.	HUNGARY
LITH.	LITHUANIA
MACED.	MACEDONIA
MOLD.	MOLDOVA
NETH.	NETHERLANDS
SERB.	SERBIA
MONT.	MONTENEGRO
SLOV.	SLOVENIA
SWITZ.	SWITZERLAND
U.A.E.	UNITED ARAB EMIRATES

J

K

A N T A R C T I C A
Ross Sea

| 9 | 10 | 11 | 12 | 13 | 14 | 15 | 16 |

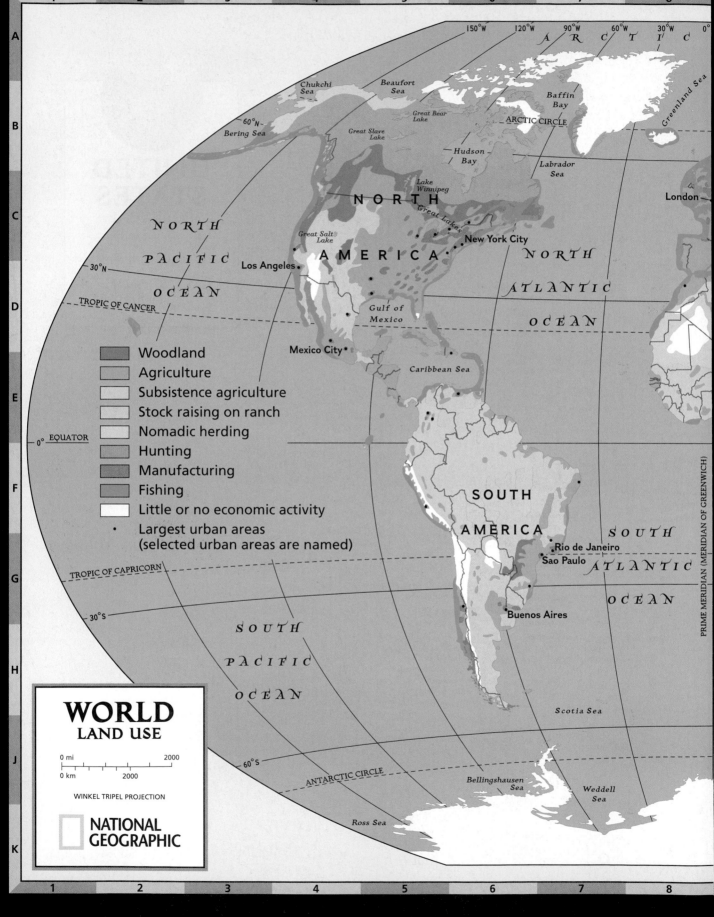

WORLD
LAND USE

Woodland
Agriculture
Subsistence agriculture
Stock raising on ranch
Nomadic herding
Hunting
Manufacturing
Fishing
Little or no economic activity
• Largest urban areas
(selected urban areas are named)

0 mi   2000
0 km   2000

WINKEL TRIPEL PROJECTION

NATIONAL GEOGRAPHIC

150°W   120°W   90°W   60°W   30°W   0°

ARCTIC

Chukchi Sea
Beaufort Sea
Baffin Bay
Greenland Sea

60°N
Bering Sea

Great Bear Lake
Great Slave Lake

ARCTIC CIRCLE

Hudson Bay
Labrador Sea

Lake Winnipeg

NORTH

London

NORTH

Great Lakes

PACIFIC

Great Salt Lake

AMERICA

New York City

NORTH

30°N

Los Angeles

ATLANTIC

OCEAN

TROPIC OF CANCER

Gulf of Mexico

OCEAN

Mexico City

Caribbean Sea

0° EQUATOR

SOUTH

AMERICA

SOUTH

Rio de Janeiro
Sao Paulo

ATLANTIC

TROPIC OF CAPRICORN

OCEAN

30°S

SOUTH

Buenos Aires

PACIFIC

PRIME MERIDIAN (MERIDIAN OF GREENWICH)

OCEAN

Scotia Sea

60°S

ANTARCTIC CIRCLE

Bellingshausen Sea

Weddell Sea

Ross Sea

UNITED STATES
LAND USE

ALBERS CONIC EQUAL-AREA PROJECTION

NATIONAL GEOGRAPHIC

N

CANADA

MINNESOTA

Lake Superior

MICHIGAN

WISCONSIN

Minneapolis • St. Paul

Mississippi

Milwaukee

Madison

IOWA

Cedar Rapids

Des Moines

Omaha

Lake Michigan

Lake Huron

Grand Rapids

Lansing

Detroit

Chicago

Gary

Fort Wayne

ILLINOIS

INDIANA

OHIO

Springfield

Indianapolis

Dayton

Cincinnati

Toledo

Akron

Cleveland

Lake Erie

Erie

PENNSYLVANIA

Pittsburgh

Harrisburg

Lake Ontario

Rochester

Buffalo

NEW YORK

Syracuse

Albany

MASS.

Montpelier

N.H.

VT.

Concord

Augusta

MAINE

Boston

Providence

RHODE ISLAND

Hartford

CONN.

Bridgeport

Newark

N.J.

New York City

Trenton

Philadelphia

Baltimore

Dover

DELAWARE

MARYLAND

Washington, D.C.

Annapolis

ATLANTIC OCEAN

Kansas City

Topeka

Jefferson City

St. Louis

Evansville

MISSOURI

Springfield

Tulsa

MA

ARKANSAS

Little Rock

KENTUCKY

Louisville

Frankfort

Ohio

WEST VIRGINIA

Charleston

Columbus

Richmond

VIRGINIA

Newport News

Virginia Beach

Norfolk

Raleigh

Knoxville

Nashville

TENNESSEE

Chattanooga

Memphis

Huntsville

Tennessee

NORTH CAROLINA

Charlotte

SOUTH CAROLINA

Columbia

Mississippi

Red

LOUISIANA

Shreveport

Beaumont

Houston

Jackson

MISSISSIPPI

Montgomery

ALABAMA

Birmingham

Atlanta

GEORGIA

Savannah

Mobile

Baton Rouge

New Orleans

Tallahassee

FLORIDA

Jacksonville

Orlando

Tampa

St. Petersburg

Fort Lauderdale

Miami

Gulf of Mexico

40°N

30°N

70°W

50°N

70°W

90°W

80°W

90°W

80°W

CUBA

TROPIC OF CANCER

20°N

Niihau

Kauai

Oahu

Honolulu

Molokai

Lanai

Kahoolawe

Maui

Hawaii

PACIFIC OCEAN

PRINCIPAL HAWAIIAN ISLANDS

0 mi 100

0 km 100

159°W

156°W

156°W

21°N

0 mi 300

0 km 300

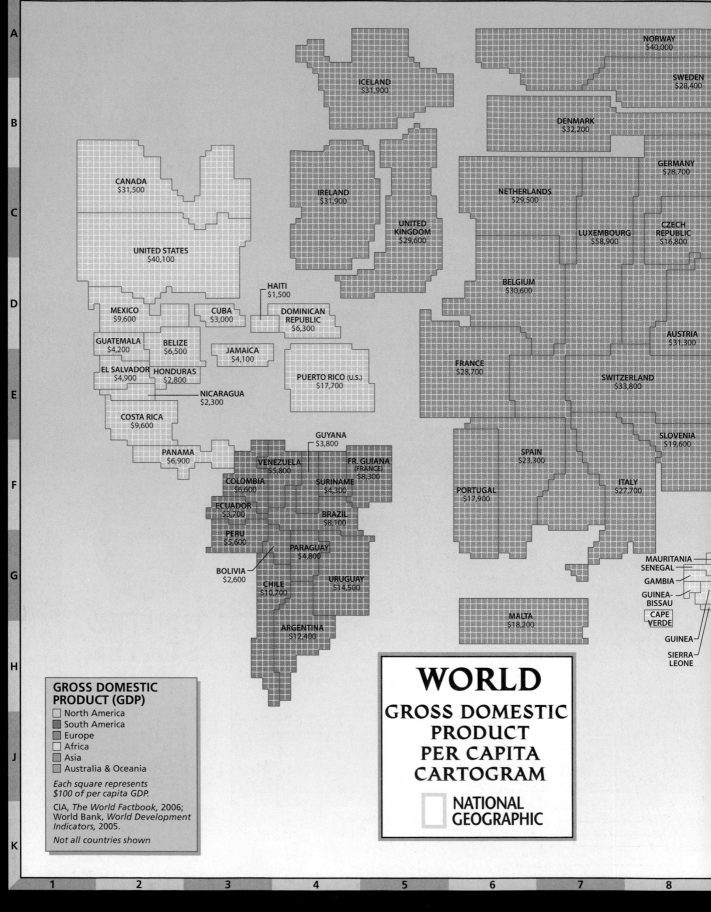

GROSS DOMESTIC
PRODUCT (GDP)
☐ North America
■ South America
■ Europe
☐ Africa
☐ Asia
☐ Australia & Oceania

*Each square represents
$100 of per capita GDP.*

CIA, *The World Factbook*, 2006;
World Bank, *World Development
Indicators*, 2005.

Not all countries shown

WORLD
GROSS DOMESTIC PRODUCT PER CAPITA CARTOGRAM

NATIONAL GEOGRAPHIC

NORWAY $40,000
SWEDEN $28,400
ICELAND $31,900
DENMARK $32,200
GERMANY $28,700
NETHERLANDS $29,500
CANADA $31,500
IRELAND $31,900
UNITED KINGDOM $29,600
LUXEMBOURG $58,900
CZECH REPUBLIC $16,800
UNITED STATES $40,100
BELGIUM $30,600
HAITI $1,500
MEXICO $9,600
CUBA $3,000
DOMINICAN REPUBLIC $6,300
AUSTRIA $31,300
GUATEMALA $4,200
BELIZE $6,500
JAMAICA $4,100
FRANCE $28,700
SWITZERLAND $33,800
EL SALVADOR $4,900
HONDURAS $2,800
PUERTO RICO (U.S.) $17,700
NICARAGUA $2,300
COSTA RICA $9,600
SLOVENIA $19,600
PANAMA $6,900
GUYANA $3,800
VENEZUELA $5,800
FR. GUIANA (FRANCE) $8,300
SPAIN $23,300
ITALY $27,700
COLOMBIA $6,600
SURINAME $4,300
ECUADOR $3,700
BRAZIL $8,100
PORTUGAL $17,900
PERU $5,600
PARAGUAY $4,800
BOLIVIA $2,600
MAURITANIA
URUGUAY $14,500
SENEGAL
CHILE $10,700
GAMBIA
GUINEA-BISSAU
CAPE VERDE
MALTA $18,200
GUINEA
ARGENTINA $12,400
SIERRA LEONE

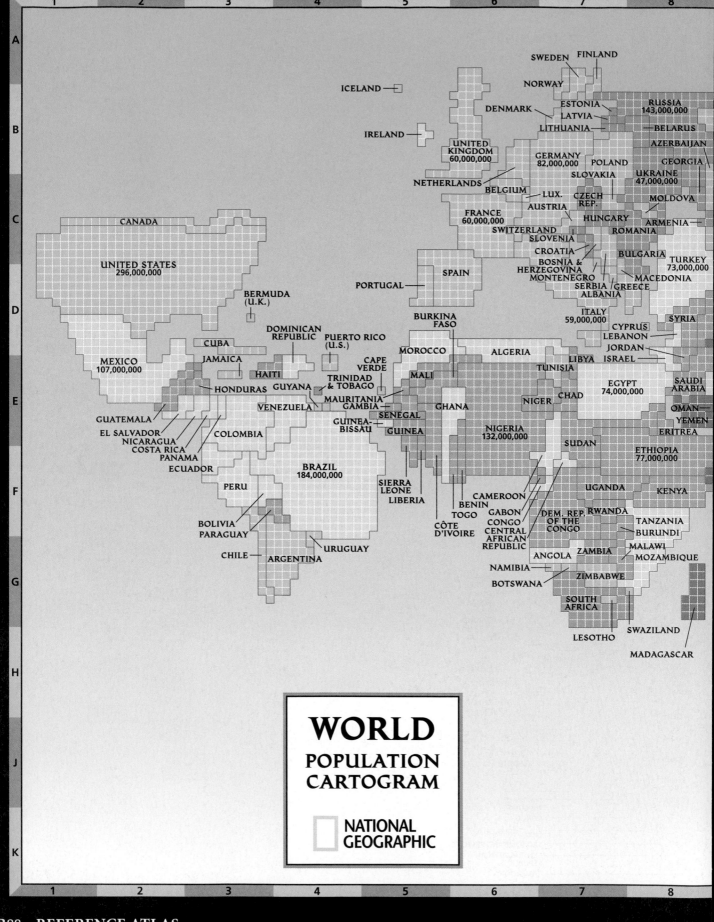

WORLD
POPULATION CARTOGRAM

NATIONAL GEOGRAPHIC

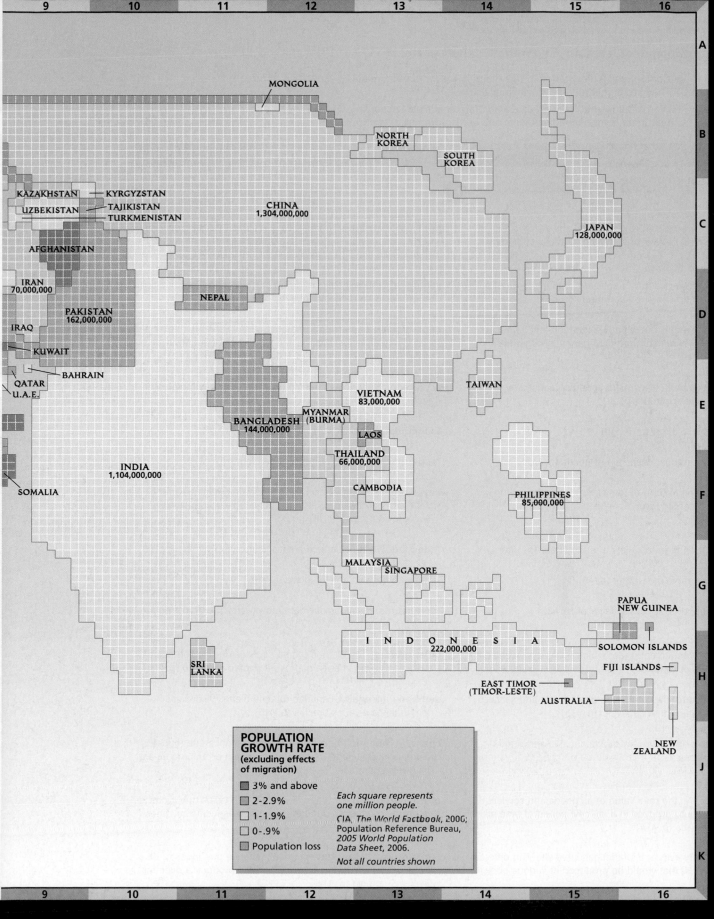

POPULATION GROWTH RATE
(excluding effects of migration)

- ■ 3% and above
- ☐ 2-2.9%
- ☐ 1-1.9%
- ☐ 0-.9%
- ■ Population loss

Each square represents one million people.

CIA, *The World Factbook*, 2006; Population Reference Bureau, *2005 World Population Data Sheet*, 2006.

Not all countries shown

MONGOLIA

NORTH KOREA

SOUTH KOREA

CHINA
1,304,000,000

JAPAN
128,000,000

KAZAKHSTAN — KYRGYZSTAN

UZBEKISTAN — TAJIKISTAN

TURKMENISTAN

AFGHANISTAN

IRAN
70,000,000

PAKISTAN
162,000,000

IRAQ

KUWAIT

BAHRAIN

QATAR

U.A.E.

NEPAL

TAIWAN

VIETNAM
83,000,000

BANGLADESH
144,000,000

MYANMAR (BURMA)

LAOS

THAILAND
66,000,000

INDIA
1,104,000,000

CAMBODIA

PHILIPPINES
85,000,000

SOMALIA

MALAYSIA

SINGAPORE

PAPUA NEW GUINEA

SOLOMON ISLANDS

INDONESIA
222,000,000

FIJI ISLANDS

SRI LANKA

EAST TIMOR
(TIMOR-LESTE)

AUSTRALIA

NEW ZEALAND

Glossary/Glosario

- Content vocabulary terms in this glossary are words that relate to economics content. They are highlighted yellow in your text.
- Words below that have an asterisk (*) are academic vocabulary terms. They help you understand your school subjects and are **boldfaced** in your text.

English	Español

ability-to-pay principle of taxation: belief that taxes should be paid according to level of income regardless of benefits received (p. 234)

principio de tributación: con base en la solvencia: creencia que los impuestos se deben pagar de acuerdo al nivel de ingresos sin considerar los beneficios recibidos (p. 234)

absolute advantage: country's ability to produce more of a given product than can another country (p. 443)

ventaja absoluta: habilidad de un país para producir más de un producto en particular que los otros países (p. 443)

accelerated depreciation: schedule that spreads depreciation over fewer years than normal to generate larger tax reductions (p. 249)

depreciación acelerada: programa que extiende la depreciación durante menos años de lo normal para generar mayores reducciones de impuestos (p. 249)

accelerator: change in investment spending caused by a change in overall spending (p. 421)

acelerador: cambio en el gasto causado por un cambio en el gasto global (p. 421)

*accommodate: to allow for (p. 46)

*acomodar: dar cabida (p. 46)

*accumulation: gradual collection of goods (p. 14)

*acumulación: colección gradual de bienes (p. 14)

acid rain: pollution in form of rainwater mixed with sulfur dioxide to form a mild form of sulfuric acid (p. 516)

lluvia ácida: contaminación en la forma de agualluvia mezclada con dióxido de sulfuro que constituye una forma leve de ácido sulfúrico (p. 516)

*adequate: just enough to satisfy a requirement (p. 108)

*adecuado: lo suficiente para satisfacer una exigencia (p. 108)

*adverse: unfavorable or harmful (p. 45)

*adverso: desfavorable o nocivo (p. 45)

*advocates: supports; speaks in favor of (p. 433)

*defensores: personas que dan apoyo; hablan en favor de (p. 433)

agency shop: arrangement under which non-union members must pay union dues (p. 204)

taller gremial: arreglo por el cual aquellos que no son miembros del sindicato tienen que pagar cuotas al mismo (p. 204)

aggregate demand: the total value of all goods and services demanded at different price levels. (p. 415)

demanda agregada: cantidad total de bienes y servicios demandados a varios precios (p. 415)

aggregate demand curve: hypothetical curve showing different levels of real GDP that would be purchased at various price levels (p. 415)

curva de demanda agregada: curva hipotética que muestra distintos niveles del PIB real que se podrían producir a distintos niveles de precio (p. 415)

aggregate supply: the total value of all goods and services that all firms would produce in a specific period of time at various price levels (p. 414)

oferta agregada: valor total de bienes y servicios que todas las empresas producirán durante un período específico a varios precios (p. 414)

aggregate supply curve: hypothetical curve showing different levels of real GDP that would be produced at various price levels (p. 414)

curva de oferta agregada: curva hipotética que muestra distintos niveles del PIB real que se podrían producir a distintos niveles de precio (p. 414)

English	Español
*allocate: to assign (p. 36)	***asignar:** adjudicar (p. 36)
*alternative: the second of two choices (p. 20)	***alternativa:** la segunda de dos opciones (p. 20)
alternative minimum tax: personal income tax rate that applies to cases where taxes would otherwise fall below a certain level (p. 249)	**impuesto mínimo alternativo:** índice de impuesto sobre la renta que se aplica a casos en los que los impuestos de otro modo caerían por debajo de cierto nivel (p. 249)
*ambiguity: uncertainty about meaning or value (p. 267)	***ambigüedad:** incertidumbre acerca del significado o valor (p. 267)
*analyze: to break down into parts and study how each part relates to one another (p. 80)	***analizar:** descomponer en partes y estudiar cómo cada parte se relaciona con las otras (p. 80)
*anticipate: to expect or be sure of in advance (p. 211)	***anticipar:** esperar o estar seguro de algo por adelantado (p. 211)
appropriations bill: legislation authorizing spending for certain purposes (p. 268)	**proyecto de ley para asignación de fondos:** legislación para asignar fondos para determinados fines (p. 268)
*arbitrarily: randomly or by chance (p. 157)	***arbitrariamente:** al azar o por casualidad (p. 157)
arbitration: agreement by two parties to place a dispute before a third party for a binding settlement; also called binding arbitration (p. 212)	**arbitraje:** acuerdo entre dos partes de anteponer la disputa ante un tercero para obtener un acuerdo obligatorio, también conocido como arbitraje obligatorio (p. 212)
ASEAN: group of ten Southeast Asian nations working to promote regional cooperation, economic growth, and trade (p. 484)	**ASEAN (siglas en inglés):** grupo de diez naciones del sudeste asiático que trabajan para promover la cooperación, crecimiento económico y comercio regional (p. 484)
*aspects: parts, phases (p. 401)	***aspectos:** partes, fases (p. 401)
*assumption: something taken for granted (p. 23)	***presunción:** algo que se da por sentado (p. 23)
automatic stabilizer: program that automatically provides benefits to offset a change in people's incomes; unemployment insurance, entitlement programs (p. 422)	**estabilizador automático:** programa que automáticamente provee beneficios para compensar por un cambio en los ingresos de la gente; seguro de desempleo, programas de derecho a gratificación (p. 422)
average tax rate: total taxes paid divided by the total taxable income (p. 235)	**tasa impositiva media:** total de impuestos pagados divididos por el total de renta imponible (p. 235)

B

English	Español
baby boom: historically high birthrate years in the United States from 1946 to 1964 (p. 332)	**auge de bebés:** período entre 1946 y 1964 durante le cual hubo un alza en la tasa de natalidad en los Estados Unidos (p. 332)
baby boomers: people born in the United States during the historically high birthrate years from 1946 to 1964 (p. 432)	**baby boomers:** personas nacidas durante el período transcurrido entre los años 1946 a 1964 en los Estados Unidos (p. 432)
balance of payments: difference between money paid to, and received from, other nations in trade; balance on current account includes goods and services, merchandise trade balance counts only goods (p. 452)	**balanza de pagos:** diferencia entre dinero que se paga o que se recibe de otras naciones en actividad comercial; el balance de cuenta corriente incluye bienes y servicios, la balanza comercial de mercancía toma en cuenta sólo los bienes (p. 452)

balanced budget • boycott

English	Español
balanced budget: annual budget in which expenditures equal revenues (p. 278)	**presupuesto balanceado:** presupuesto anual en el que los gastos están a la par con los ingresos (p. 278)
balanced budget amendment: constitutional amendment requiring government to spend no more than it collects in taxes and other revenues, excluding borrowing (p. 271)	**enmienda al presupuesto balanceado:** enmienda constitucional estatal o federal que requiere que el gobierno no gaste más de lo que recauda en impuestos y otros ingresos, a exclusión de préstamos (p. 271)
bank holiday: brief period during which all banks or depository institutions are closed to prevent bank runs (p. 395)	**cierre bancario:** breve período durante el cual todos los bancos o instituciones de depósito cierran para evitar los pánicos bancarios (p. 395)
bank holding company: company that owns and controls one or more banks (p. 407)	**compañía tenedora bancaria:** compañía que posea y controla uno o más bancos (p. 407)
bank run: sudden rush by depositors to withdraw all deposited funds, generally in anticipation of bank failure or closure (p. 395)	**pánico bancario:** prisa repentina de los depositantes por sacar todos sus fondos, generalmente en anticipación a la quiebra o cierre del banco (p. 395)
barter economy: moneyless economy that relies on trade or barter (p. 384)	**economía de trueque:** economía sin dinero que depende del comercio o trueque (p. 384)
base year: year serving as point of comparison for other years in a price index or other statistical measure (pp. 221, 321, 362)	**año base:** año que sirve como punto de comparación para otros años en un índice de precios u otra estadística (pp. 221, 321, 362)
bear market: period during which stock market prices move down for several months or years in a row (p. 310)	**mercado en descenso:** período durante el cual los precios de la bolsa bajan por varios meses o años seguidos (p. 310)
benefit principle of taxation: belief that taxes should be paid according to benefits received regardless of income (p. 234)	**principio de tributación sobre beneficios:** creencia de que los impuestos se deben pagar de acuerdo con los beneficios que se reciban independiente del nivel de ingreso (p. 234)
beneficiary: person designated to take ownership of an asset if the owner of the asset dies (p. 301)	**beneficiario:** persona designada para tomar propiedad de un bien si el poseedor del bien muere (p. 301)
Better Business Bureau: business-sponsored nonprofit organization providing information on local companies to consumers (p. 82)	**Better Business Bureau:** organización sin fines de lucro patronizada por el comercio la cual provee al consumidor información acerca de las compañías locales (p. 82)
binding arbitration: see arbitration (p. 212)	**arbitraje obligatorio:** ver arbitration (p. 212)
biomass: energy made from wood, peat, municipal solid waste, straw, corn, tires, landfill gasses, fish oils, and other waste (p. 512)	**biomasa:** energía proveniente de madera, turba, desperdicios sólidos municipales, paja, maíz, biogás, aceites de pescado y otros desechos (p. 512)
black market: market in which economic products are sold illegally (p. 491)	**mercado negro:** mercado en el cual se venden productos económicos ilegalmente (p. 491)
bond: formal contract to repay borrowed money and interest on the borrowed money at regular future intervals (pp. 69, 297)	**fianza:** contrato formal para devolver el dinero y los intereses sobre dinero prestado durante intervalos sistemáticos en el futuro (pp. 69, 297)
boycott: protest in the form of a refusal to buy, including attempts to convince others to join (p. 199)	**boicot:** protesta en la forma de rehusar a comprar, que incluye el esfuerzo para convencer a otras personas a tampoco comprar (p. 199)

English	Español
break-even point: production level where total cost equals total revenue; production needed if the firm is to recover its costs (p. 135)	**punto de equilibrio:** nivel de producción en el que el costo total iguala a la recaudación total; producción necesaria si la firma ha de recuperar sus costos (p. 135)
budget deficit: a negative balance after expenditures are subtracted from revenues (p. 269)	**déficit presupuestal:** balance negativo después de restar los gastos a la recaudación (p. 269)
budget surplus: a positive balance after expenditures are subtracted from revenues (p. 269)	**superávit presupuestal:** balance positivo después de restar los gastos a la recaudación (p. 269)
bull market: period during which stock market prices move up for several months or years in a row (p. 310)	**mercado en ascenso:** período durante el cual los precios de la bolsa suben por varios meses o años seguidos (p. 310)
business cycles: systematic changes in real GDP marked by alternating periods of expansion and contraction (p. 353)	**ciclo comercial:** cambios sistemáticos en el PIB real acentuados por periodos alternantes de expansión y contracción (p. 353)
business fluctuation: changes in real GDP marked by alternating periods of expansion and contraction that occur on an irregular basis (p. 353)	**fluctuación comercial:** cambios en el PIB acentuados por períodos alternantes de expansión y contracción que ocurren irregularmente (p. 353)

English	Español
call option: futures contract giving investors the option to cancel a contract to buy commodities, equities, or financial assets (p. 311)	**opción de compra:** contrato de futuros que da a los inversionistas la opción de cancelar un contrato para comprar productos básicos, acciones, o activos financieros (p. 311)
capital: tools, equipment, and factories used in the production of goods and services; one of four factors of production (p. 8)	**capital:** implementos, equipo y fábricas que se usan en la producción de bienes y servicios; uno de cuatro factores de producción (p. 8)
capital flight: legal or illegal export of a nation's currency and foreign exchange (p. 477)	**fuga de capitales:** exportación legal o ilegal de la moneda y las divisas de una nación (p. 477)
capital gains: profits from the sale of an asset held for 12 months or longer (p. 250)	**ganancias de capital:** ganancias de la venta de un activo después de haberlo tenido durante 12 meses o más tiempo (p. 250)
capital good: tool, equipment, or other manufactured good used to produce other goods and services; a factor of production (p. 8)	**bienes de capital:** implemento, equipo u otros bienes fabricados que se emplean para producir otros bienes y servicios; un factor de producción (p. 8)
capital-intensive: production method requiring relatively large amounts of capital relative to labor (p. 492)	**capital intensivo:** método de producción que requiere relativamente grandes cantidades de capital con relación a la mano de obra (p. 492)
capital market: market in which financial capital is loaned and/or borrowed for more than one year (p. 302)	**mercado de capital:** mercado en el que el capital financiero se presta por más de un año (p. 302)
capitalism: economic system in which private citizens own and use the factors of production in order to generate profits (pp. 38, 486)	**capitalismo:** sistema económico en el cual los ciudadanos tienen la propiedad y el uso de los factores de producción para generar ganancias (pp. 38, 486)

cartel • civilian labor force

English	Español
cartel: group of sellers or producers acting together to raise prices by restricting availability of a product; OPEC (p. 484)	**cartel:** grupo de vendedores o productores que obran conjuntamente para subir los precios al restringir la disponibilidad de un producto; OPEC (p. 484)
cash flow: total amount of new funds the business generates from operations; broadest measure of profits for a firm, includes both net income and non-cash charges (p. 73)	**flujo de efectivo:** cantidad total de nuevos fondos que el negocio genera por sus operaciones; la medida más comprensiva de las utilidades de una compañía que incluye el ingreso neto y cargos no al contado (p. 73)
*catalyst: something that stimulates activity among people or forces (p. 51)	***catalizador:** algo que estimula la actividad entre personas o fuerzas (p. 51)
cease and desist order: ruling requiring a company to stop an unfair business practice that reduces or limits competition (p. 186)	**orden de cesar y desistir:** fallo que ordena que una compañía pare una práctica comercial injusta que reduce o limita la competencia (p. 186)
census: complete count of population, including place of residence (p. 329)	**censo:** conteo total de la población, incluyendo el lugar de residencia (p. 329)
center of population: point where the country would balance if it were flat and everyone weighed the same (p. 331)	**centro de población:** punto donde el país se equilibraría si fuera plano y todo el mundo pesara lo mismo (p. 331)
central bank: bank that can lend to other banks in times of need, a "bankers' bank" (p. 394)	**banco central:** banco que le presta a otros bancos en momentos de necesidad, el "banco de los banqueros" (p. 394)
certificate of deposit: receipt showing that an investor has made an interest-bearing loan to a financial institution (p. 290)	**certificado de depósito:** recibo que indica que un inversionista ha hecho un préstamo con intereses a una institución financiera (p. 290)
chamber of commerce: nonprofit organization of local businesses whose purpose is to promote their interests (p. 81)	**cámara de comercio:** organización sin fines de lucro cuyo propósito es promover los intereses comunes de los negocios locales (p. 81)
change in demand: consumers demand different amounts at every price, causing the demand curve to shift to the left or the right (p. 99)	**cambio en demanda:** los consumidores demandan distintas cantidades en cada precio, haciendo que la curva de demanda cambie hacia la izquierda o la derecha (p. 99)
change in quantity demanded: movement along the demand curve showing that a different quantity is purchased in response to a change in price (p. 98)	**cambio en la cantidad demandada:** un movimiento en la curva de relación entre demanda y precio que demuestra que se está comprando una cantidad distinta debido a un cambio de precio (p. 98)
change in quantity supplied: change in amount offered for sale in response to a price change; movement along the supply curve (p. 119)	**cambio en la cantidad suplida:** cambio en la cantidad que se ofrece a la venta en respuesta a un cambio de precio; movimiento a lo largo de la curva de abastecimiento (p. 119)
change in supply: different amounts offered for sale at each and every possible price in the market; shift of the supply curve (p. 120)	**cambio en abastecimiento:** distintas cantidades ofrecidas a la venta a todos los precios posibles del mercado; cambio en la curva de abastecimiento (p. 120)
charter: written government approval to establish a corporation; includes company name, address, purpose of business, number of shares of stock, and other features of the business (p. 67)	**carta constitucional:** aprobación escrita del gobierno para establecer una corporación; incluye el nombre de la compañía, la dirección, propósito del negocio, número de acciones y otros aspectos del negocio (p. 67)
civilian labor force: noninstitutionalized part of the population, aged 16 and over, either working or looking for a job (pp. 204, 370)	**fuerza de trabajo civil:** parte de la población no institucionalizada, entre los 16 y 65 años, que está trabajando o buscando trabajo (pp. 204, 370)

English	Español
closed shop: arrangement under which workers must join a union before they are hired; usually illegal (p. 203)	**pacto de pertenencia:** acuerdo por el cual los trabajadores deben afiliarse al sindicato antes de ser contratados; generalmente es ilegal (p. 203)
coins: metallic forms of money such as pennies, nickels, dimes, and quarters (p. 406)	**monedas:** formas metálicas de dinero tal como el centavo, las monedas de cinco, diez y de 25 centavos (p. 406)
***coincide:** to happen or exist at the same time or in the same position (p. 268)	***coincidir:** ocurrir o existir al mismo tiempo o en la misma posición (p. 268)
collective bargaining: process of negotiation between union and management representatives over pay, benefits, and job-related matters (pp. 81, 211)	**negociación colectiva:** proceso de negociación entre el sindicato y los representantes administrativos acerca de pago, beneficios y asuntos relacionados al trabajo (pp. 81, 211)
collectivization: forced common ownership of factors of production; used in the former Soviet Union in agriculture and manufacturing (p. 490)	**colectivización:** propiedad común forzada de los factores de producción; se usó en la antigua Unión Soviética en la agricultura y en la industria manufacturera (p. 490)
***collude:** to act together in secret, especially with harmful or illegal intent (p. 180)	***coludir:** confabularse y operar en secreto con alguien, especialmente con intención de daño o ilegal (p. 180)
collusion: agreements, usually illegal, among producers to fix prices, limit output, or divide markets (p. 174)	**colusión:** acuerdos, por lo general ilegales, entre los productores para fijar los precios, limitar la producción o dividir los mercados (p. 174)
command economy: economic system characterized by a central authority that makes most of the major economic decisions (p. 35)	**economía de mando:** sistema económico que se caracteriza por una autoridad central que toma la mayoría de las decisiones económicas (p. 35)
commodity money: money that has an alternative use as an economic good; gunpowder, flour, corn (p. 384)	**dinero como producto:** dinero que tiene un uso alternativo como un bien económico; pólvora, harina, maíz (p. 384)
common stock: most common form of corporate ownership, with one vote per share for stockholders (p. 67)	**acciones ordinarias:** la forma más común de propiedad corporativa, con un voto por acción para los accionistas (p. 67)
communism: economic and political system in which factors of production are collectively owned and directed by the state; theoretically classless society in which everyone works for the common good (p. 39)	**comunismo:** sistema económico y político en el cual los factores de producción son de propiedad colectiva y dirigidos por el estado; teóricamente, una sociedad sin clases en que todos trabajan para el bien común (p. 39)
company union: union organized, supported, or run by an employer (p. 199)	**sindicato de empresa:** unión organizada, sostenida o dirigida por el patrón (p. 199)
comparative advantage: country's ability to produce a given product relatively more efficiently than another country; production at a lower opportunity cost (pp. 444, 504)	**ventaja comparativa:** habilidad del país de producir un cierto producto con relativamente más eficiencia que otro país; la oportunidad de producción al costo más bajo (pp. 444, 504)
***compensation:** something, such as money, given or received as an equivalent for goods or services, injury, debt, or high risk (p. 294)	***compensación:** algo, por ejemplo dinero, que se da o recibe como equivalente de bienes o servicios, lesiones, deuda o alto riesgo (p. 294)
competition: the struggle among sellers to attract consumers (p. 50)	**competencia:** la lucha entre vendedores para atraer consumidores (p. 50)
complements: products that increase the use of other products; products related in such a way that an increase in the price of one reduces the demand for both (p. 101)	**complementos:** productos que aumentan el uso de otros productos; productos relacionados de tal modo que el aumento del precio de uno reduce la demanda de ambos (p. 101)

English	Español
*components: parts of something (p. 325)	*componente: una parte de algo (p. 325)
composite index of leading economic indicators (LEI): composite index of 10 economic series that move up and down in advance of changes in the overall economy; used to predict turning points in the business cycle (p. 359)	índice compuesto de los principales indicadores económicos: índice compuesto de 10 series económicas que suben y bajan anticipando los cambios en la economía global; usados para predecir puntos de transición en el ciclo comercial (p. 359)
*compounded: increased, made worse (p. 509)	*compuesto: incrementado, empeorado (p. 509)
*comprehensive: covering many or all areas (p. 10)	*abarcativo: que cubre muchas o todas las áreas (p. 10)
*comprise: to be composed of (p. 62)	*abarcar: englobar, estar compuesto de (p. 62)
*concept: general idea (p. 251)	*concepto: idea general (p. 251)
*conducted: handled by way of (p. 135)	*conducido: que se maneja de cierta forma (p. 135)
*confined: kept within (p. 370)	*confinado: mantenido dentro de límites (p. 370)
conglomerate: firm with four or more businesses making unrelated products, with no single business responsible for a majority of its sales (p. 76)	conglomerado de empresas: firma con cuatro o más negocios que hacen productos no relacionados, sin ningún negocio en particular que sea responsable de la mayoría de sus ventas (p. 76)
*considerably: to a noticeable or significant extent (p. 243)	*considerablemente: en un grado significativo o visible (p. 243)
constant dollars: dollar amounts or prices that have been adjusted for inflation; same as real dollars (p. 221)	dólares constantes: las cantidades o precios al que se ajusta el dólar debido a la inflación; igual que dólares reales (p. 221)
*constituents: persons who are represented by an elected official (p. 261)	*constituyentes: personas representadas por un funcionario oficial elegido (p. 261)
*construction: creation by assembling individual parts (p. 362)	*construcción: creación a través del montaje de partes individuales (p. 362)
consumer good: good intended for final use by consumers rather than businesses (p. 13)	bienes del consumidor: bienes cuyo fin está dirigido a los consumidores en vez del comercio (p. 13)
consumer price index (CPI): index used to measure price changes for a market basket of frequently used consumer items (p. 362)	índice de precios de consumidor (CPI, siglas en inglés): índice que se usa para medir los cambios de precio de la cesta de compra de los productos que el consumidor usa con más frecuencia (p. 362)
consumer sovereignty: role of consumer as ruler of the market when determining the types of goods and services produced (p. 51)	soberanía del consumidor: papel del consumidor como soberano del mercado a la hora de determinar los tipos de bienes y servicios que se producen (p. 51)
*context: the circumstances surrounding a situation or event (p. 504)	*contexto: las circunstancias que rodean una situación o acontecimiento (p. 504)
*contributes: gives time, money, or effort (p. 130)	*contribuye: que aporta tiempo, dinero o esfuerzo (p. 130)
*controversial: disputed (p. 252)	*controversial: polémico (p. 252)

English	Español
*converted: changed into a different form (p. 387)	*convirtido: que ha cambió a una forma diferente (p. 387)
cooperative or co-op: nonprofit association performing some kind of economic activity for the benefit of its members (p. 80)	cooperativa: asociación sin fines de lucro que lleva a cabo un tipo de actividad económica para el beneficio de sus miembros; incluye las cooperativas del consumidor, de servicios y de productores (p. 80)
corporate income tax: tax on corporate profits (p. 240)	impuesto sobre la renta de corporación: impuesto que pagan las corporaciones sobre sus ganancias (p. 240)
corporation: form of business organization recognized by law as a separate legal entity with all the rights and responsibilities of an individual, including the right to buy and sell property, enter into legal contracts, sue and be sued (p. 67)	corporación: una forma de organización comercial reconocida por la ley como una entidad legal independiente con todos los derechos y responsabilidades de individuo, inclusive el derecho de comprar y vender propiedad, entrar en contratos legales, demandar y ser demandada (p. 67)
cost-benefit analysis: way of thinking that compares the cost of an action to its benefits (pp. 24, 522)	análisis de costo-beneficio: forma de pensar que compara el costo de una acción con sus ventajas (pp. 24, 522)
cost-push inflation: explanation that rising input costs, especially energy and organized labor, drive up the cost of products for manufacturers and cause inflation (p. 365)	inflación de costos: explicación que expone que el aumento de costos de producción, especialmente energía y mano de obra organizada, aumentan el costo de los productos para el fabricante y causan inflación (p. 365)
Council of Economic Advisers: three-member group that devises strategies and advises the President of the United States on economic matters (p. 433)	Consejo de Asesores Económicos: grupo de tres miembros que idea estrategias y aconseja al Presidente de los Estados Unidos acerca de asuntos económicos (p. 433)
coupon rate: stated interest on a corporate, municipal or government bond (p. 297)	tarifa de cupón: interés declarado de un bono corporativo, municipal o gubernamental (p. 297)
craft union: labor union whose members perform the same kind of work; same as trade union (p. 199)	sindicato de artesanos: gremio laboral cuyos miembros llevan a cabo el mismo tipo de trabajo; igual que un sindicato gremial (p. 199)
credit union: nonprofit service cooperative that accepts deposits, makes loans, and provides other financial services (p. 80)	unión de crédito: cooperativa de servicios sin fines de lucro que acepta depósitos, hace préstamos y brinda otros servicios financieros (p. 80)
creditor: person or institution to whom money is owed (p. 367)	acreedor: persona o institución a quien se le debe dinero (p. 367)
creeping inflation: relatively low rate of inflation, usually 1 to 3 percent annually (p. 364)	inflación reptante: índice de inflación bajo, generalmente de 1 a 3 por ciento anualmente (p. 364)
*criteria: a standard or rule on which judgment can be based (p. 145)	*criterios: normas o reglas en las que puede basarse un juicio (p. 145)
crowding-out effect: higher than normal interest rates and diminished access to financial capital faced by private investors when government increases its borrowing in financial markets (p. 281)	efecto de exclusión: tasas de interés más altas de lo normal y disminución del acceso al capital financiero al cual se enfrentan los inversionistas privados cuando el gobierno aumenta sus préstamos en los mercados financieros (p. 281)
crude birthrate: number of live births per 1,000 people (p. 474)	tasa de natalidad bruta: número de nacimientos por 1,000 personas (p. 474)

currency • demand elasticity

English	Español
currency: paper component of the money supply, today consisting of Federal Reserve notes (p. 406)	**efectivo:** componente de papel del abastecimiento de dinero, hoy consiste en billetes de la Reserva Federal (p. 406)
current dollars: dollar amounts or prices that are not adjusted for inflation (p. 219)	**dólares corrientes:** cantidades o precios del dólar que no han sido ajustados para reflejar la inflación (p. 219)
current GDP: gross domestic product measured in current prices, unadjusted for inflation (p. 322)	**PIB imperante:** producto interno bruto que se mide por los precios imperantes, sin ajustarlos para reflejar la inflación (p. 322)
current yield: bond's annual coupon interest divided by purchase price; measure of a bond's return (p. 297)	**rendimiento imperante:** el interés anual del cupón de un bono dividido por el precio de compra; medida de las ganancias de un bono (p. 297)
customs duty: tax on imported products (p. 241)	**derechos aduaneros:** impuestos sobre productos importados (p. 241)
customs union: group of countries that have agreed to reduce trade barriers and have uniform tariffs for nonmembers (p. 483)	**unión aduanera:** grupo de países que han acordado reducir las barreras de intercambio comercial entre sí y tienen aranceles uniformes para quienes no son miembros (p. 483)
cyclical unemployment: unemployment directly related to swings in the business cycle (p. 373)	**desempleo cíclico:** desempleo directamente relacionado a oscilaciones en el ciclo económico (p. 373)

D

English	Español
debtor: person who borrows money (p. 367)	**deudor:** persona que pide dinero prestado (p. 367)
default: the act of not repaying borrowed money (p. 476)	**incumplimiento:** acto de no pagar dinero prestado. (p. 476)
deficiency payment: cash payment making up the difference between the market price and the target price of an agricultural crop (p. 159)	**aportación para enjugar un déficit:** aportación en efectivo para alcanzar la diferencia entre el precio del mercado y el precio indicativo de una cosecha agrícola (p. 159)
deficit spending: annual government spending in excess of taxes and other revenues (p. 278)	**gastos deficitarios:** gastos anuales del gobierno en exceso de los impuestos y otros ingresos (p. 278)
deflation: decrease in the general level of the prices of goods and services (p. 361)	**deflación:** disminución en el nivel general de los precios (p. 361)
demand: combination of desire, ability, and willingness to buy a product (p. 91)	**demanda:** combinación de deseo, habilidad y voluntad de comprar un producto (p. 91)
demand curve: graph showing the quantity demanded at each and every possible price that might prevail in the market at a given time (p. 93)	**curva de demanda:** gráfica que ilustra la cantidad que se demanda a cada precio que puede prevalecer en el mercado en cualquier momento dado (p. 93)
demand deposit account (DDA): account whose funds can be removed by writing a check and without having to gain prior approval from the depository institution (p. 388)	**cuentas de depósito a la vista (CDV):** cuentas cuyos fondos pueden retirarse al librarse un cheque y sin previa aprobación de la institución depositaria (p. 388)
demand elasticity: a measure of responsiveness that shows how a change in quantity demanded (dependent variable) responds to a change in price (independent variable) (p. 104)	**elasticidad de demanda:** medida de responsividad que indica cómo el cambio en la cantidad demandada (variable dependiente) responde a un cambio en precio (variable independiente) (p. 104)

English	Español
demand-pull inflation: explanation that prices rise because all sectors of the economy try to buy more goods and services than the economy can produce (p. 365)	**inflación de demanda:** explicación que expone que los precios aumentan porque todos los sectores de la economía tratan de comprar más bienes y servicios que lo que puede producir la economía (p. 365)
demand schedule: listing showing the quantity demanded at all possible prices that might prevail in the market at a given time (p. 92)	**programa de demanda:** lista que indica la cantidad demandada a todos los precios posibles que pueden prevalecer en el mercado en cualquier momento dado (p. 92)
demographer: person who studies growth, density, and other characteristics of the population (p. 334)	**demógrafo:** persona que estudia el crecimiento, la densidad y otras características de la población (p. 334)
dependency ratio: ratio of children and elderly per 100 persons who are in the 18–64 working age bracket (p. 333)	**relación de dependencia:** relación de niños a población que envejece por 100 personas dentro de la categoría de trabajo de las edades entre los 18-64 años (p. 333)
depreciation: gradual wear on capital goods (p. 73)	**depreciación:** desgaste gradual de los bienes de capital (p. 73)
depression: state of the economy with large numbers of unemployed, declining real incomes, overcapacity in manufacturing plants, general economic hardship (p. 354)	**depresión:** estado de la economía con grandes números de desempleados, disminución de ingresos reales, exceso de capacidad en las plantas manufactureras, dificultades económicas generales (p. 354)
depression scrip: currency issued by towns, chambers of commerce, and other civic bodies during the Great Depression of the 1930s (p. 356)	**vale de depresión:** moneda emitida por los pueblos, las cámaras de comercio y otras entidades cívicas durante la Gran Depresión de los años 30 (p. 356)
deregulation: relaxation or removal of government regulations on business activities (p. 424)	**eliminación de restricciones:** relajamiento o eliminación de los reglamentos del gobierno sobre las actividades comerciales (p. 424)
developing country: country with relatively low average per capita income and less developed infrastructure, education, and health care system (p. 469)	**país en desarrollo:** país con promedio de ingresos per cápita relativamente bajo, e infraestructura, educación, y sistema de salud menos desarrollados (p. 469)
***devoting:** giving time or attention (p. 80)	***ferviente:** que brinda tiempo o atención (p. 80)
diminishing marginal utility: decrease in satisfaction or usefulness as additional units of a product are acquired (p. 95)	**utilidad marginal decreciente:** descenso en la satisfacción o utilidad a medida que se van adquiriendo unidades adicionales de un producto (p. 95)
diminishing returns: stage of production where output increases at a decreasing rate as more units of variable input are added (p. 130)	**rendimientos decrecientes:** etapa de producción en la que el rendimiento aumenta a un ritmo disminuyente a medida que se añaden más unidades de insumo variable (p. 130)
discomfort index: unofficial statistic that is the sum of monthly inflation and the unemployment rate; same as misery index (p. 374)	**índice de incomodidad:** estadística no oficial de la suma de la inflación mensual y el índice de desempleo; igual al índice de miseria (p. 374)
discount rate: interest rate that the Federal Reserve System charges on loans to the nation's financial institutions (p. 404)	**tasa de descuento:** tasa de interés que el Sistema de Reserva Federal cobra a las instituciones financieras por los préstamos (p. 404)
discretionary spending: spending for federal programs that must receive annual authorization (p. 270)	**gasto discrecional:** gastos para programas federales que deben recibir autorización anual (p. 270)

disposable personal income (DPI) • economic interdependence

English	Español
disposable personal income (DPI): personal income less individual income taxes; total income available to the consumer sector after income taxes (p. 324)	**ingreso personal disponible:** el ingreso personal menos los impuestos personales; todo el ingreso disponible al sector consumidor después de los impuestos (p. 324)
***distorted:** not truthfully represented (p. 212)	***distorsionado:** que no está fielmente representado (p. 212)
distribution of income: way in which the nation's income is divided among families, individuals, or other designated groups (p. 264)	**distribución de ingresos:** modo por el cual los ingresos de la nación se dividen entre familias, individuos u otros grupos designados (p. 264)
dividend: check paid to stockholders, usually quarterly, representing portion of corporate profits (p. 67)	**dividend/dividendo:** cheque que se paga a los accionistas, por lo general trimestralmente, representa una porción de las ganancias de la corporación (p. 67)
division of labor: division of work into a number of separate tasks to be performed by different workers; same as specialization (pp. 17, 504)	**división de trabajo:** división en un número de tareas específicas para llevarse a cabo por distintos trabajadores; igual que especialización (pp. 17, 504)
***dominant:** possessing the most influence and control (p. 75)	***dominante:** que tiene la máxima influencia y control (p. 75)
double taxation: feature of taxation that allows stockholders' dividends to be taxed both as corporate profit and as personal income (p. 69)	**doble impuesto:** característica de impuestos que permite que los dividendos de los accionistas sean gravados como utilidades de la corporación tanto como ganancias personales (p. 69)
Dow-Jones Industrial Average (DJIA): statistical series of 30 representative stocks used to monitor price changes (p. 310)	**Dow-Jones Industrial Average (DJIA):** serie de estadísticas representativas de 30 acciones que se usan para seguir los cambios de precio (p. 310)
durable good: a good that lasts for at least three years when used regularly (p. 13)	**bien duradero:** artículo que dura por lo menos tres años al usarse con regularidad (p. 13)
***duration:** length of time (p. 481)	***duración:** cantidad de tiempo (p. 481)

E

Earned Income Tax Credit (EITC): federal tax credits and cash payments for low-income workers (p. 343)	**Crédito Fiscal por Ingresos:** créditos impositivos federales y pagos en efectivo para los trabajadores de bajos ingresos (p. 343)
easy money policy: monetary policy resulting in lower interest rates and greater access to credit; associated with an expansion of the money supply (p. 402)	**política de dinero abundante:** política monetaria que resulta en tasas de interés más bajas y mayor acceso a crédito; se asocia con la expansión del abastecimiento de dinero (p. 402)
e-commerce: electronic business or exchange conducted over the Internet (p. 135)	**comercio electrónico:** negocio o intercambio electrónico conducido por medio de Internet (p. 135)
econometric model: macroeconomic expression used to describe how the economy is expected to perform in the future (p. 359)	**modelo econométrico:** expresión macroeconómica usada para describir cómo se espera que se comporte la economía en el futuro (p. 359)
economic growth: increase in a nation's total output of goods and services over time (p. 16)	**crecimiento económico:** aumento en la producción total de bienes y servicios de un país a través del tiempo (p. 16)
economic interdependence: mutual dependence of one person's, firm's, or region's economic activities on another (p. 17)	**interdependencia económica:** dependencia mutua de las actividades económicas de personas, compañías o regiones entre sí (p. 17)

economic model • equilibrium wage rate

English	Español
economic model: simplified version of a complex concept or behavior expressed in the form of an equation, graph, or illustration (pp. 23, 149)	**modelo económico:** versión simplificada de un concepto o comportamiento complejo expresado en forma de ecuación, gráfica o ilustración (pp. 23, 149)
economic system: organized way a society provides for the wants and needs of its people (p. 33)	**sistema económico:** manera organizada de una sociedad para proveer las necesidades de sus integrantes (p. 33)
economics: social science dealing with the study of how people satisfy seemingly unlimited and competing wants with the careful use of scarce resources (p. 6)	**economía:** ciencia social que estudia cómo la gente satisface los deseos, aparentemente ilimitados y competitivos, mediante el uso cuidadoso de escasos recursos (p. 6)
economies of scale: increasingly efficient use of personnel, plant, and equipment as a firm becomes larger (p. 176)	**economías de escala:** aumento de la eficacia del uso del personal, la planta y el equipo a medida que la empresa aumenta de tamaño (p. 176)
Efficient Market Hypothesis (EMH): argument that stocks are always priced about right, and that bargains are hard to find because they are closely watched by so many investors (p. 307)	**Hipótesis de Mercado Eficiente (HME):** argumento acerca de que las acciones siempre tienen el precio adecuado, y que las rebajas son difíciles de hallar porque muchísimos inversionistas siempre las están vigilando (p. 307)
elastic: type of elasticity where the percentage change in the independent variable (usually price) causes a more than proportionate change in the dependent variable (usually quantity demanded or supplied) (p. 104)	**elástico:** tipo de elasticidad en que el cambio de porcentaje en la variable independiente (generalmente el precio) causa un cambio más que proporcionado en la variable dependiente (generalmente la cantidad demandada u ofrecida) (p. 104)
elasticity: a measure of responsiveness that tells us how a dependent variable such as quantity responds to a change in an independent variable such as price (p. 103)	**elasticidad:** medida que nos dice cómo una variable dependiente, tal como cantidad, responde a un cambio en una variable independiente, tal como precio (p. 103)
***emphasizing:** stressing (p. 36)	***enfatizante:** que pone énfasis (p. 36)
***enabled:** made possible (p. 444)	***habilitado:** hecho posible (p. 444)
enterprise zone: area free of local, state, and federal tax laws as well as other operating restrictions (p. 344)	**zona franca:** área libre de impuestos locales, estatales y federales y de restricciones operativas (p. 344)
***entity:** unit or being (p. 63)	***entidad:** unidad o ser (p. 63)
entitlement: program or benefit using established eligibility requirements to provide health, nutritional, or income supplements to individuals (pp. 283, 422)	**titularidad:** programa o beneficio que usa los requerimientos de la elegibilidad establecida para proveer suplementos de salud, de alimentación o de ingresos a individuos (pp. 283, 422)
entrepreneur: risk-taking individual in search of profits; one of four factors of production (p. 9)	**empresario:** individuo arriesgado en busca de ganancias; uno de cuatro factores de producción (p. 9)
***equate:** to represent as equal or equivalent (p. 177)	***equiparar:** representar como igual o equivalente (p. 177)
***equivalent:** equal in value (p. 219)	***equivalente:** igual en valor (p. 219)
equilibrium price: price where quantity supplied equals quantity demanded; price that clears the market (pp. 149, 414)	**precio de equilibrio:** precio en que la cantidad ofrecida equivale a la cantidad demandada; precio que aprueba el mercado (pp. 149, 414)
equilibrium wage rate: wage rate leaving neither a surplus nor a shortage in the market (p. 209)	**índice del equilibrio salarial:** índice salarial que no deja ni exceso ni escasez en el mercado (p. 209)

equities • fact-finding

English	Español
equities: stocks that represent ownership shares in corporations (p. 306)	**capital accionario:** acciones que representan acciones de propiedad en las corporaciones (p. 306)
*equipped: prepared (p. 521)	***equipado:** preparado (p. 521)
estate tax: tax on the transfer of property when a person dies (p. 241)	**impuesto sucesorio:** impuesto por el traspaso de propiedad cuando una persona muere (p. 241)
*ethics: moral principles; generally recognized rules of conduct (p. 480)	***ética:** principios morales; normas de conducta que generalmente se reconocen (p. 480)
euro: single currency of European Union (p. 484)	**euro:** moneda única de la Unión Europea (p. 484)
European Coal and Steel Community (ECSC): group of six European countries formed in 1951 to coordinate iron and steel production to ensure peace among member countries; eventually evolved into the EU (p. 505)	**Comunidad Europea del Carbón y del Acero (CECA):** grupo de seis países europeos formado en 1951 para coordinar la producción del hierro y el acero y así asegurar la paz entre los países miembros; evolucionó para llegar a ser la UE (p. 505)
European Union: successor of the European Coal and Steel Community established in 1993 by the Maastricht Treaty (p. 483)	**Unión Europea:** la sucesora de la Comunidad Europea que estableció el Tratado de Maastricht en noviembre del 1993 (p. 483)
*evolved: developed gradually (p. 234)	***evolucionado:** que se desarrolló gradualmente (p. 234)
excess reserves: financial institution's cash, currency, and reserves not needed for reserve requirements; potential source of new loans (p. 396)	**reservas excesivas:** dinero efectivo, divisas y reservas de una institución financiera que no se necesitan por exigencias de la reserva; fuente potencial de nuevos préstamos (p. 396)
excise tax: general revenue tax levied on the manufacture or sale of selected items (p. 240)	**impuesto sobre consumo:** tributo sobre ingresos generales recaudado sobre la manufactura o venta de objetos selectos (p. 240)
*excluded: not counted or included (p. 321)	***excluido:** que no se cuenta ni se incluye (p. 321)
expansion: period of uninterrupted growth of real GDP; recovery from recession (p. 354)	**expansión:** período de crecimiento ininterrumpido del PIB real; recuperación de la recesión (p. 354)
*explicit: openly and clearly expressed (p. 427)	***explícito:** expresado abierta y claramente (p. 427)
exports: the goods and services that a nation produces and then sells to other nations (p. 442)	**exportaciones:** bienes y servicios que una nación produce y después vende a otras naciones (p. 442)
expropriation: government confiscation of private- or foreign-owned goods without compensation (p. 482)	**expropiación:** cuando el gobierno confisca bienes de propiedad privada o extranjera sin compensación (p. 482)
external debt: borrowed money that a country owes to foreign countries and banks (p. 475)	**deuda externa:** dinero prestado que un país debe a países y bancos extranjeros (p. 475)
externality: economic side effect that affects an uninvolved third party (p. 181)	**factores externos:** efecto secundario de la economía que afecta a un tercero que no está envuelto (p. 181)

F

fact-finding: agreement between union and management to have a neutral third party collect facts about a dispute and present non-binding recommendations (p. 212)	**indagación de los hechos:** acuerdo entre el sindicato y la empresa de pedirle a un tercero que reúna evidencia sobre una disputa y presente recomendaciones de manera neutral (p. 212)

English	Español
factor market: market where productive resources are bought and sold (p. 15)	**mercado de factor:** mercado en que se venden y se compran recursos productivos (p. 15)
factors of production: productive resources that make up the four categories of land, capital, labor, and entrepreneurship (p. 8)	**factores de producción:** recursos productivos que componen las cuatro categorías de tierra, capital, trabajo y espíritu empresarial (p. 8)
family: two or more persons living together that are related by blood, marriage, or adoption (p. 326)	**familia:** dos o más personas que viven juntas y que están vinculadas por sangre, matrimonio o adopción (p. 326)
federal budget: annual plan outlining proposed expenditures and anticipated revenues (p. 267)	**presupuesto federal:** plan anual que traza los gastos propuestos y las ganancias que se anticipan (p. 267)
Federal Reserve note: paper currency issued by the Fed that eventually replaced all other types of federal currency (p. 383)	**vale de la Reserva Federal:** papel moneda emitida por la Reserva Federal que con el tiempo sustituyó a todos los otros tipos de moneda federal (p. 383)
Federal Reserve System (Fed): privately owned, publicly controlled, central bank of the United States (p. 383)	**Sistema de Reserva Federal (Fed, siglas en inglés):** banco central de los Estados Unidos, de propiedad privada y cuyo control es público (p. 383)
fertility rate: number of births that 1,000 women are expected to undergo in their lifetime (p. 334)	**tasa de fecundidad:** número de alumbramientos que se espera que 1,000 mujeres experimenten en sus vidas (p. 334)
fiat money: money by government decree; has no alternative value or use as a commodity (p. 384)	**moneda fiduciaria:** dinero por decreto del gobierno; no tiene valor alternativo ni uso como producto básico (p. 384)
FICA: Federal Insurance Contributions Act; tax levied on employers and employees to support Social Security and Medicare (p. 239)	**FICA:** Acta de Contribuciones del Seguro Federal; impuesto sobre los patrones y empleados para sostener al Seguro Social y a Medicare (p. 239)
finance company: firm that makes loans directly to consumers and specializes in buying installment contracts from merchants who sell on credit (p. 292)	**compañía financiera:** firma que hace préstamos directamente a los consumidores y que se especializa en la compra de contratos a plazos de los comerciantes que venden a crédito (p. 292)
financial asset: a stock or document that represents a claim on the income and property of the borrower; CDs, bonds, Treasury bills, mortgages (p. 290)	**activo financiero:** un acción u otro documento que representa un derecho a los ingresos y la propiedad del prestatario; CD, bonos, letras del Tesoro, hipotecas (p. 290)
financial intermediary: institution that channels savings to investors; banks, insurance companies, savings and loan associations, credit unions (p. 290)	**intermediario financiero:** institución que canaliza los ahorros a los inversionistas; bancos, compañías de seguro, sociedades de ahorro y préstamo, cooperativas de crédito (p. 290)
financial system: network of savers, investors, and financial institutions that work together to transfer savings to investment uses (p. 290)	**sistema financiero:** red de ahorradores, inversionistas e instituciones financieras que colaboran para transferir los ahorros a usos de inversión (p. 290)
fiscal policy: use of government spending and revenue collection measures to influence the economy (p. 420)	**política fiscal:** el uso de las medidas que usa el gobierno para gastos y recaudación de ingresos con el fin influenciar la economía (p. 420)
fiscal year: 12-month financial planning period that may not coincide with the calendar year; October 1 to September 30 for the federal government (p. 268)	**año fiscal:** periodo de 12 meses para la planificación financiera que no necesariamente coincide con el año civil; período comprendido entre el 1 de octubre y el 30 de septiembre para el gobierno federal (p. 268)
Five-Year Plan: comprehensive, centralized economic plan used by the Soviet Union and China to coordinate development of agriculture and industry (p. 489)	**Plan Quinquenal:** plan económico centralizado y abarcante que usó la Unión Soviética y la China para coordinar el desarrollo de la agricultura y la industria (p. 489)

fixed costs • free trader

English	Español
fixed costs: costs of production that do not change when output changes (p. 133)	**costo fijo:** costo de producción que no cambia cuando cambia la producción (p. 133)
fixed exchange rates: system under which the value of currencies are fixed in relation to one another; the exchange rate system in effect until 1971 (p. 457)	**tasas de cambio fija:** sistema bajo el cual se fijan los valores de las divisas en relación al de las otras; sistema de cotización que estuvo en efecto hasta el 1971 (p. 457)
fixed income: income that does not increase even though prices go up (p. 45)	**renta fija:** ingreso que no aumenta aunque los precios suban (p. 45)
flat tax: proportional tax on individual income after a specified threshold has been reached (p. 251)	**impuesto fijo:** impuesto proporcional sobre el ingreso individual después de haber alcanzado el ingreso especificado (p. 251)
flexible exchange rates: system that relies on supply and demand to determine the value of one currency in terms of another; exchange rate system in effect since 1971, same as floating exchange rate (p. 458)	**tasas de cambio flexible:** sistema que depende de oferta y demanda para determinar el valor de una moneda en términos de otra; sistema de cotización en efecto desde el 1971, igual a tasa de cambio flotante (p. 458)
floating exchange rates: see flexible exchange rate (p. 458)	**tasas de cambio flotante:** ver flexible exchange rates (p. 458)
*fluctuates: changes continually and irregularly (p. 153)	***fluctúa:** que cambia continua e irregularmente (p. 153)
food stamps: government-issued coupons that can be exchanged for food (p. 342)	**sellos para la compra de alimentos:** cupones que emite el gobierno y que se canjean por alimentos (p. 342)
foreign exchange: foreign currencies used by countries to conduct international trade (p. 457)	**divisas:** moneda extranjera que usan los países para conducir comercio internacional (p. 457)
foreign exchange rate: price of one country's currency in terms of another currency (p. 457)	**cotización de divisas:** precio de la moneda de un país en relación a la moneda de otro país (p. 457)
401(k) plan: a tax-deferred investment and savings plan that acts as a personal pension fund for employees (p. 307)	**plan 401(k):** plan de ahorros e impuestos diferidos que actúa como una pensión personal para empleados. (p. 307)
fractional reserve system: system requiring financial institutions to set aside a fraction of their deposits in the form of reserves (p. 396)	**sistema de reserva fraccionada:** sistema que dicta que las instituciones financieras aparten una fracción de sus depósitos en forma de reservas (p. 396)
*framework: point of reference (p. 416)	***marco:** punto de referencia (p. 416)
free enterprise economy: market economy in which privately owned businesses have the freedom to operate for a profit with limited government intervention (p. 24)	**economía de libre empresa:** economía de mercado en la que los comercios privados tienen la libertad de operar para obtener ganancias con intervención limitada del gobierno (p. 24)
free-trade area: group of countries that have agreed to reduce trade barriers among themselves, but lack a common tariff barrier for nonmembers (p. 483)	**zona de comercio libre:** grupo de países que han acordado reducir las barreras comerciales entre sí, pero que carecen de una barrera arancelaria para los países no miembros (p. 483)
Free Trade Area of the Americas (FTAA): 34-nation group established in 1994 in order to set up a regional free trade area in the Americas with no internal barriers to trade (p. 506)	**Zona de Libre Comercio de las Américas (FTAA, siglas en inglés):** grupo de 34 países creado en 1994 para establecer una zona de libre comercio regional en las Américas sin barreras internas para el comercio (p. 506)
free trader: person who favors fewer or no trade restrictions (p. 450)	**comerciante libre:** persona a favor de menos restricciones al comercio, o de ninguna restricción (p. 450)

English	Español
frictional unemployment: unemployment caused by workers changing jobs or waiting to go to new ones (p. 372)	**desempleo friccional:** desempleo causado por trabajadores cuando cambian de trabajo o al esperar ir a nuevos empleos (p. 372)
*functions: roles or purposes (p. 401)	***funciones:** roles o fines (p. 401)
*fundamental: basic; an essential part of (p. 372)	***fundamental:** básico; una parte esencial de algo (p. 372)
futures contract: an agreement to buy or sell at a specific date in the future at a predetermined price (p. 311)	**futures contract/contrato de futuros:** acuerdo para comprar o vender en una fecha específica en el futuro a un precio predeterminado (p. 311)

English	Español
gasohol: mixture of 90 percent unleaded gasoline and 10 percent grain alcohol, or ethanol (p. 513)	**gasohol:** mezcla de 90 por ciento gasolina sin plomo y 10 por ciento alcohol de grano o etanol (p. 513)
GDP gap: difference between what the economy can and does produce; annual opportunity cost of unemployed resources (p. 374)	**laguna del PIB:** diferencia entre lo que la economía puede producir y lo que, de hecho, produce; costo de oportunidad anual de los recursos desempleados (p. 374)
GDP per capita: gross domestic product on a per person basis; can be expressed in current or constant dollars (p. 322)	**PIB per cápita:** producto interno bruto con base en una persona; puede expresarse en dólares corrientes o constantes (p. 322)
General Agreement on Tariffs and Trade (GATT): an international agreement signed in 1947 between 23 countries to extend tariff concessions and reduce import quotas (p. 504)	**Acuerdo General de Aranceles y Comercio (GATT, siglas en inglés):** acuerdo internacional firmado en 1947 entre 23 países para extender las concesiones arancelarias y reducir las cuotas de importación (p. 504)
general partnership: form of partnership where all partners are equally responsible for management and debts; also see partnership (p. 64)	**sociedad general:** forma de sociedad en la que todos los socios por igual son responsables del gerenciamiento y las deudas; ver también partnership (p. 64)
*generates: produces or brings into being (p. 136)	***genera:** produce u origina (p. 136)
geographic monopoly: market situation where a firm has a monopoly because of its location or the small size of the market (p. 176)	**monopolio geográfico:** situación del mercado en la que una firma tiene un monopolio debido al sitio en que está situada o a la pequeñez del mercado (p. 176)
gift tax: tax on donations of money or wealth that is paid by the donor (p. 241)	**impuesto sobre donaciones y legados:** impuesto sobre donaciones de dinero o riquezas que tiene que pagar el donante (p. 241)
giveback: wage, fringe benefit, or work rule given up when renegotiating a contract (p. 217)	**devolución de beneficios:** en la renegociación de un contrato, sueldo, beneficio complementario o regla de trabajo que se pierde (p. 217)
glass ceiling: seemingly invisible barrier hindering advancement of women and minorities in a male-dominated organization (p. 219)	**techo de cristal:** barrera aparentemente invisible que impide que las mujeres y las minorías avancen en una organización dominada por los hombres (p. 219)
globalization: the movement toward a more integrated and interdependent world economy (p. 501)	**globalización:** movimiento hacia una economía mundial más integrada e interdependiente (p. 501)
glut: substantial oversupply of a product (p. 515)	**abarrotamiento:** superabundancia de un producto (p. 515)

English	Español
gold certificate: paper currency backed by gold; issued in 1863 and popular until recalled in 1934 (p. 393)	**certificado de oro:** billete de banco respaldado por oro; emitido en 1863 y popular hasta que fue retirado en 1934 (p. 393)
good: tangible economic product that is useful, relatively scarce, transferable to others; used to satisfy wants and needs (p. 13)	**bien:** producto económico tangible y útil, relativamente escaso, transferible a otras personas; se usa para satisfacer necesidades y deseos (p. 13)
Gosplan: central planning authority in the former Soviet Union that devised and directed Five-Year plans (p. 489)	**Gosplan:** autoridad central de planificación en la antigua Unión Soviética que ideó y dirigió los planes quinquenales (p. 489)
government monopoly: monopoly created and/or owned by the government (p. 177)	**monopolio fiscal:** monopolio creado por/o de la propiedad del gobierno (p. 177)
grant-in-aid: transfer payment from one level of government to another not involving compensation (p. 263)	**donativo del gobierno:** transferencia de pago desde un nivel del gobierno a otro y que no incumbe compensación (p. 263)
Great Depression: worst period of economic decline in U.S. history, lasting from approximately 1929 to 1939 (p. 201)	**Gran depresión:** el peor periodo de disminución económica en la historia de los Estados Unidos, duró aproximadamente desde 1929 hasta 1939 (p. 201)
Great Leap Forward: China's second five-year plan begun in 1958 that forced collectivization of agriculture and rapid industrialization (p. 490)	**Gran Salto Adelante:** el segundo plan quinquenal de China que comenzó en 1958 y obligó a la colectivización de la agricultura y la rápida industrialización (p. 490)
grievance procedure: provision in a contract outlining the way future disputes and grievance issues will be resolved (p. 211)	**procedimiento para la presentación de reclamaciones:** estipulación en un contrato que define la forma en que se resolverán futuras disputas y conflictos (p. 211)
gross domestic product (GDP): dollar value of all final goods, services, and structures produced within a country's national borders during a one-year period (pp. 9, 320)	**producto interno bruto (PIB):** valor en dólares de todos los productos, servicios y estructuras finales dentro de las fronteras nacionales de un país durante el periodo de un año (pp. 9, 320)
gross national product (GNP): total dollar value of all final goods, services, and structures produced in one year with labor and property supplied by a country's residents, regardless of where the production takes place; largest measure of a nation's income (p. 324)	**producto nacional bruto (PNB):** valor total en dólares de todos los productos, estructuras y servicios finales producidos en un año con la mano de obra y la propiedad suplidas por los residentes de un país, sin importar donde toma lugar la producción; la mayor medida de los ingresos de una nación (p. 324)

H

horizontal merger: combination of two or more firms producing the same kind of product (p. 75)	**fusión horizontal:** combinación de dos o más empresas que producen el mismo producto (p. 75)
household: basic unit of consumer sector consisting of all persons who occupy a house, apartment, or separate living quarters (p. 325)	**unidad familiar:** unidad básica del sector del consumidor que consiste de todas las personas que ocupan una casa, apartamento o viviendas independientes (p. 325)
human capital: sum of peoples' skills, abilities, health, and motivation (p. 16)	**capital humano:** suma de las destrezas, habilidades, salud y motivación (p. 16)
hydropower: power or energy generated by moving water (p. 512)	**hidropotencia:** potencia o energía generada por el agua que corre (p. 512)
hyperinflation: abnormal inflation in excess of 500 percent per year; last stage of a monetary collapse (p. 364)	**hiperinflación:** inflación anormal en exceso de 500 por ciento al año; última etapa de un colapso monetario (p. 364)
*****hypothetical:** assumed but not proven (p. 128)	*****hipotético:** que se presume pero no está probado (p. 128)

English	Español

I

*ideology: a set of beliefs (p. 431)

*ideología: conjunto de creencias (p. 431)

*illustrated: shown with an image (p. 98)

*ilustrado: que se muestra con una imagen (p. 98)

*impact: effect (p. 340)

*impacto: efecto (p. 340)

imperfect competition: market structure that does not meet all conditions of perfect competition (p. 172)

competencia imperfecta: estructura de mercado que no cumple con todas las condiciones de competencia perfecta (p. 172)

*implemented: put into effect (p. 242)

*implementado: puesto en funcionamiento (p. 242)

*implication: something suggested to be naturally understood (p. 307)

*implicancia: algo que se sugiere para que se comprenda naturalmente (p. 307)

implicit GDP price deflator: index used to measure price changes in gross domestic product (p. 364)

deflactor implícito del precio PIB: índice que se usa para medir los cambios de precio del Producto Interno Bruto (p. 364)

imports: the goods and services that a nation buys from other nations (p. 442)

importaciones: bienes y servicios que una nación compra de otras naciones (p. 442)

*imposed: established; applied (p. 448)

*impuesto: establecido; aplicado (p. 448)

*incapacitated: lacking the ability to function normally (p. 523)

*incapacitado: carente de habilidad para funcionar normalmente (p. 523)

*incentive: something that motivates (p. 50)

*incentivo: algo que motiva (p. 50)

incidence of a tax: final burden of a tax (p. 231)

incidencia de un impuesto: carga final de un impuesto (p. 231)

income effect: that portion of a change in quantity demanded caused by a change in a consumer's real income when the price of a product changes (p. 98)

efecto de ingreso: aquella porción de un cambio en cantidad demandada causada por un cambio en el ingreso real de un consumidor cuando el precio de un producto cambia (p. 98)

income statement: report showing a business's sales, expenses, and profits for a certain period, usually three months or a year (p. 73)

declaración de ingreso: informe que muestra las ventas, gastos y utilidades de un negocio por un período determinado, por lo general de tres meses o un año (p. 73)

independent union: labor union not affiliated with the AFL-CIO or the Change to Win Coalition (p. 203)

sindicato independiente: gremio no afiliado con la AFL-CIO o el Change to Win Coalition (p. 203)

indexing: adjustment of tax brackets to offset the effects of inflation (p. 239)

indización: ajuste de las escalas de impuestos para contrarrestar los efectos de la inflación (p. 239)

individual income tax: tax levied on the wages, salaries, and other income of individuals (p. 232)

impuesto sobre la renta personal: impuesto sobre jornales, salarios y otros ingresos de las personas (p. 232)

Individual Retirement Account (IRA): retirement account in the form of a long-term time deposit, with annual contributions not taxed until withdrawn during retirement (p. 302)

Cuenta Personal para la Jubilación (IRA, siglas en inglés): cuenta para la jubilación en forma de un depósito a largo plazo, con contribuciones anuales que no se gravan con impuestos hasta que se retiran durante la jubilación (p. 302)

industrial union: labor union whose members perform different kinds of work in the same industry (p. 199)

sindicato industrial: unión obrera cuyos miembros realizan diferentes tipos de trabajo en la misma industria (p. 199)

English	Español
inelastic: type of elasticity where the percentage change in the independent variable (usually price) causes a less than proportionate change in the dependent variable (usually quantity demanded or supplied) (p. 104)	**no elástica:** tipo de elasticidad en el cual el porcentaje de cambio en la variable independiente (usualmente el precio) causa un cambio menos que proporcionado en la variable dependiente (usualmente la cantidad demandada u ofrecida) (p. 104)
infant industries argument: argument that new and emerging industries should be protected from foreign competition until they are strong enough to compete (p. 450)	**argumento de las industrias nacientes:** argumenta de que a las industrias nuevas que están surgiendo se les debe proteger de la competencia extranjera hasta que estén lo suficiente fuertes para competir (p. 450)
inflation: rise in the general level of prices (pp. 45, 361)	**inflación:** aumento en el nivel general de los precios (pp. 45, 361)
infrastructure: the highways, mass transit, communications, power, water, sewerage and other public goods needed to support a population (p. 332)	**infraestructura:** las carreteras, tránsito público, comunicaciones, electricidad, agua, alcantarillado y otros servicios públicos necesarios para apoyar a una población (p. 332)
***initially:** originally; at the beginning (p. 395)	***inicialmente:** originalmente; al comienzo de (p. 395)
injunction: court order issued to prevent a company or union from taking action during a labor dispute (p. 212)	**mandato judicial:** orden de la corte dictada para evitar que una compañía o: sindicato tome acción durante una disputa laboral (p. 212)
***innovation:** the creation of something new or different (p. 355)	***innovación:** la creación de algo nuevo o diferente (p. 355)
***instituted:** put into action (p. 282)	***instituido:** establecido, fundado (p. 282)
***interaction:** action of one on the actions of another (p. 120)	***interacción:** acción de uno en las acciones de otro (p. 120)
interest: payment made for the use of borrowed money; usually paid at periodic intervals for long-term bonds or loans (p. 69)	**interés:** pago que se hace por el uso de dinero prestado; por lo general se paga a intervalos periódicos para bonos o préstamos de largo plazo (p. 69)
interest rate: the price of credit to a borrower (p. 402)	**tasa de interés:** el precio del crédito para quien pide préstamos (p. 402)
intergovernmental expenditures: funds that one level of government transfers to another level for spending (p. 272)	**gastos intergubernamentales:** fondos para gastos que un nivel de gobierno transfiere a otro (p. 272)
intergovernmental revenue: funds one level of government receives from another level of government (p. 242)	**ingresos intergubernamentales:** fondos, que en el gobierno, se reciben de un nivel a otro (p. 242)
intermediate products: products that are components of other final products included in GDP; new tires and radios for use on new cars (p. 321)	**productos intermediarios:** productos que son componentes de otros productos finales incluidos en el PIB; llantas y radios nuevos para usarse en autos nuevos (p. 321)
Internal Revenue Service (IRS): branch of Treasury Department that collects taxes (p. 238)	**Servicio de Rentas Internas (IRS, siglas en inglés):** rama del Departamento de Tesorería que recauda impuestos (p. 238)
***internally:** within (p. 75)	***internamente:** dentro de (p. 75)
International Monetary Fund (IMF): international organization that offers advice, financial assistance, and currency support to all nations (p. 481)	**Fondo Monetario Internacional (FMI):** organización internacional que ofrece asesoría, asistencia financiera y ayuda de efectivos a todas las naciones (p. 481)
***intervention:** involvement in a situation to alter the outcome (p. 189)	***intervención:** participación en una situación para alterar el resultado (p. 189)
inventory: stock of goods held in reserve; includes finished goods waiting to be sold and raw materials to be used in production (p. 64)	**inventario:** abastecimiento de bienes en reserva; incluye bienes terminados esperando venderse y materias primas que se usan en producción (p. 64)
***inversely:** in the opposite way (p. 93)	***inversamente:** en la forma opuesta (p. 93)

investment tax credit • leading economic indicator

English	Español
investment tax credit: tax credit given for purchase of equipment (p. 249)	**crédito impositivo de inversión:** crédito impositivo que se da para la compra de equipo (p. 249)
***isolationism:** national policy of not interacting with other countries (p. 491)	***aislamiento:** política nacional de no interactuar con otros países (p. 491)

English	Español
junk bond: exceptionally risky bond with a Standard & Poor's rating of BB or lower that carries a high rate of return as compensation for the higher possibility of non-payment (p. 299)	**bono basura:** bono excepcionalmente riesgoso con una calificación BB o más baja de Standard & Poor, que tiene un interés alto como compensación por la mayor posibilidad de no pago (p. 299)
***justify:** to defend as warranted or necessary (p. 450)	***justificar:** defender como correcto o necesario (p. 450)

English	Español
***keiretsu:** independently owned group of Japanese firms joined and governed by an external board of directors in order to regulate competition (p. 493)	***keiretsu:** grupo de firmas japonesas de propiedad privada unidas y gobernadas por una junta directiva exterior para poder regular la competencia (p. 493)
Keynesian economics: government spending and taxation policies suggested by John Maynard Keynes to stimulate the economy; synonymous with fiscal policies or demand-side economics (p. 420)	**economía keynesiana:** políticas del gobierno para gastos e impuestos sugeridas por John Maynard Keynes para estimular la economía; sinónimo de las políticas fiscales o de la economía del lado de la demanda (p. 420)

English	Español
labor: people with all their abilities and efforts; one of four factors of production, does not include the entrepreneur (p. 8)	**trabajo:** la gente con todas sus habilidades y esfuerzos; uno de los cuatro factores de producción, no incluye al empresario (p. 8)
labor force: see civilian labor force (p. 370)	**labor force:** ver civilian labor force (p. 370)
labor union: organization that works for its members' interests concerning pay, working hours, health coverage, fringe benefits, other job related matters (p. 81)	**sindicato obrero:** organización que obra en beneficio de los intereses de sus miembros respecto a pago, horas de trabajo, seguro médico, beneficios complementarios y otros asuntos relacionados al trabajo (p. 81)
laissez-faire: philosophy that government should not interfere with business activity (p. 169)	**liberalismo:** filosofía de que el gobierno no debe interferir con las actividades comerciales (p. 169)
land: natural resources or "gifts of nature" not created by human effort; one of four factors of production (p. 8)	**tierra:** recursos naturales o "dones de la naturaleza" no creados por el esfuerzo humano; uno de cuatro factores de producción (p. 8)
Law of Demand: rule stating that more will be demanded at lower prices and less at higher prices; inverse relationship between price and quantity demanded (p. 93)	**Ley de Demanda:** principio que dicta que se demanda más a precios bajos y menos a precios altos; relación inversa entre precio y cantidad demandada (p. 93)
Law of Supply: principle that more will be offered for sale at high prices than at lower prices (p. 117)	**Ley de Oferta:** principio que dicta que se ofrece más a la venta a precios altos que a precios bajos (p. 117)
leading economic indicator: a statistical series that normally turns down before the economy turns down or turns up before the economy turns up (p. 358)	**principal indicador económico:** serie estadística que normalmente baja antes que baje la economía o sube antes que suba la economía (p. 358)

English	Español
legal reserves: currency and deposits used to meet the reserve requirement (p. 396)	**reservas legales:** moneda y depósitos que se usan para cumplir con los requisitos de reserva (p. 396)
legal tender: fiat currency that must be accepted for payment by decree of government (p. 392)	**moneda legal:** dinero fiduciario que por decreto del gobierno hay que aceptar por pago (p. 392)
***legislation:** enactment of a law (p. 198)	***legislación:** promulgación de una ley (p. 198)
life expectancy: average remaining life span in years for persons who attain a given age (pp. 334, 474)	**expectativa de vida:** promedio de la duración de vida restante en años para personas que logran una cierta edad (pp. 334, 474)
limited life: situation in which a firm legally ceases to exist when an owner dies, quits, or a new owner is added; applies to sole proprietorships and partnerships (p. 64)	**vida limitada:** situación en la cual una firma deja de existir legalmente al morir o renunciar un dueño o al agregarse uno nuevo; se aplica a propietarios únicos y a sociedades (p. 64)
limited partnership: form of partnership where one or more partners are not active in the daily running of the business, and whose liability for the partnership's debt is restricted to the amount invested in the business (p. 64)	**sociedad limitada:** forma de sociedad en la que uno o más socios no participan activamente en el funcionamiento diario del negocio y cuyas responsabilidad por la deuda de la sociedad se limita a la cantidad invertida en el negocio (p. 64)
line-item veto: power to cancel specific budget items without rejecting the entire budget (p. 282)	**veto de artículo particular:** el poder para cancelar artículos específicos en el presupuesto sin rechazar el presupuesto entero (p. 282)
lockout: management refusal to let employees work until company demands are met (p. 199)	**lockout/cierre patronal:** negativa patronal de permitir que los empleados trabajen hasta que se cumplan las demandas de la compañía (p. 199)
long run: production period long enough to change amount of variable and fixed inputs used in production (p. 129)	**largo plazo:** periodo de producción lo bastante largo para cambiar la cantidad de insumos variables y fijos que se usan en la producción (p. 129)
Lorenz curve: graph showing how much the actual distribution of income differs from an equal distribution (p. 339)	**curva de Lorenz:** gráfica que muestra cuánto difiere la distribución real de los ingresos de una distribución igual (p. 339)

English	Español
M1: money supply components conforming to money's role as medium of exchange; coins, currency, checks, other demand deposits, traveler's checks (p. 388)	**M1:** componentes del abastecimiento de dinero que se conforman al papel del dinero como medio de intercambio; monedas, divisas, cheques, otros depósitos a la vista, cheques de viajeros (p. 388)
M2: money supply components conforming to money's role as a store of value; M1, savings deposits, time deposits (p. 388)	**M2:** componentes del abastecimiento de dinero que se conforman al papel del dinero como fuente de valor; M1, depósitos de ahorros, depósitos a plazo (p. 388)
macroeconomic equilibrium: amount of real GDP consistent with a given price level; intersection of aggregate supply and aggregate demand (p. 416)	**equilibrio macroeconómico:** nivel de PIB consistente con un nivel de precio dado; intersección de oferta y demanda globales (p. 416)
macroeconomics: the branch of economic theory dealing with the economy as a whole and decision making by large units such as governments and unions (pp. 319, 413)	**macroeconomía:** esa parte de la teoría económica que trata con la economía como un total y con la adopción de decisiones por grandes unidades como los gobiernos y uniones (pp. 319, 413)
***mandate:** to order or require (p. 282)	***mandar:** ordenar o exigir (p. 282)
mandatory spending: federal spending authorized by law that continues without the need for annual approvals of Congress (p. 269)	**gasto obligatorio:** gastos federales autorizados por ley que continúan sin necesidad de aprobación anual del Congreso (p. 269)

English	Español
marginal analysis: decision making that compares the extra cost of doing something to the extra benefits gained (p. 137)	**análisis marginal:** adopción de decisión que compara el costo extra de hacer algo con los beneficios extras que se obtienen (p. 137)
marginal cost: extra cost of producing one additional unit of production (p. 134)	**costo marginal:** costo extra de producir una unidad de producción adicional (p. 134)
marginal product: extra output due to the addition of one more unit of input (p. 129)	**producto marginal:** producción extra debida a la adición de una unidad más de insumo (p. 129)
marginal revenue: extra revenue from the sale of one additional unit of output (p. 136)	**ingreso marginal:** ingreso extra de la venta de una unidad de producto adicional (p. 136)
marginal tax rate: tax rate that applies to the next dollar of taxable income (p. 235)	**tasa impositiva marginal:** tasa impositiva que se aplica al próximo dólar de ingreso sujeto a impuesto (p. 235)
marginal utility: satisfaction or usefulness obtained from acquiring one more unit of a product (p. 95)	**utilidad marginal:** satisfacción o utilidad que se obtiene de adquirir una unidad más de un producto (p. 95)
market: meeting place or mechanism allowing buyers and sellers of an economic product to come together; may be local, regional, national, or global (pp. 15, 37)	**mercado:** lugar de encuentro o mecanismo que permite que los compradores y vendedores de un producto económico se reúnan; puede ser local, regional, nacional o global (pp. 15, 37)
market basket: representative collection of goods and services used to compile a price index (p. 362)	**cesta de la compra:** colección representativa de los bienes y servicios que se usan para compilar un índice de precios (p. 362)
market demand curve: demand curve that shows the quantities demanded by everyone who is interested in purchasing a product at all possible prices (p. 94)	**curva de demanda mercadera:** curva de demanda que muestra las cantidades demandadas por todos que están interesados en comprar un producto a todos los precios posibles (p. 94)
market economy: economic system in which supply, demand, and the price system help people make decisions and allocate resources; same as free enterprise economy (pp. 37, 92)	**economía de mercado:** sistema económico en el cual la oferta y la demanda y el sistema de precios ayudan a la gente a tomar decisiones y a asignar los recursos; lo mismo que economía de libre comercio (pp. 37, 92)
market failure: market where any of the requirements for a competitive market—adequate competition, knowledge of prices and opportunities, mobility of resources, and competitive profits—are lacking (p. 180)	**fallo del mercado:** mercado que carece de cualquiera de los requisitos de un mercado competidor, como competencia adecuada, conocimiento de precios y oportunidades, movilidad de recursos y ganancias competitivas (p. 180)
market structure: market classification according to number and size of firms, type of product, and type of competition; nature and degree of competition among firms in the same industry (p. 169)	**estructura del mercado:** clasificación del mercado de acuerdo al número y tamaño de las firmas, tipo de producto y tipo de competición; naturaleza y grado de competencia entre las compañías en una misma industria (p. 169)
market supply curve: supply curve that shows the quantities offered at various prices by all firms that sell the product in a given market (p. 119)	**curva de oferta mercadera:** curva de oferta que muestra las cantidades de un producto ofrecidas a varios precios por todas las empresas que lo venden en un mercado indicado (p. 119)
market theory of wage determination: explanation stating that the supply and demand for a worker's skills and services determine the wage or salary (p. 209)	**teoría de mercado en la determinación de salarios:** explicación que expone que la oferta y demanda de las destrezas y servicios de un trabajador determinan el sueldo o salario (p. 209)
maturity: life of a bond or length of time funds are borrowed (p. 297)	**vencimiento:** plazo de un bono (p. 297)
measure of value: one of the three functions of money that allows it to serve as a common denominator to measure value (p. 387)	**medida de valor:** una de las tres funciones del dinero que le permite servir como denominador común para medir el valor (p. 387)
*mechanism: process (p. 15)	***mecanismo:** proceso (p. 15)

mediation • monetary unit

English	Español
mediation: process of resolving a dispute by bringing in a neutral third party (p. 212)	**mediación:** proceso de resolver un conflicto al incluir a un tercero neutral (p. 212)
Medicaid: joint federal-state medical insurance program for low-income people (pp. 271, 343)	**Medicaid:** programa de seguro médico del gobierno federal y el estado para personas de ingresos bajos (pp. 271, 343)
Medicare: federal health-care program for senior citizens, regardless of income (pp. 235, 270, 419)	**Medicare:** programa federal de cuidados de salud para la población que envejece, que no toma en cuenta sus ingresos (pp. 235, 270, 419)
medium of exchange: money or other substance generally accepted as payment for goods and services; one of the three functions of money (p. 387)	**medio de cambio:** dinero u otra sustancia generalmente aceptada como pago por bienes o servicios; una de las tres funciones del dinero (p. 387)
member bank: bank belonging to the Federal Reserve System (p. 400)	**banco miembro:** banco que pertenece al Sistema de Reserva Federal (p. 400)
member bank reserve (MBR): reserves kept by member banks at the Fed to satisfy reserve requirements (p. 396)	**reserva de banco miembro (MBR, siglas en inglés):** reservas que mantienen los bancos miembros en la Reserva Federal para satisfacer los requisitos de reserva (p. 396)
merger: combination of two or more business enterprises to form a single firm (p. 72)	**fusión:** combinación de dos o más empresas comerciales para formar una sola firma (p. 72)
microeconomics: branch of economic theory that deals with behavior and decision making by small units such as individuals and firms (p. 91)	**microeconomía:** rama de la teoría de la economía que trata de la conducta y las decisiones que adoptan las pequeñas unidades tales como los individuos y las firmas (p. 91)
micro loan: small, unsecured loan made primarily to women to help them undertake an income-generating project in a developing country (p. 480)	**micropréstamo:** pequeño préstamo sin garantía, se hace fundamentalmente a mujeres para ayudarlas a asumir un proyecto generador de ingreso en un país en desarrollo (p. 480)
minimum wage: lowest legal wage that can be paid to most workers (pp. 44, 158, 219)	**sueldo mínimo:** sueldo legal más bajo que se le puede pagar a la mayoría de trabajadores (pp. 44, 158, 219)
misery index: unofficial statistic that is the sum of monthly inflation and the unemployment rate; same as discomfort index (p. 374)	**índice de miseria:** estadística no oficial que es la suma de la inflación mensual y la tasa de desempleo; igual al índice de incomodidad (p. 374)
mixed economy: economic system that has some combination of traditional, command, and market economies; also see modified free enterprise economy (pp. 39, 53)	**economía mixta:** sistema económico que tiene una combinación de economía tradicional, planificada y de mercado; ver también modified economy (pp. 39, 53)
modified free enterprise economy: free enterprise market economy where people carry on their economic affairs freely, but are subject to some government intervention and regulation; also see mixed economy (pp. 53, 522)	**economía de empresa privada modificada:** economía de mercado de libre empresa donde la gente lleva a cabo sus asuntos económicos libremente, pero están sujetos a algunas intervenciones y regulaciones del gobierno (pp. 53, 522)
modified union shop: arrangement under which workers have the option to join a union after being hired (p. 204)	**empresa de exclusividad gremial modificada:** arreglo por el cual los trabajadores tienen la opción de unirse a un sindicato luego de habérseles empleado (p. 204)
monetarism: school of thought stressing the importance of stable monetary growth to control inflation and stimulate long-term economic growth (p. 426)	**monetarismo:** escuela de pensamiento que enfatiza la importancia que el crecimiento monetario estable para controlar la inflación y estimular el crecimiento económico a largo plazo (p. 426)
monetary policy: actions by the Federal Reserve System to expand or contract the money supply in order to affect the cost and availability of credit (pp. 402, 431)	**política monetaria:** acciones que toma el Sistema de Reserva Federal para ampliar o reducir el abastecimiento de dinero para afectar el costo y disponibilidad de crédito (pp. 402, 431)
monetary unit: standard unit of currency in a country's money supply; American dollar, British pound (p. 386)	**unidad monetaria:** unidad monetaria estándar del abastecimiento monetario de un país; el dólar americano, la libra británica (p. 386)

English	Español
money market: market in which financial capital is loaned and/or borrowed for one year or less (p. 302)	**mercado monetario:** mercado en el cual el capital financiero se ha prestado por un año o menos (p. 302)
monopolistic competition: market structure having all conditions of pure competition except for identical products; form of imperfect competition (p. 173)	**competición monopolística:** estructura mercantil que posee todas las condiciones de competición pura a excepción de tener productos idénticos; una forma de competición imperfecta (p. 173)
monopoly: market structure characterized by a single producer; form of imperfect competition (p. 175)	**monopolio:** estructura mercantil caracterizada por un solo productor; una forma de competición imperfecta (p. 175)
most favored nation clause: trade law allowing a third country to enjoy the same tariff reductions the United States negotiates with another country (p. 453)	**cláusula de la nación más favorecida:** derecho mercantil que permite a un país tercero disfrutar las mismas rebajas de tarifas que los Estados Unidos negocia con otro país (p. 453)
multinational: corporation producing and selling without regard to national boundaries and whose business activities are located in several different countries (pp. 76, 502)	**multinacional:** corporación que produce y vende sin importarle las fronteras nacionales y cuyas actividades comerciales están situadas en varios países (pp. 76, 502)
multiplier: change in overall spending caused by a change in investment spending (p. 420)	**multiplicador:** cambio en el gasto global causado por un cambio en el gasto de inversión (p. 420)
municipal bond: bond, often tax exempt, issued by state and local governments; known as munis (p. 299)	**bono municipal:** bono, a menudo exento de impuestos, emitido por el gobierno estatal o local; conocido como munis (p. 299)
mutual fund: company that sells stock in itself and uses the proceeds to buy stocks and bonds issued by other companies (p. 307)	**fondo mutuo:** compañía que vende acciones de sí misma y usa las ganancias para comprar acciones y bonos emitidos por otras compañías (p. 307)

N

English	Español
national bank: commercial bank chartered by the National Banking System (p. 392)	**banco nacional:** un banco comercial establecido por el Sistema Bancario Nacional (p. 392)
national currency: currency backed by government bonds and issued by commercial banks in the National Banking System (p. 392)	**moneda nacional:** moneda respaldada por bonos del gobierno y emitida por bancos comerciales en el Sistema Bancario Nacional (p. 392)
national debt: the total amount borrowed from investors to finance the government's deficit spending (p. 278)	**deuda nacional:** el monto total que pidieron prestado a los inversores para financiar el gasto deficitario del gobierno (p. 278)
national income (NI): net national product less indirect business taxes; measure of a nation's income (p. 324)	**ingreso nacional:** producto nacional neto menos los impuestos indirectos sobre las empresas; medida del ingreso de una nación (p. 324)
natural monopoly: market structure in which average costs of production are lowest when all output is produced by a single firm (pp. 176, 244)	**monopolio natural:** estructura de mercado en la cual los costos promedios de producción son más bajos cuando toda la producción es de una única compañía (pp. 176, 244)
need: basic requirement for survival; includes food, clothing, and/or shelter (p. 6)	**necesidad:** requisito básico para la supervivencia; incluye comida, ropa y/o albergue (p. 6)
negative externality: harmful side effect that affects an uninvolved third party; external cost (p. 182)	**factores externos negativos:** efectos secundarios negativos que afectan a un tercero no partícipe; costo externo (p. 182)
negative income tax: tax system that would make cash payments in the form of tax refunds to individuals when their income falls below certain levels (p. 345)	**impuesto negativo sobre la renta:** sistema de impuestos que hace pagos efectivos en forma de reembolsos de impuestos cuando los ingresos de las personas caen por debajo de ciertos niveles (p. 345)

English	Español
net asset value (NAV): the market value of a mutual fund share determined by dividing the value of the fund by the number of shares issued (p. 307)	**valor neto del activo (NAV, siglas en inglés):** valor en el mercado de una acción de un fondo mutualista de inversión determinado dividiendo el valor del fondo por el número de acciones emitidas (p. 307)
net exports of goods and services: net expenditures by the output-expenditure model's foreign sector; equal to total exports less total imports (p. 327)	**exportaciones netas de bienes y servicios:** gastos netos según el modelo de producción-gastos del sector extranjero, igual al total de las exportaciones menos el total de las importaciones (p. 327)
net immigration: net population change after accounting for those who leave as well as enter a country (p. 334)	**inmigración neta:** carga de población neta después de tomar en cuenta las personas que salen o entran del país (p. 334)
net income: measure of business profits determined by subtracting all expenses, including taxes, from revenues (p. 73)	**ingreso neto:** justificación de las utilidades de un negocio determinada substrayendo de la renta todos los gastos incluso los impuestos (p. 73)
net national product (NNP): gross national product minus depreciation charges for wear and tear on capital equipment; measure of net annual production generated with labor and property supplied by a country's citizens (p. 324)	**producto interno neto (PIN):** Producto Interno Bruto menos los cargos de depreciación por uso y desgaste del equipo capital; medida de la producción anual neta generada por la mano de obra y la propiedad suplida por los ciudadanos de un país (p. 324)
***neutral:** favoring neither side in a dispute (p. 144)	***neutral:** que no favorece a ninguna de las partes en una disputa (p. 144)
nonbank financial institution: nondepository institution that channels savings to investors; finance companies, insurance companies, pension funds (p. 292)	**institución financiera no bancaria:** institución no depositaria que canaliza los ahorros a los inversionistas; compañías financieras, compañías de seguro, fondos de pensiones (p. 292)
nondurable good: an item that wears out or lasts for fewer than three years when used regularly (p. 13)	**bien no duradero:** algo que se consume totalmente o dura menos de tres años cuando se lo usa regularmente (p. 13)
nonmarket transaction: economic activity not taking place in the market and, therefore, not included in GDP; services of homemakers, work around the home (p. 321)	**transacción fuera del mercado:** actividad económica que no toma lugar en el mercado y, por lo tanto, no está incluida en el PIB; los servicios de las amas de casa, trabajo del hogar (p. 321)
nonprice competition: competition involving the advertising of a product's appearance, quality, or design, rather than its price (p. 173)	**competición sin precio:** competencia que implica publicidad sobre el aspecto de un producto, su calidad o diseño en vez de su precio (p. 173)
nonprofit organization: economic institution that operates like a business but does not seek financial gain; schools, churches, community service organizations (p. 79)	**organización sin ánimo de lucro:** institución económica que opera como un negocio pero que no busca ganancias; escuelas, iglesias, organizaciones de servicios para la comunidad (p. 79)
nonrecourse loan: agricultural loan that carries neither a penalty nor further obligation to repay if not paid back (p. 159)	**préstamo sin recurso:** préstamo de agricultura que no lleva ni penalidad ni demás obligaciones de pago (p. 159)
nonrenewable resource: resource that cannot be replenished once it is used (p. 513)	**recurso no renovable:** recurso que no puede ser reemplazado una vez que hay sido usado (p. 513)
North American Free Trade Agreement (NAFTA): agreement signed in 1993 to reduce tariffs among the United States, Canada, and Mexico (p. 454)	**Tratado de Libre Comercio de América del Norte (NAFTA):** tratado firmado en 1993 para reducir los aranceles entre los Estados Unidos, Canadá y México (p. 454)

O

***offset:** to balance higher levels of risk with a larger payoff (p. 298)	**compensar:** balancear mayores niveles de riesgo con un retorno más elevado (p. 298)

English	Español
oligopoly: market structure in which a few large sellers dominate and have the ability to affect prices in the industry; form of imperfect competition (p. 174)	**oligarquía:** estructura mercantil en la que unos cuantos vendedores grandes dominan la industria y tienen la habilidad de afectar los precios; forma de competición imperfecta (p. 174)
open market operations: monetary policy in the form of U.S. treasury bills or bond sales and purchases, or both (p. 403)	**operaciones de mercado abierto:** política monetaria en la forma de compra y venta de bonos en el mercado de bonos (p. 403)
opportunity cost: cost of the next best alternative use of money, time, or resources when one choice is made rather than another (pp. 20, 444, 522)	**costo de oportunidad:** cuando se hace una elección en lugar de otra, el costo de la mejor alternativa que sigue para el uso del dinero, tiempo o recursos (pp. 20, 444, 522)
option: contract giving investors an option to buy or sell commodities, equities, or financial assets at a specific future date using a price agreed upon today (p. 311)	**opción:** contrato que da al inversionista una opción de comprar o vender bienes, capitales o activos financieros a una fecha específica en el futuro usando el precio acordado hoy (p. 311)
output-expenditure model: macroeconomic model describing aggregate demand by the consumer, investment, government, and foreign sectors; GDP = C + I + G + F (p. 327)	**modelo de producción-gastos:** modelo macroeconómico que describe la demanda total del consumidor, la inversión, gobierno y los sectores extranjeros; PIB = C + I + G + SE (p. 327
outsourcing: hiring outside firms to perform non-core operations to lower operating costs (pp. 372, 503)	**externalización:** subcontratar compañías externas para realizar operaciones que no son básicas y así reducir los costos operativos (pp. 372, 503)
overhead: broad category of fixed costs that includes interest, rent, taxes, and executive salaries (p. 133)	**gastos generales:** categoría amplia de gastos fijos que incluyen intereses, alquiler, impuestos y salarios de ejecutivos (p. 133)
over-the-counter market (OTC): electronic marketplace for securities not listed on organized exchanges such as the New York Stock Exchange (p. 309)	**over-the-counter market (OTC):** mercado electrónico extrabursátil para valores no anotados en casas de cambio organizadas como la New York Stock Exchange (p. 309)

P

English	Español
par value: principal of a bond or total amount borrowed (p. 297)	**valor a la par:** capital de un bono o la cantidad total pedida en préstamo (p. 297)
paradox of value: apparent contradiction between the high value of a nonessential item and the low value of an essential item (p. 14)	**paradoja de valor:** aparente contradicción entre el alto valor de elementos que no son esenciales y el bajo valor de elementos esenciales (p. 14)
partnership: unincorporated business owned and operated by two or more people who share the profits and have unlimited liability for the debts and obligations of the firm; same as general partnership (p. 64)	**sociedad:** negocio no incorporado operado por dos o más dueños quienes comparten las ganancias y que tienen responsabilidad ilimitada por las deudas y obligaciones de la firma; igual que sociedad colectiva (p. 64)
"pay-as-you-go" provision: requirement that new spending proposals or tax cuts must be offset by reductions elsewhere (p. 282)	**estipulación de "pagar según vayas surgiendo":** requerimiento de que nuevas propuestas de gasto o reducción de impuestos deben ser igualados por reducciones en otras partes del presupuesto (p. 282)
payroll tax: tax on wages and salaries to finance Social Security and Medicare costs (p. 239)	**impuesto sobre nómina de pago:** impuestos en pagos y salarios para financiar el Seguro Social y costos de atención médica (medicare) (p. 239)
payroll withholding statement: document attached to a paycheck summarizing pay and deductions (p. 248)	**estado de cuenta de retención de nómina:** documento adherido al cheque de pago que resume el pago y las deducciones (p. 248)
payroll withholding system: system that automatically deducts income taxes from paychecks on a regular basis (p. 239)	**sistema de retención de nómina:** sistema periódico que automáticamente deduce los impuestos sobre la renta del cheque de pago (p. 239)

peak • preferred stock

English	Español
peak: point in time when real GDP stops expanding and begins to decline (p. 354)	**apogeo:** punto en el tiempo cuando el PIB cesa de aumentar y comienza a declinar (p. 354)
pension: regular allowance for someone who has worked a certain number of years, reached a certain age, or who has suffered from an injury (p. 292)	**pensión:** pago regular para alguien que ha trabajado cierto número de años, ha alcanzado cierta edad o ha sufrido una lesión (p. 292)
pension fund: fund that collects and invests income until payments are made to eligible recipients (p. 292)	**fondo de pensiones:** fondo que recauda e invierte ingresos hasta que se hacen pagos a los titulares que tienen derecho (p. 292)
per capita: per person basis; total divided by population (p. 279)	**per cápita:** con base en la persona; el total dividido entre la población (p. 279)
perestroika: fundamental restructuring of the Soviet economy; policy introduced by Gorbachev (p. 490)	**perestroika:** reestructuramiento fundamental de la economía soviética; política introducida por Gorbachev (p. 490)
perfect competition: market structure characterized by a large number of well-informed independent buyers and sellers who exchange identical products (p. 170)	**competencia perfecta:** estructura del mercado que se caracteriza por un gran número de compradores y vendedores independientes bien informados que intercambian productos idénticos (p. 170)
***persistent:** continuous, without signs of weakening (p. 460)	***persistente:** continuo, sin signos de debilitamiento (p. 460)
personal income (PI): total amount of income going to the consumer sector before individual income taxes are paid (p. 324)	**ingresos personales:** cantidad total de ingresos que van al sector del consumidor antes de que se paguen los impuestos sobre la renta (p. 324)
picket: demonstrate or march before a place of business to protest a company's actions (p. 199)	**piqueteo:** manifestar o marchar ante el establecimiento comercial para protestar las acciones de la patronal (p. 199)
pollution: contamination of air, water, or soil by the discharge of a poisonous or noxious substance (p. 516)	**polución:** contaminación del aire, agua o tierra por la descarga de una sustancia venenosa o nociva (p. 516)
pollution permit: federal permit allowing a public utility to release pollutants into the air; a form of pollution control (p. 517)	**permiso de polución:** permiso federal que permite que las empresas de servicios públicos liberen poluentes en el aire; una forma de controlar la contaminación (p. 517)
population density: number of people per square mile of land area (p. 493)	**densidad demográfica:** número de personas por milla cuadrada de área de terreno (p. 493)
population pyramid: diagram showing the breakdown of population by age and gender (p. 333)	**pirámide demográfica:** diagrama que muestra la distribución de la población por edad y sexo (p. 333)
pork: a line item budget expenditure that circumvents normal budget building processes and procedures and benefits a small number of people or businesses (p. 261)	**gasto público clientelista:** gasto en el presupuesto de rubros que eluden los procedimientos normales de elaboración del presupuesto y benefician a un pequeño número de personas o empresas (p. 261)
portfolio diversification: strategy of holding different investments to protect against risk (p. 307)	**diversificación de cartera:** estrategia de retener diferentes inversiones para protección contra riesgos (p. 307)
positive externality: beneficial side effect that affects an uninvolved third party (p. 182)	**factores externos positivos:** efectos secundarios beneficiosos que afectan a un tercero no involucrado (p. 182)
poverty threshold: annual dollar income used to determine the number of people in poverty (p. 338)	**umbral de pobreza:** ingreso anual en dólares para determinar el número de personas en situación de pobreza (p. 338)
poverty guidelines: administrative guidelines used to determine eligibility for certain federal programs (p. 338)	**pautas de pobreza:** pautas administrativas usadas para determinar la elegibilidad para determinados programas federales (p. 338)
preferred stock: form of stock without vote, in which stockholders get their investments back before common stockholders (p. 68)	**acciones preferenciales:** forma del capital accionario sin voto, en el que los accionistas recuperan su inversión antes que los accionistas ordinarios (p. 68)

English	Español
premium: monthly, quarterly, semiannual, or annual price paid for an insurance policy (p. 292)	**prima:** precio que se paga mensual, trimestral, semianual o anualmente por una póliza de seguro (p. 292)
*presumed: taken for granted; supposed (p. 300)	***supuesto:** dado por sentado; conjeturado (p. 300)
*prevail: to predominate (p. 92)	***prevalecer:** predominar (p. 92)
price: monetary value of a product as established by supply and demand (p. 143)	**precio:** valor monetario de un producto establecido por la oferta y la demanda (p. 143)
price ceiling: maximum legal price that can be charged for a product (p. 157)	**precio máximo:** máximo precio legal que se puede cobrar por un producto (p. 157)
price discrimination: practice of charging customers different prices for the same product; usually illegal (p. 186)	**discriminación en el precio:** práctica de cobrarle a los clientes distintos precios por el mismo producto; por lo general ilegal (p. 186)
price-fixing: agreement, usually illegal, by firms to charge a uniform price for a product (p. 175)	**fijación de precios:** acuerdo, por lo general ilegal, que hacen las compañías para cobrar un precio uniforme por un producto (p. 175)
price floor: lowest legal price that can be charged for a product (p. 158)	**precio mínimo:** precio legal más bajo que se puede cobrar por un producto (p. 158)
price index: statistical series used to measure changes in the price level over time (p. 362)	**índice de precios:** serie estadística que se usa para medir cambios en el nivel de los precios a lo largo del tiempo (p. 362)
*primary: most important (p. 475)	***primario:** el más importante (p. 475)
primary market: market in which only the original issuer can sell or repurchase a financial asset; government savings bonds, IRAs, small CDs (p. 303)	**mercado primario:** mercado en que sólo el emisor original venderá o volverá a comprar un haber financiero; bonos de ahorros del gobierno, los IRA, pequeños CD (p. 303)
prime rate: best or lowest interest rate commercial banks charge their customers (p. 404)	**tasa preferencial:** tasa de interés mejor o más baja que los bancos comerciales cobran a sus clientes (p. 404)
primitive equilibrium: first stage of economic development during which the economy is stagnant (p. 472)	**equilibrio primitivo:** primera etapa del desarrollo económico durante la cual la economía está estancada (p. 472)
principal: amount borrowed when getting a loan or issuing a bond (p. 69)	**capital:** cantidad que se pide prestada cuando se obtiene un préstamo o se emite un bono (p. 69)
*principle: a fundamental law or idea (p. 98)	***principio:** una ley o idea fundamental (p. 98)
private property rights: fundamental feature of capitalism, which allows individuals to own and control their possessions as they wish; includes both tangible and intangible property (p. 50)	**derechos de propiedad privada:** característica fundamental del capitalismo la cual permite a los individuos a poseer y controlar sus propiedades como lo deseen, incluso las propiedades tangibles e intangibles (p. 50)
private sector: that part of the economy made up of private individuals and businesses (p. 263)	**sector privado:** aquella parte de la economía compuesta por personas privadas y negocios (p. 263)
privatization: conversion of state-owned factories and other property to private ownership (p. 487)	**privatización:** conversión de fábricas y otras propiedades del gobierno a propiedad privada (p. 487)
producer price index (PPI): index used to measure prices received by domestic producers; formerly called the wholesale price index (p. 364)	**índice de precios de productor (PPI, siglas en inglés):** índice que se usa para medir los precios recibidos de los productores domésticos; anteriormente denominado índice de precios al por mayor (p. 364)
product differentiation: real or imagined differences between competing products in the same industry (p. 173)	**diferenciación de productos:** diferencias reales o imaginadas entre productos que compiten en la misma industria (p. 173)

Glossary/Glosario

product market • protectionist

English	Español
product market: market where goods and services are bought and sold (p. 15)	**mercado de productos:** mercado donde los bienes y servicios se compran y se venden (p. 15)
production function: graphic portrayal showing how a change in the amount of a single variable input affects total output (p. 128)	**función de producción:** rendimiento gráfico que muestra cómo un cambio en la cantidad de una sola variable de insumo afecta la producción total (p. 128)
production possibilities frontier: diagram representing maximum combinations of goods and/or services an economy can produce when all productive resources are fully employed (pp. 21, 444)	**frontera de posibilidades de producción:** diagrama que representa el máximo de combinaciones de bienes y/o servicios que una economía puede producir cuando se emplean a plenitud todos los recursos (pp. 21, 444)
productivity: measure of the amount of output produced with a given amount of productive factors; normally refers to labor, but can apply to all factors of production (p. 16)	**productividad:** medida de la cantidad producción con una cantidad determinada de factores productivos; normalmente se refiere a mano de obra, pero puede aplicarse a todos los factores de la producción (p. 16)
professional association: nonprofit organization of professional or specialized workers seeking to improve working conditions, skill levels, and public perceptions of its profession (p. 81)	**asociación profesional:** organización sin fines de lucro de trabajadores profesionales o especializados que buscan mejorar las condiciones de trabajo, los niveles de habilidades y la percepción pública de su profesión (p. 81)
professional labor: workers with a high level of professional and managerial skills (p. 208)	**trabajo profesional:** trabajadores con un alto nivel de habilidades profesionales y gerenciales (p. 208)
profit: extent to which persons or organizations are better off at the end of a period than they were at the beginning; usually measured in dollars (p. 50)	**ganancias:** nivel al que personas y organizaciones mejoran al cabo de un periodo de lo que estaban al principio; por lo general se mide en dólares (p. 50)
profit-maximizing quantity of output: level of production where marginal cost is equal to marginal revenue (p. 137)	**cantidad de producto para el máximo de ganancias:** nivel de producción en que el costo marginal equivale al ingreso marginal (p. 137)
profit motive: driving force that encourages people and organizations to improve their material well-being; characteristic of capitalism and free enterprise (p. 50)	**motivo de ganancia:** fuerza motriz que anima a la gente y organizaciones a mejorar su bienestar material; característica del capitalismo y el libre comercio (p. 50)
progressive tax: tax where percentage of income paid in tax rises as level of income rises (p. 235)	**tributación progresiva:** tributación en que un porcentaje del ingreso que se paga en impuestos sube al subir el nivel de ingreso (p. 235)
*prohibited: prevented or forbade (p. 201)	***prohibido:** impedido o interdicto (p. 201)
*projected: calculated as a future outcome (p. 334)	***proyectado:** calculado como ingreso futuro (p. 334)
property tax: tax on tangible and intangible possessions such as real estate, buildings, furniture, stocks, bonds, and bank accounts (p. 244)	**impuesto sobre los bienes inmuebles:** gravámen sobre posesiones tangibles e intangibles como bienes raíces, edificios, muebles, acciones, bonos y cuentas bancarias (p. 244)
*proportion: comparative relationship between things in terms of size, quantity, etc (p. 472)	***proporción:** relación comparativa entre las cosas en términos de tamaño, cantidad, etc. (p. 472)
proportional tax: tax in which percentage of income paid in tax is the same regardless of the level of income (p. 235)	**impuesto proporcional:** tributación en la cual el porcentaje de ingresos a pagar es igual sin importar el nivel de ingreso (p. 235)
proprietorship: see sole proprietorship (p. 62)	**patrimonio:** ver sole proprietorship (p. 62)
*prospects: potential or expectations (p. 306)	***perspectivas:** potencial o expectativas (p. 306)
protectionist: person who wants to protect domestic producers against foreign competition with tariffs, quotas, and other trade barriers (p. 450)	**proteccionista:** persona que desea proteger a los productores domésticos contra la competencia extranjera con aranceles, cuotas y otras barreras comerciales (p. 450)

English	Español
protective tariff: tax on an imported product designed to protect less efficient domestic producers (p. 448)	**arancel proteccionista:** impuesto sobre un producto importado, diseñado para proteger a los productores domésticos menos eficientes (p. 448)
public disclosure: requirement forcing a business to reveal information about its products or its operations to the public (p. 188)	**revelación pública:** requisito que fuerza a un negocio a que revele al público información de sus productos u operaciones (p. 188)
public goods: economic products that are paid for and consumed collectively; such as highways, national defense, police and fire protection (p. 181)	**bienes públicos:** producto económico por el que se paga y se consume colectivamente; autopistas, defensa nacional, protección de la policía y de los bomberos (p. 181)
public sector: that part of the economy made up of the local, state, and federal governments (p. 262)	**sector público:** esa parte de la economía compuesta de los gobiernos locales, estatales y federales (p. 262)
public utility: company providing essential services such as water and electricity to consumers; usually subject to some government regulations (p. 83)	**empresa de servicios públicos:** compañía que provee servicios esenciales como el agua y la electricidad a los consumidores, por lo general sujeta a algunas regulaciones del gobierno (p. 83)
put option: futures contract giving investors the option to cancel a contract to sell commodities, equities, or financial assets (p. 311)	**opción de venta:** contrato de futuros que da a los inversores la opción de cancelar un contrato para vender productos básicos, acciones o activos financieros (p. 311)

Q

English	Español
quantity supplied: amount offered for sale at a given price; point on the supply curve (p. 119)	**cantidad ofrecida:** cantidad ofrecida en venta a un precio dado; punto en la curva de oferta (p. 119)
quantity theory of money: hypothesis that the supply of money directly affects the price level over the long run (p. 405)	**teoría de la cantidad de dinero:** hipótesis de que a largo plazo el abastecimiento de dinero afecta directamente el nivel del precio (p. 405)
quota: limit on the amount of a good that is allowed into a country (p. 448)	**cupo:** límite de cantidad de bienes que se permite en un país (p. 448)

R

English	Español
ration coupon: permit allowing holder to receive a given amount of a rationed product (p. 145)	**cupón de raciones:** permite al portador recibir una cantidad específica de un producto racionado (p. 145)
rationing: system of allocating goods and services without prices (p. 145)	**racionamiento:** sistema de distribución de bienes y servicios sin precios (p. 145)
real dollars: see constant dollars (p. 221)	**dólares reales:** ver constant dollars (p. 221)
real GDP: gross domestic product after adjustments for inflation; same as GDP in constant dollars (p. 322)	**PIB real:** Producto Interno Bruto después de ajustes para la inflación; igual que PIB en dólares constantes (p. 322)
rebate: partial refund of the original price of a product (p. 146)	**reembolso:** devolución parcial del precio original de un producto (p. 146)
recession: decline in real GDP lasting at least two quarters or more (p. 354)	**recesión:** reducción en el PIB real que dura al menos dos trimestres o más (p. 354)
*recover: to get back (p. 365)	***recobrar:** recuperar (p. 365)
regressive tax: tax where percentage of income paid in tax goes down as income rises (p. 236)	**impuesto regresivo:** impuesto en el cual el porcentaje del ingreso a pagar en imposiciones baja cuando los ingresos suben (p. 236)

English	Español
Regulation Z: provision extending truth-in-lending disclosures to consumers (p. 407)	**Regulación Z:** provisión que extiende a los consumidores revelaciones de veracidad de préstamos (p. 407)
***regulator:** someone or something that controls activities (p. 52)	***regulador:** alguien o algo que controla las actividades (p. 52)
***reluctant:** hesitant or unwilling (p. 265)	***renuente:** reacio o sin interés (p. 265)
renewable resource: natural resource that can be replenished for future use (p. 512)	**recurso renovable:** recurso natural que se puede reabastecer para uso futuro (p. 512)
reserve requirement: formula used to compute the amount of a depository institution's required reserves (p. 396)	**requisito de reserva:** fórmula que se usa para calcular la cantidad de reservas que requiere una institución depositaria (p. 396)
***residence:** the place where a person lives (p. 329)	***residencia:** el lugar donde una persona vive (p. 329)
***resource:** any available means for economic or political development (p. 6)	***recurso:** cualquier medio disponible para el desarrollo económico o político (p. 6)
***restrained:** limited the activity or growth of (p. 186)	***restringido:** limita la actividad o crecimiento de (p. 186)
revenue tariff: tax placed on imported goods to raise revenue (p. 448)	**tarifa de ingresos:** impuesto sobre bienes importados para recaudar fondos (p. 448)
***revolution:** an overthrow of government (p. 385)	***revolución:** derrocamiento del gobierno (p. 385)
right-to-work law: state law making it illegal to require a worker to join a union (p. 202)	**ley de derecho al trabajo:** ley estatal que hace ilegal el requerir que un trabajador sea miembro de un sindicato (p. 202)
risk: situation in which the outcome is not certain, but the probabilities can be estimated (p. 293)	**riesgo:** situación en la cual el resultado no es seguro, pero las probabilidades se pueden estimar (p. 293)
rural population: those persons not living in urban areas, including sparsely populated areas along the fringes of cities (p. 330)	**población rural:** aquellas personas que no viven en áreas urbanas, incluyendo zonas poco pobladas en la periferia de las ciudades (p. 330)

S

English	Español
S&P 500: see Standard & Poor 500 (p. 310)	**S&P 500:** ver Standard & Poor 500 (p. 310)
sales tax: general state or city tax levied on a product at the time of sale (p. 233)	**impuesto de ventas:** impuesto general del estado o la ciudad en un producto en el momento de venta (p. 233)
saving: absence of spending that frees resources for use in other activities or investments (p. 289)	**ahorro:** ausencia de gastos que libera los recursos para usarlos en otras actividades o inversiones (p. 289)
savings: the dollars that become available for investors to use when others save (p. 289)	**ahorros:** los dólares que se hacen disponibles para que los inversionistas los usen cuando otras personas ahorran (p. 289)
savings bond: low-denomination, non-transferable bond issued by the federal government, usually through payroll-savings plans (p. 300)	**bono de ahorros:** bono no transferible, de baja denominación emitido por el gobierno federal, usualmente a través de planes de ahorro de nómina (p. 300)
scarcity: fundamental economic problem facing all societies that results from a combination of scarce resources and people's virtually unlimited wants (pp. 6, 509)	**escasez:** problema económico fundamental que enfrentan todas las sociedades como resultado de una combinación de escasos recursos y las necesidades ilimitadas de la gente (pp. 6, 509)
seasonal unemployment: unemployment caused by annual changes in the weather or other conditions that prevail at certain times of the year (p. 373)	**desempleo estacional:** desempleo causado por cambios anuales en el clima y otras condiciones que prevalecen durante ciertas épocas del año (p. 373)

English	Español
secondary market: market in which all financial assets can be sold to someone other than the original issuer; corporate bonds, government bonds (p. 303)	**mercado secundario:** mercado en el que todos los bienes financieros se pueden vender a alguien excepto al emisor original; bonos de empresa privada, bonos del gobierno (p. 303)
secondhand sales: sales of used goods; category of activity not included in GDP computation (p. 321)	**ventas de segunda mano:** venta de bienes usados; categoría de actividad no incluida en la computación del PIB (p. 321)
***sector:** an area of the economy in which businesses offer the same or similar products or services (p. 291)	***sector:** área de la economía en la que las empresas ofrecen los mismos, o similares, productos o servicios (p. 291)
***secure:** obtain (p. 457)	***afianzar:** obtener (p. 457)
securities exchange: see stock exchange (p. 308)	**bolsa de valores:** ver stock exchange (p. 308)
seizure: temporary government takeover of a company to keep it running during a labor-management dispute (p. 212)	**incautación:** cuando el gobierno toma temporáneamente una compañía para mantenerla operando durante un conflicto obrero-patronal (p. 212)
semiskilled labor: workers who can operate machines requiring a minimum amount of training (p. 208)	**mano de obra semientrenada:** trabajadores que pueden operar máquinas que requieren la mínima cantidad de entrenamiento (p. 208)
seniority: length of time a person has been on a job (p. 210)	**antigüedad:** cantidad de tiempo que una persona ha estado en un puesto de trabajo (p. 210)
***series:** a group of related things or events (p. 358)	***serie:** un grupo de cosas o acontecimientos relacionados (p. 358)
service: work or labor performed for someone; economic product that includes haircuts, home repairs, forms of entertainment (p. 13)	**servicio:** obra o trabajo efectuado por alguien; producto económico que incluye cortes de pelo, reparaciones del hogar, formas de entretenimiento (p. 13)
set-aside contract: guaranteed contract or portion of a contract reserved for a targeted group, usually a minority (p. 219)	**contrato garantizado:** contrato o porción de un contrato respaldado con aval, reservado para un grupo objetivo, por lo general una minoría (p. 219)
shareholder: see stockholder (p. 67)	**accionista:** ver stockholder (p. 67)
short run: production period so short that only variable inputs (usually labor) can be changed (p. 128)	**corto plazo:** periodo de producción tan corto que sólo se pueden cambiar los insumos variables (por lo general la mano de obra) (p. 128)
shortage: situation where quantity supplied is less than quantity demanded at a given price (p. 151)	**escasez:** situación en donde la cantidad ofrecida es menor que la cantidad demandada a un precio dado (p. 151)
signaling theory: theory that employers are willing to pay more for people with certificates, diplomas, degrees, and other indicators of superior ability (p. 210)	**teoría de señalización:** teoría de que los empleadores estarán dispuestos a pagar más a personas con certificados, diplomas, postgrados y otros indicadores de destrezas superiores (p. 210)
silver certificate: paper currency backed by, and redeemable for, silver from 1878 to 1968 (p. 393)	**certificado de plata:** papel moneda respaldado y redimible con plata desde 1878 hasta 1968 (p. 393)
sin tax: relatively high tax designed to raise revenue and discourage consumption of a socially undesirable product (p. 230)	**impuesto de pecado:** impuesto relativamente alto diseñado para recaudar ingresos y desalentar el consumo de productos socialmente indeseables (p. 230)
skilled labor: workers who can operate complex equipment and require little supervision (p. 208)	**mano de obra adiestrada:** trabajadores que pueden operar equipo complejo y que requieren poca supervisión (p. 208)
Social Security: federal program of disability and retirement benefits that covers most working people (p. 45)	**Seguro Social:** programa federal de beneficios de invalidez y retiro que cubre a la mayoría de las personas que trabajan (p. 45)

English	Español
socialism: economic system in which government owns some factors of production and has a role in determining what and how goods are produced (p. 39)	**socialismo:** sistema económico en el cual el gobierno es dueño de algunos factores de producción y tiene un papel en la determinación de qué bienes se producirán y cómo (p. 39)
soft loan: loan that may never be paid back; usually involves loan to developing countries (p. 482)	**préstamo indulgente:** préstamo que tal vez nunca serán pagado, muchas veces hechos a países en desarrollo (p. 482)
sole proprietorship: unincorporated business owned and run by a single person who has rights to all profits and unlimited liability for all debts of the firm; most common form of business organization in the United States (p. 62)	**empresa unipersonal:** negocio no incorporado, de propiedad y operado por una sola persona quien tiene el derecho a todas las ganancias y responsabilidades sin límite por todas las deudas de la firma; la forma más común de organización comercial en los Estados Unidos (p. 62)
Solidarity: independent Polish labor union founded in 1980 by Lech Walesa (p. 491)	**Solidaridad:** gremio obrero independiente de Polonia fundado en 1980 por Lech Walesa (p. 491)
specialization: assignment of tasks to the workers, factories, regions, or nations that can perform them more efficiently (p. 17)	**especialización:** asignación de tareas a los trabajadores, fábricas, regiones o naciones que las pueden realizar más eficientemente (p. 17)
specie: money in the form of gold or silver coins (p. 385)	**especie:** dinero en forma de monedas de oro o plata (p. 385)
spending cap: limits on annual discretionary spending (p. 282)	**límites de gastos:** límites en gastos discrecionales anuales (p. 282)
spot market: market in which a transaction is made immediately at the prevailing price (p. 311)	**mercado de entrega inmediata:** mercado en el cual se hace una operación inmediatamente al precio imperante (p. 311)
***stabilize:** to make steady or unwavering (p. 159)	***estabilizar:** hacer estable o firme (p. 159)
stages of production: phases of production that consist of increasing, decreasing, and negative returns (p. 129)	**etapas de producción:** fases de producción que consisten en el aumento, disminución y rendimiento negativo (p. 129)
stagflation: combination of stagnant economic growth and inflation (p. 364)	**stagflation:** combinación de estancamiento del crecimiento económico y la inflación (p. 364)
***stagnation:** lack of movement (p. 35)	***estancamiento:** falta de movimiento (p. 35)
Standard & Poor's 500 (S&P 500): statistical series of 500 stocks used to monitor prices on the NYSE, American Stock Exchange, and OTC market (p. 310)	**Las 500 de Standard & Poor (S&P 500):** serie estadística de las 500 acciones que se usan para observar los precios en la bolsa de valores de la NYSE, American Stock Exchange y el mercado extrabursátil (p. 310)
standard of living: quality of life based on ownership of necessities and luxuries that make life easier (p. 24)	**estándar de vida:** calidad de vida basada en la propiedad de necesidades y lujos que hacen la vida más fácil (p. 24)
state bank: bank that receives its charter from the state in which it operates (p. 391)	**banco del estado:** banco que recibe su escritura de constitución del estado en el cual opera (p. 391)
stock: certificate of ownership in a corporation; common or preferred stock (p. 67)	**acción:** certificado de propiedad en una corporación; acciones preferidas y ordinarias (p. 67)
stock exchange: physical place where buyers and sellers meet to exchange securities (p. 308)	**bolsa de valores:** lugar físico donde los compradores y vendedores se encuentran para intercambiar valores (p. 308)
stockbroker: person who buys or sells securities for investors (p. 306)	**agente de bolsa:** persona que compra y vende valores para los inversionistas (p. 306)
stockholder: person who owns a share or shares of stock in a corporation; same as shareholders (p. 67)	**accionista:** La persona dueña de acciones de una corporación (p. 67)
store of value: one of the three functions of money allowing people to preserve value for future use (p. 387)	**fuente de valor:** una de las tres funciones del dinero que permite a las personas preservar el valor para uso futuro (p. 387)

English	Español
*strategy: a plan or method (p. 504)	***estrategia:** un plan o método (p. 504)
strike: union-organized work stoppage designed to gain concessions from an employer (p. 199)	**huelga:** paro del trabajo, organizado por el sindicato y diseñado para obtener concesiones del patrón (p. 199)
structural unemployment: unemployment caused by a fundamental change in the economy that reduces the demand for some workers (p. 372)	**desempleo estructural:** desempleo causado por un cambio fundamental en la economía que reduce la demanda de algunos trabajadores (p. 372)
subsidy: government payment to encourage or protect a certain economic activity (pp. 122, 264)	**subsidio:** pago del gobierno para animar o proteger cierta actividad económica (pp. 122, 264)
subsistence: state in which a society produces barely enough to support itself (p. 510)	**subsistencia:** estado en que una sociedad escasamente produce lo suficiente para sostenerse (p. 510)
substitutes: competing products that can be used in place of one another; products related in such a way that an increase in the price of one increases the demand for the other (p. 100)	**sustitutos:** productos de competición que se pueden intercambiar; productos relacionados de tal forma que un aumento en el precio de uno aumenta la demanda por los otros (p. 100)
substitution effect: that portion of a change in quantity demanded due to a change in the relative price of the product that makes other products more or less costly (p. 98)	**efecto de sustitución:** la porción de un cambio en cantidad demandada debido a un cambio en el precio relativo del producto que hace más o menos costosos a otros productos (p. 98)
*successive: consecutive (p. 518)	***sucesivo:** consecutivo (p. 518)
supply: amount of a product offered for sale at all possible prices in a market (p. 117)	**oferta:** cantidad de un producto que se ofrece a la venta a todos los precios posibles del mercado (p. 117)
supply curve: a graph that shows the quantities supplied at each and every possible price in the market (p. 118)	**curva de oferta:** gráfica que muestra las cantidades ofertadas a todos los posibles precios del mercado (p. 118)
supply elasticity: responsiveness of quantity supplied to a change in price (p. 124)	**elasticidad de oferta:** suceptibilidad de la cantidad ofrecida al cambio de precio (p. 124)
supply schedule: a table showing the quantities produced or offered for sale at each and every possible price in the market (p. 118)	**tabla de oferta:** una tabla que muestra las cantidades producidas u ofrecidas a la venta a cada precio del mercado (p. 118)
supply-side policies: economic policies designed to stimulate the economy by increasing production (p. 423)	**políticas de promoción de la oferta:** políticas económicas diseñadas para estimular la economía aumentando la producción (p. 423)
surplus: situation where quantity supplied is greater than quantity demanded at a given price (p. 150)	**superávit:** situación en que la cantidad ofrecida es mayor que la cantidad demandada a un precio dado (p. 150)
*sustain: to support or hold up (p. 181)	***sustentar:** mantener o elevar (p. 181)

T

English	Español
takeoff: third stage of economic development during which barriers of primitive equilibrium have been overcome (p. 473)	**despegue:** tercer etapa del desarrollo económico durante el cual las barreras de equilibrio primitivo han sido superadas (p. 473)
target price: price floor for agricultural products set by the government to stabilize farm incomes (p. 159)	**precio indicativo:** precio más bajo de agricultura fijado por el gobierno para estabilizar los ingresos agrarios (p. 159)
tariff: tax placed on an imported product (p. 448)	**arancel:** impuesto sobre productos importados (p. 448)
tax assessor: person who examines and values property for tax purposes (p. 244)	**tasador de impuestos:** persona que examina y evalúa propiedades para propósitos de impuestos (p. 244)

tax-exempt • trade-weighted value of the dollar

English	Español
tax-exempt: not subject to tax by federal or state governments (p. 300)	**exento de impuestos:** que no está gravado por impuestos del gobierno estatal ni federal (p. 300)
tax loophole: exception or oversight in the tax law allowing taxpayer to avoid taxes (p. 232)	**laguna tributaria:** excepción o descuido en la ley de impuestos que permite que los contribuyentes eviten impuestos (p. 232)
tax return: annual report filed with local, state, or federal government detailing income earned and taxes owed (p. 233)	**declaración de impuestos:** reporte anual que se registra con el gobierno local, el estatal o el federal y que detalla los ingresos que se ganaron y los impuestos que se deben (p. 233)
***technical:** related to a particular subject such as art, science, or trade (p. 106)	***técnico:** relacionado con un tema específico, como arte, ciencia o comercio (p. 106)
technological monopoly: market situation where a firm has a monopoly because it owns or controls a manufacturing method, process, or other scientific advance (p. 176)	**monopolio tecnológico:** situación mercantil en que una firma tiene el monopolio porque es propietaria de/o controla un método o un proceso de manufactura u otro adelanto científico (p. 176)
technological unemployment: unemployment caused by technological developments or automation that make some workers' skills obsolete (p. 372)	**desempleo tecnológico:** desempleo causado por desarrollos tecnológicos o automatización que hace que las destrezas de algunos trabajadores sean obsoletas (p. 372)
***theoretically:** existing only in theory; not practical (p. 170)	***teóricamente:** que sólo existe en la teoría; que no es práctico (p. 170)
theory of negotiated wages: explanation of wage rates based on the bargaining strength of organized labor (p. 210)	**teoría de salarios negociados:** explicación de las escalas de salarios basada en la fuerza de negociación del movimiento sindical (p. 210)
tight money policy: monetary policy resulting in higher interest rates and restricted access to credit; associated with a contraction of the money supply (p. 402)	**política de dinero escaso:** política monetaria que resulta en tasas de interés más altas y acceso restringido al crédito; se asocia con la contracción del abastecimiento de dinero (p. 402)
total cost: variable plus fixed cost; all costs associated with production (p. 134)	**costo total:** costo variable y costo fijo; todos los gastos asociados a la producción (p. 134)
total product: total output or production by a firm (p. 129)	**producto total:** rendimiento o producción total de una firma (p. 129)
total revenue: total amount earned by a firm from the sale of its products; price of goods sold times quantity sold (p. 136)	**ingreso total:** cantidad total obtenida por una compañía de la venta de sus productos; precio de los bienes vendidos multiplicado por la cantidad vendida (p. 136)
trade deficit: balance of payments outcome when spending on imports exceeds revenues received from exports (p. 460)	**déficit comercial:** resultados de la balanza de pagos cuando los gastos de las importaciones exceden los ingresos recibidos de las exportaciones (p. 460)
trade-off: alternative that must be given up when one choice is made rather than another (p. 20)	**compensación:** alternativas a las que hay que renunciar cuando se escoge una en lugar de otra (p. 20)
trade surplus: situation occurring when the value of a nation's exports exceeds the value of its imports (p. 460)	**superávit de intercambio:** la situación que ocurre cuando el valor de las exportaciones de una nación excede al valor de sus importaciones (p. 460)
trade union: see craft union (p. 199)	**sindicato gremial:** ver craft union (p. 199)
trade-weighted value of the dollar: index showing strength of the United States dollar against a market basket of other foreign currencies (p. 460)	**valor del dólar ponderado según el comercio exterior:** índice que indica la fuerza del dólar americano contra la cesta de mercado de otras divisas (p. 460)

English	Español
traditional economy: economic system in which the allocation of scarce resources and other economic activity is the result of ritual, habit, or custom (p. 34)	**economía tradicional:** sistema económico en el que la distribución de escasos recursos y otra actividad económica es el resultado de rito, hábito o costumbre (p. 34)
transfer payment: payment for which the government receives neither goods nor services in return (p. 263)	**transferencia de pago:** pago por el cual el gobierno no recibe ni bienes ni servicios de vuelta (p. 263)
*transferable: able to be moved from one person or place to another (p. 13)	***transferible:** capaz de ser trasladado de una persona o lugar a otro (p. 13)
Treasury bill: short-term United States government obligation with a maturity of 4, 13, or 26 weeks and a minimum denomination of $1,000 (p. 301)	**letra del Tesoro:** obligación de corto plazo del gobierno de los Estados Unidos que vence a las 4, 13 o 26 semanas y con denominación mínima de $1,000 (p. 301)
Treasury bond: United States government bond with maturity of 10 to 30 years (p. 301)	**bono del Tesoro:** bono del gobierno de los Estados Unidos con vencimiento de 10 a 30 años (p. 301)
Treasury note: United States government obligation with a maturity of 2 to 10 years (p. 301)	**pagaré del Tesoro:** obligación del gobierno de los Estados Unidos con vencimiento de 2 a 10 años (p. 301)
*trend: a pattern or general tendency (p. 216)	***tendencia:** un patrón o inclinación general (p. 216)
trend line: growth path the economy would follow if it were not interrupted by alternating periods of recession and recovery (p. 354)	**tendencia:** rumbo de crecimiento que seguiría la economía si no se interrumpiera por períodos alternantes de recesión y recuperación (p. 354)
trough: point in time when real GDP stops declining and begins to expand (p. 354)	**sima:** punto en el tiempo cuando el PIB real deja de descender y comienza la expansión (p. 354)
trust: illegal combination of corporations or companies organized to hinder competition (p. 186)	**sindicación:** pacto ilegal entre corporaciones o compañías que se organizan para impedir la competencia (p. 186)
trust fund: special account used to hold revenues designated for a specific expenditure such as Social Security, Medicare, or highways (p. 278)	**fondo fiduciario:** cuenta especial que se usa para retener ingresos designados para un gasto específico como el Seguro Social, Medicare o las autopistas (p. 278)
two–tier wage system: wage scale paying newer workers a lower wage than others already on the job (p. 217)	**sistema de salario de dos niveles:** escala de salario que paga a los nuevos trabajadores un sueldo más bajo que a los que ya estaban trabajando (p. 217)

U

English	Español
underground economy: unreported legal and illegal activities that do not show up in GDP statistics (p. 321)	**economía subterránea:** actividades ilegales sin reportar que no aparecen en las estadísticas del PIB (p. 321)
*undertaking: entering into an activity (p. 488)	***emprendimiento:** asumir una actividad (p. 488)
*unduly: too much (p. 417)	***excesivamente:** demasiado (p. 417)
unemployed: state of working for less than one hour per week for pay or profit in a non-family-owned business, while being available and having made an effort to find a job during the past month (p. 370)	**desempleado:** condición de trabajar por menos de una hora por semana por paga o provecho en un negocio que no es de la familia, en tanto que se está disponible y se ha hecho el esfuerzo de hallar trabajo durante el mes pasado (p. 370)
unemployment insurance: government program providing payments to the unemployed; an automatic stabilizer (p. 422)	**seguro de desempleo:** programa de gobierno que provee pagos a los desempleados; un estabilizador automático (p. 422)
unemployment rate: ratio of unemployed individuals divided by total number of persons in the civilian labor force, expressed as a percentage (p. 370)	**índice de desempleo:** relación de personas desempleadas dividida por el número total de personas en la fuerza de trabajo civil, expresado como un porcentaje (p. 370)
*unfounded: not based on fact (p. 374)	***infundado:** que no se basa en los hechos (p. 374)

English	Español
*uniform: even or consistent (p. 342)	***uniforme:** parejo o coherente (p. 342)
union shop: arrangement under which workers must join a union after being hired (p. 204)	**empresa de exclusividad gremial:** arreglo bajo el cual los trabajadores tienen que unirse a un sindicato tras ser empleados (p. 204)
unit elastic: elasticity where a change in the independent variable (usually price) generates a proportional change of the dependent variable (quantity demanded or supplied) (p. 105)	**elasticidad de la unidad:** elasticidad en que un cambio en la variable independiente (usualmente el precio) genera un cambio proporcional de la variable dependiente (cantidad demandada u ofrecida) (p. 105)
unlimited liability: requirement that an owner is personally and fully responsible for all losses and debts of a business; applies to proprietorships, general partnerships (p. 63)	**unlimited liability/responsabilidad sin límite:** requisito de que un propietario es personal y plenamente responsable por todas las pérdidas y deudas de un negocio; se aplica a propietarios y sociedades generales (p. 63)
unrelated individual: person living alone or with nonrelatives even though that person may have relatives living elsewhere (p. 326)	**individuo no relacionado:** persona que vive sola o con personas que no son sus parientes aunque esa persona tenga parientes que vivan en otro lugar (p. 326)
unskilled labor: workers not trained to operate specialized machines and equipment (p. 208)	**mano de obra no adiestrada:** trabajadores no entrenados para operar máquinas y equipos especializados (p. 208)
*unstable: unsteady (p. 420)	***inestable:** fluctuante (p. 420)
urban population: those persons living in incorporated cities, towns, and villages with 2,500 or more inhabitants (p. 330)	**población urbana:** aquellas personas que viven en ciudades incorporadas, pueblos y aldeas con 2,500 ó más habitantes (p. 330)
user fee: fee paid for the use of good or service; form of a benefit tax (p. 241)	**tarifa para el usuario:** precio que se paga por usar unos bienes o servicios; forma de un impuesto de beneficio (p. 241)
utility: ability or capacity of a good or service to be useful and give satisfaction to someone (p. 14)	**utilidad:** habilidad o capacidad de un bien o de un servicio para ser útil y darle satisfacción a alguien (p. 14)

V

English	Español
*validity: justification (p. 230)	***validez:** justificación (p. 230)
value: worth of a good or service as determined by the market (p. 14)	**valor:** valor de un bien o servicio según lo determina el mercado (p. 14)
value-added tax (VAT): tax on the value added at every stage of the production process (p. 252)	**impuesto de valor agregado:** impuesto sobre el valor agregado a cada etapa del proceso de producción (p. 252)
variable cost: production cost that varies as output changes; labor, energy, raw materials (p. 133)	**costo variable:** costo de producción que varía según cambia la producción; la mano de obra, la energía, la materia prima (p. 133)
*various: different (p. 118)	***varios:** diferentes (p. 118)
vertical merger: combination of firms involved in different steps of manufacturing or marketing (p. 75)	**fusión vertical:** combinación de firmas envueltas en distintos pasos de la manufactura o el mercadeo (p. 75)
*volume: amount; quantity (p. 443)	***volumen:** cantidad; medida (p. 443)
*voluntary: done or brought about by free choice (p. 149)	***voluntario:** realizado o iniciado por libre elección (p. 149)

English	Español
voluntary exchange: act of buyers and sellers freely and willingly engaging in market transactions; characteristic of capitalism and free enterprise (p. 49)	**intercambio voluntario:** hecho en el cual los compradores y los vendedores participan libre y voluntariamente en operaciones mercantiles; característica del capitalismo y el libre comercio (p. 49)
voucher: certificate that could be used to purchase government-owned property during privatization (p. 488)	**vale:** certificado que podría usarse para comprar propiedad del gobierno durante una privatización (p. 488)

English	Español
wage-price controls: policies and regulations making it illegal for firms to give raises or raise prices without government permission (p. 427)	**controles de salario-precio:** políticas y regulaciones que hacen ilegal los aumentos a empleados o subidas de precios de las compañías sin la aprobación del gobierno (p. 427)
wage rate: prevailing pay scale for work performed in an occupation in a given area or region (p. 208)	**escala de salarios:** escala de pago prevalente en una actividad laboral en determinada área o región (p. 208)
want: something we would like to have but that is not necessary for survival (p. 6)	**deseo:** algo que nos gustaría tener pero que no es necesario para sobrevivir (p. 6)
wealth: sum of tangible economic goods that are scarce, useful, and transferable from one person to another; excludes services (p. 14)	**riquezas:** suma de los bienes económicos tangibles que son escasos, útiles y transferibles de una persona a otra; excluye servicios (p. 14)
welfare: government or private agency programs that provide general economic and social assistance to needy individuals (p. 342)	**asistencia social:** programas del gobierno o de las agencias privadas que proveen asistencia económica y social a personas necesitadas (p. 342)
workfare: program requiring welfare recipients to work in exchange for benefits (p. 344)	**sistema de prestaciones sociales condicionadas:** programa que exige que los beneficiarios de asistencia social provean trabajo a cambio de los beneficios (p. 344)
World Bank: international agency that makes loans to developing countries; formally the International Bank for Reconstruction and Development (p. 481)	**Banco Mundial:** agencia internacional que hace préstamos a países en vías de desarrollo; antiguamente era el Banco Internacional para Reconstrucción y Desarrollo (p. 481)
World Trade Organization (WTO): international agency that administers trade agreements, settles trade disputes between governments, organizes trade negotiations, and provides technical assistance and training for developing countries (p. 453)	**Organización Mundial del Comercio (OMC):** agencia internacional que administra convenios de comercio, arregla disputas comerciales entre gobiernos, organiza negociaciones de comercio, y proporciona asistencia técnica y entrenamiento para los países en desarrollo (p. 453)

English	Español
zero population growth: condition in which the average number of births and deaths balance so that population size is unchanged (p. 474)	**crecimiento demográfico nulo:** condición en la que el número promedio de nacimientos y muertes se equilibran de modo que el tamaño de la población no cambia (p. 474)

Consumer Advisory Council, 401

consumer cooperative, 80

consumer goods, 13

consumer income, 99–100

consumer legislation, role of Federal Reserve System (FED) in preparing, 407

consumer price index (CPI), 362, *fig362*
    construction of, 362

Consumer Product Safety Commission, 185, 187

consumers, 13
    number of, 101
    role of, 51–52
    role of government as, 53

consumer sector, 325–326

consumer sovereignty, 51

consumer tastes, 100

Continental Congress, 385

continental dollars, 385, 390, 391

cooperatives, 80–81, *fig80*

copyright, 176

corporate bonds, 299

corporations, 67–71
    advantages, 68–69
    corporate structure, 67–68, *fig68*
    disadvantages, 69–70
    forming, 67
    income taxes paid by, 240
    privately-held, 70
    public, 70

corruption as obstacle to economic development, 476

corruption perception index, 476

cost(s)
    business operation and, 135
    fixed, 133, *p133*
    of idle resources, 21, 121
    of instability, 374–375
    marginal, 134
    measures of, 133–134, *fig134*
    opportunity, 20, 22, 444–445, 522
    of resources, 121
    total, 134
    variable, 133

cost-benefit analysis, 24, *crt24*, 522

cost-push inflation, 365

Council of Economic Advisers, 433

coupon rate, 297
    ration, 145

courts, attitude toward unions, 200

cowboy capitalism, 429

craft union, 199, *fig199*

Craisins, 84

credit, R10–R15, R30
    basics, R15
    establishing, R13
    and identity theft, R14
    other sources, R12

credit cards, R11, *figR11*
    antitrust suit over, 131
    statement, *figR12*

credit manager, 431

creditors, 367

credit score, R10, *figR11*, R15

credit union, 80

creeping inflation, 364

crime, unemployment and, 375

crowding-out effect, 281

crude birthrate, 474

CSL Limited, 117

Cuba, 36, 380–381, *fig380, fig381, p380–381*

currency, 406
    national, 392–393
    problems with, 391–392

current dollars, 219

current gross domestic product (GDP) versus real gross domestic product (GDP), 321–22

current yield, 297

customer insight, 434

customs, global economy and, 74

customs duties, 241, 448

customs inspector, 449

customs unions, 483, 507

cyclical unemployment, 373

D

Daewoo, 76

Danbury Hatters case, 200

Das Kapital **(Marx),** 496

Davis, Charles, 96

debates in economics, 30
    increasing of minimum wage, 166–167

debt; *see also* **national debt,** 278–283
    net interest on, 271
    private versus public, 279–280
    for student loans, R19

debtors, 367

decision making, *p521*
    economics as framework for, 521

Index

Index

Index

O

Index

Acknowledgments

McGraw-Hill would like to acknowledge the artists and agencies who contributed to illustrating this program: Argosy Publishing.

Cover i (c) Mathias Kulka/Corbis, (r) MaryBeth Thielhelm/Getty Images, (inset) Ed Bock/Corbis, (bkgd) First Light/Corbis; **iv** Tony Anderson/Getty Images; **v** Brand X Pictures/PunchStock; **vi** SW Production/Index Stock Imagery, **vii** The McGraw-Hill Companies; **ix** Joseph Van Os/The Image Bank/Getty Images; **x** Jeff Greenberg/PhotoEdit; **xi** George White Jr./Index Stock Imagery; **xvi** Syracuse Newspapers/Michelle Gabel/The Image Works; **xvii** Evan Hurd/Corbis; **xviii** Tim Fuller; **xix** Tim Wright/Corbis; **xx** Peter Beck/Corbis; **2** Jim Wark/Lonely Planet Images; **3** Jim Wark/Lonely Planet Images; **4** Masterfile; **5** Corbis; **7** Corbis; **8** (l) Corbis, (cl) Neil Beer/Getty Images, (cr) Sie Productions/Zefa/Corbis, (r) Howard Grey/Getty Images; **11** The McGraw-Hill Companies; **12** The McGraw-Hill Companies; **13** Digital Vision/PunchStock; **16** Digital Vision/Getty Images; **18** Bettmann/Corbis; **19** Icon SMI/Corbis; **23** Image Source/Getty Images; **24** REAL LIFE ADVENTURES © 2004 GarLanco. Reprinted with permission of UNIVERSAL PRESS SYNDICATE. All rights reserved.; **26** Corbis; **29** www.CartoonStock.com; **30** Peter Hvizdak/The Image Works; **31** Peter Hvizdak/The Image Works; **32** Peter Beck/Corbis; **33** David H. Wells/Corbis; **34** Gallo Images/Corbis; **35** Claro Cortes IV/Reuters/Corbis; **36** Adrian Bradshaw/EPA/Landov; **37** Mike Baldwin/Cornered/Cartoon Stock; **42** The Home Depot; **43** Getty Images; **44** Chuck Savage/Corbis; **47** Persuasive Games; **48** Silvia Otte/Getty Images; **50** Kathy Willens/AP/Wide World Photo; **51** Evan Hurd/Corbis; **52** David Young-Wolff/PhotoEdit; **54** CBS Photo Archive/Getty Images; **59** DMITRY LEBEDEV/AP Images; **60** Tony Anderson/Getty Images; **61** Marianna Day Massey/ZUMA Press; **63** Getty Images; **64** Annette Coolidge/PhotoEdit; **65** (l) Corbis, (r) Doug Menuez/Getty Images; **66** John Morris/Cartoon Stock; **69** CORNERED © 2004 Mike Baldwin. Reprinted with permission of UNIVERSAL PRESS SYNDICATE. All rights reserved.; **71** Nancy Kaszerman/Corbis; **72** Glencoe Photo; **74** Digital Vision/Getty Images; **76** (t) Brownie Harris/Corbis, (b) Robert Landau/Corbis; **78** TWPhoto/Corbis; **79** Nam Y. Huh/AP/Wide World Photos; **81** Andrew Lichtenstein/Corbis; **82** Dawn Tardif/Corbis; **84** "Courtesy of Ocean Spray Cranberries, Inc."; **87** John S. Pritchett; **88** Spencer Grant/PhotoEdit; **89** Spencer Grant/PhotoEdit; **90** AP Images; **91** AINACO/Corbis; **93** Brand X Pictures/PunchStock; **97** James Leynse/Corbis; **100** Motorola; **102** Brad Barket/Getty Images; **103** Glencoe; **106** Jeff Greenberg/PhotoEdit; **107** www.CartoonStock.com; **110** "Courtesy of Apple" www.apple.com; **113** "Chris Britt, Copley News Service."; **115** (t) "Texas Energy Museum, Beaumont, Texas", (b) Jeff Greenberg/PhotoEdit; **116** Laurence Dutton/Getty Images; **117** Robert Giroux/Getty Images; **121** Oliver Berg/dpa/Corbis; **122** LUCKY COW © 2003 Mark Pett. Reprinted with permission of UNIVERSAL PRESS SYNDICATE. All rights reserved.; **123** Spencer Grant/PhotoEdit; **127** Darryl Bush/San Francisco Chronicle/Corbis; **129** Tim Boyle/Getty Images; **131** Amilcar/Liaison/Getty Images; **132** ©2006 FedEx; **133** Bob Rowan/Progressive Image/Corbis; **135** Courtesy of Amazon.com Inc. or its affiliates. All rights reserved.; **138** Ara Koopelian; **142** WireImageStock/Masterfile; **143** Peter Horree/Alamy Images; **145** Ed Quinn/Corbis; **148** Evan Agostini/Getty Images; **151** Mike Baldwin/Cartoon Stock; **153** "Michael Newman/PhotoEdit, Inc."; **154** Jim Unger/Laughingstock Licensing; **155** Robert Harding Picture Library Ltd/Alamy; **156** "Robert W. Ginn/PhotoEdit,Inc."; **160** "McArthur,Bill/www.CartoonStock.com"; **162** Kim Kulish/Corbis; **166** Ronald Martinez/Getty Images; **167** Ronald Martinez/Getty Images; **168** Powerstock/Index Stock Imagery; **169** The McGraw-Hill Companies; **170** Mika/zefa/Corbis; **172** age fotostock/SuperStock; **173** Todd Gipstein/Corbis; **174** AP Images; **176** Ric Ergenbright/Corbis; **178** Getty Images; **179** AP Images; **181** Smiley N. Pool/Dallas Morning News/Corbis; **182** Steve Starr/Corbis; **184** Getty Images; **185** Corbis; **188** www.CartoonStock.com; **190** Photofest/Disney/Pixar; **193** www.CartoonStock.com; **194** (tl) Elizabeth Simpson/Getty Images, Larry Lee Photography/Corbis; **195** Larry Lee Photography/Corbis; **196** David Sailors/Corbis; **197** Jeff Cadge/Getty Images; **199** Bettmann/Corbis; **200** Bettmann/Corbis; **201** Bettmann/Corbis; **203** REAL LIFE ADVENTURES © 2005 GarLanco. Reprinted with permission of UNIVERSAL PRESS SYNDICATE. All rights reserved.; **206** Arthur Schatz/Time Life Pictures/Getty Images; **207** Getty Images; **210** (l) Art Vandalay/Getty Images, (r) David H. Wells/Corbis; **211** Comstock Premium/

Corbis; **455** The McGraw-Hill Companies; **456** See miscellaneous notes.; **462** Getty Images; **465** John Cole and CagleCartoons.com 2006. All rights reserved.; **466** Tim Wright/Corbis; **467** Tim Wright/Corbis; **468** Bob Daemmrich/The Image Works; **469** AP Images; **473** AP Images; **474** Karl Kummels/SuperStock; **475** Sean Sprague/The Image Works; **478** Joseph Van Os/The Image Bank/Getty Images; **479** Roger Wood/Corbis; **480** www.EconSources.com; **481** Richard Lord/The Image Works; **485** Chung Sung-Jun/Getty Images; **486** Jon Spaull/Corbis; **487** John Nordell/The Image Works; **488** Harley Schwadron/www.CartoonStock.com; **489** Amelia Kunhardt/The Image Works; **490** Iain Masterton/Alamy; **491** George White Jr./Index Stock; **493** Mark Segal/Getty Images; **494** John Nordell/The Image Works; **496** Hulton-Deutsch Collection/Corbis; **500** Macduff Everton/Corbis; **501** The McGraw-Hill Companies; **502** Justin Sullivan/ Getty Images North America/Getty Images; **504** Rajesh Nirgude/AP Images; **505** caglecartoons.com/español; **508** "Courtesy of Mahindra USA, Inc"; **509** Bob Sacha/Corbis; **512** Ocean Power Delivery Ltd.; **513** Sami Sarkis/Getty Images; **516** www.CartoonStock.com; **517** Tony Freeman/ PhotoEdit; **519** JOHN HILLERY/Reuters/Corbis; **520** Jack Kurtz/The Image Works; **521** Jeff Greenberg/PhotoEdit; **522** Corbis; **524** AP Photo/Jennifer Graylock; **527** Copyright Jeff Parker and CagleCartoons.com 2006. All rights reserved.; **528** Caroline Penn/Corbis; **529** Louie Psihoyos/ Corbis; **530** F64/Getty Images; **R1** (t) Ryan McVay/Getty Images, (c) Martyn Goddard/Corbis, (b) Getty Images; **R2** Getty Images; **R4** (t) Bumann - StockFood Munich/ Stockfood, (b) Photodisc/Getty Images; **R5** (t) Corbis, (b) Time Life Pictures/Getty Images; **R8** Bettmann/Corbis; **R9** Royalty-Free/Corbis; **R10** Noel Hendrickson/Masterfile Corporation; **R14** Simon Potter/Imagesource.com; **R16** Comstock Images/JupiterImages; **R18** www.fafsa.ed.gov; **R19** PhotoDisc/Getty Images; **R20** BananaStock/Alamy; **R21** Digital Vision; **R23** Bob Daemmrich/Photo Edit; **R24** Bettmann/Corbis; **R26** Bettmann/Corbis; **R27** Nell Redmond/ ZUMA/Corbis; **R28** age fotostock/SuperStock; **R29** Kayte M. Deioma/Photo Edit; **R30** Getty Images/SW Productions; **R32** Robert J. Bennett/age fotostock; **R35** AP Photo/Kai-Uwe Knoth; **R36** AP Photo/Steve Helber; **R38** Kayte M. Deioma/PhotoEdit; **R40** Jan Cobb Photography Ltd/Getty Images; **R42** The McGraw-Hill Companies; **R45** Munshi Ahmed/Bloomberg News/Landov; **R46** Bill Pugliano/Getty Images; **R47** (l) Scott Barbour/Getty Images, (r) Scott Barbour/Getty Images; **R58** Scott Stantis/Copley News Service

The following articles have been reprinted or adapted from BusinessWeek by special permission of the McGraw-Hill Companies:
11 "Under Armour—No Sweat," May 25, 2006; **47** "On-the-Job Video Gaming," March 27, 2006; **84** "Ocean Spray's Creative Juices," May 15, 2006; **96** "Slimmer Kids, Fatter Profits?" September 5, 2005; **138** "Steve & Barry's Rules the Mall," April 10, 2006; **155** "What's Raining on Solar's Parade?" February 6, 2006; **184** "Lord of the Rings," March 20, 2006; **222** "Twilight of the UAW," April 10, 2006; **254** "Europe Circles the Flat Tax," September 26, 2005; **266** "The NSA: Security in Numbers," January 23, 2006; **312** "Taking Their Business Elsewhere," May 22, 2006; **346** "The Rich Get (Much) Richer," August 8, 2005; 360 "Dog Days: A Frank Look at the Economy," August 21/28, 2006; **408** "Inflation: What You Foresee Is What You Get," April 3, 2006; **418** "Asia's Automakers Think Globally," March 14, 2006; **455** "The Great Firewall of China," January 12, 2006; **485** "Hands Across the DMZ," March 20, 2006; **508** "Emerging Giants," July 31, 2006